SIXTH EDITION

INTERNATIONAL BUSINESS LAW
AND ITS ENVIRONMENT

RICHARD SCHAFFER

Professor Emeritus (Ret.)
Walker College of Business
Appalachian State University

BEVERLEY EARLE

Professor
Bentley College and
McCallum Graduate School of Business

FILIBERTO AGUSTI

Attorney at Law
Steptoe and Johnson, LLP
Washington, DC

D0151258

THOMSON
SOUTH-WESTERN™

Australia · Canada · Mexico · Singapore · Spain · United Kingdom · United States

THOMSON

SOUTH-WESTERN

WEST

International Business Law and its Environment, 6e
Richard Schaffer, Beverley Earle, and Filiberto Agusti

VP/Editorial Director	**Executive Marketing Manager**	**Cover and Internal Design**
Jack W. Calhoun	Lisa Lysne	Jennifer Lambert/Jen2Design
		Cincinnati, OH
VP/Editor-in-Chief	**Sr. Production Editor**	
George Werthman	Tim Bailey	**Cover Image**
		© Getty Images, Inc.
Publisher	**Technology Project Editor**	
Rob Dewey	Christine A. Wittmer	**Production**
		Stratford Publishing Services
Acquisitions Editor	**Manufacturing Coordinator**	
Steve Silverstein	Rhonda Utley	**Printer**
		Thomson-West
Sr. Developmental Editor	**Sr. Design Project Manager**	
Susanna C. Smart	Michelle Kunkler	

ISBN: 0-324-26102-0

ISE ISBN: 0-324-22527-X

Library of Congress Control Number:
2004102433

For permission to use material from this
text or product, submit a request online
at http://www.thomsonrights.com.
Any additional questions about
permissions can be submitted by email
to thomsonrights@thomson.com.

For more information contact
West Legal Studies in Business,
5191 Natorp Boulevard,
Mason, Ohio, 45040.
Or you can visit our Internet site at:
http://www.westbuslaw.com

R. S.

To Julie, Anna, and David, for their love and infinite patience.
And to Professor William M. Champion, educator and kind friend,
for whom so many generations of law students owe so much.

B. E.

To my husband, John, for his support and to our daughter, Molly, for inspiring me
with her dedication and hard work.

F. A.

To my father, Filiberto, and my mother, Maria Luisa,
who sacrificed so much that I might be free to write and read as I wish;
and to my wife, Susan, and our daughters, Caroline,
Olivia, and Jordan, for their patience.

RICHARD SCHAFFER is Professor Emeritus (ret.), Walker College of Business, Appalachian State University, Boone, North Carolina. His primary teaching responsibilities have been in the area of business law, international business transactions, and the law of international trade and investment. Schaffer received his J.D. from the University of Mississippi and his LL.M. from New York University. A former practicing attorney, he served as visiting consultant to the United Nations Department of International Economic and Social Affairs (CSDHA/ CRIMP), New York, San Jose, and Vienna, on projects related to multinational corporations, corrupt practices and the impact of the international economic criminality on socioeconomic development (1976–1982). A founder of his college's international business program, and formerly Director of International Business Studies at his college, Schaffer has both studied and taught overseas, and has consulted with other business schools on the internationalization of their curriculum. He has served as Director for Education for the North Carolina World Trade Association, has worked with trade and industry groups, and has lectured widely on issues related to international business and international education. Now active in the international down products and home textile industries, Schaffer is involved in manufacturing, distribution, global sourcing, importing, exporting, and government compliance. He has broad experience in business, with extensive professional relationships in Western and Eastern Europe and China. Among his many interests, he is active as a K-9 handler with search and rescue dog groups in North Carolina.

BEVERLEY EARLE is a Professor in the Law Department at Bentley College and the McCallum Graduate School of Business, where she has been on the faculty since 1983. She teaches the legal environment of business and international business law at the undergraduate and graduate level. She graduated with a B.A. from the University of Pennsylvania and a J.D. from Boston University and was admitted to practice law in Massachusetts. Professor Earle received the Bentley College Scholar of the Year Award in 2001. Professor Earle won the Indiana University Center for International Business Education and Research Case Competition in 1999. She has presented papers at numerous places including Cornell University Law School Symposium in 2000, and her articles appear in law reviews published by Cornell, University of California at Berkeley, and University of Minnesota. She has also published in *The Boston Globe* and the *Philadelphia Inquirer.* She studied in Paris on a sabbatical in 1993 and 1994. Professor Earle taught at Yunnan University in Kunming, China, on a U.S.I.A. grant during May and June 1990 and in Strasbourg, France in 1992. She is a past president of the International Section of the Academy of Legal Studies in Business.

FILIBERTO AGUSTI is a partner in the Washington, DC, law firm of Steptoe & Johnson LLP, where he has practiced law since 1978. He represents major business lenders, governments, equity investors, and other participants in complex international commercial financing and corporate acquisition transactions. These representations have included negotiation, structuring, and legal drafting in international project finance and privatization transactions, cross-border corporate acquisitions, international joint ventures, and financing facilities. Mr. Agusti has authored several articles for the *Harvard Law Review* and other legal publications in the corporate arena. He also is a frequent speaker on corporate and commercial finance issues at professional and industry seminars in the United States and abroad.

Mr. Agusti was law clerk to Judge William H. Timbers, U.S. Court of Appeals for the Second Circuit, 1977–78. He is a 1977 graduate of the Harvard Law School, where he was a senior editor of the *Harvard Law Review.* He graduated summa cum laude with a B.A. from the University of Illinois in 1974.

CONTENTS IN BRIEF

v

CONTENTS

Part Two
International Sales, Credits, and the Commercial Transaction   102

Chapter Four
Sales Contracts and Excuses for Non-performance   104

CHAPTER 22
REGULATING THE COMPETITIVE ENVIRONMENT   647

APPENDICES

TABLE OF CASES

Principal cases are in **bold** type. Other cases discussed in the text are in roman type. Cases cited within the principal cases, endnotes, review questions, or other quoted materials are not included.

AD	Antidumping Duty	DOC	Department of Commerce
AGOA	African Growth and Opportunity Act	DSB	Dispute Settlement Body (WTO)
AID	Agency for International Development	DSU	Dispute Settlement Understanding (WTO)
APEC	Asia Pacific Economic Cooperation	EBRD	European Bank for Reconstruction and Development
ASEAN	Association of Southeast Asian Nations	EC	European Community
BEA	Bureau of Economic Analysis, U.S. Department of Commerce	ECJ	European Court of Justice
		EDI	Electronic Data Interchange
		EEA	European Economic Area
BIS	Bureau of Industry and Security (U.S. DOC)	EFTA	European Free Trade Association
		EMC	Export Management Company
BOP	Balance of Payments	EPO	European Patent Office
BOT	Balance of Trade	ERM	Exchange Rate Mechanism
CACM	Central American Common Market	ETC	Export Trading Company
		EU	European Union
CAP	Common Agricultural Policy of the European Union	EXIMBANK	Export-Import Bank of the U.S.
		FCIA	Foreign Credit Insurance Association
CARICOM	Caribbean Common Market	FCN	Friendship, Commerce, and Navigation treaties
CBERA	Caribbean Basin Economic Recovery Act		
CBI	Caribbean Basin Initiative	FCPA	Foreign Corrupt Practices Act
CBP	Bureau of Customs and Border Protection (U.S. DHS)	FDI	Foreign Direct Investment
		FMC	Federal Maritime Commission
CBSA	Canadian Border Services Agency	FPA	Free of Particular Average
CCC	Commodity Credit Corporation	FSC	Foreign Sales Corporation
CCC	Customs Cooperation Council	FSIA	Foreign Sovereign Immunities Act
CCL	Commerce Control List (formerly Commodity Control List)		
		FTAA	Free Trade Area of the Americas
CE	Conformité Européene	FTC	Federal Trade Commission
CET	Common External Tariff (or CXT)	FTZ	Foreign Trade Zone
CISG	Convention on Contracts for the International Sale of Goods	GATS	General Agreement on Trade in Services
CIT	Court of International Trade	GATT	General Agreement on Tariffs and Trade
CMI	Comite Maritime International		
CO	Certificate of Origin	GCC	Gulf Cooperation Council
COCOM	Coordinating Committee for Multilateral Export Controls	GDP	Gross Domestic Product
		GSP	Generalized System of Preferences
CODEX	Codex Alimentarius Commission	HTS	Harmonized Tariff Schedule (see HTSUS)
COE	Council of Europe		
COGSA	Carriage of Goods by Sea Act	HTSUS	Harmonized Tariff Schedule of the United States
CVD	Countervailing Duty		
DFAIT	Department of Foreign Affairs and International Trade (Canada)	IBRD	International Bank of Reconstruction and Development

ICC	International Chamber of Commerce	NTR	Normal Trade Relations (fomerly MFN)
ICJ	International Court of Justice (World Court)	NVOCCs	Non-Vessel Operating Common Carriers
ICSID	International Center for the Settlement of Investment Disputes	OAS	Organization of American States
		OECD	Organization for Economic Cooperation and Development
IDA	International Development Association	OFAC	Office of Foreign Assets Control (Department of Treasury)
IEEPA	International Emergency Economic Powers Act	OPIC	Overseas Private Investment Corporation
IFC	International Finance Corporation		
ILO	International Labor Organization	OSRA	Ocean Shipping Reform Act of 1998
IMF	International Monetary Fund		
IMO	International Maritime Organization	SDR	Special Drawing Rights
		SECOFI	Secretaría de Comercio y Fomento Industrial (Mexico)
IPR	Intellectual Property Rights		
ISO	International Organization for Standardization	SED	Shipper's Export Declaration
		SWIFT	Society for Worldwide Interbank Financial Telecommunications
ITA	International Trade Administration		
ITC	International Trade Commission	TAA	Trade Adjustment Assistance
JETRO	Japan External Trade Organization	TNC	Transnational Corporation (see MNC)
JIS	Japanese Industrial Standards Mark	TRIMS	Trade-Related Investment Measures
JPO	Japanese Patent Office		
LC	Letter of Credit	TRIPS	Trade Related Aspects of Intellectual Property Rights
MAC	Market Access and Compliance (U.S. Department of Commerce)		
		UCP	Uniform Customs and Practices for Documentary Credits
MERCOSUR	Mercado Common del Sur (Southern Common Market)	UNCITRAL	United Nations Commission on International Trade Law
METI	Ministry of Economy, Trade, and Industry (formerly MITI–Japan)	UNCTAD	United Nations Conference on Trade and Development
MFN	Most Favored Nation Trade Status (see NTR)	UNDP	United Nations Development Program
MNC	Multinational Corporation		
MNE	Multinational Enterprise (also MNC)	UNEP	United Nations Environmental Program
MOFTEC	Ministry of Foreign Trade and Economic Cooperation (China)	UNIDO	United Nations Industrial Development Organization
MOSS	Market-Oriented-Sector-Selective	UNIDROIT	International Institute for the Unification of Private Law
MTN	Multilateral Trade Negotiations		
NAFTA	North American Free Trade Agreement	USDA	U.S. Department of Agriculture
		USITC	U.S. International Trade Commission
NGO	Non-governmental Organization		
NIS	Newly Independent States	USTR	U.S. Trade Representative
NME	Non-market Economy Nation	WCO	World Customs Organization
NTB	Non-tariff Barrier	WIPO	World Intellectual Property Organization
NTDB	National Trade Data Bank		
NTE	National Trade Estimate Report	WTO	World Trade Organization

It has been said that America's interest in international education has peaked and ebbed with the changing tide of the American political climate, rising in times of economic expansion and ebbing during periods of political isolation or economic protectionism. Perhaps, however, the cycle has finally been broken, and industry leaders, government policymakers, and educators alike have come to understand the importance of making a permanent commitment to international education.

In the last half of the twentieth century, America faced an increasingly competitive global marketplace and a mounting trade deficit. Rather than seek protection behind often-politicized trade laws, America's leaders committed themselves and the nation to policies of free trade and open investment. American firms realized that they had no choice but to compete aggressively with international competitors, in markets both here and abroad. Witness not only America's great multinational corporations, but also the successes of the many small and medium sized companies that today do business internationally.

Among nations, the spirit of free trade has become contagious. Examples can be seen everywhere: The rush of nations to join the World Trade Organization, the growth of regional economic integration, privatization of national economies, and the opening of once tightly controlled markets in developing countries and in formerly communist countries as well. The outcome has been the globalization of the world's economy and of world markets for goods and services. It is in this climate that we have seen perhaps the greatest renewal of interest in international business education in America's history.

TRADE, INTELLECTUAL PROPERTY, AND FOREIGN DIRECT INVESTMENT: A THEMATIC APPROACH

International Business Law and Its Environment is intended for use in such courses as International Business Law, International Business Transactions, or the Law of International Trade and Investment. Our thematic approach is patterned after the basic market-entry strategies of most firms as they expand into international markets: trade in goods and services, the protection and licensing of intellectual property rights, and foreign direct investment. Through the study of law, we attempt to provide a fairly comprehensive treatment of each of these market-entry methods—and their variations and combinations—as they fit into the overall strategy of a particular firm. We begin our discussion with trade, which involves the least penetration into the international market, and progress to foreign direct investment, which immerses the firm completely in the social, cultural, and legal systems of its host country. This progression also patterns the life cycle of many firms as they mature and as they move more aggressively into new international markets.

PRIVATE AND PUBLIC INTERNATIONAL LAW

International Business Law and Its Environment emphasizes both private and public law. The private law applicable to international business transactions, for example, includes the law of international sales, trade finance and letters of credit, distribution agreements, agreements with foreign sales representatives, licensing agreements, and other governing law. Public international law includes conventions, treaties, and agreements among nations that make up the legal framework within which international business takes place. The treaties of the European Union, the GATT agreements, and NAFTA are prime examples. Public international law provides the basis for the government regulation of international business. It affects the environment within which a firm's international business strategies are developed, and the firm's responsibility under national laws and administrative regulations. Customs and tariff laws are good examples, as are laws that open markets to international investors. We also treat general principles of the law of nations, as well as the work of various intergovernmental organizations (such as UN agencies, the WTO, and the OECD), because these are fundamentals needed for study.

INTERNATIONAL AND COMPARATIVE APPROACH

No text can attempt to teach the law of every nation in which a firm might do business, and we have resisted the temptation to simply catalog foreign laws. Instead, foreign laws and foreign case decisions are presented throughout the book for comparison purposes, to illustrate differences in legal or economic systems, and differences in doing business in other countries. Where applicable, we compare civil law, common law, socialist law, Islamic law, and concepts from different legal systems. Examples include comparative sales law, labor law, advertising law, and agency law. For instance, our discussion of Chinese law provides U.S. readers with many interesting comparisons, because the United States and China are in different stages of development, with very different political systems. European law is discussed throughout the book. Of course, U.S. law and relevant international agreements, uniform codes, and the decisions of international tribunals are treated in greater detail.

THE MECHANICS AND THEORY OF INTERNATIONAL BUSINESS TRANSACTIONS

International Business Law and Its Environment not only teaches the "hands on" mechanics of international business transactions, but also provides the theory needed for businesspeople to understand the consequences of their actions. Commercial transactions are thoroughly examined and explained. This includes negotiating contracts for the sale of goods and services, negotiating contractual terms of trade, handling shipping contracts and cargo insurance, agency contracts, dealing with letters of credit and other banking arrangements, alternatives for dispute settlement, and much more. Many sample forms and documents are included. Methods for protecting one's intellectual property are closely considered, as are the handling of international investment arrangements, employing persons abroad and other issues.

Similarly, readers are taken through many thorny problems of dealing with the government, such as learning how to move goods through U.S. Customs or to fight back against unfair foreign competition or trade barriers.

A BUSINESS AND MANAGERIAL PERSPECTIVE

We begin with the premise that the world of international business is a dangerous place, and that the management of international business is the management of risk. Whether one is developing and implementing an international business strategy, or managing an international business transaction, an understanding of the special risks involved will help assure a project's success. In keeping with our thematic approach, we examine the risks of trade (e.g., managing credit or marine risk), protecting and licensing intellectual property (e.g., dealing with gray market goods or registering foreign patents), handling foreign mergers and acquisitions (e.g., unexpected differences in foreign corporate or labor law) or evaluating political risk in less stable regions of the world. We then learn how to avoid, reduce, or shift the risk to other parties or intermediaries. The case study approach is excellent for this purpose, as readers can see firsthand the mistakes others have made, and how disputes are resolved.

We also stress strategic business decision-making. For example, our chapter on imports, customs, and tariff law does not simply view importing as an isolated transaction. Rather, it addresses the importance of customs and tariff law on a firm's global operations, such as the selection of contractors or the location of overseas plants and factories. This technique is implemented throughout the book.

CULTURAL, POLITICAL, SOCIAL, AND ECONOMIC CONCERNS

New to this edition are five selected essays on living and working successfully in different foreign cultural settings. These informative essays provide information on cultural mores and corporate culture of China, Japan, Germany, Mexico, and France, and are interspersed in part throughout the text. The material continues in more depth on the text's Web site.

As with each previous edition, we have made a special effort to discuss the cultural, political, and economic aspects of international business, as they bear on differences in attitudes toward the law, their impact on trade relations, and how they affect the way we do business in another country. In discussing trade issues, it is almost impossible to separate politics, foreign policy, and trade. Thus we have devoted considerable attention to current events in many countries, including Cuba, Myanmar, China, and elsewhere. Many topics require a historical perspective, such as the Smoot-Hawley era of the 1930s, the development of GATT in the 1940s, the Iranian Revolution of 1979, forty years of U.S.-Cuba relations, or more recently, U.S. involvement in Iraq.

We also discuss U.S.-China relations and the potential impact on U.S. trade and investment there. Readers are asked to consider the impact of world current events on their strategic business decisions, particularly in unstable regions or under hostile political and economic conditions.

DEVELOPING COUNTRIES

The developing countries of Africa, Asia, Latin America, and the Caribbean present special problems for their richer trading partners. We have tried to paint a realistic picture of trade opportunities, colored by the realities of disease, poverty, and environmental degradation that threaten much of our planet.

Trade and investment issues in developing countries are incorporated in all parts of the book. Examples include the 2000 *Cotonou Agreement* that will define relations between Europe and its trading partners in the developing world for much of the century to come, the *Doha Development Agenda,* the recent U.S. trade initiatives for Africa, or negotiations for a Western Hemisphere trade agreement. Many special issues related to doing business in the independent republics of the former Soviet Union are covered. The UNCTAD *World Investment Report* is discussed, along with the impact of multinational corporations on the developing world.

ETHICS AND SOCIAL RESPONSIBILITY

Because ethical questions can arise in varying contexts, we have chosen to integrate the subject throughout the book. Examples include codes of conduct, bribery and corruption, child labor, workers' rights, protection of the environment and of wildlife, prison and forced labor, human rights issues in doing business under repressive regimes, AIDS and other world health issues, discrimination issues in foreign countries, special issues related to U.S. investment in Mexican *maquiladora* plants, the ban on asbestos products, and others. Major environmental decisions of the WTO Dispute Settlement Body are included.

TO OUR INTERNATIONAL READERS

We are pleased to know that our work is contributing to student learning at universities on virtually every continent and in every region of the world. Naturally, our audience is primarily an American one. We necessarily devote a major portion of the text to American law, to U.S. trade relations, and to the needs of the American firm. However, we have made every effort to maintain our international perspective, and to draw important international comparisons. Cases from countries other than the United States appear throughout the book, as do discussions of foreign codes and practices. Moreover, the increased reliance on uniform rules, harmonized codes, and international standards makes the book suitable for any student interested in international business law.

KEY REVISIONS TO THE SIXTH EDITION

The 6th edition covers many of the major legal and political developments that followed September 11, 2001. These include the creation of the Department of Homeland Security as a part largest reorganization of the American government in over fifty years, the USA PATRIOT Act and, where appropriate, the impact and relevance of the war on terrorism to business. The latest developments in trade negotiations, the European Community, intellectual property, global environmental protection, and investment policies are analyzed. We also gave careful attention to global public health issues related to AIDS, "mad cow" disease, "hoof and mouth" disease, genetically modified foods, asbestos and harmful products, and more. This edition has an increased focus on living and working in foreign cultures, and makes greater use of industry examples.

As with each new edition, we have included many new cases: *U.S. v. Lindh*; *U.S. v. Mead Corporation*; *Reyes-Gaona v. NC Grower's Association*; *Commission of the EC v. the Italian Republic* (the *Chocolate* case); *National Farmers' Union v. France* (the *Mad Cow* case); *Acree v. Republic of Iraq*; the *Shrimp-Sea Turtles* case; and new landmark WTO decisions on *Asbestos Products, European Steel, and Reformulated Gasoline*. There are more new cases than can be mentioned here, including four new cases interpreting international sales law (the CISG) alone.

In addition, this edition contains more foreign law decisions, and decisions of international tribunals, than did previous editions. Where possible, cases deleted from prior editions have either been discussed in the text or included as end of chapter questions, to provide continuity to users of previous editions.

PART ONE: THE LEGAL ENVIRONMENT OF INTERNATIONAL BUSINESS

- A completely new Chapter Three, "*Resolving International Commercial Disputes*." The chapter has greater emphasis on avoiding disputes and on basic principles affecting arbitration and litigation, with a focus on the special problems of international dispute settlement, such as cultural barriers to dispute resolution, obtaining jurisdiction over foreign parties in the Internet age, cross-border forum shopping and foreign judicial assistance. Conflict of laws principles are now introduced in this chapter.
- Updated trade, investment, and economic data with discussion.
- Current political and economic changes in China, Russia, Eastern Europe, and the developing countries.
- Analysis of UNCTAD's *World Investment Report* and the impact of multinational corporations on development.
- New and expanded guide to U.S. government export assistance programs.
- Greater emphasis on the basic principles of international law, with increased coverage of the law of treaties.
- Expanded comparative law coverage of privacy and criminal law.

- The international response to the "blood diamond" trade.
- Updated treatment of international affairs, including the UN and Iraq, the International Criminal Court, and more.
- Updated ethics coverage, including presentation of the Haliburton Code of Ethics for class discussion.

PART TWO: INTERNATIONAL SALES, CREDITS, AND THE COMMERCIAL TRANSACTION

- Focus on commercial and business transactions enhanced (e.g., one essay suggests *17 Steps to Take the Fear out of Letters of Credit*)
- Materials on the international sale of goods substantially updated to reflect the growth of case law under the UN CISG. Includes new cases on the applicability of the CISG, modification of contracts, warranties, and fundament breach.
- Comparative analysis of CISG and UCC now includes 2003 Amendments to Article 2.
- Updated material on electronic data interchange in international transactions.
- Updated discussion of trade terms, including a new case interpreting "*Incoterms*" under German law.
- Updated discussion of letters of credit and the rule of strict compliance.
- Complete treatment of the new *Montreal Air Convention* and the liability of air carriers, including new material on jurisdiction and air disaster litigation.

PART THREE: INTERNATIONAL AND U.S. TRADE LAW

- Covers the reorganization of the U.S. executive departments, and analyzes the impact of homeland security on U.S. importers and exporters.
- The USA PATRIOT Act is analyzed and in the *American Taliban* case presented. Changes in export controls since 2001 are discussed, and includes the *NY Times* export application case.
- Updates on the president's trade promotion authority, U.S. trade agreements, and the latest U.S. trade legislation.

- Discusses China's admission to the WTO, and current issues in doing business there.
- Latest case law on relationship between GATT/WTO and U.S. law.
- Covers latest trade negotiations, including the *Doha Agenda*
- Emphasizes rising global concerns over public health and food safety, and includes the WTO *Asbestos* decision and the EU *Mad Cow* decision. Raises issues related to genetically modified foods.
- Discusses the coming changes in global textile trade.
- Substantial rewrite of the chapter on import competition and unfair trade, with significant new case selection. Includes an analysis of safeguards, dumping, and subsidies in the global steel industry and the important WTO *European Steel* decision.
- Customs law chapter includes analysis of *Chevron*, *Haggar*, and *Mead* decisions of the U.S. Supreme Court, homeland security issues, and improved discussion of classification issues, including tariff engineering.
- Recent developments toward the *Free Trade Area of the Americas*
- EU issues updated, including changes in the euro, EU enlargement, CAP, and privacy.

PART FOUR: REGULATION OF THE INTERNATIONAL MARKETPLACE

- Covers the latest intellectual property issues and WTO TRIPS decisions. New key coverage areas include "geographical indications" on products, and patent law issues affecting the AIDS epidemic in developing countries.
- Expanded biodiversity discussion with a review of the issues and national positions.
- Addresses new attitudes toward privatization and nationalization in Russia.
- Child labor, the ILO, and other social responsibility issues expanded.
- U.S. tax consequences of foreign subsidiary operations added.
- Addresses changes in the Act of State doctrine, and a new discussion of state-sponsored terrorism issues and the *Acree* case.

- *Reyes-Gaona* decision now included, with new material on the extraterritorial application of U.S. antidiscrimination law. Explores foreign gender discrimination laws, including Japan and the Ukraine.
- Major new environmental decisions include WTO *Shrimp—Sea Turtle* and *Reformulated Gasoline*. Other highlights include new environmental treaties and "polluter pays" agreements, and issues related to the transboundary effects of industrial accidents, particularly in Eastern Europe and Central Asia.
- Presents new studies on official corruption throughout the world, new international efforts to combat it, and FCPA implications.
- Presents new case from Paraguayan Supreme Court illustrating the severity of laws governing the termination of foreign agents and representatives.
- Addresses new legal controversies in European competition law.

OUR GREATEST CHALLENGE

Perhaps the greatest challenge in preparing any edition is simply to keep up with the rapid pace of political, economic, and legal changes around the world. Revisions had to be made almost daily to keep abreast of current developments. There are countless topics that had to be included or revised at the last moment. Other issues are still outstanding. What will be the result of the *Doha Development* rounds? Will Russia be admitted to the WTO? What will be the impact of the EU's expansion? Will there be a new *Free Trade Area of the Americas?* How will the lifting of quotas on U.S. textile imports in 2005 affect jobs, and how will it affect the American political scene? How will the 2004 U.S. presidential election affect America's position on trade issues? Many questions must await the next edition.

PEDAGOGICAL FEATURES OF THE SIXTH EDITION

- Both landmark and cutting-edge cases from U.S. and foreign courts, and decisions of the WTO, NAFTA, ICSID, and other international tribunals.

- Business and industry examples, sample documents, and forms.
- *International Accents* features current real-world issues, and insight on cultural factors affecting living and working in foreign countries.
- Current economic data and statistical information
- Updated Internet links
- End-of-chapter questions
- Expanded list of frequently used acronyms in international business.

SUPPLEMENTAL MATERIALS

- The Instructor's Manual with Test Bank has been revised and enhanced by Joseph A. Zavaletta of the University of Texas, Brownsville. The Instructor's Manual contains Answers to Case Questions, end-of-chapter Questions and Case Problems, Managerial Implications, Chapter Summaries, lists of chapter cases, Supplemental Cases, Teaching Suggestions, Internet Activities, and Supplemental Exercises. In addition, the Test Bank has been revised and expanded.
- PowerPoint slides are available on the text Web site at **http://schaffer.westbuslaw.com**. These can be used by instructors as a lecture aid, and by students as a study aid.
- The text Web site at: **http://schaffer.westbuslaw.com** includes instructor materials for downloading current Internet addresses relevant to the text, Court Case Updates, and other resources. From here, you can also access NewsEdge, a news link that delivers live legal news and company data from the world's leading news sources.

West is committed to providing you with the finest educational resources available including the full complement of West resources. Because we prepare our instructor resources with a variety of teaching environments in mind, it is likely that you will need only a portion of these for your course. Before you request an item, we ask that you please read thoroughly the description of each resource on the Web site at **http://www.westbuslaw.com**. If you still need more information about resources,

we urge you to contact your local West/Thomson Learning sales representative. Many teaching and learning resources can be downloaded directly from this site. The following teaching resources are available to qualified adopters of West Legal Studies in Business textbooks:

- **Westlaw®.** Ten free hours of West's computerized legal research gives qualified instructors access to U.S. Codes, federal regulations, and numerous special libraries.
- **West Legal Studies Video Library.** West offers an extensive collection of legal studies videos developed through alliances with Court TV, The American Bar Association, CNN, and other premier institutions. Contact your Thomson Learning/West Legal Studies Sales Representative.
- **Westlaw™ Campus.** Westlaw Campus is now available to students using West Legal Studies in Business texts. Westlaw Campus is derived from Westlaw, the preferred computer-assisted legal research database of legal professionals. In addition to primary legal materials (federal and state cases, statutes, and administrative law), Westlaw Campus offers secondary resources, such as *American Law Reports (ALR)*, *American Jurisprudence 2d (Am.Jur.2d)*, and law reviews. These materials can greatly enhance research assignments, critical-thinking exercises, and term papers. Access for every student can be bundled with your text at an outstanding discount. For more information about Westlaw Campus, please visit **http://campus.westbuslaw.com**.
- **West's Digital Video Library.** Featuring 55 segments on the most important topics in Business Law, West's Digital Video Library helps make the connection between the textbook and the business world. Three types of clips are represented, **Legal Conflicts in Business** feature modern business scenarios, **Ask the Instructor** clips offer concept review, and **Drama of the Law** present classic legal situations. Together, these clips bring business law to life. Access to West's Digital Video Library can be bundled with every new text for no additional cost. For more information about West's Digital Video Library, visit **http://digitalvideolibrary.westbuslaw.com**.

ACKNOWLEDGMENTS

The authors wish to express their gratitude to the following reviewers for their help in preparing this and past editions.

Mark B. Baker
University of Texas-Austin

Patricia B. Bartscher
San Francisco State University
Nivea Castro
University of Phoenix

Larry A. Di Matteo
University of Miami

Rafi Efrat
California State University, Northridge

Joan T. A. Gabel
Georgia State University

John M. Garic
University of Central Oklahoma

David P. Hanson
Duquesne University

Michael E. Jones
University of Massachusetts, Lowell

Sandra L. Linda
University of Delaware

F. William McCarty
Western Michigan University

Sean P. Melvin
Elizabethtown College

Carol J. Miller
Southwest Missouri State University

Fred Naffziger
Indiana University at South Bend

Gregory T. Naples
Marquette University

Lynda J. Oswald
University of Michigan

Marisa Anne Pagnattaro
University of Georgia

Kimberlianne Podlas
Bryant College

Bruce L. Rockwood
Bloomsburg University

John C. Ruhnka
University of Colorado-Denver

Martin L. Saradjian
Boston University

Richard Still
Mississippi State University

Clyde D. Stoltenberg
University of Kansas

Alan R. Thiele
University of Houston

Susan M. Vance
St. Mary's College

Peter C. Ward
Millsaps College

John Wrieden
Florida International University

Norman Gregory Young
California State Polytechnic University, Pomona

We would also like to thank International Education Systems (St. Paul) and Mary Murray Bosrock, noted writer, lecturer, and author of the award-winning series, *Put Your Best Foot Forward: A Fearless Guide to International Communication and Behavior,* for her kind permission to reprint selections in our text. Ms. Bosrock's works are essential reading for any business student embarking on a career in international business. Our thanks also go to Joe Zavaletta for his work on this edition's supplements.

Each of us would like to express our sincere gratitude to our editors at West Legal Studies in Business—Rob Dewey, Susan Smart, and Tim Bailey, for their advice, support, and skill as editors, and for transforming mere words and thoughts into a valuable tool for learning. A special word of thanks is owed to Susan Smart, who has masterfully guided the development of four editions of *International Business Law,* for her dedication to our work during those years, and for her kind understanding, patience, and encouragement.

Richard Schaffer
Beverley Earle
Filiberto Agusti

SIXTH EDITION

INTERNATIONAL BUSINESS LAW
AND ITS ENVIRONMENT

PART I

The Legal Environment of International Business

Part One of *International Business Law and Its Environment* provides a framework for understanding both international business and the legal environment in which it operates. The chapters focus on how economic, social, and political forces influence the development of the law and legal institutions. Chapter One provides a conceptual framework for studying international business. The chapter explains the three major forms of international business: trade (importing and exporting); licensing agreements for the transfer and legal protection of patents, copyrights, trademarks, and other intellectual property (including franchising); and active foreign investment through mergers, acquisitions, and joint ventures.

In Chapter One, the reader is also asked to consider how the risks of international business differ from the risks of doing business at home. How does a firm deal with the added risks of doing business over great distances, the risks of language and cultural barriers, the risks of miscommunications, currency fluctuations, international hostilities and political interference, the risks of trade controls or restrictions on investment, the risks of foreign litigation, or the risks of nonpayment or breach of contract? By raising these questions, this chapter illustrates that the management of an international business transaction is, in large part, the management of risk. The remainder of the book provides the opportunity for the thoughtful reader to consider how careful business and legal planning can help to avoid or reduce these risks or shift them to another party to the transaction.

Many readers will have little familiarity with either international business or international legal principles. Chapter Two explains the nature and sources of international business law, which includes both internationally agreed-upon legal principles, such as those embodied in a treaty, convention, or other international agreement, and the rules and decisions found in the domestic law of individual nations (e.g., statutes passed by a national legislature).

In turn, each of these bodies of law can be classified as either public law or private law. If the rule of law affects a private (often commercial) transaction between two parties, such as between buyer and seller or shipper and ocean carrier, it is considered private law. If the rule of law determines the rights and responsibilities of nations in relation to one another, or places public controls on an otherwise private transaction (e.g., criminal penalties for making a false customs declaration), the law is considered public law. Chapter Two lays a foundation for understanding these basic principles.

The reader must also understand the role of intergovernmental organizations. Many international business problems can be resolved only through international or regional cooperation. Whether the problem is related to the laundering of drug money through the international banking system, setting standards for the protection of the environment from oil spills, using restrictions on business or trade with countries such as Iraq for political purposes, or developing uniform rules for international sales contracts, international organizations can be useful in bringing individual nations to agreement on difficult issues. These organizations are introduced in Chapter Two.

Chapter Three discusses how disputes are settled in an international business transaction, including litigation and arbitration. It addresses issues of jurisdiction and procedural rules for litigating international cases. For instance, the chapter attempts to answer such questions as: If a company does business in a foreign country, can the company be sued there? If a buyer purchases goods from a foreign firm that does not regularly do business in the United States, under what circumstances can the buyer sue that firm in U.S. courts? If a product that is produced in one nation injures a consumer in another nation, where should the injured party's claim be heard? If a firm obtains a court judgment in one country, can the firm enforce it against the defendant's assets held in another country? Because the costs and risks of foreign litigation are substantial, what can the parties do in advance to provide an alternative to litigation should a dispute result?

CHAPTER 1

INTRODUCTION TO INTERNATIONAL BUSINESS

ECONOMIC INTERDEPENDENCE

Many economists and business experts believe that no business can be purely domestic. The realities of the modern world make all business international. No longer can an economic or political change in one country occur without causing reverberations throughout the world's markets. The effects of the Persian Gulf War were reflected on international stock exchanges. A civil war on the African continent affects the price of commodities in London and New York. A change in interest rates in Germany affects investment flows and currency exchange rates in the United States. The European Monetary Union could have great impact on exchange rates and the cost of doing business. A deterioration in trade relations between the United States and China can affect a manufacturing plant in Canada or Australia. Terrorist attacks worldwide have affected not only international business operations, but the very ability of managers to travel and live safely in foreign lands. Perhaps nowhere is global economic interdependence more obvious than the impact of infectious disease. Whether it be Mad Cow disease affecting English cattle, or SARS affecting people from Toronto to rural China, the impact of infectious disease can now ripple through the world's economy. Indeed, in 2003, the combined effect of terrorism and infectious disease was felt by international business travel, tourism, and affected the global operations of firms on all continents. The world today is more economically interdependent than at any other time in history, which has led to the globalization of product, service, and capital markets.

Economic interdependence is the result of many factors. Precious natural resources and raw materials are located around the world. Technological advances in travel and communications have brought people closer together. Nations have moved away from protectionism and increasingly toward free trade; thus, markets for goods and services that were once closed to foreign competition are now open. The world has seen a steady movement toward economic integration and the development of free trade areas and "common markets" among nations. Greater political stability in the developing countries has led to increased foreign investment, industrialization, and the integration of those nations into the world economy. Economic interdependence also can be attributed to the sharing of technology and know-how, with patents, copyrights, and trademarks now licensed for use around the globe as freely as goods and services are sold. The interrelatedness of financial markets, the worldwide flow of capital, and the coordination of economic policies between nations have had a tremendous impact on the global economy.

Political changes in the last two decades also increased countries' interdependence. Throughout the world, countries are moving toward greater political freedom and democracy. The breakup of the Soviet Union in 1991 into independent republics, the largest of which is Russia, opened those countries to opportunities for investment by western companies. It also freed much of Eastern and Central Europe from communist oppression, leaving them open for foreign investment. This process of converting from closed communist-dominated governments to a free market economic system based on private enterprise has allowed these nations to become more economically integrated with the rest of the world. A similar phenomenon is occurring in Latin America and Asia as well. Many of these countries that were once ruled by military dictatorships have moved toward democracy. This new freedom opens them up to foreign investors and helps to integrate them into the world's economic community.

This greater economic interdependence has required nations to reach agreement on important legal issues. Thus, the global economy has been affected by the development of widely accepted legal norms and conventions, which provide a stable and consistent legal environment for firms operating on a global scale. In summary, the factors that yet hold the greatest promise for change are the growth of democracy, the resurgence of market-oriented economies, and the decline of socialism.

The Global Marketplace

Economic interdependence has caused many changes in the global marketplace. The impact on American firms has been dramatic. New competitive forces created by the emergence of economic powerhouses in Europe and Asia have transformed the modern business world. The European Union has created a single market, with a reunified Germany emerging as the continent's economic giant. The Asian countries have become increasingly industrialized and powerful. Goods from countries such as Japan and South Korea, once known only for their low cost, are now known for their quality and workmanship. Tokyo and Hong Kong now rival New York as world financial centers.

Many countries are now capable of wielding the tremendous economic clout they derive from their rich supplies of natural resources, such as bauxite, copper, and rubber. Middle Eastern nations, rich with oil, have moved from the biblical age to the industrialized age in a single generation. Mexico and the countries of Latin America possess not only precious natural resources, but also an abundant supply of labor. And the economies of Eastern Europe, Russia, and the other newly independent republics of the former Soviet Union, now in need of economic assistance, may some day themselves become competitive players in the global marketplace.

The U.S. Experience.   Americans have long been active in all aspects of international business. U.S. history is rich with stories of the "Yankee trader"—from the colonial period to the present. U.S.–owned trademarks, such as Coca-Cola, McDonald's, Disney, and Microsoft, are recognized in every culture and in every language. U.S. firms have built factories around the globe and shared their technology, know-how, and management capabilities with their investment partners.

United States involvement in international business has come chiefly from its largest companies. Small- and medium-sized manufacturing firms traditionally shied away from involvement overseas due to a provincial attitude, rooted in America's westward expansion and based on the idea that business could expand infinitely merely by tapping domestic markets. The country had a vast supply of natural resources, and domestic demand exceeded supply, so businesses felt little need to sell products overseas. The presence of vast oceans separating the nation from its trading partners made foreign trade seem even more bothersome. Furthermore, the United States was preoccupied with other matters. First came the movement westward, then the political isolationism and economic protectionism spawned by the first World War. The new European immigrants quickly sought to forget their pasts, preferring to become Americans and to adopt the language and customs of their new country.

At the close of World War II, the United States was in a preeminent political and economic position relative to the war-devastated nations of Europe and the Far East. The factories of Europe and Japan lay in rubble, with North America having virtually the only functioning industrialized economy in the world. The United States, to its credit, quickly recognized its responsibility to pull the world out of the ravages of war. It succeeded, in large part, through the creation of a massive industrial economy based on consumer goods that stimulated and strengthened the redevelopment of once-industrial Europe and Japan. In the process, however, many U.S. companies never viewed themselves as a part of a world marketplace and did not structure their market objectives or economic goals accordingly. Indeed, not until the 1980s, when the effect of mounting U.S. deficits began to be felt, and when foreign firms gained a greater share of U.S.

domestic markets, did U.S. companies realize that oceans could no longer insulate them from foreign competition.

The Education of U.S. Managers.   U.S. companies have learned about international business the hard way. Unlike their Dutch and Swiss counterparts, U.S. managers did not have a wealth of experience to draw upon. The Dutch, for instance, have always depended on trade for the very existence of their small country. Americans learned through trial and error, and, in the process, made many mistakes. A number of infamous marketing blunders and cultural *faux pas* committed by naive U.S. managers are now a part of marketing folklore.

In the early part of the last century, many U.S. firms simply lacked the commitment to international business. Some companies, for instance, viewed exporting as essential only when domestic market cycles turned downward. As a result, many ventures failed. During the time needed to gear up for the export process (e.g., identifying foreign market potential, developing a marketing plan, identifying potential buyers, participating in foreign trade shows, finding foreign sales representatives and establishing channels of distribution, arranging for trade finance, etc.), the domestic cycles would turn again, and U.S. companies would soon lose their new-found interest in selling overseas. These same firms would ship products abroad with no thought given to the problems of marketing in foreign cultures or to how they would supply parts or service for the products they sold. Without a long-term commitment, these firms were viewed by foreign buyers as unreliable suppliers. Companies that tried to find foreign buyers or investment partners soon learned that entering international markets required much patience, time, and commitment.

Recently, U.S. managers have undergone a difficult and arduous retraining process. They have had to be retrained to negotiate, sell, manage, and compete with their foreign counterparts in foreign environments. They now recognize that cultural and ethnic differences will influence their business dealings overseas. They are aware, for example, of the influence of religion on business in the Middle East, of the impact of the reunification of a once-divided Germany on the German people, and of their image as arrogant, rich Yankees when doing

business in Panama or Mexico. U.S. managers are learning to be sensitive to labor issues in Haiti and southern Africa and to the feelings of some Canadians who seek to preserve the use of the French language in Quebec.

U.S. managers are also keenly aware of the necessity of keeping abreast of the day-to-day changes in the world's economic and political events. U.S. multinational corporations, international banks and brokerage houses, insurance companies, air and ocean carriers, international architectural and construction firms, overseas branches of U.S. law firms, trading companies, and many others all feel the impact of world events. Morning television now gives nearly instantaneous foreign exchange quotations and the results of opening trading on stock exchanges around the world. International managers must scrutinize political events carefully, and their impact on business is evaluated continually. War in the Middle East can disrupt shipping, an oil spill in foreign waters means negotiations with foreign governments, and the toppling of a communist government can mean great political instability—or it can mean great opportunity. The experienced international manager is continually reassessing these global economic and political situations to gauge their impact on the firm's operations.

**http://usinfo.state.gov/products/
pubs/trade/homepage.htm**

For a glossary of international trade terms, a list of the most common acronyms used in international trade, and a chronology of major international trade events since 1916, see *The Language of Trade*, published online by the U.S. State Department.

FORMS OF INTERNATIONAL BUSINESS

This text classifies international business into three categories: (1) trade, (2) international licensing of technology and intellectual property (trademarks, patents, and copyrights), and (3) foreign direct investment. To the marketer, these broad categories describe three important methods for entering a foreign market. To the lawyer, they also represent the form of doing business in a foreign country and the legal relationship between parties to a business transaction. Each method brings a different set of problems to the firm because the level of *foreign penetration* and entanglement in that country is different. Trade usually represents the least entanglement, and thus, the least political, economic, and legal risk, especially if the exporting firm is not soliciting business overseas or maintaining sales agents or inventories there. An investment in a plant and operations overseas usually represents the greatest market penetration and thus, the greatest risk to the firm.

Considerable overlap occurs among these different forms of doing business. A business plan for the production and marketing of a single product may contain elements of each form. To illustrate, a U.S. firm might purchase the rights to a trademark for use on an article of high-fashion clothing made from fabric exported from China and assembled in offshore plants in the Caribbean for shipment to the United States and Europe. Here, a business strategy encompasses elements of trade, licensing, and investment. For firms just entering a new foreign market, the method of entry might depend on a host of considerations, including the sophistication of the firm, its overseas experience, the nature of its product or services, its commitment of capital resources, and the amount of risk it is willing to bear.

Trade

Trade consists of the import and export of goods and services. *Exporting* is the term generally used to refer to the process of sending goods out of a country, and *importing* is used to denote when goods are brought into a country. However, a more accurate definition is that *exporting is the shipment of goods or the rendering of services to a foreign buyer located in a foreign country. Importing* is then defined as *the process of buying goods from a foreign supplier and entering them into the customs territory of a different country.* Every export entails an import, and vice versa.

Trade is as old as the oldest civilization. Throughout history, countries traded to obtain needed items that were not readily available in their country. The marketplaces of Europe, Africa, Asia, and the Middle East had been the scene of trade for hundreds of years before seaborne trade became established. By the sixteenth century, the first international sea trade routes were established by the Europeans. With the advent of great naval power, Portugal and Spain opened the Americas,

India, and the Pacific to trade. Portuguese was the language of the ocean traders. Portugal purchased textiles from India and China with gold taken from Africa. They traded Chinese porcelain to Spain for gold that Spain had taken from Mexico. By the eighteenth century, the Dutch had created a great trading empire based on pepper and spices, and England relied on America for tobacco, corn, and cotton. And for more than three hundred years, trade in horses, weapons, and slaves thrived.

> **http://www.firstgov.gov**
> For easy access to all U.S. government Web sites.

Comparative Advantage. Today the products are different, but the economic concepts are the same. In theoretical terms, the concept of *absolute advantage* states that nations should concentrate their efforts on producing those goods that they can make most efficiently, with a minimum of effort and waste. Any surplus of goods left over after domestic consumption is then traded for goods that another nation has produced under the same circumstances. David Ricardo, a nineteenth-century British economist, stated that a country can gain from trading goods even though it may not have an absolute advantage in producing those goods. This notion formed the basis for the theory of *comparative advantage.* Comparative advantage exists if the costs of production and price received for the goods allow the goods to be sold for a higher price in a foreign country than at home. When countries specialize in producing goods over which they have a comparative advantage, all countries will produce more, consume more, and wealth and employment will increase. An example from the early trading days illustrates how this concept works.

By the sixteenth century, Portugal had already established outposts for trading silk, cloth, and spices throughout the Indian Ocean. The Portuguese had also found ways of trading with far-away China. Portuguese traders discovered that although they could get silk most easily from their outposts in Persia or India, it would be to their benefit to obtain these products from China. China had greater resources and more effective production methods, which made their products less costly and of a better quality than anything that Portugal could obtain elsewhere. China, on the other hand, had a great appetite for the pepper that Portugal could obtain readily from Indian outposts. China could produce its own pepper, but not of the same quantity or quality that the Portuguese traders could provide. Although Portugal had its own source of silk, and China its own pepper, their advantage came from obtaining these goods from one another. Thus, Portugal had a comparative advantage in pepper and China in silk. By focusing their capital and labor on doing what they did best, each country could produce and consume more of both products.

It is important to emphasize that this transaction was not regulated by today's barrage of tariffs, government subsidies to producers, politics, historical events, or other complicating factors. Michael Porter, in *The Competitive Advantage of Nations,* introduced a modification of this earlier concept, advocating that a nation's advantage is determined by the ability of its companies to increase productivity and continuously innovate. In today's world, the politics of protectionism or free trade could turn an economic model inside out. But world trade has developed and become the major commercial activity that it is today based upon this principle of comparative advantage.

Recent Trends in U.S. Trade. Since the 1970s, U.S. imports have increased dramatically, outpacing the growth in exports. This has led to a growing trade deficit for the nation that has continued to this day. In the early 1980s, the trade deficit was blamed on the high value of the U.S. dollar, which made U.S. goods expensive for export to foreign buyers (who had to exchange their currencies for dollars in order to buy U.S. goods). The decade of the 1980s, however, saw intense international efforts, coordinated by central banks in the United States, Japan, and Europe, to bring the value of the dollar down (to the chagrin of U.S. tourists abroad). During the 1980s, the U.S. dollar had sunk to record lows against most major foreign currencies (which boosted exports, but prompted fears of inflation due to the high cost of imported goods). In another attempt to boost U.S. exports, the U.S. government initiated a large-scale incentive and public awareness program to encourage small- and medium-sized manufacturers and service companies to enter foreign markets. During the 1980s, reports showed that a mere 250 of the

largest U.S. multinational corporations accounted for 85 percent of U.S. exports. The U.S. Department of Commerce believed that a great number of smaller U.S. firms had products suitable for export markets if they would only make the commitment needed to tap those potential customers. To assist these "new-to-export" companies, the Department of Commerce spearheaded a national effort to introduce small firms to the how-to's of exporting. By the end of the decade, many of these new-to-export companies were contributing significantly to the U.S. export base.

By 1999, according to the U.S. Department of Commerce *Exporter Database,* there were over 231,000 individual companies exporting goods from the United States, up from 112,000 in 1992. Of these, nearly 97 percent were small- or medium-sized businesses, with fewer than five hundred employees, and remarkably, almost 70 percent had fewer than twenty employees. Of course, large companies still dominate the total share of U.S. export volume. Although their largest markets are in Canada, Mexico, and Japan, the fastest growing markets for small exporters are such countries as Brazil, Malaysia, and China, and these businesses generated nearly 40 percent of U.S. exports to China and Hong Kong in 1997. These figures illustrate the success with which more and more small- to medium-sized U.S. firms are entering foreign markets, and the impact of their efforts on the U.S. economy.

Another trend also worked to increase American exports in the 1990s. Foreign firms that had invested heavily in U.S. factories were turning their attention to exporting their U.S.-made products. Honda Motor Company, for example, exports sizeable numbers of automobiles from its U.S. plants to many countries, including Japan. A study of one state, North Carolina, showed that a large percentage—more than 50 percent—of foreign-owned firms operating in that state were exporting their products abroad. In the 1990s, as U.S. firms became more competitive, and as economic growth in Europe and in the developing countries provided markets for U.S. goods and services, U.S. exports continued to increase.

Despite the actual increase in U.S. exports through the 1990s, imports of foreign goods into the United States have continued to increase at a faster rate. As a result, the United States has continued to have increasingly large trade deficits. In 2002, the U.S. Department of Commerce reported on a census basis that U.S. exports of goods amounted to $694 billion (down from 2000 and 2001). In the same year, U.S. imports of goods amounted to more than $1,164 billion, for a trade in goods deficit of $470 billion. There are many explanations for the trade deficit, including comparative rates of economic growth between nations, investment flows across national borders, changes in currency rates over time and many other factors. Despite general concern over the trade deficit, there is actually no agreement on whether trade deficits are harmful to the economy.

During the last ten years, the U.S. share of world merchandise exports remained fairly constant, at about 12 percent. The United States is still the world's largest exporter, followed by Germany, Japan, China, Canada, France, and the United Kingdom. America's top trading partner is Canada, followed by Mexico, Japan, China, Germany, the United Kingdom, South Korea, Taiwan, France, and Italy. Of these, America's trade deficit was largest with China, Japan, and Canada. The countries with whom the United States had the largest surplus in 2001 were the Netherlands, Australia, and Hong Kong. Some of the best prospects for future export growth are predicted to be in the emerging markets of developing countries.

The importance of trade to the U.S. economy cannot be overstressed. According to the U.S. Department of Commerce, U.S. exports of goods and services account for a substantial portion of real gross domestic product growth. This has been especially important during recessionary periods, when exports continued to fuel growth in the economy. Estimates are that during the mid-1990s, exports accounted for 51 percent of the new jobs in the United States, and for virtually all of the increase in manufacturing jobs. The Office of the United States Trade Representative estimates that wages paid to U.S. workers in export manufacturing industries are about 17 percent higher than average. The top-ten U.S. exporting states are Texas, California, New York, Michigan, Washington, Illinois, Ohio, New Jersey, Florida, and Pennsylvania.

Trade in Services. Trade in services includes business services such as travel, banking, insur-

ance, and securities brokerage. It also includes professional services such as law, accounting, or architecture, and technical services such as waste management, industrial and environmental engineering, software development, and management consulting. In the developed countries of Europe, Japan, Canada, and the United States, business services have actually accounted for the majority of the gross domestic product, jobs, and job growth in recent years. Cross-border trade in services accounts for over 20 percent of world trade. Exports of services by the United States have been rising steadily ($289 billion in 2002), leaving the United States with a 2002 trade surplus in services of $49 billion.

Exporting

Trade is often a firm's first step into international business. Compared to the other forms of international business (licensing and investment), trade is relatively uncomplicated. It provides the inexperienced or smaller firm with an opportunity to penetrate a new market, or at least to explore foreign market potential, without significant capital investment and the risks of becoming a full-fledged player (i.e., citizen) in the foreign country. For many larger firms, including multinational corporations, exporting may be an important portion of their business operations. The U.S. aircraft industry, for example, relies heavily on exports for significant revenues.

Firms that have not done business overseas before should first prepare an export plan, which may mean assembling an export team, composed possibly of management and outside advisors and trade specialists. Their plan should include the assessment of the firm's readiness for exporting, the export potential of its products or services, the firm's willingness to allocate resources (including financial, production output, and human resources), and the selection of its channels of distribution. The firm may need to modify products, design new packaging and foreign language labeling, and meet foreign standards for product performance or quality assurance. The firm must also gauge the extent to which it can perform export functions in-house or whether these functions should best be handled indirectly through an independent export company. Export functions include foreign marketing, sales and distribution, shipping, and handling international transfers of money.

Firms accept varying levels of responsibility for moving goods and money and for other export functions. The more experienced exporters can take greater responsibility for themselves and are more likely to export directly to their foreign customers. Firms that choose to accept less responsibility in dealing with foreign customers, or in making arrangements for shipping, for example, must delegate many export functions to someone else. As such, exporting is generally divided into two types: direct and indirect.

Direct Exporting.   At first glance, *direct exporting* seems similar to selling goods to a domestic buyer. A prospective foreign customer may have seen a firm's products at a trade show, located a particular company in an industrial directory, or been recommended by another customer. A firm that receives a request for product and pricing information from a foreign customer may be able to handle it routinely and export directly to the buyer. With some assistance, a firm can overcome most hurdles, get the goods properly packaged and shipped, and receive payment as anticipated. Although many of these one-time sales are turned into long-term business success stories, many more are not. A firm hopes to develop a regular business relationship with its new foreign customer. However, the problems that can be encountered even in direct exporting are considerable.

Many firms engaged in direct exporting on a regular basis reach the point at which they must hire their own full-time export managers and international sales specialists. These people participate in making export marketing decisions, including product development, pricing, packaging, and labeling for export. They should take primary responsibility for dealing with foreign buyers, for attending foreign trade shows, for complying with government export and import regulations, for shipping, and for handling the movement of goods and money in the transaction. Direct exporting is often done through *foreign sales agents* who work on commission. It also can

be done by selling directly to *foreign distributors.* Foreign distributors are independent firms, usually located in the country to which a firm is exporting, that purchase goods for resale to their customers. They assume the risks of buying and warehousing goods in their market and provide additional product support services. The distributor usually services the products they sell, thus, relieving the exporter of that responsibility. They often train end users to use the product, extend credit to their customers, and bear responsibility for local advertising and promotion.

Indirect Exporting.   *Indirect exporting* is used by companies seeking to minimize their involvement abroad. Lacking experience, personnel, or capital, they may be unable to locate foreign buyers or are not yet ready to be handling the mechanics of a transaction on their own. There are several different types of indirect exporting. *Export trading companies,* commonly called ETCs, are companies that market the products of several manufacturers in foreign markets. They have extensive sales contacts overseas and experience in air and sea shipping. They often operate with the assistance and financial backing of large banks, thus making the resources and international contacts of the bank's foreign branches available to the manufacturers whose products they market. Since the mid-1980s, ETCs have been able to apply for and receive a certificate from the U.S. Department of Justice that waives the application of U.S. antitrust laws to their export activities. This waiver makes it lawful for many manufacturers to cooperate in exporting to foreign markets, when such collusion might otherwise be illegal under the antitrust laws of the United States. For example, if two competing firms that manufacture similar products agree to fix prices in the U.S. market, it would be illegal. However, if they are members of an ETC, with waivers from the Department of Commerce and the Department of Justice, they may jointly establish export prices, enter into joint export marketing arrangements, allocate export territories, and do business in ways that if done with the U.S. market would be illegal. Many of the world's largest export trading companies, even those that export U.S.-made products, are Japanese owned.

Export management companies, or EMCs, on the other hand, are really consultants that advise manufacturers and other exporters. They are used by firms that cannot justify their own in-house export managers. They engage in foreign market research, identify overseas sales agents, exhibit goods at foreign trade shows, prepare documentation for export, and handle language translations and shipping arrangements. As in direct exporting, all forms of indirect exporting can involve sales through agents or to distributors.

Importing and Global Sourcing

When reading this text, the reader should keep in mind that importing is not to be viewed in the isolated context of a single transaction. True, many importers do import only on a limited or one-time basis. However, in this book importing is presented from the perspective of the global firm for which importing is a regular and necessary part of their business. *Global sourcing* is the term commonly used to describe the process by which a firm attempts to locate and purchase goods or services on a worldwide basis. These goods may include, for example, raw materials for manufacturing, component parts for assembly operations, commodities such as agricultural products or minerals, or merchandise for resale.

Government Controls over Trade: Tariffs and Nontariff Barriers

Both importing and exporting are governed by the laws and regulations of the countries through which goods or services pass. A central portion of this text will be devoted to understanding why and how nations regulate trade, known as *international trade law*. Nations regulate trade in many ways. The most common methods are *tariffs* and *nontariff barriers*. Tariffs are import duties or taxes imposed on goods entering the customs territory of a nation. Tariffs are imposed for many reasons, including (1) the collection of revenue, (2) the protection of domestic industries from foreign competition, and (3) political control (e.g., to provide incentives to import products from politically friendly countries and to discourage importing products from unfriendly countries).

Nontariff Barriers to Trade. Nontariff barriers are *all barriers to importing or exporting other than tariffs*. Nontariff barriers are generally a greater barrier to trade than are tariffs because they are more insidious. Unlike tariffs, which are published and easily understood, nontariff barriers are often disguised in the form of government rules or industry regulations and are often not understood by foreign companies. Countries impose nontariff barriers to protect their national economic, social, and political interests. Imports might be banned for health and safety reasons. Imported goods usually have to be marked with the country-of-origin and labeled in the local language so that consumers know what they are buying. One form of nontariff barrier is the *technical barrier to trade,* or *product standard*. Examples of product standards include safety standards, electrical standards, and environmental standards (e.g., German cars meeting U.S. emission standards not mandated in Europe). A *quota* is a restriction imposed by law on the numbers or quantities of goods, or of a particular type of good, allowed to be imported. Unlike tariffs, quotas are not internationally accepted as a lawful means of regulating trade except in some special cases. An *embargo* is a total or near total ban on trade with a particular country, sometimes enforced by military action and usually imposed for political purposes. An internationally orchestrated embargo was used against Iraq after its invasion of Kuwait in 1990. A *boycott* is a refusal to trade or do business with certain firms, usually from a particular country, on political or other grounds.

Tariffs and nontariff barriers have a tremendous influence on how firms make their trade and investment decisions. These decisions, in turn, are reflected in the patterns of world trade and the flows of investment capital. Consider this illustration. In 1992, the European nations lowered trade barriers between themselves. In the years prior to this event, companies from the United States, Canada, and Japan invested heavily in Europe. They purchased ongoing firms there and established new ones. If they had stayed on "outside" and remained contented to export to Europe, they would have lost competitiveness to European firms who could take advantage of the new lowered trade barriers. But by manufacturing there, they could sell within Europe on the same basis as other European firms. Similar capital investment flows occurred in Mexico in the early 1990s as a result of Mexico's closer trade ties to the United States and Canada. For example, when Japanese firms learned that Mexican-made products could be traded in North America with lowered tariffs and nontariff barriers, companies from Japan quickly sought to establish manufacturing facilities in Mexico to take advantage of changes in trade laws.

Trade Liberalization and the World Trade Organization.   *Trade liberalization* refers to the efforts of governments to reduce tariffs and nontariff barriers to trade. In the twentieth century, the most important effort to liberalize trade came with the international acceptance of the *General Agreement on Tariffs and Trade.* This is an agreement between nations, first signed in 1947, and continually expanded since that time, that sets the rules for how nations will regulate international trade in goods and services. In 1995, the Geneva-based *World Trade Organization,* or WTO, was created to administer the rules and to assist in settling trade disputes between its member nations. All WTO nations are entitled to *normal trade relations* with one another. This is referred to as *Most Favored Nation* trading status. This means that a member country must charge the same tariff on imported goods, and not a higher one, as that charged on the same goods coming from other WTO member countries. Trade liberalization has led to increased economic development and an improved quality of life around the world.

Export Controls.   Another type of restriction over trade is export control. An *export control* limits the type of product that may be shipped to any particular country. They are usually imposed for economic or political purposes and are used by all nations of the world. For instance, high-tech computers might not be allowed to be shipped from the United States or Canada to another country without a license from the U.S. or Canadian government. Before signing a contract for the sale of certain products or technical know-how to a foreign customer, U.S. exporters must consider whether they will be able to obtain U.S. licensing for the shipment.

Intellectual Property Rights and International Licensing Agreements

Intellectual property rights are a grant from a government to an individual or firm of the exclusive legal right to use a copyright, patent, or trademark for a specified time. *Copyrights* are legal rights to artistic or written works, including books, software, films, music, or to such works as the layout design of a computer chip. *Trademarks* include the legal right to use a name or symbol that identifies a firm or its product. *Patents* are governmental grants to inventors assuring them of the exclusive legal right to produce and sell their inventions for a period of years. Copyrights, trademarks, and patents compose substantial assets of many domestic and international firms. As valuable assets, intellectual property can be sold or licensed for use to others through a licensing agreement.

International licensing agreements are contracts by which the holder of intellectual property will grant certain rights in that property to a foreign firm under specified conditions and for a specified time. Licensing agreements represent an important foreign market entry method for firms with marketable intellectual property. For example, a firm might license the right to manufacture and distribute a certain type of computer chip or the right to use a trademark on apparel such as bluejeans or designer clothing. It might license the right to distribute Hollywood movies or to reproduce and market word-processing software in a foreign market, or it might license its patent rights to produce and sell a high-tech product or pharmaceutical. United States firms have extensively licensed their property around the world, and in recent years have purchased the technology rights of Japanese and other foreign firms.

A firm may choose licensing as its market entry method because licensing can provide a greater entrée to the foreign market than is possible through exporting. A firm may realize many advantages in having a foreign company produce and sell products based on its intellectual property instead of simply shipping finished goods to that market. When exporting to a foreign market, the firm must overcome obstacles such as long-distance shipping and the resulting delay in filling orders.

Exporting requires a familiarity with the local culture. Redesign of products or technology for the foreign market may be necessary. Importantly, an exporter may have to overcome trade restrictions, such as quotas or tariffs, set by the foreign government. Licensing to a foreign firm allows the licensor to circumvent trade restrictions by having the products produced locally, and it allows entrance to the foreign market with minimal initial start-up costs. In return, the licensor might choose to receive a guaranteed return based on a percentage of gross revenues. This arrangement ensures payment to the licensor whether or not the licensee earns a profit. Even though licensing agreements give the licensor some control over how the licensee utilizes its intellectual property, problems can arise. For instance, the licensor may find that it cannot police the licensee's manufacturing or quality control process. Protecting itself from the unauthorized use or "piracy" of its copyrights, patents, or trademarks by unscrupulous persons not party to the licensing agreement is also a serious concern for the licensor. The *First Flight Associates* case illustrates what can happen to a firm that fails to take proper legal steps to protect its trademark rights in a foreign country. Notice how this firm's strategy involved both exporting and licensing.

Protecting Intellectual Property Rights. Rights in property can be rendered worthless if those rights cannot be protected by law. The protection of intellectual property is a matter of national law (as in the United States where it is protected primarily under federal statutes). However, intellectual property rights granted in one nation are not legally recognized and enforceable in another, unless the owner takes certain legal steps to protect those rights under the laws of that foreign country. Most developed countries, such as Canada, Western Europe, and Japan, have laws that protect the owners of intellectual property, and they enforce those laws. However, copyrights, patents, and trademarks are widely pirated in the developing countries of Asia, Latin America, Africa, Russia, Eastern Europe, and the Middle East, whose protection laws are often nonexistent or not enforced. Indeed, some developing countries encourage piracy because of the perceived financial gains to their economies. Some products deemed indispensable to the public, such as pharmaceuticals and chemi-

cals, are often not covered by patent laws at all in these countries.

Lost profits and lost royalties to U.S. firms now amount to billions of dollars each year in counterfeited goods sold overseas. But international efforts are being made to rectify the problem. At the behest of U.S. movie and record producers, pharmaceutical manufacturers, software makers, and publishers, the United States has encouraged these countries to pass legislation protecting intellectual property and to ensure the enforcement of these laws. For instance, in 1991, the People's Republic of China acted to avert a trade war with the United States by agreeing to bring its intellectual property laws in line with those in other developing countries. The United States threatened to impose punitive tariffs on Chinese goods (toys, games, footwear, clothing, and textiles). China announced stricter enforcement efforts and a new copyright law, and a major trade war was averted. Today, the protection of property rights abroad is a principal objective of U.S. trade policy. Industry groups estimated in 2002 that U.S. firms are losing an estimated $1.8 billion per year in China and over $9 billion worldwide.

Technology Transfer. The exchange of technology and manufacturing know-how between firms in different countries through arrangements such as licensing agreements is known as *technology transfer*. Transfers of technology and know-how are regulated by government control in some countries. This control is common when the licensor is from a highly industrialized country such as the United States and the licensee is located in a developing country such as those in Latin America, the Middle East, or Asia. In their efforts to industrialize, modernize, and develop a self-sufficiency in technology and production methods, these countries often restrict the terms of licensing agreements in a manner benefiting their own country. For instance, government regulation might require that the licensor introduce its most modern technology to the developing countries or train workers in its use.

International Franchising. Franchising is a form of licensing that is gaining in popularity worldwide. The most common form of franchising is known as a *business operations franchise*, usually used in retailing. Under a typical franchising agreement, the franchisee is allowed to use a trade name

First Flight Associates v. Professional Golf Co., Inc.
527 F.2d 931 (1975)
United States Court of Appeals (6th Cir.)

BACKGROUND AND FACTS

Pro Golf, a U.S. company, manufactured and sold golf equipment under the brand name "First Flight," which had been registered in the United States and certain other foreign countries. In 1961 Pro Golf negotiated with Robert Wynn to act as their foreign sales representative in Japan. Wynn incorporated First Flight Associates, Inc. (FFA) under Japanese law for the purposes of selling Pro Golf's products there. No formal agency or distributorship agreement was ever entered into by the parties. In 1967 the parties entered into a trademark agreement, whereby FFA was permitted to use Pro Golf's "First Flight" trademark on golf soft goods, such as golf bags and clothing, in return for the payment of a royalty. FFA attempted to sublicense the trademark to another Japanese company, Teito, for a royalty much larger than that paid to Pro Golf. When Pro Golf objected, the company learned that its attempt to register the trademark in Japan had not been completely successful, but that third parties had obtained the right to use the trademark in Japan in marketing certain types of soft goods. Pro Golf terminated the agency agreement with FFA, and FFA brought this action for breach of contract.

MARKEY, CHIEF JUDGE

The issue on appeal is whether the district court erred in finding that . . . Pro Golf was entitled to terminate the sales representation contract; . . . and that FFA was not liable under the counterclaims for royalties received from Teito or for Pro Golf's expenditures relating to its trademark rights in Japan. . . .

As to the initial 1961 contract for Japanese sales representation on clubs and balls, we agree with the district court that Pro Golf effectively and lawfully terminated FFA as its representative, the termination being effective as of the end of July 1973. That termination did not breach the contract. . . .

The contract was clearly therefore one for an indefinite period of time. Contracts silent on time of termination are generally terminable at will by either party with reasonable notice. . . .

It is unnecessary to discuss the conduct of Wynn or FFA under the trademark license contract or whether "satisfactory business" was being done under the sales representation contract. The latter contract being terminable at will, Pro Golf was clearly within its rights in terminating it.

Pro Golf contends that royalties paid to FFA by Teito should have been passed through to Pro Golf. That contention is based on Pro Golf's fundamentally unsound characterization of FFA as its agent in entering into the Teito contract. As we have indicated, that contract is a trademark sub-license, wherein FFA conveyed to Teito some or all of its rights to use "First Flight" in Japan as a trademark on "soft goods," which rights FFA had under its license from Pro Golf. Nothing in FFA's trademark license contract with Pro Golf prohibited FFA from granting sub-licenses to others or required FFA to pass along to Pro Golf any royalties FFA might receive from such sub-licenses.

Pro Golf also counterclaimed for damages equal to its expenditures incurred in attempting to perfect its Japanese rights in "First Flight" as applied to certain golf soft goods. Pro Golf's difficulties stemmed from its own failure to obtain complete registration in Japan of "First Flight" in all of the relevant classes of goods. Under Japanese trademark law, rights are acquired through registration and not through use in commerce as in the United States. Although Pro Golf had exclusive rights in "First Flight" when applied to clubs and balls and to some of the classes of soft goods on which the trademark was being used by FFA, third parties had obtained Japanese registrations of "First Flight" for use on other classes of goods, including other golf soft goods. Pro Golf found it necessary to deal with those third-party registrants in seeking to acquire exclusive rights in "First Flight" as a trademark in Japan for the entire spectrum of golf soft goods. We fully agree with the district court that FFA is not liable for expenditures incurred by reason of Pro Golf's own failure to properly register its trademark in Japan.

Accordingly, the decision of the district court is in all respects affirmed.

Decision. Pro Golf was permitted to terminate its Japanese sales agency relationship with FFA because, under U.S. law, sales agency contracts are terminable at will. However, Pro Golf was not entitled to royalties earned by FFA on soft goods bearing the "First Flight" trademark because Pro Golf had failed to perfect its rights to the use of that trademark under Japanese law.

or trademark in offering goods or services to the public in return for a royalty based on a percentage of sales or other fee structure. The franchisee will usually obtain the franchiser's know-how in operating and managing a profitable business and its other "secrets of success" (ranging from a "secret recipe" to store design to accounting methods). Franchising in the United States accounts for a large proportion of total retail sales. In foreign markets as well, franchising has been successful in fast-food retailing, hotels, car rental, video rentals, educational courses, convenience stores, printing services, and real estate services, to name but a few. U.S. firms have excelled in franchising overseas, making up the majority of new franchise operations worldwide. The prospects for future growth in foreign markets are enormous, especially in developing countries such as in the Middle East or Latin America. For instance, American fast-food and retail franchises are common throughout Mexico City. Brazil now offers one of the best opportunities for franchising, with some 27,000 franchise outlets already in operation. During the 1990s, franchising had extended into the countries of Eastern Europe and the former Soviet Union as a method of introducing private enterprise to their formerly communist-dictated economies.

Some Legal Aspects of Franchising.

Franchising is a good vehicle for entering a foreign market because the local franchisee provides capital investment, entrepreneurial commitment, and on-site management to deal with local customs and labor problems. However, many legal requirements affect franchising. Franchising in the United States is regulated primarily by the Federal Trade Commission at the federal level. The agency requires the filing of extensive disclosure statements to protect prospective investors. Other countries have also enacted new franchise disclosure laws. Some developing countries have restrictions on the amount of money that can be removed from the country by the franchiser. Moreover, some countries, such as China, also require government approval for franchise operations (although many of China's restrictions will be removed by 2004, according to international agreements). Other countries might have restrictions on importing supplies (ketchup, bed linens, paper products, or whatever) for the operation of the business to protect local

companies. However, more progressive developing countries are now abandoning these strict regulations because they want to welcome franchisers, their high quality consumer products, and their managerial talent to their markets. Because of this more receptive attitude toward foreign firms, Mexico and Brazil have become home to many profitable new franchise operations.

The *Dayan v. McDonald's* case illustrates the difficulty in supervising the operations of a franchisee in a distant foreign country. Consider how any U.S. franchiser will allow its franchisees to adapt to the cultural environment in a foreign country while still providing the same consistent quality and service that is expected whenever anyone patronizes one of their establishments anywhere in the world.

Foreign Direct Investment

In this text, the term *foreign investment,* or *foreign direct investment,* refers to the ownership and active control of ongoing business concerns, including investment in manufacturing, mining, farming, assembly operations, and other facilities of production. In 1999, there was $865 billion in foreign direct investment. The United Nations estimates that in the year 2000 foreign direct investment will surpass a record $1 trillion worldwide. Throughout the text, a distinction is made between the home and host countries of the firms involved. The *home country* refers to that country under whose laws the investing corporation was created or is headquartered. For example, the United States is home to multinational corporations such as Ford, Exxon, and IBM, to name a few, but they operate in *host countries* throughout every region of the world. Of the three forms of international business, foreign investment provides the firm with the most involvement, and perhaps the greatest risk, abroad. Investment in a foreign plant is often a result of having had successful experiences in exporting or licensing, and of the search for ways to overcome the disadvantages of those other entry methods. For example, by producing its product in a foreign country, instead of exporting, a firm can avoid quotas and tariffs on imported goods, avoid currency fluctuations on the traded goods, provide better product service and spare parts, and more quickly adapt products to local tastes and market trends. Manufacturing overseas for foreign

Dayan v. McDonald's Corp.
466 N.E.2d 958 (1984)
Appellate Court of Illinois

BACKGROUND AND FACTS

In 1971, Dayan, the plaintiff, received an exclusive franchise to operate McDonald's restaurants in Paris, France. The franchise agreement required that the franchise meet all quality, service, and cleanliness (QSC) standards set by McDonald's. Dayan acknowledged his familiarity with the McDonald's system and with the need for maintaining McDonald's quality standards and controls. The franchise agreement stated that the rationale for maintaining QSC standards was that a "departure of restaurants anywhere in the world from these standards impedes the successful operation of restaurants throughout the world, and injures the value of its [McDonald's] patents, trade-marks, tradename, and property." Dayan agreed to "maintain these standards as they presently existed" and to observe subsequent improvements McDonald's may initiate. Dayan also agreed not to vary from QSC standards without prior written approval. After several years of quality and cleanliness violations, McDonald's sought to terminate the franchise. Dayan brought this action to enjoin the termination. The lower court found that good cause existed for the termination and Dayan appealed.

BUCKLEY, PRESIDING JUSTICE

Dayan also argues that McDonald's was obligated to provide him with the operational assistance necessary to enable him to meet the QSC standards.

. . . Dayan verbally asked Sollars (a McDonald's manager) for a French-speaking operations person to work in the market for six months. Sollars testified that he told Dayan it would be difficult to find someone with the appropriate background that spoke French but that McDonald's could immediately send him an English-speaking operations man. Sollars further testified that this idea was summarily rejected by Dayan as unworkable even though he had informed Dayan that sending operations personnel who did not speak the language to a foreign country was very common and very successful in McDonald's international system. Nonetheless, Sollars agreed to attempt to locate a qualified person with the requisite language skills for Dayan.

Through Sollars' efforts, Dayan was put in contact with Michael Maycock, a person with McDonald's managerial and operational experience who spoke French. Dayan testified that he hired Maycock some time in October 1977 and placed him in charge of training, operations, quality control, and equipment.

As the trial court correctly realized: "It does not take a McDonald's-trained French-speaking operational man to know that grease dripping from the vents must be stopped and not merely collected in a cup hung from the ceiling, that dogs are not permitted to defecate where food is stored, that insecticide is not blended with chicken breading; that past-dated products should be discarded; that a potato peeler should be somewhat cleaner than a tire-vulcanizer; and that shortening should not look like crank case oil."

Clearly, Maycock satisfied Dayan's request for a French-speaking operations man to run his training program. . . . The finding that Dayan refused non-French-speaking operational assistance and that McDonald's fulfilled Dayan's limited request for a French-speaking operational employee is well supported by the record. To suggest, as plaintiff does, that an opposite conclusion is clearly evident is totally without merit. Accordingly, we find McDonald's fulfilled its contractual obligation to provide requested operational assistance to Dayan.

In view of the foregoing reasons, the judgment of the trial court denying plaintiff's request for a permanent injunction and finding that McDonald's properly terminated the franchise agreement is affirmed.

Decision. Judgment was affirmed for McDonald's. McDonald's had fulfilled all of its responsibility under the agreement to assist the plaintiff in complying with the provisions of the license. The plaintiff had violated the provisions of the agreement by not complying with the QSC standards. The plaintiff is permitted to continue operation of his restaurants, but without use of the McDonald's trademarks or name.

Comment. McDonald's has recovered in France from this public relations fiasco.

http://www.bea.doc.gov
U.S. Department of Commerce Bureau of Economic Analysis provides statistics and a comprehensive analysis of U.S. economic activity.

markets can mean taking advantage of local natural resources, labor, and manufacturing economies of scale.

Multinational Corporations

Multinational corporations are firms with significant foreign direct investment assets. They are characterized by their ability to derive and transfer capital resources worldwide and to operate facilities of production and penetrate markets in more than one country, usually on a global scale. Over the past twenty years, many writers have argued over the best name to use in referring to these companies. *Multinational enterprise* has been a popular term because it reflects the fact that many global firms are not, technically speaking, "corporations." The terms *transnational corporation* and *supranational corporation* are often used within the United Nations system, in which many internationalists argue that the operations and interests of the modern corporation "transcend" national boundaries. This text makes no play on words, and places no special meaning on any of the terms used to describe these companies.

One significant trend in business during the last half of the twentieth century has been the globalization of multinational corporations. At one time, multinational corporations were simply large domestic companies with foreign operations. Today, they are global companies. They typically make decisions and enter strategic alliances with each other without regard to national boundaries. They move factories, technology, and capital to those countries with the most hospitable laws, the lowest tax rates, the most qualified workforce, or abundant natural resources. They see market share and company performance in global and regional terms.

UNCTAD's World Investment Report. The *United Nations Conference on Trade and Development* (UNCTAD) estimates that there are about 65,000 transnational corporations (or TNCs, the term used by UNCTAD) in the world, with some 850,000 foreign affiliates. The *World Investment Report* (2002), prepared by UNCTAD, gives statis-

tics on the size of the largest of these. It ranks TNCs by their foreign assets, as well as by UNCTAD's own *transnationality index*. The index is calculated as the average of three ratios: foreign assets to total assets, foreign sales to total sales, and foreign employment to total employment. Of the world's largest 100 non-financial companies, only about one-quarter are American. The others are home based in Western Europe, Japan, Scandinavia, Canada, and Australia, with five from developing countries. In terms of foreign assets alone, the ten largest of these companies include (in order) Vodafone (UK, telecommunications), General Electric (U.S.), ExxonMobil (U.S.), Vivendi Universal (France, diversified media and telecom), General Motors (U.S.), Royal Dutch Shell (the Netherlands), British Petroleum (UK), Toyota (Japan), Telefonica (Spain, telecommunications), and Fiat (Italy). But not one American company was among the top ten according to the transnationality index. According to this calculation, the ten most "globalized" companies in 2000 (in order) were Rio Tinto (UK and Australia, mining), Thomson Corporation (Canada, media/publishing), ABB (Switzerland, electrical), Nestle (Switzerland, food/beverage), British American Tobacco (UK, food/tobacco), Electrolux (Sweden, electrical equipment), Interbrew (Belgium, food/beverage), Anglo-American (UK, mining), Astrazeneca (UK, pharmaceuticals), and Phillips (the Netherlands, electrical and electronic equipment). According to the report, the most globalized U.S. firm was Coca-Cola, and it ranked only 27th on the list. UNCTAD also ranks industries according to the transnationality index, not just individual firms. By this standard, the most globalized industries are motor vehicles, electronics and computers, and petroleum. UNCTAD also ranks global companies by their foreign sales volume. The 10 companies with the highest foreign sales volume are all in the petroleum or motor vehicle industries, with the exception of IBM (U.S., computers), which ranked 9th on the list with just over $51 billion in foreign sales. It should be noted that changes in these lists are affected largely by mergers and acquisitions of existing companies, particularly in the telecommunications industry.

Many multinational corporations garner 70 percent or more of their sales or profits from foreign markets. Examples include Gillette and Colgate (not on the UNCTAD list), as well as Exxon and Coca-Cola. Switzerland's Nestle and Roche Group (pharmaceuticals) derive only a tiny portion of total sales from their home market, with about one-third of their sales from Europe, one-third from the Americas, and one-third from the rest of the world. Most all of their profits are garnered from outside Switzerland as well. Other multinationals come from developing countries in Latin America and Asia, as well as Russia and Eastern Europe.

The Impact of Multinational Corporations.

Multinationals have a tremendous impact on the world's economy. According to UNCTAD, they employ 54 million people (other estimates go as high as 90 million), with a significant percentage of them in developing countries. This amounts to trillions of dollars in wages and taxes to governments worldwide. They have a total sales volume of $19 trillion, accounting for one-third of world exports. Various other reports show that the largest multinationals account for anywhere from one-quarter to one-third of the world's production of goods and services, and perhaps 80 percent of world industrial output. The impact of these companies is huge. They have created jobs and wealth, spawned technology, fostered social development in developing countries, and improved the quality of life of people everywhere. Of course, they are not without their critics, who point to the corporate subversion of national interests, control over governments, pollution of the environment, destruction of natural resources, and other ills associated with global corporate power. Nevertheless, most modern governments of the world today recognize the benefits of hosting multinational corporations and provide many incentives to attract them.

Subsidiaries, Joint Ventures, Mergers, and Acquisitions.

Multinational corporations wishing to enter a foreign market through direct investment can structure their business arrangements in many different ways. Their options and eventual course of action may depend on many factors, in-

cluding industry and market conditions, capitalization of the firm and financing, and legal considerations. Some of these options include the start-up of a new foreign subsidiary company, the formation of a joint venture with an existing foreign company, or the acquisition of an existing foreign company by stock purchase. These arrangements are discussed in detail in Part Four of this book. For now, keep in mind that multinational corporations are usually not a single legal entity. They are global enterprises that consist of any number of interrelated corporate entities, connected through extremely complex chains of stock ownership. Stock ownership gives the investing corporation tremendous flexibility when investing abroad.

The *wholly owned foreign subsidiary* is a "foreign" corporation organized under the laws of a foreign host country, but owned and controlled by the parent corporation in the home country. Because the parent company controls all of the stock in the subsidiary, it can control management and financial decision making.

The *joint venture* is a cooperative business arrangement between two or more companies for profit. A joint venture may take the form of a partnership or corporation. Typically, one party will contribute expertise and another the capital, each bringing its own special resources to the venture. Joint ventures exist in all regions of the world and in all types of industries. Where the laws of a host country require local ownership or that investing foreign firms have a local partner, the joint venture is an appropriate investment vehicle. *Local participation* refers to the requirement that a share of the business be owned by nationals of the host country. These requirements are gradually being reduced in most countries that, in an effort to attract more investment, are permitting wholly owned subsidiaries. Many American companies do not favor the joint venture as an investment vehicle because they do not want to share technology, expertise, and profits with another company.

Another method of investing abroad is for two companies to *merge* or for one company to purchase another ongoing firm. This option has appeal because it requires less know-how than does a new start-up and can be concluded without disruption of business activity. In 2000, there were 6,000 cross-border mergers and acquisitions, totaling $594 billion.

United States Foreign Direct Investment

The United States supports open investment policies worldwide. In its negotiations with foreign nations, notably Japan, Mexico, and Canada, the United States has pressed for a reduction of barriers to investment by U.S. firms. At the end of 2001, foreign direct investment abroad by U.S. firms reached almost $1.6 trillion (valued at cost). Total U.S.-owned assets abroad, which includes FDI and other assets, was $6.2 trillion.

Similarly, the policy of the United States encourages foreign investment in this country. This policy is based on the principle of *national treatment*—that foreign investors will be treated the same as domestic firms. There are some limitations to the rule, however. For example, under the *Exon-Florio Amendments* to the *Defense Production Act,* the president can prohibit foreign investment in such industries as atomic energy, transportation, and telecommunications, or in cases involving a potential threat to national security. Unless a specific statute limits foreign investment, the courts have generally not been willing to restrict the purchase of U.S. firms.

In the past, foreign direct investment in the United States has resulted mainly from foreign firms creating their own U.S. subsidiaries. Today, it results in large part from foreign firms acquiring or merging with existing firms, many of which are publicly owned companies. Total foreign investment in the United States, or *reverse investment,* as it is often called, rose to more than $1.5 trillion, with total U.S. assets in foreign hands at $8.1 trillion in 2001. Most investment is in manufacturing, and has come from firms in the United Kingdom, Japan, the Netherlands, Germany, and Canada. Foreign firms have acquired everything from office buildings and movie studios to factories and supermarkets. Some of the best-known companies in the United States are foreign owned, and their impact on the U.S. economy has been significant.

CONDUCTING BUSINESS IN DEVELOPING COUNTRIES

Most of the more than 190 nations in the world have not reached the same state of economic advance as have the *industrialized countries,* which in-clude the United States, Canada, Japan, and Western Europe. Rather, most countries could be classified as having economies that are either (1) developing, (2) less developed, or (3) newly industrialized. For the purposes of our discussion, a fourth category includes the newly independent republics of the former Soviet Union and Eastern Europe. These groups of countries differ in culture, geography, language, religions, and in their economic, political, and legal systems as well. Two-thirds of the world's population is located in the less-developed countries—in Africa, Latin America, the Caribbean, parts of Asia and the Pacific Rim, and the Middle East.

> **http://www.worldbank.org**
> The home page for The World Bank Group.

The Developing Countries

The *developing countries* are located in every region of the world. Examples in the Americas include Mexico and Brazil, with Brazil having the tenth largest economy in the world. In Asia, examples include the People's Republic of China (referred to as China), as well as India and Pakistan. Malaysia, Indonesia, and the Philippines in the Pacific Rim are developing countries. The oil-producing countries of the Middle East, such as Saudi Arabia and Kuwait, are also included despite their tremendous wealth because they are only in the early stages of industrialization.

The "typical" developing country is impossible to describe. Most have a large agrarian population, densely populated cities, and a plentiful supply of unskilled labor. Many support high-tech industries. Although some are rich in natural resources, such as Brazil, many others have depleted their natural resources. The protection of the environment has often taken a back seat to industrialization and economic "progress," and so pollution chokes their air and water. Toxic waste dumps threaten entire communities. Crimes such as smuggling, hijacking, robberies, organized crime, and illicit drug production are major problems. Sanitation and water systems are often inadequate. Poor communication and transportation systems make business difficult. Inadequate distribution systems make it costly to get goods to market. Floods and natural disasters, exacerbated by inappropriate agricultural and industrial policies, have disrupted entire populations. Overpopulation, homelessness, malnutrition, and disease are still common. One example of how disease can affect business is the epidemic of plague that struck India in 1994. It caused workers to flee industrial communities in fear and forced the closing of many factories. A wide disparity in social and economic classes exists in many countries, with great inequality in income between the rich and poor. Political systems differ widely in developing countries. Some developing countries have stable, democratic governments; others do not. For instance, Costa Rica has the oldest continuing democracy in Central America, dating back to 1948. Other Central and South American countries have not been stable at all and have experienced varying degrees of freedom, from parliamentary rule to military dictatorship.

---

http://

http://www.cia.gov
The home page of the U.S. Central Intelligence Agency. Go to "Library and Reference" for the CIA *World Factbook,* for country-specific statistical research.

The Economic Environment in Developing Countries

Students of economics know that the economies of the developing countries have trailed those of the industrialized countries for many complex reasons, including basic geography, political instability and civil wars, ethnic and religious rivalries, a lack of an educated middle class, government corruption, and for some, the consequences of cold war clashes between the United States and the Soviet Union. Perhaps the most important factor has been government policies unfavorable to trade and investment. Governments often imposed high import duties and import licensing requirements to protect local industries from the competition of more efficient foreign firms. This protection allowed local companies to sell inferior products at higher costs than they could have if they had not been insulated from foreign competition. Developing countries also put strict controls over the inflow of capital and technology. These policies were based on the notion that government could best direct how capital and technology should be used, instead of leaving it up to free market forces. In many cases, socialist policies led to government

ownership of businesses and industry. These policies forced many multinational corporations and other investors to stay away.

Latin America is a good example. During the 1970s and 1980s, the region suffered from increased unemployment, declining personal income, financial instability, the flight of capital, low rates of savings, and high rates of inflation. Inflation was caused partly by the printing of money to cover government spending, and by automatic indexing of wage and price increases. For example, during the 1970s and 1980s, Brazil and Argentina suffered from what has been called *hyperinflation—* several thousand percent per year—that wore away the value of their currency, destroyed the buying power of their consumers, frightened investors, and damaged public confidence in their government's ability to manage its own economy. Governments were forced to cut basic services such as health care, water, and sewage. Multinational corporations pulled their capital out of the region. Investment in factories, plants, roads, and other infrastructure fell by 30 percent during the 1980s. The inflation was so severe in Latin America that, according to the U.S. International Trade Commission and the reports of international agencies, the region's economic growth rate and living standards during the 1980s actually declined. By the late 1980s, 38 percent of households were living in poverty.

By the close of the 1990s, the overall economy of Latin America started to improve. Banking and financial systems were strengthened and fiscal controls instituted. Foreign investment increased, income rose, production and exports were up, and inflation seemed under control. (While inflation averaged about 11 percent for the region as a whole in 2002, it varied from 2 or 3 percent in some countries [Panama, El Salvador, Peru, Chile] to 30 or 40 percent in others [Argentina, Venezuela, Uruguay], down drastically from the hyperinflation of earlier decades. Then in 2001 and 2002, the region suffered its worst economic decline in decades, leading economists to believe that the economic situation in the region would remain "fragile" for some time to come. There is one certainty, however, and that is that changes in GDP, incomes, rates of inflation, production and exports, and other economic indicators will continue to vary greatly from country to country and from year to year. (See Exhibit 1.1.)

EXHIBIT 1.1

Argentina

Argentina benefits from rich natural resources, a highly literate population, an export-oriented agricultural sector, and a diversified industrial base. Over the past decade, however, the country has suffered recurring economic problems of inflation, huge external debt, capital flight, and budget deficits. Growth in 2000 was a negative 0.5%, as both domestic and foreign investors remained skeptical of the government's ability to pay debts and maintain the peso's fixed exchange rate with the US dollar. The economic situation worsened in 2001 with the widening of spreads on Argentine bonds, massive withdrawals from the banks, and a further decline in consumer and investor confidence. Government efforts to achieve a "zero deficit," to stabilize the banking system, and to restore economic growth proved inadequate in the face of the mounting economic problems. The peso's peg to the dollar was abandoned in January 2002, and the peso was floated in February; the exchange rate plunged and inflation picked up rapidly, but by mid-2002 the economy had stabilized, albeit at a lower level. Output was 14.7% below the previous year's figure, and unemployment remained high, at 21.5%. In order to reverse the crisis some economists recently have advocated that Argentina adopt the US dollar as the national currency, however, others argue tieing the economy closely to the dollar was precisely what led to Argentina's current problems.

Note: In 2002, Argentina's economy declined by 10.9% and defaulted on over $60 billion in loans to foreign banks, out of its total $140 billion indebtedness. Its peso was devalued by nearly 70 percent, and foreign investment drew to a halt. In 2003, a devaluation of the peso spawned a 16% surge in exports, an increase in manufacturing, and an upturn in economic growth. The newly elected Argentine president was indicating that his country's debt should be stretched out for decades.

SOURCE: *The World Factbook 2002*, U.S. Central Intelligence Agency.

Availability of Foreign Exchange in Developing Countries. Developing countries also lack a ready reserve of foreign exchange. Keep in mind that their currencies are not generally accepted for trade around the world as are the dollar, euro, or yen. A developing country's only access to foreign exchange comes from either receiving foreign payments for the export of locally made products, foreign direct investment, or foreign aid from the United States or international community. Thus,

they often cannot afford to purchase the products or technologies they need, or to undertake public construction projects of roads, sewage, hospitals, and ports. They also do not have the ability to issue debt to foreigners in their own currency. Indebtedness to foreign banks must be in a hard currency. To provide these products and services, and to repay this indebtedness, government banking restrictions have been designed to keep as much foreign exchange as possible in the country's central bank. Local companies wanting to import foreign products often have to apply to their central bank for authority to make an overseas transfer of money to their supplier. Prior to the reforms of the 1990s, their requests were often turned down, particularly when the import was a luxury or consumer good. These restrictions made entering into foreign contracts especially risky because the money might not be available to pay one's foreign suppliers. Financial reforms have largely alleviated this problem, although the scarcity of foreign currency remains.

Controls on Trade and Licensing in Developing Countries

The protectionist policies of developing countries have been implemented by restrictions on imports and on licensing, including high tariffs and other barriers to imported products that competed with locally made goods, and barriers to goods that did not contribute to the economic goals set out in national development plans. For instance, a developing country trying to industrialize might have allowed the import of tractors, hydroelectric generators, or machine tools, but not hair dryers, cosmetics, or luxury goods. Imports of foods and pharmaceuticals have been restricted in many countries to protect local producers. Even the content of foreign television shows and advertising has been restricted. For instance, India still has some of the most severe restrictions in the world. They have high tariffs and quotas on imports, import licensing requirements, a ban on the import of practically all consumer goods, and strict control over the import of commodities. Like many other developing countries, India also has many restrictions on trade in services. Foreign lawyers cannot practice in Indian courts, and foreigners cannot own a seat on an Indian stock exchange. The banking and insurance sectors are not open to foreign firms. Licensing agreements are also restricted. During the 1970s, Coca-Cola abandoned its efforts to negotiate a licensing agreement for a bottling operation in India after the Indian government insisted that the company disclose its secret formula for making Coke and required that at least 60 percent of Coke's bottling operations there be Indian owned. Other developing countries with strict barriers to imports include China, Egypt, Indonesia, Malaysia, Pakistan, and the Philippines. They severely limit trade in both goods and services. A few countries, such as newly industrialized Singapore, have a very open trade environment. Latin America is also opening its doors rapidly.

Controls on Investment in Developing Countries

Developing countries have also maintained strict controls over investment by foreign firms. Restrictions on investment have included *local participation* requirements whereby a foreign firm would have to include local investors in any new factory or business venture; a foreign firm might be allowed to own only a portion of the stock of a business, with the remainder owned by local investors. These restrictions are most severe in petroleum and energy industries, utilities, agriculture, and transportation. For example, ocean and air freight or package delivery services are often not open to foreign companies. In many countries, broadcasting companies cannot be foreign owned. In India, insurance companies and banks are still government owned.

A foreign firm that wants to open a factory in a host developing country might face many restrictions and disincentives to investment. It might be required to employ local managers, build water treatment and sewage facilities, or pay excessive taxes on earnings or property, or export a percentage of its finished goods to other countries for foreign currency. The firm might be restricted in its *repatriation of profits;* it might be required to reinvest profits in the host country instead of removing, or repatriating, them to its stockholders in its home country. As a condition of entering into a joint venture with a local firm, a foreign investor might be required to transfer its most advanced technology and products to the joint venture partner in the host country. An extreme example of

government control occurs when a country seizes the property of a foreign company, such as factories, farms, mines, or oil refineries, and takes it for its own use. This type of activity is called *nationalization* or *expropriation.* Such harsh actions resulted from the socialist-inspired belief that the seized assets could best be operated by the government itself for the benefit of the country, rather than for private profit. Nationalization and expropriation were a greater problem twenty, thirty, or forty years ago than they are today.

Doing business in a foreign country may mean subjecting one's company to foreign laws and possibly foreign courts, and carries many risks, especially in developing countries. In the following case, *In re Union Carbide Corporation Gas Plant Disaster at Bhopal,* a U.S. corporation owned the majority of stock in an Indian corporation that operated a chemical plant in Bhopal, India. The company, Union Carbide, delegated responsibility for operating the plant to local managers. The escape of poisonous chemicals resulted in the deaths of thousands of people living near the plant—the worst industrial disaster in history. Union Carbide was placed in the position of defending itself in India. As you read, consider the legal responsibility of a corporation for negligent acts committed by its subsidiaries abroad. Also, consider the risks of a multinational corporation operating in a far-off developing country.

The Road to Free Markets, Consumer-Based Economics, and Private Ownership

In the late 1980s, the more progressive developing countries, particularly in Latin America, began to give up their isolationist policies and to loosen controls over trade and investment. Today, they are trying to attract large sources of new capital for investment, new technologies, new manufacturing techniques and business know-how, improved training for their labor force, and organizational and managerial expertise. For example, developing countries are reducing tariffs on most imported products. They are gradually ending burdensome import licensing schemes and making it easier for local companies and investors to obtain foreign currency. They are reducing many kinds of taxes on business. Some countries are lowering taxes on royalties paid to foreign companies under licensing agreements for modern

In re Union Carbide Corporation Gas Plant Disaster at Bhopal
809 F.2d 195 (1987)
United States Court of Appeals (2d. Cir.)

BACKGROUND AND FACTS

This case arose out of what has been considered the most devastating industrial disaster in history—the deaths of thousands of persons (estimates range from 2000 to 4000) and injuries of several hundred thousand caused by the release of a lethal gas known as methyl isocyanate from a chemical plant operated by Union Carbide India Limited (UCIL) in Bhopal, India, in 1984. The accident occurred on the night of December 2, 1984, when winds blew the deadly gas from the plant operated by UCIL into densely occupied parts of the city of Bhopal. UCIL is incorporated under the laws of India. Fifty-one percent of its stock is owned by Union Carbide Corporation (UCC), a U.S. corporation, 22 percent is owned or controlled by the government of India, and the balance is held by approximately 23,500 Indian citizens. The stock is publicly traded on the Bombay Stock Exchange. The company is engaged in the manufacture of a variety of products, including chemicals, plastics, fertilizers, and insecticides, at 14 plants in India and employs more than 9,000 Indian citizens. Approximately 650 people are employed at the Bhopal plant. It is managed and operated entirely by Indian citizens. All products produced at Bhopal are sold in India. The operations of the plant were regulated by more than two dozen Indian governmental agencies.

Four days after the accident, the first of some 145 actions in federal district courts in the United States was commenced on behalf of victims. In the meantime, India enacted the *Bhopal Gas Leak Disaster Act,* granting to its government (the Union of India [UOI]), the exclusive right to represent the victims in India or elsewhere. In April 1985, the Indian government filed a complaint in the Southern District of New York on behalf of all of the victims. India's decision to bring suit in the United States was attributed to the fact that although nearly 6,500 lawsuits had been instituted by victims in India against UCIL, the Indian courts did not have jurisdiction over UCC, the parent company. UCC contended that the actions are properly tried in the courts of India on the doctrine of *forum non conveniens.* The district court dismissed the action on the condition that UCC submit to the jurisdiction of the Indian courts and that UCC agree to satisfy any judgment taken against it in the courts of India.

MANSFIELD, CIRCUIT JUDGE

The plaintiffs seek to prove that the accident was caused by negligence on the part of UCC in originally contributing to the design of the plant and its provision for storage of excessive amounts of the gas at the plant. As Judge Keenan found, however, UCC's participation was limited, and its involvement in plant operations terminated long before the accident. . . . The preliminary process design information furnished by UCC could not have been used to construct the plant. Construction required the detailed process design and engineering data prepared by hundreds of Indian engineers, process designers, and subcontractors. During the ten years spent constructing the plant, its design and configuration underwent many changes.

The vital parts of the Bhopal plant, including its storage tank, monitoring instrumentation, and vent gas scrubber, were manufactured by Indians in India. Although some 40 UCIL employees were given some safety training at UCC's plant in West Virginia, they represented a small fraction of the Bhopal plant's employees. The vast majority of plant employees were selected and trained by UCIL in Bhopal. The manual for start-up of the Bhopal plant was prepared by Indians employed by UCIL.

In short, the plant has been constructed and managed by Indians in India. No Americans were employed at the plant at the time of the accident. In the five years from 1980 to 1984, although more than 1,000 Indians were employed at the plant, only one American was employed there and he left in 1982. No Americans visited the plant for more than one year prior to the accident, and during the five-year period before the accident the communications between the plant and the United States were almost nonexistent.

The vast majority of material witnesses and documentary proof bearing on causation of and liability for the accident is located in India, not the United States, and would be more accessible to an Indian court than to a United States court. The records are almost entirely in Hindi or other Indian languages, understandable to an Indian court without translation. The witnesses for the most part do not speak English but Indian languages understood by an Indian court but not by an American court. These witnesses could be required to appear in an Indian court but not in a court of the United States. Although witnesses in the

continued

continued

United States could not be subpoenaed to appear in India, they are comparatively few in number and most are employed by UCC, which, as a party, would produce them in India, with lower overall transportation costs than if the parties were to attempt to bring hundreds of Indian witnesses to the United States. Lastly, Judge Keenan properly concluded that an Indian court would be in a better position to direct and supervise a viewing of the Bhopal plant, which was sealed after the accident. Such a viewing could be of help to a court in determining liability issues.

After a thorough review, the district court concluded that the public interest concerns, like the private ones, also weigh heavily in favor of India as the situs for trial and disposition of the cases. The accident and all relevant events occurred in India. The victims, over 200,000 in number, are citizens of India and located there. The witnesses are almost entirely Indian citizens. The Union of India has a greater interest than does the United States in facilitating the trial and adjudication of the victims' claims.

India's interest is increased by the fact that it has for years treated UCIL as an Indian national, subjecting it to intensive regulations and governmental supervision of the construction, development, and operation of the Bhopal plant, its emissions, water and air pollution, and safety precautions. Numerous Indian government officials have regularly conducted on-site inspections of the plant and approved its machinery and equipment, including its facilities for storage of the lethal methyl isocyanate gas that escaped and caused the disaster giving rise to the claims. Thus India has considered the plant to be an Indian one and the disaster to be an Indian problem. It therefore has a deep interest in ensuring compliance with its safety standards. Moreover, plaintiffs have conceded that in view of India's strong interest and its greater contacts with the plant, its operations, its employees, and the victims of the accident, the law of India, as the place where the tort occurred, will undoubtedly govern.

Decision.   The district court's dismissal of the actions against Union Carbide Corporation is upheld. The doctrine of *forum non conveniens* is a rule of U.S. law, which states that where a case is properly heard in more than one court, it should be heard by the one that is most convenient. Given the facts of this case, the courts of India are the more convenient forum.

Comment.   In 1989, the Supreme Court of India approved a settlement fund of $470 million to compensate the victims of the disaster.

technology and technical assistance. China, Argentina, and other countries are lifting controls over prices and wages, allowing market mechanisms to work. Gradually, developing countries are passing new, more progressive laws—protection of intellectual property, protection of the environment, protection of consumers from fraud and abuse, protection of workers, securities laws to protect investors and increase investment opportunities, and many more. Even accounting standards are changing so that investors will be given more information about a company and can better understand its financial health. Government "red tape" is being cut, allowing a faster and easier flow of paperwork through government bureaucracies, which speeds up the application process for investment and eases the way for importers to bring goods into the country. Government agencies are applying laws and regulations to foreign firms in a fairer and more consistent manner.

Capital Investment.   Several important forces allow the developing countries to find new sources of capital investment—the globalization of financial markets, the lifting of restrictions over cross-border capital flows, and the return of once state-owned industries to private owners. Although a discussion of the globalization of financial markets is beyond the scope of this book, readers should note that many large investors already seek to maximize their investment, commensurate with risk, on a global basis. Using computers and modern communications systems, investors can quickly move money, stocks, bonds, and other financial instruments almost anywhere in the world. Advanced communications have facilitated international flows of capital into all regions of the world, including developing countries. Next, developing countries that compete in these global financial markets for sources of investment find that they must give up many of their severe restrictions on investors to get it. Multinational corporations are turning to the option of building plants or entering joint ventures with local firms. Locally owned companies are also finding greater access to foreign capital. United States mutual funds are already heavily invested in Latin American and Asian stocks and bonds. Stock markets, such as the Mexican *Bolsa,* are attracting more and more investors. Personal savings rates are increasing. One major source of capital—the pension funds of employees in developing countries that were once only invested in state-owned companies—is now beginning to be invested in private companies. This tremendous infusion of capital into developing countries is spurring the growth of modern, competitive factories, new technologies, and increased productivity. Indeed, some economists believe that most of the growth in the world's economy in the next fifty years will be in the developing countries. Capital investment flows into developing countries have increased from about $30 billion in 1986 to over $500 billion for the year 2001 (down from the two prior years). Nearly 70 percent of foreign investment by the developed countries worldwide is now taking place in the developing countries.

Developing countries have also instituted new, more prudent fiscal policies. Latin American countries have reduced government borrowing and spending. Several countries, notably Brazil and Argentina, have enacted new regulations to stabilize their exchange rates. These efforts are bringing inflation under control and returning consumer and investor confidence.

Privatization. An important development in these countries is the movement toward privatization. *Privatization* refers to the process by which a government sells or transfers government-owned industries or other assets to the private sector. Privatization is happening in the developing countries and throughout the world, including Great Britain and Western and Eastern Europe. The selling of state-owned assets to private investors has caused an infusion of new capital investment, managerial know-how, technological innovation, and entrepreneurial spirit. These issues will be discussed in greater depth in Part Four of this book.

The Results of Reform. The developing countries will continue to experience economic insta-

bility for many years to come. Financial stability and economic growth, however, are beginning to return after years of decline. Jobs and personal incomes are rising. Modern factories are increasing productivity and turning out products of greater quality. As the quality of products improves, those products are more in demand in world markets, thus, increasing export earnings and access to foreign exchange. As the economies of these countries improve, they present important emerging markets for foreign products—industrial equipment, computer and telecommunications technologies, health care, and new agricultural and environmental technologies and chemicals. The developing countries are also vast untapped consumer markets. For instance, in Brazil fewer than one out of ten people own a telephone. The market for telecommunications products ranging from fiber-optic cable to cellular phones is excellent. Indeed, the United States is Latin America's leading trading partner, with exports to that region almost tripling between 1985 and 1998 (with exports leveling off and falling slightly by 2002).

Doing business in developing countries is still not like doing business in the United States or Canada, however. They have a long way to go in opening up their product and financial markets. Investors have no guarantee that inflation will not skyrocket again, nor that the value of foreign currencies will not plummet again. Most developing countries are still experiencing considerable political instability. They are far behind in education, infrastructure, and public health. In some developing countries, such as in Latin America and the Caribbean, business prospects seem good. In others, the scourge of AIDS will almost certainly forestall the hopes of economic advance.

The People's Republic of China. China has one-quarter of the world's population and one of the world's largest economies despite its communist-dominated government and centrally planned economy. As a communist player in many world markets, China represents a special area of interest to those studying international business. In the modern period, it was not until the 1970s that China began to open its doors to outside trade and investment. Since that time, China has made many changes in its economic and legal systems necessary to doing business with the West. It has opened up opportunities for collectively and privately owned enterprises, and made it easier to set up joint ventures with foreign companies. China has increased imports of technology, modernized its banking system and other service industries, encouraged Chinese companies to adopt modern management techniques and international accounting standards, and fostered the development of quality control programs in manufacturing.

During the 1990s, China grew to become one of the most attractive markets for foreign direct investment by multinational corporations from around the world. Major investors have come from Chinese Hong Kong, Taiwan, Japan, and the United States. Indeed, over one-third of all investments flowing into developing countries worldwide has gone to China. China also has undertaken legal reform needed to attract foreign companies.

Despite the reforms, China is not a democracy and it is still a communist country with an economy that is centrally regulated and administered largely by government agencies in Beijing. Its economic and regulatory reforms take place at the government's pace, balancing the need for attracting foreign investment and trade with the need for strict social and economic control. Moreover, China has almost constantly, over the last decade, been at the verge of one "trade war" or another with the United States. One area of dispute has been China's failure to stop the infringement of U.S.-owned copyrights and trademarks (e.g., the piracy of U.S.-developed and copyrighted computer software). Another area is U.S.-imposed quotas on imports of Chinese textiles and apparel. Attempts by Chinese firms to get around these quotas have consistently led to threats of retaliation by the United States. The United States has also threatened to increase duties on Chinese products for political reasons, such as imprisonment of dissidents, the use of prison labor to manufacture consumer goods, and the sale of missiles to hostile countries. Nevertheless, in 1999, the United States completed the political and economic recognition of China that was begun by President Nixon almost three decades earlier. In that year, the United States granted permanent Normal Trade Relations (NTR) to China, a step that indicates that the United States will treat goods and services coming from China just as it treats similar goods and services coming from any other friendly nation.

Today, China is America's fourth largest trading partner, supplying about 11 percent of U.S. imports. It has been said that American consumers have become reliant on inexpensive Chinese products. If this is true, then that reliance is reflected in the trade imbalance between the two countries. From 1985 to 2002, U.S. imports of Chinese-made products increased from $3.8 billion to $125 billion, leaving a trade deficit in 2002 of a staggering $103 billion, representing nearly one-quarter of the total U.S. trade deficit with the world. The U.S. deficit with China is expected to reach $120 billion in 2003, resulting in calls from labor leaders and some legislators for greater restrictions on imports from China. In 2001, China became a full-fledged member of the world-trading community when it joined the WTO, the international organization that sets the rules for international trade in goods and services.

The Newly Industrialized Countries

The *newly industrialized countries,* primarily in southeast Asia, have made tremendous economic progress in recent years due to a highly motivated workforce and a stable climate for foreign investment. These countries export a broad mix of high-quality products, from computers to steel, attracting a reserve of foreign exchange. Their success has led to a dramatic rise in per capita gross domestic product and to improvements in jobs, wages, education, health care, living accommodations, and the overall quality of life. Most notable among these countries are the four "Asian Tigers": Hong Kong, Singapore, Taiwan, and South Korea. Hong Kong is one of the largest banking centers in the world. In 1997, Hong Kong reverted to Chinese control after having been a British colony for one hundred years. Hong Kong is a gateway for moving goods, money, and people into and out of China, and is important to China's economic future. It remains to be seen how Chinese control over Hong Kong will affect the island's social and economic future.

The Less-Developed Countries

The prospects for business in the *less-developed countries* are not as good as in those regions already discussed. The less-developed countries are located primarily in sub-Saharan Africa. Examples might be Rwanda, Ethiopia, or Somalia in Africa, Haiti in the Caribbean, or countries of Central Asia. They lack many of the basic resources needed for development and require vast amounts of foreign aid from the wealthier nations. Many of these countries have inadequate roads and bridges, inadequate public utilities and telephone systems, poor educational and health care facilities, a lack of plentiful drinking water, unstable governments, little or no technological base, illiteracy, high infant mortality, AIDS and other diseases, rampant crime, excessive armaments, ethnic and tribal warfare, and weak or nonexistent financial institutions. Their economies are often based on agriculture, mining, some assembly operations, and some manufacturing. Their reserves of foreign exchange are limited. Most of these countries lack a market-based economy that characterizes the developed world. Business opportunities for trade in consumer goods and for the products and services of most western companies are limited. Less-developed countries are in need of investments and products that will help them in dealing with these basic problems.

THE BUSINESS ENVIRONMENT IN EASTERN EUROPE, RUSSIA, AND THE NEWLY INDEPENDENT REPUBLICS OF THE FORMER SOVIET UNION

Until its breakup in 1991, the Soviet Union extended from Eastern Europe on the west, across two continents to the Pacific Ocean, and from China and Central Asia on the south to the Arctic Ocean on the north. It was the third most populated nation in the world, after China and India, comprising more than one hundred different ethnic groups. It consisted of the Slavic republics of Russia, Byelorussia, and the Ukraine; the Baltic States of Latvia, Estonia, and Lithuania; the Caucasus that includes Armenia and Georgia; and the largely Moslem Central Asian republics that extend geographically from the Caspian Sea to the Mongolian border. When the Soviet Union collapsed in 1991, it changed the political and economic landscape of Europe and much of Asia. The Soviet republics gained independence. Russia emerged as the largest

of these, called the *Russian Federation*. Eastern Europe, which borders the Soviet Union, was freed from Soviet and communist domination. Poland, Hungary, Bulgaria, East Germany, Romania, and Czechoslovakia experienced political and economic reform. The Berlin Wall fell, and communist East Germany was reunited with democratic West Germany (the Federal Republic of Germany).

The Transition from Communism to Free Markets and Private Enterprise

These countries are striving to free their economies from years of communist control by liberalizing controls over trade and investment. They are rapidly privatizing their industries, turning formerly state-owned properties over to private ownership and management. New investors from the United States, Germany, Japan, and other countries are entering joint ventures with Russian and Eastern European firms. Russian citizens are investing in their own companies. Inefficient plants are closing. Russia represents an enormous potential market for modern consumer goods, housing, and industrial equipment. Russia has a highly trained technical workforce, including superb engineers, scientists, and technicians. Russian and Eastern European managers are attending business schools in the United States for management training. International economic aid is pouring into the region. Their governments are hoping for closer ties to the United States and Western Europe.

For more than seventy years these countries operated under an economic and political system in which the state owned all natural resources, factories, farms, and other means of production. The allocation of resources, as well as production and pricing decisions, were dictated by government agencies based on their central economic plans. Because production and the supply of goods were not dictated by demand forces, consumer tastes and preferences became irrelevant. Consumer industries were totally neglected, operating with inefficient, antiquated machinery. The economy was based on military and defense industries. Illegal "black markets" provided some western consumer goods to those few who could obtain much sought-after foreign currency.

Today, the newly emerging nations of the former Soviet Union are suffering from the results of seventy years of economic neglect. Many roads, bridges, and railroads are near collapse. Transportation systems are in disrepair. Power plants are deteriorating, and the risk of a serious nuclear disaster is high. Years of communist rule have caused damaging pollution of the land, air, and waters. Toxic waste has been abandoned near populated communities, causing terrible epidemics of disease and death. Oil spills, far worse than the *Exxon Valdez,* have been reported. Food shortages exist because no distribution system exists to harvest the food and bring it to market. The state-owned industries provide no worker incentive and therefore experience low productivity. Many workers do not show for work at all. Alcoholism is a severe problem. Machinery and equipment are antiquated. Many factories have simply ceased to operate because of a lack of raw materials, constant breakdowns, and an absence of spare parts. To complicate matters, in the transition from a state-owned and state-run system, people are confused as to who is really in charge of the factories and farms. After so many years of communism, most workers lack managerial skills and the understanding of how to run a company in a free market.

The economies of these countries, especially Russia, are plagued by fraud and corruption. Criminals have preyed on unsuspecting and inexperienced foreign investors and on Russian citizens unaccustomed to doing business in a free market economy. Organized crime and gangs extort "protection money." In what some reporters have described as a "Wild West atmosphere," private businesses have resorted to armed guards to protect their assets. Laws affecting business and commercial transactions are often contradictory and unreasonably burdensome. Government agencies often "make up" rules when they feel the need to do so. Even though laws have been passed to protect intellectual property, the government has virtually no way to enforce them. Pirated brand-name goods are sold in stores and on street corners with impunity. Taxes are often imposed arbitrarily, and are so high that they discourage investment. The banking system is almost unworkable. The Russian currency, the *ruble,* has been unstable, and inflation high. This instability is making trade and investment difficult, and threatens to hold up Russia's entrance into important in-

ternational economic organizations. Many western business ventures are not profitable and are losing money. In the political realm, civil unrest among ethnic minorities in the Central Asian republics threatens to ignite the region in war. Perhaps the greatest threat to economic liberalization is that Russia is still undergoing tremendous political instability, despite democratic elections. Many people are still hostile to the United States and private enterprise and would like to return Russia to a Soviet empire. As of 1999, economic reforms were still proceeding but no one could yet predict whether they would succeed.

Managing the Risks of International Business

Readers need to keep one particular truism in mind throughout this text: *The management of international business is the management of risk.* No manager can make a strategic business decision or enter into an important business transaction without a full evaluation of the risks involved. Many of the best business plans have been ruined by a miscalculation, a mistake, or an error in judgment that could have been avoided with proper planning. This textbook is full of such cases:

- An importer of "camping tents" who thought they would be dutied at the same rate as "sporting goods," but found out too late that the U.S. Customs Service considered them to be textile products and imposed a much higher import duty.
- The owner of a yacht shipped aboard an ocean carrier from Asia, who failed to declare its real value on the shipping documents, found that when the yacht was destroyed on loading, international law allowed the yacht's owner to collect a mere $500.
- The multinational corporation that invested millions in a foreign country only to lose it amidst a revolution.
- The U.S. exporter whose goods were stranded at a foreign port, thousands of miles away, when the buyer refused to pay for them.

Advance planning could have reduced the risk in these cases. The importer of tents could have sought and received an advance ruling from U.S. Customs

Germany
The People

Germans value order, privacy and punctuality. They are thrifty, hard working and industrious. Germans respect perfectionism in all areas of business and private life. In Germany, there is a sense of community and social conscience and strong desire for belonging. To admit inadequacy—even in jest—is incomprehensible.

Meeting and Greeting
- At a business or social meeting, shake hands with everyone present when arriving and leaving.
- When introducing yourself, never use your title. Introduce yourself by your last name only.
- Never shake hands with one hand in your pocket.

Names and Titles
- Use last names and appropriate titles until specifically invited by your German host or colleagues to use their first names.
- Titles are very important. Never use titles incorrectly and never fail to use them. If unsure, err in favor of a higher title.
- A *Doktor* can be either a medical doctor or a holder of a Ph.D.
- Two titles should not be used at the same time, except when addressing a letter to someone. If a person does hold several titles, the higher one is used in speaking to him/her.

Corporate Culture
- Germans take punctuality for business meetings and social occasions seriously. Tardiness is viewed as thoughtless and rude. Call with an explanation if you are delayed.
- Send company profiles, personal profiles, etc., to German colleagues before your visit to establish credibility.
- Contacts are vital to a business success. Use a bank, German representative or the *Industrie und Handelskammer* (Chamber of Industry and Commerce) when possible.
- Rank is very important in business. Never set up a meeting for a lower ranked company employee to meet with a higher ranked person.

- The primary purpose of a first meeting is to get to know one another and to evaluate the person, to gain trust, and the check chemistry.
- Meetings are often formal and scheduled weeks in advance.
- Germans generally discuss business after a few minutes of general discussion.
- Arrive at meetings well prepared. Avoid hard-sell tactics or surprise.
- Germans take business very seriously. Levity is not common in the workplace.
- Business cards in English are acceptable.
- Germans are competitive, ambitious and hard bargainers.
- Germans value their privacy. They tend to keep their office doors closed. Always knock on doors before entering.
- Objective criticism isn't given or received easily. Compliments are seldom given for work product.
- Strict vertical hierarchy exists. Power is held by a small number of people at the top. Deference is given to authority. Subordinates rarely contradict or criticize the boss publicly.
- Organization is logical, methodical and compartmentalized with procedures and routines done "by the book."
- Decision making is slow with thorough analysis of all facts.
- Germans are not comfortable handling the unexpected. Plans are cautious with fallback positions, contingency plans, and comprehensive action steps—carried out to the letter.
- Germans produce massive written communications to elaborate on and confirm discussions.
- Written or spoken presentations should be specific, factual, technical and realistic.
- Reports, briefings and presentations should be backed up by facts, figures, tables and charts.
- Germans have an aversion to divergent opinions, but will negotiate and debate an issue fervently.
- Remain silent if the floor has not been given to you or if you are not prepared to make an informed contribution.

continued

continued

- Decisions are often debated informally and are generally made before meetings with compliance rather than consensus expected in the meeting.
- Always deliver information, products, proposals, etc., to clients on time.

Helpful Hints

- Germans are more formal and punctual than most of the world. They have prescribed roles and seldom step out of line.
- Don't be offended if someone corrects your behavior (i.e., taking jacket off in restaurant, parking in wrong spot, etc.). Policing each other is seen as a social duty.

Japan

The People

Japan is a highly structured and traditional society. Great importance is placed on loyalty, politeness, personal responsibility and on everyone working together for the good of the larger group. Education, ambition, hard work, patience and determination are held in the highest regard. The crime rate is one of the lowest in the world.

Meeting and Greeting

- A handshake is appropriate upon meeting. The Japanese handshake is limp and with little or no eye contact.
- Some Japanese bow and shake hands. The bow is a highly regarded greeting to show respect and is appreciated by the Japanese. A slight bow to show courtesy is acceptable.

Body Language

- Nodding is very important. When listening to Japanese speak, especially in English, you should nod to show you are listening and understanding the speaker.
- Silence is a natural and expected form of non-verbal communication. Do not feel a need to chatter.
- Do not stand close to a Japanese person. Avoid touching.
- Sit erect with both feet on the floor. Never sit with ankle over knee.

Corporate Culture

- Punctuality is a must in all business and social meetings.

- Japanese may exchange business cards even before they shake hands or bow. Be certain your business card clearly states your rank. This will determine who your negotiating counterpart should be.
- Bear in mind that initial negotiations begin with middle managers. Do not attempt to go over their heads to senior management.
- It is acceptable to use a Japanese company interpreter in the first meeting. Once negotiations begin, hire your own interpreter.
- Both business and personal relationships are hierarchical. Older people have higher status than younger, men higher than women and senior executives higher than junior executives.
- It is very important to send a manager of the same rank to meet with a Japanese colleague. Title is very important.
- Work is always undertaken as a group. The workgroup is strongly united with no competition; all succeed or all fail. Decision-making is by consensus. Everyone on the work team must be consulted before making decisions. This is a very slow process.
- The first meeting may focus on establishing an atmosphere of friendliness, harmony and trust. Business meetings are conducted formally, so leave your humor behind.
- It takes several meetings to develop a contract. When the time comes, be content to close a deal with a handshake. Leave the signing of the written contract to later meetings.
- Etiquette and harmony are very important. "Saving face" is a key concept. Japanese are anxious to avoid unpleasantness and confrontation. Try to avoid saying "no." Instead, say, "This could be very difficult," allowing colleagues to save face.
- Proper introduction to business contacts is a must. The introducer becomes a guarantor for the person being introduced.
- Do not bring a lawyer. It is important is to build business relationships based on trust. The Japanese do not like complicated legal documents. Write contracts that cover essential points.

Dining and Entertainment

- Restaurant entertaining is crucial to business. A person is judged by his/her behavior during and after business hours. Seldom is a business deal completed without dinner in a restaurant.
- Wait for the most important person (honored guest) to begin eating. If you are the honored

continued

prior to importing them and avoided an unexpected surprise in determining the tariff rate after they were already in the country. A better understanding of the risks of shipping goods on the high seas would have induced the yacht owner to take greater precautions in making the shipping arrangements. Had the multinational corporation evaluated the political risk in its host country, it would have been better prepared to protect its investment there. A U.S. exporter who understood the problems in collecting a debt in a foreign country would have made different arrangements for payment.

If the risk cannot be reduced through advance planning and careful execution, perhaps it can be shifted to some other party to the transaction. For example, can a seller of goods who does not want to bear the risk that the goods might be lost at sea "shift the risk" to the buyer in the process of contract negotiations? If a U.S. exporter is fearful that it may not get paid for selling merchandise to a buyer in, say, Venezuela, can it shift the transaction risk to the buyer by requiring a letter of credit from the buyer's bank? After all, in both of these cases, the parties can negotiate which one of them will bear the risk of loss to the goods, or the risk of not getting paid. Risks become a point of negotiations between parties to a transaction, be it a sale of goods contract, a patent or trademark agreement, or a joint venture contract to build a factory.

If the risk cannot be shifted to another party to

the transaction, it might be shifted to an insurance company. Many types of risks can be insured against, including the risk of damage to goods at sea, the risk of losing an investment in a developing country, and many others. Finally, a company must assess whether, after having tried to manage the risks as best as possible, the potential profits will be adequate to compensate for the risks that remain.

Risk Assessment and the Firm's Foreign Market Entry Strategy

When a firm is considering its entry or expansion in a foreign market, it must weigh all options and decide on a course of action commensurate with its objectives, capabilities, and its willingness to assume risk. As stated earlier, trade generally entails less penetration into a foreign market than licensing, and licensing less than foreign investment. To say it another way, selling to a customer in another country results in less risk to the firm than licensing patents, trademarks, and copyrights there. Licensing usually requires less risk than forming a joint venture with a foreign firm to build a factory together in China or India, for instance. A firm's global business strategy must take into account the amount of risk that the firm is willing to bear in entering the foreign market.

Consider this actual real-life example. A U.S. manufacturer of industrial equipment exported products to Europe, but faced growing competition from European firms, higher ocean freight rates, and increased European import restrictions. Moreover, the company experienced some difficulty in servicing its equipment from the United States as well as maintaining a ready supply of spare parts for Europe. It evaluated its options for overcoming the problems of exporting and for expanding its presence in the European market through a country-by-country analysis of the business climate in Europe. On the basis of labor, tax, and other factors, it determined that its best course of action was to enter the European market through Spain. Prominent in its decision was the presence of an existing firm in Spain that, with the financial and technical assistance of the U.S. firm, would have seemed to make an appropriate joint venture partner. During negotiations, the two firms preliminarily agreed that the U.S. company would take a 40 percent minority interest in the new business venture, sharing profits with their partner. The Americans had done all of the usual background checks, reviewed credit reports, and made inquiries of others with whom the Spanish company had dealt. Although everything proved to be in order, and despite many trips abroad by management, the U.S. firm wanted their auditors to visit the Spanish company and review their books. During their visit to Spain, the auditors were asked "which set of books and numbers" they wanted to review—the real financial records of the Spanish company or those used to report to Spanish tax authorities. The U.S. company became uneasy about their potential exposure as a minority partner in a foreign investment with this company. Not only were they fearful that they could be misled by their "partner," but they feared liability to Spanish legal and tax authorities for the conduct of their partner over which they had little or no control. As a result, they decided not to share ownership of a joint venture with the Spanish company, but instead decided to license their technology and know-how to the Spanish firm. They would obtain patent rights to their products in Europe, license those rights to the Spanish company, provide technical assistance, and in return receive an upfront cash payment and future royalties based on sales. This arrangement would give them the access to the European customers that they needed, without the capital costs and risks of building a plant there. This text will present many such examples of how the risks of international business will affect a firm's strategy for entering a foreign market.

Managing Distance and Communications

The risks of doing business in a foreign country are different from those encountered at home. A Texas firm, for example, will find doing business in Japan, or even neighboring Mexico, to be different from doing business in Oklahoma. The Texas firm will find Oklahoma City hardly different at all from Austin. Texas and Oklahoma share a common language and customs, a common currency, uniform commercial laws, a seamlessly networked communications system, and so on. The Texas firm would not find these similarities in a foreign country. It would encounter greater distances; problems in communications; language and cultural barriers; differences in ethical, moral, and religious codes; exposure to strange foreign laws and government regulations; and different currencies. All these factors affect the risks of doing business abroad.

Selling Face-to-Face. Parties to an international transaction must find ways of reducing the distance between them. Even though the advent of satellite communications, video teleconferencing, and fax machines has brought businesspeople closer to each other than ever before, no one has discovered a substitute for face-to-face meetings. Doing business in Asia may require many trips there and many years of ongoing negotiations in order for the parties to develop trust between them. Face-to-face meetings are essential to negotiations because they enable the parties to better describe their needs, their capabilities, and their products and services. They are better able to communicate and explain their positions, and most importantly, to gauge each other's intentions, attitudes, and integrity. These benefits of face-to-face meetings apply in banking, as well as in other industries. International bankers often travel abroad to meet foreign bankers, foreign government representatives, and foreign customers so they can personally evaluate the risks of lending money or doing other banking business.

Ask any international sales manager about the importance of face-to-face meetings, and he or she will tell you that you cannot sell your product abroad from the confines of your office. A successful sales director from a European textile firm once claimed that he had established a policy of not selling to any foreign firm that he had not visited, nor to anyone he had not met. He, thus, participated in every U.S. textile trade show and made semiannual trips across the United States to visit his customers. This policy was not just because he found it easier to sell face-to-face, but because he learned more about his customer's needs for new products, styles, and colors. He was also better able to evaluate the customer's creditworthiness and the potential for a long-term business relationship.

Attendance at International Trade Shows.
One opportunity for identifying new customers, renewing old business relationships, and expanding contacts in a given industry is to attend an international trade show, or trade fair. Most industries have these regularly scheduled exhibitions—computer and software, home textiles, restaurant products, aircraft, boats, sporting goods, clothing and apparel, paper, and industrial equipment. They are often organized by industry trade associations or convention centers. These shows give sellers from around the world the opportunity to exhibit their products and services, meet prospective buyers, and write orders.

Language and Cultural Differences

As the world's economy moves toward greater globalization, languages and cultural differences become less of a barrier to international business. Even though English is widely used in business all over the world, the language of a given transaction still depends on the type of business one is doing and on the region of the world. In the case of importing and exporting, some truth can be found in the saying that if you're the buyer, the seller will find a way to speak your language; but if you're the seller, you should find a way to communicate with your customer. One corporate CEO argued that he could not possibly know all the languages of all the countries in which he does business. That argument may not be so valid, however, for an international sales manager who does business in one or two primary foreign markets. Some positions re-

quire an even greater level of foreign language competency. For certain types of selling or contract negotiations, a mastery of a foreign language will be essential. As a firm moves toward a greater penetration of the foreign market, for instance, negotiating a licensing or investment contract, the use of native speakers or nationals of the host country becomes crucial. Contracts such as these will often be written in the languages of both parties, and so the use of foreign lawyers becomes necessary. In other cases, only social conventions are needed: to make introductions, to be courteous, and to show you took the time to learn something about their language and culture. An appreciation for the cultural environment and religious beliefs of a host is absolutely essential. In selling in a foreign country, the use of local sales agents and distributors will ease the language and cultural problems. They will also give good advice on handling the cultural differences you might face in their countries. Moreover, many countries are moving toward the use of uniform laws—laws and legal codes that are commonly agreed on and adopted by many countries (and written and made available in many languages). The following case, *Gaskin v. Stumm Handel,* illustrates what can happen by not being able to read and understand a foreign language contract.

Managing Currency and Exchange Rate Risks

Currency risk is risk a firm is exposed to as a result of buying, selling, or holding a foreign currency, or transacting business in a foreign currency. Currency risk includes (1) exchange rate risk and (2) currency control risk. (Other risks, such as inflation risk and interest rate risk, are not the subject of this book.) Most international business transactions involve the use or transfer of foreign currency. Currency risk exists when a firm must convert one currency to the currency of another country before it can be used.

Exchange Rate Risk. *Exchange rate risk* results from the fluctuations in the relative values of foreign currencies against each other when they are bought and sold on international financial markets. Virtually every international business transaction is affected by exchange rate risk. Take a simple

Gaskin v. Stumm Handel GMBH
390 F. Supp. 361 (1975)
United States District Court (S.D. N.Y.)

BACKGROUND AND FACTS

The plaintiff, a U.S. citizen, entered into an employment contract with the German firm of Stumm Handel, the defendant. The contract presented to the plaintiff was written entirely in German. Without being able to speak or read German, the plaintiff signed the contract. He never received an English language version. At the time of the signing of the contract, however, the terms of the contract were explained to him in English. One of the terms of the contract, known as a "forum selection clause" provided that any disputes that might arise between the parties would be settled in the courts of Germany. Later, when the parties reached a disagreement, the plaintiff brought this action against the defendant in the United States, contending that his failure to understand German rendered the forum selection clause invalid.

CANNELLA, DISTRICT JUDGE

With regard to such translation, Gaskin asserts that "I was never informed that by executing the (contract), I was consenting to the Republic of West Germany as the forum within which I must submit all controversies" and that "had I known this, I would not have agreed to the same, as such an obligation is onerous and unconscionable, and a deterrent to bringing any actions whatsoever." . . . We find that in making the foregoing assertions, Gaskin flies in the face of well-settled contract law principles and has failed to sustain his burden.

It is a settled proposition of contract law in this state and nation that "the signer of a deed or other instrument, expressive of a jural act, is conclusively bound thereby. That his mind never gave assent to the terms expressed is not material. If the signer could read the instrument, not to have read it was gross negligence; if he could not read it, not to procure it to be read was equally negligent; in either case the writing binds him." (citations omitted) . . .

While Mr. Gaskin's apparent "blissful ignorance" with regard to the contract under which he was to render his labors to the defendant strikes us as highly incredible as a matter of common sense, we take note of certain facts which are relevant to the disposition of this matter. It must be remembered that Mr. Gaskin is not an ignorant consumer, unlearned in the language of the contract, who has become entangled in the web of a contract of adhesion through the overreaching or other unconscionable practices of the defendant. The contract at bar does not involve the credit sale of a refrigerator or color television set, but rather compensation of some $36,000 per annum for Mr. Gaskin's services as the manager in charge of the defendant's New York operations which were to be conducted under the name Stumm Trading Company. His office (Park Avenue, New York City) is not located in an area which would have precluded his easy access to a competent translation of the involved document. There existed no emergency condition or other exceptional circumstances at the time plaintiff entered into this contract; conditions which might now serve to excuse his present plight. . . .

Thus, we find that the instant transaction was a commercial arrangement of a nature which warranted the exercise of care by Mr. Gaskin before his entry into it and that his conduct with regard to this undertaking can only be characterized as negligent, the consequences of which he must now bear. . . .

We, therefore, decline to exercise our jurisdiction over this cause in deference to the contractual forum. An order dismissing this action will be entered.

Decision. The court dismissed the plaintiff's action, holding that the plaintiff's failure to speak or read German was not grounds for invalidating any of the provisions of the contract.

example. Assume that a company based in the United States sells goods to a firm in France. In an export/import transaction, one of the parties will be dealing in the currency of the other. The one that deals in the other party's currency will bear the exchange rate risk. If the contract calls for payment in U.S. dollars upon shipment of the goods in sixty days, then the French importer bears the risk during the intervening period. If the French firm does not have a source of income in dollars, it must buy dollars from a French bank at the prevailing rate for dollars at the time it makes the purchase. If the value of the euro declines vis-à-vis the dollar during the same period, then more euros are needed to purchase the same number of dollars to pay the U.S. firm. Similarly, if the euro appreciates in value against the dollar, then the French firm will find the goods "cheaper" than it had expected. Whichever way the currencies fluctuate, the U.S. exporter will have shifted the exchange rate risk to the French side. The U.S. firm spends dollars to pay labor, utilities, taxes, and other expenses, and it will receive dollars for the goods sold to France. (Of course, even when dealing in one's own currency, a company still faces "opportunity risk"—if it had sold goods for euros, and the euro had appreciated, then the company might have reaped a windfall profit on the exchange to dollars.) On the other hand, if the U.S. firm prices its goods in euros at the request of its customer (which an exporter often must do for its customers), it will bear the exchange rate risk. As one can see from this example, currency exchange rates can have a tremendous effect on trade and investment decisions made by firms, and thus, affect the flow of money in and out of all countries.

Floating and Fixed Exchange Rates.
Floating or "hard" currencies are those currencies of the western countries and Japan freely traded on world markets. A currency's value (or price) is determined by what buyers and sellers will pay for it at any given time. Currency values can also be affected by the action of central banks (government intervention), by interest rates, or by other market factors.

Currencies with a *fixed exchange rate* are also called "soft" currencies. The Russian *ruble*, Indian *rupee*, or Chinese *renminbi* (or *yuan*) are examples of soft currencies and can only be purchased at the fixed rate established by the government.

Methods of Managing Exchange Rate Risk.
Most international bankers claim that predicting currency fluctuations is more difficult than predicting the stock market. The ability of a firm to manage its currency risk depends on the size, sophistication, and global resources of the firm. The small domestic company might "buy forward" or *hedge*. A firm hedges when it enters into a contract, usually with a bank, for the purchase of a foreign currency to be delivered at a future date at a price agreed upon in the contract. Multinational corpo-

rations have many more complex and sophisticated options for managing exchange risk. For instance, a multinational corporation's subsidiary units in foreign countries may have excess local currency derived from revenues there. These assets can be transferred to affiliated units owned by the parent company for use anywhere in the world.

Some companies engage in speculative trading of foreign currencies. These risky transactions require experience, skill, and, as traders know, "iron nerves."

Currency Control Risk.
Some countries, particularly developing countries in which access to ready foreign reserves is limited, put restrictions on currency transactions. In order to preserve the little foreign exchange that is available for international transactions, such as importing merchandise, these countries restrict the amount of foreign currency that they will sell to private companies. This limitation can cause problems for a U.S. exporter waiting for payment from its foreign customer who cannot obtain the dollars needed to pay for the goods. (The creative exporter may have to weigh alternative methods of payment in these countries, such as bartering.) The most severe form of currency restriction is the *blocked currency*. Blocked currencies, used by the former Soviet bloc countries of Eastern Europe under communism, could not legally be removed from the issuing country at all.

A multinational corporation with income earned in a country with a restricted currency, may find restrictions on its freedom to remove, or repatriate, the earnings to its home country. Repatriation of profits or dividends may be limited to a small portion of earnings or taxed at discouragingly high levels. Working in this environment presents one of the greatest creative challenges to a multinational corporation's financial managers. Industrialized countries have only rarely instituted austere currency controls in the past, and then only in times of a national monetary crisis.

Special Transaction Risks in Contracts for the Sale of Goods

A major portion of this book focuses on the special risks inherent in international transactions for the purchase and sale of goods. These transactions present special risks to both parties because the process of shipping goods and receiving payment between distant countries is riskier than when done within a single country. Because they are of special importance to international firms, these risks are described here.

Payment or Credit Risk.   The risk that a buyer will default on a sales contract and fail to pay for the goods is known as *payment risk,* often called *credit risk.* The consequences of a buyer defaulting on an international contract can be potentially disastrous. Because a company generally incurs greater expense in selling overseas, a failed contract can mean a large loss. Selling overseas adds the costs of travel, foreign marketing and advertising, procuring foreign licenses, retaining counsel overseas, distributor's fees and agent's commissions, packaging and insuring for international shipment, communications expenses, and freight forwarder's fees. One of the major considerations is the expense of international air or ocean freight. Freight costs for ocean cargo, for example, are determined by the greater of weight or volume. Thus, heavy, bulky cargo that cannot be disassembled or have its volume reduced by the removal of air or water during shipment is quite expensive to ship. In some cases, the freight costs can equal the value of replacing the goods themselves. One export manager, unable to locate a substitute buyer in a foreign country, had to abandon goods at a foreign port rather than incur the costs of bringing them home! The buyer's nonpayment or default can occur in a sales transaction for a variety of reasons. Perhaps the buyer found the goods cheaper from another source. Perhaps currency fluctuations have destroyed the buyer's anticipated profits on the purchase. Perhaps the buyer has become insolvent. Whatever the reason, a seller must plan for these potential risks. If sellers were not able to do so, all world trading would soon come to a grinding halt.

Delivery Risk.   The risk that a buyer will not receive the goods called for under a contract is called *delivery risk.* It can result from a late shipment, or no shipment at all, or from shipment of goods that do not conform to the contract specifications. It can result from adverse business conditions, labor strikes, disasters at sea, or the actions of an unscrupulous seller. Whatever the cause, buyers must assess the risk of dealing with their foreign suppliers. Business credit reports, trade references, product samples, and visits to their factory are all important in evaluating a vendor. In the words of one experienced purchasing manager for an international firm, "There is no substitute for knowing your seller."

Property or Marine Risk.   One special form of delivery risk, known as *property risk* or *marine risk,* is the potential for loss or damage to cargo or freight while in transit over great distances. Between the time that the parties initially enter their agreement and the time that the goods arrive at their destination, any number of unexpected events may cause one or more parties to incur losses under the contract. For example, goods can be damaged by the sea or salt air, ships can sink, planes can crash, refrigeration units in containers can break, food can spoil, grain can become infested with insects, and labor strikes can delay the departure of a vessel. Some of the risks can be quite surprising. Assume that an exporter is shipping goods on an ocean vessel. The ship damages its hull on rocks in the harbor because the captain had negligently left the deck. Imagine the exporter's surprise when it finds out that, not only can it not recover from the carrier, but that it must contribute to the ship's owner for the costs of towing the ship to safety, for rescuing the crew, and even for saving cargo that belonged to other shippers!

Pilferage and Containerized Freight.   Pilferage and theft has been a problem for international shippers for many years. During the days of *break-bulk* freight, when goods were loaded and unloaded on pallets or in boxes, cargo was relatively easy to steal. However, in the past twenty to thirty years shipping has changed dramatically. Today, nearly all merchandise is transported in large containers sealed by the shipper and opened only by the buyer or by customs officials. This practice has helped reduce damage and pilferage to shipments. Of course, pilferage is still a tremendous problem, especially in the ports of developing countries. One U.S. shipper of cellular phones to Latin America recently said that his firm could not mark the contents on the outside of the shipping boxes or crates because if they did the phones never reached their destinations.

Managing Political Risk

Political risk is generally defined as the risk to a firm's business interests resulting from political instability or political change in a country in which the firm is doing business. By definition, it exists in all countries and all regions regardless of political or economic system. Political risk includes risk derived from potentially adverse actions of governments of the foreign countries in which one is doing business or to whose laws and regulations one is subject. It also includes laws and government policies instituted by the firm's home country, which adversely affect the firms that do business in a foreign country. Political risk can take many forms—from war and revolution to changes in law or policy. It can affect all aspects of international business—the right to ship goods to a country or to own and operate a factory there. Although almost any adverse law or regulation of a government could be considered political risk, including restrictions on trade or currencies, this text examines political risk in more general terms.

Causes of Political Risk.
One cause of political risk is political or economic instability in a country and exposure to that country's laws or regulations, which create a hostile environment for business dealings. Instability is a particular problem in countries that experience rapid changes in government—be they democracies or less-than-democratic developing countries. As governments change, so might their trade, investment, tax, and other economic policies. When the changes result from democratic elections, the impact on business is usually gradual. Italy has undergone a succession of democratically elected governments since World War II, and firms there have had to adjust to changing economic policies. The potential for faster, more dramatic change is greater in the developing countries. Even though foreign business interests may have been welcomed under one government, its successor may take a different view. For many years, a nation may welcome foreign investment, consumer products, and Western culture, and then virtually overnight turn to resent any foreign influence at all. Cuba, Lybia, Iran, and Iraq are examples. For most of U.S. history, U.S. firms have had friendly relationships and extensive investments in these countries. Yet after political upheaval, each of these countries became hostile to Americans there.

A change in government can occur as a result of a popular revolution or military takeover, a *coup d'etat*. In the 1950s, communist-inspired revolutions forced sudden changes in some governments. Fidel Castro's takeover of Cuba is a good example. United States companies in Cuba experienced the seizure of their assets and expulsion from the island. Changes in some countries have been inspired by religious fundamentalism. The Islamic Revolution in Iran in the late 1970s and the ouster of the Shah of Iran, a dictator himself, resulted in tremendous political instability and economic uncertainty for firms that had done business there for many years. The new Islamic government retaliated against the United States for its support of the Shah of Iran. It seized the U.S. embassy in Tehran, held U.S. citizens hostage, cancelled contracts with U.S. firms, and confiscated the assets of firms operating there. The taking of privately owned assets, such as a farm or factory, by a government is called *expropriation*. The taking of ownership of a firm or of an entire industry that had been operated privately, as a part of a plan to restructure a national economy, is called *nationalization*. United States and western firms have faced the risk of expropriation and nationalization all over the world, and they have been a risk of international business since time immemorial.

The Impact on Trade Relations.
The text provides repeated examples of how trade relationships between nations are linked to their political relationships. Indeed, many nations control trade—the right to import or export goods to or from another country—as a political tool. Thus, a firm that trades with companies in a foreign country must consider the possibility of being caught up in a "trade war." Earlier, the chapter described how this has happened to U.S. firms doing business in China. Take another example: Imagine that a firm is operating in a country whose dictator decides to invade a neighboring country. If the United States and the world community take action against the invader, such as imposing economic sanctions, then the firm will be caught in the middle—and subject to those sanctions. United States firms have had to comply with U.S. embargoes of other countries on many occasions—Iraq after its invasion of Kuwait, Cuba, Nicaragua,

Haiti, countries in southern Africa, and innumerable more. Many of these cases are discussed in this text.

The Risk of International Hostilities.

Even the best laid business plans can be upset when transportation and communications are disrupted by war or revolution. Consider what happened when Egypt blocked the Suez Canal to international shipping during its 1956 war with Israel. Because this important waterway was closed, cargo ships were diverted around the Cape of Good Hope on the southern tip of the African continent, a costly journey of many thousands of miles. The loss fell upon companies that used the canal. These events present risks that the prudent businessperson must be aware of and minimize to avoid potential losses.

Handling Political Risk.

Handling political risk requires planning and vigilance. First, the firm must have an understanding of the domestic affairs of a country. Typical questions might include: Is the country politically stable? Will democracy prevail? Is the country subject to religious or ethnic strife? How are minority groups treated, and how will their treatment be viewed by the more democratic countries of the world? What is the country's economic situation? The firm must also understand regional politics. Is the region stable? Are neighboring countries in the region hostile? Are border conflicts likely to erupt? These considerations might be especially important in the Middle East. Finally, international affairs must be considered. Is the country abiding by international human rights standards? Is it a member of international organizations? Does it abide by international law?

At a minimum, international managers are well advised to keep abreast of all political affairs that could affect their operations and interests worldwide. Access to the latest information is critical. Good sources include newspapers such as *The Journal of Commerce* or *The Wall Street Journal,* and even cable news channels. Beyond that, the firm can obtain more sophisticated assessments of the political environment in a foreign country through the process known as *political risk analysis.* Professionally prepared political risk analysis reports are available, giving current assessments and forecasts of future stability. Other resources include political risk consulting firms, insurance industry reports, reports of U.S. government agencies, and informal discussions with experienced international bankers

and shipping company representatives. In some cases, *political risk insurance* is available for firms making investments in foreign countries where their exposure is great. Importantly, strategic corporate planning should take this information into consideration in developing its global business strategy and in transacting business.

Risks of Foreign Laws and Courts

You have heard the expression, "When in Rome, do as the Romans do." Whether you are trying to handle social situations with business colleagues in a foreign culture, devise marketing plans for your products there, or do business without running afoul of local laws, there is considerable truth to this old adage. We are all responsible for conforming our conduct to the laws of the state or country in which we are present. Criminal codes vary from country to country, depending on the social, political, cultural, and historical traditions there. Many acts that are perfectly legal in one country can be illegal in another. Indeed, most travelers to a foreign country could conceivably break a host of laws and not even be aware of it. The same is true for the law of contracts, employment, competition, torts, and other business laws. It is virtually impossible to catalog all of the differences between these laws from country to country. For example, consider the prohibition against charging interest on a loan under Islamic law in many Middle Eastern countries, something which is taken for granted as an everyday part of Western business. To make matters worse, many foreign laws are not made readily available or understandable to the average foreign guest. Some are unwritten and understood only by the local residents.

Consider the next case. In the United States, no one would even think about the need to apply for a government license before opening a retail store. True, in the United States a sales tax permit is required, but we do not have to seek permission to open a retail store. In the United States, "mom and pop" retail stores, as well as large-scale discount stores, open and close every day. But in many countries, including European countries with a long history of powerful trade unions, shopkeeper unions, and apprenticeships, the attitudes are very different. The following 1995 case, *DIP SpA v. Commune di Bassano del Grappa,* considered the legality of

DIP SpA v. Commune di Bassano del Grappa
October 1995
Court of Justice of the European Communities (2nd Chamber)

BACKGROUND AND FACTS

Italian law prohibits the opening of certain retail stores without first receiving a license issued by local authorities. The law requires each municipality to draw up a plan for the development of new businesses in its area. The stated purpose of the licensing scheme is to protect consumers, to achieve a balance between supply and demand, to ensure free competition, and to obtain a balance between different forms of distribution (e.g., permanent stores versus mobile vendors). A license to open a new retail store can be denied if it is believed that the market is adequately served already. The license is granted by the local mayor on the advice of a local committee. The ten- to fifteen-person committees are made up of local government representatives, local merchants, and members of local unions of shopkeepers and workers. This action was brought before the European Court of Justice by three applicants whose licenses to open new retail stores in Italy had been denied. One of the applicants was a subsidiary of a German company. The three applicants wanted to open stores that sold jewelry, hardware, and foodstuffs. The applicants maintain that the Italian retail licensing laws exclude new business, restrict competition, discriminate against non-Italian companies and imported goods, and lead to higher consumer prices. They argue that the Italian law is invalid under the laws of the European Union and the Treaty of Rome.

HIRSCH P.C., PRESIDING

According to the applicants, the Act favours and reinforces anti-competitive practices between existing traders, which is the mechanism through which the Italian retail market is said to be foreclosed. . . . While the applicants have forcefully stressed what they perceive to be the self-evidently concerted nature of the activities and common purpose of the distributor and retail representatives on these advisory committees which operate across Italy, they have not referred to any evidence which would be sufficient to justify a conclusion that, as a result of the application of the Act, such a network of collusion either subsists or has been encouraged in Italy. . . .

During the oral hearing the applicants submitted that, because the Act operated effectively to exclude new entrants, many of whom would be non-Italian

operators desirous of establishing large-scale and sometimes discount outlets which might sell more non-Italian goods than existing traders, it was likely, either actually or at least potentially, to hinder intra-Community trade.

I believe that this argument must be rejected. [W]hile the Act limits the overall number of trading licences, it does not necessarily produce an overall decrease in the number or value of goods sold on the Italian market nor does it necessarily render more difficult the sale of imports as opposed to domestic goods. I accept the Commission's observation that this type of provision is not capable of hindering intra-Community trade. . . .

Accordingly, I am of the opinion that . . .

2. legislation requiring an opinion to be obtained from a collective body, whose members include representatives of traders already operating on the market, both when the plan is drawn up and when new licences are granted, is not contrary to (the competition laws of) either Article 85 or 86 of the Treaty of Rome.
3. such legislation is not capable of hindering intra-European Community trade for the purposes of the application of Article 30 of the Treaty of Rome so long as, in law or in fact, it does not distinguish between imports and domestic (Italian) products.

The Italian Act provides that licences are to be issued by the mayor of the municipality concerned, taking into account the criteria laid down in the municipal commercial development plan. The purpose of that plan is to provide the best possible service for consumers and the best possible balance between permanent trading establishments and foreseeable demand from the population.

National rules which require a licence to be obtained before a new shop can be opened and limit the number of shops in the municipality in order to achieve a balance between supply and demand cannot be considered to put individual traders in dominant positions or all the traders established in a municipality in a collective dominant position, a salient feature of which would be that traders did not compete against one another.

On this point, it is sufficient to observe that rules such as those contained in the Italian Act make no

continued

continued

distinction according to the origin of the goods distributed by the businesses concerned, that their purpose is not to regulate trade in goods with other Member States and that the restrictive effects which they might have on the free movement of goods are too uncertain and indirect for the obligation which they impose to be regarded as being capable of hindering trade between Member States.

Decision.   The Italian law requiring the licensing of new retail stores by local committees is not invalid under the laws of the European Union and the Treaty of Rome.

Comment.   By 2003, it seemed that supermarkets and mass retailers were changing the face of Italy. Since this decision, the number of supermarkets in Italy almost doubled, and traditional family-owned businesses, with all the character, richness, and history they represent, had sadly declined. But even a country like Italy, where shoppers for generations made daily stops to the meat, produce, or dairy store, seemed to enjoy the new convenience and lower prices.

Italian law that requires applicants to gain permission from local mayors and committees before opening a retail store. American students should consider just how "foreign" this concept really is.

Settling disputes between companies can be much more difficult in international business than in domestic business. Litigation of a case in a court in a foreign country is both costly and time consuming. In addition, the laws of a foreign country can differ greatly from those laws one is accustomed to at home. Countries may exhibit vast differences in the law of contracts, crimes, torts, intellectual property, securities and investment, and more. People cannot possibly know all the laws of their own country, let alone those of every foreign country in which they do business. Language and logistical issues can be problems as well. A firm may need representation by attorneys in their own country *and* in the country of litigation. Frequent court appearances could require great travel expense. International cases also involve complex procedural problems: What country's courts should hear the case? What country's laws should apply? How does a court compel the testimony of witnesses or the production of business records not found in that country? Should the case be submitted to arbitration—perhaps in some "neutral" country? When a firm is negotiating an agreement with a foreign party, such as a contract to sell goods or to franchise a business, both parties will usually want to reach an agreement on these issues, and so the advice of an attorney at this stage in a transaction is extremely important.

Ethical Issues in International Business

Just as laws differ from country to country, so does the definition of ethical behavior. In interna-

tional business one might say that, *"the law is a floor for our behavior, but ethical codes and personal values call on us to exceed that which is required by law."* When called on to evaluate a course of action according to a code of ethics or personal value system, one must consider the decision in the cultural context. In other words, what is considered appropriate behavior in one culture may not be so in another. Readers of the situations and cases presented in this book should keep in mind, as they study international business, that managers often must evaluate their actions according to ethical codes or personal values that may or may not be commonly accepted in the country in which they are operating. The following examples serve as preparation for the consideration of ethical issues throughout this text.

http://www.state.gov
United States Department of State "Business Center" section has "Country Commercial Guides" with current economic and political information by country.

Example A: You have been negotiating with a representative of the Portuguese government to sell products to them for a new state building project. He arrives at your company's offices with a blank purchase order in hand. After negotiating a fixed price and delivery, he "suggests" that you prepare a price quotation on a "pro forma invoice"—at double the negotiated price. His government will pay the full amount shown on the invoice through a Portuguese bank, and your firm will pay him the difference as a "commission" in U.S. dollars deposited to his bank account in New York. He convincingly argues that this practice is customary in his country. The temptation for you might be great; the deal would be a profitable one.

But would it be legal or ethical? Certainly, laws and ethical standards vary from country to country. In this example, you would have to consider the laws and ethical codes of both Portugal and the United States. Even though bribery is more common in certain other countries, this transaction would clearly be illegal under U.S. law, and you would be subject to criminal prosecution, fines, and possible imprisonment.

Example B: Imagine that your firm enters into a contract to sell drilling equipment to a Korean company. The contract is closed while the Korean company president is visiting the U.S. plant. After closing, the Korean executive points out that all imports to Korea must be channeled through a registered "local agent." He quickly suggests that a wholly owned trading company *that he owns* could handle all of the paperwork—for a fee. Compare this with the first example. Should you comply with his request? Is it legal? If it is, is it ethical? The prudent manager will avoid potential legal liability and will also attempt to conform to what he or she deems to be ethical.

Example C: Your company intends to locate a plant in Mexico for the assembly of automobile engines. If the plant were in the United States, the laws require considerable expenditures for environmental controls such as antipollution equipment. United States law also mandates expensive safeguards to protect the health and safety of U.S. workers, as well as the added cost of minimum wage rules, social security contributions, health care, and other employee benefits. Assume that Mexican law is not so strict and that operating costs there are less as a result. To what extent should you conform to the legal standards applicable in the United States? Is it ethical not to? Indeed, should any firm operating in a host country carry with it the ethical codes of its home country? How does the international manager justify decisions in cross-cultural situations?

Example D: You are an international manager for a U.S. apparel designer that sells to major U.S. department stores and retailers. Several years ago your firm decided to have clothing sewn in India and Pakistan, which resulted in tremendous cost savings as opposed to having the work done in the United States. In making the decision, the firm con-

sidered its impact on U.S. families who depend on the income from these jobs. It opted for the cost savings, seeing its responsibility to produce a profit for shareholders as more important than providing jobs in the United States. Now, however, it finds that its contractor in India is overworking and abusing child labor in violation of internationally accepted standards for the treatment of children in the workplace. The Indian government shows little interest in policing its own labor practices. The sad story of the Indian children is run on national television and appears in the national press. If you decide to discontinue working with sewing contractors in India, would you do so to protect Indian children or because of the adverse publicity in the United States, or both? Consider the company's course of action and how you should react now.

> **http://www.state. gov/e/eb/tpp**
> This is the Bureau of Economic Affairs Trade Policy and Programs Division (EB/TPP) page, which links to APEC, WTO, FTAA, and NAFTA.

Receiving Professional Assistance in Going International

International managers must often rely on advice and assistance from individuals and agencies outside their own firm. Various professionals provide these necessary services: attorneys, bankers, and customs brokers. (For *U.S. Government Sources of Information and Programs to Promote Exports,* see Exhibit 1.2.)

The International Attorney. Lawyers who practice in international business can be in either private practice or employed as in-house counsel to a multinational corporation. Their work might include import/export law, customs and tariff law, immigration and nationality law, admiralty law, the licensing of intellectual property, foreign investment contracts, and other legal issues. Private practice attorneys who specialize in these areas are usually located in the larger cities and have associations with other lawyers in foreign countries. Attorneys who are employees of multinational corporations practice in these areas as well as in immigration and nationality law, tax law, and international antitrust law. They advise management on trade, licensing, and foreign investment matters; draft documents; develop internal

---

EXHIBIT 1.2

U.S. Government Sources of Information
and
Programs to Promote Exports

(See full list at http://schaffer.westbuslaw.com)

GENERAL EXPORT ASSISTANCE AND COUNSELING

International Trade Administration (ITA) provides assistance and information to exporters through domestic and overseas commercial offices, industry experts and market/economic analysts, and market access experts. **http://www.export.gov/tic**

Trade Information Center (ITA) trade specialists provide advice on how to find and use government programs; guidance on the export process, country/regional business counseling on foreign regulations, distribution channels, etc., market research and trade leads, information on trade shows/events, and sources of public and private export financing. **http://tradeinfo.doc.gov**

The Export Assistance Center Network (ITA/SBA/EXIMBANK) provides hands-on export marketing and trade finance support to small- and medium-sized American businesses.

Small Business Administration (SBA) assists U.S. companies setting up an operation, seeking financing, looking to expand, and beginning to engage in exporting. **http://www.sba.gov.**

COUNTRY SPECIFIC INFORMATION

Country Commercial Guides (ITA/STATE) gives information on the business, economic, and political climate in countries around the world. **http://www1.usatrade.gov/website/ccg.nsf**

The World Fact Book (CIA) is an authoritative source for factual information on countries around the world, including their geography, people, government, economy, transportation, etc. **http://www.odci.gov/cia/publications/factbook/**

INDUSTRY-SPECIFIC COUNSELING AND ASSISTANCE

Trade Development Industry Officers (ITA) work with U.S. firms and industry associations to identify overseas trade opportunities and obstacles by product or service, industry sector, and market.

COUNTRY-SPECIFIC COUNSELING AND ASSISTANCE

Business Information Service for the Newly Independent States (ITA) is the U.S. government's resource for commercial information on the Newly Independent States (NIS) of the former Soviet Union. **http://www.bisnis.doc.gov**

Central and Eastern Europe Business Information Center (ITA) is a business facilitation program, that provides trade leads and contacts for U.S. firms interested in expanding into Central and Eastern European markets. **http://www.mac.doc.gov/eebic/ceebic.html**

U.S. Foreign and Commercial Service Offices (ITA) provides advice and supports to U.S. firms by collecting information on trends and barriers to U.S. exports in foreign countries.

U.S. Department of State (STATE) provides political and economic briefings and advice to U.S. firms on the business culture and practices of the host country. **http://www.state.gov/**

U.S. Commercial Centers (ITA) are overseas centers that house state export development agencies, industry associations, government agencies, and other strategic partners.

Overseas Security Advisory Council (STATE) is the point of contact between the Department of State and the U.S. private sector on all overseas security-related matters such as political unrest, crime, terrorism, and the protection of information. **http://www.ds-osac.org**

continued

continued

CUSTOMIZED PROGRAMS

International Partner Search (ITA) provides a customized search to identify well-matched agents, distributors, licensees, and strategic alliance partners.

Flexible Market Research (ITA) provides customized responses to questions and issues related to a client's product or service.

ELECTRONIC MATCHMAKING AND TRADE CONTACT PROGRAMS

E-Expo USA (ITA) is a virtual trade show/online catalog of U.S. products and services where potential foreign buyers can view photos/videos of U.S. products, post leads, link to exhibitors' Web sites, and send email inquiries. **http://e-expousa.doc.gov**

MyExports.com™ (ITA and Global Publishers, LLC) allows U.S. firms to register their business to promote their products before a worldwide audience, and helps U.S. producers find export partners/export companies, freight forwarders, and other service firms.

COMPUTERIZED AND PUBLISHED MARKET INFORMATION

Export.gov (ITA) is a Web portal that brings together U.S. government export-related information organized according to the intended needs of exporters, especially small businesses. **http://www.export.gov**

Office of Trade and Economic Analysis (ITA) provides U.S. foreign trade data useful in evaluating trends in U.S. export performance by major export categories and foreign markets. **http://www.trade.gov/tradestats**

STAT-USA provides online statistical information related to business, economics, and trade. **http://www. stat-usa.gov**

TOP Trade Opportunity Program (ITA) provides companies with current sales leads from international firms seeking to buy or represent their products and services; TOP leads are also printed weekly in leading commercial newspapers.

USA Trade Online provides U.S. import and export statistics for over 18,000 commodities traded worldwide and the most current merchandise trade statistics. **http://www.usatradeonline.gov**. See also, **http://www.eurotradeonline.gov**

Export America Magazine (ITA) offers practical export advice and serves as a valuable resource for small- and medium-sized exporters (SMEs). **http://exportamerica.doc.gov.**

Webcast Library (ITA) provides an online series of video seminars and briefings on current international business topics. **http://www.usatrade.gov/webcasts**

Export and Import Trade Database/U.S. Census Bureau offers a database of U.S. export and import statistics tracked by mode of transportation and district of entry or exit. **http://www.census.gov/foreign-trade/www**

Making Contacts through Trade Promotion Events

International Buyer Program/Domestic (ITA) undertakes a worldwide promotional campaign to maximize international attendance at American trade shows, where an international business center provides export counseling, matchmaking, interpreter, and other business services. **http://www.usatrade.gov/ibp**

Trade Show Outreach Program and ShowTime/Domestic (ITA) officers provide technical advice and assistance to U.S. exporters and foreign buyers at attending U.S. trade shows.

Trade Missions (ITA) provides *commercial missions* that seek to produce export sale by scheduling appointments with officials and prospective customers, and *market access missions* that seek to create market opportunities through the removal of barriers to trade. **http://www.trade.gov/doctm/tmcal.html**

Catalog Exhbitions Program (ITA) is a program to present product literature to business prospects abroad and send trade leads directly to U.S. participants. **http://www.usatrade.gov/catalog**

corporate polices; work on external government relations at home and abroad; supervise litigation abroad; and coordinate the work of foreign counsel.

Freight Forwarder/Customs Broker.

The function of the freight forwarder or customs broker is to expedite the physical transportation of goods and the preparation of the shipping or customs documents. The documentation, or paperwork, required in an export or import shipment is quite extensive. Even though any businessperson needs to understand the legal nature and significance of all documents used to sell goods and transfer money in an international transaction, much of the paperwork is done by the forwarder. Freight forwarders act as the shipper's (the seller) agent for exporting. In doing so, they help consolidate cargo, arrange for marine insurance policies, book the least costly freight space with a carrier, and occasionally prepare the bank collection documents an exporter needs in order to be paid. When these agents represent U.S. importers, they are called customs brokers. A power of attorney is usually required for them to perform their services and to act for the importer or exporter. Customs brokerage firms are licensed and bonded under the rules of the Federal Maritime Commission and the U.S. Bureau of Customs and Border Protection.

The International Banker.

This text devotes considerable study to the role of international banks in all international business transactions. A later chapter, for example, describes how banks move money and shipping documents and, thus, make the international sales contract work. They not only provide important financing, but they also offer a range of specialized international banking services necessary to any firm going abroad. Some international bankers possess a great wealth of expertise and foreign contacts, and are, therefore, able to play an advisory role in international business.

CHAPTER SUMMARY

The business environment changed dramatically from the end of World War II to the 1990s. To be competitive in world markets today, the international manager or world trader needs to be familiar with economics, culture, politics, and law. Multinational firms have adopted business strategies that see the world, and profits, in global terms. Even small- and medium-sized manufacturing and service firms are important competitors in international markets, and will become even more important in the future.

The three basic forms of international business—trade, licensing, and investment—are methods of entering foreign markets. They are not mutually exclusive. One joint venture agreement, for instance, can have provisions for the building of a plant and the manufacture of goods, for the licensing of trademarks or patents to the joint venture for a determined period, and for the export or import of those products to other countries of distribution. The methods employed to enter a foreign market must be tailored to the type and size of the firm, the nature of its product or service, and its experience and goals.

The process of managing an international business transaction is the process of managing risk. Nowhere is that risk greater than in the rapidly changing developing world, in Eastern Europe, or in the newly independent republics of the former Soviet Union. The economic and social problems in those regions make experience and caution a prerequisite to tapping the new opportunities that wait there. Through the study of international business law, one can better prepare to identify potential risks and problems and to plan business strategies accordingly.

Questions and Case Problems

1. What factors have influenced the globalization of business?
2. Describe the "investment risk" that a multinational corporation might face in establishing a plant overseas. What were the risks faced by Union Carbide, a Connecticut-based multinational, in the ownership and operation of its plant in Bhopal, India? At the time

the investment was being planned, the government of India had made its restrictions clear: Union Carbide's Indian plant would have to have Indian joint ownership, Indian engineers and contractors would be responsible for construction, and Indian citizens would manage and operate the plant. For instance, although Union Carbide provided the basic design for the plant,

India insisted that its own firms build it. From 1972 to 1980, the construction was supervised by Indian engineers. During that time, the design was changed many times. Labor and employment polices were set by the Indian government. As the court stated, "more than 1,000 Indians were employed at the plant; only one American was employed there and he left in 1982." The court also notes that plant operations were supervised by more than two dozen Indian government agencies. Evaluate India's policies in this case. Why did they set such strict conditions? Could Indian policies have contributed to the disaster, or was Union Carbide entirely at fault? Why do you think Union Carbide agreed to the terms of the Indian government?

3. How does international business differ from domestic business? What are the risks of entering foreign markets?

4. Undertake a study of one country or one region of the world and evaluate its business climate, its attitude toward trade and foreign investment, and the level of political risk. Where would you go for sources of information? How has the breakup of the former Soviet Union affected the business climate in that region?

5. Who are the members of a firm's "export team"? Describe each of their functions.

6. Plaintiff, a Swiss corporation, entered into contracts to purchase chicken from B.N.S. International Sales Corporation. Defendant was a New York corporation. The English language contracts called for the delivery of "chicken" of various weights. When the birds were shipped to Switzerland, the 2-lb. sizes were not young broiling chickens as the plaintiff had expected, but mature stewing chickens or fowl. The plaintiff protested, claiming that in German the term *chicken* referred to young broiling chickens. The question for the court was what kind of chicken did the plaintiff order. Was it "broiling chicken" as the plaintiff argued, or any chickens weighing 2 lbs. as the defendant argued? *Frigaliment Importing Co., Ltd. v. B.N.S. International Sales Corp.,* 190 F. Supp 116 (S.D.N.Y. 1960). What could the parties have done to avoid this misunderstanding?

7. Successful international managers agree that success in entering a foreign market comes from planning and commitment. What does this mean? What kind of commitment do you think they are referring to? It is also often said that exporting is not an "elixir" for a company that is failing in its home market and is looking for new sales elsewhere. Evaluate this statement. Do you think it is true?

8. What industries in your state are the leading exporters? Who are the leading export firms? What do you think is the impact of exports on your state's economy? Where would you go for information? What role does your state government play in promoting exports?

9. U.S. firms have been very successful in foreign franchising, particularly in fast food and other retail businesses and service companies. How do you account for this success? Where do you think the best opportunities and hottest markets are for foreign franchising?

10. Multinational corporations and other firms must abide by the laws and regulations of their host countries. They must also understand the unwritten or informal rules of doing business there—rules based on culture, religious codes, and societal constraints. Sometimes these laws and rules can be very different from those in the firm's home country, or in other countries in which it operates. Pollution may be a crime in one country, and tolerated in another; bribery may be a crime in one country, and customary in another; and so on. How does the multinational manager reconcile differences like these? What is the appropriate standard of ethical conduct for a multinational manager—and how is it influenced by the laws, unwritten rules, and cultural values of the host country? How does the multinational manager balance his or her social responsibility to the people of the host country with the company's overall objective of maximizing shareholder profit? What can a multinational corporation do to aid its managers in the development of a personal ethical value system that is in keeping with the legal and cultural values of their host countries?

Managerial Implications

Your firm, SewTex, Inc., manufactures consumer and industrial sewing machinery. The consumer machines retail for $350 to $1,000 and are sold in the United States through department stores, discount stores, and home sewing stores. The industrial machines range in price from $5,000 to $50,000. The machines contain a unique computer chip that allows them to embroider words and designs on fabric in a choice of four scripts.

The firm owns the patent on the machines in the United States. Currently the industrial machines are made in the United States from components made in the United States and Taiwan. The consumer machines are assembled at plants in Texas and in the Caribbean from parts made in Taiwan. The computer chip is manufactured for SewTex by a California firm.

Currently SewTex exports about 5 percent of its production of industrial machines. Of the total exported, the most sophisticated machines went to German and Swiss textile firms. A few earlier generation models were shipped to India, Pakistan, and Brazil, although market prospects there look excellent.

The president of SewTex is concerned about the decline of the U.S. textile industry. She has asked your opinion on whether the company should consider increasing sales in foreign markets. She feels that some board members might caution against "getting involved overseas," and even she anticipates the U.S. textile market will pick up if the U.S. Congress places higher tariffs on textile imports. But she would like your thoughts. She has asked you to prepare a memorandum on the subject, and requests that you address some of the following issues.

1. She feels that she must have the support of the directors for any major overseas venture. What arguments can she offer to explain why SewTex should become active in international markets? She understands that making a commitment is important, but what does that really mean?
2. If SewTex were to consider increasing its export base, what problems might it encounter? What are the advantages and disadvantages in exporting products to Europe? Should it consider direct or indirect exporting in view of its product? If it chooses to continue exporting, how can it offer a repair service and a supply of spare parts to its customers?
3. Should SewTex consider licensing its technology to one of the other textile machinery manufacturers in Europe? Compare the advantages and disadvantages of this method of market entry to exporting.
4. The company president would like to know the options available for investment in the European market. Would this be preferable to the other market entry alternatives?
5. The company president recently read that Volkswagen and Mercedes have negotiated the purchase of automobile plants in the Czech Republic. She wonders whether the Czech government might be offering significant incentives to operate one of their mills. She knows that this country split from the Slovak Republic, in what had been Czechoslovakia, and that tension has existed between them over the years. She is concerned about the stability of a democratic government there. What sources can she turn to for more information on investment in the Czech Republic and Eastern Europe? What are the risks inherent in taking over operations there? What are the advantages?
6. SewTex's president is interested in knowing more about its market potential in Latin America for both types of machines. Can you advise her on the best methods for SewTex to penetrate that market? How would your plans for entry into the Latin American market affect SewTex's assembly operations and sales efforts worldwide?
7. Finally, can you advise SewTex on copyright, patent, and trademark issues related to its penetration of foreign markets? What are the major issues and concerns?

CHAPTER 2

INTERNATIONAL LAW AND ORGANIZATIONS

Most people are familiar with local, state, and federal or national law as it applies to their personal conduct and business behavior. For example, U.S. federal securities laws will affect the manner in which securities are traded within the United States. If the transaction crosses national borders, however, two nations' laws may apply to the transaction. The two nations may have very different legal systems and laws. Wouldn't it be simpler if once a business transaction crossed a nation's border, some international law automatically applied to the transaction? What about international law? Is there law that transcends national boundaries or is "supranational"?

International law exists and can be found in treaties or conventions and in customary international law. In addition, international organizations such as the WTO, the United Nations, and the Organization for Economic Cooperation and Development (OECD), to name only a few, have a direct impact on the conduct of transnational business. This chapter grapples with the question of what is international law. It also looks at the increasing importance of international organizations and their effect on business.

http://www.wto.org
The home page of the World Trade Organization.

PUBLIC INTERNATIONAL LAW

International law does exist. It has been defined as a "rule . . . that has been accepted as such [law] by the international community." International law includes customary international law, international agreements, and general principles common to major legal systems. Although this definition provides guidance, it also raises many questions. For example, at what point has a "rule" been accepted by the international community of states? What is a customary law? Where does one find general principles common to major legal systems?

When the term *international law* is used, people most often think of public international law. Public international law involves relationships between states (meaning nations or countries) and applies "norms regarded as binding on all members of the international community," which may be reflected in treaties, conventions, or the charters of international organizations such as the United Nations (UN). Some issues related to public international law include the following: When is it appropriate or legal for a nation to use force? How should prisoners taken pursuant to a war be treated? Is torture of prisoners ever justified? Questions of international law can be raised in national courts as well as in international fora discussed later. In a post 9-11 world, these questions seem ever pressing with a war in Afghanistan and the United Nations divided over the necessity and legality of the war in Iraq in 2003.

A famous U.S. Supreme Court case, *Paquette Habana,* illustrates how the Court discerned what was the applicable international law. The Court discusses the necessity of resorting to "customs and usage" to ascertain international law.

Public international law has been defined as the law governing relations between states. This

The Paquette Habana
175 U.S. 677 (1900)
United States Supreme Court

BACKGROUND AND FACTS

Two vessels, sailing under Spanish flags and owned by a Spanish citizen living in Cuba, were used to fish and sell the catch. The owner had no ammunition and was unaware of the hostilities with Spain nor of the 1898 blockade of Cuba. The United States seized the ship. The Spanish owner sued for damages.

The Federal District for the Southern District of Florida upheld the United States' condemnation of the vessels as prizes of war. The owner appealed to the United States Supreme Court.

JUSTICE GRAY

These are two appeals from decrees of the district court of the United States for the southern district of Florida condemning two fishing vessels and their cargoes as prize of war. . . .

We are then brought to the consideration of the question whether, upon the facts appearing in these records, the fishing smacks were subject to capture by the armed vessels of the United States during the recent war with Spain.

By an ancient usage among civilized nations, beginning centuries ago, and gradually ripening into a rule of international law, coast fishing vessels, pursuing their vocation of catching and bringing in fresh fish, have been recognized as exempt, with their cargoes and crews, from capture as prize of war. . . .

The doctrine which exempts coast fishermen, with their vessels and cargoes, from capture as prize of war, has been familiar to the United States from the time of the War of Independence. . . .

Since the United States became a nation, the only serious interruptions, so far as we are informed, of the general recognition of the exemption of coast fishing vessels from hostile capture, arose out of the mutual suspicions and recriminations of England and France during the wars of the French Revolution. . . .

In the war with Mexico, in 1846, the United States recognized the exemption of coast fishing boats from capture. . . .

International law is part of our law, and must be ascertained and administered by the courts of justice of appropriate jurisdiction as often as questions of right depending upon it are duly presented for their determination. For this purpose, where there is no treaty and no controlling executive or legislative act or judicial decision, resort must be had to the customs and usages of civilized nations, and, as evidence of these, to the works of jurists and commentators who by years of labor, research, and experience have made themselves peculiarly well acquainted with the subjects of which they treat. Such works are resorted to by judicial tribunals, not for the speculations of their authors concerning what the law ought to be, but for trustworthy evidence of what the law really is. . . .

This review of the precedents and authorities of the subject appears to us abundantly to demonstrate that at the present day, by the general consent of the civilized nations of the world, and independently of any express treaty or other public act, it is an established rule of international law, founded on consideration of humanity to a poor and industrious order of men, and of the mutual convenience of belligerent states, that coast fishing vessels, with their implements and supplies, cargoes and crews, unarmed and honestly pursuing their peaceful calling of catching and bringing in fresh fish, are exempt from capture as prize of war. . . .

This rule of international law is one which prize courts administering the law of nations are bound to take judicial notice of, and to give effect to, in the absence of any treaty or other public act of their own government in relation to the matter. . . .

Decision. The Supreme Court reversed the holding of the district court and said that under an established rule of international law, peaceful fishermen are exempt from capture as prizes of war. The Court ordered that the owner receive payment for the loss of the ship, along with damages and costs. The Court acknowledged that it was "bound" to take judicial notice of international law.

---

definition has been expanded, and public international law is now more commonly thought of as "rules and principles of general application dealing with the conduct of states and of international organizations and with their relations inter se [among themselves] as well as with some of their relations with persons, whether natural or juridical."[1]

The Law of Treaties

A *treaty* is a binding agreement, contract, or *compact* between two or more nations or international organizations that is recognized and given effect under international law. A treaty between two countries is said to be *bilateral,* and a treaty between three or more countries is *multilateral.* A *convention* is a treaty on matters of common concern, usually negotiated on a regional or global basis and open to adoption by many nations. Most treaties negotiated under the auspices of the United Nations are called *conventions.* A *protocol* is an agreement on matters less significant than those dealt with in treaties, and is usually used when referring to documents dealing with issues that are ancillary to, or amend, a treaty. A treaty is said to have been *adopted* when it is completed in its final form ready for nations to ratify. *Ratification* is the formal expression of a nation's consent to be bound by the treaty terms (ratification in the United States requires the vote of two-thirds of the U.S. Senate). Nations that join a treaty are said to be *signatories* or *contracting parties.* A treaty becomes effective on the date set out in the treaty for it to *"enter into force."* There are tens of thousands of treaties in effect worldwide. They touch on every subject affecting humankind, including peace and security, human rights, disarmament, the condition of refugees, the environment, the treatment of prisoners, and of course, trade, investment, and commerce. There are countless examples covering all aspects of international relations.

Treaties serve to make international law more uniform throughout the world. For example, one treaty facilitates the registration and protection of patent rights. The treaty provided for a uniform system of filing patent applications. In 2003, the *Madrid Protocol* became effective, enabling a trademark to be registered with one filing in all signatory countries. The World Intellectual Property Organization, an agency of the UN system, is made up of 179 member nations (2003) and administers a total of 23 treaties that facilitate the protection of intellectual property and harmonize patent, trademark, and copyright law. Another example is the *UN Convention on Contracts for the International Sale of Goods,* which sets out a uniform code defining the rights of buyers and sellers of goods sold in international commerce. In the following case, *U.S. v. Alvarez-Machain,* the Court addressed the issue of international law and the interpretation of treaty provisions.

The Vienna Convention on the Law of Treaties

Originally treaties were governed by customary international law rules. The *1980 Vienna Convention on the Law of Treaties* (*Vienna Convention*) codified many of the customary rules. With 97 countries joining the convention, legal scholars today view it as the summary statement of the law governing treaties and conventions. It covers such issues as when treaties enter into force, how they are interpreted, amended or terminated, and the rights and duties of contracting parties.

Pacta sunt servanda. The *Vienna Convention* recognizes several basic principles. One of the most important is the principle of *Pacta sunt servanda* ("the pact must be respected"), meaning that treaties are binding upon the parties by consent and must be performed by them in good faith. Other provisions deal with conflicts between treaties (i.e., when two treaties are in conflict on a particular matter, the later treaty prevails), how treaties are interpreted or terminated, the rights of the parties when it becomes impossible to continue honoring a treaty, or the effect of a fundamental change in circumstances on treaty obligations.

Jus cogens. One of the basic principles of international law is *jus cogens.* According to this principle, there are certain fundamental rights or minimum standards of state behavior that are so widely held by the community of nations that no nation may derogate from them. An example may be the norm against the execution of the mentally ill or of juveniles, norms prohibiting genocide, slavery, systematic rape as punishment, torture in prisons, or the use of children-soldiers in war. One important reason for terminating a treaty can be found in the principle of *jus cogens.* According to this principle of international law, as expressed in Article 53 of the *Vienna Convention,* a treaty is void if it violates "a peremptory norm of general international law." The convention defines *peremptory norm* as "a norm accepted and recognized by the international community of States as a whole as a norm from which no derogation is permitted. . . ."

Thus, treaty provisions are void if they violate norms commonly held by civilized nations.

http://

> **http://fletcher.tufts.edu/multilaterals.html**
> Makes available the texts of international multilateral conventions and other instruments, including the Vienna Convention.

The Impact of Treaties on Business

Treaties can have significant impact on individual rights and on business. Tax treaties are part of international law and can have a dramatic impact on business. There are numerous bilateral tax treaties that stipulate the treatment of dividends, and so forth, between signatories. An example is the *Chemical Weapons Convention,* which bans the production of chemical warfare materials and imposes significant reporting requirements on private industry including data declarations and on-site inspections to monitor enforcement of the convention. There could be countless examples.

Another example of the role of international treaties and their effect on business can be seen in the debate over the *Law of the Sea Convention.* The convention had been the subject of debate between developing and developed countries. The wealthier countries saw it as a measure to redistribute the wealth of nations. The Reagan and G.H. Bush administrations had been opposed to the treaty. Language recognizing oceans as "a common heritage of Mankind" that would be part of a "just and equitable order" was problematic. The Clinton administration successfully sought amendments to allay some of these concerns, including dropping both the fee required to explore for minerals on the ocean floor as well as the extraction of royalties to fund the oversight agency, the International Seabed Authority, in Jamaica. The advantages the treaty offered were numerous. The treaty clarified the right of passage through straits, sovereignty over twelve miles off shore, and control of fishing, oil, and gas

United States v. Alvarez-Machain
504 U.S. 655 (1992)
United States Supreme Court

BACKGROUND AND FACTS

Alvarez-Machain was a citizen and resident of Mexico. He was kidnapped from home and flown by private plane to Texas where he was arrested for participation in the kidnapping, torture, and murder of a U.S. Drug Enforcement Agent (DEA) and the agent's pilot. Although the DEA agents did not themselves abduct Alvarez-Machain, the Court concluded that they were responsible. The torture and murder had been videotaped, and the agent had been given drugs by the accused to prolong his consciousness during torture. Mexico protested a violation in the extradition treaty with the United States. The district court dismissed the indictment based on the conclusion that the abduction violated the extradition treaty and ordered the accused be returned to Mexico. The court of appeals affirmed. The Supreme Court granted certiorari.

REHNQUIST, CHIEF JUSTICE

The issue in this case is whether a criminal defendant abducted to the United States from a nation with which it has an extradition treaty thereby acquires a defense to the jurisdiction of this country's courts. We hold that he does not and that he may be tried in federal district court for violations of criminal laws of the United States. . . .

[O]ur first inquiry must be whether the abduction of Alvarez from Mexico violated the extradition treaty. . . . In construing a treaty as in construing a statute we first look to its terms to determine its meaning. . . . The Treaty says nothing about the obligations of the United States and Mexico to refrain from forcible abductions of people. In the absence of an extradition treaty, nations are under no obligation to surrender those in their country to foreign authorities for prosecution. . . . Extradition treaties exist so as to impose mutual obligations to surrender individuals in certain defined sets of circumstances, following established procedures. [The Treaty thus provides a mechanism which would not otherwise exist, requiring, under certain circumstances, the United States and Mexico to extradite individuals to

continued

continued

the other country, and establishing the procedures to be followed when the Treaty is invoked.]

The history of negotiation and practice under the Treaty also fails to show that abductions outside of the Treaty constitute a violation of the Treaty. . . .

Thus, the language of the Treaty, in the context of its history, does not support the proposition that the Treaty prohibits abductions outside of its terms. The remaining question, therefore, is whether the Treaty should be interpreted so as to include an implied term prohibiting prosecution where the defendant's presence is obtained by means other than those established by the Treaty.

Respondent contends that the Treaty must be interpreted against the backdrop of customary international law, and that international abductions are "so clearly prohibited in international law" that there was no reason to include such a clause in the Treaty itself. The international censure of international abductions is further evidenced, according to respondent, by the United Nations Charter and the Charter of the Organization of American States. Respondent does not argue that these sources of international law provide an independent basis for the right respondent asserts not to be tried in the United States, but rather that they should inform the interpretation of the Treaty terms. . . .

Respondent would have us find that the Treaty acts as a prohibition against a violation of the general principle of international law that one government may not "exercise its police power in the territory of another state." There are many actions which could be taken by a nation that would violate this principle, including waging war, but it cannot seriously be contended an invasion of the United States by Mexico would violate the terms of the extradition treaty between the two nations.

In sum, to infer from this Treaty and its terms that it prohibits all means of gaining the presence of an individual outside of its terms goes beyond established precedent and practice. . . . By contrast, to imply from the terms of this Treaty that it prohibits obtaining the presence of an individual by means outside of the procedures the Treaty establishes requires a much larger inferential leap, with only the most general of international law principles to support it. The general principles cited by respondent simply fail to persuade us that we should imply in the United States-Mexico Extradition Treaty a term prohibiting international abductions.

The judgment of the Court of Appeals is therefore reversed, and the case is remanded for further proceedings consistent with this opinion.

STEVENS, BLACKMUN, AND O'CONNOR, JUSTICES DISSENTING

The Court's admittedly "shocking" disdain for customary and conventional international law principles, is thus entirely unsupported by case law and commentary.

As the Court observes at the outset of its opinion, there is reason to believe that respondent participated in an especially brutal murder of an American law enforcement agent. That fact, if true, may explain the Executive's intense interest in punishing respondent in our courts. Such an explanation, however, provides no justification for disregarding the Rule of Law that this Court has a duty to uphold. That the Executive may wish to reinterpret the Treaty to allow for an action that the Treaty in no way authorizes should not influence this Court's interpretation. Indeed, the desire for revenge exerts "a kind of hydraulic pressure . . . before which even well-settled principles of law will bend," but it is precisely at such moments that we should remember and be guided by our duty "to render judgment evenly and dispassionately according to law, as each is given understanding to ascertain and apply it." . . . I suspect most courts throughout the civilized world will be deeply disturbed by the "monstrous" decision the Court announces today. For every Nation that has an interest in preserving the Rule of Law is affected, directly or indirectly, by a decision of this character. As Thomas Paine warned, an "avidity to punish is always dangerous to liberty" because it leads a Nation "to stretch, to misinterpret, and to misapply even the best of laws." To counter that tendency, he reminds us: "He that would make his own liberty secure must guard even his enemy from oppression; for if he violates this duty he establishes a precedent that will reach to himself."

Decision. The Court held the defendant did not have a basis to object to jurisdiction. Thus, he could be tried by the lower court.

Comment. After almost three years in custody, Alvarez was acquitted at trial and returned to Mexico. The American Civil Liberties Union has pressed a $20 million civil lawsuit against the United States government on his behalf. His right to bring this suit was upheld by the U.S. Court of Appeals, and as of 2003, was being reviewed by the U.S. Supreme Court. In 1994 the United States and Mexico signed a new treaty to prohibit the kidnapping of criminal suspects wanted for trial.

rights within two hundred miles off shore. The treaty had sixty-one country ratifications and took effect in 1994. Although Clinton signed it, the U.S. Senate has not ratified the treaty. This illustrates the difficulty in developing international agreements when an important nation like the United States remains so divided on the issue.

International Court of Justice

Some public international law disputes may be heard by the World Court. The International Court of Justice or ICJ (also known as the World Court) was formed in 1945 with its statute attached to the United Nations charter. Its precursor, called the Permanent Court of Justice, was established in 1920 as part of the League of Nations. The World Court has fifteen judges who are elected by the United Nations General Assembly and the Security Council for a term of nine years. If a state is a party to a dispute before the court and no judge of that nationality is sitting on the court, a sixteenth and possibly seventeenth judge will be temporarily elected. The court sits in The Hague, The Netherlands, and

---

Exhibit 2.1

Statute of the International Court of Justice

Article 36

1. The jurisdiction of the Court comprises all cases which the parties refer to it and all matters specially provided for in the Charter of the United Nations or in treaties and conventions in force.

2. The states parties to the present Statute may at any time declare that they recognize as compulsory *ipso facto* and without special agreement, in relation to any other state accepting the same obligation, the jurisdiction of the Court in all legal disputes concerning;

    a. the interpretation of a treaty;

    b. any question of international law;

    c. the existence of any fact which, if established, would constitute a breach of an international obligation; and

    d. the nature or extent of the reparation to be made for the breach of an international obligation.

3. The declarations referred to above may be made unconditionally or on condition of reciprocity on the part of several or certain states, or for a certain time.

4. Such declarations shall be deposited with the Secretary-General of the United Nations, who shall transmit copies thereof to the parties to the Statute and to the Registrar of the Court.

5. Declarations made under Article 36 of the Statute of the Permanent Court of International Justice and which are still in force shall be deemed, as between the parties to the present Statute, to be acceptance of the compulsory jurisdiction of the International Court of Justice for the period which they still have to run and in accordance with their terms.

6. In the event of a dispute as to whether the Court has jurisdiction, the matter shall be settled by the decision of the Court.

Article 38

1. The Court, whose function is to decide in accordance with international law such disputes as are submitted to it, shall apply:

    a. international conventions, whether general or particular, establishing rules expressly recognized by the contesting states;

    b. international custom, as evidence of a general practice accepted as law;

    c. the general principles of law recognized by civilized nations;

    d. subject to the provisions of Article 59, judicial decisions and the teachings of the most highly qualified publicists of the various nations, as subsidiary means for the determination of rules of law.

2. This provision shall not prejudice the power of the Court to decide a case *ex aequo et bono* if the parties agree thereto.

bases its decisions on the Statute of the International Court of Justice. (See Exhibit 2.1.) The ICJ also uses three to five member chambers to hear some cases. This practice allows for a quicker, less cumbersome process.

Problems of Jurisdiction.   The World Court has not been a major force in settling world disputes, particularly commercial ones, for several reasons. First, only states can be parties before the court, although a state may bring an action before the court on behalf of an individual or individuals, alleging that some infringement of an individual's right is an infringement against the sovereign state. Secondly, decisions are binding only on the parties involved; however, some unofficial case precedent has been developed through the evolution of general principles of law. Third, before a nation can be brought before the court, it must accept jurisdiction of the court because no compulsory process forces a state

see Liechtenstein case

to come before the court. Many communist, and formerly communist, countries have not accepted the jurisdiction of the court by filing declarations of acceptance with the court; thus, they preserve their right to pick and choose when they will consent to the jurisdiction of the court on matters related to them. This selective acceptance of jurisdiction limits the World Court's ability to assume as prominent a role as it otherwise could. Lastly, the enforcement powers of the court, although detailed in the statute as well as in the United Nations charter, rely in large part on good faith compliance of the parties.

> **http://www.icj-cij.org/**
> Offers text of official judgments, advisory opinions, and orders from the International Court of Justice.

The   following case examines the first problem—that only states may be parties—and how the court may address individual or corporate injury despite this limitation.

Liechtenstein v. Guatemala (Nottebohm Case)
1955 I.C.J. REP.4 (1955)
International Court of Justice

BACKGROUND AND FACTS
Nottebohm was born in Germany in 1881. He moved to Guatemala for business reasons in 1905 and lived there until 1943 except for business trips and visits to his brother in Liechtenstein.

In 1939, Germany attacked Poland. Visiting Liechtenstein that year, Nottebohm applied to be naturalized as a citizen and asked Liechtenstein to waive the three-year residency requirement. He paid taxes to Liechtenstein and filed the requisite forms, and in 1939 Liechtenstein waived the required time period, swore him in as a citizen, and issued him a passport.

In 1943 Guatemala entered World War II, siding with the United States. Guatemala seized Nottebohm as a German enemy, turned him over to the United States for internment, and seized his property for the government. Nottebohm was released in 1946, but his property was not returned.

Liechtenstein filed a "memorial," as it is called, before the International Court of Justice (ICJ), claiming that Guatemala had violated international law and was obligated to pay damages.

Guatemala has referred to a well-established principle of international law, which it expressed in Counter-Memorial, where it is stated that "it is the bond of nationality between the State and the individual which alone confers upon the State the right of diplomatic protection."

. . . Counsel for Liechtenstein said: "The essential question is whether Mr. Nottebohm, having acquired the nationality of Liechtenstein, that acquisition of nationality is one which must be recognized by other States."

The Court does not propose to go beyond the limited scope of the question which it has to decide, namely, whether the nationality conferred on Nottebohm can be relied upon as against Guatemala in justification of the proceedings instituted before the Court. It must decide this question on the basis of international law.

International arbitrators have . . . given their preference to the real and effective nationality, that which accorded with the facts, that based on stronger factual ties between the person concerned and one of the States whose nationality is involved.

The character thus recognized on the international level as pertaining to nationality is in no way inconsistent with the fact that international law leaves it to each State

continued

---

continued

to lay down the rules governing the grant of its own nationality.

At the time of his naturalization, does Nottebohm appear to have been more closely attached by his tradition, his establishment, his interests, his activities, his family ties, his intentions for the near future to Liechtenstein than to any other State?

Naturalization was asked for not so much for the purpose of obtaining a legal recognition of Nottebohm's membership in fact in the population of Liechtenstein, as it was to enable him to substitute for his status as a national of a belligerent State with that of a national of a neutral State, with the sole aim of thus coming within the protection of Liechtenstein but not of becoming wedded

to its traditions, its interests, its way of life or of assuming the obligations—other than fiscal obligations—and exercising the rights pertaining to the status thus acquired.

Guatemala is under no obligation to recognize a nationality granted in such circumstances. Liechtenstein consequently is not entitled to extend its protection to Nottebohm vis-à-vis Guatemala, and its claim must, for this reason, be held to be inadmissible.

Decision.   The World Court held that the claim was inadmissible because Guatemala was not required to recognize the citizenship granted by Liechtenstein in a way that did not follow well-established principles of international law

---

Although only a state can be a party before the court, sometimes a state will itself take up the cause of a person or company, often only after attempts to resolve the matter through diplomatic channels have failed. The *Nottebohm* (1955 ICJ4) case illustrates this point.

As noted in the preceding case, a state must accept the jurisdiction of the court before a case can be brought before the court. Many communist countries have not accepted the jurisdiction of the court, and many other nations, particularly Western ones, have filed declarations accepting the court's jurisdiction with various limitations. For example, France, Norway, and the United States filed statements accepting the jurisdiction of the ICJ. The United States stated that the declaration did not apply to

a. disputes the solution of which the parties shall entrust to other tribunals by virtue of agreements already in existence or which may be concluded in the future; or
b. disputes with regard to matters which are essentially within the domestic jurisdiction of the United States of America as determined by the United States of America; or
c. disputes arising under a multilateral treaty, unless (1) all parties to the treaty affected by the decision are also parties to the case before the Court, or (2) the United States of America specially agrees to jurisdiction.

Because of hostilities and philosophical differences between the United States and Nicaragua, on

April 6, 1984, the United States amended its declaration to exempt matters dealing with Central America. The declaration stated in part that the aforesaid declaration shall not apply to disputes with any Central American State or arising out of or related to events in Central America, any of which disputes shall be settled in such manner as the parties to them may agree.

Notwithstanding the terms of the aforesaid declaration, this proviso shall take effect immediately and shall remain in force for two years, so as to foster the continuing regional dispute settlement process which seeks a negotiated solution to the interrelated political, economic and security problems of Central America.

Three days later, Nicaragua filed an action with the ICJ, claiming that the United States had mined Nicaraguan harbors and committed other covert acts designed to destabilize the government of Nicaragua.

The United States claimed on the basis of its amended declaration that the court did not have jurisdiction. The court did not agree with the United States because the previous declaration had contained a six months' notice provision, and issued a decision stating that it had jurisdiction and would proceed to hear arguments in the case. The United States withdrew and refused to participate in the hearings on the merits. The United States noted that nine of the fifteen judges came from states that did not accept compulsory jurisdiction. The court proceeded to hear the case in the absence of the United States, but tried to anticipate and address arguments that the United States might have raised had it participated. Not surprisingly, the court voted in 1986 that the United States had not acted in self-defense, that it had breached "customary international law not to intervene in the affairs of another state" by arming the "contra forces," and that it violated the sovereignty of another state. The court ordered the United States to cease all acts that constituted a breach of international law and to make reparation to Nicaragua for any injury caused. The decision included sixteen separate findings in which the judges' votes ranged from 11–1 to 14–1. In the latter case, only the United States' judge voted against the finding. Only the final finding, "to seek a solution to their disputes by peaceful means in accordance with international law," was unanimous.

The near-unanimous sentiment expressed by the judges, with the exception of the United States and British judges, underscores how differently other nationalities view the United States's interpretation of actions permissible under international law, particularly in Central America.

It also underscores how "politicized" the court had become. The future of the court was in question, because the United States, a long-time proponent of the court, now questioned its purpose and utility. Due to a political change in Nicaragua from the Sandinista regime to an elected government, the G. H. Bush administration began negotiations about the resumption of financial aid. Following these discussions, Nicaragua asked the ICJ to discontinue the proceedings and the court, in 1991, entered such an order.

Developments Since the Nicaragua Case.   The United States has signaled a shift in policy since it amended its declaration and walked out on the Nicaragua case proceeding in the World Court. Thereafter, the United States agreed to submit a case involving the expropriation (or taking over by a state) of a Raytheon subsidiary, ELSI, in Italy to five agreed-upon judges, illustrating the use of a chamber proceeding. In 1987, Italy and the United States agreed to go forward with the case. Nevertheless, the United States lost the case. More recently the World Court, in 2003, ordered the United States to take "all measures necessary" to prevent the execution of three Mexican nationals,

pending the court's final judgment. Many countries are concerned that foreign nationals arrested by the United States never have the opportunity to consult with embassy/consular officials of their home country, in contravention of the *Vienna Convention on Consular Relations.* In the past, the United States has executed foreign nationals who did not have the benefit of a consultation with consular officials, claiming that due process rights were sufficient. The ICJ has also adjudicated disputes between Benin and Niger, Congo and Rwanda, El Salvador and Honduras, and France and the Congo. These cases may be reviewed at the court's Web site.

THE ROLE OF THE UNITED NATIONS IN THE PUBLIC INTERNATIONAL LAW

The original fifty-one founding states' purpose for establishing the United Nations is stated in the Charter, as shown in Exhibit 2.2. Since the fall of the Berlin Wall and the demise of communism, the member countries have been able to use the United Nations more as its founders originally envisioned.

Currently, the United Nations has 191 members. Most countries, both communist and democratic, are members. Switzerland recently joined in 2002.

> **http://www.un.org**
> Provides the full text of the Charter of the United Nations.

The General Assembly and the Security Council

The United Nations is structured with a General Assembly, the Security Council, and the Secretary General, who tries to lead both of them. Each member nation sends a delegate to the General Assembly and has one vote. In the General Assembly, all countries have equal votes; thus, the United States, the United Kingdom, and Japan share the same position as the Republic of Burkina Faso. The Secretary General functions as the chief administrative officer within a Secretariat designed to provide an apolitical supranational civil service. In practice, this has not always been the case. The Secretary General is recommended by the Security Council and elected by the General Assembly.

Historically, the Secretaries General have tried to exercise a leadership role in achieving the United Nations' goal of international peace.

The Security Council is composed of fifteen member states with five permanent members. The People's Republic of China, France, the United Kingdom, now Russia, and the United States each have a permanent representative, and ten nonpermanent members are elected by the General Assembly every two years.

Permanent members of the Security Council have a veto over nonprocedural issues, thereby ensuring that a superpower can block an action proposed by the Security Council. The use of the veto exercised by the former Soviet Union or the United States had effectively rendered the Security Council impotent and unable to take any action during the Cold War. This changed when the Berlin Wall fell in 1989. The end of the Cold War and the establishment of trade relations with China opened the opportunity for the permanent five members to begin to work more cooperatively on political issues.

The *United Nations Charter* delineates the powers of the Security Council, which include the severance of diplomatic relations, and military action via blockades or air, sea, and land operations (see Exhibit 2.3).

The UN Security Council and Iraq. Political events in the Middle East in recent years highlight the importance of the UN and of international law in world affairs. In the period leading up to the first Gulf War in 1991, there was clear agreement by the nations of the Security Council that Iraq had wrongfully invaded its neighbor, Kuwait, and that it had to withdraw. A UN Security Council resolution to that effect was passed. Armed with this resolution, the United States led a coalition of military forces to enforce the will of the international community. This ushered in what came to be known as the "decade of international law," reflecting the importance of law in enforcing international peace and security. The second conflict with Iraq in 2003 did not result from a similar international consensus. The nations of the Security Council had differing views on whether Iraq was in violation of its resolutions on weapons inspection and disarmament. There was great argument as to whether economic sanctions would force Iraq into compliance

or whether military force was necessary. Although legal arguments were made for and against the use of force, in the end the United States, Britain, and their closest allies launched a preemptive attack on Iraq leading to a change in government there. While the legality of the war may well be decided only by historians, the one thing that is clear is that nations prefer to act with the support of the international community whenever possible, but when not possible, they will act to protect their own national interests.

International Law and the World of Business

This introduction to public international law, and to the UN system, helps build the foundation for our later study of legal and political issues affecting businesses worldwide. Throughout the book we will look at how companies operate in a global environment, subject to international law and internationally accepted rules for trade, commerce, and investment. Moreover, we will often see how the realities of the political world will affect businesses and the decisions that managers make as they operate in the far reaches of the globe. A manager who understands these issues will be better able to assess the risk of international transactions and of doing business on a global scale.

PRIVATE INTERNATIONAL LAW

Up to this point, our discussion has focused on public international law and not specifically on international business law. Scholars and practitioners often divide international law into two categories: public international law and private international law. *Private international law,* defined as the laws applying to private parties in international transactions, is sometimes described as *conflict of laws* or the "domain of rights, duties, and disputes between and among persons from different places," and often involves commercial transactions.[2] In other words, private international law concerns how a nation's courts deal with a different nation's laws. Different national legal systems may compete for jurisdiction, and the laws they choose conflict.

Private international law is a misnomer in that it suggests that a separate body of law governs private transactions. Just as in public international law, private international law has no uniform codified set of accepted law. The field of conflict of laws consists of three areas: choice of law (which law applies to the transaction), choice of forum (who has jurisdiction or the power to hear the case), and recognition and enforcement of judgments. Private international law is also affected by multilateral conventions that provide a base for initial unification of substantive law.

Examples of these conventions include the *Recognition and Enforcement of Foreign Arbitral Awards* (1958); *Service Abroad of Judicial and Extra-Judicial Documents* (1965); *Taking of Evidence Abroad; Inter-American Convention on Letters Rogatory* (1975); *Hague Convention on International Child Abduction* (1980); and the *Convention on Contracts for the International Sale of Goods* (1980).

Through these conventions, some progress has been made in securing national agreement that arbitration awards should be honored and that foreign courts should be assisted by national courts in collecting evidence, although not necessarily in exact compliance with the requesting legal system. In other words, although France might assist a party in a dispute in New York to gather evidence in France, it will not necessarily comply with every deposition, interrogatory, or motion to produce documents that would be honored in the United States.

Historically, law evolved to deal with the growth of trade. Early regional attempts at codification of mercantile law include the *Sea Law of Rhodes,* adopted in 300 B.C., and the Amalfitan Table, adopted after the First Crusade by the Republic of Amalfi. The expansion of agriculture and the rise of cities in the twelfth and thirteenth centuries led to the development of special courts for merchants, which were familiar with their business practices. The noted thirteenth-century English judge and legal scholar Henry de Bracton noted that such courts were essential for merchants because they had special requirements, such as a need for speedy justice, which could be aided by a reduced time to answer a summons. The law administered by these courts, the *Law Merchant* or *Lex Mercatoria,* derived from ancient codes developed among merchants, some of which can be traced back to the Chaldeans in Mesopotamia (Iraq) and to the Babylonian king Hammurabi, who issued a code of laws around 2,000 B.C. The *Lex Mercatoria* represents the earliest form of private international law.

These special mercantile courts disappeared in England by the eighteenth century (although they lingered on in France, Germany, and Switzerland), and thereafter merchants were forced to prove the *Lex Mercatoria* as if it were some foreign law, such as Turkish or French law, in regular courts. In English and U.S. courts, the *Law Merchant* has been absorbed into the common law.

In his *Commentaries,* the great eighteenth-century English jurist Sir William Blackstone said of the *Law Merchant*:

> The affairs of commerce are regulated by a law of their own called the law merchant or *lex mercatoria,* which all nations agree in and take notice of, and it is particularly held to be part of the law of England which decides the causes of merchants by the general rules which obtain in all commercial countries, and that often even in matters relating to domestic trade, as for instance, in the drawing acceptance and the transfer of Bills of Exchange.

Another English jurist, Lord Mansfield, noted:

> Mercantile law is not the law of a particular country, but the law of all nations.

Lord Blackburn, another English jurist, observed:

> The general law merchant for many years has in all countries caused bills of exchange to be negotiable; there are in some cases differences and peculiarities which by the municipal law of each country are grafted on it.

National law is a major factor in private international law, because in dealing with conflicts of law problems (e.g., which state's law applies), the national legal system takes center stage.

Comparison of National Legal Systems

For the student who is not widely traveled, the great differences between national legal systems may come as a surprise. These systems may be classified in many ways: for example, by origin, cultural similarity, or political ideology. For the purposes of this text, a few examples follow:

- *Civil law countries:* France, Germany, and Japan. Communist and Islamic legal systems are also based upon a code, but because of their unique national aspects, they will be treated separately.
- *Common law countries:* United States, Canada (except Quebec), Great Britain, and Nigeria.

One should be cognizant of the limits of generalizations, however, because the legal environment of any country is continually evolving. In Japan, companies are not subjected to the same volume of product liability and negligence lawsuits and subsequent punitive damage awards as they are in the United States. However, there are small signs that change is coming to Japan, as heretofore unheard of plaintiff victories, albeit with small monetary awards, have been recorded. Recently, a Japanese district court reportedly awarded a woman employee approximately $12,000 for the sexual harassment inflicted upon her by her boss. The harassment was repetitive, lewd comments and sexually derogatory statements about her. Thus, even though one can fairly say that Japan has less litigation than the United States, and that this type of suit is not common in Japan, their legal environments show emerging similarities.

There are striking national legal differences relevant to businesspeople. For example, Canadian law precludes the patenting of a mouse. Canadian law requires that 50 percent of a cigarette pack contain a warning about the dangers. France passed a law that legalized same sex unions. Much to the surprise of the country, more heterosexual couples registered under the provisions dubbed "marriage lite." This law will impact on business' employee benefit plans.

Common and Civil Law

To start at a basic level, the civil law system established in continental Europe is based on a comprehensive code, whereas the common law system, established in England and carried on in its former colonies, evolves through case precedent.

Civil law came from the Roman tradition and was codified in the sixth century in the Justinian Code. In the eighteenth century, France codified the law into a civil, commercial, penal, civil procedure, and criminal procedure code. Other European countries, such as Germany and Switzerland,

followed with a codification of their law. The colonization of Africa, Asia, and Latin America spread the civil law system. However, some countries such as Japan and Taiwan simply adopted law based upon the civil law model.

This explanation could be amplified by contrasting the role of judge and lawyer in civil and common law systems. The judge in a civil law system takes on many of the functions of the lawyer in deciding what evidence needs to be developed or produced. In a common law jurisdiction, the judge is more neutral and rules more on requests by the parties' lawyers. Thus, in a common law system, the person one hires as a lawyer arguably plays a more critical role in the outcome. However, this difference should not be interpreted in the extreme because in civil law states, lawyers are still important.

The jury in both criminal and civil cases in the United States, a common law country, is not used comparably in civil law countries. In some civil law countries, the citizens assist the judge in criminal cases in determining guilt and imposing sentence.

Legislative proposals in the U.S. Congress to reform civil litigation by adopting a version of "loser pays" did not pass, leaving reform to the states. Many states have passed laws with caps on noneconomic damages. Once again, there are efforts at the national level to pass legislation capping damages on so-called "pain and suffering" in certain tort cases. The results of this effort are not known as of this writing.

Socialist Law

Socialist law is based upon a code, so it can be classified as civil law, but its ideological basis produces some fundamental differences. One cannot conclude, however, that all socialist legal systems are the same; both the People's Republic of China and Cuba could be classified as socialist, yet they differ in significant ways.

The political and economic philosophy of a communist society, in which the state traditionally owns and controls the means of production, is reflected in its legal system. These countries exhibit no great need for commercial law because any dispute can be solved bureaucratically or politically. Until recently, private ownership ran counter to established principles of law in both the former

Soviet Union and China. Hungary led the experiment by passing legislation to encourage foreign investment and provide a legal framework that would encourage businesspeople. China followed suit in 1978, and the former Soviet Union, approximately ten years later, passed a law authorizing the establishment of joint ventures as well as privately owned cooperatives. The nagging concern from a non-communist perspective is whether reform is temporary, an idiosyncrasy that might be eradicated as quickly as it was implemented, or whether it will endure and provide a secure legal environment for lasting economic partnerships.

Law under communist rule serves a different function than in a democracy. Initially, the individual's rights are of less concern in a communist country because the emphasis is on the collective or society. Likewise, the concept of law as a limit on governmental power is not embraced, but, rather, the state is permitted to limit even rights it has granted, for example, speech or the right to assemble.

The dramatic changes in Eastern Europe and the breakup of the Soviet Union demonstrate that changes in the law follow political transformation. These countries are now struggling with the universal issues, such as states' rights, freedom, rights of property owners, taxation, and price control.

Islamic Law

Too often, students, and professors as well, look at a problem or issue through an exclusively Western perspective. The power and importance of nations adhering to Islam compel other countries to have some basic understanding of this different system. Many Persian Gulf countries are adopting new commercial codes, in the civil law tradition, to encourage business, but they are to be interpreted in harmony with Shari'a (or God's rules) and the Koran. The Koran is not a code of law, but the expression of the Islamic ethic; it contains general injunctions to honor agreements and to observe good faith in commercial dealings. Shari'a describes the Islamic legal system, and the Koran is based on the Sunnah (sayings or decisions of the prophet Muhammad). Tenth-century scholars concluded that the early scholars had interpreted the divine law sufficiently and "ijtihad" or independent reasoning was finished. Therefore, harmoniz-

ing commercial reality and Shari'a can be a minefield because so many developments have occurred since the tenth century and yet theoretically, new law is not needed. Moral conduct is the preeminent concern. For example, because Shari'a embraces a concept called "riba," which prohibits "unearned or unjustified profits," interest on loans can be problematic. Some countries acknowledge that interest can be legitimate and have found ways to comply with the scripture and still secure financing. "Mudaraba" allows the bank to buy shares in the enterprise and receive a portion of the profits or share the loss. Through Mudaraba, the bank loans money to purchase assets and could be paid in a year or two, not with interest, but with an additional payment to show thanks and appreciation. Although it sounds like interest, according to the country legal experts it is not. Similarly, "gharar" prohibits any gain that is not clearly outlined at the time of the contract because it is likened to gambling. Many countries have adopted civil codes that define contracts and cover commercial transactions. Business can still be conducted in these countries, but only with sensitivity to and ingenuity in dealing with the national legal systems.[3] Even countries that adhere to Shari'a are changing; for example, the Sudan reportedly modified the sentences of several convicted criminals, deleting the mandatory limb amputation for stealing. One should be aware of the differences between countries that adhere to the teachings of Islam. Iran's and Saudi Arabia's legal systems are not identical. Before doing business in any one country, one should familiarize oneself with the particular characteristics of that country's system.

Comparative Law

Comparative law is the name of the discipline that examines differences between legal systems. (Chapter Three continues this discussion, particularly with regard to litigation.) Within national systems, international legal principles and standards can be noted. For example, in 1989, the Zimbabwe Supreme Court found that a sentence of whipping a juvenile violated both the Zimbabwean constitutional provision of "inhuman or degrading punishment" and international human rights norms. The youth convicted of assault had been sentenced to "receive a moderate correction

In Some Countries Dangerous Legal Pitfalls Await the Unwary Visitor

Tuesday, January 28, 2003
By David Koeppel

An American telecommunications executive on business in Venezuela is involved in an automobile accident that severely injures the other driver. Even though he is not at fault, he is arrested.

A businessman traveling in the Middle East is arrested at the airport for possessing a pornographic magazine.

A Connecticut dealer in meteorites is jailed in Brazil, accused of stealing a meteorite.

While the vast majority of business conducted by Americans abroad is relatively problem-free, security specialists, lawyers and diplomats all recommend taking great care in countries where navigating an array of obscure and often byzantine laws can be perilous. The State Department estimates that about 3,000 Americans are arrested in foreign countries every year, and most experts say the true figure is probably higher. In many cases, guilt or innocence is irrelevant.

"When you're traveling abroad for business or pleasure you need to understand something about the country's legal and cultural background," said Alexander Tabb, the associate managing director of the Security Services Group of Kroll Inc. "Just because you're an American doesn't make you safe, and it doesn't mean some cop won't beat the living daylights out of you."

Even innocent gestures like taking photographs can court trouble. And reckless driving or possession of even a small amount of drugs can land you in jail for years. Prison conditions in most developing nations are at best squalid and at worst extremely dangerous.

Ronald Farrell, 48, a buyer and seller of meteorites in Bethany, Conn., discovered how dangerous. Mr. Farrell spent 75 days in a Brazilian federal prison in 1997 after he and an associate were accused of stealing a meteorite from a museum, a charge he said was baseless.

Mr. Farrell said he was locked in an 18-by-20-foot cell with 16 other prisoners, including convicted murderers, given inedible meals and threatened by guards with beatings. In his second month of captivity, he said, he managed to bribe officials into giving him better food and letting him make cellphone calls to his wife back home. After his lawyers bought his freedom for $25,000, he said, he was forced to remain in Brazil for two months. He said that throughout the ordeal the American consulate offered little assistance.

"I still suffer from trauma when I travel," he said. "I can wake up in a strange hotel and think I'm still back in that Brazilian cell."

Kelly Shannon, a State Department spokeswoman, declined to comment on Mr. Farrell's case, but said that the help that consular officers could give to jailed Americans was limited. The officers generally visit the prisoners and can bring food, medication and reading material; making legal recommendations; insist on proper treatment; notify the prisoners' families; and file protests about prison conditions. But, she said, they cannot demand a detainee's release or provide a lawyer.

The State Department recommends that travelers check its Web site (www.travel.state.gov) for specific warnings and advisories.

While most business travelers are smart enough not to bring illegal drugs or firearms into foreign countries, they can be caught unaware by some local regulations. Many countries prohibit taking photos of government buildings and airports, for example; Ms. Shannon said a woman was detained in Zimbabwe for photographing a government mansion last year. And Japan bans such commonplace over-the-counter medications as Tylenol Cold Medicine and Nyquil.

Bruce McIndoe, chief executive of IJet, a Maryland company that provides legal, cultural and security information about 182 countries to mostly corporate and government clients, urges travelers to be alert to local mores, like whether police will seek a bribe or bristle at one. In Thailand, he said, it is not unheard-of for drugs to be planted in a traveler's suitcase.

About the worst thing that can happen is to be

continued

continued

arrested for drug possession. Scores of Americans have been imprisoned in Thailand on drug charges in recent years, for example, most of them claiming they were coerced or duped.

In one highly publicized case, Stephen Roye, an American journalist, was arrested in 1994 at the Bangkok airport and charged with possessing about six pounds of heroin. Mr. Roye, now 57, said he had been doing research for an article on the drug trade and was forced into concealing the contraband in his luggage by heroin smugglers who threatened to kill his mother and son. He received a life sentence that was later commuted to 40 years; last month, he was allowed to return home and complete his sentence in the United States.

Richard Atkins, the vice president of International Recoveries, a Philadelphia organization that works with Americans arrested abroad, says a more common risk is being detained in car accidents, especially if there are serious injuries. Drivers and passengers alike can "wind up in a hellhole of a prison cell," Mr. Atkins said.

"Investigations can sometimes last several months," he added.

He strongly recommends carrying a charged cellphone and having adequate travel insurance that includes a 24-hour legal-consultations service. He recalled a client who was arrested several years ago in Venezuela after his car was struck in the rear by another driver, who was seriously injured. The client, an American telecommunications executive, grabbed his cellphone and called his travel-assistance company's hot line even as he was being taken away by police, Mr.

Atkins said. The company then called International Recoveries with his insurance information, the name of co-workers and Venezuelan officials to contact immediately, he said. The client was released from custody within several hours.

Other experts recommend finding a reliable and licensed car service in unfamiliar countries. Gladson I. Nwanna, a finance professor at Morgan State University in Baltimore and author of "Americans Traveling Abroad: What You Should Know Before You Go" (World Travel Institute, 1996), says that in any third world country it is a good idea to check in with the American consulate and with the country's tourism ministry on potential pitfalls.

"Bribery is a common way of doing business in many parts of the world," Dr. Nwanna said. "But if you give money to the wrong person, it can get you into trouble."

Giving it to the right person does not have to be expensive, though. John Briley, the senior managing editor for Ijet and a freelance writer, said $5 freed him from a speeding charge in Panama and $10 bought off a border guard when he wandered into Costa Rica by mistake.

Mr. Tabb, the Kroll official, advises Americans who think they are about to be arrested abroad to keep a cool head—and a soft voice. "Let them know you're an American citizen and ask to speak to the consulate," he said. "Don't be demanding or arrogant. The squeaky wheel will not get the grease."

of four cuts with a light cane, which was to be administered in private by a prison officer."

The comparison of foreign criminal law is of increasing concern to businesspeople who find themselves under the control of a foreign government and accused of crimes. Assuming that in every country one is innocent until proven guilty or will be afforded all of the procedural guarantees familiar to anyone who watches U.S. TV crime shows is a mistake.

The differences between two common law countries are illustrated in the following case, on page 63, where a U.S. court denied enforcement of a British judgment because of the differences in libel law.

The legal environment of the country is an important part of any businessperson's briefing before assignment. Looking at legal systems out of sociocultural context can be a mistake, however. For example, U.S. businesspeople may successfully adopt an aggressive litigation strategy in the United States, but find this tactic not only unworkable but actually detrimental in Germany or Japan. Therefore, simply knowing the law is not enough.

Another area of comparison is how different countries handle the issue of jurisdiction over matters involving the Internet. Three cases (Exhibit 2.2) illustrate the viewpoint of France, the United States, and Australia.

correct refering

EXHIBIT 2.2		

France	United States	Australia
UEJF et LICRA v. Yahoo!, (2000) order of Nov. 20, 2000, No. Rg 00/05308 (The County Court of Paris).	*Yahoo! v. Ligue Contre le Racisme et L'Antisemitisme*, 169 F.Supp.2d 1181 (N.D.Cal. 2001)	*Dow Jones v. Gutnick*, 2002 HCA 56 (2002), (1994 A.L.R. 433)
Issue: Does a French court have jurisdiction to prohibit Yahoo! from allowing individuals to post Nazi memorabilia for sale over the Internet that is available to persons within France in contravention of French law?	Issue: Yahoo! sought a declaratory judgment in U.S. federal court that the French order violated U.S. law (First Amendment and Constitution) and could not be enforced in the United States. Yahoo! did this even though it had already complied.	Issue: Gutnick, an Australian citizen, claimed Dow Jones defamed him by publishing on a Web site an article that "implied he had laundered money." Seventeen hundred subscribers to the Web site lived in Australasia. He filed suit in Victoria, Australia. Dow Jones argued that the case should be heard in New York or New Jersey.
Result: The French court ordered Yahoo! to remove such items.	Result: The U.S. court agreed and found the French order unenforceable in violation of the Constitution and cited *Matusevitch v. Telnikoff*, discussed on page 63.	Result: The Australian court dismissed the appeal of Dow Jones, allowing the case to go forward in 2002. (This case is discussed further in Chapter Three.)
Update: Yahoo! removed some items, but left the book, *Mein Kampf*, for sale.	Update: The French party appealed the ruling, but there has been no action.	Update: Dow Jones filed a complaint about Australia's libel law with the United Nations' Human Rights Committee. The *Gutnick* case is scheduled to be heard later in 2003.

France and Britain, as well as Australia, have more restrictive views of libel than the United States. For example, an editor of a French magazine was sued in France because he compared a French wine to excrement. The winemakers sued and won the equivalent of $375,000 for denigration of a product. Compare this result to one in the United States where popular Oprah Winfrey was sued for trade disparagement by a group of Texas cattlemen. However, with the help of the general population as well as the jury consultant, "Dr. Phil" McGraw, Ms. Winfrey was victorious, in contrast to the French journalist.

In the civil environment, a comparison of how countries have reacted to the threats of terrorism is instructive. In Spain, suspects can be held for five days and in France, suspects can be held twenty-four hours without speaking to a lawyer. In many countries, the police routinely carry machine guns. In Britain, for example, closed circuit television is used by many municipalities to control and deter crime. (See Exhibit 2.3.)

Comparative law highlights the different approaches taken by nations. Even when two countries share the same framework, such as common law, there can be significant differences. Globalization and the Internet have brought nations closer together and may eventually bring such diverse entities into convergence on major issues like jurisdiction over the Internet.

Foreign Investment Codes

Foreign investment law is another area of law that can be compared. Many countries, including Eastern European, Latin, and South American ones, have been changing their laws to attract foreign investment, including laws on government approval for foreign investment and technology transfer agreements. Some countries have removed restrictions on repatriation of profits, movement of capital, and foreign ownership, and have lowered tax rates as an incentive.

EXHIBIT 2.3							
A Global Privacy Checklist							

Asian and European nations place varying demands for information on their inhabitants.

	Belgium	Britain	China	France	Germany	Japan	Netherlands	Spain
Are people required to carry ID cards?	Yes	No	Yes	Yes	No	No	Yes	Yes
	Note: In Japan foreigners are requied to carry alien-registration cards; in Germany the police can require proof of identity in some cases.							
Is closed-circuit TV used by the police to watch streets and other public places?	N.A.	Yes	Yes	Yes	Yes	No	Yes	Yes
	Note: In Germany only in limited areas; in Japan Tokyo police plan to use CCTV in certain areas starting next year; in Spain only with court authorization, and signs must be posted to inform passersby.							
Do people need to register their home address with the local police station or other authorities?	Yes	No	Yes	No	Yes	Yes	Yes	No

SOURCE: WSJ research. Copyright © 2001, *The Wall Street Journal*. Reprinted with permission. Dow Jones Co. All rights reserved worldwide.

Matusevitch v. Telnikoff
877 F. Supp.1 (D.D.C. 1995)
United States District Court, District of Columbia

BACKGROUND AND FACTS

Mr. Telnikoff and Mr. Matusevitch are both Russian emigrants. Mr. Telnikoff wrote an opinion editorial for a London newspaper criticizing the BBC for hiring Russian "minorities." Mr. Matusevitch, a U.S. citizen, wrote a letter to the editor of the London paper stating that the use of "minority" in conjunction with Russian was anti-Semitic because it referred to Jewish people in the Russian context. Mr. Telnikoff sued for libel and was awarded $416,000 by a London court. He sought to enforce the judgment in the United States where Mr. Matusevitch had assets. Mr. Matusevitch asked the U.S. court to declare the British libel law judgment unenforceable because it violated the First and Fourteenth Amendments of the U.S. Constitution.

URBINA, DISTRICT JUDGE

British law on libel differs from U.S. law. In the United Kingdom, the defendant bears the burden of proving allegedly defamatory statements true and the plaintiff is not required to prove malice on the part of the libel defendant. . . . As a result, a libel defendant would be held liable for statements the defendant honestly believed to be true and published without any negligence. In contrast, the law in the United States requires the plaintiff to prove that the statements were false and looks to the defendant's state of mind and intentions. In light of the different standards, this court concludes that recognition and enforcement of the foreign judgment in this case would deprive the plaintiff of his constitutional rights.

continued

continued

Speech similar to the plaintiff's statements have received protection under the First Amendment to the Constitution and are thereby unactionable in U.S. courts. . . . The Supreme Court held that hyperbole is not actionable. Plaintiff contends that his statements were plainly hyperbolic because they were stated in an attempt to portray defendant's extremist position.

In addition, in the United States, courts look to the context in which the statements appeared when determining a First Amendment question. . . .

In the case at hand, the court notes that the British judgment was based on jury instructions which asked the jury to ignore context. Therefore, this court finds that if the statements were read in context to the original article or statement and in reference to the location of the statements in the newspaper, a reader would reasonably be alerted to the statements' function as opinion and not as an assertion of fact.

The defendant in this case has described himself as a prominent activist for Human Rights in the Soviet Union since 1955. Therefore, for purposes of his article about the composition of Russian personnel hired by Radio Free Europe/Radio Liberty, the court finds that the defendant was a limited public figure. In light of defendant's status as a limited public figure, the plaintiff is entitled to all the constitutional safeguards concerning speech used against public figures.

For the reasons stated herein, the court grants summary judgment in favor of the Plaintiff.

Decision.   The court refused to recognize the English judgment because it would deprive the plaintiff of his constitutional rights.

Each country, depending upon its stage of development as well as past experience with foreign investment, will develop unique investment codes. Assumptions about what is permissible for business in a particular country are dangerous because while one country allows wholly owned foreign companies, other countries may require some level of local participation.

INTERNATIONAL ORGANIZATIONS

International organizations, both governmental and non-governmental (NGO), play an increasingly important role in today's global society as forums for legal, political, and economic issues. NGOs include environmental and labor groups too, and their numbers have grown dramatically in the last ten years, no doubt a by-product of the Internet age. A recent example of an NGO's influence can be found in the World Diamond Congress' action to block the trade in gems for weapons (see International Accents article). The remainder of this chapter examines the structures and functions of several of these organizations, and pays particular attention to how they impact on international business.

Organizations Affiliated with the United Nations

The United Nations is an important organization that has been discussed in a previous section. A number of organizations affiliated with the United Nations undertake activities affecting the international business environment. The United Nations Economic and Social Council consists of members elected by the General Assembly for three-year terms and coordinates the efforts of all specialized agencies "established by Governmental agreement and having wide international responsibilities . . . in economic, social, cultural, educational, health, and related fields."

The following list provides a sense of the types of work many of the agencies perform:

- Food and Agriculture Organization
- International Labor Organization
- IBRD (World Bank)
- IMF (International Monetary Fund)
- UNESCO (United Nations Educational, Scientific, and Cultural Organization)
- World Health Organization (WHO)
- WIPO (World International Property Organization)

Numerous commissions have also been established to deal with special issues. The objective of the United Nations Commission on International Trade Law (UNCITRAL) is to promote international trade through the harmonization of trade law between nations. This agency includes members from many nations. One of its major achievements has been the entry into force of the *Convention on Contracts for the International Sale of Goods*

international accents

Prosecutor deplores 'blood diamond' trade: Al-Qaeda uses gems to launder terror cash

Al-Qaeda continues to use "blood diamonds" from Sierra Leone to fund its international operations, says the chief prosecutor for the special United Nations court for the West African country.

"I'm aware there is a connection. That connection is specific. They are moving diamonds as a commodity to launder their funds," David Crane told the Ottawa Citizen in an exclusive interview.

Crane also criticized the UN process to eradicate the trade of blood diamonds and questioned whether the international diamond industry is sincerely committed to finding solutions.

Blood diamonds have been used to finance civil wars in several African countries, including Sierra Leone and Angola, leading to millions of deaths.

Since the Sept. 11, 2001, terrorist attacks on the United States, reports have emerged that al-Qaeda has used the trade in the illicit rough stones, culled from mines in areas controlled by rebel militias, to finance its own international operations.

Crane's comments appear to be the firmest to date linking al-Qaeda to the blood diamond trade of Sierra Leone. Last fall, the RCMP concluded that it could not say for sure whether al-Qaeda was connected to the trade, but "it is probably one of the many financing schemes used by al-Qaeda."

Crane's court was established six months ago to prosecute crimes related to Sierra Leone's civil war.

The first criminal charges are still months away, he said. And while he predicted major indictments, such as crimes against humanity and war crimes, will be brought against those directly responsible for the carnage wrought on civilians, Crane also said his tribunal would take aim at those who profited through the blood diamond trade.

"The economic side of this investigation is huge. It's international in scope," he told the Citizen.

"They're all inter-connected. They all work together. They know each other. It's a common plan, a scheme, to move diamonds as a commodity, to do whatever they need to trade it for cash, arms, or to launder money."

Critics have noted that the United States had little interest in supporting the battle against blood diamonds prior to the Sept. 11 attacks.

The Kimberly Process involves 48 governments and the diamond industry in an attempt to create a certification system that would label legitimate stones thereby blocking the sale of conflict diamonds and protecting the integrity of the $7.8-billion annual trade. About four per cent of that trade is in conflict diamonds.

Material reprinted with the express permission of The Ottawa Citizen Group, Inc., a CanWest partnership.

Material reprinted with the express permission of: "The Ottawa Citizen Group Inc.," a CanWest Partnership.

(CISG, which is discussed in Chapter Four). The United Nations *Convention on the Carriage of Goods by Sea of 1978* was initiated by UNCITRAL and addresses international bills of lading used in the shipment of goods. In 1976, UNCITRAL adopted arbitration rules, which have been widely used. Other projects involve the drafting of model laws to be used by countries, such as the *Model Law on Electronic Funds Transfer*. Two other organizations are complementary to UNCITRAL in that they also strive to unify international law: the Hague Conference on Private International Law and the International Institute for the Unification of Private Law (UNIDROIT).

> **http://www.ngocongo.org**
> Lists and describes the roles of non-governmental organizations (NGOs) in partnership with the U.N.

History and Development of the "Bretton Woods" Institutions

After World War I, a confluence of economic conditions resulted in many countries facing dramatically similar problems, including inflation, high unemployment, and currency fluctuations. Many nations turned toward protectionism as a way to deal with these problems. Although these measures were largely unsuccessful, the onset of World War II absorbed the world's attention. While World War II was still in progress, several major meetings were held laying the groundwork to prevent future economic and military catastrophes. A multinational conference was convened at Bretton Woods, New Hampshire, in 1944 to focus on short-term financial problems, ways to promote free trade, and the creation of a bank that would help finance the necessary rebuilding after the war. The conference culminated in the creation of the International Monetary Fund (IMF) and the International Bank for Reconstruction and Development (World Bank).

International Monetary Fund

In general, the objectives of the IMF are "to promote international monetary cooperation, exchange stability and orderly exchange arrangements, to foster economic growth and high levels of employment and to provide temporary financial assistance to countries to help ease balance of payments adjustments." The fund lends money to developing countries to assist them with fundamental problems blocking development, such as high interest rates and inflated oil prices. The fund works closely with commercial banks in this process.

Membership in the IMF (currently 184 states) obliges a nation to adhere to the initial goals of Bretton Woods as reflected in the articles. Members must act in a way that promotes stable exchange rates and must pursue economic and fiscal policies that foster growth in an orderly way. The purpose here is to avoid the chaos of the 1930s. Members must also be careful not to pursue policies with another member that may discriminate against a third member. The fund headquarters are located in Washington, D.C.

The IMF and the World Bank

Many people have difficulty distinguishing the IMF from the World Bank. This difficulty is understandable because these international organizations do have much in common. Both institutions were created at the Bretton Woods Conference of 1944, have the same membership, and are concerned with international economic issues. In addition, the two organizations, although distinct entities, work together in close cooperation and hold joint annual meetings.

Despite their similarities, the IMF and the World Bank are separate entities. The IMF, as noted, oversees the international monetary system and promotes exchange stability and orderly exchange relations among its members. The IMF assists all members, rich or poor, that have balance of payments difficulties. On the other hand, the World Bank seeks to promote economic development of poorer countries and is concerned with assisting developing countries through the financing of specific development projects and programs. The World Bank and the IMF have been the target in 2000 of environmentalists and other groups who argued their policies have had a deleterious effect on poverty around the world. The agencies' lending practices have been targeted as encouraging projects that negatively affect the environment.

> http://www.worldbank.org
> The home page of the World Bank Group.

International Bank for Reconstruction and Development

The name "World Bank" encompasses two institutions, the International Bank for Reconstruction and Development (IBRD) and the International Development Association (IDA). These institutions should not be confused with EBRD (European Bank for Reconstruction and Development). The IBRD was established in 1945, but due to the beginning of the Cold War (the postwar tension between the Soviet Union and the United States), when it opened in 1946, the USSR did not join.

The IBRD does not make high-risk loans, and the loans it makes are generally at market terms. Thus, it cannot achieve its goals as much as it might hope. The IDA was created in 1960 to bridge this gap between IBRD objectives and reality. The IDA makes loans to the world's poorest countries with average per capita GDP of $875 or less (2003) on more favorable terms than the IBRD. Loans can be made only to governments, however, which stifles some private initiatives. The IDA and the IBRD share staffs.

A separate entity, the International Finance Corporation (IFC), was created in 1956 to address the issue of loans to private enterprises in developing countries. The IFC works jointly with commercial banks and also advises countries on developing capital markets. The IFC does not have the backing of a governmental guarantee when it borrows.

The idea behind the IBRD and the IDA is that countries should "graduate," moving first from the assistance of the IDA to the assistance of the IBRD and then eventually becoming a contributor to the IBRD. Japan is the sterling example of a country that has "graduated" from borrower to contributor.

GATT and WTO

In the aftermath of World War II, many nations reflected on recent history and tried to devise ways to avoid repeating past mistakes. The 1930s had brought a wave of protectionism and high tariff rates to keep foreign goods out. The United States joined this trend by passing the *Smoot Hawley Tariff Act of 1930,* thereby exacerbating the Depression. As part of the postwar examination, in 1947–48, fifty-three nations negotiated the *Havana Charter,* which established the International Trade Organization (ITO). The United States, although a participant in the conference, changed its mind about signing as a result of ensuing Cold War tensions. The GATT *(General Agreement on Tariffs and Trade)* came into force on January 1, 1948, as a temporary measure to salvage some of the principles of the ITO.

The purpose of GATT was to commit member countries to the principles of nondiscrimination and reciprocity, meaning that if a bilateral trade treaty is negotiated between two GATT members, those provisions will be extended to other members. Countries that are members are granted "most favored nation" (MFN) status. All member nations must harmonize their laws with GATT or face sanctions. The organization became the WTO in 1995 with one hundred and forty-six current members and is discussed in Chapter Nine.

Bilateral trade talks are replaced (though not entirely) with talks with all contracting parties participating. Countries designated as LDCs (less-developed countries) receive additional breaks. The group offices are headquartered in Geneva. China joined in 2001.

OECD

The Organization for European Economic Cooperation (OEEC), born out of General Marshall's plan to aid recovery of Europe after World War II, was formed in 1948 by the Western European nations, with the United States and Canada as associate members. The Organization for Economic Cooperation and Development (OECD) replaced the OEEC in 1961 and added the United States, Canada, and Japan as full members. The goals remained the same but included coordinating efforts to aid less-developed countries.

Recently the OECD drafted a *Convention on Combating Bribery of Foreign Public Officials in International Business Transactions,* which went into effect in 1999. Thirty-five countries that signed the Convention have agreed to conform their national legislation to the international treaty, including the United States, Japan, and Germany, to name just a few. The Convention adopts the extraterritorial approach from United States law, the *Foreign Corrupt Practices Act* (see Chapter Sixteen), making it illegal to bribe a foreign official of another country.

Other NGOs have worked on this issue as well. Perhaps the most important group is Transparency International, modeled after Amnesty International, based in Germany but with chapters all over the world. They have educated the public about the connection between corruption and economic development.

> **http://www.oecd.org**
> The home page of the Organization for European Economic Co-operation and Development

International Chamber of Commerce

The International Chamber of Commerce (ICC) is a worldwide organization that draws its members from all sectors of the business community. The basic purposes of the organization are listed as follows:

1. Permanently represent business vis-à-vis the major intergovernmental institutions and conferences.
2. Harmonize, codify, and standardize international business practices.
3. Provide practical services for its members and for the international business community.
4. Provide a link between countries with different economic systems, or a meeting place for sectors of economic activity with different interests.

The ICC can point to many achievements that have facilitated the development of multinational business. It developed the *Uniform Customs and Practice for Documentary Credits,* which are used in financing international sales, and *Incoterms,* the uniform definitions used in trade. The ICC also created a forum for the settlement of disputes, the International Court of Arbitration. The ICC serves as a liaison with the United Nations and its agencies to help advocate the views of the private sector.

The Rome Statute of the International Criminal Court

[1998 — handwritten annotation above "Statute"]

During the 1990s, the UN Security Council created temporary tribunals to prosecute war criminals from the former Yugoslavia in Eastern Europe, and Rwanda in Africa (taken in principle from the Nuremburg and Tokyo war crimes trials that followed World War II). This broadened into efforts to create a permanent international criminal court that would be universally accepted by all countries for the trial of "the most serious crimes of international concern," including those accused of genocide, crimes against humanity, war crimes, and the controversial, yet-to-be-defined, "crime of aggression." Such a court was brought into being by the *Rome Statute (Treaty) of the International Criminal Court* (1998). Today the *International Criminal Court* is based in The Hague, the Netherlands. Interestingly, both terrorism and drug trafficking were not included in the court's jurisdiction because of the magnitude of those problems. As of 2003 ninety-two nations had ratified the Rome treaty. Both China and the United States, among others, have refused to join a treaty that would subject their citizens, or military personnel, to trials for war crimes in foreign countries, or that would subject their government leaders to frivolous prosecutions. The United States also maintains that the court's powers are inconsistent with the UN Charter. As a compromise, the UN Security Council has granted temporary immunity from prosecution from peacekeeping troops acting under UN authorization. The U.S. government has also entered into many bilateral agreements with foreign countries exempting U.S. military personnel from prosecution under the treaty.

Other Organizations

Numerous other organizations with countries as members impact on business. For example, the International Whaling Commission, based in Cambridge, England, was established in 1946. It has thirty-six country members dedicated to regulating whaling to promote conservation. The commission helps to fund studies and compiles statistics regarding the whale populations.

Private organizations also play a significant role in international business. For example, professional groups can be involved in standard-setting for a particular industry, thus having far-reaching impact on business.

HUMAN RIGHTS, ETHICS, AND BUSINESS' RESPONSE

Agreeing about human rights or ethics in a diverse global environment is not an easy task. Human rights, by definition, incorporates values about which people may disagree. For example, many Europeans believe the United States routinely violates fundamental human rights when it executes convicted criminals. Others believe that Kuwait violates basic principles when it denies women the right to vote. Yet every day, multinationals choose to do business in these countries as well as many others and, thus, confront a number of human rights "issues." Corporations find themselves besieged by environmental, labor, and human rights activists who can now organize very effectively on the Internet. Yet, many corporations have found that the best way to address the potential problems is to confront them head on. Nike hired former ambassador and civil rights activist Andrew Young to investigate and report on its subcontractors overseas. Despite his stature, this effort was criticized as window dressing and many activists publicly attacked the company, tarnishing its reputation. More recently, Reebok, with a vice president for human rights, conducted its own investigation of conditions in its contractors' factories in Indonesia and issued a report. Because the workers did not understand the term sexual harassment, they answered there was none. In response, the factories are training workers to understand the concept of sexual harassment as well as attempt to remedy other problems. It is reported that $250,000 was spent on training at each of the two factories.

A new effort is reflected in corporate and NGO alliances. In 2000, fifty companies and twelve labor groups, in conjunction with the United Nations, signed a "Global Compact" committing their support to human rights, eliminating child labor, allowing free trade unions, and refraining from polluting the environment wherever they do business. Signatories include Nike, Dupont, Unilever, Amnesty International, and the World Wildlife Fund. Greenpeace did not sign. Some criticized the efforts of the multinationals as trying to use the good name of the other organizations to shield them from review or criticism. The companies are trying to blunt the anti-sweatshop movement active on college campuses and other grassroots campaigns that have a negative effect on sales. The diamond industry's response to rebel forces use of diamonds is another example of the multinationals trying to police themselves with various voluntary pacts and ethics codes.

In the United States, there has been a greater interest in ethics codes and codes of conduct for corporations and industries since the adoption of the *U.S. Federal Sentencing Guidelines*. If the company adopts a code and has a compliance program to reduce the chance of criminal conduct, and if it later discovers wrongdoing (such as environmental, tax, antitrust, or bribery problems), it can use the code as a basis to argue for a reduced fine under the *Guidelines*. The number of corporate

ethics officers in the United States has grown from twelve in 1992 to over eight hundred. Thus, corporations have inaugurated ethics programs to demonstrate their intent to comply with the law and to mitigate any fine in the event of corporate transgression. Yet, this increased emphasis on ethics has not deterred or prevented some of the most recent cases of alleged corporate misconduct at WorldCom, Enron, Arthur Anderson, Adelphi, and others. Examples of these codes include Responsible Care in the chemical industry and the CERES *Principles (Coalition for Environmentally Responsible Economies)*. Thomas Dunfee of the Wharton School has proposed that corporations adopt the "C^2 principles," which call for companies to adopt anti-bribery policies, and monitor and disclose the results. An example of a corporate code of ethics is Halliburton's *Ethical Business Practices,* seen in Exhibit 2.4.

Corporations may pay attention to ethics and human rights issues both because it is the right thing to do and because it is prudent from a business perspective. However, they may also pay attention because if they don't, they will be sued. See the International Accents article, "Making a Federal Case Out of Overseas Abuse."

The use of the statute, the *Alien Tort Claims Act,* is discussed in more detail in a later chapter.

EXHIBIT 2.4

Halliburton Corporations Code of Ethical Business Practices

Company policy requires Directors, employees and agents to observe high standards of business and personal ethics in the conduct of their duties and responsibilities. Directors and employees must practice fair dealing, honesty and integrity in every aspect of dealing with other Company employees, the public, the business community, shareholders, customers, suppliers, competitors and government authorities. When acting on behalf of the Company, Directors and employees shall not take unfair advantage through manipulation, concealment, abuse of privileged information, misrepresentation of material facts, or other unfair-dealing practices. Company policy prohibits unlawful discrimination against employees, shareholders, Directors, officers, customers or suppliers on account of race, color, age, sex, religion or national origin. All persons shall be treated with dignity and respect and they shall not be unreasonably interfered with in the conduct of their duties and responsibilities.

No Director or employee should be misguided by any sense of loyalty to the Company or a desire for profitability that might cause him or her to disobey any applicable law or Company policy. Violation of Company policy will constitute grounds for disciplinary action, including, when appropriate, termination of employment.

Sensitive Transactions

Company policy prohibits its Directors, employees and agents from entering into sensitive transactions. If such a transaction occurs, the Company and its officers, Directors and employees directly involved may be subject to fines, imprisonment and civil litigation.

continued

continued

Commercial Bribery

Company policy prohibits commercial bribes, kickbacks and other similar payoffs and benefits paid to any suppliers or customers.

Accounting Controls, Procedures & Records

Applicable laws and Company policy require the Company to keep books and records that accurately and fairly reflect its transactions and the dispositions of its assets.

Use & Disclosure of Inside Information

Company policy prohibits disclosure of material inside information to anyone other than persons within the Company whose positions require them to know such information.

Confidential or Proprietary Information

Company policy prohibits employees from disclosing confidential or proprietary information outside the Company, either during or after employment, without Company authorization to do so.

Conflicts of Interest

Company policy prohibits conflicts between the interests of its employees and the Company.

Fraud & Similar Irregularities

Company policy prohibits fraud and establishes procedures to be followed concerning the recognition, reporting and investigation of suspected fraud.

SOURCE: Haliburton Corporation. Reprinted with permission.

international accents

Making a Federal Case Out of Overseas Abuses

An obscure law paves the way for suits against multinationals

by Paul Magnusson

Should U.S. multinationals be held liable for the human-rights abuses of foreign governments? Victim advocates charge, for instance, that Burma's military rulers forced peasants at gunpoint to help build a pipeline for Unocal Corp., torturing and killing those who resisted. The company knew and approved, they claim. Unocal denies it.

This emotional issue lies at the heart of a dozen lawsuits that seek to hold companies liable if they work with repressive regimes. Plaintiffs in several of these suits, including the one against Unocal, recently have made strides in establishing legal grounds for such claims under an arcane 1789 statute called the

Alien Tort Claims Act. Early courtroom victories have set off alarms among business groups, which worry that the likes of IBM, Citibank, and Coca-Cola may be socked with huge jury damages for the misdeeds of Third World governments. Ultimately, up to 1,000 U.S. and foreign companies could be named as defendants in the pending suits, experts on both sides say.

To head them off, business groups have called a closed-door strategy session in Washington on Nov. 18 to consider everything from possible legislation to filing a slew of *amicus curiae* briefs. Already, some companies have been lobbying the Justice Dept. to intervene. Last summer, the State Dept. warned a judge that a case against Exxon Mobil Corp. in Indonesia

continued

continued

"could potentially disrupt" the fight against terrorism and should be dropped. Business groups fear that further plaintiffs' successes could chill U.S. companies' activities around the globe. "Large jury awards will send a message that if you are going to do business in a country where the government is violating human-rights or labor standards, you may be sued," warns J. Daniel O'Flaherty, vice-president at the National Foreign Trade Council, which represents U.S. exporters.

The Alien Claims act on which the suits are based was originally intended to reassure Europe that the fledgling U.S. wouldn't harbor pirates or assassins. It permits foreigners to sue in U.S. courts for violations of "the law of nations." It remained little used until 1976, when a Paraguayan doctor brought suit in U.S. court against a former Paraguayan police official for the murder of the doctor's son. In 1980, a federal appeals court ruled that the law allowed foreigners to bring suit in U.S. court over acts committed abroad.

In the early 1990s, human-rights lawyers began applying the law to U.S. corporations. Their contention: that companies can be liable for aiding wrongdoing by authorities or can be "vicariously liable" for the damages caused. For example, a Colombian labor union has brought a U.S. lawsuit against Coca-Cola Co. for allegedly hiring paramilitary units that murdered union organizers. And South Africans have sued Citigroup and other as-yet-unnamed companies for allegedly profiteering from apartheid. "These lawsuits hold the corporate world responsible for the ultimate actions of what their products and money do," says Edward Fagan, a New York lawyer helping the plaintiffs.

Human-rights activists think they have the best shot in the Unocal case. It was filed in Los Angeles in 1996 on behalf of Burmese citizens who claim that the California energy giant used the army of Burma to force villagers to clear jungle for the company's natural-gas pipeline. A lower court dismissed the case, but in September the often liberal Ninth Circuit U.S. Court of Appeals reinstated it. The court suggested that Unocal could be liable if it "provided practical assistance or encouragement" to the Burmese military—or even if Unocal simply knew that crimes were occurring.

The case still faces plenty of legal hurdles, but it has progressed to the point where Unocal may soon have to face torture survivors in court—a publicity nightmare. If that happens activists are sure to bring more grievances to U.S. courts.

Reprinted from November 25, 2002, *Business Week* by special permission. Copyright © 2002 by the McGraw-Hill Companies, Inc.

Cultural and Ethical Environment

The multinational company faces a dilemma when doing business in developing countries with much less strict environmental, safety, and work regulations. Is complying with local law sufficient? Is setting a standard higher than local law, but lower than U.S. law sufficient? Many multinationals do this by paying their workers overseas more than the prevailing local wages, but much lower than U.S. wages. After all, low wages is one of the major reasons the company chose to manufacture overseas. How does one define sufficient? What is the difference between legally sufficient and ethically defensible? Can a company realistically commit to a "first-world standard" for labor and the environment in Third World countries? Does it advance human rights if a company cracking down on child labor fires everyone under the age of fourteen? These are difficult questions that cause much disagreement. Some people from de-

veloping countries argue that the U.S. companies' concern with human rights and the environment is really protectionism in disguise. However, companies should be concerned because they may be subjected to litigation with all its attendant bad publicity and cost.

CHAPTER SUMMARY

Doing business internationally requires an understanding of international (public and private) law, national law, and organizations. Trade between entrepreneurs from different countries can never be totally divorced from the relationships of the home countries of the businesspeople. Political allegiances shift and trade is affected. For example, just as trade between the former Soviet Union and the United States increased during the late 1970s, the Soviet incursion into Afghanistan and President Jimmy Carter's consequent grain embargo chilled all business ventures. A businessperson must be able to assess astutely the environment and formulate an effective business plan. Knowledge of the host country's legal system and its ramifications for business is essential.

International business law draws from both public and private law as they relate to business transactions. Some of the distinction between public and private international law has been blurred, however,

organizations such as the United Nations, WTO, and various treaties have expanded their effect on business transactions. Treaties such as bilateral tax treaties or multilateral conventions create obligations for private parties. Similarly, national law, such as investment codes, can play a substantial role in business decisions. All of these issues together then are considered international business law.

Questions and Case Problems

1. What is public and private international law? What is international business law?

2. Why aren't there more treaties dealing with international business issues?

3. Does the U.S. Constitution's First Amendment protection of freedom of speech extend overseas? Do all nations have similar national legal provisions?

4. You overhear someone say, "International law does not exist." What do they mean? What evidence can you provide to persuade them that they are mistaken?

5. Review the Halliburton Ethical Business Practices code (Exhibit 2.4). What problems can you identify? Go online and compare this code with Johnson and Johnson's. What differences do you find? Has Halliburton had any difficulties in the last year that might conflict with its code?

6. Do corporations have to be concerned about human rights issues when doing business internationally?

7. The United States has refused to sign the International Criminal Court Treaty as well as a number of others. Why?

8. May the Bacardi and Co. Ltd. buy the trademark for Havana Club Rum from the Arechabala family who registered it in the United States in 1994? The Cuban government had seized all assets in 1959 and had given a French company permission to use the name. See the *Havana Club Holding S.A. v. Galleon, S.A.,* 203 F.3d 116 (2d Cir. N.Y. 2000).

9. In 2000, British Law Lords ruled, "Former heads of state are not immune from prosecution for torture and crimes against humanity." Nevertheless, the British Home Secretary, Jack Straw, decided Pinochet, the former ruler of Chile residing in Britain, was too ill to be extradited to Spain to stand trial for human rights abuses including torture and murder of dissidents during his rule in Chile. Pinochet was allowed

to leave the country and return to Chile. Is it possible he could face trial in Chile? Explain. Search the Internet and see if anything happened when Pinochet returned to Chile.

10. How do you reconcile the French court's ruling in Yahoo! and the U.S. federal court's ruling in Yahoo!? Would an international treaty be helpful in this area? Is that likely? Why or why not?

11. Do NGOs represent an important citizen check on corporations and governments, which will help to build a "civil society," or do they portend a dangerous new direction of unchecked influence and power and an erosion of national sovereignty?

12. What was the basis for the United States' and Britain's argument about the legality of the second Gulf War? What were the arguments made opposing this view by France and Germany? Which argument do you find more persuasive and why? Does this disagreement mean that international law is too vague?

13. Does the United Nations' Human Rights Committee have a jurisdiction over a dispute between Gutnick, an Australian, and Dow Jones, a corporation based in the United States?

14. The International Court of Justice (in February 2003) ordered the United States to stay the executions of three Mexicans imprisoned in the United States. Mexico claimed the United States had violated the *Vienna Convention* on consular relations because the imprisoned were not told they had a right to consult with a representative from their country's consulate. The court previously made similar rulings regarding convicted Paraguayan and German nationals. Those rulings were ignored by the United States and the executions were carried out. How is the ICJ ruling different, if at all, from the previous ones? Has the United States moved to execute these Mexican individuals?

Managerial Implications

1. You are CEO of a small privately held company, JayzTogs, Inc. You have decided to expand your sales to include Eastern Europe, including Bulgaria and Japan. What difference does it make that both countries have ratified the OECD Anti-Bribery Convention? Could this be a factor in your business expansion plans?

2. You subcontract most of your manufacturing to suppliers in developing countries. What responsibility, legally and ethically, do you have to monitor conditions there? Is there any accountability?

3. Your company in Makonobo uses a number of toxic cleaning solvents to clean manufacturing equipment. You could sell empty solvent containers and make money, or pay to have them disposed of in an environmentally safe way. Makonobo has very little environmental regulation and the first option is legal in Makonobo, but would violate U.S. law. What is your decision? Does your answer change if the profit or expenses of each option changes?

Notes

1. Restatement (Third) of the Law, §101, Copyright 1987 by the American Law Institute.
2. David D. Siegel, *Conflicts,* p. 2 (West, 1986).
3. For additional reading on one example of a legal system, see Nabil Saleh, *The Law Governing Contracts in Arabia,* 38 Int'l. & Comp. L.Q. 761, 775, 788 (1989).

RESOLVING INTERNATIONAL COMMERCIAL DISPUTES

AVOIDING BUSINESS DISPUTES

Long-term business relationships are generally the most profitable ones. Experienced executives and international managers know this, and they work very hard to foster them, both at the personal and organizational levels. Long-term relationships are based on trust. In a world where we do business with people who look, speak, and act differently from ourselves and who live and work oceans away, trust takes on a new and even more important significance. Indeed, it has been said that all of international business is based on trust. Any dispute that threatens the bonds of trust can threaten future business opportunities, do irreparable harm to individual and corporate reputations, and permanently damage long-term relationships. Moreover, when disputes become combative, it can be costly, time consuming, and physically and mentally exhausting for all parties. After all, there is the real possibility that one or both of the parties will have to litigate in a protracted and expensive trial in a foreign court, before a foreign judge in a foreign language, and have their rights determined under foreign procedural rules and possibly foreign law. Quite often the parties must retain attorneys in more than one country. So, when disagreements break out, amicable settlements are usually the best outcome and offer the best hope of salvaging a business relationship. It is always helpful if the parties have a reservoir of trust and goodwill that they can draw on to settle the dispute in a friendly way. But, of course, this is not always possible, and the prudent international business person, in any contract or any venture, will seek good legal advice and always "hope for the best and plan for the worst." Nowhere is this more important than in negotiating and drafting business contracts. The contract is the basis of any bargain and its importance cannot be overstated. If and when a dispute arises, the terms of the contract provide the basis for dispute resolution.

Cultural Attitudes Toward Disputes

Keep in mind that cultural factors will influence a party's attitude toward how disputes are settled. Americans are notorious litigators, quickly turning to the courts to redress grievances. Their combative stance can result in a "win or lose" mentality. On the other hand, Asians are notable for going to great lengths to seek an amicable settlement. After all, by tradition, it is a virtue to seek harmony and a vice to seek discord. These differences are evident in the way American and Japanese businesspeople approach contract or business negotiations. It is quite common for Americans to include their attorney or corporate counsel as a member of the negotiating team. Indeed, many Western managers and executives would never dream of it being any other way. But to the Japanese side, this may seem a little confrontational, a little unnecessary, and a bad omen or a sign that disagreement is inevitable. All too often, Americans view the negotiating process as something to be gotten out of the way so the deal can be closed, the contract signed, and all can go back home. People of many other cultures, from Asia to Latin America, might see the negotiating process as a time to build a relationship and new friendships. Of course, these attitudes differ throughout the world, and from country to country, and no generalizations should really be made. But one thing is certain, and that is that the rest of the world views Americans as confrontational and quick to call in the lawyers. Perhaps the words of the English Lord Denning best sum up the foreign view.

> As the moth drawn to the light, so is a litigant drawn to the United States. If he can only get his case into their courts, he stands to win a fortune. At no cost to himself; and at no risk of having to pay anything to the other side. . . . The lawyers will charge the litigant nothing for their services but instead they will take forty percent of the damages. . . . If they lose, the litigant will have nothing to pay to the other side. The courts in the United States have no such cost deterrents as we have. There is also in the United States a right to trial by jury. These are prone to award fabulous damages. They are notoriously sympathetic and know that the lawyers will take their forty percent before the plaintiff gets anything. All this means that the defendant can be readily forced into a settlement. *Smith Kline and French Laboratories v. Bloch*, 1 W.L.R. 730, 733–4 (Eng. C.A.1982).

The resolution of disputes between citizens of different countries, with business transactions that span continents and cultures, raises many complicated legal and tactical problems. Consider a dispute involving an American manufacturer that purchases thousands of meters of cloth from a Chinese supplier. The cloth is shipped to Vietnam where the manufacturer contracted to have it embroidered and sewn into pillow shams. When the finished goods arrive in the United States, it is discovered that they are damaged. Apparently the fabric was shipped from China in a defective condition, but the Vietnamese firm failed to inspect for damage as it normally did. The Chinese company claims that the time for bringing the defective fabric to its attention has long passed. The Vietnamese company says it was not its responsibility. Consider all the questions presented. To whom does the manufacturer look for remuneration? Is the relationship between the parties worth keeping, and is the case capable of being settled or should the manufacturer "take the gloves off"? Was there a contract with either party and did it specify the method of resolution, such as mediation, arbitration, or litigation, and if so, where

and under what law? If the contract does not specify, what legal rules apply to determine where the case should be heard and what law should govern (two entirely different issues)? Finally, if a judgment is obtained through litigation, how will it be enforced across international borders? These are some of the questions discussed in this chapter.

Methods of Resolution

This chapter presents several alternatives for dispute resolution, including mediation, arbitration, and litigation. Consider a domestic dispute in which a New York supplier tries to sue a Texas distributor. This situation raises several questions: Should the parties settle, mediate, arbitrate, or litigate? Where should the dispute be heard—in which forum, New York or Houston? In federal or state court? Which law applies to the transaction—the law of New York, Texas, or some other jurisdiction? Finally, if a resolution is reached (be it a settlement, a verdict, or a judgment), how will it be enforced?

Changing the parties to an American supplier and a foreign distributor adds several dimensions to the problem. Many of the same questions that are relevant to a domestic dispute are equally relevant to an international dispute, but they become infinitely more complex. This chapter examines these questions as they apply to commercial disputes in international business.

ALTERNATE DISPUTE RESOLUTION

Alternate dispute resolution (ADR) usually offers a faster, cheaper, and more efficient alternative to resolving international commercial disputes than litigation. Unlike litigation, ADR requires that the parties voluntarily submit to the resolution process.

Mediation

Mediation is a voluntary, nonbinding, conciliation process. The parties agree on an impartial mediator who helps them amicably reach a solution. The final decision to settle rests with the parties themselves. It is private, and there are no public court records or glaring articles in the local press to influence local opinion about the firms. The parties reserve all legal rights to resort to binding arbitration or litigation.

Arbitration

Arbitration is a more formalized process resulting in a binding award that will be enforced by courts of law in many countries. The parties must agree to arbitration, but once they do, they may not withdraw. Arbitration is frequently used in international business because it "levels the playing field" since the case may be heard in a more impartial tribunal. First, arbitration permits the resolution of the case in a third "neutral" country, rather than in the country of one of the parties. The parties are generally free to choose the location for arbitration that is mutually convenient. For example, a dispute between an American company and a Russian company might be arbitrated in Paris or Stockholm. Disputes between American companies and Chinese companies are often arbitrated in Hong Kong (not only is Hong Kong still considered a neutral site, but its awards are enforceable by the courts of both the United States and China). Secondly, the arbitrator may be chosen by the parties from a roster of impartial industry experts or distinguished lawyers, who may also be from a third country. Finally, the case may be resolved using the impartial and straightforward *arbitration rules* of the arbitrating organization, rather than the procedural rules buried in the statutes or rules of the court of the country of one of the parties. There are other advantages to arbitration besides this neutrality. Pretrial discovery is faster and more limited than that available in the United States, resulting in less expense and delay. The process is private and not publicly available as are court records. Arbitration fees are far less than litigation, as are attorney fees. The rules of evidence admissibility are more flexible than in many national courts. And finally, a party's right to appeal is more limited.

Although parties can always agree to arbitration, a requirement to submit to arbitration is often set out in many international contracts. Arbitration clauses might be used in contracts for the sale of goods, commodities, or raw materials. They are used in international shipping contracts, employment contracts, international construction contracts, financing agreements, and cruise ship tickets,

to name a few, as well as in multimillion or billion dollar contracts. Today, arbitration is being used more to resolve disputes over intellectual property and licensing agreements. Despite its reputation for being less costly than litigation, arbitration is not cheap. The International Chamber of Commerce (ICC) estimates that for a $1 million claim before its International Court of Arbitration in Paris, the average arbitrator's fee would be approximately $32,000, with about $19,000 in administrative expenses, for a total of approximately $49,000 in costs—or about 5 percent. For a $100,000 claim, the costs would be closer to 13 percent.

National Arbitral Laws. Most commercial nations today have laws permitting arbitration and specifying the effect of an arbitral award (see Exhibit 3.1). The *British Arbitration Act* went into effect in 1996. The *Arbitration Law of the People's Republic of China* became effective in 1994 (it provides that arbitrators must have eight years' prior legal experience), and the Russian law was enacted in 1993 (it provides that arbitration may be conducted in Russia in any language agreed upon). The laws of many countries, such as China, Russia, Mexico, and Canada, were patterned after the *1985 Model Law on International Commercial Arbitration* of the UN Commission on International Trade law (UNCITRAL). The U.S. *Federal Arbitration Act* dates back to 1925, but has been modernized. It applies to both domestic and international arbitration and defers to the

---

EXHIBIT 3.1

Some Arbitration Treaties in Force Worldwide

Arab Convention on Commercial Arbitration (1987)

Convention on the Recognition and Enforcement of Foreign Arbitral Awards (New York, 1959)

Convention on the Settlement of Investment Disputes Between States and Nationals of Other States (Washington Convention, 1966)

European Convention Providing a Uniform Law on Arbitration (Strasbourg Convention, 1966)

Geneva Protocol on Arbitration Clauses (1923)

Geneva Convention on the Execution of Foreign Arbitral Awards (1927)

Inter-American Convention on International Commercial Arbitration (Organization of American States, Panama Convention, 1975)

specific procedural rules of the arbitral body conducting the arbitration proceedings. Many U.S. states (e.g., California, Connecticut, Illinois, Oregon, and Texas) have enacted statutes on international commercial arbitration, some patterned after the UNCITRAL model.

Arbitration Bodies. There are many organizations worldwide providing arbitral services. The choice is up to the parties, and this is often decided in advance and set out in the terms of the contract. Some of the leading private arbitral organizations for arbitration of commercial disputes are the following:

- China International Economic and Trade Arbitration Commission
- American Arbitration Association
- International Court of Arbitration of the International Chamber of Commerce (ICC)
- London Court of Arbitration
- Arbitration Institute of the Stockholm Chamber of Commerce
- St. Petersburg International Commercial Arbitration Court
- Hong Kong International Arbitration Centre and the HK Mediation Centre
- Singapore International Arbitration Centre
- Japan Commercial Arbitration Association
- World Intellectual Property Organization (WIPO) Arbitration and Mediation Center

Two additional organizations provide dispute resolution between private parties and national governments:

- *The International Centre for Settlement of Investment Disputes* (ICSID, a part of the World Bank group) (providing arbitration for the settlement of disputes between member countries and investors who qualify as nationals of other member countries).
- *The Permanent Court of Arbitration at The Hague* (providing arbitral services for commercial disputes to states, private parties, and intergovernmental organizations, including handling mass claims and environmental disputes where one of the parties is a national government).

Each of these organizations operates under a different set of procedural rules. The ICC uses its own rules that are highly respected. Many other arbitral bodies use the widely accepted rules drafted by UNCITAL, which take into account the various legal systems and countries in which they might be used. The UNCITRAL rules, for example are used by the *Hong Kong Arbitration Center,* by the WIPO, and by other organizations throughout the world.

---

http://www.globalarbitrationmediation.com/
For a survey of world arbitration laws, including the laws of the United States, Canada, Great Britain, Russian, China, and Japan, see this private commercial site.

http://www.iccwbo.org/index_court.asp
A guide to dispute resolution services of the International Court of Arbitration of the International Chamber of Commerce, including the Rules of Arbitration, Arbitration Cost Calculator, and Small Claims Guidelines.

Arbitration Clauses. Many contracts contain clauses requiring that disputes be submitted for arbitration because it removes much of the uncertainty in the event of a breach of contract or other dispute. Here is a typical example:

> Any disputes or claims arising out of this contract, or breach thereof, shall be resolved by arbitration before [name of arbitral body], and according to the rules of that body. Any award rendered thereby may be entered in any court of competent jurisdiction

While the validity of these clauses is now generally accepted, that was not always clear. In the following case, *Scherk v. Alberto-Culver,* the U.S. Supreme Court considered an arbitration clause in an international contract calling for arbitration in Paris.

Enforcement of Arbitration Awards. Arbitral awards are recognized and enforceable by the courts of most nations. In the United States, they will usually be enforced if they were enforceable under the local law of the country where the award was made if the defendant was properly subject to the jurisdiction of the arbitral tribunal, if the defendant was given notice of the arbitration proceeding and an opportunity to be heard, and if the enforcement is not contrary to public policy. An arbitral award will not be enforced, however, if the contract with the arbitration clause would be unlawful under applicable law, if it is void for reasons of fraud or the incapacity of one of the parties, or if the arbitration procedures violate the

Scherk v. Alberto-Culver
417 U.S. 506 (1974)
United States Supreme Court

Read!

BACKGROUND AND FACTS

Alberto-Culver Co., a Delaware corporation with its principal office in Illinois, manufactures toiletries and hair products in the United States and abroad. In February 1969, Alberto-Culver signed in Austria a contract to purchase three businesses of Fritz Scherk (a German citizen) that were organized under German and Liechtenstein law, as well as the trademarks to related cosmetics. In the contract, Scherk warranted that he had the sole and unencumbered ownership of these trademarks. The contract also contained a clause that provided that "any controversy or claim [that] shall arise out of this agreement or the breach thereof would be referred to arbitration before the International Chamber of Commerce in Paris, France, and that the laws of Illinois shall govern." One year after the closing, Alberto-Culver discovered that others had claims to Scherk's trademarks. Alberto-Culver tried to rescind the contract; Scherk refused, and Alberto-Culver filed suit in Illinois Federal District Court claiming that the misrepresentations violated the Securities and Exchange Act, Sec. 10(b) and the SEC rule 10b-5. Scherk moved to dismiss or to stay the action pending arbitration. In the U.S. District Court, the motion to dismiss was denied and arbitration was enjoined. The Court of Appeals affirmed. The Supreme Court granted certiorari.

JUSTICE STEWART

The *United States Arbitration Act*, now 9 U.S.C. 1 et seq., reversing centuries of judicial hostility to arbitration agreements, was designed to allow parties to avoid "the costliness and delays of litigation," and to place arbitration agreements "upon the same footing as other contracts. . . . "

Alberto-Culver's contract to purchase the business entities belonging to Scherk was a truly international agreement. Alberto-Culver is an American corporation with its principal place of business and the vast bulk of its activity in this country, while Scherk is a citizen of Germany whose companies were organized under the laws of Germany and Liechtenstein. The negotiations leading to the signing of the contract in Austria and to the closing in Switzerland took place in the United States, England, and Germany, and involved consultations with legal and trademark experts from each of those countries

and from Liechtenstein. Finally, and most significantly, the subject matter of the contract concerned the sale of business enterprises organized under the laws of and primarily situated in European countries, whose activities were largely, if not entirely, directed to European markets.

Such a contract involves considerations and policies significantly different from those found controlling in *Wilko*. In *Wilko*, quite apart from the arbitration provision, there was no question but that the laws of the United States generally, and the federal securities laws in particular, would govern disputes arising out of the stock-purchase agreement. The parties, the negotiations, and the subject matter of the contract were all situated in this country, and no credible claim could have been entertained that any international conflict-of-laws problems would arise. In this case, by contrast, in the absence of the arbitration provision considerable uncertainty existed at the time of the agreement, and still exists, concerning the law applicable to the resolutions of disputes arising out of the contract.

Such uncertainty will almost inevitably exist with respect to any contract touching two or more countries, each with its own substantive laws and conflict-of-laws rules. A contractual provision specifying in advance the forum in which disputes shall be litigated and the law to be applied is, therefore, an almost indispensable precondition to achievement of the orderliness and predictability essential to any international business transaction. Furthermore, such a provision obviates the danger that a dispute under the agreement might be submitted to a forum hostile to the interests of one of the parties or unfamiliar with the problem involved.

A parochial refusal by the courts of one country to enforce an international arbitration agreement would not only frustrate these purposes, but would invite unseemly and mutually destructive jockeying by the parties to secure tactical litigation advantages. In the present case, for example, it is not inconceivable that if Scherk had anticipated that Alberto-Culver would be able in this country to enjoin resort to arbitration he might have sought an order in France or some other country enjoining Alberto-Culver from proceeding with its litigation in the United States. Whatever recognition the courts of this country

continued

continued

might ultimately have granted to the order of the foreign court, the dicey atmosphere of such a legal no-man's-land would surely damage the fabric of international commerce and trade, and imperil the willingness and ability of businessmen to enter into international commercial agreements. . . .

For all these reasons we hold that the agreement of the parties in this case to arbitrate any dispute arising out of their international commercial transaction is to be respected and enforced by the federal courts in accord with the explicit provisions of the Arbitration Act.

Decision. Reversed and remanded.

Comment. The Court understood that an arbitration agreement was the ultimate type of forum selection clause. The Court made reference to national legislation that indicated an acceptance of arbitration (the Arbitration Act, 9 U.S.C I et. seq.). Other countries have similar national legislation or are signatories to the *New York Convention* and/or the *European Convention on International Arbitration*.

---

law where arbitration took place. More than 130 nations have signed the 1958 *United Nations Convention on the Recognition and Enforcement of Foreign Arbitral Awards,* known as the *New York Convention,* further strengthening the ability to enforce awards in those countries.

LITIGATION

Litigation is the final step in attempting to resolve a dispute. It is used more frequently in the United States than in virtually any other country. Many countries have different procedural rules for litigating cases. First, many concepts familiar to American and English students, such as trial by jury and other traditions, may not be used in the civil law countries. While we take jury trials in criminal and civil cases almost for granted in America, the same is not true throughout the world. The role of the judge may be very different; in some countries, the judge is an impartial arbiter of fairness and procedure, while in other countries, he may examine witnesses and take an active role in the search for the truth. The *discovery* process, by which the parties attempt to uncover evidence in advance of trial, can be different. For instance, oral depositions taken under oath outside of court may be routinely done in the United States, while in China and some other countries, their use is prohibited. There are different rules for compensating lawyers; in the United States, for instance, contingent fees are widely used in tort cases, while in other countries, they are barred. The entire issue of damages is frequently handled

differently; the United States is famous for its whopping punitive damage awards that serve to punish a losing party for its especially egregious conduct, while in many other countries, such as Japan, punitive damages are not used. Finally, appeals are handled differently in many countries, with some, like the United States, limiting appeals to reconsidering issues of law applied by the trial courts. In other countries, appellate courts will consider new or additional evidence.

There can also be many differences in substantive law—the law of the case, although this topic is certainly too broad for this chapter. Suffice it to say that almost every body of law—contracts, torts, crimes, property, business regulation, intellectual property, and so forth—can vary from legal system to legal system and country to country. Some of these differences were highlighted in the last chapter in our discussion of *comparative law,* and so you should be well aware that this will have a tremendous impact on the outcome of litigation. Certainly, parties to a contract can have some control over the choice of substantive law and procedural rules by incorporating *choice of law clauses* and *forum selection clauses* in their contracts. And they may be able to have control over where the litigation takes place. These are critical issues that must be kept in mind as you read on.

Jurisdiction

Jurisdiction, one of the key concepts of jurisprudence, is the power of a court to hear and decide a case. A court that has jurisdiction is said to be a "competent" court. The term has different meanings depending on how it is used. For example, *territorial jurisdiction* refers to the power of criminal courts to hear cases involving crimes committed within their territory. *Universality jurisdiction* refers to the power of any court to hear crimes committed against humanity. *In rem* jurisdiction refers to a court's power over property within its geographical boundaries. *Subject matter jurisdiction* refers to the court's authority to hear a certain type of legal matter, such as tort cases or breach of contract. In the United States, for example, federal courts have subject matter jurisdiction of cases involving federal statutes and federal government agencies, constitutional issues, and cases arising between citizens of different states or between citizens of the United States and citizens of foreign countries (where the amount in controversy exceeds $75,000). The latter is known as *diversity of citizenship* jurisdiction. Thus, we see that the term "jurisdiction" can be used in many different ways. But one thing is certain—without it, lawful courts are powerless to act.

In Personam Jurisdiction.

In personam jurisdiction or "jurisdiction over the person" refers to the court's power over a certain individual or corporation. No party can be made to appear before a court unless that court has personal jurisdiction. If there is no personal jurisdiction, the case will be dismissed. Typically, jurisdiction is obtained by having a summons served on an individual or on the legal agent of a corporation. While the serving of a summons on a party is the best way for a court to obtain jurisdiction over the person, there are many substitute methods, such as those used to summon parties not personally present in the court's territory (this subject will be discussed later in this chapter). In certain types of cases, service over those not present in the territory can be done by registered mail or even through publication in the "legal notices" section of approved newspapers. In the United States, the requirement of obtaining service of process on a defendant in a case, and of having jurisdiction over them, is required by the Due Process Clause of the 5th and 14th Amendments. The method used must be authorized by statute and be fundamentally fair. The basic concept is that one should not be "hauled into court" in some distant state or country unless that person has some connection to that place. Every national legal system has its jurisdictional requirements. For example, the *French Civil Code* states, "a foreigner, even if not residing in France, may be cited before French courts for the execution of obligations by him contracted in France with a citizen of France." In Germany, the presence of property owned by the defendant, whether the property is insignificant or even if it is not related to the case, can still be the basis of jurisdiction. Similarly, in the United States, there are many federal and state statutes that define when a court is competent to hear and decide a case over a defendant.

Requirement for In Personam Jurisdiction: Minimum Contacts.

At one time in U.S. legal history, the U.S. Supreme Court had interpreted the Due Process Clause to limit personal jurisdiction to people physically present in the court's territory. As the nation grew and as interstate commerce expanded, the concept was broadened to allow jurisdiction over persons not present within the court's geographical territory, but for reasons of justice and fairness should be held to answer a complaint there. A modern example are state "implied consent" statutes, by which one operating a motor vehicle on the highways of a state "impliedly consents" to submitting to the jurisdiction of the courts of that state for all suits arising out of the operation of the vehicle there. The due process requirements for *in personam* jurisdiction over persons absent from a state or territory have been carefully considered by the courts. In the now famous language of U.S. Supreme Court decisions dealing with both interstate and international commerce "due process requires only that in order to subject a defendant to a judgment *in personam*, if he be not present within the territory of the forum, he have *certain minimum contacts with it such that the maintenance of the suit does not offend traditional notions of fair play and substantial justice*." *International Shoe Co. v. Washington*, 326 U.S. 310 (1945). [Emphasis added]

But just how much of a connection to a foreign state or country does it take for the courts to require one to defend a case there? The courts have answered the question on a case-by-case basis, looking to see whether it would be fair to ask a nonresident to come to their jurisdiction to defend a case. The courts have looked at many factors, including the extent of the defendant's presence in the state, what business he may have conducted there, the burden on the defendant, fairness to the plaintiff, and the interest of the state in having the case resolved there. Did the defendant have an office, branch location, or salespeople in the territory of the forum? Did any of its employees or agents travel there on business? Did it advertise or otherwise solicit business there? Did it ship goods there? Did it enter into a contract there, or was the contract to be performed there? In *Worldwide Volkswagen Corp. v. Woodson*, 444 U.S. 286 (1980), the U.S. Supreme Court stated that a New York automobile distributor was not required to appear in Oklahoma to defend a products liability suit based on the sale of a vehicle that took place in New York and was later involved in a serious accident in Oklahoma.

Petitioners carry on no activity whatsoever in Oklahoma. They close no sales and perform no services there. They avail themselves of none of the privileges and benefits of Oklahoma law. They solicit no business there either through salespersons or through advertising reasonably calculated to reach the State. Nor does the record show that they regularly sell cars at wholesale or retail to Oklahoma customers or residents or that they indirectly, through others, serve or seek to serve the Oklahoma market. In short, respondents seek to base jurisdiction on one, isolated occurrence and whatever inferences can be drawn therefrom: the fortuitous circumstance that a single Audi automobile, sold in New York to New York residents, happened to suffer an accident while passing through Oklahoma.

A similar concept exists in the international context. The following case, *Asahi Metal Ind. v. Superior Ct. of California*, 480 U.S. 102 (1987), questions whether a Japanese manufacturing

Asahi Metal Ind. v. Superior Court of California, Solano
107 S.Ct. 1026 (1987)
United States Supreme Court

BACKGROUND AND FACTS
Asahi Metal, a Japanese corporation, manufactured valve assemblies in Japan and sold them to tire manufacturers including Cheng Shin (a Taiwanese corporation) from 1978 to 1982. Cheng Shin sold tires all over the world, including in California. On September 23, 1978, in Solano County, California, Gary Zurcher was injured riding his motorcycle. His wife was killed. He filed a product liability action against Cheng Shin (Taiwan), the manufacturer of his motorcycle tire, alleging that the tire was defective. Cheng Shin filed a cross-complaint seeking indemnification from Asahi Metal Industry. Cheng Shin settled with Zurcher. However, Cheng Shin (Taiwan) pressed its action against Asahi (Japan), and Asahi petitioned for certiorari to the United States Supreme Court. The case presented the question of whether a dispute between a Taiwanese company and a Japanese company with the preceding relationship to California should be heard by the California courts. In other words, did the California court have jurisdiction over the matter?

JUSTICE O'CONNOR
The placement of a product into the stream of commerce, without more, is not an act of the defendant purposefully directed toward the forum State. Additional conduct of the defendant may indicate an intent or purpose to serve the market in the forum State, for example, designing the product for the market in the forum State, advertising in the forum State, establishing channels for providing regular advice to customers in the forum State, or marketing the product through a distributor who has agreed to serve as the sales agent in the forum State. But a defendant's awareness that the stream of commerce may or will sweep the product into the forum State does not convert the mere act of placing the product into the stream into an act purposefully directed toward the forum State.

Assuming, *arguendo*, that respondents have established Asahi's awareness that some of the valves sold to Cheng Shin would be incorporated into tire tubes sold in California, respondents have not demonstrated any action by Asahi to purposefully avail itself of the California market. It has no office, agents, employees, or property in California. It does not advertise or otherwise solicit business in California. It did not create, control, or employ the distribution system that brought its valves to California. Cf. *Hicks v. Kawasaki Heavy Industries*, 452 F. Supp.

continued

continued

130 (1978). There is no evidence that Asahi designed its product in anticipation of sales in California. Cf. *Rockwell International Corp. v. Costruzioni Aeronautiche Giovanni Agusta,* 553 F. Supp. 328 (ED Pa. 1982). On the basis of these facts, the exertion of personal jurisdiction over Asahi by the Superior Court of California exceeds the limits of Due Process.

The strictures of the Due Process Clause forbid a state court from exercising personal jurisdiction over Asahi under circumstances that would offend "traditional notions of fair play and substantial justice." *International Shoe Co. v. Washington,* 326 U.S., at 316, 66 S.Ct., at 158.

We have previously explained that the determination of the reasonableness of the exercise of jurisdiction in each case will depend on an evaluation of several factors. . . .

Certainly the burden on the defendant in this case is severe. Asahi has been commanded by the Supreme Court of California not only to traverse the distance between Asahi's headquarters in Japan and the Superior Court of California in and for the County of Solano, but also to submit its dispute with Cheng Shin to a foreign nation's judicial system. The unique burdens placed upon one who must defend oneself in a foreign legal system should have significant weight in assessing the reasonableness of stretching the long arm of personal jurisdiction over national borders.

When minimum contacts have been established, often the interests of the plaintiff and the forum in the exercise of jurisdiction will justify even the serious burdens placed on the alien defendant. In the present case, however, the interests of the plaintiff and the forum in California's assertion of jurisdiction over Asahi are slight. All that remains is a claim for indemnification asserted by Cheng Shin, a Taiwanese corporation, against Asahi. The transaction on which the indemnification claim is based took place in Taiwan; Asahi's components were shipped from Japan to Taiwan. Cheng Shin has not demonstrated that it is more convenient for it to litigate its indemnification claim against Asahi in California rather than in Taiwan or Japan.

Because the plaintiff is not a California resident, California's legitimate interests in the dispute have considerably diminished. The Supreme Court of California argued that the State had an interest in "protecting its consumers by ensuring that foreign manufacturers comply with the state's safety standards." . . . The State Supreme Court's definition of California's interest, however, was overly broad. The dispute between Cheng Shin and Asahi is primarily about indemnification rather than safety. Moreover, it is not at all clear at this point that California law should govern the question whether a Japanese corporation should indemnify a Taiwanese corporation on the basis of a sale made in Taiwan and a shipment of goods from Japan to Taiwan.

Considering the international context, the heavy burden on the alien defendant, and the slight interests of the plaintiff and the forum State, the exercise of personal jurisdiction by a California court over Asahi in this instance would be unreasonable and unfair.

Because the facts of this case do not establish minimum contacts such that the exercise of personal jurisdiction is consistent with fair play and substantial justice, the judgment of Supreme Court of California is reversed, and the case is remanded for further proceedings not inconsistent with this opinion.

It is so ordered.

Decision. Reversed and remanded. The United States Supreme Court found that there was no jurisdiction, reversing the California Supreme Court. This Supreme Court case is significant because it lists several factors that will be taken into account in determining whether the court will take jurisdiction.

company should be forced to defend a lawsuit in California for an accident that occurred there. As you read, keep in mind that these cases are resolved on a case-by-case basis after a consideration of all of the facts. A decision on jurisdiction may depend on one or more different factors not present in other cases. In other words, it is very difficult for lawyers to counsel whether your actions will or will not subject you to a foreign court's jurisdiction some time in the future. In reading, think about what factors, if they had been present, might have forced Asahi to appear in court in California.

Jurisdiction in the Internet Age. As electronic commerce brings the world closer together, there will likely be more disputes between parties in distant countries. How will the courts fashion rules for deciding when a party must defend itself against litigation in foreign courts? Just as the meaning of "minimum contacts" adapted to the rise of interstate commerce in the United States over fifty years ago, so too is it adapting to the rise of the Internet age. The following case, *Graduate Management Admission Council v. Raju,* involves a case that many readers may well appreciate. In this case,

involving several different tort actions including trademark infringement and unfair competition, the Indian defendant must have simply decided not to show up in the United States to answer a complaint against him. Perhaps he thought that the U.S. courts would have no jurisdiction over him if he stayed away. He did not appear and a default judgment was entered against him.

Graduate Management Admission Council v. Raju
241 F. Supp.2d 589 (2003)
United States District Court (E.D.Va.)

BACKGROUND AND FACTS

Plaintiff GMAC is a nonprofit corporation located in Virginia. It develops and owns all rights to the Graduate Management Admission Test (GMAT), used for admittance to about 1700 graduate business programs in the United States and elsewhere. The GMAT forms and questions are original, copyrighted materials. GMAC routinely registers its material with the Register of Copyrights and has registered "GMAT" as trademark with the U.S. Patent and Trademark Office. Defendant Raju is a citizen of India. Raju registered the domain names "gmatplus.com" and "gmatplus.net" in 2000 and operates a Web site under the former name. The Web site sells, for as much as $199, seven books containing "100 percent actual questions" never before published. The books were sold to customers in India, China, Korea, Singapore, France, Australia, Japan, Taiwan, and to at least two individuals in Virginia. The Web site contained ordering information for customers in the United States. Orders placed on the site are paid for by a money transfer through Western Union or MoneyGram. GMAC filed a complaint against Raju for infringement, cyber piracy, unfair competition, and other torts. The defendant failed to appear, and the court entered a default judgment against him on the basis of having personal jurisdiction over him.

ELLIS, DISTRICT JUDGE

* * *

Under the well-established *International Shoe* formulation, the exercise of personal jurisdiction over a defendant requires that the defendant "have certain minimum contacts with [the forum] such that the maintenance of a suit does not offend 'traditional notions of fair play and substantial justice.'" See *Inter-*

national Shoe Co. v. Washington, 326 U.S. 310, 316, 66 S.Ct. 154 (1945), *ALS Scan, Inc. v. Digital Service Consultants, Inc.,* 293 F.3d 707, 710 (4th Cir. 2002). Personal jurisdiction can be established under either general or specific jurisdiction. Where, as here, the defendant's contacts with the forum are also the basis for the suit, specific jurisdiction is appropriate. In determining whether specific jurisdiction exists, courts must consider "(1) the extent to which the defendant 'purposefully availed' itself of the privilege of conducting activities in the State; (2) whether the plaintiff's claims arise out of those activities directed at the State; and (3) whether the exercise of personal jurisdiction would be constitutionally 'reasonable.'" *Id.*

As the Fourth Circuit noted in *ALS Scan,* this due process analysis must take account of the modern reality of widespread Internet electronic communications. Accordingly, the Fourth Circuit recently adopted the *Zippo* "sliding-scale" approach for determining whether Internet activity can serve as a basis for personal jurisdiction. (Discussing *Zippo Manufacturing Co. v. Zippo Dot Com, Inc.,* 952 F. Supp. 1119 [W.D.Pa. 1997]).

Under the now-familiar *Zippo* test, the likelihood that personal jurisdiction can be constitutionally exercised is determined by focusing on "the nature and the quality of commercial activity that an entity conducts over the Internet." Passive websites, that do "little more" than make information available to users in other jurisdictions, cannot support personal jurisdiction everywhere that information is accessed. At the other end of the spectrum are situations where a defendant "clearly does business over the Internet," for example through the "knowing and repeated transmission of files over the Internet,"

continued

continued

which clearly do support personal jurisdiction. In between is the "middle ground" of "interactive Web sites" which are not passive, because they allow a user to exchange information with the host computer, but also do not constitute "clearly doing business over the Internet." To determine whether an "interactive" website is grounds for personal jurisdiction, a court must consider the "level of interactivity and the commercial nature of the exchange of information that occurs on the Web site." * * * *

Rule 4(k)(2), *Federal Rules of Civil Procedure* . . . provides for personal jurisdiction through nationwide service of process over any defendant provided (i) exercise of jurisdiction is consistent with the Constitution and the laws of the United States, (ii) the claim arises under federal law, and (iii) the defendant is not subject to the jurisdiction of the courts of general jurisdiction of any state. Rule 4(k)(2) was added in 1993 to deal with a gap in federal personal jurisdiction law in situations where a defendant does not reside in the United States, and lacks contacts with a single state sufficient to justify personal jurisdiction, but has enough contacts with the United States as a whole to satisfy the due process requirements. Precisely this situation is presented here. The first element of the Rule 4(k)(2) analysis requires the same minimum contacts due process analysis as is conducted under Rule 4(k)(1)(A), with the significant difference that the relevant forum is the United States as a whole, not an individual State. * * *

In considering Raju's contacts with the United States in this case, the *ALS Scan* test for determining personal jurisdiction based on electronic activities must be adapted for the purpose of national contacts analysis. Substituting the United States as the relevant forum, the test requires a showing in this case (i) that Raju directed his electronic activity into the United States, (ii) that he did so with the manifest intent of engaging in business or other interactions within the United States, and (iii) that his activity creates a potential cause of action in a person within the United States that is cognizable in the United States' courts.

Raju's alleged activity plainly creates a potential cause of action in a person within the United States which is cognizable in federal courts, satisfying the third element of the *ALS Scan* test. GMAC is a Virginia non-profit corporation and thus a "person" within the United States. GMAC's causes of action are based on federal law, and thus are clearly cogniz-able in federal courts. It is also clear that Raju's intent is to "engage in business," namely the business of selling his GMAT test preparation materials to buyers for a substantial fee. Thus, the second element of the *ALS Scan* test is fulfilled in part. All that remains is a showing that Raju "directed his electronic activity" into the United States, with the intent of engaging in business "within the United States," as required by the first and second elements of the *ALS Scan* test.

The record clearly indicates that Raju directed his activity at the United States market and specifically targeted United States customers. The intended market for business conducted through a website can be determined by considering the apparent focus of the website as a whole. *See Young v. New Haven Advocate,* 315 F.3d 256 (4th Cir. 2002) (Examining the "general thrust and content" of the newspapers' websites, including the local focus of the stories, local advertisements and classifieds, local weather and traffic information, and links to local institutions, in determining that "the overall content of both websites is decidedly local"). The relevant question is whether the website is "designed to attract or serve a [United States] audience." *Id.*

There is ample evidence that Raju targeted the United States market. First, and most significantly, the *GMATplus* site provides specific ordering information for United States customers. The ordering information page directs customers who "live in the United States or Canada" to contact Western Union or MoneyGram, and provides the toll free numbers for use by those customers. . . . No other countries apart from the United States and Canada are mentioned by name on the ordering information page. Thus, ordering information for customers in the United States (and Canada) is provided first and with more specificity than for customers from other countries. Second, the ordering information page informs customers that materials will "reach most parts of the world (including the US) within 3-5 working days." Third, the prices for the products are listed in dollars, presumably United States dollars. Fourth, three of the six testimonials are purportedly from United States citizens. Fifth, the promotional text on the site suggests that Raju's materials will allow American citizens and others to catch up with test takers from "India, China, Korea, Japan, and Taiwan," who purportedly score better on the test as a group than "their American or European counterparts . . .

continued

continued

because most of them have access to 100 percent of unpublished previous questions in these countries." Finally, Raju confirmed his apparent intent to serve United States customers by shipping his materials to the two Virginia residents mentioned in the record.

In sum, it is quite clear upon review of the *GMATplus* website and the record as a whole that while Raju may have aimed his website at the entire, worldwide market of GMAT test takers, he specifically directed his electronic activity at the United States market and did in fact ship materials in the United States. Thus, GMAT has shown under the *ALS Scan* test that Raju "directed his electronic activity into [the United States] with the manifested intent of engaging in business . . . within [the United States]," satisfying the remaining elements of the *ALS Scan* test. It follows that the exercise of personal juris-

diction based on nationwide contacts under 4(k)(2) comports with constitutional due process requirements in this case. * * * To find otherwise would not only frustrate GMAC's attempts in this case to vindicate its rights under United States law, by requiring GMAC to turn to foreign courts to vindicate those rights against a likely elusive defendant, it would also provide a blueprint whereby other individuals bent on violating United States trademark and copyright laws could do so without risking suit in a United States court.

Decision. Raju had sufficient minimum contacts with the United States to justify personal jurisdiction here over him under the federal rules. The magistrate judge was directed to take whatever steps deemed necessary to determine the appropriate relief to be awarded GMAC in this matter.

Obtaining Jurisdiction by Service of Process. As we have learned, a court must have personal jurisdiction over individuals or corporate entities before they can be made to appear and defend a civil case. Personal jurisdiction is obtained through lawful service of process. Without proper service, any judgment that might be taken will not be enforceable. This is especially problematic when attempting to enforce a judgment internationally. To illustrate, imagine that an American plaintiff files suit in a U.S. court against a resident of France for a contract that was performed in the United States. Assume that the plaintiff's attorney is able to obtain service of process over the defendant in France. The French citizen does not appear in the United States and a default judgment is taken. When the American attempts to enforce the U.S. judgment in the courts of France, the defendant will claim that the method of service of process over him was unsatisfactory under French law. If the French courts agree, the plaintiff's judgment may be worth nothing if the defendant's only assets are in France. Thus, international lawyers trying to obtain process over a foreign defendant are advised to consult an attorney in the defendant's country and to follow the requirements of both U.S. and French law to the letter.

Obtaining service of process over a foreign de-

fendant is addressed in *The Hague Convention on the Service Abroad of Judicial and Extra-Judicial Documents in Civil and Commercial Matters*, in force in about 75 countries. Authorized methods of service are different even for countries that are members of the treaty. Some countries permit service through the use of registered or certified mail, with a return receipt signed by the defendant being served, although other countries (e.g., Germany, Norway, Egypt, China, and others) do not permit this method. Some countries permit personal service by an agent or attorney of the plaintiff located in the defendant's country who signs an "affidavit of service" at a nearby U.S. embassy affirming that he has served the defendant with notice and a copy of the complaint. Most countries require the complaint to be in the local language as well as in English. Perhaps the safest method, but one that can cause very long delays (up to a year according to the U.S. State Department) is a formal request for service made through a *letter rogatory* (a "letter of request" sent through diplomatic channels) that results in personal service on the defendant by the courts of the country in which he is found. Defendants located in countries not parties to this convention can also be served with process with a *letter rogatory*. Letters rogatory are discussed later in this chapter.

Venue

Jurisdiction is often confused with the concept of venue. *Venue* refers to the geographical location of a court of competent jurisdiction where a case can be heard. While the courts of several different states, or countries, may have proper jurisdiction, the concept of venue helps decide which one of these should actually hear the case. For instance, in some civil lawsuits between citizens of different states, we know that the federal courts may have jurisdiction. But in which federal district should it be tried? Imagine an automobile accident in which the passengers of one car are residents of Pennsylvania, while the driver of the other vehicle is a resident of North Carolina, and the accident occurs while they're both on vacation in California. We know that jurisdiction is proper in the federal courts (and it may also be proper in some state court). But we certainly would not expect that the case could be tried in a federal court located in Montana. So, federal rules generally permit the case to be heard either where all of the plaintiffs reside, where all of the defendants reside, or where the cause of action arose. (In complex transnational litigation, it is not unusual that courts in several countries might attempt to exercise jurisdiction over the matter.) While typically the plaintiff will initially choose where to file its suit, it is not unusual for a defendant to request a change of venue, asking that the case be removed to a location that is more convenient and that has a closer connection to the facts of the particular case.

international accents

Case Sails Back to a U.S. Court
A cruise line's bid to have suit tried in Italy is stymied—for now.

By David E. Rovella
National Law Journal Staff Reporter

Latin for "inconvenient forum," *forum non conveniens* is a term that causes lawyers to cringe—one with the power to conjure up memories of civil procedure classes brimming with fun cases such as *Erie Railroad* and *International Shoe.*

But for Miami lawyer Michael S. Olin, it just evokes anger. Mr. Olin and his clients, three elderly couples who were injured while traveling the South Pacific in 1994 on an Italian cruise liner, were forced to go to federal court after a Florida appeals panel cited the obscure legal concept in moving their negligence lawsuit to Italy.

A common-law principle, *forum non conveniens* allows a judge to dismiss a case if the venue is inconvenient or unjust.

Despite the plaintiffs' being Americans—from Washington state and California—and the Florida business contacts of the Genoa, Italy-based defendant—Costa Crociere S.p.a.—Mr. Olin said, the court was intent on keeping a "provincial" attitude toward out-of-state litigants.

But the U.S. district court in Miami recently ruled for Mr. Olin's clients, saying that the plaintiffs' private interests, when taken with Costa's part-ownership by Miami-based Carnival, bar a move to Italy, *Bestor v. Costa Crociere,* No. 99–1914.

"This case stands for the notion that it is unreasonable for a cruise line . . . to get away with saying that a country that has nothing to do with the cruise should be the venue," said Mr. Olin, a partner at Miami's Podhurst Orseck Josefsberg Eaton Meadow Olin & Perwin.

Mr. Olin admitted, though, that these days most tickets have forum selection clauses that are usually enforced—a point noted by Costa lawyer Stephanie Hurst Wylie. Ms. Wylie, of Miami's Horr, Linfors & Skipp, said that the federal court should have followed the state court ruling because both were applying the same federal balancing test. In her motion to reconsider, filed on March 27, she argued that the court was also wrong to make Costa's ownership by Carnival part of the equation because insurance coverage protects Carnival and its shareholders from liability.

Sword or a shield? "The Florida court system is exhausted," said Ms. Wylie, who said that the state court's acerbic ruling reflected judicial frustration with travel industry litigation. "Judicial resources are being expended on cases that have nothing to do with Florida," she said.

continued

continued

But Mr. Olin argued that *forum non conveniens* has been used as a sword by the travel industry to send tort suits to foreign jurisdictions—and oblivion.

Mr. Olin's clients, who were injured during a 1994 stopoff in Vietnam while on a Hong Kong-to-Singapore cruise aboard Costa's Ocean Pearl, alleged that Costa was liable for the injuries caused them by the Vietnamese driver who put their van in a ditch near Da Nang.

"[Costa] arranged the van tour through the tour director, who made all the arrangements and even introduced them to the driver," said Mr. Olin, who is seeking $1 million. Ms. Wylie countered that the driver was an independent contractor, and thus not an agent of the cruise line for purposes of liability.

But the trial court first had to deal with Costa's attempt to move the case to Italy. Although that court rejected Costa's motion, the appeals court granted it because the defendant is based in Italy and the plaintiffs are not from Florida.

"[There is] no meaningful relationship to Florida whatever . . . maintenance of this case involves the epitome of the abuse of our courts." *Pearl Cruises v. Bestor,* 678 So. 2d 372.

The importance of staying on U.S. soil cannot be understated, said David W. Robertson, an expert on *forum non conveniens.* "When a plaintiff loses a forum case, generally that means the case has gone to zero value. No juries, no contingency fees," said Mr. Robertson, of Baton Rouge, La.'s Due, Caballero, Price & Guidry. "Mostly plaintiffs just give up at this point."

Forum Non Conveniens

The legal doctrine of *forum non conveniens* (meaning "inconvenient forum") refers to the discretionary power of a court to refuse to hear a case, even though it otherwise has proper jurisdiction and venue, because a court in another jurisdiction or location would be more convenient and justice better served. According to this doctrine, whenever a case is properly heard in the courts of more than one jurisdiction, it should be heard in the jurisdiction that is more convenient and has the closer connection to the cause of action that led to the case. In deciding on where to hear a case, the courts will examine both "private factors" (factors affecting the convenience of the parties and their ability to pursue their claims) and "public factors" (factors related to the public interest). For example, it may be more convenient to hear a case where the action arose, where witnesses and evidence are located, where the parties reside, or in the state or country whose law applies to the case. Imagine an airline disaster in the United States, with many plaintiffs and one airline. Venue may be proper in any number of locations—including the airline's principle place of business. But would it not be more convenient to hold the trial where the crash occurred? After all, that is where the wreckage is located, and where the controllers and other witnesses live and work. *Forum non conveniens* is applied by courts in the United States, as well as in many other countries. In the United States, it is applied by the federal courts in determining where to hear lawsuits between citizens of different states. It is also used in determining whether an international case should be heard by U.S. courts or by the courts of some other country. It is not unusual for one of the parties to a case to ask a court to transfer the case to another judicial district or location for reasons of convenience. The factors generally considered were described by the U.S. Supreme Court in *Gulf Oil v. Gilbert,* 330 U.S. 501 (1947).

Important considerations are the relative ease of access to sources of proof; availability of compulsory process for attendance of unwilling [witnesses] and the cost of obtaining attendance of willing witnesses; . . . and all other practical problems that make trial of a case easy, expeditious and inexpensive. There may also be questions as to the enforceability of a judgment if one is obtained. . . . It is often said that the plaintiff may not, by choice of an inconvenient forum, "vex," "harass," or "oppress" the defendant by inflicting upon him expense or trouble not necessary to his own right to pursue his remedy. But unless the balance is strongly in favor of the defendant, the plaintiff's choice of forum should rarely be disturbed. . . . There is a local interest in having localized controversies decided at home. There is an appropriateness, too, in having the trial of a diversity case in a forum that is at home with the state law that must govern the case, rather than having a court in some other forum untangle problems in conflict of laws, and in law foreign to itself.

Forum Shopping.

It is not unusual that requests to transfer on the basis of *forum non conveniens* are in truth attempts by counsel to "shop around" for a better legal deal. They may be looking for a law that is more favorable to their case or for a jury that might be more sympathetic to their side. After all, in federal lawsuits between residents of different states, such as in tort cases, the federal courts apply the law of the state in which they sit. Although there are procedural rules that discourage "forum shopping," it still weighs on the minds of most trial lawyers. The same is true, perhaps even more so, in international cases. In the following case, *Iragorri v. United Technologies,* the appellate court had to decide whether a case for wrongful death should be heard in Connecticut or in Cali, Colombia. The plaintiffs wanted the case heard in Connecticut because, as one would expect, the possibility of winning a large damage award was much greater than in Colombia.

Iragorri v. United Technologies Corp. & Otis Elevator Co.
274 F. 3d 65 (2001)
United States Court of Appeals (2nd Cir.)

BACKGROUND AND FACTS

Iragorri and his family had been residents of Florida since 1981, and naturalized citizens of the United States since 1989. In 1993, while visiting his mother in Cali, Colombia, he fell to his death through an open elevator shaft. Iragorri's children had been attending school there as exchange students from their Florida high school. His surviving wife and children brought this action in United States District Court in Connecticut for damages against two American companies, Otis Elevator and its parent corporation, United Technologies. They alleged that employees of International Elevator had negligently wedged a door open with a screwdriver during repairs, leaving the shaft open. International Elevator was a Maine corporation doing business in South America. Both Otis and United had their principle place of business in Connecticut. The complaint alleged that Otis and United were liable because (1) International had acted as their agent in negligently repairing the elevator, and (2) Otis and United were liable under Connecticut's products liability statute for the defective design and manufacture of the elevator which had been sold and installed by their affiliate, Otis of Brazil. Otis and United moved to dismiss the case on the basis of *forum non conveniens,* arguing that it should be heard in the Colombian courts. The District Court dismissed the case, and the plaintiffs brought this appeal.

OPINION BY PIERRE N. LEVAL AND JOSÉ A. CABRANES, CIRCUIT JUDGES FOR THE COURT SITTING *EN BANC*

We regard the Supreme Court's instructions that (1) a plaintiff's choice of her home forum should be given great deference, while (2) a foreign resident's choice of a U.S. forum should receive less consideration, as representing consistent applications of a broader principle under which the degree of deference to be given to a plaintiff's choice of forum moves on a sliding scale depending on several relevant considerations.

The Supreme Court explained in *Piper Aircraft Co. v. Reyno,* 454 U.S. 235, 102 S. Ct. 252 (1981) that the reason we give deference to a plaintiff's choice of her home forum is because it is presumed to be convenient. ("When the home forum has been chosen, it is reasonable to assume that this choice is convenient.") In contrast, when a foreign plaintiff chooses a U.S. forum, it "is much less reasonable" to presume that the choice was made for convenience. In such circumstances, a plausible likelihood exists that the selection was made for forum-shopping reasons, such as the perception that United States courts award higher damages than are common in other countries. Even if the U.S. district was not chosen for such forum-shopping reasons, there is nonetheless little reason to assume that it is convenient for a foreign plaintiff.

continued

continued

Based on the Supreme Court's guidance, our understanding of how courts should address the degree of deference to be given to a plaintiff's choice of a U.S. forum is essentially as follows: The more it appears that a domestic or foreign plaintiff's choice of forum has been dictated by reasons that the law recognizes as valid, the greater the deference that will be given to the plaintiff's forum choice. Stated differently, the greater the plaintiff's or the lawsuit's bona fide connection to the United States and to the forum of choice and the more it appears that considerations of convenience favor the conduct of the lawsuit in the United States, the more difficult it will be for the defendant to gain dismissal for *forum non conveniens*. Thus, factors that argue against *forum non conveniens* dismissal include the convenience of the plaintiff's residence in relation to the chosen forum, the availability of witnesses or evidence to the forum district, the defendant's amenability to suit in the forum district, the availability of appropriate legal assistance, and other reasons relating to convenience or expense. On the other hand, the more it appears that the plaintiff's choice of a U.S. forum was motivated by forum-shopping reasons— such as attempts to win a tactical advantage resulting from local laws that favor the plaintiff's case, the habitual generosity of juries in the United States or in the forum district, the plaintiff's popularity or the defendant's unpopularity in the region, or the inconvenience and expense to the defendant resulting from litigation in that forum—the less deference the plaintiff's choice commands and, consequently, the easier it becomes for the defendant to succeed on a *forum non conveniens* motion by showing that convenience would be better served by litigating in another country's courts.

* * *

We believe that the District Court in the case before us, lacking the benefit of our most recent opinions concerning *forum non conveniens*, did not accord appropriate deference to the plaintiff's chosen forum. Although the plaintiffs had resided temporarily in Bogota at the time of Mauricio Iragorri's accident, it appears that they had returned to their permanent, long-time domicile in Florida by the time the suit was filed. The fact that the children and their mother had spent a few school terms in Colombia on a foreign exchange program seems to us to present little reason for discrediting the bona fides of their choice of the Connecticut forum. Heightened deference to the plaintiffs' chosen forum usually applies even where a plaintiff has temporarily or intermittently resided in the foreign jurisdiction. So far as the record reveals, there is little indication that the plaintiffs chose the defendants' principal place of business for forum-shopping reasons. Plaintiffs were apparently unable to obtain jurisdiction in Florida over the original third defendant, International, but could obtain jurisdiction over all three in Connecticut. It appears furthermore that witnesses and documentary evidence relevant to plaintiffs' defective design theory are to be found at the defendants' installations in Connecticut. As we have explained, "live testimony of key witnesses is necessary so that the trier of fact can assess the witnesses' demeanor." *Alfadda v. Fenn*, 159 F.3d 41, 48 (2d Cir. 1998). Also, in assessing where the greater convenience lies, the District Court must of course consider how great would be the inconvenience and difficulty imposed on the plaintiffs were they forced to litigate in Cali. Among other factors, plaintiffs claim that they fear for their safety in Cali and that various witnesses on both sides may be unwilling to travel to Cali; if these concerns are warranted, they appear highly relevant to the balancing inquiry that the District Court must conduct.

Decision. Remanded to the District Court for a determination in accordance with this opinion. In deciding whether to hear the case, the District Court should consider the degree of deference to which plaintiffs' choice is entitled, the hardships of litigating in Colombia versus the United States, and the public interest factors involved.

In re Union Carbide Gas Plant Disaster at Bhopal. In Chapter One, we read about the Bhopal disaster litigation. After a chemical leak at a plant in India killed almost 2,000 people, Indian citizens filed suit in the United States against Union Carbide. At one point, almost 145 legal actions on behalf of some 200,000 plaintiffs had been consolidated for trial in federal court in New York. However, the case was subsequently dismissed on the basis of *forum non conveniens* in favor of the case being heard in India. The judge gave many reasons for the decision: The Indian legal system was better able to determine the cause of accident and fix liability; the overwhelming majority of witnesses and evidence were in India; the records of plant design, safety procedures, and training were located in India; most records were not in English and many witnesses did not speak English; the court would be unable to compel witnesses to appear and the cost to transport them to the United States would be prohibitive; visits to the plant might be necessary; there was the likelihood that the U.S. court would have to apply Indian law (the tort law of the jurisdiction where the tort occurred); and the undue burden of this immense litigation would unfairly tax an American tribunal (see Exhibit 3.2). Also considered was the fact that India had a substantial interest in the accident and the outcome of the litigation (the Indian government and Indian citizens owned 49 percent of the plant, with Union Carbide owning the rest). As the judge expressed in the opinion:

> To retain litigation in this forum would be another example of imperialism, another situation in which an established sovereign inflicted its rules, its standards and values on a developing nation. This Court declines to play such a role. The Union of India is a world power in 1986, and its courts have the proven capacity to mete out fair and equal justice. To deprive the Indian judiciary of this opportunity to stand tall before the world and to pass judgment on behalf of its own people would be to revive a history of subservience and subjugation from which India has emerged. India and its people can and must vindicate their claims before the independent and legitimate judiciary created there since the Independence of 1947. This Court defers to the adequacy and ability of the courts of India. Their interest in the sad events . . . in the City of Bhopal, State of Madhya Pradesh, Union of India, is not subject to question or challenge. *In re Union Carbide Gas Plant Disaster at Bhopal*, 634 F. Supp. 842 (S.D.N.Y. 1986).

The case was settled in India in 1989 prior to trial when Union Carbide agreed to pay $470 million in compensation, although the government of India is still attempting to assert criminal jurisdiction over former Union Carbide officers.

Forum Selection Clauses

Businesspeople and lawyers negotiating international contracts can avoid much of the uncertainty over venue by including a forum selection clause in their contracts. A *forum selection clause* is a provision in a contract that fixes in advance the jurisdiction in which any disputes will be arbitrated or litigated. It provides certainty because the parties know where and how a dispute will be resolved in the event of a breach. One of the major advantages of their use is that they eliminate the last minute attempt by lawyers to go "forum shopping" by filing suits in jurisdictions that offer the best law for their case. The last chance for forum shopping may very well be during contract negotiations. This allows both parties to agree on a forum, perhaps the courts of a certain country, that they find acceptable. Of course, the reality is that these clauses are often not open for negotiation at all—the party to the contract with the greatest bargaining power will simply include a fine print provision calling for disputes to be resolved in the courts of the country where it is located (this is discussed further in the next chapter when we consider "standard term" contracts).

Historically, any attempt by private parties to control jurisdiction was viewed with hostility by the courts as an effort to usurp their authority. However, the realities of the international marketplace and the need to reduce uncertainty in a dispute has persuaded many courts to accept forum selection clauses. Today, they are generally accepted as valid provided that the forum chosen has some reasonable connection to the transaction. In the following case, *M/S Bremen v. Zapata*, 407 U.S. 1 (1972), the Supreme Court of the United States upheld a clause calling for disputes to be resolved before the English courts, noting that U.S. courts can no longer remain geocentric in light of modern day international trade.

EXHIBIT 3.2
Why Do Plaintiffs Seek Access to the U.S. Legal System?

Contingent fee lawyers
Jury trials in civil cases
Larger jury awards
Class action suits permitted
Discovery process is wide open
Punitive damages are permitted
Treble damages in antitrust cases
Award of attorney fees possible
Ability to attach property in United States
Integrity of judicial system

M/S Bremen v. Zapata Off-Shore Co.
407 U.S. 1 (1972)
United States Supreme Court

BACKGROUND AND FACTS

In 1967, Zapata, a Houston-based corporation, entered into a contract with Unterweser, a German corporation, to tow Zapata's drilling rig from Louisiana to Ravenna, Italy. The contract the parties signed contained the clause "Any dispute arising must be heard before the London Court of Justice." During a storm, the rig was damaged, and Zapata instructed Unterweser's tug, the *Bremen,* to tow instead to Tampa, Florida, the nearest port. Immediately thereafter, Zapata filed suit in federal district court in Tampa, Florida, on the basis of admiralty jurisdiction seeking $3,500,000 damages *in personam* against Unterweser and *in rem* against the *Bremen.* Unterweser moved to dismiss for:

1. Lack of jurisdiction on the basis of the forum clause
2. *Forum non conveniens* (not a convenient forum)
3. A stay of action pending resolution in the London Court of Justice

Unterweser filed suit in London for breach of contract. The U.S. District Court and Court of Appeals had denied the motion to stay, thus allowing the case to proceed in U.S. court despite the forum selection clause. Unterweser filed a petition of certiorari to the Supreme Court.

CHIEF JUSTICE BURGER

We hold, with the six dissenting members of the Court of Appeals, that far too little weight and effect were given to the forum clause in resolving this controversy. For at least two decades we have witnessed an expansion of overseas commercial activities by business enterprises based in the United States. The barrier of distance that once tended to confine a business concern to a modest territory no longer does so. Here we see an American company with special expertise contracting with a foreign company to tow a complex machine thousands of miles across seas and oceans. The expansion of American business and industry will hardly be encouraged if, notwithstanding solemn contracts, we insist on a parochial concept that all disputes must be resolved under our laws and in our courts. Absent a contract forum, the considerations relied on by the Court of Appeals would be persuasive reasons for holding an

American forum convenient in the traditional sense, but in an era of expanding world trade and commerce, the absolute aspects of the doctrine of the *Carbon Black* case have little place and would be a heavy hand indeed on the future development of international commercial dealings by Americans. We cannot have trade and commerce in world markets and international waters exclusively on our terms, governed by our laws, and resolved in our courts.

Forum-selection clauses have historically not been favored by American courts. Many courts, federal and state, have declined to enforce such clauses on the ground that they were "contrary to public policy," or that their effect was to "oust the jurisdiction" of the court. Although this view apparently still has considerable acceptance, other courts are tending to adopt a more hospitable attitude toward forum-selection clauses. This view, advanced in the well-reasoned dissenting opinion in the instant case, is that such clauses are prima facie valid and should be enforced unless enforcement is shown by the resisting party to be "unreasonable" under the circumstances. We believe this is the correct doctrine to be followed by federal district courts sitting in admirality. . . .

This approach is substantially what followed in other common-law countries including England. It is the view advanced by noted scholars and that adopted by the *Restatement of the Conflict of Laws.* It accords with ancient concepts of freedom of contract and reflects an appreciation of the expanding horizons of American contractors who seek business in all parts of the world. . . . The choice of that forum was made in an arm's length negotiation by experienced and sophisticated businessmen, and absent some compelling and countervailing reason it should be honored by the parties and enforced by the courts.

The elimination of all such uncertainties by agreeing in advance on a forum acceptable to both parties is an indispensable element in international trade, commerce, and contracting. There is strong evidence that the forum clause was a vital part of the agreement, and it would be unrealistic to think that the parties did not conduct their negotiations, including fixing the monetary terms, with the consequences of

continued

continued

the forum clause figuring prominently in their calculations.

Thus, in the light of present-day commercial realities and expanding international trade we conclude that the forum clause should control absent a strong showing that it should be set aside. Although their opinions are not altogether explicit, it seems reasonably clear that the District Court and the Court of Appeals placed the burden on Unterweser to show that London would be a more convenient forum than Tampa, although the contract expressly resolved that issue. The correct approach would have been to enforce the forum clause specifically unless Zapata could clearly show that enforcement would be unreasonable and unjust, or that the clause was invalid for such reasons as fraud or overreaching. Accordingly, the case must be remanded for reconsideration.

Decision. Vacated and remanded for proceedings consistent with the opinion. The Court vacated the Court of Appeals judgment stating, "Thus in light of present-day commercial realities and expanding international trade we conclude that the forum clause should control absent a strong showing that it should be set aside."

Comment. The Court noted the possible reasons that a forum selection clause could be unenforceable: (1) if it contravenes strong public policy and (2) if the forum is seriously inconvenient. These reasons still hold today. Other reasons forum selection clauses may be ignored by the courts are because parties are of unequal bargaining power, counsel was not consulted, the clause was written in a foreign language, the clause violates federal law, changed circumstances (where the forum is the site of a revolution hostile to one party's country—for example, a forum selection of Iran after the Iranian revolution could be held invalid). Many other countries also support the validity of forum selection clauses, including Austria, England, France, Germany, Italy, and many Latin American and Scandinavian countries.

CONFLICT OF LAWS

As a general rule, courts apply the law in force in their jurisdiction to the cases before them. In the United States, state courts usually apply their own state's law. Federal courts hearing diversity of citizenship cases, such as breach of contract or tort actions between residents of different states, generally apply the law of the state in which they sit (unless a federal statute or treaty controls). But these are general rules only, and there are many cases where courts apply the law of another state, or even of a foreign country. The term *conflict of laws* refers to the rules by which courts determine which jurisdiction's laws apply to a case and how differences between laws will be reconciled. In turn, the choice of law will ultimately determine whether a court has jurisdiction, the rights and liabilities of the parties, and how a judgment or monetary award will be enforced.

The *Restatement (Second) of the Conflict of Laws*

Conflict of laws rules are some of the most complex in procedural law, with different jurisdictions following different rules. However, the concepts found in the *Restatement (Second) of the Conflict of Laws,* drafted under the auspices of the American Law Institute in 1971, provide a clear and widely accepted explanation of these rules. As a general rule, courts will apply the law of the state, country, or jurisdiction that has the closest relationship to the action before them. The *Restatement (Second)* addresses different types of actions, including actions for a breach of contract and for torts.

Contracts. It has been said that deciding which law governs a contract is like finding its "center of gravity." In other words, in the absence of an agreement by the parties, contracts should be governed by the law of the jurisdiction that *has the most significant relationship* to the transaction and the parties. The *Restatement (Second)* sets out five factors to be considered: (1) the place of contracting (i.e., where the acceptance took place); (2) the place where the contract was negotiated (particularly if the parties met and negotiated at length); (3) the place where the contract will be performed; (4) the location of the subject matter of the contract; and (5) the domicile, residence, nationality, place of incorporation, and place of business of the parties. If the contract was both negotiated and performed in the same jurisdiction, then the law of that jurisdiction will apply (except for contracts involving real estate or life insurance, which have special rules). Of these, the place of negotiation and performance (especially if both parties are performing within the same jurisdiction) is often the most important. The place of contracting and the domicile of the parties, while not critical by themselves, are important when supporting other factors.

Torts. Traditionally, the law in the United States and in most countries has been that tort actions, including personal injuries, product liability, wrongful death, fraud, business torts such as libel, and others, should be governed by the law of the place *where the injury or damage occurred* (known as *lex loci delicti*). In the United States, many courts are adopting the broader view taken by the *Restatement (Second)*: that tort liability should be governed by the law of the jurisdiction that has the *most significant relationship to the tort and to the parties*. The *Restatement (Second)* lists the following factors to be considered: (1) the place where the injury occurred; (2) the place where the conduct causing the injury occurred; (3) the domicile, residence, nationality, place of incorporation, and place of business of the parties; and (4) the place where the relationship between the parties is centered. The courts of New York apply the law of the state or country that has the "greatest interest" in having its law applied.

Choice of Law Clauses

Choice of law clauses are contract provisions that stipulate the country or jurisdiction whose law will apply in interpreting the contract or enforcing its terms. Lawyers are quite aware that laws can be very different from state to state or country to country and will consider this in contract negotiations. Indeed, the choice of law may well become a bargaining point in international contract negotiations. As a general rule, the choice of law selection will be upheld as long as there is a reasonable relationship between the transaction and the jurisdiction chosen. As one court put it, parties today have several choices of law that could apply to their dealings, but they could not choose to have their disputes decided under the *Code of Hammurabi*. For example, imagine a Japanese manufacturer who enters into a contract with a buyer in New York for the shipment of goods to New York. Both parties have offices in California and sign the contract there. A clause making California law applicable to the contract would be valid, because there is a sufficient nexus, or connection, between the contract and the state of California.

The Application of Foreign Law in American Courts

If an American court determines that it should apply foreign law to the case, how does it know what that law is? At one time foreign law was required to be proven in court as fact. Today, in the federal courts that has changed. Courts are free to make their own determinations *as a matter of law* what the foreign law is. The federal courts will follow the *Federal Rules of Civil Procedure*. Rule 44.1 states that:

> A party who intends to raise an issue concerning the law of a foreign country shall give notice by pleadings or other reasonable written notice. The court, in determining foreign law, may consider any relevant material or source, including testimony, whether or not submitted by a party or admissible under the *Federal Rules of Evidence*. The court's determination shall be treated as a ruling on a question of law.

Accordingly, judges may conduct their own research on foreign law, they may request briefs provided by the parties' lawyers, or they may rely on the testimony of foreign lawyers in or out of court. The following case, *Finnish Fur Sales Co., Ltd. v. Juliette Shulof Furs, Inc.,* involves a U.S. court in New York that had to decide a case under the laws of Finland. It offers an explanation of how a choice of law clause works and shows how a U.S. court applies the law of a foreign country to resolve a contract dispute. Notice the interplay of federal and state law, and the application of Rule 44.1.

Judicial Assistance: Discovery and the Collection of Evidence

Countries have their own rules governing pretrial discovery, obtaining access to documents and other evidence, and the admissibility of that evidence at trial. In the United States, this is governed

Finnish Fur Sales Co., Ltd. v. Juliette Shulof Furs, Inc.
770 F. Supp. 139 (1991)
United States District Court (S.D.N.Y.)

BACKGROUND AND FACTS

Juliette Shulof Furs (JSF) is a New York corporation that has been in the fur dealing business for 15 years. George Shulof, an officer of JSF, attended two auctions conducted by Finnish Fur Sales (FFS) in Finland in 1987. He purchased more than $1.2 million worth of skins at the auctions. Shulof attended each auction and was the actual bidder. The conditions of sale were listed in the auction catalog in English. JSF paid for the majority of the skins purchased, leaving an unpaid balance of $202,416.85. FFS brought this action to recover the contract price of the skins from Shulof, claiming he is personally liable for payment under Finnish law. Shulof responds that he was acting only as the agent for JSF and that under New York law he is not personally responsible for the contracts of the corporation he represented at the auction.

LEISURE, DISTRICT JUDGE

Section 4 of the *Conditions of Sale* provides:

> Any person bidding at the auction shall stand surety as for his own debt until full payment is made for purchased merchandise. If he has made the bid on behalf of another person, he is jointly and severally liable with the person for the purchase.

George Shulof denies any personal liability on the grounds that the provision is unenforceable under both New York and Finnish law.

Section 15 of the *Conditions of Sale* provides that "[t]hese conditions are governed by Finnish law." Choice of law clauses are routinely enforced by the courts of this Circuit, "if there is a reasonable basis for the choice." *Morgan Guaranty Trust Co. v. Republic of Palau*, 693 F. Supp. 1479, 1494 (S.D.N.Y. 1988). New York courts also generally defer to choice of law clauses if the state or country whose law is thus selected has sufficient contacts with the transaction. Under those circumstances, "New York law requires the court to honor the parties' choice insofar as matters of substance are concerned, so long as fundamental policies of New York law are not thereby violated." *Woodling v. Garrett Corp.* 813 F.2d 543, 551 (2d Cir. 1987). Finland's contacts with the transactions at issue are substantial, rendering the choice of law clause enforceable unless a strong public policy of New York is impaired by the application of Finnish law. Plaintiff FFS is a Finnish resident, which held auctions of Finnish-bred furs in Finland. All bids were made in Finnish marks, with payment and delivery to take place in Finland. Mr. Shulof voluntarily traveled to Finland in order to partake in FFS's auctions. Thus, virtually all of the significant events related to these transactions took place in Finland. Finland also has an obvious interest in applying its law to events taking place within its borders relating to an important local industry, and in applying uniform law to numerous transactions with bidders from foreign countries.

Mr. Shulof argues that the choice of Finnish law provision should be held invalid. . . . According to Mr. Shulof, New York has the following interests in this action: it is the place of business and of incorporation of JSF; FFS has a representative with a New York office who communicated with Mr. Shulof about the fur auctions; and that New York is, allegedly, "the economic and design center for the world's fur industry." Mr. Shulof also argues that, under New York law, Section 4 of the *Conditions of Sale* would be invalid as contravening New York's policy against imposing personal liability on corporate officers. . . .

Under Federal Rule of Civil Procedure 44.1, a court, "in determining foreign law, may consider any relevant material or source, including testimony." Both parties have submitted affidavits of Finnish attorneys on the issue of Mr. Shulof's liability under Finnish law. FFS's expert, Vesa Majamaa, a Doctor of Law and Professor of the Faculty of Law at the University of Helsinki, gives as his opinion that the provision of Section 4 of the *Conditions of Sale* imposing personal liability upon the bidder, regardless of whether he bids on behalf of another, is valid both as a term of the particular auctions at issue and as a general principle of Finnish and Scandinavian auction law. According to Majamaa, it is "commonly accepted in Scandinavia that a bidder, by making a bid, accepts those conditions which have been announced at the auction." Further, he states: According to the Finnish judicial system, no one may use ignorance of the law as a defense. . . . This same principle is also . . . applicable when the matter in question concerns . . . terms of trade. . . . If the buyer

continued

---

continued

is not familiar with the terms observed in an auction, he is obliged to familiarize himself with them. In this respect, failure to inquire will result in a loss for the buyer. . . . If a businessman who has been and is still active in the fields falls back on his ignorance in a case in which he has been offered an actual opportunity to find out about the terms of the auction, his conduct could be considered to be contrary to equitable business practices [and] the "Principle of Good Faith." . . . Majamaa also notes that under Danish law, which he maintains would be applied by a Finnish court in the absence of Finnish decisional or legislative law on point, "It is taken for granted that someone who has bid on merchandise on someone else's account is responsible for the transaction, as he would be for his own obligation, together with his superior. . . . Hence the auction buyer's responsibility is not secondary, as is, for example, the responsibility of a guarantor." . . .

Majamaa also opines that the terms of Section 4 are neither unexpected nor harsh because "the liability has been clearly presented in the terms of the auction," and because the same rule of liability would apply under Finnish law in the absence of any provision.

. . . [T]he Court concludes that a Finnish court would enforce the provisions of Section 4 and impose personal responsibility upon George Shulof for his auction bids on behalf of JSF.

Moreover, even if a New York court would not enforce such a provision in a transaction to which New York law clearly applied, this Court does not find New York's interest in protecting one of its residents against personal liability as a corporate officer to constitute so fundamental a policy that New York courts would refuse to enforce a contrary rule of foreign law. Indeed, the New York Court of Appeals has held that "foreign-based rights should be enforced unless the judicial enforcement of such a contract would be the approval of a transaction which is inherently vicious, wicked or immoral, and shocking to the prevailing moral sense." *Intercontinent Hotels Corp. v. Golden* 146 N.Y. 2d. 9, 13, 254 N.Y.S. 2d 527, 529, 203 N.E. 2d 210 (1964). Given the lack of a clear conflict with either New York law or policy, this Court concludes that a New York court would apply Finnish law to the issue before the Court. The Court also notes that a similar result has often been reached under New York conflict rules even in the absence of a contractual choice of law clause. Thus, Mr. Shulof must be held jointly and severally liable with JSF for any damages owed to FFS for the furs purchased.

Decision.   Under conflict of law rules, the U.S. court applied Finnish law to hold the defendant Shulof personally liable for the contract debt.

---

by the *Federal Rules of Civil Procedure*. The United States has very liberal rules permitting the pretrial oral deposition of witnesses out of court and the submission of written interrogatories that the parties must answer under oath. The courts have broad subpoena powers over documents and other tangible evidence. When that evidence is located outside the jurisdiction of the court, such as in a foreign country, special problems arise. The *1970 Hague Convention on the Taking of Evidence Abroad in Civil or Commercial Matters* provides methods for collecting foreign evidence via formal requests made by the courts of one country to the courts of another country through diplomatic channels (such as the government Ministry of Justice). Although only thirty countries are party to the convention, most countries cooperate in the collection of civil evidence, some to a greater or lesser degree than others.

Letters Rogatory.   When a court in one country wants to make a request of a court in another country for judicial assistance, it does so in writing through a formal request known as a *letters rogatory* (letters of request). It can be used to request a deposition, a response to written interrogatories, or the production of documents. Most countries do not have the liberal rules of discovery like the United States. Japan and China are notable examples. Many countries do not permit oral depositions to be taken before trial. For example, China has declared that it does not recognize the right of foreign attorneys to take depositions, even of willing witnesses. Any foreigner caught attempting to do so without prior authorization is subject to arrest, detention, or deportation. Moreover, only certain government officials may administer an oath, and anyone else caught doing so is committing a crime. Requests for obtaining evidence from U.S. courts must be addressed in the form of letters rogatory to the Chinese Ministry of Foreign Affairs. The last time a U.S. party was permitted to take a deposition in China was in 1989. Japan has a slightly more liberal view. According to the U.S. State Department, Japanese law permits the taking of a deposition of a willing witness for use by a court in the United States only if the deposition is presided over by a U.S. consular officer pursuant to a court order and only if it is conducted on U.S. consular premises. It is a violation of Japanese law for anyone to travel to Japan for the purpose of taking a deposition unless they have a special "deposition visa" from a Japanese consulate.

Some countries, on the other hand, such as Canada, are very cooperative with foreign requests for judicial assistance. According to the U.S. State Department, there are no rules in Canada that prohibit taking evidence from a willing person in private civil matters. Parties in a private civil case in the United States may arrange to depose a willing witness in Canada without prior consultation or permission from the Canadian government. The party seeking to take the deposition must arrange for a court reporter/stenographer and facilities in which to take the deposition.

Antisuit Injunctions

U.S. courts have the power to enjoin a party over whom they have jurisdiction from bringing a lawsuit in a foreign country. This is known as an *antisuit injunction*. The purposes are to prevent a party already involved in U.S. litigation from circumventing the American court system and American law, preventing the other party in the dispute from being subjected to undue harassment and expense, and protecting the integrity of American courts. While this may seem to invite a confrontation between U.S. and foreign courts, the injunction is not directed at any foreign court but at the individual involved. A U.S. court may enjoin foreign litigation if at the time it has jurisdiction over the party in a case currently pending before it, if the parties are the same in both cases, and if the issues are so similar that resolution of the domestic case will resolve the issues that could be brought in the foreign case. As of 2003, there was some disagreement between the U.S. Courts of Appeal on how to apply these rules, with some Cir-

cuits being less willing to grant injunctions than others. A case illustrating the more liberal view is *Kaepa, Inc. v. Achilles Corp.*, 76 F.3d 624 (5th Cir. 1966). Achilles, a Japanese corporation, signed a contract with a provision calling for disputes to be settled in Texas and under Texas law. Achilles then filed suit in Japan. Kaepa requested an antisuit injunction. In permitting the injunction, the appellate court said, "The prosecution of the Japanese action would entail an absurd duplication of effort, and would result in unwarranted inconvenience, expense and vexation. Achilles' belated ploy . . . smacks of cynicism, harassment and delay."

Enforcement of Foreign Judgments

At the close of a judicial proceeding, a winning party might obtain a judgment for damages or some other award. Once a judgment is taken against a defendant it must be enforced. If necessary, it can be done through a legal process, including the seizure of the losing party's property. But what if a judgment is won in a state or country where that party has no money or property? This is where some good detective work comes in handy. In the United States, judgments taken against a party by a court of competent jurisdiction in one state will be enforced by all other states under the *Full Faith and Credit* provision of the U.S. Constitution. This provision, however, does not apply to the recognition of judgments from foreign countries. Nevertheless, as a general rule, the judgments of foreign countries will be recognized by the courts of the United States when the requirements of comity between nations are satisfied.

Many states have statutes specifically permitting the enforcement of foreign judgments. About thirty states have adopted the *Uniform Recognition of Foreign Money Judgments Act* (see Exhibit 3.3). U.S. courts will usually recognize a foreign judgment based on a full and fair trial on the merits of the case by an impartial tribunal. The foreign court must have had jurisdiction over the subject matter and over the parties or property involved, and the defendant must have been given notice of the action and an opportunity to appear. Judgments will not be enforced where they violate public policy or were procured by fraud, where they contradict an earlier final judgment, where the original proceeding contravened a forum selection clause in the contract, or where the foreign court was a seriously inconvenient forum. Japan's rules are very similar. An example of a U.S. court's refusal to honor a foreign judgment is seen in *Stiftung v. V.E.B. Carl Zeiss,* 433 F.2d 686 (2d Cir. 1970). There, a U.S. court refused to enforce a judgment from (then) communist East Germany because, in the federal judge's view, the procedures were not fair and because the (former) East German judiciary would "orient their judgments according to the wishes of the leaders of the socialist state."

Judgments of U.S. courts will often be enforced by foreign courts on the basis of reciprocity and comity in countries where the losing party or its property can be found. Foreign courts, including several in Europe, have been known to refuse to honor the judgments of American courts where in

---

EXHIBIT 3.3
Jurisdictions Adopting the Uniform Recognition of Foreign Money Judgments Act

Alaska
California
Colorado
Connecticut
Delaware
District of Columbia
Florida
Georgia
Hawaii
Idaho
Illinois
Iowa
Maine
Maryland
Massachusetts
Michigan
Minnesota
Missouri
Montana
New Jersey
New Mexico
New York
North Carolina
Ohio
Oklahoma
Oregon
Pennsylvania
Texas
Virginia
Virgin Islands
Washington

---

the view of the foreign court the amount of money awarded was excessive, or for punitive or treble damages, or where in the opinion of the foreign judge the American court extended its net of jurisdiction too widely. To ensure that U.S. judgments will be enforceable in foreign courts, or foreign judgments enforceable in the United States, it is a good idea for the plaintiff's counsel here to coordinate with counsel in the foreign country. That way they can develop some reasonable assurance that the procedures used to obtain the judgment will satisfy the courts of the country in which property is located or it will otherwise be enforced. In Europe, there are a number of multilateral and bilateral conventions, as well as resolutions of the Council of Europe intended to promote uniformity in the recognition of judgments.

Uniform Foreign Money Claims Act. As a general rule, courts award money judgments in their own currency. For many years, U.S. courts were only able to award judgments in dollars. This rule was rooted in English law dating back several hundred years. However, it created some problems. If an international contract called for payment in the year 2000, in say, Japanese yen, and a judgment for a breach of the contract is awarded in 2003 in dollars, fluctuations in currency exchange rates may have distorted the value of the judgment relative to the contract terms. One of the parties may be greatly disadvantaged, while the other may receive a windfall profit. The question of whether or not a foreign money judgment can be awarded is, in the United States, a matter of state law, not federal law. In recent years, about half of the states have enacted the *Uniform Foreign Money Claims Act.* This statute gives state courts the authority to issue a judgment in a foreign currency. Some state courts have permitted foreign money awards by judicial decision, acknowledging the need to make the parties whole. Foreign money awards have been available in Great Britain since 1975. The following case, *Manches & Co. v. Gilby,* considers issues related to foreign money judgments.

COMMERCIAL DISPUTES WITH NATIONS

This chapter has dealt with commercial disputes between private parties. Of course, governments too are players in commercial transactions as the

Manches & Co. v. Gilby
646 N.E. 2d 86 (1995)
Supreme Judicial Court of Massachusetts

BACKGROUND AND FACTS
On August 20, 1992, the Queen's Bench Division of the High Court of Justice in London entered a default judgment in favor of Manches & Co., a London firm of solicitors, against Suzanne Gilby and Peter Thorton totaling £30,138.35. On November 9, 1992, Manches commenced this action in the Superior Court in Barnstable County to enforce the foreign judgment pursuant to G.L. c. 235, § 23A (1992 ed.), the *Uniform Recognition of Foreign Money Judgments Act.* Manches's underlying claim was that the defendants were liable for legal services rendered to Gilby in England following the death of her father.

The principal issue in this appeal concerns the amount of the judgment that should have been entered in Massachusetts in view of changes in the exchange rate between the British pound and the American dollar. It appears that on August 20, 1992, the date that judgment was entered in London, approximately $58,450 equaled the amount stated in pounds in the English judgment (£30,138.35). On December 13, 1993, the date on which summary judgment was granted in favor of Manches in Barnstable Superior Court, approximately $45,130 would have purchased £30,138.35. Thus, because of the decline in the British pound in relation to the American dollar, the defendants could satisfy their obligation to Manches, expressed in pounds, by paying out considerably fewer dollars in late 1993 than they could have sixteen months earlier when the English default judgment was entered.

JUSTICE WILKINS
Because the motion judge entered judgment in dollars using the latter exchange rate (the one more beneficial to the defendants), Manches has appealed. Because the motion judge entered judgment in favor of Manches, the defendants have appealed, arguing that, for various reasons, the English judgment is not worthy of enforcement in Massachusetts. We transferred the cross appeals to this court on our own motion. If the defendants are correct in their claim that the English judgment is unenforceable, the question of the proper amount of any judgment that should be entered in favor of Manches in Massachusetts is unimportant. Therefore, we shall discuss the defendants' appeal first. We conclude that the English judgment is enforceable in Massachusetts and that the appropriate judgment is one that reflects the exchange rate at the time of the payment of the judgment.

None of the defendants' arguments in opposition to the enforcement of the English judgment has merit. The defendants rely on grounds set forth in G.L. c. 235, § 23A, that, if they exist, would deny enforcement of a foreign judgment: lack of jurisdiction over them in England, denial of due process in the English justice system, and a form of *forum non conveniens.*

The English court had jurisdiction over the defendants. Manches received court permission to serve the defendants outside the jurisdiction. The contract for legal services to be rendered in England was governed by English law, and thus under English law the court there had jurisdiction over the parties.

There is no showing that the English system lacked "procedures compatible with the requirements of due process" or that the defendants were denied due process in their attempt to claim an appeal from the default judgment. England was not a "seriously inconvenient forum" and that statutory basis for denial of enforcement of a foreign judgment has no application in any event, because it applied when, unlike this case, jurisdiction in the foreign court was based "only on personal service."

The obligation to pay pounds, expressed in the English judgment, should be enforced by a judgment that orders the defendants at their option either (a) to pay £30,138.35 (with interest) or (b) to pay the equivalent in dollars of £30,138.35 (with interest), determined by the exchange rate in effect on the day of payment (or the day before payment). Manches is entitled to be restored to the position in which it would have been if the defendants had paid their obligations, but it is not entitled to more. The so-called payment day rule achieves this result.

There is no guiding Massachusetts law on this point. The decided cases in this country have adopted various positions. Some have followed the breach day rule, the one Manches advocates, in which the conversion of foreign obligations is made as of the date of breach of the obligation. Others

continued

continued

have used the judgment day rule, converting the foreign obligation into dollars based on the exchange rate on the date the judgment is entered. We prefer a third option, the payment day rule.

The Restatement (Third) of Foreign Relations Law advises that the conversion to dollars should be "made at such rate as to make the creditor whole and to avoid rewarding a debtor who has delayed in carrying out the obligation." The Restatement becomes more specific and tentatively adopts the breach day rule if, as here, the foreign currency has depreciated since the breach, and, if the foreign currency has appreciated since the breach, it adopts the exchange rate on the date of judgment or the date of payment. "The court is free, however, to depart from those guidelines when the interests of justice require it."

The *Uniform Foreign–Money Claims Act,* which has been enacted in eighteen American jurisdictions (but not in Massachusetts), adopts the payment day rule. It is this rule that, for the circumstances of this case, we apply as a matter of common law. That rule will award Manches in pounds (or the equivalent in dollars on or near the day of payment) the amount it would have recovered had it been able to collect on the judgment in Great Britain. Satisfaction of the judgment in present day pounds will make Manches whole. In entering judgments, courts do not normally reflect changes in the purchasing power of local currency between the date of a breach and the date of the award of judgment. As the prefatory note to the Uniform Act states: "The principle of the Act is to restore the aggrieved party to the economic position it would have been in had the wrong not occurred. . . . Courts should enter judgments in the money customarily used by the injured person." Manches incurred its expenses in England, expected to be compensated in pounds, and sustained its loss in pounds. The payment day rule is fair in this case because its application meets the reasonable expectations of the parties in this case.

Decision. Judgment shall be entered ordering that Manches & Co. shall recover from the defendants, at the defendants' option, either (a) the amount of the English judgment (£30,138.35) or (b) the equivalent in dollars of the English judgment determined at the exchange rate in effect on the day of or the day before payment, with interest on that amount (in each instance), payable in pounds or dollars, at the Massachusetts rate of interest from the date of entry of the action until the date of payment.

---

largest purchasers of goods and services in the world. Resolving disputes with nations is quite a different matter. In the last part of this book, we will see that when governments act in their capacity as a sovereign, it is very difficult to bring them to answer in court. When they act in a commercial capacity, it is easier. Later in the book, we will examine issues related to the settlement of investment disputes, including the *Convention on the Settlement of Investment Disputes Between States and Nationals of Other States* (*Washington Convention,* 1966) that created the *International Centre for the Settlement of Investment Disputes.*

Chapter Summary

When negotiating international transactions, the prudent businessperson or lawyer will hope for the best but always plan for the worst. Planning for disputes in advance is a proper method of minimizing risk in a transaction. This planning includes obtaining expert legal advice in negotiating and drafting business contracts. The importance of the contract cannot be overstated because if and when a dispute arises, the terms of the contract provide the basis for dispute resolution.

Alternate dispute resolution usually offers a faster, cheaper, and more efficient alternative to litigation. Mediation is a voluntary, nonbinding, conciliation process. Arbitration is a more formalized process, resulting in a binding award that will be enforced by courts of law in many countries. The parties must agree to arbitration, but once they do, they cannot withdraw. Most commercial nations today have laws permitting arbitration and specifying the effect of an arbitral award. There are many organizations worldwide that provide arbitral services. Many arbitral bodies use the widely accepted rules of the United Nations Commission on International Trade Law. Arbitration clauses will be enforced by the courts, as will arbitral awards.

Litigation is the final step in attempting to resolve a dispute. It is used more frequently in the United States than in virtually any other country.

Jurisdiction, one of the key concepts of jurisprudence, is the power of a court to hear and decide a case. A court that has jurisdiction is said to be a "competent" court. *In personam* jurisdiction, or "jurisdiction over the person," refers to the court's power over a certain individual or corporation to a suit. No court can enter a judgment against an individual or corporate defendant unless they have jurisdiction over them. When a defendant is not physically present in the state, a court can obtain jurisdiction over them only if the party has had sufficient minimum contacts with the territory of the forum such that it is fair for them to answer in court there. The Internet is leading to new jurisdictional issues.

Jurisdiction is often confused with the concept of venue. Venue refers to the geographical location of a court of competent jurisdiction where a case can be heard. According to the legal doctrine of *forum non conveniens,* whenever a case is properly heard in the courts of more than one jurisdiction, it should be heard in that jurisdiction that is most convenient.

The term conflict of laws refers to the rules by which courts determine which state or country's laws will apply to a case and how differences between laws will be reconciled. To avoid the uncertainties of conflict of laws problems, many international contracts contain forum selection and choice of law clauses. A forum selection clause is a provision in a contract that fixes in advance the jurisdiction in which any disputes will be litigated. A choice of law clause is a contract provision that stipulates which country or jurisdiction's law will apply in interpreting the contract or enforcing its terms.

Countries have their own rules governing pretrial discovery, obtaining access to documents and other evidence, and the admissibility of that evidence at trial. As a general rule, the judgments of foreign countries will be honored by the American courts when the requirements of comity between the nations are satisfied and when the foreign judgment was rendered by an impartial tribunal in a fashion that would not offend American notions of fundamental fairness and due process of law. Judgments of U.S. courts will often be enforced by foreign courts on the basis of reciprocity and comity in countries where the defendant or its property can be found. Some foreign courts have been known to refuse to honor the judgments of American courts where, in the view of the foreign court, the amount of money awarded was excessive.

Questions and Case Problems

---

1. Explain the concepts of jurisdiction and minimum contacts. What applications do they have in international disputes?

2. Should a South Dakota court enforce a Hong Kong Court's judgment awarding the plaintiff $98,438 in money damages for failure to pay for shipments of fireworks? What relevance, if any, is it that Hong Kong is formally under mainland China's control? Does it matter that South Dakota is not one of the jurisdictions adopting the *Uniform Recognition of Foreign Money Judgments Act*? *Kwongyuen Hagkee Co., Ltd. v. Starr Fireworks Inc.,* 634. N.W.2nd 95 (S.D. 2001).

3. In 1992, a picture of George Noonan, a Boston police officer, was used in a Winston cigarette ad in France. Noonan had not given permission. Noonan in fact is an antismoking crusader. The picture was included in a CLB book (a British company). CLB sold the rights to the picture to Lintas, a French ad agency, which was working for RJR France. Noonan sued the French ad agency and the tobacco company. Does

U.S. Federal court have jurisdiction over this matter? *Noonan v. Winston,* 135 F.3d 85 (1st Cir. 1998).

4. Dickson Marine owned a ship *Dickson IV.* It needed repairs off the coast of Africa. Panalpina Inc., a N.J. corporation with an office in New Orleans, suggested Air Sea Ltd., which suggested Panalpina Gabon SA in Gabon could help. Panalpina Gabon subcontracted the work. The ship capsized. Panalpina Gabon is a Gabonese corporation and Air Sea is a Swiss corporation. Plaintiff sued them in Federal district court. The district court dismissed for lack of personal jurisdiction as to Panalpina and *forum non conveniens* as to Air Sea. How did the court decide? *Dickson v. Panalpina* 179 F.3d 331 (5th Cir. 1999).

5. What are the risks associated with arbitration? Why might a company prefer to settle disputes by litigation? What are the advantages of arbitration?

6. How would a choice of law clause and a clause clearly delineating the power of the arbitrator help to address some of a party's concerns?

7. Why do companies have to be careful about their employees' use of email?

8. Why do so many litigants, "like moths to a flame," want to litigate in the United States? Does that suggest that the United States needs to alter its court system?

9. Will a U.S. court enforce a Mexican judgment dealing with a loan agreement and collateral on a promissory note if the note violates Texas usury laws? Texas does have the *Texas Uniform Country Money Judgment Recognition Act.* What is the impact of this statute? Discuss the arguments on both sides. Which one is stronger? What did the court decide? *Southwest Livestock & Trucking Co. v. Ramon,* 169 F.3d 317 (5th Cir. 1999).

10. Compare the enforceability of a foreign country court judgment and an arbitration decision. What effect will a treaty have on enforcement?

11. What can a party do to compel a foreign country to assist in gathering evidence related to a case in the party's country?

12. Compare the different results in *Alfadda v. Fenn,* 966 F. Supp 1317 (S.D.N.Y. 1997), (U.S. court found French judgment precluded U.S. proceedings) with *Alesayi Beverage Corp. v. Canada Dry Beverage Corp,* 947 F. Supp. 658 (S.D.N.Y. 1996), *affd.* 122 F.3d. 1055 (2nd Cir. 1997) (denying preclusive effect of Saudi judgment in United States). Why do parties initiate such parallel proceedings?

13. A businessman, Wyser–Pratte, met with Mr. Lederer at the Four Seasons Hotel in New York City. Mr. Lederer made a presentation about a German corporation, Babcock, and its plans to acquire 100 percent of HDW. Wyser–Pratte invested $20 million, but shortly thereafter, Babcock sold its 50 percent stake in HDW rather than increase it. Mr. Lederer left to run HDW and Babcock became insolvent. May Wyser–Pratte bring suit in New York? Discuss.

Managerial Implications

1. You are CEO of a large publicly traded company called Microtech. You are negotiating several contracts with foreign governments in Vietnam, India, and Brazil to provide hardware and software to government agencies. Are you interested in including an arbitration clause in the contract? What are the plusses and minuses of such a clause? What alternatives do you have?

   How does your plan change, if at all, if you are dealing with a corporation in the same countries? What about a corporation in England and one in New York? Discuss how these variables may affect your decision.

2. You have started a small hi-tech company in New York.

   a. You are running an informational Web site. Customers must call your 800 number to place an order. A customer in Alaska is very unhappy with your product. Can they successfully sue you in Alaska?

   b. You decide you want to be clear in all your future dealings, so you insert a choice of forum clause in all of your contracts with your customers that stipulates arbitration in New York under the rules of the American Arbitration Association. Would this be enforceable?

   c. What if the forum clause stated that all disputes would be heard in Tibet?

   d. What ramifications are there to changing your Web site and making it more interactive so that people can place orders there?

   e. What if your competitor is using your trade secrets and your patents without your permission or payment, would you be interested in arbitrating this dispute? Explain.

   f. What difference would it make if your competitor were a Dutch company?

   g. The CEO has asked you to outline a comprehensive strategy to deal with customers, suppliers, and citizen groups complaining about a myriad of issues as well as employee complaints (both domestic and foreign). Prepare a short memo addressing key principles, major concerns, and suggested actions.

PART 2

International Sales, Credits, and the Commercial Transaction

In Part Two of *International Business Law and Its Environment,* we turn our attention to more traditional commercial law topics: the rights of buyer and seller under a contract for the international sale of goods, the legal mechanism for transferring title to the goods sold and for allocating the risk of loss or damage to the goods between buyer and seller, the methods of financing the sale and assuring payment for the goods, the rights and responsibilities of the ocean carrier, and the methods for resolving international commercial disputes.

In this area of study, the law is derived primarily from the domestic law of individual nations, including statutes and court decisions. However, the impact of international law is still quite great because many of the domestic laws are derived from international conventions, codes, or agreements. For instance, international sales law in the United States, as well as U.S. statutes governing the rights and responsibilities of air and ocean carriers, is largely based on international conventions to which many nations of the world subscribe. There are also many court decisions affecting international commercial law. These are particularly relevant to our study in the field of contracts, negotiable instruments, documents of title, and letters of credit. Some of the decisions are rooted in those of the English *Law Merchant* of hundreds of years ago, although none in this text is so old. The

decisions appearing in the following chapters, whether English or American cases, are composed of both classic, or "landmark," cases offered to explain long-standing principles of commercial law, and illustrative cases designed to demonstrate common day-to-day problems faced by merchants and other international traders.

In Chapter Four we will study basic principles of international sales law as they are illustrated by the provisions of the *United Nations Convention on Contracts for the International Sale of Goods.* Although this is not the applicable law for all international sales, it does provide us with the opportunity to study the first widely accepted body of international sales law. It also provides many opportunities to engage in a comparative analysis of sales law, so as to see how different legal systems might address the same legal problem in different ways.

In many international sales, the movement of the goods and the exchange of money are inextricably connected to the transfer of the document of title and other shipping documents. This is easily explained. Because the risks of buying or selling goods across great distances are considerable, a special mechanism has developed in the law to assure the maximum protection to both parties. As a result, ownership and control over the goods passes from the seller to the buyer only upon some assurance that the seller will receive payment. Similarly, the exchange of money, from the buyer to the seller, will be conditioned upon some assurance that delivery of the goods is imminent. These topics are discussed in Chapter Five.

Chapter Six deals with the liability of ocean and air carriers for damage or loss to cargo. It also covers some interesting problems of maritime and marine insurance law. No area of international business has engendered as much litigation in the courts as has the carriage of goods. Goods are subjected to a wide range of risks during international shipment—from storms to piracy at sea. This is a fascinating and important area of study.

In Chapter Seven we begin with a discussion of how international payments are handled in a transaction for the sale of goods. From there we will look generally at the law of letters of credit and at the role that banks play in international commercial transactions. Many exporters find that they are successful in selling to foreign customers not because they necessarily offered the best product at the best price, but because they provided trade finance to the customer to make the sale possible. Thus, Chapter Seven looks at trade finance alternatives in the banking industry and the legal relationship between the parties to the transaction.

CHAPTER 4

SALES CONTRACTS AND EXCUSES FOR NONPERFORMANCE

THE DEVELOPMENT OF INTERNATIONAL SALES LAW

In the twelfth century, medieval Europe experienced a renaissance of trade and commerce. Merchants from the cities, many traveling by caravan, met at trade fairs and city markets to exchange goods such as wool, salted fish, cotton cloth, wine, fruit, and oils. Trade routes to the East were opening, with access to silk and new spices. Rudimentary banking systems were founded so that money could be used as payment in long-distance transactions. New legal instruments—the forerunners of today's bank checks—were created. Over time, the merchants developed a set of customs for exchanging goods—an unwritten code of how to bargain, barter, and sell goods at market. For instance, merchants decided that if one bought goods at a city market and later discovered that the goods had been stolen, then the innocent buyer took ownership of the goods anyway. By relying on custom, they knew what was expected of both parties to a transaction and how to avoid or resolve a disagreement. These customs of the marketplace became known as the *lex mercatoria* or *law merchant,* and they were "enforced" by the merchants themselves. Similar customs were developing in the maritime trade. In the centuries to follow, the local courts recognized the *law merchant* and used juries made up of other merchants to decide cases. As trade spanned greater distances, and nations created colonies, merchants took on greater risks, and transactions required more complex legal rules. In England, by the eighteenth century, the *law merchant* became a part of the *common law* of England when a famous English judge, Lord Mansfield, ruled that it was up to the English courts to say what the *law merchant* was and not merely what merchants thought it to be.

More than one hundred years later, in 1894, England enacted its *Sale of Goods Act* that codified many rules for merchants, thus adapting the common law to business needs of the time. In Europe, the *law merchant* gave way to stricter legal codes enacted by local lawmakers and legislatures, based on legal concepts dating to the Roman period. In 1906, in the United States the *Uniform Sales Act* (although no longer in effect) was passed in many states codifying the law of sales. The result, by the dawn of the twentieth century, was that nations had developed very different commercial codes. As the business world became more complex, and with the dawn of air travel and worldwide communications, there was a need for a clearer set of modern rules, and for more uniformity in the application of commercial laws around the world. Virtually all trading nations of the world today have modern commercial codes governing the sale of goods.

> **http://www. lexmercatoria.org**
> The International Trade and Commercial Law Monitor

Modern Sales Law in the United States: The UCC and CISG

In 1951, a new commercial law was proposed in the United States. Known as the *Uniform Commercial Code* (UCC), it is the primary body of commercial law for domestic transactions in the United States. The purposes of the UCC are

1. To simplify, clarify, and modernize the law governing commercial transactions.
2. To permit the continued expansion of commercial practices through custom, usage, and agreement of the parties.
3. To make uniform the law among the various jurisdictions (states). UCC 1–102.

The UCC has been adopted (with some minor differences) in all fifty states. It covers many areas of commercial law, ranging from bank deposits to secured transactions. It does not, however, cover the sale of real estate or services, insurance, intellectual property, bankruptcy, or many other areas. Many subjects covered in the UCC are traditional areas of study in college courses in Business Law. For instance, Article 2 of the UCC applies to "transactions in goods"—*sales* and *contracts of sale*. A contract of sale includes both the present sale of goods and contracts to sell goods at a future time. Contracts not governed by the UCC or other codes are governed by the common law, and where the UCC is silent, the common law of contracts applies to the transaction. Many early principles of the *law merchant* are still found in Article 2 in a modern, codified form. Important amendments to UCC Article 2 were drafted by the National Conference of Commissioners on Uniform State Laws and approved by the American Law Institute in 2003. They will become effective when enacted into law by state legislatures.

For many international transactions involving U.S. companies, the UCC has been supplanted by a new law, the *United Nations Convention on Contracts for the International Sale of Goods* (CISG). The CISG is the uniform international sales law in effect in countries that account for over two-thirds of all world trade. It was drafted under an effort led by the United Nations and has been adopted as law by countries from five continents. Its purpose is to unify the law of sales between nations. The CISG became effective in the United States in 1988. It now applies to many international sales when buyer or seller are located in countries that have adopted the convention. Many provisions of the UCC and the CISG are similar, but many are different. This chapter discusses international contracts for the sale of goods with an

eye toward comparing relevant portions of these two laws.

---

http://www.law.cornell.edu/
Cornell Law School Legal Information Institute. Select "Law by Source or Jurisdiction" link to "State Law" and "Commercial Code" for access to the UCC.

Conflicts of Law

The sales contract is universally recognized as the legal mechanism for conducting trade in goods. It is essential to trade because an international agreement to buy and sell goods, like many domestic agreements, takes time to perform. If buyer and seller could fully perform the contract at the moment the agreement was reached, or if every seller handed over the goods when the purchase price was paid, they would not need binding agreements. But few merchants or traders, from any country, would enter a potentially risky long-term transaction without a contract. Thus, the contract's importance stems from its embodiment of the agreement of the parties, which provides assurances that each party will perform its part of the bargain. If the agreement breaks down, and a court must resolve a dispute, the rights and obligations of the parties will be based on the law applicable to the case. In an international transaction, at least one party is likely to have its rights decided under the law of a foreign country. Thus, when a firm enters a contract governed by foreign law, it is undertaking an added risk. The interpretation of the terms of the contract under that law or a firm's rights and obligations according to the contract may be surprising.

To know what law applies to a contract, courts will resort to *conflict of laws* rules. Should the applicable law be that of the country in which the contract was made, in which it was to be performed, or in another country with a close connection to the contract? Consider the following example. Assume a French subsidiary of a U.S. company enters into a contract with a company from Zaire for the purchase of copper. The contract is negotiated and signed in Switzerland and calls for the copper to be shipped from Zaire to the parent company in the United States. If the copper is impure or of the wrong grade—where will the case be heard? Once the case does go to court, which country's law will decide the buyer's damages? This uncertainty and lack of predictability over how the case will be resolved increases the risk of an international sale.

Choice of Law Clauses.   Many international contracts designate the parties' *choice of law* that is to apply in case of dispute. The laws of most countries, within limits, allow this designation. The choice of law that they agree upon may depend on the relative bargaining position of the parties and on each party's ability to extract this choice as a concession from the other side.

By agreeing which law will govern a contract, the parties are attempting to reduce the uncertainty of conflict of law rules. They, or their lawyers, will be able to predict in advance their rights and obligations in the event one of them were to breach the contract. They are managing their legal risk. Even though one of the parties will be subjecting themselves to foreign law, it is assumed that this was a rational act for which they will be compensated by the profits of the deal (although in reality they may have just "signed the bottom line" and never even realized the consequence of this decision).

However, a choice of law provision does not mean that the case will be heard in the courts of that country. These are very different issues. It is very common that a court situated in one country will have to apply the law of yet one or more other countries. This makes the resolution even more uncertain and complicated. In cases before the federal courts of the United States, a party who is suing under a contract with a choice of law provision involving foreign law must give notice to the court of the foreign law. The U.S. court may then determine for itself, as a matter of law, by using any relevant material, source, or testimony, what it believes the foreign law to be (Rule 44.1 of the *Federal Rules of Civil Procedure*). Thus, federal judges have great authority to determine what the foreign law is. Of course, this may often require the court to listen to experts on foreign law or engage in research on foreign law subjects. This can make trials governed by foreign law very time consuming and expensive.

Development of the CISG

The CISG was drafted to avoid two of the major problems associated with the conflict of laws—un-

certainty and unpredictability. Companies doing business throughout the world can benefit from knowing what their rights will be under a sales contract. And lawyers can more easily advise their clients when laws are uniform. But the task of producing one international sales law to satisfy the needs and interests of every country was enormous. The many differences between national laws had to be resolved. Some differences date back to the time when the law merchant was incorporated into English common law, while the European countries moved toward Roman civil law. Even greater differences occurred in those countries with legal codes based on Islamic religious beliefs or on socialist principles derived from Marxist ideology. As a result, the function and nature of sales law are viewed differently in different legal systems. Each system has its individual rules for deciding the validity of a contract, for interpreting its terms, and for defining the remedies available to a party upon a breach. As the European Union (EU) moves toward greater economic integration, it is also seeking to standardize those principles that are used to interpret contracts and to determine appropriate remedies for nonperformance by a party. Somewhat akin to the *Restatement of the Law of Contracts* in the United States, the *Principles of European Contract Law* have been drafted by lawyers from each of the EU member countries. Exhibit 4.1 provides some general information about this recent statement regarding contract law in Europe. The following sections look at contract law from the perspective of the developing countries, the socialist countries, and the People's Republic of China in particular.

---

http://www.cisg.law.pace.edu/
For the text of the CISG cases, and materials, also see the
Guide for Managers and Counsel.

Contract Law in the Developing Countries

The developing countries' concern over the governing of contracts stems directly from their economic position relative to the industrialized countries. Although all developing countries cannot be lumped into the same category, and they are not all in the same state of development or industrialization, developing countries have long

EXHIBIT 4.1

European Contract Law

The Principles of European Contract Law 1997

In response to the expanding volume of laws regulating specific types of contracts in the European Union a body of lawyers drawn from all of Europe have prepared a code of contract law. The lawyers who have prepared the Principles are known as the *Commission on European Contract Law*. The Principles are intended to be applied as general rules of contract law in the European Union. The Principles apply when contracting parties have agreed to incorporate them into their contracts or have specified that their contract is to be governed by them.

The official publication of the text was published at the end of 1997. It contains nine chapters dealing with topics ranging from the Scope of the Principles (Chapter 1 includes sections on the freedom of contract, usages and practices, and the good faith obligation) to the Formation of Contracts (Chapter 2) and Remedies for Non-performance (Chapters 8 and 9).

The provisions of *The Principles of European Contract Law* may be viewed by visiting the Web site at: http://www.jus.uio.no/lm/eu.contact.principles.1998/index.html or by conducting a search of the topic on almost any international law Web site.

faced three related problems in their business relationships with the wealthier industrialized nations. First, they often do not have a cadre of trained professionals, such as economists, engineers, lawyers, or business managers, to help their governments in contract negotiations. Consequently, some developing countries have been at a negotiating and bargaining disadvantage in dealing with experienced representatives of Western multinational corporations. Secondly, these countries have often found themselves in desperate need of hard currency to fund their socioeconomic development programs, such as health care, education, irrigation, or foreign debt repayment. As a result, they have lacked the economic bargaining power of their trading partners in carrying out contract negotiations.

Representatives of developing countries are quick to point out that many contract provisions were forced on them even though the provisions were not in their best interest. For instance, the developing countries contend that they have often been victims of unconscionable contracts. They point to cases in which they were sold shoddy equipment, tainted foods, or goods unsuitable for sale or banned in Western countries, such as expired pharmaceuticals. They also point to contracts for the sale of inappropriate technology and equipment. They argue that for many years their development funds were squandered on needless weaponry purchased by local political officials who had been willing to accept the cash bribes of Western companies. Consider this dramatic example from 1992. It was disclosed that an American firm had contracted to export needed chemicals to an African country, whose purchase received financial backing from the U.S. Agency for International Development. When the drums which were to contain the chemicals arrived, the buyers discovered, incredibly, that they were victims of a fraud. Instead of the needed chemicals, they had been sent a shipment of toxic waste for which the owners could not find a dumping site in the United States.

A third problem in contract negotiations, particularly in southern Africa, is that in the past many developing countries simply did not have the sophisticated legal system for dealing with contract disputes, such as those needed to enforce a buyer's rights against a seller of defective equipment. These developing countries were eager for an international agreement that would modernize and strengthen their sales laws and make them more attractive for foreign investment.

Contract Law in Socialist Countries

Many countries contributed to the development of the CISG, including the socialist and communist countries of the time. Today most of these countries have abandoned communism and have moved toward greater democracy, private enterprise, and free markets. Despite these vast changes, socialist principles and central economic planning remain influential in many countries. Socialist legal principles still exert a profound impact on the development of international law.

Socialist contract law serves primarily to protect national interests, to achieve state goals for the production and distribution of goods to individuals, and to regulate foreign trade contracts with outside companies. Socialist countries generally conduct foreign trade through state trading organizations instead of through private companies. State trading organizations, such as those in the People's Republic of China (China), are heavily bureaucratic. Because of their strict organizational structure, state trading organizations seek as much certainty and predictability in the law as possible. As a result, sales law in socialist countries differs greatly from sales law in Western countries. Generally speaking, socialist law is more mechanical and far more cumbersome than law in Western countries. For instance, although many Western countries do not require that contracts for the sale of goods be in writing, the socialist countries do. Where the West might favor a law that would allow courts to "fill the gaps" in a contract by looking to the customs and usages of the trade, the socialist countries do not do so. Where Western countries do not require that the parties specify the exact price to be paid for the goods, provided that a reasonable price could later be ascertained (i.e., a "market price"), the socialist countries generally do insist that the parties specify the price by writing it into the contract.

Contract Law in the People's Republic of China: An Illustration

China's business laws changed remarkably in the last quarter of the twentieth century. Today, China has many modern legal codes covering the law of contracts, investments, commercial transactions, and others that are necessary for a modern nation involved in a globalized economy. However, this is relatively new for China. In the years after World War II, China's legal system was dominated by principles derived from strict Marxist/Communist dogma. As a result of the Cold War, China and its legal system had been isolated by the West for much of the last century. In the early 1950s, China adopted a system of centrally controlled state planning similar to that in effect in the Soviet Union at that time. There was, and still remains, strong central planning of most economic activity, with few market mechanisms for regulating the factors of production, the use of natural resources, or pricing. State policy, and not consumer demand, largely dictated how much and what kinds of goods were to be produced. Historically, there was little need for private contracts, or for a body of contract law to protect private rights. After all, under Marxist principles, the law was seen as an

instrument of class warfare, as a means of establishing state authority and ensuring socialist market principles. Contracts served only to implement government policy. In other words, domestic contract law ensured that state doctrine was followed and that commitments made to and between state agencies were upheld. Interestingly enough, in sharp contrast to what lawyers in the West were accustomed to, "breach of contract" actions more closely resembled quasi-criminal prosecutions for breaching one's obligation to the state. This difference is reflected in the remedies most commonly used. In the West, when a party breaches a contract, a court typically awards damages to the nonbreaching party as a form of compensation. In China, the focus was on protecting the interests of the state through legal rules that compelled a breaching party to do what it had promised. Penalties and other forms of punishment were also routinely used.

---

http://www.qis.net/Chinalaw/
China Law Web contains English translation and in-depth analysis of all areas of Chinese law, in effect in the PRC, Taiwan, Hong Kong, and Macau.

Today, China's legal system is based on both socialist and Western civil law principles. (An exception is the *Hong Kong Special Administrative Region,* which takes many of its legal principles from Great Britain. Hong Kong was a British colony from 1898 until 1997, when the island reverted to Chinese control. The Chinese have established a "one country, two systems" policy for Hong Kong, preserving Hong Kong's capitalist economic system, while making it clear that Hong Kong is a part of China. Although no one can predict Hong Kong's future, it seems that British influence will remain for a very long time). As China opened its doors to Western business in the late 1970s and early 1980s, it recognized that modern commercial laws were essential to attracting buyers for Chinese-made goods and foreign investors to Chinese industry. In the 1980s and 1990s, China enacted many modern codes including codes of banking, joint ventures and investments, copyrights and patents, foreign trade, consumer protection, taxation, aviation and transportation, advertising, insurance, accounting regulations, and many others. By enacting these laws, China hoped to demonstrate to other nations that it deserved to be treated as an equal trading partner by other nations, and that it deserved membership in the WTO. These laws reflected China's transition from a purely socialist state to a nation with a mixed economy—partially state owned, partially privately owned, albeit with great central state control. During this period, China also enacted two modern codes of contract law. One of these applied exclusively to contracts between domestic individuals or companies and the other applied to contracts involving foreign ones. But these laws were repealed in 1999 with the enactment of a single, comprehensive *Contract Law for the People's Republic of China* by the Ninth National People's Congress, the main legislative body in China.

> http://www.CCLAW.net
> See the Chinese Civil Law Forum for the English version of the Chinese Contract Law of 1999.

The 1999 Contract Law of China.

The *Contract Law for the People's Republic of China* covers many areas traditionally associated with contract law that would be familiar to lawyers from Western countries. It applies not only to the sale of goods, the subject of this chapter, but also to contracts for the sale of electricity, water, and gas; loan agreements; leasing contracts; contracts with independent contractors; construction contracts; contracts for carriage and the transportation of people and cargo; contracts involving the sale or transfer of patents and other technology; warehousing contracts; agency contracts; and brokerage agreements. The law clearly recognizes that contracts may be made through electronic data interchange, the Internet, or email. Keep in mind what a step forward this is for a nation whose Internet communications are still tightly controlled by the government.

Given the breadth of subjects covered in the Chinese code, its 428 articles seem remarkably short and concise by American law standards, although that is probably in keeping with Chinese thinking. Its provisions would be easily recognized by almost any American lawyer or businessperson. But this is to be expected because the Chinese legal scholars and government representatives that drafted the law had spent years studying generally accepted legal principals in the rest of the world, and adapted them to the Chinese economic and political sys-

tems. Indeed, the Chinese drew on many of the concepts found in the CISG, which will be covered in detail in the next section. Of course, China does not benefit from the plethora of court decisions found in American or English law that interpret, define, and expand the commercial codes in those countries. In China, the opinions of most judges in deciding cases are not usually publicly reported and do not serve as precedent for future cases (although in 1981, the National People's Congress gave the Supreme Court the power to issue interpretive pronouncements on statutes. Unlike in the United States, where courts only act upon cases brought before them by litigants, the Chinese highest court can issue interpretations of Chinese statutes on its own initiative). The judge's role is to apply the code law as written and not to define or expand its principles beyond the case at hand. Chinese judges, like judges throughout the world, are schooled in the application of their own law.

> http://english.mofcom.gov.cn
> China's Ministry of Commerce, English language translations of Chinese laws on trade, banking, insurance, customs, taxation, labor and employment, intellectual property and others.

THE CONVENTION ON CONTRACTS FOR THE INTERNATIONAL SALE OF GOODS

Early attempts at constructing an international law of sales actually began in the late 1920s with the work of the *International Institute for the Unification of Private Law,* or UNIDROIT, an organization of European lawyers that was working closely with the League of Nations. It successfully developed two conventions in 1964. However, the effort was primarily a European one (the United States and many other countries did not participate in drafting these documents), and the conventions never received wide acceptance.

In 1966, the United Nations created the *U.N. Commission on International Trade Law,* or UNCITRAL. UNCITRAL consists of thirty-six representatives from nations in every region of the world. Supported by a highly respected staff of lawyers, it is headquartered at the U.N. Vienna International Centre in Austria. UNCITRAL has drafted several widely accepted legal codes for international business, including the CISG. Unlike many other UN codes that are not binding, the CISG is a convention or agreement between nations that is binding once the legislature of a country adopts it. It then becomes a part of the country's domestic law. In the United States, a convention must be ratified by the Senate. The CISG received Senate ratification in 1986 and became U.S. law on January 1, 1988.

Now, if a U.S. buyer or seller contracts for the sale of goods with a company whose place of business is in a country that has also ratified the convention, then the CISG will determine their rights under the contract. To say it another way, if a U.S. buyer brings an action for the delivery of defective merchandise purchased from a seller in France or China, or if the seller brings an action for nonpayment, their rights will be determined in court by the CISG—and not the *Uniform Commercial Code* (UCC) or French or Chinese law—regardless of the country in which the case is heard.

The CISG has already been adopted by the countries shown in Exhibit 4.2 and is being considered by others. Translations are available in Arabic, Chinese, English, French, Russian, and Spanish. A copy of the CISG appears in the appendix, and students are encouraged to refer to it often in this chapter.

This chapter examines the following aspects of the CISG: (1) the applicability of the CISG to international sales, (2) its general provisions, including the rules for interpreting and forming contracts, (3) provisions related to the warranty of goods, (4) provisions regarding performance of the contract and remedies available to the injured party on breach, and (5) excuses for nonperformance of a contract.

---

http://www.unidroit.org/
The International Institute for the Unification of Private Law.
http://www.uncitral.org/
The site of the United Nations Commission on International Trade Law. Complete guide to the CISG and other UNICTRAL work. Headquartered in Vienna, Austria.

Applicability of the CISG to International Transactions

In the United States, UCC Article 2 applies to purely domestic sales of goods. The CISG, however, applies if the following three conditions are met:

EXHIBIT 4.2

Countries that Have Ratified or Acceded to the CISG

Argentina	Kyrgyzstan
Australia	Latvia
Austria	Lesotho
Belarus	Lithuania
Belgium	Luxembourg
Bosnia and Herzegovina	Mauritania
Bulgaria	Mexico
Burundi	Moldova
Canada	Mongolia
Chile	Netherlands
China	New Zealand
Colombia	Norway
Croatia	Peru
Cuba	Poland
Czech Republic	Romania
Denmark	Russian Federation
Ecuador	St. Vincent-Grenadines
Egypt	Serbia and Montenegro
Estonia	Singapore
Finland	Slovakia
France	Slovenia
Georgia	Spain
Germany	Sweden
Ghana	Switzerland
Greece	Syrian Arab Republic
Guinea	Uganda
Honduras	Ukraine
Hungary	United States
Iceland	Uruguay
Iraq	Uzbekistan
Israel	Yugoslavia
Italy	Zambia

---

1. The contract is for the commercial sale of *goods* (the term "goods" is not defined in the CISG).
2. It is between parties whose places of business are in different countries (nationality or citizenship of individuals is not a determining factor).
3. The places of business are located in countries that have ratified the convention.

Place of Business Requirement.   In the case of buyers or sellers with places of business in more than one country, such as a multinational corporation, its "place of business" would be considered to be in the country that has the closest relation to the contract and where it will be performed. This could mean that if two American companies negotiated a contract entirely within the United States, but one of them had a place of business outside of the United States and the contract was to be *performed outside* the United States (e.g., the contract calls for delivery of the goods to a point outside the United States), then the CISG might govern the transaction.

The following case, *Asante Technologies, Inc. v. PMC-Sierra, Inc.*, discusses three important provisions of the CISG: the place of business requirement, the ability of the parties to "opt out" of the CISG by using a choice of law clause, and the concept that in international transactions the CISG preempts the contract laws of U.S. states.

Asante Technologies, Inc. v. PMC-Sierra, Inc.
164 F.Supp.2d 1142 (2001)
United States District Court (N.D. Cal.)

BACKGROUND AND FACTS
The plaintiff, Asante, purchased electronic parts from the defendant, PMC, whose offices and factory were in Canada. Asante placed its orders through defendant's authorized distributor, Unique Technologies, located in California. Asante's order stated that the contract "shall be governed by the laws of the state shown on buyer's address on this order." PMC's confirmation stated that the contract "shall be construed according to the laws of Canada." Invoices were sent from Unique, and payment remitted to Unique, either in California or Nevada. Asante claimed that the goods did not meet its specifications, and filed suit in California state court to have its claim decided under California law. When the case was transferred to a U.S. federal court, Asante requested that the case be remanded back to state court.

WARE, DISTRICT JUDGE
Place of Business Requirement
The *Convention on Contracts for the International Sale of Goods* ("CISG") is an international treaty which has been signed and ratified by the United States and Canada, among other countries. . . . The CISG applies "to contracts of sale of goods between parties whose places of business are in different States . . . when the States are Contracting States." CISG Art. 1 (1) (a). Article 10 of the CISG provides that "if a party has more than one place of business, the place of business is that which has the closest relationship to the contract and its performance." CISG Art. 10. . . .

It is undisputed that plaintiff's place of business is Santa Clara County, California. It is further undisputed that . . . defendant's corporate headquarters, inside sales and marketing office, public relations department, principal warehouse, and most of its de-

sign and engineering functions were located in Canada. However, plaintiff contends that, pursuant to Article 10 of the CISG, defendant's "place of business" having the closest relationship to the contract at issue is the United States. . . .

Plaintiff asserts that Unique acted in the United States as an agent of defendant, and that plaintiff's contacts with Unique establish defendant's place of business in the U.S. for the purposes of this contract. Plaintiff has failed to persuade the Court that Unique acted as the agent of defendant. . . . To the contrary, a distributor of goods for resale is normally not treated as an agent of the manufacturer. . . . Furthermore, while Unique may distribute defendant's products, plaintiff does not allege that Unique made any representations regarding technical specifications on behalf of defendant. . . . Plaintiff's dealings with Unique do not establish defendant's place of business in the United States.

Plaintiff's claims concern breaches of representations made by defendant from Canada. Moreover, the products in question are manufactured in Canada, and plaintiff knew that defendant was Canadian, having sent one purchase order directly to defendant in Canada by fax. . . . Moreover, plaintiff directly corresponded with defendant at defendant's Canadian address. . . . In contrast, plaintiff has not identified any specific representation or correspondence emanating from defendant's Oregon branch. For these reasons, the Court finds that defendant's place of business that has the closest relationship to the contract and its performance is British Columbia, Canada. Consequently, the contract at issue in this litigation is between parties from two different Contracting States, Canada and the United States. This contract therefore implicates the CISG.

continued

continued

Choice of Law Clause

Plaintiff next argues that, even if the Parties are from two nations that have adopted the CISG, the choice of law provisions in the [buyer's purchase order and seller's confirmation] reflect the Parties' intent to "opt out" of application of the treaty. The Court finds that the particular choice of law provisions in the "Terms and Conditions" of both parties are inadequate to effectuate an "opt out" of the CISG.

Although selection of a particular choice of law, such as "the California Commercial Code" or the "Uniform Commercial Code" could amount to implied exclusion of the CISG, the choice of law clauses at issue here do not evince a clear intent to opt out of the CISG. For example, defendant's choice of applicable law adopts the law of British Columbia, and it is undisputed that the CISG is the law of British Columbia. Furthermore, even plaintiff's choice of applicable law generally adopts the "laws of" the State of California, and California is bound by the Supremacy Clause to the treaties of the United States. Thus, under general California law, the CISG is applicable to contracts where the contracting parties are from different countries that have adopted the CISG. . . .

Federal Preemption

It appears that the issue of whether or not the CISG preempts state law is a matter of first impression. In the case of federal statutes, "the question of whether a certain action is preempted by federal law is one of congressional intent. . . . The Court concludes that the expressly stated goal of developing uniform international contract law to promote international trade indicates the intent of the parties to the treaty to have the treaty preempt state law causes of action. The availability of independent state contract law causes of action would frustrate the goals of uniformity and certainty embraced by the CISG. Allowing such avenues for potential liability would subject contracting parties to different states' laws and the very same ambiguities regarding international contracts that the CISG was designed to avoid. As a consequence, parties to international contracts would be unable to predict the applicable law, and the fundamental purpose of the CISG would be undermined.

Finally, plaintiff appears to confuse the matter of exclusive federal jurisdiction with preemption. . . . Even where federal law completely preempts state law, state courts may have concurrent jurisdiction over the federal claim if the defendant does not remove the case to federal court [citation omitted]. This Court does not hold that it has exclusive jurisdiction over CISG claims.

Decision. The federal court had concurrent jurisdiction over this case because the applicable law was the CISG, an international convention ratified by the United States (even though the case could also have been heard in state court).

Sales Excluded from the CISG. The following types of sales have been specifically excluded from the convention:

1. Consumer goods sold for personal, family, or household use.
2. Goods bought at auction.
3. Stocks, securities, negotiable instruments, or money.
4. Ships, vessels, or aircraft.
5. Electricity.
6. Assembly contracts for the supply of goods to be manufactured or produced wherein the buyer provides a "substantial part of the materials necessary for such manufacture or production."
7. Contracts that are in "preponderant part" for the supply of labor or other services.
8. Liability of the seller for death or personal injury caused by the goods.
9. Contracts where the parties specifically agree to "opt out" of the convention or where they choose to be bound by some other law.

In the United States, Article 2 of the UCC applies to both consumer and commercial transactions. Consumer sales were excluded from the CISG because consumer protection laws are so specific to every country that it would have been very difficult to harmonize them. Further, consumer sales are usually domestic in nature.

---

http://www.unilex.info
A user-friendly database on the CISG, with case law organized by country, date, and article or arbitral award.

The parties to a sales contract are free to negotiate other terms that might differ from the CISG. If they feel unsure about the code, they may "opt out" entirely, simply by specifying that the UCC (or the law of some other nation) will apply. Article 6 of the CISG states, "The parties may exclude the application of this Convention or . . . derogate from or vary the effect of any of its provisions."

VALIDITY AND FORMATION OF INTERNATIONAL SALES CONTRACTS

Under the common law, a *valid contract* is an agreement that contains all of the essential elements of a contract. As students of business law well know, a contract contains a number of elements.

1. It is an agreement between the parties entered into by their mutual assent (e.g., an offer and acceptance of the contract's material terms).
2. The contract must be supported by legally sufficient consideration (e.g., the exchange in the contract as bargained for by the parties).
3. The parties must have legal capacity (e.g., that the parties are not minors, legally incompetent, or under the influence of drugs or alcohol).
4. The contract must not be for illegal purposes or to carry on an activity that is illegal or contrary to public policy.

If a contract is missing any one of these essential elements, it is a *void contract*. It will not be enforced by the courts. The CISG only governs the formation of a contract and the rights and obligations of the seller and buyer. The Convention does not provide rules for determining whether a contract is valid, for determining whether a party to a contract is legally competent, nor for determining whether a party is guilty of fraud or misrepresentation. These rules are left to individual state or national laws. In China, for example, contracts must be concluded voluntarily and the parties must act in good faith and fairly toward each other.

Enforcement of Illegal Contracts

A generally recognized principle of contract law is that, in all legal systems, contracts that violate the laws of a state or nation are void. A void contract is of no legal effect and will not be enforced by a court. As you read the following case, *Tarbert Trading, Ltd. v. Cometals, Inc.*, consider both the legality of the sales contract in question and the ethical behavior of the parties.

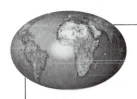

Tarbert Trading, LTD. v. Cometals, Inc.
663 F. Supp. 561 (1987)
United States District Court (S.D.N.Y.)

BACKGROUND AND FACTS
Cometals purchased Kenyan red beans from Tarbert Trading, an English commodities trading company. Agrimen, a South African company engaged in commodities trading, acted as an agent for Tarbert in connection with the sale. The beans were held in a warehouse in Rotterdam, the Netherlands. Cometals had purchased the beans for resale to a buyer in Colombia. Colombia would only allow the beans to be imported if the seller could provide a certificate of origin (issued by a Chamber of Commerce) proving the beans were a product of a country in the European Economic Community (EEC). Cometals requested that Tarbert supply such a certificate and Tarbert agreed. Both parties understood that it was impossible to honestly furnish the certificate since

the Kenyan red beans originated in Africa. Later, the defendant refused the beans claiming that they were of poor quality and the plaintiff sued. Defendant also maintains that the agreement should be declared void and unenforceable because plaintiff could not, except through fraud, supply defendant with an EEC certificate of origin for the beans.

NEWMAN, SENIOR JUDGE
We first address the issue concerning conflict of laws. As to that matter, the court agrees with the contention of Tarbert that the law of New York is applicable in this case rather than the law of the Netherlands, as urged by Cometals. The court has considered various facts: Cometals resides in New

continued

continued

York; negotiations took place between Cometals in New York and Agrimen in South Africa; the formal letter agreement was prepared by Cometals in New York; and the physical location of the beans in Rotterdam was not a significant factor in the parties' transaction. . . . However, in view of the result reached in this case, it is immaterial whether the law of the Netherlands or of New York is applied.

Under the law of the Netherlands a contract that calls for the doing of an illegal or tortious act is absolutely void and unenforceable. See Martindale-Hubbell, *Netherlands Law Digest*, p. 5 (1985).

Insofar as New York law is concerned: *Stone v. Freeman*, 298 N.Y. 268, 271, 82 N.E.2d 571, 572 (1948),

> it is the settled law of this State (and probably of every other State) that a party to an illegal contract cannot ask a court of law to help him carry out his illegal object, nor can such a person plead or prove in any court a case in which he, as a basis for his claim, must show forth his illegal purpose. . . . For no court should be required to serve as paymaster of the wages of crime, or referee between thieves. Therefore, the law "will not extend its aid to either of the parties" or "listen to their complaints against each other, but will leave them where their own acts have placed them.

Concededly, both Tarbert and Cometals were cognizant of the fact that an EEC certificate of origin stating that the Kenyan beans were of the origin of an EEC member would be false and would be shown to third persons. Simply put, [Cometals] intended to deceive the Colombian customs officials with a false certificate as to the beans' country-of-origin so that they would allow the importation of the beans by Cometals' customer. . . .

Irrespective of the rather incredible explanations of [Tarbert's employees] as to what they understood to be the purport of the requested certificate of origin, they finally and grudgingly conceded that an EEC certificate stating that the goods were of the origin of an EEC member would be understood by anyone reading it to mean that the beans were grown in an EEC country and not simply shipped from such country. Consequently, it is completely understand-

able why [Agrimen's employees] expressed shock, dismay and disapproval of the oral agreement concerning the EEC certificate between [Cometals and Tarbert]. . . . The fact that the agreement drafted by Cometals duplicitously described the subject commodity simply as "Small red beans, 1982 crop," . . . does not avoid the illegality of the contract inasmuch as both parties understood from the prior communications and intended that the Kenyan beans stored in [a Rotterdam] warehouse were the subject of the contract.

It is evident from the Kenyan origin of the beans that it would have been impossible for Tarbert to honestly obtain from a Chamber of Commerce and furnish Cometals with a bona fide EEC certificate of origin stating that the goods were of the origin of a member of the EEC since concededly Kenya is not an EEC member. Thus, the only way in which Tarbert could have complied with the agreement would have been to convince an official of a Chamber of Commerce to issue a fradulent certificate or to obtain a forged certificate. Both acts are obviously illegal.

No one shall be permitted to profit by his own fraud, or take advantage of his own wrong, or to found any claim upon his own iniquity, or to acquire property by his own crime. These maxims are dictated by public policy, have their foundation in universal law administered in all civilized countries, and have nowhere been superseded by statutes. Plaintiff maintains that the furnishing of the EEC certificate of origin was a non-essential and separable part of the bargain, and that therefore the court may hold only that portion of the agreement unenforceable. However, the court finds that the illegality is inseparable from and goes to an essential ingredient of the bargain between the parties, because Cometals insisted upon the EEC certificate in the requested form with an eye to its . . . surreptitious importation of the beans into Colombia. Plainly, enforcement of the agreement for either party would be contrary to public policy. . . . [T]he complaint and counterclaim are dismissed.

Decision.   Contracts that violate the law are void and will not be enforced by a court. In this case, a contract calling for the delivery of a fraudulent certificate of origin is illegal and contrary to public policy.

The Writing Requirement

The laws of many nations differ as to whether contracts for the sale of goods must be in writing. Under the UCC, American law requires that contracts for the sale of goods of $500 ($5,000 under the 2003 proposed amendments) or more must be in writing (see Exhibit 4.3). Such writing requirements in common law countries date back to an act of the English Parliament in 1677. Today,

---

EXHIBIT 4.3

Requirement of Writing or Record

CISG Article 11
A contract of sale need not be concluded in or evidenced by writing and is not subject to any other requirement as to form. It may be proved by any means, including witnesses.

UCC § 2-201 Formal Requirements; Statute of Frauds (2003 Amendments)*

(1) A contract for the sale of goods for the price of $5,000 or more is not enforceable by way of action or defense unless there is some record sufficient to indicate that a contract for sale has been made between the parties and signed by the party against which enforcement is sought or by the party's authorized agent or broker. A record is not insufficient because it omits or incorrectly states a term agreed upon but the contract is not enforceable under this subsection beyond the quantity of goods shown in the record.

(2) Between merchants if within a reasonable time a record in confirmation of the contract and sufficient against the sender is received and the party receiving it has reason to know its contents, it satisfies the requirements of subsection (1) against the recipient unless notice of objection to its contents is given in a record within 10 days after it is received.

UCC § 2-103 Definitions and Index of Definitions

"Record" means information that is inscribed on a tangible medium or that is stored in an electronic or other medium and is retrievable in perceivable form.

*Subject to enactment by state legislatures.

---

however, the many exceptions to this UCC rule make most oral sales contracts quite enforceable. In 1954, Great Britain repealed its law. Civil law countries for the most part never had any writing requirement at all. In China, contracts may either be written or oral, unless some other statue or administrative regulation requires that they be in writing. Under the CISG, contracts for the sale of goods need not be in writing. The code states what is probably obvious, that the contract may be proven by any means, including witnesses, which is in keeping with modern trends toward flexibility in contracting and the necessity of speed in modern commercial transactions. Several countries, including Russia, have elected to omit this provision from their version of the CISG.

Digital Signatures in Electronic Commerce.
As of the year 2000, the United States, Japan, China, and the European countries had enacted laws recognizing the validity of electronic or digital signatures. The U.S. law, the *Electronic Signatures in Global and National Commerce Act,* or E-Sign, as it is commonly known, makes an electronic signature on a contract as legally binding as a handwritten one on a paper document. The United Nations is preparing a model law for elec-

tronic signatures that would be especially helpful to developing countries interested in enacting such legislation of their own.

Problems of Interpretation

No contract can be written in such precise terms that its meaning will never be in question. The best lawyers cannot possibly craft a written contract in such perfect form, especially when language barriers affect the negotiation and drafting of an international contract. Oral agreements can have even more ambiguity.

The Parol Evidence Rule. The *parol evidence rule* states that where the parties have entered into a written sales contract that is intended to be the final expression of the parties' agreement, the written agreement may not, under most circumstances, be contradicted by any prior agreement or contemporaneous oral agreement (parol evidence). Parol or extrinsic evidence may be introduced to clarify an ambiguity, to prove additional terms of the agreement not covered in the written contract, or to prove fraud. The CISG allows a court, when considering the intent of the parties to a contract, to consider "all relevant circumstances of the case, including the negotiations, any practices which the parties have established between themselves, usages, and any subsequent conduct of the parties."

In *MCC-Marble Ceramic Center, Inc. v. Ceramica Nuova D'Agostino, S.P.A.*, 144 F.3d 1384 (11th Cir. 1998), an American had signed a contract for the purchase of Italian ceramic tile while at a trade fair in Bologna. The document consisted of the seller's order form, and included preprinted terms on the front and reverse sides. The terms stated that if the goods did not conform to the contract, notice had to be given to the seller within ten days. When the tile arrived, the buyer believed it was inferior, but never gave notice of this fact to the seller. There was uncontradicted evidence that, at the time of signing the contract, all parties had had a verbal understanding that the preprinted terms would not be applicable. The court ruled that parol evidence *could* be considered to contradict the written terms of the contract. In other words, the trial court could consider the subjective intent of the parties, as well as their verbal understanding at the time of signing the contract, in order to invalidate the preprinted terms. With no preprinted terms, the buyer would be permitted to withhold payment because the goods did not conform to the contract specifications. The case was decided under the CISG. Courts apparently have wide leeway in using parol evidence under the CISG.

Customs, Practices, and Trade Usages.

The courts of the United States and many other common law countries will often look to the past dealings of the parties and to *trade usages* for guidance in interpreting contracts or filling the gaps. Trade usages are derived from the customs of an industry, the practices of merchants in their past dealings, and the usages of trade terminology and language. For example, the Tampa Cigar Co. contracts to buy an ocean container of "Sumatra tobacco" from an independent broker in Mexico City. Tampa Cigar, and indeed most of the industry, believes that Sumatra tobacco is grown on the island of Sumatra. Unless agreed otherwise, this term becomes a part of the contract. If the broker delivers tobacco grown in Honduras from Sumatra seed, he may be in breach of contract if the law recognizes "Sumatra tobacco" as a valid trade usage.

Take another example of a trade usage. Suppose that a buyer sues a seller for delivery of defective goods. The seller points to a guarantee in the contract that the goods "will be of average and acceptable quality for the kind and type of goods sold in the trade." How would a court interpret this provision? It could look to testimony and evidence attesting to what the trade considers "average and acceptable."

Courts, lawyers, and trade negotiators in some developing countries do not rely on trade usages to interpret contracts because of their widespread belief that many customs and trade usages were derived from the practices of European trading nations and colonial powers. In the early history of international trade, they were able to establish mercantile practices that favored the English, Dutch, and other colonial traders. A good example might be the cocoa trade, which was dominated by London merchants. When they traded in Africa, the Mediterranean, or the Caribbean, these merchants established their trade usages and practices there. Some developing countries still believe that a trade usage derived from European traders and in use by modern Western firms could only be to their disadvantage.

Trade Usages under the CISG.

The CISG provisions of Article 9 more closely resemble the way trade usages are handled under American law. The only trade usages that can be used to interpret or fill in the gaps in a contract are (1) those to which the parties agree to be bound or that derive from their past dealings, or (2) those usages of which the parties knew or ought to have known and that are regularly observed in the industry or trade involved.

Entering the Agreement: The Offer

The contract laws of all countries require that the parties reach a mutual agreement and understanding about the essential terms of a contract. This agreement is reached through the bargaining process between offeror and offeree. The offeror, by making the offer, creates in the offeree the power of acceptance, or the power to form a contract.

The Intention to Be Bound.

Under Article 14 of the CISG, a communication between the parties is considered an offer when (1) it is a proposal for concluding a contract, and (2) it is "sufficiently definite and indicates the intention of the offeror to be bound." An offer is considered sufficiently definite if it (1) indicates or describes the goods,

(2) expressly or implicitly specifies the quantity, and (3) expressly or implicitly specifies the price for the goods.

However, one should not think that the presence of these three terms always indicates a contract. In many international contracts involving a great deal of money, no firm would make a commitment without reaching an agreement on many other terms, such as methods of payment, delivery dates, quality standards, etc. Take the following example. Buyer and seller are negotiating the sale of ten industrial knitting machines for five million Deutsche marks. The buyer states, "Everything seems agreeable. I'll take the machines." The agreement probably is not a contract even though it seems "sufficiently definite" under the CISG. The lack of any agreement on other matters indicates that the parties might not as yet have demonstrated their intention to be bound to a contract. However, if the court does find that the parties had the intention to be bound, it can supply many of the missing terms by looking at the past dealings of the parties and at customs in the trade or industry, or by referring to the applicable provisions of the CISG.

Public Offers. The laws of some nations hold that an offer must be addressed to one or more specific persons. In those countries, an advertisement can never create the power of acceptance in a member of the public who reads the ad. In Germany, for instance, advertisements addressed to the public in general are mere invitations to deal. Other countries, such as the United States and China, while treating most advertisements as mere invitations to deal, do recognize that specific advertisements that describe the goods, their quantity, and price may be considered an offer. In China a price list sent to a customer is considered an invitation to deal. The CISG takes a middle position by creating a presumption that an advertisement or circular is not an offer "unless the contrary is clearly indicated by the person making the proposal." Consequently, a seller may want to include in all of its price sheets and literature a notice that the material does not constitute an offer.

Open Price Terms. Merchants often fail to include price terms in the chain of correspondence or communications making up a contract. Perhaps they were relying on some external market factor or course of dealings to determine price. A contract may even make reference to a market price on a date that is months or even years away. If the price is left "open," is the parties' understanding sufficiently definite to constitute a valid contract? In the United States, most state UCC laws provide that if price is not specified, a "reasonable price" will be presumed. Under this flexible approach, the contract does not fail. On the other hand, such a provision would not be found in a socialist legal system in which prices are dictated by government central planning. Open price terms are not favored in developing countries either because they are major exporters of agricultural commodities, minerals, and other raw materials subject to a highly fluctuating market. Even in most civil law nations, such as France, a sales price must be sufficiently definite in order for a contract to be valid. Chinese law takes an approach in keeping with its socialist system. If the price of goods is not stated in the contract, then a market price will be presumed. However, where Chinese law or administrative rulings specify a required or suggested price for the goods in question, then the government-established price must be used.

Although some conflict stems from the language of the CISG regarding open price terms (see Articles 14 and 55), the CISG provisions seem similar to those of U.S. state law. Article 55, found under the section on the obligations of the buyer, states that where price is not fixed, the price will be that charged "for such goods sold under comparable circumstances in the trade concerned." Accordingly, if the buyer and seller fail to specify the price of the goods, a court might look to the trade or to the market price of comparable goods to make its own determination of price, and the contract and all its other provisions will remain in effect.

Firm Offers. As a general rule, an offer may be revoked at any time prior to acceptance. Under the UCC, as between merchants, an offer may not be revoked if it is made in a signed writing (or *record,* as defined in the 2003 amendment in Exhibit 4.3) that gives assurance that it will remain open for a stated period of time, not to exceed three months. Under the CISG, firm offers are valid even if they are not in writing. Moreover, an offer may not be revoked if the offeree reasonably relies on the offer as being irrevocable and the offeree has acted in reliance on the offer. Consider a buyer who states to a supplier, "Within the next month, I will be placing an order for one hundred computers, so please give me your best price." The supplier responds, making no reference as to whether the offer will remain open. If the buyer then quotes a price on the computers for resale to a customer, the offer will be irrevocable during that month. Some civil law countries, such as Germany, France, Italy, and Japan, go even further in limiting the offeror's power to revoke. In civil law countries, the offeror may not revoke during the period of time normally needed for the offeree's acceptance to arrive.

Entering the Agreement: The Acceptance

A contract is not formed until the offer is accepted by the offeree. The acceptance is the offeree's manifestation of the intention to be bound to the terms of the offer. Modern legal rules give great flexibility to the offeree as to the manner and method of accepting; certainly greater flexibility than under the common law. Under the CISG, an acceptance may take the form of a statement or *conduct* by the offeree that indicates the offeree's intention to be bound to the contract. CISG Article 18 states that "a statement made by or other conduct of the offeree indicating assent to an offer is an acceptance." (UCC 2-206 states that "an offer to make a contract shall be construed as inviting acceptance in any manner and by any medium reasonable in the circumstances.") This rule has day-to-day applicability. It is very common for a prospective buyer to place an order to purchase goods, with the seller responding not with a verbal or written confirmation, or not by initialing the order and returning it to the buyer, but simply by shipping the goods called for. For instance, the seller may be shipping urgently needed replacement parts for a stopped assembly line. Similarly, it is not uncommon for a buyer to accept the delivery of goods by simply remitting payment (as in the case where the seller ships blue widgets instead of the red ones ordered; if the buyer pays for the nonconforming red ones, there is a contract). Both the UCC and the CISG cover these situations. CISG Article 18 states that an offeree may accept by "dispatching the goods or payment of the price, without notice to the offeror" provided that the parties have established this as a practice or it is routinely accepted in the trade, and if the act is

performed within the time for acceptance fixed by the offeror or within a reasonable time.

> http://www.jus.uio.no/lm//un.contracts.international
> .sale.of.goods.convention.1980/index.html
> See for the Articles in Part II: Formation of the Contract.
> **or**
> http://www.cisg-online.ch/
> A complete guide to the CISG and searchable case database
> for German-speaking countries.

Silence as Acceptance. The general rule in most countries is that the offeree's silence should not be interpreted as an acceptance. If you unexpectedly receive goods that you did not order, you should not have to pay for them (although in most legal systems, you might have to safeguard them until retrieved by the sender). Moreover, it would be unfair if a seller could force you to take goods simply by stating, "If I don't hear from you, I assume you will keep them and pay for them." On the other hand, there are situations where the parties can agree that silence is an acceptance. If seller makes an offer to you, and you reply, "If you do not hear from me by 5:00 p.m., ship the goods," then you have made your silence an acceptance.

Another exception occurs when the parties' previous dealings obliges them to speak up and not remain silent. Consider this case: For the past five years, DownPillow, Inc. regularly ordered quantities of white goose down from Federhaus, GmbH that were to be shipped within three months. At first, Federhaus confirmed all orders. Soon, Federhaus stopped sending written confirmations of orders and just shipped. This time, DownPillow placed the order and Federhaus never shipped. DownPillow suffered damages when it unexpectedly ran out of feathers. It can sue Federhaus for breach of contract on the basis that the established practice of the parties presumed Federhaus' acceptance of DownPillow's order.

Time of Acceptance. Under the common law, and in virtually all legal systems, the offeree may accept at any time until the offer is revoked by the offeror, until the offer expires due to the passage of time, until the original offer is rejected by the offeree, until the offeree makes a counteroffer in return, or until the offer terminates (such as through the death of one of the parties or destruction of the subject matter). Thus, it is often important to know when an acceptance becomes valid because it is at that point in time when contractual rights and obligations arise. Time constraints can be even more critical in international transactions between buyers and sellers located in different time zones and using several different means of communications—next-day letters, email, telephone, and facsimile transmissions.

Under the common law, a contract is formed when the acceptance is dispatched by the offeree. In the case of an acceptance by letter, the time of dispatch is the time the letter is put into the hands of the postal authorities. This rule assumes that the correct mode of transmission is used (i.e., one that the offeror specifies or, if none, one that is reasonable under the circumstances). This assumption makes sense, for if a fax arrives offering to sell fresh roses sitting on the tarmac in Colombia, one does not accept by letter and expect a contract to be formed on dispatch. Hence, if a buyer submits a purchase order to a seller, a contract is formed upon the dispatch of the seller's order confirmation. The buyer's power to withdraw the purchase order ended at that time. Furthermore, the effect of this rule is that the seller is also bound to the contract upon dispatch and may no longer withdraw the offer after that time.

The CISG follows a somewhat different approach. Under Article 18, an acceptance is not effective upon dispatch, but is effective when it reaches the offeror (or in the case of electronic transmission, appears on the offeror's fax machine or in his email inbox). Article 16 protects the offeree by stating that the dispatch of an acceptance cuts off the offeror's right to revoke the offer. Thus, an acceptance may possibly be withdrawn if the withdrawal reaches the offeror before or at the same time as the acceptance does (Article 22). Recall that under the common law, the offeree would not have had the same right because the contract would have been formed at the moment of dispatch. This CISG rule follows the basic rules in effect in China and civil law countries. The following case, *Chateau des Charmes Wines, Ltd. v. Sabaté,* discusses the making of a verbal contract and one party's futile attempt to modify it.

Chateau des Charmes Wines Ltd. v. Sabaté
2004 WL 2012551 (2003)
United States Court of Appeals (9th Cir.)

BACKGROUND AND FACTS

Sabaté France sold wine corks to Chateau, a winery in Canada. The sale took place through Sabaté's California subsidiary, Sabaté USA. In talks, Sabaté claimed that the corks would not distort the taste of wine. The parties agreed by telephone on the quantity, price, and payment and shipping terms. No other terms were discussed, and the parties had never done business before. After a second order, totaling eleven shipments, a total of 1.2 million corks had been sold. An invoice accompanied each shipment stating that "Any dispute arising under the present contract is under the sole jurisdiction of the Court of Commerce of the City of Perpignan." Chateau took delivery, remitted payment, and after bottling the wine, discovered that the cork had tainted the wine's flavor. When Chateau sued for breach of warranty, Sabaté argued that the forum selection clause required that the case be heard in France. Chateau countered, claiming that a valid and enforceable verbal contract had already existed, and that the subsequent forum selection clause was not a part of it. The district court held for Sabaté.

Before Fletcher, Kozinski, and Trott, Circuit Judges

PER CURIAM

The question before us is whether the forum selection clause in Sabaté France's invoices was part of any agreement between the parties. The disputes in this case arise out of an agreement for a sale of goods from a French party and a United States party to a Canadian party. Such international sales contracts are ordinarily governed by a multilateral treaty, the *United Nations Convention on Contracts for the International Sale of Goods* (CISG), which applies to "contracts of sale of goods between parties whose places of business are in different States . . . when

continued

continued

the States are Contracting States." The United States, Canada, and France are all contracting states to the CISG . . . [T]here is no doubt that the CISG is valid and binding federal law. . . .

Under the CISG, it is plain that the forum selection clauses were not part of any agreement between the parties. The Convention sets out a clear regime for analyzing international contracts for the sale of goods: "A contract of sale need not be concluded in or evidenced by writing and is not subject to any other requirement as to form." CISG, art. 11. A proposal is an offer if it is sufficiently definite to "indicate the goods and expressly or implicitly fix or make provision for determining the quantity and the price," *id.,* art. 14, and it demonstrates an intention by the offeror to be bound if the proposal is accepted. In turn, an offer is accepted if the offeree makes a "statement . . . or other conduct . . . indicating assent to an offer." *Id.,* art. 18. Further, "A contract is concluded at the moment when an acceptance of an offer becomes effective." *Id.,* art. 23. Within such a framework, the oral agreements between Sabaté USA and Chateau as to the kind of cork, the quantity, and the price were sufficient to create complete and binding contracts.

The terms of those agreements did not include any forum selection clause. Indeed, Sabaté France and Sabaté USA do not contend that a forum selection clause was part of their oral agreements, but merely that the clauses in the invoices became part of a binding agreement. The logic of this contention is defective. Under the CISG, a "contract may be modified or terminated by the mere agreement of the parties." *Id.,* art. 29(1). However, the Convention clearly states that "[a]dditional or different terms relating, among other things, to . . . the settlement of disputes are considered to alter the terms of the offer materially." *Id.,* art. 19(3). There is no indication

that Chateau conducted itself in a manner that evidenced any affirmative assent to the forum selection clauses in the invoices. Rather, Chateau merely performed its obligations under the oral contract.

Nothing in the CISG suggests that the failure to object to a party's unilateral attempt to alter materially the terms of an otherwise valid agreement is an "agreement" within the terms of Article 29. *Cf.* CISG, art. 8(3). ("In determining the intent of a party or the understanding a reasonable person would have had, due consideration is to be given to all relevant circumstances of the case including the negotiations, any practices which the parties have established between themselves, usages and any subsequent conduct of the parties.") Here, no circumstances exist to conclude that Chateau's conduct evidenced an "agreement." We reject the contention that because Sabaté France sent multiple invoices it created an agreement as to the proper forum with Chateau. The parties agreed in two telephone calls to a purchase of corks to be shipped in eleven batches. In such circumstances, a party's multiple attempts to alter an agreement unilaterally do not so effect [citation omitted].

Decision. The verbal contract for the purchase of corks was valid and binding. The attempt by the seller to later include a new and material term (the forum selection clause) in the invoices was not effective. The buyer did not assent to the new term simply by receiving and paying for the goods. Reversed and remanded.

Comment. Here the seller attempted to add a new "surprise" term after the contract had already been formed, and indeed, after the goods had been shipped. Distinguish this case from cases where the new term is incorporated into the seller's written confirmation sent in reply to a buyer's purchase order form (the typical "battle of the forms" situation).

The Mirror Image Rule. Most countries of the world follow the *mirror image rule.* The rule requires that an offeree respond to an offer with an acceptance that is definite and unconditional, and that matches the terms of the offer exactly and unequivocally. Under these laws, a purported acceptance that contains different or additional terms is considered a counteroffer and thus, a rejection of the original offer.

The Manner of Offer and Acceptance: Buyer's and Seller's Forms

In the real world, the chain of correspondence or exchange of documents between buyer and seller often makes it difficult to tell which one is the offer and which one is the acceptance. When an agreement is put into one document, signed by both parties, it is easier to tell. But this one-document agreement is not always the practice. In reality, the offer might come from either buyer or seller. The only way to tell which is the offer and which is the acceptance is to understand basic contract rules. A correspondence can be an offer if it is "sufficiently definite and indicates the intention of the offeror to be bound" (Article 14). The other party's response might be an acceptance, or if it contradicts the terms of the offer, it might be a counteroffer. For instance, a buyer might have looked at the seller's catalogs and samples. On that basis, he requests a price quote from the seller. If the price quote is sufficiently definite in its terms, then the seller has made an offer, and the buyer may accept or reject. Formal price quotes used in international trade are often done in the form of a seller's *pro forma invoice,* as shown in Exhibit 4.4. In another case, a buyer might have enough price and product information at hand to send a *purchase order* to the seller. If it is sufficiently definite in its terms then it would be the offer (and presumed to be such in most jurisdictions), and the sellers' reply, via an *order confirmation,* would be the acceptance (assuming it meets the legal requirements for an acceptance and is not a counteroffer).

The *Pro Forma* Invoice. One common method of offering products for sale to a foreign buyer is through the *pro forma* invoice. It is a formal written offer to a specified buyer to sell the products described. It sets out the price for the goods in the currency stated, plus any additional charges payable by the buyer's account, including the cost of packing and crating; the cost of inland freight; the cost of ocean or air freight, freight forwarder's fees, and pier delivery charges; wharfage and warehouse charges; and insurance. (Most exporters rely heavily on their freight forwarders to obtain this cost information and, later, to make these shipping arrangements.) The *pro forma* invoice specifies the mode of shipment, the method of payment, the length of time for which the quoted terms will be valid, and any and all other terms required by the seller as a condition of sale. Sellers usually require the buyer to accept the offer by signing it and returning it to them before shipment. In other cases, a buyer might accept by sending their own purchase order form. *Pro forma*

invoices are often required by a buyer's bank or by the customs authority in the buyer's country prior to importation of the goods so that import licenses can be issued in advance. Pro forma invoices are used in all types of industries, manufacturing firms in particular. The pro forma invoice should not be confused with the *commercial invoice,* which is the final bill for the goods that accompanies the request for payment.

Contract Terms and Conditions and the "Battle of the Forms"

The mirror image rule requires that an acceptance be unconditional and that it not attempt to change any of the terms proposed in the offer. These requirements present special problems when both parties, buyer and seller, negotiate back and forth via "standard" business forms. The seller might quote prices by letter or by formal pro forma invoice. The buyer might use a preprinted purchase order form to place orders with all vendors. The seller might rely on an order confirmation form or sales acknowledgement form. Typically, these forms leave room on the front so the parties may insert important contract terms—those that they "bargained for," such as price, quality, or ship date. The reverse side often contains detailed "fine-print" provisions or standard clauses, often called *terms and conditions,* or *general conditions of sale,* as shown in Exhibit 4.5.

Their use is common in international trade. They are often drafted by attorneys to protect their client's rights, placing greater liability on the other party. Often they are adapted from recommended standard clauses provided by industry or trade associations. For instance, one set of standard clauses might be utilized by the steel industry, another by grain merchants, and yet another by the chemical industry. The parties may not even be aware of the legal significance of these seldom read fine-print provisions. For the most part, a seller would only read the most crucial provisions on the front page of a buyer's purchase order to see what was ordered. A buyer may only glance at the key provisions of the seller's confirmation to see when the goods will be shipped. Usually, the preprinted terms on these forms differ, sometimes in significant ways.

EXHIBIT 4.4

Pro Forma Invoice

DownPillow International, Inc.
Pro Forma Invoice
Boone, North Carolina, U.S.A.

Invoice to:	Japanese Retailer Osaka, Japan	Date of pro forma invoice: Oct. 12, 2000
Ship/Consign to:	as per buyer's instructions	This pro forma no. 000044372
Shipment via:	U.S. port to destination Kobe	Terms of Payment:
Notify Party:	Buyer to advise	Cash against documents,
Country-of-Origin:	U.S.A.	irrevocable LC payable in U.S. dollars
Total weight (est.):	9405 lbs/4266 kg.	Shipment Date
Shipping volume (est.):	3000 cu.ft./85 cu.m.	45 days after receipt of LC

Quantity	Item Code	Description	Price	Amount
5000	5WGD-1	Bed pillows of white goose down total fill weight 26oz./0.74kg, contents sterilized shell: 100% cotton, with piping size 26" x 26", 66cm x 66cm	$32.00	$160,000
		PRICE Ex Works, Domestic packing		$160,000
		Export packing/vacuum pack charges		850
		Cartage/Inland freight charge		1250
		Pier delivery charge		150
		Freight forwarder's fees		200
		PRICE F.A.S. NC PORT		$162,450
		Ocean freight charges port to port		$3355
		Container rental charge		450
		Marine insurance charges		640
		PRICE C.I.F. Port of KOBE, Japan		$166,895

DownPillow International, Inc.

_____   _____

by, Export Sales Manager   Authorized buyer's signature

All terms of sale interpreted by _Incoterms_ 2000. This quotation is valid for a period of 60 days from above date. Any changes in the actual cost of shipping, handling, packaging, insurance or other charges not a part of the actual cost of the goods are buyer's responsibility.

SEE OTHER SIDE FOR ADDITIONAL TERMS AND CONDITIONS

EXHIBIT 4.5

Seller's Terms and Conditions of Sale

(Seller's Order Confirmation—Reverse Side)
Pro Forma Invoice or
TERMS AND CONDITIONS OF SALE

1. Acceptance

This constitutes acceptance by Seller of Buyer's purchase order. This acceptance is expressly made conditional upon Buyer's assent, express or implied, to the terms and conditions set forth herein without modification or addition. Buyer's acceptance of these terms and conditions shall be indicated by any part of the following, whichever first occurs: (a) Buyer's written acknowledgment hereof; (b) Buyer's acceptance of shipment of the goods herein described; (c) Buyer's failure to acknowledge or reject these terms and conditions in writing within five business days after delivery; or (d) any other act or expression of acceptance by the Buyer. Seller's silence or failure to respond to any such subsequent term, condition or proposal shall not be deemed to be Seller's acceptance or approval thereof.

2. Price and Delivery

The quoted price for the goods may be varied by additions upwards by the Seller according to market conditions at the date of shipment and the Buyer shall pay such additions in addition to the quoted price, including but not limited to increases in the cost of labor, material, operations, and/or transport. Delivery and payment terms shall be made according to this order confirmation. Trade formulas used herein (e.g., CIF, CPT, FAS or FOB) shall be interpreted according to *Incoterms* (2000). Payment in the currency and at the conditions of this confirmation.

3. Force Majeure

Seller shall not be liable for loss or damage due to delay in manufacture, shipment, or delivery resulting from any cause beyond Seller's direct control or due to compliance with any regulations, orders, acts, instructions, or priority requests of any government authority, acts of God, acts or omissions of the purchaser, fires, floods, epidemics, weather, strikes, factory shutdowns, embargoes, wars, riots, delays in transportation, delay in receiving materials from Seller's usual sources, and any delay resulting from any such cause shall extend shipment or delivery date to the extent caused thereby and Seller shall be reimbursed its additional expenses resulting from such delay. In the case of delay lasting more than eight weeks, Seller has the right to cancel contract. Receipt of merchandise by the Buyer shall constitute a waiver of any claims for delay.

4. Warranties

The Seller makes no representations or warranties with respect to the goods herein. Seller hereby disclaims warranties, express or implied, as to the products, including but not limited to, any implied warranty of quality or merchantability or fitness for any particular purpose, and the Buyer takes the goods on the Buyer's own judgment. Seller not liable for any damage or loss for a breach of warranty.

5. Limitation of Liability

Seller is not liable for any special, consequential, or incidental damages arising out of this agreement or the goods sold hereunder, including but no limited to damages for lost profits, loss of use or any damages or sums paid by Buyer to third parties, even if Seller has been advised of the possibility of such damages.

6. Governing Law

In respect of any standard, test, mode of inspection, measurement, or weight, the practice governing the same adopted for use in United States shall prevail. This agreement shall be governed by the Laws of North Carolina and in the event of any dispute arising whether touching on the interpretation hereof or otherwise, the same shall be resolved before the General Court of Justice of the State of North Carolina.

Here are several examples of how they might differ:

- Buyer's purchase order allows the buyer to bring suit for consequential damages if the seller breaches the contract. Seller's confirmation specifically excludes consequential damages.
- Buyer's purchase order calls for disputes to be resolved in the buyer's country. Seller's confirmation calls for disputes to be heard in the courts of the seller's country.
- Buyer's purchase order requires shipment by a certain date named in the order. Seller's confirmation allows a grace period for late shipping or provides for excuses for late shipment.
- Buyer's purchase order is silent about whether the buyer has to notify the seller in the event of problems with the merchandise. Seller's confirmation requires buyer to notify the seller of any problems in the order within seven days.

The potential for conflict is almost endless. When this occurs, lawyers call it a *battle of the forms*. In the following sections, assume that the buyer is the offeror and that the buyer's purchase order is the offer. Assume also that the seller is the offeree and that the seller's confirmation of that order is the (attempted) acceptance. The assumptions serve to simplify the discussion for understanding. Keep in mind that the seller could possibly make an offer first, such as in a pro forma invoice, in which case the buyer's purchase order might actually be an attempted acceptance.

The Battle of the Forms under the Common Law and Civil Law.

If a seller sends a confirmation in response to a buyer's purchase order, and the seller's form contains differing or additional terms, no matter how minor, then no contract would exist. The mirror image rule has been violated. Each form or correspondence between them is considered a counteroffer, canceling the previous one. If the parties do not perform (e.g., the seller does not ship the goods), then no contract is formed. Indeed, the buyer cannot force the seller to ship because no contract exists. If the parties do perform—the seller ships the goods—then that action is an acceptance of the terms on the other party's last form. The result usually is that the form sent last in time will prevail as the contract. Consider the following two examples:

- Suppose that a U.S. company, DownPillow International, Inc., sends a purchase order to Federhaus, a German supplier of feathers. Federhaus replies with a confirmation stating that the buyer has only ten days to notify the seller in the event of a problem with the shipment. DownPillow faxes back that it must have thirty days. With no more said, Federhaus ships. This action is an acceptance—and the contract terms are those in DownPillow's last correspondence. DownPillow has thirty days. If the ten-day provision was important to Federhaus, it should have gotten an affirmative response from DownPillow before shipping.

- Now assume that Federhaus's confirmation states that a charge of 1 percent per month will be applied to outstanding balances if the account is not paid within thirty days. DownPillow does nothing more. If the seller ships, it might not have recourse against DownPillow for refusing the goods—the new term was not a mirror image of the buyer's order, and thus, no contract was formed to protect the seller. On the other hand, if DownPillow accepts the feathers and then fails to pay within thirty days, it will be liable for the interest penalty because the confirmation was a counteroffer that DownPillow accepted by receiving the merchandise. These determinations would be the result if the case were heard in a court that applied the common law or civil law rules. These results are not the case in the United States today.

The Battle of the Forms and Mirror Image Rule under the UCC.

In the United States the mirror image rule has been modified by statute to deal with modern business practices and to avoid the problems in the preceding examples. Under subsections 1 and 2 of the original UCC 2–207:

1. A written confirmation which is sent within a reasonable time operates as an acceptance even though it states terms additional to or different from those in the purchase order, unless the confirmation "is expressly made conditional on assent to the additional or different terms."
2. If both parties are merchants, any additional terms contained in the seller's confirmation automatically become a part of the contract *unless:*
   a. The buyer's purchase order "expressly limits acceptance" to the terms in that order;
   b. The additional terms in the confirmation "materially alter" the terms of the order; or

c. The buyer notifies the seller of an objection to the additional terms within a reasonable time after receiving the confirmation containing the new terms.

A careful reading of UCC 2–207 shows that the UCC attempts to uphold the intentions of the parties by keeping the contract in existence where there are only *minor differences* between the forms used by the parties. The UCC states that, between merchants, an acceptance by a confirmation that contains additional terms that reflect only minor changes from the buyer's order will be effective to produce a contract, and the minor terms become a part of it (unless the buyer notifies the seller of an objection to the new term). A minor term might be one that is in *usual and customary usage* in the trade. Adding a provision that calls for an interest penalty for late payment is an example of a minor term (such penalties are common in sales contacts).

Now, reconsider our example under the UCC. DownPillow faxes its purchase order for feathers; its order does not expressly limit the acceptance to the terms of the order. All the "bargained" terms such as price, quality, and ship date are agreed upon. Seller Federhaus's confirmation states, however, that a charge of 1 percent per month will be applied to outstanding balances if the account is not paid within thirty days. DownPillow does nothing more. This time, under the UCC, a contract is formed. The seller is safe in shipping and DownPillow will have breached it if it refuses delivery of the goods. Moreover, if DownPillow is late in paying, interest will run on its open account. DownPillow could have objected to the inclusion of the late payment fee term, but it did not.

The situation is different in the case of new terms in the acceptance that attempt to *materially alter* the offer. A material term is generally considered to be one that is not commonly accepted in the trade and that would result in *surprise hardship* to one party if unilaterally included in the contract by the party. Such new terms do not become a part of the contract unless accepted by the other party. Suppose that DownPillow sends a purchase order to Federhaus in Germany. The order does not expressly limit an acceptance to the terms of the order. The confirmation is identical as to price, quality, ship date, and other bargained terms. However, the standard clause on the reverse side of the confirmation from Federhaus states that "all disputes are to be resolved in arbitration before the International Chamber of Commerce in Paris." A term that affects the rights of the parties in the event of a breach, such as an arbitration clause like this, is a material term. A contract will be formed without Federhaus's new terms. *Sellers who wish to be assured that their order confirmation will comprise the entire agreement should request that the buyer show its acceptance of the new terms by signing the confirmation and returning the completed contract to them.*

See Exhibit 4.6 for the 2003 amendments to UCC 2-206 and 2-207.

Confirmation Notices—German Law and the CISG. As stated earlier, these determinations would not be the result under the civil codes of European countries that strictly follow the mirror image rule. However, some special rules in effect in some European countries take into account the special formalities and formal business practices of the European firms. In Germany, for example, manufacturing firms regularly confirm purchase orders with their *Auftragsbestätigung,* or "order confirmation." These documents are given special treatment under German law. If this formal confirmation alters the terms of a buyer's purchase order, the terms of the confirmation prevail unless the buyer specifically rejects them in a prompt and timely fashion. However, although Germany applies this law in contracts between parties in Germany, a German court has held that the confirmation notice principle does not apply under the CISG. Thus, the failure to respond to a confirmation note has no effect if a contract with a German firm is governed by the CISG.

The Battle of the Forms under the CISG. The CISG rules fall somewhere between the rules set out by the common and civil law and the UCC. In an international sales transaction governed by the CISG, an acceptance containing new terms that do not materially alter the terms of the offer becomes a part of the contract, *unless the offeror promptly objects to the change.* However, a purported acceptance that contains additional or different terms that do materially alter the terms of the offer *would constitute a rejection of the offer and a counteroffer.* No contract would arise at all unless the offeror in return accepts all of the terms of the

---

EXHIBIT 4.6

2003 Amendments to UCC 2-206 and 2-207*

§ 2-206. Offer and Acceptance in Formation of Contract.

(3) A definite and seasonable expression of acceptance in a record operates as an acceptance even if it contains terms additional to or different from the offer.

§ 2-207. Terms of Contract; Effect of Confirmation.

If (i) conduct by both parties recognizes the existence of a contract although their records do not otherwise establish a contract, (ii) a contract is formed by an offer and acceptance, or (iii) a contract formed in any manner is confirmed by a record that contains terms additional to or different from those in the contract being confirmed, the terms of the contract, subject to Section 2-202, are:
  (a) terms that appear in the records of both parties;
  (b) terms, whether in a record or not, to which both parties agree; and
  (c) terms supplied or incorporated under any provision of this Act.

Preliminary Official Comment

1. This section applies to all contracts for the sale of goods, and it is not limited only to those contracts where there has been a "battle of the forms."

*Subject to enactment by state legislatures.

---

counteroffer (recall that under the UCC a contract would arise, albeit without the new terms). Continuing the previous example, no contract would be formed between DownPillow and Federhaus under the CISG, and Federhaus's new material terms would amount to no more than a counteroffer.

Under the CISG, an acceptance of the counteroffer may arise by assent or *by performance.* In other words, if the original offeror takes some steps toward performing the contract after having received a counteroffer, the offeror will be deemed to have accepted the counteroffer and a contract will be created on the new terms. So, if DownPillow remits payment for the feathers without having read the fine-print provisions of Federhaus's confirmation (a counteroffer), it implies acceptance of Federhaus's terms, including the arbitration terms. By way of example, a draft commentary to Article 19 states:

> For example, an offeree might reply to an offer stating that the offeror has fifty tractors available for sale at a certain price by sending a telegram that accepts the offer but adds "ship immediately." . . .
> . . . [T]he additional or different terms contained in [this] reply would constitute material alteration since the terms "ship immediately" would change the time of delivery (since no shipping date had been specified, a "reasonable time" for shipment would have been presumed under the CISG). . . .

If the reply contains a material alteration, the reply would not constitute an acceptance but would constitute a counteroffer. If the original offeror responds to this reply by shipping the goods . . . a contract may eventually be formed by notice to the original offeree of the shipment. . . .

Unlike the UCC, the CISG states those key elements of a contract that will materially alter a contract: *price, payment, quality and quantity of goods, place and time of delivery, extent of one party's liability to the other, and settlement of disputes.* This list is so broad that almost any term could conceivably be interpreted as "material." Thus, under the CISG, almost any new or different term in the acceptance could constitute a counteroffer. The effect is that many businesspeople may believe that they are "under contract" when they really are not. Consequently, those businesspeople negotiating an international contract must make certain that all material terms of the contract are understood and agreed upon by the parties.

The Validity of Standard Contract Terms: A Comparison. Today, so-called "fine print" or standard terms in contracts are widely used. They offer many advantages to businesses by eliminating the need to negotiate all the details of a contract every time goods are sold. For large firms selling to hundreds or thousands of customers around the world, the use of standard forms reduces costs, saves time, and allows the firm's legal department to maintain centralized control over contract terms and negotiations. As the potential for disputes increases with an ever-growing volume of business, the large firm can ensure some control over how those disputes will be resolved. In the United States, standard terms are generally permitted in business-to-business contracts unless in violation of a statute or struck down by the courts for other reasons. However, in some civil law countries, such as China or Germany, to take two examples, the statutes are quite specific about the kinds of standard contract terms that are permissible.

China takes a simplistic, yet clear, legal approach to the validity of standardized terms. Chinese law requires standardized terms to be fair in limiting the rights and liabilities of the parties. The terms must be brought to the attention of the other party, and they must be explained if requested. Caution should be used when using standardized terms in China at all, because if they are not fairly negotiated between both parties they might be declared invalid.

The *German Civil Code* has even more detailed provisions dealing with standard contract terms. The *Standard Contract Terms Act (Gesetz zur Regelung des Rechts der Allgemeinen Geschäftsbedingungen)* provides that standard terms are void if they unreasonably disadvantage the other party to the contract by depriving them of their essential rights under the contract or prevents them from performing their part of the contract. Contract terms are deemed invalid in a number of other instances: If they are contrary to the basic terms of a statute; if they give the drafting party an unreasonably long period of time to accept an offer or to perform their part of a contract; if they permit a party to escape all obligations without cause or reason; if they call for the payment of a stated amount of money as damages in the event of a breach (liquidated damage provisions) where the stated damages are unjustified, excessive or not related to the actual harm suffered; if they permit one party to pass through price or cost increases to the other party for deliveries made within four months of the contract date (continuing supply contracts excepted); if they release a party from giving notice of receipt of defective goods; if they attempt to require a party to buy or sell goods on a continuing basis for more than two years, and many others.

EXPRESS AND IMPLIED WARRANTIES

Express warranties are contractual terms that define a product's design and performance characteristics, quality, or workmanship. These terms need to be spelled out clearly so that no confusion arises over what the seller is responsible for doing. A misunderstanding here can permanently injure the long-term relationship between the parties. Consequently, warranties are often subject to intensive bargaining. Typically, sellers will want to limit the scope of their liability, place a ceiling on the amount of damages for which they can be liable, and place a limit on the time that the warranty will run. Buyers will want to negotiate the broadest provisions and gain the most legal protection.

Sometimes the parties might not realize that they are negotiating warranty terms. International contracts for the sale of goods are often not embodied in formal written documents carefully drafted by experienced lawyers. Due to the great distances involved in international business, contracts often arise through a chain of correspondence and catalogs sent through the mail, by telex, or by facsimile over the telephone wires. Plagued with potential language problems and the possibility of a misunderstanding, international companies and experienced traders tend to place greater reliance on the use of models, diagrams, spec sheets, and samples to explain their product's quality, packaging, and ability to perform. Each communication might contain some warranty about the product that also becomes an important part of the bargain between the parties.

Implied Warranties

Implied warranties are those warranties that are not expressly given by the seller but are "read into the contract" by the law. In the United States, the law governing express and implied warranties is found in the UCC. The provisions of the CISG are similar to those in the UCC. Under CISG Article 35, the seller must deliver goods that are of the quantity, quality, and description required by the contract, and that

1. Are fit for the purposes for which goods of the same description would ordinarily be used.
2. Are fit for any particular purpose expressly or impliedly made known to the seller at the time of the conclusion of the contract.
3. Possess the qualities of goods which the seller has held out to the buyer as a sample or model.
4. Are contained or packaged in the manner usual for such goods or, where there is no such manner, in a manner adequate to preserve and protect the goods.

Clearly, items 3 and 4 reflect two important features of international business—the greater use of samples and models and the greater need for packaging that protects goods during ocean shipment.

Nonconforming goods are those that do not conform to the express or implied terms of a contract. In *United Trade Associates Limited v. Dickens & Matson,* 848 F. Supp. 751 (E.D. Mich. 1994), a U.S. court decided a case involving a breach of warranty for nonconforming telephones shipped from the United States to Russia. A choice of law provision in the contract called for it to be governed by the law of England. After you read the case, compare and contrast the meaning of *merchantablility* under English law with that found in the CISG and the UCC of the United States.

Trade usages and custom are also used by courts to determine whether a product is merchantable under a contract. *T. J. Stevenson v. 81,193 Bags of Flour,* 629 F.2d 338 (5th Cir. 1980), is a U.S. case decided under the UCC (see Exhibit 4.7 for applicable UCC provisions). In the case, the court looked to trade usages and custom in the agricultural commodities business to determine whether flour that was infested with beetles was *merchantable and fit for human consumption.* The court stated,

> . . . [W]e observe that finding what the parties meant by "merchantability" requires some evaluation of standards in the commercial market and the state of the art in flour manufacturing. The merchantability of infested flour to be sold to con-

sumers is a question of degree and kind. We have often recognized that no food is completely pure. The FDA has long permitted very small amounts of insect fragments and other dead infestation in food products. To declare that any contamination of flour—even by small amounts of insect fragment— renders the flour unmerchantable would no doubt be out of step with commercial reality and would wreak havoc on food manufacturers and distributors while affording little or no additional protection to the consumer. What this case involves, however, is significant amounts of live infestation, by flour beetle eggs, larvae, pupae, and adults. Here the question is: How much live infestation renders consumer-destined flour unfit for the ordinary purposes for which it is used?

Judicial interpretation, trade usage, and course of dealing point to but one conclusion as to flour infested with significant amounts of live flour beetles: although the flour may be "fit for human consumption" in the sense that it can be eaten without caus-

EXHIBIT 4.7
UCC Implied Warranties, Merchantability, and Usage of Trade

§2–314(2) Goods to be merchantable must be at least such as

    (a) pass without objection in the trade under the contract description; and

    (b) in the case of fungible goods, are of fair average quality within the description; and

    (c) are fit for the ordinary purposes for which such goods are used; and

    (d) run, within the variations permitted by the agreement, of even kind, quality, and quantity within each unit and among all units involved; and

    (e) are adequately contained, packaged, and labeled as the agreement may require; and

    (f) conform to the promises or affirmations of fact made on the container or label if any.

§2–314(3) (a) Unless excluded or modified other implied warranties may arise from course of dealing or usage of trade.

ing sickness, it is nonetheless not of merchantable quality. Such flour is not what is normally expected in the trade.

Disclaiming Implied Warranties.
One notable difference between the UCC and the CISG is that U.S. law places restrictions on the parties' ability to limit the implied warranties of the UCC. For instance, under the UCC, a seller may "disclaim" an implied warranty only by using conspicuous, or specified, language to that effect, such as the words "as is." However, the CISG contains no provisions limiting disclaimers for several reasons: International sales contracts take place between more sophisticated and experienced buyers and sellers; the CISG does not apply to consumer sales, where the greatest chance of fraud and abuse might occur; and the nations participating in the drafting of the CISG wanted to preserve as much freedom of contract as possible for the merchants or companies involved. As such, any form of disclaimer will suffice under the CISG.

Schmitz-Werke GmbH & Co. v. Rockland Industries, Inc.
37 Fed.Appx. 687
United States Court of Appeals

BACKGROUND AND FACTS
The seller is an American fabric manufacturer that sold "Trevira" drapery fabric to the plaintiff (buyer) in Germany. During negotiations, the seller stated that the fabric was particularly suited to be a printing base for transfer printing. The buyer had another German company, PMD, experiment with printing on a sample. The buyer informed the seller that although they were satisfied with the material, there were some problems. After receiving 15,000 meters of fabric, the buyer noted additional problems but was encouraged by the seller to continue printing. A second shipment of 60,000 meters was received. When PMD complained about problems in printing on the fabric, another German company was asked to inspect the fabric. Their report indicated that over 15 percent of the fabric was lower grade or seconds. The buyer returned the unused portion, and after negotiations broke down, this suit was brought for breach of warranty.

Before Widener and King, Circuit Judges, and Garwood, Sr. Circuit Judge (5th Cir.) sitting by designation.

Affirmed by unpublished PER CURIAM opinion.

Seller argues that buyer must demonstrate both the existence and the nature of the defect in the fabric before it can recover for breach of warranty—and that to show the nature of that defect, expert testimony is required. Article 35 of the CISG governs the duty of the seller to deliver goods that conform with the contract. Article 35(2) lists various reasons goods may not conform with the contract, including goods which were expressly or impliedly warranted to be fit for a particular purpose. Under Article 35(2)(b) goods are unfit unless they "are fit for any particular purpose expressly or impliedly made known to the seller at the time of the conclusion of the contract, except where the circumstances show that the buyer did not rely, or that it was unreasonable for him to rely, on the seller's skill and judgment." In response, buyer argues that all it need show is that the goods were unfit for the particular purpose warranted—transfer printing—and that it need not show precisely why or how the goods were unfit if it can show that the transfer printing process the goods underwent was performed competently and normally. Seller is correct that buyer did not provide any evidence at trial that would establish the exact nature of the defect in the Trevira fabric. The text of the CISG is silent on this matter.

Under either the CISG or Maryland law, buyer may prevail on a claim that the fabric was unfit for the purpose for which it was expressly warranted (transfer printing) by showing that when the fabric was properly used for the purpose seller warranted, the results were shoddy—even if buyer has introduced no evidence as to just why or how the fabric was unfit. Buyer has shown that the fabric was defective—the fabric's defect was that it was unfit for transfer printing. Seller attempts to counter this argument by claiming that this improperly shifts the burden of proof. Seller's concerns are misplaced—buyer still must prove that the transfer printing

continued

continued

process was ordinary and competently performed, and still must prove that the fabric was defective—it just permits buyer to do so without proving the exact nature of the defect.

There was significant evidence regarding PMD's transfer printing process presented at trial. . . . The district court found that seller warranted its fabric to be fit for transfer printing, that the fabric was transfer printed in a normal and competent way, and that the resulting printed fabric was unsatisfactory. This is enough to support the district court's factual finding in favor of buyer on the warranty claim—the fabric was not fit for the purpose for which it was warranted. . . .

Seller also argues that even if the court properly found that the Trevira fabric was not particularly well suited for transfer printing as warranted, buyer cannot recover on such a warranty because it did not in fact rely on seller's advice as required under CISG Article 35(2)(b). Seller is correct that Article 35(2)(b) of the CISG requires that the buyer reasonably rely on the representations of the seller before liability at-

taches for breach of a warranty for fitness for a particular purpose. The district court explicitly found that buyer relied on the statements of seller's representative that the Trevira fabric was particularly well suited for transfer printing. The court also found that buyer continued to print the fabric with the express consent of seller after it discovered and reported problems with the fabric. The district court's finding that buyer relied on seller's statements proclaiming the Trevira fabric's suitability for transfer printing is supported by the evidence and was not clearly erroneous.

Accordingly, the judgment of the district court is affirmed.

Decision. Under the CISG, the fabric was not fit for the purposes for which it was intended. The exact nature of the fabric's defect need not be proved. It was sufficient that the plaintiff prove that it had reasonably relied on the defendant's representations that the fabric was suitable for transfer printing, and that it was not.

Notice of Nonconforming Goods

If the shipment is nonconforming, or if the goods that are delivered are in some way deficient in quality, quantity, description, packaging, or warranties, both parties must understand what is expected of them and what their alternative courses of action may be. Most legal systems require that notice be given by a buyer to a seller in the event of a breach. In many European countries, that period is fairly short, often a year or less.

During the drafting of the CISG, the developing countries objected to such a short period. Many products imported by developing countries might contain defects that are not readily discoverable, such as with mechanical equipment or pharmaceuticals. They usually required some time to obtain technical assistance from abroad in order to test the imported products for quality or performance. In some cases, products might remain aboard ship,

perhaps anchored offshore, for months or years waiting for a strike to be settled or for government red tape to clear before delivery becomes possible.

The CISG reflects the concerns of developing countries and requires that the buyer examine the goods "within as short a period as is practicable" after they are received. Unless some reasonable excuse prevents doing so, the buyer must give notice of a nonconformity or defect in the goods within a reasonable time after it is discovered or should have been discovered. In any event, however, notice must be given within two years from the date on which the goods were "handed over" to the buyer. When there is a fundamental breach, the notice should state that the contract is avoided. If the buyer fails to give proper notice, the results are clear: the buyer loses the right to assert the breach against the seller.

The notice of nonconformity should specifically, and in necessary detail, state how the goods are nonconforming. This is necessary so a breaching party will be able to send substitute goods or otherwise correct the problem. In one German case, a German fashion retailer purchased clothing from an Italian manufacturer. The buyer refused to pay, and noti-

http://www.cisg.law.pace.edu/cisg/text/e-text-35.html
See for Article 35 of the CISG.

fied the seller that the clothes were of "poor workmanship and improper fitting." The German court, applying the CISG, ruled that the buyer had lost his breach of warranty claim because the notice did not precisely specify the defect in the goods.

REMEDIES FOR BREACH OF CONTRACT

The remedies available to a buyer or seller under the CISG are drawn from both common law and civil law systems. They are intended to give the parties the benefit of their bargain and to put the parties into the economic position they would have been in had the breach not occurred. The remedies outlined in the CISG include (1) avoidance of the contract, (2) seller's right to remedy or cure, (3) seller's additional time to perform, (4) price reduction, (5) money damages, and (6) specific performance.

---

http://www.jus.uio.no/lm//un.contracts.international
.sale.of.goods.convention.1980/index.html
See Part III, Sale of Goods, for Articles 45–52 and 61–65 on
breach of contract.

Avoidance and the Fundamental Breach

Both the UCC and the CISG have provisions that allow the buyer to refuse deliveries of nonconforming or defective goods, or to return them once the defects are discovered. Under the UCC, these remedies are called "rejection" and "revocation of acceptance," and under the CISG they are referred to as *avoidance of the contract*. The term refers to a party's right to cancel the contract.

Fundamental Breach. A buyer's right of rejection of defective goods under the UCC is somewhat broader than a buyer's right of avoidance under the CISG. Under the "perfect tender" provisions of the UCC, the buyer has greater rights in rejecting a shipment for minor nonconformities. Thus, if the seller is under an obligation to deliver twenty-five computer chips, and one or two are defective, the buyer may reject the entire lot. Once the delivery is accepted, the buyer may reject only if the goods show substantial nonconformity.

The CISG goes further to keep the parties in their bargain. In the case of a dispute under the CISG, a buyer can avoid the contract only in the case of a *fundamental breach* by the seller. The

CISG distinguishes between a serious or fundamental breach of the contract and one that is minor or less than fundamental. Article 25 defines a fundamental breach as one that will "substantially deprive him of what he is entitled to expect under the contract." The seller's shipment of seriously defective goods that cannot be repaired, or that have no value to the buyer under the contract, is probably a fundamental breach. So too would be the seller's failure and refusal to ship at all. A partial shipment may also amount to a fundamental breach if it presents a serious problem for the buyer and one that cannot quickly be remedied. Any further interpretation of fundamental breach will have to be left up to the courts.

Buyer's Right to Avoidance. If the breach is fundamental, the buyer need not take delivery nor pay for the goods, nor find a buyer to take them. A buyer may simply cancel the contract by notifying the seller of avoidance of the contract, taking care that the goods are temporarily protected and preserved, and returning them for a full refund of monies already paid. When the goods can rapidly deteriorate or decay, such as with certain foods, the buyer may notify the seller and then take steps to sell them. These rights are especially important to a buyer in an international transaction because of the hardships associated with having to accept delivery and then reselling or disposing of imported goods in a foreign (i.e., the buyer's) market. A buyer who avoids a contract may still sue the seller for damages resulting from the seller's breach.

In *Medical Marketing International v. Internazionale Medico Scientifica, S.R.L.*, a U.S. court held that an Italian seller was in fundamental breach of contract for shipping goods to the United States that did not conform to U.S. government safety standards.

Notice of Avoidance. The buyer's avoidance rights are not effective until the seller is given notice. A buyer who has already accepted the goods, and then discovers their nonconformity, loses the right to avoid the contract, if the buyer does not notify the seller of the intention to avoid within a reasonable time after the buyer knew or should have known of the breach. Thus, if the defect can be discovered only upon use, the buyer has a reasonable period from then on to notify the seller. In

Medical Marketing International, Inc. v. Internazionale Medico Scientifica, S.R.L.
1999 WL 311945 (1999)
United States District Court (E.D.La.)

BACKGROUND AND FACTS

Medical Marketing (MMI) , the plaintiff, entered into an exclusive licensing agreement for the U.S. distribution of mammography units manufactured by the defendant (IMS) in Italy. The U.S. Food and Drug Administration seized the equipment because it did not comply with U.S. safety regulations. MMI argued that the defendant was responsible to assure that its equipment met U.S. standards. When the defendant denied responsibility, MMI declared the contract avoided (terminated) on the grounds of nonconformity of the goods. The dispute was submitted to arbitration, and an award of $357,000 was given to MMI who brought this court action to enforce the award.

DUVAL, DISTRICT J.

The FAA outlines specific situations in which an arbitration decision may be overruled: . . . (4) if the arbitrators exceeded their powers. Instances in which the arbitrators "exceed their powers" may include violations of public policy or awards based on a "manifest disregard of the law." See *W.R. Grace & Co. v. Local Union 759*, 461 U.S. 757, 766, 103 S.Ct. 2177, 2183 (1983).

IMS has alleged that the arbitrators' decision violates public policy of the international global market and that the arbitrators exhibited "manifest disregard of international sales law." Specifically, IMS argues that the arbitrators misapplied the *Convention on Contracts for the International Sale of Goods* (CISG), and that they refused to follow a German Supreme Court case interpreting the CISG.

MMI does not dispute that the CISG applies to the case at hand. Under the CISG, the finder of fact has a duty to regard the "international character" of the convention and to promote uniformity in its application. CISG Article 7. The Convention also provides that in an international contract for goods, goods conform to the contract if they are fit for the purpose for which goods of the same description would ordinarily be used or are fit for any particular purpose expressly or impliedly made known to the seller and relied upon by the buyer. CISG Article 35(2). To avoid a contract based on the nonconformity of goods, the buyer must allege and prove that

the seller's breach was "fundamental" in nature. CISG Article 49. A breach is fundamental when it results in such detriment to the party that he or she is substantially deprived of what he or she is entitled to expect under the contract, unless the party in breach did not foresee such a result. CISG Article 25.

At the arbitration, IMS argued that MMI was not entitled to avoid its contract with IMS based on nonconformity under Article 49, because IMS's breach was not "fundamental." IMS argued that the CISG did not require that it furnish MMI with equipment that complied with the United States GMP regulations. To support this proposition, IMS cited a German Supreme Court case, which held that under the CISG Article 35, a seller is generally not obligated to supply goods that conform to public laws and regulations enforced at the buyer's place of business. *Entscheidunger des Bundersgerichtshofs in Zivilsachen* (BGHZ), 129, 75 (8 March 1995). In that case, the court held that this general rule carries with it exceptions in three limited circumstances: (1) if the public laws and regulations of the buyer's state are identical to those enforced in the seller's state; (2) if the buyer informed the seller about those regulations; or (3) if due to "special circumstances," such as the existence of a seller's branch office in the buyer's state, the seller knew or should have known about the regulations at issue.

The arbitration panel decided that under the third exception, the general rule did not apply to this case. The arbitrators held that IMS was, or should have been, aware of the GMP regulations prior to entering into the 1993 agreement, and explained their reasoning at length. IMS now argues that the arbitration panel refused to apply the CISG and the law as articulated by the German Supreme Court. It is clear from the arbitrators' written findings, however, that they carefully considered that decision and found that this case fit the exception and not the rule as articulated in that decision. The arbitrators' decision was neither contrary to public policy nor in manifest disregard of international sales law.

Decision.   The arbitration panel did not exceed its authority when it found that the Italian seller was in funda-

continued

continued

mental breach of contract. As a general rule, the fitness of goods sold under an international contract will be determined by reference to standards for such goods in the seller's country, unless, as in this case, the seller knew or should have known that the goods would not conform to the standards in the buyer's country.	**Comment.** The district court's opinion is notable for its discussion of German case law. This seems in keeping with the basic principles of the CISG that state that the convention should be interpreted according to its "international character" and to "promote uniformity in its application."

the case of goods that have been delivered late so that they no longer have any value to the buyer (i.e., a fundamental breach), the buyer can lose the right to avoid the contract, unless the buyer does so within a reasonable time after becoming aware of the late delivery.

Seller's Right to Remedy

A seller who has delivered some goods to the buyer prior to the delivery date, even if the goods are nonconforming or the shipment is not complete, has the chance to remedy (also called *cure*), or correct the problem in the shipment. The seller maintains this right to cure, and the buyer may not avoid, until the time for performance expires. Thus, if the buyer receives a defective shipment, or missing parts, or a quantity less than what was ordered, the seller has the right to cure by sending substitute or replacement goods if it can be done by the date for performance called for in the contract. Article 37 states that the seller may exercise this right only if it does not cause unreasonable inconvenience or expense to the buyer.

Unless the parties specify otherwise, the "date for delivery" under the contract (and for the purposes of determining the seller's right to cure), is the date the seller hands the goods over directly to the first carrier (truck, rail, air, or ocean carrier). Consider the following example: DownPillow, Inc., enters a contract to buy 4,000 pounds of feathers from Federhaus, GmbH. The contract calls for delivery by October 1. Federhaus ships 3,000 pounds on September 1 that arrive on October 15. Federhaus also ships 1,000 pounds on September 30, one day prior to the delivery date. This shipment does not arrive until November 15. Federhaus has successfully remedied the short shipment of September 1 by delivering the remaining 1,000 pounds to a carrier before the October 1 date. If the con-

tract did not permit two shipments, then Federhaus could cure the defect only if the second shipment does not cause unreasonable inconvenience or expense to DownPillow. This example should serve as a warning to all international buyers. Businesses that require the goods to be in their hands by a certain date had better clearly specify an arrival date as well as a shipment date in the contract.

Seller's Additional Time to Perform

Both the UCC and the CISG allow the seller to cure a nonconforming shipment if it can be done within the time for performance called for in the contract. Unlike the UCC, however, civil law systems traditionally grant an additional period of time, *beyond the date called for* in the contract, within which the parties may perform. This grace period is often referred to in French civil law as *mise en demeur* and in German law as *nachfrist,* meaning "the period after." The CISG adopts the civil law rule. In the event that the seller has failed to deliver the goods, and the time for their shipment or delivery has passed, the buyer may grant the seller extra time to do so. During this time, the buyer may not avoid the contract or resort to a breach of contract action. If the seller does not perform within the *nachfrist* period, the buyer may avoid the contract whether or not the breach was fundamental.

Article 48 contains a provision entitling the seller to invoke a *nachfrist* period, which allows a seller who fails to perform on time, or who delivers nonconforming goods, to cure performance if it does not cause the buyer "unreasonable delay" or "unreasonable inconvenience." If a seller asks a buyer to agree to an extension of time for delivery and the buyer fails to respond within a reasonable time, the seller may perform within the time requested.

These provisions of the CISG attempt to encourage the parties to stay in their contract rather than to repudiate it in the event of a dispute. The parties will be more likely to negotiate, and where commercially reasonable, resolve their disputes in a manner that will keep the contract together and give each of them the benefit of their bargain. The CISG goes far beyond the UCC in achieving this goal.

Seller's Avoidance.   The seller also may avoid a contract. A seller may avoid a contract if a buyer either fails to take delivery, pay the purchase price, or otherwise commits a fundamental breach (CISG Article 64). The effect of avoidance is that the seller is released from the contract, need not deliver the goods still in the seller's possession, and may claim their return if they have already been delivered. The seller also may seek damages under CISG Article 74.

Price Reduction

One solution for the buyer in the event that the seller makes only a partial shipment, or if the goods are nonconforming, is that of *price reduction*. A buyer who would like to retain the goods may (unilaterally and without notice to the seller) adjust the amount paid by withholding a proportionate part of the purchase price in order to offset the shortage or to reflect the reduced value of the nonconforming goods. If the buyer can repair the goods, or bring them up to contract specifications, the buyer may adjust the price paid accordingly. If the goods have already been paid for, the buyer may ask that the seller return a portion of the amount paid. Obviously, the amount of price reduction is far easier to calculate when the seller delivers less than the quantity promised, than if the goods are damaged or are of inferior quality. The amount of reduction, then, is within the discretion of the buyer. A seller who disputes the buyer's calculation can only resort to legal action.

The remedy of price reduction may be used by the buyer whether or not the seller's breach has been fundamental. In the case of fundamental breach, price reduction is an alternative to the buyer's other remedies. In the case of a minor breach (one not fundamental), price reduction is often the buyer's best remedy because the parties can more easily come to an amicable solution. As-

sume a contract for the sale of 4,000 pounds of white goose down at $60 per pound. If the seller commits a fundamental breach by delivering only 1,000 pounds, the buyer may avoid the contract entirely. But if the seller delivers only 3,800 pounds, the buyer probably will want to deduct $12,000 (200 pounds x $60) and keep the delivered goods. Price reduction is not available if the seller has already delivered substitute goods or if the buyer has refused to accept the seller's attempt to remedy or cure the breach.

Money Damages

In breach of contract cases, the usual remedy granted by common law courts is the legal remedy of money damages. The CISG provides that a breaching party shall be liable for damages in an amount sufficient to make the injured party whole in the event of a breach. Article 74 states that damages to an injured party shall consist of a "sum equal to the loss."

The method of measuring money damages depends on whether the buyer has been able to purchase substitute goods from another supplier. If the seller fails to perform and the buyer does purchase substitute goods, the buyer may claim damages if the substitute goods cost more than the contract price. If the buyer has not purchased substitute goods, damages are measured by the difference between the contract price and the current market price. As under the UCC, damages under the CISG may also include an amount for *lost profits* and other *consequential damages* arising as a "reasonably foreseeable" consequence of the breach. These consequential damages are limited under Article 74 to those that the parties "foresaw or ought to have foreseen at the time of the conclusion of the contract." For the wording or remedies for breach of contract in the CISG and the UCC, see Exhibit 4.8. Note that the UCC provisions are more detailed and specific than the CISG articles.

In the following case, *Delchi Carrier SpA v. Rotorex Corp.*, the buyer incurred many expenses as a result of the seller's delivery of nonconforming goods: repair expenses, storage expenses, assembly line downtime, sourcing substitute merchandise, and lost profits. As you read, consider how the court determines which expenditures are consequential damages and which are not.

EXHIBIT 4.8

Comparison of Consequential Damage Provisions of the CISG and the UCC

Convention on Contracts for the International Sale of Goods

Article 74
Damages for breach of contract by one party consist of a sum equal to the loss, including loss of profit, suffered by the other party as a consequence of the breach. Such damages may not exceed the loss which the party in breach foresaw or ought to have foreseen at the time of the conclusion of the contract, in the light of the facts and matters of which he then knew or ought to have known, as a possible consequence of the breach of contract.

UCC 2–715
Buyer's Incidental and Consequential Damages

1. Incidental damages resulting from the seller's breach include expenses reasonably incurred in inspection, receipt, transportation and care and custody of goods rightfully rejected, and commercially reasonable charges, expenses or commissions in connection with effecting cover and any other reasonable expense incident to the delay or other breach.
2. Consequential damages resulting from the seller's breach include
    a. any loss resulting from general or particular requirements and needs of which the seller at the time of contracting had reason to know and which could not reasonably be prevented by cover or otherwise; and
    b. injury to person or property proximately resulting from any breach of warranty.

Delchi Carrier, SpA v. Rotorex Corp.
1994 WL 495787 (1994)
United States District Court (N.D.N.Y.)

BACKGROUND AND FACTS
Rotorex, a New York corporation, agreed to sell air compressors to Delchi, an Italian company. The compressors were for use in producing Ariele air conditioners. The first shipment reached Delchi, and Delchi paid $188,000. In preparation Delchi had spent 39 million *lire* for special tooling, and 27 million *lire* for special insulation and tubing for use in making Arieles. Delchi expended 18 million *lire* in shipping and customs duties. Delchi then paid $130,000 to Rotorex for a second shipment. While the second shipment was en route, Delchi discovered that the first lot was nonconforming. It rejected the compressors and canceled the contract. Delchi spent several million *lire* to replace problem grommets, inspect, repair, and retest the compressors in an effort to make them usable. During this time, Delchi's assembly line shut down incurring unproductive assembly worker wages. Delchi was able to obtain some substitute compressors from other sources in time for the selling season, which it had to adapt for Ariele units at additional expense. It arranged to have a shipment of Sanyo compressors, which it has

previously ordered, sent to it by air freight so that it could fill some orders. Delchi was also unable to fill some orders, amounting to millions of *lire* in lost profit. Delchi brought this action for damages.

MUNSON, SENIOR DISTRICT JUDGE
The governing law of the instant case is the United Nations Convention on Contracts for the International Sale of Goods ("CISG").

* * *

Rotorex breached its contract with Delchi by failing to supply 10,800 conforming compressors. Under CISG Delchi is entitled to collect monetary damages for Rotorex's breach in "a sum equal to the loss, including loss of profit," although not in excess of the amount reasonably envisioned by the parties. (CISG, article 74). This provision seeks to provide the injured party with the benefit of the bargain, including both its expectation interest and its reliance expenditure.

continued

continued

CONSEQUENTIAL DAMAGES

i. Plaintiff's Attempts to Remedy Nonconformity.
Delchi is entitled to recover damages incurred as a result of its attempts to remedy the nonconformity of Rotorex's compressors. These were not anticipated costs
of production, but were costs that would not have been
incurred without Rotorex's breach. Further, such damages were a foreseeable result of Rotorex's breach.
Hence Delchi is entitled to recover for unreimbursed
expenses [for repairing the units], . . . for labor costs relating to replacing original, problematic grommets with
substitutes, . . . for extraordinary reinspection and testing of units after [repair].

ii. Expedited Shipment of Sanyo Compressors.
Once Delchi's attempts to remedy the nonconformity
failed, it was entitled to expedite shipment of previously
ordered Sanyo compressors to mitigate its damages. Indeed, CISG requires such mitigation. (CISG, article 77):
"A party who relies on a breach of contract must take
such measures as are reasonable in the circumstances to
mitigate the loss." The shipment of previously ordered
Sanyo compressors did not constitute cover under
CISG article 75, because the Sanyo units were previously
ordered, and hence cannot be said to have replaced the
nonconforming Rotorex compressors. Nonetheless,
Delchi's action in expediting shipment of Sanyo compressors was both commercially reasonable and reasonably foreseeable, and therefore Delchi is entitled to
recover . . . the net cost of early delivery of Sanyo compressors [the cost of air shipment less the expected
cost for ocean shipment].

iii. Handling and Storage of Rejected Compressors.   Delchi is further entitled to collect costs incurred for handling and storage of nonconforming
compressors. . . .

iv. Lost Profits.   CISG permits recovery of lost
profit resulting from a diminished volume of sales. In
conformity with the common law, to recover a claim for
lost profit under CISG, a party must provide the finder
of fact with sufficient evidence to estimate the amount
of damages with reasonable certainty. Delchi proved
with sufficient certainty that it incurred, as a foreseeable
and direct result of Rotorex's breach, . . . a total of
546,377,612 lire in lost profit in Italy. Delchi did not
prove with sufficient certainty any lost sales from "indi-

cated [anticipated] orders" in Italy. Delchi's claim of
4,000 additional lost sales in Italy is supported only by
the speculative testimony of Italian sales agents who
averred that they would have ordered more Arieles had
they been available. . . . Delchi provides no documentation of additional lost sales in Italy, and no evidence that
if any such lost sales did exist, that Delchi's inability to fill
those orders was directly attributable to Rotorex's
breach. Delchi can not recover on its claim for additional
lost profits in Italy because the amount of damages, if
any, cannot be established with reasonable certainty.

Delchi is not entitled to recover . . . for modification
of electrical panels for use with substitute Sanyo compressors. Delchi failed to prove that this cost was directly attributable to Rotorex's breach, and that the cost
was not part of the regular cost of production of units
with Sanyo compressors.

Decision.   The plaintiff was awarded compensatory
damages for those expenses incurred in repairing the
nonconforming goods, obtaining substitution goods, and
for lost profits. Lost profits does not include profits that
may arise from anticipated sales that cannot be established by reasonable certainty.

Comment.   Although not reprinted in the above excerpt, the District Court denied Delchi's claim for damages based on other expenses, including: (i) shipping,
customs, and incidentals relating to the two shipments
of Rotorex compressors; (ii) the cost of obsolete insulation and tubing that Delchi purchased only for use with
Rotorex compressors; (iii) the cost of obsolete tooling
purchased only for production of units with Rotorex
compressors; and (iv) labor costs for four days when
Delchi's production line was idle because it had no compressors to install in the air-conditioning units. The court
denied an award for these items on the ground that it
would lead to a double recovery because "those costs
are accounted for in Delchi's recovery on its lost profits
claim." On appeal, the Court of Appeals for the Second
Circuit disagreed. It held that,

An award for lost profits will not compensate
Delchi for the expenses in question. . . . The expenses incurred by Delchi for shipping, customs, and
related matters for the two returned shipments of
Rotorex compressors, including storage expenses
for the second shipment at Genoa, were clearly foreseeable and recoverable incidental expenses. These
are up-front expenses that had to be paid to get the

continued

continued

goods to the manufacturing plant for inspection and were thus incurred largely before the nonconformities were detected. To deny reimbursement to Delchi for these incidental damages would effectively cut into the lost profits award. The same is true of unreimbursed tooling expenses and the cost of the useless insulation and tubing materials. These are legitimate consequential damages that in no way duplicate lost profits damages.

The labor expense incurred as a result of the production line shutdown of May 16–19, 1988 is also a reasonably foreseeable result of delivering nonconforming compressors for installation in air conditioners. However, Rotorex argues that the labor costs in question were fixed costs that would have been incurred whether or not there was a breach. The district court labeled the labor costs "fixed costs," but did not explore whether Delchi would have paid these wages regardless of how much it produced. Variable costs are generally those costs that "fluctuate with a firm's output," and typically include labor (but not management) costs. Whether Delchi's labor costs during this four-day period are variable or fixed costs is in large measure a fact question that we cannot answer because we lack factual findings by the district court. We therefore remand to the district court on this issue.

Delchi Carrier SpA v. Rotorex Corp., 71 F.3d 1024 (2nd Cir. 1995), *aff'g in part and rev'g in part*, 1994 WL 495787 (N.D.N.Y. 1994).

The power to avoid a contract is even more important in a fluctuating market for the goods. If the buyer chooses to accept the goods and sues for damages for the seller's breach of contract, the money damages the buyer could collect would be equal to the difference between the value of the nonconforming goods and the contract price. However, if a buyer avoids the contract under Article 49, and refuses to take delivery at all, *and the value of the goods falls greatly in the marketplace,* the buyer may be able to purchase the goods for much less than the amount agreed to under the contract. Alternatively, *if the value of the goods increases in the marketplace,* the buyer may still sue for the difference between the contract price and the higher market price at which it purchased substitute goods.

Specific Performance in Common Law and Civil Law Systems

The usual legal remedy in contract cases in common law countries is an award for money damages. The usual remedy in civil law countries, on the other hand, is that of *specific performance.* Specific performance is used when a court requires a party to the contract to perform, or carry out its part of the bargain. To be sure, courts in the United States and other common law countries hesitate to require parties to specifically perform. It is considered a harsh remedy to be used only where money damages cannot be calculated or are inadequate, which may occur when the subject matter of the contract is unique. For example, in a dispute over the sale of a prized race horse or a famous work of art, a common law court may specifically require a seller to deliver the item to the buyer because of the "unique" nature of the goods. Money damages would not have been sufficient to remedy the buyer in such a case; the buyer wants the goods contracted for. But in civil law countries, the use of specific performance is not only more common, it is preferred.

Specific Performance under the CISG. The CISG draws strongly on the civil law's acceptance of specific performance as a remedy in contract cases. This is based on the idea that the buyer wants what was ordered and not just the right to sue for those injuries that the seller's nondelivery may have caused. Under Article 46, a court may grant specific performance only if all of the following conditions are met: (1) the buyer had not resorted to another remedy, such as avoidance or price reduction; (2) the seller had failed to deliver or, in the case of nonconforming goods, the nonconformity was so serious that it constituted a fundamental breach; (3) the buyer gave timely notice to the seller that the goods were nonconforming; and (4) the buyer had made a timely request that the seller provide substitute goods. As in the civil law nations, the court may grant specific performance without regard to whether money damages are inadequate.

The provisions of the CISG probably will not have much effect on the law in common law countries. Article 28 places a limit on the buyer's right to specific performance by providing that a court need not grant specific performance unless "it would do so under its own law." Thus, the CISG will have little effect on the use of specific performance in the United States.

Anticipatory Breach

Anticipatory breach occurs when one party clearly sees that the other party to the contract either will not perform a substantial part of its obligations or that it will commit a fundamental breach. The breach may occur as a result of one party repudiating the contract and notifying the other that it will not perform, or it may be determined from the conduct of the breaching party.

---

http://www.law.cornell.edu
Cornell Law School Legal Information Institute, select "Law by Source or Jurisdiction" and choose "Law from Around the World." Links to legal reference sources, constitutions, statutes, and case decisions in countries worldwide.

Right to Suspend Performance.   Either party may *suspend performance* under a contract if one party realizes that the other party will not perform a "substantial part" of its obligations. A buyer may suspend payment when aware of evidence that the seller cannot or will not ship. A seller may suspend shipment when the buyer obviously cannot pay or take delivery of the goods. A seller who has already shipped may stop the goods in transit. The right to suspend performance ends when the other party provides adequate assurance that it will perform. If adequate assurance becomes impossible, the other party may then avoid the contract entirely.

Consider this example: Assume that seller is required to deliver goods by March 15. Seller learns that buyer is insolvent and about to declare bankruptcy. On February 1, seller suspends performance and halts shipment. On March 1, buyer provides bank guarantees to seller that it can pay for the goods. The market price of the goods has risen significantly and seller refuses to ship. Seller is correct in suspending performance, but commits a breach of contract by not accepting buyer's assurance of performance.

Right to Avoidance.   If one of the parties is likely to commit a fundamental breach, the other party may avoid the contract. In contrast to the right to suspend, just discussed, avoidance is allowed where one party will *never* be able to perform. For instance, if the seller's plant burns down, or if an embargo in the seller's country makes it legally impossible to ship the contracted goods, then the buyer may avoid the contract.

Avoidance of Installment Contracts.   When a contract calls for the delivery of goods by installments, the rules of avoidance apply to each individual delivery. Therefore, a single nonconforming shipment may be refused by a buyer if the seller has committed a fundamental breach. Assume that buyer and seller have a contract for 160,000 pounds of peanuts to be shipped from Georgia to Denmark in twenty shipments over a five-year period. One shipment arrives in Denmark and is unfit for human consumption. In terms of the entire contract, the one shipment may not amount to a fundamental breach, but because it is an installment contract, the buyer may avoid the contract with respect to this shipment.

Where the breach of one installment indicates strong grounds that a party will breach future installments, the nonbreaching party may declare the contract avoided if done within a reasonable time. So, if a buyer refuses to pay for one or two installments, the seller may avoid the remainder of the contract.

Events Beyond the Control of the Parties: Excuses for Nonperformance

Occasionally, a party will find that circumstances make carrying out its part of the contract difficult, unprofitable, or even impossible. As a defense to an action for breach of contract, it may claim that it has been excused because intervening events beyond its control have made performance impossible or financially impracticable. But it will have a difficult time convincing a court. Courts generally do not allow a party to escape contractual obligations merely because it becomes unable to perform, even though inability to perform was through no fault of its own. When a seller's employees go on strike, when suppliers fail to deliver raw materials on time, when equipment breaks down, when crops are destroyed due to bad weather, or when a party simply becomes financially distressed, its failure to deliver on time will generally not be excused. This common ruling is in keeping with generally accepted legal principles, which hold that contracts are binding. After all, when parties enter into agreements, do they not weigh these contingencies in setting their prices and establishing their terms? Yet, in the real world in which international transactions are conducted, the parties are liable to find many roadblocks in their path to performance.

Whether an intervening event will cause a party to be excused and discharged from its contractual promise depends on the reasoning used by the court. Some courts reason that a party's performance is excused (1) if performance of the contract has been rendered physically or legally impossible, (2) if the underlying purposes of the contract no longer exist, or (3) if a change in circumstances has rendered the contract commercially or financially impracticable.

Impossibility of Performance

Under English law, a court may excuse a party's nonperformance where it becomes *objectively impossible* for it to perform. The courts hold that it must be impossible for *anyone* to perform, not just this particular party, and that the parties did not expressly assume such risk. Impossibility would therefore excuse nonperformance in cases involving the death of one of the parties, the destruction of the specific subject matter of the contract, or when performance of the contract has been rendered illegal or made impossible due to the fault of the other party. Impossibility is usually recognized only where performance becomes a physical impossibility. The inability to pay money is usually never accepted as an excuse.

Supervening Illegality. A contract becomes impossible to perform and the parties excused when performance becomes illegal or prohibited by su-

pervening government regulation. For instance, suppose that a U.S. company is under contract to ship computers to Iraq. After Iraq's invasion of Kuwait, the U.S. government declared that conducting business with Iraq or shipping goods there was illegal. Because the contract has been rendered illegal, nonperformance is excused.

Frustration of Purpose

Does a contract to purchase a diamond engagement ring from a jeweler become unenforceable because the intended bride jilts her boyfriend? Under the English common law, a party's performance could be excused if some unforeseen event occurred that frustrated the purposes of the contract. This event, called *frustration of purpose,* would have to destroy totally the value of the contract to the party relying on the excuse. Moreover, both parties must have known what the purposes of the contract were. To understand, one might ask the question, "Had this event existed at the time of the contract, would the parties have gone through with it?" In a leading English case, *Knell v. Henry,* 2 K.B. 740 (1903), a party leased a room overlooking the coronation route of the king. When the king took ill and the coronation canceled, the court ruled that the party was excused from paying rent on the room because the coronation was essential to the purposes of the contract. Although it had been *possible* to perform, the party would have realized *no value* in doing so.

However, frustration of purpose is not widely recognized in the United States today.

This is illustrated in the case of *Coker International v. Burlington Industries,* 935 F.2d 267 (4th Cir. 1991). Coker had contracted to purchase textile looms from Burlington for export to Peru. Subsequently, the government of Peru banned the import of this type of machinery and Coker sued Burlington for a return of its deposit. In denying Coker's claim, the court stated, "The contract is not conditioned on any resale by Coker. . . . Coker had both the possibility of profit and the risk of loss from resale. . . . The actions of the government of Peru may have frustrated Coker's intended resale, but it is not the same as the purpose of its contract with Burlington, which was the conveyance of the looms from Burlington to Coker."

Would the case be different if it were the U.S. government prohibiting the export? Probably not. In cases going back at least to 1920, U.S. courts have held that where the buyer's intended purpose was to resell the goods overseas, and it subsequently becomes illegal to export the goods, the contract is not invalid *where the U.S. seller's obligation was to deliver the goods to the buyer within the United States.* The courts reason that the contract only requires delivery of the goods to the buyer within the United States. Where the export provision was never a part of the contract, the buyer will not be let off the hook just because he can no longer make his expected profit on resale outside the country.

Commercial Impracticability

A party to a contract that is prevented from performing may attempt to be excused under the doctrine of *commercial impracticability*. This modern doctrine is used in the United States today. It dates back to 1916 when a court stated, "A thing is impossible in legal contemplation when it is not practicable; and a thing is impracticable when it can be done only at an excessive and unreasonable cost." Today, impracticability in the United States has been codified in the UCC (see Exhibit 4.9) and in Article 79 of the CISG (found in the appendix). Remember, courts hesitate to excuse parties from contracts. Accordingly, the breaching party will be excused only if performance would result in extreme hardship, difficulty, or unreasonable expense as a result of an unforeseen event.

Extreme Hardship, Difficulty, or an Unreasonable Expense. The courts have experienced some difficulty in determining what is a "hardship" and how much additional cost is "unreasonable." If the cost of performing the contract becomes so excessive that performance is rendered unrealistic and senseless, and threatens the viability of the business itself, performance may be excused. Of course, what is a lot of money to one company, may be a drop in the bucket to another. Thus, if a large multinational corporation contracts to deliver goods at a contract price, and discovers that wage increases or an increase in the price of raw materials will cause it to lose millions of dollars on the deal, the courts still may not release the company from its obligation.

EXHIBIT 4.9

Excuse by Failure of Presupposed Conditions

Uniform Commercial Code

2–615. Except so far as a seller may have assumed a greater obligation and subject to the preceding section on substituted performance:

a. Delay in delivery or nondelivery (performance or nonperformance, 2003 amendments) in whole or in part by a seller who complies with paragraphs (b) and (c) is not a breach of his duty under a contract for sale if performance as agreed has been made impracticable by the occurrence of a contingency the nonoccurrence of which was a basic assumption on which the contract was made or by compliance in good faith with any applicable foreign or domestic governmental regulation or order whether or not it later proves to be invalid.

b. Where the causes mentioned in paragraph (a) affect only a part of the seller's capacity to perform, the seller must allocate production and deliveries among its customers but may at its option include regular customers not then under contract as well as its own requirements for further manufacture. The seller may so allocate in any manner which is fair and reasonable.

c. The seller must notify the buyer reasonably that there will be delay or nondelivery and, when allocation is required under paragraph (b), of the estimated quota thus made available for the buyer.

Unforeseen Events. Courts also look to see whether the party claiming the excuse should have foreseen the likelihood of its occurrence. If the event was foreseeable, the nonperforming party will not be released from its obligations. This does not mean that the parties had to foresee the *specific event* that actually occurred. Rather, the parties *should have* foreseen that an event *of this kind* could occur. Thus, if a party is a sophisticated business, experienced and familiar with the risks of entering into this kind of contract, they might have difficulty in proving that they should not have foreseen a particular risk. Consider the following examples:

- A mining company should foresee the possibility of a cave-in.
- A farming conglomerate should foresee the possibility of bad weather.
- An oil company should foresee the possibility of oil price increases in the Middle East.

The courts generally feel that if a particular risk was foreseeable, then the parties would have provided in their contract to be excused if it occurs—if they did not provide for the excuse in the contract, then they must have intended to bear this risk.

Shortages and Market Price Fluctuations.

For the most part, shortages, inflation, and even dramatic fluctuations in market prices are to be anticipated by parties to a contract. Such a result is illustrated by *Eastern Air Lines, Inc. v. Gulf Oil Corp.*, 415 F. Supp. 429 (S.D.Fla. 1975), a case arising out of the oil price increases caused by the Arab oil embargo in 1973. In 1972, Eastern Airlines contracted with Gulf Oil Corporation for a supply of jet aviation fuel. In the following year, the Middle East war and Arab oil embargo of the United States resulted in a 400 percent increase in the price of crude oil. These events caused Gulf to demand a price increase from Eastern and to threaten a cutoff in supply. Eastern brought an action under the UCC to ensure its supply of oil at the contract price. Gulf claimed that the contract as it had been negotiated was commercially impracticable. The court disagreed, noting that not only had Gulf not suffered a sufficient hardship to claim impracticability, but that the actions of the OPEC oil cartel and the resulting energy crisis were reasonably foreseeable by a multinational oil company such as Gulf.

The CISG Exemptions for Impediments Beyond Control

CISG Article 79 provides that a party is not liable for a failure to perform any obligations if (1) it was due to an *impediment beyond control*; (2) the impediment was not reasonably foreseeable at the time the contract was concluded; (3) the impediment was unavoidable and could not be overcome, and (4) notice was given to the other party of the impediment and of its effect on the contract. An impediment does not entirely excuse performance, but merely suspends it during the time that the impediment exists.

---

http://www.cisg.law.pace.edu/ cisg/text/e-text-79.html
This is the site of UN Contracts and International Sale of Goods. See Section IV, Article 79, Exemptions.

Force Majeure Clauses

Courts do not like to release parties from a contract on the basis of an excuse. Under the rule of commercial impracticability, a party will not be excused if the risk was foreseeable because the party is assumed to have provided for that excuse in the contract itself. As a result, lawyers frequently advise their clients to incorporate a *force majeure* clause into a contract.

The term *force majeure* means "superior force." A *force majeure* clause in a contract is an exculpatory clause. It excuses a party from failing to perform on the occurrence of an event specified in the clause itself—a *force majeure*. Of course, this assumes the party claiming the *force majeure* did not cause the event and could not control it. These clauses usually list, specifically, those events that will excuse nonperformance. These events might include war, blockades, fire, acts of governments, inability to obtain export licenses, acts of God, acts of public enemies, failure of transportation, quarantine restrictions, strikes, and others. (For an example of a *force majeure* clause, see the *Terms and Conditions of Sale*, Exhibit 4.5.)

Lawyers advise that *force majeure* clauses should not just provide for standard contingencies such as those listed, but should be tailored to the special nature of the contract and the type of businesses involved. *Force majeure* clauses for the mining industry would not be the same as for the steel or textile industries, for example. A clause in a shipping contract issued by an ocean carrier would be different too because the risks differ. In major contracts, the drafting of a *force majeure* clause requires skilled lawyers. Language that is too narrow may not provide sufficient protection, and language that is too broad may leave too many outs in the contract.

In practice, most *force majeure* clauses do not excuse a party's nonperformance entirely, but only suspend it for the duration of the *force majeure*. Another special type of *force majeure* clause, is the *government approval* clause. Because government permission is often needed to transact business across national borders, many companies include a provision in their contract stating that the contract is subject to obtaining government approval or licenses. The *Harriscom Svenska, AB* case illustrates the operation of a *force majeure* clause.

Harriscom Svenska, AB v. Harris Corp.
3 F.3d 576 (1993)
United States Court of Appeals (2nd Cir.)

BACKGROUND AND FACTS

RF Systems, a division of Harris Corporation, manufactures radio communications products in New York. It appointed Harriscom, a Swedish firm, as its exclusive distributor to the Islamic Republic of Iran. The contract contained a force majeure clause. In 1985 the U.S. Customs Service detained a shipment of radios ordered by Harriscom and bound for Iran. The government prohibited all sales to Iran of goods it categorized as military equipment. In 1986 RF Systems negotiated a compromise under which it agreed to "voluntarily withdraw from all further sales to the Iranian market." Harriscom brought this action for a breach of contract against RF Systems. The District Court granted judgment for the defendants on the basis of commercial impracticability and force majeure, and the plaintiff appealed.

CARDAMONE, CIRCUIT JUDGE

One of the issues before us is whether the manufacturer's refusal to ship the spare parts was a voluntary act on its part, subjecting it to liability to its distributor for damages for breach of contract. We think it a foregone conclusion that a government bureaucracy determined to prevent what it considers military goods from leaving this country and with the will to compel compliance with its directives is an irresistible force, one that cannot reasonably be controlled. The government in these circumstances may be likened to the wife of "Rumpole of the Bailey," John Mortimer's fictional barrister, who describes his wife as "she who must be obeyed." . . .

What appellant ignores is the overwhelming and uncontradicted evidence that the government would not allow RF Systems to continue sales to Iran. RF Systems established the affirmative defense of commercial impracticability because it complied in good faith with the government's informal requirements. Further, for RF Systems to have failed to comply would have been unusually foolhardy and recalcitrant, for the government had undoubted power to compel compliance. Like commercial impracticability, a force majeure clause in a contract excuses nonperformance when circumstances beyond the control of the parties prevent performance. The contracts between these parties specifically contained force majeure clauses to excuse RF Systems' performance under the present circumstances, namely, "governmental interference."

Decision. Summary judgment for the defendant, RF Systems, was affirmed. The *force majeure* clause in the distributorship agreement excused the manufacturer from performance on the grounds of "government interference."

CULTURAL INFLUENCES ON CONTRACT NEGOTIATIONS

Lawyers and businesspeople in different countries treat their approach to negotiating and drafting contracts quite differently. First, Americans tend to approach contract negotiations in an aggressive, adversarial manner. They often view contracting as a win–lose proposition, taking pride in having driven the hardest bargain. This attitude leads them to attempt to gain legal and business advantages over the other party. Similarly, U.S. lawyers, who are accustomed to practicing in a highly litigious society, press for every legal advantage. They draft their contracts in calculated, technical, and detailed language, setting forth exactly how the parties are to perform and what their legal rights are if the deal falls apart.

Negotiating Contracts in Japan

By contrast, contract negotiations in many countries take a much different form. Japan presents perhaps the best example. The role of a contract in Japanese society is influenced tremendously by three aspects of Japanese culture and ancient Confucian thinking. First, every person must strive to maintain harmony and accord in society. From childhood, individuals are taught to avoid disputes and acrimony in their personal and business relationships with others. Second, the maintenance of harmony and the importance placed on personal dignity stress the importance of not causing others to "lose face" or become embarrassed. The considerable social pressure to avoid dishonor works in all aspects of life, including negotiating contracts and resolving contract disputes. Third, the Japanese attach the utmost importance to the social group to which one belongs, particularly to one's school or company. Thus, Japanese businesspeople may be characterized by their group loyalty and their desire for group harmony and consensus.

---

http://www.ita.doc.gov/td/tic/
For the business traveler, information about culture, customs, people, holidays, and political situations in other countries.

These attributes make doing business in Japan, and indeed throughout Asia, different from doing business anywhere else. They also affect the way the Japanese view contractual relationships. A contract is a relationship, and as much a social one as a business one. Therefore, the desire to maintain harmony in society has a dramatic effect on how the Japanese view their business contracts. Instead of the combative approach of U.S. lawyers, Japanese negotiators view the contract as an expression of a common goal and of a desire for a long-lasting business relationship.

These cultural and societal influences affect the manner in which contracts are negotiated and drafted. Because lawyers must do all they can to protect their own clients' interests, they are necessarily adversarial. Japanese firms normally prefer that lawyers not be involved in negotiating, because they feel that lawyers interfere with the parties' concentrating on their mutual business interests. Western negotiators also must remember that they must never put the other parties in a situation in which losing face is the only out. One must be careful not to create embarrassment by making demands without offering something in exchange. By avoiding a loss of face, the parties strengthen their business relationships and reduce the likelihood of misunderstanding and contract disputes.

In addition, a Western company must be prepared to carry out negotiations for an extended period of time. In many cases, the Japanese firm requires a long period of time to reach a group consensus before a decision can be made. Many U.S. senior managers have gone abroad to negotiate a contract only to face frustration at the other party's apparent refusal or unwillingness to conclude an agreement. The U.S. managers simply may not realize that, while they have the authority to bind their firms to the agreement, the foreign party does not. The foreign negotiator may require approval from superiors or from a working group. In doing business in Asia, the watchwords are not only "trust" and "respect," but "patience" as well.

When the contract is finally put into writing, it is typically short and written in little detail. The Japanese consider this necessary because a long-term relationship requires a flexible agreement, and one that the parties can easily modify in the future. Many U.S. lawyers are unaccustomed to this Japanese practice.

The desire to maintain social harmony and to avoid the embarrassment of litigation also affects the manner in which contract disputes are resolved. Unlike contracts between Americans, contracts with the Japanese might state that, in the event of a dispute, "the parties will resolve their disagreement harmoniously and in mutual consultation with each other." If the contract breaks down and the parties disagree over an issue, they are more likely to want to settle the matter through private conciliation. Litigation, while on the increase in Japan as elsewhere, is still to be avoided if at all possible.

---

http://www.ita.doc.gov/
http://www.meti.go.jp/english/index.html
Information on doing business in Japan.

Another factor that U.S. contract negotiators should be aware of is that foreign firms, more so than U.S. firms, rely on technical experts during contract negotiations. More than one U.S. company has failed to obtain an important order because its negotiating team lacked credibility because it did not include the necessary engineers, specialists, or technicians. This is true not only in Japan, but also in many European countries and much of the rest of the world.

China

The People

Deeply rooted in Chinese society is the need to belong and conform to a unit, whether the family, a political party or an organization. The family is the focus of life for most Chinese. Age and rank are highly respected. However, to the dismay of older people, today's young people are rapidly modernizing, wearing blue jeans and sunglasses, drinking Coke, and driving motorbikes.

Meeting and Greeting
- Shake hands upon meeting. Chinese may nod or bow instead of shaking hands, although shaking hands has become increasingly common.
- When introduced to a Chinese group, they may greet you with applause. Applaud back.
- Senior persons begin greetings. Greet the oldest, most senior person before others. During group introductions, line up according to seniority with the senior person at the head of the line.

Names and Titles
- Use family names and appropriate titles until specifically invited by your Chinese host or colleagues to use their given names.
- Address the Chinese by Mr., Mrs., Miss plus family name. Note: married women always retain their maiden name.
- Chinese are often addressed by their government or professional titles. For example, address Li Pang using his title: Mayor Li or Director Li.
- Names may have two parts; for example: Wang Chien. Traditional Chinese family names are placed first with the given name (which has one or two syllables) coming last (family name: Wang; given: Chien).
- Chinese generally introduce their guests using their full titles and company names. You should do the same. Example: Doctor John Smith, CEO of American Data Corporation.

Corporate Culture
The Chinese are practical in business and realize they need Western investment, but dislike dependency on foreigners. They are suspicious and fearful of being cheated or pushed around by foreigners, who are perceived as culturally and economically corrupt. It is very difficult to break through the "them vs. us" philosophy (foreign partner vs. Chinese). In personal relationships, the Chinese will offer friendship and warm hospitality without conflict, but in business they are astute negotiators.

- Punctuality is important for foreign businesspeople. Being late is rude.
- Business cards are exchanged upon meeting. Business cards should be printed in English on one side and Chinese on the other.
- English is not spoken in business meetings, although some Chinese may understand English without making it known. Hire an interpreter or ask for one to be provided.
- Be prepared for long meetings and lengthy negotiations (often ten days straight) with many delays.
- The Chinese will enter a meeting with the highest-ranking person entering first. They will assume the first member of your group to enter the room is the leader of your delegation. The senior Chinese person welcomes everyone. The foreign leader introduces his/her team, and each member distributes his/her card. The leader invites the Chinese to do the same.
- Seating is very important at a meeting. The host sits to the left of the most important guest.
- There may be periods of silence at a business meeting; do not interrupt these.
- A contract is considered a draft subject to change. Chinese may agree on a deal and then change their minds. A signed contract is not binding and does not mean negotiations will end.
- Observing seniority and rank are extremely important in business.
- The status of the people who make the initial contact with the Chinese is very important. Don't insult the Chinese by sending someone with a low rank.
- Chinese negotiators may try to make foreign negotiators feel guilty about setbacks; they may

continued

continued

then manipulate this sense of guilt to achieve certain concessions.

- Two Chinese negotiating tricks designed to make you agree to concessions are staged temper tantrums and a feigned sense of urgency.
- If the Chinese side no longer wishes to pursue the deal, they may not tell you. To save their own face, they may become increasingly inflexible and hard-nosed, forcing you to break off negoti-

ations. In this way, they may avoid blame for the failure.

The continuation of this document is at http://schaffer.westbuslaw.com, Chapter 4.

Reprinted with permission. Excerpted from *Put Your Best Foot Forward* series by Mary Murray Bosrock. © 2003 International Education Systems, St. Paul, MN. For more information about IES products, please visit http://www.MaryBosrock.com.

CHAPTER SUMMARY

All commerce and trade require a stable and predictable legal environment in which to prosper. In recent years, the international community has agreed on a common body of international sales law, the *U.N. Convention on Contracts for the International Sale of Goods*. The CISG is important not only because it governs transactions for the trade in goods between parties in those nations that have adopted it, but also because it represents internationally accepted legal principles of sales law.

The CISG was drafted under the aegis of the United Nations by skilled lawyers representing countries with diverse political, economic, and legal systems. It has already achieved wide international acceptance, and more countries are expected to adopt it in the years to come.

This chapter does not purport to cover all aspects of international sales law. For example, the actual mechanics of the transaction to see how the contract is carried out by the parties is yet to be discussed. The next two chapters look at how goods are shipped, paid for, and what happens if the goods are lost at sea. These chapters also examine the responsibility of the carrier for transporting the goods, and the carrier's relationship to buyer and seller.

Questions and Case Problems

1. Bende had a contract to sell boots to the government of Ghana for $158,500. Bende promised to deliver the boots "as soon as possible." Bende then contracted with Kiffe who agreed to make the boots in Korea and to deliver them in Ghana within sixty to ninety days at a price of $95,000. The contract contained no *force majeure* clause. Kiffe knew that Bende was going to resell the boots. Kiffe failed to deliver the boots on the agreed date because a train had derailed carrying the boots in Nebraska. Bende brought this action against Kiffe for breach of contract. *Bende and Sons, Inc. v. Crown Recreation and Kiffe Products*, 548 F. Supp 1018 (E.D.N.Y. 1982).

   a. Kiffe claims that the contract had been rendered commercially impracticable and that performance was excused. Do you agree? Why or why not? Was the train wreck foreseeable or unforeseeable?

   b. What could Kiffe have done in negotiating the contract to protect itself from this contingency?

   c. If Bende would have incurred an additional $18,815 in freight charges and miscellaneous costs had the breach not occurred, what would be its measure of damages? Is Bende entitled to lost profits? How are damages measured in a case such as this?

   d. In this case, the risk of damage or loss to the boots while in transit remained with the seller, Kiffe. How would the case differ if the parties had agreed that Kiffe would merely ship the goods by a certain date (instead of deliver) and that Kiffe would bear the risk of loss during transit? (You may have to wait until the next chapter to answer this one.)

2. The defendant purchased sewing machines from a Swiss manufacturer in Swiss francs. The machines were imported into the United States for sale

through distributors. The importer's contract with a distributor contained an "open-price term" that allowed it to pass cost increases in the machines to the distributor. The open-price term worked well until fluctuation in the exchange rate between the U.S. dollar and the Swiss franc became extreme. When the Swiss franc rose in value against the dollar, the importer's profit margin was cut in half. The importer then imposed a 10 percent surcharge to protect itself. The distributor did not feel that this additional "cost" fell under the term used in the contract. The importer believed that increased costs due to currency fluctuations were covered by the open-price term, and further, that the exchange risk had rendered performance under the contract commercially impracticable. The distributor brought this action to have the contract enforced at its original price. Judgment for whom, and why? *Bernina Distributors v. Bernina Sewing Machine Co., 646 F.2d 434 (10th Cir. 1981).*

3. The CISG contains no provisions that a contract for the sale of goods be supported by consideration. Further, the CISG does not address questions related to the validity of the contract, including legality, mistake, fraud, duress, or undue influence. How will national courts handle these issues in cases that they might be called upon to decide under the CISG? In common law countries? In civil law countries of Europe? How has this been addressed by courts in the United States?

4. CISG Articles 71–73 contain legal rules on anticipatory breach. Article 77 contains rules on the mitigation of damages. These articles can be found in the appendix. Consider the following case: Contract provides that Mexicana Fabricators, S.A., deliver 1,000 personal computer housings by December 1 to AES Computer, Inc., in Austin, Texas, for a total price of $50,000. On July 1, Mexicana faxed AES that due to a rise in prices they could not deliver for less than $60,000. AES replied that it would insist that Mexicana deliver at the $50,000 price. From July 1 through September, AES could have bought the housings from other suppliers for $55,000 for December 1 delivery. On December 1, AES covered and purchased the housings for $64,000 for delivery on February 1. Because of the delay until February 1, AES Computer suffered additional damages of $2,000. What is the measure of AES's damages? Was AES under any duty to mitigate damages? Why or why not?

5. An importer of children's toys, Fun 'N Games, Inc., receives a price quotation from a German toy maker offering toy train sets: "KBG train sets. Locomotive. Four cars. Transformers. Thirty pieces of track. Minimum order thirty sets. $7,500 C.I.F.

Baltimore." Fun 'N Games, Inc., sends an order stating: "Ship 30 KBG train sets: to include locomotive, four cars, transformer, forty pieces of track," along with a check for $7,500. Was the price quotation from the German toy maker an offer? If it was, how does Fun 'N Games' change in terms—"forty pieces of track"—affect acceptance? If the German toy maker ships the thirty sets with "thirty pieces of track," does a contract exist? Decide the case under the common law, the UCC, and the CISG.

6. A computer printer distributor in Argentina receives an offer by mail from Epson, a U.S. company, in reply to an inquiry. The offer arrives in Argentina on June 2. On June 12, the Argentinean company sends its acceptance by mail. On June 8, Epson sends a revocation of its offer that was received on June 13 in Argentina. The acceptance from Argentina arrives in the United States on June 17. Did a valid contract arise? When was the offer valid? When was the acceptance valid? When was the revocation valid? Decide the case under the common law and under the CISG.

7. Your company, Acme Widgets, sells its widgets worldwide. Acme has a contract for 250,000 widgets to be shipped to the Czech Republic. The price stated in the offer and acceptance is $1 per widget, C.I.F. Prague. During the production of the widgets, the price of one component increases 250 percent due to a shortage. In addition these widgets are due for shipment on June 15 and arrival in Prague no later than July 1. On June 15, a stevedores' strike begins, which lasts for sixty days. Are either or both of these factors—material price increase and the stevedores' strike—an excuse for Acme's nonperformance? What legal theory might Acme use under U.S. common law as an excuse? Under the CISG?

8. A German seller brought a claim against a Russian buyer because the buyer failed to pay for the equipment supplied to the buyer pursuant to their contract. The buyer acknowledged it had received the goods but said its nonpayment should be excused as it was due to the failure of the bank responsible for the buyer's foreign currency transactions to make payment to the seller. The buyer claimed the fact it lacked the available currency resources should be regarded as a *force majeure*, discharging it from liability for nonpayment to the buyer. The contract did include a *force majeure* clause but it did not refer to the buyer's lack of foreign currency. Do you agree with the buyer? *Tribunal of International Commercial Arbitration at the Russian Federation Chamber of Commerce and Industry 17 October 1995. (See case law on UNICTRAL texts*

Abstract No. 142; it is reproduced with permission on Pace University's CISG Web site.)

9. Henri Ramel, a French wine merchant, contracted to purchase Italian wine from Sacovini, a firm with a place of business in Italy. The wine delivered by Sacovini became chaptalized (it turned to vinegar) and the French buyer sought to avoid the contract claiming the wine it received was not of merchantable quality. The seller said it did deliver the wine specified so it did not breach its contract obligation. The CISG applies to the contract and the buyer claims Article 35 requires the seller to deliver goods conforming to the contract (wine the buyer could sell as drinking wine). Did the seller's delivery of chaptalized wine meet the requirements of the CISG Article 35? *Societe Sacovini v. Societe Les fil de Henri Ramel 23 January 1996 Cour de Cassation (French Supreme Court)*. (The Abstract of this case found in the UNICTRAL case Abstracts, No. 150. Consult the Pace University CISG Web site.)

10. An Austrian buyer brought a claim against a Ukrainian seller for damages resulting from the seller's refusal to deliver a certain quantity of goods. The seller claimed it never reached a contract with the buyer. The seller had sent a telex to the buyer regarding the nature of the goods, their quantity, and period for delivery. The telex stated the price could be agreed to ten days prior to the new year.

The buyer confirmed the contents of the telex but said nothing regarding the price. The parties did not subsequently agree as to the price. Did the lack of agreement on an established price prevent the parties from reaching a valid contract under the CISG? (The CISG controlled because the parties elected Austrian law and that law referred to the CISG for international sales contracts.) *Tribunal of International Commercial Arbitration at the Russian Federation Chamber of Commerce and Industry 3 March 1995*. (The Abstract of this case is found in the UNICTRAL case Abstracts. Consult the Pace University CISG Web site.)

Managerial Implications

You are the vice president of sales for DownPillow International, Inc., a U.S. manufacturer of bed pillows. The raw materials needed for making pillows are all sourced from suppliers overseas. Your firm purchases feathers from exporters in China who maintain large flocks of geese and ducks for breeding. Cotton ticking and other textiles are purchased from mills in Germany. Every year you show your products at the International Bed Show in New York. This year, a delegation of Japanese buyers, representing several well-known Tokyo stores, showed interest in your best quality pillows. The president of your firm expressed interest in these contacts because although Americans use the same old cruddy pillow forever, the Japanese are fastidious about their bedding. You followed up with samples, product, and pricing information. After several discussions and months of correspondence, you now expect to be receiving your first overseas orders.

You are to meet with legal counsel next week to discuss this opportunity. What questions might you want to ask about entering a sales contract with a Japanese buyer? If a buyer shows interest in purchasing large quantities, should you consider a visit to their Tokyo office? What would you accomplish? Should your attorney conduct negotiations there for you? If you and your buyer agree to put your agreement in writing, what terms might the document contain? Your customers want assurances that their pillows will be made of the

finest white goose down, with less than 10 percent feathers. What assurance will you be able to give them regarding product quality and specifications? What factors might influence the selection of a choice of law clause? Do you think your lawyer will insist on a *force majeure* clause? Can you suggest some of the things DownPillow might want in its clause?

If you anticipate that you may have several accounts in Japan, and each of them will be sending in purchase orders for each order, will you need a confirmation form? Will your attorney recommend that you develop a standard form to use for confirming all export orders? How will this form differ from the form you use for domestic shipments? What kind of provisions should it have?

How might negotiating your supply contracts with the Chinese differ from dealing with the German textile mills? You have some concern about making sure that the quality of the down from China remains consistent. How can you be assured that you will receive goose down and not duck down? What other precautions should you take? The German mill has asked that your orders be mailed in or faxed. Your lawyer recommends that certain terms be put into your purchase order form. What might they be? Your purchase order states that the seller is liable for consequential damages for late shipment. The mill's confirmation states that "the liability of the seller is limited to the replacement of returned goods." In the event of a dispute, which will prevail under U.S. law? Under German law? Under the CISG?

Your contract with the Japanese buyer specifies that the CISG is to govern the transaction. Your pillows arrive in Japan and the buyer discovers that they contain only 13 oz. of down instead of the full 16 oz. of down as promised. You goofed and want to resolve the problem. But, the buyer has just been offered the same quality pillow at considerably lower prices from a firm in Taiwan and wants out. Discuss the rights of each of the parties under the CISG.

CHAPTER 5

THE DOCUMENTARY SALE AND TERMS OF TRADE

Chapter Four discussed how the contract represents the agreement of the parties to an international sale. Their agreement typically includes the description and price of the goods, warranties, and other essential terms. The contract also can specify other important terms and conditions of sale, including the conditions of payment, the shipping and insurance terms, and the responsibility for damage to the goods while in transit. These terms and conditions are even more important in an international sale than in a sale to a domestic customer because of the greater distances involved, the time and costs of transportation, and the added dangers of an air or sea journey. Each party must be aware of the risks of moving goods and money over great distance and be prepared to negotiate terms that are mutually acceptable to both parties.

The first part of this chapter looks at how the parties use secure payment terms that provide assurance that the seller will be paid and that the buyer will receive the goods. This assurance helps them to manage significant transaction risks. The discussion provides the opportunity to study the documentary sale and the law of negotiable bills of lading.

Next, the text examines how to allocate, to either the buyer or seller, the risk of damage to the goods while in transit. Despite the importance of air transport today, the greatest volume of cargo is still carried by sea. Although all forms of transportation put cargo at risk, ocean cargo can be imperiled by time, moisture, storms, shipwrecks, and, even today, piracy. Both parties want to know exactly when the risk of loss to the goods passes from the seller to the buyer.

The text also discusses how the parties can allocate the responsibility for shipping arrangements and charges. In international trade, the shipping terms are an integral part of the price terms. Because of the high cost of freight, the parties typically negotiate the invoice price for the goods and the shipping terms as a package deal. A seller may then offer the goods for one price at the factory, another at a seaport, and yet another for the goods delivered to the buyer's warehouse. This chapter describes how the parties negotiate these terms as a part of the terms of sale.

PAYMENT AND DELIVERY RISK

The discussion begins by looking at how seller and buyer might manage both payment and delivery risk in an international sale. The risk that the buyer will fail to pay is called the seller's *payment risk* (often called *credit risk*). The risk that the buyer will fail to receive the goods is called the buyer's *delivery risk*. The buyer will want assurance that the goods will be shipped on time, properly packaged, and adequately insured.

No seller would want to ship goods overseas and place them into the hands of a foreign buyer without some assurance of payment. Once the goods leave the seller's control, any remedies to recover from the buyer can be costly and time-consuming. If the buyer fails or refuses to pay, the seller might have to resort to litigation in the buyer's country in order to recover the money owed. Even then, recovery might become impossible, such as where the buyer becomes insolvent or bankrupt.

Ideally, if they could have their way, sellers would like to have *cash in advance* from foreign buyers before the goods leave their hands. On the other hand, few buyers would part with their money merely in the hope that the goods they ordered would ever arrive. Once the seller has the cash, what motivation would induce the seller to ship conforming goods, or goods that are not defective, or any goods at all? The seller may have no long-term interest in exporting to a foreign market, or may just be dishonest. Cultural and language barriers might make it especially hard to gauge a seller's honesty or intentions. So, this payment option, cash in advance, usually will not serve to bring buyer and seller together.

On the other hand, all buyers would like to be able to buy on open credit terms, or on *open account*. In domestic sales, for the seller who has had an opportunity to learn the creditworthiness of the buyer, sales are often made on, say, 30-day open account terms. However, few sellers would risk shipping their goods to a foreign market, giving up possession, control, and even ownership of the goods, to a buyer so far away. Perhaps after a long relationship has developed between them, they may agree to do business this way; but an open account sale is usually not secure enough for most larger international transactions. In addition, a seller who quotes on open account in a foreign currency bears considerable currency risk during the open credit period. Thus, if cash in advance or open account were the only payment options, buyer and seller would be at an impasse. To bring them together, some other methods of assuring that the seller will ship and the buyer will pay as promised are required. One method that provides such assurance is the documentary sale.

THE DOCUMENTARY SALE

The *documentary sale* is a type of contract for the sale of goods in which the buyer is required to pay upon the presentation of a negotiable document of title by the seller (see Exhibit 5.1). It serves to reduce the transaction risks between a buyer and a seller who are great distances apart by assuring that if one releases the title to the goods the other will release the money.

The documentary sale is a unique method of exchange devised by early traders as their sailing vessels traveled medieval trade routes. The method spread by custom and practice, and eventually became recognized in early English law—in the modern common law countries and in the civil law countries of Europe. Today, the documentary sale is a common type of contract for the sale of goods.

The Document of Title

The key to understanding the documentary sale is understanding the nature of a *document of title*. Documents of title are legal instruments that evidence the ownership of goods. Common documents of title include dock receipts, warehouse receipts, and bills of lading. They are issued by a party (known as the *bailee*) in receipt for goods taken into its possession from a *bailor*. Documents of title may be either negotiable or nonnegotiable. A *negotiable document* is one that can legally be transferred from one party to another in return for value or payment. Negotiable documents of title are used to transfer ownership of goods from one party to another without the necessity of transferring physical possession of the goods themselves. The property can stay in the possession of the bailee, while the owner can safely trade, barter, pledge, or deal with it in the commercial world.

The Bill of Lading

A *bill of lading* is a document of title issued by a *carrier* to a shipper upon receiving goods for transport (see Exhibit 5.2). Having first been used in the sixteenth century, the bill of lading has played a vital role in international trade. It serves three purposes:

1. A receipt for the goods from the carrier, indicating any damage to the goods that was visible at the time of loading.
2. The contract of carriage between the shipper and the carrier (i.e., a *transport document*).
3. The document of title to the goods described in it.

Other types of transport documents will serve as a contract of carriage, but do not act as a document of title.

Order and Bearer Documents. Only negotiable bills of lading are used in documentary sales. To be negotiable, they must state that the goods are

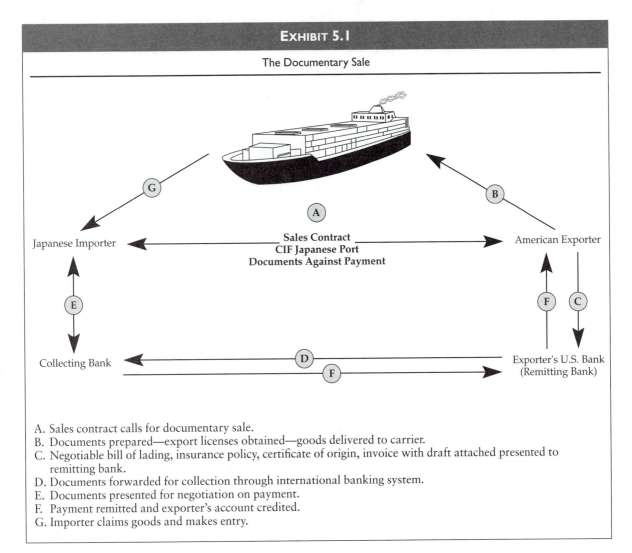

EXHIBIT 5.1

The Documentary Sale

Japanese Importer

Sales Contract
CIF Japanese Port
Documents Against Payment

American Exporter

Collecting Bank

Exporter's U.S. Bank
(Remitting Bank)

A. Sales contract calls for documentary sale.
B. Documents prepared—export licenses obtained—goods delivered to carrier.
C. Negotiable bill of lading, insurance policy, certificate of origin, invoice with draft attached presented to remitting bank.
D. Documents forwarded for collection through international banking system.
E. Documents presented for negotiation on payment.
F. Payment remitted and exporter's account credited.
G. Importer claims goods and makes entry.

to be delivered "to the bearer" or "to the order of" a named person. Negotiable bearer documents can be transferred to another party by mere delivery of the document. Because of the danger that they might fall into the wrong hands, bearer documents are not used for foreign trade.

Because of the protection they provide to the seller, order bills of lading are the most common type of bill used in international transactions. Once a carrier issues a bill of lading, the carrier may surrender the goods only to the holder of the bill. If the carrier delivers to anyone else, it will be liable to the holder for *misdelivery of the goods*.

Because the carrier is required to deliver the goods only to the holder of the bill of lading, the seller may make the bill payable to its own order

so that the buyer is prevented from gaining possession of the goods before payment is made. After receiving payment, the seller then endorses the bill of lading to the order of the buyer or the bank that is financing the transaction. Unfortunately, however, mistakes may prevent the process of exporting from running smoothly.

In the United States, the laws governing the negotiability of bills of lading are the *Federal Bills of Lading Act* (for bills originating in the United States for export shipments) and the *Uniform Commercial Code*.

> **http://www.forwarderlaw.com**
> A comprehensive resource for legal information on freight forwarding.

EXHIBIT 5.2

Ocean Bill of Lading

OCEAN BILL OF LADING

Shipper/Exporter	Export References
Shipper's name Address	Invoice or order number (Not negotiable unless consigned to order)

Consignee: (Complete Name and Address) To the order of: Shipper	Forwarding Agent – References Shippers Freight Forwarder

	Forwarding Agent – References U.S.A.	Forwarding Agent – References

Notify Party (Complete Name and Address) Buyer or buyer's import agent	Domestic Routing/Export Instructions Pre-carriage These commodities licensed by U.S. for ultimate destination Japan and for resale to any destination except North Korea, Iraq, Cambodia, or Cuba.

Pier	Onward Inland Routing	Place of delivery
Ocean Vessel	Flag	Port of Loading	
Port of Discharge	For Transshipment To	

Carrier's Receipt — **Particulars Furnished By Shipper**

Marks and Numbers	No. of Cont. or Other Pkgs.	Description of Goods	Gross Weight	Measurement
Container No. UP 362459 Seal # 2398112 Shipping Marks: Down Bedding	95	1 x 40' container said to contain down pillows on invoices to be as per proforma invoices nos. 2368714, 2368715 dated April 15, 2006. "Shipper Load, Stuff & Count" Clean Shipped on board 5/10/2006 "Freight Prepaid" House to port basis Signed _____ Title of Company Official	1,550 Kg (Net)	

ON BOARD

Received in apparent good order and condition except as otherwise noted hereon the goods, containers, or other packages, or units mentioned above for transportation from the place of receipt if named above or (if not named) the port of loading to the port of discharge or place of delivery (as the case may be) subject to exceptions, limitations, conditions and liberties hereof and there to be delivered to the consignee or his or their assigns.

(TERMS OF THIS BILL OF LADING CONTINUED ON REVERSE SIDE HEREOF)

Freight Charges	Prepaid	Collect
Land Charges		
Port Charges		
Ocean Charges		
Container Rental		
Total	4850.00	

B/L No.

IN WITNESS WHEREOF, The Master or Agent of said vessel has affirmed to THREE (3) _____ Bills of Lading, all of this tenor and date, one of which being accomplished, the others stand void.

Carrier: TAMPA BAY STEAMSHIP JACKSONVILLE, FLA.

By _____
Agent (for the Master) TBS

Dated at Port of Shipment	Mo. 5	Day 10	Yr. 02

Importance of Negotiability to Trade. The negotiability of the bill of lading is what makes it so important to trade. As the document is bought and sold, so too are the goods it represents. Negotiability permits merchants to trade in cargo while it is still afloat. With a bill of lading, goods can be bought and sold, time and again, while they are still on the high seas, with the bill of lading circling the globe from one buyer to the next. This practice is, in fact, quite common. Persian Gulf oil can change hands twenty or thirty times in the six weeks that it takes a tanker to reach U.S. waters.

The negotiability of bills of lading was recognized in most European trading centers at least as early as the sixteenth century. Early records of them have been found in many languages. In 1883, Lord Justice Bowen described the bill of lading in this time-honored description from *Sanders Brothers v. Maclean & Co.,* 11 Q.B.D. 327 at 341 (1883).

> The law as to the indorsement of bills of lading is as clear as in my opinion the practice of all European merchants is thoroughly understood. A cargo at sea while in the hands of the carrier is necessarily incapable of physical delivery. During this period of transit and voyage, the bill of lading by the law merchant is universally recognized as its symbol, and the indorsement and delivery of the bill of lading operates as a symbolical delivery of the cargo. Property in the goods passes by such indorsement and delivery of the bill of lading, whenever it is the intention of the parties that the property should pass, just as under similar circumstances the property would pass by an actual delivery of the goods. And for the purpose of passing such property in the goods and completing the title of the indorsee to full possession thereof, the bill of lading, until complete delivery of the cargo has been made on shore to some one rightfully claiming under it, remains in force as a symbol, and carries with it not only the full ownership of the goods, but also all rights created by the contract of carriage between the shipper and the shipowner. It is a key which in the hands of a rightful owner is intended to unlock the door of the warehouse, floating or fixed, in which the goods may chance to be.

As the vessel bearing the goods proceeds out of the harbor and onto the open ocean, the seller safely retains the title to the merchandise, literally held in hand. The seller can sell the goods as planned by sending the bill of lading ahead to the buyer, divert the shipment to another buyer around the globe, pledge it for a loan, or bring it home. This unique flexibility has made the documentary sale essential to world trade and the international economy.

Documentary Collections

The *documentary collection* is the process by which banking institutions serve as intermediaries between seller and buyer to handle the exchange of the bill of lading for payment. The documentary collection is an integral part of the documentary sale. It provides a safer alternative for payment than either cash in advance or sale on open account. The parties might indicate their desire for a documentary collection by specifying in the contract that payment terms are "cash against documents" or "documents against payment." Such an indication is not always essential because the collection process is implied in most documentary sales contracts.

Typically, the documentary collection works like this: Seller places the goods in the hands of a carrier and receives a bill of lading in return. Seller endorses the bill of lading and presents it to the bank for collection. Along with the bill of lading, the seller will include other essential documents, such as a *marine insurance* policy on the goods covering the risks of the ocean voyage. A *certificate of origin* (see Exhibit 5.3) may be required by customs regulations in the buyer's country. The seller's *commercial invoice* describing the goods and showing the price to be paid is always required. Finally, a *documentary draft* will be needed to expedite the exchange of money. The draft is a negotiable instrument used to make payment for the invoice and for the bill of lading. As described in a later chapter, the draft is a negotiable "order to pay" made out by the seller, drawn on the buyer for collection, and payable to the order of the seller. Its purpose is to tell the parties how much to pay when purchasing the bill of lading. The draft will also be needed by the bank if financing is to be provided for the sale. Other documents may be required, as well, depending on the needs of the parties or the export-import regulations of their countries.

EXHIBIT 5.3

Certificate of Origin for U.S. Export Sale

CERTIFICATE OF ORIGIN

SHIPPER/EXPORTER	DOCUMENT NO.
ABC Company 123 Elm St. Anytown, NC 12345	EXPORT REFERENCES Shipper Ref: PO# 0001

CONSIGNEE	FORWARDING AGENT – REFERENCES
XYZ Corporation 456 Wind St. Anycity, France	Smith Forwarders/REF 10001
	POINT AND COUNTRY OF ORIGIN NC, USA

NOTIFY PARTY	DOMESTIC ROUTING/EXPORT INSTRUCTIONS
Foreign Custom Broker 1001 Maple Ave. Anycity, France	

PIER OR AIRPORT
Charlotte

EXPORTING CARRIER (Vessel/Airline) US Air	PORT OF LOADING Charlotte	DESCRIPTION
AIR/SEA PORT OF DISCHARGE Paris	FOR TRANSHIPMENT TO Anycity	

PARTICULARS FURNISHED BY SHIPPER

MARKS AND NUMBERS	NO. OF PKGS.	DESCRIPTION	NET KILOS OR POUNDS	GROSS KILOS	GROSS POUNDS
MKD: AS ADDR PO# 0001	10	Cartons Leather Aprons	97 KG	109	240

The undersigned _ ABC Company _ _ _ _ (Owner or Agent), does hereby declare for the above named shipper, the goods as described above were shipped on the above date and consigned as indicated and are products of the United States of America.

Dated at _ _ _ _ _ _ Anytown, NC _ _ _ _ _ _ _ _ on the _ 01 _ _ day of _ _ _ _ _ _ June _ _ _ _ _ _ _ _ _ 20 06 _ _ .

Sworn to before me this _ 01 _ _ day of _ _ _ _ _ June _ _ _ _ _ _ _ _ _ 20 06 _ _ .

_ _
SIGNATURE OF OWNER OR AGENT

The_ _ _ _ _ _ _ _ _ Anytown Chamber of Commerce _ , a recognized Chamber of Commerce under the laws of the State of _ _ _ _ North Carolina _ _ _ _ , has examined the manufacturer's invoice or shipper's affidavit concerning the origin of the merchandise, and, according to the best of its knowledge and belief, finds that the products named originated in the United States of America.

Secretary _

The seller's bank forwards the draft and documents to a *collecting bank* in the buyer's country, with instructions that the documents can be released to the buyer only upon payment of the draft. The collecting bank negotiates the documents to the buyer upon payment of the draft, and remits the money back to the seller's bank. In addition to the many variations of the collection process, banks offer a range of *trade finance* services to help finance the deal between buyer and seller.

Rights of Purchasers of Bills of Lading

Although some readers may be familiar with the rights of parties that purchase *negotiable instruments,* such as checks and promissory notes, the law regarding the transfer and sale of *negotiable documents* is somewhat different because their functions are different. Negotiable instruments serve as a substitute for money, while negotiable documents are used to move goods.

Good-Faith Purchasers of Bills of Lading.

In order for documents of title to be freely accepted in commerce and trade, the law gives special protection to purchasers of bills of lading (and other documents of title as well). Purchasers take their documents free from the adverse claims of other parties to the goods. The rights of the purchaser of a document depends on whether the case is governed in the United States by Article 7 of the *Uniform Commercial Code,* or by the *Federal Bills of Lading Act.* This discussion generally applies to both laws. Under the UCC, special protection is accorded to holders by due negotiation, also called good-faith purchasers.

A *holder by due negotiation* or a *good-faith purchaser* is one who purchases the document (1) for value (and not in settlement of a past debt), (2) in good faith and without any notice of any adverse claim against it, and (3) in the ordinary course of business or financing. If it is an order instrument, then the *good-faith purchaser* must take it by endorsement. When a buyer, bank, or other party takes a document as a good-faith purchaser, it acquires even greater rights in the document than the one from which it had been negotiated. In other words, the good-faith purchaser takes the document free from any claims that other parties might have against either the document or the goods.

Consider the following case: A entrusts goods to B for storage. B delivers the goods to a carrier, obtains a bill of lading, negotiates the document to C, and absconds with the money. C, who is a good-faith purchaser, takes title to both the document and the goods. A may not reclaim them because C takes *paramount title.* C's rights are paramount even to the original owner because B had been entrusted with the goods and then wrongfully sold them. There are many cases where the good-faith purchaser takes greater rights than the transferor of the document had. But in other instances, a good-faith purchaser would not enjoy greater rights. For instance, when a thief steals goods and obtains a bill of lading, a purchaser of the document does not obtain paramount title over the original owner. In the following case, *Banque de Depots v. Ferroligas,* the court addresses the rights of a party who takes a bill of lading by "due negotiation." Notice how the court attempts to protect the rights of these purchasers of negotiable documents.

Different rules apply to transferees of *nonnegotiable* bills of lading and to transferees of negotiable bills of lading who did not take them by due negotiation or as good-faith purchasers. In these cases, the holder receives only those rights that the transferor had, or which the transferor had the actual authority to convey, and no more. Recall the example in which A entrusted goods to B for storage. Here, B transfers a nonnegotiable bill of lading to C and absconds with the money. A can reclaim the goods from C.

Carrier's Misdelivery.

The carrier may deliver the goods only to the holder of an original bill of lading. Assume that A entrusts a shipment of animal skins to an ocean carrier and obtains a bill of lading. The carrier delivers the goods to B without asking B to produce the document. Without knowledge of what has occurred, A sells the bill to C, who takes it for value and in good faith. C is the good-faith purchaser and the owner of the goods, and may bring an action to reclaim the goods from B. C also has a cause of action against the carrier for misdelivery of the goods because the carrier violated the terms of the contract of carriage.

Shipside Bonds.

If a consignee is expecting an ocean shipment, but the bill of lading either has not yet arrived or is lost or destroyed, the consignee can claim its goods by posting a *shipside*

Banque de Depots v. Ferroligas
569 So. 2d 40 (1990)
Court of Appeals of Louisiana, 4th Circuit

BACKGROUND AND FACTS

Banque de Depots, a Swiss banker, brought an action against Bozel, a Brazilian exporter, seeking a money judgment because Bozel had allegedly misapplied the bank's funds. The bank obtained an order seizing 1,300 metric tons of calcium silicon located in a Louisiana port. The calcium silicon was shipped under ocean bills of lading by Bozel from Rio de Janeiro to New Orleans for transit to three purchasers, none of whom were domiciled in Louisiana. The documents were still in the hands of the collecting banks, and had not yet been negotiated to the buyers. Bozel asked the court to free the goods because he was not the owner of the bills of lading.

LOBRANO, JUDGE

Bozel asserts that . . . title to the cargo follows the bills of lading, and once those were transferred to the collecting banks, they [Bozel] were no longer the owner of the cargo.

The Bank asserts that . . . only bills of lading which are "duly negotiated" transfer ownership of goods. . . . They contend that the bills of lading may have been transferred to the collecting banks, but they were not "duly negotiated" . . . since there was no value given prior to the attachment. . . .

We agree that Louisiana law governs the ownership of the cargo when it reached Chalmette, La. Article 2 of the UCC has not been adopted in Louisiana, hence the courts must look to the Louisiana Civil Code in determining the ownership of movables. . . .

The holder of a duly negotiated bill of lading acquires title to the document and title to the goods described therein. It is clear that once a carrier has issued a negotiable bill of lading for goods being placed in commerce, the intent of the law is to protect those who subsequently become holders through "due negotiation." Part and parcel of that intent is the protection afforded the [carrier] in relinquishing possession of the goods to the holder of the document. Thus, although goods in the possession of a [carrier] may have been seized, if the document's negotiation has not been enjoined or the document is not in its possession, [Louisiana law] permits the [carrier] to surrender the goods to the duly negotiated holder. The law protects that holder from acquiring goods that are subject to a seizure. Any other conclusion would lead to the absurd result of requiring the holder, prior to his purchase of the bill of lading, to check every jurisdiction through which the goods passed to determine if it has been seized by judicial process. This would defeat the purpose of our commercial laws.

The record is clear that on May 14, 1990, the date of the seizure, the negotiable bill of lading were outstanding. They were not in the hands of the carrier and their negotiation had not been enjoined. As discussed, the validity of the attachment must be determined as of the date it was issued. The Bank cannot cure this defect by seeking to impound the bills of lading after it obtained the seizure. To hold otherwise would create an impossible contradiction in our commercial laws since the "seized" goods would still be subject to the legal effects of the unimpaired "due negotiation" of the corresponding bills of lading. The legal "capture" of the bills of lading is a prerequisite to the seizure of the goods.

We order that the writ of attachment be dissolved.

Decision.   A court-ordered seizure of goods in transit cannot stand when the title to the goods is represented by a bill of lading and the bill of lading itself was not seized by the court order.

Comment.   The Swiss bank was attempting to assert jurisdiction over Bozel by seizing its cargo in the United States. Although this attempt failed, the court stated that the bank was free to continue to find other ways to get Bozel.

bond. A shipside bond, sometimes called a *steamship guarantee,* is a guarantee issued by a commercial bank that promises to indemnify an ocean carrier who releases goods to a consignee who cannot produce a bill of lading.

Carrier's Lien.   All carriers have a lien on the cargo covered by the bill of lading, while it is in their possession, to cover the payment of freight, storage, or other fees. If the carrier is not paid for these expenses, it may, if necessary, sell the cargo at auction and remit any balance to the holder of the bill of lading.

http://www.export.gov/documentation.html
U.S. government export portal. Explains export basics, pricing, quotes, and negotiations, with sample shipping documents explained.

Responsibilities of Buyer and Seller in a Documentary Sale

Now that the documentary collection process has been explained, the next area to examine is exactly what is expected of the buyer and seller in fulfilling their responsibilities under the contract.

The exact responsibilities of buyer and seller depend on their agreement. In many documentary sales, the seller must not only tender a bill of lading to the buyer for payment, but also must provide marine insurance on the goods and must prepay the freight to the foreign port. These contracts are called *CIF contracts,* standing for "cost, insurance, and freight." This and other *trade terms* are discussed later in the chapter. In the following case involving a CIF contract, the seller in San Francisco tendered the documents to the buyer in London even before the goods were shipped. Wanting to inspect the merchandise first, the buyer refused to pay until delivery was made. The seller claimed that payment was due upon presentation of the documents alone.

The Kennedy dissent in *Biddell Brothers* represents a virtually universal view of CIF and other documentary sales contracts today. This rule has been adopted by both the UCC and the *United Nations Convention on Contracts for the International Sale of Goods,* and it has long been recognized by courts in the United States.

Biddell Brothers v. E. Clemens Horst Co.
I King's Bench 934 (1911)
Court of Appeal

BACKGROUND AND FACTS
The defendant entered into a contract to sell hops to the plaintiff in London, as follows:

> ... one hundred bales, equal to or better than choice brewing Pacific Coast hops of each of the crops of the years 1905 to 1912 inclusive. The said hops to be shipped to Sunderland. The [buyer] shall pay for the said hops at the rate of ninety shillings sterling per 112 lbs. CIF to London, Liverpool, or Hull. Terms net cash.

The seller wrote to the buyer stating that they were ready to ship and that they expected payment upon presentation of a negotiable bill of lading. The buyer replied that it was prepared to take delivery, but insisted that the seller either submit samples for prior inspection or that it be permitted to inspect each bale prior to payment. The buyer was unwilling to accept a certificate of inspection from the San Francisco Merchant's exchange as assurance of quality. The seller refused to ship and the buyer brought this action. The seller counterclaimed for the buyer's refusal to pay on the documents. The lower court ruled in favor of the defendant buyer. The Court of Appeals affirmed, with Kennedy, L.J., dissenting. On appeal to the House of Lords, the judgment was reversed in favor of the seller.

LORD JUSTICE KENNEDY, DISSENTING
The plaintiffs' case is that the price was not to be paid until they had been given an opportunity of inspecting the shipment, which could not be given until after its arrival in this country. The defendants contend that the plaintiffs' obligation was to pay for the hops, whether they arrived or not, against tender of the shipping documents. The Court, therefore, has in the present case to decide what are the true conditions of the right of the seller to payment under a CIF contract, if that commercial contract is to be performed strictly according to its tenor.

Let us see, step by step, how according to those principles and rules the transactions as in such a CIF contract as that before us is and, I think, must be carried out in order to fulfill its terms.

At the port of shipment—in this case San Francisco—the vendor ships the goods intended for the purchaser under the contract. Under the Sale of Goods Act, 1893, s. 18, by such shipment the goods

continued

continued

are appropriated by the vendor to the fulfillment of the contract, and by virtue of s. 32 the delivery of the goods to the carrier—whether named by the purchaser or not—for the purpose of transmission to the purchaser is prima facie to be deemed to be a delivery of the goods to the purchaser. Two further legal results arise out of the shipment. The goods are at risk of the purchaser, against which he has protected himself by the stipulation in his CIF contract that the vendor shall, at his own cost, provide him with a proper policy of marine insurance intended to protect the buyer's interest, and available for his use, if the goods should be lost in transit. How is such a tender to be made of goods afloat under a CIF contract? By tender of the bill of lading, accompanied in case the goods have been lost in transit by the policy of insurance. The bill of lading in law and in fact represents the goods. Possession of the bill of lading places the goods at the disposal of the purchaser. . . . But then I understand it to be objected on behalf of the plaintiffs: "Granted that the purchaser might, if he pleased, take this constructive delivery and pay against it the price of the goods; what is there in the 'cost freight and insurance' contract which compels him to do so? Why may he not insist on an option of waiting for a tender of delivery of the goods themselves after having had an opportunity of examining them after their arrival?"

There are, I think, several sufficient answers to such a proposition. In the first place, an option of a time of payment is not a term which can be inferred, where the contract itself is silent. So far as I am aware, there is no authority for the inference of an option as to times of payment to be found either in the law books or in the Sale of Goods Act. Secondly, if there is a duty on the vendor to tender the bill of lading, there must, it seems to me, be a corresponding duty on the part of the purchaser to pay when such tender is made. For thereunder, as the bill of lading with its accompanying documents comes forward by mail, the purchaser obtains the privilege and absolute power of profitably dealing with the goods days or weeks, or, perhaps, in the case of shipments from a distant port, months, before the arrival of the goods themselves. This is, indeed, the essential and peculiar advantage which the buyer of imported goods intends to gain under the CIF contract according to the construction which I put upon it.

Finally, let me test the soundness of the plaintiffs' contention that according to the true meaning of this contract their obligation to pay arises only when delivery of the goods has been tendered to them after they have an opportunity of examination, in this way. Suppose the goods to have been shipped, the bill of lading taken, and the insurance for the benefit of the buyer duly effected by the seller, as expressly stipulated in the contract. Suppose the goods then during the ocean transit to have been lost by the perils of the sea. The vendor tenders the bill of lading, with the insurance policy and the other shipping documents (if any) to the purchaser, to whom from the moment of shipment the property has passed, and at whose risk, covered by the insurance, the goods were at the time of loss. Is it, I ask myself, arguable that the purchaser could be heard to say, "I will not pay because I cannot have delivery of and an examination of the goods?" But it is just this which is necessarily involved in the contention of these plaintiffs. The seller's answer, and I think conclusive answer, is, "You have the bill of lading and the policy of insurance."

In my judgment, the judgment of Hamilton, J., was right, and this appeal, so far as relates to the plaintiffs' claim, should be dismissed.

Decision.   Under a CIF sales contract, the buyer has no right to inspect the goods, but is obligated to pay upon the presentation of the proper documents.

Seller's Duty to Tender Documents

If the documents are in good order, then the collection process normally works smoothly, with buyer and seller each getting what had been bargained for in the contract. The process may not be so smooth, however, if the documents tendered to the buyer contain one or more obvious defects. If the documents appear improper, the buyer may reject them. For instance, if the documents show that the goods were shipped later than the date called for in the contract, or on an improper vessel, or if they are improperly or inadequately insured, or if the documents on their face appear fraudulent, the buyer may have grounds for refusal. The buyer's refusal could come as quite a surprise to the seller, who, in good faith shipped and tendered documents to the buyer, only to find

---

EXHIBIT 5.4

2003 Amendments to UCC 2-513*

§ 2-513 Buyer's Right to Inspection of Goods

(1) Unless otherwise agreed and subject to subsection (3), where goods are tendered or delivered or identified to the contract for sale, the buyer has a right before payment or acceptance to inspect them at any reasonable place and time and in any reasonable manner. When the seller is required or authorized to send the goods to the buyer, the inspection may be after their arrival.

(2) Expenses of inspection must be borne by the buyer but may be recovered from the seller if the goods do not conform and are rejected.

(3) Unless otherwise agreed, the buyer is not entitled to inspect the goods before payment of the price when the contract provides
   (a) for delivery on terms that under applicable course of performance, course of dealing, or usage of trade are interpreted to preclude inspection before payment; or
   (b) for payment against documents of title, except where such payment is due only after the goods are to become available for inspection.

---

*Subject to enactment by state legislatures.

---

that they have been rejected and the draft unpaid, due to some "technicality." Of course, the point of contention may be more than just a technicality from the buyer's point of view, who may feel the rejection was based on good cause. But the effect is to leave the seller with a good deal of exposure while goods remain in a distant foreign port. Learning to manage these risks, however, will have to wait for a later chapter.

Seller's Additional Risk of Nonpayment

Although the documentary sale considerably reduces the seller's payment risk in an international sale, the possibility remains that the buyer may simply become insolvent or may find the goods cheaper from another source, and refuse to pay for the documents when they arrive. Even though the seller can control the goods through the bill of lading, the seller may still be burdened with getting rid of unneeded goods. For protection against these circumstances, the seller may require in the contract, as a precondition of shipment, that the buyer's bank irrevocably promise to buy the documents when presented to it.

Certificates of Inspection or Analysis

The documentary sales transaction serves to protect not only the seller, but also the buyer. The bill of lading assures that the goods have been loaded aboard ship for transport on the date shown, and the insurance policy serves to protect against covered marine losses. However, is not the buyer taking the description of the goods in the bill of lading, and in the invoice that usually accompanies it, at face value? If the goods are nonconforming or defective, the buyer's only remedy may be an action for breach of contract. In many industries, buyers will require that bills of lading be accompanied by a *certificate of inspection*, a *certificate of weight*, or perhaps a *certificate of analysis* from a reputable inspection company, usually located in the seller's country. Inspections are common in the chemical, extraction, and commodities business, as well as throughout other types of international trade. For instance, even major apparel retailers in the United States have garments inspected for defects in Hong Kong before they are shipped from the Orient.

In the *Basse* case, the buyer claimed that its bank should have been more diligent in accepting an inspection certificate that the seller had obtained from a chemist by fraud and trickery.

Measuring Damages for Breach of the Documentary Sale

The last chapter discussed the remedies available to a buyer and seller for breach of contract. Here, the text turns to the unique problem presented by the documentary sale. If the buyer sues the seller for nondelivery or other breach of contract, the buyer's damages may be measured by the difference between the contract price for the goods and their fair market value. How is market value determined in a documentary sale? Is it the market value at the time that the goods are shipped, the time of delivery of the goods, or the time of payment? Under the English view, damages would be based on the date that the buyer would have paid for the goods had the seller not breached. In *Sharpe & Co., Ltd. v. Nosawa & Co.,* 2 K.B. 814 (1917), a Japanese seller entered into a contract to ship peas to an English buyer under a documentary sale, CIF London. Neither the goods nor the documents were ever sent and the buyer sued for damages. The question was whether the buyer's damages should have been calculated on the basis of the difference between the contract price (£10.15 sterling per ton) and the market price of peas at the time of the anticipated August delivery (£17.10 sterling per ton) or the market price of peas at the time the documents would have been tendered in London July 21 (£12.00 sterling per ton). The court held that the seller's responsibility in this contract would have not been completed until he delivered the shipping documents to the buyer in London, at which time he would have been paid, and that the damages should therefore be measured by the price of peas on that date, July 21. Obviously, in a market with highly fluctuating prices, this question becomes especially important.

Seaver v. Lindsay Light Co., 135 N.E. 329 (N.Y. 1922) illustrates how the American courts have taken a different view. The seller and buyer entered a CIF contract for the shipment of thorium from Chicago to London. After the seller refused to ship, the buyer brought an action for breach of contract. Contrary to the English rule, the New York court looked at the nature of a shipment contract and stated, "Where was the delivery of the thorium in the present case to be made? Was it at Chicago or at London dock? When the correspondence and cablegrams are all construed together, as they must be, then it seems to me they clearly indicate an intention on the part of both parties that the delivery was to be made at Chicago, and when defendant delivered to a carrier at that point, paid the freight to point of desti-

nation, and forwarded the other necessary documents, he had fully completed his part of the contract." The court then concluded that damages for breach of a shipment contract should be measured by the market price of the goods *at the port of shipment on that date.*

Types of Ocean Bills of Lading

Bills of lading can take a variety of forms with different functions and usages in trade. The legal significance of each is important to all parties to the document.

Clean Bills of Lading.   In addition to being a document of title, the bill of lading is also a receipt for the goods. A *clean bill* is one that contains no notations by the carrier that indicate any visible damage to the goods, packages, drums, or other containers being loaded. A bill of lading that is not clean is *foul.* Normally, this description applies only to the external appearance of the goods. For instance, leaking containers, rust on metal products, and external evidence of infestation by insects must be noted on the bill of lading. As a generally accepted practice, the bill of lading must state the condition of the goods themselves, even if they are not externally observable, if the carrier nonetheless *knows or should have known* that the goods are damaged. This type of inspection serves to protect the carrier from responsibility for *preshipment* damage. Buyers should insist that all contracts call for the seller to provide a clean bill.

A buyer who receives a clean bill still has no assurance that the goods will arrive in good condition. A clean bill of lading means only that the carrier noted no obvious or visible damage to the goods when they were loaded aboard ship. Of course, a clean bill of lading is also no guarantee as to the quality of the goods or whether the goods conform to the description in the sales contract. And it is no guarantee that the goods will not be damaged during the voyage.

Onboard Bills of Lading.   An *onboard bill of lading,* signed by the ship's master or other agent of the carrier, states that the goods have actually been loaded aboard a certain vessel. In most documentary sales, the buyer would want to specify that payment is conditioned upon receipt of a negotiable, clean, onboard bill of lading. This document gives

Basse and Selve v. Bank of Australasia
90 Law Times 618 (1904)
King's Bench

BACKGROUND AND FACTS

The plaintiff had purchased ore from Oppenheimer. The plaintiff requested that the defendant bank negotiate documents on its behalf from Oppenheimer covering a shipment of "cobalt ore analysis not less than 5 per cent pertoxide." The plaintiff specified that the bill of lading must be accompanied by a policy of insurance and a certificate of analysis from Dr. Helms, a Sydney chemist. Oppenheimer submitted for analysis phony samples of ore to the chemist, who, on the basis of this small sample, issued his certificate indicating the quality to be as described in the bill of lading. In fact, the ore contained in the actual shipment was worthless. The plaintiff brought this action in order to recover amounts paid by the bank against the documents.

JUSTICE BIGHAM

It was no part of their duty to verify the genuineness of the documents; the duty was not cast upon them of making inquiries at the office of the ship's agent as to whether the goods had, in truth, been received on board; nor were they to examine the contents of the packages to see whether they were right; nor were they to communicate with Dr. Helms in order to ascertain whether he had properly made the analysis mentioned in the certificate. The plaintiffs' mandate amounted in business to a representation to the defendants that upon all such matters they might rely on Oppenheimer, and the legal effect of such a representation is now to preclude the plaintiffs from questioning the validity of any apparently regular documents which Oppenheimer might tender. If this is so, then the only question left on this part of the case is whether the documents were apparently regular. It is admitted by the plaintiffs that the bill of lading and the policy of insurance were apparently regular, but an objection is made on this score to Helms's certificate. It is said that it professes to show merely the test of the contents of a sample packet with a mark upon it, and does not purport to show a test of the bill of lading of 100 tons of ore. This, I think, is a fanciful objection. Large quantities of produce are necessarily tested by means of samples. Such samples are drawn either by the servants of the owner of the goods or (as it seems) by the servants of the analyst, and if the samples are carefully and skillfully drawn they generally fairly represent the bulk. But in this case it would be no part of the bank's duty to see to the sampling or to ascertain that it was fairly done. The bank was entitled to assume that it was so just as they were entitled to assume that the analyst had acted skillfully in making the analysis. The certificate is, in my opinion, regular on its face, and comes within the meaning of the mandate under which the bank was acting, and the bank in taking it acted carefully and properly.

Judgment for defendants.

Decision. The court ruled that because the certificate on its face was regular, the bank had acted properly in paying the seller. The bank had no duty to inspect the ore itself.

---

some assurance that the goods described in the bill of lading have actually been loaded on board and are underway to the buyer. It also insulates the exporter from loss of the goods before loading. An importer who buys an onboard bill also has an approximate idea of when the goods will arrive.

Received-for-Shipment Bills of Lading.

A *received-for-shipment bill of lading*, on the other hand, is issued by a carrier only upon having received goods for transport. It has limited use in cases of a time delay between the delivery of the goods to the carrier and their being loaded on-board ship. Imagine a buyer who is asked to pay for a received-for-shipment bill of lading for bananas being shipped from Honduras to the United States. The buyer has no guarantee that they won't be sitting on the sun-parched dock for weeks waiting to be loaded. Most documentary sales contracts will require that sellers tender onboard (and clean) bills of lading. A received-for-shipment bill of lading can be converted into an onboard bill of lading by the carrier's noting the vessel name and date of loading on the face of the bill.

Straight Bills of Lading. The bill of lading used in a documentary sale is negotiable. In nondocumentary sales, a nonnegotiable or *straight bill of lading* will suffice. They are used by ocean carriers only if the seller intends that the goods be delivered directly to a *consignee,* a specific person, named in the bill. The consignee may be the foreign buyer, as in the case of a sale on open account terms. It also may be the buyer's bank or customs agent. The consignee is not required to produce the actual bill in order to receive delivery.

Straight bills of lading are also used when the exporter is shipping to its own agent (or subsidiary company) in the foreign country, with the expectation that the agent will make direct arrangements with the buyer for payment before the goods are turned over. As in the case of negotiable documents, the carrier may deliver only to the party named in the bill. If the carrier delivers the goods to anyone else, it will be liable for misdelivery. Straight bills do not represent transferable title to the goods and cannot, alone, be used as collateral for a loan. Thus, typically, straight bills of lading are used when there is no financing involved.

Other Types of Transport Documents

Many specialized types of transport documents are in use today. The ocean bills of lading just described are only a few of the most common. Transport documents have specific uses, depending on the type of carrier and the function the document is to perform. Many new types of transport documents have been developed because of modern shipping techniques. The following summary describes the different types of transport documents.

---

http://www.cargolaw.com

Reference materials and articles on air and ocean transport law and logistics. Analysis of statutes, case law, and conventions. See Transportation Law Navigator, photos of historic bills of lading, and more.

Air Waybills. Most airfreight is handled through nonnegotiable *air waybills* issued by air cargo carriers (see Exhibit 5.5). The carrier will make delivery only to the consignee named in the bill. The importance of negotiability in airfreight is not as important as in ocean freight because the goods

are not out of the control of the parties for long periods. The air waybill contains a mechanism by which the seller can guarantee payment, even though the sale is not a documentary sale. The air waybill can name a foreign bank as consignee and specify that the goods be held at the point of destination until payment is guaranteed by the bank or until the bank approves release to the buyer. COD services are also available.

International law applicable to air waybills is found in the *Warsaw Convention* of 1929 and in subsequent amendments. The convention is applicable to all international transportation by air of persons, baggage, or goods by commercial aircraft. The convention places limits on the liability of air carriers for injuries to air travelers and damage to cargo, and a two-year statute of limitations on the filing of claims. Because not all nations have ratified the amendments, a great deal of inconsistency between nations is apparent in the laws regarding air transportation.

Forwarder's Bill of Lading. Bills of lading, either straight or order, can be issued by freight forwarders. They allow claims only against the forwarder itself, not the carrier. The carrier is liable only to the forwarder who holds the carrier's bill of lading. These bills must be distinguished from forwarder's receipts that are mere acknowledgements that the forwarder has received goods for shipment. Such receipts are nonnegotiable and usually will not be accepted for payment under a draft unless specifically allowed.

Multimodal Transport Documents. When goods are transported by only one mode of transportation, the transport is referred to as *unimodal.* If the transport is executed by using more than one mode of transportation, the transport is *multimodal.* Multimodal transport or *combined transport operators* represent shippers whose cargo will be sent via several different carriers in one journey—truck, rail, barge, or ship. Multimodal transport has been made possible by new methods of containerizing freight that replaced "break bulk" cargo for all but the smallest shipments. The *combined transport document* is a single contract between the shipper and the operator, who, in turn, contracts with each of the carriers involved. The operators become responsible for the shipment of goods throughout the time of their transport.

EXHIBIT 5.5

International Air Waybill

AIRPORT OF DEPARTURE		INTERNATIONAL AIR WAYBILL		
037- 0226 0123			**037-** 0226 0123	

SHIPPER'S NAME AND ADDRESS	SHIPPER'S ACCOUNT NUMBER	NOT NEGOTIABLE	US△IR
ABC Company 123 Elm St. Anytown, NC 12345		**AIR WAYBILL** (AIR CONSIGNMENT NOTE) Copies 1, 2 and 3 of this Air Waybill are originals and have the same validity.	USAir, Inc. NATIONAL AIRPORT, WASHINGTON, D.C. 20001

CONSIGNEE'S NAME AND ADDRESS	CONSIGNEE'S ACCOUNT NUMBER
XYZ Corporation 456 Wind St. Anycity, France	

It is agreed that the goods described herein are accepted in apparent good order and condition (except as noted) for carriage SUBJECT TO THE CONDITIONS OF CONTRACT ON THE REVERSE HEREOF. THE SHIPPER'S ATTENTION IS DRAWN TO THE NOTICE CONCERNING CARRIERS' LIMITATION OF LIABILITY. Shipper may increase such limitation of liability by declaring a higher value for carriage and paying a supplemental charge if required.

TO EXPEDITE MOVEMENT, SHIPMENT MAY BE DIVERTED TO MOTOR OR OTHER CARRIER AS PER TARIFF RULE UNLESS SHIPPER GIVES OTHER INSTRUCTIONS HEREON.

ISSUING CARRIER'S AGENT NAME AND CITY	ALSO NOTIFY NAME AND ADDRESS *(OPTIONAL ACCOUNTING INFORMATION)*
	Foreign Custom Broker 1001 Maple St. Anycity, France

AGENT'S IATA CODE	ACCOUNT NUMBER	ACCOUNTING INFORMATION	(SHIPPER CHECK ONE)
1-5678		XX AIR FREIGHT	☐ AIR EXPRESS ☐ COMAT

AIRPORT OF DEPARTURE (ADDR OF FIRST CARRIER) AND REQUESTED ROUTING
Charlotte

ROUTING AND DESTINATION						CURRENCY	CHGS CODE	WT/VAL PPD COLL	OTHER PPD COLL	DECLARED VALUE FOR CARRIAGE	DECLARED VALUE FOR CUSTOMS
TO CDG	BY FIRST CARRIER US		TO	BY	TO	BY	USD		X	X	NVD	5000

AIRPORT OF DESTINATION	FOR CARRIER USE ONLY	AMOUNT OF INSURANCE	INSURANCE– If shipper requests insurance in accordance with conditions on reverse hereof, indicate amount to be insured in figures in box marked amount of insurance.	TC
	FLIGHT/DATE US 8/15/06 — FLIGHT/DATE	NIL		

HANDLING INFORMATION These commodities licensed by US for ultimate destination. Diversion contrary to US law is prohibited.

MKD: AS Addr.   PO# 0001

NOTIFICATION (PERSON NOTIFIED)	BY
DATE/TIME	DISPOSITION

NO. OF PIECES RCP	GROSS WEIGHT	Kg lb	RATE CLASS COMMODITY ITEM NO.	CHARGEABLE WEIGHT	RATE / CHARGE	TOTAL	NATURE AND QUANTITY OF GOODS (INCL. DIMENSIONS OR VOLUME)
10	109	K		109	2.10	228.90	Leather aprons

PREPAID / WEIGHT CHARGE / COLLECT	P-UP ZONE	PICK-UP CHARGES	ORIGIN ADVANCE CHARGES	DESCRIPTION OF ORIGIN ADVANCE	ITEMS PREPAID
A. 228.90	B.	25.00	K.		
VALUATION CHARGE /	DEL. ZONE		DEST. ADVANCE CHARGES	DESCRIPTION OF DESTINATION ADVANCE	ITEMS COLLECT
D.	C.		L.		
TAX	SHIPPER'S R.F.C. (AMOUNT TO BE ENTERED BY SHIPPER)	OTHER CHARGES AND DESCRIPTION			
I.		F.			
TOTAL OTHER CHARGES DUE AGENT					
58.00	SHIPPER CERTIFIES THAT THE PARTICULARS ON THE FACE HEREOF ARE CORRECT AND THAT INSOFAR AS ANY PART OF THE CONSIGNMENT CONTAINS RESTRICTED ARTICLES, SUCH PART IS PROPERLY DESCRIBED BY NAME AND IS IN PROPER CONDITION FOR CARRIAGE BY AIR ACCORDING TO APPLICABLE NATIONAL GOVERNMENT REGULATIONS, AND FOR INTERNATIONAL SHIPMENTS THE CURRENT INTERNATIONAL AIR TRANSPORT ASSOCIATION'S RESTRICTED ARTICLES REGULATIONS.				
TOTAL OTHER CHARGES DUE CARRIER					
10.00					
I. COD → CURRENCY	SIGNATURE OF SHIPPER OR HIS AGENT				
TOTAL PREPAID	TOTAL COLLECT	EXECUTED ON			
	296.00				
CURRENCY CONVERSION RATES	TOTAL COLLECT IN DEST. CURRENCY	(Date) (Time) at (Place) SIGNATURE OF ISSUING CARRIER OR ITS AGENT			
FOR CARRIERS USE ONLY AT DESTINATION	CHARGES AT DESTINATION	TOTAL COLLECT CHARGES	CARRIER CERTIFIES GOODS DESCRIBED ABOVE WERE RECEIVED FOR CARRIAGE SUBJECT TO THE CONDITIONS ON THE REVERSE HEREOF, THE GOODS THEN BEING IN APPARENT GOOD ORDER AND CONDITION EXCEPT AS NOTED HEREON.		
(ALL COLLECT CHARGES IN DESTINATION CURRENCY)			**037-** 0226 0123		

Electronic Data Interchange

There is a growing trend to replace written documents with a computer-to-computer messaging system. This practice has been referred to as *electronic data interchange* or EDI. Under this practice, trade documents, such as bills of lading, letters of credit, and certificates of origin, may be filed electronically at a central database.

The electronic transfer of documents has several advantages over paper-based transfers. First, it allows buyers and sellers to track goods that are in transit and enables the parties to make necessary adjustments when the goods are delayed. Second, the faster transmission of bills of lading and other documents enables the seller to obtain faster payment for goods, which in turn translates into an improved cash flow for the seller. Third, the elimination of the need to manually prepare multiple copies of documents reduces the redundancy of paperwork and improves efficiency and accuracy.

EDI however, also raises several issues. A principal concern is security. Traditionally, the buyer has been required to present an original signed bill of lading in order to receive the goods. Although the written signature requirement may be replaced by a "digital signature," such documents may not be protected against unauthorized access. Not all geographic regions have reliable telecommunication networks. Another issue is liability. Who bears responsibility for electronic transfers that are sent but not received? Who bears responsibility for unauthorized access to the documents? The answers to these questions depend on how such electronic transfers are characterized. A third obstacle to the global paperless system of trade is the lack of standardization. A particular trade document, such as a bill of lading, may have several different formats depending on the country and practices used. In order for a global system to work, the format of trade documents must be standardized.

SHIPPING TERMS AND THE RISK OF LOSS

The *shipping terms* in a sales contract are those provisions that define the seller's and buyer's responsibilities for making the shipping arrangements, paying transportation charges, procuring insurance on the goods, paying port charges, and bearing the risk that the goods may be lost or damaged in transit. In contract negotiations, the parties often consider these terms as important as the quality of the merchandise or its price. Indeed, the shipping terms are integral to the price term itself. Because of the risks of international trade and the high cost of air and ocean freight, a contract price without shipping terms is nearly meaningless. If the parties cannot reach agreement on the shipping terms, the entire deal may fail.

Allocating the Risk of Loss

The parties to a contract must know when they are responsible for damage or loss to goods and when they are not. Clearly, the seller is responsible if the goods are destroyed by fire during production at the seller's plant. Likewise, if the goods are destroyed after they have been moved into the buyer's warehouse, then the buyer is responsible. But when does the risk pass from one party to the other? In some countries, including the United Kingdom, the party who bears the risk of loss is the party who has "title" to the goods—the party who owns them at that moment. However, because the document of title does not move physically with the goods, a determination of who owned the goods at the exact time of their destruction is often difficult. This "title" method was employed in the United States until the adoption of the UCC decades ago.

Ideally, the seller wants to be free of the risk of loss as soon as the goods leave the back door. The buyer would like to delay it for as long as possible. The ability to negotiate, of course, stems from the relative bargaining position of the parties. If the seller's products contain superior technology, or if they are commodities in short supply, or patented products that the buyer needs, then the seller may be in a stronger position to shift the risk to the buyer. Similarly, if the buyer is in a dominant economic position, such as by being able to order in large quantities, the buyer may be able to dictate the terms of the contract. For example, the owner of a rare 1927 Rolls Royce in London may say to a U.S. buyer, "You may purchase my Rolls in London and drive it away, but if you want it shipped to you, you must bear all the risks of the journey from the moment it leaves my door."

Buyer and seller are always free to decide in their contract when the risk of loss will pass from one to the other. But if the parties fail to do so, and a dispute arises, the courts will be forced to decide on the basis of whether the contract is of the shipment type or of the destination type.

Destination Contracts. The question of whether a contract is a shipment or a destination contract will be determined by how the responsibilities of the parties are defined: Who has responsibility for shipping or transporting the goods? Who is paying the freight charges? By what means will the buyer remit payment? If the contract calls for the seller to deliver the goods to a particular destination, such as the buyer's city or place of business, the contract is a *destination contract* (sometimes referred to an "arrival" contract). Under the UCC §2–509 (see Exhibit 5.6), the risk of loss in a destination contract passes to the buyer when the goods are tendered to the buyer at the point of destination.

Shipment Contracts. If the contract calls for the seller to ship the goods by carrier, but does not require the seller to deliver the goods to a named place, then it is a *shipment contract* (sometimes referred to as a "departure" contract). In a shipment contract, the risk of loss or damage to the goods passes to the buyer when the goods are given to the first carrier—be it truck, airline, or ocean carrier. Shipment contracts are more common in international trade because sellers usually prefer not to be responsible for the goods at sea.

The Risk of Loss in International Sales under the CISG

The CISG contains provisions that allocate the risk of loss in Articles 66–70, reproduced in the appendix. Like the UCC, CISG provisions apply only if the parties do not specify by agreement when the risk shifts from seller to buyer. Article 67 applies to sales in which the goods will be transported by carrier. If the contract calls for the goods to be *handed over to a carrier at a particular place*, then the risk passes to the buyer at that place. However, if the seller is simply expected to ship, but not bound to hand over the goods *at a particular place*, the risk passes to the buyer when the goods are *handed over to the first carrier* for shipment to the buyer. For instance, assume that a company located in Boone, North Carolina, confirms an order for the export of its product to a foreign customer. The contract reads simply that "Seller will handle all transportation charges and arrangements." The seller arranges for a trucking company to pick up the goods and deliver them to the air carrier's terminal at the Charlotte airport, one hundred miles away. The risk of loss will pass from seller to buyer when the goods are

---

EXHIBIT 5.6

2003 Amendments to UCC 2-509*

§ 2-509 Risk of Loss in the Absence of Breach

(1) Where the contract requires or authorizes the seller to ship the goods by carrier
    (a) if it does not require the seller to deliver them at a particular destination, the risk of loss passes to the buyer when the goods are delivered to the carrier even though the shipment is under reservation (Section 2-505); but
    (b) if it does require the seller to deliver them at a particular destination and the goods are there tendered while in the possession of the carrier, the risk of loss passes to the buyer when the goods are there so tendered as to enable the buyer to take delivery.

    * * *

(3) In any case not within subsection (1) or (2), the risk of loss passes to the buyer on the buyer's receipt of the goods.

(4) The provisions of this section are subject to contrary agreement of the parties and to the provisions of this Article on sale on approval (Section 2-327) and on effect of breach on risk of loss (Section 2-510).

*Subject to enactment by state legislatures.

first handed over to the trucking company at the seller's factory or warehouse in Boone. If the goods are damaged from that point forth, on land or in the air (or sea, in the case of ocean shipment), the loss falls on the buyer. Of course, the seller is responsible for properly packaging and preparing the merchandise for shipment. The buyer would be relieved from any obligation to pay for the goods if the loss was due to an act or omission of the seller (see Article 66).

> http://www.cisg.law.
> pace.edu
> Link to the annotated text of the CISG. Choose Articles 66–70 for the text on risk of loss.

Freight and Transportation Charges

A buyer and seller must do more than merely agree on a price for the goods; they must also agree on who is going to pay the transportation charges. For the price quoted, will the seller deliver the goods to the buyer, or will the seller also put them aboard a ship, or just make them available to a common carrier at the factory door? For instance, a seller might say, "This is the price if you come to my factory and pick up the goods. If you want me to pay to get them to the seaport in my country, or even across the ocean to your country, I will; but this is what the price of the goods will be then." Moreover, the seller also has an opportunity to negotiate the passing of the risk of loss. Seller may say, "I'll be glad to ship these to you in the United States, and I'll arrange their carriage on the SS *Anna Star,* freight prepaid, but you must bear the risk of loss from the moment the goods are loaded on board."

A seller will frequently present a proposal to a buyer offering a choice of shipping terms. For instance, one proposal may show a price with ocean freight, another without. These choices provide the buyer with a breakdown of the costs and responsibility for those costs within the transaction. Buyers who have an itemized breakdown of the various transportation, handling, and insurance charges from the seller can compare those with the costs of making the shipping arrangements themselves. The document prepared by the seller and sent to the buyer that shows the description of the goods and a breakdown of the charges is called a pro forma invoice (see Chapter Four). Furthermore, transportation costs are needed if the buyer is comparing price quotations on similar goods from two different foreign suppliers. A buyer who requests all suppliers to quote prices on the same terms is able to compare "apples to apples."

A party to a contract doesn't negotiate shipping terms only on the basis of cost or the passing of the risk of loss. Sales decisions are more likely to be based on how these terms fit into a buyer's overall business needs. A buyer who imports regularly may have buying agents in the seller's country who can handle the details of moving the goods. Similarly, some buyers may take full responsibilities for chartering their own ships, as in the case of a country making a large purchase of grain for its own population. They may want the grain made available to them alongside their ship, and they will pay all expenses and bear all risks from that point. In many cases, a seller that maintains a warehouse in the buyer's country will price the goods for pickup there.

Unless a seller is in such a dominant position in the market that it can dictate terms, it may want to offer more flexible shipping terms in order to land a contract. Even if one seller offers a lower price, a competitor with better shipping terms may get the order. The buyer may be inexperienced at moving cargo, or may just not want to be bothered dealing with cargo in the seller's country. For instance, imagine a Japanese buyer who attends a trade fair in New York and concludes a contract with a company from Boone, North Carolina. The buyer may not want to bother with getting the goods from "the Boonedocks" to a U.S. seaport and then on to Japan. The buyer may just want the best price for the goods delivered and unloaded from a ship at a Japanese seaport nearest the buyer's factory.

Trade Terms

Shipping terms, as with other terms of sale, are often drafted into contracts in detail by experienced attorneys. However, many sales contracts use trade terms as a shorthand method of expressing shipping terms as well as allocating the risk of loss. Trade terms are usually expressed in the form of abbreviated symbols, such as FOB or CIF. They permit the parties to express their agreement quickly, with little confusion, and with few language problems. If the parties use a trade term in their contract, they must define it. If it is not defined in the contract, a court would have to look to the applicable law for its interpretation. The most common method of defining trade terms, however, is to incorporate them into the contract by reference to some independent source or publication.

International Rules for the Interpretation of Trade Terms

The most important set of trade term definitions are the *International Rules for the Interpretation of Trade Terms*, or *Incoterms* (2000), published by the Paris-based *International Chamber of Commerce*.[1] These definitions have the support of important business groups, including manufacturing, shipping, and banking industries worldwide. First published in 1936, the newest revision was released in 2000. The new terms accommodate the changes in airfreight, modern multimodal shipping, containerized cargo, and electronic data interchange.

Incoterms include approximately thirteen trade terms (more with the variations). They are classified into four groups—E, F, C, and D—according to the relative responsibilities of each party and to the point at which the risk of loss passes from seller to buyer. The terms are grouped in Exhibit 5.7 (see pages 170–171). (Consult the appendix for more complete definitions.) Exhibit 5.7 arranges the terms with the minimum responsibility of the seller and the maximum responsibility of the buyer appearing at the top; the minimum responsibility of the buyer and maximum responsibility of the seller appearing at the bottom. International salespeople, export managers, and world traders benefit from a working knowledge of these terms. *Incoterms* are not automatically part of a contract for the sale of goods. To ensure that the *Incoterms* definitions will be applied to their contract, parties should include a clause such as "This contract is to be interpreted in accordance with *Incoterms*."

The following case, *St. Paul Guardian Ins. Co. v. Neuromed Medical Systems & Support, GmbH.*, illustrates the wide acceptance of *Incoterms*. Here an American court was called upon to decide who was responsible for goods damaged at sea, the German seller or U.S. buyer. The contract used a common trade term: CIF ("cost, insurance, and freight," see Exhibit 5.6), but did not define CIF. The contract also specified that it was governed by the laws of Germany. The court stated that under German law the CIF term, and thus the rights of the parties, would be defined by *Incoterms*. The court reasoned that *Incoterms* were so commonly used that they had become a trade usage to which the parties were bound in the absence of their agreement to the contrary.

The following section looks at some hypothetical illustrations to see how these terms are used. Keep in mind that the terms represent years of work by their authors to reflect how companies actually do business. Selecting a term for incorporation in a contract is more than just bargaining over who will pay freight costs or bear the risk of loss. Certain terms may fit better with the needs of the parties. Some are suited for ocean carriage, some for airfreight, or cases in which the seller will use many modes of transport—truck to a railhead, rail to the port, and finally an ocean voyage—known as *multimodal transport*. Some terms are suited for a documentary form of payment; others are suited to open account payment terms. Be sure to study Exhibit 5.7 before reading the following summary. As you read, keep in mind that the following terms are for maritime and inland waterway transport only: FAS, FOB, CFR, CIF, DES, and DEQ. Others are for any mode of transport.

---

http://www.iccwbo.org

The site of the International Chamber of Commerce, with information on global business issues such as advertising and marketing, arbitration, commercial crime, extortion and bribery, intellectual property, international trade, piracy, and many others.

"E" Terms. *E Terms* represent the least amount of responsibility for the seller. In the following hypothetical situation, assume a buyer in the Netherlands is placing an order with a supplier in Albany, New York. The buyer states that its U.S. subsidiary will pick up the goods at the Albany plant and arrange export. Therefore, the seller would probably quote its price in terms *EXW Albany factory*. Under this term, the seller need only make the goods available at its factory (or mill, farm,

St. Paul Guardian Ins. Co. v. Neuromed Medical Systems & Support, GmbH
WL 465312 (2002)
United States District Court (S.D.N.Y.)

BACKGROUND AND FACTS

Shared Imaging, an American company, agreed to purchase an MRI machine from Neuromed, a German seller. The one-page contract of sale stated that the delivery terms were "CIF New York Seaport, the buyer will arrange and pay for customs clearance as well as transport to Calumet City." In addition, under "Disclaimer" it stated, "system including all accessories and options remain the property of Neuromed till complete payment has been received." Payment was to be made when the machine was received in Calumet City. The contract also stated that it was to be governed by the laws of Germany. The MRI was loaded aboard the vessel *Atlantic Carrier* undamaged and in good working order. When it reached its destination of Calumet City, Illinois, it had been damaged and was in need of extensive repair, which led plaintiff to conclude that the MRI had been damaged in transit. Shared Imaging filed its claim for insurance with St. Paul Guardian, who brought this action against Neuromed for damages. Neuromed argues that the case should be dismissed because it is not liable under German law.

STEIN, DISTRICT J.

Neuromed contends that because the delivery terms were "CIF New York Seaport," its contractual obligation, with regard to risk of loss or damage, ended when it delivered the MRI to the vessel at the port of shipment and therefore the action must be dismissed because plaintiff has failed to state a claim for which relief can be granted. Plaintiff responds that the generally accepted definition of the "CIF" term, as defined in *Incoterms 1990,* is inapplicable. Moreover, the plaintiff suggests that other provisions of the contract are inconsistent with the "CIF" term because Neuromed, pursuant to the contract, retained title subsequent to delivery to the vessel at the port of shipment and thus Shared Imaging manifestly retained the risk of loss.

Applicable German Law

The parties concede that pursuant to German law, the *U.N. Convention on Contracts for the International Sale of Goods* ("CISG") governs this trans-

action because (1) both the U.S. and Germany are Contracting States to that Convention, and (2) neither party chose, by express provision in the contract, to opt out of the application of the CISG. . . . (citations hereinafter omitted). Germany has been a Contracting State since 1991, and the CISG is an integral part of German law. To hold otherwise would undermine the objectives of the Convention which Germany has agreed to uphold.

CISG, INCOTERMS and "CIF"

"CIF," which stands for "cost, insurance and freight," is a commercial trade term that is defined in *Incoterms 1990,* published by the International Chamber of Commerce ("ICC"). The aim of INCOTERMS, which stands for international commercial terms, is "to provide a set of international rules for the interpretation of the most commonly used trade terms in foreign trade. . . ." INCOTERMS are incorporated into the CISG through Article 9(2) which provides that, "The parties are considered, unless otherwise agreed, to have impliedly made applicable to their contract or its formation a usage of which the parties knew or ought to have known and which in international trade is widely known to, and regularly observed by, parties to contracts of the type involved in the particular trade concerned." CISG, art. 9(2). . . . INCOTERMS defines "CIF" (named port of destination) to mean the seller delivers when the goods pass "the ship's rail at the port of shipment." The seller is responsible for paying the cost, freight and insurance coverage necessary to bring the goods to the named port of destination, but the risk of loss or damage to the goods passes from seller to buyer upon delivery to the port of shipment. . . .

Plaintiff's legal expert contends that INCOTERMS are inapplicable here because the contract fails to specifically incorporate them. Nonetheless, he cites and acknowledges that the German Supreme Court (Bundesgerichtshof)—the court of last resort in the Federal Republic of Germany for civil matters—concluded that a clause "FOB" without specific reference to INCOTERMS was to be interpreted according to

continued

continued

INCOTERMS "simply because the INCOTERMS include a clause 'FOB'."

Conceding that commercial practice attains the force of law under section 346 of the German Commercial Code (citing the German Court), plaintiff's expert concludes that the opinion of the German Court "amounts to saying that the INCOTERMS definitions in Germany have the force of law as trade custom." As encapsulated by defendant's legal expert, "It is accepted under German law that in case a contract refers to CIF-delivery, the parties refer to the INCOTERMS rules . . ." Thus, pursuant to CISG art. 9(2), INCOTERMS definitions should be applied to the contract despite the lack of an explicit INCOTERMS reference in the contract.

Effect of Transfer of Title Contract Provisions

Plaintiff argues that Neuromed's explicit retention of title in the contract to the MRI machine modified the "CIF" term, such that Neuromed retained title and assumed the risk of loss. INCOTERMS, however, only address passage of risk, not transfer of title. Under the CISG, the passage of risk is . . . independent of the transfer of title. Moreover, according to Article 67(1), the passage of risk and transfer of title need not occur at the same time, as the seller's retention of "documents controlling the disposition of the goods does not affect the passage of risk." CISG, art. 67(1).

* * *

Effect of Other Delivery Terms

Plaintiff next contends that . . . the other terms in the contract are evidence that the parties' intention to supercede and replace the "CIF" term such that Neuromed retained title and the risk of loss. That is incorrect. Citing the "Delivery Terms" clause in the contract, plaintiff posits that had the parties intended to abide by the strictures of INCOTERMS there would have been no need to define the buyer's obligations to pay customs and arrange further transport. Plaintiff's argument, however, is undermined by *Incoterms 1990,* which provides that "[i]t

is normally desirable that customs clearance is arranged by the party domiciled in the country where such clearance should take place." The "CIF" term as defined by INCOTERMS only requires the seller to "clear the goods for export" and is silent as to which party bears the obligation to arrange for customs clearance. The parties are therefore left to negotiate these obligations. As such, a clause defining the terms of customs clearance neither alters nor affects the "CIF" clause in the contract.

Plaintiff also cites to the "Payment Terms" clause of the contract, which specified that final payment was not to be made upon seller's delivery of the machine to the port of shipment, but rather, upon buyer's acceptance of the machine in Calumet City. These terms speak to the final disposition of the property, not to the risk for loss or damage. INCOTERMS do not mandate a payment structure, but rather simply establish that the buyer bears an obligation to "[p]ay the price as provided in the contract of sale." Inclusion of the terms of payment in the contract does not modify the "CIF" clause.

The terms of the contract do not modify the "CIF" clause in the contract such that the risk of loss remained with Neuromed. The fact remains that the CISG, INCOTERMS, and German law all distinguish between the passage of the risk of loss and the transfer of title. Thus, because (1) Neuromed's risk of loss of, or damage to, the MRI machine under the contract passed to plaintiff upon delivery of the machine to the carrier at the port of shipment and (2) it is undisputed that the MRI machine was delivered to the carrier undamaged and in good working order, Neuromed's motion to dismiss for failure to state a claim is hereby granted.

Decision. The U.S. court, interpreting German law, held that a delivery term in a sales contract (here CIF) should be defined according to *Incoterms,* in the absence of contractual provisions specifying otherwise. The court reasoned that under the CISG, merchants impliedly agree to trade usages of which they should have known. *Incoterms* are so widely used that they have become a trade usage, or international custom, applicable to this contract. The risk of loss passed to the buyer at the port of shipment.

warehouse, or other place of business) and present the buyer with an invoice for payment. The buyer must arrange all transportation and bear all risks

and expenses of the journey from that point. The buyer would also have to clear the goods for export by obtaining export licenses from the U.S.

EXHIBIT 5.7

Explanation of *Incoterms 2000*: ICC Official Rules for the Interpretation of Trade Terms

Group and Type	Term Abbreviation/In Full	Mode of Transportation	Seller's Responsibilities*	Buyer's Responsibilities*	Passage of Risk
E Group	EXW *Ex Works* (works: mill, factory, mine, warehouse, etc.)	Up to buyer (all modes)	Have the goods ready for pickup at the location specified in the contract, usually seller's place of business.	Provide vehicle or rail car and load goods. Obtain export licenses. Enter goods thru customs.	When the goods are made available by seller at named location.
F Group *Shipment Contract*	FCA *Free Carrier* (named place)	Ocean, air, truck, rail, or multimodal (all)	Place the goods in the hands of a carrier (usually inland) named by the buyer at the place specified. Provide export license.	Choose carrier, arrange transport, and pay freight charges. On arrival, enter goods thru customs.	When the goods are delivered to the carrier or terminal operator at the named place of shipment.
	FAS *Free Alongside Ship* (named port of shipment)	Ocean or water only	Place the goods alongside the ship specified by the buyer (on the dock or barge) within the time called for in the contract, ready for loading. Obtain export license.	Choose ocean carrier, arrange transport and pay freight. Enter goods thru customs.	When the goods are delivered alongside the ship specified by buyer.
	FOB *Free on Board* (named port of shipment)	Ocean or water only	Load the goods on board the ship specified by the buyer within the time called for in the contract. Pay costs of loading. Obtain export license.	Choose ocean carrier and pay freight charges. Enter goods thru customs.	When the goods cross the ship's rail at port of shipment.
C Group *Shipment Contract*	CFR *Cost and Freight* (named port of destination)	Ocean or water only	Contract for transport and pay freight charges to the named port of destination. Arrange for loading goods on board ship, usually of seller's choice, and pay costs of loading. Obtain export license. Notify buyer of shipment. Documentary sale is assumed. Tender documents to buyer.	Purchase document of title and take delivery from ocean carrier. No date of delivery at buyer's port is implied. Pay import duties. Enter goods thru customs.	When the goods cross the ship's rail at port of shipment. Buyer must procure own insurance or else use CIF term.
	CIF *Cost, Insurance and Freight* (named port of destination)	Ocean or water only	Same as CFR, with added requirement that seller purchase marine insurance in amount of invoice price plus 10%. Insurance policy is assigned to buyer. Documentary sale is assumed.	Same as CFR, except seller supplies insurance. Buyer may ask for additional insurance coverage at own expense.	When the goods cross ship's rail at port of shipment. If damage or loss, buyer files claim for insurance.

Sellers: Least Responsibility ⟶
Buyers: Most

Term	Transport modes	Seller's obligations	Buyer's obligations	Transfer of risk
CPT *Carriage Paid To* (named place of destination)	Ocean, air, truck, rail, or multimodal (all)	Similar to CFR, but for all modes of transport. Deliver goods to truck, rail or multimodal carrier, or to ship, and arrange for transport to destination. Freight charges prepaid. Obtain export license. Notify buyer of shipment. Seller need not insure goods. Documentary sale is assumed.	Similar to CFR. Purchase document of title and take delivery of goods from carrier. Enter goods thru customs. Pay import duties.	When goods are delivered by the seller to the first carrier. Buyer must procure own insurance or use CIP term.
CIP *Carriage and Insurance Paid To* (named place of destination)	Ocean, air, truck, rail, or multimodal (all)	Same as CPT, with added requirement that seller purchase policy of marine insurance in amount of invoice plus 10%. Insurance policy assigned to buyer.	Same ast CPT. Purchase document of title and take delivery of goods from carrier. Enter goods thru customs. Pay import duties.	When goods are delivered by the seller to the first carrier. If damage or loss, buyer files claim for insurance.
D Group *Destination Contract*				
DAF *Delivered at Frontier* (named place)	Usually for int'l. rail shipments (can be used for all modes)	Contract for transport and pay freight expenses to the "frontier" point in the country of importation. Buyer clears goods for import by customs authorities.	Pay freight charges from frontier point. Enter goods thru customs. Pay import duties.	When the goods are ready to be handed over to the buyer at the named (frontier point) in buyer's country.
DES *Delivered Ex Ship* (named port of destination)	Ocean or water only (often used when ship is chartered by seller)	Arrange transport and pay all freight charges to port of foreign destination. Notify buyer of expected arrival date. Place goods at disposal of buyer aboard ship within time called for in contract.	Arrange and pay cost of unloading goods from ship and land transport. Enter goods thru customs.	When the goods are ready for unloading by the buyer at port of destination.
DEQ *Delivered Ex Quay;* (named port of destination)	Ocean or water only	Contract for transport and pay freight charges to put the goods on the quay (dock) beside the ship at specified port of destination. Notify buyer of arrival date. May be used for documentary sale.	Take delivery of goods at dock and enter goods thru customs. Pay import duties. Arrange land transport to buyer's place of business.	When the goods are placed on the dock or in terminal. Seller should insure goods for own protection.
DDU *Delivery Duty Unpaid* (named place of destination)	Ocean, air, truck, rail, or multimodal (all)	Similar to DEQ, except used for all modes of transport. Seller usually contracts for carriage to inland port of entry in importing country. May be used for documentary sale.	Purchase document of title if required. Take delivery at specified location and enter goods thru customs. Pay import duties.	When goods are delivered at location specified. Seller should insure for own protection.
DDP *Delivery Duty Paid* (named place of destination)	Ocean, air, truck, rail, or multimodal (all)	Same as DDU, except that seller obtains import licenses, pays import duties, and clears goods thru customs. Place of destination specified is usually buyer's place of business.	Purchase document of title if required. Take delivery of goods at specified location.	When the goods are delivered to buyer at specified location. Seller should insure for own protection.

*In all cases, seller is required to provide goods in conformance with contract; buyer is to pay invoice according to contract. Time for shipment or delivery is determined by contract. Trade term must be stated in contract and reference made therein to *Incoterms 2000* in order for these definitions to apply.

SOURCE: Based on ICC No. 560, *Incoterms 2000.* For more on the *Incoterms 2000* or the ICC, visit http://www.incoterms.org or http://www.iccbooksusa.com.

government. This term is most often used when the buyer will pick up the goods by truck or rail. Therefore, for international shipments, EXW terms are common in Europe where goods frequently move across national boundaries by ground transportation. This term is likely to become more popular in trade between Canada, the United States, and Mexico in the future. But unless this term has been requested by the buyer, use of it may show that the seller is not really interested in exporting and is unwilling to accommodate a foreign buyer.

"F" Terms. The *F terms* are shipment contracts similar to those studied earlier. Under F terms, the seller is required to deliver the goods to the designated point of departure "free" of expense or risk to the buyer. At that point, the risk of loss passes from seller to buyer. The buyer arranges the transportation and pays all freight costs. However, if it is convenient and the parties agree, the seller may pay the freight and add that amount to the invoice price already quoted. F terms are often used when the buyer has contracted for a complete shipload of materials or commodities and thus had reason to assume the responsibility for arranging carriage. F terms may also be used because the buyer feels that it can obtain better freight rates than the seller. Some F terms are for ocean shipment only. Others can be used for all modes of transport.

Assume that the buyer in the Netherlands wants to arrange its own ocean transportation. The seller in Albany would like to deliver the goods to a carrier near it, for transportation to the Port of New York, so different forms of transportation will be required. For instance, the seller might deliver the goods to a barge hauler for a trip down the Hudson, or to a railroad or trucking company. The seller may want to hand over the goods to a multimodal terminal operator nearby and let it handle the goods from there. This inland carrier will then transport the goods to the Port of New York for shipment to the foreign destination. If this inland carrier is in Albany, then the seller should quote prices *FCA Albany*. Here, for the contract price, the seller bears the costs and assumes all risks of getting the goods from its factory to the carrier or terminal in Albany. The seller then has the responsibility to obtain any government export licenses that are required. This term could also be used for airfreight. A term *FCA JFK*

Airport means that the seller has agreed, for the contract price, to deliver the goods from Albany to the airline in New York for shipment.

Assume now that the Dutch buyer is purchasing a bulk cargo, such as agricultural commodities, and will be chartering a full ship for the overseas voyage—*a voyage charter*—departing from New York to Rotterdam. The buyer may find the voyage charter more convenient and cheaper to arrange than leaving the shipping up to the seller. The buyer would like the seller to place the goods on barges or on the pier alongside the ship, *Queen Anna E,* docked at the Port of New York. The appropriate contract terms would be *FAS Queen Anna E.* (If the name of the vessel is not yet known, the parties can contract on terms *FAS New York.*) The risk of loss passes from seller to buyer at the time the goods are placed alongside the ship. The buyer, having arranged the ocean transport, will pay the separate costs of loading the vessel they have provided or have chosen. The seller must obtain an export license and clear the goods for export. An FAS buyer should also provide the seller with notice of the ship's departure date and loading times. The seller's obligation is to place the goods alongside the vessel within the time called for in the contract.

Under FOB (free on board) contracts, the seller bears slightly more responsibility. In addition to obtaining export clearance, the seller is required to place the goods aboard the ship. Risk of loss passes to the buyer only when the goods cross the ship's rail. Therefore, if the contract were on terms *FOB New York* or *FOB Queen Anna E,* the seller would be required to secure export licenses, pay all costs of loading and deliver the goods over the ship's rail. Notice that under *Incoterms,* the seller's responsibility does not end until the goods have actually passed the ship's rail. Exporters should always use the FOB term as a shipment contract as it was intended. Using it in conjunction with a destination location (e.g., *FOB foreign port*) would contradict the *Incoterms* definition and would shift the risk of the voyage to the exporter.

"C" Terms. *C terms* are also shipment contracts. The letter *C* indicates that the seller is responsible for certain costs after the goods have been delivered to the carrier. Like the FOB term, however, risk of loss passes to the buyer when the goods cross the ship's rail at the point of shipment. Assume that our Dutch buyer requests pricing information from Albany. As an experienced exporter, the seller might understand that the buyer has little interest in arranging transportation, let alone coming to pick up the goods. The buyer simply wants the goods delivered to the port of entry in its country closest to its company. If ocean shipment is required, the seller will prepare a price quotation *CFR Port of Rotterdam* (formerly called *C & F*) or *CIF Port of Rotterdam*. For the price quoted the seller will deliver the goods to an ocean carrier, arrange shipment, prepay the freight charges to the agreed upon port of destination, obtain a clean, onboard bill of lading marked *freight prepaid*, and forward it along with the invoice to the buyer for payment.

The only difference between CFR and CIF terms is that under CIF terms the seller must also procure and forward to the buyer a policy of marine insurance to cover the risk of loss once it passes to the buyer. (This amount is the minimum coverage; the buyer may want to request additional insurance be purchased for its own protection.) By providing both carriage and insurance coverage, the seller is able to earn additional profit yet retain its rights in the goods until payment is made against documents. Upon presentation of the bill of lading, the Dutch buyer is required to make payment, but once it receives the bill of lading, it can resell the goods, or if the goods are lost, it is entitled to collect the insurance money. However, both *Incoterms* and maritime practice seem to indicate that, *if the seller desires,* it may forego its right to collect on the documents and negotiate the bill of lading directly to the buyer and make other arrangements for payment or credit.

If the seller intends to arrange ocean transportation, but will be delivering the goods to a road or rail carrier, inland waterway, or to a multimodal terminal operator for transit to the seaport, the seller may wish to quote *CPT, Port of Rotterdam.* Here, the risk of loss shifts to the buyer when the goods are delivered to the first carrier. CIP terms are the same as under CPT, with the added requirement that the seller procure insurance to cover the buyer's risk of loss.

"D" Terms. Contracts with *D terms* of sale are destination contracts. If the seller in Albany is willing to enter into a destination contract, then it must be willing to accept far greater responsibility than under any other terms. For the price stated in the contract, the seller must not only deliver the goods at the port of destination, but bear the risk of loss throughout the journey. Thus, if the goods are lost in transit, the Dutch buyer would not be entitled to claim the insurance money although the buyer may have lost profits it was hoping to make on the goods.

DES and DEQ are destination terms used for ocean cargo. If the contract terms are *DES Rotterdam,* the seller must pay the ocean freight to Rotterdam, but the buyer pays the unloading charges at the Rotterdam terminal. Under *DEQ Rotterdam,* the seller will pay the ocean freight, import duties, and unloading charges to place the goods on the *quay* (pronounced "kee," meaning the dock or wharf) in Rotterdam. When specifically stated in the sales contract, the seller may also agree to obtain import licenses from the government of the Netherlands, and pay the import duties and taxes at the port of entry. DES and DEQ terms are commonly used with open account payment terms, although the seller may tender a negotiable bill of lading accompanied by all necessary documents to clear the goods through Dutch customs. Clearly, the seller will not want to take on the responsibility and risks of a DEQ shipment unless it is experienced in importing into the Netherlands and familiar with customs regulations and tariff laws there.

Today, destination contracts are actually becoming increasingly popular due to an increasingly competitive and globalized marketplace. Many manufacturers and other shippers find they must do more and more to win and keep customers. In other words, shippers often have to provide credit terms to their customers by shipping on open account and giving the customer time to pay. Shippers are also being forced to take greater responsibility for getting the goods into the customer's hands. For these reasons, more and more shippers are quoting prices on D terms than ever before. Still others are quoting prices on C terms to shift the risk of the voyage, but voluntarily foregoing the documentary collection and sending the bill of lading directly to the customer for payment on open account.

Modification of Trade Terms

On occasion, the parties may be tempted to alter the meaning of a trade term in their contract to meet their own business requirements. The International Chamber of Commerce and many experienced lawyers usually recommend that buyer and seller do not attempt to add to, explain, or change the meaning of any trade term without legal advice. This "customizing" only causes needless confusion. The problem usually arises in CIF contract cases. The general rule is that if the additional shipping terms added by the parties to a CIF contract do not contradict the usual terms of a CIF contract, then the contract will still be considered a CIF contract.

On the other hand, if the parties insert additional terms that are contrary to the usual meaning of CIF, then it can destroy the CIF terms. For instance, assume that the parties enter into a contract labeled "CIF." They then add that "payment is not due until the goods are sold by the buyer." A court would then have to decide, looking at all the evidence, whether the contract was on CIF terms. This issue was one discussed by the court in the *Kumar* case. As you read, notice that the court decides the case on the basis of the seller's failure to obtain insurance on the cargo as required under CIF terms.

---

http://www.tradeport.org
California's gateway to global trade. Take the export tutorial, "Focusing on Detail." Examines pricing issues in export marketing, price quotations, freight strategies, Incoterms, and terms of sale.

Kumar Corp. v. Nopal Lines, Ltd.
462 So.2d 1178 (1985)
District Court of Appeals of Florida, Third District

BACKGROUND AND FACTS
Kumar sold 700 television sets to one of its largest customers, Nava, in Venezuela. The contract was on CIF terms, Maracaibo. However, they agreed that Nava would not pay Kumar until Nava actually sold the merchandise. Kumar obtained the televisions from its supplier, received them in its Miami warehouse, loaded them on a trailer, delivered the trailer to its freight forwarder, Maduro, in Florida, and obtained the shipping documents. The trailer was stolen from the Maduro lot and found abandoned and empty. Kumar had failed to obtain marine insurance on the cargo. Kumar sued Maduro and the carrier. The defendants argued that, since the risk of loss had passed from Kumar to Nava, Kumar did not have standing to sue. The trial court agreed with the defendants and dismissed Kumar's case. Kumar appealed.

DANIEL S. PEARSON, JUDGE
Kumar's argument that it is the real party in interest proceeds . . . from the premise that its agreement to postpone Nava's obligation to pay for the goods modified the ordinary consequence of the CIF contract that the risk of loss shifts to the buyer. A CIF contract is a recognized and established form of contract, the incidents of which are well known. Thus, if a buyer and seller adopt such a contract, "they will be presumed, in the absence of any express term to the contrary, to have adopted all the normal incidents of that type of contract," D. M. Day, *The Law of International Trade*, 4 (1981), one of which is that the buyer, not the seller, bears the risk of loss when the goods are delivered to the carrier and the seller's other contractual obligations are fulfilled. A CIF contract is not a contract "that goods shall arrive, but a contract to ship goods complying with the contract of sale, to obtain, unless the contract otherwise provides, the ordinary contract of carriage to the place of destination, and the ordinary contract of insurance of the goods on that voyage, and to tender these documents against payment of the contract price." C. Schmitthoff, *The Law and Practice of International Trade*, 26–27 (7th ed. 1980).

It is clear, however, that parties may vary the terms of a CIF contract to meet their own requirements. But where the agreed-upon variation is such that it removes a vital ingredient of a CIF contract, then the contract ceases to be a CIF contract. Thus, "if according to the intention of the parties the actual delivery of the goods [to the buyer] is an essen-

continued

continued

tial condition of performance, the contract is not a CIF contract." C. Schmitthoff, *supra*.

In the present case, Kumar and Nava agreed to payment upon Nava's sale of the goods in Venezuela . . . [thereby negating an essential ingredient of the CIF contract]. . . . [T]he use of the term CIF does not ipso facto make the contract a CIF contract if the contract has been altered in a manner that is repugnant to the very nature of a CIF contract. Therefore, because the record before us does not . . . conclusively show that the contract remained a true CIF contract despite the agreement between Kumar and Nava concerning the payment for the goods, it was improper for the trial court to conclude as a matter of law that the risk of loss passed to Nava when Kumar delivered the goods to the shipper.

But even assuming, arguendo, that we were to conclude, as did the trial court, that the risk of loss passed to Nava merely by virtue of the label CIF on

the contract, Kumar must still prevail. Under the CIF contract, Kumar was obliged to procure insurance, and by not doing so, acted, intentionally or unintentionally, as the insurer of the shipment. As the insurer of the shipment, Kumar was obliged to pay Nava, the risk bearer, for the loss when the goods were stolen. Being legally obliged to pay Nava's loss, Kumar would thus be subrogated to Nava's claims against the appellees. Since a subrogee is the real party in interest and may sue in its own name, Kumar would have standing to sue under this theory.

Reversed and remanded for further proceedings.

Decision.   The court held that where, under a CIF contract, the seller fails to obtain marine cargo insurance on behalf of the buyer, the risk of loss remains with the seller, who becomes a self-insurer of the property. As such, the seller has standing to sue the carrier for the cargo loss.

CHAPTER SUMMARY

In an international contract for the sale of goods, the terms of sale are as essential to the contract as the quality of the goods themselves. Moving goods around the world is expensive and risky. If a contract does not specify the terms of sale and who bears the risk of loss, the parties may be in for a tremendous surprise. Moreover, because of the risk of nonpayment and nondelivery, the parties may not wish to do business on cash or open account terms until a business relationship is established. Thus, an understanding of the documentary sale, as well as of the most common trade terms, is necessary for any international sales specialist or export manager.

Despite the continued widespread use of the documentary sale, its use has declined greatly in the past thirty years due to a number of factors. First, the greater reliability of international credit reporting makes open account transactions between foreign parties much safer than in previous years. Second, the increasing globalization of markets means that foreign manufactured goods are now no longer available only from foreign sources. Many of the same products can be easily purchased from domestic sources, such as domestic subsidiaries of foreign manufacturers, or through local distributors. Nevertheless, the documentary sale is often used when the credit risk is high or when the goods will be resold while in transit.

No reader should be left with the impression that the documentary sale eliminates the risk of foreign shipments. For example, the buyer might refuse the documents when they are presented by its bank, or the buyer might buy documents that appear to be in order, only to find defective merchandise in the containers. To minimize these risks, a seller can insist in the contract that the documents will be purchased, not by the buyer, but by the buyer's bank, as discussed in a later chapter.

Questions and Case Problems

1. Bruitrix held a bill of lading covering a shipment of washing machines that it had purchased. The washing machines were placed into a bonded warehouse operated by the British Transport Commission. Bruitrix pledged the bill of lading to its creditor, Barclay's Bank, as security for an outstanding debt. Two months later, the defendant, the Commissioners of Customs, obtained a judgment against Bruitrix for a delinquent tax. The bank attempted to take possession of the goods in order to satisfy Bruitrix's outstanding debt. On the same day, the Commissioners attempted to take possession of the goods to satisfy their judgment. The bank brought this action claiming that the pledge had transferred title to the goods to it, and that as the holder of the bill of lading it was entitled to the goods. Who has a greater right in the property, Barclay's Bank or the Commissioners? Why? How does the bill of lading serve as a financing device? The bill of lading is a contract of carriage. When does the carrier discharge its performance under the contract? *Barclay's Bank, Ltd. v. Commissioners of Customs and Excise,* 1 Lloyd's 81, Queen's Bench (1963).

2. Colorado Fuel sold caustic soda to a buyer in Bombay under a CIF contract. The soda was fully loaded aboard ship when a labor strike made it impossible for the vessel to sail. As a result, the soda arrived in Bombay six months late. The buyer sued for the late shipment. Was Colorado Fuel liable for damages? Does it matter that Colorado Fuel may have known that a strike was imminent? *Badhwar v. Colorado Fuel and Iron Corp.,* 138 F. Supp. 595 (S.D.N.Y. 1955).

3. Buyer and seller entered into a contract for the sale of sugar from the Philippines to New York on CIF terms. They added language to the contract that delivery was to be "at a customary safe wharf or refinery at New York, Philadelphia, or Baltimore to be designated by the buyer." Before the sugar arrived, the United States placed a quota on sugar imports. The sugar was not allowed to be imported and was placed in a customs warehouse. The buyer refused the documents and the seller sued, claiming that the import restriction was no excuse for the buyer's nonpayment. The buyer argued that the language calling for delivery to a U.S. port converted a shipment contract into a destination contract. Was this a CIF contract or a destination contract? What was the effect of the additional shipping language used by the parties? Why should the parties not attempt to modify a trade term or add other delivery language? *Warner Bros. & Co. v. A.C. Israel,* 101 F.2d 59 (2nd Cir. 1939).

4. Phillips contracted to buy naphtha from Tradax for shipment from Algeria to Puerto Rico on C&F terms. Shipment was to be made between September 20 and 28, 1981. The agreement incorporated the ICC *Incoterms.* It also contained a *force majeure* clause that stated, "In the event of any event delaying shipment or delivery of the goods by the seller, the unaffected party may cancel the unfulfilled balance of the contract." On September 16, Tradax shipped on the *Oxy Trader.* While enroute, the *Oxy Trader* was detained by maritime authorities at Gibraltar, deemed unsafe, and was not allowed to proceed. Tradax informed Phillips, which telexed back on October 1 that October 15 was the last acceptable delivery date. On October 7, its cargo had to be off-loaded in Portugal for shipment on another vessel. On October 13, Phillips refused payment of the documents due to the delay. In November, the cargo was sold by Tradax to a third party at a loss. Phillips brought this action in the United States. Tradax claimed that it had ceased to bear responsibility for the goods when it transferred the goods to the carrier for shipment. Phillips maintained that it was excused from performance because the ship's delay constituted *force majeure.* Judgment for whom and why? *Phillips Puerto Rico Core, Inc. v. Tradax Petroleum Ltd.,* 782 F.2d 314 (2nd Cir. 1985).

5. Design Inc., in Newport, Rhode Island, entered into a contract with Buenavista, S.A. in Barcelona, Spain to buy 1,000 sheets of stained glass. The contract contained a delivery clause which read, "FOB Hasta Luego." The contract also stated that it was to be interpreted in accordance with *Incoterms.* While the glass was being loaded onto the ship (*Hasta Luego*), one of the crates slipped from the loading mechanism and landed in the water before it crossed the ship's rail. Who bears the risk of loss of the glass? Would the answer change if the contract was governed by the UCC?

6. The defendant agreed to sell watches to the buyer in Mexico. A notation was printed at the bottom of the contract, which, translated into English, reads as follows: "Please send the merchandise in cardboard boxes duly strapped with metal bands via air parcel post to Chetumal. Documents to Banco de Commercio De Quintana Roo S.A." There were no provisions in the contract that specifically allocated the risk of loss on the goods sold while in the possession of the carrier. When the goods were lost in transit, the buyer sued for a refund of his purchase price. Judgment was entered for the defendant and the buyer appealed. Judgment for whom and why? Was this a shipment or destination contract? When or where did the risk of loss pass? *Pestana v. Karinol Corp.,* 367 So.2d 1096 (Fla. Dist. Ct. App. 1979).

Managerial Implications

You receive a fax transmittal from Japanese buyers you met in New York. They indicate that they would like to place an order for 5,000 down bed pillows. The pillows must contain no less than 85 percent cluster prime white goose down. In order to make the transportation as cost effective as possible, they would like to have pricing for a full ocean container. Before placing the order, they do have some questions about the details of the sale.

Their fax has indicated that although they would prefer to pay for the pillows on open account terms, they would consider your suggestions for payment options. They have indicated that they are unwilling to purchase against the documents unless they can first inspect the pillows on their arrival in Japan. They want this right of inspection to find out if the quality is what they had ordered and to look for possible freight damage. They feel strongly about this issue and insist on these conditions, unless you can show them that they can be adequately protected. In addition, they also would like to consider the cost of alternative shipping arrangements before they decide whether they want to handle this themselves.

1. Prepare a pro forma invoice giving your buyer several options for shipping the pillows. Consider how they will be packed and transported to the closest or best seaport. What facilities are available for handling containerized cargo or for multimodal transport in your region? Utilizing *Incoterms,* present a breakdown of the shipping alternatives and costs involved in the transaction. Contact a freight forwarder and inquire as to what services it can provide. Can it assist you in obtaining the information you need to prepare your pro forma invoice?

2. In determining your export price, what other factors must be taken into consideration in addition to freight costs? Do you consider additional communication expenses, port fees, trade show expense, forwarder fees, sales agents, and clerical expenses? Discuss your export pricing with your marketing team and decide on your pricing strategy.

3. Prepare a letter to accompany the pro forma invoice explaining why payment by "cash against documents" would be fair to both parties. What can you propose to address their concerns that the goods shipped will conform to their quality specifications? How will they be protected from marine risks?

Notes

1. For the complete text of *Incoterms,* explanation, and graphical presentation, see Jan Ramberg, *ICC Guide to Incoterms* 2000. ICC Publishing S.A., ICC Publication No. 620A (2000), available through ICC Publishing Corporation, New York, N.Y.

CHAPTER 6

THE CARRIAGE OF GOODS AND THE LIABILITY OF AIR AND SEA CARRIERS

The last two chapters examined the legal relationship between the seller and buyer in a contract for the international sale of goods. Introduced were some basic concepts about the relationship between the seller and the carrier that undertakes to transport the goods to the buyer, such as the function and importance of transport documents. This chapter discusses the liability of the carrier for damage or loss to cargo while it is in transit. It includes the following subjects: (1) the liability of carriers for misdelivery of goods, (2) the liability of international air carriers, (3) the liability of ocean carriers, (4) transport intermediaries, and (5) selected issues in maritime and marine cargo insurance law.

CARRIER'S LIABILITY FOR MISDELIVERY OF CARGO

In the last chapter, we learned that a bill of lading is a transport document and a contract of carriage. Under the terms of that contract, the carrier may release cargo only to the authorized holder of the original bill of lading, in the case of a negotiable order bill of lading, or to the consignee named in a straight bill of lading. But the practicalities of day-to-day business are such that occasionally cargo is released to the wrong party. For instance, in many reported cases, cargo has been released to the notify party instead of the consignee. The notify party, usually an agent of the importer—such as a customs broker, warehousing firm, banker, or business associate—is supposed to be notified when the cargo arrives at its destination, but it is not entitled to take possession. In

other cases, the cargo may be released improperly to the right party. For example, if the payment terms are "cash on the documents," but the cargo is released to the buyer without demanding presentation of the bill of lading, it is very possible that the seller may never be paid.

In the following case, *Allied Chemical International Corp. v. Companhia de Navegacao Lloyd*, involving an order bill of lading, the carrier released cargo to the buyer in Brazil on presentation of a tax certificate, but not the bill of lading. Unfortunately for the seller, the bill of lading was still in the hands of the negotiating bank. The circumstances of this case illustrate a practice that is not uncommon in some regions of the world.

BAILMENTS AND COMMON CARRIERS

An understanding of the legal arrangement between the one shipping the goods and the one carrying the goods is important. When a carrier accepts cargo for transport a bailment situation is created. A *bailment* is a legal arrangement whereby the owner of property, the *bailor*, transfers possession of the property to the *bailee*. One example of a bailment occurs when a bailor places goods in a warehouse for storage. The owner of the warehouse is the bailee. In the context of shipping goods, the bailor is the *shipper* who places goods in the hands of a *common carrier*, the bailee, for transport to a *consignee*. A common carrier is a carrier that contracts with the public for transportation services, and might include road, rail, air, ocean, and inland waterway carriers. As discussed in the last chapter, the contract between

Allied Chemical International Corp. v. Companhia De Navegacao Lloyd Brasileiro
775 F.2d 476 (1985)
United States Court of Appeals (2nd Cir.)

BACKGROUND AND FACTS

Allied Chemical, a U.S. exporter, received an order from Banylsa, a Brazilian importer, for a shipment of caprolactam, terms C&F Salvador, Brazil. Allied delivered the bags to Lloyd, the carrier, at the Port of Norfolk and received clean order bills of lading showing that the goods were consigned to the order of Banylsa. Banylsa was also listed as the notify party. Allied sent the bill of lading, draft, and invoice to a Brazilian bank for collection, together with a letter of instruction to deliver the documents only on payment of the sight drafts. In the meantime, the goods had been put into a warehouse under the supervision of the port authority. However, in order to obtain the goods from a state warehouse, one may produce either the bill of lading or a *carta declaratoria*, a letter from the carrier stating that Brazilian import fees had been paid. Banylsa obtained a *carta declaratoria* from Lloyd and used it to obtain possession of the goods from the warehouse. Banylsa never purchased the bill of lading and never paid for the goods. Banylsa then became insolvent and filed for receivership in Brazilian civil court. Allied sued Lloyd for misdelivery in New York.

MESKILL, CIRCUIT JUDGE

The liability question in this case inextricably involves the critical importance of the documentary transaction in overseas trade. . . . "Delivery to the consignee named in the bill of lading does not suffice to discharge the [carrier] where the consignee does not hold the bill of lading." 2 T.G. Carver, *Carriage by Sea* P. 1953 (R. Colinvaux 13th ed. 1982). If the carrier delivers the goods to one other than the authorized holder of the bill of lading, the carrier is liable for misdelivery. The ocean carrier's liability arises from rights of property and "[d]elivery to a person not entitled to the goods without production of the bill of lading is prima facie a conversion of the goods and a breach of contract." . . .

While it is clear . . . that Lloyd retained some responsibilities after discharge, the bill of lading did not specify what they might be. Therefore, "the law steps in to fill the lacuna" and provides that when Lloyd discharged the cargo, it assumed the status of a bailee. The transfer of the cargo to the port authority, without more, did not alter this status; thus Lloyd remained presumptively responsible for the proper delivery of the goods. We have previously articulated the applicable standard of responsibility under admiralty law: "a bailee is absolutely liable for misdelivering cargo, unless his mistake as to the person entitled to receive the goods was induced by the bailor" or the contract of carriage otherwise reduced or eliminated his liability. There is no suggestion in the record that Allied induced the misdelivery. Allied was not even aware until well after the event that Banylsa had acquired possession of the goods. . . .

Pursuant to the Pomerene Act (Federal Bills of Lading Act), a carrier operating under an order bill of lading is justified in delivering the goods to one lawfully entitled to them or to one in possession of an order bill "by the terms of which the goods are deliverable to his order; or which has been indorsed to him, or in blank by the consignee." When Lloyd caused the goods to be released to Banylsa, by means of the *carta declaratoria*, the bill of lading was still in the custody of the Brazilian bank because payment had not been made on the sight draft. Not having paid on the draft, Banylsa was neither lawfully entitled to the goods nor in possession of the bill. Delivery to Banylsa, therefore, was not justified. . . .

The fact that the government-controlled port authority, rather than Lloyd itself, physically delivered the goods to Banylsa does not in any way relieve Lloyd from liability. As previously noted, it is undisputed that unless Banylsa presented to the port authority either the original bill of lading or a *carta declaratoria* issued by the carrier, the port authority would not have permitted Banylsa to take the cargo. Because Banylsa did not pay the sight draft and take possession of the bill of lading, Lloyd retained control over the goods. Thus, Lloyd acted at its peril when it authorized the release of the goods to Banylsa without demanding production of the bill. . . .

The judgment of the district court is affirmed. Appellant is liable for costs.

Decision. The court held that the carrier was liable for misdelivery of the goods for two reasons. First, a bill of lading is a contract of carriage that must be strictly construed against the party that drafted it, the carrier.

continued

---

continued

Secondly, the court determined that the carrier was liable as a bailee of property belonging to another (the bailor). Thus, if the carrier delivers the goods to someone other than the authorized holder of the bill of lading, the carrier is liable for misdelivery, resulting in the tort of conversion of the goods and a breach of contract.

Comment. Although the court allowed the shipper to recover from the carrier, this case should still serve as a word of caution to U.S. export managers. Beware of maritime customs and shipping practices in countries in which one is inexperienced in doing business.

---

shipper and carrier is called a *contract of carriage,* and it is evidenced in the written *transport document.* In ocean carriage, this contract is the *bill of lading.* In air carriage it is the *air waybill.* (Copies of these documents appear in Chapter Five.) The rights and responsibilities of shipper and carrier to one another depends on the contractual provisions in the transport document and on the law applicable to that contract. In any case involving damage to cargo, the plaintiff is usually the person or party who has title to the goods, whether it is the original shipper, the consignee, or other party who has acquired title to the goods.

Under the traditional law of bailments, a carrier must return the property to the bailor (or deliver it to the consignee or holder of the bill of lading) in the same condition in which it was received. Thus, common carriers are held strictly liable for damage or loss to goods. If goods are destroyed or stolen, the carrier is liable even if it was not at fault. Common carriers, however, are not liable for damage or loss caused by (1) acts of God, such as an earthquake, (2) an act of a public enemy or terrorist, (3) an act of government intervention or court order, (4) an act of the shipper, such as improper packaging or mislabeling, or (5) an inherent characteristic of the goods such as perishability or chemical reaction, that causes its own destruction or waste. Historically, carriers could also limit their liability through *disclaimers.* A disclaimer is an exculpatory clause written into the bill of lading or air waybill that limits or relieves the carrier of liability for injuries or damage. Air and ocean carriers are in powerful positions vis-à-vis passengers and shippers. They are capable of saying, "If you wish to fly with us, or sail aboard our ship, here are the terms—we will not be liable for any damages at all to you or your property, take it or leave it." To redress this difference in bargaining power between international carriers and their customers, in the 1920s and 1930s, nations took action to prohibit the use of disclaimers, and to set forth in laws exactly when carriers will be liable and in what amount.

In the United States, the liability of a carrier for damage or loss to cargo in domestic shipments is determined by a combination of the common law of bailments, and state and federal statutes (including the *Uniform Commercial Code* and regulations of U.S. government agencies). International shipments are treated much differently. They are governed primarily by international law.

The Liability of International Air Carriers: From Warsaw to Montreal

The liability of air carriers for loss or damage to baggage and cargo, as well as for bodily injury or death of passengers, is governed by a host of international treaties and national laws. Indeed, air disasters can lead lawyers to many conflict-of-law questions. For example, in the United States alone, the extent of an air carrier's liability in an accident depends on whether the injured or deceased passenger was on a domestic or international trip, whether the accident occurred over land or sea, whether it was within 12 miles of the U.S. shoreline, or whether it was over the high seas in "international waters." As a result, air disasters often result in protracted legal arguments over where cases are to be heard and under which law they will be decided. Nevertheless, there are many common principles governing the area that are derived from international treaties that date back to the early days of aviation. Our discussion is thus limited to concepts that would apply to most international flights, although not necessarily all. Remember that these rules do not apply to passengers ticketed solely for domestic travel.

The Warsaw and Montreal Conventions

Since 1929 the most important multilateral treaty defining the liability of air carriers has been the *Warsaw Convention*. This agreement was adopted by the United States and has been the law in almost 150 nations. The *Warsaw Convention* has been amended many times since 1929, including the important *Protocol 4 of 1999* that was adopted by fifty-four countries, including the United States and other major air transport nations. However, the most important change to air transportation law in seventy years occurred with the adoption of the *1999 Convention for the Unification of Certain Rules for International Carriage by Air,* known as the *1999 Montreal Convention*. This treaty has been ratified by those countries shown in Exhibit 6.1, and by the United States in 2003, supplanting the *Warsaw Convention,* and making it applicable to flights between these signatory nations. The newer *Montreal Convention* generally modernized the law (including provisions for issuing tickets and air waybills electronically), and eliminated many of the criticisms of the older treaty. While the focus of the 1929 treaty was on the protection of the air industry, the *Montreal Convention* focuses on the protection of air travelers. The *Warsaw Convention* will continue to remain an important source of law until more nations ratify the newer treaty. Therefore we will discuss its provisions, noting changes brought about by *Protocol 4* and the *Montreal Convention* where appropriate.

As you read, keep in mind that international treaties often take the name of the city in which they were signed. There can be other "Montreal

ExHIBIT 6.1
Countries that have ratified the Montreal Convention (as of 2003)

Bahrain	Mexico
Barbados	Namibia
Belize	New Zealand
Botswana	Nigeria
Canada	Panama
Cameroon	Paraguay
Colombia	Peru
Cyprus	Portugal
Czech Republic	Romania
Estonia	Slovakia
Greece	Slovenia
Japan	Syria
Jordan	Tanzania
Kenya	United Arab Emirates
Kuwait	United States
Macedonia	

Conventions," such as the famous treaty on the protection of the environment, so be careful of the context in which you are speaking when you refer to the convention by name.

Limitations on Air Carrier Liability and Special Drawing Rights

At the beginning of air travel in the early part of this century, the risk of an air disaster was far greater than today. The risk was so great that investors feared entering the aviation industry in which their fortunes could be wiped out in one disaster. Insurance companies also feared insuring the new air carriers. Governments soon realized that firms entering the fledgling aviation industry required protection from catastrophic loss in order for the industry to flourish. The delegates to the *Warsaw Convention* recognized the need for a uniform monetary limit on the liability of an air carrier for loss or damage to baggage or cargo, or for bodily injuries or loss of life. In the interest of uniformity, the delegates decided to express the limit not in the currency of any one nation, but in an amount of currency relative to the value of gold. This method worked well until the 1970s when gold was no longer used as a standard value for currencies. For some years after that, in the United States, the limitation on liability was determined by a ruling of the

U.S. Supreme Court. Today, the limitation of an air carrier's liability is set in *Special Drawing Rights* (SDRs). SDRs represent an artificial "basket" of currency values developed by the International Monetary Fund (IMF). The value of an SDR on any given day can be found by consulting the IMF (available online). At the close of 2003, one SDR was worth approximately $1.46. Under the *Montreal Convention* nations will review the limitation on liability periodically, and will be able to adjust it upward to account for inflation.

Liability for Death or Bodily Injury

A plaintiff in an air accident is usually the injured passenger or the estate or heirs of a deceased passenger. An airline is liable for death or injury to a passenger ticketed for international travel (including a passenger who is injured or killed in an accident in their own country, provided that their ticket included travel to or from another country) and which occurs as a result of *an accident* aboard an aircraft or in the process of boarding or disembarking. There are many court decisions discussing the meaning of "accident." It generally requires that the injury be caused by some event that is a peculiar risk of air travel and "external" to the passenger. This might include injuries resulting from a bomb threat, skyjacking, the spilling of hot coffee on a passenger, or a crash landing. A blood clot in a passenger's leg is not an "external" event, and thus not an accident. However, in *Olympic Airways v. Husain*, 2004 WL 329950 (2004) an asthmatic passenger died from an allergic reaction to secondhand smoke aboard the aircraft. The United States Supreme Court ruled that the flight attendant's refusal to move him away from the smoke was an "unusual and unexpected event external to the passenger" and thus, an "accident" under the Warsaw Convention. In the following case, *El Al Israel Airlines, Ltd. v. Tseng*, the United States Supreme Court considers whether a passenger may bring a claim against an air carrier under New York law for psychological damages arising out of a search of her person by a security guard, where her claim could not otherwise be brought under the *Warsaw Convention.*

Limitations on Liability for Death or Bodily Injuries.

Under the *Warsaw Convention* an air carrier is protected by a $75,000 maximum limit on damages. A plaintiff can collect a higher amount only if it proves that the damage resulted from an act of the carrier, its employees or agents, done with the intent to cause damage or done recklessly and with knowledge that injuries or death would likely result ("willful misconduct"). As amended by *Protocol 4,* the carrier is not liable if it proves that it, or its employees or agents, have taken "all measures to avoid the damage or that it was impossible for them to take such measures." While most cases do not involve "willful misconduct" this was found in several notable cases. In the case of Pan Am Flight 103 that went down over Lockerbie, Scotland, the courts found willful misconduct where the carrier failed to stop a bomb from being smuggled aboard the aircraft. Willful misconduct by the carrier was also found in the case of Korean Airlines Flight 007 traveling from New York to South Korea. After refueling in Alaska, the crew had strayed several hundred kilometers off course when it was shot down by the former Soviet Union while in its airspace over the Sea of Japan. The limitation on liability and the willful misconduct requirement became unpopular in recent years, and became one of the most controversial subjects in air transportation law. It was considered totally inadequate by modern standards to compensate air disaster victims.

As of 2003, the *Montreal Convention* abolishes the $75,000 limit and sets out a new framework for the carrier's liability. First, the carrier is *strictly liable* for all damages up to 100,000 SDRs (about $146,000 in 2003) arising out of an accident, whether the carrier was at fault or not (subject to the defense of contributory negligence). The carrier is then liable for all proven damages above 100,000 SDRs unless it can show either 1) that the damages were not due to its negligence, or to the negligence of its agents or employees, or 2) that the damages were *solely* due to the negligence or wrongful acts of third parties. If the carrier is even partly at fault, it is liable for the entire sum of damages. Recognizing that plaintiffs in air disaster litigation have often had to wait many years before receiving any money from settlements or judgments, countries may now require carriers to make advance payments to individuals to meet the immediate economic needs of those entitled to compensation.

Punitive damages cannot be collected and are prohibited. By national law and court decision, damages for mental anguish or psychological injury

El Al *Israel Airlines, Ltd. v. Tseng*
525 U.S. 155, 119 S.Ct. 662 (1999)
United States Supreme Court

BACKGROUND AND FACTS
Tseng purchased a ticket on an *El Al* flight from New York to Tel Aviv in 1993. Prior to boarding, an *El Al* security guard questioned her about her travel plans. The guard considered her response "illogical" and ranked her as a "high risk" passenger. Tseng was taken to a private security room, told to remove her shoes and to lower her blue jeans to mid-hip. A female guard then searched her body outside her clothing by hand. Nothing was found, and she was allowed to board. Tseng sued *El Al* for damages in a New York state court, asserting her claim under New York law for assault and false imprisonment, claiming mental and psychosomatic injuries. She did not claim any bodily injury. *El Al* removed the case to the federal district court, which dismissed the claim on the basis of the *Warsaw Convention*. On appeal, the Court of Appeals concluded that no "accident" had occurred under the meaning of the *Warsaw Convention,* and therefore the Convention did not apply. The court then ruled that national law was intended to provide a remedy for the passenger where the Convention did not expressly apply. *El Al* then appealed to the U.S. Supreme Court.

JUSTICE GINSBURG DELIVERED THE OPINION OF THE COURT
[Tseng's] case presents a question of the Convention's exclusivity: When the Convention allows no recovery for the episode-in-suit, does it correspondingly preclude the passenger from maintaining an action for damages under another source of law, in this case, New York tort law? The exclusivity question before us has been settled prospectively in a *Warsaw Convention* protocol *(Montreal Protocol 4)* recently ratified by the Senate. . . . We conclude that the protocol, to which the United States has now subscribed, clarifies, but does not change, the Convention's exclusivity domain. We therefore hold that recovery for a personal injury suffered "on board [an] aircraft or in the course of any of the operations of embarking or disembarking," if not allowed under the Convention, is not available at all. [citations omitted] * * *

At the outset, we highlight key provisions of the treaty we are interpreting. The *Warsaw Convention* . . . declares . . . that the "[C]onvention shall apply to all international transportation of persons, baggage, or goods performed by aircraft for hire."
* * * Article 17 establishes the conditions of liability for personal injury to passengers: "The carrier shall be liable for damage sustained in the event of the death or wounding of a passenger or any other bodily injury suffered by a passenger, if the accident which caused the damage so sustained took place on board the aircraft or in the course of any of the operations of embarking or disembarking." * * * We accept it as given that *El Al*'s search of Tseng was not an "accident" within the meaning of Article 17, for the parties do not place that Court of Appeals conclusion at issue. . . . The parties do not dispute that the episode-in-suit occurred in international transportation in the course of embarking.

Our inquiry begins with the text of Article 24, which prescribes the exclusivity of the Convention's provisions for air carrier liability. * * * Article 24 provides that "cases covered by article 17" . . . may "only be brought subject to the conditions and limits set out in the Convention." In Tseng's view, and in the view of the Court of Appeals, [Article 17] means those cases in which a passenger could actually maintain a claim for relief under Article 17. So read, Article 24 would permit any passenger whose personal injury suit did not satisfy the liability conditions of Article 17 to pursue the claim under local law.

In *El Al*'s view, on the other hand, and in the view of the United States as *amicus curiae,* [Article 17] refers generically to all personal injury cases stemming from occurrences on board an aircraft or in embarking or disembarking, and simply distinguishes that class of cases from cases involving damaged luggage or goods, or delay. So read, Article 24 would preclude a passenger from asserting any air transit personal injury claims under local law, including claims that failed to satisfy Article 17's liability conditions, notably, because the injury did not result from an "accident," or because the "accident" did not result in physical injury or physical manifestation of injury.

Respect is ordinarily due the reasonable views of the Executive Branch concerning the meaning of an international treaty. See *Sumitomo Shoji America,*

continued

continued

Inc. v. Avagliano, 457 U.S. 176, 102 S.Ct. 2374 (1982) ("Although not conclusive, the meaning attributed to treaty provisions by the Government agencies charged with their negotiation and enforcement is entitled to great weight."). We conclude that the Government's construction of Article 24 is most faithful to the Convention's text, purpose, and overall structure.

The cardinal purpose of the *Warsaw Convention,* we have observed, is to "achiev[e] uniformity of rules governing claims arising from international air transportation." *Eastern Airlines, Inc. v. Floyd,* 499 U.S. 530, 111 S.Ct. 1489 (1991). The Convention signatories, in the treaty's preamble, specifically "recognized the advantage of regulating in a uniform manner the conditions of . . . the liability of the carrier." To provide the desired uniformity, the Convention sets out an array of liability rules which, the treaty declares, "apply to all international transportation of persons, baggage, or goods performed by aircraft." * * * Given the Convention's comprehensive scheme of liability rules and its textual emphasis on uniformity, we would be hard put to conclude that the delegates at Warsaw meant to subject air carriers to the distinct, nonuniform liability rules of the individual signatory nations. * * *

Construing the Convention, as did the Court of Appeals, to allow passengers to pursue claims under local law when the Convention does not permit recovery could produce several anomalies. Carriers might be exposed to unlimited liability under diverse legal regimes, but would be prevented, under the treaty, from contracting out of such liability. Passengers injured physically in an emergency landing might be subject to the liability caps of the Convention, while those merely traumatized in the same mishap would be free to sue outside of the Convention for potentially unlimited damages. The Court of Appeals' construction of the Convention would encourage artful pleading by plaintiffs seeking to opt out of the Convention's liability scheme when local law promised recovery in excess of that prescribed by the treaty. Such a reading would scarcely advance the predictability that adherence to the treaty has achieved worldwide. * * *

Tseng . . . argues that air carriers will escape liability for their intentional torts if passengers are not permitted to pursue personal injury claims outside of the terms of the Convention. But we have already cautioned that the definition of "accident" under Article 17 is an "unusual event . . . *external to the passenger,*" and that "[t]his definition should be flex-

ibly applied." *Air France v. Saks,* 470 U.S. 392, 397, 105 S.Ct. 1338 (1985). In *Saks,* the Court concluded that no "accident" occurred because the injury there—a hearing loss—"indisputably result[ed] from *the passenger's own internal reaction* to the usual, normal, and expected operation of the aircraft." As we earlier noted, Tseng and *El Al* chose not to pursue in this Court the question whether an "accident" occurred, for an affirmative answer would still leave Tseng unable to recover under the treaty; she sustained no "bodily injury" and could not gain compensation under Article 17 for her solely psychic or psychosomatic injuries. * * *

Montreal Protocol 4, ratified by the Senate in 1998, amends Article 24 to read, in relevant part: "In the carriage of passengers and baggage, any action for damages, however founded, can only be brought subject to the conditions and limits set out in this Convention. . . ." Both parties agree that . . . the Convention's preemptive effect is clear: The treaty precludes passengers from bringing actions under local law when they cannot establish air carrier liability under the treaty. Revised Article 24 . . . merely clarifies, it does not alter, the Convention's rule of exclusivity. * * *

Courts of other nations bound by the Convention have also recognized the treaty's encompassing preemptive effect. The "opinions of our sister signatories," we have observed, are "entitled to considerable weight." *Saks.* The text, drafting history, and underlying purpose of the Convention, in sum, counsel us to adhere to a view of the treaty's exclusivity shared by our treaty partners.

Decision. The decision of the Court of Appeals is reversed. Under the *Warsaw Convention* a passenger may not bring an action for personal injury damages under local law when his or her claim does not satisfy the conditions for liability under the Convention. Recourse to local law would undermine the uniform regulation of international air carrier liability that the Convention was designed to foster.

Comment. In *Air France v. Saks,* (cited herein) the Court ruled that a passenger's permanent loss of hearing caused by the pressurization of the aircraft was not a result of an "accident" because the injury had resulted from the passenger's own internal reaction to the unusual, normal, and expected operation of an aircraft. Compare and contrast this with the more recent holding by the Court in *Olympic Airways v. Hussain,* mentioned prior to this case.

are generally not permitted in the absence of bodily injuries. Damages can be reduced if a passenger's own negligence contributed to the injury, but only if this defense is permitted under national law. (This would generally be the case in the United States and other countries that recognize principles of comparative and contributory negligence.) The conventions do not prohibit suits against third parties; thus a plaintiff can sue the manufacturer of a defectively designed or manufactured airplane that caused the accident.

Jurisdiction. Under the *Warsaw Convention* lawsuits can be brought only in a country that is party to the convention, and either in the country where the tickets were purchased, the country of the passenger's final destination, or the country where the air carrier is incorporated or has its principle place of business. The *Montreal Convention* also permits lawsuits for passenger death or injury to be brought in the country of the passenger's "principal and permanent residence," if the carrier operates or conducts business there. This will prevent passengers or their families from having to litigate cases in far off countries of the world where air disasters might occur.

Time Limitations. Where baggage or cargo are damaged, the carrier must be notified immediately, and no later than seven days from the date of receipt in the case of checked baggage and fourteen days from the date of receipt in the case of cargo. Claims for damages for delayed baggage or cargo must be made *in writing* and at the latest within twenty-one days from the date on which the baggage or cargo was actually delivered. Legal actions against air carriers for damages must be brought *within two years*.

Liability for Air Cargo and Baggage Losses

The *Montreal Convention* maintains many of the provisions of the earlier treaties with regard to liability of air carriers for loss to cargo or baggage. The *Warsaw Convention*, as amended by *Protocol 4*, holds an air carrier liable for all cargo damage unless caused by (1) an inherent defect, quality, or vice of the cargo, (2) defective packing performed by someone other than the carrier, (3) an act of war or armed conflict, or (4) an act of public authority, such as customs authorities. The air car-

rier is not liable for any cargo damage caused by the contributory negligence of the shipper.

---

http://www.joc.com
The Journal of Commerce. Established and authoritative daily reporting on all matters affecting international air and sea transportation, customs, and trade issues.

Cargo Losses. Cargo losses in the United States are limited to an amount in dollars equal to 17 SDRs per kilogram, unless the shipper has declared a higher value on the air waybill and paid an additional fee if required. This limit does not apply if it can be shown that the damage resulted from an intentional act of the air carrier or its employees, or from an act that was done recklessly and with knowledge that damage would probably result from such an act.

Baggage Losses. The liability of the carrier in the case of loss, damage or delay to baggage is limited to 1,000 SDRs for each passenger unless the passenger has declared a higher value and paid any additional fees required (but in no case greater than the actual value of the baggage).

Delay. The carrier is liable for delays in transporting passengers, baggage or cargo. However, the carrier is not liable if it proves that it and its servants and agents took *reasonable measures* to avoid the damage or that it was impossible for it or them to take such measures. Liability for delays is limited to 4150 SDRs per passenger.

The U.S. Death on the High Seas Act

The U.S. *Death on the High Seas Act* is a federal statute dating back to 1920 that gives U.S. federal courts jurisdiction over wrongful death cases arising on or above (as in the case of air disasters) the high seas. The act applies only to cases arising beyond the 12-mile territorial limit of U.S. waters. The act permits compensation for economic losses (not punitive damages). Recent amendments permit the spouse, child or other dependent relative to also recover noneconomic damages for the loss of a deceased passenger's "care, comfort and companionship" in a commercial aircraft disaster.

LIABILITY FOR THE CARRIAGE OF GOODS BY SEA

Ocean-going cargo is constantly at risk. Damage can result from any number of causes, including external forces, the inherent nature of the goods, the passage of time, or any combination of factors. Typical examples of cargo damage include infestation from insects or molds, contamination from chemicals previously held in the ship's hold, rust and other moisture damage from condensation inside the hold, damage from broken refrigeration units and other equipment, storm damage from rain and seawater, losses from fire or the sinking of the ship, damage done to cargo while rescuing the ship from peril, damage resulting from cargo being improperly stowed above deck, losses from theft and modern day piracy on the seas, damage from acts of war, and so on.

One of the greatest dangers to cargo has traditionally been pilferage and theft. This problem was particularly troublesome during the time when goods were moved by break-bulk freight. With the advent of containerization, particularly in the last twenty-five years, pilferage has been greatly reduced. The impact of containerization was described by the court in *Matsushita Electric Corp. v. S.S. Aegis Spirit,* 414 F. Supp. 894 (W.D. Wash. 1976):

> The emergent use of these cargo-carrying containers marks a significant technological stride within the maritime industry, and their use seems certain to expand in years to come because of the substantial advantages they provide over conventional modes of ocean carriage for shippers and carriers alike. Their increasing popularity finds its source in the enhanced economy and efficiency they offer in the handling, loading, stowing, and discharge of most types of seagoing cargo. Their value to shippers lies in the greater protection they afford cargo from pilferage, rough handling, and the elements. Use of containers will frequently permit the shipper to substitute lighter, more economical packaging materials without increased risk to the cargo. Furthermore, the shipper can, in most container operations, personally ensure a tight stow and the careful handling of his goods, because he has the responsibility to stuff the containers under the carriage contract. The carrier, for its part, enjoys tremendous

savings in labor by eliminating slow, manual handling and stowing of individual packages, and in claim payments by reason of reduced cargo loss and damage. Although shippers and freight forwarders sometimes acquire their own fleet of containers, carriers are the predominant owners of containers used in maritime commerce.

Despite the impact of containerization on international trade, damage and loss to cargo must be anticipated by any international shipper. In the event of a loss, inevitably the owner of the goods or the insurer will look to the carrier for recovery. But carriers enjoy considerable protection under the law.

---

http://www.mgn.com/
The "Maritime Global Net" contains information and communication resources for the international maritime community, links to ocean carriers, carrier shipping schedules, and ocean ports worldwide.

History of Carrier Liability

The law governing an ocean carrier's liability for damage or loss to cargo is rooted in the history of transportation and trade. As goods moved across the high seas on sailing ships, they were under the exclusive control of the ship's captain for months at a time. Shippers had no way of proving that goods were lost or destroyed as a result of a natural disaster, the negligence of the carrier, or from the crew's pilferage or theft. As a result, the maritime laws of both England and the United States held carriers to be absolutely liable for all loss or damage to cargo in their possession. Although a few exceptions to this liability were recognized, carriers were virtual insurers of their cargo. With the growth of trade and the advent of steamships, carriers became more economically powerful. They began to include provisions in their bills of lading (which is a contract between the shipper and carrier) that would limit their liability. These limitation-of-liability clauses attempted to free the carrier from all responsibility, including liability for its own negligence or even for providing an unfit vessel. The small shippers were at the mercy of the steamship companies. The result was a period of great uncertainty over the liability of ocean carriers.

The *Harter Act*. In 1892, the U.S. Congress first addressed the problem in the *Harter Act*, a federal law still in effect today. This act set out the liability of a carrier for the care of its cargo, and imposed restrictions on the use of exculpatory clauses in bills of lading. Subsequent developments in the law have resulted in the *Harter Act's* limited application. Today, the *Harter Act* remains applicable to contracts for the carriage of goods only from one U.S. port to another U.S. port. For international shipments, the *Harter Act* has been superseded by a new statute. The *Harter Act* also applies to the liability of the carrier for caring for the goods before they are loaded and after they are unloaded from the ship (e.g., during warehousing).

The *Hague Rules*. At the end of the first World War, other nations attempted to develop similar rules. The result was the near universal acceptance of a 1924 international convention on bills of lading known as the *Hague Rules*. These rules represent an international effort to achieve uniformity of bills of lading, and were intended to reduce the uncertainties concerning the responsibilities and liabilities of ocean carriers. The *Hague Rules* define the liability of ocean carriers for damage or loss to goods on the seas. Virtually every trading nation of the world today has incorporated them into its national law.

The *Carriage of Goods by Sea Act*

The *Hague Rules* were codified in the United States in 1936 in the *Carriage of Goods by Sea Act* or COGSA. COGSA is applicable to every bill of lading for the carriage of goods by sea, to or from ports of the United States in foreign trade. COGSA governs the liability of a carrier from the time goods are loaded onto the ship until the time the cargo is unloaded. COGSA does not apply to losses that occur prior to loading or after discharge from the vessel (during which the *Harter Act* applies). Thus, it is commonly said that COGSA applies from "tackle to tackle." However, COGSA does permit the shipper and carrier to extend the application of COGSA beyond the "tackle to tackle" period by including a provision to that effect in the bill of lading. Thus, COGSA often applies to damage losses outside the "tackle to tackle" period and to some domestic shipments

as well. Because virtually all bills of lading issued in the United States provide that they are controlled by COGSA, the discussion here concentrates on that statute.

Limitations of Liability under COGSA. COGSA invalidates all clauses in the bill of lading that try to exonerate a carrier from liability for damage or loss to cargo, or that attempt to lessen a carrier's liability beneath that set by the statute itself. For instance, a carrier is liable under COGSA if refrigeration units are inadequate to prevent spoilage of perishable fruit during a journey. A carrier cannot put a "fine print" provision in a bill of lading that says they are not liable for inadequate refrigeration; such an attempted provision is void.

Forum Selection Clauses. Prior to 1995, U.S. carriers were protected from having to defend themselves in cargo lawsuits filed in foreign countries. In that year, the U.S. Supreme Court decided *Vimar Seguros y Reaseguros, S.A. v. M/V Sky Reefer*, 115 S.Ct. 2322 (1995). The case involved over $1 million in damaged oranges shipped from Morocco to a customer in New York aboard a ship owned by a Japanese company. The bill of lading stated that any dispute would have to be resolved in Japan. In a surprising decision, the Court held that the forum selection clause was valid. The decision threw U.S. shippers into a panic because of the fear of being subjected to lawsuits in foreign countries and under foreign laws. Indeed, the unpopular decision has led the shipping industry to call for a complete repeal of COGSA by the U.S. Congress.

Nautical Liability of the Carrier

The liability of a carrier for damage or loss to ocean-going cargo is strictly defined and limited by COGSA. COGSA provides considerable protection to the carrier for cargo damage resulting from negligence in navigating or managing the ship, or from fire or storms. The carrier, however, is liable for its failure to use due diligence in providing a seaworthy ship at the beginning of the voyage.

> **http//www. admiraltylawguide.com.**
> A complete guide to legal matters affecting ocean shipping and the maritime industry.

Establishing the Carrier's Liability. When cargo is found to be damaged upon delivery, COGSA requires that written notice be given to the carrier at the port of discharge. If the damage is visible, the notice must be given before or at the time that the goods are taken from the carrier's custody. If the loss is not visible or apparent, written notice must be given to the carrier within three days of delivery. Failure to give notice in writing creates a rebuttable presumption that the goods were delivered in good condition. The statute of limitations for filing claims under COGSA is one year.

Proving liability leads to complex litigation and has resulted in untold numbers of cases in the law reports. In the event of a dispute, suits are generally brought by the shipper, owner of the cargo or holder of the bill of lading, or their insurer. The plaintiff must show that the goods were loaded in good condition and unloaded in damaged condition, or lost while in the carrier's custody. A clean bill of lading received from the carrier at the time of shipment establishes a rebuttable presumption that the goods were delivered to the carrier in good condition. The plaintiff does not have to prove that the carrier was at fault nor explain how the loss occurred. The burden shifts to the carrier to prove that it is not liable.

There is a problem in relying on a clean bill of lading in establishing the carrier's liability where the goods were shipped in a sealed ocean container. Recall that a clean bill of lading is one that contains no notations from the ship's master that there was visible evidence of damage at the time the goods were turned over to the carrier. If the goods are in closed containers or packages, damage may not be observable, and there may be no way for the carrier to know the condition of the goods inside. Here the clean bill only establishes the external condition of the outer containers. In these cases, the courts generally require the plaintiff to show more than just a clean bill. The plaintiff must prove the nature and extent of the damage, loss, or shortage and the likelihood that it occurred while in the carrier's custody. Courts generally require the shipper to introduce other evidence, such as inspection certificates or testimony from people who have knowledge of the condition of the goods before or at the time of loading. For example, there might be testimony that the damage was of the type that normally occurs at sea and not on land. In *Allied Signal Technical Services Corp. v. M/V Dagmar Maersk*, 234 F. Supp.2d 526 (D.Md. 2002), the shipper brought action against the carrier to recover for damages to a space telescope shipped to Italy. Although the court considered the testimony of the plaintiff's insurance investigators, outside experts, and employees, and of independent surveyors who supervised the loading and unloading, it found that the plaintiff's evidence was not sufficient to show that the goods were delivered to the carrier in good condition.

Carrier's Due Diligence. Once the shipper establishes that the goods were turned over to the carrier in good condition and delivered in damaged condition, it becomes the carrier's burden to show that it was not legally responsible for the damage or loss. In the case of losses at sea, the carrier does this by proving either that the damage was not caused by its failure to use *due diligence* in providing a *seaworthy ship at the beginning of the voyage* or that the loss occurred from one of the specific exemptions shown in Exhibit 6.2. This exhibit shows the specific exceptions to a carrier's liability set out in COGSA. The carrier is not liable if it can prove that the cargo was damaged as a result of an act of war or terrorism, fire, an error in navigation or management of the ship, an accident, a peril of the sea, or other exemption listed.

Seaworthiness of the Ship. The carrier is liable for damage to cargo resulting from its failure to use due diligence to make the ship seaworthy at the time of its departure on the voyage. This assurance has been called the "warranty of seaworthiness." A vessel is *seaworthy* if it is reasonably fit to carry the cargo it has undertaken to carry on the intended journey. In other words, the carrier must not only use due diligence to inspect the vessel for repair, but it must be sure the vessel is the proper type for carrying this specific type of cargo on this particular voyage. The standard of seaworthiness includes a number of factors, including the type of ship and the condition and suitability of its equipment, the competence of its crew, the type of cargo being carried and the manner in which it is stowed, the weather (e.g., was the ship prepared for the type of weather expected?), and the nature of the voyage. Some courts will recognize a presumption of *un*seaworthiness at the time of depar-

---

EXHIBIT 6.2

Carriage of Goods by Sea Act
Specific Exceptions to Liability

Carriers are not liable for losses resulting from a number of specific causes listed in the statute. These exceptions include the following:

1. Errors in the navigation or in the management of the ship

2. Fire, unless caused by the actual fault of the carrier (the corporate owner of the ship)

3. Perils, dangers, and accidents of the sea

4. An act of God (a natural disaster)

5. An act of war

6. An act of public enemies

7. Legal seizures of the ship

8. Quarantine restrictions

9. An act or omission of the shipper or owner of the goods

10. Labor strikes or lockouts

11. Riots and civil commotions

12. Saving life or property at sea

13. An inherent defect, quality, or vice of the goods that causes wastage in bulk or weight or other damage or loss

14. Insufficiency of packing

15. Inadequate marking of goods or containers

16. Latent defects in ship or equipment (which might render the ship unseaworthy) that were not discoverable by due diligence

---

ture if the ship breaks down shortly after departure in clear weather and calm seas.

The carrier is responsible for properly manning, equipping, and supplying the ship, and making the refrigerating and cooling chambers, and all other parts of the ship in which goods are carried, fit and safe for receiving, carrying, and preserving the goods. The carrier must also properly load, store, and carry the goods. For instance, the cargo holds must not be in such a condition that they cause moisture damage to the goods through condensation. Cargo should not be stowed in a manner that causes it to shift and be crushed. Cargo should not be exposed to rain and seas. Refrigeration units must be in working order, and so forth.

The carrier must also properly unload the cargo and hand it over to the party entitled to it.

Errors in Navigation or Mismanagement of the Ship. Exhibit 6.2 shows those situations in which a carrier is not liable for damage to cargo. One of the most important is that the carrier—the corporate ship's owner—is not liable for errors in navigation or mismanagement of the ship caused by the master, mariner, pilot, or a crew member (except for the crew's negligence in the care and custody of the cargo, such as during loading and unloading, for which the carrier is liable).

Understand that an error in the "navigation and management of the ship" by the crew is a very different thing than when the ship's corporate owner fails to use due diligence in providing a seaworthy ship at the beginning of the voyage. Although carriers are not liable for the former, they are liable for the latter—for failing to provide a seaworthy ship. Thus, some courts have held carriers liable for their crew's negligence by reasoning that a crew that errs in navigating or managing a ship is not competent, and a ship is not seaworthy without a competent crew. As a result, carriers are often held liable despite the protection they receive from this defense.

Damage from Fire Aboard Ship. Fire aboard ship has the potential to cause catastrophic losses at sea. Ocean carriers are not liable unless the actual negligence of the carrier—the corporate owner of the ship—caused the fire or prevented it from being extinguished. Although the U.S. federal courts disagree as to how to handle fire cases, they tend to rule that carriers will be liable for fire damage only if the corporate owner of the ship was actually at fault. The negligence of the crew is not enough to make the carrier liable. For instance, the carrier is liable if it allows the ship to leave port with inadequate firefighting equipment or with a crew untrained to fight fires.

In this instance, the carrier (i.e., the company that owned the ship) would have had control over installation of the equipment or training of the crew in firefighting. Thus, the law holds them responsible. However, once at sea, the corporate owner loses control of the ship—it becomes at the mercy of the elements and the ocean. Here, the corporate owner is not liable for losses due to fire. Once the carrier proves in court that fire damaged the cargo, the burden shifts to the plaintiff (the shipper or cargo owner) to prove that actual negligence of the ship's owner caused the fire or prevented it from being extinguished. In one of the leading fire cases, *Asbestos Corp. Ltd. v. Compagnie de Navigation,* 480 F.2d 669 (2nd Cir. 1973), a fire broke out in an engine room where large quantities of hot oil are expected to be present. The firefighting equipment was located in the engine room, and thus could not be used to extinguish the fire there. The court ruled that the ship's owner was negligent in installing the equipment at that location, and liable for the loss to cargo as a result.

Perils of the Sea. COGSA exempts carriers from liability for damage resulting from "perils, dangers, and accidents of the sea." A *peril of the sea* is a fortuitous action of the sea or weather of sufficient

international accents

High Seas Terrorism Alert in Piracy Report
London, 29 January 2003

The vulnerability of shipping to terrorist attacks is highlighted in a report on piracy and other criminal attacks at sea issued by the ICC International Maritime Bureau (IMB).

The IMB annual piracy report for 2002 says that attacks like the one in the Gulf of Aden last October, when the French tanker Limburg was rammed by a boat packed with explosives, were difficult to prevent. "No shipboard response can protect the ship in these circumstances."

The only answer was for coastal states to make sure that approaches to their ports were secure. IMB recommended that port authorities designate approach channels under coast guard or police supervision from which all unauthorized craft would be banned. . . .

Commenting on last year's tally of 370 attacks on shipping at sea worldwide—up from 335 in 2001—IMB noted that most occurred while ships were at anchor. A marked increase in successful boarding by pirates combined with a drop in the number of attempted attacks suggested that many ships were complacent about the need for additional precautionary measures. "Vigilant anti-piracy watch is still the best deterrent," the report said.

There was a substantial rise in hijackings, up from 16 to 25 incidents. Many involved smaller boats, such as tugs, barges and fishing boats, in the Malacca Straits and Indonesian waters. Crime syndicates in the area were believed to be targeting vessels carrying valuable palm oil and gas oil.

IMB Director Pottengal Mukundan commented: "In some parts of the world it is all too easy to board a merchant vessel unlawfully. Against the current concern in respect of maritime terrorism, it is vital that coastal states allocate resources to patrolling their waters more effectively. Failing this, we do not foresee a reduction in these incidents."

Although the number of crew killed in 2002 was down to 10 compared with 21 in 2001, that figure concealed a chilling statistic—24 passengers or crew were missing, and most of these must be considered dead. The report's summary of attacks on ships frequently noted that pirates threw crew members into the sea, leaving them to drown.

Indonesia again experienced the highest number of attacks, with 103 reported incidents in 2002. Piracy attacks in Bangladesh ranked second highest with 32 attacks and India was third with 18 attacks.

In South America, Brazil, Colombia, Dominican Republic, Ecuador and Guyana all showed a marked increase in attacks.

The waters off Somalia are among the most dangerous in the world. "The risk of attack to vessels staying close to the coastline from Somali armed militias has now increased from one of possibility to certainty," the IMB said.

"Any vessel, not making a scheduled call in a Somali port, which slows down, or stops close to the Somali coast will be boarded by these gangs." They had extorted substantial sums from owners for the return of the vessel and crew.

SOURCE: Copyright 2003 International Chamber of Commerce, Piracy Reporting Centre, International Maritime Bureau, Commercial Crime Services. Reprinted with permission.

force to overcome the strength of a seaworthy ship or the diligence and skill of a good crew. The defense often depends on the severity of the storm and the manner in which the cargo was damaged. The courts will consider the force of the wind, the height of the waves, the foreseeability of the storm when the ship set sail, the ability of the ship to avoid the storm, whether other ships in the same storm suffered damage, the type of damage to the cargo, and other factors. The negligence or lack of competence on behalf of the crew will void the perils of the sea defense. But if the ship was seaworthy when it left port, and was operated in a competent manner, the carrier is not liable for cargo damage from a storm so strong that it represents a peril of the sea. In the case that follows, *J. Gerber & Co. v. S.S. Sabine Howaldt,* the court ruled that the carrier had used due diligence to maintain a seaworthy ship and that the damage had resulted from a peril of the sea. Ships encounter tremendous forces of water and weather on the high seas. As the court

notes, just because a ship is seaworthy does not mean that it can withstand every form of violent weather and turbulent sea that ocean-going ships might encounter.

The Q-Clause Defense. Even if a carrier cannot prove one of the sixteen exceptions shown in Exhibit 6.2, it still may be exonerated from liability under a seventeenth defense, the *Q-clause defense.* This provision states that a carrier is not liable for "any other cause arising without the actual fault and privity of the carrier . . . but the burden of proof shall be on the [carrier] to show that neither the actual fault . . . nor the fault or neglect of the agents or servants of the carrier contributed to the loss or damage." The carrier must therefore prove that it was free from any fault whatsoever contributing to the loss, damage, or disappearance of the goods entrusted to it, and it must also prove what the actual cause of the loss was. This burden is difficult for the carrier to

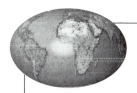

J. Gerber & Co. v. S.S. Sabine Howaldt
437 F.2d 580 (1971)
United States Court of Appeals (2d Cir.)

BACKGROUND AND FACTS
The SS *Sabine Howaldt,* a small cargo vessel, was chartered for a voyage from Antwerp, Belgium, to Wilmington, Delaware. The ship was carrying a quantity of steel products consigned to the plaintiff. The cargo was in good condition when loaded at Antwerp. On arrival at the port of destination in the United States, however, the steel showed extensive salt water damage from rust and pitting. In the course of her voyage across the North Atlantic, the *Sabine Howaldt* encountered extremely heavy weather. Water penetrated the ventilators and damaged the cargo. The carrier argued that the damage was caused solely by a peril of the sea, and that the ship was not unseaworthy. The trial court found that the ship was unseaworthy due to the negligence of the defendant and that the winds and seas that the vessel encountered did not constitute a peril of the sea.

ANDERSON, CIRCUIT JUDGE
The ship's log records that . . . the ship was badly strained in her seams and sea water was breaking

over forecastle deck, hatches, and upper works. It was necessary for the vessel to heave to and she so remained for 12 hours. The hull of the *Sabine Howaldt* was twisted and strained in the turbulent cross seas; she rolled from 25 degrees–30 degrees; waves constantly broke over her; and she shuddered and vibrated as she was pounded and wrenched by the heavy seas. . . . Subsequently it was discovered that during this period of hurricane . . . a porthole in the galley was smashed; the catwalk or gangway from the amidships housing aft over the hatches and the well-deck to the poop was destroyed when it was torn loose and landed against a ventilator, which it dented.

The district court not only found that the character and nature of the winds and seas were not sufficiently severe to constitute a peril of the sea in fact, but it also found that the *Sabine Howaldt* was unseaworthy due to the neglect of the defendant carrier. It concluded that the defendant was negligent in permitting the ship to proceed on the voyage with defective hatch

continued

continued

covers without tarpaulins over them and also because its ventilators were insufficiently protected. . . .

On arrival at Wilmington, Delaware, on January 3, 1966, the chief officer examined the hatches and found no damage to the hatches, the hatch covers, or their rubber gaskets—all were in good condition. . . . There was no evidence that there was a customary or usual standard in the exercise of good seamanship that called for the use of canvas tarpaulins over MacGregor hatchcovers. It was quite apparent that the customary practice of most steamship lines was not to use tarpaulins over such hatchcovers. . . . As there was no evidence in the case that the MacGregor hatchcovers on the *Sabine Howaldt* were not properly maintained and as there was substantial, uncontradicted evidence that they were, it was plain error to hold there was negligence in regard to a failure to cover the hatchcovers with tarpaulins.

The standard of seaworthiness must remain uncertain because of the imponderables of the forces exerted upon a ship by the winds and seas. Ship design and construction over many centuries of experience have evolved to meet the dangers inherent in violent winds and tempestuous seas. But for the purpose of deciding whether or not they constitute perils of the sea for a particular vessel for the purpose of the statutory exception there is the question of how violent and how tempestuous. These are matters of degree and not amenable to precise definition. . . . Other indicia are, assuming a seaworthy ship, the nature and extent of the damage to the ship

itself, whether or not the ship was buffeted by cross-seas which wrenched and wracked the hull and set up unusual stresses in it and like factors. While the seaworthiness of a ship presupposes that she is designed, built, and equipped to stand up under reasonable expectable conditions, this means no more than the usual bad weather which is normal for a particular sea area at a particular time. It does not, however, include an unusual combination of the destructive forces of wind and sea which a skilled and experienced ship's master would not expect and which the ship encountered as a stroke of bad luck. Hurricane-force winds and turbulent cross-seas generating unpredictable strains and pressures on a ship's hull are an example.

We are satisfied that the *Sabine Howaldt* was a seaworthy vessel when she left Antwerp on December 15, 1965. . . . Throughout the voyage she was operated in a good and seamanlike manner. There was no negligence on the part of the carrier. The damage to the cargo was caused by violence of the wind and sea and particularly by the resulting cross-seas which, through wrenching and twisting the vessel, set up torsions within the hull which forced up the hatchcovers and admitted sea water to the holds.

Decision.   The Court of Appeals reversed the decision of the trial court. The defendant carrier met its burden of proof that the vessel was seaworthy when it left port, was operated in a seamanlike manner, and the damage to the cargo resulted solely from a peril of the sea.

---

bear, and relatively few cases in the literature describe carriers that have been successful using this defense.

Shipper's Liability for Hazardous Cargo

Thus far we have been discussing the liability of the ocean carrier. Now consider the liability of a shipper of hazardous cargo for damage caused to a ship at sea. The *M/V Tokyo Senator* was transporting 300 barrels of thiourea from Korea to Norfolk. Thiourea is a white, odorless powder used as a reducing agent and in the bleaching of protein fibers such as paper, paper pulp, and textiles. The chemical spontaneously ignited at sea, damaging the ship. The carrier brought an action

against the shipper for damages. The shipper did not know that thiourea was hazardous, and at the time of the shipment, thiourea was considered a stable compound under normal conditions. At trial, the carrier failed to prove the actual cause of the fire or that the shipper was responsible. There was evidence, however, that the combustion was caused by the inherently dangerous nature of the chemical itself. The district court granted summary judgment for the shipper, holding that COGSA does not impose liability on a shipper of inherently dangerous goods unless it can be shown that the shipper actually or constructively knew of the dangerous nature of the cargo prior to shipment and failed to disclose that nature to the carrier. The carrier appealed. In *Senator Linie GmbH*

& Co. Kg v. Sunway Line, Inc., 291 F.3d 145 (2nd Cir. 2002), the court reversed, stating:

> We conclude—[as have the British courts]—that COGSA established a rule of strict liability for a shipper of inherently dangerous goods when neither the shipper nor the carrier had actual or constructive preshipment knowledge of the danger. This construction of COGSA is consonant with COGSA's goals of fostering international uniformity in sea-carriage rules and allocating risk between shippers and carriers in a manner that is consistent and predictable. . . . [W]e conclude today that a strict-liability construction will foster fairness and efficiency in the dealings of commercial maritime actors. In contrast to a carrier, which typically is in the position of taking aboard its vessel a large quantity and variety of cargoes, a shipper can be expected to have greater access to and familiarity with goods and their manufacturers before those goods are placed in maritime commerce. If an unwitting party must suffer, it should be the one that is in a better position to ascertain ahead of time the dangerous nature of shipped goods. That party in many cases will be the shipper.

The case stands as a warning to a shipper of hazardous materials. Be certain that your marine insurance policy covers such losses.

> **http://www.fmc.gov**
> The official site of the Federal Maritime Commission, the U.S. agency responsible for regulating shipping in the foreign trades of the United States.
>
> **http://www.comitemaritime.org**
> The Comité Maritime International is a nongovernmental organization devoted to the unification of maritime law.

Carrier's Liability for Cargo Shortages

Ocean containers are generally loaded and sealed at the shipper's place of business and not opened until they are in the hands of the consignee. Even so, cargo shortages are a regular occurrence in the maritime trade. The legal problems here are somewhat different from the problems of damaged cargo. As the first step in any litigation, the owner of the cargo or the insurer must establish that a shortage actually occurred while the goods were in the carrier's custody. Then, under the catch-all Q-clause

defense that limits the carrier's liability (as discussed in the previous section), the carrier may attempt to prove that the shortage resulted despite its having exercised due care to safeguard the cargo.

A consignee can prove a shortage by showing that the quantity or weight of the cargo at the destination is less than that listed on the bill of lading. This issue can also be problematic, however. Under COGSA, a bill of lading usually lists the number of packages, the quantity, or weight of the cargo that the carrier receives for shipment; but the quantity or weight is usually supplied by the shipper. Because shipping containers are sealed at the shipper's place of business, the carrier doesn't really have the opportunity to physically count the number of packages inside. The carrier will customarily insert a disclaimer in the bill of lading stating that the cargo inside the container is the "shipper's weight, load, and count" (i.e., not weighed, loaded, or counted by the carrier). Thus, carriers claim that they should not be liable for "missing cargo"—for delivering less cargo than described in the bill of lading. Recent cases have not recognized these disclaimers and, as in the *Westway Coffee* case, are holding carriers liable for shortages in sealed containers where the weight or quantity stated on the bill of lading was verifiable by the shipper. In *Westway Coffee v. M.V. Netuno*, the carrier was held liable for a loss of some twenty tons of coffee in 419 cartons, despite the disclaimer in the bill of lading stating that the weight and quantity were provided by the shipper, because the weight of the sealed container had been verifiable by the carrier. The liability of the carrier in *Westway* stems from the carrier's option of weighing the container when it is received in order to confirm the existence of cargo inside, and then weighing it again at its destination in order to prove delivery.

> **http://www.iccwbo.org**
> The International Chamber of Commerce Commercial Crime Services. Includes sites for the International Maritime Bureau, Commercial Crime Bureau, Counterfeiting Intelligence Bureau, Cybercrime Unit and the Piracy Reporting Centre.

In *Plastique Tags, Inc. v. Asia Trans Line, Inc.*, 83 F.3d 1367 (1996), the 11th Circuit Court of Appeals, citing *Westway Coffee*, held that a carrier

Westway Coffee Corp. v. M.V. Netuno
528 F. Supp. 113 (1981), aff'd, 675 F.2d 30 (2d Cir. 1982)
United States District Court (S.D.N.Y.)

BACKGROUND AND FACTS

Westway, the consignee, purchased 1,710 cartons of coffee from Dominium, S.A., of Sao Paulo, Brazil. The cartons were loaded into six cargo containers under the supervision of a government officer who inspected and counted the cartons going into the containers. Dominium sealed and padlocked the containers. The containers were then driven from Sao Paulo to the port of Santos, where they were stored in a customs bonded warehouse prior to loading onto the *MV Netuno,* a vessel owned by Netumar. Netumar issued an onboard bill of lading listing the serial numbers of the containers, along with the gross weight of the containers filled with coffee and the number of cartons within them. Netumar did not count the cartons. The bill of lading contained disclaimers stating that the containers were "said to contain" a quantity of cargo described by the shipper, that the cargo was the "shipper's load, and count," and that the "contents of packages are shipper's declaration." After the *Netuno's* arrival in New York, the padlocked containers were opened, revealing a shortage of 419 cartons or approximately twenty tons of coffee. Westway purchased the bill of lading and then brought this action against the carrier under the *Carriage of Goods by Sea Act.*

SAND, DISTRICT JUDGE

Plaintiff contends that the weights stated in the bill of lading constitute prima facie evidence of the receipt by the carrier of the goods as therein described; that it was entitled to rely on the weights stated in the bill of lading which was duly negotiated to it; and that Netumar is estopped from claiming that the missing cartons of coffee were not in the containers when Netumar took possession of them.

Defendant contends that plaintiff has failed to prove delivery of the full quantity to the carrier, and thereby has failed to establish a prima facie case; and alternatively, that defendant has established that it exercised proper care, and that plaintiff's estoppel theory does not apply to cases involving sealed containers. These contentions are based largely on the disclaimers contained in the bill of lading, and on the fact that the goods were "hidden" within the containers.

COGSA provides the answer to defendant's contention. Section 1303(3) provides:

After receiving the goods into his charge the carrier . . . shall, on demand of the shipper, issue to the shipper a bill of lading showing among other things,

(b) Either the number of packages or pieces, or the quantity or weight, as the case may be, as furnished in writing by the shipper.

(c) The apparent order and condition of the goods: Provided, that no carrier, master, or agent of the carrier, shall be bound to state or show in the bill of lading any . . . quantity, or weight which he has reasonable ground for suspecting not accurately to represent the goods actually received, or which he has had no reasonable means of checking.

As our Court of Appeals has said of this section: "The Act specifically provides a method for avoiding carrier liability for false information given by the shipper, by not stating it in the bill. . . . The carrier must utilize that method, rather than the quite general reservation attempted here." *Spanish American Skin Co. v. The Ferngulf,* 242 F.2d 551, 553 (2d Cir. 1957). Thus, if defendant has reason to doubt the shipper's weights, it was required to use the method for limiting liability expressly provided by COGSA and cannot now advance the general statement in the bills, "said to weigh," against the consignee. Since plaintiff relied on the weights specified in the bills in purchasing the consignment, defendant is estopped from denying the accuracy of the description contained therein.

We thus find that despite the disclaimers stamped on the bill of lading, the weights recited in the bill established prima facie receipt by the carrier of the entire shipment of coffee.

Plaintiff having satisfied its initial burden, the burden thus shifts to defendant to establish the applicability of a COGSA exception. Defendant contends that it has satisfied this burden by demonstrating that it exercised "proper care," relying on the catchall exception contained in COGSA. Defendant must therefore prove that it was free from negligence. We find the testimony produced by defendant with respect to the loading of the containers on the *Netuno,* their stowage on the ship, and the operation of Pier 36 insufficient to satisfy that burden. We find as a matter of fact that there were significant periods of time when the container could have been pilfered . . . most notably during loading and the voy-

continued

continued

age (which included stops in three other ports), and during discharge. Moreover, we find the testimony with respect to the general security measures taken on Pier 36 insufficient to establish defendant's freedom from negligence, especially in view of the testimony that coffee was an item in high demand on Pier 36 and easily saleable to salvors during this period of time. Finally, the fact that the unnumbered seals and locks were intact when the loss was discovered is not conclusive. First, the seals, which consist of wire and a seal stamped IBC but have no identifying number or unique characteristic, could be easily duplicated. Second, as the testimony indicated and as other courts have recognized, the locks used on these containers could have been picked.

If defendant had succeeded in showing that the extent of surveillance, fending, internal security measures, and other security measures were such that pilferage could not readily have been accomplished on the pier or during the voyage, we would conclude that, although the precise technique utilized by the thief is still unknown, the defendant had absolved itself of any negligence. But defendant's showing falls far short of this, and the extent of pilferage, especially of coffee, is a matter of record. Since defendant is estopped from denying that the coffee was within the container when it came into its custody, and has not shown that it adopted security measures which would have effectively precluded the inference that the cargo was stolen, plaintiff's prima facie case has not been adequately rebutted, and plaintiff is therefore entitled to recover its damages.

So ordered.

Decision. The District Court ruled that the consignee was entitled to recover for the missing coffee. The carrier was not permitted to relieve itself of liability for the shortage by claiming that the weight or quantity of cargo stated on the bill of lading was the weight or count of the shipper. Further, the court held that the carrier had failed to meet its burden of proof under COGSA that it had used due care in protecting the cargo during shipment.

Comment. This case illustrates the carrier's predicament. If it refuses to put the shipper's quantity or weight on the bill of lading, it runs the risk that a consignee might refuse to purchase it. After all, the buyer wants assurance that the goods are actually in the container. Opening every container to check the shipper's count would be impracticable, costly, and contrary to maritime practice. Thus, the only practical alternative for the carrier might now be to omit all reference on the bill of lading to the shipper's quantity and to simply weigh the container on receipt and on discharge. On appeal, the Second Circuit confirmed that the carrier would have had a defense against a claim for shortage of weight if it had weighed the container at loading, listed that weight on the bill of lading, and then weighed it again at unloading and found the same weight.

was not liable for shortages in a shipment of plastic bags from Korea to the United States in a container sealed by the shipper. The bill of lading recited that the container was the "Shippers Load and Count" and that it was "Said to Contain 5600 boxes/4,437,500 plastic bags." The court apparently believed that because only a number of units was given on the bill of lading, and no weight, that it was impossible for the carrier to verify the accuracy of the shipper's representation.

The Per Package Limitation

In the United States, COGSA also provides that carriers are not liable in amounts in excess of $500 "per package" where the shipper has had a "fair opportunity" to indicate the nature and value of the shipment on the bill of lading. Typically, the bill provides blank spaces on the front in which to declare a value for the goods, and a notice to the shipper on the reverse side of its right to do so. Shippers will be charged a higher rate for cargo of greater value.

Where the shipper has not declared the value of the cargo, any loss or damage to the goods is likely to lead to litigation over what constitutes a "package," as in the *Z.K. Marine, Inc.* case on the next page. Where the goods are not shipped in packages, the $500 limit applies to a *customary freight unit* for goods of that type. For instance, when a large corrugated container is strapped to a wooden skid, the courts usually hold that the $500 limitation applies to each of the smaller boxes inside. In one case, the shipper entered a claim for losses to 4,400 men's suits being transported by container. Each suit was on a hanger in its own plastic wrapper. The court looked to the bill of lading, which stated that 4,400 suits were being shipped, and set the limitation of liability at a maximum of $2.2 million.

A number of carriers have tried to claim that an ocean container, in which large quantities of goods can be transported, constitutes a "package." The courts have not agreed. In *Mitsui & Co. v. American Export Lines,* 636 F.2d 807 (2nd Cir. 1980), the court considered whether an ocean container is a "package" for purposes of the $500 COGSA limitation. Steel ocean containers resemble truck trailers without the wheels. They are usually 8′ x 8′ x 20′ long, or 8′ x 8′ x 40′ long. In this case, Armstrong had shipped 1,705 rolls of floor covering to Japan. Each roll was six feet long, contained sixty square yards of material wrapped around a hollow cardboard roll, and weighed about three hundred pounds. Each was wrapped in brown paper. The rolls were packed and sealed in thirteen containers at Armstrong's factory. The bill of lading described the shipment as "13 containers, said to contain 1,705 rolls of floor covering." It also gave the weight and measurement of the rolls, but stated no value. The containers were lost at sea during a storm. Armstrong claimed damages in excess of $350,000 for the CIF value of the merchandise. The carrier claimed it was liable for only $6,500 ($500 x 13 containers). In awarding Armstrong full value for its loss, the court stated that, "Certainly, if the individual crates or cartons prepared by the shipper and containing his goods can rightly be considered 'packages' standing by themselves, they do not suddenly lose that character upon being stowed in a carrier's container. I would liken these containers to detachable stowage compartments of the ship. They simply serve to divide the ship's overall cargo stowage space into smaller, more serviceable loci. . . . A container is not a COGSA package if its contents and the number of packages or units are disclosed (on the bill of lading)."

These cases give due warning to the export sales manager. The shipper should always be certain that the goods are correctly described, weighed, and counted, and that their value is cor-

---

Z.K. Marine, Inc. v. M/V Archigetis
776 F. Supp. 1549 (1991)
United States District Court (S.D. FL.)

BACKGROUND AND FACTS
The plaintiff, Z.K. Marine, is an importer of yachts for sale in the United States. In 1987, five yachts were shipped from Taiwan to the United States aboard the MV *Archigetis*. Each yacht was shipped under a clean negotiable bill of lading. Each of the five bills of lading provided on its face that one unit only was being shipped, that the yacht was being shipped on deck at the shipper's risk, and that the value of the goods could be declared with prior notice. On the back of each bill of lading, the liability for danger or loss was limited to $500 per package or customary freight unit. All five yachts were secured by cradles and shipped on deck. During transit, one yacht was lost and the other four were damaged. The bills of lading were purchased by the plaintiffs while the yachts were in transit. The defendant claims that it is liable only in the amount of $500 per yacht.

HOEVELER, DISTRICT JUDGE
Defendants argue that pursuant to the *Carriage of Goods by Sea Act,* and the explicit provisions of the bills of lading, damages are limited to $500 per package. Because the bills of lading are clearly stamped "one unit," defendants contend that their liability is limited to $500 per yacht. Alternatively, defendants argue that if the yachts are not one package, they are each a customary freight unit—since the freight charges were based upon a customary freight unit and yacht was used as the basis of a single freight charge—and consequently subject of the $500 limitation.

Plaintiffs argue that the terms of the bills of lading should be given no effect because the consignees had no opportunity to declare a higher value for the yachts, they now argue that the carrier cannot now limit its liability. Plaintiffs urge the Court to disre-

continued

continued

gard the explicit limitation because they had no chance to bargain over this clause. Alternatively, plaintiffs argue that the limitation is for $500 per package, not per yacht, and thus the limitation does not apply to this situation. . . .

First, [plaintiffs] argue that there is no opportunity to declare a higher value because the bills of lading themselves provide no space to do so. A cursory inspection of the bills of lading reveals that this is not the case, however. On the face of the bills, in capital letters, it states that the "VALUE OF GOODS MAY BE DECLARED PROVIDED MERCHANT GIVES PRIOR NOTICE AND AGREES TO PAY GREATER FREIGHT AD VALOREM BASES SEE CL 18 ON BACK HEREOF." Clause 18 limits the value to $500 per package unless a higher value is declared and higher freight paid. Although there is no specific slot for the shipper to write in its higher value, there appears plenty of space on the face of the bills for it to do so, if desired. The bills plainly afford space and, by their terms, opportunity for the shipper to declare a higher value.

Plaintiffs argue in the alternative that even if the bills of lading offer the shipper opportunity to declare a higher value, the plaintiffs, as purchasers of the negotiable bills, had no such opportunity. Therefore, they argue that the limitation provisions should not be enforced. Purchasers of a negotiable bill of lading, however, purchase only those rights which the shipper had. The right to declare a higher value and pay higher freight ended when the goods were delivered on board the ship. Therefore, the purchasers of the bills cannot now complain if a higher value was not declared.

Plaintiffs' next contention is that each yacht is not a package so that the limitation to $500 per package does not apply. Plaintiffs contend that the cradles attached to the yachts for ease in transporting them do not suffice as packaging because the cradles do not enclose the yachts. Plaintiffs are mistaken in this regard. A package is some class of cargo, irrespective of size or weight, which has been prepared for transportation by the addition of some packaging that facilitates handling, but which does not necessarily enclose the goods. . . . In the instant case, the yachts were all transported on cradles, analogous, for purposes of the package analysis, to skids. Accordingly, this court finds that each yacht constituted a package within the purview of COGSA's liability limitation provisions. Therefore the limitation of $500 per package on the bills of lading applies to limit liability of the carrier to $500 per yacht. . . .

Decision. The court held that each yacht had constituted one package unit, that the shipper had been given a fair opportunity to declare a higher value, and that the carrier had validly limited its liability to $500 per package. The purchasers of the bills of lading are bound by the terms of the bills of lading, including the limitation provisions.

Comment. COGSA's limitation of liability generally does not apply to goods carried above deck, however, in this case, a provision in the bill of lading stated that it would be governed by COGSA. This type of statement is known as a *clause paramount*. Thus, the court held that the COGSA package limitation applied to these yachts.

---

rectly stated on the bill of lading. Moreover, a shipper must never knowingly or fraudulently misstate the identity of cargo or its value on the bill of lading, or the carrier cannot be held liable for any damage to the goods.

Liability for a Material Deviation

In the nineteenth century, steamships commonly interrupted a voyage and detoured from their customary or shortest route if presented with the opportunity to profit by loading or discharging cargo or passengers. Today, COGSA largely prevents this practice by prohibiting a carrier from

deviating from the journey unless necessary to save lives or property at sea.

Any material deviation from the terms of the bill of lading can cause the carrier to lose any immunity or protection it may have under the act. For instance, in one case an Israeli-owned vessel was transporting clock movements through the Gulf of Mexico from Israel to Louisville, Mississippi. It was ordered to unload at Mobile and return to Israel in order to join in the war effort. The clocks were left to be damaged on an unsheltered dock. The court held that this action was a material deviation for which the carrier is liable. If the material deviation is unreasonable, the carrier becomes a virtual insurer of the cargo. When a material deviation occurs, most U.S. courts have held that the carrier cannot claim protection of the $500 per package limitation.

Most courts have also held that stowage of cargo *above deck* under a clean bill of lading without the consent of the shipper is deemed to be an unreasonable material deviation from the terms of the bill of lading. Accordingly, goods can generally not be stowed above deck, where they are exposed to the weather and seas, unless the bill of lading specifically allows it, or unless the shipper knew that it was the common practice of the carrier to stow the particular type of goods in question above deck.

Several court cases have distinguished between carrying exposed cargo above deck and stowing it in a sealed ocean container. The courts noted that transporting cargo in a sealed ocean container on the deck of a modern container ship is not an unreasonable deviation because containers stowed on deck are not necessarily subject to greater risks than containers stowed below deck (although as a practical matter, ocean containers are not entirely watertight). The courts also considered the fact that many ships and loading terminals are designed exclusively for handling containerized cargo.

Himalaya Clauses.   If a carrier is relieved from liability under COGSA, such as for an error in navigation, can a plaintiff recover against the captain, crew, or other agents of the carrier? Would stevedores be responsible to the owner of cargo for damage caused by the negligent operation of a crane? In many countries, the *Hague Rules,* from which COGSA was derived, do not apply to parties other than the carrier. These countries exclude stevedores, who are generally independent contractors of the carrier. To protect these other parties, carriers include exculpatory clauses in their bills of lading extending the protection of the *Hague Rules* to their agents, employees, and independent contractors. These *Himalaya clauses,* named after a famous case, are recognized in some countries, including the United States, and are invalid in others (e.g., the United Kingdom and Canada).

The Hamburg Rules

In 1978, the United Nations completed drafting a new Convention on the *Carriage of Goods by Sea,* known as the *Hamburg Rules.* These rules are different from the *Hague Rules* and COGSA. They do not relieve the carrier for errors in navigation or in the management of the ship, and they make ocean carriers liable for losses resulting from negligence. They also make it easier for cargo owners to win their cases against carriers. These rules were drafted by the United Nations to serve the interests of cargo owners and shippers in developing countries that do not have large carrier fleets. The rules are also supported by shippers in other countries who believe they will reduce insurance costs. As of 2000, only twenty-five countries (mostly developing countries) had sanctioned the new rules, making them legally binding in those countries only. However, higher insurance rates for shipowners who sail to or from these countries are already being charged by international marine insurance pools. The rules are strongly opposed by carriers and insurance companies worldwide, and adoption of the *Hamburg Rules* in the United States and other ocean-going nations seem unlikely.

The Visby Amendments

The *Visby Amendments* are amendments to the original 1924 *Hague Rules.* They are already in effect in many countries, including the United Kingdom, Canada, most of Western Europe, Japan, Hong Kong, and Singapore. The *Visby Amendments* raise the per package limitation of carriers to an amount based on special drawing rights of the IMF, or approximately $1,000, and make them liable for all losses resulting from the carrier's "recklessness" in the operation and navigation of the ship. The carrier is reckless if it knew or should have known that its conduct would be likely to cause damage. The *Visby Amendments* have not been adopted in the United States.

> *http://*
>
> **http://www. maritimeadvocate.com**
> A maritime law magazine. Past issues are free to access and read.

THE LIABILITY OF OCEAN TRANSPORTATION INTERMEDIARIES

Thus far, this chapter has discussed the liability of air and ocean carriers. However, many companies that ship or receive goods internationally often use the services of intermediaries—service companies that handle the cargo, arrange transportation with air or ocean carriers, assist shippers in clearing legal hurdles in moving freight internationally, and provide many other services. These ocean transportation intermediaries include *freight forwarders* and *non-vessel operating common carriers.*

Freight Forwarders

Transporting goods over great distances and across national borders is often costly, complex, and highly susceptible to error and unexpected delays. Most exporters (as well as importers) rely on the services of a professional *freight forwarder* for assistance. *Freight forwarders* are persons or firms that act as agents for shippers in contracting with land or sea carriers for the transportation of goods to a place of destination. Forwarders contract with carriers for transportation of cargo by land and sea, obtain cargo insurance, assist in packing and containerizing cargo, arrange warehousing of goods pending shipment or delivery, prepare many different legal documents, assist shippers in getting paid for their goods, handle customs and other legal matters when moving goods across national borders, track shipments around the world, and offer many other services. Shippers utilize the freight and insurance cost calculations of their forwarders in order to prepare price quotations for foreign customers. Many forwarders specialize in moving complex or dangerous cargo, such as explosives. Some have foreign offices and are familiar with foreign import regulations. Freight forwarders that operate in the United States are licensed and regulated by the Federal Maritime Commission and the International Air Transport Association. They must post a bond in order to assure financial security in handling their customer's money and cargo. States and municipalities in the United States are prohibited from regulating freight forwarders. In order to act on behalf of their customer, freight forwarders must have a written *power of attorney* form filled out by their customer and kept on file in their offices. This permits them to sign legal documents on their customer's behalf and thus helps to expedite imports and exports. When forwarders receive cargo for shipment, they issue "forwarder's receipts" or "house bills of lading"

(called "consignment notes" in some countries). These do not have the same legal effect as an ocean bill of lading, and are not negotiable. Most freight forwarders also act as *customs brokers.* A customs broker represents an importer by arranging for the receipt and customs clearance of shipments into a country.

http://www.FIATA.com
The International Federation of Freight
Forwarders Association
http://www.NCBFAA.org
The National Customs Brokers and Forwarders
Association of America

The following case, *Prima U.S. Inc. v. Panalpina, Inc.,* discusses the liability of a freight forwarder for damage to cargo that occurred on the high seas.

Non-Vessel Operating Common Carriers

Most international cargo today moves by containerized freight. Shippers who can fill an entire ocean container with goods can receive favorable shipping rates as opposed to those shippers whose must move smaller amounts of cargo without a container (known as "break-bulk" freight). *Non-vessel operating common carriers* (commonly referred to as NVOCCs) act as freight consolidators for smaller shippers, permitting them to take advantage of lower freight rates. NVOCCs combine the cargo of several small shippers into one container and book space with an ocean carrier at a lower rate. An NVOCC is a common carrier that functions like an ocean carrier, but does not operate the vessels by which transportation is provided. It issues bills of lading and assumes liability for goods due to loss or damage during transport. It also performs many of the same services as does a freight forwarder.

The *Ocean Shipping Reform Act of 1998*

Ocean carriers, freight forwarders, and NVOCCs are regulated by the *Ocean Shipping Reform Act of 1998* (OSRA). OSRA represents an attempt by the U.S. Congress to bring sweeping reform to ocean shipping regulation. OSRA amends the *Shipping Act of 1984* by allowing carriers greater

Prima U.S. Inc. v. Panalpina, Inc.
233 F.3d 126 (2000)
United States Court of Appeals (2d Cir.)

BACKGROUND AND FACTS

Westinghouse contracted with Panalpina, a freight forwarder, to arrange for the transportation of an electric transformer from the manufacturer in Italy to 3M Corporation in Iowa. Panalpina stated to Westinghouse, "rest assured your shipment will receive door to door our close care and supervision...." Westinghouse paid Panalpina $21,785.00 for its services. As is the industry custom, Panalpina did not issue a bill of lading for the shipment.

The standard "Terms & Conditions" listed on the reverse side of its contract stated that Panalpina would use "reasonable care" in the selection of those who would actually carry or handle the goods. The terms also limited Panalpina's liability for losses to $50 per shipment, and they disclaimed liability for all consequential or special damages in excess of this amount. These were the same terms utilized in the prior ten-year course of dealing involving over 1,000 transactions between Westinghouse and Panalpina.

Panalpina hired an Italian customs broker to coordinate the movement of the transformer through Italy. The Italian broker hired CSM, a local stevedore, to load the transformer aboard the ship for the voyage to the United States. Panalpina never inquired of CSM how the transformer was lashed for the ocean voyage. Nor did it supervise the endeavor. CSM improperly secured and lashed the transformer onto a "flat-rack" container for shipment. During the ocean voyage, the ship encountered heavy seas and the transformer broke loose, crushing a laser-cutting machine owned by Prima. Prima sued the owner of the ship, Westinghouse, and Panalpina for damages to the laser. The district court held Panalpina liable and Panalpina appeals.

MCLAUGHLIN, CIRCUIT JUDGE

The job of a non-vessel operating common carrier ("NVOCC") is to consolidate cargo from numerous shippers into larger groups for shipment by an ocean carrier. A NVOCC—as opposed to the actual ocean carrier transporting the cargo, issues a bill of lading to each shipper. If anything happens to the goods during the voyage the NVOCC is liable to the shipper because of the bill of lading that it issued.

A freight forwarder like Panalpina, on the other hand, simply facilitates the movement of cargo to the ocean vessel. The freight forwarder secures cargo space with a steamship company, gives advice on governmental licensing requirements, proper port of exit and letter of credit intricacies, and arranges to have the cargo reach the seaboard in time to meet the designated vessel. Freight forwarders generally make arrangements for the movement of cargo at the request of clients and are vitally different from carriers, such as vessels, truckers, stevedores or warehouses, which are directly involved in transporting the cargo. Unlike a carrier, a freight forwarder does not issue a bill of lading, and is therefore not liable to a shipper for anything that occurs to the goods being shipped. As long as the freight forwarder limits its role to arranging for transportation, it will not be held liable to the shipper. Panalpina did not issue a bill of lading and it did not consolidate cargo. It was hired by Westinghouse simply as a freight forwarder to arrange for the transportation of a transformer from Italy to Iowa. By analogy, Panalpina was hired to act as a "travel agent" for the transformer: it set things up and made reservations, but did not engage in any hands-on heavy lifting. Admittedly, Panalpina did state that Westinghouse's "shipment [would] receive door to door our close care and supervision . . . ". However, because of the well settled legal distinction between forwarders and carriers, that statement—mere puffing—cannot transform Panalpina into a carrier, and bestow liability upon it.

Panalpina hired CSM as a stevedore to load and lash the transformer. CSM was the same stevedore that was used by United Arab Shipping, and was the designated official Port of Genoa stevedore. Panalpina clearly acted reasonably in hiring CSM on behalf of Westinghouse, fulfilling its duties as a freight forwarder. Panalpina is not liable to Westinghouse for CSM's negligent actions.

Decision. Judgment reversed for Panalpina. Panalpina was a freight forwarder hired by Westinghouse to arrange for transportation and other services. It was not a carrier and is not liable for the cargo during shipment. Freight forwarders must use due diligence and reasonable care in performing their functions. Panalpina was reasonable in its selection of CSM as stevedore to load the ship.

flexibility in contracting with shippers and establishing shipping rates.

Prior to OSRA, carriers could only charge their publicly posted freight "tariff" rates and had to offer the same rates to all "similar" carriers. OSRA now permits carriers and shippers to enter confidential "service contracts," with freight rates and terms being bargained between them. Thus, large shippers, or associations of several shippers, will gain lower rates on volume cargo and preferred cargo space. These service contracts will serve as a contract of carriage, and so no bill of lading need be issued. Because these agreements are considered private contracts (with no bill of lading), and the carriers are not acting as "common carriers," they are not subject to COGSA. Instead, the parties are free to negotiate their own liability terms. Exclusive agreements by a shipper to use one carrier in return for reduced rates are no longer illegal. OSRA provides that ocean carriers are not subject to the antitrust laws. Freight rates for regular common carriage need no longer be filed with the Federal Maritime Commission, but may be made publicly available, for instance, on a carrier's Web site. The carriers must treat freight forwarders and NVOCCs, called "Ocean Transportation Intermediaries" in OSRA, just as they would treat shippers under the law.

Carriers may not unreasonably or unjustly refuse to deal or negotiate with shippers and ocean transportation intermediaries. With regard to shipments based on a published tariff under a bill of lading (as opposed to the "service contracts" discussed previously), carriers may not unjustly discriminate against any shipper or ocean transportation intermediary in terms of rates, cargo accommodations, or other services. No person may willfully engage in false billing, false weighing, or otherwise attempt to unjustly obtain a lower freight rate. Civil penalties for violations of OSRA may be as high as $5,000 per day for each violation, unless the violation was willfully and knowingly committed, in which case the penalty may be up to $25,000 per violation.

MARINE CARGO INSURANCE

As is evident from the foregoing discussions, the insuring of cargo is an essential element of international trade. The potential for damage and loss to goods, particularly during ocean shipments that are more lengthy and more hazardous than air shipments, is tremendous. The last chapter demonstrated how the risk of loss can be allocated between buyer and seller, often through the use of trade terms. If loss does occur, the party bearing the risk (perhaps the holder of the bill of lading) will surely seek to shift its financial burden to an insurer. Sellers, buyers, and even banks that finance international sales will want to be certain that their interest in the goods is fully insured. If not, the property risks will prove unacceptably high.

---

http://www.forwarderlaw.com
Resource for legal information on freight forwarding.
http://www.tradeport.org
A comprehensive site covering all aspects of international trade. Log on to "Tradeport," go to the section on "Moving the Goods." Online shipping tutorial, export documentation, links to shipping companies and freight forwarders, seaports, and ocean shipping schedules.

Marine Insurance Policies and Certificates

Although policies of insurance are issued to cover individual shipments, many shippers who do large volumes of business overseas maintain *open cargo policies*. An open policy offers the convenience and protection of covering all shipments by the shipper of certain types of goods to certain destinations and over specified routes. With an open policy in effect, the exporter is authorized by the insurance company to issue a certificate of insurance on a form provided by the company. Open cargo policies are often used by exporters shipping on CIF terms. These certificates are negotiable and are transferred along with the bill of lading to the party who purchases and takes title to the goods. The type or form of the certificate is determined by the contract between the parties or by the requirements of the bank that is providing financing for the sale. The insurance company must be notified as soon as possible after shipment under an open policy.

When a sales contract calls for the seller to obtain a marine insurance policy or certificate on behalf of the buyer, the certificate is universally understood to be acceptable. When the parties state only that a contract is CIF, however, and make no reference to insurance, some confusion can arise as to whether a certificate will be accepted.

The English view is that a certificate of insurance will not substitute for an insurance policy. In the 1924 case, *Kunglig Jarnvagsstyrelsen v. Dexter & Carpenter, Inc.,* 299 F. 991 (S.D.N.Y. 1924), a U.S. court rejected the English view. The court based its argument on the fact that insurance certificates are so widely recognized in commerce that they should be recognized in the law. This rule has been adopted by the UCC.

General Average and FPA Losses

Marine insurance policies cover several different types of loss: (1) total losses of all or part of a shipment, (2) general average losses, and (3) partial or particular average losses.

The term *average* in marine insurance law means loss. A *general average* is a loss that results when extraordinary expenses or losses are incurred in saving the vessel or its cargo from danger at sea. This ancient principle of maritime law, which was developed long before insurance was available, spreads the risk of a disaster at sea by making all parties to the voyage contribute to any loss incurred. Under this rule, if A's cargo is damaged or "sacrificed" in the process of saving the ship, and B's cargo is saved as a result, B or its insurer must contribute to A for the loss. A's claim is a general average. In other words, the owner of the cargo that was sacrificed would have a general average claim for contribution against the owner of the cargo that was saved. For example, when fire threatens an entire ship, and certain cargo is damaged by water in putting the fire out, the owners of all of the cargo must contribute to the loss of the cargo that was damaged by the water. The owners of cargo that is thrown overboard to save a sinking ship may have a claim against those whose cargo was thereby saved. General average claims are typically covered by marine insurance.

In order to prove a general average claim, the claimant must show that (1) the ship, cargo, and crew were threatened by a common danger; (2) the danger was real and substantial (the older cases required that the danger also be "imminent"); and (3) the cargo or ship was voluntarily sacrificed for the benefit of both, or extraordinary expenses were incurred to avert a common peril.

The *York-Antwerp Rules*.   The *York-Antwerp Rules* are a set of standardized rules on general average. An effort to develop commonly accepted principles of general average began in England as early as 1860, with work on the rules being completed in 1890. Following World War II, an international effort to achieve universally accepted general average rules resulted in the revised *York-Antwerp Rules* of 1950. The rules have achieved widespread acceptance by the maritime industry; the latest version was agreed to in 1994. The rules are not the subject of treaty or convention, and have not been enacted into national laws. They traditionally have become a part of the contract of carriage because their provisions are generally incorporated into all modern bills of lading.

General Average Claims by the Carrier.   Surprisingly enough, ocean carriers can bring general average claims against the owners of cargo. The principles of general average apply when a carrier incurs extraordinary expenses in rescuing, saving, or repairing an endangered ship.

The results of general average law must have been quite surprising to the plaintiff in *Amerada Hess Corp. v. S/T Mobil Apex,* 602 F.2d 1095 (2nd Cir. 1979). Plaintiff shipped gasoline and naphtha. When the cargo was destroyed by an explosion and fire that had been started by sparks from machinery in the engine room, the plaintiff sued the carrier for damages. The carrier counterclaims for general average losses. The court denied recovery to the cargo owner under COGSA, holding that the carrier was not liable for the fuel because the ship was not unseaworthy. The court then held, much to the chagrin of the plaintiff, that it was actually liable to the carrier for towing and salvage expenses incurred in arresting the fire and saving the ship.

Real and Substantial Danger.   Historically, the courts have allowed a general average claim only where the loss occurred as a result of the ship being in imminent peril. Today, that concept has been broadened to include instances of *real and substantial danger.* In *Eagle Terminal Tankers, Inc. v. Insurance Co. of USSR,* 637 F.2d 890 (2nd Cir. 1981), the ship had traveled for more than a day with a damaged propeller. It dry-docked, unloaded the cargo, had the damage repaired at a cost of $127,000 (which included the crew's expenses during that time), reloaded, and completed its voyage to Leningrad. The court awarded the carrier the general average claim. It noted that "a ship's master should not be discouraged from taking timely action to avert a disaster," and need not be in actual peril to claim general average.

Particular Average Losses

Although total and general average losses are ordinarily covered up to the policy amount, special problems result from partial or particular average losses. A *particular average loss* is a partial loss to the insured's cargo. Many insurance policies limit the insurer's liability for particular average losses. Because many losses only partially damage the cargo, a shipper must understand the particular average terms of the policy. A policy designed *free of particular average (FPA)* will not cover any partial losses. A policy FPA, followed by certain specified losses, will not pay for any partial or particular average losses of that nature. As such, an "FPA fire" policy will not pay for partial losses to the cargo due to fire.

Types of Coverage

Marine cargo insurance is available for virtually any type of risk, for any cargo, destined for almost any port (see Exhibit 6.3). The only limitations are the willingness of the insurer to undertake the risk and the price. The types of risk covered in a policy are described in the perils clause.

The Perils Clause.   The *perils clause* covers the basic risks of an ocean voyage. It generally covers extraordinary and unusual perils that are not expected during a voyage. Examples of perils that are included are bad weather sufficient to overcome a seaworthy vessel, shipwreck, stranding, collision, and hitting rocks or floating objects. (An example of a perils clause follows in the next case.) But not every event that can damage goods is covered by this clause. Damage due to the unseaworthiness of the vessel is not included in a perils clause; neither is loss from explosion or pilferage, and the clause only covers losses while at

sea. Moreover, only *fortuitous losses* are covered. Fortuitous is a concept that runs throughout insurance law. It means that the loss occurred by chance or accident and could not have reasonably have been predicted. For example, damage due to predictable winds or waves are generally *not* held to be fortuitous. Thus, if a ship sinks in calm seas and good weather, it is presumed that the loss was caused by the ship's own unseaworthiness. Only if it is proven that the ship was seaworthy can it then be shown that the loss was due to a fortuitous event. Courts have held that damage from seawater due to improper stowage of goods is not fortuitous.

A shipper who desires additional coverage can purchase it from the insurer at an added charge. This is called a *specially to cover clause*. For instance, damage resulting from explosion is not generally covered in a standard perils clause, but insurance to cover it can be obtained in the form of an explosion clause. Similarly, additional coverage can be purchased to protect against the risks of fresh water damage, moisture damage, and rust or contamination of the cargo from chemicals, oil, or fuel. Many insurers have recently offered specially designed import–export insurance packages for shippers of perishable foodstuffs, tobacco, steel, and other products and commodities.

The *Shaver* case discusses a standard perils clause and several additional types of coverage purchased by the insured. Unfortunately, none of them covered the loss that the plaintiffs had incurred.

All Risks Coverage.   An *all risks policy* covers all risks except those specifically excluded in the policy. These policies usually exclude damage from acts of war through a "free of capture and seizure" clause, damage or loss from delay in reaching the destination, or damage resulting from strikes and civil commotion. Coverage for strikes is available, but only at additional cost.

EXHIBIT 6.3

Marine Cargo Insurance Policy

CHUBB GROUP
of Insurance Companies   **CARGO POLICY OF INSURANCE**
CHUBB **100 William Street, New York, N.Y. 10038**

$ Number   Issued by the stock insurance company
                                                                   shown below

Open Policy No.   **FEDERAL INSURANCE COMPANY**
In consideration of a premium as agreed, the Company   Incorporated under the Laws of New Jersey
Does insure (lost or not lost)
to the amount of   Dollars,
on

valued at   to be shipped on board of the   B/L Date
at and from
to
and it is hereby understood and agreed, that in case of loss, such loss is payable to the order of
                                                                   on surrender of this Policy.

(continued)

Touching the Adventures and Perils which said Assurers are contented to bear, and take upon themselves, in this Voyage, they are of the Seas, Fires, Assailing Thieves, Jettisons, Barratry of the Master and Mariners, and all other like Perils, Losses and Misfortunes that have or shall come to the Hurt, Detriment or Damage of the said Goods and Merchandise, or any part thereof except as may be otherwise provided for herein or endorsed hereon. AND in case of any Loss or Misfortune, it shall be lawful and necessary to and for the Assured, his or their Factors, Servants and Assigns, to sue, labor and travel for, in and about the Defense, Safeguard and Recovery of the said Goods and Merchandise, or any part thereof, without Prejudice to this insurance; nor shall the acts of the Assured or Assurers, in recovering, saving and preserving the property insured, in case of disaster, be considered a waiver or an acceptance of an abandonment; to the charges whereof, the said Assurers will contribute according to the rate and quantity of the sum hereby insured.

In case of loss, such loss to be paid in thirty days after proof of loss and proof of interest in the property hereby insured.

In case the interest hereby insured is covered by other insurance (except as hereinafter provided) the loss shall be collected from the several policies in the order of the date of their attachment, insurance attaching on the same date to be deemed simultaneous and to contribute pro rata; provided, however, that where any fire insurance, or any insurance (including fire) taken out by any carrier or bailee is available to the beneficiary of this policy, or would be so available if this insurance did not exist, then this insurance shall be void to the extent that such other insurance is or would have been available. It is agreed, nevertheless, that where these Assurers are thus relieved of liability because of the existence of other insurance, these Assurers shall receive and retain the premium payable under this policy and, in consideration thereof, shall guarantee the solvency of the companies and/or underwriters this clause, but not exceeding, in any case, the amount which would have been collectible under this policy if such other insurance did not exist.

In all cases of damage caused by perils insured against, the loss shall, as far as practicable, be ascertained by a separation and a sale or appraisement of a damaged portion only of the contents if the packages so damaged and not otherwise.

Losses arising from breakage and/or leakage and/or loss of weight and/or loss of contents are excluded from this insurance unless caused by stranding or collision with another vessel, or unless this insurance has been expressly extended to include such losses.

Warranted free from Particular Average unless the vessel or craft be stranded, sunk or burnt, but notwithstanding this warranty these Assurers are to pay any loss of or damage to the interest insured which may reasonably be attributed to fire, collision or contact of the vessel and/or conveyance with any external substance (ice included) other than water, or to discharge of cargo at port of distress. The foregoing warranty, however, shall not apply where broader terms of average are provided for herein or by endorsement hereon.

If the voyage aforesaid shall have been terminated before the date of this policy, then there shall be no return of premium on account of such termination of the voyage.

Wherever the words "ship", "vessel", "seaworthiness", "ship or vessel owner" appear in this Policy, they are deemed to include also the words "aircraft", "airworthiness", "aircraft owner".

THIS INSURANCE IS SUBJECT TO THE AMERICAN INSTITUTE CARGO CLAUSES (FEB. 1949) (INCLUDING THE WAREHOUSE TO WAREHOUSE CLAUSE), SOUTH AMERICAN 60 DAY CLAUSE WHEN APPLICABLE. ALSO SUBJECT TO THE AMENDED F. C. & S. AND S. R. & C. C. WARRANTIES (OCT. 1959) (*SEE REVERSE*)

(continued)

EXHIBIT 6.3

Marine Cargo Insurance Policy—(continued)

Original and Duplicative issued, one of which being accomplished the other to stand null and void

SPECIAL CONDITIONS	**Marks and Numbers**
ON DECK—Merchandise and/or goods shipped on deck to an On Deck Bill of Lading *which must be so specified in this policy* are insured.—Free of particular average unless caused by the vessel being stranded, sunk, burnt, on fire, or in collision, but including jettison and/or washing overboard, irrespective of percentage.	

Where the words "including M. E. C." are typed in the space below at the time the policy is issued, this insurance is subject to the American Institute Marine Extension Clauses.	**Where the words "including Strike Risks"** are typed in the space below at the time the policy is issued, this insurance is subject to the Current American Institute S. R. & C. C. Clauses.	**Where the words "including War Risk"** are typed in the space below at the time the policy is issued, this insurance is subject to the Current War Risk Clauses.

In Witness Whereof, the Company issuing this policy has caused this policy to be signed by its authorized officers, but this policy shall not be valid unless signed by a duly authorized representative of the Company.

FEDERAL INSURANCE COMPANY

Date:

Henry G Gubel
Secretary

Henry L. Harlon
President _____
Authorized Representative

The following Warranties shall be paramount and shall not be modified or superseded by any other provision included herein or stamped or endorsed hereon unless such other provision refers specifically to the risks excluded by these warranties and expressly assumes the said risks.

(A) "Notwithstanding anything herein contained to the contrary, this insurance is warranted free from capture, seizure, arrest, restraint, detainment, confiscation, preemption, requisition or nationalization, and the consequences thereof or any attempt thereat, whether in time of peace or war and whether lawful or otherwise; also warranted free, whether in time of peace or war, from all loss, damage or expense caused by any weapon of war employing atomic or nuclear fission and/or fusion or other reaction or radioactive force or matter or by any mine or torpedo, also warranted free from all consequences of hostilities or warlike operations (whether there be a declaration of war or not), but this warranty shall not exclude collision or contact with aircraft, rockets or similar missiles or with any fixed or floating object (other than a mine or torpedo), stranding heavy weather, fire or explosion unless caused directly (and independently of the nature of the voyage or service which the vessel concerned or, in the case of a collision, any other vessel involved therein, is performing) by a hostile act by or against a belligerent power; and for the purposes of this warranty 'power' includes any authority maintaining naval, military or air forces in association with a power.

Further warranted free from the consequences of civil war, revolution, rebellion, insurrection, or civil strife arising therefrom, or piracy."

(B) Warranted free of loss or damage caused by or resulting from strikes, lockouts, labor disturbances, riots, civil commotions or the acts of any person or persons taking part in any such occurrence or disorder.

NOTE: It is necessary for the assured to give prompt notice to these Assurers when they become aware of an event for which they are "held covered" under this policy and the right to such cover is dependent on compliance with this obligation.

SOURCE: Sample policy provided courtesy of Chubb Group of Insurance Companies.

Shaver Transportation Co. v. The Travelers Indemnity Co.
481 F. Supp. 892 (1979)
United States District Court (D. Or.)

BACKGROUND AND FACTS

Shaver, a barge company, contracted with Weyerhauser, the shipper, to transport caustic soda to a buyer. Shaver arranged for marine cargo insurance with Travelers. Several different types of coverage were discussed. Shaver decided on "free from particular average" and "standard perils" provisions, supplemented with "specially to cover" clauses. Shaver loaded the first shipment of caustic soda on one of its barges and transported it to the buyer. The buyer refused delivery because it had been contaminated with tallow. The contamination occurred as Shaver was loading the caustic soda aboard the barge. The barge had previously carried a load of tallow, and Shaver had not thoroughly cleaned the barge input lines. The barge was returned to Shaver's dock. Shaver and Weyerhauser filed a claim with Travelers. Travelers argued that the contamination did not represent a recoverable loss under the policy. Shaver and Weyerhauser brought this action against Travelers.

SKOPIL, CIRCUIT JUDGE, SITTING BY DESIGNATION

Although the plaintiffs request recovery under several theories, there is only one major issue in the case: Are the losses incurred by the plaintiffs the consequences of an insured event under the marine cargo insurance policy? If the losses are not insured against, no recovery is possible.

Recovery under the Perils Clause and Free from Particular Average Clause

The perils clause, almost identical to ancient perils provisions dating back several hundred years, defines the risks protected by the policy. In addition to a long list of "perils of the sea," the clause concludes with "and all other perils, losses, and misfortunes, that have or shall, come to the hurt, detriment, or damage to the said goods and merchandise." Plaintiff argues that the "forced" disposition of the caustic soda was like jettison (an enumerated peril) and is covered by the concluding language of the clause. That language has been interpreted to include only perils that are similar to the enumerated perils.

Whether or not I conclude the forced disposition was a type of jettison, plaintiffs are unable to show an insurable loss due to jettison. The loss contamination of the cargo occurred at the time of loading. . . . plaintiffs cannot recover under the perils clause of the policy. The term "jettison" also appears in the Free from Particular Average clause. If jettison did occur, this clause affords coverage regardless of the amount of cargo damage. However, I find that a jettison did not occur in this instance. Jettison is the act of throwing overboard from a vessel a part of the cargo, in case of extreme danger, to lighten the ship. The orderly unloading and sale of the cargo to a chemical salvage company is not "jettison." Plaintiff cannot recover under the Free from Particular Average clause.

Recovery under the . . . Shore Coverage Clause

The shore coverage clause provides coverage for enumerated risks occurring on shore. Plaintiffs argue that contamination while loading is a shore accident. However, since the contamination occurred within the barge's intake lines, the incident arose "on board." Therefore shore coverage does not apply. Even if it were to apply, contamination of cargo is not within the enumerated risks covered by the shore coverage clause. . . .

Recovery under the Inchmaree Clause

The purpose of the Inchmaree clause is to expand the coverage of the policy beyond the perils provision. Federal law allows a vessel owner to become exempt from liability for fault or error in navigation or management of the ship. In contrast, the shipowner must retain liability for negligence in the care and custody of the cargo. The Inchmaree clause is intended to provide coverage to a cargo owner when a loss is due to error in navigation or management of the vessel since the carrier is exempt from liability. Plaintiffs argue the contamination was the result of an error in management and therefore covered under the Inchmaree clause. Defendant naturally urges the court to find the loss caused by fault in the care and custody of the cargo.

The United States Supreme Court has addressed the distinction between error in management and error in care of cargo but has not articulated a clear test. The Ninth Circuit, noting that no precise defini-

continued

continued

tions exist, advocates a case-by-case determination using the following test: "If the act in question has the primary purpose of affecting the ship, it is "in navigation or in management;" but if the primary purpose is to affect the cargo, it is not "in navigation or in management." *Grace Line, Inc. v. Todd Shipyards Corporation,* 500 F.2d 361, 374 (9th Cir. 1974).

Using this test, I find that the contamination of the cargo in this case was caused by fault in the care, custody, and control of the cargo. The Inchmaree clause will not provide coverage for plaintiffs' losses under the facts of this case.

Recovery under Negligence Clause

The Negligence clause provides coverage against losses due to enumerated perils caused by the unseaworthiness of the vessel. . . . This unseaworthiness must then cause a loss through one of the enumerated perils: "sinking, stranding, fire, explosion, contact with seawater, or by any other cause of the nature of any of the risks assumed in the policy." . . .

Since contamination is not an enumerated peril, plaintiff urges coverage . . . by suggesting the barge was in imminent danger of sinking. Although there is evidence that the caustic soda would have eventually corroded through the barge and caused it to sink, the process would have taken three to five years. This possibility is too far removed to find coverage under a provision providing for loss due to sinking. No recovery is possible under the Negligence clause of this policy. . . .

Plaintiffs suggest a number of theories of recovery under the marine cargo insurance policy. None is suited to this case. I am aided in my construction of this policy by one additional fact. Shaver rejected insurance coverage costing more but did not believe contamination was covered under the policy. Plaintiffs' present attempt to include this type of loss within the coverage of the policy is an afterthought.

Judgment shall be entered for the defendant.

Decision. The plaintiffs' loss due to contamination was not covered under any of the clauses of the insurance policy.

Comment. The following clauses were at issue in this case.

The Perils Clause

"Touching the adventures and perils which the said Assurers are contended to bear, and take upon themselves, they are of the seas and inland waters, man of war, fires, enemies, pirates, rovers, assailing thieves, jettisons, letters of mart and countermart, reprisals, taking at sea, arrests, restraints and detainments of all kings, princes of people of what nation, condition or quality soever, barratry of the master and mariners, and all other perils, losses, and misfortunes, that have or shall come to the hurt, detriment, or damage to the said goods and merchandise, or any part thereof."

The Shore Clause

"Including while on docks, wharves, or elsewhere on shore and/or during land transportation, risks of collision, derailment, fire, lightning, sprinkler leakage, cyclones, hurricanes, earthquakes, floods, the rising of navigable waters, or any accident to the conveyance and/or collapse and/or subsidence of docks and/or structures, and to pay loss or damage caused thereby, even though the insurance be otherwise FPA."

The Inchmaree Clause (named after a famous British case)

"This insurance is also specially to cover any loss of or damage to the interest insured hereunder, through the bursting of boilers, breakage of shafts, or through any latent defect in the machinery, hull, or appurtenances, or from faults or errors in the navigation and/or management of the vessel by the Master, Mariners, Mates, Engineers, or Pilots; provided, however, that this clause shall not be construed as covering loss arising out of delay, deterioration, or loss of market, unless otherwise provided elsewhere herein."

The Negligence Clause

". . . [T]he Assurers agree that in the event unseaworthiness or a wrongful act or misconduct of shipowner, character, their agents or servants, shall, directly or indirectly, cause loss or damage to the cargo insured by sinking, stranding, fire, explosion, contact with seawater, or by any other cause of the nature of any of the risks assumed in the policy, the Assurers will [subject to the terms of average and other conditions of the policy] pay to an innocent Assured the resulting loss."

War Risk.   Typically, marine insurance policies do not cover the risks of war. *War risk insurance* is available for ocean shipments. If war risk insurance is desired, the shipper will have to purchase it separately from the insurer. Under CIF terms, the seller is not expected to provide war risk insurance. If the buyer wants war risk coverage, it will have to agree on the price separately from the marine insurance provisions. The rates for war risk insurance are relatively stable in peacetime, but fluctuate almost daily in times of war.

Chapter Summary

The greatest portion of trade in the world today still moves on the ocean. The contract of carriage between the shipper and the ocean carrier is set forth in the bill of lading. The transport document used in the air cargo business is known as the air waybill.

The liability of an air carrier for death or personal injury of a passenger traveling internationally, or for loss or damage to cargo or baggage, is determined by the *Warsaw and Montreal Air Conventions.* Air carriers are liable for damage to cargo up to 17 SDRs per kilogram, unless the shipper declared a higher value on the air waybill. In 1999, fifty-two nations, including the United States, signed the *Montreal Convention,* the most important change in air transportation law in seventy years. This convention is replacing the *Warsaw Convention,* and has increased the liability of air carriers for injuries and loss to human life, and generally modernized air transport law. The provisions of Protocol 4 with regard to the liability for damage or loss to cargo, have been included in the *Montreal Convention.*

The liability of the carrier for damage or loss to ocean-going goods, in most nations of the world, is governed by the *Hague Rules,* adopted in the United States as the *Carriage of Goods by Sea Act.* COGSA provides many limitations on the liability of shipowners. The carrier's primary obligation is to provide a seaworthy ship. Its liability for damage to cargo resulting from errors in navigation, perils of the sea, and fire is limited. A tremendous amount of litigation in the United States concerns cargo that has been lost or damaged during ocean transport. The losses usually fall on the insurers of the cargo and vessel, who often become embroiled in the litigation.

The activities of ocean carriers and "ocean transportation intermediaries" (freight forwarders and non-vessel operating common carriers) are regulated by the *Ocean Shipping Reform Act of 1998.* OSRA permits carriers to grant special lower freight rates to large volume shippers by utilizing a service contract to govern the shipment in lieu of a bill of lading.

Maritime and marine insurance law is a complicated and specialized area of the law, with concepts dating back to the days of the ancient mariners. Under the law of general average, a carrier can assert a general average claim against the owners of cargo demanding that they (or their insurers) contribute to expenses incurred in saving a vessel from a common peril on the seas. Marine insurance policies are complex contracts. Shippers must exercise caution in insuring their goods for ocean transport, seeking professional advice when deemed prudent.

Questions and Case Problems

1. Hanson suffered from asthma and was allergic to second-hand smoke. He boarded an Olympic Airways flight with his wife, Rubina Husain, and was seated three rows in front of the smoking section. As her husband struggled to breathe, Mrs. Husain asked desperately that her husband be moved away from the smoke. Her requests were ignored by the flight attendant. Hanson died of an asthma attack during the flight. Mrs. Husain sued for damages under the *Warsaw Convention,* claiming that his death was an "accident" as defined by the treaty. The District Court agreed and awarded $1.4 million in damages. The Court of Appeals affirmed in *Husain v. Olympic Airways,* 316 F.3d 829 (9th Cir. 2002). The U.S. Supreme Court granted *Certiorari.* Find the Court's opinion and explain whether the Court ruled Hanson's death an "accident." The *Warsaw Convention* only permitted damages above $75,000 if the air carrier was guilty of willful misconduct (a limit abolished by the later *Montreal Convention*). Do you think that the $75,000 limit should apply in this case?

2. What are the policy reasons underlying the protection that the *Carriage of Goods by Sea Act* (COGSA) offers to ocean carriers? Explain.

3. Tradex Petroleum Services negotiated for the carriage of oil well equipment with West India. West India's agent confirmed by letter that freight rates would be based on the greater of weight or volume. The bill of lading indicated that the freight would be based on tonnage and would amount to $44,800. After reaching its destination, the cargo was unloaded and the rate recalculated on the basis of volume, a sum equal to $108,000. West India, the carrier, claims that it is due the larger amount. What was the result? *West India Industries v. Tradex Petroleum Services,* 664 F.2d 946 (5th Cir. 1981).

4. Sony Corp. packed a shipment of video cassette tapes into a forty-foot ocean container for transport to England. Sony put the tapes into 1,320 cardboard cartons, then strapped the cartons onto 52 wooden pallets. The pallets were put into one shipment container. The bill of lading stated: "1 × 40 container: 1,320 ctns. magnetic tape." The value of the tapes shown on the export certificate was $400,000. On loading, the ship's deck crane dropped the container sixty feet to a concrete deck. Sony claims it can recover the value of the tapes. The ship maintains that under COGSA its liability is limited to 52 pallets. Does COGSA apply in this situation? Why would the carrier want to make this type of argument? What would be the limits of liability for 1,320 cartons versus 52 pallets under COGSA? How many "packages" were involved here and what do you think should be the outcome? *Sony Magnetic Products Inc. of America v. Merivienti O/Y,* 863 F.2d 1537 (11th Cir. 1989).

5. A shipper of fruits and vegetables delivered a refrigerated van of produce to the S.S. *Bayomon* at the port of Elizabeth, New Jersey, on September 22 for shipment to San Juan, Puerto Rico. The ship was supposed to sail that day, but was unable to do so because of repairs needed to correct a boiler problem. The ship sailed on September 25 and arrived in Puerto Rico on September 27. A clause paramount incorporated COGSA into the bill of lading. Upon arrival in Puerto Rico, part of the produce was found to be rotten. The shipper claims that the carrier is liable because the ship was not "seaworthy." COGSA states that the carrier shall not be liable unless it shows a failure to make the ship seaworthy before and at the beginning of the voyage. Does COGSA apply here considering that the port is domestic rather than foreign? Is the carrier liable for an unseaworthy vessel? What is the outcome? *Squillante & Zimmerman Sales, Inc. v. Puerto Rico Marine Management,* Inc., 516 F. Supp. 1049 (D. Puerto Rico 1981).

6. ICC, a Korean corporation, sold down garments to Down in the Village (D/V) of New York. In order to assure payment, however, the garments were consigned to Kologel, an American subsidiary of ICC, with D/V being specified on the air waybill as "notify party" only. Upon their arrival in New York, however, Northwest Airlines delivered the garments to a delivery service representing D/V. Kologel, being unable to recover either the goods or payment from D/V, is attempting to recover from the air carrier for misdelivery. What is the result? *Kologel v. Down in the Village,* 539 F. Supp. 727 (1982).

7. New York Merchandising Company (NYMCO) imported goods produced by C-ART in Hong Kong. The goods were shipped on the Hong Kong Island Lines (carrier). The parties' prior course of dealings had been for the carrier to release the goods to NYMCO on its presentation of a "bank guarantee." These bank guarantees released the carrier from liability for any misdelivery. On this occasion, however, the carrier released the goods upon NYMCO's corporate guarantee of payment. Soon thereafter, NYMCO filed for Chapter 11 bankruptcy. C-ART sued the carrier to recover the money owed for the goods. The carrier argued that it was not liable for misdelivery because NYMCO had good title to the goods from the time they were shipped in Hong Kong. Do you agree with this argument? The carrier also claims that the bills of lading are not valid because the importer NYMCO was insolvent. What is wrong with this argument? *C-ART, Ltd. v. Hong Kong Islands Line America, S.A.,* 940 F.2d 530 (1991).

8. Dazo entered the San Jose, California, airport to board a flight to St. Louis, where she was to take a connecting flight to Toronto. At the security checkpoint, then operated by Globe Airport Security Services, she placed her bag on the x-ray machine conveyor belt. After proceeding through the metal detector, she discovered that her bag had been stolen. She sued Globe and the air carrier for $100,000 worth of jewelry in the bag. The trial court dismissed her suit and she appealed. Was the decision affirmed or reversed on appeal? For the purposes of the *Warsaw Convention,* was this an international or domestic flight? Did the theft of the bag occur "during the transportation by air"? If the *Warsaw Convention* caps the limit of liability of an air carrier, does it also cap the liability of Globe? Do you think that Globe is an "agent" of the air carrier? If so, how would this be different now that airport security is handled by the U.S. Transportation Security Administration? What about other types of air carrier agents? *Dazo v. Globe Airport Security Services,* 268 F.3d 671 (9th Cir. 2001).

Managerial Implications

You are CEO of a firm that regularly imports raw materials from Thailand, Malaysia, Indonesia, and the Philippines. They are shipped to you by ocean carrier through the South China Sea. Your finished goods are sold in the United States and exported to ports in Europe and the Middle East. What kind of information do you need in assessing the risk potential to your cargo passing through these dangerous waters? What will the source of your information be? What sources are available in your library? Which are commercially available? If part of your job is to keep abreast of developments on a daily basis, where will you obtain that information? What types of information might be available from freight forwarders, steamship companies, local port authorities, and insurers?

CHAPTER 7

BANK COLLECTIONS, TRADE FINANCE, AND LETTERS OF CREDIT

Chapter Four discussed the law governing contracts for the sale of goods. Chapter Five described how the parties can define and allocate the risks of shipping and transporting the goods sold under a sales contract. Part of that discussion covered how a negotiable document of title can be used to transfer ownership of the goods sold from one party to another. This chapter examines how the international banking system is used to move money from one party in a transaction to another—how sellers collect for their shipments and how buyers remit payments for their purchases. It also explains how banks guarantee that sellers will be paid for their goods through the use of bank letters of credit and how they provide commercial financing for the international sale. Keep in mind that most of the concepts covered here apply not just to collecting money for the sale of goods, but are equally applicable to many different types of international transactions involving the movement of money internationally and the use of banks to provide an assurance of contractual commitments.

http://www.sba.gov/oit/
U.S. Small Business Administration Office of International Trade. Link to their Trade Finance Program, Export Capital Program, and SBA Exporting Guide.

http://www.law.cornell.edu/ucc/3/overview.html
See the text of the UCC, Article 3 for U.S. negotiable instruments law.

THE BILL OF EXCHANGE

The *bill of exchange* is a specialized type of *negotiable instrument* commonly used to expedite foreign money payments in many types of international transactions. A bill of exchange is often called a *draft*, or *international draft*. A *documentary draft* is used to expedite payment in a documentary sale. The word *draft* is more frequently used in U.S. law and banking practice, while the term *bill of exchange* is more frequently used outside the United States, particularly in England. Generally, the term *draft* is used in this text except when referring specifically to an English bill of exchange. These negotiable instruments can serve two purposes: (1) they act as a substitute for money; and (2) they act as a financing or credit device.

Although it is beyond the scope of this text to offer a thorough treatment of the law of negotiable instruments, an understanding of the importance of the draft is essential to anyone engaged in international trade.

The Origin of Bills of Exchange

The origin of the bill of exchange lies in the history of the merchants and traders of fourteenth- and fifteenth-century Europe. As merchants visited the markets of distant cities to buy and sell their wares, they sought a safer means of transferring their gold or money than by carrying it in their caravans. It might have worked like this: Assume Merchant A delivered goods to Merchant B in a distant city, who became indebted to A for the amount of the purchase. Later Merchant A desires to purchase goods from Merchant C. Merchant A could pay Merchant C for the goods with a written piece of paper—an order—addressed by A to B to pay that money to C. Of course, Merchant B was probably wealthy and respected in the trade—one whose credit was highly regarded. Merchant C could present the written order to B for payment immediately, or if he wished, he could simply ask B to sign (or "accept") the order for future payment. Thus, the written order to pay became an *acceptance*. With the acceptance in hand, Merchant C could purchase new wares from yet another merchant, and use the acceptance in payment. Eventually, merchants turned to wealthy families, Italian banking societies, or medieval bankers spread throughout Europe to transfer money over great distances by issuing payment orders to their correspondents living in distant cities. As merchants recognized that these orders could be bought and sold, the concept of negotiability evolved and negotiable instruments were born. At first, English law did not recognize the validity of negotiable instruments. But merchants accepted them as substitutes for money, and they were enforceable in the merchant's private courts under the Law Merchant. As their importance and use evolved, so did their validity and treatment under the law. They became formally recognized by statute in England in 1822 in the *English Bills of Exchange Act* and in the United States in 1866 in the *Uniform Negotiable Instruments Law.*

Bills of exchange or drafts are today governed in the United States by the *Uniform Commercial Code,* in England by the *Bills of Exchange Act,* and in more than twenty other countries by the 1930 *Convention on Bills of Exchange and Promissory Notes.* Despite their common history, these laws differ in their treatment of the creation and transfer of negotiable instruments, as well as the rights of the parties should an instrument be dishonored or refused.

http://www.UNCITRAL.org
For the United Nations Convention on International Bills of Exchange and International Promissory Notes, follow links from "Adopted Texts" to "International Payments."

Brief Requirements of a Bill of Exchange

The *English Bills of Exchange Act* requires that the bill of exchange be (1) an unconditional order in writing, (2) addressed by one person to another, (3) signed by the person giving it, (4) with a requirement that the person to whom it is addressed pay on demand or at a fixed or determinable future time,

(5) a sum certain in money, (6) to or *to the order of* a specified person, or to bearer. These characteristics are similar to the requirements for a draft set out in the *U.S. Uniform Commercial Code* (UCC). (The *Convention on Bills of Exchange* requires that the words "bill of exchange" appear on the instrument, but English and U.S. laws do not.)

Basically, a bill of exchange or international draft is similar to a check, in that it is an unconditional order to pay a sum of money. (Drafts can be made payable in any currency.) In the case of a check, the *drawer* orders its bank, the *drawee*, to pay the amount of the check to the *payee*. However, instead of being drawn against funds held on deposit in a bank (as with a check), an international draft is an order from the seller to the buyer or buyer's bank to pay the seller upon the delivery of goods or the presentation of shipping documents (e.g., an ocean bill of lading or air waybill). Thus, the seller is both the drawer (the one giving the order to pay) and the payee (the one entitled to payment under the instrument). The drawee is either the buyer or its bank, depending on the arrangements made for payment.

Negotiation and Transfer of Negotiable Instruments.   The commercial use of a draft or other negotiable instrument is derived from its negotiability, the quality that allows it to act as a substitute for money. *Negotiation* is the transfer of an instrument from one party to another so that the transferee (called a *holder*) takes legal rights in the instrument. The correct manner of negotiation depends on whether the instrument is a *bearer* or *order* instrument. Most drafts used in international trade are order instruments because they are payable to a named payee. In order to negotiate an order instrument, *endorsement* (by signature) *and delivery* of the instrument to the holder must take place. References to the negotiation of international drafts appear throughout this chapter.

The Documentary Draft and the Bank Collection Process

Drafts come in several different types. A draft that is to be paid upon presentation or demand is known as a *sight draft* because it is payable "on sight." The sight draft is prepared by the seller and is sent to the buyer along with the shipping documents (e.g., the bill of lading) through banking channels, moving from the seller's bank in the country of export to a foreign correspondent bank in the buyer's country and city. The draft is being sent "for collection," known as a *documentary collection.* The banks act as the agent of the seller for collection purposes. The draft and documents are accompanied by a *collection letter* that provides instructions from the seller on such matters as who is responsible for bank collection charges, what to do in the event the buyer dishonors the draft, and instructions for remittance of the proceeds back to the seller. Thus, the collection letter may specify that in the event of the buyer's dishonor of the draft, the seller's agent in the buyer's country is to be notified, and that the goods are to be properly warehoused and insured pending resolution of the problem or sale of the goods to another party.

Essentially, documentary collections function like a cash-on-delivery (C.O.D.) transaction. When the sight draft is presented to the buyer at its bank or place of business, it is paid, and the payment remitted back to the seller. Only then does the bank turn over the shipping documents with which the buyer can claim its cargo from the carrier. The transaction is somewhat risky however, because when presented with documents, there is no guarantee that the buyer will actually pay. Assuming the buyer does pay, the average cycle for completing a documentary collection is approximately three weeks (although most banks offer accelerated schedules). If a sales contract between buyer and seller calls for payment upon presentation of a sight draft, the contract terms commonly call for *cash against documents* (recall Chapters Four and Five).

---

http://www.royalbank.com/trade
Take a self-guided tour of a trade transaction from both the importer's and exporter's views. Covers managing risk, financing options, foreign exchange, credit insurance, getting paid, etc., from a Canadian perspective.

The SWIFT System. International banking transactions are handled through an industry-owned cooperative known as the SWIFT system, or *Society for Worldwide Interbank Financial Telecommunication.* This worldwide telecommunications system has greatly expedited the remission of payments in a documentary collection. SWIFT is a private, high-speed communications network between banks, set up to transfer funds worldwide.

It originated through the cooperative efforts of major banks in Europe, the United States, and Canada in the mid-1970s and is now in use in more than fifty nations. Due to its speed and cost effectiveness, it has largely replaced the use of the telex and mail-in fund transfers. Currently, SWIFT is involved in the *Bolero Project* that is designed to eventually replace the paper-based transfer of trade documents with electronic transmissions on a global scale.

---

http://money.cnn.com
cnnfn.com/market/currencies
CNN site performs exchange rate calculations between 164 countries.

TRADE FINANCE

Banks and other financial institutions involved in commercial lending provide a wide range of financing packages for international trade, commonly called *trade finance.* Trade finance not only assists the buyer in financing its purchase, but also provides immediate cash to the seller for the sale, and is profitable for the lending institution.

The documentary draft can serve as an important financing or credit device, providing the seller and buyer with a mechanism for financing the international sale. In a competitive marketplace, an exporter must be able to offer its customers credit or other financing for their purchase. Many firms consider their ability to arrange credit a crucial component of their marketing strategy. If an exporter can prearrange financing for the buyer, it has an advantage over a competitor who cannot.

---

http:www.wachovia.com
Many commercial bank Web sites offer an excellent source of information on international payments, trade finance, and letters of credit. From the home page, go to "Corporate and Institutional," then to "International Banking."

The Use of Time Drafts and Acceptances

The use of the draft in trade finance works like this: Seller agrees to issue a draft that is due, say, sixty days after shipment of the goods. The draft states that it is due in sixty days, or on a future date specified on the instrument. A draft due at a future date or after a specified period of time is known as a *time draft,* as shown in Exhibit 7.1. The time

EXHIBIT 7.1

Time Draft Drawn Under Letter of Credit with Banker's Acceptance

AT SIGHT _____ DATE _____ CITY_____
(INDICATE ABOVE WHETHER PAYABLE ON DEMAND OR OTHER TIME LIMIT)

PAY TO THE ORDER OF_____ U.S.$ _____
(NAME OF EXPORTER, EXPORTER'S BANK OR PAYEE)

_____ U.S. DOLLARS

FOR VALUE RECEIVED AND CHARGED TO THE ACCOUNT OF NATIONAL BANK LETTER OF CREDIT NO. _____

ACCEPTED
Date
National Bank, N.A.
Per Authorized Signature

THE TRANSACTION WHICH GIVES RISE TO
THIS INSTRUMENT IS THE:
☐ IMPORT ☐ DOMESTIC SHIPMENT
☐ WAREHOUSING
OF_____
FROM _____ TO _____

TO: NATIONAL BANK, N.A.
         ANYTOWN, U.S.A.
(IMPORTER, BUYER OR DRAWEE)

_____
DRAWER'S SIGNATURE (EXPORTER)

draft is sent to the buyer for its *acceptance*. Typically, the acceptance is done by stamping the date and the word "accepted" across the face of the draft, together with the name and signature of the drawee—no party is obligated on a draft unless its signature appears on it. Under the UCC, the acceptance "may consist of the drawee's signature alone." The buyer has thus created a *trade acceptance*. The buyer's acceptance indicates the buyer's unconditional obligation to pay the draft on the date due. A draft payable at "sixty days after date" is payable by the drawee sixty days after the original date of the instrument. A draft payable at "sixty days sight" means that it is due to be paid sixty days after the date of the acceptance.

As with a sight draft, a seller usually sends the time draft together with the shipping documents to the buyer through banking channels with instructions to the banks that the shipping documents should be handed over to the buyer only upon acceptance of the draft. The sales contract would have indicated the parties' agreement to this arrangement by calling for "documents against acceptance," or other clear language of similar meaning. After acceptance, the draft is then returned through banking channels to the seller. The seller can then hold the draft to maturity, or sell it at a discount to a local bank or commercial lending institution for immediate cash. The commercial lender takes the acceptance by negotiation. The greater the creditworthiness of the buyer, the greater the marketability of the trade acceptance. Where the foreign buyer is unquestionably creditworthy, such as a major multinational corporation, the trade acceptance carries little risk and is easily saleable.

http://www.tradeport.org
Commercial site offering trade information and leads. Enter and use their Trade Expert Tutorial and test your knowledge of exporting. See section on "Financing Your Exports."

Banker's Acceptances and Acceptance Financing

A *banker's acceptance* is a negotiable instrument and short-term financing device widely used to finance international (as well as domestic) sales. The purpose of an acceptance is to substitute a bank's credit for that of the buyer in order to finance the sale. A banker's acceptance is a time draft drawn on and accepted by a commercial bank. The bank stamps its name, date, and signature on the face of the draft to create the acceptance, and thereby becomes obligated to pay the amount stated to the holder of the instrument on the date specified. The holder of the acceptance can convert it to cash immediately at a discounted rate or hold it until it matures.

Banker's acceptances are flexible instruments, with many creative uses. Acceptance financing can be done by either the buyer's or seller's bank. Importing buyers can use a banker's acceptance for short-term borrowing until they can resell and liquidate the goods being purchased. Sellers to export markets can use a banker's acceptance for short-term, preexport, financing of raw materials and production costs until the goods are sold to the foreign customer and payment received. Exporters can also use acceptances to grant credit terms to foreign customers. For instance, in a sale on open account, an exporter might draw a time draft on its own bank for the amount of its overseas sale. The draft is accepted by the exporter's bank, the discounted amount is paid to the exporter, and the acceptance negotiated and discounted in the credit markets. When the importer pays the invoice amount to the exporter, the proceeds are used to satisfy the acceptance at maturity. In another arrangement, the exporter's draft may be accepted by the importer's bank then discounted in the credit markets. In any case, the acceptance is satisfied at maturity through the proceeds of the sale.

In essence, the acceptance financing is self-liquidating because repayment is made from the underlying sales transaction, using credit market monies to finance business. The bank charges the borrower a commission and the discount rate for acceptance financing, which is usually deducted from the face amount of the acceptance when paid to the borrower. Depending on market conditions, acceptance financing is often cheaper for companies than regular credit borrowing.

Banker's acceptances are generally short-term instruments because they must be for a period of six months or less. An *eligible* banker's acceptance is one that qualifies for discount at the U.S. Federal Reserve Bank, which will buy it if it is not sold privately. Acceptances thus serve to finance international trade with outside capital. Because they are created by commercial banks, the use of banker's acceptances is subject to banking laws and Federal Reserve regulations in the United States.

Credit Risk in Trade Finance Programs

Institutions regularly involved in trade lending commonly prearrange these financing terms by agreeing in advance to purchase the trade acceptances of the foreign buyer. They must first perform an analysis and evaluation of the buyer's financial position. Thorough credit checks are done on the buyer, utilizing trade and banking information, the reports of U.S. or foreign credit reporting agencies, and even site visits to the foreign firm. (Although obtaining and verifying credit information is relatively easy in the United States, Canada, Japan, and Western Europe, it is somewhat more difficult, and the information is less reliable, in other regions of the world.) To reduce the credit risk and lower the cost of trade finance, several government agencies, in the United States and other countries, provide credit guarantees to back trade finance lending by commercial institutions. In the United States, these agencies include Eximbank, the Commodity Credit Corporation, and the Agency for International Development (discussed later in this chapter).

Credit Risk in Acceptance Financing: Rights of the Holder in Due Course

One of the primary reasons for the popularity of the acceptance as a financing device is the protection provided to the financial institution or other party who purchases it, provided that party is a *holder in due course*. The detailed requirements to become a holder in due course are spelled out in the UCC. A holder in due course is a holder in possession of a negotiable instrument (such as a draft or acceptance) that has been taken: (1) for value, (2) in good faith, (3) without notice that it is overdue or has been dishonored, and (4) without notice that the instrument contains an unauthorized signature or has been altered (UCC 3–302). If all of the requirements for transferring a negotiable instrument are met, and the transferee qualifies as a holder in due course, the transferee can take greater rights in the instrument than the transferor had.

According to the *holder in due course rule,* the purchaser of an acceptance, or any negotiable instrument, takes it free from most disputes that might arise between the drawer and drawee—the original parties to the underlying transaction. The most common type of dispute that might arise is breach of contract. For example, assume that DownPillow sells pillows to a Japanese buyer and forwards documents and a draft for acceptance. DownPillow discounts the trade acceptance to a U.S. bank, who discounts the instrument in the credit markets. If the pillows turn out to be molded and worthless, the Japanese buyer must still honor and pay the acceptance upon presentation in Japan. It may then assert its separate claim for breach of contract against the seller. This rule ensures the free transferability of commercial paper in international commerce. A financial institution can discount an international draft without fear that it will be caught up in the middle of a breach of contract action between buyer and seller. If a draft did not come with this protection, banks might not be so willing to finance international sales.

Credit Risks in Factoring Accounts Receivable: The Rights of the Assignee

As firms become more globalized, and as credit information becomes more widely available, many firms are offering open account terms to their better, long-term foreign customers. These sellers are giving their customers an open credit period of usually thirty days to several months to pay for goods received. But companies engaged in exporting products are not in business to loan money. Thus, banks are providing open account trade finance services, including the factoring of foreign accounts receivable.

An account receivable is no more than a representation of a *contract right* belonging to the seller—the right to collect money owed by the buyer under the contract for goods shipped. Contract rights can be *assigned* to another party. In a typical financing arrangement, the seller (*assignor*) assigns its right to collect the account to the finan-

cial institution (*assignee*). This is also called *factoring,* and the *assignee* is sometimes called the *factor.* Under basic contract law, the assignee "steps into the shoes" of the assignor and acquires only those rights under the contract that the assignor had against the other party to the contract (e.g., the buyer of the goods). Take the following example: Assume that DownPillow ships an ocean container of pillows to Japan and factors the account receivable with a U.S. bank (the assignee). DownPillow now has its money and the bank is awaiting payment directly from Japan (of course, it is important for the Japanese buyer to be notified of the assignment and instructed to pay only the assignee bank). If a dispute later breaks out over the quality of the pillows, the Japanese buyer may legally assert any claims and defenses against collection by the bank that it otherwise would have had against DownPillow. Thus, for example, the buyer can successfully argue that it does not have to pay the bank because of the breach of warranty by DownPillow. DownPillow will have to repay the bank for money received, and resolve the breach of contract suit with the buyer. For this reason, banker's acceptance financing offers some advantages over accounts receivable financing. Unlike a factor, a holder in due course of a banker's acceptance is protected by the holder in due course rule. Thus, the fact that the products are defective does not provide a defense against payment to one liable on the negotiable instrument. Some insurance companies today offer commercial *credit insurance* to protect against accounts receivable that become bad debts and cannot be collected.

THE DOCUMENTARY LETTER OF CREDIT

As discussed in preceding chapters, a seller to foreign markets assumes less credit risk in the documentary sale than in a sale on open account terms. Nevertheless, a seller still faces the possibility that the buyer might breach its contract and not honor the documentary draft when it is presented for payment. Any number of reasons might cause a buyer to breach a contract, including the buyer's inability to pay or to obtain financing. The buyer also might have found the merchandise at a cheaper price from another supplier. This situation could easily happen in a depressed market in which the price of the

How Well Do You Know Your Customers?

Fraudulent business and/or credit propositions may include any or combinations of the following characteristics. Have any of the following happened to you?

International Fraud/Credit Red Flags

- Requests for blank letterhead and proforma invoices, stamped and signed, as well as bank account information from the U.S. firm for the alleged purpose of transferring funds from a foreign account.
- Supposed urgent need for products or samples to be shipped immediately, before payment can be secured or verified, or with promise of later payment; requests to ship goods by air freight from stock immediately upon receipt of a "certified bank draft."
- Requests for payment by a U.S. citizen of an alleged foreign tax, registration or legal fee, or service charge to finalize a transaction.
- Efforts to acquire a U.S. visa under the pretext of visiting the United States for legitimate business purposes by requesting letters of invitation.
- Promises to the U.S. firm of contracts to supply goods or services to the foreign government, often through the "Federal Tenders Board," which does not exist.
- Requests that correspondence and shipment be sent via air/express courier services, although the solicitation letter came by regular mail.
- Requirement that U.S. company representative travel to a foreign country to sign contract and money transfer documents, or alternatively, that the U.S. company provide power of attorney to a lawyer to sign said papers. The latter involves hefty (and phony) legal fees.
- Vague or implausible explanation of how the sender obtained the company's name as a contact.
- Termination of an existing agent/distributor due to either poor performance or lack of market knowledge.

If so, then you need to know your customer better. Selection of an international agent or distributor is one of the most important business decisions that the exporter will make. The international success of the firm is dependent upon that decision as well as the potential for significant financial loss. In addition to asking your prospective business partner to complete a questionnaire detailing current business partners, the U.S. company may wish to obtain at least two supporting business and credit reports to ensure that the distributor or representative is reputable. By using a second credit report from another source, the U.S. firm may gain new or more complete information. Reports are available from commercial firms and from the Department of Commerce's International Contact Program (ICP) previously known as World Traders Data Report program. The cost of the report is $100 and it contains on average 25 distinct data points about your prospective customer including business reputation, existing trade disputes, business ownership, number of employees, branch locations, assets, bank references, business capitalization and others.

Commercial firms and banks are also sources of credit information on overseas representatives. They can provide information directly or from their correspondent banks or branches overseas. Directories of international companies may also provide credit information on foreign firms. For additional information, you may wish to contact the international division of your bank or ask for a referral from your domestic bank to their international correspondent bank.

If the U.S. company has the necessary information, it may wish to contact a few of the foreign firm's U.S. clients to obtain an evaluation of their representative's character, reliability, efficiency, and past performance. To protect itself against possible conflicts of interest, it is also important for the U.S. firm to learn about other product lines that the foreign firm represents. Contacts through business colleagues and associations can often prove invaluable to U.S. exporters. A colleague with firsthand experience in an international market may give a personal recommendation for an agent, distributor, or potential buyer. Conversely, the recommendation against the use of a representative for credit or reliability reasons may save the firm a number of problems. Attending export seminars and industry trade

continued

goods or commodities has dropped sharply since the time the buyer signed the contract.

Another problem is that an act of the buyer's country might prevent the buyer from making payment on the documents. Although not likely in the case of exports to Japan, Canada, or Western Europe, currency controls imposed on importers by their governments might make it impossible for their companies to obtain the foreign currency needed to purchase foreign goods from their central banks. If such an event occurs, the seller may have to wait extended periods to receive payment. Thus, a seller could quite possibly have its goods arrive at a foreign port only to find that the buyer, for one reason or another, is unable or unwilling to pay for them.

Ideally, the seller would prefer not to relinquish title to the goods until it is certain that it will be paid. The buyer, on the other hand, ideally would want to postpone payment until it is assured that the goods are what was contracted for and are no longer subject to the seller's control or disposition. In order to reconcile these conflicting objectives and reduce the risks involved in an international sale of goods transaction, the parties may arrange for payment under a letter of credit.

The Letter of Credit Defined

Letters of credit are flexible commercial instruments adaptable to a broad range of commercial uses. They are the most common form of payment for the international sale of goods. This chapter covers two types of letters of credit: (1) *documentary* letters of credit (also called *documentary credits* or *commercial credits*), and (2) *standby* letters of credit. "In business, letters of credit are generally referred to as letters of credit." Documentary credits are used in sale of goods transactions, and so the discussion begins with this type.

The documentary *letter of credit* is defined as a conditional undertaking by a bank, issued in accordance with the instructions of the account party, addressed to or in favor of the beneficiary wherein the bank promises to pay, accept, or negotiate the beneficiary's draft up to a certain sum of money, in the stated currency, within the prescribed time limit, upon the presentation of stipulated documents. In a sales transaction, the *account party* is the buyer, the *beneficiary* is the seller, and the *issuing bank* (or *issuer*) is the buyer's bank (see Exhibit 7.2). In a letter of credit transaction, the promise of an internationally recognized bank is substituted for that of the buyer. As long as the seller complies with all conditions in the letter of credit, such as tendering the documents called for in the letter of credit within the time allowed, the seller has more assurance of being paid than in any other form of sale except by receiving cash in advance. Letters of credit specify whether the issuing bank will pay sight drafts or accept time drafts presented by the beneficiary. Typically, bank letters of credit call for the seller's draft to be accompanied by shipping documents together with a number of other collateral documents. The shipping documents could be a negotiable ocean bill of lading, a nonnegotiable or straight ocean bill of lading, an air waybill, or a multimodal transport document. Collateral documents that might be required in the letter of credit include a commercial invoice describing the goods, a marine insurance policy, a consular invoice, a country of origin certificate, a certificate of analysis or inspection, various customs declarations, packing slips, and almost any other documentation demanded by the buyer.

The use of the letter of credit in international trade is well described by the court in *Voest-Alpine International Corp. v. Chase Manhattan Bank,* 707 F.2d 680 (2d Cir. 1983).

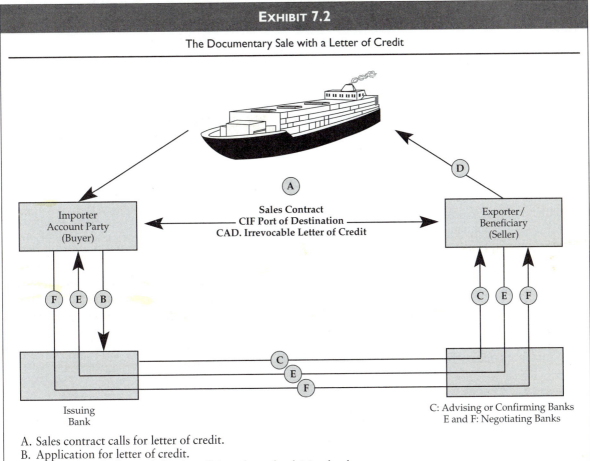

EXHIBIT 7.2

The Documentary Sale with a Letter of Credit

A. Sales contract calls for letter of credit.
B. Application for letter of credit.
C. Letter of credit forwarded to beneficiary through advising bank.
D. Documents prepared according to letter of credit—goods shipped.
E. Documents negotiated for payment against sight draft through negotiating or confirming bank.
F. Payment after documents checked for discrepancies.

Originally devised to function in international trade, a letter of credit reduced the risk of nonpayment in cases where credit was extended to strangers in distant places. Interposing a known and solvent institution's (usually a bank's) credit for that of a foreign buyer in a sale of goods transaction accomplished this objective. A typical letter of credit transaction, as the case before us illustrates, involves three separate and independent relationships—an underlying sale of goods contract between buyer and seller, an agreement between a bank and its customer [buyer] in which the bank undertakes to issue a letter of credit, and the bank's resulting engagement to pay the beneficiary [seller] provided that certain documents presented to the bank conform with the terms and conditions of the credit issued on its customer's behalf. Significantly, the bank's payment obligation

to the beneficiary is primary, direct, and completely independent of any claims which may arise in the underlying sale of goods transaction. . . .

Letters of credit evolved as a mercantile specialty entirely separate from common-law contract concepts and they must still be viewed as entities unto themselves. Completely absorbed into the English common law by the 1700s along with the Law Merchant—of which it had become an integral part by the year 1200—letter of credit law found its way into American jurisprudence where it flourishes today. Its origins may be traced even more deeply into history. There is evidence letters of credit were used by bankers in Renaissance Europe, Imperial Rome, ancient Greece, Phoenicia, and even early Egypt. These simple instruments survived despite their nearly 3,000-year-old lineage because of their inherent reliability, convenience, economy, and flexibility.

Law Applicable to Letters of Credit

Letters of credit are recognized in all legal systems of the world. In the United States, the law governing letters of credit has been codified in Article 5 (1995 revision) of the UCC. In addition, in some states, notably New York, letters of credit make up a great body of case law. Perhaps the most important rules affecting letters of credit are not laws at all, but a privately developed set of guidelines based on the customs and commonly accepted practices of merchants and bankers, known as the *Uniform Customs and Practice for Documentary Credits.*

The Uniform Customs and Practice for Documentary Credits. The *Uniform Customs and Practice for Documentary Credits* (UCP) is a document that international bankers know well. It is a set of standardized rules for issuing and handling letters of credit, drafted and published by the *International Chamber of Commerce* (which also publishes *Incoterms*) with the assistance of the international banking community. The UCP establishes the legal format of letters of credit, sets out rules by which banks process letter of credit transactions, and defines the rights and responsibilities of all parties to the credit. Because the UCP has been drafted primarily by banks, its provisions primarily protect them in any transaction. The UCP was first introduced in the early 1930s, with the latest revision (UCP No. 500) published in 1993. The UCP is in use in virtually every nation of the world (including, for example, the People's Republic of China).

> http://www.iccwbo.org
> http://www.iccbookusa.com
> International Chambers of Commerce, publishers of the UCP

Legal Effect of the UCP. The International Chamber of Commerce is not a government or lawmaking body, and the UCP is not law. The UCP "governs" letters of credit only if its provisions are incorporated into the letters of credit by reference. The great majority of international letters of credit issued today state that they are to be interpreted according to the UCP. The UCP is widely recognized by judges in deciding letter of credit cases; reference to it appears in virtually every reported decision on international letters of credit. UCC Article 5 (1995 revision) now defers to the UCP, and specifically states that the UCC is *not* applicable to any letter of credit to the extent that it is in conflict with the UCP. As a result, the UCP has a far greater impact on the law of international letters of credit than does the UCC.

Letters of Credit Are Independent of the Underlying Transaction

As the previous quote from the *Voest-Alpine* case states, the letter of credit is a separate contract between the account party and the issuing bank. Under this *principle of independence,* the letter of credit is separate from the underlying contract between buyer and seller on which it is based. The following case, *Maurice O'Meara Co. v. National Park Bank of New York,* is generally considered by writers in the United States to be the classic statement of the legal nature of letters of credit.

The rule of *Maurice O'Meara* is recognized in UCP 500, Article 3.

> Credits, by their nature, are separate transactions from the sales or other contracts on which they may be based and banks are in no way concerned with or bound by such contracts. . . .
>
> Consequently, the undertaking of a bank to pay, accept and pay drafts or negotiate and/or fulfill any other obligation under the credit, is not subject to claims or defenses by the applicant [account party] resulting from his relationships with the issuing bank or the beneficiary.
>
> A beneficiary can in no case avail himself of the contractual relationships existing between the banks or between the applicant (account party) and the issuing bank.

Rights of the Account Party in Cases of Fraud

Under the UCC, a partial exception has been created to the preceding rule if the letter of credit is fraudulent, forged, or *fraud in the transaction* exists in the underlying sales contract. This exception is governed by the UCC because the UCP is silent on the question of fraudulent documents. Under this exception, if a seller presents documents

Maurice O'Meara Co. v. National Park Bank of New York
146 N.E. 636 (1925)
Court of Appeals of New York

BACKGROUND AND FACTS

National Park Bank issued a letter of credit addressed to Ronconi & Millar, beneficiary, at the request of its account party, Sun Herald, "covering the shipment of 1,322 tons of newsprint paper in 72½ inch and 36½ inch rolls to test 11–12, 32 lbs. at 8½ cents per pound net weight—delivery to be made in December 1920, and January 1921." The letter of credit did not require that a testing certificate from an independent laboratory accompany the documents. When Ronconi & Millar's invoice and draft were presented to the bank, the documents described the paper as was required in the letter of credit. But the bank refused payment because it had no opportunity to test the tensile strength of the paper. (Interestingly, the market price of newsprint paper had fallen sharply in the time period between the contract of sale and the presentation of documents, amounting to over $20,000 in this case.) Ronconi & Millar transferred their rights to collect payment to Maurice O'Meara, a financial institution, who brought this action to collect the full amount of the drafts. Maurice O'Meara claims that the issuing bank had no right to test or inspect the paper.

MCLAUGHLIN, JUDGE

[The letter of credit] . . . was in no way involved in or connected with, other than the presentation of the documents, the contract for the purchase and sale of the paper mentioned. That was a contract between buyer and seller, which in no way concerned the bank. The bank's obligation was to pay sight drafts when presented if accompanied by genuine documents specified in the letter of credit. If the paper when delivered did not correspond to what had been purchased, either in weight, kind or quality, then the purchaser had his remedy against the seller for damages. Whether the paper was what the purchaser contracted to purchase did not concern the bank and in no way affected its liability. It was under no obligation to ascertain, either by a personal examination or otherwise, whether the paper conformed to the contract between the buyer and seller. The bank was concerned only in the drafts and the documents accompanying them. This was the extent of its interest. If the drafts, when presented, were accompanied by the proper documents, then it was absolutely bound to make the payment under the letter of credit, irrespective of whether it knew, or had reason to believe, that the paper was not of the tensile strength contracted for. This view, I think, is the one generally entertained with reference to a bank's liability under an irrevocable letter of credit of the character of the one here under consideration.

The defendant had no right to insist that a test of the tensile strength of the paper be made before paying the drafts; nor did it even have a right to inspect the paper before payment, to determine whether it in fact corresponded to the description contained in the documents. The letter of credit did not so provide. All that the letter of credit provided was that documents be presented which described the paper shipped as of a certain size, weight, and tensile strength. To hold otherwise is to read into the letter of credit something which is not there, and this the court ought not to do, since it would impose upon a bank a duty which in many cases would defeat the primary purpose of such letters of credit. This primary purpose is an assurance to the seller of merchandise of prompt payment against documents.

It has never been held, so far as I am able to discover, that a bank has the right or is under an obligation to see that the description of the merchandise contained in the documents presented is correct. A provision giving it such right, or imposing such obligation, might, of course, be provided for in the letter of credit. The letter under consideration contains no such provision. If the bank had the right to determine whether the paper was of the tensile strength stated, then it might be pertinent to inquire how much of the paper must it subject to the test. If it had to make a test as to tensile strength, then it was equally obligated to measure and weigh the paper. No such thing was intended by the parties and there was no such obligation upon the bank. The documents presented were sufficient. The only reason stated by defendant in its letter of December 18, 1920, for refusing to pay the draft, was that— "There has arisen a reasonable doubt regarding the quality of the newsprint paper. . . . Until such time as we can have a test made by an impartial and unprejudiced expert we shall be obliged to defer payment."

This being the sole objection, the only inference to be drawn therefrom is that otherwise the documents

continued

---

continued

presented conformed to the requirements of the letter of credit. All other objections were thereby waived.

Judgment should be directed in favor of the plaintiff.

Decision. National Park Bank's obligation to pay the beneficiary's drafts submitted under its letter of credit is separate and distinct from the contract of sale between the buyer and seller. Banks deal in documents only. Therefore the defendant, National Park Bank, cannot withhold payment of the drafts even if it believes that the paper is not of the weight, kind, or quality ordered by Sun Herald. Defendant also has no right to demand testing of the paper or to inspect it prior to payment.

---

for a nonexistent shipment of goods, fraud in the transaction occurs. If the bank does choose to honor a demand for payment despite being notified of fraud, the buyer may petition a court for an injunction that would prevent the bank from paying on the credit. The court may order the injunction where necessary to protect the buyer from *irreparable harm*. If the demand for payment is made by a holder in due course, however, then the bank *must* honor the demand for payment.

Compare the last case, *Maurice O'Meara,* with the following case, *Sztejn v. J. Henry Schroder Banking Corp.* It presents a clear distinction between a mere breach of warranty and fraud. *O'Meara* involved a breach of warranty—the seller shipped newsprint paper of inferior quality. *Sztejn* involves fraud in the transaction—the presentation of documents covering goods, and the shipment of bales of worthless rubbish. The *Sztejn* case is one of the most widely cited cases in U.S. letter of credit law.

Compare the rule holding in *Sztejn* regarding fraud in the transaction with the circumstances that arise in the English case, *United City Merchants (Investments) Ltd. v. Royal Bank of Canada* (see page 224). Notice how the English court distinguishes American precedent and narrows the application of the fraud exception.

Fraud in the transaction can take many forms, as illustrated by a not uncommon situation. In *Regent Corp., U.S.A. v. Azmat Bangladesh, Ltd.,* 686 N.Y.S.2d 24 (N.Y.A.D. 1 Dept. 1999), a textile company located in Bangladesh represented to a U.S. buyer that bed sheets and pillow cases were to be manufactured in Bangladesh. In fact, the seller knew that the goods were a product of Pakistan, but nevertheless provided a fake certificate of origin. The seller was trying to circumvent U.S. import quotas on Bangladeshi linens. The New York court ruled that this was sufficient fraud in the transaction to justify the bank's refusal to honor the draft under the letter of credit.

A Letter of Credit Transaction

The following discussion examines how a letter of credit is used in a sale of goods transaction. For ease in understanding, the parties are referred to as "buyer" and "seller" instead of their banking terms, *account party* and *beneficiary.*

Once the sales contract calls for payment under a letter of credit, the buyer becomes responsible for applying to its bank for the letter of credit. The application is prepared on the bank's form. The application requests that the issuing bank honor the seller's drafts by paying or accepting them (as the case may be) up to a specified amount (usually the contract price), but *only if the drafts are accompanied by specified documents.* The buyer will specify in the application which documents must be presented in order for the bank to rightfully honor the draft. It will also specify exactly what those documents must say. For instance, the buyer might call for the letter of credit to require that the bill of lading be negotiable, or marked "freight prepaid," or that the packing slip or certificate of analysis contain certifications as to quality, weight, or markings. It probably would require the bank to honor the letter of credit only if the documents are accompanied by a marine insurance policy (such as in a CIF contract), or a country-of-origin certificate. The application may also specify any other requirements for honoring the draft desired by the buyer. To illustrate, suppose the buyer does not want the seller to make partial shipments because of the increased risk of damage or loss to the goods. It knows that unless the letter

Sztejn v. J. Henry Schroder Banking Corp.
31 N.Y.S.2d 631 (1941)
Supreme Court, Special Term, New York County

BACKGROUND AND FACTS

The plaintiff contracted to purchase hog bristles from Transea Traders in India. The defendant bank issued an irrevocable letter of credit to Transea covering a shipment of hog bristles and payable upon presentation of the proper documents. Transea filled 50 cases with cow hair and other worthless rubbish in order to obtain an ocean bill of lading from the steamship company showing the shipment of 50 cases of hog bristles. The documents and draft were presented to the defendant bank by The Chartered Bank of India, acting as agent for Transea. The plaintiff brought this action against the issuing bank to restrain it from paying on the letter of credit.

SHIENTAG, JUSTICE

One of the chief purposes of the letter of credit is to furnish the seller with a ready means of obtaining prompt payment for his merchandise. It would be a most unfortunate interference with business transactions if a bank before honoring drafts drawn upon it was obliged or even allowed to go behind the documents, at the request of the buyer and enter into controversies between the buyer and the seller regarding the quality of the merchandise shipped. . . . Of course, the application of this doctrine presupposes that the documents accompanying the draft are genuine and conform in terms to the requirements of the letter of credit. However, I believe that a different situation is presented in the instant action. This is not a controversy between the buyer and seller concerning a mere breach of warranty regarding the quality of the merchandise; on the present motion, it must be assumed that the seller has intentionally failed to ship any goods ordered by the buyer. In such a situation, where the seller's fraud has been called to the bank's attention before the drafts and documents have been presented for payment, the principle of the independence of the bank's obligation under the letter of credit should not be extended to protect the unscrupulous seller. It is true that even though the documents are forged or fraudulent, if the issuing bank has already paid the draft before receiving notice of the seller's fraud, it will be protected if it exercised reasonable diligence before making such payment. However, in the instant action

Schroder has received notice of Transea's active fraud before it accepted or paid the draft. . . .

Although our courts have used broad language to the effect that a letter of credit is independent of the primary contract between the buyer and seller, that language was used in cases concerning alleged breaches of warranty; no case has been brought to my attention on this point involving an intentional fraud on the part of the seller which was brought to the bank's notice with the request that it withhold payment of the draft on this account. The distinction between a breach of warranty and active fraud on the part of the seller is supported by authority and reason. As one court has stated: "Obviously, when the issuer of a letter of credit knows that a document, although correct in form, is, in point of fact, false or illegal, he cannot be called upon to recognize such a document as complying with the terms of a letter of credit." . . .

While the primary factor in the issuance of the letter of credit is the credit standing of the buyer, the security afforded by the merchandise is also taken into account. In fact, the letter of credit requires a bill of lading made out to the order of the bank and not the buyer. Although the bank is not interested in the exact detailed performance of the sales contract, it is vitally interested in assuring itself that there are some goods represented by the documents.

Accordingly, the defendant's motion to dismiss the supplemental complaint is denied.

Decision.   The court held in favor of the plaintiff and enjoined the bank's payment. A court can enjoin an issuing bank from honoring a draft if the bank learns that its customer will suffer irreparable harm as a result of fraud.

Comment.   Under the UCC (Section 5–114), a bank "may honor the draft . . . despite notification from the customer (the buyer) of fraud . . . but a court . . . may enjoin such honor." As an interesting note, the California legislature chose to omit the words "but a court . . . may enjoin such honor." Therefore, in California, courts have held that no injunction can be issued against a letter of credit for fraud in the transaction.

United City Merchants (Investments) Ltd. v. Royal Bank of Canada
2 Weekly Law Reports 1039
House of Lords, 1982

BACKGROUND AND FACTS

The buyer, a Peruvian company, entered into a contract to purchase glass fibers at a price of $662,082 from an English seller. Payment was to be made under an irrevocable letter of credit confirmed by Royal Bank of Canada. The letter of credit called for a bill of lading dated no later than December 15, 1976. The goods were in fact loaded onto the vessel (*The American Accord*) on December 16, but the loading brokers issued a bill of lading which was dated December 15, 1976. Unaware of the false statement, the sellers submitted documents to Royal Bank who refused to pay on the credit because it suspected fraud in the documents.

LORD DIPLOCK

If on their face, the documents presented to the confirming bank by the seller conform with the requirements of the credit as notified to him by the conforming bank, that bank is under a contractual obligation to the seller to honour the credit, notwithstanding that the bank has knowledge that the seller at the time of presentation of the conforming documents is alleged by the buyer to have, and in fact has already, committed a breach of his contract with the buyer for the sale of the goods to which the documents appear on their face to relate, that would have entitled the buyer to treat the contract of sale as rescinded and to reject the goods and refuse to pay the seller the purchase price. The whole commercial purpose for which the system of confirmed irrevocable documentary credits has been developed in international trade is to give to the seller an assured right to be paid before he parts with control of the goods that does not permit of any dispute with the buyer as to the performance of the contract of sale being used as a ground for non-payment or reduction or deferment of payment.

To this general statement of principle as to the contractual obligations of the confirming bank to the seller, there is one established exception: that is where the seller, for the purpose of drawing on the credit, fraudulently presents to the confirming bank documents that contain, expressly or by implication,

material representations of fact that to his knowledge are untrue. . . . [*Sztejn v. J. Henry Schroder Banking Corporation* (1941) 31 N.Y.S.2d 631]. This judgment of the New York Court of Appeals was referred to with approval by the English Court of Appeal in *Edward Owen Engineering Ltd. v. Barclays Bank International Ltd.* [1978] Q.B. 159. . . . The courts will not allow their process to be used by a dishonest person to carry out a fraud.

The instant case, however, does not fall within the fraud exception. [The trial judge] found the sellers to have been unaware of the inaccuracy of Mr. Baker's notation of the date at which the goods were actually on board *American Accord*. They believed that it was true and that the goods had actually been loaded on or before December 15, 1976, as required by the documentary credit.

* * *

It has so far as I know, never been disputed that as between confirming bank and issuing bank and the buyer, the contractual duty of each bank under a confirmed irrevocable credit is to examine with reasonable care all documents presented in order to ascertain that they appear on their face to be in accordance with the terms and conditions of the credit, and, if they do so appear, to pay to the seller/beneficiary by whom the documents have been presented the sum stipulated by the credit. . . . It is equally clear, and is so provided by Article 9 of the Uniform Customs, that confirming banks and issuing banks assume no liability or responsibility to one another or to the buyer "for the form, sufficiency, accuracy, genuineness, falsification or legal effect of any documents."

Decision. Confirming banks are not permitted to refuse a demand payment when the documents, on their face, comply with the letter of credit. Under the English view, fraud perpetuated by a third party does not constitute fraud in the transaction so as to permit the confirming bank to deny payment. Here it was not established that the beneficiary had committed or had knowledge of the fraud.

of credit states otherwise, the issuing bank is permitted to honor drafts on partial shipments. Therefore, it must indicate on the application that drafts drawn under the letter of credit are not to be honored in the event that the documents show a partial shipment.

Thus, the application for the letter of credit forms a *contract between the buyer and its bank* (not between buyer and seller), with the buyer agreeing to reimburse the bank for any sums properly paid out according to the terms of the letter of credit. If the bank does not act according to its contract with its customer, it may not be entitled to reimbursement.

Irrevocability of Letters of Credit. According to UCP 500, credits may be either revocable or irrevocable, but "in the absence of such indication the credit shall be deemed to be *irrevocable*." Revocable letters of credit are seldom used in international commerce (except perhaps between some corporate subsidiaries) because they do not provide sufficient protection to the beneficiary. An example of an irrevocable documentary letter of credit is shown in Exhibit 7.3.

Advising the Letter of Credit. The letter of credit will be issued and sent to the seller via a foreign correspondent bank located in the seller's country. This bank, known as the *advising bank,* merely informs or "advises" the seller that a letter of credit has been issued in its favor and that the letter of credit is available for the seller. Under UCP 500, the letter of credit is advised "without engagement" by the advising bank, which is not liable on the letter of credit and makes no promise to pay the seller. It provides only a banking service by transmitting the letter of credit to the seller. The bank is responsible, however, for using reasonable care to authenticate the letter of credit, which is often done by comparing the signature on the credit with the authorized signature kept on file in the bank's signature books. UCP 500 states that letters of credit can be transmitted from issuing bank to advising bank electronically, and that no mail confirmation need be sent.

Seller's Compliance with the Credit. Until the seller receives the letter of credit, it may not want to package the goods, arrange transportation, or prepare the documentation. This reluctance is because the seller must first read the letter of credit and follow its instructions carefully in order to be paid by the bank.

First, the seller will want to compare carefully the terms of the letter of credit with the terms of the underlying contract of sale. If the documents show significant differences, the seller would want to contact the buyer to inquire why and resolve the difference. For instance, assume that a sales contract called for shipment of "4,000 lbs. washed white goose down in machine-compressed bales," and the letter of credit reads "3,000 lbs. washed white goose down in machine-compressed bales." The seller must stop and inquire why a difference appears in the quantities expressed. Did the buyer change its mind and decide to purchase only 3,000 lbs. instead of the 4,000 lbs. agreed to? If so, why wasn't the seller contacted to reconfirm the new order? Perhaps the bank erred in transmitting the letter of credit. Whatever the reason, the seller should do nothing until the problem is resolved or until an *amended* letter of credit is received. If the seller ships 4,000 lbs., its drafts may be refused and it may only get paid for 3,000 lbs.; if it ships 3,000 lbs., it may be losing a sale for the 1,000 lbs. difference.

The seller would want to examine many other provisions of the letter of credit before shipping; the letter of credit might prompt other questions for which the seller would want answers. In the above example, can the seller ship the goods within the time called for in the letter of credit? Can the down be washed, sorted, baled, delivered to the carrier, and an onboard bill of lading received within the time limits set in the letter of credit? If an export license is needed in order to export goose down from the seller's country, can it be processed and received on time? (Although obtaining a license is not so much a problem for exporters of products such as down, corn, or pencils, it can be a real headache for exporters of high-tech products!) A letter of credit that calls for shipment aboard a certain vessel sailing on a certain date may not be possible, and the seller may want to request an extension in an amended letter of credit. Is the total amount of the letter of credit sufficient to cover the drafts? Is it in the currency called for in the sales contract? Do the provisions for insurance and the payment of freight charges meet the terms of the contract of sale, or

EXHIBIT 7.3	

Irrevocable Documentary Letter of Credit

IMPORTER'S BANK CONFIRMATION OF BRIEF CABLE	Irrevocable Documentary Letter of Credit

Importer's Bank	Date of Issue
Charlotte, NC	February 1, 2004

	Issuing Bank Letter of Credit No.	Advising Bank Letter of Credit No.
	78346	

Advising Bank	Applicant
German Bank F.R.G.	Downpillow, Inc. North Carolina

Beneficiary	Expiratory Date (For Negotiation)		
Federhaus, GMBH F.R.G.	Day	Month	Year
	30	April	2004

Currency	Amount	
U.S.A.	35,000.00	Thirty-Five Thousand Dollars

Gentlemen:

We hereby issue this documentary Letter of Credit in your favor which is available against your draft at sight drawn on Importer's Bank, Charlotte, North Carolina for 100% of the invoice value bearing the clause "Drawn under documentary letter of Credit Number 78346" Accompanied by the following documents:

1. Commercial invoice in triplicate
2. U.S. special customs form #1111 in triplicate
3. Insurance policy/certificate in duplicate covering all risks
4. Certificate of origin "form A" in duplicate
5. Full set 3/3 clean on-board bills of lading issued
   to the order of Importer's bank, marked "Freight prepaid,"
   notify applicant.

   Purporting to cover: 3000 lbs washed white goose down in machine
   compressed bales, CIF Norfolk, Va.

Shipment from	Partial Shipments	Transshipments
F.R.G. To Norfolk, Va.	Prohibited	Prohibited

Special conditions

Documents must be presented to negotiating bank within 10 days of issuance of shipping documents but within the validity of the credit.
Latest ship date March 15, 2004.

Negotiating bank is authorized to forward all documents to us via airmail.   All banking charges outside the United States are for account of the beneficiary.

We hereby engage with the bona fide holders of all drafts under and in compliance with the terms of this letter of credit that such drafts will be duly honored upon presentation to us. The amount of each drawing must be indorsed on the reverse side of this letter of credit by the negotiating bank.	Indications of the Advising Bank
B. D. DeWoolfson Authorized Signature	Place, Date, Name, and Signature of the Advising Bank

Except so far as otherwise expressly stated this documentary letter of credit is subject to the Uniform Customs and Practices for Documentary Credits (1993 Revision) the International Chamber of Commerce Document No. 500.

are they agreeable to the seller? Does the letter of credit allow partial shipments? Has the buyer made any last-minute changes to the order that should be included in a new letter of credit? Finally, can the documents and the draft be presented to the issuing bank before the date of expiration of the letter of credit?

If the seller is unable to comply with the letter of credit for any reason, the buyer must be contacted immediately so that an amended credit can be issued. In one case, for instance, a U.S. furniture manufacturer received a letter of credit from Kuwait calling for the shipment of furniture in "one 40' ocean container." Only after packaging and loading did the manufacturer realize that a few pieces would not fit into the container. If the manufacturer's documents had shown less furniture than was called for in the letter of credit, its draft might not have been paid. An amended credit had to be issued covering the new quantity before it was safe for the furniture manufacturer to ship. Due to the added cost of small shipments, the potential for damage, and the difficulty of handling break-bulk cargo in modern Middle Eastern ports, the buyer simply reduced its order rather than have the pieces shipped separately.

Collecting on the Credit. Once the seller knows that it is able to meet the terms of the letter of credit, it is ready to prepare the draft and shipping documents and present them to a *negotiating bank* in its city to be forwarded to the issuing bank. The UCP permits the issuing bank to "nominate" a negotiating bank. If not, the documents may be negotiated through the advising bank or another bank of the seller's choice. The beneficiary must present the documents within a specified number of days after shipment, or prior to the expiration of the letter of credit (known as the *expiry date*), whichever is earlier. If no time period is specified, the UCP requires submission of shipping documents to banks within twenty-one days of shipment. Both the expiration and presentment dates must be met or the documents will be rejected (unless the defect is waived by the buyer). This requirement is an assurance to the buyer that the goods have been shipped on time.

The negotiating bank then transmits the documents to the issuing bank, which then inspects them for accuracy, irregularities, and discrepancies against the letter of credit. Documents that are not in order may be rejected. If the issuing bank decides to reject, it must notify the negotiating bank within seven banking days. If the issuing bank pays out on documents that do not conform to the letter of credit, then the bank will be liable to its customer, the buyer, for doing so. If the documents are in order, the bank will normally pay the draft at sight or at maturity, or accept the time draft, and then negotiate the shipping documents to the buyer. Thus, with bill of lading in hand, properly indorsed by the bank, the buyer may claim its goods from the carrier.

Examination of the Documents Under the UCP

From this overview of a letter of credit transaction, the next section performs a more careful analysis of how the seller's documents must conform to the requirements of the letter of credit. According to the independence principle, the obligation of the issuing bank to honor the beneficiary's draft under a letter of credit is not dependent on the contract of sale between the buyer and seller. Rather, the obligation of the bank to honor drafts is conditional solely upon the beneficiary's doing exactly what is requested in the letter of credit. This notion is clear throughout the UCP. Article 4 states that "in credit operations all parties concerned deal with documents, and not with goods, services and/or other performances to which the documents may relate." Indeed, banks deal mainly in the appearance of documents. Article 14 requires that the issuing bank "determine on the basis of the documents alone whether or not they appear on their face to be in compliance with the terms and conditions of the credit." As long as the documents are in apparent good order, appear valid on their face, and correspond to the terms of the letter of credit, the bank must honor the beneficiary's draft, and will be able to seek reimbursement from its customer, the buyer, regardless of the quality or condition, or even the existence, of the goods. The banks are not concerned whether the documents serve any commercial purpose or as to why their account party wanted the documents in any particular form. That the goods might have gone to the bottom of the ocean during their voyage is irrelevant to the bank's obligation. That the goods inside the container are not even close to what the buyer ordered is irrelevant. The bank has no obligation to check the quality or condition of the goods, nor to investigate rumors about them. The UCP does not require the bank to examine any documents not called for in the letter of credit. Of course, the issuing bank would want to check the documents carefully for any apparent signs that they are not genuine or that they might have been forged.

The Rule of Strict Compliance.   As you have learned, the letter of credit will specify which documents must be presented for payment and exactly what terms the documents must contain. Recall why this is important. This is the beneficiary's assurance that when it presents documents in compliance with the letter of credit, it will be paid on a timely basis by the bank that issued the credit. Similarly, the buyer is assured that it is purchasing documents that purport to cover the goods it ordered. If there is no fraud, and the goods indeed exist, it can be fairly satisfied that the cargo will arrive, fully insured, at the port of destination and that it can then exchange the bill of lading for the goods. However, in order for a bank to pay out on documents presented by the beneficiary, the documents must appear exactly as required in the letter of credit. The goods must be described in the invoice as described in the letter of credit, the bill of lading must be clean, and marked "on board," and dated within the time for shipment called for in the letter of credit, the draft must be in the amount specified, presentment must be prior to the expiry date set in the letter of credit, and so on. If these conditions are not met, then the bank will most likely reject the documents as nonconforming. This rule is as old as letter of credit law itself. It was stated quite aptly by Lord Sumner in *Equitable Trust Co. of New York v. Dawson Partners Ltd.* 2 Lloyd's Rep 49 (1927): "There is no room for documents which are almost the same, or which will do just as well." Today, that statement is embodied in UCP Article 13:

> Banks must examine all documents stipulated in the credit with *reasonable care to ascertain whether or not they appear, on their face, to be in compliance* with the terms and conditions of the credit. . . . Documents *which appear on their face to be inconsistent* with one another will be considered as not appearing on their face to be in compliance with the terms and conditions of the credit. . . .

The prevailing rule established by the courts for examining documents is the *strict compliance rule.* According to this view, the terms of the documents presented to the issuing bank must strictly conform to the requirements of the letter of credit. When a document contains language or terms different from the letter of credit, or some other apparent irregularity, it is said to contain a *discrepancy*. Documents that do not conform are *discrepant*. The documents and letter of credit are literally put side by side by a document checker at the issuing bank and the terms are matched. This does not mean that every "i" must be dotted and every "t" crossed. (As one court stated, it's not a discrepancy if Smith is spelled "Smithh.") Some typographical errors are excusable, of course. But the thrust of the rule is that every provision of the bill of lading, commercial invoice, insurance policy, and other required shipping documents must match the letter of credit. Even a small discrepancy can cause the bank to reject the documents. If the issuing bank pays against documents that contain a discrepancy, then the bank cannot seek reimbursement from the account party, its customer. A summary of common discrepancies appears in Exhibit 7.4. In the following case, *Courtaulds North America, Inc. v. North Carolina National Bank,* the court considered a discrepancy between the description of the goods on the letter of credit and on the invoice.

Apply the strict compliance rule of the *Courtaulds* case to the following situation: Suppose that a seller receives a letter of credit from a foreign buyer covering "1,000 standard-size bed pillows." Seller's export manager completes an invoice for "1,000 bed pillows, size 20 x 26 in." A discrepancy would exist. Bankers are not expected to know that a "standard" bed pillow is 20 x 26 inches, and even if the banker did know, he would still have to refuse the document because of the discrepancy (although in practice, the bank would call its customer to get a waiver of the discrepancy). Assume now that the invoice matches the letter of credit, but that the bill of lading shows shipment of "1,000 pillows." On this point, the UCP is very clear:

> The description of the goods in the commercial invoice must correspond with the description in the credit. In all other documents, the goods may be described in general terms not inconsistent with the description of the goods in the credit. (Article 37c)

EXHIBIT 7.4

Common Discrepancies Found in Documentation

Bill of Lading/Air Waybill

- An incomplete set of bills (originals missing)
- Onboard notations not dated and signed or initialed
- Time for shipment has expired
- Unclean bill of lading shows damage
- Indorsement missing
- Evidence of forgery or alteration
- Does not show freight prepared if required under the letter of credit
- Description of goods differs substantially from letter of credit
- Name of vessel differs
- Shows partial shipment or transshipment where prohibited by the letter of credit

Commercial Invoice

- Description of goods does not conform to description in letter of credit
- Does not show terms of shipment
- Amount differs from that shown on draft
- Amount exceeds limits of letter of credit
- Weights, measurements, or quantities differ

Draft

- Draft and invoice amounts do not agree
- Draft does not bear reference to letter of credit

- Evidence of forgery or alteration
- Draft not signed
- Maturity dates differ from letter of credit
- Currency differs from letter of credit

Insurance Policy

- Description of goods differs from invoice
- Risks not covered as required by the letter of credit
- Policy dated after date of bill of lading
- Amount of policy insufficient
- Certificate or policy not indorsed
- Certificate presented instead of policy, if required in letter of credit

General Discrepancies

- letter of credit expired
- letter of credit overdrawn
- Draft and documents presented after time called for in letter of credit
- Incomplete documentation
- Changes in documents not initialed
- Merchandise description and marks not consistent between documents

---

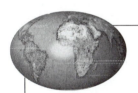

Courtaulds North America, Inc. v. North Carolina National Bank
528 F.2d 802 (1975)
United States Court of Appeals (4th Cir.)

BACKGROUND AND FACTS

The defendant bank issued an irrevocable letter of credit on behalf of its customer, Adastra Knitting Mills. It promised to honor 60-day time drafts of Courtaulds for up to $135,000 covering shipments of "100% Acrylic Yarn." Courtaulds presented its draft together with a commercial invoice describing the merchandise as "Imported Acrylic Yarns." The packing lists that were stapled to the invoice contained the following description: "Cartons marked: 100% Acrylic." The bank refused to accept the draft because of the discrepancy between the letter of credit and the commercial invoice. (The buyer had gone into bankruptcy, and the court appointed

trustee would not waive the discrepancy.) The documents were returned and the plaintiff brought this action. The lower court held that the bank was liable to the plaintiff for the amount of the draft because the packing lists attached to each carton stated that the cartons contained "100% Acrylic," and the bank appealed.

BRYAN, SENIOR CIRCUIT JUDGE

The defendant denied liability chiefly on the assertion that the draft did not agree with the letter's conditions, viz., that the draft be accompanied by a "Commercial invoice in triplicate stating (inter alia) that it covers . . . 100% acrylic yarn"; instead, the

continued

continued

accompanying invoices stated that the goods were "Imported Acrylic Yarn."

. . . [T]he District Court held defendant Bank liable to Courtaulds for the amount of the draft, interest, and costs. It concluded that the draft complied with the letter of credit when each invoice is read together with the packing lists stapled to it, for the lists stated on their faces: "Cartons marked: 100% Acrylic." After considering the insistent rigidity of the law and usage of bank credits and acceptances, we must differ with the District Judge and uphold Bank's position.

In utilizing the rules of construction embodied in the letter of credit—the *Uniform Customs* and state statute—one must constantly recall that the drawee bank is not to be embroiled in disputes between the buyer and the seller, the beneficiary of the credit. The drawee is involved only with documents, not with merchandise. Its involvement is altogether separate and apart from the transaction between the buyer and seller; its duties and liability are governed exclusively by the terms of the letter, not the terms of the parties' contract with each other. Moreover, as the predominant authorities unequivocally declare, the beneficiary must meet the terms of the credit—and precisely—if it is to exact performance of the issuer. Failing such compliance there can be no recovery from the drawee. That is the specific failure of Courtaulds here.

. . . [T]he letter of credit dictated that each invoice express on its face that it covered 100% acrylic yarn. Nothing less is shown to be tolerated in the trade. No substitution and no equivalent, through interpretation or logic, will serve. Harfield, *Bank Credits and Acceptances* (5th ed. 1974), commends and quotes aptly from an English case: "There is no room for documents which are almost the same, or which will do just as well." Although no pertinent North Carolina decision has been laid before us, in many cases elsewhere, especially in New York, we find the tenent of Harfield to be unshaken.

At trial Courtaulds prevailed on the contention that the invoices in actuality met the specifications of the letter of credit in that the packing lists attached to the invoices disclosed on their faces that the packages contained "cartons marked: 100% acrylic." . . . But this argument cannot be accepted.

The district judge's pat statement adeptly puts an end to this contention of Courtaulds: "In dealing with letters of credit, it is a custom and practice of the banking trade for a bank to only treat a document as an invoice which clearly is marked on its face as 'invoice.' " This is not a pharisaical or doctrinaire persistence in the principle, but is altogether realistic in the environs of this case; it is plainly the fair and equitable measure. (The defect in description was not superficial but occurred in the statement of the quality of the yarn, not a frivolous concern.) Bank was not expected to scrutinize the collateral papers, such as the packing lists. Nor was it permitted to read into the instrument the contemplation or intention of the seller and buyer. . . .

Had Bank deviated from the stipulation of the letter and honored the draft, then at once it might have been confronted with the not improbable risk of the bankruptcy trustee's charge of liability for unwarrantably paying the draft monies to the seller, Courtaulds, and refusal to reimburse Bank for the outlay. Contrarily, it might face a Courtaulds claim that since it had depended upon Bank's assurance of credit in shipping yarn to Adastra, Bank was responsible for the loss. In this situation Bank cannot be condemned for sticking to the letter of the letter.

Nor is this conclusion affected by the amended or substituted invoices which Courtaulds sent to Bank after the refusal of the draft. No precedent is cited to justify retroactive amendment of the invoices or extension of the credit beyond the August 15 expiry of the letter.

For these reasons, we must vacate the decision of the trial court, despite the evident close reasoning and research of the district judge. . . .

Reversed and remanded for final judgment.

Decision.   The judgment is reversed for the defendant bank. The description of the goods in the invoice did not match the description of the goods in the credit, and the defect was not cured by a correct description in the packing list.

Here the documents show no discrepancy. The language used in the bill of lading, "1,000 pillows," is a more general statement "not inconsistent with" the full language used to describe the pillows in the letter of credit.

The rule of strict compliance seems to make commercial sense. Bankers are involved every day with letters of credit from all industries, comprising all sorts of goods and services. They cannot be expected to be experts in all areas—textiles, steel, agriculture commodities, electronics, or as in our examples, the bedding business.

Other Views on Strict Compliance

While the strict compliance rule remains the prevailing view in most jurisdictions, it may be interpreted more liberally in some jurisdictions than in others. *Voest-Alpine Trading Co. v. Bank of China,* 167 F.Supp.2d 940 (S.D.Tex. 2000), *aff'd* 288 F.2d 262 (5th Cir. 2002) involved a shipment of styrene from Voest-Alpine to a customer in China under a $1.2 million letter of credit issued by the Bank of China. Apparently, the market value of the styrene at the time the documents were presented for payment had fallen well below the contract price. Voest-Alpine refused a price concession requested by the buyer, and the bank started looking for discrepancies. The court ruled that the Bank of China must honor the letter of credit. Although the basis of the ruling was that the bank had taken longer (just one day longer!) than the seven days permitted by the UCP to inspect the documents for compliance and to give notice of dishonor to the seller describing specific discrepancies, the district court's opinion is notable for its discussion of the strict compliance problem. The beneficiary's name, Voest-Alpine *Trading USA,* was transposed to "*USA Trading.*" While the letter of credit required three "original" bills of lading, none were stamped "original," one was stamped "duplicate" and another "triplicate." All three, however, contained original hand signatures in blue ink. The survey report for damage was dated a day after the bill of lading, even though the report stated that the goods had been inspected upon loading. While the reference number of the letter of credit was incorrect on the cover letter prepared by Voest-Alpine, it was correct elsewhere. Finally, the name of the port city, Zhangjiagang, was spelled several different ways in various documents. The Bank of China argued that if the documents contained discrepancies on their face, it was justified in rejecting them. Voest-Alpine argued for a "functional standard" of compliance, contending that the bank should have looked at the whole of the documents. In agreeing with Voest-Alpine, the court rejected the notion that the documents should be a "mirror image" of those called for in the letter of credit, and adopted a more moderate approach. The district court stated:

> A common sense, case-by-case approach would permit minor deviations of a typographical nature. . . . While the end result of such an analysis may bear a strong resemblance to the relaxed strict compliance

standard, the actual calculus used by the issuing bank is . . . whether the documents bear a rational link to one another. In this way, the issuing bank is required to examine a particular document in light of all documents presented and use common sense but is not required to evaluate risks or go beyond the face of the documents. The Court finds that in this case the Bank of China's listed discrepancies should be analyzed under this standard by determining whether the whole of the documents obviously relate to the transaction on their face.

Avoiding and Handling Discrepancies. Actually, estimates are that *more than half* of the letter of credit transactions in the United States involve discrepant documents. Many discrepancies occur because of clerical errors. Thus, the seller's export clerks should follow the letter of credit when preparing their invoice and shipping documents— more than one export manager has suggested that "any words found misspelled in the letter of credit, should be misspelled in the documents." Other discrepancies might occur as a result of documents prepared by an insurance agent, by the seller's freight forwarder, or by the carrier. For instance, if the letter of credit requires an onboard bill of lading, and the representative of the carrier that issued the bill of lading forgot to sign, initial, or date it to indicate that the goods have been loaded, the bank will rightfully reject the documents. This type of error should be caught and corrected early.

The best advice is that all parties use extreme care in preparing documents. Sellers should request that as few documents as possible be required in the letter of credit, to lessen the chance of mistake. The seller should be certain that the freight forwarder is experienced in documentation. In addition, the seller should be sure that all deadlines are met—that the goods are shipped on time and the documents promptly presented. Finally, the seller's international banker should review the documents and give an opinion as to whether they are in compliance with the letter of credit. The seller should not ship until all mistakes in the documents are corrected.

An Ethical Issue in Handling Letters of Credit. In most cases, where a minor discrepancy occurs, the issuing bank will obtain a written waiver from the buyer, and the transaction will proceed as anticipated, but the world of international business is a perilous place. The lore of international trade is filled with stories of the unwary being taken in by the unscrupulous. Sellers and bankers beware: If a buyer is looking for a reason to reject the documents (for instance, if the market price of the goods falls, or if the buyer's country has entered a period of civil war, or if it learns that the ship has gone to the bottom of the sea during the voyage), a seller who errs in preparing the documents is giving the savvy (or unscrupulous) buyer a way out. Although banks must preserve and protect their international reputations for honoring their credits, if they realize that the buyer is going to back out of the deal, their first reaction will be to try to find a justifiable reason for rejecting the documents—the best reason is, of course, to uncover a discrepancy. (An old adage states that any banker who cannot find a discrepancy isn't worth her salt.) Then, when the buyer's bank refuses to honor the draft, the buyer graciously offers to waive the discrepancy—but only for a huge discount off the contract price! Of course, almost all discrepancies are honest accidents or commercial mistakes and are easily resolved.

Procedures for Dishonor

When documents are submitted to an issuing bank for payment, the bank has a responsibility to its customer to examine the documents with care. The bank would prefer that all documents are perfect and the transaction go as planned. If it must dishonor a request for payment, it risks a lawsuit from the beneficiary, but if the dishonor is wrongful, it risks possibly far greater damage to its reputation for honoring its letters of credit. On the other hand, if it pays out on discrepant documents, then it may not be able to seek reimbursement for the goods—and no bank wants to be stuck with having to sell or liquidate goods that it knows nothing about. However, if a bank must dishonor, there are exact procedures that it must follow, or it will be precluded from asserting the discrepant documents as a defense against a suit for wrongful dishonor. This is known as the rule of *issuer preclusion.*

Issuer Preclusion. If a bank discovers discrepancies when comparing documents to the terms of

the letter of credit, the first step is normally to ask the purchaser if it wants to waive them. If the bank and purchaser decide to refuse the documents, the bank must give notice of its refusal to the presenting bank or beneficiary by telecommunication, no later than the close of the seventh banking day following receipt of the documents. The notice must describe the discrepancies specifically and must contain an unambiguous refusal or dishonor (see *Voest-Alpine Trading Co. v. Bank of China,* cited earlier). The notice must inform the presenter whether the documents are being held pending further instructions or are being returned. If the issuing bank fails to do this, they cannot later argue that the documents were discrepant.

Confirmed Letters of Credit

For the most part, a letter of credit will serve to adequately assure payment of the seller's drafts. In certain instances, however, the credit of the issuing bank may be insufficient to assure payment. This lack of assurance may occur when shipments are exported to countries that have shortages of foreign currencies, large foreign debts, and a poor balance of payments record. In such a situation, government currency restrictions imposed between the time the contract is agreed to and the time the drafts are tendered for payment could prevent the issuing bank from honoring its letter of credit in dollars. A U.S. seller may want to include as part of the sales contract that the buyer will furnish a letter of credit *confirmed* by a bank in the United States.

Sellers have other reasons for insisting on a confirmed letter of credit. In some instances, the seller may be unsure of the soundness of the buyer's bank and wants the backing of some reputable U.S. bank on the letter of credit. Additionally, should legal action ever be necessary to collect on a letter of credit, a seller can much more easily sue a U.S. confirming bank in the United States than a foreign bank in foreign courts. Of course, a confirmed credit is far more expensive than one that is unconfirmed because two banks are exposed to the risk of the transaction. These costs must be weighed by the parties in determining the level of acceptable risk in the transaction.

Banks in the United States that confirm foreign letters of credit try to be aware of the economic and political conditions in those foreign countries.

17 Steps Take the Fear Out of Letters of Credit

Letters of credit can be a major headache for export professionals. Banking industry statistics show that up to 80% of letter of credit documents are rejected by the bank upon presentation. If you aren't preparing these crucial documents correctly—and checking and double-checking them for errors—your firm will soon experience unanticipated bank fees and payment delays that will significantly erode the export bottom line. In worst-case scenarios, you can suffer complete loss of payment.

Because letters of credit are such a major source of concern, the following checklist of procedures can help eliminate—or at least greatly minimize—letter of credit problems.

1. Match incoming letters of credit against purchase orders and quotations. Prior to receiving the letter of credit, you should match the PO against the quotation.
2. Send copies of the letter of credit to your sales and shipping departments for immediate review to ensure that it matches the order and that you can meet the dates in the document.
3. Show a copy of the letter of credit to your banker to make sure there are no obvious banking errors.
4. If you find discrepancies, ask your customer to make the appropriate changes, since in most cases your customer will have a better relationship with the issuing bank. Also, not waiting until the eleventh hour will put you in a better negotiating position—something that could be especially important if your goods have already shipped.
5. As a matter of practice, make your initial quote through a proforma invoice. Proforma invoices help eliminate many of the misunderstandings that can creep into international sales.
6. Check that the letter of credit is from an American bank—if it comes directly to you from a foreign bank, there's a good chance it's phony.
7. Ask for a confirmed letter of credit only if the confirmation is truly needed. Otherwise you may be wasting money, since the confirming bank could be less creditworthy than the institution being confirmed. If the dollar amount is large, however, get a confirmation—confirmed letters of credit are generally paid faster. Also, check whether the country you're dealing with requires a confirmation.
8. Be aware that a bank that confirms a letter of credit is not required to confirm amendments. This is another reason to check your letters of credit quickly. If a political situation suddenly changes, such confirmations may be withheld. In such circumstances, letters of credit will be examined microscopically, since the confirming bank knows it will not be paid and will look for any way out it can find.
9. Make sure your letters of credit are confirmed by a bank you're comfortable with. If this means a bank from another country, rather than a U.S. bank, that's not a problem.
10. Never have your freight forwarder handle your letters of credit.
11. Make sure all your letters of credit specify that they're covered by UCP 500. This should be acceptable in all countries—with the possible exception of Vietnam.
12. Fill out a sample letter-of-credit application and send it to your customer. Most bank applications are similar, and your sample should work well in most instances. Doing this will start your customer off on the right foot.
13. Make sure the letter of credit is for 110% of the CIF or CIP value, unless the individual letter of credit specifies otherwise.
14. Note that a full set of documents means three originals and three copies—unless the shipping line issues it. Also be aware that a deck bill of lading is not usually acceptable if a clean bill of lading is required.
15. Remember that all letters of credit permit partial shipments unless they specifically state otherwise.
16. Make sure the shipping terms specified in the letter of credit agree with those actually used.
17. The words "about," "approximately," or "circa" in a letter of credit modify only what immediately follows and only by plus or minus 10%. Such

continued

---

continued

language can be used in the case of goods that cannot be measured precisely, when the container size is not precise, or when quoting far in advance, where flexibility for changes is required. If the letter of credit is silent on this issue, tolerances of 5% will be allowed. If the word "exactly" is used, no variations will be permitted.

. . .

Also, please keep in mind that letters of credit arriving from countries affiliated with either the Organization of African States or the Arab League (and supporting countries including Indonesia and Brunei) in support of boycotts against selected African countries and/or Israel may contain certain clauses which are illegal for you to comply with. These guidelines are contained in the Boycott Section of the US Export Adminis-

tration Regulations. Most of these will be headed off by your bank and/or freight forwarder, but you are still legally liable for substantial fines if you comply.

Likewise, you should never receive a letter of credit directly from your customer. All letters of credit should be advised by a US (or in some instances foreign) bank. Anything else should be considered suspicious and is probably fraudulent. As always, if you want to have your letter of credit as well as any supporting documentation reviewed, please call the nearest office of the **US Commercial Service** for an appointment.

If a buyer is unable to have a letter of credit from its country confirmed, then the U.S. bank is signaling that it deemed the political and credit risks too high. Certainly this type of high risk is not one an exporter wants to assume if its bank would not. In these cases, U.S. sellers often request that their foreign customer have the letter of credit issued from a bank in a country with less risk, such as Switzerland, Great Britain, or Japan.

Liability of Confirming Bank.

Unlike an advising bank, a confirming bank *does* become liable on the letter of credit. Under the UCP, payment is made immediately to the seller upon its presentation of the documents. A confirming bank that negotiates documents from the seller is entitled to reimbursement from the issuing bank if the documents presented to it are in order. The confirming bank also bears the risk that the issuing bank or the buyer will become unable to reimburse it. If the confirming bank pays for documents that are not in order, it generally cannot seek reimbursement from the beneficiary. A confirming bank that cannot obtain reimbursement may be left holding

title to the goods purchased. (And if the shipment contains toaster ovens or clock radios, they can give them away to people who open new accounts at their branch offices!)

Standby Letters of Credit

The standby letter of credit can be used to guarantee that a party will fulfill obligations under a service contract, construction contract, or sales contract. Standby letters of credit can also be used to ensure the repayment of a loan. Suppose, for example, that a subsidiary of a U.S. company operating in Latin America borrows money from a local bank. The bank can require a standby letter of credit from a U.S. bank that would allow it to draw against the credit should the subsidiary default on its obligation.

Standby Credit as Performance Guaranty.

Most standby credits are used, however, not in sale-of-goods transactions, but as guaranties of performance under consulting and performance contracts. Unlike a regular letter of credit in which the beneficiary of the credit is the seller, a standby credit is issued in favor of the buyer to guarantee the seller's performance.

For example, if an engineering firm enters into a contract with a foreign government to perform engineering services related to a major public works project, the engineering firm could apply for a standby credit to be issued that would guar-

---

http://www.tdcommercialbanking.com/tradefinance/index.jsp

A Canadian commercial bank site with step-by-step guides to documentary collections, letters of credit, and trade finance. See the "Crash Course in International Trade" slide show.

antee its performance to the foreign government. A standby credit however, does not usually require the same type of documentation such as a bill of lading that would be required by a traditional letter of credit. Instead the bank is required to honor a demand for payment under a standby credit upon receiving a signed statement by the beneficiary (buyer) that the seller has not performed the contract. In this case, the government would simply have to submit a signed statement that states that the engineering firm failed to perform its services. Because all that is required for the beneficiary to receive payment is a statement that a default has occurred, a standby letter of credit is sometimes referred to as a *suicide* credit for the buyer.

Not surprisingly, standby letters of credit, which are so common in international business transactions, have led to a great deal of litigation in the courts. To protect an account party under a standby credit from an "unfair" demand by the beneficiary, many international business lawyers will require that the beneficiary's request for payment be accompanied by an independent confir-

mation of the account party's default by a third party.

Middle East Politics and Standby Letters of Credit: The Iranian Claims.

The politics of the Middle East have caused a great deal of litigation in this area. Prior to 1979, U.S. companies enjoyed lucrative business contracts with the Imperial Government of Iran, under the rule of the Shah of Iran. Many of these contracts involved the supply of the latest armaments, consumer goods, and construction projects to this Islamic nation. These contracts had often been obtained through the use of illegal payments to the Shah and his family. At the time of the revolution, and the seizing of hostages at the U.S. embassy in Tehran, many U.S. firms had outstanding commitments to the government of Iran that were guaranteed with standby letters of credit. For example, in 1978, five banks alone had $12.6 billion in outstanding standby letters of credit. The following *American Bell* case clearly illustrates that the political risks of international business can even affect letter of credit transactions.

American Bell International Inc. v. Islamic Republic of Iran
474 F. Supp. 420 (1979)
United States District Court (S.D.N.Y.)

BACKGROUND AND FACTS
In 1978, American Bell International, a subsidiary of AT&T, entered into a contract with the Imperial Government of Iran to provide consulting services and telecommunications equipment. The contract provided that all disputes would be resolved according to the laws of Iran and in Iranian courts. The contract provided for payment to Bell of $280 million, including a down payment of $38 million. Iran had the right to demand return of the down payment at any time and for any reason, with the amount returned to be reduced by 20 percent of the amounts that Bell had invoiced for work done. At the time of this action, about $30 million remained callable. In order to secure the return of the down payment on demand, Bell had been required to arrange for Manufacturers Bank to issue a standby letter of credit to the Bank of Iranshahr, payable on the demand of the Iranian government. However, in 1979, a revolution resulted in the overthrow of the imperial government. The Shah of Iran fled the coun-

try, and a revolutionary council was established to govern the country. The nation was in a state of chaos and Westerners fled the country. Having been left with unpaid invoices, Bell ceased its operations. Fearing that any monies paid to Iran would never be recouped, Bell brought this action asking the court to enjoin Manufacturers Bank from honoring Iran's demands for payment under the letter of credit.

MACMAHON, JUDGE
Plaintiff has failed to show that irreparable injury may possibly ensue if a preliminary injunction is denied. Bell does not even claim, much less show, that it lacks an adequate remedy at law if Manufacturers makes a payment to Bank Iranshahr in violation of the Letter of Credit. It is too clear for argument that a suit for money damages could be based on any such violation, and surely Manufacturers would be able to pay any money judgment against it. . . .

continued

continued

To be sure, Bell faces substantial hardships upon denial of its motion. Should Manufacturers pay the demand, Bell will immediately become liable to Manufacturers for $30.2 million, with no assurance of recouping those funds from Iran for the services performed. While counsel represented in graphic detail the other losses Bell faces at the hands of the current Iranian government, these would flow regardless of whether we ordered the relief sought. The hardship imposed from a denial of relief is limited to the admittedly substantial sum of $30.2 million.

But Manufacturers would face at least as great a loss, and perhaps a greater one, were we to grant relief. Upon Manufacturers' failure to pay, Bank Iranshahr could initiate a suit on the Letter of Credit and attach $30.2 million of Manufacturers' assets in Iran. In addition, it could seek to hold Manufacturers liable for consequential damages beyond that sum resulting from the failure to make timely payment. Finally, there is no guarantee that Bank Iranshahr or the government, in retaliation for Manufacturers' recalcitrance, will not nationalize additional Manufacturers' assets in Iran in amounts which counsel, at oral argument, represented to be far in excess of the amount in controversy here.

Apart from a greater monetary exposure flowing from an adverse decision, Manufacturers faces a loss of credibility in the international banking community that could result from its failure to make good on a letter of credit.

Bell, a sophisticated multinational enterprise well advised by competent counsel, entered into these arrangements with its corporate eyes open. It knowingly and voluntarily signed a contract allowing the Iranian government to recoup its down payment on demand, without regard to cause. It caused Manufacturers to enter into an arrangement whereby Manufacturers became obligated to pay Bank Iranshahr the unamortized down payment balance upon receipt of conforming documents, again without regard to cause.

Both of these arrangements redounded tangibly to the benefit of Bell. The contract with Iran, with its prospect of designing and installing from scratch a nationwide and international communications system, was certain to bring to Bell both monetary profit and prestige and goodwill in the global communications industry. The agreement to indemnify Manufacturers on its Letter of Credit provided the means by which these benefits could be achieved. One who reaps the rewards of commercial arrangements must also accept their burdens. One such burden in this case, voluntarily accepted by Bell, was the risk that demand might be made without cause on the funds constituting the down payment. To be sure, the sequence of events that led up to that demand may well have been unforeseeable when the contracts were signed. To this extent, both Bell and Manufacturers have been made the unwitting and innocent victims of tumultuous events beyond their control. But, as between two innocents, the party who undertakes by contract the risk of political uncertainty and governmental caprice must bear the consequences when the risk comes home to roost.

So ordered.

Decision. The court refused to issue the injunction. The letter of credit was not enjoined because there was no clear showing of irreparable injury and because the plaintiff had an adequate legal remedy against Iran for the return of the monies that would be paid. Such a rule protects the sanctity of a bank's reputation for honoring its letters of credit. The plaintiff was aware of the risks involved and must bear the consequences.

In *KMW International v. Chase Manhattan Bank,* 606 F.2d 10 (2d Cir. 1979), the court held that the unsettled situation in Iran was insufficient reason for releasing the bank from its obligation under a letter of credit. The court in *KMW* gave perhaps the real reason for the decision in the Iranian cases when it stated, "Both in the international business community and in Iran itself, Chase's commercial honor is essentially at stake. Failure to perform on its irrevocable letter of credit would constitute a breach of trust and substantially injure its reputation and perhaps even American credibility in foreign communities. Moreover, it could subject Chase to litigation in connection with not only this matter, but also other banking affairs in Iran."

Other Specialized Uses for Letters of Credit

Many specialized types of letters of credit provide a mechanism for financing a sale or other business transaction. Some of these types are discussed here.

Transferable Credits. *Transferable credits* are usually used by international traders. Traders buy and sell goods in international trade—quickly and with no view to actually using the goods themselves. They bear considerable risk every day. Traders operate on little capital, buying merchandise or commodities in one country, taking title through the documents, and then, through their business contacts built up over years of experience, selling at a profit. Some traders specialize in trade with the developing world, often trading commodities for raw materials or merchandise when dollars or hard currency are not available there. For instance, a Swiss bank issues a letter of credit for the account of an African country in favor of the trader, with a part of the credit transferred to the trader's supplier in the Philippines for the cost of the goods it is supplying to the African country. This letter of credit can be split up among many suppliers around the world, each presenting documents for payment, with the trader taking its profit out of the balance of the credit. Shipments of crude oil are often bought and sold in this fashion.

Red Clauses in Credits. The *red clause* is a financing tool for smaller sellers who need capital to produce the products to be shipped under a letter of credit. A red clause in a letter of credit is a promise (usually written or underlined in red ink) by the issuing bank to reimburse the seller's bank for loans made to the seller. The loan, then, is really an advance on the credit. Loans can be used only for purchasing raw materials or for covering the costs of manufacturing or shipping of the goods described in the credit. Ultimately, the liability will fall on the buyer if the seller defaults on shipment or repayment of the amounts taken under the credit. This form of financing is very risky for the buyer and its bank.

> **http://www.USAID.gov**
> The home page for the U.S. Agency for International Development.

Revolving and Evergreen Credits. When a buyer is planning on purchasing on a regular basis from a foreign seller, a *revolving letter of credit* may be used. Instead of having to use several different credits, one may be used with a maximum amount available during a certain period of time. As the draws against the credit are paid, the full amount becomes available again and continues until the expiration of the credit. An *evergreen* clause provides for automatic renewal of the letter of credit until the bank gives "clear and unequivocal" notice of its intent not to renew.

Back-to-Back Letter of Credit Financing. A *back-to-back letter of credit* is a special type of financing device. In certain circumstances, an exporter is selling goods to a buyer in one transaction and is buying supplies in another. Under a back-to-back credit, the exporter can use its credit with the buyer to finance the purchase of goods from the supplier. Thus, a back-to-back credit is really two credits, one representing the security for the second. The bank that issues the second credit requires that it be assigned the proceeds of the original credit. Many banks will issue the second credit only if they had opened the first (known as a countercredit). Back-to-back letters of credit are usually used by traders who are not manufacturers, or by other intermediaries with minimal capital resources who buy and sell goods for delivery to others.

Electronic Data Interchange and the "eUCP"

Like funds transfers, letters of credit have been issued and transmitted to advising banks electronically for many years (and from advising bank to beneficiary usually by mail). Now it appears that the use of electronic documentation will soon increase, and that beneficiaries in the near future will also be presenting documents electronically to banks for payment.

In 2002, the International Chamber of Commerce published the eUCP, a set of rules that extends the UCP to electronic documents. When documents are submitted electronically, eUCP rules apply by agreement of the parties. The eUCP addresses the format for electronic documents (the rules are flexible and include signed email attachments or secured transfer), authentication and digital signatures, transmission errors, the manner of presentation, and other issues.

Bolero is a technical infrastructure created by the world's banking and logistics firms for exchanging electronic documents in a common format, including bills of lading, letters of credit, and other bank documents. *Identrus* is a private company founded by a small consortium of the world's largest banks to provide secure "digital identities" or signatures for confidentiality and authentication of financial and legal documents. Both *Identrus* and *Bolero* represent technological innovations necessary to move the centuries-old banking and shipping industries to the paperless age.

Letters of Credit in Trade Finance Programs

Letter of credit financing plays an important role in export financing by government and intergovernmental agencies. U.S. exports are financed by such agencies as the *Agency for International Development* (AID), the *World Bank* (which provides financial and technical assistance to developing countries to stimulate economic growth), the *Commodity Credit Corporation* (covering surplus agricultural products), and the *Export-Import Bank of the United States (Eximbank)*. These agencies often ensure payments made to U.S. sellers under letters of credit that are confirmed by U.S. banks through the use of a letter of commitment from the agency to the issuing bank.

> **http://www.exim.gov**
> Home page
> of the Export-
> Import Bank of
> the United States.

AID Financing. A typical AID financing situation might include a letter of credit. A country wishing to import U.S. products, usually to be used in developmental projects such as building roads, power-generating facilities, and the like, applies to AID for financing. AID then issues its commitment to a U.S. bank that issues its letter of credit for the benefit of the U.S. supplier of eligible goods used in the project. The issuing bank receives reimbursement for payments under its letter of credit from AID.

Eximbank Financing. Eximbank is the largest U.S. export financing agency. It can provide guarantees on loans made by commercial banks, and insurance on credit extended by U.S. exporters to their foreign customers. It also makes loans directly from Eximbank funds. Under an Eximbank loan program, a U.S. bank, designated by the foreign buyer, opens a letter of credit on behalf of the buyer for the benefit of a U.S. supplier. Eximbank guarantees the issuing bank repayment of sums that it pays out under the credit. Eximbank then receives its payments under the loan agree-

ment worked out in advance between it and the foreign buyer. Despite the importance of the U.S. Eximbank, only a small percentage of U.S. exports are financed by Eximbank (about 3 percent). Eximbank has been subject to much criticism for failing to assist with the special needs of small business exporters. Recently, Eximbank has increased its lending guarantees for U.S. goods going to developing countries. The largest foreign market for U.S. goods financed by Eximbank guarantees is China, with over $1 billion in guarantees there in 1994. Other countries have export–import banks of their own to assist in financing their exports.

Commodity Credit Corporation. The Commodity Credit Corporation provides payment assurances to U.S. sellers of surplus agricultural products to approved foreign buyers. Standby letters of credit are often used, whereby the seller can draw under the credit for invoices that remain unpaid by the overseas buyer.

Foreign Credit Insurance Association. The Foreign Credit Insurance Association (FCIA) is an association of private insurance companies that insure U.S. exporters from political and commercial risk. It works in partnership with Eximbank. Commercial risk includes losses due to the default of the buyer and the inability of the buyer to pay because of natural disasters. Political risk (covered by Eximbank) covers the confiscation of goods by the government, nonconvertibility of the buyer's currency, war expropriation, and the inability of the buyer to obtain an import license. Typically, the FCIA provides coverage for up to 100 percent of the political risk and 90 percent of the commercial risk. The cost of this insurance is based on an analysis of the country and the foreign importer.

Another benefit to small- and medium-sized exporters is that their foreign accounts receivable are more valuable to commercial banks due to the insurance protection. As such, exports sold on open account to foreign buyers can more readily be sold or assigned to a financial institution. FCIA policies are also available to cover losses under confirmed letters of credit issued in favor of U.S. exporters by U.S. commercial banks.

COUNTERTRADE

The focus of this chapter has been on payment by documentary collection and letters of credit.

Many other methods of effectuating payment between buyer and seller have developed in recent years. Firms trading with the independent states of the former Soviet Union, China, the countries of Eastern Europe, and the developing countries often have to find a substitute for hard cash if they want to sell their products there. Many nations in all regions of the world, from Mexico to Poland, have a shortage of foreign currency, a high debt burden to foreign banks that must be paid in dollars, and little currency left over to purchase the products needed for consumption by their people. As a result, they may have instituted exchange controls that make normal trade difficult or impossible. The foreign currency that is available will be allocated by central planning authorities or central banks to the purchase of only the most essential goods. As a result, many countries will attempt to find other means of paying for the products they need. They may require, for instance, that a seller take goods in return, or that every import be "offset" by the seller with an export sale of similar value. These alternatives are generally known as countertrade.

---

http://www.countertrade.org
American Countertrade Association site includes reference library and overview of countertrade techniques.

What Is Countertrade?

Countertrade is the term for several different types of transactions, arising from agreement between buyer and seller, and involving an exchange of goods rather than an exchange of currency. Although a large portion of the world's countertrade occurs between private firms and governments or state trading organizations, much of it takes place between private parties.

Countertrade deals span all sectors of the world economy and all regions of the globe. Given that approximately 70 percent of the world's population lives in countries with nonconvertible currencies, it is no surprise that countertrade accounts for nearly 30 percent of world trade. Such deals can be large or small transactions, running into the hundreds of millions of dollars, or larger. General Electric, for example, succeeded in obtaining a $150 million power-generating project in Romania against firms from Germany and Japan, not because its technology or price were any better, but because it agreed to take $150 million in Romanian products in exchange. In the largest trade deal ever signed between the former Soviet Union and an American corporation, Pepsi-Cola agreed to trade its concentrate syrup for Stolichnaya Russian vodka until the year 2000, a deal worth $3 billion in total retail sales. Other industries active in countertrade include aerospace, weapons systems, and construction.

Counterpurchase

The most common type of countertrade is the *counterpurchase agreement.* Counterpurchase involves the sale of goods to a buyer, often a foreign government, who requires as a condition of the sale that the seller buy other goods produced in that country. For example, the People's Republic of China may agree to purchase a firm's machine tools, but will require in return that the firm either purchase a quantity of Chinese-made products— or find someone who will. These deals are usually two separate contracts where each party is paid in currency when its products are delivered to the other party. Often, the private firm is given a period of several years in which to fulfill its purchase obligation. Usually, the seller will be given a selection of items for export so that if the particular Chinese products do not fit into the seller's channels of distribution, the seller can choose other products instead. The goal of a counterpurchase arrangement, however, is for export transactions to offset the "cost" of import transactions.

Barter

Another form of countertrade is barter. *Barter* is the direct exchange of goods for goods (or services). Unlike counterpurchase transactions, which involve payment in currency, barter transactions are not pegged to market prices and therefore it is difficult to compensate for changes in the value of the goods exchanged. Barter transactions can involve a wide range of items, from pharmaceuticals and aircraft to agricultural commodities, oil, and natural resources. Some firms that specialize in barter transactions have developed creative schemes for minimizing risks for exporters.

Buy-Back

A *buy-back agreement* is often associated with the sale of machinery or industrial equipment, or the construction of plants and factories. Here the provider of the equipment or technology will receive, as its payment, a portion of the goods manufactured by the equipment or in the factory. For example, under the Israel Cooperation Program, any foreign company that sells products to the Israeli government is required to purchase 35 percent of the value of the contract from Israeli companies in return. Consequently, when El Al (the Israeli government-owned airline) agreed to buy approximately $90 million worth of engines for its Boeing 757 jets from Rolls Royce, Rolls Royce agreed to buy Israeli technological products and engine components worth 35 percent of El Al's purchases. One of the problems for firms that enter into buy-back agreements is that they cannot effectively control the quality of the goods taken back. Another problem arises when the firm that provides the equipment also manufactures the same products as those for which the equipment will be used. The goods produced may possibly compete with those that the firm manufactures itself.

Countertrading is generally left to the more experienced multinationals, exporters, or traders, as it is considered one of the more risky ventures of international trade. Many stories tell of smaller firms that suffered great losses in countertrading, particularly when they did not have the foresight to arrange for a buyer for their countertraded products in advance. Because of the rapidly expanding market, countertrade specialists, who purchase traded goods at a discount and resell them for a profit, have emerged.

CHAPTER SUMMARY

This chapter describes some of the legal issues involved in moving money from one party to another in an international transaction. The reader should understand why bills of exchange, or drafts, are the primary instrument for effectuating payment in an international transaction, and how they are used. Drafts are commonly classified as sight drafts or time drafts. When a draft is accepted by a merchant in the trade it becomes a trade acceptance. When it is accepted by a bank, it becomes a banker's acceptance. These negotiable instruments are used as substitutes for money, as well as in acceptance financing. By discounting an acceptance in the credit markets, outside capital is used by buyer and seller to finance their trade sale. A holder in due course of an acceptance is protected from disputes that might arise between buyer and seller in the underlying transaction. The ability of a seller to provide trade finance to a buyer is important in a competitive market.

Although most of the discussion focused on transactions involving the sale of goods, the same negotiable instruments and legal concepts discussed apply to moving money in many different types of transactions, including licensing and investment contracts, the sale of services and construction contracts.

Drafts can be used to collect payment under a bank letter of credit. Letters of credit are not bank guarantees, but they are assurances to the seller of payment, if the seller complies with all the terms and conditions stated in the credit. Courts in most jurisdictions rely on the UCP to interpret the rights of the parties to a letter of credit. Under the independence principle, a letter of credit is separate from the underlying sales transaction. Banks are required to honor a demand for payment upon presentation of documents that conform to the requirements of the letter of credit. Standby letters of credit are guarantees of the seller's performance to the buyer. Like traditional letters of credit, the beneficiary of a standby credit is entitled to payment upon presentation of the required documents to the bank.

Countertrade is a business practice involving the exchange of goods, as a substitute for money. It is used by experienced traders in all regions of the world, but especially in Russia, Eastern Europe, China, and other developing countries that are subject to a scarcity of hard currency. Countertrade accounts for a large share of world trade.

Questions and Case Problems

1. Wade entered into a contract to sell irrigation equipment to Ribadalgo, its Ecuadorian distributor. Ribadalgo obtained an irrevocable letter of credit in the amount of $400,000 from Banco General Runinahui, S.A. (Banco), a bank in Quito, Ecuador. The letter of credit provided that Wade was to ship by June 30, 1992. Wade was to present documents for payment "no later than 15 days after shipment, but within the validity of the credit." The expiry date of the letter of credit was August 4, 1992. Partial shipments were acceptable. The letter of credit stated that it was governed by the UCP. Citibank confirmed the letter of credit. Later, the letter of credit was amended to extend the shipment date to July 30 and the expiry date to August 21. Wade shipped a portion of the goods on July 7. On July 21, just before the document presentment deadline, Wade presented the requisite documents to Citibank for payment. Two days later, on July 23, Citibank informed Wade that the documents contained discrepancies and that it therefore would not honor Wade's request for payment. In response, Wade forwarded amended documents to Citibank on July 24 and July 27. Although Citibank conceded the documents as amended contained no discrepancies, it nevertheless rejected them as untimely because they were not received within fifteen days of the July 7 shipment date as required by the credit. On July 17, the Ecuadorian government issued an order freezing all Ribadalgo's assets and precluding payment on any lines of credit made available to Ribadalgo due to alleged drug trafficking. Four days later, Ecuadorian banking authorities entered an order barring Banco from making payment under the letter of credit. In turn, Banco advised Citibank not to honor any request for payment made by Wade thereunder. Is Wade entitled to payment under the letter of credit from Citibank? Did Wade submit conforming documents as required under the terms of credit? Wade argues that the documents did not have to be conforming before the presentment deadline, but only before the expiry date of the credit. Is Wade correct? *Banco General Runinahui, S.A. v. Citibank*, 97 F.3d 480 (11th Cir. 1996).

2. The rule of strict compliance in New York is best illustrated by *Beyene v. Irving Trust Co.*, 762 F.2d 4 (2d Cir. 1985). The letter of credit specified that payment be made on presentation of a bill of lading naming "Mohammed Sofan" as the party to be notified when the goods arrive. But the actual bill of lading submitted to the bank with the demand for payment misspelled the name as "Mohammed Soran." The

confirming bank refused payment because of this discrepancy and the beneficiary sued. Is this a "material" discrepancy, or is it "so insignificant as not to relieve the issuing and confirming bank of its obligation to pay"? The court compares and contrasts the misspelling of "Sofan" as "Soran" to the misspelling of "Smith" as "Smithh." The court stated that the misspelling of "Smith" is not a discrepancy because the meaning is "unmistakably clear despite what is obviously a typographical error." How did the court decide? Is there a difference between the misspellings of the two different names?

3. Habib Bank issued a letter of credit on the instructions of its account party calling for the payment of drafts upon the presentation of documents showing shipment by a certain date. The bank examined the documents and paid the beneficiary's draft. The account party refused to take the documents and reimburse the bank because the shipping date was incorrectly stated in the documents. The bank sued the beneficiary for a return of its money for presenting nonconforming documents. The bank brought its action under the UCC, Article 5–111, which states that a presenting beneficiary warrants that "the necessary conditions of the credit have been complied with." The beneficiary claims that under the UCP the bank was precluded from complaining about the discrepancies because the bank had failed to object to the documents in a timely fashion. UCP 500, Article 14, states that an issuing or nominated bank must notify the beneficiary (or another bank from which it is receiving the documents) of the rejection *without delay but no later than the close of the seventh banking day following the day of receipt of the documents.* Judgment for whom and why? Which rule will apply, the UCC rule or the UCP rule? *Habib Bank Ltd. v. Convermat Corp.*, 554 N.Y.S.2d 757 (N.Y.Sup. 1990).

4. Hambro Bank, Ltd., an English bank, received a cable from a Danish company, A.O., requesting that an irrevocable letter of credit be opened in favor of J. H. Rayner and Company. A.O. instructed Hambro Bank that the letter of credit be for ". . . about \P16,975 [pounds] against invoice full straight clean bills of lading . . . covering about 1,400 tons Coromandel groundnuts." The bill of lading presented to Hambro by J. H. Rayner stated ". . . bags machine-shelled groundnut kernels," with the abbreviation C.R.S. in the margin. Hambro refused to pay on the letter of credit. J. H. Rayner sued Hambro. The custom of trade holds that C.R.S. is short for Coromandel groundnuts. Why did the bank not want to pay

on this letter of credit? Was the bank correct in denying payment on this letter of credit? *J. H. Rayner and Co., Ltd. v. Hambro's Bank, Ltd.,* 1 K.B. 36 (1943).

5. The seller of goods has a right to proceed judicially against an issuing bank that dishonors its obligation under an irrevocable letter of credit, just as the seller has the right to proceed directly against the buyer. Should the issuing bank also be liable for consequential damages that are reasonably foreseeable? See *Hadley v. Baxendale,* 9 Ex. 341 (1854).

6. Lotsa Music has signed a contract to buy "2,000 new CD players, with manufacturer's warranties" from Phoney, Inc., in Korea. Phoney is shipping the CD players CIF, and requires an irrevocable letter of credit. First Faithful Bank has issued a letter of credit on Lotsa Music's behalf promising to honor a draft accompanied by a clean onboard bill of lading and an invoice showing "2,000 new CD players, with manufacturer's warranties." Hamsung, a competitor, informs you that even though Phoney obtained a bill of lading for "2,000 new CD players, with manufacturer's warranties," the CD players are all used and partly inoperable. What can your company do? Would it make any difference if Phoney's bank had confirmed the letter of credit and already paid the amount of the draft before you learned about this problem? See *United Bank Ltd. v. Cambridge Sporting Goods Corp.,* 360 N.E.2d 943 (N.Y. 1976).

7. A South African firm applied for a revolving letter of credit at Barclays Bank, Johannesburg, in favor of a German exporter. The letter of credit was issued covering shipments of pharmaceuticals, and was confirmed by Deutsche Bank, Germany. After a number of shipments, the amount of the letter of credit was increased. To the best knowledge of Barclays, their account party had always taken possession of the goods and sold them quickly for a profit. In the last shipment, Deutsche Bank honored the seller's sight draft for the full amount of the letter of credit, and presented the documents to Barclays. While Barclays was inspecting the documents, it learned that the South African buyer had ceased business. In the meantime, Deutsche Bank discovers that the seller has ceased business also. On inspection by Barclays, the cargo containers contained only worthless junk. Reports placed both buyer and seller in Brazil. What happened? What are the rights and liabilities of the advising and confirming bank? How do banks handle problems like this?

8. Pursuant to the instructions of the buyer, a Chicago bank issued its credit in favor of a bicycle exporter in Hong Kong covering "HPO 360 bicycles." The operative credit was by cable, with no mail confirmation to follow. The Hong Kong bank confirmed. On receipt of the documents, the confirming bank paid the seller and forwarded the documents to the Chicago bank. On receipt, the Chicago bank rejected the documents, claiming that the invoices showed the merchandise as "NOOHPO 360 bicycles." The confirming bank claims that the documents complied with the credit because the cable containing the credit called for "NOOHPO 360 bicycles." Later, the banks realized that although the Chicago bank had sent the cable correctly (describing HPO 360 bicycles), the Hong Kong bank had received the credit with the description "NOOHPO 360 bicycles." Investigation revealed that the error was caused by sunspots affecting satellite transmission. Under the transmission agreement, the satellite company is liable only for $250. The confirming bank in Hong Kong seeks reimbursement. What is the confirming bank's argument? What claim does the confirming bank have against the beneficiary? What is the argument of the issuing bank in Chicago? What legal or ethical responsibilities do the buyer and seller have to each other and to the two banks?

Managerial Implications

1. Your firm regularly sells to customers in Germany, Poland, Japan, Canada, and Venezuela. How would you evaluate the creditworthiness of firms in each of these countries? How would the credit risk differ in each of these countries? What sources of information would you use? Under what circumstances would you consider selling to firms in these countries without a letter of credit? In which of these countries would you want the buyer's letter of credit to be confirmed by an American bank? Why? What additional protection does the confirmed credit provide?

2. An advising bank presents documents to you for payment. How would you respond to each of the following discrepancies? Explain your answer.
   a. The letter of credit calls for an ocean bill of lading. The seller presents a trucker's bill of lading showing shipment to an ocean port.
   b. The sales contract and the letter of credit call for shipment of "Soda Ash Light." The invoice shows shipment of "Soda Ash Light," but the bill of lading describes the shipment as "Soda Ash."
   c. The letter of credit calls for shipment of 1,000 kilo-

grams. The invoice shows shipment of an equal amount in pounds.

d. The CIF contract with the letter of credit calls for onboard bill of lading to be dated by December 20. The bill of lading is dated December 20, but the insurance policy is dated December 21.

3. Your firm has contracted to purchase silk from overseas suppliers on letter of credit terms. After contracting, but before presentment of the seller's documents, China expands its production and floods the market with raw silk. The price of silk plummets on world markets. Comment on whether you should try to find a minor discrepancy in the documents to justify rejecting the documents. Is it ethical for a buyer to reject documents presented under a letter of credit that contains only a minor discrepancy between the documents and the credit? Do the reasons matter? Does it matter that the buyer may know that the shipment actually conforms to the requirements of the contract and of the letter of credit?

PART 3

International and U.S. Trade Law

Part Three turns from the study of the private law of international business transactions to a study of the public law of international trade. These are actually two very different areas of the law. As we saw in the preceding chapters, the law of international business transactions is a type of private law that determines the rights and responsibilities of two or more parties in their business relationship. The law of international contracts for the sale of goods was one example. *International trade law,* on the other hand, is a body of public law used to determine the responsibilities that nations have to one another in their trade relations. An agreement between two nations to charge a certain rate of duty on imported goods would be governed by international trade law.

Before one can understand how nations agree upon and implement international trade law, one must first understand the national lawmaking process. Chapter Eight explains how the various branches of the U.S. government share the responsibility for regulating foreign commerce and trade. Once the role of the executive and legislative branches of government in regulating trade activity is explained, the discussion of public law can be extended to international trade relations.

Chapters Nine, Ten, and Eleven cover the basics of international trade law: Chapter Nine examines the *General Agreement on Tariffs and Trade 1994,* GATT, and the *World Trade Organi-*

zation. Since its inception in 1947, GATT has provided the framework for regulating most world trade in goods. We will examine in detail the major GATT principles as enacted in 1994 as a result of the *Uruguay Round* trade negotiations. Many current events issues will be covered in this chapter, giving the reader an inside look at the trade negotiations behind some of the headline news stories of the 1990s. Chapter Ten examines laws that help assure access to foreign markets. The focus of the chapter is on how the U.S. government has used its economic and political leverage to force other countries to remove nontariff barriers to the import of U.S. goods and services. Here, we will have the chance to examine many "sectoral issues," including trade in services, agriculture, textiles, steel, and other areas.

In Chapter Eleven we move on to special GATT problems involving the issues of free trade versus protectionism, and the regulation of import competition. Many of these topics, such as dumping and subsidies, may be familiar to the reader from courses in economics. Here we look at the very interesting legal aspects and political ramifications of these issues.

Chapter Twelve examines customs and tariff laws that govern the importing of goods into the United States and the relationship between a U.S. importer and the U.S. government. We will take a hands-on look at how to enter goods through U.S.

Customs and how to determine the dutiable status of goods. The chapter focuses on importing as an integral part of the global strategy of the firm, in the context of global sourcing and the location of factories and assembly plants in different regions of the world.

Chapter Thirteen covers the *North American Free Trade Agreement* (NAFTA) and trade issues affecting the Western Hemisphere. This subject is covered near the end of this part because it builds upon the principles of global trade covered in the earlier chapters. The European Union (EU) is covered in Chapter Fourteen, near the end of this part because it represents one extreme on the continuum of economic integration. Although NAFTA is a "free trade area," the EU takes the process of economic integration several steps further and is both a "customs union" with common tariff laws and a "monetary union" with a common currency. Finally, Chapter Fifteen discusses U.S. export law and regulations necessary to move goods across the American borders to customers in foreign countries.

CHAPTER 8

NATIONAL LAWMAKING POWERS AND THE REGULATION OF U.S. TRADE

The U.S. Constitution provides for a separation of powers between the executive and legislative branches of government. In the field of international economic affairs, however, the role of Congress and the president is not always clearly defined. We know that Congress has the authority to impose tariffs, to regulate commerce with foreign nations, and to declare war. But what of the president? We know that the president appoints ambassadors, negotiates with foreign nations, and is the commander-in-chief of the armed services. Of course, we should not forget that the president makes treaties, albeit only with the advice and consent of the Senate. Thus, it would seem that most of the authority to regulate U.S. trade rests with Congress, and not with the president. This is true. As we will see in this chapter, however, much of the president's role in regulating U.S. trade is delegated to him by Congress itself. This puts tremendous responsibility in the hands of the president and his cabinet, most importantly the U.S. Trade Representative, the Secretary of Treasury, and the Secretary of Commerce. In this chapter, we will examine the role of the legislative and executive branches in regulating U.S. trade and how their respective functions are affected by their separation of powers. Most importantly, the reader should consider the impact of their decisions on American firms doing business around the world. An understanding of this chapter will assist the reader later in understanding America's role in solving global trade problems.

U.S. TRADE LAW AND AMERICAN FOREIGN POLICY

U.S. trade law is that body of public law that governs America's trade relations with foreign countries, including the import and export of goods and services. Trade law is used to implement American trade policies. These policies are determined by Congress and the president, often after protracted public debate of the issues. The debates usually focus on the economic and political objectives for the nation. One possible economic objective of U.S. trade policy might be to affect the balance of trade, perhaps by promoting exports or by reducing consumption of imports. Other objectives might be to affect the strength of the U.S. dollar, to aid in promoting the economic and social development of poorer developing countries, to force foreign countries to permit U.S. goods to enter their markets freely, or to foster growth in an American industry, such as automobiles, semiconductors, or steel.

Trade law is used to implement not only economic policy but also foreign policy. Trade law can be used to encourage trade with a political ally or to discourage trade with a potential foe. It can determine those countries with which Americans will trade and do business and those with which they will not. It is trade policy that determines where on the globe U.S. firms will source raw materials, where their contract labor will be done, where their complex finished goods will be assembled, and to whom these goods will be shipped. For example, the U.S. Congress might want to restrict trade by imposing higher tariffs on the goods from countries that are nondemocratic or that violate human rights. Congress might be willing to grant favorable tariff treatment to goods coming from countries that promise to protect the global environment. The president also might ban trade altogether with countries that sponsor international terrorism or an illegal drug trade. Examples of the use of trade controls for political purposes have occurred throughout U.S. history. President Kennedy embargoed trade and travel to Cuba when communist leader Fidel Castro came to power. President Nixon imposed import surcharges on U.S. imports to address an international monetary crisis. President Carter banned trade and travel to Iran after its takeover of the U.S. embassy there. President Reagan imposed trade sanctions on Panama in response to its government's sponsorship of international drug trafficking, and on Libya for sponsoring international terrorism. President G.H. Bush granted favorable trading status to Hungary and other formerly communist countries when they eased their emigration policies. President G.H. Bush and President Clinton both have imposed UN–backed sanctions on Iraq for invading Kuwait and for developing weapons of mass destruction.

Many critics claim that trade policy often "falls victim" to foreign policy. They argue that trade will suffer if it is used as a tool for implementing foreign policy in an unstable political world. They claim that trade should not be used as a political carrot and stick because in a global economy trade restrictions are seldom effective. They argue that if U.S. companies cannot sell to a country because it is governed by a cruel dictator, then that foreign country will simply purchase the needed products elsewhere. Unless all countries are willing to participate in an embargo of a rogue nation's products, the embargo is unlikely to be effective. Cuba is a good example: communism has lasted for over forty years there, despite Cuba's near total isolation from the United States. Critics also point out that trade sanctions seldom work against "third world dictators" because the population that suffers the most, for instance the people of Iraq, is not in a position to rise up and oust the government anyway. An excellent example of how trade sanctions can backfire on the United States occurred during the late 1970s. President Carter ordered a halt of all shipment of U.S. grain to the Soviet Union when that country invaded Afghanistan. The trade ban did send a message to the Soviet Union—that the United States objected to the invasion. But the Soviets simply purchased their grain from other global suppliers—to the chagrin of the American farmers, who lost a good-paying customer. Of course, these moves also involve important moral decisions that are actually supported by many members of Congress and the American public, and the sacrifice for the sake of morality is considered by many to be worth the price. This quandary leads us to an important point. Quite often U.S. firms are caught in the middle of international disputes. Any action by the United States involving trade sanctions against another country is liable to hurt some American interest. Therefore, it is essential that companies be able to manage the risk of doing business in a political world. In the following case, *B-West Imports, Inc. v. The United States* (1996), ten U.S. firms that had been doing business in China learned that they no longer could do so. These companies had been importing arms and munitions from China for sporting use, when they learned that their import licenses had been revoked. The revocation was based on foreign policy grounds. The court rejected their argument that they had an established right to continue importing.

For a very real example of how a U.S. firm can be affected by foreign policy, give some thought to the "managerial implications" problem at the end of this chapter. This problem involves America's relations with the poorest country in the Western Hemisphere, the island nation of Haiti, and the impact of U.S. policies on companies doing business there. Consider both the effectiveness of the trade sanction in achieving foreign policy and the firm's reaction to the ensuing crisis.

> **http://www.state.gov**
> Home page of the U.S. Department of State, the lead U.S. foreign affairs agency.

THE SEPARATION OF POWERS

At the time the Constitution was drafted, people were greatly concerned with how foreign commerce would be regulated. During this period of U.S. history, each state was interested primarily in its own economic well-being. States imposed regulations on

B-West Imports, Inc. v. the United States
75 F.3d 633
United States Court of Appeals (C.A.F.C. 1996)

BACKGROUND AND FACTS

The U.S. *Arms Export Control Act* (AECA) prohibits the import of arms and munitions from countries on the "proscribed list" without a license. Although China had been on the proscribed list, prior to 1994 exemptions had been made for China and import licenses issued. On May 26, 1994, however, President Clinton announced a ban on the import of arms and munitions from China, and other trading sanctions because of "continuing human rights abuses" and other foreign policy reasons. The law was enforced by the U.S. Customs Service and the Bureau of Alcohol, Tobacco and Firearms (BATF). The agencies detained all shipments of arms from China and revoked all import permits. B-West Imports (the appellants), together with nine other importers, challenged the government's actions in the Court of International Trade. They argued that the AECA does not authorize the president or his delegates to impose an arms embargo and that the revocation of the permits violated the Due Process and Takings Clauses of the Fifth Amendment to the Constitution.

BRYSON, CIRCUIT JUDGE

In this court, the appellants renew their argument that the AECA does not authorize an arms embargo. Although the Act, 22 U.S.C. § 2778, grants the president the authority to "control" arms imports, the appellants argue that the term "control" limits the president to creating and operating a licensing system for arms importation, and does not allow the president to ban the importation of arms for which import permits have been granted.

The appellant's statutory argument is unconvincing. They concede that the term "control" is broad enough to allow the president to ban imports by denying licenses or permits for future imports. Their contention is thus limited to the assertion that "control" does not include the right to revoke licenses and permits after they are granted. . . . As the court noted in *South Puerto Rico Sugar Co. v. U.S.,* 167 Ct.Cl. 236, 334 F.2d 622 (1964), presidents acting under broad statutory grants of authority have imposed and lifted embargoes, prohibited and allowed exports, suspended and resumed commercial intercourse with foreign countries. Thus, the broad statutory delega-

tion in the AECA incorporates the historical authority of the president in the fields of foreign commerce and of importation into the country. We therefore agree with the Court of International Trade that the AECA authorizes the president not only to regulate arms importation through a licensing system, but also to prohibit particular importations altogether when the circumstances warrant. . . .

Finally, the appellants challenge the government's actions as violative of the Takings and Due Process Clauses of the Fifth Amendment. In the *Legal Tender Cases,* 79 U.S. (12 Wall.) 457 (1870), the Supreme Court rejected just such an argument, noting that an embargo would not give rise to a compensable taking or a valid due process claim:

> A new tariff, an embargo, a draft, or a war inevitably bring upon individuals great losses; may, indeed, render valuable property almost valueless. They may destroy the worth of contracts. But whoever supposed that, because of this, a tariff could not be changed, or a non-intercourse act, or an embargo be enacted, or a war be declared. . . . [W]as it ever imagined this was taking private property without compensation or without due process of law? Id. 79 U.S. (12 Wall.) at 551.

While it is true that takings law has changed significantly since 1870, the principles that the Supreme Court articulated in the *Legal Tender Cases* have remained valid, particularly as they apply to governmental actions in the sphere of foreign relations. . . .

The same principle is directly applicable here. While an individual who obtains a permit to import arms may make commitments in the arms market on the assumption that the permit will not be revoked before the importation is completed, that assumption does not constitute a "reasonable investment backed expectation" of the type necessary to support a takings claim. That is particularly true with respect to importations of arms from a country with which the United States has an arms embargo that is subject to an exemption that could be terminated at any time.

The appellants' due process claim fares no better. They assert that the implementation of the Chinese arms embargo deprived them of property without

continued

continued

due process of law by denying them the opportunity to sell in the United States the munitions for which they had obtained permits prior to the announcement of the embargo. As we have discussed, however, the appellants' right to import and sell Chinese arms in the United States was subject at all times to the hazard that their permits would be revoked, pursuant to statute and regulation, on foreign policy grounds or for other reasons. The Due Process Clause does not require the government to stand as a surety against the adverse consequences sometimes suffered by persons who knowingly undertake that kind of commercial risk.

Decision. Judgment affirmed for the United States. Under the *Arms Export Control Act,* the president has wide latitude to enforce this law by prohibiting the import of controlled items. A statute that deprives one of the opportunity to import goods does not violate or "take" one's property under the Fifth Amendment without compensation, nor does it deprive the importer of due process of law.

commerce designed to protect their own local industries, their ports, and their agricultural interests. To ensure that states would not erect barriers to commerce between them, and to guarantee a source of revenue to the federal government in the form of import duties, the drafters of the Constitution placed the power to regulate international commerce in the hands of the federal government. The drafters believed, for example, that economic disintegration could result if states were free to tax exports, or if states located along the seacoast could tax imports passing through to states located inland. Moreover, the concern was that the United States be able to deal with foreign nations from a position of political strength and unity. The framers of the Constitution understood that trade relations with foreign nations could not be handled successfully by each state on its own, but only by a strong federal government that could speak for the economic and political interests of the nation as a whole.

The Executive–Legislative Debate

Today, the fact that the power over both foreign affairs and foreign trade rests with the federal government arouses little controversy. Considerable debate arises, however, over how the Constitution divides that power between Congress and the president. Indeed, in recent years, both branches of government have sought greater control over international affairs.

One argument in favor of a strong executive branch is that the nation must "speak with one voice" in international affairs. If each senator or representative, perhaps motivated by the local interests of her own constituents, attempted to negotiate agreements with foreign nations on matters such as tariff reductions, trade in agriculture, or, say, trade in computer chips, provisions for military assistance, or even nuclear disarmament, the process would be encumbered by local interests and would be ineffective and potentially disastrous.

On the other hand, in recent years, Congress has exercised greater oversight and control over the president's conduct of foreign affairs. For a number of historical reasons, Congress has come to view the executive branch with an element of suspicion and mistrust. During the 1960s and 1970s, Congress passed several statutes attempting to limit the president's powers over foreign affairs. These laws were enacted partially as a result of the president's unpopular use of U.S. troops in the Vietnam War, and partially as a result of the illegal and unethical conduct of the president and his closest advisers during the Watergate scandal. More recently, Congress has kept strict watch over the president's actions in the Middle East and Central America to ensure that the president complies with all provisions of U.S. law in the handling of U.S. foreign policy.

The executive and legislative branches of government and their roles in setting and carrying out foreign economic and trade policies of the United States will be examined briefly now.

The Congress

Article I of the Constitution confers "all legislative powers" upon Congress, including the power "to regulate commerce with foreign nations, and among the several states" (Section 8, clause 3). In addition, Congress has broad power to pass domestic laws, declare war, appropriate monies, lay and collect taxes, and give advice and consent to the president in making treaties with foreign nations. Considering these powers as a whole, the U.S. Supreme Court has consistently held that Congress has wide-ranging constitutional power to establish overall economic policy for the United States and to put it into effect through legislation. Congress has recognized, however, that the day-to-day conduct of trade relations with foreign nations is often best conducted through a strong executive branch. As a result, Congress has delegated the authority to the president to carry out trade policies set by statute.

The President

Article II of the Constitution confers executive power on the president. The executive power is not clearly specified, and many court decisions interpret what the Constitution meant to confer. However, the courts and writers have said that the president has greater and wider-reaching power over foreign affairs than over domestic matters at home. One of the most famous statements about the power of the president is found in *United States v. Curtiss-Wright Export Co.*, 299 U.S. 304 (1936).

> Not only, as we have shown, is the federal power over external affairs in origin and essential character different from that over internal affairs, but participation in the exercise of the power is significantly limited. In this vast external realm, with its important, complicated, delicate and manifold problems, the President alone has the power to speak or listen as a representative of the nation. He makes treaties with the advice and consent of the Senate; but he alone negotiates. Into the field of negotiation the Senate cannot intrude; and Congress itself is powerless to invade it. As Marshall said in his great argument of March 7, 1800, in the House of Representatives, "The President is the sole organ of the nation in its external relations, and its sole representative with foreign nations." . . .
>
> It is quite apparent that if, in the maintenance of our international relations, embarrassment—perhaps serious embarrassment—is to be avoided and success for our aims achieved, congressional legislation which is to be made effective through negotiation and inquiry within the international field

must often accord to the President a degree of discretion and freedom from statutory restriction which would not be admissible were domestic affairs alone involved. Moreover, he, not Congress, has the better opportunity of knowing the conditions which prevail in foreign countries, and especially is this true in time of war. He has his confidential sources of information. He has his agents in the form of diplomatic, consular and other officials. Secrecy in respect of information gathered by them may be highly necessary, and the premature disclosure of it productive of harmful results.

The president's powers over foreign affairs are derived from (1) the treaty power; (2) inherent executive power, including the power to appoint ambassadors and to act as commander-in-chief of the armed forces; and (3) powers delegated by Congress. Each of these is addressed here in turn, to provide a better understanding of the interplay between the president and Congress in setting trade policies and carrying out trade relations with foreign countries.

THE TREATY POWER

Sovereign governments have been entering into military and trade alliances with one another for thousands of years. As modern nations see the growing need to come to terms with one another on important global issues, these agreements take on an even greater significance. The interdependence of all peoples of the world is expanding. Scientific and technological advances are proceeding more rapidly than ever before. Air and water pollution know no national boundaries. Toxic waste from one nation is dumped in another. Endangered wildlife slaughtered in one country is sold in another. Illegal drug trafficking, terrorism, and other forms of criminal behavior have taken on multinational dimensions. Products designed and produced in one country cause injuries to consumers in others. All of these problems have one thing in common: Resolving each of them requires the cooperation, understanding, and joint efforts of all nations of the world. In a global economy, in which the economic and financial well-being of all nations is interrelated, economic cooperation thus becomes absolutely necessary.

The primary instrument for implementing foreign political and economic affairs is the *inter-*

national agreement. International agreements include treaties and executive agreements. International agreements are either *bilateral* (between two nations) or *multilateral* (between many nations).

A *treaty* is an agreement, contract, or *compact* between two or more nations that is recognized and given effect under international or domestic law. Treaties can cover almost any subject of mutual concern to nations—from ending war and conflict to the elimination of nuclear weapons testing to enhancing the free movement of trade and investment across national borders. In the United States, the treaty power is found in Article II of the Constitution. Treaties are negotiated by the president with the "advice and consent" of the Senate, requiring passage by a two-thirds senatorial vote. A *convention* is a treaty on matters of common concern, usually negotiated on a regional or global basis and open to adoption by many nations. Many conventions discussed in this book, such as the *Convention on Contracts for the International Sale of Goods* or the *Warsaw Convention,* function to make otherwise diverse national laws uniform. A *protocol* is a common term for a draft treaty prior to ratification or an agreement used to supplement or amend an existing treaty. *Executive agreements,* made by the president without the formal treaty process in the Senate, are discussed in the next section.

Treaty Powers and the Constitution

The *treaty power* of the United States is derived from the Constitution. Under the Constitution, a treaty is considered the "Law of the Land." It is binding on both the federal and state governments with the same force as an act of Congress. Treaties are said to be either *self-executing* or *non-self-executing* (also known as *executory* treaties). The United States is party to both types. In the United States and other countries with written constitutions, a self-executing treaty has a "domestic law effect." Thus, once the treaty has been ratified, no further presidential or legislative action is required for it to become binding law. Self-executing treaties therefore provide to individuals specific rights, which the courts will enforce.

An executory or non-self-executing treaty requires an act of Congress or of the president to give it legal effect. In many other nations, including Great Britain, all treaties must be put into force through legislation. Whether a treaty is self-executing or not depends on how a U.S. court interprets the language of the treaty and the history surrounding its negotiation and approval.

One self-executing treaty well known to all travelers is the *Warsaw Convention.* This international agreement determines the rights and remedies available to those who are injured or whose property is damaged during travel on commercial aircraft. Similarly, the *Convention* determines the liability and limitations on liability of the airline. On the other hand, treaties that merely express a nation's desire to cooperate with other nations in achieving broad social, economic, cultural, humanitarian, or political objectives may not be self-executing. *The Charter of the United Nations,* for example, is a non-self-executing international "pledge" to abide by common values for the betterment of humankind, and is generally considered by U.S. courts *not* to grant enforceable rights to private parties.

Treaties of Friendship, Commerce, and Navigation

Treaties of Friendship, Commerce, and Navigation (FCN treaties) are self-executing bilateral agreements that provide a broad range of protection to foreign nationals doing business in a host country. Although each treaty is different, they all typically state that each country will allow the establishment of foreign branches or subsidiary corporations; the free flow of capital and technology; the equitable and nondiscriminatory treatment of foreign firms, individuals, and products; the right of travel and residence; the payment of just compensation for property taken by the state; the privilege of acquiring and owning real estate; and most-favored-nation trading status for goods.

The self-executing nature of FCN treaties is illustrated in *MacNamara v. Korean Air Lines.* This case involved a conflict between a federal statute that protects workers against discrimination in employment and the FCN treaty between the United States and Korea that allows foreign firms to give preference in hiring their own foreign nationals for executive, managerial, and technical positions.

Other self-executing treaties (in the United States) discussed elsewhere in this text include the

MacNamara v. Korean Air Lines
863 F.2d 1135 (1988)
United States Court of Appeals (3rd Cir.)

BACKGROUND AND FACTS

MacNamara brought this action against his former employer, Korean Air Lines (KAL), for discrimination under Title VIII of the Civil Rights Act of 1964 and the U.S. Age Discrimination in Employment Act. KAL is a Korean company. MacNamara, an American citizen, was a district sales manager in Philadelphia who had worked for the defendant airline since 1974. In 1982, at age 57, he was dismissed from employment. KAL claimed that his dismissal was part of KAL's reorganization plan, which included merging the Philadelphia and Atlanta offices into one office located in Washington, D.C. KAL had also dismissed six American managers and replaced them with four Korean citizens. The Korean citizen who replaced MacNamara was 42 years old. After exhausting his administrative remedies, MacNamara filed suit claiming that KAL had discriminated against him on the basis of race, national origin, and age. KAL moved to dismiss on the ground that its conduct was protected by the Treaty of Friendship, Commerce, and Navigation between the United States and Korea. The motion to dismiss was granted and the plaintiff appealed.

CIRCUIT JUDGE STAPLETON

The Korean FCN treaty is one of a series of friendship, commerce and navigation treaties the United States signed with various countries after World War II. Although initially negotiated primarily for the purpose of encouraging American investment abroad, the treaties secured reciprocal rights and thus granted protection to foreign businesses operating in the United States. The specific provision of the Korean FCN treaty relied upon by KAL in this case provides as follows:

> Nationals and companies of either party shall be permitted to engage, within the territories of the other party, accountants and other technical experts, executive personnel, attorneys, agents, and other specialists of their choice.

We agree with the Courts of Appeals for the Fifth and Sixth Circuits that Article VIII(1) goes beyond securing the right to be treated the same as domestic companies and that its purpose, in part, is to assure foreign corporations that they may have their business in the host country managed by their own nationals if they so desire. We also agree with the conclusion of the Sixth Circuit Court of Appeals that Article VIII(1) was not intended to provide foreign businesses with shelter from any law applicable to personnel decisions other than those that would logically or pragmatically conflict with the right to select one's own nationals as managers because of their citizenship. Insofar as Title VII and the ADEA proscribe intentional discrimination on the basis of race, national origin, and age, we perceive no theoretical or practical conflict between them and the right conferred by Article VIII(1). Thus, for example, we believe that a foreign business may not deliberately undertake to reduce the age of its workforce by replacing older Americans with younger foreign nationals. On the other hand, to the extent Title VII and the ADEA proscribe personnel decisions based on citizenship solely because of their disparate impact on older managers, a particular racial group, or persons whose ancestors are not from the foreign country involved, we perceive a potential conflict and conclude that it must be resolved in favor of Article VIII(1).

Having concluded that KAL cannot purposefully discriminate on the basis of age, race, or national origin, we now turn to the most difficult aspect of this case. To this point we have confined our analysis to liability for intentional discrimination. The reach of Title VII and the ADEA, however, extends beyond intentionally discriminatory employment policies to those practices fair in form, but discriminatory in operation. *Griggs v. Duke Power Co.*, 401 U.S. 424, 91 S.Ct. 849, 28 L.Ed.2d 158 (1971). Accordingly, Title VII and ADEA liability can be found where facially neutral employment practices have a discriminatory effect of "disparate impact" on protected groups, without proof that the employer adopted these practices with a discriminatory motive.

The fact that empirical evidence can satisfy the substantive standard of liability would pose a substantial problem in disparate impact litigation for corporations hailing from countries, including perhaps Korea, whose populations are largely homogeneous. Because a company's requirement that its

continued

continued

employees be citizens of the homogeneous country from which it hails means that almost all of its employees will be of the same national origin and race, the statistical disparity between otherwise qualified noncitizens of a particular race and national origin, and citizens of the foreign country's race and national origin is likely to be substantial. As a result, a foreign business from a country with a homogeneous population, by merely exercising its protected treaty right to prefer its own citizens for management positions, could be held in violation of Title VII. Thus, unlike a disparate treatment case where liability cannot be imposed without an affirmative finding that the employer was not simply exercising its Article VIII(1) right, a disparate impact case can result in liability where the employer did nothing more than exercise that right. For this reason we conclude that disparate impact liability under Title VII and the ADEA for a foreign employer based on its practice of engaging its own nationals as managers cannot be reconciled with Article VIII(1). Accordingly, we hold that such liability may not be imposed.

Decision. The Court of Appeals reversed and remanded for a trial on the question of whether KAL's dis-

criminatory treatment was intentional. The court ruled that the FCN treaty that authorized foreign employers to engage executives and technical specialists "of their choice" permits discrimination on the basis of citizenship. Although the treaty does not grant foreign employers a blanket exception to the civil rights laws, and employers are liable for *intentional* discrimination (disparate treatment) on the basis of race, national origin, or age, the treaty *does permit* foreign employers to retain their own nationals in executive and technical positions even where the *effect* of such personnel decisions is discriminatory and would otherwise subject the employer to disparate impact liability under the law.

Comment. In a U.S. Supreme Court decision, relied upon by the *MacNamara* court, *Sumitomo v. Avagliano,* 457 U.S. 176, 102 S.Ct. 2374 (1982), it was held that the FCN treaty between the United States and Japan did not provide immunity to a Japanese trading company for liability under Title VII of the *Civil Rights Act of 1964.* In *Sumitomo* the Court ruled that because the employer was a wholly owned U.S. subsidiary of a Japanese company, incorporated under the laws of the United States, it was not a Japanese company but a U.S. one. Thus, it was not entitled to protection under the treaty.

Hague Convention, the *Convention on Contracts for the International Sale of Goods,* and the *U.N. Convention on Recognition and Enforcement of Foreign Arbitral Awards.* Tax treaties are also considered self-executing in that the provisions of these treaties, like those of the others mentioned, need no further legislation to make them a binding source of law in U.S. courts.

THE EQUAL-DIGNITY RULE

Self-executing treaties have the same legal effect as statutes passed by both houses of Congress. How, then, do we resolve conflicts between treaties or statutes, the terms of which are inconsistent with one another? In these cases, the rule is that the *last in time prevails.* A treaty will override an inconsistent prior act of Congress. Similarly, an act of Congress can override an inconsistent prior treaty, provided that Congress had expressed its intention to do so. The rule is easy to understand and based on the idea that statutes and treaties are of equal legal importance or of *equal dignity.*

EXECUTIVE AGREEMENTS

Executive agreements are international agreements between the president and a foreign country, entered into without resort to the treaty process. They are binding obligations of the U.S. government and have the effect of law in the United States. Executive agreements are not provided for in the Constitution, as are treaties. Yet, throughout U.S. history, presidents have utilized executive agreements to conduct foreign affairs. For many practical and political reasons, presidents often favor the executive agreement over the treaty. Since World War II, most international agreements of the United States have not been treaties; they have been executive agreements.

Of the two types of executive agreements, a *sole-executive agreement* is one that the president can negotiate and put into legal effect without congressional approval. The *congressional–executive agreement* is based on authority granted by Congress to the president in a joint resolution or statute, or by treaty.

Sole-Executive Agreements and the President's Inherent Power

The president's authority to enter a sole-executive agreement is based on powers inherent in the executive office. *Inherent powers* are either stated expressly in the Constitution or found to be there by judicial interpretation. The president may only rely on this inherent power when Congress has not passed a law directing otherwise. If Congress has passed a statute on a subject, the president's inherent power does not grant "license" to violate that law. Sole-executive agreements are usually reserved for agreements with foreign countries that do not affect the broad interests of the nation as a whole. Most sole-executive agreements, such as the one in *Dole v. Carter,* are between two countries on specific matters.

Dole v. Carter
444 F. Supp. 1065 (1977)
United States District Court (D.Kan.)

BACKGROUND AND FACTS

This action was brought by a U.S. senator against the president to enjoin him from returning the Hungarian coronation regalia to the People's Republic of Hungary. The Holy Crown of St. Stephen had been held by the Hungarian people as a treasured symbol of their statehood and nationality for nearly 1,000 years. At the close of World War II, it was entrusted to the United States for safekeeping by Hungarian soldiers. In 1977, the governments of the United States and Hungary entered into an agreement returning the crown to Hungary. Many Hungarians living in the United States were opposed to the return of the crown. The plaintiff filed this action seeking an injunction against delivery of the crown to Hungary on the ground that such action was tantamount to a treaty undertaken by the president without the prior advice and consent of the Senate.

DISTRICT JUDGE O'CONNOR

We turn now to the plaintiff's argument that the agreement to return the coronation regalia to Hungary in and of itself constitutes a treaty which must be ratified by the Senate. It is well established, and even plaintiff admits, that the United States frequently enters into international agreements other than treaties. Indeed, as of January 1, 1972, the United States was a party to 5,306 international agreements, only 947 of which were treaties and 4,359 of which were international agreements other than treaties. These "other agreements" appear to fall into three categories: (1) so-called congressional-executive agreements, executed by the president upon specific authorizing legislation from the Congress; (2) executive agreements pursuant to treaty, executed by the president in accord with specific instructions found in a prior, formal treaty; and (3) executive agreements executed pursuant to the president's own constitutional authority (hereinafter referred to as "executive agreements"). Defendant contends that his agreement to return the coronation regalia to Hungary falls into the latter category, and the court agrees.

Since the *Curtiss-Wright* decision, the Supreme Court has twice upheld the validity of an executive agreement made by President Franklin Roosevelt with the Soviet Union. In the Litvinov Agreement, the president recognized and established diplomatic relations with that nation. In addition, for the purpose of bringing about a final settlement of claims and counterclaims between the Soviet Union and the United States, it was agreed that the Soviet Union would take no steps to enforce claims against American nationals, but all such claims were assigned to the United States with the understanding that the Soviet Union would be notified of all amounts realized by the United States. In speaking for the Court in *United States v. Belmont,* 301 U.S. 324, 57 S.Ct. 758, 81 L.Ed. 1134 (1937), Justice Sutherland, who also authored the majority opinion in *Curtiss-Wright* . . . stated:

> (A)n international compact, as this was, is not always a treaty which requires the participation of the Senate. There are many such compacts, of which a protocol, a *modus vivendi,* a postal convention, and agreements like that now under consideration are illustrations.

continued

continued

The United States enters into approximately 200 executive agreements each year, and it has been observed that the constitutional system "could not last a month" if the president sought Senate or congressional consent for every one of them. *L. Henkin, Foreign Affairs and the Constitution . . .* Congress itself recognized this fact in passing P.L. 92–403, 1 U.S.C. § 112b, requiring the secretary of state to transmit for merely informational purposes the text of all international agreements other than treaties to which the United States becomes a party. The House Committee on Foreign Affairs stated in recommending passage of that statute that while it wished to be apprised of "all agreements of any significance," "[c]learly the Congress does not want to be inundated with trivia." 1972 *U.S. Code Cong. and Admin. News,* p. 3069. While the president's understanding to return the Hungarian coronation regalia is hardly a "trivial" matter to either the United States or the people of Hungary, the court is yet convinced that the president's agreement in this regard lacks the magnitude of agreements customarily concluded in treaty form. The president's agreement here involves no substantial ongoing commitment on

the part of the United States, exposes the United States to no appreciable discernible risks, and contemplates American action of an extremely limited duration in time. The plaintiff presented no evidence that agreements of the kind in question here are traditionally concluded only by treaty, either as a matter of American custom or as a matter of international law. Indeed, while the court has not exhaustively examined all possibly pertinent treaties, the court can hardly imagine that any such examination would lend support to the plaintiff's position. Finally, the agreement here encompasses no substantial reciprocal commitments by the Hungarian government. As a matter of law, the court is therefore persuaded that the president's agreement to return the Hungarian coronation regalia is not a commitment requiring the advice and consent of the Senate under Article II, Section 2, of the Constitution.

Decision. The plaintiff's motion for a preliminary injunction is denied. The agreement to return the coronation regalia was not a treaty requiring ratification by the Senate, but a valid executive agreement based on the president's inherent power.

Congressional–Executive Agreements

In performing its duties, Congress has broad legislative power to establish policy for the nation. It passes laws and enters treaties to implement that policy. Then, Congress delegates to the president and the executive branch the responsibility to carry out or enforce those laws, which is known as the president's *delegated power.* If the president enters into an executive agreement pursuant to this delegated authority, the agreement is valid and has the effect of binding law. This action is known as a *congressional–executive agreement.*

Congressional–executive agreements serve much the same purpose as treaties. Their legal nature, however, is different. Unlike treaties, congressional–executive agreements are not described in the Constitution. Their use grew out of the constitutional history of the United States during the present century. For the most part, they were born of the Roosevelt era of the 1930s and 1940s, when the president was seeking new and more flexible ways of dealing with

the nation's economic problems during the Great Depression and World War II. By the close of World War II, the House and Senate had informally agreed with the president to provide a substitute process for approving international agreements—one that would not require a two-thirds vote of approval of the Senate, as do treaties. Instead, they agreed on a substitute process permitting international agreements to be approved either by statute or by joint resolutions of both houses of Congress. Statutes and joint resolutions can pass on a *simple majority vote* of both houses. Presidents usually prefer the congressional–executive agreement process to the treaty process because it is often easier for them to obtain congressional approval by majority vote of both houses than by a two-thirds vote of one house. (Thus, the legislature and president become partners in forming international agreements—a real "balance of power.") Today, congressional–executive agreements, based on the majority vote of both houses of Congress, are recognized as having the same binding legal effect as treaties.

TRADE AGREEMENTS

Like treaties, executive agreements cover a wide range of subjects. For instance, bilateral agreements might attempt to open investment opportunities in one nation for citizens of the other. *Trade agreements,* discussed here, are executive agreements between countries on matters involving international trade and related issues. They are used to implement the trade policies of a nation. If, for instance, a nation takes a liberal, open-market view of trade, then it might seek to enter agreements with foreign nations to further that goal (e.g., reducing tariffs and nontariff barriers to trade). If it seeks to protect key domestic industries from foreign competition, it can try to negotiate trade agreements for that purpose (e.g., imposing quotas or increased tariffs). Trade agreements can be either bilateral or multilateral. The United States' first trade agreement was with France in 1778. Today, the United States participates in many trade agreements, affecting virtually every major industry and sector of the American economy. For instance, the United States is a party to nearly fifty bilateral trade agreements affecting trade in textiles alone. Other industries regulated by trade agreements include semiconductors, steel, and automobiles. Companies that import and export these products are directly affected by the trade and tariff regulations outlined in these agreements. The most important trade agreements are of the congressional–executive type. Some of the most important trade agreements (FTA) of the United States since World War II include:

- General Agreement on Tariffs and Trade, 1994 (GATT Uruguay Round Agreement), including the Agreement Establishing the World Trade Organization
- General Agreement on Tariffs and Trade, 1947 (and subsequent GATT agreements)
- U.S.–Israel FTA
- North American FTA
- U.S.–Chile FTA

http://www.ustr.gov
The home page for the U.S. Trade Representative, a cabinet-level post that advises the president on trade issues, directs negotiations with foreign countries, and acts as the president's spokesperson on trade.

- U.S.–Jordan FTA
- U.S.–Singapore FTA
- U.S.–Central American FTA (ready for Congressional approval in 2004)
- U.S.–China Bilateral Market Access Agreement

http://www.mac.doc.gov/tcc
For a quick, concise explanation of what trade agreements do for American firms, see "Exporter's Guide to U.S. Trade Agreements." From the U.S. International Trade Administration's Market Access and Compliance Center.

The Smoot–Hawley Tariff Act of 1930

The United States has had trade and tariff laws since its founding. In the 1800s, these laws gave virtually no authority to the president other than to collect taxes; Congress established tariff rates. Shortly after World War I, as a result of isolationist sentiments at home, the United States began to increase tariffs on imported goods. In 1930, the U.S. Congress imposed the highest tariff levels in the nation's history when it enacted the *Smoot–Hawley Tariff Act.* The bill was signed by President Herbert Hoover. Under *Smoot–Hawley,* tariffs on more than one thousand items were increased to levels so high that other nations raised their tariffs in retaliation. Some tariff rates reached nearly 100 percent of the cost of the goods. Economic activity declined precipitously. It is generally accepted today that these high tariffs worldwide contributed to the Great Depression of the 1930s. The newly elected president, Franklin Roosevelt, recognized the immediate need to reduce tariffs and "liberalize" trade. At that time, however, the president simply did not have the legal authority to take any significant action without congressional approval, and the treaty process was too cumbersome. Roosevelt thus worked with Congress to pass the *Reciprocal Trade Agreements Act of 1934,* which provided the president with the authority needed to lower tariffs.

The Reciprocal Trade Agreements Act of 1934

Prior to 1934, the president had little or no discretion in setting tariff rates. The *Reciprocal Trade Agreements Act* provided the president with a mechanism not only for lowering U.S. tariffs, but also for encouraging other countries to lower their rates as well. This Act granted the president far more flexible powers to adjust tariffs than under any prior legislation. The president was granted the authority to negotiate tariff reductions on a product-by-product basis with other countries on the basis of *reciprocity.* The United States would reduce a tariff on a foreign product if the foreign country would reciprocate by lowering its tariffs. An agreement to reduce a tariff to a specified level is known as a *tariff concession.* If the United States was to lower an existing tariff on an imported product from, say, France, then France would have to make similar concessions on the same or other products coming from the United States.

The 1934 law also introduced what is known as *unconditional most-favored-nation (MFN) trade,* now commonly referred to as *normal trade relations (NTR).* It provided that a lower tariff rate negotiated with one nation would automatically be granted to like products imported from all other nations that had signed an MFN agreement with the United States, without any concession being requested from those nations in return. Moreover, if two other nations reached an agreement to lower tariffs on a given product, then that new rate would apply to U.S. products imported into those nations as well. This system served to quicken and expand the process of lowering duties worldwide.

In the following case, *Star-Kist Foods, Inc. v. United States,* the constitutionality of the tariff-setting process of the *Reciprocal Trade Agreements Act* was upheld against a charge that it was an unconstitutional delegation of power by Congress to the president.

Star-Kist Foods, Inc. v. United States
275 F.2d 472 (1959)
United States Court of Customs and Patent Appeals

BACKGROUND AND FACTS

Star-Kist Foods, a U.S. producer of canned tuna, instituted a lawsuit to protest the assessment of duties made by the collector of customs on imported canned tuna fish. The canned tuna was assessed at the rate of 12.5 percent pursuant to a trade agreement with Iceland. Prior to the agreement, the tariff rate had been set by Congress in the *Tariff Act of 1930* at 25 percent *ad valorem.* The trade agreement with Iceland, which resulted in lowering the rate of duty, was executed pursuant to the *Reciprocal Trade Agreements Act of 1934.* That act authorized the president to enter into foreign trade agreements for the purpose of expanding foreign markets for the products of the United States by affording corresponding market opportunities for foreign products in the United States. To implement an agreement, the president was then authorized to raise or lower any duty previously set by Congress, but not by more than 50 percent. Star-Kist brought this action contending that the delegation of authority under the 1934 act and the agreement with Iceland were unconstitutional.

JUDGE MARTIN

A constitutional delegation of powers requires that Congress enunciate a policy or objective or give rea-

sons for seeking the aid of the president. In addition the act must specify when the powers conferred may be utilized by establishing a standard or "intelligible principle" which is sufficient to make it clear when action is proper. And because Congress cannot abdicate its legislative function and confer carte blanche authority on the president, it must circumscribe that power in some manner. This means that Congress must tell the president what he can do by prescribing a standard which confines his discretion and which will guarantee that any authorized action he takes will tend to promote rather than flout the legislative purpose. It is not necessary that the guides be precise or mathematical formulae to be satisfactory in a constitutional sense.

In the act before us the congressional policy is pronounced very clearly. The stated objectives are to expand foreign markets for the products of the United States "by regulating the admission of foreign goods into the United States in accordance with the characteristics and needs of various branches of American production so that foreign markets will be made available to those branches of American production which require and are capable of developing such outlets by affording corresponding

continued

continued

market opportunities for foreign products in the United States. . . . "

Pursuant to the 1934 act the presidential power can be invoked "whenever he [the president] finds as a fact that any existing duties or other import restrictions of the United States or any foreign country are unduly burdening or restricting the foreign trade of the United States and that the [purpose of the act] will be promoted." . . .

Under the provisions of the 1934 act the president by proclamation can modify existing duties and other import restrictions but not by more than 50 percent of the specified duties nor can he place articles upon or take them off the free list. Furthermore, he must accomplish the purposes of the act through the medium of foreign trade agreements with other coun-

tries. However, he can suspend the operation of such agreements if he discovers discriminatory treatment of American commerce, and he can terminate, in whole or in part, any proclamation at any time. . . .

In view of the Supreme Court's recognition of the necessity of flexibility in the laws affecting foreign relations . . . we are of the opinion that the 1934 act does not grant an unconstitutional delegation of authority to the president.

Decision. The court held in favor of the United States. The congressional delegation of authority under the 1934 statute was constitutional because Congress had provided the president with a sufficiently discernible standard to guide any decisions in carrying out the purposes of the Act.

More Recent U.S. Trade Legislation

The *Reciprocal Trade Agreements Act of 1934* provided the basic system for trade negotiations until 1962. In that year Congress passed the *Trade Expansion Act of 1962* that authorized the president to negotiate *across-the-board* tariff reductions instead of using the tedious product-by-product system set up in 1934. This law also created the *Office of Special Trade Representative* (today the *U.S. Trade Representative*), empowered to conduct all trade negotiations on behalf of the United States. The *Trade Reform Act of 1974* replaced most provisions of the 1962 law, and delegated even more authority to the president. The president was given wide latitude in reducing or eliminating duties (with authority to reduce duties by up to 60 percent and simply end any import duties of less than 5 percent), and in negotiating a reduction of nontariff barriers during the *Tokyo Round*. The *Trade Agreements Act of 1979* continued congressional support for expanding free trade by approving the president's trade agreements to reduce nontariff barriers. The *Trade and Tariff Act of 1984* authorized the president to negotiate agreements related to high-technology products, trade in services, and barriers to foreign investment. It also authorized the free trade area between the United States and Israel. In 1988, President Reagan signed a bill into law ratifying

the *U.S.–Canada Free Trade Agreement*, creating a duty-free trade area between the two countries. In 1988, Congress passed the *Omnibus Trade and Competitiveness Act* that extended the president's authority to negotiate trade agreements, including an expansion of the U.S.–Canadian free trade area to include Mexico in the *North American Free Trade Agreement* (NAFTA). It also gave even broader powers to the president to "pry open" foreign markets that have unfair barriers to the entry of U.S. goods and services (through both negotiations and sanctions). In addition, Congress has also passed a number of trade agreements dealing with specific issues or affecting U.S. trade with specific world regions. For instance, as we will study in later chapters, Congress has passed the *Trade Act of 2002* (which reauthorized an important trade program that promotes imports from developing countries), the *Caribbean Basin Economic Recovery Act of 1983*, the *Andean Trade Program and Drug Eradication Act of 2002*, the *African Growth and Opportunity Act of 2000*, as well as other important trade laws. As can be seen, many of the basic principles and programs established in the 1930s and 1940s are, in a modern form, still in existence today. To this day, every U.S. president has returned to Congress to ask for needed authority to negotiate congressional–executive agreements on trade and investment issues with foreign nations.

The *General Agreement on Tariffs and Trade*

The *General Agreement on Tariffs and Trade,* or GATT, became effective in 1947 for the purpose of promoting and expanding trade through multilateral trade negotiations between member nations. As the most important trade agreement of the twentieth century, it has provided a global framework for reducing tariffs and nontariff barriers to trade. Today, more than one hundred nations are signatories of GATT. The most recent GATT, the *General Agreement on Tariffs and Trade 1994* (commonly called the *Uruguay Round Agreement*), led to the creation of the new *World Trade Organization* (WTO), the subject of the next chapter.

The Legal Status of GATT 1947.
The original *General Agreement on Tariffs and Trade* of 1947 was not a treaty, nor was it a typical congressional–executive agreement. Rather, it was an international agreement adopted only by a proclamation of the president. Despite no explicit congressional approval, GATT 1947 was accepted as a binding agreement of the United States, and its legal status today is completely accepted because GATT 1994 was approved by Congress.

Presidential Authority for GATT Multilateral Trade Negotiations.
GATT succeeded in liberalizing trade in this century because it provided a forum for bringing nations together in *multilateral trade negotiations.* GATT negotiations are called "rounds." The most notable GATT rounds were the *Dillon Rounds* (1950s), the *Kennedy Rounds* (1960s), the *Tokyo Rounds* (1970s), and the *Uruguay Rounds* (1980s and 1990s). Each set of rounds resulted in improvements in the world trading environment. The president has sought congressional approval for trade agreements negotiated under GATT, granted under the statutes listed in the preceding sections.

Trade Promotion Authority

Congressional–executive trade agreements require the approval of Congress in order to be legally binding on the United States. However, a foreign nation might be less willing to enter trade negotiations with the president's negotiating team if it thought that any agreement might later be rejected by Congress because of domestic political pressures in the United States. Imagine the U.S. government taking years to negotiate trade agreements with dozens of countries, covering thousands of products affecting hundreds of industries—only to have a senator or member of Congress vote against it because it reduced import duties on foreign products that compete with those made by his or her "special interests" back home. To avoid this, the *Trade Reform Act of 1974* set up a "fast-track" process for approving trade agreements. The statute gave the president authority to negotiate trade agreements pursuant to the objectives set out by Congress. If those objectives were met, and negotiations concluded within the set period of years, Congress had to vote yes or no, by simple majority, to either accept or reject the agreement in its entirety without amendment. This helped to assure the passage of trade agreements into U.S. law because it eliminated the possibility that it would be affected by special interests. The fast-track process has been used by presidents since that time to negotiate many important trade agreements, until it expired in 1994. It was renewed in the *Bipartisan Trade Promotion Authority Act of 2002* (Title XXI of the *Trade Act of 2002*), and is now known as the president's *Trade Promotion Authority.* The authority under the Act expires in 2005, with an automatic extension through 2007 unless Congress objects. During negotiations, the president must consult with Congress and notify it of proposed changes to U.S. trade laws. Congress can then comment on the negotiations before there is a final agreement and while there is still time for the president to modify it. This makes the president and Congress partners in furthering America's trade interests. In 2003, the Bush Administration had concluded free trade agreements with Singapore and Chile, and was negotiating trade issues with Central America, Bahrain, Morocco, Australia, and the countries of southern Africa. Negotiations for a *Free Trade Area of the Americas* were also ongoing at that time.

Trade Negotiating Objectives.
The 2002 act asks the president to negotiate agreements that will:

- reduce tariff and nontariff barriers to trade in goods, agricultural products, and services on a reciprocal basis

- eliminate trade barriers that decrease market opportunities for U.S. exports
- promote respect for worker rights and the protection of child labor, considering the labor standards of the International Labor Organization
- consider the impact of trade on the environment and natural resources and promote adherence to global environmental standards
- assure that trade agreements afford small businesses equal access to international markets and expanded export market opportunities
- reduce barriers to foreign investment by U.S. firms

- protect intellectual property rights
- prohibit government officials in foreign countries from accepting bribes or engaging in corrupt practices that affect or distort international trade
- assure that global rules for furthering trade apply to electronic commerce

In the following case, *Made in the USA Foundation v. United States*, a U.S. federal court upheld the fast-track trade promotion authority used by President Clinton to negotiate the *North American Free Trade Agreement.*

Made in the USA Foundation v. United States
56 F. Supp.2d 1226 (1999)
United States District Court (N.D. Ala.)

BACKGROUND AND FACTS
In 1990, the United States, Mexico, and Canada initiated negotiations with the intention of creating a "free trade zone" through the elimination or reduction of tariffs and other barriers to trade. After two years of negotiations, the leaders of the three countries signed the North American Free Trade Agreement ("NAFTA" or the "Agreement") on December 17, 1992. The negotiations were undertaken by the president pursuant to his responsibility to conduct the foreign affairs of the United States, and pursuant to "fast-track" negotiating authority granted by Congress under the *Trade Act of 1974* and the *Omnibus Trade and Competitiveness Act of 1988*. Fast-track legislation vests the president with authority to negotiate a trade agreement with a foreign nation according to the basic goals and objectives set by Congress. Once the agreement is signed and submitted to Congress for approval by majority vote, Congress cannot amend or change the terms of the agreement, but can only vote it "up or down." This prevents individual legislators from trying to "pick it apart" by proposing amendments for their constituents and increases the likelihood of passage. On December 8, 1993, Congress approved NAFTA and passed the implementation act by a vote of 234 to 200 in the House and 61 to 38 in the Senate. The implementation act included a number of laws to permit enforcement of NAFTA's provisions in the United States. The enactment of the implementation act brought to a close a lengthy period of rancorous debate over NAFTA. The plaintiffs in this case, the Made

in the USA Foundation (along with the United Steelworkers of America and others), claim that NAFTA and the implementation act are unconstitutional. It argues that NAFTA is a treaty and as such can only be approved by two-thirds vote of the Senate, as required by the Treaty Clause, contained in Article II, Section 2 of the U.S. Constitution.

PROPST, SENIOR DISTRICT JUDGE
To be certain, the [Constitution] does not explicitly state that the Treaty Clause procedure is the exclusive method by which the federal government may conclude an international agreement that constitutes a "treaty." Given the absence of express textual proscriptions of Presidential or Congressional power in the area of international agreement-making, the Government suggests that the text of the Constitution clearly allows the political branches to conclude international agreements through alternative methods. Thus the Government contends that the Supreme Court has sanctioned the federal government's use of international agreements that "do not constitute treaties in the constitutional sense." [Citations Omitted] According to the Government, *United States v. Belmont,* 301 U.S. 324, 57 S. Ct. 758 (1937), establishes that the President may, on his own authority or in tandem with Congress, enter into international agreements without adhering to the strictures of the Treaty Clause. Finally, the Government maintains that the Supreme Court's deci-

continued

continued

sion in *Field v. Clark,* 143 U.S. 649, 12 S. Ct. 495 (1892), stands for the proposition that Congress as a whole may direct and participate in the making of international agreements.* * *

Plaintiffs contend that the powers of the President and Congress in the areas of foreign affairs and commerce do not authorize them to adopt treaties without the concurrence of two-thirds of the Senate. Citing Emmerich de Vattel's *The Law of Nations,* which the Framers allegedly relied upon to some degree in forming their conceptions of the term "treaty," the plaintiffs argue that the Framers certainly considered the term "treaty" to include commercial agreements. They again note that the supermajority requirement was included in the Constitution as a result of the Framers' fear that "commercial Treaties may be so framed as to be partially injurious." The plaintiffs note the fact that the concern surrounding commercial treaties was so focused that when a proposal was made at the Constitutional Convention to exempt peace treaties from the supermajority requirement, the proposal was objected to solely on the grounds that peace treaties could be worded so as to influence commercial interests.* * *

The most significant issue before the court is whether the Treaty Clause is an exclusive means of making an international agreement under the circumstances of this case. It is clear that there is no explicit language in the Constitution which makes the Treaty Clause exclusive as to all international agreements. On the other hand, the broad breadth of the Commerce Clause, particularly the Foreign Commerce Clause, has been repeatedly emphasized. The inability of the Congress under the *Articles of Confederation* to regulate commerce was one of the main weaknesses which led to the call of the Constitutional Convention. The *Annapolis Convention of 1786* was called to discuss problems which had resulted from this weakness. This meeting, in turn, led to the Constitutional Convention. The Commerce Clause was clearly intended to address this concern. The "Power" to regulate commerce, foreign and interstate and with Indian Tribes, was specifically given to Congress. The Treaty Clause makes no specific reference to commerce of any type.

Thus, while the reasons for the existence and adoption of the Treaty Clause and its scope are debatable, the plenary scope of the Commerce Clause is clear. There exists no reason to apply a limiting construction upon the Foreign Commerce

Clause or to assume that the Clause was not meant to give Congress the power to approve those agreements that are "necessary and proper" in regulating foreign commerce. It is impossible to definitively conclude that the Framers intended the regulation of foreign commerce to be subject to the rigors of the Treaty Clause procedure when commercial agreements with foreign nations are involved. Given the Court's language in *Gibbons v. Ogden,* 9 Wheat. 1, 22 U.S. 1 (1824) the power of Congress to regulate foreign commerce with foreign nations is so extensive that it is reasonably arguable, as earlier discussed, that no "treaty" affecting commerce with foreign nations is valid unless adopted by Congress as a whole. In the absence of specific limiting language in or relating to the Treaty Clause, I am led to conclude that the Foreign Commerce power of Congress is at least concurrent with the Treaty Clause power when an agreement, as is the case here, is dominated by provisions specifically related to foreign commerce and has other provisions which are reasonably "necessary and proper" for "carrying all others into execution. . . ." Further, I note that the President, in negotiating the Agreement in connection with the fast track legislation, was acting pursuant to his constitutional responsibility for conducting the Nation's foreign affairs and pursuant to a grant of authority from Congress.

Saying that the President has the power to make treaties by and with the advice and consent of the Senate is not saying that agreements with foreign nations cannot otherwise be made and implemented. The plaintiffs argue that nothing in the Constitution empowers Congress to enact as legislation an agreement with a foreign country. Citing Federalist No. 75 (Hamilton), they argue that the Framers believed that "contracts with foreign nations" could not be made through "the legislative authority . . . to enact laws." The Government does not contest the plaintiffs' assertion. However, it should be noted that the Supreme Court has upheld the power of Congress to delegate to the President the ability to negotiate and conclude agreements with foreign nations or to implicitly approve the President's actions with respect to such agreements. *See Dames & Moore v. Regan,* 453 U.S. 654, 668, 101 S. Ct. 2972 (1981). Under such circumstances, the President is said to "exercise not only his powers but also those delegated by Congress," and has been allowed to conclude international agreements settling claims of

continued

continued

United States citizens. Thus, although Congress itself may not be empowered to conclude an international agreement, Congress may delegate its authority in a given field to the President, creating a combination of powers that allows the President to conclude an international agreement in an area otherwise reserved to Congress or where the President's authority might be questionable.

The foregoing, considered in light of at least some degree of presumption of constitutionality to which the Agreement is entitled, leads me to ultimately conclude that NAFTA and the Implementation Act were made and approved in a constitutional manner. One thing is clear. This court does not have jurisdiction to review the wisdom of NAFTA or to determine whether it is in the best interest of the Nation.

Thus, I hold that the President had the authority to negotiate and conclude NAFTA pursuant to his executive authority and pursuant to the authority granted to him by Congress in accordance with the terms of the *Omnibus Trade and Competitiveness Act of 1988,* and the *Trade Act of 1974,* and as further approved by the Implementation Act.

Decision. In an eighty-four page opinion, complete with 354 textual footnotes, the U.S. District Court upheld the *North American Free Trade Agreement* and in so doing recognized that trade agreements negotiated by the president pursuant to fast-track legislative authority and passed into law by a majority vote of both houses of Congress are a valid alternative to the treaty process.

Expanded Powers.   Today, the president is not just authorized to reduce duties on products, but to take a wide range of executive actions to deal with the complexities of the modern business world. This authority is in keeping with the modern notion that the president needs increased flexibility in handling matters related to international trade and foreign affairs. For example, under the *Trade Act of 1974* and the *Omnibus Act,* the president has been given authority to negotiate special trade relations with developing countries; to negotiate rules for dealing with agricultural trade problems; to coordinate international monetary policies; to negotiate better mechanisms for protecting copyrights, patents, and trademarks in foreign countries; to negotiate a reduction of barriers to trade in high technology; and to ensure equal access to foreign high technology by U.S. firms.

In addition, the president has been given broader powers to deal with a range of complex economic problems. For example, the president may take certain authorized measures (tariffs, quotas, and the like) designed to protect U.S. industry from foreign competition under certain well-defined situations, such as when U.S. industry is being injured by increased imports of particular foreign products. The president is also authorized to invoke emergency regulations to deal with severe international economic problems, such as U.S. balance of payments shortages. These problems are discussed in later chapters.

http://www.ita.doc.gov
See for country-by-country expertise from the U.S. Department of Commerce (DOC).

THE PRESIDENT'S EMERGENCY POWERS

The president can also justify executive actions by invoking far-reaching *emergency powers.* Dating back to the time of the Civil War, Congress has granted extraordinary powers to the president to deal with a variety of "national emergencies." Although originally conceived to allow the president to deal with the economic problems arising during wartime, the concept of a *national emergency* has gradually been expanded to include a broad range of situations affecting international trade.

Trading with the Enemy Act

The *Trading with the Enemy Act* (TWEA) was passed in 1917 for the purposes of punishing Americans who trade with the enemy during times of war. In 1933, however, President Roosevelt used this statute during a domestic economic crisis to declare a national banking emergency, close the nation's banks, and prevent the hoarding of gold. Congress ratified the president's actions and expanded the president's emergency powers to include peacetime crises determined by the president to be a "national emergency."

In the 1970s, Congress generally came to believe that the TWEA provided the president with far more sweeping powers to regulate nonwartime emergencies than had ever been intended by the law. After all, this was the time of the Vietnam War. The excesses of presidential power were becoming evident as the Watergate disclosures and abuses of public office were made public. Executive actions of the president were considered suspect. In this climate, Congress sought to increase its role in making U.S. foreign policy and to impose new controls on the president's actions during national emergencies. By 1977, Congress had passed new emergency powers statutes that repealed the TWEA with the exception of the provisions restricting trade with Cuba and North Korea.

National Emergencies Act

In 1976, Congress passed the *National Emergencies Act* (NEA), which ended four existing states of emergency and established new procedures for declaring new ones. (Ironically, the banking emergency declared by President Roosevelt during the Great Depression had remained in effect until 1976.) Under the NEA, the president can still declare a state of emergency, although the authority to act under it lasts for only one year. At the end of that period, the president must ask Congress to renew authority over that situation. The president must consult with Congress prior to declaring an emergency and report to Congress every six months while the emergency continues. Congress votes every six months on whether to continue the emergency and may terminate a national emergency declared by the president through a joint resolution of both houses of Congress.

Although the procedures for congressional oversight are set out in the *National Emergencies Act,* the powers and the scope of remedies available to the president are set out in the 1977 *International Emergency Economic Powers Act* (IEEPA).

International Emergency Economic Powers Act

This statute provides the current grant of authority to the president to regulate economic and financial

transactions, and to place restrictions on importing or exporting during a peacetime (or wartime) national emergency. The statute states that the president may declare a national emergency in the event of "any unusual and extraordinary threat, which has its source in whole or substantial part outside the United States, to the national security, foreign policy, or economy of the United States." IEEPA allows the president wide discretion in controlling international financial transactions, including the transfer of monies, goods, and securities to and from the United States. It allows the president to seize foreign assets held in U.S. banks or foreign branches of U.S. banks. The statute also allows the president to impose a trade embargo with a foreign country and to take a wide range of other economic sanctions. The president's policy decisions under IEEPA are often implemented by the U.S. Treasury, whose regulations are published in the *Federal Register.*

---

http://www.ustreas.gov/ofac
The U.S. Department of Treasury, Office of Foreign Assets Control, publishes OFAC-enforced trade sanctions against targeted foreign countries, organizations that sponsor international terrorism, and international narcotics traffickers.

Economic Sanctions under IEEPA. Since its enactment, IEEPA has been used to impose economic sanctions against Nicaragua, South Africa, Panama, Libya, Haiti, Serbia, Sudan, Burma, Afghanistan (under the Taliban), and Iraq in response to the political situations in those and other countries. These sanctions, tailored to the special problems presented by each individual country, have included a ban on the import and export of goods (computers, arms, and nuclear equipment to South Africa), prohibitions on financial transactions (a ban on the import of South African gold krugerrands and a prohibition on U.S. loans to South Africa), a ban on air flights between the United States and Nicaragua, and a ban on Nicaraguan and Panamanian ships entering U.S. ports. The embargo against Libya, in the wake of Libyan-sponsored terrorism, included a ban on travel to that country by U.S. citizens and a freeze on all Libyan property in the United States. President Clinton and President Bush both have used IEEPA as a major weapon in the war on terrorism, using the law to seize the assets of terrorist groups and cutting off their funding.

As of 2003, the United States had maintained economic and trade restrictions with the following countries:

- Burma (also called Myanmar)—ban on imports to the United States, prohibition of U.S. foreign investment, and freeze of U.S. assets of senior government officials due to government's suppression of human rights, its unwillingness to give up power after elections, and arrest of pro-democracy demonstrators (see International Accents on page 271)
- Iran, Syria, Sudan, Libya, Cuba—for support of international terrorism
- Balkans—blocking of property with individuals promoting violence and disrupting peace
- Sierra Leone—U.S. prohibition on imports of diamonds (proceeds used to fund civil war)
- Liberia—diamonds
- North Korea—for violating international atomic energy rules and for missile testing
- Zimbabwe—for politically motivated violence

Other restrictions were being enforced against those persons, firms, or governments affiliated with terrorist organizations—any country attempting to interfere with the Middle East peace process; certain named individuals and organizations associated with the proliferation of weapons of mass destruction; and certain persons identified by the president as significant foreign drug traffickers under the *Foreign Narcotics Kingpin Designation Act of 1999*.

USA PATRIOT Act

One of the major U.S. legal responses to the terrorist attacks of September 11, 2001, was the enactment of a statute with a rather cumbersome title, *Uniting and Strengthening America by Providing Appropriate Tools Required to Intercept and Obstruct Terrorism (2001)*, commonly called the *USA PATRIOT Act*. The act made significant changes to IEEPA and to other U.S. criminal statutes, and gave far-reaching powers to law enforcement to deal with the threat of terrorism in America. First, the act created new federal crimes and penalties for terrorism. These include new crimes (or increased penalties for existing crimes)

for attacks on mass transportation, for harboring terrorists, for possession of biological toxins or weapons, for fraudulent charitable solicitation, and for providing material support to terrorists. The act also modified the immigration laws by giving the government greater freedom to detain and deport noncitizens where the U.S. Attorney General has reasonable grounds to believe that an individual belongs to a terrorist group or jeopardizes U.S. national security. The act amends IEEPA to give the government greater flexibility to seize property of those who commit terrorist acts or who provide material support to terrorists. It permits the president to order the confiscation of foreign property belonging to any individual, group, or country that planned, authorized, aided, or engaged in any attack against the United States. Moreover, it allows assets of an individual or organization to be frozen *pending* an IEEPA investigation into their links to terrorists.

The *PATRIOT Act* amends U.S. laws on financial transactions and bank secrecy, so the government can better follow the trail of money supporting terrorists. The act expands the record-keeping requirements for financial institutions (including banks, brokers, dealers, and other financial institutions) and calls for greater government scrutiny over international business transactions. Financial institutions are placed in the position of "knowing their customer." By consulting the *Specially Designated Nationals and Blocked Person's List* they can determine if any transaction includes persons or organizations whose assets have been seized under the law. Financial transactions, both inside and outside the United States, must be tracked and reported to the government when there is suspicion of money laundering for terrorist groups. Cash transactions over $10,000 must also be reported. The law is enforced by the Department of Treasury (*Office of Foreign Assets Control* and the *Financial Crimes Enforcement Network* or *FinCen*), the Department of Justice, and various other government agencies.

The *USA PATRIOT Act* also provides law enforcement with greater investigative tools to fight terrorism, with less judicial supervision and oversight. It expands law enforcement's authority to conduct searches, permits nationwide execution of search warrants against terrorists or those who harbor them, allows the "roving" electronic surveillance of criminal suspects, permits monitoring of some email and computer messages without a warrant, and eases restrictions on law enforcement when national security is at stake. The act also expands the extraterritorial application of federal criminal law to terrorist acts committed against Americans or American property overseas. While the act is considered crucial in the government's effort to prevent future terrorist attacks in the United States, it is also criticized by many Americans for its broad and sweeping powers, especially those authorizing electronic eavesdropping, that some believe infringe on basic American liberties.

---

http://www.fincen.gov

Financial Crimes Enforcement Network (FinCen) U.S. government agency that brings people and information together to fight the complex problem of international money laundering and financial crimes. Links federal, state, local, and international law enforcement, regulatory, and financial communities.

IEEPA and UN Sanctions Against Iraq. In 1990, shortly after the Iraqi invasion of Kuwait, President G.H. Bush used his authority under IEEPA to impose economic sanctions on Iraq. In an effort to block Iraq from seizing Kuwait assets, the Treasury Department used IEEPA to freeze all assets of both countries held in U.S.-owned or -controlled banks, or by U.S. firms. The sanctions were administered by the Treasury's Office of Foreign Assets Control. All sales between Iraq and U.S. companies were halted.

The Iraqi case presented a unique situation under IEEPA. The authority for U.S. action against Iraq in 1991 was broadened by international cooperation and by the force of international law. The United States was not acting unilaterally against Iraq; it was, rather, responding to calls from the UN for sanctions against Iraq. This case was also unique in that IEEPA sanctions were used to aid in the protection of foreign assets (those belonging to the government and people of Kuwait), not just to punish an offending country. The sanctions resulted in lost business, disruption of the international oil markets, blocked letter-of-credit transactions, and a regulatory nightmare for U.S. companies doing business in the Middle East. The first Gulf War began when the U.S. administration

determined that the sanctions would not be effective. The sanctions were lifted in 2003 at the end of the second war with Iraq. Trade in arms, stolen cultural artifacts, and transactions with Baath party officials remained prohibited, and blocked Iraqi money was to be used in the rebuilding of Iraq.

Court Challenges to IEEPA

When Libya was implicated in supporting international terrorism in the late 1980s, the president prohibited U.S. citizens from performing any contract in support of commercial, industrial, or governmental projects there. In *Herman Chang v. United States*, 859 F.2d 893 (Fed. Cir. 1988), a group of petroleum engineers brought suit against the United States alleging that the termination of their employment with a Libyan oil company by an executive order under IEEPA violated their constitutional protection against the taking of private property without the payment of just compensation. In upholding the president's order, the court dismissed the argument that the U.S. government may not act in an emergency situation in a way that causes economic harm to individuals or companies. The court stated,

> A new tariff, an embargo, a [military] draft, or a war may inevitably bring upon individuals great losses; may, indeed, render valuable property almost valueless. They may destroy the worth of a contract. But whoever supposed that, because of this, a tariff could not be changed . . . or an embargo be enacted, or a war be declared?

IEEPA and the 1979 Iranian Revolution. In the late 1970s, the government of Iran was overthrown during an Islamic Revolution. Islamic militants, angry at the United States for its support of the prior government, seized the U.S. embassy in Tehran and held the Americans there hostage for 444 days. At the time, Americans and American firms had considerable business interests and property in Iran. That property was also seized by the new government. In response, President Carter declared a national emergency under IEEPA and froze all Iranian property ($12 billion) held by U.S. banks, or by U.S. corporations, both here and abroad. All trade was halted and travel restricted between the two countries. In order to free the hostages, the United States and Iran signed the *Algiers Agreement,* by which the United States agreed to place the blocked Iranian money in trust accounts in British banks, pending the settlement of claims by the newly created U.S.–Iranian Claims Tribunal (at The Hague, Netherlands). Chas. T. Main International, Inc., a U.S. engineering firm that had been doing work on an Iranian hydroelectric power plant, brought a legal action of its own in a U.S. court against Iran seeking compensation for its lost property, and a declaration that the *Algiers Agreement* exceeded the president's powers under the Constitution. In *Chas. T. Main International, Inc. v. Khuzestan Water & Power Authority*, 651 F.2d 800 (1st Cir. 1981), the Court of Appeals ruled that the president had the authority to enter an agreement for the settlement of all claims between U.S. firms and Iran, and that such agreement prevailed over all other attempts by Americans to regain their property in courts of law. In ruling that the president had the constitutional power to create the tribunal to settle international claims, the court stated: "This case well illustrates the imperative need to preserve a presidential flexibility sufficient to diffuse an international crisis, in order to prevent the crisis from escalating or even leading to war." Chas. T. Main had to proceed with its claim at

The Hague, and it ultimately won an award against Iran there.

The Case of the "American Taliban." In 1999, President Clinton declared a national emergency to deal with the threat posed by the *al Qaeda* terrorist organization and by the *Taliban* (meaning "student of Islam") government of Afghanistan where *al Qaeda* training camps were located. The executive order prohibited the making or receiving of any contribution of funds, goods, or services to or for the benefit of the *Taliban*. The state of emergency was continued by President Bush and was in effect until after the successful U.S. military action in Afghanistan. During the war in Afghanistan, an American citizen by the name of John Walker Lindh was captured when it was discovered that he had undergone terrorist training in Pakistan and was fighting with the *Taliban*. He was charged in the United States with conspiracy to murder Americans, providing material support to foreign terrorist organizations, and with violating IEEPA. The following case illustrates one of the most recent legal attacks on the *International Emergency Economic Powers Act*.

United States v. Lindh
212 F.Supp.2d 541 (2002)
United States District Court (E.D.Va.)

BACKGROUND AND FACTS
Beginning in 1995, both Presidents Clinton and Bush issued several executive orders under the *International Emergency Economic Powers Act* (IEEPA) declaring a national emergency in dealing with terrorism. Pursuant to those orders, the Department of Treasury issued regulations prohibiting transactions with terrorist groups or providing services to them. *Al Qaeda* was named as a terrorist organization, along with the *Taliban* government of Afghanistan that supported them. Shortly after September 11, 2001, the United States invaded Afghanistan to locate and destroy *al Qaeda* terrorist training camps and to overthrow the *Taliban* government. During the war, it was discovered that the defendant was an American citizen fighting for the *Taliban*. He had undergone terrorist training in Pakistan and had allegedly met

Osama bin Laden. He was charged in the United States under criminal statutes with conspiracy to murder Americans and with providing material support to foreign terrorist organizations in violation of the president's IEEPA orders. Lindh argued that IEEPA applied only to commercial transactions with terrorist groups and not to his conduct.

ELLIS, District Judge

* * *

Lindh argues that Counts Six through Nine of the Indictment should be dismissed because they charge violations of regulations that were promulgated in excess of the statutory authority provided by IEEPA.

continued

continued

Specifically, these four counts charge Lindh with "Contributing Services to *al Qaeda*, Supplying Services to the Taliban," and conspiracy to do each of these. . . . Lindh argues that IEEPA cannot be construed to authorize promulgation of any regulations prohibiting his voluntary and noncommercial donation of services to the Taliban and *al Qaeda*.

The IEEPA is a relatively recent addition to this country's arsenal of sanctions to be used against hostile states and organizations in times of national emergency. For much of the twentieth century, this country's sanctions programs were governed by the Trading with the Enemy Act (hereafter "TWEA"), enacted in 1917. As amended in 1933, TWEA granted the President broad authority "to investigate, regulate, . . . prevent or prohibit . . . transactions" in times of war or declared national emergencies. *See Dames & Moore v. Regan*, 453 U.S. 654, 672, 101 S.Ct. 2972, 69 L.Ed.2d 918 (1981). Congress changed this statutory scheme in 1977 to limit TWEA's application to periods of declared wars, but created IEEPA to provide the President similar authority for use during other times of national emergency. . . .

Despite the breadth of the Regulations and Executive Orders issued pursuant to IEEPA, Lindh asserts that IEEPA does nothing more than permit the President to freeze the assets of a foreign state or foreign national and prohibit certain international financial transactions during times of a declared national emergency. Lindh argues, moreover, that neither the plain meaning of IEEPA, nor its legislative history, indicate that it provides a basis for the wide-ranging regulations here in issue. Thus, Lindh argues, the Regulations he is charged with violating exceed IEEPA's statutory grant of power.

The straightforward question presented, therefore, is whether the Regulations are within the scope of IEEPA. As this is a question of statutory construction, analysis must begin "as always with the language of the statute."

The IEEPA language in issue is as follows:

[T]he President may, under such regulations as he may prescribe, by means of instructions, licenses, or otherwise—
(A) investigate, regulate, or prohibit—
   (i) any transactions in foreign exchange,
   (ii) transfers of credit or payments between, by, through or to any banking institution, to the extent that such transfers or payments involve any interest of any foreign country or a national thereof,
   (iii) the importing or exporting of currency or securities; and
(B) investigate, regulate, direct and compel, nullify, void, prevent or prohibit, any acquisition, holding, withholding, use, transfer, withdrawal, transportation, importation or exportation of, or dealing in, or exercising any right, power, or privilege with respect to, or transactions involving, any property in which any foreign country or a national thereof has any interest; by any person, or with respect to any property, subject to the jurisdiction of the United States. 50 U.S.C. § 1702.

This language manifestly sweeps broadly, as courts have consistently recognized in according deference to various sanctions programs under IEEPA and TWEA (see, . . . *United States v. McKeeve*, 131 F.3d 1, 10 (1st Cir. 1997) ("IEEPA codifies Congress's intent to confer broad and flexible power upon the President to impose and enforce economic sanctions against nations that the President deems a threat to national security interests.") See also *United States v. Curtiss-Wright Export Corp.*, 299 U.S. 304, 320, 57 S.Ct. 216, 81 L.Ed. 255 (1936) (noting that generally the President's actions are entitled to greater deference when acting in the fields of foreign affairs or national security). This sweeping language provides ample authority for the issuance of the Regulations and also easily reaches Lindh's alleged conduct. This conduct—which includes, for example, attending Taliban and *al Qaeda* training camps, using and transporting Taliban and *al Qaeda* weapons and ammunition, and using Taliban and *al Qaeda* transportation and residence facilities—plainly involves "use" of Taliban and *al Qaeda* "property." And, given the breadth of the common dictionary meanings of "use," "dealing," "transactions" and "property," there is similarly no doubt that Lindh's provision of combatant services to the Taliban and *al Qaeda* also falls within the IEEPA and the Regulations.

* * *

Lindh seeks to avoid the result reached here by arguing that IEEPA concerns only commercial or economic conduct. In support, he cites the statute's title and the fact that many cases involving IEEPA and TWEA address solely economic or commercial activity. This argument, while not implausible, is again contradicted by the statute's sweeping broad language. As

continued

continued

noted, the plain dictionary meanings of statutory terms like "transaction," "dealing," "use," and "property" do not limit their use to commercial transactions; these terms are sufficiently broad to cover the conduct alleged here, including the donations of combatant services.

Decision. The provisions in the indictment alleging violations of IEEPA are valid. The plain language of IEEPA indicates congressional intent to grant broad powers to the president in times of a declared national emergency. The regulations issued pursuant to IEEPA apply to the rendering of combatant services to the terrorist organizations concerned.

Comment. In 2002, John Walker Lindh, known as the "American Taliban," pled guilty to the charges and was sentenced to 20 years in prison.

U.S. Sanctions on Trade with Cuba

Prior to 1959, the United States had strong ties to Cuba, an island nation just ninety miles off the coast of Florida. Many Americans had business investments there, and the country was a mecca for tourists from around the world. In 1952, an army general seized power in a military *coup d'etat*. Political unrest fermented, culminating with the 1959 overthrow of the government by Fidel Castro's Marxist guerrilla army. Castro set up a communist government, with strong ties to the Soviet Union. Cuba nationalized the assets of American citizens and U.S. firms (including farms, factories, hotels, bank accounts, real estate, etc.) without compensation. Castro began an effort to "export communism" to other countries in Latin America and he played center stage during the Cold War between the United States and the Soviet Union. So began forty years of anger between the United States and Cuba, beginning with President Kennedy's failed Bay of Pigs invasion in 1963 and the Cuban Missile Crisis.

In 1963, the United States passed the *Cuban Assets Control Regulations,* under the authority of the *Trading with the Enemy Act.* The purpose of the law was to isolate Cuba economically and politically. It banned all trade and financial transactions between Cuba and the United States, and froze all U.S.-held assets of the Cuban government and of private Cuban citizens. It also prohibited almost all travel to Cuba by U.S. citizens (certain researchers, student groups, journalists, athletes, and those traveling to see immediate family members in humanitarian need excepted).

The *Helms–Burton Act.* After the fall of the Soviet Union in the early 1990s, the U.S. Congress wanted to pressure Cuba for democratic change. This led to the passage of the *Cuban Liberty and Democratic Solidarity Act,* commonly called the *Helms–Burton Act,* named after its key sponsors. The law toughened the Cuban sanctions. It also authorized U.S. citizens with claims to confiscated property in Cuba to file private lawsuits in U.S. courts against any person, including a citizen of a foreign country, that "traffics" (engaging in any commercial activity) in that property. The most controversial part of the law requires the United States to deny an entry visa to any foreign citizen who traffics in property that was confiscated by Cuba after 1959. This would include many Mexican, Canadian, and European businesspeople who do business in Cuba.

The passage of *Helms–Burton* caused a worldwide protest, primarily from Mexico, Canada, and the European Union, who argued that *Helms–Burton* violated international law. A protest was filed with the World Trade Organization by the European Union, but was suspended when the Clinton Administration gave assurances that the visa restrictions of *Helms–Burton* would not be enforced against citizens of third countries. *Helms–Burton* calls for sanctions on Cuba to end once Cuba has a democratically elected government, abides by human rights conventions, opens its prisons to international inspection, returns Cuban citizenship to Cuban exiles living in the United States, and makes progress in returning expropriated property to its rightful owners. In 2000, for the first time in four decades, the U.S. government legalized some food and medicine sales to Cuba.

The Effectiveness of Trade Sanctions.   Many people have condemned the Cuban trade sanctions for their harshness. Even the Vatican protested *Helms–Burton,* claiming that it increased the economic suffering of the Cuban people. Many trade groups have argued against the law because they believe that economic engagement promotes freedom in totalitarian countries. United States firms wishing to do business in Cuba also seek an end to U.S. sanctions. Indeed, 157 member nations of the UN called on the United States to end the sanctions. Ironically, surveys of American public opinion show that the vast majority of Americans favor ending sanctions as well, and recognizing the government of Fidel Castro. Forty years of communism have left the island nation an economic ruin. But a lack of basic necessities and few consumer goods has not resulted in a democratic uprising. Moreover, a study by the U.S. International Trade Commission released in 2001 revealed that the U.S. embargo has had only a minimal impact on Cuba, noting that Castro tends to make trade and investment decisions based on ideology and political factors, not on economic considerations (see, USITC Publication 3398, February 2001). Perhaps the argument against modern-day Cuban sanctions was expressed best by Arthur Schlesinger Jr., noted U.S. historian and close advisor to President Kennedy, when he stated, "A better policy . . . would be to repeal *Helms–Burton,* lift the embargo and drown the [Castro] regime in American tourists, investments, and consumer goods." *Letter to the Editor, New York Times,* February 21, 1997, cited in *Havana Club Holding v. Galleon,* 961 F. Supp. 498 (S.D.N.Y. 1997).

---

http://www.usaengage.org

For an opposing view of U.S. trade sanctions, see USAEN-GAGE, a coalition of American businesses committed to sustained U.S. involvement in world affairs and economic engagement with foreign countries.

FEDERAL–STATE RELATIONS

Thus far our discussion has focused on the relation between the executive and legislative branches of the federal government. But the notion of "federalism" also implies that the United States has two levels of government—state and federal. The Constitution has several provisions that touch upon the relations between the state and federal governments and that determine a state's authority to regulate international (as well as interstate) trade. These include the *Supremacy Clause,* the *Import–Export Clause,* and the *Commerce Clause.*

The Supremacy Clause

When a law or regulation of the federal government directly conflicts with those of the state (or local) government, the federal law will still generally prevail when Congress either expresses the intention that the federal law shall prevail or when it is implied in the legislation or from the circumstances. For example, when Congress enacts a comprehensive scheme of legislation, such as regulations governing commercial aviation, it includes an implication, known as *federal preemption,* that the federal rule will prevail over an inconsistent state rule. The inconsistent state law will be void to the extent of the conflict.

Burma, Human Rights, and Federal Preemption

Burma (officially known as Myanmar) is a poor Asian country, about the size of Texas, with a population of about 48 million. It is bordered by China, India, and Thailand. Its major economic activities are agriculture, textiles and footwear, wood and wood products, and minerals. It benefits from a cheap labor supply and rich natural resources. It is a place of natural beauty, ancient culture, and Buddhist temples. English is widely spoken, and the government works heartily to attract more foreign tourists. But since 1962, a military dictatorship, or *junta,* has ruled Burma with an iron hand. Military rule and mismanagement have resulted in widespread poverty, with an annual per capita income of less than $300. There is state monopolization of leading industries, a bloated bureaucracy, arbitrary laws and regulations, corruption, an inadequate infrastructure, a shortage of foreign exchange, and disproportionately large military spending at the expense of social programs. For most Western firms, these problems outweigh Burma's business opportunities.

In 1990, the military junta permitted a free election for a parliament, with the National League for Democracy (NLD) winning more than 60 percent of the popular vote and 80 percent of the parliamentary seats. The junta, however, refused to relinquish power. Throughout the 1990s, the junta systematically violated human rights in Burma to suppress the pro-democracy movement and to thwart repeated efforts by the representatives elected in 1990 to convene. Antigovernment guerrilla groups continued to fight an insurrection war in parts of the country.

According to reports from the U.S. State Department, the military government uses violence, torture, intimidation, harassment, and fear to remain in power. The U.S. State Department's *Consular Information Sheet* shows how dangerous travel in Burma can be. For example, medical facilities are inadequate for even routine medical care. Common drugs, such as insulin, are often adulterated and unsafe to use. HIV/AIDS is rampant, as is malaria and hepatitis. The harshest prison sentences can be handed out, even to foreigners, for unknowingly violating Burmese law. It is illegal to own or possess an unregistered computer modem, and foreigners entering Burma with a computer are likely to have it confiscated. There are reports of tourists being harassed for taking pictures of men in uniform. U.S. citizens have been detained, arrested, tried, and deported for distributing pro-democracy literature and for visiting the homes and offices of Burmese pro-democracy leaders. With the increase of the drug trade in Burma, individuals carrying automatic weapons on the street are not uncommon. Crimes such as vehicle hijacking have been reported.

Economic Sanctions against Burma.   In 1996, the Commonwealth of Massachusetts, several major U.S. cities, and the U.S. Congress sought to ban U.S. business with Burma. Massachusetts passed a law prohibiting all Commonwealth agencies from buying goods or services from any person or firm that does business in Burma. By contrast, Congress took a different strategy. The federal statute banned all economic aid to the Burmese government except for humanitarian assistance, denied U.S. entry visas to Burmese citizens, and authorized the president to prohibit "new invest-

ment" in Burma if the Burmese government continues its violent suppression of democracy. The powers delegated to the president were specific, and also directed him to work diplomatically with other Asian countries to promote democracy in Burma. In 1997, the president issued an executive order and imposed further restrictions on new investment as Congress had directed (the president's order was based both on the 1996 statute and the *International Emergency Economic Powers Act* as well). Criminal penalties for violations range from up to ten years' imprisonment and up to $500,000 in corporate fines and up to $250,000 in individual fines.

In *Crosby v. National Foreign Trade Council,* 530 U.S. 363 (2000), the U.S. Supreme Court struck down the Massachusetts law on the basis of federal preemption. Justice Souter explained why the state law must give way to the federal statute. He noted the difference between the federal and state sanctions. The Massachusetts sanctions were immediate and direct in prohibiting business in Burma. The federal sanctions were more flexible, gradually allowing the president to increase pressure on Burma as needed and to do so through both specific legal and diplomatic means. The court reasoned, "If the Massachusetts law is enforceable the President has less to offer and less economic and diplomatic leverage as a consequence." Thus, the state law undermined the intended purpose and "natural effect" of the federal act. In preempting the state statute, the Court repeated that the federal government must "speak with one voice" in foreign policy matters and that Congress had left no room for states or municipalities to become involved.

---

http://www.state.gov/www/global/human_rights/ hrp_reports_mainhp.html

Annual Country Reports on Human Rights Practices submitted to Congress by the State Department detailing the status of internationally recognized human rights practices.

Many U.S. and European companies—Eddie Bauer, Levi Strauss, Liz Claiborne, Pepsi, and others—have stopped doing business in Burma. Only time will tell whether this economic pressure, and international diplomatic efforts aided by U.S. sanctions, will help to bring democracy to Burma.

The Import–Export Clause

The *Import–Export Clause* prohibits the federal government from taxing *exports* and prohibits the states from taxing either *imports* or *exports*. Historically, three reasons prompted such a provision. First, the federal government must be able to "speak with one voice" on matters related to foreign affairs. Second, import duties provided an important source of revenue for the federal government. And third, seaboard states were prevented from imposing burdensome regulations and taxes on "in transit" goods that were destined for inland states.

In *Michelin Tire Corp. v. Wages,* 423 U.S. 276 (1976), the U.S. Supreme Court addressed the issue of the state's power to tax imports. Michelin Tire Corporation imported tires manufactured in France and Nova Scotia, Canada, by Michelin Tires, Ltd. The company maintained a distribution warehouse in Georgia. The state assessed an *ad valorem* property tax against the tires being held in inventory. The tax was nondiscriminatory in nature in that the same tax was imposed upon all property similarly being held for resale in Georgia. The petitioner filed suit to have the collection of the tax enjoined as being unconstitutional under the Import–Export Clause. The Supreme Court ruled that the tax was permitted under the Import–Export Clause because the tax was imposed on all products for the purpose of supporting the cost of public services, the tax was nondiscriminatory, and did not interfere with the federal government's regulation of international commerce.

In 1978, the Supreme Court considered the constitutionality of a Washington state tax on stevedoring (the process of loading and unloading

international accents

Country Reports on Human Rights Practices—2002 [edited]

Burma (*Myanmar*)

Burma is ruled by a highly authoritarian military regime. In 1988 the armed forces brutally suppressed prodemocracy demonstrations, and a junta composed of military officers, called the State Peace and Development Council (SPDC), took control. Since then the SPDC has ruled by decree. The judiciary was not independent, and there was no effective rule of law.

The regime's human rights record remained extremely poor, and it continued to commit numerous serious abuses. Citizens did not have the right to change their government. In ethnic minority areas, security forces continued to commit extrajudicial killings and rape, forcibly relocated persons, used forced labor, and conscripted child soldiers. Disappearances continued, and members of the security forces tortured, beat, and otherwise abused prisoners and detainees. Citizens were subjected to arbitrary arrest without appeal. Arrests and detention for expression of dissenting political views occurred on numerous occasions. Prison conditions remained harsh and life threatening, although conditions improved in some prisons since the International Committee of the Red Cross (ICRC) was allowed access.

Disappearance.   Private citizens and political activists continued to "disappear" for periods ranging from several hours to several weeks or more, and many persons never reappeared. . . . Family members generally learned of their relatives' fates only if fellow prisoners survived and later reported information to the families.

Torture and Other Cruel, Inhuman, or Degrading Treatment or Punishment.   There are laws that prohibit torture; however, members of the security forces reportedly tortured, beat, and otherwise abused prisoners, detainees, and other citizens. They routinely

continued

continued

subjected detainees to harsh interrogation techniques designed to intimidate and disorient. There were reports in past years that prisoners were forced to squat or assume stressful, uncomfortable, or painful positions for lengthy periods. There continued to be many credible reports that security forces subjected citizens to harassment and physical abuse. The military forces routinely confiscated property, cash, and food, and used coercive and abusive recruitment methods to procure porters. . . . In the past, numerous farmers were held in custody for failing to meet local production requirements, although there were no such reports during the year.

Corruption among local government officials was widespread and included complicity in the trafficking of persons. Prison and labor camp conditions generally remained harsh and life threatening. In the prisons, food, clothing, and medical supplies reportedly were in very short supply. Bedding consisted of a single mat on the floor. Prisoners were forced to rely on their families, who were allowed to visit once every 2 weeks for 15 minutes per visit, for basic necessities. HIV/AIDS infection rates in prison reportedly were high due to communal use of single syringes for injections. During the year, the health of several political prisoners deteriorated, and at least three political prisoners died in custody.

Arbitrary Interference with Privacy, Family, Home, or Correspondence.   The Constitution does not provide for these rights, and authorities infringed on citizens' privacy rights. The law requires that any person who spends the night at a place other than his registered domicile inform the police in advance, and that any household that hosts a person not domiciled there to maintain and submit to the police a guest list.

Telephone service also was controlled tightly. Security personnel regularly screened private correspondence and telephone calls. The authorities generally continued to discourage citizens from subscribing directly to foreign publications. The regime continued to control closely the licensing and rationing of all electronic communication devices, which were monitored closely. Possession of an unregistered telephone, facsimile machine, or computer modem was punishable by imprisonment. In June 2000, Myanmar Posts and Telecommunications also announced that users of non-registered cordless telephones in the country would face up to 3 years' imprisonment . . .

The law does not permit private ownership of land. . . . A September report by a highly respected private citizen in Thailand estimated more than 2,500 villages have been destroyed or forcibly relocated by SPDC troops since 1996, displacing more than 600,000 citizens. The report estimated that more than 350,000 of these citizens were moved to SPDC-controlled "relocation centers," while the remainder lived in hiding.

Military units also routinely confiscated livestock, fuel, food supplies, fishponds, alcoholic drinks, vehicles, or money. Such abuses have become widespread since 1997, when the junta ordered its regional commanders to meet their logistical needs locally, rather than rely on the central authorities. In violation of humanitarian law, both army and insurgent units used forced conscription, including conscription of children.

The regime's intelligence services also monitored the movements of foreigners and questioned citizens about conversations with foreigners. Government employees generally were required to obtain advance permission before meeting with foreigners. Marriages between female citizens and foreigners officially were banned; however, the ban was not enforced.

Use of Excessive Force and Violations of Humanitarian Law in Internal Conflicts.   In May (women's groups) alleged the military used rape as a systematic weapon of war against the ethnic populations in Shan State. According to Human Rights Watch (HRW), SPDC troops conscripted children as young as the age of 11, especially orphans and street children.

Freedom of Speech and Press.   The law allows the regime to restrict freedom of speech and freedom of the press. . . . The regime continued to arrest, detain, convict, and imprison citizens for expressing political opinions critical of the junta. . . . Many prominent writers and journalists remained in prison for expressing their political views. Between April and June 2000, the junta arrested 11 persons for distributing anti-junta leaflets and allegedly planning attacks on government buildings. The regime owned and controlled all daily newspapers and domestic radio and television broadcasting facilities.

Freedom of Movement Within the Country, Foreign Travel, Emigration, and Repatriation.   The regime also carefully scrutinized prospective travel abroad. Such control facilitated rampant corruption, as many

continued

continued

applicants were forced to pay large bribes. Bribes for passports were sometimes as high as $3,000 (approximately 3.6 million kyat), the equivalent of more than 10 years' salary for the average citizen. The official board that reviews passport applications has denied passports on political grounds. All college graduates who obtained a passport (except for certain government employees) were required to pay a special fee to reimburse the regime for the cost of their education.

Children. The regime continued to allocate minimal resources to public education. Child prostitution and trafficking in girls for the purpose of prostitution—especially Shan girls who were sent or lured to Thailand—continued to be a major problem. The official age of enlistment in the ostensibly all-volunteer army is 18 years. However, the authorities reportedly rounded up orphans and street children in Rangoon and other cities and forced them into military service.

The Right to Organize and Bargain Collectively. Workers did not have the right to organize and bar-

gain collectively. According to the law, workers generally are prohibited from striking, although a small number of workers purportedly are accorded the right to strike. The last reported strike was in 2000, when an employer retracted a promise to pay piece rates. Subsequently 30 employees were detained, many for up to 3 months. All employees lost their jobs.

Trafficking in Persons. Trafficking of women and girls to Thailand and other countries, including China, India, Bangladesh, Taiwan, Pakistan, Malaysia, Singapore, Japan, and countries in the Middle East, for sexual exploitation, factory labor, and as household servants was a problem. While most observers believed that the number of these victims was at least several thousand per year, there were no reliable estimates of the total number.

Released by the Bureau of Democracy, Human Rights, and Labor U.S. Department of State, March 31, 2003. See full text at http://www.state.gov/g/drl/rls/hrrpt/2002/18237.htm

---

cargo on ships). Relying on the *Michelin* decision, the Court in *Department of Revenue of the State of Washington v. Association of Washington Stevedoring Cos.*, 435 U.S. 734 (1978) held that

> the tax does not restrain the ability of the federal government to conduct foreign policy. As a general business tax that applies to virtually all businesses in the state, it has not created any special tariff. The assessments in this case are only upon that business conducted entirely within Washington. No foreign business or vessel is taxed. . . . The tax merely compensates the state for services and protection extended by Washington to the stevedoring business.

In discussing interstate rivalries, the Court concluded that if it were to strike down the tax, then the state of Washington would be forced to subsidize the commerce of inland consumers. The tax was upheld under the Import–Export Clause.

The Commerce Clause

As discussed earlier in the chapter, the broadest power of the federal government to regulate business activity is derived from Article I, Section 8 of the Constitution. The *Commerce Clause* vests the

federal government with exclusive control over foreign commerce. Conversely, in what is known as the *negative implication doctrine,* state governments may not enact laws that impose a substantial burden on foreign commerce. Where there is an existing federal law governing some aspect of foreign commerce, a conflicting state statute may be invalid (preempted) under the Supremacy Clause.

The Commerce Clause and Multiple Taxation.

A state's authority to tax a business engaged in foreign commerce is also determined by whether or not the tax imposed results in *multiple taxation*. Multiple taxation occurs when the same service or property is subjected to the same or a similar tax by the governmental authorities of more than one nation.

The following case, *Japan Line, Ltd. v. County of Los Angeles,* discusses the problems of multiple taxation.

The purpose of restricting multiple taxation is to strengthen the government's ability to foster domestic participation in the international marketplace. By not prejudicing foreign companies operating in the United States, this country does not risk retaliation by foreign governments against U.S. firms operating abroad.

Japan Line, Ltd. v. County of Los Angeles
441 U.S. 434 (1979)
United States Supreme Court

BACKGROUND AND FACTS

The state of California imposed an *ad valorem* property tax upon cargo containers owned by Japanese companies and temporarily located in California ports. The containers were used exclusively for transporting goods in international commerce. They were based, registered, and subjected to property taxes in Japan. The containers spent, on average, only three weeks a year in California. Japan Lines contended that the tax was invalid because it subjected the containers to multiple taxation in Japan and the United States.

The California Supreme Court upheld the statute and the ship owners appealed.

JUSTICE BLACKMUN

This case presents the question whether a state, consistently with the Commerce Clause of the Constitution, may impose a nondiscriminatory *ad valorem* property tax on foreign-owned instrumentalities (cargo containers) of international commerce. . . .

In order to prevent multiple taxation of commerce, this Court has required that taxes be apportioned among taxing jurisdictions, so that no instrumentality of commerce is subjected to more than one tax on its full value. The corollary of the apportionment principle, of course, is that no jurisdiction may tax the instrumentality in full. "The rule which permits taxation by two or more states on an apportionment basis precludes taxation of all of the property by the state of the domicile. . . . Otherwise there would be multiple taxation of interstate operations." The basis for this Court's approval of apportioned property taxation, in other words, has been its ability to enforce full apportionment by all potential taxing bodies.

Yet neither this Court nor this Nation can ensure full apportionment when one of the taxing entities is a foreign sovereign. If an instrumentality of commerce is domiciled abroad, the country of domicile may have the right, consistently with the custom of nations, to impose a tax on its full value. If a state should seek to tax the same instrumentality on an apportioned basis, multiple taxation inevitably results. Hence, whereas the fact of apportionment in interstate commerce means that "multiple burdens" logically cannot occur, the same conclusion, as to

foreign commerce, logically cannot be drawn. Due to the absence of an authoritative tribunal capable of ensuring that the aggregation of taxes is computed on no more than one full value, a state tax, even though "fairly apportioned" to reflect an instrumentality's presence within the state, may subject foreign commerce "to the risk of a double tax burden to which [domestic] commerce is not exposed, and which the commerce clause forbids."

Second, a state tax on the instrumentalities of foreign commerce may impair federal uniformity in an area where federal uniformity is essential. Foreign commerce is preeminently a matter of national concern. "In international relations and with respect to foreign intercourse and trade the people of the United States act through a single government with unified and adequate national power." *Board of Trustees v. United States.* . . .

A state tax on instrumentalities of foreign commerce may frustrate the achievement of federal uniformity in several ways. If the State imposes an apportioned tax, international disputes over reconciling apportionment formulae may arise. If a novel state tax creates an asymmetry in the international tax structure, foreign nations disadvantaged by the levy may retaliate against American-owned instrumentalities present in their jurisdictions. Such retaliation of necessity would be directed at American transportation equipment in general, not just that of the taxing state, so that the Nation as a whole would suffer. . . .

It is stipulated that American-owned containers are not taxed in Japan. California's tax thus creates an asymmetry in international maritime taxation operating to Japan's disadvantage. The risk of retaliation by Japan, under these circumstances, is acute, and such retaliation of necessity would be felt by the Nation as a whole. . . .

We hold the tax, as applied, unconstitutional under the Commerce Clause.

Decision. The Supreme Court reversed, holding that the tax was unconstitutional. The Court ruled that an *ad valorem* property tax applied to cargo containers used exclusively in foreign commerce violates the Commerce Clause because it results in multiple taxation of instrumentalities of foreign commerce.

State Income Taxation of Multinational Corporations. The issue of multiple taxation was recently considered in *Barclays Bank PLC v. Franchise Tax Board of California,* 114 S.Ct. 2268 (1994). This important case upheld the constitutionality of California's "unitary" method of assessing income tax on companies in California that are subsidiaries of foreign multinational corporations.

Barclays Bank of California (Barcal), a California banking institution, was a subsidiary of the Barclays Group, a multinational banking enterprise based in the United Kingdom. The Barclays Group included more than 220 corporations doing business in sixty nations. In 1977, Barcal reported taxable income only from its own operations within California. California claimed that Barcal was a member of a multinational "unitary" business, and that the *entire worldwide income* of the unitary business—the income of all of the subsidiaries within the Barclays Group operating anywhere in the world—was taxable in California. Under the unitary method, taxes were assessed on the percentage of worldwide income equal to the average of the proportions of worldwide payroll, property, and sales located in California. Thus, if a multinational corporation had 8 percent of its payroll, 3 percent of its inventory and other property, and 4 percent of its sales in California, the state imposed its tax on 5 percent of the multinational's total income. (The weight given to each category can vary under different formulas.) California used the unitary method because it believed that under traditional methods of tax accounting, conglomerates had the ability to manipulate transactions between affiliated companies so as to shift income to low-tax jurisdictions (although to guard against such manipulation, transactions between affiliated corporations are generally scrutinized to ensure that they are reported on an "arm's length" basis). Barclays claimed that California's tax resulted in multiple taxation, in violation of the Commerce Clause.

Citing its previous decisions, the U.S. Supreme Court upheld the California tax because seven requirements were met: (1) the tax applied to an activity with a substantial connection to California; (2) the tax was "fairly apportioned"; (3) the tax did not discriminate against interstate commerce; (4) the tax was fairly related to the services provided by the state; (5) the tax did not result in

multiple taxation; (6) the tax did not impair the federal government's ability to "speak with one voice when regulating commercial relations with foreign governments"; and (7) compliance with the formula was not so impossible as to deprive the corporation of its due process of law.

Even before this case went to court, foreign corporations doing business in California had objected strongly to the unitary tax. Foreign governments also objected, claiming it violated international law. In response to this outcry, the state of California in 1986 dropped its unitary tax requirement and substituted a *water's edge election* allowing corporations the option of being taxed only on their California income—up to the "water's edge." Nevertheless, the case is important because it stands for the principle that unitary taxation is constitutional. It is still used in a few states.

State Restrictions on Exports. The Commerce Clause prohibits state governments from restricting, taxing, or otherwise imposing undue burdens on exports. In *South-Central Timber Development, Inc. v. Wunnicke,* 467 U.S. 82 (1984), the Supreme Court considered an Alaska regulation that required that all timber taken from state lands be processed within the state prior to being exported. South-Central was an Alaskan company engaged in purchasing timber and shipping logs overseas. It filed suit claiming that the regulation violated the negative implications of the Commerce Clause. Alaska argued that the Commerce Clause did not apply because the state was acting as a "market-participant" (a vendor of lumber), not as a regulator. The Court agreed with South-Central. The Court concluded,

> The limit of the market-participant doctrine must be that it allows a State to impose burdens on commerce within the market in which it is a participant, but allows it to go no further. The State may not impose conditions, whether by statute, regulation, or contract, that have a substantial regulatory effect outside of that particular market. . . . [A]lthough the state may be a participant in the timber market, it is using its leverage in that market to exert a regulatory effect in the processing market, in which it is not a participant.

In addressing the Commerce Clause question directly, the Court also noted, "In light of the substantial attention given by Congress to the subject of export restrictions on unprocessed timber, it would be peculiarly inappropriate to permit state regulation of the subject."

State Restrictions on Imports. State government restrictions on imports are severely limited. User fees for the use of port facilities are generally permitted. Also, states may impose restrictions directly related to the protection of the public health and safety. For example, Florida could limit, restrict, or ban the import of fruits or vegetables suspected of carrying a disease that could contaminate the local crop. In one case, however, a labeling and licensing statute was invalidated by the courts even though its alleged purpose was the protection of the public health and safety. Tennessee had enacted a statute calling for the licensing of all persons who deal in foreign meat products in the state and the labeling of all foreign meats sold in the state as being of foreign origin. The court, in *Tupman Thurlow Co. v. Moss*, 252 F. Supp 641 (M.D. Tenn. 1961), concluded that "The regulation here involved cannot fairly be construed as a consumer protection measure, and if it should be, it would be interdicted by the Commerce Clause because it unreasonably discriminates against foreign products in favor of products of domestic origin."

FEDERAL AGENCIES AFFECTING TRADE

Thus far, this chapter has discussed the constitutional role of government in regulating international trade. The remainder of the chapter briefly discusses the various agencies and executive branch departments of government that carry out the functions of government on a daily basis. U.S. government agencies that provide technical and financial assistance for exporters, such as the Small Business Administration, the Export–Import Bank, the Overseas Private Investment Corporation, the Commodity Credit Corporation, the Agency for International Development, the Trade and Development Program, the U.S. Department of Agriculture, and others are discussed elsewhere in the text. The role of the Department of Treasury was, in part, addressed earlier in this chapter. The following agencies are primarily concerned with the establishment of trade policy and the handling of trade disputes.

United States Department of Commerce

The U.S. Department of Commerce has broad authority over many international trade issues. The department's functions include fostering trade and promoting exports of U.S. goods and services (trade promotion), investigating and resolving complaints by U.S. firms that foreign governments are unfairly blocking access to foreign markets (market access), administering U.S. unfair import laws (import administration), issuing export licenses for certain products, developing U.S. international trade statistical information, and many other functions. The *International Trade Administration* (ITA), housed within the department, performs many of the trade promotion, market access, and import administration functions. Within the ITA, the *U.S. Commercial Service* maintains a network of offices at home and abroad to assist U.S. firms in developing export opportunities. The *U.S. Bureau of Industry and Security* regulates the export of sensitive goods and technologies for national security, enforces the export control laws, and assists U.S. industry in complying with international arms control agreements.

United States Department of Homeland Security

The *Department of Homeland Security* was created as an executive department of government in 2003. Its creation was part of the largest reorganization of the American government in over a half-century. The new department brought together many existing agencies of government with a common responsibility for protecting the American homeland. The department is organized into four directorates: Border and Transportation Security, Emergency Preparedness and Response, Science and Technology, and Information Analysis and Infrastructure Protection. Its primary mission is to prevent terrorist attacks within the United States.

Border and Transportation Security. This directorate brings together the major border security and transportation security functions of the department. This includes the following agencies relevant to this book: the *Bureau of Customs and Border Protection,* the *Bureau of Citizenship and Immigration Services,* and the *Transportation Security Administration,* the *Secret Service,* and the

U.S. Coast Guard. Many of the functions of these agencies were previously handled by the Treasury Department, the Justice Department, and the Transportation Department. The agency with the greatest impact on our reading is the *Bureau of Customs and Border Protection* (CBP*)*. This agency brings together many functions of the former U.S. Customs, the Border Patrol, and the Immigration and Nationality Service. Its functions include preventing terrorists from entering the United States; apprehending individuals attempting to enter the United States illegally; stemming the flow of illegal drugs and other contraband; protecting our agricultural and economic interests from imported pests and diseases; preventing the illegal import of goods in violation of U.S. copyright, patent, and trademark laws; enforcing U.S. import and export laws; and collecting import duties.

The Impact of Homeland Security on American Importers and Exporters.

In a free society, the protection of the American homeland from possible terrorist attack, or from the smuggling of terrorist weapons, requires a balance between maintaining public security and the needs of American companies to move goods swiftly across national borders. Consider that CBP estimates that it takes a team of four inspectors about four hours to search one container. Inspecting every shipment arriving by truck or aircraft, and each of the over 6 million ocean containers arriving annually at U.S. ports, would be difficult and cause extensive delays at the border. So CBP is implementing several projects to enhance security while speeding delivery of goods. These include advance notice of cargo shipments bound to U.S. ports (the *24-hour rule*), foreign inspections of high-risk containers (*Container Security Initiative*), a CBP program for reviewing security measures in a U.S. importer's foreign supply-chain security (C-TPAT), and a special cooperative arrangement between the United States and Canada for the FAST clearance of cross-border trade (*Free and Secure Trade*). Clearly, the war on terrorism will have a tremendous effect in the years to come not only on the movement of goods in international trade, but on the entire world of international business.

United States Trade Representative

The *United States Trade Representative* (USTR) is a cabinet-level post reporting directly to the president. The USTR carries on all bilateral and multilateral trade negotiations on behalf of the United States, serves as the principal adviser on trade matters to the president, represents the United States at all WTO meetings, coordinates the trade agreements program, and coordinates all U.S. trade policies, including those related to agricultural, textile, and commodity trade and unfair trade practices. Much of the responsibility for trade matters once held by the Department of State has been transferred to the USTR.

International Trade Commission

The *International Trade Commission* (ITC), formerly called the U.S. Tariff Commission, is an independent agency of government created by Congress in 1916. The ITC maintains a highly trained cadre of professional economists and researchers who conduct investigations and prepare extensive reports on matters related to international economics and trade for Congress and the president. The role of the ITC (along with that of the International Trade Administration) in investigating unfair trade practices will be thoroughly discussed in future chapters. Because of the highly political nature of many of the investigations related to the impact of imported goods on U.S. domestic industry, the ITC is a bipartisan agency. The members of the commission are appointed by the president from both political parties and subject to Senate confirmation.

The U.S. Court of International Trade

The *Court of International Trade* (CIT) consists of nine judges who hear cases arising from the trade or tariff laws of the United States. Appeals from the U.S. Customs Service regarding duties assessed on imported goods and appeals from decisions of the ITC in unfair import cases are heard by the CIT. Appeals from the CIT go to the Court of

Appeals for the Federal Circuit and, where appropriate, to the U.S. Supreme Court.

The court has exclusive jurisdiction over all civil actions commenced against the United States involving (1) revenue from imports or tonnage; (2) tariffs, duties, fees, or other taxes on importation of merchandise for reasons other than the raising of revenue; (3) embargoes or other quantitative restriction of the importation of merchandise for reasons other than the protection of the public health or safety; and (4) administration or enforcement of the customs laws. The court is located in New York City.

> **http://www.uscit.gov**
> The home page of the U.S. Court of International Trade.

Chapter Summary

Although the roles of the legislative and executive branches of government are set forth in the Constitution, considerable debate in recent years has surrounded the power of the president in regulating foreign commerce and foreign affairs. The president's power in these areas is derived from the treaty power, the inherent power under Article II, and the power delegated by Congress.

Trade policies are implemented through treaties or executive agreements. Treaties are negotiated and made by the president with the advice and consent of the Senate. Many treaties, such as FCN treaties, are self-executing. They require no act of the legislature to become effective, binding law.

Sole-executive agreements relating to international affairs are valid if undertaken pursuant to the president's inherent power. Congressional–executive agreements are binding upon approval of both houses. Most major trade agreements today, such as those creating free trade areas, are negotiated under fast-track authority. Congress has set trade policies for the United States in the *Tariff Act of 1930* and in subsequent acts that authorize the president to enter into trade agreements with foreign countries to reduce tariffs on imports. These agreements have helped achieve today's level of global prosperity.

The role of the states in regulating trade is limited. They may not tax imports or otherwise obstruct international commerce. States may levy reasonable fees to cover the cost of inspecting imports in the interest of the public health and safety.

Questions and Case Problems

---

1. North Carolina, South Carolina, and Georgia produce a large amount of cotton each year. In an effort to protect their farmers from overseas competition, the governors of these three states met and agreed on a uniform "inspection fee" to be imposed on all foreign cotton coming into their states through their ports. They vowed to do their best to get their state legislatures to adopt this fee as law. Would any problem arise with such a fee?

2. From what four sources does the president draw the power to regulate foreign commerce or international trade? Explain each source.

3. The U.S. State Department negotiated directly with European and Japanese steel producers to limit their exports to the United States. This was done as a result of threats by the president to set import quotas. No foreign government was party to the agreement. Although the president had been granted express authority to limit imports by an act of Congress, this act required that he either hold public hearings through the Tariff Commission about setting import quotas or deal directly with foreign governments about limiting imports. The Consumers Union of U.S., Inc., felt that when Congress gave the president this express power, it preempted any other action by the president. They brought an action against the secretary of state to have the president's agreement with private steel producers in Europe and Japan declared illegal. What should be the result of such an action? *Consumers Union of U.S., Inc. v. Kissinger,* 506 F.2d 136 (D.C. Cir. 1974).

4. The *Trade Expansion Act of 1962* as amended by the *Trade Act of 1974* stated that if the secretary of the treasury finds that an "article is being imported into the United States in such quantities or under such circumstances as to threaten to impair the national security," the president is authorized to "take such action . . . as he deems necessary to adjust the imports of the article . . . so that [it] will not threaten to impair the national security." Does this grant of

power to the president by Congress allow the president to establish quotas? If importation of foreign oil were determined to be "a threat to national security," could the president implement a $3–4 per barrel license fee? See *Federal Energy Administration v. Algonquin SNG, Inc.,* 426 U.S. 548 (1976).

5. What is a treaty? Where does the treaty power of the United States come from? What is the difference between a self-executing treaty and a non-self-executing treaty? How does the treaty approval process differ from the approval process for congressional–executive agreements?

6. Future U.S. trade negotiations will focus both on the U.S. trade relationships with the world through the World Trade Organization, as well as special trade relationships with countries in Latin America. Some leaders of Congress want to use trade negotiations to push Latin American countries to protect worker's rights, conserve tropical forests, and protect the environment. Such issues may dominate U.S. trade relations for most of this decade. As of today, what is the status of the president's fast-track authority? What has Congress required of the president in leading current or future U.S. trade negotiations? To what extent has Congress included these "side-issues," such as labor rights or the environment? Research the topic and discuss the pros and cons of linking trade relations to these and other social and political "side-issues."

7. During the 1940s, the U.S. government instituted a price support system for domestic potatoes. In order to protect the potato market from imported Canadian potatoes, the U.S. secretary of state entered into an executive agreement with the Canadian ambassador in which they agreed that Canada would permit the export of potatoes into the United States only if they were to be used for seed and not for food. The agreement was not submitted to or approved by Congress. The Agricultural Act of 1948 permitted the president to restrict potato imports by requesting an investigation by the Tariff Commission and considering its recommendations. Guy W. Capps, Inc., the importer, assured the Canadian exporter that the potatoes were destined for planting, but while they were in transit, they were sold to A&P grocery stores for resale. The United States brought suit against Guy Capps for damages. The court entered judgment for Guy Capps and the government appealed. Was the U.S.–Canadian agreement valid under the U.S. Constitution? Was the president acting under his inherent constitutional authority, power delegated from Congress, or neither? What did Congress say the President could do to restrict agricultural imports? *See United States v. Guy W. Capps, Inc.* 204 F.2d 655 (4th Cir. 1953).

8. Xerox manufactured parts for copy machines in the United States that were shipped to Mexico for assembly. The copiers were designed for sale exclusively in Latin America. All printing on the machines was in Spanish or Portuguese. The copiers operated on a 50-cycle electric current unavailable in the United States. The copiers had been transported by a customs bonded warehouse in Houston, Texas, where they were stored pending their sale to Xerox affiliates in Latin America. The copiers had previously been stored in Panama. Under federal law, goods stored in a customs bonded warehouse are under the supervision of the U.S. Customs Service. Goods may be brought into a warehouse without the payment of import duties and stored for up to five years. At any time they may be reexported duty-free or withdrawn for domestic sale upon the payment of the duty. Harris County and the city of Houston assessed a nondiscriminatory *ad valorem* personal property tax on the copiers. Xerox claims that the local tax is preempted by the federal legislation. How did the Court hold? Does it make any difference whether the goods are needed for domestic use or intended for re-export? See *Xerox Corporation v. County of Harris, Texas,* 459 U.S. 145, 103 S. Ct. 523 (1982).

9. The state of Tennessee passed legislation requiring that any person selling or offering for sale in the state of Tennessee any meats that are the products of any foreign country shall so identify such product by labeling it "This meat is of foreign origin." The state law did not require a higher standard of purity and sanitation than that required by the U.S. Department of Agriculture. A New York corporation selling imported meats to customers in Tennessee challenged this state statute in U.S. District Court. The corporation's sales of imported meat to customers in Tennessee was one-half its volume prior to enactment of the statute. What do you think the legal basis was for this challenge to the Tennessee law? What do you think Tennessee's legal argument was for passing the law? What do you think the court decided? See *Tupman Thurlow Co. v. Moss,* 252 F. Supp. 641 (M.D. Tenn. 1966).

10. Name the federal agencies that deal with the day-to-day functions of U.S. trade.

11. Both the *North American Free Trade Agreement* (NAFTA) and the 1994 *Uruguay Round* GATT Agreement were negotiated according to fast-track authority from Congress. They were passed by slim margins, and only after much heated debate. Research the history of fast-track authority stemming from the *Trade Reform Act of 1974* through today. Then examine the political and economic issues that were the focus of this debate.

Managerial Implications

Your firm, Day-O Shoes, Inc., manufactures deck shoes in the Caribbean island country of Haiti. Haiti is the poorest nation in the Western Hemisphere. Your plant there employs more than four hundred workers, and has always considered itself a good citizen of both Haiti and the United States. Most of the shoes are imported for sale into the United States, where you maintain a 30 percent share of a competitive market. In 1991, the freely elected president of Haiti is removed from office by military officers who install a dictator of their choice. In response, the president of the United States exercises authority under the *International Economic Emergency Powers Act* and issues an executive order imposing a complete embargo on trade with Haiti. The Treasury Department's Office of Foreign Assets Control is charged with enforcing the embargo. Facing the impending embargo, your firm shuts down its production operations there, one week prior to the date set for the embargo. Feeling some obligation to the unemployed workers, your company's chief executive ships over ten tons of food and clothing to the people who have lost their jobs.

Believing that the United States is serious about the embargo, and that it would remain in effect until the rightful president was returned to Haiti, your firm ships its U.S.-made raw materials, such as rubber soles and leather uppers, from Haiti to your other factory in Costa Rica. But you soon discover, much to your surprise, that your competitors are continuing to produce and stockpile their shoes in Haiti in the belief that the embargo would soon be lifted. Three months after you had ceased

operations, the U.S. government decides to lift the embargo because it has resulted in the loss of 50,000 Haitian jobs. With no inventory of finished shoes, and your raw materials enroute to Costa Rica, your firm is unable to fill existing orders. Your competitors are ready, however, to ship their shoes from Haiti immediately.

1. Evaluate the course of action taken by Day-O Shoes. How did Day-O Shoes balance its responsibility under U.S. law to comply with the embargo with its need to remain competitive in the industry? What could it have done differently? Evaluate the ethics of Day-O's actions.
2. Was Day-O Shoes required to stop producing in Haiti? Were its competitors violating U.S. law by continuing to produce and stockpile their inventories? Were they violating any moral code, or even the "spirit of the law" by continuing to produce there? Evaluate the risks taken by the competitors in continuing their operations in Haiti during the embargo.
3. The embargo was intended to put economic pressure on Haiti so as to encourage political reform. Is the U.S. government saying that the embargo worked too well? Do you think that the embargo was lifted because of its impact on the Haitian workers or on U.S. firms doing business there? Critics argue that the U.S. government's attempts to use trade policy as a means of conducting foreign policy lead to confusion and uncertainty, and are counterproductive. Evaluate this argument.

CHAPTER 9

GATT LAW AND THE WORLD TRADE ORGANIZATION: BASIC PRINCIPLES

The last chapter discussed how the responsibility for formulating and implementing the trade policies of the United States is shared between the legislative and executive branches of government, but the United States is only one nation in the world community. Every nation establishes its own trade policies and has its own best national interests at heart when dealing with other nations. Nowhere is this clearer than in the post-World War I policies of isolationism and protectionism. The Great Depression of the 1930s showed what can happen when nations try to isolate themselves economically and politically from the world solely for their own economic interests.

Yet from the economic and industrial ruin of the Great Depression and World War II came a renewed belief in free trade and a new international approach to dealing with common economic problems. Nations learned that their mutual interests could be best served if they could find a way to encourage free trade in goods, unfettered by high tariffs and other barriers, by enacting "liberalized" trade rules. However, they first needed to reach an agreement on trade issues of common concern, and then to find a way to resolve their disputes when they occurred.

Today's global framework for liberalizing trade rules and reducing barriers to the free movement of goods was established shortly after World War II by the *General Agreement on Tariffs and Trade* (GATT)—and the modern global trading system was born. GATT today provides the framework for most multilateral (many nations) trade negotiations aimed at reducing trade barriers. For nearly fifty years, GATT has functioned to set the rules of international trade and provide a forum for settling international disputes. In 1994, a new world-trade agreement was reached, called the *General Agreement on Tariffs and Trade 1994* that enhanced the role of international law in regulating trade and created the *World Trade Organization* (WTO), an international organization charged with administering the GATT world-trade system.

IMPORT BARRIERS TO TRADE

A *trade barrier* is any impediment to trade in goods or services. An *import* trade barrier is any impediment, direct or indirect, to the entrance or sale of imported goods or services existing in the country of importation. A *trade barrier* usually refers to *laws or government regulations* that make selling foreign-made goods more difficult or costly than competing domestic-made goods. The term may also include *many other nonlegal* factors that discourage the sale or purchase of imported products.

All countries have trade barriers. Although the United States is generally considered to be a "free-trade" nation, with relatively few barriers to imports as compared to some other countries, it too has many trade barriers. The United States has accused Japan of having many unfair barriers to the import of U.S.-made products; however, Japan has responded with similar accusations against the United States. The United States has also accused many developing countries of erecting barriers to U.S. goods and services. Even countries such as Canada and the United States, which have many similar interests, have come to blows over trade—

including such products as beer, lumber, and automobiles. When nations are unable to resolve these
disputes through negotiated agreements, *trade wars*
can erupt.

Anatomy of a Trade War: Auto Parts to Japan

To understand how a trade war can develop, let us
use automotive trade as an example. Remember
that the automobile industry is one of the most, if
not the most, economically important manufacturing industries in the world—and also one of the
most competitive. A trade war here can cause tremendous economic hardship. Our example involves
a long standing dispute between the United States
and Japan in which the U.S. government and U.S.
car manufacturers claimed that Japan unfairly
restricts the import and sale of U.S. cars and car
parts there.

At the end of World War II, the Japanese government wanted to rebuild its ruined economy. In
order to foster the growth of its own automobile
industry, the Japanese government restricted the
import and sale of foreign automobiles. The problem never made much noise outside of U.S. automobile circles until the late 1960s when more and
more Japanese cars started to be sold in the United
States. Ever since then, the United States has tried
to persuade the Japanese government to make it
easier for U.S. cars and car parts to be sold in
Japan. But by 1994, U.S. cars had made up less
than 3 percent of all cars sold in Japan. Also in
that year, the U.S. government reported that of the
total $62 billion trade deficit that the United
States had with Japan, $36 billion was attributa-
ble to automobile trade. The United States claimed
that this was largely due to actions of the Japanese
government and its failure to permit U.S. companies to have free and fair access to its market. In
1995, the U.S. Trade Representative called for
Japan to agree to opening its car market—or else.

The U.S. Position.
The United States pointed
out that U.S.-made cars were selling in Japan at
prices nearly 40 percent higher than similar cars in
the United States and far higher than similar
Japanese models. The United States blamed the
Japanese distribution system that favors Japanese
products and the excessive costs required to make

U.S.-made cars comply with Japanese requirements. The United States felt that the Japanese
government as well as Japanese car manufacturers
had pressured car dealers in Japan to not carry
U.S. brands. For example, all Japanese car dealers
were bound by a "prior consultation clause" in
their franchise contracts that required them to
"consult" with Japanese car manufacturers before
selling U.S. brands.

The United States wanted Japanese car manufacturers to purchase more "original equipment" parts
from U.S. companies for use in their auto assembly
plants both in Japan and in North America. Also,
the United States argued that Japanese regulations
restricted the sale of U.S.-made replacement parts
such as mufflers. The United States argued that
Japanese requirements affecting the sale of car parts
were unreasonable and anticompetitive. The United
States cited Japanese regulations that required most
repairs to be done in a government-licensed garage.
Virtually all of the licensed garages in Japan are
either owned or controlled by the Japanese automobile and automobile parts manufacturers, limiting the opportunities for U.S.-made parts to break
into the market.

http://www.trade.gov/td/auto
The U.S. International Trade Administration Office of
Automotive Affairs. Industry data, country reports,
U.S./Japan trade agreements, and other issues of
interest to the automotive industry.

The problem is part of a larger dilemma in
Japan's highly integrated vertical distribution system resulting in part from Japan's *keiretsu* system
of business relationships. A *keiretsu* is the Japanese practice of having interlocking directorships,
joint ownership, and other linkages between Japanese companies. *Keiretsu* companies share corporate directors and develop long-term contractual
relationships that favor *keiretsu* members, thus
keeping foreign firms from many business opportunities. The United States maintained that many
keiretsu relationships are actually illegal collusion,
which would violate antitrust laws if they occurred
in the United States. Japanese new car manufacturers have vertically integrated *keiretsu* relationships with Japanese parts manufacturers, and thus
purchase parts only from them. The large parts
manufacturers also control the distribution of after-

market parts to the wholesalers and to the licensed garages that make repairs, inspections, sell, and install the parts for retail customers. Moreover, many of the garages are owned by Japanese parts manufacturers and carry only Japanese parts. Inspections are rigorous and expensive (the installation and inspection of even minor parts, such as trailer hitches or shock absorbers, can run many hundreds or thousands of dollars). The system effectively prohibited U.S. firms from the parts market in Japan. The United States had for years called on Japan to deregulate its inspection and licensing system.

The Japanese Position.   The Japanese tell a different story. Reports of the *Japan Fair Trade Commission* and the *Japanese Ministry of Economy, Trade and Industry (METI)*, claimed that U.S.-made cars did not sell in Japan simply because of the preferences of Japanese consumers. For instance, they argued that U.S. manufacturers did not make enough right-hand drive models (for driving on the left-hand side of the road). With regard to the U.S. demands, Japan argued that the United States' insistence that Japanese car manufacturers commit to purchase specified quantities of U.S. parts was a "results based" strategy that put the United States in the position of "managing trade" in violation of free market principles. They refused to submit to purchasing quotas imposed by the United States. They also argued that any agreement with the United States would discriminate against European, Mexican, and other parts suppliers in violation of international law. Moreover, the Japanese government claimed that *keiretsu* relationships were based on Japanese tradition, on cultural and social norms, and on business decisions—not on conspiracy and collusion. They argued that car parts were purchased from long-standing Japanese suppliers in order to ensure consistent quality control. The Japanese also pointed out that their requirements are based on safety considerations, with which the United States should not interfere.

A Breakdown in Negotiations.   In 1995, trade talks between the United States and Japan took place in Canada. The United States refused to accept the few concessions made by the Japanese (e.g., the Japanese government offered to write a letter to sellers of car parts in Japan telling

them that they may offer U.S. parts for sale). The issue reached the boiling point when the U.S. Trade Representative threatened to impose trade sanctions against Japan by increasing tariffs on Japanese luxury cars entering the United States to 100 percent of their value. U.S. car dealers worried that prices of Japanese cars could nearly double as a result, and that hundreds or thousands of dealerships could close and that tens of thousands of U.S. jobs would be lost. Japanese government officials threatened counter sanctions against a list of U.S. products, including aircraft and farm products, and fears of an all out economic war with Japan loomed.

Japan immediately filed a petition with the WTO in Geneva, Switzerland, to have the matter resolved before an international tribunal.

---

http://www.meti.go.jp/english
For the Japanese view of WTO and trade issues, see the home page of the Ministry of Economy, Trade and Industry. Contains reports, publications and Japanese policy information, and links to well over 100 Japanese Web sites, most in English.

An "Eleventh Hour" Settlement.   Trade negotiations were moved to Geneva, Switzerland, to the headquarters of the WTO, where in June of 1995 they continued virtually 24 hours a day. For weeks, U.S. negotiators continued to threaten to impose the punitive tariffs of 100 percent on Japanese luxury cars if a deal was not reached. Japanese negotiators, bolstered by Japanese public opinion, steadfastly maintained their markets were open, and refused to give in to "unreasonable" U.S. pressure. But, with only a few hours left before U.S. tariffs became effective, an agreement was reached.

The settlement called for Japanese auto manufacturers to purchase more U.S.-made auto parts, increase the number of Japanese-model cars made in the United States, and to increase the number of Japanese dealerships carrying U.S. models. The agreement called for reform to the distribution system in Japan. For example, the Japanese government agreed to tell all car dealers that they were free to carry U.S. brands. The government agreed to aid in the marketing and promotion of U.S. cars through trade shows and exhibitions. Japan also agreed to speed up the delivery of imported cars to dealerships by sending inspectors (e.g., to inspect for compliance with safety and emission standards) directly to the dealerships. With regard to the repair-parts market, the agreement called for Japan to permit more small, independently owned garages to do repair work and to sell and install U.S.-made parts. For example, Japan decreased the square footage requirement for garages to service large cars, thus allowing more garages to service bigger U.S. cars. The agreement also called for Japan to eliminate restrictions on the use of accessories, such as roof racks. With regard to Japanese transplant companies in the United States, the Japanese government agreed to get them to do more than just assemble cars in the United States by encouraging them to build research and development facilities here as well. Japan also pledged itself to expand its investigations and prosecutions of violations of the *Japanese Antimonopoly Act,* which prohibits restrictive and anticompetitive business practices.

The United States had to abandon its insistence on enforceable, mandatory requirements for Japanese imports and instead agree to voluntary goals that would be monitored in the future. The agreement did little to affect the Japanese *keiretsu* system. At the same time, U.S. automakers announced that they were going to be more aggressive marketing in Japan. For instance, Chrysler announced a major capital investment in Japan and the opening of new dealerships. All the U.S. auto companies announced that they would build more cars with right-hand drive for export to Japan. In the end, U.S. public opinion saw the Clinton administration as being "tough on Japan." Also, many observers noted that Japanese negotiators are famous for stalling, and then reaching a last minute compromise. On the other hand, the opinion of many commentators and of the world trade community was that the Japanese commitment was an empty promise. The United States was criticized for resorting to threats and intimidation. They argued that if the United States had actually imposed sanctions against Japan—a "trading partner"—without the full approval of the world community, it would have destroyed the spirit of cooperation and negotiation on which the world trading system is built. They also argued that it set a dangerous precedent for brinkmanship in future trade relations. The U.S.–Japan pact expired at the end

of 2000, as U.S. automotive sales to Japan continued to decline. In 2001, dark clouds loomed on the trade horizon once again.

The U.S.–Japanese auto dispute was important because of the volume of trade that would have been affected, but the problems and principles are the same regardless of the product, industry, or money involved. With this dispute as our introduction, this chapter will examine the basic international legal principles affecting trade and the legal mechanisms for resolving trade disputes and preventing trade wars before they occur.

Reasons for Regulating Imports

Nations impose import trade barriers for many economic and political reasons. Several broad policy reasons prompt the regulation of import or export of goods and services. These include the following:

1. *Collection of revenue* (taxing imports).
2. *Regulation of import competition* (the protection of domestic industry, agriculture, or jobs).
3. *Retaliation against foreign government trade barriers.*
4. *Implementation of foreign policy* (prohibition on allowing the import of goods from a country that violates international norms or is a military adversary).
5. *Implementation of national economic policies* (preservation of foreign exchange; implementation of industrial policy).
6. *Protection of the national defense* (erection of barriers to foreign firms selling defense-related equipment or essential products such as machine tools; protection of strategic national industries such as aerospace or telecommunications).
7. *Protection of natural resources or of the environment* (ban on export of scarce minerals; a requirement that imported cars be equipped with antipollution devices; or ban on import of tuna caught in fishing nets that trap dolphins).
8. *Protection of public health, safety and morals, and plant and animal life* (ban on the import of disease-carrying fruit, explosives, or obscene materials; use of safety requirements for construction equipment or consumer goods).
9. *Protection of local cultural, religious, or ethnic values* (limitations on foreign television programming; prohibition of the import of religiously offensive materials in fundamentalist

Middle Eastern countries; ban on export of artifacts or antiques).

Import trade barriers can take many different forms and are usually classified as either tariff barriers or nontariff barriers.

> **http://www.ustr.gov**
> The home page for the U.S. Trade Representative.

Tariffs

The most common device for regulating imports is the *tariff* or *import duty*. (Note: these terms are used interchangeably in this text.) A tariff is a tax levied on goods by the country of importation. It is usually computed either as a percentage of value (*ad valorem* tariffs) or on the basis of physical units (also called specific or flat tariffs). Goods that are fungible (e.g., crude oil, wheat, or standard-size graded lumber) are usually subject to a specific or flat-rate tariff, while goods that vary in value (e.g., chairs, machinery, or specialized steel) are usually subject to an *ad valorem* tariff. Tariffs are generally considered to be one of the least restrictive types of trade barriers.

Nontariff Barriers to Trade

Nontariff barriers to trade are any impediment to trade other than tariffs. This rather broad definition can be broken down into *direct* and *indirect* nontariff barriers. *Direct nontariff barriers* include those barriers that specifically limit the import of goods or services, such as embargoes and quotas. *Indirect nontariff barriers,* discussed in the next section, are those that on their face seem perfectly neutral and nondiscriminatory against foreign-made products, but which in their actual use and application make it difficult or costly to import foreign-made goods.

Embargoes. The most restrictive of the direct nontariff barriers is the embargo. An *embargo* can be either a complete ban on trade with a certain foreign nation (e.g., the United States embargo on trade with Iraq or North Korea) or a ban on the sale or transfer of specific products (e.g., ivory) or technology (e.g., nuclear). The embargo can be both on imports from, or exports to, that nation. Al-

though a quota is used for economic purposes, the embargo is usually reserved for political purposes. The use of this extraordinary remedy is usually designed to implement foreign policy objectives, such as to "punish" another country for some offensive conduct in world affairs. In recent years, the United States has imposed embargoes on Cuba, Iran, Iraq, North Korea, Libya, and a few other countries.

Quotas. Perhaps the direct nontariff barrier that most people think of first is the *quota*. A quota is a quantitative restriction on imports. It can be based either on the value of goods or on quantity (weight, number of pieces, etc.). A quota can also be expressed as a percentage share of the domestic market for that product. Quotas can be placed on all goods of a particular kind coming from all countries, a group of countries, or only one country. Thus, a quota to protect U.S. garment manufacturers could limit imports of men's trousers either to a specified number of trousers or to a given percentage of the U.S. market for men's trousers. *Global quotas* are imposed by an importing nation on a particular product regardless of its country of origin. They are filled on a first-come, first-serve basis. *Bilateral quotas* are placed on a particular product on the basis of its country of origin. A *zero quota* is a complete ban on the import of a product by permitting *zero* quantities to be imported.

Quotas are used either to protect domestic industry from foreign competition or as a tool for implementing a nation's economic policy of reducing imports. Governments sometime prefer the use of quotas to tariffs because quotas work more quickly in restricting imports. Quotas can work quickly to protect a domestic industry threatened with increased imports of competing goods. A country that experiences a domestic economic crisis caused by excessive imports (such as during a *balance-of-payments crisis,* when an excessive amount of foreign exchange leaves the country to purchase imported products) can use quotas immediately to restore economic equilibrium.

Because of the ease in administering and applying a quota, it is a more flexible tool for regulating imports than a tariff. It can, therefore, be used to reduce imports on a specific product or commodity to correct short-term market conditions. Also, government policy makers can more easily assess the potential impact of a quota than of a tariff because no one can predict with absolute certainty what the economic effect of a tariff will be. Another advantage is that quotas can either be applied across the board to all imports from a particular nation or be applied to the products of several nations. These *allocated quotas* can thus serve important foreign policy objectives because the ability to allocate additional quota rights to certain countries can become a powerful economic incentive in world politics. Quotas have been widely used in regulating trade in textiles and agricultural products, although these will soon be phased out by international agreement.

Quotas, of course, also have several disadvantages. First, a costly governmental *licensing scheme* is necessary to enforce them. Imports may need to be tracked on the basis of their country of origin, requiring complex recordkeeping. Second, most quotas provide no revenue to the importing nation. Third, they are often politically unpopular because they deprive importers and consumers of the ability to make a choice of products in the marketplace. Fourth, the imposition of quotas often can lead to retaliation by foreign governments whose products have been restricted. Fifth, the complex licensing schemes used to enforce quotas are difficult for many foreign exporters to understand, so they may not know what barriers they will face when their goods reach the foreign country. Sixth, and most importantly, quotas interfere with the *price mechanism* in the marketplace, affecting prices by reducing supply. Firms able to import the product under the quota receive a monopoly profit, which contributes to considerable price increases to consumers. Indeed, the reduced supply and increased prices attributable to quotas and other restraints on imported products restrict competition and allow the price of competing domestic products to increase correspondingly.

Historically, U.S. presidents have not favored the use of quotas to protect U.S. industry for fear that the foreign nations affected would retaliate, giving rise to trade wars. Import quotas are more likely to be used when increased foreign imports threaten national security. For instance, in the 1980s, quotas were placed on imported machine tools for this reason. This quota prompted foreign manufacturers to invest in factories in the United States to avoid these restrictions.

Auctioned Quotas.   A quota that is sold to the highest bidder is known as an *auctioned quota*. One advantage of auctioned quotas is that they allocate import rights by price, rather than by government restrictions on supply. Moreover, auctioned quotas minimize the cost of relief to the economy by transferring the profits gained from owning quota rights from the foreign producer or importer to the country imposing the quota.

Tariff-Rate Quotas.   A *tariff-rate quota* is not really a quota at all, but a tariff that increases according to the quantity of goods imported. It is a limitation or ceiling on the quantity of goods that may be imported into a country at a given tariff rate. Let's use bedspreads as an example. A country that wants to protect its domestic textile industry might impose a tariff rate of, say, 7 percent on the first 500,000 bedspreads to be imported into the country in a given year; 14 percent on the next 500,000 bedspreads; and an even higher rate, perhaps, 25 percent, on all bedspreads imported above 1,000,000 pieces. The use of tariff-rate quotas is quite common worldwide.

Indirect Nontariff Barriers

Indirect nontariff barriers include laws, administrative regulations, industrial or commercial practices, or even social and cultural forces that have the *effect of limiting or discouraging the sale or purchase of foreign goods or services in a domestic market,* regardless of whether the barrier is intended as a measure to control imports. All countries have indirect nontariff barriers of some sort. Many indirect barriers are intended to protect domestic industries from foreign competition. Consider some examples.

To restrict imports, countries may impose *monetary and exchange controls* on currencies that limit the amount of foreign currency available to purchase foreign goods. Foreign *government procurement* policies may encourage government agencies to buy goods and services primarily from domestic suppliers. Foreign administrative regulations can impose *technical barriers to trade,* including performance standards for products, product specifications, or product safety or environmental engineering standards. Examples might include national standards for electrical appliances, health standards for food or cosmetics, safety standards for industrial and consumer goods, and even automotive emission requirements. Unless foreign suppliers of goods can meet these standards in the same fashion as domestic suppliers, they will be frozen out of the foreign market. The refusal to allow the import of beef containing growth hormones would effectively shut down imports of beef from countries in which virtually all beef produced contains such chemicals. Governmental restrictions on the use of food preservatives, such as those that have been imposed by Japan, are another excellent example of a trade barrier in disguise—as foods without preservatives cannot be transported long distances. Other common examples might include requirements that instruction manuals for consumer goods be written in the language of the importing nation, that only metric sizes appear on the product or packaging, or that imported goods be subject to stringent inspections or fees that are not applicable to domestic products. In recent years, U.S. firms such as L.L. Bean and Lands' End have made successful inroads into the Japanese catalog business despite restrictive Japanese postal regulations.

The *Japanese Large-Scale Retail Stores Law.*

Another good example of an indirect nontariff barrier in Japan was the *Japanese Large-Scale Retail Stores Law.* This controversial law, now repealed, protected the small "mom and pop" retail stores by limiting the location and operations of large retail stores and supermarkets in Japan. Because large retail chains are high-volume purchasers and large U.S. exporters are set up to sell to high-volume buyers, this law had the effect of limiting U.S. imports. Moreover, it perpetuated the vertically integrated distribution system in Japan and allowed large Japanese manufacturers greater control over the distribution of their products sold through many small retail stores. The effect was to strengthen their market position to the exclusion of foreign firms. The problem was exacerbated because of high land prices in Japan that make it costly for foreign companies to obtain suitable real estate for large-scale retail operations. This law was an excellent example of a nontariff barrier that on its face was completely neutral. It did not discriminate against products because they are of foreign origin, yet it had the

effect of limiting access to the Japanese retail market by American and other foreign discount chains.

The *Japanese Large-Scale Retail Stores Law* protected retailers with stores as small as five hundred square meters by giving them a voice in determining whether any large stores could come into their locale. The Japanese METI refused to accept a retailer's notification that it planned to open a new store unless there was also a document indicating the terms under which local merchants agreed to the large store's opening. Negotiations between new store owners and local merchants frequently took seven or eight years to reach an accord.

---

http://www.jetro.org

The Japanese External Trade Organization's U.S.-based Web site. Enter and link to "Business Information" section. Contains practical information on distribution and marketing in Japan, the Japanese consumer, Japanese retailing, negotiating with the Japanese and setting up businesses there.

Both domestic and international pressure led to changes in the law and in its application in the 1990s. Effective June 1, 2000, the Japanese legislature abolished this law and replaced it with the *Large-Scale Retail Store Location Law.* The new law provides that approval of large stores will no longer be based on whether there is a competitive need for additional stores in the local market, but rather on the degree to which a new large store would impact the local environment, particularly traffic, noise, parking, and trash removal. The environmental standards will be developed by the Japanese government and implemented by the local municipalities. Although the United States welcomed the abolition of the original law, the manner in which the new law will be implemented at the local level will determine whether it will really afford greater market access for large stores. The new law requires public notification by companies applying to open stores over 1,000 square meters, and a review period during which local residents, businesses, local governments, and others can present their views on the environmental impact of the store. Any firm attempting to open a supermarket, department store, or discount store in Japan will almost certainly face many bureaucratic hurdles, local regulations, and resentment from owners of small stores in the community. By the end of the 1990s, many American retailers were succeeding in the Japanese market. Examples include the GAP, Office Depot, Eddie Bauer, Amazon, Toys "R" Us, and Costco. Wal-Mart is opening stores there also, as American-style "volume discounters" begin to transform retailing in Japan.

Import Licensing Schemes and Customs Procedures as Trade Barriers.   Some of the most insidious indirect barriers to trade are import licensing schemes and customs procedures. Some governments require importers to apply for permission to import products, subject to meeting many complex and often discriminatory requirements. The licensing is often expensive and time consuming. For instance, an importer may have to make a deposit of foreign exchange in order to get the license, or the license may be based on a discriminatory quota system.

A host of governmental red tape, administered by entrenched bureaucracies, can also cause delays of days or weeks in bringing goods into a country. Import documentation and inspection requirements, for instance, can be so unreasonable that firms cannot comply without incurring delays and unanticipated expense. Bribery and corruption in a foreign government office can stall an importer's paperwork endlessly. Administrative regulations might be impossible to comply with. For instance, imagine a country that requires all foreign-made jewelry be marked with the country of origin, but provides no exemption for jewelry too small for engraving. Inspection procedures have also been used to stall shipments. To illustrate, in 1995, the United States accused Korea of using delaying tactics, in the form of "inspections," to hold shipments of U.S.-grown fresh produce on the docks until it rotted.

Transparency

When a foreign government's import regulations are not made readily available to the public, or are hidden or disguised in bureaucratic rules or practices, the regulations are not *transparent*. For instance, government procurement policies *lack transparency* when the requirements for bidding on a project are made available only to select domestic firms. A licensing scheme used to enforce a quota is not transparent when the "rules of the game" are not made known to foreign exporters.

When a nation's import regulations or procedures lack transparency, foreign firms cannot easily gain entrance to its markets. Many trade laws today incorporate transparency by requiring nations to publish all regulations directly or indirectly affecting imports.

Impact of Trade Barriers on Managerial Decisions

In making import–export decisions, the international manager needs to assess the impact of trade barriers on a business strategy. For example, the decision to ship goods into a foreign market, or to license or produce there, might be made on the basis of government policies that either restrict or promote trade. To the exporter of manufactured goods, regulations of the importing country may determine whether the firm's products can be successfully imported and marketed at all. To the importer, regulations may dictate those countries from which the firm may "source" raw materials, purchase machine parts, or locate finished goods. To the service provider, governmental regulations may determine when and on what terms it can successfully enter the banking, insurance, architectural, or engineering market. And to the investor who is considering building a plant, entering into a joint venture, or forming a subsidiary abroad, governmental regulations and trade barriers may indicate how suitable the economic and political climate is for the enterprise.

talked in 1944 , completed in 1947 , rvsd in 1994

THE GENERAL AGREEMENT ON TARIFFS AND TRADE

Most nations have come to realize that trade barriers are damaging to the international economy—and ultimately to their own. Moreover, they have realized that if they restrict the products of their trading partners in order to protect one segment or sector of their economy, then another sector will suffer. For instance, restrictions on the import of steel benefit domestic steel producers, but injure the automakers that use the finished product (as well as increase automobile prices to consumers). Similarly, import restrictions that protect one sector sometimes result in foreign retaliation against another sector. For instance, Korea might put strict quotas on U.S. beef imports, but the United States might respond by placing retaliatory tariffs on Samsung appliances or Hyundai cars. So, in order to limit the snowball effect of protectionism, nations have established certain rules.

Even while World War II was being fought, the United States and its allies were charting a course to rebuild and revitalize the world's economy and to ensure that the economic mistakes of the 1930s would not be repeated. In 1944, the allied nations met at the *Bretton Woods Conference* in New Hampshire and established several important international economic institutions, including the *International Monetary Fund* and the *International Bank for Reconstruction and Development,* or *World Bank.* At that time, a third specialized agency was planned to promote and stabilize world trade by reducing tariffs. In international meetings held in the United States and in Geneva, Switzerland, in 1947 a *General Agreement* was reached that reduced tariffs and set rules to hold countries to their tariff commitments.

After World War II, national leaders and policy makers stressed a more international view of the world's economy. At the same time, the UN and other new international organizations were born. Led by the United States, other nations embraced free trade and open market policies; they wanted to continue to reduce tariff and nontariff barriers to trade. But most importantly, they wanted to ensure that the world would never again fall victim to the forces of protectionism that existed in the 1930s. Their efforts to establish new rules for conducting their trade relations resulted in the creation of an international legal system to handle trade matters, complete with international law, dispute settlement mechanisms, and agreed-upon codes for regulating trade. This system is based on GATT.

GATT has been the most important multilateral agreement for liberalizing trade by reducing tariffs, opening markets, and setting rules for promoting freer and fairer trade. The original GATT agreement, completed in 1947, governed most of the world's trade in goods for almost fifty years.

Twenty-three nations, including the United States, were the original signatories to GATT in 1947. The agreement became effective through the signing of the *Protocol of Provisional Application.* Although GATT 1947 was never ratified by the U.S. Congress as a treaty, it has consistently been accepted as a binding legal obligation of the United States under international law. Until January 1, 1995, the GATT agreement was administered by *The GATT,* a multilateral trading organization based in Geneva, Switzerland, composed of countries that were signatories to the GATT agreement.

In 1994, after nearly a decade of negotiations, the world community adopted a new *General Agreement on Tariffs and Trade* that made many changes to the original 1947 agreement. GATT 1994 was signed by 125 nations on April 15, 1994, as a result of the *Uruguay Round* of multilateral negotiations that had begun in 1986. The United States negotiated and adopted GATT 1994 under "fast-track" negotiating authority as a congressional–executive agreement. The agreement was negotiated by three U.S. presidents, and was submitted to Congress by President Clinton. Congress approved the agreement at the close of 1994 to become effective on January 1, 1995.

GATT 1994 establishes rules for regulating trade in goods and services that are broader in scope than those of GATT 1947. It also resulted in the creation of the WTO, which replaced the original GATT organization that had operated for nearly fifty years. Countries that were signatories to GATT 1947 were called *contracting parties* to reflect that GATT is a contract between nations. Under GATT 1994, signatory nations are called *members.* Selected provisions of GATT 1994, which includes GATT 1947, are reproduced in the appendix.

The GATT Framework

GATT provides an organized global structure to improve the economic, political, and legal climate for trade, investment, and development. Its primary goal is to achieve distortion-free trade through the removal of artificial barriers and restrictions imposed by self-serving national governments. The GATT system includes an international legal system with rules, a mechanism for interpreting those rules, and a procedure for resolving disputes under them.

GATT rules are created by international agreement and become guiding principles of international trade law, upon which a WTO member nation's own trade regulations are to be based. In theory, the GATT legal system exists side by side with the domestic legal systems of sovereign nations. GATT anticipates that national legislatures and government agencies will comply with GATT's principles in setting tariffs and regulating imports. For instance, when a nation imposes a tariff or quota on imported products, it is to use guidelines established by GATT. If it does not follow the GATT principles, the offending nation may suffer economic or political sanctions imposed by other GATT members. Although absolute enforcement of international law is not possible except through war between nations, international trade law is to some extent enforceable because it is in the best economic and political interests of nations to comply with it. In essence, then, international trade law serves as a check upon the actions of governments that might otherwise severely and unnecessarily restrict the free flow of trade and commerce between nations. At the close of the *Uruguay Round,* the United States implemented the GATT 1994 agreement in the *Uruguay Round Agreements Act,* effective January 1, 1995.

GATT and U.S. Law

The GATT agreement does not provide individual rights and remedies to private parties. It cannot be used by private litigants to assert rights or claims for compensation in lawsuits against the U.S. government, nor to challenge the legality of a federal statute. For instance, in *Suramerica v. U.S.* 466 F.2d 660 (Fed. Cir. 1992) the federal appellate court stated that "GATT does not trump domestic legislation." The *Uruguay Round Agreements Act* stated that "No state law ... may be declared invalid ... on the ground that the provision or application is inconsistent with any of the *Uruguay Round Agreements,* except in an action brought by the United States for the purpose of declaring such law or application invalid."

The 1995 *Uruguay Round Agreements Act* states that "No provision of the Uruguay Round Agreements (GATT) ... that is inconsistent with any law of the United States shall have effect. Nothing in this Act shall be construed to amend or modify any law of the United States relating to the protection of human ... life, the protection of the environment, or worker safety." If a private firm or industry in the United States believes that its rights under GATT are being violated by a foreign com-

pany or foreign government, then it may seek redress either with the appropriate federal administrative agency or before the courts *on the basis of a U.S. statute,* but not under GATT. Of course, it can also communicate its grievance to the U.S. government, which can at its discretion negotiate with the foreign government under GATT rules in an attempt to resolve the trade dispute—nation to nation.

GATT Agreements as a Basis for Interpreting U.S. Trade Statutes.   There may be occasions where a U.S. court is called upon to interpret a U.S. statute whose wording is ambiguous or unclear. If the subject of the statute is addressed in an international treaty to which the United States is a party, the courts of the United States may look to the treaty for guidance in interpreting the statute. In establishing an important rule for interpreting statutes, the U.S. Supreme Court in *Murray v. Schooner Charming Betsy,* 6 U.S. 64 (1804) said, "[A]n act of Congress ought never to be construed to violate the law of nations, if any other possible construction remains. ..." This rule was recently restated by a lower federal court in a case involving U.S. trade statutes and GATT. *Timken Co. v. United States,* 240 F. Supp.2d 1228 (CIT, 2002) involved the dumping of Japanese roller bearings at an unfairly low price in the U.S. market. The plaintiffs argued that the U.S. Department of Commerce's application and interpretation of the antidumping statute was contrary to the GATT *Antidumping Agreement.* In deciding the case, the court had the opportunity to examine the U.S. statute and stated, "The interaction between international obligations and domestic law is interesting and complex. While an unambiguous statute will prevail over a conflicting international obligation, an ambiguous statute should be interpreted so as to avoid conflict with international obligations." As such, GATT and other treaties do influence the judicial interpretation of U.S. statutory law.

Scope and Coverage of GATT 1947

Before examining GATT's major principles, a reader needs to understand generally the scope and coverage of the GATT agreements. The rules of GATT 1947 applied only to trade in goods. Because most of the major trading nations of the world have been members, GATT has controlled more than 80 percent of the world's trade in goods. GATT 1947 was successful in reducing tariffs and nontariff barriers to trade worldwide. However, nations encountered many trade issues over which GATT had no responsibility. Trade in services, such as banking or insurance, was specifically excluded from GATT 1947. It also failed to regulate agricultural trade, an area of constant dispute between nations. Trade in textiles and apparel was also not covered because of the politically sensitive nature of these industries. (Trade in textiles and apparel has been regulated by other international agreements between textile producing and textile importing nations.) Because GATT 1947 only dealt with trade in goods, it did little or nothing to protect intellectual property rights, such as copyrights and trademarks. GATT 1947 also did not regulate the use of restrictions on foreign investment that interfered with the free movement of goods. GATT 1947 failed to provide adequate standardized rules for nations to deal with "unfair trade" problems. Finally, the dispute settlement process set up under GATT 1947, used to resolve trade conflicts between countries, was filled with loopholes and was often ineffective. Many of these deficiencies were remedied in GATT 1994.

Scope and Coverage of GATT 1994

GATT 1994 is much broader in scope and coverage than the original 1947 agreement, and addresses many of the latter's limitations. The two most important agreements included in GATT 1994 are the *Final Act Embodying the Uruguay Round of Multilateral Trade Negotiations* and the *Agreement Establishing the World Trade Organization* (see appendix). In addition to the original provisions of GATT 1947, GATT 1994 includes the following multilateral trade agreements on specific issues:

- *General Agreement on Tariffs and Trade 1994*
- Agreement on Agriculture
- Agreement on the Application of Sanitary and Phytosanitary Measures
- Agreement on Textiles and Clothing
- Agreement on Technical Barriers to Trade
- Agreement on Trade-Related Investment Measures

- Agreement on Implementation of Article VI (Dumping)
- Agreement on Implementation of Article VII (Customs Valuation)
- Agreement on Preshipment Inspection
- Agreement on Rules of Origin
- Agreement on Import Licensing Procedures
- Agreement on Subsidies and Countervailing Measures
- Agreement on Safeguards (Import Relief)
- General Agreement on Trade in Services (GATS)
- Agreement on Trade-Related Aspects of Intellectual Property Rights
- Understanding on Rules and Procedures Governing the Settlement of Disputes
- Trade Policy Review Mechanism
- Understanding on Commitments in Financial Services
- Agreement on Government Procurement, and miscellaneous sectoral trade agreements
- Understanding on Balance-of-Payments

This chapter examines the basic principles of GATT trade and tariff law and the role of the WTO. Most of these principles are applicable to all of the agreements shown above. Later chapters deal with more specific GATT issues, such as those related to agricultural trade, trade in textiles, and trade in services.

THE WORLD TRADE ORGANIZATION

As of January 1, 1995, the WTO replaced the original GATT organization. It provides an umbrella organization that sets the rules by which nations regulate trade in manufactured goods, services (including banking, insurance, tourism, and telecommunications), intellectual property, textiles and clothing, and agricultural products. The role of the WTO is to facilitate international cooperation to open markets, provide a forum for future trade negotiations between members, and provide a forum for the settlement of trade disputes. The WTO will have a stature equal to that of the IMF or World Bank, and will cooperate with those agencies on economic matters. The WTO's membership includes those countries that previously belonged to GATT, and is now open

http://www.wto.org
The home page of the World Trade Organization.

to other countries, if accepted by a two-thirds majority vote of the members. As of April 2003, there were 146 members of the WTO.

Organization of the WTO

The organization of the WTO is shown in Exhibit 9.1. The WTO is overseen by the *Ministerial Conference,* made up of high-ranking representatives from all WTO member countries. They plan to meet at least once every two years to direct the policies, activities, and future direction of the WTO. The Ministerial Conference appoints the WTO *Director-General* and specifies his duties. The work of the Director-General is supported by the WTO *Secretariat* staff. Beneath the Ministerial Conference is the *General Council,* made up of representatives of each nation and responsible for overall supervision of the WTO's activities. The General Council also oversees the work of the lower councils, which carry out the work of the WTO in specialized areas. As of 2003, the WTO had 550 employees at its headquarters in Geneva, Switzerland, and a $108 million budget.

The *Trade Policy Review Body* periodically reviews the trade policies and practices of member countries for transparency and to ensure that member nations adhere to the rules and commitments of GATT. The body is a policy body only and has no enforcement powers. The *Council for Trade in Goods* oversees the functioning and implementation of the multilateral trade agreements. The *Committee on Trade and Development* reviews the treatment received by least-developed countries under GATT, considers their special trade problems, and makes recommendations to the General Council for appropriate action.

Decision making by the WTO is by consensus. If the countries cannot agree by consensus, voting is by majority vote, with each member having one vote (each EU country also has one vote). The Ministerial Conference and the General Council have the authority to adopt interpretations of the GATT agreements. For countries that experience extraordinary circumstances, the Conference may grant a temporary waiver of an obligation imposed under GATT by three-fourths vote of the members.

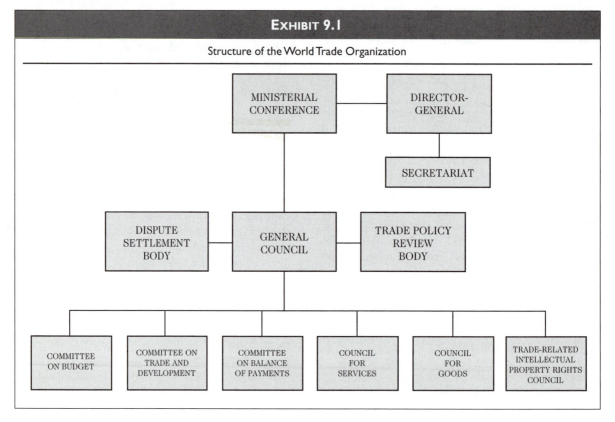

EXHIBIT 9.1

Structure of the World Trade Organization

GATT/WTO Dispute-Settlement Procedures

GATT 1994 envisions that one nation will not take unilateral retaliatory action against another nation in a trade dispute, but that the parties will rely on GATT *dispute-settlement procedures* to avert a trade war. GATT's dispute-settlement procedures are a quasi-judicial process for resolving trade disputes when attempts by the countries involved to reach a settlement become deadlocked. This process is intended to resolve conflicts before "trade wars" erupt. For instance, if nation **A** imposes a "GATT illegal" quota on nation **B**'s products, then nation **B** may file a complaint with GATT. In the meantime, nation **B** is not supposed to unilaterally retaliate with quotas or tariffs on **A**'s products and, in fact, needs GATT approval to do so. Only a government can bring a GATT complaint against another government. Complaints are not filed by or against firms or individuals (although as a practical matter, GATT cases are often brought by nations upon the instigation of private industry).

WTO Dispute-Settlement Procedures

Under GATT 1947, panel decisions were released only to the countries involved to give them another chance to resolve the issue. Panel decisions did not have the force of international or domestic law. Decisions did not acquire legal effect until they were adopted by the GATT Council of Ministers. Under the rules, valid through 1994, panel decisions were effective only if both sides in the dispute agreed to be bound. Either party could "block" or veto a panel's decision before it was sent to the Council. (Many nations chose not to block GATT panel decisions because they did not want to undermine a process for resolving disputes that they might want to use in the future. Furthermore, GATT/WTO panel decisions do carry the voice of world opinion and serve as an international conscience for determining which trade practices are acceptable and which are not.)

---

http://www.wto.org

For WTO dispute settlement reports, like these appearing in this book, go to the "Dispute Settlement" page and search or browse the "online document database."

Under GATT 1994, the dispute-settlement process has been strengthened and the deficiencies remedied. The WTO is given far more authority in handling trade disputes than the former GATT organization had, and individual countries can no longer block panel decisions from going into force. Among the most important changes are new procedures and timetables to assure prompt handling of disputes. The following provisions are expressed in the WTO *Understanding on Rules and Procedures Governing the Settlement of Disputes* known as the *Dispute-Settlement Understanding* (DSU).

- Responsibility for dispute settlement now rests with the WTO's General Council, which oversees the work of the *Dispute Settlement Body*. The Dispute Settlement Body appoints panels, adopts panel decisions, and authorizes the withdrawal or suspension of concessions.

- A complaining party can request *consultations* to seek a solution. If no solution is found within 60 days, the complaining party may request that a panel hear the case. In urgent cases, such as in cases involving perishable goods, members must enter into consultations within 10 days, and if they fail to reach agreement within 20 days thereafter, they may request that a panel be convened. The panel will consist of three to five individuals nominated by the Secretariat, but subject to rejection by a party for compelling reasons.

- Other member nations with a "substantial interest" in the case may make written submissions and an oral argument before the panel. More than one member nation may join in bringing a related complaint to a single panel established by the Dispute Settlement Body.

- A panel must make an *objective assessment* of the facts of the case and determine whether the terms of a GATT agreement have been violated. It may call on experts for advice on scientific and technical matters. All panel deliberations are confidential. The panel must submit a written report to the parties and to other members within six months (three months in urgent cases). Unless the parties file for an appeal to the Appellate Body, the panel's report will be adopted by the Dispute Settlement Body. However, the Dispute Settlement Body may vote by consensus not to accept the report. Thus, the offending nation in a dispute settlement case can no longer "block" the decision of the panel without a unanimous vote of all members.

- An *Appellate Body* of three people will hear appeals from a panel case. They may uphold, modify, or reverse a panel decision. People serving on the Appellate Body will be chosen by the Dispute Settlement Body on the basis of their expertise in law and international trade to serve for four-year terms. Other member nations with a substantial interest in the case may file written submissions and appear before the Appellate Body. Appeals are limited to issues of law covered in the panel report and legal interpretations considered by the panel. The appellate report is final unless the Dispute Settlement Body rejects it by consensus vote within 30 days.

- If the panel report finds that the offending party has violated a GATT agreement, the Dispute Settlement Body can recommend ways for the offending party to come into compliance. The offending party has 30 days in which to state how it plans to comply with the panel's ruling. Compliance must be within a reasonable time. If no immediate solution is available, the offending party can voluntarily make compensatory adjustments to the complaining party as a temporary measure.

- If no settlement is reached, or if the trade violation is not removed, the panel may authorize the complaining party to impose a retaliatory trade sanction against the offending party by withdrawing or suspending a concession. The sanction should be imposed on the same type of goods imported from the offending nation, or on goods from the same type of industry or economic sector. Sanctions should be in an amount equal to the impact that the GATT violation had on the complaining party. Sanctions are to be temporary and in force only until the offending party's violation is removed.

http://europa.eu.int/comm/trade/index_en.htm
See Europa (The EU online) for the European perspective on WTO disputes and other trade issues, or use

http://www.europa.eu.int
and navigate to the home page for the European commission and reference "trade" under the alphabetical index.

The following WTO Appellate Body Report, *European Communities—Regime for the Importation, Sale and Distribution of Bananas*, involves a long-running trade dispute between the European Community, Latin America, and the United States. It addresses the issue of who may request a WTO panel in a trade dispute.

European Communities—Regime for the Importation, Sale & Distribution of Bananas
WT/DS27/AB/R
September 9, 1997
Report of the Appellate Body World Trade Organization

BACKGROUND AND FACTS
In recent years the European Community (EC) has been the world's largest importer of bananas, accounting for 38 percent of world trade in bananas. In 1991, the EC imported over 3.65 million tons, two-thirds of which was grown in Latin America. Almost 19 percent came from developing countries that were once colonies of Britain, Spain, and France, located in Africa, the Caribbean, and the Pacific (known as ACP countries). Growers in the ACP countries could not compete with the highly efficient non-ACP producers, most of which are in Latin America. In order to encourage the import of ACP-grown bananas, and to aid in the development of ACP economies, the EC devised a host of tariff and non-tariff barriers aimed at non-ACP bananas. For example, a complex quota scheme was used permitting only a limited quantity of non-ACP bananas to be imported each year. While licenses to import ACP bananas were granted routinely, only importers who met strict requirements could receive licenses to import Latin American and other non-ACP bananas. While most ACP bananas entered duty free, other bananas had a very substantial tariff rate. Several Latin American countries requested consultations, claiming that the EC regula-

continued

continued

tions violated GATT by discriminating against bananas grown in their countries. The United States joined with the Latin Amerian countries arguing that it too had a substantial interest in the issue. While the United States was not an exporter of bananas, the U.S. government felt that U.S. companies, such as Chiquita Brands and others, conducted a wholesale trade in bananas amounting to hundreds of millions of dollars a year and would lose market share because of the EC's actions. The EC maintained that the United States had no grounds for complaining about the EC regulations because it was not a producer and grower. A WTO panel was convened, and its decision was appealed to the WTO Appellate Body.

REPORT OF THE APPELLATE BODY

The EC argues that the Panel infringed Article 3.2 of the Dispute Settlement Understanding (DSU) by finding that the United States has a right to advance claims under the GATT 1994. The EC asserts that, as a general principle, in any system of law, including international law, a claimant must normally have a legal right or interest in the claim it is pursuing. . . . The EC asserts that the United States has no actual or potential trade interest justifying its claim, since its banana production is minimal, it has never exported bananas, and this situation is unlikely to change due to the climatic and economic conditions in the United States. In the view of the EC, the panel fails to explain how the United States has a potential trade interest in bananas, and production alone does not suffice for a potential trade interest. The EC also contends that the United States has no right protected by WTO law to shield its own internal market from the indirect effects of the EC banana regime. . . .

We agree with the Panel that no provision of the DSU contains any explicit requirement that a member must have a "legal interest" as a prerequisite for requesting a panel. We do not accept that the need for a "legal interest" is implied in the DSU or in any other provision of the WTO Agreement. . . . [We believe] that a member nation has broad discretion in deciding whether to bring a case against another member nation under the DSU. . . .

The participants in this appeal have referred to certain judgments of the International Court of Justice and the Permanent Court of International Justice relating to whether there is a requirement, in international law, of a legal interest to bring a case. We do not read any of these judgments as establishing a general rule that in all international litigation, a complaining party must have a "legal interest" in order to bring a case. Nor do these judgments deny

the need to consider the question of standing under the dispute settlement provisions of any multilateral treaty, by referring to the terms of that treaty.

We are satisfied that the United States was justified in bringing its claims under the GATT 1994 in this case. The United States is a producer of bananas, and a potential export interest by the United States cannot be excluded. The internal market of the United States of bananas could be affected by the EC banana regime, in particular, by the effects of that regime on world supplies and world prices of bananas. We also agree with the Panel's statement that: " . . . with the increased interdependence of the global economy, . . . member nations have a greater stake in enforcing WTO rules than in the past since any deviation from the negotiated balance of rights and obligations is more likely than ever to affect them, directly or indirectly."

Accordingly, we believe that a member nation has broad discretion in deciding whether to bring a case against another member under the DSU. The language of Article XXIII:1 of the GATT 1994 and of the DSU suggests, furthermore, that a member is expected to be largely self-regulating in deciding whether any such action would be "fruitful."

Decision. The Appellate Body held that the United States could call for the convening of a WTO panel to question EC import barriers even though its exports were not directly affected.

Comment. The United States sought WTO authorization to "suspend concessions" (i.e., impose retaliatory tariffs) on a wide range of EU products, the value of which was equivalent to the nullification or impairment sustained by the United States. In 1999, the Dispute Settlement Body authorized the United States to impose 100 percent *ad valorem* duties on a list of EU products with an annual trade value of $191.4 million. The range of European products included bath preparations, handbags of plastic, paperboard, lithographs not over twenty years old, cotton bed linens that are printed and do not contain any embroidery or trimming, certain lead-acid batteries, "articles of a kind normally carried in the pocket or handbag, with outer surface of reinforced or laminated plastics," folding cartons of noncorrugated paper, and electric coffeemakers. In 2001, an agreement was reached to end the trade dispute. The EU restrictions were dismantled, and U.S. tariffs lifted. The "Banana Wars" were the largest trade war to date with tremendous economic and political ramifications. Current information on this and other trade issues is available from the U.S. Trade Representative's Web site.

WTO Reports as Legal Precedent

The issue arises as to whether WTO reports carry precedential value for future panels as case decisions do in common law courts. According to the language of GATT and recent WTO reports, the answer seems to be no. The Appellate Body, in *Japan—Taxes on Alcoholic Beverages* (1996) addressed the status of a report that is adopted by the Dispute Settlement Body, as follows:

> We do not believe that the contracting parties [WTO member nations] in deciding to adopt a panel report, intended that their decision would constitute a definitive interpretation of the provisions of GATT 1947. Nor do we believe that this is contemplated under GATT 1994. . . . Adopted panel reports can play an important part of the GATT *acquis*. They are often considered by subsequent panels. They create legitimate expectations among WTO members, and, therefore should be taken into account where they are relevant to any dispute. *However, they are not binding. . . .*

> http://www.useu.be
> The U.S. Mission to the EU.
> Includes information on
> U.S.–EU trade issues.

This statement is reaffirmed in the actual language of GATT 1994, which states that interpretations of the agreement may only be made by the Ministerial Conference and the General Council. Nevertheless, WTO Appellate Body reports continue to cite prior reports for their precedential value.

In the United States, WTO Panel and Appellate Body decisions are not binding on the courts. However, there are several cases in which the federal courts have cited WTO decisions for their persuasive authority. For example, in *Hyundai Electronics Co., Ltd. v. United States,* 53 F.Supp.2d 1334 (CIT, 1999), the court stated, "Thus, the WTO panel report does not constitute binding precedential authority for the court. Of course, this is not to imply that a panel report serves no purpose in litigation before the court. To the contrary, a panel's reasoning, if sound, may be used to inform the court's decision." In application, this means that a U.S. court cannot strike down a U.S. law or regulation merely because a WTO decision has ruled that it is in violation of an international agreement. For instance, if a WTO panel rules that a U.S. Department of Energy regulation regarding the sale of imported oil is held to be in violation of GATT's nondiscrimination provisions, a U.S. court cannot rely on that decision in striking down the regulation. It would be a matter for the U.S. Congress, or the executive branch of government, to bring that regulation into compliance with a WTO decision, and not the judiciary.

GATT 1994: Major Principles of Trade Law

In addition to member nations' commitments to consult with each other over trade differences and to resort to dispute settlement, GATT 1994 continues five basic principles of international trade law.

1. *Multilateral trade negotiations:* nations will meet periodically to reduce tariffs and nontariff barriers to trade.
2. *Predictability of trade opportunities:* By commiting themselves to specific, negotiated tariff rates, or "bindings," nations permit exporters and importers to know the highest tariff rate applicable to that product or commodity. This enhances the stability of the world's trading system.
3. *Nondiscrimination and unconditional most-favored-nation trade:* members will not give any import advantage or favor to products coming from one member over the goods of another member.
4. *National treatment:* members will not discriminate in favor of domestically produced goods and against imported goods, nor treat the two differently under their internal tax laws, regulations, and other national laws.
5. *Elimination of quotas and other nontariff barriers:* nations first "convert" their nontariff barriers to tariffs (through a process called *tariffication*), and then engage in negotiations to reduce the tariff rates.

In addition, GATT contains provisions to promote trade with developing nations and special rules allowing the establishment of free-trade areas and customs unions. Other special rules allow restrictions on imports when necessary to protect the public health and safety or to protect domestic firms from unfair trade practices or increased levels of imports that cause serious economic injury to domestic industries.

Multilateral Trade Negotiations

Since 1947, the GATT organization has served to bring member nations together to negotiate tariff reductions and the opening of markets. Under the auspices of GATT, the contracting parties have completed eight major *rounds,* or *multilateral negotiating sessions.*

1. Geneva, Switzerland, in 1947
2. Annecy, France, in 1948
3. Torquay, England, in 1950
4. Geneva, Switzerland, in 1956
5. *Dillon Round,* 1960–1961
6. *Kennedy Round,* 1964–1967
7. *Tokyo Round,* 1973–1979
8. *Uruguay Round,* 1986–1994
9. *Doha Development Agenda,* 2003–2004

The *Kennedy Round.* In the early rounds, countries negotiated on a product-by-product basis by simply presenting lists of tariff reductions that they desired from other countries, who submitted requests for concessions that they wanted in return. These rounds resulted in lowering *ad valorem* tariffs from roughly 40 percent in 1945 to approximately 20 percent in 1961. The *Kennedy Round,* which took place from 1964 to 1967, resulted in even larger across-the-board tariff cuts, particularly in manufactured goods, averaging nearly $40 billion in trade. More than sixty nations participated in the *Kennedy Round.* During this period, many developing countries joined GATT.

The *Tokyo Round.* By the 1970s, GATT's efforts had proven so successful that tariffs ceased to be the world's greatest barrier to trade in goods. Indeed, without GATT, decades of bilateral negotiations may have been necessary to achieve the reductions that multilateral negotiations reached within a few years. In the *Tokyo Round* more than one hundred participating nations agreed to tariff cuts averaging 34 percent and covering $300 billion in trade, which effectively lowered the average level of tariffs to about 5 percent. In addition, the parties established a number of GATT *codes* that attempted to remove nontariff barriers. These codes have addressed issues such as subsidies, technical barriers to trade, government procurement rules, customs valuation, and dumping (discussed in Chapter Eleven).

The *Uruguay Round.* The *Uruguay Round* negotiations lasted from 1986 to 1994 and resulted in GATT 1994 and the creation of the WTO. Its *market access provisions* are expected to add trillions of dollars to the world's economy in the years to come. It is expected to increase total U.S. employment, at a minimum, by hundreds of thousands of jobs and increase U.S. labor productivity and wages (United States Trade Representative, Office of Chief Economist, January 31, 1994). The market access negotiations resulted in worldwide tariff cuts averaging 35 to 40 percent on merchandise, farm products, and industrial goods.

Some products have much greater tariff reductions, including 50 to 100 percent on electronic items such as semiconductors and computers. In addition to tariff cuts, tariffs have been *bound,* or capped, at their rate effective at the time of the agreement. A country that raises a bound tariff will have violated GATT and would have to withdraw the increase or reach an agreement with the affected countries to lower tariffs on some other product.

The *Doha Development Agenda.* The *Doha Development Agenda* are trade rounds that began in 2001. The agenda for the meetings was set by the *Doha Declaration,* drafted by the WTO's Ministerial Conference. The focus of trade negotiations is on the following:

- Assisting the developing countries implement the trade rules that came out of the *Uruguay Rounds.*
- Reaching an agreement to reduce or end agriculture subsidies (domestic price supports and export incentives) by developed countries (an area of disagreement between the rich and poor countries because they encourage cheap exports of farm products from developed to poorer developing countries).
- Freeing trade in services, such as banking and insurance, to better allow these firms to operate globally.
- A reduction of high tariffs on products that countries consider "sensitive imports," and generally limiting them to 15 percent. Also, elimination of "escalating tariffs" in which higher import duties are applied on semi-processed products than on raw materials, and higher still on finished products.

- Negotiation of a higher level of copyright protection on products with "geographical names," especially for wine and cheese, such as *Champagne, Burgundy, Parma* ham, or *Feta* cheese.
- Trade issues related to investment, government procurement, patent protection, electronic commerce, trade and the environment, foreign investment rules, and more.

The Seattle and Cancun Meetings. The world was witness to the failure of two Doha meetings (Seattle 1999 and Cancun, Mexico 2003) as television coverage showed protestors demonstrating against what they perceived as a growing "struggle" of the rich versus the poor, developed versus developing country, corporations versus consumers and environmentalists, and so on. Indeed, in Cancun, a Korean farmer, the head of the South Korean Federation of Farmers and Fishermen, committed suicide atop a wire barrier in protest over agricultural trade issues. In actuality, the talks failed to reach their goals because of the inability of the rich and poor nations to reach agreement on controversial and highly politically charged trade issues. Agriculture trade and the protection of domestic farmers was one of the main reasons. Negotiations will continue through 2005.

Tariffication

Tariffication refers to the process by which quotas, licensing schemes, and other nontariff barriers to trade are "converted" to tariffs. Tariff rates can then be reduced through negotiation and the global economic environment for trade improved. For example, under GATT 1994, quotas on agricultural products will be converted to tariffs and gradually reduced. Tariffication has been a GATT policy since 1947.

Zero-for-Zero Tariff Elimination. During the *Uruguay Round,* the United States adopted a *zero-for-zero* tariff reduction policy. U.S. negotiators sought reciprocal tariff elimination in key industry sectors. The agreement eliminates tariffs in ten product areas over time (averaging five years): agricultural equipment, medical equipment, construction equipment, beer, distilled spirits, chemicals, furniture, paper, and printed matter; tariffs on pharmaceuticals and toys were eliminated in 1995. Each nation's tariff schedules deposited with

the WTO reflect the new rates. Current U.S. legislation grants the president the authority to negotiate additional market access agreements in future WTO negotiations on a zero-for-zero basis.

Tariff Concessions, Bound Rates, and Tariff Schedules

Article II of GATT calls for member nations to cooperate in lowering tariffs through negotiations. In a *tariff concession,* one country promises not to levy a tariff on a given product at a level higher than agreed upon. In essence, each country makes a concession to the products of the other country and receives reciprocal treatment. This process does not set the same tariff rate on a particular product for every nation, but determines a tariff rate that is said to be *bound.* A country may not arbitrarily raise its tariff above its "bound" rate. The rates are arrived at through compromise, and these concessions are recorded in *tariff schedules,* which are detailed product-by-product listings of all tariff obligations for a particular nation. Tariff schedules for the United States are found in the *Harmonized Tariff Schedule of the United States* (HTSUS). GATT calls for its members to negotiate reciprocal reductions in tariffs, either on a product-by-product basis or across the board.

The case, *European Economic Community—Import Regime for Bananas,* illustrates the importance of countries honoring their tariff rates granted by concession to foreign countries. As the case shows, government and business planners alike rely on access to foreign markets. If an importing nation unexpectedly raises its tariff rate, contrary to its concession, this would cause market disruption and injury to foreign exporters. The GATT Panel ruled that the change in EC tariff schedules had "nullified and impaired" the rights of foreign banana exporters who should have been able to rely on the existing tariff structure.

NONDISCRIMINATION, MOST FAVORED NATION TRADE, AND NATIONAL TREATMENT

The principle of *nondiscrimination* has long been a guiding concept of international economic relations and of trade liberalization. Defined most

European Economic Community—Import Regime for Bananas
34 I.L.M 177 (1995)
Report of the GATT
Dispute Settlement Panel (not adopted by the Council)

BACKGROUND AND FACTS

This case was decided in 1995 by a GATT Dispute Settlement Panel prior to GATT 1994 and the creation of the WTO. It resulted from the same "Banana Trade Wars" as a case appearing earlier in this chapter. Since 1963 the EEC had negotiated tariff rates with the developing countries that export bananas, and these concessions were bound in the tariff schedules at 20 percent *ad valorem*. In 1993 the EEC took over banana import regulation from the individual countries. The EEC set up uniform rules on quality, marketing standards, and tariffs. Under the EEC regime the tariff rates on bananas from the Latin American countries were increased between 20 and 180 percent. A complex licensing scheme was also set up to limit foreign banana traders (e.g., Chiquita, Dole, and DelMonte) access to sell in the EEC. The Latin American countries claimed that the regulations impaired their Article II tariff concessions, violated Article I, MFN principles, and other GATT provisions.

REPORT OF THE PANEL

Article II—Schedules of Concessions: [Central and South American] banana producers had assessed their competitive position on the basis of the bound tariff level. They had made strategic decisions and investments on that basis; they had cultivated substantially more land specifically for this export trade; and they had pursued marketing ties with European importers. The new tariff quota undermined the legitimate expectations upon which these actions were based and severely disrupted the trade conditions upon which these producers had relied, regardless of the actual protective effect of the new regime.

The Panel noted that Article II required that each contracting party "accord to the commerce of the other contracting parties treatment no less favourable than that provided for in the . . . *Schedule of Concessions*." The Panel then considered whether the introduction of a specific tariff for bananas in place of the *ad valorem* tariff provided for in its *Schedule* constituted "treatment no less favourable" in terms of Article II. . . . The Panel consequently found that the new specific tariffs led to the levying of a duty on imports of bananas whose *ad valorem* equivalent was, either actually or potentially, higher than 20 percent *ad valorem*. . . .

The Contracting Parties had consistently found that a change from a bound specific to an *ad valorem* rate was a modification of the concession. A working party examining a proposal by Turkey to modify its tariff structure from specific to *ad valorem* had stated: "The obligations of contracting parties are established by the rates of duty appearing in the schedules and any change in the rate such as a change from a specific to an *ad valorem* duty could in some circumstances adversely affect the value of the concessions to other contracting parties. Consequently, any conversion of specific into *ad valorem* rates of duty can be made only under some procedure for the modification of concessions." . . .

Decision. The panel held that the EEC had deprived (also called "nullified and impaired") the complaining Latin American countries of the benefits to which they were entitled under the bound tariff schedules.

---

broadly, nondiscrimination means that in every aspect of economic life, all nations should be treated equally and without discrimination. For example, if a nation taxes wire transfers of money sent to a recipient in a foreign country, then it should tax similar transfers equally, regardless of what country will receive the money. In terms of international trade, nondiscrimination means that the products of all nations should be treated equally and without discrimination by importing

and exporting nations. Simply put, nations should not "play favorites" with each others' goods or services. Although this ideal has rarely, if ever, been achieved, the concept of nondiscrimination runs throughout GATT law. It is most evident in the following areas: (1) the concept of *most favored nation trade,* that favorable tariff treatment on goods and services imported from one country shall be extended to similar goods and services from all other countries; (2) the concept of *national treatment,* that an importing country shall treat imported goods and services the same as its own domestic goods and services for purposes of all internal (domestic) laws, regulations, and taxes; and (3) that although GATT calls for countries to not regulate trade with quotas or other quantitative restrictions on imports, if a country does use them, they must be employed without discrimination and without regard to the country of origin of the goods or services imported.

Most Favored Nation Trade

Nondiscrimination is the principle behind *unconditional most favored nation* (MFN) trade. MFN principles require that any trade advantage or privilege granted by one GATT member to the goods or services of another member should be granted to all. Any tariff, tax, or other restriction on imports should be applied equally to products, without regard to origination. Because the products of all MFN countries are treated equally, products shipped from both economically powerful countries and small countries will be treated the same in the foreign market. Although MFN trade has been in use for at least three hundred years, it is now a basic principle of GATT law, found in Article I:

> With respect to customs duties and charges of any kind imposed on or in connection with importation or exportation . . . and with respect to the method of levying such duties and charges, and with respect to all rules and formalities in connection with importation and exportation . . . Any advantage, favour, privilege, or immunity granted by any other member to any product originating in or destined for any other country shall be accorded immediately and unconditionally to the like product originating in or destined for the territories of all other members.

Unconditional MFN Trade. *Unconditional* MFN trade requires that when a nation extends some privilege or right to one of its trading partners, such as a reduced tariff rate, that privilege *automatically* becomes applicable to all other trading partners. So, if nation **A** negotiates a reduced tariff rate on a particular product imported from nation **B**, that new rate becomes applicable to like products imported from MFN nation **C** and from all nations that have MFN status with the importing country. Unconditional treatment is granted merely because nation **C**'s product is "entitled" to be treated equally and without discrimination, and does not require further concessions to be in effect.

Unconditional MFN trade is different from conditional MFN trade. *Conditional* treatment requires that a trading partner give something in return for a tariff concession. Conditional MFN trade was used by the United States in its first trade pact made in 1778 with France and through the end of World War I. Then, the United States found out that conditional MFN trade allowed other countries to discriminate against U.S. exports, and the practice was phased out. MFN trade today is unconditional.

MFN treatment for imported goods greatly influences trade flows between nations. If a country's products do not qualify for MFN tariff rates in an importing nation, then it may not be economically practical to import those products at all. For example, assume that a company desires to import products into nation **A** that originated in nation **B**. If nation **B**'s goods do not qualify for MFN tariff treatment in nation **A**, then the transaction may not be profitable because of the high tariff rates. For instance, an MFN rate on a particular product might typically be 5 percent of the value of the import. Without MFN treatment, however, the rate on the same goods might be 90 percent on the value of the import. The importer may actually have to find substitute products in some other country that is an MFN trading partner of nation **A**.

Most people understand MFN trade as special treatment given to products imported from a nation's best trading partners. Actually, it is the norm. In the United States, MFN is now referred to as *Normal Trade Relations,* or NTR. Both terms are used in this book. Europe, Japan, and most developed countries of the world are MFN trading partners with the United States. However, products of some countries can receive *less favorable than* MFN treatment and others can receive *more favorable than* MFN treatment. Some developing countries' products can be imported into a developed country at tariff rates *even lower* than the MFN rate—such as when the United States or European Union is trying to encourage imports from poorer developing countries. Similarly, some countries' products come into the United States at a rate higher than the MFN rate—such as when the United States is restricting trade with another country, usually one considered to be a political "rogue" or outlaw nation.

Each nation's law determines the qualifications for granting MFN status to a trading partner, as long as those laws comply with GATT's general provisions. However, membership in the WTO does not automatically guarantee MFN treatment. For example, the United States denied MFN treatment to imports of Polish goods in the period from 1982 to 1987—because of the Polish communist government's tough stand against economic and political reform—even though Poland was a GATT member. Also, a trading partner that is not a GATT member may still be granted MFN status.

Normalization of U.S. Trade Relations with Russia and Vietnam.

The 1990s saw improvement in bilateral trade relations between the United States and many of its former enemies and political adversaries. Perhaps the best examples come from Russia and the newly independent republics of the former Soviet Union, the formerly communist countries of Eastern Europe and the countries of Indochina, including Vietnam.

With the collapse of Soviet communism in Russia, and Eastern Europe in the early 1990s, America wanted to assist these countries in their transition to democracy. Today, almost all of these formerly communist countries have normal trade relations with the United States. Many of these countries, notably Russia, actually have "better than normal" trade relations with the United States and their products enter the United States at preferred rates of duty that are even lower than the MFN rate. As of 2003, Russia held only "observer" status at the WTO. Membership requires a lengthy negotiating process (sector by sector, industry by industry, and sometimes product by product), where the applying country must demonstrate that its markets are sufficiently open to goods, services and investment from other WTO countries and that they will not be subject to discrimination. Some of the Eastern European countries have been

granted membership in both the WTO and the European Union as well.

The scars of the Vietnam War are taking decades to heal. In 1994, the United States ended the trade embargo with Vietnam and in 1995 reestablished diplomatic relations. By 1997, the United States had normalized trade relations with Cambodia and Laos, Vietnam's neighbors in Indochina. In 2000, President Clinton became the first U.S. president to visit Vietnam since 1969, and the first ever to visit its capitol, Hanoi. Although Vietnam is a socialist country run by a communist government, the signs of American economic capitalism are apparent everywhere. News reports of the president's trip from the Associated Press and CNN showed Ho Chi Minh City crowded with billboard advertising for Coke, American music blaring from sidewalk cafes, and counterfeit Nike and Calvin Klein products being sold on the streets. Obviously, America has had a tremendous impact on Vietnamese popular culture to this day. During the president's visit, the United States and Vietnam signed a trade agreement normalizing trade relations between the two countries. Vietnam promised to protect U.S. copyrights and trademarks from infringement and to open its borders to U.S. investment. Vietnam's normal trade status will be renewable annually. NTR status was continued by President Bush.

NTR and Human Rights

The use of NTR tariff treatment is subject to several exceptions. U.S. laws authorize the president to deny NTR status to any nation on the basis of national security, foreign policy, or a foreign government's denial of fundamental human rights to its citizens. The *Jackson–Vanik Amendment* to the *Trade Act of 1974* (Title IV) is a statute that grew out of the Cold War. It prohibits the granting of NTR status to any nation whose government unreasonably restricts the right of its citizens to emigrate. The statute was primarily aimed at the former Soviet Union and other communist countries. It requires the president to review the human rights records of foreign countries and to make reports to Congress annually. The president may grant *temporary* NTR status only if the country improves its human rights record. Permanent NTR status can be granted by Congress (exempting a country from annual review by the president).

Normalization of U.S. Trade Relations with China

In recent years, an important political debate in the United States has surrounded the issue of normalizing trade with the People's Republic of China. China has been ruled by a communist government for over fifty years. Although China was an original party to GATT 1947, it withdrew in 1950 as a result of the communist takeover. In 1951 China lost its normal trade status with the United States, resulting in prohibitively high import duties on Chinese goods. From 1974 to 1980, China's human rights record was watched closely under the *Jackson–Vanik Amendment*. In 1980, China's emigration policies improved, and since that time has received annual waivers from the *Jackson–Vanik Amendment*, granting temporary normal trade status to Chinese goods entering the United States. Throughout the 1990s, U.S. relations with China improved, and it seemed that annual renewal of China's normal trade status would be "virtually automatic." In 2000, Congress granted permanent normal trade status to China, effective on China's admission to the WTO in December 2001.

---

http://www.mac.doc.gov/china
The home page of China Gateway, containing all of the China resources of the U.S. International Trade Administration. Includes U.S.–China trade agreements, market access information, and ITA export services.

The United States and China have strong economic ties, despite many political differences. China has a population of approximately 1.3 billion people, and represents the largest potential market for U.S. goods and services in the world. There are tremendous opportunities for United States exports to China, particularly in agriculture, computers, automobiles, financial services, and telecommunications. The United States also relies heavily on Chinese imports. It is sometimes said that U.S consumers have become "addicted" to inexpensive Chinese products. In 2002, the United States imported $125 billion in goods from the Chinese mainland, and exported $22 billion in goods there. In that year, the United States had a larger trade deficit with China than with any other country except Japan.

More than one-third of China's exports are shipped to the United States. As a normal trading partner, China's products enter the United States with an average 3 percent import duty. If China did not have normal trade status, import duties on many Chinese goods would exceed 70 percent, resulting in a tremendous cost to U.S consumers. Thus a continued normal trade relation between the two countries is important to both nations.

---

http://www.chinaonline.com
An on-line business information service offering resources, news, original articles, and analysis for understanding the business climate in China.

Normalization of trade relations with China has always been linked to U.S. foreign policy. China's trade status was called into question in 1989 when the Chinese government used military force to stop pro-democracy demonstrations against the government at Tiananmen Square (during which student demonstrators were arrested as political prisoners or killed). Americans who oppose normal trade relations with China make the following arguments: China's human rights record has not improved. It has suppressed religious and other freedoms in Tibet; it does not treat prisoners humanely; it has used forced sterilization and abortion to control population growth; it uses prisoners in forced labor camps to manufacture goods (some of which have been exported to the United States); it has used the Chinese army to manufacture goods sold at unfairly low prices in world markets; it has allowed shipments of textile and apparel products to the United States in violation of U.S. import quotas, and it has allowed violations of U.S.-owned patents, copyrights, and trademarks. In addition, China has been accused of supporting communist North Korea, of exporting nuclear technology in violation of international agreements, and of selling Scud missiles in the Middle East.

Arguments for the normalization of relations with China are based on the fact that China has made many economic and political reforms. It has improved its human rights record, released many political prisoners, and has permitted greater freedom of travel and emigration. It has strengthened its intellectual property laws, reformed its tax laws, opened its borders to foreign direct investment, and made many economic reforms. Another argument is that trade is ineffective as a political weapon. Depriving China—or any nondemocratic country—of normal trade status will not effectively change its domestic or foreign policies. By closing the doors to trade with China, the United States would lose its ability to influence the Chinese economically. It would hinder economic development in China, making it harder for China to move from a socialist economy to a free market economy. Most people agree that trade leads to greater interpersonal contact, more openness in society and democratization. Moreover, history teaches us that if the United States denies normal trade status to China, China will still be able to trade with other nations around the world. The argument, then, is that trade should not be "held hostage to politics" and should not be used as a tool of foreign policy. For these reasons, even many of China's critics support continued normalization of trade relations.

Perhaps the greatest threat to U.S.–Chinese relations is China's claim to the island nation of Taiwan (see the Managerial Implications problem at the end of this chapter). The United States has supported a free and independent Taiwan (called "Chinese Taipei" in the WTO system) and is pledged to its defense. There is concern in the United States that a takeover of Taiwan would allow China to have excessive economic, political, and military influence over Japan and the rest of Asia. China maintains that Taiwan is a "renegade province" and that it is a part of China. In 2001, just as the U.S. administration was considering weapon sales to Taiwan, a U.S. spy plane and its crew were detained in China. This international incident again called U.S.–Chinese trade relations into question and a few U.S. lawmakers suggested revoking China's normal trade status and imposing economic sanctions. The United States insisted that Taiwan's admission to the WTO be granted simultaneously with that of China.

> http://www1.moftec.gov.cn/moftec_en/
>
> The official English-language site for the Ministry of Foreign Trade and Economic Cooperation of the People's Republic of China.

international accents

Country Commercial Guide: CHINA

Executive Summary

U.S. business' romance with China lay dormant for thirty years after WWII, but the love affair was rekindled in the late 1970s when China adopted a policy of "reform and opening up." Since the initiation of that policy, China's economy has grown at an average annual rate of nearly 9%, and the number of foreign firms doing business in or with China has grown exponentially. According to Chinese statistics, U.S. firms have invested over $25 billion in China—90% of it within the last ten years.

Despite this interest and investment, China remains a medium-sized market, albeit one with vast potential. Last year, China's Gross Domestic Product (GDP) was $1.08 trillion. This is about the size of the economy of Italy. Spread over a population of 1.2 billion, this does not represent a large amount of disposable income for the people of China. Since 1990, U.S. exports to China have grown almost 12% annually. Nevertheless, China consumes less than 2% of total U.S. exports, and U.S. investments in China represent only a tiny portion of the total U.S. holdings overseas. In spite of this, China holds huge potential for certain American exporters. In 2000, exports from China to the rest of the world were up 28%. Imports in the same time period, however, were up 36%. This shows that in key sectors, such as energy, telecommunications, medical equipment, construction, services, franchising, and many others. China is an interesting and viable market. With China's accession to the WTO, the number of sectors with market potential will expand dramatically.

American companies continue to have mixed

continued

continued

experiences in China. Some have been extremely profitable, while others have struggled. To be a success in China, American companies must thoroughly investigate the market, pre-qualify potential business partners, take steps to assure that they will be paid, and craft contracts which minimize misunderstandings between the parties. The problems of doing business in China can be grouped in four large categories:

1. China often lacks predictability in its business environment. Predictability can be provided by a transparent and consistent body of laws and regulations. China lacks both. Its current legal and regulatory system can be opaque, inconsistent, and often arbitrary.
2. China has a government that tends to be mercantilist and protectionist. China has made significant progress toward a market-oriented economy, but parts of its bureaucracy still tend to protect local firms and state-owned firms from imports, while encouraging exports.
3. China has the remnants of a planned economy. In many sectors of the Chinese business community, the understanding of free enterprise and competition is incomplete. The Chinese economy is often prone to over-investment and over-production, for reasons not related to supply and demand.
4. Foreign businesses have been over-enthusiastic about China. Encouraged by a government eager for foreign capital and technology, and entranced by the prospect of 1.2 billion consumers, thousands of foreign firms have charged into the Chinese market. These companies often do not fully investigate the market situation, don't perform the necessary risk assessment, and fail to get counsel. Without the necessary preparation, these companies often stumble into bad business deals, resulting in trade complaints and lost investments.

It is important to understand that while reform is absolutely essential for China to fully participate in the world trading community, in many areas, these changes have not yet taken place. Companies must deal with the current environment in a realistic manner. Risk must be clearly evaluated. If a company determines that the risk is too great, it should seek other markets. Remember, there is nothing noble about losing money in China . . . it is just the same as losing money anywhere else.

China's accession to the WTO brings new opportunities. Some have described it as "the beginning of time" for trade relations. Problems will not disappear overnight, but after WTO accession, the tools become available to address protectionism in China's market. As disposable income grows (up 6.4% last year) China's market potential will expand as well. This will be a gradual process, but the combination of WTO and an expanding economy bode well for U.S. business in the years ahead.

Other Exceptions to Normal Trade Status. Returning to our discussion of the GATT principles, the GATT Agreement provides for trade relations that may be even more favorable than normal (MFN) treatment. These include allowance of even lower tariffs for goods traded within a free-trade area (e.g., the largest of which is the *North American Free Trade Agreement*) and common markets such as the EU. GATT also provides for special trade "preferences" for developing countries under which their products qualify for better-than-normal tariff treatment.

For other interesting views on Chinese issues, see the following:

http://www.gio.gov.tw/
Taiwan's official government information office

http://www.chinapost.com.tw/
Taiwan's leading English language newspaper

http://www.info.gov.hk/eindex.htm
Official site of the Hong Kong Administrative Region of the PRC

http://www.tdctrade.com
Home page of the Hong Kong Trade Development Council

NATIONAL TREATMENT

The *national treatment* provisions of GATT are intended to ensure that imported products will not be subjected to discriminatory treatment under the laws of the importing nation. Under Article III, imported products must not be regulated, taxed, or otherwise treated differently from domestic goods once they enter a nation's stream of commerce. GATT Article III:2 provides that imports shall not be subject to internal taxes or charges in excess of those applied to like domestic products.

Article III

1. The contracting parties recognize that internal taxes and other internal charges, and laws, regulations and requirements affecting the internal sale, offering for sale, purchase, transportation, distribution or use of products, and internal quantitative regulations requiring the mixture, processing or use of products in specified amounts or proportions, should not be applied to imported or domestic products so as to afford protection to domestic production.

2. The products of the territory of any contracting party imported into the territory of any other contracting party shall not be subject, directly or indirectly, to internal taxes or other internal charges of any kind in excess of those applied, directly or indirectly, to *like domestic products*. Moreover, no contracting party shall otherwise apply internal taxes or other internal charges to imported or domestic products in a manner contrary to the principles set forth in paragraph 1.

Ad Article III (Annex) to Paragraph 2

A tax conforming to the requirements of the first sentence of paragraph 2 would be considered to be inconsistent with the provisions of the second sentence only in cases where competition was involved between, on the one hand, the taxed product and, on the other hand, a *directly competitive or substitutable product* which was not similarly taxed.

The even broader provisions of Article III:4 state that imported products shall be given "treatment no less favourable than that accorded to like products of national origin in respect of all laws, regulations, and requirements affecting their internal sale." This provision has been interpreted as prohibiting discrimination against imports resulting from a wide range of nontariff barriers to trade, including discriminatory customs procedures, government procurement policies, and product standards. In the following case, *Japan—Taxes on Alcoholic Beverages,* the WTO Appellate Body undertook a thorough analysis of Japan's *Liquor Tax Law* and found that the Japanese tax violated GATT Article III. As you read, look not only for its interpretation of national treatment, but also look at the Appellate Body's reflections on GATT as international law.

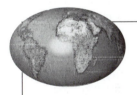

Japan—Taxes on Alcoholic Beverages
WT/DS11/AB/R
October 4, 1996
Report of the Appellate Body World Trade Organization

BACKGROUND AND FACTS

The Japanese *Liquor Tax Law,* or *Shuzeiho,* taxes liquors sold in Japan based on the type of beverage. There are ten categories of beverage (the categories are *sake, sake compound, shochu, mirin,* beer, wine, whiskey/brandy, spirits, liqueurs, and miscellaneous. *Shochu* is distilled from potatoes, buckwheat, or other grains. *Shochu* and vodka share many characteristics. However, vodka and other imported liquors fall in categories with a tax rate that is seven or eight times higher than the category for *shochu.* Foreign spirits account for only 8 percent of the Japanese market, whereas they account for almost 50 percent of the market in other industrialized countries. The United States, the European Union, and Canada called for consultations before the WTO. The panel held that the Japanese tax law violated GATT, and Japan appealed to the Appellate Body.

continued

continued

REPORT OF THE APPELLATE BODY

The WTO Agreement is a treaty—the international equivalent of a contract. It is self-evident that in an exercise of their sovereignty, and in pursuit of their own respective national interests, the Members of the WTO have made a bargain. In exchange for the benefits they expect to derive as Members of the WTO, they have agreed to exercise their sovereignty according to the commitments they have made in the WTO Agreement. One of those commitments is Article III of the GATT 1994, which is entitled *National Treatment on Internal Taxation and Regulation.*

The broad and fundamental purpose of Article III is to avoid protectionism in the application of internal tax and regulatory measures. More specifically, the purpose of Article III is to ensure that internal measures not be applied to imported or domestic products so as to afford protection to domestic production. Toward this end, Article III obliges Members of the WTO to provide equality of competitive conditions for imported products in relation to domestic products. "[T]he intention of the drafters of the Agreement was clearly to treat the imported products in the same way as the like domestic products once they had been cleared through customs. Otherwise indirect protection could be given. Moreover, it is irrelevant that "the trade effects" of the tax differential between imported and domestic products, as reflected in the volumes of imports, are insignificant or even non-existent; Article III protects expectations not of any particular trade volume but rather of the equal competitive relationship between imported and domestic products. Members of the WTO are free to pursue their own domestic goals through internal taxation or regulation so long as they do not do so in a way that violates Article III or any of the other commitments they have made in the WTO Agreement. . . .

[I]f imported products are taxed in excess of like domestic products, then that tax measure is inconsistent with Article III. . . . [We must determine first] whether the taxed imported and domestic products are "like" and, second, whether the taxes applied to the imported products are "in excess of" those applied to the like domestic products. If the imported and domestic products are "like products," and if the taxes applied to the imported products are "in excess of" those applied to the like domestic products, then the measure is inconsistent with Article III:2.

We agree with the Panel also that the definition of "like products" in Article III:2 should be construed narrowly. How narrowly is a matter that should be determined separately for each tax measure in each case. [A 1970 GATT Report] set out the basic approach for interpreting "like or similar products":

> [T]he interpretation of the term should be examined on a case-by-case basis. This would allow a fair assessment in each case of the different elements that constitute a "similar" product. Some criteria were suggested for determining, on a case-by-case basis, whether a product is "similar": the product's end-users in a given market; consumers' tastes and habits, which change from country to country; the product's properties, nature and quality.

The concept of "likeness" is a relative one that evokes the image of an accordion. The accordion of "likeness" stretches and squeezes in different places as different provisions of the WTO Agreement are applied. [The definition of "likeness" must be narrowly interpreted.] The Panel determined in this case that *shochu* and vodka are "like products."

A uniform tariff classification of products can be relevant in determining what are "like products." Tariff classification has been used as a criterion for determining "like products" in several previous adopted panel reports. . . . There are risks in using tariff bindings that are too broad as a measure of product "likeness." . . . It is true that there are numerous tariff bindings which are in fact extremely precise with regard to product description and which, therefore, can provide significant guidance as to the identification of "like products." Clearly enough, these determinations need to be made on a case-by-case basis. However, tariff bindings that include a wide range of products are not a reliable criterion for determining or confirming product "likeness" under Article III:2.

The only remaining issue under the first sentence of Article III:2 is whether the taxes on imported products are "in excess of" those on like domestic products. If so, then the Member that has imposed the tax is not in compliance with Article III. Even the smallest amount of "excess" is too much. The prohibition of discriminatory taxes in Article III is not conditional on a "trade effects test" nor is it qualified by a *de minimis* standard.

If imported and domestic products are not "like products" . . . those same products may well be

continued

continued

among the broader category of "directly competitive or substitutable products" that fall within the domain of the second sentence of Article III:2. How much broader that category of "directly competitive or substitutable products" may be in any given case is a matter for the panel to determine based on all the relevant facts in that case. In this case, the Panel emphasized the need to look not only at such matters as physical characteristics, common end-uses, and tariff classifications, but also at the "market place." This seems appropriate. The GATT 1994 is a commercial agreement, and the WTO is concerned, after all, with markets. It does not seem inappropriate to look at competition in the relevant markets as one among a number of means of identifying the broader category of products that might be described as "directly competitive or substitutable." Nor does it seem inappropriate to examine elasticity of substitution as one means of examining those relevant markets. In the Panel's view, the decisive criterion in order to determine whether two products are directly competitive or substitutable is whether they have common end-uses, *inter alia*, as shown by elasticity of substition. We agree.

Our interpretation of Article III is faithful to the "customary rules of interpretation of public international law." WTO rules are reliable, comprehensible and enforceable. WTO rules are not so rigid or so inflexible as not to leave room for reasoned judgements in confronting the endless and ever chang-ing ebb and flow of real facts in real cases in the real world. They will serve the multilateral trading system best if they are interpreted with that in mind. In that way, we will achieve the "security and predictability" sought for the multilateral trading system by the Members of the WTO through the establishment of the dispute settlement system.

Decision. The Japanese *Liquor Tax* Law violated the national treatment provisions of GATT Article III. *Shochu* is a "like product" and is "directly competitive and substitutable" with other imported spirits. The imported spirits were taxed higher than the *Shochu*. The decision of the panel was upheld and Japan was requested to bring its tax law into compliance with GATT.

Comment. In 1997, the United States was forced to seek binding arbitration when it became apparent that Japan did not intend to bring its liquor tax into WTO compliance within a "reasonable period" as required by WTO rules. The arbitration ruling supported the U.S. position. Japan agreed to revise its tariff system in stages, and to eliminate tariffs on all brown spirits (including whisky and brandy) and on vodka, rum, liqueurs, and gin by April 1, 2002. The U.S. distilled spirits industry reported that, as expected, the change in taxation has increased exports of U.S. distilled spirits to Japan. The United States continues to "monitor" Japan's compliance.

GATT AND THE ELIMINATION OF QUOTAS

The GATT Agreement permits the use of tariffs as the acceptable method of regulating imports, but not quotas or other quantitative restrictions. Since 1947, the agreement has called for countries to give up using quotas. Of course, many countries still utilize them—because they are a sure and certain way of keeping out foreign-made goods. The GATT prohibition of quotas is found in Article XI:

No prohibitions or restrictions other than duties, taxes, or other charges, whether made effective through quotas, import or export licenses, or other measures, shall be instituted . . . on the importation of any product . . . or on the exportation or sale for export of any product.

The use of quotas, even where they are permitted by GATT, is subject to the principle of non-discrimination. GATT Article XIII states that an importing nation may not impose any quantitative restriction on a product unless it imposes the same restriction on all like or similar products coming from all other WTO member nations.

Despite the prohibition on the use of quotas, countries still do use them for many economic and political reasons. Quotas have been used to protect essential industries from foreign competition and to implement national economic policies. They are used by virtually all countries, including (although to a lesser extent) the United States. GATT permits the use of quotas to relieve food shortages and to restrict the import of agricultural and fishery products subject to governmental price support mechanisms. Quotas are also widely used to regulate world trade in textiles and apparel. Also, quotas are used by importing countries facing severe balance-of-payments deficits in order to temporarily preserve needed foreign exchange.

Quantitative Restrictions: The Balance-of-Payments Exception and Developing Countries

From 1947 to this day, the GATT agreements have provided for the special needs of developing countries. One burden that developing countries face is the need for readily acceptable international currency for use in trading in world markets. Historically, many developing countries were agrarian economies, some with only a few "cash crops" that could be sold for export. Others were able to develop basic industries in steel or textiles that provided export revenues. Often this was their only source of scarce foreign exchange, which was needed to purchase essential foreign goods such as medicine, fertilizer, or farm equipment or to repay international debts. After all, dollars, pounds, or yen could be used for trade anywhere on the globe, but usually their local currency could not. When a nation's payments of foreign exchange exceed receipts, a *balance-of-payments* deficit can arise. This happens to both developed and developing countries, and both can face these crises. However, the problem is usually exacerbated in developing countries because their international transactions are almost always done with one of the major currencies, not their own. The fastest way to halt the outflow of foreign exchange by local companies is to place quantitative restrictions on imports of goods and service through the use of quotas or licensing schemes (tariffs, obviously, would take much longer to have the same desired effect).

Despite GATT's prohibition of quotas, any nation (including developed nations) may resort to quantitative restrictions in a balance-of-payments crisis. Article XII applies to a developed country "with very low monetary reserves" and allows the use of quantitative restrictions in order to "safeguard its external financial position and its balance-of-payments . . . necessary to forestall the imminent threat of, or to stop, a serious decline in its monetary reserves." Article XVIII applies to a developing country that "can only support low standards of living and is in the early stages of development." For a developing country, the rule is more liberal, allowing the use of quantitative restrictions "in order to safeguard its external financial position and to ensure a level of [foreign exchange] reserves adequate for the implementation of its program of economic development." In both cases, the restrictions must be temporary and phased out as economic conditions improve, as they are no longer required.

GATT 1994 instituted a new requirement that a WTO member must use the least-restrictive means possible for correcting a balance-of-payments emergency, preferably a price-based measure, such as a surcharge or tariff increase, rather than a pure quantitative limit on imports. Restrictions should not be targeted at individual products, but should affect the "general level" of all imports to the country. The restrictions must be transparent and the government must publicly announce its timetable for removing them. Justification for the measure must be given to the WTO *Balance-of-Payments Committee,* and the action is subject to WTO surveillance and periodic review. Exporters who do business in developing countries should pay particular attention to this issue. In the following WTO Panel Report, *India—Quantitative Restrictions on Imports of Agricultural, Textile, & Industrial Products,* the United States sought to have India remove a complex scheme of import restrictions that had existed for almost 50 years.

India—Quantitative Restrictions on Imports of Agricultural, Textile, & Industrial Products
WT/DS90/R (April 6, 1999)
Report of the Panel World Trade Organization

BACKGROUND AND FACTS

India is a rapidly developing country of over 1 billion people, one-third of which are under the age of 15. Over 80 percent are of the Hindu religion. Although its per capital GDP is only about $2,500, with almost 25 percent of the population living below the poverty line, during the late 1990s its economy grew at an annual rate of about 6 percent. While its economy is largely agricultural based, it is strong in the areas of textiles, chemicals, food processing, steel, industrial goods, financial services, technology, and computer software. It has a rapidly growing consumer sector. For the past 50 years, India has placed complex restrictions on the import of agricultural, industrial, and consumer goods from other countries. Goods placed on the "negative list" could only be imported by special license, which was generally only granted to the "actual user," rather than to firms in the normal chain of distribution. Many goods could only be imported by state agencies. The restrictions were, in many cases, applied arbitrarily and in the discretion of Indian government officials on a case-by-case basis. As a result, it was often impossible to know at any given time what goods might be allowed into the country. In 1997, the United States filed a dispute with the WTO against India requesting that restrictions on 2,714 products be removed. India claimed that without restrictions its foreign exchange would leave the country, upsetting its balance of payments and inhibiting its economic development.

REPORT OF THE PANEL

The United States contended that . . . persons wishing to import an item on the Negative List had to apply for a license and explain their "justification for import": the authorities provided no explanation of the criteria for judging applications, and no advance notice of the volume or value of imports to be allowed. In fact, licenses were routinely refused on the basis that the import would compete with a domestic producer. The leading item on the Negative List was consumer goods (including many food items), and for many consumer goods inclusion on the Negative List had amounted to an import ban or close to it.

The United States considered that the restrictiveness of India's licensing of consumer goods imports

was demonstrated by the trade statistics . . . *zero imports for 1995/96*, including meat; fish; cereals; malt and starches; preparations of meat or fish; cocoa, chocolate and cocoa preparations; nuts, canned and pickled vegetables and fruits, and fruit juices; wine, beer, spirits and vinegar; leather articles; matting and baskets; carpets; knitted fabrics; clothing; headgear; umbrellas; and furniture. [Imports of hundreds of other products were allowed in only minute quantities for a population of 1 billion.] Thus, in many cases import licensing amounts to an import ban, or close to it.

The United States noted that . . . the "Actual User condition" ruled out any imports by wholesalers or other intermediaries, and itself was a further quantitative restriction on imports.

* * *

Thus, according to the United States, the generally applicable import licensing process was a complete black box for the importer and for the foreign exporter. No information was provided on the Government's sectoral priorities with respect to products or on what its views of "merit" might be. All that the United States knew was that the Indian licensing authority generally refused to grant import licences for "restricted" items when it was considered prejudicial to the state's interest to do so.

The United States added that the broad definition of "consumer goods," and the fact that some goods were *only* restricted if they were consumer goods, created considerable confusion, commercial uncertainty and distortion of trade. * * * The 1996 study on *Liberalisation of Indian Imports of Consumer Durables* by the Export–Import Bank of India had noted that the only two commonly-used consumer durable goods that were freely importable were cameras and nail cutters.

* * *

India said that it needed to use discretionary licensing on a case-by-case basis for the following reasons. India's economy had been almost totally closed to imports barely 15 years ago. Because of the size and structure of the economy, it was impossible for India to estimate precisely the level of demand for imports, the import elasticity of demand for a huge number of

continued

continued

products, as well as the elasticity of substitution of domestic products by consumers, and the effective rate of protection for all these products. Accordingly, India considered recourse to discretionary licensing to be unavoidable. Further, India was progressively phasing out its import restrictions. As part of its autonomously initiated programme of economic liberalization, India had already reduced the number of items on which there were import restrictions to just 2,296 as of 1998, from about 11,000 HS-lines in 1991.

* * *

The United States stated that India's quantitative restrictions and licensing regimes had damaged and continued to damage U.S. trade interests. . . . In 1996, the United States exported $1.3 billion to India in goods subject to quantitative restrictions. However, while the ASEAN area had a population half the size of India's, U.S. exports to ASEAN were eight times the value of U.S. exports to India. As the panel on *Japanese Measures on Imports of Leather*" noted, "the fact that the United States was able to export large quantities of leather to other markets [than Japan] . . . tended to confirm the assumption that the existence of the restrictions [on leather imports] had adversely affected United States' exports."

The nature and operation of India's import licensing regimes also damaged and continued to damage U.S. trade interests. The uncertainty and limitations imposed by India's licensing regime deterred or prevented exporters from undertaking the investments in planning, promotion and market development necessary to develop and expand markets in India for their products. No exporter would put resources into developing a product's market in India without some assurance that it would be able to export some minimum amount per year, and the Indian system provided no such assurance—only a guarantee of continuing uncertainty—if the product in question was on the Negative List of Imports.

* * *

In light of the foregoing, we note that it is agreed that India's licensing system for goods in the Negative List of Imports is a discretionary import licensing system, in that licences are not granted in all cases, but rather on unspecified "merits." We note also that India concedes this measure is an import restriction under Article XI:1.

* * *

Having determined that the measures at issue are quantitative restrictions within the meaning of Article XI:1 and therefore prohibited, we must examine . . .

India's defence under the balance-of-payments provisions of GATT 1994.

* * *

In this connection, we recall that the IMF reported that India's reserves as of 21 November 1997 were $25.1 billion and that an adequate level of reserves at that date would have been $16 billion. While the Reserve Bank of India did not specify a precise level of what would constitute adequacy, it concluded only three months earlier in August 1997 that India's reserves were "well above the thumb rule of reserve adequacy" and although the Bank did not accept that thumb rule as the only measure of adequacy, it also found that "[b]y any criteria, the level of foreign exchange reserves appears comfortable." It also stated that "the reserves would be adequate to withstand both cyclical and unanticipated shocks."

* * *

For the reasons outlined . . . we find that . . . India's monetary reserves of $25.1 billion were not inadequate as that term is used in Article XVIII:9(b) and that India was therefore not entitled to implement balance-of-payments measures to achieve a reasonable rate of growth in its reserves.

* * *

The institution and maintenance of balance-of-payments measures is only justified at the level necessary to address the concern, and cannot be more encompassing. Paragraph 11, in this context, confirms this requirement that the measures be limited to what is necessary and addresses more specifically the conditions of evolution of the measures as balance-of-payments conditions improve: at any given time, the restrictions should not exceed those necessary. This implies that as conditions improve, measures must be relaxed in proportion to the improvements. The logical conclusion of the process is that the measures will be eliminated when conditions no longer justify them.

* * *

In conclusion . . . we have found that India's balance-of-payments situation was not such as to allow the maintenance of measures for balance-of-payments purposes under the terms of Article XVIII:9, that India was not justified in maintaining its existing measures under the terms of Article XVIII:11, and that it does not have a right to maintain or phase-out these measures on the basis of other provisions of Article XVIII:B which it invoked in its defence. We therefore conclude that India's measures are not justified under the terms of Article XVIII:B.

* * *

continued

continued

This panel suggests that a reasonable period of time be granted to India in order to remove the import restrictions which are not justified under Article XVIII:B. Normally, the reasonable period of time to implement a panel recommendation, when determined through arbitration, should not exceed fifteen months from the date of adoption of a panel or Appellate Body report. However, this 15-month period is "a "guideline for the arbitrator," not a rule," and . . . "that time may be shorter or longer, depending upon the particular circumstances."

* * *

Decision. India's quantitative restrictions and licensing scheme at issue were no longer justified to preserve its balance of payments and should be quickly phased out.

Comment. The panel's decision was upheld by the WTO Appellate Body in its report of August 1999 and adopted by the Dispute Settlement Body in September of that year.

CHAPTER SUMMARY

The *General Agreement on Tariffs and Trade* has provided a framework for the international trading system since the close of World War II by establishing the principles of international trade law upon which national trade laws are based. GATT prevented reactionary forces from drawing the world back into the isolationism and protectionism of the 1930s. GATT's multilateral trade negotiations have resulted in tariff concessions and a worldwide lowering of duties. Today, GATT has succeeded in reducing tariffs to levels that no longer act as a barrier threatening world trade. GATT's trade liberalization rules have also opened markets for foreign goods by reducing nontariff barriers to trade.

The *Uruguay Round,* completed in 1994, resulted in worldwide tariff reductions of almost 40 percent and will gradually eliminate many duties entirely under the zero-for-zero tariff concessions. The MFN and national treatment principles are based on the concept of nondiscrimination. These important principles ensure that importing nations will treat the goods of all GATT members equally in terms of taxes, charges, and administrative regulations. GATT provides for the eventual elimination of all quotas, although the balance-of-payment exception allows countries to impose temporary quantitative measures in a financial emergency.

GATT 1994 consists of the original 1947 agreement, numerous multilateral agreements negotiated since 1947, and the *Uruguay Round Agreements.*

GATT 1994 created the new WTO. This institution took over the responsibilities of the former GATT organization (1947–1994) effective in 1995. As of 2003, there were 146 members of the WTO. Despite some controversy, China was admitted to the WTO in 2001. If Russia's economic reforms continue, it is likely to gain entrance to the WTO.

GATT also provides a dispute settlement mechanism by which nations can settle their differences before a trade war begins. As of mid-2003, approximately 300 trade disputes had been brought to the WTO for consultation. Dispute settlement under the WTO has made many improvements over GATT 1947 methods. The WTO has greater power to enforce the decisions of the panel because no single country can veto their adoption.

This chapter focused on the basic principles of GATT international trade law and dispute settlement. However, the *Uruguay Round* also addressed many other specialized areas of trade relations. GATT 1994 contains agreements related to trade in agriculture, services, and textiles; these are trade-related investment measures and aspects of intellectual property rights; government procurement; technical barriers to trade; and more.

Questions and Case Problems

1. Visit the WTO Web site at http://www.wto.org. It is a practical, user-friendly guide, offering complete information on its role and organizational structure, access to the GATT legal texts, and dispute settlement cases.

   a. As a beginning point, and for an easy-to-understand introduction to the WTO, consider navigating to the section entitled *Resources > Resource Gateway,* and click on *Webcasting.* The page provides webcasting of major world trade events and a series of excellently produced training films. Be sure to watch *Basic Principles of the WTO System* by Pieter Jan Kuijper.

   b. To understand the importance of the WTO to world trade, from the organization's viewpoint, click on *The WTO > What Is the WTO.* For an interactive training module covering the technical aspects of the WTO, from this page link to *The WTO—A Training Package.*

   c. For links to all GATT/WTO agreements, from 1947 to the present, from the home page link to *Documents* and choose either *Legal Texts* or *Official Documents.* Accessing WTO materials through the link to *Legal Texts* is quick and easy. The latter page leads to http://docsonline.wto.org/, an alternative address for locating WTO materials where you can find documents either by browsing or searching.

   d. For access to WTO trade issues, including trade in goods, services, intellectual property, electronic commerce, investment, government procurement, trade and the environment, and dispute settlement, from the home page link to *Trade Topics > Trade Topics Gateway.*

   e. The topmost decision-making body of the WTO is the Ministerial Conference, which brings together all members of the WTO for meetings every two years. The Ministerial Conference can make decisions on all matters under any of the multilateral trade agreements. Ministerial Conferences were held in Cancún (2003), Doha (2001), Seattle (1999), Geneva (1998), and Singapore (1996). From the *Trade Topics Gateway,* link to *Ministerial Conference.* What is on the agenda of the most recent meeting?

   f. For access to the reports of WTO dispute settlement panels and the Appellate Body, from the home page link to *Trade Topics > Dispute Settlement > The Disputes.* Follow the link either *Chronologically, By Country,* or *By Subject.* Notice that the disputes are cited as *DS* followed by a number. The numbers are sequential, so that DS1 was the first dispute filed in 1995. Citations for panel reports will generally appear as WT/DS#/R, and reports of the Appellate Body will appear as WT/DS#/AB/R.

2. One of the most controversial areas for the WTO and its member governments has been relationship between trade and the environment. What are the overlapping issues? What impact does trade, or trade negotiations, have on environmental issues? How do these issues affect the developing countries, and what is their position? Explain the relationship between protection of the environment and economic development.

   a. Consider the following major trade-related environmental disputes at the WTO: *U.S.—Standards for Reformulated and Conventional Gasoline* (provisions of the U.S. *Clean Air Act,* DS52); *U.S.—Import Prohibition of Certain Shrimp and Shrimp Products* (selling of shrimp caught in nets without turtle extractors, DS58); *Measures Affecting Asbestos and Asbestos-Containing Products* (DS135); *European Communities—Measures Concerning Meat and Meat Products* (containing growth hormones, DS26, DS48, DS39); *European Communities—Measures Affecting the Approval and Marketing of Biotech Products* (genetically engineered foods, DS 291). Select one of these cases, and use it as a basis for a case study on the relationship between trade and environmental issues. Be sure to explore both sides of the debates.

   b. For alternative views on trade and the environment, see http://www.citizen.org/trade, http://www.sierraclub.org/trade, and a highly educational site offered by the Center for Strategic and International Studies (Washington, DC) aptly called http://www.globalization101.org/. To learn more about the important Shrimp/Turtle case at the WTO, see the National Wildlife Federation's site, http://www.nwf.org/trade/learnmore.html.

3. Every year the U.S. Trade Representative issues a report of foreign government trade barriers to U.S. goods and services. Locate these reports and describe the nature of these trade barriers. Which countries are the greatest "offenders"? What industries are most affected?

4. The term "most favored nation trade" is widely used throughout the world. In the United States, lawmakers and politicians prefer to use the term "Normal Trade Relations." Why do you suppose that they prefer this term?

5. In 1990, a Korean law established two distinct retail distribution systems for the sale of beef: one system for the retail sale of domestic beef and another system for the retail sale of imported beef. A small retailer (a non-supermarket or non-department store) designated as a "Specialized Imported Beef Store" may sell any beef *except domestic beef;* any other small retailer may sell any beef *except imported beef.* A large retailer (a supermarket or department store) may sell both imported and domestic beef, as long as the imported beef and domestic beef are sold in separate sales areas. A retailer selling imported beef is required to display a sign reading "Specialized Imported Beef Store." The dual retail system resulted in a reduction of beef imports. By 1998, there were approximately 5,000 imported beef shops as compared with approximately 45,000 shops selling domestic beef. Korea claims that stores may choose to sell either domestic or imported beef, and that they have total freedom to switch from one to another. Moreover, Korea argues that the dual system is necessary to protect consumers from deception by allowing them to clearly distinguish the origin of the beef purchased. Is the Korean regulation a valid consumer protection law? Do you think this system is necessary to protect consumers from fraudulent misrepresentation of the country of origin of the beef? Does it matter that scientific methods are available to determine the country of origin of beef? How do you think the dual system might affect the prices of imported beef versus domestic beef? Assuming that countries have the right to protect consumers from deception, what other methods might be available to accomplish this goal? *Korea—Measures Affecting Imports of Fresh, Chilled and Frozen Beef, World Trade Organization Report of the Appellate Body,* WT/DS161/AB/R, WT/DS169/AB/R (11 December 2000).

6. One of the central obligations of WTO membership is a limit on tariffs on particular goods according to a nation's tariff commitments. If a member does not abide by its agreement, can another WTO member unilaterally raise its agreed-upon tariff? Explain.

7. The U.S. auto industry has had its problems in the past from foreign competition. If the auto industry lobbied the president and Congress for implementation of a quota on the total number of imported automobiles and trucks, would such a quota be in violation of GATT 1994? Under what circumstances may a country impose a quota?

8. The WTO comprises many nations from all regions of the world. As such, the GATT/WTO system takes a global view of trade liberalization based on nondiscrimination, unconditional MFN, national treatment, tarrification, and multilateral trade negotiations. The GATT agreement recognizes that nations may form free-trade areas and customs unions. Yet a free-trade area only has free trade between the countries that belong to it. How does the concept of a free-trade area, such as the *North American Free Trade Agreement* (NAFTA) fit into the GATT/WTO global framework? Do free-trade areas violate the principle of nondiscrimination and MFN trade? Evaluate these arguments.

Managerial Implications

Your firm designs, manufactures, and markets children's toys for sale in the United States. Almost 90 percent of your production is done in the People's Republic of China. During the 1990s, U.S. relations with China improved. Even though there were many disagreements between the two countries, the United States granted normal trade status to China and continued to support China's application for membership in the WTO. Your firm invested heavily in China during that time. You have developed close ties to Chinese suppliers and have come to depend greatly on inexpensive Chinese labor and the lower costs of doing business there. You are now concerned, however, about increasing political tension between China and the United States over a variety of issues. The U.S. president has criticized the Chinese government, arguing that it has supported communist North Korea and sold missile technology to Middle Eastern countries. Most worrisome is China's claim to Taiwan under its "One-China" reunification policy, yet China continues to aim more missiles at Taiwan, accusing the United States of fostering "independence" there. The United States indicates that it may sell the newest navy destroyers and aegis radar systems to Taiwan. As China warns that sales of military equipment to Taiwan could lead to "serious danger," the president publicly reaffirms the importance of trade with China.

1. Describe the impact that a trade dispute would have on your firm.

2. Describe the impact on your firm if China were to lose its MFN trading status.

3. What strategic actions might you consider to reduce your firm's exposure to political risk?

4. What are the current areas of agreement or disagreement between the United States and China and how do you think they will affect future trade relations between the two countries?

5. In the wake of a communist victory in the late 1940s, the nationalist Chinese fled mainland China for the security of the island of Formosa. Today the island is known as Taiwan, and has its own independent, multiparty government and popularly elected president. It is industrialized and considered one of the Asian economic "Tigers." One of the pillars of American foreign policy during the Cold War was that the island of Taiwan should remain independent. But political and economic realities have caused the United States to remain pragmatic in its relationships with both the government of the People's Republic of China and Taiwan over the last thirty years. Taiwan joined the WTO under the name "Chinese Taipei," encompassing the "separate customs territory of Taiwan, Penghu, Kinmen, and Matsu." Examine the history of Taiwan and its relationship to China. What do you think of U.S. policies toward the region? While both mainland China and Taiwan are "Chinese," doing business there differs greatly. Describe that difference. How do business opportunities differ on the mainland versus the island? What do you think of the prospects for reunification, and what would be the impact on firms operating there?

CHAPTER 10

LAWS GOVERNING ACCESS TO FOREIGN MARKETS

The process of opening a country's markets to competition by foreign firms is often a slow and painful one, burdened by local political concerns. Many trade disputes over foreign market access have lasted for years. But as more and more industries become dependent on export sales, they become more vulnerable to foreign trade barriers. Open access to foreign markets thus becomes critical to business survival.

This chapter examines specific GATT agreements that open markets for goods and services in the following areas: (1) technical barriers to trade, including product standards; (2) import licensing procedures; (3) government procurement of goods and services; (4) trade in services, including consulting, engineering, banking and financial services, insurance, telecommunications, and the professions; (5) trade in agricultural products; (6) trade in textiles and apparel; (7) trade-related investment measures; and (8) trade-related aspects of intellectual property rights. The United States has implemented these GATT obligations in the *Uruguay Round Agreements Act*. The chapter concludes with a look at the U.S. response to foreign trade barriers that deny access to U.S. products and services or that treat U.S. firms unfairly. This includes U.S. laws that permit the country to retaliate against illegal foreign barriers to fair trade.

THE GENERAL PRINCIPLE OF LEAST RESTRICTIVE TRADE

We begin with one of the broadest and most important legal concepts in the body of international trade law: the *principle of least restrictive trade*. The principle states that WTO member countries, in setting otherwise valid restrictions on trade, shall make them no more restrictive than necessary to achieve the goals for which they were imposed. For example, if a country requires inspections of foreign fruit arriving from countries affected by a plant disease, the inspection procedures must be no more arduous, no more rigorous, and no more expensive than necessary to achieve those ends. In essence, they may not be a trade barrier in disguise.

A corollary is that national laws and regulations passed for purely internal purposes, such as the protection of the general health, welfare, and safety of its citizens, must also be as least restrictive to trade as possible. The principle might apply to health codes, environmental regulations, worker safety laws, or to uniform technical specifications for a wide range of industrial or consumer products. Examples might include laws regulating the sale of alcohol or tobacco, or banning the sale of beef containing hormones, of genetically modified foods, or toxic lead paint. It might include testing requirements for the flammability of fabrics or safety of childrens' toys, or set mandatory standards for the practice of law or medicine. The list could be endless; the concept is the same. Countries may protect their citizens to the extent they deem necessary, but must choose those methods that do not unduly burden international trade and do not single out foreign goods or service providers for unfair or discriminatory treatment. The WTO Appellate Body has stated that this is a balancing test: weighing the necessity of protecting the public against the restrictions on free trade. The principle of least restrictive trade appears throughout GATT law and applies to most of the discussions in this chapter.

The following case, *Thailand— Restrictions on*

Importation of Cigarettes, is an early GATT panel decision that is still cited by the WTO Appellate Body today. It considers Thailand's options for reducing tobacco use.

Thailand—Restrictions on Importation of Cigarettes
GATT Basic Instruments and Selected Documents, 37th Supp. 200 (Geneva, 1990).
Report of the Dispute Settlement Panel

BACKGROUND AND FACTS

The Royal Thai government maintains restrictions on imports of cigarettes. The *Tobacco Act of 1966* prohibited the import of all forms of tobacco except by license of the Director-General of the Excise Department. Licenses have only been granted to the government-owned Thai Tobacco Monopoly, which has imported cigarettes only three times since 1966. None have been imported in the ten years prior to this case. The United States requested the Panel to find that the licensing of imported cigarettes by Thailand was inconsistent with GATT Article XI and could not be justified under Article XX(b) since, as applied by Thailand, the licensing requirements were more restrictive than necessary to protect human health. Thailand argued that cigarette imports were prohibited to control smoking and because chemical and other additives contained in U.S. cigarettes might make them more harmful than Thai cigarettes.

REPORT OF THE PANEL ADOPTED ON 7 NOVEMBER 1990

The Panel, noting that Thailand had not granted licences for the importation of cigarettes during the past 10 years, found that Thailand had acted inconsistently with Article XI:1, the relevant part of which reads: "No prohibitions or restrictions . . . made effective through . . . import licenses . . . shall be instituted or maintained by any [country] on the importation of any product of the territory of any other [country]." . . .

The Panel proceeded to examine whether Thai import measures affecting cigarettes, while contrary to Article XI:1, were justified by Article XX(b), which states in part:

[N]othing in this Agreement shall be construed to prevent the adoption or enforcement by any [country] of measures: . . .

(b) necessary to protect human, animal or plant life or health.

The Panel then defined the issues which arose under this provision. . . . [The] Panel accepted that smoking constituted a serious risk to human health and that consequently measures designed to reduce the consumption of cigarettes fell within the scope of Article XX(b). The Panel noted that this provision clearly allowed [countries] to give priority to human health over trade liberalization; however, for a measure to be covered by Article XX(b) it had to be "necessary." . . .

The Panel concluded from the above that the import restrictions imposed by Thailand could be considered to be "necessary" in terms of Article XX(b) only if there were no alternative measure consistent with the GATT Agreement, or less inconsistent with it, which Thailand could reasonably be expected to employ to achieve its health policy objectives. The Panel noted that [countries] may, in accordance with Article III:4 of the GATT Agreement, impose laws, regulations and requirements affecting the internal sale, offering for sale, purchase, transportation, distribution or use of imported products provided they do not thereby accord treatment to imported products less favourable than that accorded to "like" products of national origin. The United States argued that Thailand could achieve its public health objectives through internal measures consistent with Article III:4 and that the inconsistency with Article XI:1 could therefore not be considered to be "necessary" within the meaning of Article XX(b). The Panel proceeded to examine this issue in detail. . . .

The Panel then examined whether the Thai concerns about the quality of cigarettes consumed in Thailand could be met with measures consistent, or less inconsistent, with the GATT Agreement. It noted that other countries had introduced strict,

continued

continued

non-discriminatory labeling and ingredient disclosure regulations which allowed governments to control, and the public to be informed of, the content of cigarettes. A non-discriminatory regulation implemented on a national treatment basis in accordance with Article III:4 requiring complete disclosure of ingredients, coupled with a ban on unhealthy substances, would be an alternative consistent with the GATT Agreement. The Panel considered that Thailand could reasonably be expected to take such measures to address the quality-related policy objectives it now pursues through an import ban on all cigarettes whatever their ingredients.

The Panel then considered whether Thai concerns about the quantity of cigarettes consumed in Thailand could be met by measures reasonably available to it and consistent, or less inconsistent, with the GATT Agreement. The Panel first examined how Thailand might reduce the demand for cigarettes in a manner consistent with the GATT Agreement. The Panel noted the view expressed by the World Health Organization (WHO) that the demand for cigarettes, in particular the initial demand for cigarettes by the young, was influenced by cigarette advertisements and that bans on advertisement could therefore curb such demand. At the Forty-third World Health Assembly a resolution was approved stating that the WHO is: "Encouraged by . . . recent information demonstrating the effectiveness of tobacco control strategies, and in particular . . . comprehensive legislative bans and other restrictive measures to effectively control the direct and the indirect advertising, promotion and sponsorship of tobacco."

A ban on the advertisement of cigarettes of both domestic and foreign origin would normally meet the requirements of Article III:4. . . . The Panel noted that Thailand had already implemented some non-discriminatory controls on demand, including information programmes, bans on direct and indirect advertising, warnings on cigarette packs, and bans on smoking in certain public places.

The Panel then examined how Thailand might restrict the supply of cigarettes in a manner consistent with the GATT Agreement. The Panel noted that

[countries] may maintain governmental monopolies, such as the Thai Tobacco Monopoly, on the importation and domestic sale of products. The Thai Government may use this monopoly to regulate the overall supply of cigarettes, their prices and their retail availability provided it thereby does not accord imported cigarettes less favourable treatment than domestic cigarettes or act inconsistently with any commitments assumed under its Schedule of Concessions. . . .

For these reasons the Panel could not accept the argument of Thailand that competition between imported and domestic cigarettes would necessarily lead to an increase in the total sales of cigarettes and that Thailand therefore had no option but to prohibit cigarette imports.

In sum, the Panel considered that there were various measures consistent with the GATT Agreement which were reasonably available to Thailand to control the quality and quantity of cigarettes smoked and which, taken together, could achieve the health policy goals that the Thai government pursues by restricting the importation of cigarettes inconsistently with Article XI:1. The Panel found therefore that Thailand's practice of permitting the sale of domestic cigarettes while not permitting the importation of foreign cigarettes was an inconsistency with the GATT not "necessary" within the meaning of Article XX(b).

Decision. The licensing system for cigarettes was contrary to Article XI:1 and is not justified by Article XX(b). The Panel recommended that Thailand bring its laws into conformity with its obligations under the GATT.

Comment. GATT Article XVII permits a country to create state agencies and "marketing boards" that have the authority to import and export goods. The Thai Tobacco Monopoly is an example. State trading enterprises are often used in developing countries and usually have the exclusive rights to import or export certain classifications of goods. Products traded by state enterprises might include foodstuffs, medicines, liquor, or in this case, tobacco. Article XVII requires that state enterprises not discriminate against the purchase of foreign goods, or treat them differently than domestic goods.

TECHNICAL BARRIERS TO TRADE

A *technical regulation* is a law or regulation affecting a product's characteristics—such as performance, design, construction, chemical composition, materials, packaging, labeling, etc.—that must be met before a product can be sold in a country. A *product standard,* or *standard,* is a voluntary guideline for product characteristics established by a recognized private or administrative body. Technical regulations are mandatory and imposed by government regulations, whereas standards are usually voluntary and issued by either private industry groups or government agencies. Although a standard may be "voluntary," it may very well be that a product will not be accepted by consumers in the marketplace unless it complies with the standard. Technical regulations and standards that apply to imported foreign products, even if they also apply equally to domestic products, are called *technical barriers to trade*.

The Protection of Public Health, Safety, or Welfare

Almost all products are subject to technical regulations or standards set by either government regulators or private standard-setting groups. They are generally imposed for the protection of public health, safety, or welfare. Examples might include standards for the safe design and manufacture of consumer or industrial goods, applied to an endless list of products, from machine lathes or automobiles to infant car seats or toothpaste. Imagine multinational companies such as Ford, General Electric, or Procter & Gamble and the incredibly diverse product standards they must meet in each country in which their products are sold. Other standards might protect consumers from fraud or deception; environmental standards on appliances and other products, such as the widely used restrictions on ozone-damaging refrigerants; fuel economy or exhaust emission standards for automobiles; packaging requirements on products such as plastic bottles to aid in recycling; technical specifications to standardize electrical power or telecommunications; building and construction standards such as common sizes for lumber and building materials; and many others.

Restrictions on Sale and Distribution: Testing and Inspections. Regulations can require the

inspection of the factory or plant where a product is made. Some products must be tested prior to sale and certified by a government agency or independent laboratory. For instance, in the United States, the *Flammable Fabrics Act* places technical restrictions on the sale of all bed mattresses. The law is administered through regulations of the Consumer Products Safety Commission. Six prototypes are subjected to a controlled cigarette burn test under laboratory conditions to determine whether they meet federal safety requirements. If the length of the char is longer than allowed or if the mattress ignites, then it does not pass. The manufacturer usually arranges to have the test performed by an independent laboratory. They are required to keep photographs and records of the results at their place of business, and to make them available to retailers, customers, or agency regulators when requested. Importers are also subject to the regulations; any of their products entering into the United States must meet these standards. If they cannot produce the certification, the goods will be denied entry. Thus, foreign manufacturers and importers alike must be familiar with the regulations of the countries to which their products will be shipped.

Because they often cause delays in getting goods to market, inspection and testing requirements can prove to be a tremendous barrier to trade. This is especially true if the product has a short shelf life, as with produce or other food products, or a short technological life (semiconductors or computer parts). In 1989, the European Community complained that the United States was delaying the inspection of perishable products by making them wait in turn behind nonperishable goods such as steel products, causing the perishables to spoil in the process. Entire shipments of citrus fruit from Spain had to be dumped, and the importer received no compensation.

In the United States, technical regulations and product standards are set by many federal agencies, including the Department of Agriculture, the Consumer Product Safety Commission, the Food and Drug Administration, the Federal Communications Commission, the Department of Energy, and the Department of Transportation. To illustrate, the U.S. Department of Agriculture is required by law to review meat inspection standards in foreign countries to ensure that imported meat products comply with USDA standards. The Federal Communications Commission promulgates uniform standards for telecommunications equipment that apply to foreign products. The Consumer Product Safety Commission's rules apply to all consumer products, regardless of where they are made. In 1994, the Commission learned that children's crayons imported from China contained hazardous amounts of lead in violation of U.S. regulations. The crayons were removed from stores.

Why Technical Regulations and Standards Are Barriers to Trade

Of course, a regulation or standard that applies only to foreign goods and not to domestic goods discriminates against the foreign goods. However, many technical barriers do not discriminate on their face, only in their application. As a result, discrimination may occur even when imported and domestic products are treated the same. A manufacturer whose product meets local regulations may find that building another product specially to meet foreign regulations is cost prohibitive. For instance, if U.S. wallboard manufacturers produce wallboard that is 3/8" thick, and Europe requires wallboard to be 1.5 cm. thick, then the firm will have to produce specially made wallboard for export to Europe. Certainly the European nations have the right to determine safety standards for construction, but the regulation does not allow the U.S. firm to take advantage of economies of scale and is, thus, an indirect technical barrier to trade. Another problem is that many technical barriers are not disclosed to foreign firms. Either they are not published or are made known only to domestic firms. Moreover, foreign companies are generally not a part of the standard-setting process. Domestic firms are typically invited to participate in developing and writing regulations or standards; foreign firms are not. Thus, they often experience delays in adapting their products for sale in the foreign market, causing them to lose competitive advantage to local firms. The U.S. Department of Commerce maintains a collection of international standards so that U.S. exporters have access to foreign technical regulations and standards applicable to their industries.

http://www.scc.ca (Canada)
http://www.jisc.go.jp/eng (Japan)
(Japan Industrial Standards Committee)
http://www.gost.ru (Russia)
http://www.sac.gov.cn
Other National Standard Organizations

Technical Barriers in the European Union. The problem of technical barriers is critical to firms operating in the EU where national standards vary tremendously. Consider the impact of these barriers on a firm such as Phillips, a Dutch electronics company, which has had to manufacture twenty-nine different types of electrical outlets. Thus, the standards policy of the EU is designed to balance the health and safety interests of member countries with the need for the free flow of goods. Despite decades of work by the EU Commission to reduce technical barriers to trade, thousands of new national standards have arisen. Even after years of debating detailed standards for thousands of products, companies wishing to sell their products in Europe still face a maze of complex regulations, applicable to a wide range of products from beer to hair dryers, automobiles to plywood. However, EU countries understand that uniform standards are essential to achieving a unified market.

The EU's effort to reduce technical barriers is reflected in many opinions of the European Court of Justice. In one case, arising over the sale of liquor made in France and sold in Germany, the Court ruled that an EU member country cannot prohibit the sale of a product produced in another EU member country when that product had already met the technical specifications of the producing country. In decisions handed down in the 1980s, the court rejected attempts by two EU countries to protect centuries-old industries. Disregarding consumer protection arguments, the Court of Justice struck down Germany's beer purity law that had kept out foreign beers containing preservatives and required that beer only be made from wheat, barley, hops, and yeast (beer made in other European countries often contains rice and other grains), and Italy's pasta content regulations. In one long-standing dispute with the United States, the EU prohibited the import of beef with hormones, and because the hormones are widely used in the United States, U.S. beef was kept out of European markets.

Most standard setting in the EU takes place through the *European Committee for Standardization,* which sets voluntary standards for non-electrical products, the *European Committee for Electrotechnical Standardization,* and the *European Telecommunications Standards Institute.* These intergovernmental agencies work with manufacturers, including some European subsidiaries of U.S. firms, and scientists to develop workable product standards. When adopted by directive of the European Council, the standards become legally binding for products sold in Europe (see Exhibit 10.1).

> **http://www.cenorm.be**
> Web site of the *European Committee for Standardization.*

The EU has attempted to increase its standardization through the use of the *"CE Mark,"* meaning *Conformité Européene.* The CE Mark is an internationally recognized symbol for quality and product safety for many different types of products, such as children's toys, gas appliances, machinery and medical and electrical equipment. European manufacturers are inspected and audited by an EU authorized body. The product itself must be tested by an independent laboratory. Once the mark is received, a European manufacturer may sell its products throughout the EU without undergoing inspections in each individual country. Manufacturers outside the EU may submit their products to an independent laboratory for testing before attaching the CE Mark. The U.S. government estimates that by 2004, half of the U.S. products shipped to Europe will require CE Mark compliance.

> **http://europa.eu.int/ecolabel**
> The home page of the EU "Eco-Label" provides information and assistance for producers seeking certification for eco-labeling. The label is valid for three years and demonstrates that a product is environmentally friendly.

Technical Barriers in Japan. Japan and the United States have had a long history of disputes over Japanese technical barriers to trade. U.S. and other non-Japanese firms have lodged many complaints against Japan's technical barriers, most of which involve unreasonable and burdensome inspection procedures or import licensing requirements, and the arbitrary enforcement of overly strict standards. Japan has maintained complex technical regulations on thousands of important products, including electrical appliances, telecommunications and medical equipment, lumber, electronic components, pharmaceuticals, and food. The prolific use of technical requirements in Japan is rooted in Japan's protective attitude toward consumers, the historical role of the Japanese government in economic life, and the Japanese people's acceptance of governmental regulation of business. Products standards in Japan have been generally based on *design* characteristics—how a product should be designed and manufactured. U.S. standards, by contrast, are usually based on *performance.* Thus, products designed according to foreign regulations can pass U.S. regulations if they perform according to standards. Products capable of inflicting injury on consumers or that affect public health are more highly regulated than other products. For example, for many years Japan banned the import of cosmetics containing colorants and preservatives for health reasons, despite the fact that they are approved for use in the United States.

Japanese agencies that enforce technical regulations include the *Japanese Ministry of Economy, Trade, and Industry,* which has the widest authority, and the ministries that oversee the health, agriculture, and transportation sectors. Many products require testing and *prior approval* before they can be sold. For instance, prior to the mid-1980s, foreign products could not be inspected for preclearance at the foreign factory, but could only be inspected, shipment by shipment, as they arrived in Japan. Items had to be individually inspected and tested for compliance with the technical regulations or standards. Legal changes have now made it possible for a foreign firm to register with the appropriate regulatory ministry and to obtain advance product approval without going through a Japanese importer or intermediary. Another problem occurs when Japanese technical regulations and standards lack transparency. Their agencies still generally do not permit foreign input into

EXHIBIT 10.1

EU Council Directive Concerning the Safety of Toys*

Article 1.1. This Directive shall apply to toys. A "toy" shall mean any product or material designed or clearly intended for use in play by children of less than 14 years of age.

2. Taking account of the period of foreseeable and normal use, a toy must meet the safety and health conditions laid down in this Directive.

Article 5.1. Member states shall presume compliance with the essential requirements referred to in Article 3 in respect of toys bearing the EC mark provided for in Article 11, hereinafter referred to as "EC mark," denoting conformity with the relevant national standards which transpose the harmonized standards the reference numbers of which have been published in the Official Journal of the European Communities.

Article 7.1. Where toys bearing the EC mark are likely to jeopardize the safety and/or health of consumers, it shall withdraw the products from the market.

Article 8.1. Before being placed on the market, toys must have affixed to them the EC mark by which the manufacturer or his authorized representative established within the Community confirms that the toys comply with those standards;
. . .

3. The approved [inspection firm] shall carry out the EC type-examination in the manner described below:
   -it shall check that the toy would not jeopardize safety and/or health, as provided for in Article 2.
   -it shall carry out the appropriate examinations and tests—using as far as possible the harmonized standards referred to in Article 5 (1).

Article 11.1. The EC mark shall as a rule be affixed either to the toy or on the packaging in a visible, easily legible and indelible form.

2. The EC mark shall consist of the symbol "CE."

3. The affixing to toys of marks or inscriptions that are likely to be confused with the EC mark shall be prohibited.

Article 12.1. Member States shall take the necessary measures to ensure that sample checks are carried out on toys which are on their market and may select a sample and take it away for examination and testing.

ANNEX II ESSENTIAL SAFETY REQUIREMENTS FOR TOYS

II. PARTICULAR RISKS

1. Physical and mechanical properties:

(a) Toys must have the mechanical strength to withstand the stresses during use without breaking at the risk of causing physical injury.

(b) Edges, protrusions, cords, cables, and fastenings on toys must be so designed and constructed that the risks of physical injury from contact with them are reduced as far as possible.
. . .

(d) Toys, and their component parts, and any detachable parts of toys which are clearly intended for use by children under thirty-six months must be of such dimensions as to prevent their being swallowed or inhaled.

(e) Toys, and their parts and the packaging in which they are contained for retail sale must not present a risk of strangulation or suffocation.
. . .

(h) Toys conferring mobility on their users must, as far as possible, incorporate a braking system which is suited to the type of toy and is commensurate with the kinetic energy developed by it.

2. Flammability: (a) Toys must not constitute a dangerous flammable element in the child's environment. They must therefore be composed of materials which . . . irrespective of the toy's chemical composition, are treated so as to delay the combustion process.

ANNEX IV WARNINGS AND INDICATIONS OF PRECAUTIONS TO BE TAKEN WHEN USING TOYS

1. Toys which might be dangerous for children under thirty-six months of age shall bear a warning, for example: "Not suitable for children under thirty-six months."
. . .

5. Skates and skateboards for children. If these products are offered for sale as toys, they shall bear the marking: "Warning: protective equipment should be worn."

---

*Exhibit text was edited for student use by the authors.
Council Directive 88/378/EEC of 3 May 1998 concerning the safety of toys. *Official Journal* L 187, 16/07/1988, p. 0001–0013; Document 388L0378
SOURCE: EU Web site. http://europa.eu.int/eur-lex/en/lif/dat/1988/en_388L0378.html

the drafting of the regulations, although on occasion U.S. industry groups, under pressure, have succeeded in being heard by Japanese standard-setting groups. During the 1980s, new Japanese regulations provided that advance announcements of product standards be made by the *Japan External Trade Organization.*

The symbol of an approved product in Japan is the government-authorized *Japan Industrial Standards Mark,* or JIS Mark. Its appearance on a product, although voluntary, indicates that the manufacturer has submitted to on-site inspections by the appropriate Japanese ministry and has met accepted standards for quality control, production techniques, and research methods. Because this mark has become widely recognized, foreign products without it are often not competitive in the Japanese market.

International Organization for Standardization

The most internationally accepted standards are those promulgated by the *International Organization for Standardization,* based in Geneva. The standards have become widely recognized throughout the world and have become required in many industries. The most commonly known standard is ISO 9000. Since 1987, ISO 9000 is the standard used for assuring product quality through product design and manufacturing process. Companies become certified through a costly and rigorous inspection of their facilities and documentation of their quality control systems. They are audited on a regular basis for compliance. In order to sell in Europe, many U.S. firms have obtained ISO certification. By meeting ISO requirements, the firms no longer have to certify each product individually in every European country. ISO certification is required under EU law for certain regulated products, such as medical devices and construction equipment. Market demands make compliance for other products equally essential. In the United States, a number of firms offer assistance to U.S. companies seeking ISO certification. New ISO 9000 standards were issued in 2000. They are tougher and more demanding, and require a greater commitment from executives and senior management. By 1999 almost 350,000 companies worldwide had received ISO quality certification. ISO 14000 standards will provide guidelines for environmental management and labeling (e.g., advertising claims that a product is "environmentally safe," etc.).

> **http://www.iso.ch/**
> The home page of the ISO. Links to "Standards and World Trade" and to the ISO 9000: 2000 Quality Standards.

The GATT 1994 *Agreement on Technical Barriers to Trade*

The GATT 1994 *Agreement on Technical Barriers to Trade* is one of the *Uruguay Round* agreements. It governs the use of technical regulations, product standards, testing, and certifications by WTO member countries. It improves on the older standards code that had been in effect since the *Tokyo Round* in 1979. Unlike the 1979 code that was signed by about only thirty countries, the new agreement is binding on all WTO member countries. Remember that this agreement does not contain standards of its own. It makes no attempt to say how a product should perform or be designed, or when a product is safe or unsafe. These are matters for nations and local governments to decide. But the GATT *Agreement on Technical Barriers* does prohibit countries from using their regulations or standards to discriminate against the import of foreign goods.

> **http://www.wto.org/**
> For information on the WTO *Agreement on Technical Barriers to Trade,* and other WTO agreements discussed in this chapter, link from WTO home page to "Trade Topics."

The 1994 *Agreement on Technical Barriers to Trade* builds on the 1979 agreement. It applies to all products, including agricultural, industrial, and consumer goods. The agreement's main provisions can be outlined as follows:

1. All technical regulations shall be applied on a nondiscriminatory basis, without regard to the national origin of the products.
2. Regulations must not be made or applied to create an *unnecessary obstacle* to trade, and they must not be more trade restrictive than necessary to fulfill a legitimate objective such as national security, preventing fraud or deception of consumers, protecting public health or safety, or protecting the environment.

3. The agreement requires that countries take into account available scientific and technical information in writing their standards. This provision is intended to assure that standards are not made just to keep out foreign goods, but that they have some scientific foundation.

4. Wherever possible, product requirements should be based on performance abilities of the product rather than on design or descriptive characteristics.

5. The agreement recommends that countries develop and use internationally accepted standards where they exist. International standards will be presumed to be in compliance with GATT.

6. Proposed standards must be published and made available to foreign countries, and an opportunity be given to those countries to make written comments prior to adoption.

7. Final regulations must be published, with a reasonable time given before they become effective so that foreign producers have time to adapt their products.

8. Testing and inspection procedures should restrict trade as little as possible and should not discriminate. The agreement encourages on-site factory inspections instead of port-of-entry inspections for foreign goods.

9. Nations should try to see that states and local governments, as well as private standard-setting groups, comply with the agreement.

10. Disputes between countries may be referred to the WTO for negotiation and settlement.

The following case, *European Communities—Measures Affecting Asbestos & Asbestos-Containing Products,* is considered a landmark case in world trade law. Not only is it the first case to interpret the *Agreement on Technical Barriers to Trade,* but it addresses a country's right to pass laws protecting the public health and safety under this agreement and under general GATT principles.

European Communities—Measures Affecting Asbestos & Asbestos-Containing Products
WT/DS135/AB/R (2001)
World Trade Organization Report of the Appellate Body

BACKGROUND AND FACTS

Asbestos is a natural mineral product in use since the 1800s. It is inexpensive, resistant to heat and flame, and has been used in many industrial applications. It has been used in making fireproof materials, fireproof insulation, and brake linings, and is used today in construction materials such as asbestos cement boards and pipes. It has been known for some time that exposure to asbestos fibers and particles can cause deadly lung disease, including a form of cancer for which the death rate is 100 percent. Signs of disease may not manifest themselves for thirty years after exposure. Although most uses of asbestos are now banned, it is still used in certain forms. Today, deposits are still mined in Russia, Canada, China, Brazil, and a few other countries. There are substitutes for asbestos such as glass or cellulous whose fibers are not as dangerous.

The asbestos at issue in this case involves Canadian chrysotile exports to France. Prior to 1997, Canada was exporting up to 40,000 tons of asbestos to France each year. Citing the health risk, France imposed a virtual ban on its manufacture, import, sale, and use, subject to a few limited and temporary exceptions. The Canadian asbestos industry responded that chrysotile fibers can be used without incurring any detectable risk because the fibers become encapsulated in the hardened products into which it is made, such as heat-resistant cement blocks. Canada requested WTO dispute settlement. France claims that it can restrict asbestos both under GATT Article XX(b) (general provisions that a country may protect public health) and under similar provisions in the *Agreement on Technical Barriers to Trade* (the TBT). The Canadian government argued that the French law was not a "technical regulation" as permitted under the TBT, but a total prohibition. It also argued that under GATT Article III:4 (the general principle of nondiscrimination) a country may not treat imported products differently than "like products" of domestic origin. Canada maintained that the restrictions on asbestos discriminated against other less harmful substitute products made of

continued

continued

glass or cellulous. Finally, Canada argued that the restrictions went beyond what was "necessary" to protect human health, as set forth in GATT Article XX(b) [see appendices to this text]. It claimed that less restrictive measures, such as "controlled use" of the product, were enough to guarantee safety. The Appellate Body report upholds the French law, although for different reasons than those stated by the original panel.

REPORT OF THE APPELLATE BODY
* * *

Are the restrictions on asbestos a technical regulation? [added for understanding]
The heart of the definition of a "technical regulation" is that a "document" must "lay down"—that is, set forth, stipulate or provide—"product characteristics." The word "characteristic" has a number of synonyms that are helpful in understanding the ordinary meaning of that word in this context. Thus, the "characteristics" of a product include, in our view, any objectively definable "features," "qualities," "attributes," or other "distinguishing mark" of a product. Such "characteristics" might relate . . . to a product's composition, size, shape, colour, texture, hardness, tensile strength, flammability, conductivity, density, or viscosity. . . . The definition of a "technical regulation" also states that "compliance" with the "product characteristics" laid down in the "document" must be "mandatory."
* * *

"Product characteristics" may, in our view, be prescribed or imposed with respect to products in either a positive or a negative form. That is, the document may provide, positively, that products must possess certain "characteristics," or the document may require, negatively, that products must not possess certain "characteristics." In both cases, the legal result is the same: the document "lays down" certain binding "characteristics" for products, in one case affirmatively, and in the other by negative implication.

With these considerations in mind, we examine whether the measure at issue is a "technical regulation." [The French law] aims primarily at the regulation of a named product, asbestos [and imposes] a prohibition on asbestos fibers, as such. This prohibition on these fibers does not, in itself, prescribe or impose any "characteristics" on asbestos fibers, but simply bans them in their natural state. Accordingly, if this measure consisted only of a prohibition on

asbestos fibers, it might not constitute a "technical regulation."

There is, however, more to the measure than this prohibition on asbestos fibers. . . . It is important to note here that, although formulated negatively—products containing asbestos are prohibited—the measure, in this respect, effectively prescribes or imposes certain objective features, qualities or "characteristics" *on all products*. That is, in effect, the measure provides that *all products must not contain* asbestos fibers [emphasis added]. . . . We also observe that compliance with the prohibition against products containing asbestos is mandatory and is, indeed, enforceable through criminal sanctions. * * * For these reasons, we conclude that the measure constitutes a "technical regulation" under the TBT Agreement.
* * *

Do the restrictions on asbestos imports, but not on less harmful domestic substitutes, violate GATT's nondiscrimination provisions? Are they "Like Products"?
We are very much of the view that evidence relating to the health risks associated with a product may be pertinent in an examination of "likeness" under Article III:4 of the GATT 1994. This carcinogenicity, or toxicity, constitutes, as we see it, a defining aspect of the physical properties of chrysotile asbestos fibers. The evidence indicates that [cellulous, glass, and other less harmful fibers] in contrast, do not share these properties, at least to the same extent. We do not see how this highly significant physical difference *cannot* be a consideration in examining the physical properties of a product as part of a determination of "likeness" under Article III:4 [general principles of nondiscrimination] of the GATT 1994.
* * *

We also see it as important to take into account that, since 1977, chrysotile asbestos fibers have been recognized internationally as a known carcinogen. . . . This carcinogenicity was confirmed by the experts consulted by the Panel, with respect to both lung cancers and mesotheliomas. . . . "In contrast . . . [t]he experts also confirmed, . . . that current scientific evidence indicates that [cellulous and glass] do "not present the same risk to health as chrysotile" asbestos fibers. * * * It follows that the evidence relating to properties indicates that, physically, chrysotile asbestos and [its substitutes] are very different. . . .

continued

continued

Is the French law valid under GATT Article XX(b), which provides that a country may adopt measures necessary to protect human life or health, provided that it is not a disguised restriction on trade?

[W]e have examined the seven factors on which Canada relies in asserting that the Panel erred in concluding that there exists a human health risk associated with the manipulation of chrysotile-cement products. We see Canada's appeal on this point as, in reality, a challenge to the Panel's assessment of the credibility and weight to be ascribed to the scientific evidence before it. Canada contests the conclusions that the Panel drew both from the evidence of the scientific experts and from scientific reports before it. As we have noted, we will interfere with the Panel's appreciation of the evidence only when we are "satisfied that the panel has *exceeded the bounds of its discretion,* as the trier of facts, in its appreciation of the evidence." In this case, nothing suggests that the Panel exceeded the bounds of its lawful discretion. To the contrary, all four of the scientific experts consulted by the Panel concurred that chrysotile asbestos fibers, and chrysotile-cement products, constitute a risk to human health, and the Panel's conclusions on this point are faithful to the views expressed by the four scientists. In addition, the Panel noted that the carcinogenic nature of chrysotile asbestos fibers has been acknowledged since 1977 by international bodies, such as the International Agency for Research on Cancer and the World Health Organization. In these circumstances, we find that the Panel remained well within the bounds of its discretion in finding that chrysotile-cement products pose a risk to human life or health. Accordingly, we uphold the Panel's finding that the measure [protects human life or health], within the meaning of Article XX(b) of the GATT 1994.

Does GATT mandate the level of protection necessary to protect life and health or the means of achieving it?

As to Canada's argument, relating to the level of protection, we note that it is undisputed that WTO Members have the right to determine the level of protection of health that they consider appropriate in a given situation. France has determined, and the Panel accepted, that the chosen level of health protection by France is a "halt" to the spread of *asbestos*-related health risks. . . . Our conclusion is not altered by the fact that [glass and cellulose] fibers might pose a risk to health. The scientific evidence before the Panel indicated that the risk posed by

[these substitutes] is, in any case, *less* than the risk posed by asbestos, although that evidence did *not* indicate that the risk posed by [glass or cellulose substitutes] is non-existent. Accordingly, it seems to us perfectly legitimate for a Member to seek to halt the spread of a highly risky product while allowing the use of a less risky product in its place. In short, we do not agree with Canada's third argument.

Canada asserts that [France could achieve the same level of public safety through a "controlled use" policy instead of a complete prohibition and that this] represents a "reasonably available" measure that would serve the same end. The issue is, thus, whether France could reasonably be expected to employ "controlled use" practices to achieve its chosen level of health protection—a halt in the spread of asbestos-related health risks.

In our view, France could not reasonably be expected to employ *any* alternative measure if that measure would involve a continuation of the very risk that the [French law] seeks to "halt." Such an alternative measure would, in effect, prevent France from achieving its chosen level of health protection. On the basis of the scientific evidence before it, the Panel found that, in general, the efficacy of "controlled use" remains to be demonstrated. Moreover, even in cases where "controlled use" practices are applied "with greater certainty," the scientific evidence suggests that the level of exposure can, in some circumstances, still be high enough for there to be a "significant residual risk of developing asbestos-related diseases." "Controlled use" would, thus, not be an alternative measure that would achieve the end sought by France.

Decision. The French restrictions on asbestos are a valid technical regulation under the TBT Agreement. GATT requires that national laws not discriminate between imports and domestic "like products." Asbestos and its less harmful domestic substitutes are not "like products" because their effects on human life and health are very different. This impact on health may be taken into account in determining if the products are "like" each other. The restrictions are permitted both under the TBT Agreement and under the general right of a country under Article XX(b) to protect public health. Given the deadly long-term effects of asbestos inhalation, France need not use a less restrictive means of controlling asbestos, but is free to decide the level of health protection for its citizens. Future disputes over the health and safety of other imported products must be considered by panels on a case-by-case basis.

IMPORT LICENSING PROCEDURES

The case of Thailand's cigarette restrictions earlier in the chapter is an example of how an import licensing scheme can work to block foreign imports. Of course, Article XI does permit a country to use licensing in a nondiscriminatory, MFN, and transparent fashion in order to regulate imports in certain cases. For instance, a country may use licensing to enforce its technical regulations or standards laws. Thus, in such a case, a health department would appropriately permit importation of say, pillows and mattresses *only* upon a license indicating that the products were made from sterilized materials. Customs officials might request to see this license at the border. Revenues from license fees could go to support the costs of inspection and administering the law. Import licenses are also used to track the quantities of imported goods subject to a quota. For instance, textile products from certain countries enter the United States under a quota. The textile importer must hand over the license for the given quantity to U.S. Customs. The license appears in the precise form (including typeface and color) as agreed between the United States and foreign governments so it can be authenticated. The license information is then sent to Washington, where the Customs Service tracks the quantity of each type of textile product entered from each foreign country so far in that year.

Imagine if you were trying to ship to a foreign customer in, say, Burkina Faso, Slovenia, or Japan. Suppose that country maintained complex licensing requirements for your products. Imagine now that you and your customer are told that the application and conditions for import are not set out in the local law books or regulations, but in some internal "back office" manuals—or even worse, they are made up by local government bureaucrats on a case-by-case basis. Both you and your customer might very well throw up your hands and give up. This is what we mean by licensing requirements that lack "transparency." GATT requires that import license procedures be transparent. Under WTO rules, a licensing scheme is *transparent* if the procedures to obtain the license are not unduly complicated, and the licensing rules are published and openly available to business parties in all countries. GATT requires

that applications for import licenses should be handled within thirty to sixty days.

The GATT 1994 *Agreement on Import Licensing Procedures*

The GATT 1994 *Agreement on Import Licensing Procedures* sets guidelines for countries issuing import licenses. It calls for the procedures to be fair, reasonable, and nondiscriminatory, and that application procedures to obtain a license should be as simple as possible. Applications should not be refused because of minor errors in paperwork. In other words, governments should see that clerical workers and bureaucracies do not use the licensing procedures to stand in the way of trade. Where licenses are used to administer quotas, the amount of the quota already used must be published for all importers to see. The WTO *Import Licensing Committee* must be notified if any new products will become subject to licensing requirements.

Trade Facilitation

Anyone experienced in moving goods from one country to another has had to suffer through arcane foreign regulations, reams of paperwork, miles of "government red tape," and what sometimes seems like endless delays at the border. The WTO estimates that these "hidden" costs can often be greater than the cost of tariffs themselves. *Trade facilitation* refers to the WTO's effort to simplify and standardize government regulations and procedures affecting the movement of goods across national borders. Although many of the specific trade agreements, such as the *Agreement on Import Licensing Procedures,* deal with certain aspects of this problem, trade facilitation is a broader effort to reduce the costs of cross-border shipments and to speed the movement of goods through the use of streamlined procedures, computerization and automation, and increased communication between customs agencies in different countries.

GOVERNMENT PROCUREMENT

Governments are among the largest business customers in the world. GATT Article III permits an exception from its national treatment provision for government procurement, allowing governments to favor domestic suppliers. Article III, which normally prohibits laws that discriminate against foreign goods, states that,

> [T]his article shall not apply to laws, regulations or requirements governing the procurement by governmental agencies of products purchased for governmental purposes and not with a view to commercial resale or with a view to use in the production of goods for commercial sale.

Most nations of the world have laws that require their own government agencies to give some preference to domestically made products. The laws often apply to goods purchased by defense-related agencies or by the military. Other laws might require that the purchased product contain a certain proportion of domestically made component parts or raw materials. In the United States, the *Federal Buy American Act* as well as state and local Buy American laws allow preferences for the purchase of domestic goods. The federal government is required to buy domestic products unless such purchases are not in the public interest or the costs are unreasonable. The U.S. Department of Defense must purchase domestic products unless those products are more than 50 percent more expensive than competing foreign goods. Japan has come under criticism for its discriminatory procurement rules. For the company that is considering bidding on a foreign government procurement contract, knowledge of the specific rules applicable to that bid is essential.

The GATT 1994 *Agreement on Government Procurement*

The *Uruguay Round Agreement on Government Procurement* (AGP) is causing many changes in procurement practices in the United States and other countries. The AGP requires fair, open, and nondiscriminatory procurement practices and sets up uniform procurement procedures to protect suppliers from different countries. It applies to the purchase of goods or services worth more than $185,000 (as of June 2003) or to construction contracts (building, dams, power plants, etc.) worth more than $7 million. Unlike the other GATT agreements, the AGP applies only to those coun-

tries that have signed it. (As of 2001, there were twenty-eight nations, including the United States and the EU, participating in the AGP.) The countries negotiated with each other as to how the AGP will be applied among them, and so the rules can differ depending on the countries involved in a purchase. For instance, the AGP says that Japan will not receive the benefit of the agreement if it wants to sell goods or services to NASA because Japan has not treated U.S. companies equally in procuring satellite technology. The purpose of the agreement is to bring competition to world procurement markets. The ITC estimates that the agreement will open up export markets for U.S. companies worth hundreds of billions of dollars.

Agencies Excluded from the Procurement Rules. The agreement applies to almost ninety U.S. federal agencies, large and small—from the Department of Labor to the American Battle Monuments Commission—and includes the executive branch departments. Several exclusions from the procurement rules include purchases to be sent to foreign countries as foreign aid; purchases by the Department of Agriculture for food distribution or for farm support programs; and some purchases made by the Federal Aviation Administration, the Department of Energy, and the Department of Defense that are related to national security or to the military. In the United States, thirty-seven states have also agreed to comply, and more will do so in the future. Many states—based on political reasonings—opted to exclude certain items: New York excluded subway cars and buses, and South Dakota excluded purchases of beef. Thus, state agencies in these states may give preferences to local producers when awarding procurement bids for these products.

Procurement Rules. The new AGP reverses the general GATT rules that allow government agencies to favor domestic products. It brings the principles of MFN trade, nondiscrimination, and transparency to government procurement. A procuring agency must treat the products, services, and suppliers from all other countries that have signed the agreement equally *and no less favorably than* if they were from its own country. Moreover, a government agency may not discriminate against local suppliers just because they are foreign-owned. The agreement prohibits *offsets,* which occur when a firm is awarded a contract only when it gives something to the government in return. Contracts cannot be awarded to a firm because it had agreed to utilize domestic materials, parts, or labor. Offsets also can be complex. For instance, assume that Aeroflop, a U.S. firm, wants to sell several million dollars worth of airplanes to a government-owned airline in a European country famous for cheese. In order to get the contract it agrees to pay a 5 percent kickback to another U.S. company, Cheezy, if Cheezy agrees to buy all of its cheese from a seller in that European country. If the cheese-producing country requires Aeroflop to make the offset, it violates the AGP.

Other rules state how the country-of-origin of products sold to a government agency is to be determined. For instance, a supplier that sells a product that is fraudulently labeled with the incorrect country-of-origin may be subjected to severe penalties under the law of the country involved.

Transparency in Procurement Procedures. To ensure that the new rules are applied fairly, the AGP sets up procedures for governments to follow. When a government agency intends to make a purchase by inviting suppliers to "bid on the job," the agency must give adequate notice to potential bidders when the contract is announced and disclose all the information necessary for them to submit their bid. The agreement requires fairness in qualifying foreign companies to bid (e.g., countries can disqualify companies that are not technically or financially capable of delivering). In the event of a disagreement between a supplier and a procuring agency, countries must allow the supplier to challenge the contract either before an independent administrative review board or the courts.

Administering Government Procurement Rules in the United States

Congress has placed responsibility for implementing the AGP with the president. Basically, the president may waive the requirements of the *Buy American Act* for suppliers from any country that is party to the AGP *and* that complies with its terms in its own procurement practices. Suppliers from a least-developed country also receive the waiver. This waiver entitles those foreign suppliers to nondiscrimination and equal treatment with U.S. domestic suppliers.

The president must compile an annual report of those countries that have adopted the AGP but that do not abide by it. The USTR negotiates with violating countries to get them to end their unfair practices and give equal access to U.S. firms. If no agreement is reached, then the USTR must present the case to the WTO for dispute settlement. If an agreement or resolution is still not reached within eighteen months of initiating dispute settlement, then the president must revoke the waiver of the *Buy American Act,* and preferences for domestic suppliers will be allowed.

In certain cases, the president must completely prohibit U.S. government agencies from procuring products from suppliers in a foreign country, such as where the country "maintains a significant and persistent pattern or practice of discrimination against U.S. products or services which results in identifiable harm to U.S. business." The prohibition also applies to a country that has not joined the AGP—but from whom the U.S. government buys significant amounts of goods or services—that fails to provide U.S. firms with equal access to its procurement markets, or that permits its agencies to engage in bribery, extortion, or corruption in procuring goods or services. This severe sanction can only be used if the president has first consulted interested U.S. companies and if it will not harm the public interest of the United States and does not unreasonably restrict competition.

Other Procurement Agreements. The United States has negotiated several other procurement agreements with foreign nations. On behalf of the U.S. telecommunications industry, it entered into an agreement with Japan to help open opportunities for U.S. firms bidding on contracts there. A 1993 agreement between the United States and the EU opened up the $15 to $20 billion heavy electrical equipment (power plant) market in Europe. The *North American Free Trade Agreement* (NAFTA) also contains its own provisions to guarantee U.S., Canadian, and Mexican firms "equal access" and "equal opportunity" to government contracts over $25,000.

TRADE IN SERVICES

Service industries such as travel and tourism; transportation and distribution; professional services, finance, banking, and insurance; and telecommunications account for the majority of the gross domestic product in the United States and most developed countries. Indeed, in 2002, service industries accounted for over 80 percent of U.S. GDP, according to the U.S. Department of Commerce. Although much attention is given to the U.S. merchandise trade deficits, the United States consistently runs a trade surplus in services. In 2002, U.S. exports of services amounted to $292 billion, or 30 percent of total U.S. trade volume, generating a trade surplus in services of $65 billion. According to the WTO, total cross-border services accounted for about 25 percent of world trade or about $1.5 trillion annually. Although the GATT agreement regulated trade in goods for more than forty-five years, it did not regulate trade in services until the *Uruguay Round* agreements. (Also, the *North American Free Trade Agreement* permits a free flow of services between the United States, Canada, and Mexico.)

---

http://europa.eu.int/comm/trade/services/
index_en.htm
Presents the EU view on trade services.
http://www.trade.gov/td/sif
The U.S. government's most comprehensive information site for trade in services.

The GATT 1994 *General Agreement on Trade in Services*

As a result of the *Uruguay Round,* the *General Agreement on Trade in Services,* or GATS, is the first multilateral, legally enforceable agreement to establish rules for international trade in services. It is a part of the WTO system, and is overseen by the *Council for Trade in Services.* The agreement is largely patterned after the concepts that GATT applies to trade in goods. The agreement covers trade in most services, including health services, architecture, engineering and construction, travel and tourism, legal and other professional services, rental and leasing, distribution and courier services, education, management and environmental consulting, market research and advertising consulting, computer services, repair and maintenance, sanitation and disposal, franchising, entertainment, and others. GATS applies to the federal government as well as to state and local governments. Two areas,

telecommunications and financial services, are treated in separate GATS agreements. GATS defines four different ways of providing an international service:

- services supplied from one country to another (e.g., international telephone calls), officially known as "cross-border supply."
- consumers or firms making use of a service in another country (e.g., tourism), officially known as "consumption abroad."
- a foreign company setting up subsidiaries or branches to provide services in another country (e.g., foreign banks setting up operations in a country), officially known as "commercial presence."
- individuals traveling from their own country to supply services in another (e.g., fashion models or consultants), officially known as "presence of natural persons."

GATS principles are similar to the GATT principles studied in previous chapters. Rules affecting service providers must be transparent and made readily available. Signatory countries to the agreement can place no limit on the number of service providers or on the number of people they may employ. The agreement also prohibits a requirement that local investors own any percentage of the service company (although they may if the parties choose). Like GATT, the GATS agreement also contains MFN trade and national treatment (nondiscrimination) provisions. Countries may not treat foreign service providers less favorably than they treat domestic providers. Laws and regulations must be transparent, reasonable, objective, and impartial. Also, countries may not unreasonably restrict the international transfer of money by service industries or the movement of people across borders for the purpose of providing a service.

GATS contains a set of schedules, or commitments, wherein each country lists its specific commitments for each type of service, which amounts to an exception to the nondiscrimination provision for certain types of services. For example, the United States excluded transportation services from GATS. Japan excluded repair services for certain automobiles and motorcycles, as well as courier services with respect to letters. In Canada, GATS applies to legal services only for law firms or attorneys advising on foreign or international law. Many countries excluded printing and publishing services. Thus, a country may not treat foreign services or service providers any less favorably than promised in the schedules. As a result, no new or additional restrictions may be imposed in the future. Countries also are bound to negotiate an eventual elimination of the exceptions made in the schedules.

Recognition of Licensing and Professional Qualifications.
GATS also has special provisions governing the qualifications of service providers set by national or local governments. Most governments license certain service providers at some level; in the United States, licensing generally occurs at the state level. Of course, areas such as law, nursing, architecture, and accounting will continue to have more strict professional licensing requirements than, say, management consulting. Countries can continue to license professionals and other service providers as necessary to ensure the quality of the service provided that it is not made overly burdensome just to restrict trade. Licensing must be based on objective criteria, such as education or ability. It must not discriminate on the basis of the person's citizenship. Countries may recognize the licenses of other countries, but only if they choose to do so.

---

http://www.wto.org

For GATS and other WTO agreements discussed in this chapter, see WTO home page and link to "Trade Topics." Contains easy to read explanations, statistics, and coverage of new multilateral trade negotiations on services and other topics.

To illustrate the impact of GATS licensing provisions, in 1999 the Japanese Ministry of Finance held national accreditation examinations for foreign certified public accountants for the first time since 1975. From 1950 through 1975, only seventy-four foreign CPAs had been certified to practice in Japan. Typically, foreign CPAs in Japan only provide auxiliary services to clients in Japan through Japanese CPA offices because of the requirements to register as a member of the Japan Institute of CPAs and laws that allow only Japanese nationals to own and run CPA offices. Japan announced that it plans to follow international standards and eventually sign mutual recognition agreements with other countries.

The GATS *Agreement on Trade in Financial Services.*
Over one hundred nations, including the EU and the United States, have joined the GATS *Agreement on Trade in Financial Services.* The agreement applies free trade principles to the commercial banking, securities, and insurance industries by opening domestic markets to foreign competition. The agreement is intended to promote efficiency, reduce costs, and provide consumers with a greater choice of service providers, while still permitting countries to regulate these industries for the protection of investors, depositors, and consumers. Exhibit 10.2 illustrates some of the different types of commitments made by individual nations, in addition to the general principles of MFN trade and nondiscrimination.

The GATS *Agreement on Basic Telecommunications.*
The services included under the GATS *Agreement on Basic Telecommunications,* are voice and facsimile telephone systems, data transmission, fixed and mobile satellite systems and services, cellular telephone systems, mobile data services, paging, personal communications systems, and others. The agreement binds eighty-six countries, including the United States, Canada, the EU, and Japan, to MFN trade and to honor their specific commitments to open their telecommunications markets to foreign competitors. Local, long distance, and international communications are included.

---

http://www.trade.gov/

For the ITA Office of Telecommunications Technologies, go to the ITA home page, link to "Trade Development," then "Industry Programs." Contains telecom market information by industry sector or region, trade agreements, and trade promotion activities.

TRADE IN AGRICULTURE

Agricultural exports are an important part of world trade, accounting for 9 percent of world exports. According to the U.S. Department of Agriculture, about one-third of U.S. crop acreage is exported, accounting for 25 percent of all agricultural revenues. The United States exports almost 20 percent of its agricultural production, worth over $55 billion in 2001. However, agricultural products are among the most heavily protected

---

EXHIBIT 10.2

Opening Global Financial Services Markets
Examples of the Types of Commitments Made by 14 of the 102 Countries
Under the *General Agreement on Trade in Services*

Australia
- Eliminates a prohibition on the acquisition of control of any of Australia's four main banks.

Egypt
- Removes the 51 percent foreign equity limit in Joint Venture Banks allowing up to 100 percent foreign owner-ship; ownership of more than 10 percent is subject to approval on a nondiscriminatory basis;
- Relaxes a nationality requirement on the General Managers of banks by replacing it with a ten-year experience requirement;
- Introduces a commitment to allow 51 percent foreign ownership in insurance companies, as of 1 January 2000 for life insurance companies and 1 January 2003 for non-life insurance companies.

Iceland
- Removes a citizenship requirement on the manager of a leasing company.

Jamaica
- Allows up to 100 percent foreign ownership in insurance and reinsurance companies.

Korea
- Allows the establishment of subsidiaries in credit card services and all forms of commercial presence in finan-cial leasing;
- Eliminates the approval requirements on the establishment of representative offices of foreign securities com-panies;
- Extends the types of securities allowed to be brokered for foreigners;
- Allows the establishment of all types of credit rating companies;
- Allows the establishment of independent insurance agencies.

Kuwait
- Allows up to 40 percent foreign participation in Kuwaiti banks.

Netherlands
- Elimination of a requirement that only companies incorporated according to the law and regulations of an EC Member State may become members of the Amsterdam Stock Exchange.

Philippines
- Increases the allowable additional branches of foreign banks to 6 from the current 4, with the first three in locations of the bank's choice, and the remaining three at designated locations;
- Allows cross-border trade in marine hull and marine cargo insurance.

Poland
- Allows investment abroad of no more than 5 percent of insurance funds.

Singapore
- Allows eligible finance companies to deal in foreign currencies, gold or other precious metals, and acquire for-eign currency stocks, shares or debt and convertible securities.

United States
- Removes some restrictions at the state level in relation to the issuance of licenses to nonresidents, for example, residency or citizenship requirements, in insurance and services auxiliary to insurance (brokers, agencies, con-sultancies, etc.);
- Removes some state restrictions in relation to the issuance of branch or agency licenses to foreign banks, as well as some state restrictions on the opening of representative offices by foreign banks;
- Provides market access and national treatment to foreign firms with respect to interstate banking and interstate branching of banks.

SOURCE: Non-attributable summary of the main improvements in the new financial services commitments. World Trade Organiza-tion, Geneva, 6 February 1997.

products traded in the world. No nation wants to be dependent on other nations for its food supply. Also, agriculture represents a politically powerful and important constituency in most countries. To protect farmers, many governments control the domestic pricing structure in order to provide market stability. These agricultural price supports set prices at higher-than-world-market prices and contribute to the buildup of food surpluses. To avoid disrupting their price support systems, many countries impose import restrictions on both raw and processed food products. The United States, Japan, and the EU provide farming subsidies and controls on prices. GATT Article XI, which prohibits quantitative restrictions, contains a loophole allowing quotas on agricultural imports when necessary to protect government price support programs. Thus, prior to 1995, agricultural products had really escaped control by GATT.

Agricultural price supports in the EU are handled through a *Common Agricultural Policy,* which uses a variable levy to bring the world price of an agricultural import up to the domestic price level. Expenditures for agricultural subsidies and price supports cost billions of dollars each year, constituting nearly three-quarters of the annual total budget of the EU. In the United States, the Farm Bill provides billions of dollars to subsidize farm exports.

No other single trade issue has created so much international disagreement and controversy as trade in agriculture. The United States has generally demanded that EU farm subsidies, including direct payments to European farmers, be reduced. France, Europe's largest grain exporter, has been unwilling to reduce farm subsidies because French farmers are politically powerful. (Pictures of rioting French farmers setting trucks afire in the early 1990s to contest their government's negotiations with the United States over agricultural subsidies filled the TV screens around the world.)

The largest purchaser of U.S. agricultural products is Japan, and farmers in Japan have been highly protected. The *Japanese Staple Food Control Law* put strict limitations on the import of foreign agricultural products. One of the most protected items has been rice. One small, but vivid example of protectionism occurred in 1991 when U.S. rice exhibitors at a Japanese trade fair were threatened with arrest for merely exhibiting U.S.

rice products there. The U.S. rice had to be removed from the show. Although the United States does ship rice to Japan today, it is still not treated equally with domestic rice.

The GATT 1994 *Agreement on Agriculture*

The *Uruguay Round* resulted in many significant changes in government control of agricultural trade. The GATT *Agreement on Agriculture,* effective in 1995, attempts to bring fair trade and competition to the farming sector, and to end government programs that distort normal market conditions. The agreement aims at three main areas: (1) cutting domestic programs that support higher than normal food prices, (2) cutting programs that subsidize exports of farm products, and (3) converting quotas and other nontariff barriers to trade.

Domestic Support Programs.   Domestic support programs artificially manipulate farms prices in a way that protects domestic farmers and encourages cheap exports. The agreement prohibits programs that distort farm production, prices, trade, but permits support for research, disease control, environmental protection, and other national concerns. Cash payments to farmers who have had a loss of income from unexpected emergencies or disasters would be permitted. Domestic support programs will have been cut in developed countries by 20 percent by 2001, and will be cut to a lesser extent in developing countries by 2004.

Agricultural Export Subsidies.   These export subsidies are payments or any other benefits to farmers that directly encourage, or are conditional upon, the export of food or agricultural products. Even indirect benefits are included, such as where a government subsidizes the cost of shipping food products to foreign customers. Export subsidies will have been reduced 36 percent in developed countries by 2001, and by a lesser extent in developing countries by 2004. Food aid to poorer countries is not considered an export subsidy and will not be affected by the agreement.

Making Export Markets Accessible.   An important step in making agricultural markets accessible was to alleviate the quotas, licensing schemes, and nontariff barriers that existed prior to 1995. This was done through *tariffication,* the converting of nontariff barriers to trade, and then gradually reducing the tariff rates. By 2001, developed countries reduced their tariff rates by an average 36 percent and developing countries will cut their rates 24 percent by 2004 to a lesser extent. The agreement permitted special import and inspection procedures on very sensitive products, such as rice imports in Japan, but even that was lifted in 1999 (although as a practical matter there are still other more subtle barriers to rice sales in Japan).

Food, Animal, and Plant Safety

Trade in agricultural goods has been impeded because some countries use food safety as an excuse for blocking agriculture imports. No one doubts the right of a government to take extraordinary measures to protect the people from contagious disease or to protect food or agricultural products from infestation. If a blight, fungus, or insect were found in orange groves in Mexico, no one argues against the right of the United States to keep out Mexican oranges to protect the U.S. crop. The GATT *Agreement on the Application of Sanitary and Phytosanitary Measures* (SPS Agreement) is specifically designed to allow governments to protect human, animal, and plant life from infestation, contaminants, pesticides, toxins, harmful chemicals, or disease-carrying organisms. However, the restrictions may not be used as an excuse to keep out foreign goods.

The agreement opens markets for agricultural exports by requiring that: (1) the measures must not be more trade-restrictive than required and may be applied only to the extent necessary for the protection of human, animal, or plant life; (2) measures may not be a disguised restriction on trade; (3) measures must be based on a risk assessment made according to scientific principles and scientific evidence; (4) the measures may not unjustifiably discriminate between countries where similar threatening conditions prevail; and (5) countries must ensure that inspections or controls are fair and reasonable, and that they are instituted without delay. Consider an example: If an Asian country sets a short shelf life for a food product, say hot dogs, then hot dogs shipped from the United States will be discriminated against because their shelf life has been "used up" in the time it takes to ship across the Pacific. Under the *Sanitary and Phytosanitary Agreement,* however, the shelf life restrictions cannot stand unless they are based on scientific evidence. Another novel case might be the strict Japanese laws prohibiting thoroughbred race horses from entering Japan—this prohibition would violate the agreement if the laws are unnecessary, discriminatory toward the United States, or not backed by scientific evidence. Citing the GATT agreement, the U.S. Department of Agriculture in 1995 partially repealed an eighty-one-year-old prohibition against the import of Mexican avocados.

Codex Alimentarius. Whenever possible, countries must rely on internationally accepted standards or recommendations for the protection of their plants, animals, and foodstuffs. The most notable are found in the *Codex Alimentarius.* This "food code" for the protection of the world's food supply developed slowly over most of the last century. Today, the *Codex Alimentarius* Commission develops these important standards on the basis of worldwide scientific studies, and disseminates them to government agencies and lawmakers. The commission is based in Rome and is made up of countries that belong to the UN World Health Organization and the UN Food and Agricultural Organization. If a country's national standards are based on the *Codex Alimentarius,* they are deemed to be in compliance with the SPS Agreement.

---

http://www.codexalimentarius.net/
The home page of the *Codex Alimentarius* Commission. Trace the history of international food safety laws. The universally accepted *Codex Alimentarius* is accessible from this site.

In the following 1997 WTO panel decision, *EC Measures Concerning Meat & Meat Products (Hormones),* the panel held that the European ban on the sale of beef containing residues of growth hormones violated the *Sanitary and Phytosanitary Agreement.*

---

http://www.fao.org/
The UN Food and Agricultural Organization promotes international agricultural development, nutrition, and food security. Information and links on biosecurity, global warming, controlling "hoof-and-mouth" disease, pesticide management, etc.

EC Measures Concerning Meat and Meat Products (Hormones)
WT/DS26/R/USA (1997)
Complaint by the United States
World Trade Organization

BACKGROUND AND FACTS

Throughout the 1970s European consumers became more concerned over the use of hormones to speed the growth of livestock. Their fears were in part based on the fact that some people had been injured by the illegal use of certain banned hormones. Some consumer organizations boycotted meats. By 1986 the EC had banned the sale of beef from cattle given growth hormones. The EC maintained that such measures were necessary to protect public health (primarily from hormone related illnesses and cancer), and necessary to restore confidence in the meat industry. The United States began contesting the hormone ban in 1987 at GATT. In January 1989, the United States introduced retaliatory measures in the form of 100 percent ad valorem duties on a list of products imported from the European Communities. The United States, together with Canada, Australia, and New Zealand, maintained that the ban was unlawful under the 1994 *Agreement on the Application of Sanitary and Phytosanitary Measures* ("SPS Agreement"). The United States argued that the ban was not based on an assessment of risk, not based on scientific principles, more trade-restrictive than necessary, and a disguised restriction on trade. In June 1996, the European Communities requested the establishment of a panel to examine this matter, and the United States terminated its retaliatory action entirely. Prior to the ban U.S. firms exported hundreds of millions of dollars annually to Europe. After the ban exports plummeted to nearly zero. The European Communities argued that its measures offered equal opportunities of access to the EC market for all third-country animals and meat from animals to which no hormones had been administered for growth promotion purposes. Of the 31 countries which were authorized to export meat to the European Communities, only six apparently allowed the use of some or all of these hormones for growth promotion purposes.

REPORT OF THE PANEL

Article 3.1 requires Members to base their sanitary measures on international standards, guidelines or recommendations [where they exist]. We note, therefore, that even if international standards may not, in their own right, be binding on Members, Article 3.1 requires Members to base their sanitary measures on these standards. . . . We shall therefore, as a first step, examine whether there are international standards, guidelines or recommendations with respect to the EC measures in dispute and, if so, whether the EC measures are *based on* these standards, guidelines or recommendations in accordance with Article 3.1. . . .

Article 3.1 of the SPS Agreement reads as follows:

To harmonize sanitary and phytosanitary measures on as wide a basis as possible, Members shall base their sanitary and phytosanitary measures on international standards, guidelines or recommendations, where they exist, except as otherwise provided for in this Agreement. . . .

. . . For food safety . . . the SPS Agreement defines "international standards, guidelines or recommendations" as "the standards, guidelines and recommendations established by the Codex Alimentarius Commission relating to food additives, *veterinary drug* and pesticide *residues,* contaminants, methods of analysis and sampling, and codes and guidelines of hygienic practice" (emphasis added). . . . [The Codex Alimentarius Commission is an advisory body to the World Health Organization. The purpose of this programme is to protect the health of consumers and to ensure fair practices in food trade by establishing food standards. These standards, together with notifications received from governments with respect to their acceptance or otherwise of the standards, constitute the *Codex Alimentarius* . . . a collection of internationally adopted food standards presented in a uniform manner]. . . . We note that [there are] five Codex standards . . . relating to veterinary drug residues . . . with respect to five of the six hormones in dispute when these hormones are used for growth promotion purposes. . . . We find, therefore, that international standards exist with respect to the EC measures in dispute. . . .

The amount of residues of these hormones administered for growth promotion purposes allowed by these Codex standards is . . . higher than zero (a maximum level of such residues has not even

continued

continued

been prescribed). The EC measures in dispute, on the other hand, do not allow the presence of any residues of these three hormones administered for growth promotion purposes. The level of protection reflected in the EC measures is, therefore, significantly *different* from the level of protection reflected in the Codex standards. The EC measures in dispute are . . . therefore, *not based on* existing international standards as specified in Article 3.1. . . .

[For those sanitary measures for which no international standards exist] . . . a Member needs to ensure that its sanitary measures are based on an assessment of risks. The obligation to base a sanitary measure on a risk assessment may be viewed as a specific application of the basic obligations contained in Article 2.2 of the SPS Agreement which provides that "Members shall ensure that any sanitary . . . measure is *applied only to the extent necessary to protect* human, animal or plant life or health, is *based on scientific principles* and is *not maintained without sufficient scientific evidence* . . . " (emphasis added). Articles 5.1 to 5.3 sum up factors a Member needs to take into account in making this assessment of risks. . . . [A]n assessment of risks is, at least for risks to human life or health, a *scientific* examination of data and factual studies; it is not a policy exercise involving social value judgments made by political bodies. . . .

We recall that under the SPS Agreement a risk assessment should, for the purposes of this dispute, identify the adverse effects on human health arising from the presence of the specific hormones at issue when used as growth promoters in meat or meat products and, if any such adverse effects exist, evaluate the potential or probability of occurrence of these effects. We further recall that a risk assessment should be a scientific examination of data and studies and that the SPS Agreement sets out factors which need to be taken into account in a risk assessment.

[The panel conducted a review of the scientific studies.] All of the scientific studies outlined above came to the conclusion that the use of the hormones at issue for growth promotion purposes is safe; most of these studies adding that this conclusion assumes that good practice is followed. We note that this conclusion has also been confirmed by the scientific experts advising the Panel. Accordingly, the European Communities has not established the existence of any identifiable risk against which the EC measures at issue . . . can protect human life or health.

Decision. The EC's ban on the sale of beef containing residues of growth hormones violates the *Agreement on the Application of Sanitary and Phytosanitary Measures*. Where an existing internationally accepted standard permits beef to contain a residue of a certain growth hormone, an EC regulation permitting zero residue is in violation of the agreement. Where no internationally accepted standard exists on the residue of a certain hormone, the EC ban on that hormone is not permitted because it is not based on a risk assessment made using scientifically accepted principles.

Comment. The panel's decision was upheld by the WTO Appellate Body in January 1998.

Trade in Textiles and Clothing

Textiles and clothing comprise an important part of total world trade, amounting to over $340 billion in 2001, or 6 percent of world exports of merchandise. The textile and apparel industries are among the most "import sensitive" sectors of the world economy. They are labor intensive, allowing developing countries quickly to become major competitors in world markets. China is the world's longest producer, and the United States is the world's largest importer (consuming over one-fifth of all cotton textiles sold worldwide). In 2002, the United States had a trade deficit in textiles of almost $61 billion, to the chagrin of U.S. textile workers and politicians in textile producing states (according to the U.S. Office of Textiles and Apparel, International Trade Administration). Until 1995, the textile trade remained outside of the GATT system, thus allowing strict regulation of textile imports into the United States.

The process of "managing" trade in textiles and apparel began in the early 1960s when the developed countries were flooded with textile imports from low-wage developing countries, such as China, India, Turkey, the Philippines, Egypt, Pakistan, Hong Kong, Indonesia, Korea, Taiwan, and Mexico. Indeed, textiles account for nearly one-half of the total Chinese exports to the United States, so the regulation of trade in textiles has a considerable impact on U.S. relations with that country. Now countries in Eastern Europe, such as the Czech Republic and Bulgaria, have joined in the export of textile products.

Trade in textile products made from cotton, wool, and other natural and synthetic fibers was governed by the 1974 *Multifiber Arrangement* (MFA), an international agreement between textile importing countries and more than forty textile-producing nations. The purpose of the MFA was to promote exports from developing countries, while avoiding market disruption in developed importing countries. The MFA was a system of bilateral agreements between importing and pro-ducing countries setting quota limits on a country-by-country basis for each product category (e.g., silk blouses from India, cotton sweaters from Pak-istan, down-filled comforters from China). A com-plex licensing system was established to track shipments and monitor quota limits. In the United States, textile negotiations were, and still are, con-ducted by the *Committee for the Implementation of Textile Agreements* (CITA). CITA is a U.S. agency made up of members from five departments of government. The agency also administers the tex-tile quota system. (Under the *North American Free Trade Agreement*, Mexican-made textiles entering the United States or Canada are not subject to quotas.) A complete list of all textiles and articles of apparel, broken down by country of export, showing the percentage of quota filled for the year, is available at the U.S. Customs Web site.

The GATT 1994 *Agreement on Textiles and Clothing*

The *Uruguay Round* resulted in the *Agreement on Textiles and Clothing*. During the period of the agreement, from 1995 through 2005, it will put an end to the previous MFA quota system, reduce tariffs on textiles, reduce barriers to foreign mar-kets, and liberalize trade in textiles. A ten-year period was chosen to phase in the reforms in order to minimize economic disruption in textile import-ing countries, like the United States and the EU. The agreement will end in 2005 when textiles and clothing are brought completely within the scope of normal GATT rules, under the auspices of the WTO. All textiles and clothing will be covered by the basic GATT principles of MFN trade and nondiscrimination. Quotas on textiles will be abolished (with some exceptions) by that date. A U.S.–China agreement will permit the United States to continue special quotas on Chinese tex-tiles through the end of 2008 to further ease the economic shock to U.S. industry. After 2005, tex-tiles will be subject to normal WTO rules on safe-guards and unfair trade. As with other goods, a country will still be able to impose temporary safeguard measures if "increased textile imports cause serious injury to a domestic industry making like products" (see Chapter Nine), and antidump-ing and countervailing duty actions would apply. The agreement created the WTO *Textile Monitor-ing Body* to oversee trade in textiles and to assist countries in complying with the new rules. Dis-putes not resolved here can be settled before the WTO Dispute Settlement Body.

---

http://otexa.ita.doc.gov/
ITA Office of Textiles and Apparel. Find textile trade agree-ments, import quotas, statistics, legislation affecting textile trade, and necessary information for U.S. textile exporters and importers. Also at http://trade.gov/ and link to "Trade Development," then "Industry Programs."

OTHER WTO TRADE AGREEMENTS

Two other agreements that will have an effect on world trade are the *Agreement on Trade-Related Investment Measures* and the *Agreement on Trade-Related Aspects of Intellectual Property Rights*. These issues are mentioned only briefly here because they are discussed more fully in Part Four of this book.

Trade-Related Investment Measures

There is no question today that trade and foreign direct investment are interrelated. To be competi-tive in a global market, firms must do more than just produce in one country and sell in another. They must be able to supply services or conduct procurement, manufacturing, assembly, and distri-bution operations on a global scale. This requires the freedom to build foreign factories, to open new foreign subsidiaries, or to merge with foreign firms. The link between investment and trade becomes even more obvious when looking at the volume of trade between related companies. According to UNCTAD's *World Investment Report* (2002), there are 65,000 multinational corporations, with 850,000 foreign affiliated companies, worldwide. Intracompany trade—trade between foreign affiliated companies or between subsidiaries and their parent company—accounts for over one-third of world trade. Government controls that hamper the freedom of firms to make these investment decisions will have an adverse effect on trade in goods and services, especially between these multinational affiliates.

The *Uruguay Round* agreements resulted in the *Agreement on Trade-Related Investment Measures* (commonly called *TRIMS*). The agreement does not set broad rules for local investing, such as rules affecting domestic stock exchanges. It does attempt to reduce restrictions on foreign investment that might restrict cross-border trade in goods and services. It also eliminates discrimination against foreign firms and their goods and services to the extent that those restrictions distort or restrict trade. For example, TRIMS prohibits *trade balancing requirements*—laws that condition a company's right to import foreign goods on the basis of the volume of goods that company exports. TRIMS also prohibits *local content requirements*—regulations that dictate that a foreign company or other producer must use a certain minimum percentage of locally made parts or components in the manufacture of a product. For instance, Argentina may not say to a U.S. multinational corporation: "We will finance the construction of a new automobile factory for you, but only if you guarantee us that 25 percent of the component parts used in assembling cars are made in this country," or "You may only import foreign raw materials on condition that you export an equal volume of finished goods from our country." These requirements would violate the prohibition of quantitative restrictions of GATT Article XI. Also prohibited are laws that condition the receipt of foreign exchange on the company's foreign exchange revenues. Thus, Argentina may not demand: "Our central bank will only permit you to transfer U.S. dollars out of the country if you have brought into the country an equivalent amount this year in dollars, yen, or other hard currency."

Trade-Related Aspects of Intellectual Property Rights

Intellectual property rights (IPRs) include copyrights, trademarks, and patents. The economic value of an IPR lies in the right of its owner to the sole use of the IPR or to license its use to someone else, but it only has worth if the owner can prevent its unauthorized use. Because IPRs are not "goods," they did not fall within the bounds of the 1947 GATT agreement. However, IPRs are often attached to, and used to sell, goods. Thus, if IPRs are not protected from unauthorized use, then trade in goods and services suffer as a result. For this reason, the *Uruguay Round* negotiations focused on IPRs and resulted in the *Agreement on Trade-Related Aspects of Intellectual Property Rights,* or TRIPS.

TRIPS sets new, comprehensive standards for the protection of IPRs in all member countries of the WTO. It requires every WTO country to abide by the most important international intellectual property conventions and then calls on countries to grant even greater protection to inventors, authors, and trademark owners. The agreement requires that all domestic and foreign IPR owners, regardless of their citizenship, be treated the same under a country's IPR laws. It prohibits countries from imposing requirements on foreign firms in exchange for being granted a trademark, patent, or copyright. For instance, a WTO country will not be able to condition the award of a patent on the basis of the inventor's promise to manufacture the item in that country. Countries must publish all laws, regulations, and administrative rulings that pertain to the availability, application, protection, or enforcement of IPRs. Enforcement efforts will be strengthened worldwide to reduce the billions of dollars worth of losses every year due to counterfeit and pirated goods (e.g., fake Rolex watches or Microsoft software). WTO member countries will bring their IPR laws into compliance with TRIPS, as the United States has already done. For example, in 1995 the United States increased the patent period from seventeen years to twenty years to comply with TRIPS' longer period. The TRIPS Council of the WTO will monitor compliance with TRIPS, and after the year 2000, disputes may be settled by the WTO Dispute Settlement Body.

Information Technology Agreement

There are fifty-five nations that have signed the *International Technology Agreement* of 1996. The agreement includes the United States, Canada, the EU, Japan, Hong Kong, Singapore, and other countries accounting for virtually all of world trade in information technology products. The agreement calls for the elimination of tariffs on computers, semiconductors, telecommunications equipment, software, scientific instruments, and other information technology products and component parts by the year 2000 (with some extensions until 2005).

TRADE SANCTIONS AND U.S. SECTION 301: THE THREAT OF RETALIATION

One of the most important weapons in the U.S. arsenal against foreign trade barriers and unfair trade practices is commonly known to businesspeople and lawyers alike as *Section 301*. *Section 301* refers to the provisions found in that section of the *Trade Act of 1974*, although it has been amended by Congress several times since then. The law permits the United States to retaliate unilaterally against other countries—not against foreign *companies*—that violate GATT, that are unfair in restricting the import of U.S. goods or services, or that maintain unreasonable or discriminatory policies or practices. Congress believed that other countries would only comply with GATT if the United States could threaten retaliation for violations. After all, if other countries were threatened with being denied access to the vast U.S. market, they would be less likely to discriminate against U.S. goods or services. Although most experts think that the law has been successful in achieving its goals, many others do not. The law really contains four different provisions: (1) *Basic Section 301*, (2) *Special 301*, (3) *Telecommunications 301*, and (4) *Super 301*.

Basic Section 301

In *Basic Section 301*, Congress instructs the United States Trade Representative (USTR) when retaliatory action against a foreign country in a trade dispute is *discretionary*, and when it is *mandatory*. Retaliatory action may be taken at the discretion of the USTR against any foreign country whose policies or actions are *unreasonable* or *discriminatory* and which *burdens* or *restricts* U.S. trade or foreign investment. A foreign country acts unreasonably if its policies toward U.S. firms are unfair and inequitable, even though not in violation of any international agreement. This includes the unfair restriction of foreign investment, denial of equal access to their markets, failure to protect U.S. IPRs, or the subsidization of a domestic industry. *Section 301* gives the president sufficient flexibility to attack a wide variety of foreign unfair trade practices. Retaliation by the USTR in these instances is discretionary. The USTR also has the discretion to take retaliatory action when a foreign government (1) fails to allow workers the right to organize and bargain collectively; (2) permits forced labor; (3) does not provide a minimum age for the employment of children; or (4) fails to provide standards for minimum wage, hours of work, and the health and safety of workers.

Retaliation is *mandatory* if the USTR determines that (1) a foreign country has denied the United States its rights under any trade agreements; or (2) a foreign country's actions or policies are unjustifiable, violate the legal rights of the United States, *and* burden or restrict U.S. commerce. Unjustifiable acts or policies include illegal tariffs or quotas, denial of MFN treatment, illegal import procedures, overly burdensome restrictions on U.S. foreign investment, and IPR violations. In a case of a violation of GATT, the "burden" to U.S. commerce is presumed. Mandatory action is waived if a WTO panel has upheld the foreign government action, if the foreign country has agreed to eliminate the illegal policy, if the USTR believes that a negotiated solution is imminent, or if in extraordinary cases the USTR believes that retaliation would have a greater adverse impact to the U.S. economy than benefit.

Section 301 **Procedures.** A *Section 301* action begins with the filing of a petition by an interested

international accents

301 Alert
A Service of the U.S. Department of Commerce

The U.S. Department of Commerce welcomes you to its "301 alert" service, which delivers timely alerts concerning retaliatory actions taken by the United States Trade Representative (USTR) under Section 301 of the 1974 Trade Act (USA). This notification will provide U.S. businesses an opportunity to protect their economic interests by participating in the public comment process. These retaliatory actions may include the publication of a list of imported products that could potentially be subject to increased duties. If your business imports an item that is selected for increased import duties under Section 301, you could pay substantially more for the imported product. This service will provide alerts via electronic mail when such retaliatory actions by the United States Government are pending and have the possibility of affecting the level of duties on products imported into the United States.

"301 alert" is completely Internet-based, in line with Secretary Evans's commitment to a "Digital Department." There are two components: this World Wide Web site and an electronic-mail list. They are designed to be complementary, but either one by itself is useful.

How Does the Web Site Work?

Businesses can join the site's automatic e-mail service. After joining the service, businesses will receive updates via e-mail on pending Section 301 actions. For example,

- If negotiations with the country are successful, 301 Alert will notify all registered users of the concessions and/or settlement reached.
- If negotiations fail, 301 Alert sends an automatic e-mail to all registered users informing them of the preliminary list and the public comment period.
- When USTR publishes the final list, 301 Alert will notify all registered users of the final retaliation list of products to be subject to higher import duties.

Alternatively, if businesses choose not to register for the e-mail service, they can visit the site regularly to determine the status of a Section 301 case.

The Department of Commerce provides this service as a courtesy to users of the web site. Although the Department attempts to deliver up to date messages regarding Section 301 matters to all subscribers, these informal messages do not replace the Government's official notice published in the Federal Register. Subscribers should continue to review the Federal Register for all official notices regarding Section 301 matters.

Source: http://www.ita.doc.gov/301alert (http://www.trade.gov/301alert)

---

party, such as a U.S. company, or on the initiative of the USTR. The petition asks the USTR to conduct an investigation of the foreign unfair trade practice. The USTR has forty-five days in which to decide whether to conduct the investigation. Petitions for investigation are usually granted only when an entire U.S. industry is affected. An opportunity must be provided for interested parties to submit their views in writing, and a hearing must be provided if requested. All petitions and decisions to investigate are officially published in the *Federal Register*. A new online service from the Department of Commerce informally notifies interested parties (see the International Accents box). Once an inves-

tigation is begun, the USTR must also begin negotiations with the foreign government involved. If the petition claims that the foreign government has violated GATT, and the dispute is not resolved within 150 days or within the time required in the agreement, then the USTR must invoke the formal WTO dispute settlement procedures. The USTR must complete its investigation and determine whether to impose sanctions within eighteen months of having initiated the investigation, or within thirty days after the conclusion of WTO dispute procedures, whichever occurs first. When sanctions are authorized by the WTO, *Section 301* is used to carry them out under U.S. law.

Sanctions and Retaliatory Measures. Investigations are conducted not on behalf of the petitioning firm, but on behalf of the U.S. government itself. The purpose of *Section 301* is to end the illegal foreign practice, not to compensate the petitioning U.S. firm. No benefits accrue directly to the petitioning firm other than those that affect all U.S. companies or industries in a similar position. The USTR has a wide range of retaliatory measures, or *trade sanctions,* that can be used. Generally, the most common form of retaliation is to assess additional import duties on products from the offending nation in an amount that is equivalent in value to the burden imposed by that country on U.S. firms. The sanctions may be imposed against any type of goods or against any industry. A country might put quotas on U.S. food products, and the United States can retaliate against their electronic parts. For instance, when the United States threatened trade sanctions against Japan for unfairly keeping out U.S. auto parts, the USTR proposed 100 percent import duties on imports of Japanese luxury automobiles. When China refused to protect U.S. copyrights, the United States threatened to impose over $1 billion a year in trade sanctions on Chinese imports. When the EU refused to comply with a WTO panel decision and lift its ban on U.S. beef containing growth hormones in 1999, the United States imposed 100 percent duties on $117 million in European imports. The duties were still in effect in 2003.

The *Trade and Development Act of 2000: The Carousel Law*

Section 407 of the *Trade and Development Act of 2000* amends *Section 301* by requiring the USTR to periodically review the list of products subject to retaliatory tariffs and to revise them 120 days after their initial effective date and every 180 days thereafter. This has become commonly known as the *"Carousel law,"* referring to the periodic rotation of products on and off the retaliation "hit list." The law was enacted in part to the EU's refusal to comply with WTO rulings to end their restrictions on imports of bananas and on imports of beef from cattle fed growth hormones. The U.S. Congress felt that this law would hasten Europe's compliance with the WTO rulings in those cases. The purpose of regularly changing the list of prod-

ucts subject to retaliatory tariffs every 180 days, instead of simply continuing the tariffs on one group of products, is to "spread the pain" across more companies in the offending country, causing them to put greater political pressure on their governments to conform to WTO requirements. The EU has criticized the Carousel law as violating WTO rules. American importers are opposed to the Carousel law because of the uncertainty as to whether their products will unexpectedly end up on the retaliatory list and be subjected to punitive tariffs. For example, the *Journal of Commerce* reported in 2000 that, according to Warner-Lambert, a 100 percent duty on cough drops would lead to the loss of 200 company jobs. The article also quoted a small Minnesota firm as stating that if candles, sweet biscuits and lingonberry preserves are hit, "our company of 28 years would have to close its doors." Clearly, the uncertainty of the Carousel law has many U.S. firms concerned.

---

http://www.meti.go.jp/english
The official Web site of Japan's Ministry of Economy, Trade, and Industry contains METI's report on foreign trade barriers facing Japanese products, Japanese trade statistics, and statements of Japanese trade policy.

Special 301

Special 301 is used by the United States against countries that fail to protect U.S. intellectual property rights (IPR). Each year the USTR must identify foreign countries that deny adequate and effective IPR protection. The worst offenders will be designated as *priority foreign countries* and placed on either the *watch list* or the *priority watch list.* The USTR must begin *Section 301* investigations of the *priority watch* countries. The USTR has six months to decide whether to invoke sanctions according to *Basic Section 301.* In 2002, the focus was on counterfeiting of CD-ROMs, and on Internet piracy. In that year, the USTR identi-

---

http://www.ustr.gov/
The home page of the U.S. Trade Representative. Contains links to all trade agreements negotiated by the United States, the National Trade Estimate Report on Foreign Trade Barriers, and the report on the Identification of Trade Expansion Priorities.

United States—Sections 301–310 of the Trade Act of 1974
WT/DS152/R (22 December 1999)
World Trade Organization
Report of the Panel

BACKGROUND AND FACTS
The European Communities requested a WTO panel to decide whether U.S. Sections 301–310 [the Act] violate GATT dispute settlement procedures. The Act permits the USTR to investigate possible violations of GATT or other international trade agreements, to negotiate a settlement of the dispute, and to request a WTO dispute settlement panel if necessary. The Act also permits the USTR to impose retaliatory tariffs or other trade sanctions either unilaterally or if authorized by the WTO Dispute Settlement Body. The EC argues that the Act violates WTO rules.

REPORT OF THE PANEL
The European Communities argues that [WTO rules] prohibit unilateralism in the . . . dispute settlement procedures. Members must await the adoption of a panel or Appellate Body report by the Dispute Settlement Body, or the rendering of an arbitration decision . . . before determining whether rights or benefits accruing to them under a WTO agreement are being denied. . . .

The European Communities . . . took the position in the Uruguay Round that a strengthened dispute settlement system must include an explicit ban on any government taking unilateral action to redress what that government judges to be the trade wrongs of others.

The United States argues that nothing in Sections 301–310 requires the US government to act in violation of its WTO obligations. To the contrary, the Act requires the USTR to undertake WTO dispute settlement proceedings when a WTO agreement is involved, and provides that the USTR will rely on the results of those proceedings when determining whether US agreement rights have been denied. Likewise, [the Act] explicitly indicates that the USTR need not take action when the DSB has adopted a report finding no denial of US WTO rights.

Under well-established GATT and WTO jurisprudence and practice which the European Communities appears to accept, a law may be found inconsistent with a Member's WTO obligations only if it precludes a Member from acting consistently with those obligations. The European Communities must therefore demonstrate that Sections 301–310 do not permit the United States government to take action consistent with US WTO obligations—that this legislation in fact mandates WTO-inconsistent action. The European Communities has failed to meet this burden. Its analysis of the language of Sections 301–310 ignores pertinent statutory language and relies on constructions not permitted under US law. Sections 301–310 of the Trade Act of 1974 are fully consistent with US WTO rights and obligations.

* * *

Decision. Sections 301–310 of the U.S. *Trade Act of 1974* are valid under the GATT 1994 agreements. The panel clarified that the United States may impose retaliatory trade sanctions against other WTO members only where the United States strictly followed WTO dispute settlement rules and when authorized by the Dispute Settlement Body.

fied 51 countries that denied protection to U.S. patents, trademarks, and copyrights.

Telecommunications 301

Telecommunications 301 is another special statute that calls for an annual review, by March 31st of each year, of foreign barriers to U.S. telecommunications firms. It requires *mandatory* retaliation against countries that block access to their markets by U.S. telecommunications companies.

Super 301

The so-called *Super 301* law is the most controversial piece of trade legislation that the United States ever enacted. It was passed in 1988 by a Congress vowing to "get tough" on trade issues. The law has been extended through 2001 by executive orders of President Clinton. It requires the USTR to identify and report to Congress those *priority trade practices* that pose the greatest barriers to U.S. trade in foreign countries. The USTR also has to identify those *priority countries* that exhibit a pervasive pattern of discrimination against U.S. firms. Within twenty-one days of the report, the USTR must initiate investigations of the countries named. If a priority country does not remove a trade barrier, then retaliation by the USTR is required. The act provides a real threat to other countries—if they block U.S. firms from their markets they will lose access to the U.S. market. The *Report on Trade Expansion Priorities* is based on the USTR's *National Trade Estimate Report on Foreign Trade Barriers*, prepared annually for Congress and the president. The latter is a "laundry list" of U.S. complaints about trade barriers in foreign countries. The 2000 *Trade Estimate* focused on Brazil, India, Europe, Japan, Korea, and China.

Assessing the Impact of Unilateral Action.

Many experts believe that *Section 301, Special 301,* and *Super 301* have been successful in getting other countries to open their markets to U.S. goods and services. A look at the reports of the USTR, and its announcements in the *Federal Register* reveal many cases in which *Section 301* has resulted in increased market access. In the early 1990s, *Section 301* was helpful in getting Japan to reduce its restrictions on the import of citrus products, glass, wood products, medical technology, supercomputers, and satellites. Korea, China, Brazil, Poland, Saudi Arabia, Thailand, and countries in every region of the globe, agreed to provide greater protection to IPRs; Taiwan reduced import barriers on foreign tobacco, beer, and wine; Brazil improved market access for the U.S. software industry; Canada agreed to change its marketing restrictions on the sale of U.S. beer. Market access has been improved in dozens of countries around the world. Yet, the use of trade sanctions in these cases is actually rare. In virtually all cases, trade disputes have been resolved through negotiation or panel decisions. The very existence of the law has provided the USTR with the "negotiating leverage" needed to resolve a dispute and avoid a trade war. The threat of action has prompted other nations to open markets for U.S. products and to protect U.S. IPRs. Many problem areas remain, however. The USTR cites Japanese restrictions inherent in their distribution system that discriminate against foreign suppliers, Japanese standards that discriminate against U.S.–

designed products, and Japanese government procurement practices. In terms of product areas, Japan is still criticized by the USTR for unfair treatment of U.S. auto parts, fish, and steel. Europe is criticized for quotas on U.S. television programming, and intellectual property violations continue worldwide. Long-running disputes over Korean restrictions on imports of U.S. products continue. Almost all observers believe that *Section 301* will continue to be used in the future, and that it will aid in the enforcement of WTO dispute panel decisions.

Most countries, especially Japan, India, and those in Europe, have criticized *Section 301* and *Super 301* as a one-sided "strong-arm" tactic that violates U.S. commitments to settle trade wars through WTO dispute resolution. They will surely continue to press the United States not to use *Section 301* without authorization by the WTO.

CHAPTER SUMMARY

As industries become more dependent on export sales, they become more vulnerable to foreign trade barriers that deny them access to export markets. The *Uruguay Round* trade negotiations resulted in many important GATT 1994 agreements designed to remove trade barriers and improve access to foreign markets, including agreements on technical barriers, import licensing, government procurement, services, agriculture, textiles, intellectual property, and foreign investments. For the first time, GATT now governs trade in services, textiles, agriculture, and intellectual property. Most economists predict that the impact will be felt by U.S. firms, and by firms around the world, stimulating economic growth for years to come.

The *Agreement on Technical Barriers to Trade* will guide WTO nations in their use of technical regulations and product standards. It does not set standards of its own for product performance, design, safety, or efficiency, but it guides nations in the application of their own regulations and standards through legal principles of nondiscrimination, transparency, and MFN trade. The agreement applies broadly to regulations imposed to protect the public health, safety, and welfare, including consumer and environmental protection. Health and safety regulations may not be used unless they are "trade neutral" and restrict trade no more than necessary, according to the principle of least-restrictive trade.

France

The People

The French adhere to a strong and homogeneous set of values. They cherish their culture, history, language and cuisine, which is considered an art. The French have been and are today world leaders in fashion, food, wine, art and architecture. They embrace novelty, new ideas and manners with enthusiasm as long as they are elegant.

Meeting and Greeting

- At a business or social meeting, shake hands with everyone present when arriving and leaving. A handshake may be quick with a light grip.
- Men may initiate handshakes with women.
- When family and close friends greet one another, they often kiss both cheeks.

Names and Titles

- Use last names and appropriate titles until specifically invited by your French host or colleagues to use their first names. First names are used only for close friends and family.
- Colleagues on the same level generally use first names in private but always last names in public.
- Address people as *Monsieur, Madame* or *Mademoiselle* without adding the surname.
- *Madame* is used for all adult women, married or single, over 18 years of age (except for waitresses, which are addressed as *Mademoiselle*).
- Academic titles and degrees are very important. You are expected to know them and use them properly.

Body Language

- Do not sit with legs spread apart. Sit up straight with legs crossed at knee or knees together.
- Keep your hands out of your pockets.
- Do not yawn or scratch in public. Sneeze or blow your nose as quietly as possible using a handkerchief or tissue. If possible, leave the room.
- Do not slap your open palm over a closed fist (this is considered a vulgar gesture).
- The "okay" sign, made with index finger and thumb, means "zero."
- The French use the "thumbs up" sign to say "okay."

Corporate Culture

- Professionalism is highly valued in business and is the key to acceptance of outsiders.

- France enjoys a skilled, well-educated labor force. Hard work is admired, but workaholism is not.
- Be on time. The French appreciate punctuality.
- Give business cards to the receptionist or secretary upon arrival to an office and to each person you meet subsequently. Print cards in English or French. Include academic degree and/or title.
- Many French speak and understand English, but prefer not to use it. An interpreter will probably not be necessary, but check ahead of time. Use French only for greetings, toasts and occasional phrases unless your French is perfect.
- Government plays a major role in business. Find a local representative (banker, lawyer or agent) to help you through regulatory obstacles.
- Business people tend to be formal and conservative. Business relationships are proper, orderly and professional.
- Don't discuss personal life with business people. Personal lives are kept separate from business relationships.
- The French get down to business quickly, but make decisions slowly after much deliberation.
- Organizations are highly centralized with a powerful chief executive. Bosses are often dictatorial and authoritative.
- French are leaders in the area of economic planning. Plans are far-reaching and detailed.
- Entering a room and seating is done by rank.
- Meetings follow an established format with a detailed agenda.
- The purpose of meetings is to brief/coordinate and clarify issues. State your intentions directly and openly.
- The French dislike the hard sell approach.
- Things actually get done through a network of personal relationships and alliances.
- Avoid planning business meetings during August or two weeks before and after Christmas and Easter period.

The continuation of this document is at http://schaffer.westbuslaw.com, Chapter 10.

Government procurement is a key sector of the world's economy. *The Agreement on Government Procurement* provides an exception to the rule that governments may treat goods and services from domestic suppliers more favorably than those from foreign suppliers. Countries must "free up" their procurement policies and practices by giving foreign firms equal access in bidding on government contracts, and providing transparent and easily obtained rules for submitting bids.

About 20 percent of world trade is in services. The GATS applies basic GATT principles to service industries for the first time since 1947. This agreement has already opened access to foreign markets in construction, engineering, health care, law, banking, insurance, securities, and transportation.

Trade in agriculture has been distorted by billions of dollars' worth of government subsidies granted to farming interests worldwide, and restrictions on food imports. Attempts to limit government support of agriculture have been met by attacks from politically powerful farm groups, particularly in France and other European countries. The *Agreement on Agriculture* is expected to reduce government subsidies on farm products by 20 to 36 percent and to open access to markets. Exports of farm products have suffered because of discriminatory trade barriers imposed under the guise of health standards. Under the *Sanitary and Phytosanitary Agreement,* countries cannot impose restrictions to protect animal and plant life from pests or contagious diseases unless those restrictions are applied fairly and equally to goods from all countries that present a risk of infection. Restrictions must be supported by scientific evidence and be the least restrictive to trade as possible. These issues are critical to all humankind, as we face potential scourges like "mad cow" and "hoof-and-mouth" disease.

Textiles are one of the most import sensitive industries of all. Many jobs in developed countries have been lost to low-wage jobs in the textile-producing developing countries. Quotas are used to control and monitor textile and apparel shipments for each product category. The quota is administered through a licensing system. Textiles imported from most countries cannot enter without a license. The *Agreement on Textiles* is intended to eliminate quotas over a ten-year period. When quotas close on Chinese textiles, some shippers illegally transship or reroute Chinese textiles through other countries whose quota allotment is still open. They are subject to severe criminal penalties in the United States. Textile trade negotiations will continue for many years, in the *Doha Rounds,* and likely well into the future.

GATT 1994 also sets new rules on *Trade-Related Investment Measures* that limit the use of trade-restrictive conditions on investment. The rules on *Trade-Related Aspects of Intellectual Property* Rights change the copyright, patent, and trademark laws of many nations, including the United States. It makes them more uniform and provides greater protection to the holders of IPRs. (These topics will be discussed in greater detail in Part Four.)

No one knows whether the WTO will be able to ensure that the world will enjoy full trade in the future. The ability of the WTO to resolve countries' disputes before trade wars erupt will surely be critical to its overall success.

One of the new issues likely to appear is the link between trade and the environment—trade in tropical products, trade in endangered species, the destruction of the world's forests, pollution, and degradation of the air and water. These environmental issues may reach the WTO's agenda in the not-too-distant future. Another difficult issue is that of labor and workers' rights. The WTO, as a trade organization that functions by consensus, may be rigorously tested as it addresses such a political issue as this.

Questions and Case Problems

1. The United States, along with Canada and Argentina, is one of the leading producers and proponents of *genetically modified foods;* that is, bioengineered organisms (GMOs). The U.S. government believes that GMOs are important for the world's food supply because they can boost food production and nutrition and lead to both disease-resistant crops and more tasteful foods. Many respected scientific studies vouch for the safety of GMOs for human and animal consumption and on the earth's environment. GMOs are important to U.S. agriculture economically. According to the U.S. Department of Agricul-

ture, approximately three-quarters of U.S. soybean and cotton production and over one-third of corn production is genetically modified. However, many consumer groups and countries argue that the dangers to humans, wildlife, and the environment are unknown. Genetically modified corn and soy had been approved for sale in the EU prior to 1998, but the European countries ceased new approvals after that time. In addition, the EU and several other countries adopted regulations requiring the tracing of biotech crops through the chain of distribution, and they imposed strict labelling requirements on all foods and animal feed containing more than 1 percent GMO. European consumers who fear GMO foods will not purchase products with these labels. The United States claims that the requirements are expensive and unnecessary and have cost U.S. farm exporters hundreds of millions of dollars in lost revenues. In 2003, the United States requested a WTO panel to decide whether the moratorium and labelling requirements violate the WTO *Phytosanitary agreement*. Research the case at the WTO. What was the outcome? Can you find any decisions of the European Court of Justice on GMOs? What is the current state of EU legislation on GMOs?

2. In 2001, an outbreak of "hoof-and-mouth" disease threatened the meat supply of Europe. The virus is spread through the air or by contact. To control its spread, millions of cattle, sheep, and pigs were slaughtered and burned; export and transportation of British livestock, meat, and dairy products were halted; and many areas of Great Britain were placed off limits to travelers. Certain areas of the country were quarantined, with "Keep Out" notices posted on the roads. Officials sprayed chemicals to kill the virus on the soles of shoes and automobile tires. The virus quickly spread to continental Europe, and even the United States banned the import of meat from Europe. Explain the WTO *Agreement on Sanitary and Phytosanitary Measures*. Does the agreement tell countries specifically what actions to take? What action does the agreement permit nations to take to fight a disease like this? Do you think that the agreement gave sufficient latitude to countries to fight the disease? For additional information, see the Web sites listed in this chapter, or http://www.oie.int/ the World Organization for Animal Health, a Paris-based government organization comprised of 157 nations.

3. Immediately after India was targeted under *Super 301* for restricting market access by U.S. firms, it began a public relations campaign against the United States. Its representatives stated that India would not negotiate "at the point of a gun." Evaluate this statement. Do you agree that unilateral retaliation by the

United States has been the best way to improve access to foreign markets and to protect U.S. IPRs?

4. What are the real economic impacts and long-term effects of trade sanctions? Assume that the United States imposes punishingly high tariffs of 100 percent on, say, Japanese cars. Immediate costs might be borne by the Japanese manufacturers, U.S. dealerships, or consumers; but what does such a measure do to the long-term health and competitiveness of the U.S. car industry? Could you see any impact on the U.S. lead in innovation, design, and quality? Discuss.

5. Research the term *managed trade*. Do you agree or disagree that trade can be "managed"? Give examples from the text, and from your reading, of how governments manage trade. Can you cite successful or unsuccessful cases? What is the position of recent U.S. administrations in regard to "managing" trade?

6. Do you think that the United States has been guilty of "Japan Bashing" in the automotive trade? What have been the key issues affecting trade between the United States and Japan? How has their relationship been affected by political considerations?

7. At the request of the Canadian owner of a country music channel, Canada removed from the air a Nashville-based country music channel. This effort is only one in a series made by Canada to restrict U.S. programming. Canadians argue that their country is dominated by U.S. culture on television and want it restricted. The U.S. firm petitions the USTR for trade sanctions unless the Canadian policy is changed. After an investigation, the USTR threatens the Canadian government with $500 million in punitive tariffs. Discuss whether the USTR should have threatened sanctions before the case is heard by the WTO. See *Initiation of Section 302 Investigation Concerning Certain Discriminatory Communications Practices*, 60 FR 8101 (February 10, 1995).

8. The marketing and sale of beer and alcoholic beverages in Canada are governed by Canadian provincial marketing agencies or "liquor boards." In most of the ten Canadian provinces, these liquor boards not only regulate the marketing of domestic beer in the province, but serve as import monopolies. They also warehouse, distribute, and retail imported beer. Canada imposed restrictions on the number of locations at which imported beer could be sold; authorization from the liquor board was needed to sell a brand of beer in the province; and higher markups were required on the price of foreign beer than on domestic beer sold by the liquor boards. Do the regulations violate the nondiscrimination provisions of GATT? May Canada use state trading monopolies to regulate imports of this kind? Are Canada's provisions valid public health regulations or illegal

discrimination? If trade statistics showed that foreign beer sales have actually increased, could an exporting country's rights under GATT still be subject to "nullification and impairment"? Would *Section 301* apply to this case? See, 56 FR 60128 (1991). See *GATT Dispute Settlement Panel Report: Canada Import, Distribution and Sale of Alcoholic Drinks By Canadian Provincial Marketing Agencies*, Document I-B-38, International Economic Law Documents (1988).

9. Thailand has been slow to protect copyrights. Although the Thai government has conducted raids and taken other steps that have reduced pirated goods on the market, prosecution of pirates of U.S. works in the Thai courts has not been successful. Of the cases filed, many have been pending for nearly two years with little result. Evidentiary requirements, limits on raids and other problems make enforcement difficult. Under the Thai copyright law, computer software is not protected. Unauthorized public performances of copyrighted recordings are also not controlled. Although Thailand passed a patent law in 1992, it allows the government extremely broad authority in using foreign patents without compensation. The law also establishes a Pharmaceutical Patent Board with extraordinary authority requiring owners of pharmaceutical patents to provide sensitive cost and pricing information; it also imposes draconian fines for failure to provide such information. What recourse would U.S. intellectual property owners have under *Special 301*? Is this case actionable at the WTO? See *Identification of Priority Foreign Countries*, 58 FR 26991 (May 6, 1993); *Thailand: Revocation of Priority Foreign Country Designation* (September 21, 1993). For additional information, see Chapter Seventeen.

Managerial Implications

I. Your company is a U.S. multinational corporation with a 40 percent share of the world market for its product. Over the past decade management has invested more than $500 million dollars trying to get its products into Japanese stores. After all of its efforts the company has less than a 10 percent share of the Japanese market, and only 15 percent of Japanese stores carry its products. Company investigations show that its major Japanese competitor has a virtual monopoly there and has violated Japanese antitrust laws by fixing prices and refusing to sell to any store that carries your firm's products. Most distributors and retailers are linked to your competitor through *keiretsu* relationships. Management believes that by "having the Japanese market all to themselves," the competitor is able to maintain prices sufficiently high in Japan to permit them to undersell your company in the United States. Apparently, the Japanese government simply "looks the other way." Moreover, your firm has been effectively restrained by the bureaucracy that administers government procurement contracts in Japan. As a result, management estimates that it has lost several billion dollars in exports since the company first entered the Japanese market. Your competitor responds that they are not the only producer in Japan, that the market there is very competitive, and besides, they also outsell your firm's products in several other Asian countries.

1. If you petition for a *Section 301* action, do you think the USTR will begin an investigation? What political factors in the United States might affect the USTR's decision to investigate? What is the attitude of the current U.S. administration toward the use of *Section 301*?

2. Management thinks that the Japanese government should require distributors to agree to import a given quantity of U.S.-made products in a year's period. How would the Japanese government mandate this? Do you think the Japanese distribution system or its *keiretsu* practices can be reformed? What other remedies or sanctions might be appropriate in this case? What is the likelihood that the threat of sanctions by the United States will affect the Japanese position? Given the history of U.S.–Japanese trade relations, and authority of the new WTO, what do you think is the likely outcome of this case? Based on your study of the last two chapters, what provisions of the GATT agreement, if any, might apply to this case?

3. Are the market share statistics relevant to your case? What other data or information will be important?

II. The Asian country of Tamoa imports large quantities of down pillows each year. DownPillow, a U.S. company, would like to do more business there, but it has a problem. Tamoa has a number of regulations affecting the importation and sale of down bedding. Consider the following five regulations:

1. Pillows made from down harvested from Tamoan flocks may be labeled as "goose down" even

though they contain up to 25 percent duck down. (Down is taken from both geese and ducks, but duck down is considered inferior.) If the pillow is made from foreign down, then a pillow labeled "goose down" may contain no more than 5 percent duck down. U.S. regulations recognize that geese and ducks often get plucked together, and therefore permit goose down to contain up to 10 percent duck down. DownPillow believes the 10 percent "tolerance" is reasonable, but given farming methods in most countries it is not possible to sort out the geese and the ducks any better than that. Tamoa believes that the stricter standard for imported pillows is justified to protect Tamoan consumers from fraud, and because Tamoan farmers do not raise any ducks, the 25 percent domestic standard is irrelevant anyway.

2. Tamoa also requires that the cotton coverings of all pillows be certified to meet certain ecology and human health standards for textiles—that they not contain any harmful chemicals such as formaldehyde or chlorine and that they have been tested according to minimum standards set by the International Organization for Standardization. Certifications are accepted from qualified testing laboratories in any country. U.S. regulations do not require certification.

3. All pillow imports must be inspected on arrival in Tamoa. No inspections are permitted at the for-

eign factory. Tamoa has only one full-time inspector, who must remove down from at least three pillows from every shipment and subject it to laboratory analysis. Given the current backlog, inspections and analysis are taking up to four weeks, during which time the pillows are often damaged by Tamoa's high humidity.

4. Tamoan regulations also require that Down-Pillow's plant be inspected and that the sterilization process be approved by Tamoan officials. In the United States the down is washed, sanitized, and subjected to hot air heat several hundred degrees in temperature, all under health department supervision. The Tamoan ministry of agriculture refuses to accept the sterilization permits, inspections, and approvals from state health departments in the United States. Tamoa does not pay the overseas travel expenses of its inspectors.

5. Tamoan regulations prohibit pillows and comforters from being compressed or vacuum packed for shipment to assure the down will not be damaged in shipment. DownPillow ships smaller orders by airfreight and larger orders by ocean container.

DownPillow and other U.S. firms are not pleased with these requirements. Evaluate the legality of the regulations and their impact on DownPillow. What course of action should DownPillow take?

CHAPTER 11

REGULATING IMPORT COMPETITION AND UNFAIR TRADE

The last two chapters examined the basic principles of GATT law found in the *General Agreement on Tariffs and Trade* 1994. The key principles dealt with nondiscrimination, MFN trade, national treatment, and the elimination of quotas and nontariff barriers. A knowledge of this material is essential here because these concepts are carried throughout this chapter as well as the remainder of the book. Chapter Ten also described how the World Trade Organization has become the primary international body for liberalizing trade, and how the WTO's dispute-settlement procedures work. Chapter Ten looked at specific GATT agreements related to opening access to foreign markets. It also examined trade regulation in different sectors, such as agriculture services and textiles.

This chapter covers two areas: The first is the regulation of import competition through laws that "safeguard" domestic industries. These laws protect industries that say, "We're trying as best we can to compete, but foreign competitors seem more efficient and more productive. They're shipping ever-greater quantities of products here, and we need time to adjust—to retool our plants and retrain our workers to become more competitive again. Just give us some time!"

The second area covers the regulation of "unfair trade," more specifically, the two most common unfair trade practices of dumping and government subsidies. Here, domestic industries might say, "Foreign firms compete unfairly. They dump their goods in our market at ridiculously low prices. They absorb the losses until they drive us all out of business so they'll have the whole U.S. market to themselves!" Or, "How can we expect to sell our products here at home when we can't match the price of imports. Our overseas competitors are subsidized; they're paid by their own government, with their taxpayers' money, to build products and ship them here. We've got to stop this!"

THE DOUBLE-EDGED SWORD OF IMPORT REGULATION

Trade wars are often depicted in nationalistic terms as an us-against-them problem. Pictures of unemployed factory workers fill the television screens. Politicians call for greater protectionist measures. Of course, these familiar stories have two sides: U.S. auto workers and manufacturers scream for the president to put high tariffs on imported cars and trucks. Yet, the Japanese government claims that the Japanese manufacturers are only producing cars that Americans want. The few remaining U.S. manufacturers of display screens for portable computers call for protection against an onslaught of imports. Yet, U.S. computer manufacturers who use the screens threaten to close shop in the United States and move overseas if more duties are placed on the imported screens. U.S. steelmakers want higher tariffs on imported steel, while high-tech companies fear that they will pay the price in higher tariffs placed on their products in return. Examples such as these come from every agricultural, industrial, and service sector of the world's economy. Amid the clamoring for protection against imports, calls for free trade come from the heads of those firms whose exports might suffer from foreign retaliation, or by leaders of consumer groups concerned about the rising price of imported consumer products. The discussion in this chapter attempts to break through this protectionism-versus-free-trade morass by focusing on how international rules serve as a check on these competing national political interests.

Even purely domestic firms that do not import or export must have an understanding of how governments regulate import competition. Virtually all domestic products compete with products made abroad, and U.S. managers require a knowledge of how U.S. trade policies and trade laws affect their firms' competitive positions. Managers may need to determine whether legal action could forestall a flood of competing imports, and on what grounds such a lawsuit could be based. Would an action for relief be brought in the courts or before an administrative agency? Do any government programs exist to provide benefits to workers whose jobs are lost due to import competition? In the United States, many industries have sought protection against foreign competition. Some notable examples include apparel, shoes, gloves, motorcycles, steel, chemicals, foodstuffs, microwave ovens, typewriters, minivans, glass, and automobiles.

---

http://www.wto.org
From the home page, link to "Trade Topics" and find both introductory and technical explanations of the subjects covered in this chapter.

SAFEGUARDS AGAINST INJURY

Economic and political realities often force nations to take temporary corrective action to protect a domestic industry from severe market disruptions and dislocations of the workforce resulting from increased imports. A country takes legal action to protect a domestic industry by granting *import relief* or *adjusting imports,* commonly known as a *safeguard against injury.* Safeguards are generally used to protect a domestic industry from increasing volumes of imported goods (regardless of any wrongdoing or unfair trade practice by a foreign firm or foreign government). These safeguards include temporarily increasing tariffs, imposing quotas, or by some other (lawful) method to restrict or discourage imports. The legal authority for a GATT

member nation to safeguard its firms from injury comes from the GATT escape clause.

The GATT Escape Clause

If a nation reduces its tariffs, the result is frequently increased imports and possibly serious market disruption to a domestic industry. Article XIX of GATT 1947, known as the *GATT escape clause,* authorizes a country to take temporary corrective action to adjust import levels of a certain product and thus safeguard domestic industry. The escape clause is so named because it temporarily permits a country to "escape" from previous promises (tariff concessions) it may have made to lower tariffs on that product. Article XIX was included in the GATT agreement at the insistence of the United States, which had previously used similar provisions in bilateral treaties. Today, the GATT 1994 *Agreement on Safeguards* establishes additional rules for safeguarding domestic industry and providing import relief.

The GATT 1994 *Agreement on Safeguards*

The *Agreement on Safeguards* provides that a member may apply a temporary safeguard measure (e.g., increase tariffs) to a product only if that product "is being imported in such increased quantities and under such conditions as to cause or threaten to cause serious injury to the domestic industry that produces like or directly competitive products." The term *serious injury* is defined as a "significant overall impairment in the position of a domestic industry." A threat of serious injury must be *imminent.* The term *domestic industry* means "producers as a whole," as opposed to just one firm within the industry.

In order to apply a safeguard, a country must first undertake an administrative investigation, which includes a public hearing at which importers, exporters, and other interested parties can present evidence and their views of whether the safeguard would be in the public interest. The investigating body is required to evaluate all relevant economic factors bearing on the industry's position, and it must find that the increased imports are the actual cause of the domestic industry's decline. If other factors are shown to be causing injury simultaneously, then the increased imports are not considered to be the cause. Emergency action can be taken without the investigation if clear evidence justifies the safeguards, but any additional tariffs imposed must be lifted within two hundred days.

Limits on the Use of Safeguards.

GATT places limits on safeguards because they are a temporary remedy to be used only until the problem is resolved. They may not exceed four years (with an extension to eight years). The restrictions on imports must be gradually lifted as conditions warrant. Imposing safeguards on a product can only be done without discrimination, regardless of the product's country of origin, and only as is necessary to prevent or remedy serious injury. WTO Appellate Body reports have ruled that a safeguard "may not be more restrictive than necessary to prevent or remedy a serious injury and to facilitate adjustment." Tariffs are the preferred safeguard. A quota, if used, may not reduce the quantity of imports below the average level of imports of the prior three years. Quotas should be allocated between supplying nations based upon their proportion of the total quantity of imports during the preceding years. Governments may not attempt to protect domestic industries by pressuring foreign firms to voluntarily hold back shipments. Although once a popular method of restraining imports, these *voluntary restraint agreements* are no longer permitted under GATT rules. Nations must follow certain limits when imposing safeguards on products from developing countries.

Safeguards can only be applied to imports from developing countries if a particular developing country is supplying more than 3 percent of the total imports of that product.

Trade Compensation.

GATT 1994 encourages a country imposing a safeguard to compensate a supplying nation for the burden the safeguard measure has imposed on it. For instance, if the United States imposes safeguard tariffs on imported bicycles, and Taiwan supplies large numbers of bicycles to the United States, then the United States should make *trade compensation* to Taiwan by reducing tariffs on other Taiwanese imports in an equivalent amount. The countries are expected to negotiate trade compensation; if they fail to reach agreement, then the supplying nation may "suspend . . . substantially equivalent concessions"—or raise tariffs in retaliation.

The WTO Committee on Safeguards.

Countries must notify the *Committee on Safeguards* when taking safeguard actions. The Committee reports to the WTO *Council for Trade in Goods*. It monitors compliance with GATT safeguard provisions and assists countries in negotiating trade compensation.

Safeguards against Injury under U.S. Law

The U.S. escape clause is found in *Section 201* of the *Trade Act of 1974* as amended by the *Omnibus Trade and Competitiveness Act of 1988* and the *Uruguay Round Agreements Act*. U.S. law does not follow the guidelines of GATT Article XIX and the *Agreement on Safeguards* completely, but is similar. U.S. law does not refer to the term *safeguards*, but rather to the "positive adjustment to import competition" or import relief.

Standard for Import Relief.

Under U.S. law, import relief can be granted when "an article is being imported into the United States in such increased quantities as to be a substantial cause of serious injury or threat thereof to the domestic industry producing an article like or directly competitive with the imported article." The president may make an adjustment to imports (e.g., impose tariffs or quotas) only after an investigation by the U.S. International Trade Commission (ITC), and if, in the president's discretion, it will "facilitate efforts by the domestic industry to make a positive adjustment to import competition and provide greater economic and social benefits than costs." Because of this discretionary power, a president who adopts free trade or free market concepts might be reluctant to apply a safeguard remedy at all. Although largely political in nature, a president's decision is usually based on the national interest.

ITC Safeguard Investigations.

A petition for relief may be filed with the ITC by any firm, trade association, union, or group of workers, or by Congress or the president, or it may be initiated by the commission itself. The ITC gives public notice in the *Federal Register* of its investigation and hearings. If it finds that the requirements of the law are

Argentina—Safeguard Measures on Imports of Footwear
WT/DS121/AB/R
14 December 1999
Report of the Appellate Body World Trade Organization

BACKGROUND AND FACTS

In 1997, Argentina initiated a safeguard investigation and determined that increased imports were the cause of serious injury to Argentine producers. Increased import duties were placed on imports of foreign-made footwear greater than those previously bound in Argentine tariff concessions. In effect, the import duty went from the bound rate of 35 percent to 200 percent. The increased duties were imposed on imports of footwear from all countries except from South American countries that are members of the regional MERCOSUR common market. After consultations failed, the European Communities (EC) requested a WTO panel to decide if Argentina had complied with the GATT agreements. The United States joined as a third party. The EC made several arguments. First, that Argentina's administrative safeguard proceedings had failed to show that the surge in imports was the cause of injury to domestic producers and had failed to consider whether the injury to the domestic footwear industry was actually caused by other economic factors. Second, the EC argued that Argentina must impose safeguards without regard to the country of origin, and not solely on non-MERCOSUR countries. Third, that GATT Article XIX required that safeguard measures be imposed only if the increase in imports results from "unforeseen developments." The EC maintained that the increases in imports resulted from lowered rates of duty that were freely negotiated between countries, as a part of their tariff concessions, then the increases could not be "unforeseen." Argentina defended that the 1994 GATT *Agreement on Safeguards* abandoned this requirement. The panel held that the Argentine safeguards had violated the GATT agreements, but expressed its view that there was no requirement that the increases in imports be unforeseeable. Argentina appealed to the WTO Appellate Body.

REPORT OF THE APPELLATE BODY

Article XIX of the GATT 1994 and "Unforeseen Developments"

The provisions of Article XIX: 1(a) of the GATT 1994 and Article 2.1 of the *Agreement on Safeguards*, which together set out the conditions for applying a safeguard measure under the *WTO Agreement*, read as follows:

GATT 1994 Article XIX
Emergency Action on Imports of Particular Products

1.(a) If, *as a result of unforeseen developments and of the effect of the obligations incurred by a Member under this Agreement, including tariff concessions,* any product is being imported into the territory of that Member in such increased quantities and under such conditions as to cause or threaten serious injury to domestic producers in that territory of like or directly competitive products, the Member shall be free, in respect of such product, and to the extent and for such time as may be necessary to prevent or remedy such injury, to suspend the obligation in whole or in part or to withdraw or modify the concession. (emphasis added)

Agreement on Safeguards Article 2 Conditions

1. A Member may apply a safeguard measure to a product only if that Member has determined, pursuant to the provisions set out below, that such product is being imported into its territory in such increased quantities, absolute or relative to domestic production, and under such conditions as to cause or threaten to cause serious injury to the domestic industry that produces like or directly competitive products.

* * *

As to the meaning of "unforeseen developments," we note that the dictionary definition of "unforeseen," particularly as it relates to the word "developments," is synonymous with "unexpected." "Unforeseeable," on the other hand, is defined in the dictionaries as meaning "unpredictable" or "incapable of being foreseen, foretold or anticipated." Thus, it seems to us that the ordinary meaning of the phrase "as a result of unforeseen developments" requires that the developments which led to a product being imported in such increased quantities and under such conditions as to cause or threaten to cause serious injury to domestic producers must have been "unexpected." With respect to the phrase "of the effect of the obligations incurred by a

continued

continued

Member under this Agreement, including tariff concessions . . . ," we believe that this phrase simply means that it must be demonstrated, as a matter of fact, that the importing Member has incurred obligations under the GATT 1994, including tariff concessions.

* * *

In our view, the text of Article XIX:1(a) of the GATT 1994, read in its ordinary meaning and in its context, demonstrates that safeguard measures were intended by the drafters of the GATT to be matters out of the ordinary, to be matters of urgency, to be, in short, "emergency actions." And, such "emergency actions" are to be invoked only in situations when, as a result of obligations incurred under the GATT 1994, a Member finds itself confronted with developments it had not "foreseen" or "expected" when it incurred that obligation.

Imposition of Safeguard Measures by a Member of a Customs Union

Argentina claims on appeal that the Panel erred by "imposing an obligation" on a member of a customs union to apply any safeguard measure on other members of that customs union whenever imports from all sources are taken into account in a safeguards investigation. Article 2 of the *Agreement on Safeguards* provides that "Safeguard measures shall be applied to a product being imported irrespective of its source." On the basis of this reasoning, and on the facts of this case, we find that Argentina's investigation, which evaluated whether serious injury or the threat thereof was caused by imports from *all* sources, could only lead to the imposition of safeguard measures on imports from *all* sources. Therefore, we conclude that Argentina's investigation, in this case, cannot serve as a basis for excluding imports from other MERCOSUR member States from the application of the safeguard measures.

Serious Injury

We agree with the Panel that Articles 2.1 and 4.2(a) of the *Agreement on Safeguards* require a demonstration not merely of *any* increase in imports, but, instead, of imports "in such increased quantities . . . and under

such conditions as to cause or threaten to cause serious injury." . . . And this language in both Article 2.1 of the *Agreement on Safeguards* and Article XIX:1(a) of the GATT 1994, *we believe, requires that the increase in imports must have been recent enough, sudden enough, sharp enough, and significant enough, both quantitatively and qualitatively, to cause or threaten to cause "serious injury"* [emphasis added].

With respect to the requirement relating to "serious injury," Article 4.2(a) of the *Agreement on Safeguards* provides, in relevant part:

> In the investigation to determine whether increased imports have caused or are threatening to cause serious injury to a domestic industry under the terms of this Agreement, the competent authorities *shall evaluate all relevant factors of an objective and quantifiable nature having a bearing on the situation of that industry, in particular, . . . the share of the domestic market taken by increased imports, changes in the level of sales, production, productivity, capacity utilization, profits and losses, and employment.*

As the Panel found that Argentina had not evaluated two of the listed factors, capacity utilization and productivity, the Panel concluded that Argentina's investigation was not consistent with the requirements of Article 4.2(a).

We agree with the Panel's interpretation that Article 4.2(a) of the *Agreement on Safeguards* requires a demonstration that the competent authorities evaluated, at a minimum, each of the factors listed in Article 4.2(a) as well as all other factors that are relevant to the situation of the industry concerned. Furthermore, we do not dispute the Panel's finding that Argentina did not evaluate all of the listed factors, in particular, capacity utilization and productivity.

Decision. The Appellate Body upheld the Panel's conclusion that Argentina had not shown that the increased imports were the cause of serious harm to the domestic footwear industry. Safeguards, where justified, must be imposed on imports without regard to the country of origin, and only where the increased imports resulted from "unforeseen developments."

met, it may advise the president as to what action to take. The commission conducts public hearings at which interested parties may present evidence and make suggestions as to the form of import relief. The ITC prepares a detailed economic analysis of the affected market and then makes its determination. The factors that the commission considers in determining whether increased imports are a substantial cause of serious injury include:

---

http://www.usitc.gov

For information on ITC safeguard investigation, as well as ITC investigations under other unfair import laws discussed in this chapter, link from home page to "Information Center."

---

1. A significant idling of productive facilities in the industry.
2. The inability of firms to operate at a reasonable profit.
3. Unemployment or underemployment in the industry.
4. Growing inventories.
5. A decline in sales, market share, production, wages, or employment.
6. A firm's inability to generate capital for plant and equipment modernization or for research and development.
7. An actual increase in imports or in market share held by imports.
8. Other factors that may account for the serious injury to the domestic industry (e.g., incompetent management or lack of technological innovation).

U.S. law defines *substantial cause* as "a cause which is important and not less than any other cause." (Review the requirements for applying a safeguard measure as set out by the WTO Appellate Body in the *Argentina Footwear* case.) The ITC may not consider overall economic trends, such as the impact of a recession on the industry, but must look at the impact of the increased imports. In the ITC report on the U.S. motorcycle industry (see next case), Commissioner Eckes found that increased imports of heavyweight motorcycles threatened serious injury to the petitioner, Harley-Davidson, despite the severe impact of a long recession on total sales in the industry.

In the event that a foreign country requests a WTO panel to review a U.S. safeguard decision, the entire investigative process comes under scrutiny. If a WTO panel reviews the fact-finding decisions of the ITC or of an investigative agency in another country, what is the standard of review? Several Appellate Body decisions have addressed this (including the *Argentina Footwear* decision in this chapter) and concluded that Article 11 of the *Dispute Settlement Understanding* obligates a panel to make an "objective assessment" of the facts, not by trying to determine the facts of the case anew, but by looking to see whether domestic agencies have evaluated all relevant facts and have provided an adequate and reasonable explanation about how the facts supported their determinations. This is a practical realization that judges in Geneva cannot gather facts and information from industries around the world.

Available Remedies under U.S. Law. Any relief granted by the president must be temporary (limited to four years, with an extension to eight years if the firms in the industry are making needed changes), and designed to allow those firms sufficient time to regain their competitive position in the market. Relief should only provide time to retool, modernize, streamline, recapitalize, improve quality, or take other actions to better meet new competitive conditions in the market. The president's options for adjusting imports include (1) tariff increases subject to a maximum increase of 50 percent; (2) tariff-rate quotas, which allow a certain number of articles to be imported at one tariff rate, while all excess amounts enter at a higher rate; (3) absolute quotas; (4) quotas administered through the auctioning of import licenses; (5) negotiated agreements with foreign countries that limit their exports to the United States (the latter is not permitted under WTO rules, and is no longer used); or (6) trade adjustment assistance for the domestic industry.

Trade Adjustment Assistance

Workers who are unemployed as a result of increased imports of foreign goods may be entitled to federal *trade adjustment assistance* (TAA). Petitions for TAA are filed with the U.S. Department of Labor. Assistance to workers, in the form of direct cash payments, tax credits, or vouchers, is intended to cover the expenses of job search, retraining and relocation, and health insurance coverage. As of 2002, benefits can extend up to 78 weeks, with extensions for remedial job training. For workers to be eligible to apply for TAA, the Secretary of Labor must determine that a significant number or group of workers in a firm have become, or are threatened to become, partially or totally separated; that the firm's sales or production have decreasd absolutely; and that increases in like or directly competitive imported products contributed importantly to the separation and to a decline in the firm's sales or production. There are also provisions permitting assistance to workers, irrespective of whether there are increased quantities of foreign imports, whose employer has shifted production to a foreign country that is a party to a free trade agreement with the United States (this includes Mexico, Canada, and countries in the Andean, Caribbean, and African regions). The program is administered by state job agencies. It is not uncommon to see them sponsor announcements in local newspapers asking workers to contact them about assistance if their employer has moved their jobs to foreign factories.

---

http://www.doleta.gov
For information on TAA, see U.S. DOL Employment and Training Administration. Link to "Dislocated Workers," then "Trade Act Programs." For an example of a state's role see http://www.texasworkforce.org and link to "Boards," and then "Program Information."

Workers have been certified in many TAA programs. The six industries with the largest concentration of certified workers during the last two decades were: automotive equipment, apparel and other finished products made from fabrics and similar materials, primary metal industries, oil and gas production and services, leather and leather products, and electrical and electronic machinery equipment and supplies. In 2002, the benefits were made available to the farm and fishing industries.

Federal Assistance to Firms. Trade adjustment assistance is not just available for U.S. workers, but also for U.S. companies. This program is administered by the U.S. Department of Commerce through the Economic Development Administration. It is intended to help U.S. companies become more competitive. To qualify, a firm must

be certified under the law that increased imports contributed importantly to a decline in sales and to the unemployment of a significant number of its workers. Twelve assistance centers nationwide help certified companies develop business recovery plans over a two-year period. The plans include such things as improving production capabilities, marketing, computer systems and Web site development, and standards certification. In order to receive financial assistance, the certified firm must contribute its own matching funds. On average, about 150 firms have been certified annually to receive assistance.

The U.S. Steel Industry: A Case Study in Protectionism

The U.S. steel industry presents a classic example of the problems and politics of protectionism versus free trade. As is usually the case in so many industries, tariffs to protect one industry from foreign competition can adversely affect another. Trade remedies such as quotas or retaliatory tariffs may protect a U.S. industry from low-cost imports, but they also raise the price of goods to consumers. In the case of steel, cheaper imported steel benefits steel users and consumers because it lowers the price of everything made from steel—cars, home appliances, bridges, and so on. The modern history of the steel industry has seen steel producers and the steelworkers' union pitted against industry users of steel and consumer groups. Moreover, countries around the world have subsidized steel producers in their countries through an endless scheme of tax breaks and favors, hoping to give them an advantage in world markets. In the United States, lawmakers and presidents from both parties have weighed in, and the result is that during the last thirty or forty years, American steel has benefited from a range of protective actions, to the ire of consumer groups and foreign governments alike.

After World War II, the United States dominated the world steel industry. But with their steel industries in ruin, Europe and Japan had the opportunity to rebuild with modern plants and techniques. Gradually, developing countries like Taiwan, Korea, India, and Brazil, and later even Russia, also found it easy to spur development by exporting steel. On the other hand, the large American mills did not modernize, and by the late 1960s

Heavyweight Motorcycles & Engines & Power-Train Subassemblies
Report to the President on Investigation No. TA-201–47
United States International Trade Commission 1983

BACKGROUND AND FACTS

In 1982, the ITC instituted an investigation to determine if motorcycles having engines with displacement more than 700 cubic centimeters are being imported into the United States in such increased quantities as to be a substantial cause of serious injury, or threat thereof, to domestic industry producing like or directly competitive articles. The investigation was in response to a petition for relief filed by Harley-Davidson Motor Co., a U.S. firm. The investigation showed that from 1977 to 1981, U.S. shipments of motorcycles grew by 17 percent, with domestic productive capacity increasing by nearly 82 percent (largely as a result of American Honda's increased production in the United States). During that same period the number of U.S. jobs increased by 30 percent. In 1982, however, consumption fell, domestic shipments declined, and employment dropped. In the first nine months of 1982, domestic shipments fell by 13 percent and inventories rose, leaving large numbers of unsold motorcycles. Production during that period showed a decline of 36 percent, profits were down by 20 percent, and employment was down by 12 percent. Inventories of imported motorcycles doubled in that period, representing a tremendous threat to Harley-Davidson. The country as a whole was in the midst of a recession, and demand for heavyweight motorcycles was depressed.

VIEWS OF CHAIRMAN ALFRED ECKES

* * *

It is evident that inventories of imported motorcycles have increased significantly during the most recent period. These increases exceed growth in consumption and surpass historical shipment trends for importers. The mere presence of such a huge inventory has had and will continue to have a depressing effect on the domestic industry. Also, given the natural desire of consumers for current design and up-to-date performance capabilities, motorcycles cannot be withheld from the market indefinitely. They must be sold. And given the realities of the market place, there is a strong incentive to liquidate these inventories as quickly as possible. The impact of such a massive inventory build-up on the domestic industry is imminent, not remote and conjectural.

I have seen no persuasive evidence that would suggest imports of Japanese heavyweight motorcycles will decline in the near future. Instead, the Japanese motorcycle industry is export oriented—exporting in 1982 some 91 percent of the heavyweight motorcycles produced in Japan. Because motorcycles of more than 750cc, which include the merchandise under investigation here, cannot be sold in Japan under current law, Japanese producers cannot consider domestic sales as a replacement for exports. The other option, which they apparently pursued in 1982, is to push export sales in the face of declining demand in the U.S. market. This tactic helps to maintain output and employment in the producing country but it shifts some of the burden of adjustment to competitors in the importing country. Evidence that the Japanese producers will seek to maintain a high level of export sales to the U.S. is found in an estimate of the Japanese Automobile Manufacturer's Association. This organization estimated that exports of 700cc or over motorcycles to the United States for 1982 and 1983 would average 450,000 units or less for both years combined. That figure results in import levels higher than recent levels.

Finally, imports of finished heavyweight motorcycles pose a "substantial cause" of threat of serious injury. Under section 201(b)(4), a "substantial cause" is a "cause which is important and not less than any other cause." In my view, there is no cause more important than imports threatening injury to the domestic motorcycle industry.

In reaching this conclusion I have considered the significance of the present recession in my analysis. Without a doubt the unusual length and severity of the present recession has created unique problems for the domestic motorcycle industry. Without a doubt the rise in joblessness, particularly among blue-collar workers, who constitute the prime market for heavyweight motorcycles, has had a severe impact on the domestic industry. Nonetheless, if the Commission were to analyze the causation question in this way, it would be impossible in many cases for a cyclical industry experiencing serious injury to obtain relief under section 201 during a recession. In my opinion Congress could not have intended for the Commission to interpret the law this way.

continued

continued

There are other reasons for doubting the domestic recession is a substantial cause of injury or threat to the U.S. industry. During the current recession, imports from Japan have increased their market share from domestic producers, gaining nearly six percentage points. Imports have taken market share from the domestic facilities of Honda and Kawasaki as well as Harley-Davidson.

Moreover, while the current recession has undoubtedly depressed demand for heavyweight motorcycles, economic conditions are beginning to improve in this country. . . . As demand responds to this improvement, the domestic industry will be pre-empted from participating in any growth because of the presence of a one-year supply of motorcycles poised and ready to capture market share. Consequently, not the recession, but the inventory of motorcycles coupled with anticipated future imports constitute the greatest threat of injury in the months ahead.

Decision.   The commission recommended that incremental duties be imposed for five years at the declining rate of 45, 35, 20, 15, and 10 percent, in addition to the existing rate of 4.4 percent *ad valorem*.

Comment.   The president followed the commission's recommendations, but added tariff-rate quotas of 5,000 units in order to keep the U.S. market open to European firms that exported to the United States in smaller quantities. The remedy has been considered one of the most successful uses of safeguards. Under protection, Harley-Davidson recapitalized, introduced quality control processes and just-in-time inventory control, and regained its competitiveness. By 2003, Harley was one of the most demanded motorcycles in the world, including in Japan. In that year, Harley exported over 50,000 units worldwide.

found themselves operating inefficiently and at a competitive disadvantage to the new foreign mills. As foreign plants increased capacity, they ate into former export markets for U.S. steel companies while increasing market share in the United States itself. U.S. companies also faced higher wage rates, as well as loss of market share to plastics, aluminum, and newer technologies.

In the 1960s and 1970s, the steel industry worldwide, including America and Europe, underwent a financial crisis. Since that time, every U.S. president has tried to limit foreign steel to a small percentage of U.S. consumption, generally from 15 to 18 percent. But for decades, it seemed that every time a restriction on steel imports was lifted, imports of foreign steel surged (sometimes to over one-quarter of U.S. consumption), followed by a string of plant closings, layoffs, and bankruptcies. Routinely, the steel industry filed for protection under the safeguard laws, antidumping laws, and countervailing duty laws, all the while amassing a tremendous lobbying effort in Washington calling for "toughening" of U.S. unfair trade statutes. Indeed, for the past two decades, the American government has imposed added import duties on foreign steel under its "unfair trade" laws (see the discussion later in this chapter on dumping and subsidies). Critics and consumer groups long maintained that the decades of protection have resulted in tens of billions of dollars in higher prices for steel products while doing little to encourage steel industry modernization and efficiency.

During these decades, U.S. steel producers maintained that they have attempted to compete in a market that is rigged against them. They have argued that foreign countries are subsidizing the sale of cheap foreign steel in the United States, that foreign firms are dumping steel in the United States at unfairly low prices, and that the additional duties imposed on them are really just necessary to "level the playing field." Unless the U.S. government protects the U.S. steel industry, they argue, to give it time to modernize, restructure, and compete, America as a nation will be left without essential steel producing capabilities. Those opposed to steel industry protection (which includes foreign governments in steel exporting nations) maintain that competition is not the reason for the decline of the U.S. industry. They point out that America's large, traditional mills (known as "integrated" mills) have become dependent on protection, while America's more competitive "mini mills," producing specialty steel products, are very profitable.

By the 1990s, it seemed that the industry was actually becoming more competitive. Those plants that remained were modernizing, corporate mergers and consolidations were improving cost efficiencies, foreign mills were making ownership investment in U.S. mills, and the new "mini mills" were succeeding in the specialty steel market. But in the late 1990s, the Asian financial crisis dried up many markets for steel. With a glut of steel on the world market, foreign producers found it more important than ever to ship to the United States. Steel imports jumped, prices plummeted, high energy prices made manufacturing more costly, tens of thousands of steelworkers were laid off, and dozens more U.S. steel firms closed or filed for bankruptcy. The Bush administration found itself under tremendous pressure to again protect the industry, and it initiated a Section 201 safeguard investigation. The ITC found that the imports were "a substantial cause of serious injury or threat thereof" and recommended additional tariffs (on top of those already in place). In 2002, President Bush imposed tariffs of up to 30 percent on the majority of imported steel coming from all countries except Canada, Mexico, Jordan, and Israel, to be effective for three years. In the same year, the European Union, Japan, Korea, China, Switzerland, Norway, New Zealand, and Brazil brought dispute cases to the WTO. In a 1,000-page report, the panel ruled that (1) the U.S. measures were not a result of "unforeseen developments" as required under the WTO rules (the United States maintained that the Asian financial crisis was unforeseen); (2) for most steel products, the ITC could not show that the imported quantities have increased; (3) the United States has not shown that the imports caused the serious injury to the U.S. steel industry; and (4) excluding imports from Canada, Mexico, Israel, and Jordan was inconsistent with the nondiscrimination WTO rules. The EC claimed a "full victory." In 2003, the Appellate Body upheld the panel's decision against the United States. *United States—Definitive Safeguard Measures on Imports of Certain Steel Products— Report of the Appellate Body, WT/DS 248/AB/R (10 November 2003).* The EC and Japan had threatened over $2 billion in retaliatory tariffs on U.S. products unless the United States backed down, singling out U.S. products from states key to Bush's 2004 reelection campaign, such as Florida orange juice. Citing his belief that the steel industry was quickly recovering, President Bush lifted the tariffs in December 2003.

UNFAIR IMPORT LAWS: DUMPING AND ANTIDUMPING DUTIES

In importing, *dumping* is the unfair trade practice of selling products in a foreign country for less than the price charged for the same or comparable goods in the producer's home market. It is a form of price discrimination causing injury to domestic competitors through artificially low prices against which domestic producers cannot compete at a profitable level. GATT has prohibited dumping since 1947, and in the United States, it has been illegal since 1916.

Virtually all developed nations have statutes, patterned after GATT, that permit the importing country to impose antidumping duties on dumped products to offset the unfair low price and to prevent injury to a domestic producer. The United States, the EU, Canada, and Australia all have antidumping laws. China enacted its antidumping law in 1997. In the EU the antidumping laws are imposed only on trade between a member country and a nonmember country. The Japanese have similar laws, although they are not widely enforced. Developing countries, such as Mexico, Brazil, Argentina, and Korea, are currently enacting antidumping codes. Antidumping laws are used more frequently than any other trade law in the United States and Europe.

The Economics of Dumping

The theories that explain the economic motivation for dumping fill entire volumes and are certainly beyond the scope of this book. At first glance, one might wonder what is wrong with consumers of one country being able to buy the products of another nation cheaply. As long as the products remain available at a reasonable market price, nothing is wrong. But the lower prices charged in an importing country are often not related to superior efficiencies in production. Rather, dumping is often intended to drive competitors out of business so that the dumping firms will ultimately be free to raise their prices to monopoly levels.

Dumping has become a fairly persistent problem in international trade, often practiced by those firms wishing to sell their excess production capacity at bargain prices to cover fixed costs and to avoid cyclical worker layoffs. As long as dumped products are not sold in the producer's own country, causing price suppression in the producer's home market, then the dumping firm has everything to gain and little to lose. Some economists point out that dumping is not always predatory, but may be related to market conditions. An exporting firm may not be able to command the same prices from foreign buyers as in its domestic market, where it has brand-name recognition and greater market power.

Critics of antidumping laws claim that they injure consumers by "fixing prices" at high levels. Once the prices rise for imported products, domestic manufacturers follow suit by raising their prices as well. Critics cite the fact that antidumping laws are designed to *correct* an unfair trade practice and not to *protect* domestic companies. They also maintain that antidumping laws do not require the United States to assess the impact of additional duties on the public interest (i.e., the cost to consumers), and do not provide an exception for goods that are in short supply in the United States.

The GATT 1994 *Antidumping Agreement*

The GATT provisions on dumping are found in GATT 1994 Article VI and in the *1994 Antidumping Agreement*. The 1994 agreement provides complex rules for determining when dumping has occurred and for resolving dumping disputes.

Every WTO member country is expected to see that its national antidumping laws comply with the WTO rules. These national laws are reported annually to the WTO in Geneva and are easily accessed by anyone interested in a foreign country's dumping laws at the WTO Web site. In the United States, the *Uruguay Round Agreements Act* amended U.S. antidumping laws to reflect the new GATT provisions, and they are incorporated into U.S. tariff law generally in Title 19 of the *United States Code*. In this section, our discussions apply generally to both the GATT antidumping agreement and to U.S. antidumping laws. However, laws or procedures specific to the United States are noted as such.

---

http://www.wto.org

For an explanation of dumping, the offical text of the WTO Antidumping Agreement, and antidumping dispute documents, link from the WTO home page to "Trade Topics."

The GATT agreement provides that dumping occurs when foreign goods are imported for sale at a price less than that charged for comparable goods in the exporting or producing country. Antidumping duties may be imposed only when the dumping threatens or causes *material injury* to a domestic industry producing *like products*. GATT requires that an importing country resort to antidumping duties only after conducting a formal investigation to determine both the amount of the dumping and the extent of material injury. In the United States, there are two federal agencies involved in the investigation. The United States International Trade Administration (ITA) of the U.S. Department of Commerce determines whether the merchandise has been sold in the United States at a price less than its normal value and the International Trade Commission (ITC) determines whether this has caused, or threatens to cause, a material injury to U.S. producers of like products. Petitions for an investigation may be filed by producers of "like" and competing domestic products, including manufacturers, sellers, or labor groups who produce at least 25 percent of domestic U.S. production. Investigations must be concluded within 18 months.

Calculating the Dumping Margin.   Antidumping laws are designed to prevent foreign manufacturers from injuring domestic industries by selling their products in the United States below the prices that they charge for the same products in their home markets. The U.S. statute provides that antidumping duties may be imposed on imported merchandise if that merchandise is sold or likely to be sold in the United States *at less than fair value*. Contrary to popular belief, dumping does not require that the foreign products be sold for less than the cost to produce it, although a sale at below cost is certainly "less than fair value." In order to determine whether merchandise is sold at less than fair value, the ITA compares the *normal value* of the merchandise, or the price at which it is first sold for consumption in the exporting or producing country, to the *export price,* or the price of the good when sold in or for export to the United States. If the export price is less than the normal value of the product in the home market, then the sale is *below normal value*, or in the language of the U.S. statute, at *less than fair value*.

The price differential is known as the *dumping margin*. GATT rules require that the dumping margin use price and value figures that will result in a *fair comparison*. When dumping causes or threatens material injury to domestic producers of like products, the importing nation may equalize the price differential by imposing an additional tariff, above the normal tariff charged for that product. These *antidumping duties* are assessed in an amount equal to the dumping margin and are calculated for each individual exporter. Thus, if a Korean company sells a widget in Korea at $100, and sells the same widget in the United States at $80, then the dumping margin is $20 and an antidumping duty of $20 can be imposed on the imported widget. If the dumping margin is less than 2 percent of the value of the products, the dumping is considered *de minimis* and no duties are imposed.

Calculating the Export Price.

The *export price* is the price (usually the *ex factory* price without shipping charges) at which a product is sold to an unaffiliated or unrelated buyer in the importing country. When a price charged for a product does not reflect an "arms length," or freely negotiated transaction, a *constructed export price* must be used. A constructed export price is used when the exporter and importer are affiliated or related companies or the product price is "hidden" in some other type of compensatory arrangement (such as barter). In these cases, the constructed price is deemed to be the price at which the imported product is first resold in its original condition to an independent buyer. An "affiliated buyer" is a U.S. company or corporation in which the foreign seller owns a 5 percent equity ownership or more, or one over which the foreign seller is in a position to control, manage, or direct. This may also include companies where the seller has a degree of control as a result of having an exclusive supplier arrangement or where the same individuals sit on the boards of directors of both companies.

Calculating the Normal Value of Like Products in the Exporting or Producing Country.

Normal value is the price at which *foreign like products* are sold for consumption in the exporting or producing country in usual commercial quantities and the ordinary course of business, and at the same level of trade—in other words, comparing wholesale sale to wholesale sale, or retail to retail—as the dumped product. If insufficient quantities of like products are sold in the exporting country with which to make a fair comparison, then normal value is calculated on the basis of sales to third countries, or on the basis of a constructed value. Constructed value is calculated on the basis of what it might actually cost to produce the product in the exporting country, plus an amount for selling, administrative, packaging, and other expenses, and a reasonable profit.

What Is a "Like Product"? One common problem in comparing the price of the dumped product to "like products" sold for normal value in the exporting country is defining what that "like product" is. First, many antidumping actions are taken against an entire category, kind, or classification of merchandise, not just on a single item or product. The ITA will have to determine what products to include in its price analysis and which not to include. Also keep in mind that in many cases the products sold by a manufacturer or producer in one country are not like those sold in foreign countries. For example, the range of qualities, specifications, or dimensions may differ. The goods may be packaged differently or in different quantities and bulk packs. There are endless examples. Steel tubing sold in one country may be different from that sold in another. Building materials may differ according to local construction codes. Electrical standards can require that products be assembled differently or use varying component parts. Consumer preferences often dictate significant changes in products when they are sold for export. All of these factors make it very difficult to compare the export price with the normal value of a "like product" in the exporting country. Generally speaking, the ITA will look at many factors, including whether the products identical in physical characteristics, whether they are produced by the same or different firms, whether they are made of the same or similar component materials, whether they are of equal commercial value, and whether they are used for the same purpose. The following case, *Pesquera Mares Australes Ltda. v. United States,* illustrates a typical problem that might face the ITA in determining a "like product." It's actually one of the more readable opinions in this area of the law. Most cases deal with far more complex industrial product classifications

Pesquera Mares Australes Ltda. v. United States (Chilean Salmon)
266 F.3d 1372 (2001)
United States Court of Appeals (Fed. Cir.)

BACKGROUND AND FACTS

Pesquera Mares Australes, a Chilean salmon exporter, was accused of dumping salmon in the U.S. market at less than fair value. An antidumping petition was filed in 1997 by the Coalition for Fair Atlantic Salmon Trade. The U.S. Department of Commerce (ITA) conducted an investigation to compare the price of the salmon sold in the United States with its "normal value" in the home market. Finding no sales of Mares Australes' salmon in Chile during that time, ITA based normal value on the price of the salmon sold in Japan. However, while the salmon sold in the United States was of the "premium" grade, the salmon sold in Japan was of both "premium" and "super-premium" grades. Nevertheless, ITA found that the salmon sold in Japan and in the United States had "identical physical characteristics" and thus were "like products" as defined by the U.S. statute. ITA then included the price of the super-premium Japanese grade in its determination of normal value. This resulted in the ITA finding a larger dumping margin and imposing higher antidumping duties. The duties were affirmed by the Court of International Trade and Mares Australes appealed to the Court of Appeals for the Federal Circuit.

DYK, CIRCUIT JUDGE

* * *

[T]he antidumping statute specifically defines "foreign like product," as . . . merchandise *which is identical in physical characteristics.* . . . In this case ITA . . . sought to identify salmon sold by Mares Australes to Japan that was "identical in physical characteristics" to salmon exported by that company to the United States. It is ITA's interpretation of the phrase "identical in physical characteristics" that is at issue.

* * *

Mares Australes argued that the super-premium salmon it sold to Japan could not be considered "identical in physical characteristics" to the premium grade salmon it sold to the United States. As evidence of this distinction, the company stressed . . . that certain physical defects (such as external lacerations to the salmon) were present in premium but not super-premium salmon; that super-premium salmon enjoyed a darker, redder color than premium salmon; and that its customers in Japan, recognizing these physical and

color distinctions, paid higher prices for premium-grade salmon. . . . But ITA noted that "the record also contains evidence that the distinctions between the two grades were, in practice, nominal. . . ."

As support for its conclusion that super-premium was not a commercially recognized separate grade, ITA also pointed to commercial practice in countries (other than Chile) exporting to Japan, whose salmon industries did "not recognize any grade higher than 'superior'." [In its final determination] ITA stated: ". . . The Norwegian, Scottish, Canadian, and U.S. salmon industries do not recognize any grade higher than "superior." The "superior" grade is consistent with the premium grade and permits minor defects. . . . Nonetheless, all salmon in this range are graded equally (*i.e.*, as "superior"/"premium"), and are comparable products in the market place. [*Notice of Final Determination of Sales at Less Than Fair Value: Fresh Atlantic Salmon From Chile*, 63 Fed. Reg. 31411 (June 9, 1998)]. ITA thus determined that "salmon reported as super-premium are in fact of premium grade," and accordingly compared the sales of both super-premium and premium salmon to Japan to corresponding sales of premium salmon only in the United States. The practical consequences of ITA's decision to classify the two grades of salmon as "identical in physical characteristics" was to increase Mares Australes' dumping margin from the de minimis level (1.21%) to a final dumping margin of 2.23%.

* * *

This case requires us to interpret the phrase "identical in physical characteristics" as that phrase appears in the definition of "foreign like product" [U.S. Code]. In order to ascertain the established meaning, of a term such as the word "identical," it is appropriate to consult dictionaries. There are a variety of dictionary definitions of "identical." Some require exact identity. *See, e.g., American Heritage Dictionary,* 896 (3d ed. 1996) (defining "identical" as "being the same" and "exactly equal and alike"). . . . Others allow "minor differences" so long as the items are "essentially the same." *See, e.g., The American Heritage Dictionary,* 639 (2d ed. 1991). . . . We find nothing in the statute to suggest that Congress intended to depart from the ordinary definition of

continued

continued

the term "identical." But that leaves the question of which of the two common usages was intended by Congress: *exactly the same* or *the same with minor differences?*

We conclude that Congress intended the latter usage. . . . As Coalition for Fair Atlantic Salmon Trade points out, Congress could hardly have intended to require ITA in each and every instance to compare *all* the physical characteristics of the goods. It might not be possible, for example, with certain types of merchandise to "account for every conceivable physical characteristic" of that merchandise.

Despite our conclusion that Congress intended to allow identical merchandise to have minor differences, the phrase "identical in physical characteristics" [as used in the U.S. statute] remains ambiguous, and, as we learn from *Chevron U.S.A., Inc. v. Natural Resources Defense Council, Inc.*, 104 S.Ct. 2778 (1984), ITA has discretion to define the term.

* * *

ITA has concluded that merchandise should be considered to be identical despite the existence of minor differences in physical characteristics, if those minor differences are not commercially significant. We conclude that this standard adopted by ITA constitutes "a permissible construction of the statute." . . . We conclude that this finding is supported by substantial evidence, and that it has been adequately explained.

* * *

Decision.   The Chilean salmon exporter (Mares Australes) violated the antidumping laws of the United States by selling foreign salmon in the United States at less than fair value. The super-premium salmon sold by Mares Australes in Japan was similar enough to the premium grade sold in the United States to be considered a "foreign like product," the price of which should be included in determining the normal value for purposes of calculating the dumping margin.

---

than salmon. As you read, consider how the agency made its decision, and the deference given to that decision by the Court of Appeals for the Federal Circuit.

Adjustments to Value and Price.   Calculating the dumping margin requires a *fair comparison* of the price of the dumped product in the export market with the price of a like product sold in the ordinary course of trade in the exporting or producing country (i.e., the normal value). A fair comparison often requires adjustments to either the export price or to normal value to compensate for differences in the sale—comparing "apples to apples." For example, if the German manufacturer of ball bearings must pay a sales commission to sales representatives for ball bearings sold in Germany, but does not pay commissions on sales to the United States, then the difference must be accounted for in the calculation. Adjustments can be made for differences in the terms and conditions of sale, for the cost of ocean containers and packaging, for freight and warehouse expenses, customs brokerage fees, insurance on the goods in transit, and other expenses. Adjustments should also be made for differences in taxes, advertising and sales commission expenses, quantity dis-

counts, and other factors that might legitimately cause the export price to be lower than normal value. The rules for making adjustments in U.S. dumping cases are spelled out in U.S. law.

---

http://www.ita.doc.gov

To learn more about U.S. unfair import laws, link from the ITA home page to "Learn About ITA Import Administration." Includes introductory explanations about dumping and subsidies, reports and current investigations.

Market Viability Test and Constructed Value. A price comparison between the export price in the foreign market and the normal value of the product in the exporting country only works if the exporting country has a *viable market*. If the exporting country has insufficient sales of a like product, then the *normal value* is difficult to determine. When aggregate sales volume in the exporting country (the home market) is less than 5 percent of the aggregate sales volume of the dumped product in the U.S. market, the dumping margin is calculated by comparing the dumped product to the price of a like product when it is exported to a third country—provided that this price is representative of a normal value. If sales to a third country are also insufficient, then a constructed value for the product is substituted for normal value. In this case, the price of the dumped product is compared to the cost of producing the product in the exporting country plus a reasonable amount for administrative, selling, and other costs, and for profits. The amount of profit to be added into constructed value is based on (1) actual profits in the transaction, (2) average profits on sales of the same product made by other producers, *or* (3) profits made on different products sold by the same producer.

Sales Below Cost. If substantial quantities of a product are sold in the exporting country (or in a third country if that is used for comparison purposes) at a price below per unit cost of production (including fixed and variable costs plus administrative and selling costs), the below-cost sales may be disregarded in determining a dumped product's normal value. A product is sold in "substantial quantities" if, over the period of one year, 20 percent or more of the sales in question are below cost. Normal value is then calculated on the basis of the remaining above-cost sales.

The Level-of-Trade Problem. A producing firm that sells to its local market at a different level in the chain of distribution than in foreign markets presents a common problem in the evaluation of dumping cases. For example, a higher normal value frequently occurs when the producer sells directly to retailers or to end-users in the home country, whereas in the export market the producer may be selling to distributors or to wholesalers. The dumping margin would be attributed to the different costs of sale and different markups required. In a *level-of-trade problem* such as this, the ITA adjusts the price differential so that figures for normal value and export price are comparable.

http://

http://europa.eu.int/comm/trade

For an overview of European Union unfair trade laws against dumping and subsidies, follow the link from the EU Commission Web site to "Trade Policy Instruments." Include the official text of legislation, reports, and statistics.

GATT Dispute Settlement in Dumping Cases

Prior to the WTO agreement in 1994, GATT was sometimes criticized for its inability to control

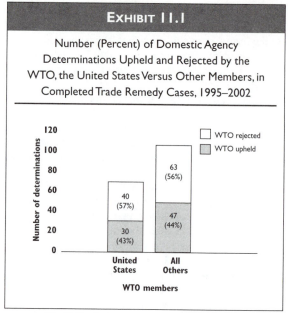

EXHIBIT 11.1

Number (Percent) of Domestic Agency Determinations Upheld and Rejected by the WTO, the United States Versus Other Members, in Completed Trade Remedy Cases, 1995–2002

SOURCE: *World Trade Organization, Standard of Review and Impact of Trade Remedy Rulings,* U.S. General Accounting Office, GAO-03-824, July 2003

dumping or resolve dumping disputes. The 1994 agreement creates the *WTO Committee on Antidumping Practices,* which is responsible for assisting countries in implementing the agreement.

Dumping disputes may be taken to the WTO *Dispute Settlement Body* for negotiation or resolution. (The procedures for WTO dispute settlement were discussed in Chapter Nine.) The parties to dispute settlement, of course, are the nations involved and not the sellers and buyers of the dumped products—although individual companies often have considerable influence in initiating dumping investigations.

The WTO panel may review a final antidumping order of an administrative agency in the importing country to determine if it is consistent with the GATT *Antidumping Agreement.* The panel can look to see if the agency misinterpreted the provisions of the agreement, or whether it properly followed all administrative procedures in an "unbiased and objective" manner as called for in the GATT agreement. If the panel finds that an antidumping order violates GATT, the panel can recommend measures to be taken against the importing country. However, the scope of review of an agency's investigation and antidumping order is limited.

A dispute panel cannot reconsider issues of fact determined during a dumping investigation or overturn an interpretation of the agreement made by the investigating agency. Thus, in reviewing U.S. dumping cases, a panel must accept the facts as found by the ITA and ITC in their investigations and look only to see whether the agencies correctly applied GATT law. This standard of review is similar to the process found in the United States in which courts of law review decisions of administrative agencies.

Dumping and Non-market Economy Countries in Transition

The United States has special rules for calculating the dumping margin of products imported from countries whose political and economic systems rely heavily on government central control, rather than on free market forces. These *non-market economy countries* (NME) have political and economic systems that are still rooted in the socialist principles of a state controlled economy. Almost all are in some degree transitioning to a private free market economy (with a couple of exceptions, of course). Many still have extensive government control over the allocation of resources or the price of raw materials or energy. They can control labor costs or provide transportation, insurance, or other services as an indirect government service to government industries. The governments can set quotas for production output or for export volume. Investment may be heavily regulated, involving a mixture of government ownership with private interests, and so on. Remember, these governments are in a position to see that their exports sell at almost any price they desire. It is impossible to ask a private firm to compete on a level playing field under these circumstances. Thus, in terms of the law of dumping, it is impossible to compare the "normal value" of a product in the NME market to the export price in the United States. U.S. law requires the ITA to investigate and to determine a "surrogate" normal value. The *surrogate normal value* is the value of the *factors of production,* including materials, labor, energy, capital costs and depreciation, packaging, and other general expenses, *in a market economy country that is at a level of economic development comparable to that of the NME and that is a sig-*nificant producer of comparable merchandise. Added to that is an estimated amount for profit. If information is inadequate or not provided, which may be the case if the government does not want it released, surrogate normal value is *the price* at which comparable merchandise produced in market economy countries that are a level of economic development comparable to that of the NME *is sold in the United States or other countries.* Today, the U.S. government uses the NME method of finding normal value only for China and certain countries of the former Soviet Union.

Market-Oriented Industries. The ITA understands that the transition to free markets cannot happen overnight. Rather, it might take place in steps, with the government freeing certain market sectors to competition or by selling state-owned factories or property through privatization. So, even if the exporting country is an NME, the ITA may look to see if the particular industry producing the dumped products in that country is a market-oriented industry. A *market-oriented industry* is one in which resources (materials, energy, etc.) and labor costs are procured at free market prices, where there is little government involvement in controlling production and capacity decisions, where prices are set by markets, and where the producers are mostly privately owned. Even where an industry is found not to be market oriented, it is still possible to find that an individual firm or firms are operating freely. In the following case, *Bulk Aspirin from the People's Republic of China,* a French-owned chemical giant with a plant in the United States petitioned the government for antidumping duties against its Chinese competitors. The case will give you a good feel for the administrative process and the combative nature of the proceedings. As you read the case, and especially the comment that follows, consider the ironies in the case. Consider the impact of the antidumping laws on workers and consumers, and the place of dumping laws in the future of the global economy.

> **http://www.ccra-adrc.gc.ca**
> For information on Canadian antidumping duty laws and investigation, go to "customs, business" or search on "Special Import Measures Act."

Bulk Aspirin from the People's Republic of China
(Notice of Preliminary Determination of Sales at Less Than Fair Value) 65 FR 116 (2000)
International Trade Administration, U.S. Department of Commerce

BACKGROUND AND FACTS

Rhodia Pharma Solutions is one of the world's leading manufacturers of specialty chemicals, including acetylsalicylic acid (bulk aspirin). With corporate headquarters in France, it has about 25,000 employees in offices and manufacturing plants in the United States and throughout the world. In 1999, Rhodia filed a petition with the Department of Commerce ("ITA" herein) alleging that imports from the People's Republic of China (PRC) are being dumped in the United States for less than fair value. Based on industry information, Rhodia believed that their customers were paying less than half of Rhodia's price for the same product. No other firms joined the petition, and Rhodia is apparently the only producer of aspirin in the United States. Rhodia's petition identified several potential Chinese exporters of bulk aspirin. Only two Chinese firms, Jilin and Shandong, responded to the petition. The ITA sent questionnaires to Jilin and Shandong, and to the Chinese government, asking that it be forwarded to other Chinese producers. Jilin and Shandong responded with the price and market information requested by the ITA. No other Chinese firms responded. After an investigation, the agency issued this preliminary determination.

PRELIMINARY DETERMINATION

The ITA has treated the PRC as a nonmarket economy ("NME") country in all past antidumping investigations. A designation as an NME remains in effect until it is revoked by the ITA.

Separate Rates: Both Jilin and Shandong have requested separate company-specific rates. These companies have stated that they are privately owned companies with no element of government ownership or control. To establish whether a firm is sufficiently independent from government control to be entitled to a separate rate, the ITA analyzes each exporting entity. Under the separate rates criteria, the ITA assigns separate rates in NME cases only if the respondents can demonstrate the absence of both *de jure* and *de facto* governmental control over export activities.

Absence of De Jure Control ["by law"]: The respondents have placed on the record a number of documents to demonstrate absence of *de jure* gov-

ernment control, including the *Foreign Trade Law of the People's Republic of China* and the *Company Law of the People's Republic of China*. The ITA has analyzed these laws in prior cases and found that they establish an absence of *de jure* control . . . over export pricing and marketing decisions of firms.

Absence of De Facto Control ["in fact or reality"]: . . . Shandong and Jilin have each asserted the following: (1) They establish their own export prices; (2) they negotiate contracts without guidance from any governmental entities or organizations; (3) they make their own personnel decisions; and (4) they retain the proceeds of their export sales and use profits according to their business needs without any restrictions. Additionally, these two respondents have stated that they do not coordinate or consult with other exporters regarding their pricing. This information supports a preliminary finding that there is no *de facto* governmental control of the export functions of these companies. Consequently, we preliminarily determine that both responding exporters have met the criteria for the application of separate rates.

Use of Facts Available: The PRC-Wide Rate: U.S. import statistics indicate that the total quantity of U.S. imports of aspirin from the PRC is greater than that reported by Jilin and Shandong. . . . Accordingly, we are applying a single antidumping deposit rate—the PRC-wide rate—to all exporters [other than Jilin and Shandong] based on our presumption that the export activities of the companies that failed to respond to the ITA's questionnaire are controlled by the PRC government. The PRC-wide antidumping rate is based on adverse facts available. The exporters that decided not to respond in any form to the ITA's questionnaire failed to act to the best of their ability in this investigation. Thus . . . we are assigning the highest margin in the petition, 144.02 percent, which is higher than any of the calculated margins.
* * *

Normal Value [NV]: Surrogate Country: Section 773(c)(4) of the Act requires the ITA to value the NME producer's factors of production, to the extent possible, in one or more market economy countries that: (1) Are at a level of economic development

continued

continued

comparable to that of the NME, and (2) are significant producers of comparable merchandise. The ITA has determined that India, Pakistan, Sri Lanka, Egypt, Indonesia, and the Philippines are countries comparable to the PRC in terms of overall economic development. We have further determined that India is a significant producer of comparable merchandise. Accordingly, we have calculated NV using mainly Indian values, and in some cases U.S. export values, for the PRC producers' factors of production.

* * *

Factors of Production: [W]e calculated NV based on factors of production reported by the companies in the PRC which produced aspirin and sold aspirin to the United States. Our NV calculation included amounts for materials, labor, energy, overhead, SG&A, and profit. To calculate NV, the reported unit factor quantities were multiplied by publicly available Indian and U.S. export price values.

Decision. Based on the calculations of normal value, two producers, Jilin and Shandong, were able to show that their export pricing was not under government control and received separate antidumping duty rates

based on their individual dumping margins (from 4 to 42 percent). Bulk aspirin imports from all other Chinese exporters received the PRC-wide rate of 144 percent.

Comment. The final determination of dumping was made in 2000, the same year that the U.S. International Trade Commission found injury to the U.S. producers. In 2001–2002, the Court of International Trade reversed parts of the ITA's methodology of obtaining surrogate values for certain factors of production because it was not based on substantial evidence. The ITA then changed its methods of calculating overhead, labor, and other factors. For example, instead of using a higher weighted average overhead factor, the ITA used figures from the lowest Indian producer. Subsequently, Jilin and Shandong's antidumping duties were cut to zero. In 2003, a Rhodia representative stated in testimony before the U.S. House of Representatives that at first the new duties had helped it regain customers and become profitable again, but when ITA changed its methodology and the antidumping duties disappeared, so did its customers. Rhodia's business in the United States had been devastated. And with that, Rhodia closed the last remaining aspirin plant in America—and moved it to—you guessed it, China.

UNFAIR IMPORT LAWS: SUBSIDIES AND COUNTERVAILING DUTIES

A second type of unfair trade practice is subsidies. *Subsidies* are financial contributions or benefits conferred by a government to a domestic firm or industry to achieve some economic or social objective. Subsidies might be granted to assist the startup of new companies, to retire old factories, to help firms meet new environmental regulations, or to protect industries such as steel, aircraft, or agriculture that are essential to national security. They may take many forms, including low interest loans, direct cash payments, export financing and credit assistance, favorable tax treatment, and so on. Subsidies are granted by all industrialized nations to virtually all segments of their economies, and not just to manufacturing firms. The EU, the United States, and Japan each spend tens of billions of dollars annually on agricultural subsidies alone, including direct payments to farmers.

Subsidies have long been recognized as damaging to the international economy. Subsidized industries are able to sell their products in foreign markets at prices lower than would otherwise be possible, which distorts trade patterns based on comparative advantage, and gives an unfair competitive advantage to subsidized industries. Subsidies also encourage private industries to embark on commercial ventures that, once the subsidy ends, may prove unprofitable or commercially disastrous. These drawbacks of subsidies can be illustrated in the case of the *Concorde* supersonic aircraft, which flies from Europe to the United States in less than half the time of a regular jet. The aircraft's development by a consortium of European companies was spurred not by demand, but by a host of EU subsidies. In commercial use, the plane turned out to be highly unprofitable and was taken out of service in 2003. Without the subsidy, the plane would have proved too costly to merit production.

http://www.wto.org

For an explanation and official text of the WTO Argument on Subsidies and Countervailing Duties, link from the WTO home page to "Trade Topics."

GATT 1994 *Agreement on Subsidies and Countervailing Measures*

Subsidies have been regulated by GATT since 1947. The current law is found in the GATT 1994 *Agreement on Subsidies and Countervailing Measures,* negotiated during the *Uruguay Round.* The basic terms of the new GATT agreement have been incorporated into federal law in the *Uruguay Round Agreements Act.*

Under the GATT agreement, subsidies may be dealt with in several ways. First, a WTO member country may appeal to the WTO for dispute resolution. The WTO may recommend that the subsidy be discontinued, that its harmful effects be eliminated, or that some countermeasure be taken by the importing country. Secondly, an importing country may initiate its own administrative proceedings, similar to antidumping proceedings, to impose a countervailing duty on the subsidized goods in order to eliminate their unfair price advantage. A *countervailing duty* (CVD) is a special tariff, in addition to the normal import tariff, imposed on imports of subsidized goods in an amount equal to the amount of the countervailable subsidy. A CVD action may be brought at the same time as the WTO dispute settlement action. However, only one form of relief—either the CVD or a countermeasure approved by the WTO—is available.

Definition of a Subsidy

A subsidy exists if a government *confers a benefit* on a domestic firm or industry by providing any form of income or price support *or* provides a *financial contribution* by

1. Providing funds, grants, or making loans at less than prevailing commercial interest rates, or loan guarantees that allow the company to receive loans at rates more favorable than nonguaranteed commercial loan rates;
2. Not collecting revenue or taxes otherwise due;
3. Providing investment capital if the investment decision is inconsistent with the usual practices of private investors;
4. Furnishing goods or services other than general infrastructure, such as building a road or bridge;
5. Purchasing goods from firms at a higher price than would be paid in the marketplace.

GATT 1994 provides for three types of subsidies: prohibited subsidies, domestic or adverse effects subsidies, and nonactionable or socially beneficial subsidies. All three types must meet the preceding definition.

Prohibited Subsidies

Prohibited subsidies include export subsidies or import substitution subsidies. An *export subsidy* is made available to domestic firms upon the export of their product, or is contingent upon export performance. An *import substitution subsidy* is a governmental subsidy whose payment is contingent on its recipient using or purchasing domestically made goods over imported goods. Both of these are completely prohibited under GATT. An importing country that is a WTO member can request dispute settlement before a WTO panel regardless of whether the subsidy causes injury to any of its firms or industries. WTO dispute resolution should take less than a year to complete. CVDs may be imposed on export subsidies through administrative or legal proceedings in the importing country. In CVD proceedings, export subsidies must be shown to have caused or threatened material injury to a domestic industry producing a like product.

Examples of an export subsidy include money paid on the basis of the number of exported goods, free or subsidized transportation provided for export shipments, rebates of taxes paid on the export of products, export credit guarantees at below market rates, and special tax treatment of income earned through export sales. In an interesting example of an export subsidy, Germany assisted the development, manufacture, and export of the European Airbus (a jumbo jet that competes with U.S. planes) by providing no-interest loans and currency stabilization guarantees to the manufacturers. These subsidies allowed the manufacturers to enter contracts to sell planes to U.S. airlines without assuming any currency fluctuation risk. In 1992, a GATT panel ruled that the German currency stabilization guarantees violated GATT.

Domestic Subsidies

Many subsidies take the form of government programs designed to achieve some greater social or national economic objective, ranging from health care to national defense, and indirectly give firms an advantage in world markets. After all, when a government makes large purchases of overpriced military jets, it subsidizes (and lowers the cost of) passenger aircraft. These purchases generally fall in the category of *domestic subsidies,* and must be distinguished from export subsidies. Examples include the provision of capital or low-cost loans for modernizing factories or for buying land on which to build new factories; providing industry with low-cost oil, chemicals, or other raw materials at discount prices from government-owned stockpiles; government defense spending on military aircraft or ships; grants for research and development of medicines; cash payments for apprentice programs or tax deductions to employers that pay college tuition for employees; government-supplied utilities; tax deductions or tax credits to encourage investment in capital equipment. Domestic subsidies such as these are generally permissible as a part of the legitimate responsibility of government to direct its industrial growth and fund social programs.

Remedies for Adverse Effects of Domestic Subsidies.   Some domestic subsidies, however, give unfair competitive advantage to domestic firms and are known in GATT as *adverse effects subsidies.* They are actionable at the WTO only if they (1) cause injury to a domestic industry of another WTO member country, (2) cause nullification and impairment of rights accruing to a member country under GATT, or (3) cause serious prejudice to another member. *Serious prejudice is presumed to exist* if the subsidy of a product exceeds 5 percent of its value, if the subsidy covers a firm's operating losses, or if the government forgives a debt owed to it. Serious prejudice may exist if (1) the subsidy impedes world trade in similar products produced in member countries; (2) the subsidy causes lost sales or price undercutting by the subsidized product; or (3) in the case of a subsidy of a primary product or commodity, it causes an increase in the subsidizing country's world market share of that product. In these cases, the WTO may recommend that the subsidizing country remove the prohibited subsidy or that the complaining country take some countermeasures against it. In a CVD proceeding conducted by an administrative agency in the importing country, as opposed to WTO panel proceedings, the requirement is different; a complaining party need only show that the domestic subsidy caused or threatens to cause *material injury* to domestic producers of like products.

What Makes a Subsidy Specific?   The second requirement, for both WTO actions and CVD administrative actions, is that the domestic subsidy be *specific. All* prohibited (export and import substitution) subsidies are presumed to be specific. All other subsidies are specific if they are limited to helping an enterprise or industry. A government's objective criteria for eligibility for a domestic subsidy is *not* specific if eligibility is automatic and does not favor one enterprise or industry over another. For instance, suppose that tax authorities allow all taxpayers to deduct $50,000 of the cost of new machinery as an ordinary operating expense in the year of purchase instead of $25,000 that had been allowed. Because the tax reduction does not favor one industry over another, it is not specific. However, if the companies receiving the subsidy are limited in number, if one firm or industry is the predominant user of the subsidy, or if the subsidy is limited to firms within a certain geographical region, then the subsidy is probably specific. In *Cabot Corp. v. United States,* 620 F. Supp. 722 (CIT, 1985), the court adopted the "specificity test." The test was enacted into law by Congress in 1988 and subsequently brought to the *Uruguay Round Agreement* by the United States.

Upstream Subsidies.   An *upstream subsidy* is one that is granted by a government to a firm or industry that produces raw materials or component parts (input products) that are used in an exported product. For instance, a subsidy on coal might also be considered a subsidy on steel made in furnaces that burn that coal. A subsidy on European wheat might be considered a subsidy upon Italian pasta made from that wheat. Similarly, a subsidy on live swine might be considered an upstream subsidy of unprocessed pork exports. A subsidy of semiconductors would amount to a subsidy of computers in which they are installed. Upstream subsidies are subject to CVDs if the input product is made available at a below-market price and has a significant effect on the cost of manufacturing the final product. Under the U.S. *Uruguay Round Agreements Act,* upstream subsidies include only domestic subsidies, and not export subsidies. Upstream subsidies may be countervailed only when they bestow a competitive benefit on the goods in question.

Nonactionable or Socially Beneficial Subsidies

Socially beneficial subsidies are not actionable under the WTO and not countervailable if they meet the requirements of the GATT agreement. They include (1) certain subsidies granted to industry or universities for expanding knowledge through research and development, provided it does not directly create an unfair competitive advantage to exported products; (2) certain subsidies to poor, depressed, or underemployed geographic regions— U.S. law requires that per capita GDP or income does not exceed 85 percent of the national average or that unemployment be at least 110 percent of the rate in the subsidizing country; and (3) certain subsidies granted on a one-time basis to help companies meet costly environmental or antipollution regulations, provided it is limited to 20 percent of the cost and made available to all companies that require the new pollution control equipment or technology. Member countries should notify the WTO Committee on Subsidies and Countervailing Measures in advance of granting a socially beneficial subsidy. A socially beneficial subsidy is not countervailable if the country that granted it notified the WTO Committee on Subsidies and Countervailing Measures in advance. An importing country's only recourse in this case is at the WTO which uses binding arbitration in these cases.

Subsidies and State Owned Enterprises

Applying the principles of CVD law to goods exported by state owned enterprises presents several problems, especially when those enterprises are owned by countries that have a non-market economy. In *Georgetown Steel Corp. v. United States,* 801 F.2d 1308 (Fed. Cir. 1986), the court ruled that the U.S. CVD statute could not be applied to imports from non-market countries. The court believed Congress had designed the statute to remedy subsidies that distort the free market process by altering the market decisions of

manufacturers and exporters. In non-market economy countries, the subsidy is, in a sense, made only to the government itself, with no resulting effect on market decision making.

Exports from Newly Privatized Enterprises. What happens when a state owned enterprise is transitioned into private ownership? Do the subsidies once provided when the enterprise was government owned continue to benefit the now privately owned firm? Understand that state owned enterprises exist not just in non-market economy or socialist countries, but in many countries that we think of as being "free market" or "capitalist." These include Western nations like the UK, Sweden, and France, as well as developing countries such as Mexico, Chile, and Brazil. For example, government ownership of communications or energy industries is not unusual. However, since the late 1980s, there has been a worldwide trend away from government ownership of industry and toward private investment. This is known as privatization. The term *privatization* refers to the process by which a government sells or transfers government owned industries or other assets to the private sector.

The next case, *United States—Countervailing Measures Concerning Certain Products from the European Communities* (European Steel), sees the largest European steel mills go from their days of near financial collapse in the late 1960s, through a government bailout and takeover of ownership, to a subsequent return to private hands decades later. The United States believed that the financial contributions made to the firms while they were government owned were benefits that passed through to the newly privatized companies. This, in turn, continued to permit low-cost steel exports to the United States. The issue reached the WTO Appellate Body in Geneva.

---

http://www.globalization101.org
Provides an interesting and cogent analysis of the economics and politics of trade and trade regulation.

When a Remedy Becomes a Subsidy: The Controversy over the *Continued Dumping and Subsidy Offset Act of 2000*

Normally, antidumping and countervailing duties collected on imports by the Bureau of Customs and

*United States—Countervailing Measures Concerning Certain Products from the
European Communities (European Steel)*
WT/DS212/AB/R (9 December 2002)
World Trade Organization Report of the Appellate Body

BACKGROUND AND FACTS

During the 1960s and 1970s, the European steel industry
was near financial collapse. With the support of labor
groups, the largest firms were kept alive with cash, low-
interest loans, and equity investments from European
governments. Many mills became government owned. In
the early 1980s, the equivalent of tens of billions of dollars of public money was used to keep the mills running.
The money financed operations, revitalized equipment,
lowered the firms' debt, trained steelworkers, and permitted the export of low-priced steel. The United States
responded with a host of trade remedies, including countervailing duties. When the political climate changed in
Europe, governments decided to sell off their interests to
private investors in free market stock sales. From 1988
to date, many large steel mills were privatized. This
included British Steel (today Corus), Germany's Saarstahl,
France's Usinor, and others. The new privately-owned
companies continued to sell steel in America.

The U.S. Department of Commerce ("ITA" herein)
imposed countervailing duties on European steel imports
despite the fact that the European mills had been privatized. It believed that the benefits endowed by the subsidies while the companies were government owned
continued to "pass through" to the same steel companies (arguing that the companies were still the "same
legal person") even after the change in ownership. After
all, it was assumed, the new shareholders received the
modern equipment, trained workers, and other assets
paid for by the government. The European Communities
maintained that the privatizations took place at arm's
length and for fair market value, that the government no
longer had any ownership interest or control, and thus
that public monies were no longer subsidizing steel production. The EC argues that the U.S. "same person" rule
violates the *WTO Agreement on Subsidies and Countervailing Measures [SCM Agreement]*. Consultations between
the governments failed, and in 2001, the EC requested
that the WTO Dispute Settlement Body convene a dispute panel. After the decision of the panel, the United
States appealed to the Appellate Body.

REPORT OF THE APPELLATE BODY

* * *

[W]e find that the Panel erred in concluding that
"[p]rivatizations at arm's length and for fair market
value *must* lead to the conclusion that the privatized
producer paid for what he got and thus did not get
any benefit or advantage from the prior financial contribution bestowed upon the state-owned producer."
(emphasis added) Privatization at arm's length and
for fair market value *may* result in extinguishing the
benefit. Indeed, we find that there is a rebuttable presumption that a benefit ceases to exist after such a
privatization. Nevertheless, it does not *necessarily* do
so. There is no inflexible rule *requiring* that investigating authorities, in future cases, *automatically* determine that a "benefit" derived from pre-privatization
financial contributions expires following privatization
at arm's length and for fair market value. It depends
on the facts of each case.

* * *

With all this in mind, we now turn to the administrative practice of the ITA that is the source and
subject of this dispute. . . . Generally, the ITA applies
the "same person" method to countervailing duty
determinations following a change in ownership.

* * *

The Panel stated, and the United States agreed
before the Panel and on appeal, that the "same person" method *requires* the ITA to "consider that the
benefit attributed to the state-owned producer can
be automatically attributed to the privatized producer without any examination of the condition of
the transaction" when the agency determines the
post-privatization entity is not a new legal person. It
is only if the ITA finds that a new legal person has
been created that the agency will make a determination of whether a benefit exists, and, in such cases,
the inquiry will be limited to the subject of whether a
new subsidy has been provided to the new owners.

Thus, under the "same person" method, when
the ITA determines that no new legal person is created as a result of privatization, the ITA will conclude from this determination, *without any further
analysis,* and irrespective of the price paid by the

continued

continued

new owners for the newly-privatized enterprise, that the newly-privatized enterprise continues to receive the benefit of a previous financial contribution. This approach is contrary to the *SCM Agreement* that the investigating authority must take into account in an administrative review "positive information substantiating the need for a review." Such information could relate to developments with respect to the subsidy, privatization at arm's length and for fair market value, or some other information. The "same person" method impedes the ITA from complying with its obligation to examine whether a countervailable "benefit" continues to exist in a firm subsequent to that firm's change in ownership. Therefore, we find that the "same person" method, *as such*, is inconsistent with . . . the *SCM Agreement*.

* * *

Decision. In countervailing duty actions, national administrative agencies must consider a broad range of criteria on a case-by-case basis in determining whether prior subsidies to a former government-owned company have "passed through" to the newly privatized company. The "same person" test used by the U.S. Department of Commerce violates the *SCM Agreement*.

Comment. In 2003, the ITA announced a new rule based on the presumption that a government subsidy can benefit a company over a period of time, corresponding to the useful life of the assets. However, the presumption is rebuttable if it can be shown that the government sold its ownership of all or substantially all of a company or its assets, retaining no control, and that the sale was an *arm's-length transaction* for *fair market value.*

Border Protection are paid to the U.S. Treasury. To toughen U.S. unfair trade laws, the U.S. Congress enacted the *Continued Dumping and Subsidy Offset Act of 2000*. It provides that the offset duties be paid directly to the petitioning companies in the action. Early Senate reports indicated that about $40 million would be collected and distributed in the first ten years. In 2001 and 2002 alone, Customs paid over $500 million directly to U.S. firms. The industries receiving the largest payments were steel, candles, and computer chips. It prompted immediate protests by eleven WTO members, including some of America's closest trading partners from across the globe. They argued that the law would prompt firms to file unfair import cases, give them an unfair competitive advantage, and that transferring duties to individual firms amounts to the making of subsidy payments that are not a permitted remedy in unfair import cases under WTO rules. In *United States—Continued Dumping and Subsidy Offset Act of 2000*, Report of the Appellate Body, World Trade Organization, WT/DS217/234/AB/R (16 January 2003), the WTO Dispute Settlement Body recommended that the U.S. law be brought into compliance. Later that year, President Bush announced that he would seek the repeal of the law.

Material Injury in U.S. Unfair Import Cases

In unfair trade actions between WTO members, the importing country must find that a domestic industry has been materially injured, threatened with material injury, or that the establishment of an industry has been materially retarded. This requirement applies to both antidumping actions and CVD actions.

The "material injury" requirement under the unfair import statutes prescribes a finding of less harm than does the "serious injury" requirement in the safeguard actions. Material injury has generally been defined as injury that is not inconsequential or unimportant. In determining material injury under the unfair trade laws, the ITC must consider all relevant economic factors. Factors used to determine material injury include (1) the volume of the dumped or subsidized imports (Have dumped imports increased significantly?); (2) the effect of the imports on prices in the domestic market for like products (Have prices been undercut significantly? Have prices been depressed? Are domestic firms unable to raise prices to cover increased costs?); and (3) the impact of the imports on the domestic industry, including all relevant economic data reflecting industry sales, profits, market share, productivity, return on investment, utilization of capacity, cash flow, wages, unemployment, growing inventories, and so on. A finding of material injury must be reviewed every five years if the antidumping order is still in effect at that time.

JUDICIAL REVIEW IN INTERNATIONAL TRADE CASES

Decisions of the ITA or ITC in both CVD cases and antidumping duty cases are reviewable in the U.S. Court of International Trade if they are final decisions or if they are negative determinations. A *negative determination* is a decision by the agency either to not initiate an investigation or that a material injury does not exist. If an antidumping determination involves Canadian or Mexican goods, appeals may be made to a binational arbitration panel established under NAFTA.

CHAPTER SUMMARY

A nation's choice either to protect its domestic industries from foreign competition or to adopt free trade policies is an economic and political decision. A country that joins the WTO pledges to protect domestic industries from foreign competition only within the guidelines and international legal standards set out in the GATT. This chapter discussed how GATT permits countries to "safeguard" domestic industries from increasing imports and offset the price advantage of "unfairly" imported goods. The *Uruguay Round Agreements* significantly changed international trade rules. The United States has implemented the GATT 1994 rules in the *Uruguay Round Agreements Act,* effective January 1, 1995.

A country may safeguard a domestic industry from serious injury caused by increasing imports, by providing import relief or adjusting import competition. In the United States, the president may provide import relief in the form of temporary tariff increases only upon investigation by the ITC and its finding that increasing imports are the substantial cause of serious injury to a domestic industry producing like products. The purpose of the relief is to give the domestic industry time to adjust to market conditions. The willingness of the president to protect an industry depends on national interests as well as the president's own economic and trade philosophies. Trade adjustment assistance is available to workers whose jobs are lost to

foreign imports or by the relocation of factories to foreign countries.

The U.S. steel industry provides a classic example of the interplay between international economics and unfair trade law. It shows the steps that a government can take to protect what it perceives as an industry necessary for the national defense, the opposing views of "big steel" interests versus firms that buy steel for manufacturing, and consumer groups. For decades, the steel industries of both the United States and Europe benefited from heavy subsidies. At the same time, their exports were subjected to restraint agreements, safeguards, antidumping duties, and countervailing duties.

Unfair trade includes dumping and subsidies. Both practices allow foreign products to be imported at unfairly low prices. Dumping is the practice of selling goods in a foreign country for less than the normal value of like products in the home market. The producer or exporter in this case is the "wrongdoer." The GATT *Antidumping Agreement* permits the collection of additional duties to offset this practice. Much of the litigation in this area involves determining normal value, and the calculation of the dumping margin. There are special rules for handling dumped imports from nonmarket (or mixed economy) countries, such as China. A subsidy is a financial contribution made by the government of the exporting country that confers a benefit on a firm, directly or indirectly. The GATT *Subsidies Agreement* permits countervailing duties on subsidized imports to offset the value of the benefit. Remedies in unfair trade cases may be imposed only where the domestic industry has suffered material injury as a result. Throughout this area, the decisions of the WTO Appellate Body in Geneva, Switzerland, are becoming increasingly important. In several cases, the United States has had to reform or repeal its laws and administrative practices to comply with WTO rules.

It appears that the number of trade cases taken to the WTO for resolution will continue to increase. As WTO panels and the Appellate Body have the opportunity to consider future trade issues, their rulings will have a growing impact on domestic laws and regulations in all countries. Already, there have been trade regulation cases in which the WTO Appellate Body and the U.S. federal courts have come to different opinions on the "legality" of a U.S. law. Of course, the Dispute Settlement Body can "recommend" that a national law be brought into compliance with WTO rules. And since American courts have generally stated that they are not bound to follow or enforce WTO Appellate Body decisions, U.S. compliance with a WTO ruling becomes a matter for the legislative or executive branches to remedy, not the judiciary. Moreover, U.S. law does not permit private parties to sue in U.S. courts to enforce rights under the WTO agreements. But the two tribunals, an ocean apart, are surely influencing each other already. The interrelationship between the American judiciary and the WTO dispute tribunals will certainly be debated and reevaluated in the years to come.

Questions and Case Problems

1. Consider how *Section 201* (safeguard against injury) has been used in the United States in recent years. Safeguard measures were applied by President Reagan in the *Harley-Davidson* case, and by President Bush to protect the U.S. steel industry in 2002. Based on your research, on what other occasions has a U.S. president imposed safeguard measures to protect an American industry since 1980? Evaluate the government's use of safeguard measures. What are the pros and cons of using safeguards? What are the effects on domestic industry in the short term? How might it affect a firm's competitiveness in the long term? Although the administrative process is handled through a bipartisan, independent commission (the ITC), why is the process still very political?

2. The U.S. *Revenue Act of 1916* also contains special provisions that make certain types of dumping illegal. It allows for private claims against and criminal prosecutions of parties that regularly and systematically import goods into the United States at a price substantially less than actual market value or wholesale price. Civil suits against dumping firms can result in treble damages for the winning petitioner. Both Japan and the EU challenged the act as being inconsistent with article VI of GATT 1994 and the GATT *Antidumping Agreement*. The United States contended that the act is not an antidumping act at all, but merely outlaws predatory pricing with the intent to destroy, injure, or prevent the establishment of an American industry or to restrain trade in or monopolize a particular market. What do you think the panel held? What other information would you like to know about the 1916 act to help you decide? *United States—Anti-Dumping Act of 1916,* Report of the Appellate Body, World Trade Organization, WT/DS136/162/AB/R (28 August 2000).

3. What makes an import practice "unfair"? What remedies are available under U.S. law to protect domestic industries from unfair imports?

4. Describe the different functions of the ITA and the ITC in regulating import competition.

5. The plaintiff, Smith Corona, was the last remaining manufacturer of portable electric typewriters in the United States. This action was brought to challenge the method used by the International Trade Administration to determine whether the Japanese typewriter companies, Brother and Silver Seiko, had engaged in dumping in the United States. The typewriters in question were sold in Japan (the home market) under different circumstances of sale than in the United States. In Japan, Silver Seiko provided volume rebates to its customers based on total sales of all merchandise sold. Brother incurred advertising expenses in Japan, as well as expenditures for accessories that accompany typewriters sold in Japan but not in the United States. The ITA subtracted these amounts from foreign market value in calculating the dumping margin. Was the ITA correct? See *Smith-Corona Group v. United States,* 713 F.2d 1568 (Fed. Cir. 1983).

6. The American Grape Growers alleged that imports of wine from France and Italy were being subsidized and sold in the United States at less than fair value. The ITC's preliminary review found no reasonable indication that a United States industry was threatened with material injury by reason of those imports. The American growers said the ITC decision did not cumulate the imports from France and Italy as they should have been. It instead had considered the two products different because the French wines were primarily white wines, and the Italian wines were primarily red and effervescent. The growers also said the ITC was wrong to base its decision on whether an injury had been proved, as opposed to whether there was a possibility of injury. Do you agree with the grape growers that the ITC preliminary decision was wrong?

7. Plaintiff, Cabot Corporation, is contesting the International Trade Administration's finding that the Mexican government's provision of carbon black feedstock and natural gas to Mexican producers at below-market prices did not constitute a countervailable subsidy. Carbon black feedstock and natural gas

are used in the production of paints, inks, plastics, and carbon paper. The feedstock is a by-product of crude oil and sold in Mexico through PEMEX, the government-owned oil company. Pursuant to a comprehensive economic development plan, PEMEX supplied the feedstock and natural gas at below-market prices to two Mexican producers of carbon black.

The plaintiff, U.S. producer of carbon black, contends that under U.S. law the actions of the Mexican government amount to a countervailable domestic subsidy. What is the correct legal test to determine if the supply of feedstock to Mexican manufacturers was a countervailable domestic subsidy? *Cabot Corp. v. United States,* 620 F. Supp. 722 (CIT, 1985).

Managerial Implications

Your firm manufactures optic transistors (OTs) used as a component part of personal computers. U.S. firms control 60 percent of the U.S. market for OTs. The market has done well overall, but recently, Japanese manufacturers of computers have increased their market share. Over the past two years the Japanese have been exporting OTs to the United States in larger quantities. You have noticed that in the past two years your share of the U.S. market for OTs has dropped from more than 25 percent to less than 20 percent. In addition, your total sales have declined, your inventories are at their largest levels, and you have had to postpone hiring new employees. You have been informed by one of your better customers that it can purchase imported OTs for $0.95 each, ex factory, or $1.00, CIF American port. Your U.S. price has been $1.20, FOB your factory, with your costs at $0.90. The same OTs are sold to Japanese computer firms at $1.15. Furthermore, you have learned that the Japanese government assists OT manufacturers by rebating the value-added tax normally assessed on all products manufactured in Japan.

To complicate your problems, you have experienced difficulty cracking export markets. You noticed that countries in which personal computers are now being assembled, such as Brazil, Korea, and Taiwan, have restricted your imports through a maze of complex regulations. These regulations require that you disclose important manufacturing and design techniques before import licenses will be granted. You are also concerned that your design patents will not be protected there, because Korean patent protection laws are not enforced. Korea has imposed quotas on OTs that make it virtually impossible to export to that market.

What remedies are available to your firm under U.S. law? What factors (economic, political or other) will affect the outcome of the case? Discuss.

CHAPTER 12

IMPORTS, CUSTOMS, AND TARIFF LAW

Importing is the process of entering goods into the customs territory of a country. The study of importing should not be approached from the perspective of an isolated transaction. Rather, importing should be viewed as an integral part of a global company's operations. For instance, a chemical company might find that raw materials can be sourced from foreign suppliers at a net cost far less than if purchased at home. A leading apparel designer might ship garments to the United States that had been assembled in Honduras, from parts of clothing that were cut and sewn at plants in Hong Kong, from fabric that had been woven in China. An automobile company might ship cars to the United States from assembly plants in Mexico that used component parts sourced from Japan or Europe. A Japanese-owned electronics company might assemble televisions in the Caribbean using both Japanese and U.S. parts, with the finished products shipped back to U.S. markets. A large retailer might import foreign-made consumer goods, such as toys or appliances, because they are cheaper from overseas sources. U.S. distributors of Swiss watches, Danish cheese, or French wine might import these foreign brands because customers perceive them to be of superior quality. Each of these companies views the operation of their firm in a global context, and they are aware that their global strategy will be affected by the customs and tariff laws applicable to their products as these goods cross national borders.

Whereas the preceding chapters discussed the process by which nations regulate international trade, this chapter focuses on the specific problems of importing goods into the United States. It exam-ines U.S. regulations governing the admission of goods into the country, the calculation of import duties, tariff preferences for developing countries, the marking requirements for goods, and the use of many duty-saving devices, such as foreign trade zones. The chapter begins with an explanation of how imports into the United States are supervised by U.S. Customs and how the customs and tariff laws are administered.

> **http://www.cbp.gov**
> The official site of
> the U.S. Bureau of Customs and
> Border Protection.

THE ADMINISTRATION OF CUSTOMS AND TARIFF LAWS

The customs and tariff laws of the United States are enacted by the U.S. Congress and implemented and enforced by the *U.S. Bureau of Customs and Border Protection,* referred to as Customs. Customs is an agency within the Department of Homeland Security, and is headed by the Commissioner of Customs. The creation of the Department of Homeland Security in 2003 was a part of the largest reorganization of the American government in over fifty years. The Bureau of Customs and Border Protection was created by merging the functions related to border security that had previously been handled by the Department of Agriculture, the Immigration and Naturalization Service, the Border Patrol, and U.S. Customs (formerly a part of the Department of Treasury). The agency's functions are to prevent terrorists and terrorist weapons from entering the United States, enforce border security, assess and collect the tariff revenue of the United States, enforce the customs laws, which includes regulating the entry of products under quota, enforcing the labeling statutes, supervising exports, administering of duty-free zones, and other functions. As a law enforcement agency, U.S. Customs combats smuggling of narcotics and contraband and investigates tariff fraud cases. Customs has the authority to bar the entry of goods that violate the patent, trademark, or copyright laws. The agency is responsible for the administration of customs laws throughout the customs territory of the United States, which includes Puerto Rico. U.S. Customs officers are assigned to U.S. embassies in many foreign countries to assist in the administration of U.S. Customs laws.

Customs is divided into seven geographic regions, each headed by a regional commissioner. The regions are further divided into Customs districts, headed by a district director. Customs offices are located at the *ports of entry,* including major seaports, airports, inland ports, and border crossings. Within each district are *field import specialists,* who make initial determinations as to the entry of goods. They can seek advice from the *national import specialists.* Some officers are specialists in particular types of products, such as textiles. The district director supervises all imports within the district and makes sure that imported goods are entered in accordance with the rules of the agency and decisions of the courts.

Locating Customs and Tariff Laws.
The primary tariff laws enforced by Customs related to this chapter are found in Title 19 ("Customs Duties") of the *United States Code.* Customs regulations that interpret and explain Title 19 are found in *Customs Regulation of the United States* and printed in the *Code of Federal Regulations.* The *Customs Bulletin and Decisions* is a weekly publication that contains decisions, rulings, proposed regulations, notices, news, and other information related to customs law and the operation of the agency. It also contains related court decisions. The U.S. Customs Web site

http://www.access.gpo.gov
The U.S. Government Printing Office. Follow instructions for access to U.S. Customs Regulations under Title 19.

now provides easy access to many of the same materials. U.S. Customs also has many pamphlets, videos, and books written in simple English to aid importers' compliance with the laws.

The Formal Entry Process

The *formal entry process* refers to the administrative process required to import goods into the stream of commerce of a country. There are four basic requirements:

1. the goods have arrived at a U.S. "port of entry,"
2. the goods are not of a type that are not permitted entry or from an embargoed country,
3. delivery is authorized by Customs after inspection and release, and
4. estimated duties have been paid or a customs bond posted.

The process begins upon the arrival of the merchandise at a U.S. port of entry. Goods not entered within fifteen days are sent to a warehouse as "unclaimed freight." The goods may be entered by the owner, purchaser, consignee (the party to whom the goods are shipped or to be delivered), or customs broker. A *customs broker* is an authorized agent, licensed by federal law, to act for and on behalf of importers in making entry of goods. Over 90 percent of all entries are made by customs brokers. A broker is not needed to import goods for yourself. A customs broker must possess a written power of attorney from the party making entry. Nonresident individuals and foreign corporations may make entry, but they are bound by much stricter rules. The entry process is not merely transporting the goods into the United States; it includes the filing of customs documents and the payment of duties.

Required Documentation.
When goods are entered, the entry documents must be filed within five days. The documents necessary to enter goods generally include the following items:

1. An entry manifest or merchandise release form (see the *Entry/Immediate Delivery Form* in Exhibit 12.1).
2. U.S. Customs *Entry Summary Form* (Exhibit 12.2).
3. Proof of the right to make entry (a bill of lading, air waybill, or Carrier's Certificate).

EXHIBIT 12.1

Entry/Immediate Delivery Form

DEPARTMENT OF THE TREASURY
UNITED STATES CUSTOMS SERVICE

FORM APPROVED
OMB NO. 1515-0069

ENTRY/IMMEDIATE DELIVERY

19CFR 142.3, 142.16, 142.22, 142.24

1. ARRIVAL DATE	2. ELECTED ENTRY DATE	3. ENTRY TYPE CODE/NAME	4. ENTRY NUMBER
060902		01 ABI/S	ABI CERTIFIED 669-2242260-6

5. PORT	6. SINGLE TRANS. BOND	7. BROKER/IMPORTER FILE NUMBER	
1512	X 891	617795E	

	8. CONSIGNEE NUMBER		9. IMPORTER NUMBER
			12-34567 SAME

10. ULTIMATE CONSIGNEE NAME

Importer's Company
Anytown, NC 20000

12. CARRIER CODE	13. VOYAGE/FLIGHT/TRIP	14. LOCATION OF GOODS–CODE(S)/NAME(S)
111	444	L362

15. VESSEL CODE/NAME

LUFTHANSA

16. U.S. PORT OF UNLOADING	17. MANIFEST NUMBER	18. G.O. NUMBER	19. TOTAL VALUE
1704			$3331

20. DESCRIPTION OF MERCHANDISE

Bedding

21. IT/BL/AWB CODE	22. IT/BL/AWB NO.	23. MANIFEST QUANTITY	24. H.S. NUMBER	25. COUNTRY OF ORIGIN	26. MANUFACTURER ID.
I	22069456995		6304.99.60107	DE	DEBILRHE4044KRA
M	22069456995				
H	48502287	5			

27. CERTIFICATION

I hereby make application for entry/immediate delivery. I certify that the above information is accurate, the bond is sufficient, valid, and current, and that all requirements of 19 CFR Part 142 have been met.

SIGNATURE OF APPLICANT

X   Importer's Customs Broker

PHONE NO.	DATE
	6/11/02

29. BROKER OR OTHER GOVT. AGENCY USE

28. CUSTOMS USE ONLY

☐ OTHER AGENCY ACTION REQUIRED, NAMELY:

☐ CUSTOMS EXAMINATION REQUIRED.

☐ ENTRY REJECTED, BECAUSE:

JUN 12 8 23 AM '02

DELIVERY AUTHORIZED:	SIGNATURE WRL	DATE 6-12-02

Customs Form 3461 (010189)

EXHIBIT 12.2

Entry Summary Form

DEPARTMENT OF THE TREASURY
UNITED STATES CUSTOMS SERVICE

Importer's Broker
P.O. Box 123
Charlotte, N.C. 28219

(1) Entry No. 2242260-6	(1) Entry No. 01 ABI/S	3. Entry Summary Date 6/26/02 ABI APPROVED	414

4. Entry Date	(5) Port Code 1512		

6. Bond No. 891	7. Bond Type Code SEB -9	8. BROKER/IMPORTER FILE NO. 123456ab-6	

9. Ultimate Consignee Name and Address	10. Consignee No.	(11) Importer of Record Name and Address	(12) Importer No. 12-34567
Importer's Company Anytown, NC 20000		Same	

		(13) Exporting Country DE GERMANY	14. Export Date 06/06/02
		(15) Country of Origin DE	6. Missing Documents
		(17) I.T. No. 22069456995	(18) I.T. Date 6/06/02

(19) BL or AWB No. 22069456995	20. Mode of Transportation 40	21. Manufacturer I.D. DEBILRHE4044KRO	22. Reference No.
(23) Importing Carrier LUFTHANSA	24. Foreign Port of Lading Frankfurt	25. Location of Goods/G.O. No. L362	
26. U.S. Port of Unlading 1704 ATLANTA	(27) Import Date 06/06/02		

(28). Line No.	30. (A) T.S.U.S.A. No. B. ADSA CVD Case No.	31. (A) Gross Weight B. Manifest Qty.	(32) Net Quantity in T.S.U.S.A. Units	33. (A) Entered Value B. CHGS C. Relationship	34. (A) T.S.U.S.A. Rate B. ADA/CVD Rate (C) I.R.C. Rate D. Visa No.	(35) Duty and I.R. Tax Dollars	Cents
48502287							
INV. NO. 9999/99/89591							
001	FURN ARTICLES:N/KNIT:WOOL/HAIR						
	6304.99.60107	193	193KG	3331 709	6.4%	213	18
		MERCHANDISE PROCESSING FEE			.17%	5	66
INV VAL 4039.98							
LESS NDC 709.00							
3330.98	US DOLLAR AT 1.00000000						
ENT. VAL 3330.98 AS	3331 TOTAL						
				3331		234	18
5 PCS TOTAL							
BLOCK 39 SUMMARY:							
MPF 499	21.00						
TOTAL:	21.00		TEV:	3331			

(36) Declaration of Importer of Record (Owner or Purchaser) or Authorized Agent	↓ **U.S. CUSTOMS USE** ↓	TOTALS

I declare that I am the
[ ] importer of record and that the actual owner, purchaser, or consignee for customs purposes is as shown above. OR [X] owner or purchaser or agent thereof.

I further declare that the merchandise
[X] was obtained pursuant to a purchase or agreement to purchase and that the prices set forth in the invoice are true. OR [ ] was not obtained pursuant to a purchase or agreement to purchase and the statements in the invoice as to value or price are true to the best of my knowledge and belief.

I also declare that the statements in the documents herein filed fully disclose to the best of my knowledge and belief the true prices, values, quantities, rebates, drawbacks, fees, commissions, and royalties are true and correct, and that all goods or services provided to the seller of the merchandise either free or at reduced cost are fully disclosed. I will immediately furnish to the appropriate customs officer any information showing a different state of facts.

Notice require by Paperwork Reduction Act of 1980. This information is needed to ensure that importers/exporters are complying with U.S. Customs laws, to allow us to compute and collect the right amount of money, to enforce other agency requirements, and to collect accurate statistical information on imports. Your response is mandatory.

A. Liq. Code	B. Ascertained Duty	(37) Duty 213.18
	C. Ascertained Tax	(38) Tax .00
	D. Ascertained Other	(39) Other 21.00
	E. Ascertained Total	(40) Total 234.18 -17.09

(41) Signature of Declarant, Total and Date
Importer's Broker   6/11/02

STATISTICAL

Customs Form 7501 (030984)

4. The commercial invoice obtained from the seller (or a pro forma invoice when the commercial invoice is temporarily delayed by the seller).
5. Packing slips to identify the contents of cartons.
6. Other documents required by special regulations (e.g., certificate of origin, quota visa, textile declaration, etc.).

The Commercial Invoice.

A seller must provide a separate invoice for each commercial shipment entering the United States. The *commercial invoice* is required for all shipments greater than $500 and intended for sale or commercial use in the United States. The invoice must provide all pertinent information about the shipment, in English, and be signed by the seller. One invoice can be used for installment shipments to the same consignee if the shipments arrive within ten days of each other. The invoice must include the following information:

- Name of the port of shipment and the destined port of entry.
- Name of buyer and seller or consignee.
- Common or trade name for the goods and their detailed description.
- Country-of-origin.
- Currency of payment.
- Quantity and weight of the goods shipped.
- Value of the goods accurately and correctly stated, including a breakdown of all itemized charges such as freight, insurance, packing costs, the costs of containers, and any rebates and commissions paid or payable.
- A packing list stating in detail what merchandise is in each individual package.
- Special information for certain classes of merchandise (e.g., bedspreads must indicate whether they contain any embroidery, lace, braid, or other trimming).

The Entry Summary and Immediate Delivery Forms.

Within ten working days the importer must file these completed documents with Customs at the port of entry. The information on the form is used to determine the amount of duties owed, to gather import statistics, and to determine if the goods conform to other U.S. regulations.

Payment of Duties.

If import duties are assessed on the goods by U.S. Customs, the importer must deposit estimated duties with Customs at the time of filing the entry documents or the entry summary form. The duties must be in an amount determined by U.S. Customs, pending a final calculation of the amount actually owed. Payment to a customs broker does not relieve the importer of liability to pay the duties. The liability for duties constitutes a personal debt of the importer, and a lien attaches to the merchandise. In lieu of paying duties immediately, an importer may post a customs bond. This is more convenient for companies needing immediate delivery of their goods. A customs bond can be purchased for a single shipment or for all shipments over the course of a year and up to the amount stated in the bond. The purpose of the bond is to ensure the payment of duties on final calculation. In some cases, goods can be released for transportation or storage *in-bond,* with the payments of duties suspended until the goods are released for sale or use in the United States. There is no liability for duties on unordered or unclaimed merchandise.

Informal Entries.

Personal and some smaller commercial shipments valued at $2,000 or less may be cleared through an *informal entry* process. A bond is not required for entry, and import duties are payable immediately at the time of entry. Informal entries may be processed through the U.S. Postal Service. The letter carrier acts as the agent for U.S. Customs for the purpose of collecting import duties. This practice has several advantages. Postal rates can be far less for smaller packages than commercial airfreight. The entry process is quicker and less expensive, with no customs broker needed. The documentation and marking requirements are still strict, however, and the importer should check with the postal service before attempting a postal entry. A commercial invoice must accompany the shipment. In addition, many products have a $250 limit on postal entries; these include furniture, flowers, textiles, leather goods, footwear, toys, games and many other items. Wool products and wearing apparel from the Pacific Rim countries require a formal customs entry regardless of value. If a mail article is found to contain merchandise subject to an import duty, and the article is not accompanied by a customs declaration and invoice, it is subject to seizure and forfeiture.

Electronic Entry Processing.

In the late 1990s, Customs instituted a paperless entry process, known as the *Automated Commercial System*. It is designed to reduce costs to business and government and to speed the entry process. The system allows entry documents to be filed electronically through an automated hook-up between importers, customs brokers, and Customs via the *Automated Broker Interface.* Many companies, primarily the largest and more sophisticated importers and brokers, are already filing electronically.

Remote Location Filing. Until recently entry processing had to take place at the same port that the goods were located. Thus, importers had to rely on the services of a broker at the port of entry, even if the goods were being entered in a distant location. Large importers who move goods through different ports asked Congress to permit entry processing from remote locations. The Remote Location Filing system allows brokers in all parts of the country to make remote entries at distant ports.

Liquidation and Protest

In a normal import transaction, assuming no errors or penalties are at issue, the entry will be liquidated. *Liquidation* is the final computation and assessment of the applicable duty on entered goods by Customs. This "closes the book" and the entry is complete. If Customs accepts the entry as submitted on the importer's documents, liquidation occurs immediately. However, when Customs at the port of entry determines that additional duties are owed, a *notice of adjustment* is sent to the importer. The importer must respond to the notice, or the duty will be assessed as corrected. If a question or dispute arises concerning the goods themselves, as in the case of technical or unusual products, or in complex cases, the case may be referred to an *import specialist* familiar with that type of product. Either the importer or Customs officials may seek internal advice from the agency's headquarters. Officially, the liquidation becomes effective, and the entry closed, when it is posted at the "customshouse" at the port of entry. A courtesy notice is sent to importers advising them of the liquidation, although this notice is not legally effective. If actual duties owed exceed the estimated duties paid at the time of entry, the importer must pay them within fifteen days of the posting of the notice of liquidation.

Time Limits on Liquidation. Liquidation must occur within one year of entry. The time can be extended for good cause. An entry not liqui-

dated within one year is "deemed liquidated" by operation of law. Under a *deemed liquidation,* the goods are dutied at the rate accepted on the entry summary form. A liquidation can be reopened within two years if there is evidence to suspect that the importer committed fraud.

Protesting Liquidations. An importer that wants to dispute a liquidation made by Customs may file a protest with Customs at the port where the goods were entered within ninety days. An importer may not file a protest where no change was made by Customs to the entry as filed by the importer. Customs has thirty days to respond in cases where the goods have been denied entry; otherwise they have two years to act. Appeals can be made to Customs' headquarters in Washington, D.C.

Judicial Review of Protests. If Customs denies a protest—as most are—the importer may seek judicial review in the Court of International Trade. All duties assessed must first be paid, and the appeal must be filed within 180 days. The Court of International Trade is a specialized federal court located in New York City. Appeals from the Court of International Trade are made to the U.S. Court of Appeals for the Federal Circuit in Washington, D.C.

Enforcement and Penalties

The Bureau of Customs and Border Protection is a law enforcement agency charged with enforcing the tariff laws of the United States. U.S. Customs has broad powers to establish regulations, carry out investigations, and impose penalties. All care must be used in complying with Customs' requirements, and many experienced importers will tell you that they would no sooner make an error on a customs form than they would on their own tax returns.

The basic enforcement and penalty provisions of the customs laws are found in Title 19, Section 1592. The offenses set out here are civil violations calling for civil penalties imposed administratively by Customs. Criminal violations are addressed elsewhere in the U.S. Criminal Code. Section 1592 begins by setting out an importer's basic responsibility: "No person may enter or attempt to enter any merchandise into the United States by means of any written document, electronic transmission of information, oral statement, or other act that is both *material and false* or which omits any material information affecting the entry."

Making Materially False Statements to Customs.

An act or statement is "material" if it refers to the identity, quality, value, source, or country-of-origin of the merchandise, or if it affects the rate of duty charged, or the item's right to be imported into the United States. For instance, stating that cigars are from Honduras, rather than from Cuba, might allow them to pass through Customs when they otherwise would be denied entry. Stating that a textile product contains embroidery, when it actually does not, might mean a considerable decrease in the lawful rate of duty. And a statement or omission can be material even if it doesn't actually cause a change in the rate of duty. Identifying an imported fabric as "100 percent cotton," when in fact it is made of a blend of cotton and silk, would be material even though it may or may not actually result in a change in the rate of duty collected. The statement or omission must also be false. There is no violation if the falsity resulted from simple clerical errors or mistakes of fact (such as where a foreign supplier unexpectedly includes merchandise in a sealed container that you were not aware was being shipped to you, and you had no way to find out) as long as the errors are not part of a pattern of negligent conduct. The violation occurs whether the false statement or omission was made intentionally or by accident. The penalty, however, does depend on whether the offense resulted from negligence, gross negligence, or fraud.

Negligent Violations.

A *negligent violation* is one in which the importer fails to use *reasonable care, skill, and competence* to ensure that all customs documents and statements are materially correct and all laws are complied with. It might result because the importer failed to accurately ascertain the facts or information required by Customs when making an entry. It could also result from a misinterpretation of Customs' regulations or a mistake in completing the customs documents. Negligence penalties can seem pretty severe: If duty has been lost, the penalty can be up to two times the loss of duty, but no more than the value of the goods. If no duty is lost, then the penalty can be as high as 20 percent of the value of the goods, depending on whether there were mitigating or aggravating circumstances.

In the following case, *United States v. Golden Ship Trading Co.*, the importer was found negligent in misstating the country-of-origin of t-shirts even though she based her information on assurances made by her supplier.

Gross Negligence.

An importer commits *gross negligence* if there is "clear and convincing evidence" that the act or omission was done with actual knowledge or reckless disregard for the relevant facts, and with disregard for the importer's obligations under the law. The penalty is approximately twice that for negligent violations.

Civil Fraud.

Customs *fraud* is far more serious. A fraudulent violation exists where there is "clear and convincing evidence" that the importer *knowingly* made a materially false statement or omission while entering or attempting to enter goods into the United States. This might include intentionally giving a phony description of the goods being imported, understating their value by submitting a fake seller's invoice or by concealing money paid to the seller, or altering the country-of-origin listed on a document. Although the act must have been done knowingly, it does not matter whether the importer intended to evade paying import duties. According to Customs' guidelines the agency will normally seek a penalty equal to 100 percent of the value of the goods, reduced to five to eight times the total loss of duty for mitigating circumstances. Where the fraud did not result in a loss of duty to the government, the minimum penalty sought will be 50 percent of the value of the goods to a maximum of 80 percent. Even greater penalties may be imposed where there has been an egregious violation, a risk to public health or safety, or the presence of aggravating factors. In no case may the penalty exceed the value of the merchandise. In many cases, Customs may seize the merchandise and either have it destroyed or sold at auction.

It should be mentioned that customs fraud is also a separate *criminal offense*. Title 18 of the United States Code specifies a range of criminal activities, including the use of fraudulent customs documents, making false statements to a Customs officer, smuggling, conspiracy, money laundering, and many other acts. The law provides a maximum sentence of two years imprisonment, a fine, or both, for each violation. Anyone who willfully, and with the intent to defraud the United States,

United States v. Golden Ship Trading Co.
2001 WL 65751 (2001)
Court of International Trade

BACKGROUND AND FACTS

J. Wu entered three shipments of t-shirts purchased from Hui who claimed that he operated a factory in the Dominican Republic. Hui furnished all the relevant information necessary for the importer's customshouse broker to prepare the import document and to obtain a visa permit for entry of wearing apparel into the United States. Wu signed the entry papers stating that the country-of-origin of the t-shirts was the Dominican Republic. Customs discovered that Hui produced the body of the t-shirts in China and shipped them to the Dominican Republic where sleeves were attached and "Made in Dominican Republic" labels inserted. The finished shirt was then transshipped to the United States. According to law, merely attaching the sleeves does not make the shirt a product of the Dominican Republic. Chinese-made shirts could not have been imported without a textile visa, which Hui may not have been able to obtain. The government alleges that Wu acted without due care in determining the country-of-origin, and seeks penalties of $44,000. Wu does not dispute that the country-of-origin is China, but denies that she was negligent and claims that Hui had duped her.

BARZILAY, J.

Section 1592(e) describes the burden of proof that each side bears in a penalty action based on negligence. The United States bears the burden of establishing that the material false act or omission occurred; the burden then shifts to the defendant to demonstrate that the act did not occur as a result of negligence. See 19 U.S.C. §1592(e)(4). In this action, Customs has adequately demonstrated that the material false act occurred.

Since the court holds that the statements on the entry papers were both material and false, the only remaining issue is whether Ms. Wu has carried her burden that "the act or omission did not occur as a result of negligence." To decide if the mismarking was the result of Ms. Wu's negligence the court must examine the facts and circumstances to determine if Ms. Wu exercised reasonable care under the circumstances.

Ms. Wu admits she relied on the information provided by the exporter and accepted his representations that the Dominican Republic was the country of origin of the t-shirts because "all the documents that the exporter provided prior to entry stated the country of origin was the Dominican Republic." Further, she claims that she was the victim of the exporter's fraudulent scheme which was so elaborate that even Customs had difficulty discovering it. Ms. Wu points out that the exporter did have a t-shirt factory in the Dominican Republic and that the factory did perform some manufacturing operations on the imported t-shirts. Ms. Wu also claims "figuring out which (t-shirts) qualified as country of origin Dominican Republic and which did not required an entire team of Customs investigators, special agents and import specialists. Obviously, the exporter's fraud in this case was well-concealed." Furthermore, she contends, if Customs had difficulty investigating and uncovering the exporter's falsifications, how could Ms. Wu, with far fewer resources and less expertise, be expected to know that the entry papers falsely reflected the country of origin of the imported t-shirts? Therefore, Ms. Wu claims, she was justified in relying on the exporter's entry information.

The court finds that Ms. Wu failed to exercise reasonable care because she failed to verify the information contained in the entry documents. Under the regulation's definition of reasonable care, Ms. Wu had the responsibility to at least undertake an effort to verify the information on the entry documents. There is a distinct difference between legitimately attempting to verify the entry information and blindly relying on the exporter's assertions. Had Ms. Wu inquired as to the origin of the imported t-shirts or, at minimum, attempted to check the credentials and business operations of the exporter, she could make an argument that she attempted to exercise reasonable care and competence to ensure that the statements on the entry documents were accurate. Instead, Ms. Wu applies circular reasoning to prove she was not negligent. She assumes she would not have been able to discover that the exporter was misrepresenting the county of origin and therefore was not negligent even though she made no attempt to verify. The critical defect with Ms. Wu's argument is that it removes the reasonable care element from the negligence standard. The exercise of reasonable care may not have guaranteed success, but the failure to attempt any verification undercuts the argument that she would have been unable to determine the truth.

continued

continued

Ms. Wu failed to "exercise" reasonable care because she utterly failed to attempt to verify the exporter's information. Indeed, Ms. Wu admits, and the evidence is uncontraverted, that she relied solely on the word of the exporter.

Q. What information did you rely on when you signed this document that indicates that the single country of origin of the imported items was the Dominican Republic?

A. I believe [sic] Pedro. He said he sent me all the documents and the documents said it's made in the Dominican Republic so I just signed them.

Furthermore, Ms. Wu openly admits she did not inquire at all about the origin of the imported merchandise.

Q. Did you discuss with Mr. Hui (the exporter) where the fabrics from the t-shirts were made?

A. I never asked. I don't [sic] know how to ask. I never asked it.

Although it is apparent Ms. Wu did not directly research the authenticity of the exporter's claims, she argues that she employed the services of a licensed customs house broker and relied on the broker's expertise to properly prepare the import documents. However, Ms. Wu did not attempt to verify or ascertain the correctness of the information prepared by the broker.

Q. Did you discuss with the broker where he got the information from?

A. I did not discuss it with him.

Even though Ms. Wu did not attempt to verify the country of origin, she still signed and certified the accuracy of the information contained in the entry documents. Ms. Wu's reliance on the exporter and the broker does not remove the obligation to exercise reasonable care and competence to ensure that the statements made on the entry documents were correct.

The court finds that Ms. Wu's failure to attempt to verify the entry document information shows she did not act with reasonable care and did, therefore, attempt to negligently introduce merchandise into the commerce of the United States in violation of 19 U.S.C. §1592(a)(1)(A) and, therefore, must pay a civil penalty for her negligence pursuant to 19 U.S.C. §1592(c)(3)(B).

With regard to the amount of the penalty, the court directs the parties to attempt to settle the matter by consultation guided by the court's opinions in *United States v. Complex Machines Works Co.*, 83 F. Supp.2d 1307 (1999) and *United States v. Modes, Inc.*, 826 F. Supp. 504 (1990) regarding mitigation.

Decision. Wu did not exercise reasonable care because she failed to verify the information contained in the entry documents. Customs may assess a penalty that takes into account the mitigating circumstances of the case. Once the government proves the false act occurred, the burden shifted to Ms. Wu to prove that she was *not* negligent.

---

smuggles or attempts to smuggle goods into the country can receive a five-year prison sentence. Special criminal offenses apply to drug smuggling and to travelers entering the United States with merchandise in their baggage or on their person.

Aggravating and Mitigating Circumstances. The following are examples of the types of additional factors that Customs will consider in determining the amount of a penalty:

- *Aggravating Factors:* Obstructing the investigation, withholding evidence, providing misleading information, prior improper shipments, illegal transshipments of textiles to hide their actual country-of-origin.

- *Mitigating Factors:* Errors committed by Customs itself that contributed to the violation, erroneous advice from a Customs official, cooperation with the investigation, immediate remedial reaction (e.g., payment of the duty voluntarily and immediately, discharge or retraining of an offending employee), inexperience in importing (except in fraud cases), a prior good shipment record. In addition, Customs may consider the inability of the importer to pay the penalty.

Informed Compliance and Shared Responsibility.   Unless the majority of U.S. importers voluntarily comply with the customs laws, enforcement would be impossible. Congress recognized this when it passed the 1993 *Customs Modernization and Informed Compliance Act* (called "the Mod Act"). It introduced the doctrine of *informed compliance* that shifted to the importer a major responsibility to comply with all customs laws and regulations. It requires that importers, customs brokers, and carriers use reasonable care in complying with the law, in handling all import transactions, and in preparing all documentation for entered goods. Reasonable care means more than simply being careful. It means that those handling import transactions must be properly trained, that companies must establish internal controls over import operations to ensure compliance. When requirements are not understood, the importer should consult a licensed broker, customs law attorney, or Customs itself. Importers are expected to have enough information and knowledge in order to comply with the law. This includes having accurate information about the type of merchandise being imported, its value and origin, the identity of the seller, and so forth. It also requires importers to have a working knowledge of statutes, regulations, and rulings of Customs and U.S. Customs' procedures.

In order to make informed compliance work, Customs recognizes that it has an equal responsibility to provide information, advice, technical assistance, and clear regulations to importers. As a part of its *Trade Enforcement Plan,* Customs works closely with high-volume importers and those in problem or sensitive industries (e.g., textiles, automobiles, and steel) to assist them in developing their own corporate compliance programs.

The Reasonable Care Checklist. In 1997, U.S. Customs published a "checklist" to give smaller or less experienced importers a better understanding of their obligation to use reasonable care (see Exhibit 12.3). Customs understood that a "black and white" definition of reasonable care is impossible because the concept depends on individual circumstances. The checklist is not a law or regulation; it merely helps importers to understand what is expected of them. Importers who fail to meet the reasonable care requirements on the checklist may be subjected to penalties for negligence.

Reporting Errors to Customs before an Investigation. Congress has enacted a statute to encourage importers to voluntarily report their own possible violations of the customs laws. This is called a *prior disclosure*. If an importer admits

---

Exhibit 12.3

Just How Informed Do You Have to Be? Reasonable Care Checklist for Importers

1. If you have not retained an expert to assist you in complying with U.S. Customs requirements, do you have access to the *Customs Regulations* (Title 19 of the *Code of Federal Regulations*), the *Harmonized Tariff Schedule of the United States,* and the GPO publication *Customs Bulletin and Decisions*? Do you have access to the *Customs Internet Website, Customs Electronic Bulletin Board* or other research service to permit you to establish reliable procedures, and facilitate compliance with customs laws and regulations?
2. Have you consulted with a customs "expert" (e.g., lawyer, broker, accountant, or customs consultant) to assist in preparation of documents and the entry of the merchandise?
3. If you use an expert to assist you in complying with U.S. Customs requirements, have you discussed your importations in advance with that person and have you provided that person with full, complete, and accurate information about the import transactions?
4. Has a responsible and knowledgeable individual within your organization reviewed the customs documentation prepared by you or your expert to ensure that it is full, complete, and accurate?
5. Are identical transactions or merchandise handled differently at different ports or customs offices within the same port? If so, have you brought this to the attention of the appropriate customs officials?
6. Have you established reliable procedures within your organization to ensure that you provide complete and accurate documentation to U.S. Customs?
7. Have you obtained a customs ruling regarding the importation of the merchandise?
8. Do you know the merchandise that you are importing and have you provided a detailed and accurate product description and tariff classification of your merchandise to U.S. Customs? Is a laboratory analysis or special procedure necessary for the classification?

continued

Exhibit 12.3—(continued)

9. Have you consulted the tariff schedules, U.S. Customs' informed compliance publications, court cases, or U.S. Customs rulings to assist you in describing and classifying the merchandise?

10. If you are claiming a free or special tariff treatment for your merchandise (e.g., GSP, HTS Item 9802, NAFTA, etc.), have you established a reliable program to ensure that you reported the required value information and obtained any required or necessary documentation to support the claim?

11. Do you know the customs value of the imported products? Do you know the "price actually paid or payable" for your merchandise?

12. Do you know the terms of sale; whether there will be rebates, tie-ins, indirect costs, additional payments; whether "assists" were provided, commissions or royalties paid? Have all costs or payments been reported to U.S. Customs? Are amounts actual or estimated? Are you and the supplier "related parties" and have you disclosed this to U.S. Customs?

13. Have you taken reliable measures to ascertain the correct country-of-origin for the imported merchandise? Have you consulted with a customs expert regarding the country-of-origin of the merchandise?

14. Have you accurately communicated the proper country-of-origin marking requirements to your foreign supplier prior to importation and verified that the merchandise is properly marked upon entry with the correct country-of-origin?

15. If you are importing textiles or apparel, have you developed reliable procedures to ensure that you have ascertained the correct country-of-origin and assured yourself that no illegal transshipment (rerouting through a third country for illegal purposes) or false or fraudulent documents or practices were involved? Have you checked the U.S. Treasury's published list of manufacturers, sellers, and other foreign persons who have been found to have illegally imported textiles and apparel products? If you have obtained your textiles from one of these parties have you adequately verified the country-of-origin of the shipment through independent means?

16. Is your merchandise subject to quota/visa requirements and, if so, have you provided or developed a reliable procedure to provide a correct visa for the goods upon entry?

17. Have you determined or established a reliable procedure to permit you to determine whether your merchandise or its packaging bear or use any trademarks or copyrighted matter or are patented and, if so, that you have a legal right to import those items into, and/or use those items in, the United States?

18. If you are importing goods or packaging which contain registered copyrighted material, have you checked to ensure that it is authorized and genuine? If you are importing sound recordings of live performances, were the recordings authorized?

19. Have you checked to see that your merchandise complies with other government agency requirements (e.g., FDA, EPA/DOT, CPSC, FTC, Department of Agriculture, etc.) prior to or upon entry and procured any necessary licenses or permits?

20. Have you checked to see if your goods are subject to a Commerce Department dumping or countervailing duty determination and reported that to U.S. Customs?

SOURCE: Excerpted and adapted by the authors from TD 97–96 (1997), United States Customs.

his mistake and informs Customs of a possible violation *before* learning of an investigation against him, the penalties are limited. The importer must *completely disclose the materially false statements or omissions and the circumstances of the violation.* Any unpaid duties must be remitted immediately or within thirty days. However, an attorney should be consulted before doing so. Some prior disclosures have reportedly saved companies many millions of dollars in potential fines.

The Statute of Limitations.   The government is barred from bringing any action to collect an import duty after five years from the *date of the* *violation* involving negligence or gross negligence, or five years from the *date of discovery* of a violation involving fraud.

Record Keeping Requirements.   Importers are required to keep records of all import transactions for five years from the date of entry and to give Customs access to those documents on demand. The records include all documents "normally kept in the ordinary course of business," including sales contracts, purchase orders, government certificates, letters of credit, internal corporate memoranda, shipping documents, correspondence with suppliers, and any other documents bearing on the entry of the merchandise. It is highly recommended that any corporate importer establish a customs records compliance program to avoid penalties. The willful failure to keep records about the entry is punishable by the lesser of a $100,000 fine or 75 percent of the value of the merchandise. Even negligent record keeping is punishable by fines up to $10,000, or 40 percent of the value of the goods, whichever is less. There is an exception if the records were destroyed by an act of God. Concealment or destruction of records carries an additional $5,000 fine or up to two years' imprisonment or both. U.S. Customs conducts audits to verify business records. Inspections can take place on reasonable notice to the importer. Documents can be seized by court order.

Judicial Enforcement of Penalty Actions.

In any action to collect a penalty, U.S. Customs acts as plaintiff in bringing suit in the Court of International Trade. Quite often Customs will ask the court to consider all levels of culpability—negligence, gross negligence, and fraud—hoping to win on one or the other. The burden of proof in court depends on the violation. Fraud and gross negligence must be proved by "clear and convincing evidence." In negligence cases, the government must prove only that the act or omission occurred, and the burden shifts to the defendant-importer to show that it did not occur as a result of negligence.

Binding Rulings

Imagine that you have an opportunity to sell imported women's boxer shorts to a leading U.S. department store chain. They would like you to quote "your best price." You learn that some women will wear the boxers as short pants, while others will wear the shorts as underwear. If you underestimate your costs, you'll end up eating your shorts on the deal. The problem is that you are not sure whether Customs will consider the boxers to be "outerwear" and dutied at almost 18 percent, or "women's slips and briefs" that are dutied at less than 12 percent. Importers faced with a situation like this may make a written request for a *binding ruling* or the *ruling letter* from Customs in advance of an entry. The ruling represents the "official position" of Customs with respect to that transaction and is binding on Customs personnel until revoked.

Customs does not publish public notice in advance of a ruling, and there is no opportunity for the public to comment on the issue. Rulings are important to importers, especially those dealing in new or unusual merchandise that they have not imported before. It relieves them of the uncertainty of how the product will be treated by Customs, or how much duty they will have to pay.

Binding rulings can be even more important where companies are considering the tariff consequences of restructuring their global manufacturing operations. Take another simple example. Assume you are trying to choose between Mexico and China as a site to produce bicycles for sale in the United States. The parts will come from many suppliers around the world. Among all the factors to be considered—labor costs, quality control issues, local tax rates, access to the U.S. market—there is also the tariff consequences. Will there be a difference in the tariff rate between producing in China and importing a completed bicycle into the United States as opposed to importing the parts into Mexico, assembling the bicycle there, and shipping to customers in the United States? This requires a working knowledge of complex tariff code provisions, and a ruling letter from Customs in advance will mean one less surprise later on.

A request for a ruling letter should be submitted in writing. It should contain all relevant information, and in some cases—like the boxer shorts case—the importer should send a sample of the article. The ruling is issued only on the basis of the exact facts given, and assures that the products described will be entered according to the terms set out in the letter. The letter applies only to the importer to whom it is addressed. (You can research ruling letters on Customs' Web site.) Most rulings are issued within thirty to sixty days, although especially difficult ones can take up to nine months. Rulings are published in the *Custom's Bulletin*.

Judicial Review

The role of the courts in reviewing the decisions and actions of U. S. Customs depends on whether Customs was involved in formal rulemaking applicable to the public at large or whether it was an informal action, such as the issuance of a binding ruling or an action affecting a single shipment of goods belonging to a single importer.

Judicial Review of Formal Rulemaking   In *United States v. Haggar Apparel Co.,* 526 U.S. 380, 119 S.Ct. 1392 (1999), Haggar shipped U.S.-made fabric to Mexico where it was cut and sewn into pants, then permapressed and returned to the United States for sale. According to U.S statutes (Section 9802 of the U.S. tariff schedules) component parts or materials made in the United States may be shipped to certain foreign plants for assembly and returned to the United States with a partial duty exemption. However, the materials may only be assembled and must not undergo further manufacturing or processing in the foreign country. Customs issued a regulation interpreting the statute, stating that permapressing was an additional step in manufacturing and "not incidental to the assembly process." Customs issued the regulation using a formal rulemaking process (called "notice and comment" rulemaking) and it was applicable to all importers. In other words, as a formal rule it was more than just a ruling regarding a single entry by an individual importer. It was promulgated only after a public comment period, it was embodied in the *Code of Federal Regulations,* and had the "force of law." The Supreme Court held for the government, stating that Custom's decision to define permapressing as "not incidental to the assembly process" was perfectly reasonable. The Supreme Court held that courts must give "judicial deference" to the formal regulations of U.S. Customs where those regulations are a "reasonable interpretation" of an ambiguous statute. This is known as "Chevron deference" taken from the important case of *Chevron U.S.A. Inc. v. Natural Resources Defense Council, Inc.,* 467 U.S. 837, 104 S.Ct. 2778 (1984).

> **http://www.uscit.gov**
> The home page for the U.S. Court of International Trade.

Judicial Review of Binding Rulings.   *Haggar* did not address the scope of judicial review of informal decisions such as binding rulings. These and other routine decisions are made on a case-by-case basis every day—thousands every year—by Customs officials around the country. It might be a binding ruling about the tariff classification of imported merchandise or a decision about an entry when the goods arrive at a U.S. port. If an importer seeks review of a Customs' decision in the courts, to what extent will the court give deference to Customs' decision? Should the court consider that the agency is an expert on customs matters and simply defer to its original decision? Or should the court undertake its own analysis and reach its own decision independent of the agency's determination? The following U.S. Supreme Court decision, *United States v. Mead,* defines the scope of judicial review over binding rulings, tariff classifications, and other "informal" day-to-day decisions of Customs.

United States v. Mead Corp.
533 U.S. 218 (2001)
United States Supreme Court

BACKGROUND AND FACTS

Mead had imported "day planners" for several years. They had entered duty free. The planners included a calendar, a section for daily notes, a section for telephone numbers and addresses, and a notepad. The larger models also included a daily planner section, plastic ruler, plastic pouch, credit card holder, and computer diskette holder. A loose-leaf ringed binder held the contents, except for the notepad, which fit into the rear flap of the day planner's outer cover. In a binding ruling, Customs changed the classification of the planners to "bound diaries" under the *Harmonized Tariff Schedules,* with a 4 percent import duty. Mead argued that the day planners were not diaries and were not bound, and that the planners should be classified in an "other" subcategory that was duty free. After entering the goods and paying the duties, Mead filed a protest. When the protest was denied, Mead appealed. The Court of International Trade issued a summary judgment for the government. The Court of Appeals reversed, holding that the planners

continued

continued

were not "bound diaries" on the basis of the dictionary meaning of those terms. The court held that it owed no deference to Customs' classification rulings under the *Chevron* and *Haggar* court decisions, but was free to decide the classification issue anew, as a matter of law. The court noted that those cases involved formal regulations that carried the force of law, while classification rulings apply only to the specific transaction at issue. The U.S. Supreme Court agreed to hear the case.

JUSTICE SOUTER

We agree that a tariff classification has no claim to judicial deference under *Chevron U.S.A. Inc. v. Natural Resources Defense Council, Inc.,* 467 U.S. 837, 104 S.Ct. 2778, 81 (1984) there being no indication that Congress intended such a ruling to carry the force of law, but we hold that under *Skidmore v. Swift & Co.,* 323 U.S. 134, 65 S.Ct. 161 (1944), the ruling is eligible to claim respect according to its persuasiveness [most citations omitted].

* * *

"[T]he well-reasoned views of the agencies implementing a statute 'constitute a body of experience and informed judgment to which courts and litigants may properly resort for guidance,' *Skidmore,* and [w]e have long recognized that considerable weight should be accorded to an executive department's construction of a statutory scheme it is entrusted to administer . . ." *Chevron.* The fair measure of deference to an agency administering its own statute has been understood to vary with circumstances, and courts have looked to the degree of the agency's care, its consistency, formality, and relative expertness, and to the persuasiveness of the agency's position. . . . Justice Jackson summed things up in *Skidmore:*

> The weight [accorded to an administrative] judgment in a particular case will depend upon the thoroughness evident in its consideration, the validity of its reasoning, its consistency with earlier and later pronouncements, and all those factors which give it power to persuade, if lacking power to control.

* * *

There is room at least to raise a *Skidmore* claim here, where the regulatory scheme is highly detailed, and Customs can bring the benefit of specialized experience to bear on the subtle questions in this case: whether the daily planner with room for brief daily entries falls under "diaries," when diaries are grouped with "notebooks and address books, bound; memorandum pads, letter pads and similar articles," HTSUS subheading 4820.10.20; and whether a planner with a ring binding should qualify as "bound," when a binding may be typified by a book, but also may have "reinforcements or fittings of metal, plastics, etc.," *Harmonized Commodity Description and Coding System Explanatory Notes to Heading 4820.* A classification ruling in this situation may therefore at least seek a respect proportional to its "power to persuade," *Skidmore.* Such a ruling may surely claim the merit of its writer's thoroughness, logic, and expertness, its fit with prior interpretations, and any other sources of weight.

* * *

Since the *Skidmore* assessment called for here ought to be made in the first instance by the Court of Appeals for the Federal Circuit or the CIT, we go no further than to vacate the judgment and remand the case for further proceedings consistent with this opinion. It is so ordered.

Decision. The Court of International Trade and the Court of Appeals for the Federal Circuit must grant a limited degree of deference to the tariff classification ruling letters issued by U.S. Customs, according to the *Skidmore* standard. The degree of deference depends on the agency's thoroughness, the validity of its reasoning, its expertise, and its "power to persuade."

Comment. On remand back to the Court of Appeals, the court found Customs' ruling somewhat "unpersuasive" under the *Skidmore* standard. Noting that it was the court's job to determine the meaning of language used in the tariff schedules, the court relied on the dictionary definitions of "bound" and "diary," and, for a second time, entered a judgment for Mead.

Pre-Importation Judicial Review in Emergency Circumstances. Normally, an importer cannot seek court review until a shipment has been entered and a protest denied by Customs. Under limited circumstances, they may seek review in the courts prior to entry where there exists *extraordinary circumstances that could cause irreparable injury* to the importers and severe business disruption and substantial costs would result. Other cases have stated that if an importer can show that a Customs' ruling threatens to "close the importer's doors," then review will be permitted in advance of entering the goods.

DUTIABLE STATUS OF GOODS

Tariffs are applied to goods according to the item's *dutiable status*. The dutiable status of goods is determined by (1) the classification of the merchandise (What is it?), (2) the value of the merchandise, and (3) the country-of-origin of the merchandise (What country does it come from for purposes of determining the tariff rate or applicability of a quota?). An accurate estimate of the duties owed on imports provides essential information for business planning, for the development of cost estimates, and for pricing and marketing decisions.

Determining the dutiable status of merchandise can require importers to negotiate a maze of regulations. For importers who enter a wide variety of products or materials, or who enter them from many different countries, the potential for problems increases significantly. For U.S. exporters trying to enter goods into foreign countries, the regulatory headaches can become nightmarish. Lessons learned from importing into one country are not necessarily transferable when importing into another.

In recent years, worldwide efforts have attempted to make customs procedures and import regulations more uniform, more understandable, and easier to follow, so that even foreign firms can comply more easily. These efforts have resulted in the development of uniform rules for classifying and valuing imports and for determining their country-of-origin. These include a standardized system for classifying products (the *Harmonized Commodity Description and Coding System,* or *Harmonized System*), the GATT *1994 Rules on Customs Valuation,* and the GATT *1994 Agreement on Rules of Origin.*

---

http://www.usitc.gov
For the HTS go to the U.S. International Trade Commission and select "Information Center." Take the quick index to "Trade Matters" and choose "HTSA By Chapter." In popular PDF file format. See also, **http://www.customs.treas.gov** and link to "Importing and Exporting."

The *Harmonized Tariff Schedule*

All goods entering the United States are dutiable unless specifically exempted. Duties and restrictions on imports are based on the exact type and classification of goods being imported. Since 1989, goods entering the United States have been classified according to the *Harmonized Tariff Schedule of the United States* (HTSUS or HTS). The harmonized system was part of a worldwide effort, spanning nearly two decades, to standardize tariff nomenclature according to the *Harmonized Commodity Description and Coding System.* Under this uniform system, a company that knows the classification of its product in the United States. The harmonized system provides the mechanism for defining all commodities, materials, and articles sold in international trade, but does not set the tariff rate. Tariff rates are set by each nation in its own statutes. The system was developed by the World Customs Organization, an international organization located in Brussels, representing approximately 150 nations.

---

http://dataweb.usitc.gov
A pilot program of the ITC providing a searchable, interactive version of the HTS. Convenient and in summary form, but not legally binding. Be sure to try the "General Staged Tariff Reduction" and "NAFTA/Mexico Staged Tariff Reductions" to find new reduced rates for future years, if applicable.

Using the *Harmonized Tariff Schedule*.   The HTSUS divides products into approximately 5,000 tariff classifications, ranging from basic commodities and agricultural products to manufactured goods. It is organized into twenty-two sections, covering products from different industries. Sections are broken down into ninety-nine chapters, each covering the commodities, materials, and products of a distinct industry. The chapters are arranged in a progression from crude and natural products, such as livestock and agricultural products through advanced manufactured goods, such as vehicles and aircraft. The following list provides a few examples:

Chapter 1   Live animals
Chapter 9   Coffee, tea, spices

Chapter 22	Beverages, spirits, vinegar
Chapter 25	Salt, sulfur, earths, and stone
Chapter 30	Pharmaceuticals
Chapter 44	Wood and articles of wood
Chapter 51	Wool, fine or coarse animal hair
Chapter 52	Cotton
Chapter 62	Articles of apparel, accessories not knitted
Chapter 63	Other textile articles, sets, worn clothing
Chapter 76	Aluminum and articles thereof
Chapter 84	Nuclear reactors, boilers, machinery and mechanical appliances
Chapter 85	Electrical machinery, sound recorders, television image
Chapter 88	Aircraft, spacecraft, parts thereof
Chapter 94	Furniture, bedding, lamps
Chapter 97	Works of art, collectors' pieces
Chapter 98/99	Reserved for special tariff classifications (e.g., imports that enter the United States only temporarily or for service and repair, etc.)

Chapters are broken down into headings, subheadings, and tariff items. Tariff items are denoted by eight-digit codes. In the United States, the schedules break out to ten digits to allow for compiling of statistical data on imports.

Chapter: first two digits
Heading: four digits
Subheading: five or six digits
Tariff items: eight digits
Statistical break: ten digits

Consider the example in Exhibit 12.4. Tents made of synthetic fibers—such as nylon—used for backpacking are classified as item 6306.22.10. They are found within subheading 6306.22, for tents of synthetic fibers, and heading 6306 for "Tarpaulins, awnings and sunblinds, tents, sails for boats . . ." and within chapter 63 for "Other textile articles." Countries that use this international coding system have "harmonized" their classifications to six digits—at the subheading level. After the first six digits, each country assigns its own numbers.

After locating the article in the schedule, the importer can determine the tariff rate. The schedule is divided into two columns (see Exhibit 12.4). Column 1 contains a *general rate* applicable to imports from NTR (formerly MFN) nations, and a *special rate* applicable to one or more special tariff programs. The special rate applies to goods coming from developing countries under the *Generalized System of Preferences,* to goods coming from Canada or Mexico under the *North American Free Trade Agreement,* or to goods imported from the Caribbean Basin or Israel. Column 2 rates are the original *Smoot–Hawley* rates applicable to non-NTR countries under the Tariff Act of 1930, although few countries fall in this category today.

Tariffs are imposed on imports either on the basis of *ad valorem,* specific, or compound rates. The most common type of tariff is the *ad valorem* rate, based on a percentage of the value of the materials or articles imported. A specific rate is a specified amount per unit of weight or measure. A compound rate is a combined *ad valorem* and specific rate.

The Classification of Goods

Tariff rates are based on an article's HTS classification. To classify a product, you must know what your product is, or how it will be used, and where it falls in the tariff schedules. This is not as easy a task as it might seem. The schedules include every kind and category of product on earth. They include consumer goods ranging from "Articles for Christmas festivities and parts thereof" to "Electromechanical domestic appliances;" textile products ranging from "Cotton, not carded or combed, having a staple length under 28.575 mm" to "Men's or boys suits . . . of worsted wool fabric . . . having an average fiber diameter of 18.5 microns or less;" industrial equipment ranging from "Bookbinding machinery" to "Nuclear reactors;" and electronic products from "Ballasts for discharge lamps or tubes" to "Laser imaging assemblies." Finding your product among these is like walking a maze.

The problem is compounded because many products can seemingly appear to fit into more than one classification. For example, should sleeping bags be classified as "Camping goods," "Sporting goods," or as "Articles of bedding and similar furnishing . . . fitted with springs or stuffed?" This is an area where reasonable minds can differ. Naturally, importers will argue that their products should fall into the classification that carries the lowest tariff rate. U.S. Customs, whose job it is to collect the tariff revenue of the United States, will

EXHIBIT 12.4

Harmonized Tariff Schedule of the United States (2003—Supplement 1)

Annotated for Statistical Reporting Purposes

Heading/ Subheading	Stat. Suf- fix	Article Description	Unit of Quantity	Rates of Duty 1 General	Rates of Duty 1 Special	Rates of Duty 2
6306		Tarpaulins, awnings and sunblinds; tents; sails for boats, sailboards or landcraft; camping goods: Tarpaulins, awnings and sunblinds:				
6306.11.00	00	Of cotton (369)	kg	8.8%	Free (CA,IL,MX) 4.4% (JO)	90%
6306.12.00	00	Of synthetic fibers (669)	kg	8.9%	Free (CA,IL,MX) 2.3% (JO)	90%
6306.19.00		Of other textile materials	. . . .	5.2%	Free (CA,E*,IL, MX)	40%
	10	Of artificial fibers (669)	kg		1.3% (JO)	
	20	Other (899)	kg			
		Tents:				
6306.21.00	00	Of cotton	kg	8.8%	Free (CA,IL,MX) 4.4% (JO)	90%
6306.22		Of synthetic fibers:				
6306.22.10	00	Backpacking tents	No. . . . . . . kg	0.5%	Free (A,CA,E,IL, J,MX)	90%
6306.22.90		Other	. . . .	8.9%	Free (CA,IL,MX) 2.3% (JO)	90%
	10	Screen houses	kg			
	30	Other (669)	kg			
6306.29.00	00	Of other textile materials	kg	3.2%	Free (CA,E*,IL, J*,JO,MX)	40%
		Sails:				
6306.31.00	00	Of synthetic fibers	kg	0.4%	Free (A,CA,E,IL, J,MX)	30%
6306.39.00	00	Of other textile materials	kg	0.4%	Free (A,CA,E,IL, J,MX)	30%
		Pneumatic mattresses:				
6306.41.00	00	Of cotton	kg	3.8%	Free (CA,IL,JO,MX)	25%
6306.49.00	00	Of other textile materials	kg	3.8%	Free (A,CA,E,IL, J*,JO,MX)	25%
		Other:				
6306.91.00	00	Of cotton	kg	3.8%	Free (C AIL,JO,MX)	40%
6306.99.00	00	Of other textile materials	kg	5%	Free (CA,E*,IL, J*,MX) 1.5% (JO)	78.5%

General Notes [edited for student use]

3. *Rates of Duty.* The rates of duty in the "Rates of Duty" columns designated 1 ("General" and "Special") and 2 of the tariff schedule apply to goods imported into the customs territory of the United States as hereinafter provided in this note:

(a) *Rate of Duty Column 1.*

(i) The rates of duty in column 1 are rates which are applicable to all products other than those of countries enumerated in paragraph (b) of this note. Column 1 is divided into two subcolumns, "General" and "Special," which are applicable as provided below.

(ii) The *"General"* subcolumn sets forth the general or normal trade relations (NTR) rates which are applicable to products of those countries described in subparagraph (i) above which are not entitled to special tariff treatment as set forth below.

(iii) The *"Special"* subcolumn reflects rates of duty under one or more special tariff treatment programs described in paragraph (c) of this note and identified in parentheses immediately following the duty rate specified in each subcolumn. These rates apply to those products which are properly classified under a provision for which a special rate is indicated and for which all of the legal requirements for eligibility for such program or programs have been met. Where a product is eligible for special treatment under more than one program, the lowest rate of duty provided for any applicable program shall be imposed. Where no special rate of duty is provided for a provision, or where the country from

continued

continued

which a product otherwise eligible for special treatment was imported is not designated as a beneficiary country under a program appearing with the appropriate provision, the rates of duty in the "General" subcolumn of Column 1 shall apply.

(iv) Products of Insular Possessions (omitted)

(v) Products of the West Bank or Gaza Strip (omitted)

(b) *Rate of Duty Column 2.* Notwithstanding any of the foregoing provisions of this note, the rates of duty shown in Column 2 shall apply to products, whether imported directed or indirectly, of the following countries and areas:

Cuba   Laos   North Korea

(c) *Products Eligible for Special Tariff Treatment.*

(i) Programs under which special tariff treatment may be provided, and the corresponding symbols for such programs as they are indicated in the "Special" subcolumn, are as follows:

Generalized System of Preferences ....A, A* or A+
Automotive Products Trade Act ....B
Agreement on Trade in Civil Aircraft..C
North American Free Trade Agreement:
    Goods of Canada, under the terms of
    general note 12 to this schedule..CA
    Goods of Mexico, under the terms of
    general note 12 to this schedule..MX
African Growth and Opportunity Act ....D
Caribbean Basin Economic Recovery Act ....E or E*
United States–Israel Free Trade Area IL
Andean Trade Preference Act or
    Andean Trade Promotion and Drug Eradication Act ....J, J* or J+
United States-Jordan Free Trade Area Implementation Act...........................JO
Agreement on Trade in Pharmaceutical Products...........................K
Uruguay Round Concessions on Intermediate
    Chemicals for Dyes L
United States–Caribbean Basin Trade Partnership Act ....R

want to classify the products at the highest rate. (Initially, the importer makes the classification by listing it on the entry form filed with Customs, who must then accept or reject the classification. Of course, the importer is bound by the informed compliance standard to use reasonable care in making its classification.) It is especially difficult for importers to classify a product if they are importing it for the first time or if it is a newly designed product. The problem is complicated by the fact that at any time Customs can "change its mind" and decide to reclassify an article, despite having accepted another classification of the same article in the past.

To illustrate how difficult it is to classify an article, consider the following case, *Camel Manufacturing Co. v. United States,* 686 F. Supp 912 (Ct. Int'l. Trade 1988), involving the import of camping tents. At the time, the tariff schedules had no category specifically for "tents." The importer and Customs disagreed over the other possibilities: sporting

goods or miscellaneous textiles. Incredibly, the decision turned on the judge's definition of what is a "sport." Although the case was decided under the old schedules (now replaced by the harmonized schedule), it remains one of the authors' favorites. No case better illustrates the unpredictability of customs classifications and the importance of advance planning.

Understanding Tariff Descriptions: The Common Meaning Rule. Articles are described in the tariff schedules in several ways: by common name (known as an *eo nomine* description), by a description of the article's physical characteristics, by a description of their component parts, or by a description of the article's use.

To understand the meaning of terms used in the tariff schedules, the courts look to the common meaning of the articles described. According to the cases, the *common or popular meaning* of terms used in the tariff schedules applies unless Congress

Camel Manufacturing Co. v. United States
686 F. Supp. 912 (1988)
Court of International Trade

BACKGROUND AND FACTS

The plaintiff imported nylon tents into the United States. The tents were designed to hold up to nine people and weighed over thirty pounds, including carrying bag, stakes, and frames. The floor sizes ranged from eight feet by ten feet to ten feet by fourteen feet, and when folded for carrying were approximately fifty inches long. It was undisputed that the tents were used as shelter by people who wish to camp outdoors, either purely for that purpose or for the purpose of engaging in other outdoor activities such as fishing, hunting, and canoeing. The importer entered the tents as "sports equipment" carrying a 10 percent *ad valorem* import duty. U.S. Customs ruled that the tents were properly classifiable as "Textile articles not specially provided for" and imposed a duty of 25 cents per pound plus 15 percent *ad valorem*. Upon liquidation, the importer appealed.

JUDGE WATSON

The basic question before the court is whether or not the activity in which the tents are used, which we shall call by the name of "camping out" is a sport, which would then lead to the conclusion that these tents are sporting equipment.

In a previous opinion, *The Newman Importing Co., Inc. v. United States,* 415 F. Supp. 375 (1976), this court decided that certain light tents used in backpacking were sports equipment because the activity of backpacking was found to be a sport. In this action, the court was given a generous range of opinions regarding what it is that makes an activity a sport. Seven witnesses testified on behalf of the plaintiff and two witnesses testified on behalf of the defendant. The witnesses had a wide range of familiarity with the use and manufacture of tents. Although these opinions were extremely interesting, the fact remains that in the end the question of defining the term "sporting equipment" is really one of legal interpretation for the court.

The rationale used in the *Newman Importing* case will not suffice here because these tents are not suitable for backpacking. The court finds that these tents are too heavy for that particular activity and, in fact, are generally used by persons who are camping in the outdoors and are not subject to strict limitations of weight in the tenting equipment which they can take with them. In the absence of persuasive proof regarding any special attributes of these tents which may contribute to their use in backpacking, the court finds it quite reasonable for the Customs Service to have excluded them from the category of backpacking tents on the basis of their weight and carrying size.

The basic question before the court is whether the general activity of camping out, i.e., taking up temporary residence in the outdoors, is a sport within the meaning of the Tariff Schedules.

The court is unable to expand its view of the term "sports" to include the activity of camping out. To do so would require a definition of the term so loose that it would cover almost any purposeful activity engaged in by humans in a natural setting. If it were simply a question of whether an activity had a certain degree of challenge and skill then the activity of gardening, which has in it a good measure of challenge, skill, and struggle and offers in innumerable ways the "joy of victory and agony of defeat," would also have to be considered a sport. This tells us that as a matter of simple logic and meaning, it does not appear that the term "sport" can be carried past the point which was expressed in the *Newman* case.

It follows that these tents are not "sports equipment" within the meaning of the tariff law.

For the reasons given above, it is the opinion of the court that plaintiff's claim for classification must be denied and judgment must issue dismissing that claim.

Decision. The importer's classification was rejected and the decision of the government upheld. The tents were not properly classifiable as "sporting goods" because the tents were designed for camping out, which was held not to be a sport. Affirmed by the U.S. Court of Appeals for the Federal Circuit, 861 F.3d 1266 (1988).

clearly intended a *commercial meaning* or *scientific meaning* to apply or unless there is a different commercial meaning that is definite, uniform, and in general use throughout the trade. Courts will often examine the legislative history of the tariff act and will consult dictionaries and encyclopedias to determine the common meaning of the terms used (e.g., is an *anchovy* commonly understood to be the same thing as a *sardine*?). The courts also rely on scientific authorities and expert witnesses during the trial.

Determining the common meaning is not always so simple. In *Texas Instruments v. United States,* 518 F. Supp. 1341 (Ct. Int'l. Trade 1981), *aff'd.* 673 F.2d 1375 (C.C.P.A. 1982), the court was faced with determining the common meaning of a watch movement. The plaintiff, Texas Instruments, Inc., had entered solid-state electronic watch modules and electronic watches. The articles consisted of an integrated circuit chip, a capacitor, a quartz crystal, a liquid crystal display for digital readouts, and plastic cases within which the modules were encased. Because digital watches had not yet been invented at the time the tariff schedule was enacted by Congress, the court upheld Customs' determination that the common meaning of watch movement in the horological industry did not include these electronic modules. The court believed that Congress could not have intended the term "movement" to include the mere vibration of a quartz crystal in a digital watch. In addressing the impact of technological development on Customs law, the Court of International Trade stated that

> The courts cannot be asked to restructure the tariff schedules by judicial fiat in order to accommodate scientific and engineering innovations which far transcend the vision and intent of the Congress at the time of the enactment of the tariff schedules. It is true . . . that it is an established principle of customs law that tariff schedules are written for the future as well as for present application and may embrace merchandise unknown at the time of their enactment. It must be borne in mind, however, that . . . in applying a tariff provision to an article, unknown at the time of the enactment thereof, such an article must possess an essential resemblance to the characteristics so described by the applicable tariff provision.

Accordingly, the court ruled that the solid-state electronic module was not a "watch movement."

Dictionary definitions are often used to interpret the tariff schedules. In *C. J. Van Houten & Zoon v. United States,* 664 F. Supp. 514 (Ct. Int'l. Trade 1987), the court ruled that tariff schedule items for "bars or blocks" of chocolate weighing ten pounds or more did not apply to imports of molten, liquid chocolate imported into the United States in tank cars. Rather, the molten chocolate

was to be classified as "sweetened chocolate in any other form." After consulting several dictionaries for the common meaning of the terms "bars and blocks," the court concluded that this meant only solid materials.

Determining the Classification of Products: Questions of Law and Fact. Determining an article's tariff classification typically involves two steps. The first step requires you to interpret the common meaning of the terms described in the tariff schedules. Second, you must look at the facts to determine if the imported articles in question fall within the particular category described in the schedules. Courts like to say that the first step in defining tariff language is a "question of law," and the second step is a "question of fact."

Classification by Actual or Principal Use. The tariff schedules describe articles by name, physical characteristics, or by use. When an article is described by both its use and by name, the use provision is generally deemed to be more specific, and often controls. *Principal use* is that use to which articles of the kind being imported are usually put. When an article might have several uses, the principal use controls. Principal use is the use that is greater than any other single use of the article.

An article may be classified according to the actual use intended for the article. To classify according to *actual use,* the product must be used for the purposes listed in the schedule. The actual use must be stated to Customs at the time of entry, and the imported article must actually be used in that manner. Proof of actual use must be furnished to Customs within three years of entry.

Using the General Rules of Interpretation

The *General Rules of Interpretation* (GRI rules) are an integral part of the HTSUS and govern its use. Anyone attempting to locate a product in the schedule must first consult the six required GRI rules. A summary of the rules is given later in this section.

The six rules must be applied in numerical order. To determine how an article is classified, first consult GRI 1. This requires that an article be classified *according to the four-digit heading under which it is specifically and completely described, or according to any relative section or chapter notes.* Most imported goods can be classified according to GRI 1. Consider Exhibit 12.4. Heading 6306 includes

"Tarpaulins, awnings and sunblinds; tents; sails for boats. . . ." If the article is specifically and completely stated in the heading, as are "tents," then you may proceed to look at the six-digit subheading and eight-digit tariff-item levels. Thus, "backpacking tents" would be classified under 6306.22.10.

Notice that GRI 1 also requires that you consult the official *Notes* found at the beginning of each of the twenty-two sections and ninety-nine chapters. The notes define specific terms used in the section or chapter (such as the terms "suit" or "ensemble" when used in reference to sets of apparel). They also list specific goods that are either included or excluded from that section or chapter. For instance, Chapter 94 covers "Furniture, bedding, mattresses, mattress supports, cushions. . . ." But the notes to Chapter 94 state: "This chapter does not cover . . . pneumatic or water mattresses . . . dentists' chairs . . . toy furniture. . . ."

In the event that the goods cannot be classified solely on the basis of GRI 1, the remaining rules may then be consulted. They must be applied in sequence beginning with GRI 2 and proceeding in order through GRI 6. The rules deal with problems that arise when an article could conceivably be classified under more than one heading, and for classifying mixtures and articles made up of component parts.

The following rules have been edited for ease of study. Consult the GRI for the official text. Study them carefully, and be sure you are able to apply them.

GRI 1. Classification shall be determined *according to the terms of the headings* and any relative section or chapter notes and, provided such headings or notes do not otherwise require, according to GRI 2–6.

GRI 2. (a) An article described in a four-digit heading includes the completed, finished article as well as one that is incomplete or unfinished, provided that the incomplete or unfinished article has the essential character of the complete or finished article. Articles that are entered unassembled shall be classified as the assembled article [e.g., a shipment of an unassembled bicycle will be dutied as a finished bicycle, provided that all of the parts needed to make a completed bicycle arrive in one shipment].

(b) Any reference in a heading to a material or substance shall include mixtures or combinations of that material or substance. Any reference in a heading to goods made from a certain material shall include goods made wholly or partly of that material. Goods consisting of more than one material shall be classified according to GRI 3.

GRI 3. When goods are classifiable under two or more headings, the article shall be classified as follows:

(a) The heading that provides the *most specific description* shall be preferred to headings that provide more general descriptions. [This is known as the *Rule of Relative Specificity*.]

(b) Mixtures, composite goods consisting of different materials or made up of different components, and goods put up in sets for retail sale, which cannot be classified by referring to 3(a), shall be classified as if they consisted of the material or component that gives them their *essential character*.

(c) When goods cannot be classified by reference to 3(a) or (b), they shall be classified under the heading *that occurs last* in numerical order among those that equally merit consideration.

GRI 4. Goods that cannot be classified according to the above rules shall be classified under the heading for goods to which they are *most akin*.

GRI 5. In addition to the foregoing, the following rules apply:

(a) Camera cases, musical instrument cases, gun cases . . . and similar containers, specially shaped or fitted to contain a specific article, suitable for long-term use and entered with the article for which they are intended, shall be classified with such articles when of a kind normally sold therewith.

(b) Packing materials and containers entered with the goods therein shall be classified with the goods, unless the materials or containers are clearly suitable for repetitive use.

GRI 6. The classification of goods in the subheadings shall be determined according to the terms of the subheading and any related notes, and only subheadings at the same level are comparable.

The Rule of Relative Specificity. Recall that GRI 1 requires us to classify a product according to the four-digit heading. But suppose a product could arguably be classified under more than one heading? The *rule of relative specificity,* found in GRI 3(a), provides that where an article could be classified under more than one heading, it must be classified under the one *that most specifically describes* the item. Moreover, we must only compare the language of the headings, without reference to any of the subheadings. Only after determining that an article is classifiable under a certain heading can you then proceed to find the proper subheading. For instance, assume you are importing electric toothbrushes. There are two possible classifications. Heading 8509 includes *"electromechanical domestic appliance with self-contained motor"* dutied at 4.5 percent. Heading 9603 includes *"brooms, brushes, including brushes constituting parts of machines"* that are duty free. Which is the correct classification? The answer is heading 8509 because it more specifically describes the items than does 9603. And this is despite the fact that at the eight-digit level, 9603.10.90 includes *"tooth-brushes, shaving brushes, hairbrushes..."* We must first determine the most specific four-digit heading, and the description *"electromechanical domestic appliance with self-contained motor"* is more specific than *"brooms, brushes...."* In addition, where items could be classified under more than one heading, a description by name is more specific than a description of a class of merchandise. For example, tools used by a hair stylist would be classified as *"shavers and hair clippers with self-contained electric motor"* under heading 8510 because this description is more specific than *"electromechanical tools for working in the hand with self-contained electric motor"* under 8508.

Classification by Essential Character. Suppose an article is made of two or more different materials or components. There is no heading that specifically and completely describes the entire article, but there are several headings that describe the individual materials or components. If two or more headings each describe only certain materials or components of the article, GRI 3(b) requires that the article be classified under the heading that describes those materials or components that give the article its *essential character.* This method is helpful to determine the classification of mixtures of chemicals, foodstuffs, and other substances or materials blended together, assuming that there is no classification that fits the mixture. The rule also applies to *composite goods.* For instance, imagine a typical notebook computer that also contains a standard AM/FM radio receiver. Should it be classified as "Reception apparatus for radio telephony" under heading 8527, or as "Automatic data processing machines" under 8471? If the notebook computer imparts the essential character to this odd contraption, it would probably be classified under 8471. In *Pillowtex Corp. v. United States,* 171 F.3d 1370 (Fed. Cir. 1999), the court considered the tariff classification of comforters made from a 100 percent cotton shell and filled with white duck down. The court held that the down fill should control the classification because the essential character of the comforters was derived from the insulating ability of the filling, not from the shell. Cases involving the essential-character test are very fact-intensive; they turn on a detailed analysis of the facts of the case.

Classification of Items Packaged for Retail Sale as a Set. The essential-character test is also used when "goods are put up in sets" for retail sale. In order for a product to qualify as "goods put up in sets," there must be *two or more different materials or articles packaged together for retail sale to the user without further repacking,* and there must be no heading in the tariff schedules providing for the set as a whole. The items must have been packaged together to meet a particular need or for use in a specific activity or function, rather than each item serving divergent functions.

In the following case, *Better Home Plastics Corp. v. United States,* 916 F. Supp. 1265 (Ct. Int'l. Trade 1996), the court had to determine whether a shower curtain set was classified under the heading for *"Curtains"* or under the heading for *"Tableware,*

---

http://www.mof.go.jp/english/index.htm
For English language access to Japanese customs and tariff laws, including Japan's version of the HTS, see the Japan Ministry of Finance. Use the site above or go to MOF home page, choose "English" and then "Customs and Tariff."

Better Home Plastics Corp. v. United States
916 F. Supp. 1265 (1996)
Court of International Trade

BACKGROUND AND FACTS

Plaintiff, Better Home Plastics Corp., imported shower curtain sets. The shower curtain sets consisted of an outer textile curtain, inner plastic magnetic liner, and plastic hooks. The plastic liner prevents water from escaping the shower while the shower is in use. The liner is color coordinated to match the outer curtain, and adds to the set's decorative appearance. The textile curtain is intended to be decorative, and does not block the water from getting out on the floor. The curtain is also semi-transparent, permitting the color of the plastic liner to show when the curtain and the liner are drawn. Better Home Plastics sells the sets to budget stores at prices ranging from $5.00–$6.00, and retailers resell them at prices from $9.00–$12.00. Customs classified the merchandise under the provision for the set's outer curtain at a duty of 12.8% according to Chapter 63, Subheading 6303.92.0000 of the *Harmonized Tariff Schedule* (HTSUS). Better Home Plastics asserts classification of the set is properly determined by the set's inner plastic liner under Chapter 39, Subheading 3924.90.1010, HTSUS, at a duty of 3.36% *ad valorem*.

DICARLO, CHIEF JUDGE

The *General Rules of Interpretation* (GRI) govern the classification of the imported shower curtain sets under the HTSUS. GRI 1 establishes the general presumption for classification under the rules. GRI 1 provides that the headings and relative section or chapter notes determine the classification of the imported merchandise, so long as those headings or notes do not require otherwise.

GRI 3 governs where the merchandise at issue consists of more than one material or substance, such as a textile curtain and an inner plastic liner, as here. GRI 3 mandates that, when "goods are, prima facie, classifiable under two or more headings," the court must classify the merchandise in question pursuant to the heading providing the most specific description. This is known as the *rule of relative specificity*. An exception to this rule exists. When, however, two or more headings each refer . . . to part only of the items in a set put up for retail sale, those headings are to be regarded as equally specific . . . even if one heading provides a more complete or precise description of the goods. Accordingly, the rule of relative specificity does not apply when two of the headings each refer only to part of the items within the set.

Goods put up in sets for retail sale, which cannot be classified according to the most specific heading, are classified by the "component which gives them their essential character" (the *essential character test*). Better Home Plastics contends the court must apply the essential character test, in classifying the applicable merchandise. Application of the test, Better Home Plastics asserts, would mandate classification of the set on the basis of its inner plastic liner pursuant to Subheading 3924.90.1010, HTSUS. . . .

Defendant contends the essential character of the curtains are embodied in the textile curtain. Defendant raises numerous arguments to support its position, particularly that (1) the plastic liner is replaceable at 1/3 to 1/4 the price of the set; (2) the consumer purchases the set because of the decorative function of the outer curtain, and not for the protection afford by the liner; and (3) the liner is only employed for the limited period that someone is utilizing the shower, whereas the decorative outer curtain is employed, at a minimum, when the bathroom is in use, and as much as 24 hours a day. Defendant also contends Better Home Plastics' invoice description supports Customs' classification. Pursuant to the invoice description, the set is sold as "Fabric Shower Curtain and Liner." Therefore, defendant argues, this description serves as an admission that the curtain provides the essential character of the set.

Although the court agrees that the curtain in the imported set imparts a desirable decorative characteristic, nonetheless, it is the plastic liner that provides the indispensable property of preventing water from escaping the shower enclosure. The liner (1) prevents water from escaping when the shower is in use; (2) protects the fabric curtain from mildew and soap scum; and (3) conceals the shower and provides privacy when the shower is in use. Further, the plastic liner can serve its intended function without the outer curtain and contributes to the overall appearance of the set. The outer curtain, in contrast, merely furthers the set's decorative aspect. The court therefore concludes the essential character of the set is derived from the plastic liner.

continued

---

continued

Defendant's other contentions are also unpersuasive. The manner in which the set is invoiced does not definitively determine which component provides the essential character of the set. The invoice description is intended to characterize the shipped item; it is not a declaration of the relative importance of its component parts. Finally, while the court takes into consideration the relative cost of the component parts, this point alone is not dispositive, nor very persuasive against the competing arguments.

It is the essential character of the set—derived in part from the plastic's ability to repel water—that denotes the set's utility, purpose, and accordingly, character. Inclusion of the textile curtain within the classification for the plastic liner does little to change the qualities or the basic nature of the set in meeting this purpose.

The court finds Better Home Plastics has overcome the presumption of correctness accorded to Customs, and the shower curtain sets were improperly classified under subheading 6303.92.0000, HTSUS. In addition, the court agrees with Better Home Plastics' proposed classification of the sets under subheading 3924.90.1010, HTSUS.

This decision is limited to its facts, i.e., that the set at issue is at the low end of the shower curtain market. The court does not offer an opinion on the proper classification of sets targeted to a different market segment.

Decision. When articles are made up of component parts, or are in sets, and their parts are referred to in two equally specific headings, then the rule of relative specificity does not apply, and their classification must be determined by which part gives the article its essential character. In this case, the shower liner imparts the essential character to the set.

Comment. Judge DiCarlo's opinion was affirmed by the U.S. Court of Appeals in *Better Home Plastics Corp. v. United States*, 119 F.3d 969 (Fed. Cir. 1997).

---

kitchenware, other household articles and toilet articles, of plastics . . . Other: Curtains and drapes including panels and valances." Notice how the court applies the *General Rules of Interpretation* and the essential-character test.

Classification at the Subheading Level. Only after an article has been classified at the heading level, should the subheadings be consulted. When comparing two or more different subheadings within the same heading, the rules set out in GRI 1–5 (i.e., relative specificity, essential character, etc.) must still be followed. Articles must be compared at equal subheading levels, so that only six-digit subheadings are compared to other six-digit subheadings, and so on.

Tariff Engineering. *Tariff engineering* is the process of modifying or engineering your product prior to importation for the purposes of obtaining a lower rate of duty. The general rule established by the U.S. Supreme Court for well over a hundred years is that an article is to be classified according to its condition at the time it is imported. Thus, generally, tariff engineering is an acceptable practice. As far back as 1881, the Supreme Court stated that "if the manufacturer uses . . . bleaching processes in order to make his sugars more saleable, why may he not omit to do so in order to render them less dutiable; nay, why may he not employ an extra quantity of molasses for that purpose?" *Merrit v. Welsh*, 104 U.S. 694 (1881). In *United States v. Citroen*, 223 U.S. 407, 32 S.Ct. 259 (1912), an importer unstrung pearls and then restrung them in the United States, achieving a lower rate of duty. The Court stated:

The [tariff classification] reads "pearls set or strung." It does not say pearls that can be strung, or that are assorted or matched so as to be suitable for a necklace, but pearls "set or strung." We are not concerned with the reason for the distinction; it is enough that Congress made it. Had these pearls never been strung before importation, no one would be heard to argue . . . because they could be strung, or had been collected for the purpose of stringing or of being worn as a necklace. Loose pearls—however valuable the collection—however carefully matched or desirable for a necklace—are not "pearls set or strung."

Tariff engineering permits importers to design their products, or to enter their goods at any step in the manufacturing or assembly process, in order to obtain a lower rate of duty.

Of course, there are some limits on tariff engineering. There must be no fraud or deception, the goods must be correctly described on the entry documents, and they must be honestly presented to Customs for inspection if requested. In *Heartland By-Products, Inc. v. United States*, 264 F.3d 1126 (Fed. Cir. 2001), the importer added molasses to sugar syrup in Canada and removed it after the syrup was imported into the United States. The syrup with molasses entered free from U.S. tariff-rate quotas on sugar syrup imports. Customs maintained that there was no other purpose for adding molasses except to avoid the quota, that the molasses was a "foreign substance," and that adding it was not a genuine step in the manufacturing process. Since the molasses was later returned to Canada to be reused for the same purpose, Customs maintained that the process was done for "disguise or artifice" to circumvent the customs laws. There was no evidence that Heartland ever falsified or concealed the identity of its sugar syrup, its method of manufacture, or its use. The Court of Appeals yielded to the persuasiveness of Customs' argument and upheld its reclassification of the syrup. The impact of Heartland's imports on the American beet sugar industry and its subsequent loss in this case were widely discussed in the media.

http://rulings.customs.gov
Searchable database of the Customs Rulings Online Search System (CROSS)

Customs Valuation

The customs value, often called *dutiable value,* of all goods entered into the United States must be established and reported to U.S. Customs at the time of entry. All relevant facts and terms of the contract of sale that affect value must be disclosed. Dutiable value is defined by U.S. law as the *transaction value* of the goods. The transaction value of the merchandise is *the price actually paid or payable* for the merchandise when sold for exportation to the United States, plus the following amounts if not included in the purchase price: (1) packing costs (including containers, covers, and labor for packing) incurred by the buyer, (2) any selling commission incurred by the buyer, (3) the value of any assist, (4) any royalty or license fee that the buyer is required to pay as a condition of sale, and (5) the proceeds of any subsequent resale of the merchandise that accrues to the seller. Transaction value does not include international freight charges, insurance or customs brokerage fees, inland freight after importation, charges for assembling or maintaining the goods after importation, or import duties. Charges for transporting the goods in the country of exportation (e.g., from the seller's factory to the port) are also excludable when these charges are identified separately on the seller's invoice. Transaction value is not affected by whether the sales contract called for CIF or FOB payment terms. If the price is expressed as CIF, the freight and insurance will be deducted; if FOB, the freight and insurance were not included anyway.

When a seller provides financing on goods exported to the United States, the interest payments are not includable in the transaction value of the goods when the interest is identified separately (rather than as a part of the purchase price), the financing contract or note is in writing, and the interest rate is not unusual.

Importers are often required to pay royalties or license fees to the holders of copyrights, trademarks, or patents for the privilege of importing merchandise subject to those rights. Design and engineering fees may have to be paid to foreign firms separate from payments to the actual producer of the product. Sometimes these payments are made through the seller or exporter of the merchandise. When such payments are made "as a condition of sale of the imported merchandise for exportation to the United States," they are includable in transaction value. For instance, if a firm imports blue jeans manufactured in Hong Kong, and as a condition of sale makes royalty payments to the designer of the jeans in Paris, the royalty would be includable in the transaction value of the merchandise.

The GATT 1994 *Agreement on Customs Valuation* attempts to unify the various nations' methods of calculating dutiable value on the basis of transaction value. It also attempts to toughen rules for dealing with importer fraud in stating value. Its greatest effect will be in assuring U.S. exporters that their goods will be fairly valued in foreign countries according to international principles.

Agency Commissions. The importance of transacting business through a foreign agent is stressed many times in this text. Agents are used both by sellers attempting to export to foreign markets and by buyers attempting to source materials or goods from foreign suppliers. The terms of the relationship between the importer and the agent can have a distinct impact on the calculation of transaction value. Although commissions paid to a buying agent (an agent of the buyer/importer) are generally not included in transaction value, payments made to, or for the benefit of, the seller or seller's agent are included. Customs carefully scrutinizes the relationship between U.S. importers and their buying agents to be sure that dutiable value is accurately reported.

In *Monarch Luggage Co. v. United States,* 715 F. Supp. 1115 (Ct. Int'l. Trade 1989), the importer successfully structured a business transaction so that the buying commissions were excludable from transaction value. Although representatives of Monarch traveled to the Far East several times a year to meet with their suppliers, inspect their facilities, and place orders for luggage, they nevertheless maintained a local agent there. Under a written agreement, the agent was to locate the best sources for luggage and visit the suppliers to determine the quality of the luggage, but could place orders only at Monarch's direction. The agent coordinated payment for the luggage and arranged transportation according to Monarch's explicit instructions. The supplier and not the agent absorbed the loss of defective merchandise. The agent bore no risk of loss to the goods and never took title to them. The agreement further stated that "the agent shall never act as a seller in any transaction involving the principal." Most importantly, Monarch made the payments to its agent directly and separately and not as a part of the invoice price paid to the supplier of the luggage. In other words, the agent was in fact a representative of the buyer, and not an agent of the seller. The fees paid to the agent were not included in dutiable value.

Assists. Importers will often provide some form of assistance to a foreign manufacturer from whom they are purchasing goods. If this *assist* is provided free of charge or at a reduced cost, for use in the production of or sale of merchandise for export to the United States, the value of the assist is includable in transaction value. Assists generally include (1) raw materials and component parts incorporated in or used in the production of the imported merchandise; (2) tools, dies, or molds; and (3) engi-

neering, development, artwork, and design, or plans and sketches performed by a foreign firm or person not domiciled within the United States.

In *Texas Apparel Co. v. United States,* 698 F. Supp 932 (Ct. Int'l. Trade 1988), the importer provided sewing machines to a Mexican manufacturer and paid the cost of repairs to the machines. The machines were used to produce garments sold to the importer in the United States. The court held that if the machines were supplied to the Mexican firm free of charge, or at a reduced cost, then the value of the machines had to be included in the dutiable value of the garments as an assist. In *Salant v. United States,* 86 F. Supp.2d 1301 (Ct. Int'l. Trade 2000) the importer provided free rolls of fabric to a foreign shirt manufacturer for use in making shirts for sale back to the importer. The court upheld Customs' regulations that the value of the assist included both the value of the fabric that went into the shirts as well as the value of the scrap fabric discarded as waste because including all of the fabric was more in keeping with "generally accepted accounting principles."

Other Methods of Calculating Dutiable Value. When the transaction value of imported merchandise cannot be determined, Customs will look to the value of identical merchandise. If identical merchandise cannot be found, then the value of similar merchandise will be used. The identical or similar merchandise used in the comparison must have been recently sold for export to the United States at the same level of trade (manufacturer to distributor, distributor to retailer, for example) and in quantities similar to the entry being valued.

If dutiable value cannot be determined by any of these methods, Customs will utilize the deductive value or computed value methods. *Deductive value* is the resale price of the goods (including packaging costs) in the United States after importation, less international and inland freight, insurance, customs duties, brokerage fees, commissions, and expenses of refining, assembling, or further manufacturing incurred in the United States. The final method for calculating the value of imports gives the computed value. *Computed value* is calculated by adding the costs of raw materials, processing or fabricating, overhead, labor costs, packing costs, the value of any assist, and an amount for profit.

Currency Exchange Rates. If imported products are invoiced in a foreign currency, customs valuation is not based on the actual amount paid to the foreign supplier in U.S. dollars according to the exchange rate obtained by the importer. Rather, the goods will be valued in dollars based on the exchange rate certified by the Federal Reserve Bank of New York on the day of export from the foreign country.

Country-of-Origin

Imagine that it's 1989 and that your trading company has firm commitments from buyers in the United States to take all of the ostrich chicks that you can provide during the next year. After considerable searching and time spent traveling the world, you find an ostrich hatchery in England. You enter into a sales contract with the hatchery, with payment to be made under a confirmed letter of credit. Your bank pays the seller cash on the documents and the chicks arrive peeping and squawking at a U.S. port of entry. The chicks are entered with their country-of-origin listed as Great Britain. An astute Customs inspector realizes that the chicks could not possibly have "originated" in that country and corrects the country-of-origin to South Africa, where the eggs obviously originated. You agree that the fertilized eggs originated in South Africa, but argue that their incubation and hatching in Great Britain amounts to a "substantial transformation" and that Great Britain therefore became the country-of-origin. U.S. Customs rules that the processing of the eggs in Great Britain was a natural biological consequence of the initial fertilization of the eggs in South Africa, that the chicks continued to be a product of South Africa, and that they are prohibited from entering the United States under a U.S. law banning the import of products from South Africa (the ban, of course, was lifted with the end of *apartheid* and political changes in South Africa in the early 1990s). This not-so-hypothetical case illustrates how critical it is to know the lawful country-of-origin of imported goods.

Rules of Origin. No country will permit goods to be imported unless the country-of-origin of the goods is properly determined and reported to Customs authorities. The country-of-origin determines the tariff rate on imported products, the applicability of quotas, and, as in the above example, the effect of embargoes or other restrictions on trade. The country-of-origin is *not simply* the country from which the goods were purchased, or from where they were shipped. If that were the case, one could enter Italian leather or leather products into the United States at the lower Mexican tariff rate by simply routing them through Mexico. Where a product is made in one country, entirely from raw materials and components originating there, the country-of-origin is not difficult to determine. Bananas grown in Honduras and shipped directly to supermarkets in the United States are products of Honduras. Plywood sheets glued and pressed in Brazil, from trees grown in Brazil, are obviously products of Brazil. Men's shirts that were cut and sewn in China, from fabric woven and yarn spun there, that were made from cotton grown there, are obviously a product of China. In these cases, the general rule applies: the country-of-origin is *that country where an article was grown, mined, or wholly and completely produced or manufactured entirely from materials originating in that country.*

But few products today are wholly made in one country entirely from materials derived there. More and more products are subjected to manufacturing, processing, and assembly operations on a global scale. Agricultural commodities grown in one country may be processed into food in another. Steel produced in one country may be processed into wire, steel plates, girders, or automobile parts in another country. An automobile destined for the United States may be assembled in Latin America or Canada from parts and materials that may have originated or been assembled in dozens of countries. Some products can involve hundreds or thousands of component parts that have been manufactured and assembled in plants located on several continents. Nevertheless, importers are expected to accurately track the movement of materials and understand the complex manufacturing or assembly processes to accurately know the product's country-of-origin. Where goods are not wholly and completely manufactured in one country, the country-of-origin can only be determined by referring to the appropriate *rules of origin*.

The Substantial-Transformation Test. There can be only one country-of-origin for customs purposes, even for products that undergo manufacturing operations in several different countries. In this case, the generally accepted rule is that the country-of-origin is *that country where a product last underwent a substantial transformation.* But there is no easy definition of "substantial transformation." The definition largely depends on the rules of origin applicable to the products and countries involved. In the United States, there are currently four basic sets of rules of origin, each with its own test for what amounts to a substantial transformation. The fifth rule is one currently being developed by the WTO.

1. The *name, character, or use test* is used to determine the country-of-origin for most goods entering the United States from NTR (formerly MFN) countries with whom the United States has normal trade relations. The rule applies when determining the tariff rate, the applicability of quotas or other trade restrictions, and the country-of-origin marking or labeling requirements. For example, if steel is made in Korea and shipped to Germany (or any other NTR country) where it is turned into fine cutlery, it can enter the United States under the tariff rate for German cutlery, and be labeled "Made in Germany" only if the processing in Germany amounted to a substantial transformation that created a new and different article of commerce with a new "name, character, or use" as defined by U.S. law.

2. The rules of origin of the *North American Free Trade Agreement* (NAFTA) between the United States, Canada, and Mexico permit goods that are *wholly produced or obtained* in North America to be sold in North America at favorable NAFTA rates. "Wholly produced or obtained," as some writers have said with a little exaggeration, means that the goods cannot have "one atom" that did not originate in North America. Goods that are made from materials or components that originated outside North America qualify for free-trade status only if each and every non-North American material or component (called *inputs*) has undergone a change in tariff classification as described in NAFTA Annex 401. For example, a product manufactured in Canada from raw material inputs originating in Europe can be

shipped to the United States as a product of North America (at the tariff rate applicable to Canadian imports and labeled "Made in Canada") only if every single one of the European materials or components underwent a change in tariff classification set out in the NAFTA agreement when they were made into the new product in Canada. This is known as the NAFTA *tariff-shift rule.* The United States, Canada, and Mexico each have their own tariff-shift rules. Each country's rules are based on the principles of Annex 401, and found in the notes to their national tariff schedules.

3. *Trade-preference rules* are used to determine if goods qualify for favorable tariff treatment (a "preference") as a result of having originated in the Caribbean, Africa, a country with whom the United States has a free trade pact (e.g., Israel, Jordan, Chile), or a developing country from some other region that has qualified under U.S. law. For example, if an article originates in China and is sent to a Caribbean processing plant to be made into a finished product destined for customers in the United States, the finished product can be entered under the preferential tariff rates for Caribbean-made products only if the processing that took place in the Caribbean country met the specific "substantial-transformation" requirements as defined by the *U.S.–Caribbean Basin Economic Recovery Act.* Similar laws apply to products of Africa and to developing countries in all regions of the world.

4. *Textile and apparel rules of origin.* Special rules apply to U.S. imports of textile and apparel products.

5. The WTO is currently developing a uniform set of rules of origin under the authority of the 1994 *Agreement on Rules of Origin.* These new rules are still several years away from completion, but if adopted will significantly change the rules of origin in the United States and other countries. The rules are similar to the *tariff-shift rules of NAFTA.*

We begin our discussion with the rule of origin that currently has the broadest impact on the customs laws in the United States: *the name, character, or use test.* (The other rules will be discussed later in this chapter, except for the NAFTA rules that are the subject of the next chapter.)

Substantial Transformation: The "Name, Character, or Use" Test. For almost one hundred years, the courts of the United States have held that a substantial transformation occurs *when the original article or product loses its identity as such and is transformed into a new and different article of commerce having "a new name, character or use" different from that of the original item.* In 1908, the U.S. Supreme Court ruled that imported cork had not been substantially transformed when it was dried, treated, and cut into smaller sections for use in bottling beer. The Court stated, "Something more is necessary . . . There must be a transformation; a new and different article must emerge, having a distinctive name, character or use. This cannot be said of the corks in question. A cork put through the claimant's process is still a cork." *Anheuser-Busch Brewing Association v. United States,* 207 U.S. 556 (1908). Since then, many courts have tried to interpret this phrase and to apply it to many different products and manufacturing operations.

The *name, character, or use test* is used to determine the country-of-origin for tariff purposes (other than in specialized cases, such as those falling under the *North American Free Trade Agreement*), as well as to determine how foreign-made products are to be marked or labeled. Customs uses the "name, character, or use" test to determine the country-of-origin for marking and labeling purposes. U.S. law strictly requires that every foreign-made article imported into the United States be marked or labeled in English so as to indicate to the *ultimate purchaser* the country-of-origin of the article. Suppose an article is taken from Country A to Country B where it is subjected to a refining process that combines it with other materials. If the process in Country B amounts to a substantial transformation so that a new product emerges with a new "name, character, or use," then the article may be imported into the United States and marked as "Made in Country B." Similarly, if foreign raw materials are imported into the United States and put through a manufacturing process that substantially transforms them into a product with a new "name, character, or use," the new product need not be marked as of foreign origin when sold to the ultimate purchaser. In other words, the foreign raw materials have been transformed into a product of the United States.

The landmark case, *Gibson-Thomsen Co. v.*

United States, 27 C.C.P.A. 267 (1940), involved the application of the *name, character, or use test* under the marking and labeling laws of the United States. The court ruled that when wooden handles and blocks were imported into the United States from Japan, drilled with holes into which American bristles were inserted, with the final product being sold in the United States as toothbrushes and hairbrushes, that the imported wooden components had "lost their identity in a tariff sense" and had been transformed into products of the United States. The court took account of the fact that the bristles, which had been of U.S. origin, were a key component of the new product. Because the transformation took place in the United States, the wooden handles did not have to be marked as having originated in Japan. *Gibson-Thomsen* is often cited by courts today.

Since 1940, the courts have interpreted and refined the "name, character, or use" concept. Some courts have looked to see if a "new article of commerce" emerges from the transformation. For instance, in a 1970 case, a court ruled that unfinished furniture chair parts were substantially transformed by the importer into chairs that were new and different articles of commerce. Similarly, wooden sticks imported into the United States and then set into liquid ice cream and frozen have been held to be substantially transformed into a new product having a new name, character, and use. In a 1960 case, a court ruled that the winding of typewriter ribbon onto imported spools resulted in a substantial transformation of the spools because the imported spool became an integral part of the whole product with which it was combined. In 1984, Customs used the same rationale for deciding not to impose country-of-origin marking requirements on the plastic spools and shells in which audiocassette tape is wound. Although many cases look to see if the name commonly given the transformed article has changed, a product's name is generally considered to be only one of several factors to take into account. Greater emphasis is usually placed on whether the *essential character*—sometimes said to be the "essential nature" of the product—or its *use* has changed.

Many of the modern cases also look to see whether the substantial transformation has resulted in an increase in value, called the *value-added test.* In *National Juice Products Association v. United States,* 628 F. Supp. 978 (Ct. Int'l. Trade

1986), a U.S. company had imported evaporated orange concentrate and blended it with water, orange oils, and fresh juice to make frozen orange concentrate. The blending and processing in the United States had added only a 7 percent value to the orange juice. The court held that the orange juice sold to consumers had to be labeled with the foreign country-of-origin.

In *Uniroyal, Inc. v. United States,* 542 F. Supp. 1026 (Ct. Int'l. Trade 1982), *aff'd. per curiam,* 702 F.2d 1022 (Fed. Cir. 1983), the court ruled that a substantial transformation had not occurred when the leather upper portion of a shoe was imported and then attached to the preformed rubber sole in the United States and sold as a "Sperry Topsider." The court relied heavily on evidence that the time and cost of producing the leather upper in Indonesia were much greater than the time and cost of attaching it to the rubber sole

(called a "minor assembly operation"). The court also considered that the fashioning of the leather uppers in Indonesia required far greater skill than was required to attach the sole in the United States. The court stated that "[I]t would be misleading to allow the public to believe that a shoe is made in the United States when the entire upper—which is the very essence of the completed shoe—is made in Indonesia and the only step in the manufacturing process performed in the United States is the attachment of an outsole." The court noted that unlike the earlier case involving typewriter spools, the upper leather portion of the shoe was not just a vehicle for selling something else, but was the major reason that consumers selected this shoe.

The *Ferrostaal Metals* case illustrates the difficulty in determining whether a substantial transformation has occurred. As this case shows, the

---

Ferrostaal Metals Corp. v. United States
664 F. Supp. 535 (1987)
Court of International Trade

BACKGROUND AND FACTS
Plaintiff attempted to enter steel products at the Port of Seattle. They consisted of unpainted steel sheets that had originated in Japan but had been hot-dip galvanized in New Zealand. Plaintiff's entry documents identified New Zealand as the country-of-origin. Customs ruled that the country-of-origin was Japan and that the steel was therefore subject to a voluntary restraint agreement between the United States and Japan. Customs contended that hot-dip galvanizing of Japanese steel sheets in New Zealand was merely a "finishing process" carried out to improve certain performance characteristics of the steel sheets and not a process that results in a substantial transformation so as to change the country-of-origin. The plaintiff disagreed and brought this action for review.

JUDGE DICARLO
Substantial transformation is a concept of major importance in administering the customs and trade laws. In addition to its role in identifying the country-of-origin of imported merchandise for purposes of determining dutiable status, or, as in this case, the applicability of a bilateral trade agreement, substantial transformation is the focus of many cases involving country-of-origin markings. . . .

The essence of these cases is that a product cannot be said to originate in the country of exportation if it is not manufactured there. The question, therefore, is whether operations performed on products in the country of exportation are of such a substantial nature to justify the conclusion that the resulting product is a manufacture of that country. "Manufacture implies a change, but every change is not manufacture. . . . There must be transformation; a new and different article must emerge, 'having a distinctive name, character, or use.' " *Anheuser-Busch Brewing Ass'n. v. United States,* 207 U.S. 556, 562, 28 S.Ct. 204, 206 (1908). The criteria of name, character, and use continue to determine when substantial transformation has occurred, and the prior cases of this court and our predecessor and appellate courts provide guidance in the application of this test.

* * *

Whether galvanizing and annealing change the character of the merchandise depends on the nature of these operations and their effect on the properties of the materials. . . . To produce one of the types of imported sheet . . . the sheet must be heated to 1,350 degrees F, at which point recrystallization of the

continued

continued

grains of steel occurs. The sheet is then brought down to 880 degrees F, before galvanizing begins. At 880 degrees F, the sheet enters a pot of molten zinc and is dipped. The molten zinc reacts immediately with the solid steel, and begins a process known as "alloying." Alloying constitutes a chemical change in the product, characterized by the formation of iron-zinc alloys at the interface between the steel and the zinc. The galvanized steel sheet emerging from the bath has a mixed zinc-steel surface with an identifiable atomic pattern. The formation of a galvanized surface is an irreversible process which provides electrochemical protection to the sheet. As a result of the galvanic protection, the steel will last up to twenty years, or ten times as long as ungalvanized steel. . . .

The alloy-bonded zinc coating affects the character of the sheet by changing its chemical composition and by providing corrosion resistance. The court also finds that the hot-dip galvanizing process is substantial in terms of the value it adds to full hard cold-rolled steel sheet. The evidence showed that the Japanese product is sold for approximately $350 per ton, while the hot-dipped galvanized product is sold for an average price of $550 to $630.

Taken as a whole, the continuous hot-dip galvanizing process transforms a strong, brittle product which cannot be formed into a durable, corrosion-resistant product which is less hard, but formable for a range of commercial applications. Defendant's witness stated that the imported sheet has a "different character from the standpoint of durability." The court finds that the annealing and galvanizing processes result in a change in character by significantly altering the mechanical properties and chemical composition of the steel sheet.

The court also finds substantial changes in the use of the steel sheet as a result of the continuous hot-dip galvanizing process. Testimony at trial overwhelmingly demonstrated that cold-rolled steel is not interchangeable with steel of the type imported, nor are there any significant uses of cold-rolled sheet in place of annealed sheet.

The name criterion is generally considered the least compelling of the factors which will support a finding of substantial transformation. Nonetheless, the satisfaction of the name criterion in this case lends support to plaintiffs' claim. The witnesses for both parties testified that the processing of full hard cold-rolled steel sheet results in a product which has a different name, continuous hot-dip galvanized steel sheet.

The court also considers relevant whether the operations underlying the asserted transformation have effected a change in the classification of the merchandise under the Tariff Schedules of the United States. Change in tariff classification may be considered as a factor in the substantial transformation analysis. Here this factor supports a substantial transformation. Full hard cold-rolled steel sheet is classified under item 607.83, TSUS, while continuous hot-dip galvanized steel sheet is classifiable under item 608.13, TSUS. (The TSUS was the forerunner to the *Harmonized Tariff Schedule*.)

Based on the totality of the evidence, showing that the continuous hot-dip galvanizing process effects changes in the name, character, and use of the processed steel sheet, the court holds that the changes constitute a substantial transformation and that hot-dipped galvanized steel sheet is a new and different article of commerce from full hard cold-rolled steel sheet.

Decision. Japanese steel that had been galvanized in New Zealand prior to its importation into the United States was substantially transformed so that it had become a product of New Zealand and thus was not subject to voluntary restraint agreements between the United States and Japan.

Comment. "Voluntary restraint agreements" such as those described in this case to restrict steel imports from Japan are no longer used as a method of limiting imports of foreign goods into America, as they do not fall under the permissible rules of the WTO. Nevertheless, this case serves well to illustrate the use of the substantial-transformation test in tariff cases. The case was cited in 2003 by U.S. Customs in a ruling determining the country-of-origin of fiber optic cable.

precise definition of substantial transformation is unclear because so many factors can be considered. Faced with complex cases, courts have developed rules on a case-by-case basis. The courts have recognized that it is difficult to take legal concepts applicable to products such as textiles and apply them to combinations of liquids or the fabrication of steel articles. As you read, consider the actual process of hot-dip galvanizing described here. Would you agree that the operations performed on the steel in New Zealand created a product with a new "name, character, or use"? The unpredictable nature of these court rulings increases importers' difficulties in interpreting and applying the rules of origin, as evidenced by the large number of customs cases appealed to the courts.

GATT 1994 *Agreement on Rules of Origin*

GATT 1994 calls on countries to harmonize and clarify their rules of origin. According to the *Agreement on Rules of Origin,* the country-of-origin will be defined as either where the article and all of its constituent materials have been wholly obtained, or if the article is produced in more than one country, it is that country where the article last underwent a change in tariff classification. This provision is known as the *tariff-shift rule.* These rules will apply to all trade between countries that are members of the WTO. The United States is moving toward the use of the tariff-shift rule. Rules of origin based on the tariff-shift rule state precisely—for every given category of product in the HTS—what tariff classification changes will result in a substantial transformation. This rule is already in effect under the NAFTA for trade between Canada, Mexico, and the United States. (See Chapter Thirteen for a detailed discussion of North American rules of origin.)

As of 2003, the WTO had agreed on rules covering many non-agricultural products. The goal is to complete a single set of rules of origin covering over 5,500 products in both the agricultural and non-agricultural sectors that would be applied by all WTO member countries.

Special Rules of Origin for Textiles and Apparel

The world's textile and apparel industry operates on a global scale. Textile firms shift the site of spinning, weaving, cutting, sewing, and other operations from country to country, and region to region, to take advantage of low-cost labor and materials, and to benefit from customs and tariff laws in the country in which the goods will be sold. For instance, cotton might be grown and spun into yarn in China, where it is woven into cloth. The cloth might be sent to Hong Kong where it is cut to form pieces of garments (e.g.,

sleeves, collars, etc.), and then sent to Honduras for assembly. Textile and apparel manufacturers must consider the rules of origin in sourcing yarn, fabric, and other raw materials, or in locating textile dyeing and finishing operations, cut and sew plants, or assembly operations.

Textile and apparel imports to the United States are governed by specialized rules of origin. They are more restrictive than rules applicable to other products, making it more difficult to import textiles than almost any other product. The rules are not only complex and arcane, but have undergone significant changes several times in the last ten years. Many factors determine the country-of-origin of products made in more than one country: the type of product (e.g., yarn, fabric, clothing and apparel, or textile products for the home), the fiber content (e.g., silk, wool, cotton, etc.), and the steps or processes that take place in the transition from yarn to cloth to final product. The origin of certain items, for example, might be the country where the fabric was woven or knitted, regardless of where it was cut and assembled into a finished product. Other items are said to have originated where the fabric from which they were made was dyed and printed, and not where they were woven. Yet other items, such as apparel, originate where they were wholly assembled, or where the most important assembly operation took place. There is no logical method to the rules and many commentators believe they derive primarily from political considerations. For example, prior to 2000, silk scarves made from Chinese silk entered the United States as products of China, subject to quota limits on Chinese scarves. And they had to be labeled "Made in China" despite the fact that they were dyed, printed, and finished in Italy by premier Italian textile converters with exclusive brand names and a reputation for sophisticated designs and quality. It was not until the EU threatened WTO action that the United States changed the rule. Now, scarves and some other items that are made from Chinese silk may be entered as a product of that country in which they were subjected to dyeing, printing, plus two other finishing operations. Today, the silk scarves could carry the prestigious label "Made in Italy."

The rules of origin create unique problems for U.S. textile importers. Consider this example. Textiles from developing countries are still limited by annual quotas that apply to every category of product according to its country-of-origin. For instance, U.S. quotas for 2002 may limit imports of "women's blouses from Pakistan" or "quilts and comforters from China" to only so many units or pieces per year. Thus, a rule of origin that determines where a product "originates" also determines the quota limit for that product. Imagine that cotton fabric from China is taken to Hong Kong, cut and sewn into an unfilled comforter shell, and filled with goose down. Despite the fact that the greater value of the finished comforter was derived from operations in Hong Kong, the comforter enters the United States under the down comforter quota limit and tariff rate for China, and would have to be labeled as "Made in China." This is known as the *fabric-forward rule* that applies to many home textile products: the country-of-origin is the country where the fabric was woven, regardless of where the comforter was cut, sewn, and filled. In the 1990s, this created a crisis for U.S. importers of home textiles. China produced much of the fabric used for home textiles, and as a result of these rules, the annual quotas on Chinese home textile products filled up rapidly. Meanwhile, quota allowances for the countries where the products were cut and sewn remained "unused." As a result, the tariffs were higher and the exhausted quota limits prevented U.S. consumers from getting all the home textiles they wanted at fair market prices.

To complicate matters, U.S. imports of textiles from Canada or Mexico are treated differently under NAFTA. Take the exact same situation as above, but now imagine that you are going to have your cotton fabric woven and made into unfilled comforter shells in China, then shipped to Canada where they are filled with goose down. The unfilled comforter shells fall under HTS subheading 6307.90. They are shipped to Canada to be filled with goose down from China or Europe. Goose down is classified under HTS subheading 0505.10. On shipment to the United States, the finished comforter, classified under HTS subheading 9494.90, is entered under NAFTA's zero-tariff rate for Canadian comforters, and with none of the problems of Chinese quotas. The NAFTA rules of origin, based on the tariff-shift rule, specifically provide that a transformation of articles from headings 6307 or 0505 to heading 9404 allows the final product to enter the United States at a zero-tariff rate, and to be marked "Made in Canada."

Textile imports from Israel, Jordan, Chile, Africa, the Caribbean, or other developing countries all may be subject to different rules. Moreover, there are separate tariff and marking rules for U.S. fabrics that are taken to a foreign country (usually in the Caribbean); processed; cut and sewn into jeans, t-shirts, and other clothing; and returned to the United States for sale. These contradictory and confusing rules often stymie the most experienced importers. So, textile and apparel manufacturers and importers rely heavily on attorneys and customs brokers that specialize in textile imports. They also frequently obtain binding ruling letters from U.S. Customs in advance of setting up operations to be certain that they comply with law.

Opportunities for Business Planning. The rules of origin can provide a resourceful importer with significant opportunities for good business planning. With proper legal advice, a firm can structure its global operations so as to minimize tariffs and to take advantage of the favorable trade and tariff treatment granted to goods coming from particular foreign countries. After all, trade and tariff laws are designed in part to either encourage or discourage trade with particular nations. Many firms, particularly multinational corporations, are therefore capable of shifting global resources and production facilities to those countries whose goods receive the most favorable trade and tariff treatment in the United States or other major importing nations. But to do this, the corporation must follow the importing nation's rules of origin meticulously. The tariff savings can be so great that some unscrupulous U.S. importers have been tempted to transship articles through developing countries, repackage or relabel them, and then enter them into the United States at the lower tariff rate. The penalties for furnishing false information to U.S. Customs authorities are quite severe.

Marking and Labeling of Imports

The United States has two primary laws that require imports to be labeled with the country-of-origin: the marking rules of U.S. Customs and the Federal Trade Commission (FTC) rules. The rules of U.S. Customs apply to country-of-origin markings of all imported products sold in the United States. The FTC rules apply primarily to the term "Made in

U.S.A." or similar terms. To be labeled "Made in U.S.A.," a label must meet the requirements of both agencies.

Customs Marking Rules. We have already learned that the marking rules require that every article of foreign origin imported into the United States must be indelibly and permanently marked in English in a conspicuous place and in such a manner as to indicate to the *ultimate purchaser* in the United States the name of the country-of-origin of the article. For example, the ultimate purchaser of frozen airline meals has been held to be the airline and not the passenger. Thus, only the packages containing the meals, which were seen only by the airline, had to be marked with the country-of-origin.

If the imported article is converted, processed, or combined with other articles or ingredients in the United States, so that it undergoes a substantial transformation resulting in a new article of commerce, with a new name, character, or use, as defined by the *Gibson-Thomsen* case, then the U.S. firm that transformed the article is considered the ultimate purchaser. As a result, the new product need not be labeled with a foreign country-of-origin. Does that mean that it can be labeled "Made in U.S.A."? Perhaps not. As we will see in the next section, the FTC rules take over—and they will not allow that claim unless the new product is "all or virtually all" made in America. Because the product was only "transformed" in the United States from foreign materials, it might be labeled "Made in U.S.A. of Imported Materials."

Items Not Requiring Marks. Customs regulations specify many articles by name that are exempt from marking requirements. These are generally objects that are incapable of being marked because of their size or special characteristics. Examples include works of art, unstrung beads, rags, nuts and bolts, screws, cigarettes, eggs, feathers, flowers, cellophane sheets, livestock, bamboo poles, maple sugar, vegetables, newsprint, and many others. In addition, the following general exemptions exist for certain categories of products: (1) products incapable of being marked; (2) products that cannot be marked without injury; (3) crude substances; (4) articles produced more than twenty years prior to importation; (5) products of possessions of the United States; (6) articles imported solely for the use of the importer and not intended for resale (e.g., personal articles purchased abroad by a tourist); (7) products of American fisheries that are entered duty free; and (8) certain products of the United States that are exported and returned. In addition, articles used by an importer as samples in soliciting orders and that are not for sale are exempted from the marking requirements. When an item is exempted from markings, the container in which it is sold to the consumer must be marked. To illustrate, imported carpentry nails need not be marked, but the box in which they are sold to the consumer must be.

Federal Trade Commission "Made in U.S.A." Rules

In the United States, the FTC and U.S. Customs have overlapping jurisdiction with regard to country-of-origin claims. While Customs oversees foreign country-of-origin marking ("Made in China"), the FTC regulates the use of the term "Made in U.S.A." Customs rules apply only to product marking, while the FTC rules apply to all claims, including those on product labels, catalogs, packaging, and all forms of advertising. Customs rules are more complex and detailed, while the "Made in U.S.A." rules of the FTC are more flexible and based on whether or not the claims would mislead or cause deception in the minds of the average consumer. The FTC bases its rules on its authority under the *Federal Trade Commission Act* to prevent unfair or deceptive trade practices.

There is no rule that requires a U.S.-made product to be labeled as such. Except for special rules applicable to automobiles and textile and fur products, U.S content need not be disclosed. However, a seller may not claim that a product is "Made in U.S.A." unless *all or virtually all* of the materials, processing, or component parts are made in the United States and that their final assembly or processing took place there. It means that all significant parts and processing that go into the product must be of U.S. origin. That is, the product should contain only negligible foreign content. For instance, the FTC has held that a gas barbecue grill assembled from all U.S. parts could be labeled as "Made in U.S.A." despite the fact that the knobs were of foreign origin. The knobs were said to make up a small portion of the product's total cost and an insignificant part of the final product.

The FTC origin rules apply also to other more indirect forms of marketing and promotion that may be deceptive. In one case, a company packaged its Chinese-made product in a package covered with an American flag and eagle. Despite the statement "Made in China" in small print on the bottom and side panels of the package, the FTC held that the labeling was deceptive.

Partly Made in the U.S.A.?   Products that cannot be labeled as "Made in U.S.A." may still bear qualified claims. A qualified claim is one that indicates that the product was partially made or processed in the United States. An example would be a down comforter labeled "Shell made in Germany with filling and further processing in the U.S.A." To use a qualified claim, there must still be a significant amount of U.S. content. A product that is invented in the United States and made in India could *not* claim "Created in U.S.A.," as this would be deceptive. The term "Assembled in U.S.A." may be used only where the product has undergone a substantial transformation in the United States and where the use of the term would not be deceptive. For example, according to the FTC, component parts for computers made in Singapore and assembled in Texas with only a screwdriver and screws may *not* be labeled as "Assembled in U.S.A." Here there was no substantial transformation in the United States and the statement is deceptive.

www.ftc.gov
For the FTC "Made in U.S.A."
rule see the home page of
the Federal Trade Commission
Web site.

U.S. TRADE PREFERENCES FOR DEVELOPING COUNTRIES

The United States has recognized that trade with developing countries, and particularly with the poorer nations of the Western Hemisphere, is essential to the economic development and political stability of these countries. U.S. law provides trade and investment incentives in the form of *trade preferences* for goods imported from these countries. These preferences generally take the form of reduced tariffs or duty-free status for goods. These laws include the *Generalized System of Preferences and the Caribbean Basin Economic Recovery Act.*

The Generalized System of Preferences

Under the *Generalized System of Preferences* (GSP), the United States aids in the economic development of certain developing countries by allowing their products to enter the United States at reduced rates of duty, or duty-free, until such time as these countries establish their own competitive industries. Such a trade preference is allowed under the terms of GATT and is similar to programs that other industrialized nations offer developing countries (notably the preferences granted by European nations to the products of many African nations). The program was begun in the United States in 1976 and has been renewed regularly by Congress. Mexico no longer qualified for the GSP when it joined NAFTA in 1994. There are approximately 140 countries receiving GSP status. Examples include Brazil and Argentina in South America, India and Thailand in Asia, Indonesia and the Philippines in the Pacific Rim, Poland and Hungary in Eastern Europe, as well as Russia and most of Africa. In 2002, imports worth more than $17.5 billion entered the United States duty free under the GSP.

Eligibility for GSP Status.   In order for a country to be eligible for GSP status, it must be designated a *beneficiary developing country.* Countries are not eligible for GSP status if they (1) have participated in an organized embargo of oil against the United States, (2) do not cooperate with the United States in the enforcement of narcotics laws, (3) aid and abet international terrorism, (4) have unlawfully expropriated the property of U.S. citizens, (5) do not recognize or enforce the arbitral awards of U.S. citizens, or (6) are controlled by communist governments. In addition, the president has wide authority under the GSP statute to deny duty-free treatment on political and economic grounds. For instance, the president can deny GSP status to any country that does not protect the patents, trademarks, and copyrights of U.S. citizens; maintains unreasonable restrictions on U.S. investment; does not grant internationally

http://www.ustr.gov/gsp/index.shtml
The "Trade and Development" section of the USTR's Web
site. Contains information on U.S. trade preference programs.

recognized worker rights to its workers; or whose exports to the United States injure a U.S. industry.

The product must also be eligible for duty-free treatment; over 4,600 products are eligible. Many of the eligible products are agricultural. Other typical products admitted under the GSP include sugar, jewelry, leather shoe uppers, wooden furniture, Christmas tree lighting, and telephones. Certain import-sensitive products such as textiles, footwear, steel, watches, and some electronic items are not eligible. A country may lose GSP benefits for specific products under competitive need limits. *Competitive need* is determined by an annual review process conducted on a product-by-product basis. Usually the duty-free status of a country's product will be terminated when more than half of the total U.S. imports of that product are imported from one GSP country or when imports of that product from the GSP country exceed a level established by Congress. Competitive need limits do not apply to sub-Saharan Africa. U.S. firms, labor unions, and even foreign governments may petition that products be added to, or removed from, the GSP list.

Once a developing country reaches a per capita gross national product of $8,500, it becomes ineligible for GSP treatment, and is considered *graduated*. By the close of the 1980s, the four "Asian tigers" of Hong Kong, Singapore, South Korea, and Taiwan were graduated from the GSP.

GSP Rules of Origin.   In order for an article to qualify for duty-free treatment, it must meet the following requirements: (1) it must be imported into the United States directly from the beneficiary developing country; (2) it must be the "growth, product, or manufacture" of the beneficiary developing country (or substantially transformed there into a product with a new name, character and use); and (3) at least 35 percent of the value of materials and the direct cost of processing operations must have been added to the article in a single beneficiary developing country (or in any two or more GSP countries that are members of the same free trade association, such as ASEAN, CARICOM, or Andean Group). A special rule applies when raw materials are brought to the GSP country from another country and then made into a finished article and shipped to the United States. In this case, the law requires a *dual transforma-*

tion. The raw materials brought from another country into the GSP country must first undergo a substantial transformation in the GSP country resulting in a new and different article of commerce in order to be included in the 35 percent value-content requirement. Then that article must undergo a second transformation into another new and different article of commerce, which is then shipped to the United States.

To better illustrate, consider the following example of a dual transformation adapted from the *Code of Federal Regulations*:

http://www.eurunion.org
The "European Union in the U.S." For EU Customs and tariff information, go to "EU Law and Policy Overviews"

A raw, perishable skin of an animal grown in a nonbeneficiary country is sent to a beneficiary country where it is tanned to create nonperishable leather. The tanned leather is then cut, sewn, and assembled with a metal buckle imported from a nonbeneficiary country to create a finished belt that is imported directly into the United States. Because the operations performed in the beneficiary country involved both the substantial transformation of the raw skin into a new or different article (tanned leather) and the use of that intermediate article in the production or manufacture of a new or different article imported into the United States, the cost or value of the tanned leather used to make the imported article *may be counted* toward the 35 percent value requirement. The cost or value of the metal buckle imported into the beneficiary country *may not be counted* toward the 35 percent value requirement because the buckle was not substantially transformed in the beneficiary country into a new or different article prior to its incorporation in the finished belt.

Caribbean Basin Economic Recovery Act

According to the U.S. Department of Commerce, U.S. imports from the Caribbean for 2002 were $21 billion. Under the *Caribbean Basin Economic Recovery Act* (CBERA), enacted in 1983, the president has the authority to grant tariff reductions and duty-free status to imports from twenty-four eligible countries in order to increase imports from the region. (See Exhibit 12.5.) This law was part of a larger program to stimulate investment in the Caribbean known as the *Caribbean Basin Initiative*. These nations include

---

EXHIBIT 12.5

Caribbean Basin Beneficiary Countries

Antigua	Haiti
Aruba	Honduras
Bahamas	Jamaica
Barbados	Montserrat
Belize	Netherlands Antilles
British Virgin Islands	Nicaragua
Costa Rica	Panama
Dominica	St. Kitts & Nevis
Dominican Republic	St. Lucia
El Salvador	St. Vincent
Grenada	& Grenadines
Guatemala	Trinidad & Tobago
Guyana	

Central America and the island nations of the Caribbean, although communist Cuba is excluded from eligibility. A few of the leading participants in the CBERA program are the Dominican Republic, Costa Rica, and Guatemala. A few of the most important products benefiting from CBERA are cigars, cane sugar, communications equipment, electrical and non-electrical machinery, medical appliances, orange juice, bananas and tropical fruits, ethyl alcohol, baseballs, and rum. In 2000, preferences were extended to footwear, certain leather goods such as handbags and gloves, luggage, oil, canned tuna, watches, and certain textile products.

Many countries that qualify for favorable CBERA treatment also receive GSP treatment. Also, many products qualify under both laws. However, the criteria are not the same for eligibility. Unlike the GSP, CBERA has no provisions for graduating Caribbean countries on the basis of any economic criteria. The CBERA applies to a greater variety of products than the GSP, and the competitive need requirements of the GSP are not applicable. CBERA is a permanent program with no date set for expiration of the law.

The objective of CBERA was to encourage investment in the Caribbean by allowing goods made there to be imported into the United States at preferential tariff rates. Any program like this naturally engenders fear in some quarters that it will have an adverse impact on American labor and manufacturing. However, some statistics are revealing. In 1983, the United States had a $3.2 billion trade deficit with the Caribbean countries. By the late 1990s, the United States reversed that and had a small trade surplus with the region. Although imports rose 92 percent since 1983, exports actually increased by 237 percent. And in 1999, the U.S. Department of Labor announced that the CBERA trade preferences have had no adverse impact on, and have constituted no significant threat to, U.S. employment. Apparently, the United States has benefited at least as much as the Caribbean has.

CBERA Rules of Origin. CBERA rules of origin are similar to those of the GSP. In addition, CBERA grants duty-free entry into the United States for articles that have been "assembled or processed" in CBERA countries from U.S.-made "components, materials, or ingredients." In other words, U.S.-made parts that have been subjected to minor assembly, finishing, and processing operations in the CBERA country, and then shipped back to the United States qualify for duty-free entry. For these products, the substantial transformation requirement has been eliminated.

---

http://europa.eu.int/comm/development/body/cotonou/index_en.htm

For the 2000 *Cotonou Agreement* providing EU tariff preferences and a trading partnership for the least developed countries of Africa, the Caribbean, and the Pacific (ACP countries), see this site, or link from the Europa home page.

The 2000 *Caribbean Basin Trade Partnership Act*. This law significantly increases the trade benefits that the Caribbean countries have had under CBERA. Under the *Caribbean Basin Trade Partnership Act,* many products formerly excluded from CBERA, such as footwear, luggage, and watches, now receive trade preferences. Apparel made in the Caribbean may now be shipped to the United States both duty and quota free, provided the garments are made from U.S. fabrics woven or knitted from yarn spun in the United States, or that are made from fabrics, such as silk or batiste, that are deemed to be in short supply.

To receive the additional benefits, the President of the United States must certify that each of the twenty-four Caribbean countries is adequately recognizing the rights of workers to organize and bargain collectively; prohibiting forced labor; eliminating child labor abuses; setting a minimum age for employing children; and setting an acceptable minimum wage, hours of work, and occupational safety and health standards. The reason for this is illustrated in the case of Guatemala, where murders of labor organizers have been reported. In 1999, armed thugs kidnapped leaders of a banana workers' union who were protesting the illegal dismissal of nine hundred workers. The United States pressured Guatemala to recognize the rights of the nine hundred fired workers, prosecute those responsible, enact changes in its labor laws, and provide adequate law enforcement and legal protection for workers' rights in the future. As of 2003, all fourteen countries have been certified eligible for benefits.

Africa Growth and Opportunity Act of 2000.

This statute (AGOA) is intended to aid in the economic growth and the establishment of political freedom in forty-eight poor countries in sub-Saharan Africa where the per capita annual income averages about $500 per year. The law encourages U.S. trade and investment there and improves access for African products to U.S. markets. To qualify for the benefits of the act, the African countries must try to improve their own conditions through progressive economic and social policies. The country must abide by human rights standards, eliminate abuses of child labor, and not support terrorism. Almost forty countries are now eligible. AGOA broadens the GSP for Africa and extends it through 2008. It includes duty-free status for 6,400 eligible products. For certain countries, AGOA removes all quotas on apparel as well.

In order to qualify for AGOA duty-free status, an article must be produced or manufactured in an AGOA country and meet the rules of origin. For most products, the rules are similar to, but more lenient than, the GSP rules with which you are already familiar. African-made apparel generally qualifies for duty-free treatment if it is made from African or U.S.-made fabric that was woven from U.S.-made yarn and assembled with U.S.-made thread, or from fabrics in short supply (e.g., linen, silk, batiste, velveteen, and some others).

---

http://www.agoa.gov
The official home page for the Africa Growth and Opportunity Act, presented by the U.S. Department of Commerce, Office of Africa.

Andean Trade Program. The *Andean Trade Program* is part of an effort by the United States to promote economic development in the Andean countries while combating drug trafficking and encouraging democracy. These countries include Peru, Colombia, Ecuador, and Bolivia, and their major exports are natural gas, minerals, certain metal products (of copper, zinc, etc.), jewelry, forestry and wood products, coffee, cocoa, fruits, cut flowers, sugar, handicrafts, leather accessories, footwear and textile products, to name a few. The program permits the duty-free import of over 6000 different kinds of products into the United States. The program was renewed by the United States Congress in the *Andean Trade Program and Drug Eradication Act of 2002.*

OTHER CUSTOMS LAWS AFFECTING U.S. IMPORTS

This section examines three other laws affecting U.S. imports: drawback provisions allowing a refund of duties paid, the duty-free return of U.S. exports, and foreign trade zones.

Drawbacks

A *drawback* is a refund of duties already paid. The most common type is the *manufacturing drawback,* designed to encourage U.S. manufacturers to export. A manufacturing drawback is a 99 percent refund of duties and taxes paid on merchandise that is imported, subjected to manufacture or production, and then exported within five years. U.S. firms are becoming increasingly sophisticated in using manufacturing drawbacks. For instance, duties paid on imported yarn will be refunded to the importer who exports a finished fabric made from that yarn. Similarly, a poultry farm that imports chicken feed can receive a drawback on duties paid on the imported feed when the chickens are slaughtered and exported. Drawbacks such as these allow the exporter to purchase materials from low-cost foreign suppliers, including non-MFN countries, without having to pay prohibitively high duties. The use of drawbacks in U.S.–Canadian trade was eliminated in 1996. In U.S.–Mexican trade, drawbacks will be eliminated by 2001.

Same-condition drawbacks are utilized when the imported goods are not processed or manufactured, but are reexported in the "same condition" as they were imported. These products are not significantly altered while in the United States (although they may be repackaged, cleaned, tested, or displayed). For example, nuts and bolts can be entered in bulk, and sorted and repackaged in packages with foreign-language labeling. On export, the drawback applies. Many trading companies utilize same-condition drawbacks.

In certain cases, an importer may export U.S.-made goods in the substitution of imported goods that are of the "same kind and quality" (i.e., interchangeable) and receive the drawback on the imported items. This practice is known as a *substitution drawback*. Substitution drawbacks are applicable to both manufacturing and same-condition drawback situations. For instance, assume that a U.S. manufacturer imports semiconductors for use in making computers. The manufacturer may receive a drawback on duties paid if it exports, within three years, products containing U.S.-made semiconductors of the same kind and quality. If the company exports only 40 percent of its production, it can claim a drawback for 40 percent of the duties paid (a manufacturing/substitution situation). To take another example, the importer of soda ash can decide to resell the foreign soda ash in this country and export the same quantity of U.S.-made soda ash to a foreign buyer, and then receive a drawback on duties paid on the imported soda ash (a same-condition/substitution situation). In most instances, these substitution drawbacks deal with fungible goods or commodities such as agricultural products.

A drawback of 99 percent is also allowed for imported merchandise that does not conform to specifications or to samples (e.g., zippers that do not zip; receipt of cotton sweaters instead of wool), provided that the error was the fault of the foreign shipper (not of the importer) and the merchandise is returned to U.S. Customs within ninety days for inspection and return to the seller under Customs' supervision. A similar drawback is allowed for merchandise shipped to a U.S. firm without its consent. If a U.S. firm imports foreign goods and finds that they are useless and cannot be returned, the importer can receive a drawback on the duties paid on the merchandise, which is subsequently destroyed.

A drawback is essentially a contract with U.S. Customs. Firms wishing to arrange a drawback need competent advice in doing so. The procedures, time limits, documentation, and accounting requirements for obtaining all drawbacks are complex and exact, and many U.S. companies use the services of specialist firms for advice on structuring drawback transactions. Some firms utilize specially developed software to help track and document a drawback transaction. Civil penalties are imposed for violating the provisions of the law. Many firms do not file for drawbacks for fear of being assessed a penalty for clerical errors. The criminal penalties for fraudulently claiming a drawback are severe.

Returns of U.S. Exports

If U.S. exports are returned to the United States, they are dutiable just as though they were foreign products. This rule has three general exceptions: (1) U.S.-made products that were exported and returned to the United States and that were not substantially transformed or advanced in value while outside the United States (e.g., samples sent to a prospective buyer and returned; articles such as equipment leased to a foreign firm and returned at the end of the lease term; articles subjected to minor processing); (2) articles exported for repair or alteration, which are dutiable on the value of the repair or alteration provided that they were not substantially transformed while outside the United States; and (3) component parts made in the United States and assembled in a foreign country under special provisions of the tariff laws designed to promote economic development in certain developing countries. (This provision is discussed in the next chapter.)

http://www.naftz.org
The home page of the National Association of Foreign Trade Zones

Foreign Trade Zones

Foreign trade zones (FTZs) are legally defined areas outside the customs territory of the country in which they are located. They are monitored by, and under the control of, the customs authorities of that country. Foreign trade zones exist under the laws of most nations, including the United States and European countries. In the United States, FTZs operate under a license from the FTZ

Board. They must be within a 60-mile radius of a U.S. port of entry. Imported goods may be brought into an FTZ without being subjected to tariffs until such time as the goods are released into the stream of commerce in the United States.

FTZs are operated by state or local governments, airports or seaports, or specially chartered corporations who charge private firms for their use. Originally, FTZs were intended to encourage U.S. firms to participate in international trade by providing a "free port" into which foreign-made goods could be transported, stored, packaged, and then reexported without the payment of import duties. Today, FTZs are used for many different purposes, ranging from warehousing to actual manufacturing. The length of time that these goods can be held in a zone is not limited.

The flexibility offered to an importer through the use of FTZs provides many opportunities for creative importing strategies. For example, firms can ship goods to their zone duty-free and hold them for later entry and sale in the United States pending buyer's orders or more favorable market conditions. Foreign goods can also be held for exhibition and display in the zone for unlimited periods without the payment of duties. Foreign goods that arrive damaged or defective may be destroyed without the payment of duties. Goods in an FTZ are not subject to quotas, and may remain in the FTZ until the quota opens and their entry is permitted. Title to goods held in an FTZ may be transferred to another party without the payment

of duties (although not to a retail customer for consumption outside of the FTZ). Other permitted activites include cleaning, relabeling, repackaging, or testing goods. Opportunities for creative business planning are almost endless. For instance, in certain cases it is possible that foreign component parts can be assembled in an FTZ, and the duties payable when the finished product is sold are less than what the duties would have been on the individual components. As another example, if a commodity is duted by weight, it may be brought into an FTZ for drying and may be entered without the excess weight caused by the moisture. But perhaps the most unusual use of an FTZ is the Cape Canaveral Zone in Florida. There, foreign payloads can be imported into the United States, processed and made ready for a space launch, and "exported" to space without the payment of U.S. import duties! Over two hundred general purpose foreign trade zones and more than two hundred and fifty subzones exist in the United States.

In addition to general purpose zones, firms are able to establish their own special purpose *subzones*. Subzones can be placed anywhere in the United States with U.S. Customs approval. Most automotive manufacturers and oil refineries use subzones. They are also widely used in chemicals, pharmaceuticals, computer assembly, electronics, shipbuilding, and as retail distribution centers. The following case arose out of Nissan's importation of equipment into an automotive manufacturing subzone in Tennessee.

Nissan Motor Mfg. Corp., U.S.A. v. United States
884 F.2d 1375 (1989)
United States Court of Appeals (Fed. Cir.)

BACKGROUND AND FACTS
Nissan operates a foreign trade zone subzone at its automotive manufacturing and assembly plant located in Smyrna, Tennessee. Nissan imported production machinery for use in the subzone consisting of industrial robots, automated conveyor systems, and a computerized interface. The machinery was to be assembled and tested in the zone, and if it proved unsatisfactory it was to be replaced, redesigned, or scrapped. Customs ruled that production equipment was not "merchandise" as

defined under the FTZ act and was therefore dutiable. Duties were liquidated at $3 million and Nissan filed a protest. On denial, the Court of International Trade ruled that the equipment was dutiable and this appeal was filed.

CIRCUIT JUDGE ARCHER
The activities performed by Nissan in the foreign trade zone subzone with the imported equipment are not among those permitted by a plain reading of the

continued

continued

statute. Section 81c provides that merchandise brought into a foreign trade zone may be "stored, sold, exhibited, broken up, repacked, assembled, distributed, sorted, graded, cleaned, mixed with foreign or domestic merchandise, or otherwise manipulated, or be manufactured. . . ."

The act does not say that imported equipment may be "installed," "used," "operated" or "consumed" in the zone, which are the kinds of operations Nissan performs in the zone with the subject equipment. Alternative operations of a different character should not be implied when Congress has made so exhaustive a list.

Nissan relies upon the case of *Hawaiian Indep. Refinery v. United States*, 460 F. Supp. 1249 (Cust. Ct. 1978), in support of its position. The merchandise there involved was crude oil which was entered into a foreign trade zone for manufacture into fuel oil products. This, of course, is an activity delineated by the act and entry into the zone was exempted from Customs duties. Thereafter, a portion of the crude oil was consumed in the manufacturing process and Customs assessed duty on the theory that there had been a "constructive" entry into the Customs territory of the United States. In holding that the assessment was improper, the Court

of International Trade did not have to deal with the question at issue here of whether the initial entry into the zone was exempt. Clearly, in that case the crude oil was exempt at the time of entry. Thus, the Court of International Trade properly concluded that the *Hawaiian Indep. Refinery* case was not dispositive of this case.

We are convinced that the Court of International Trade correctly determined that the importation by Nissan of the machinery and capital equipment at issue into the foreign trade zone subzone was not for the purpose of being manipulated in one of the ways prescribed by the statute. Instead it was to be used (consumed) in the subzone for the production of motor vehicles. Under the plain language of the 1950 amendment to the act and the legislative history of that amendment, and Customs' published decision interpreting the act as amended, such a use does not entitle the equipment to exemption from Customs duties. Accordingly, the judgment of the Court of International Trade is affirmed.

Decision.   The decision of the lower court is affirmed. Machinery entered into a foreign trade zone for use in the manufacture and assembly of automobiles is not "merchandise" under the act and may not be entered duty-free.

Chapter Summary

The Bureau of Customs and Border Protection, formerly the U.S. Customs Service, is a part of the Department of Homeland Security. It is responsible for securing America's borders from terrorist threat, interdicting contraband and narcotics smuggling, collecting tariff revenue, enforcing the customs and tariff laws of the United States, and enforcing the export control laws.

The entry process is used to determine the dutiable status of goods. Information needed by Customs to enter goods is obtained from the commercial invoice and other required documents. Importers are required to maintain proper business records of all customs transactions. Enforcement actions and penalties can be severe for violating customs laws, depending on whether it was done negligently or intentionally. The concept of informed compliance means that importers must use reasonable care in handling entries, and either must be adequately trained or should rely on trained professionals.

Customs issues binding ruling letters applicable only to the importer and transaction to which it is addressed. When courts review Customs' letters and other informal rulings, they will defer to Customs' decisions when the ruling is persuasive and in accordance with law. Formal regulations are granted a higher degree of deference by the courts.

The dutiable status of goods is determined by classification, valuation, and country-of-origin. Many protests are filed with Customs over these issues. In many countries, including the United States, goods are classified according to the *Harmonized Tariff Schedules*. All importers must know how to research their products in the schedules to find the applicable rate of duty. Determining the country-of-origin requires understanding complex "rules of origin." These rules are different for general merchandise imports into the United States, imports from within North America, imports from developing countries, and textile imports. The WTO is working to develop uniform rules of origin. Goods must be marked with the country-of-origin for the ultimate purchaser to see. For goods subject to assembly or manufacturing in more than one country, the country-of-origin for marking purposes is where the goods last underwent a substantial transformation so as to become a new product with a new "name, character, or use."

The United States grants trade preferences to goods from developing countries, and maintains special programs to encourage trade with the Caribbean, Andean, and African countries. These programs not only encourage imports from these countries, but also indirectly promote U.S. investment there. Businesses can plan their operations in ways that take advantage of these and other duty reducing mechanisms in the customs laws, including drawbacks and the use of foreign trade zones.

Most importantly, importers must plan their business strategies to take advantage of opportunities in the customs laws. Multinational companies must also coordinate import strategies with their manufacturing, assembly, and other operations. Customs laws in the United States and elsewhere, like tax or labor laws, will affect where multinationals build their plants, where they source their materials or component parts, how they move goods from country to country, and how they structure their overall global operations. Careful customs planning is essential to the success of any international business plan.

Questions and Case Problems

1. Acquaint yourself with the Web site for the Bureau of Customs and Border Protection, http://www.cbp.gov. What resources does it contain for the trade community?

   a. The *Customs Rulings Online Search System* (CROSS) is a searchable database of about 100,000 ruling letters. Try your hand at locating rulings on some of the issues discussed in this chapter. For example, enter "country origin" together with the name of a product or class of products and see what you can find. Remember, these letters are binding only for the individual to whom they are written and only for that transaction. But they are interesting and helpful to importers that use this service frequently.

   b. Go to the *Legal* section and look at the *Customs' Bulletins and Decisions*. This is a weekly diary of all official acts of the agency. What type of information does it contain, and who might want to follow this on a regular basis?

   c. Go to the *Import* section, and look at the *Container Security Initiative*. Six million ocean containers enter U.S. ports every year. Only a tiny fraction can be inspected by hand. Any one of them could be used to hide a weapon of mass destruction. Look at the *Customs-Trade Partnership Against Terrorism* (C-TPAT), a process for enhancing security between U.S. importers and their foreign supply chains. How do you think the threat of terrorism and Customs' security programs will affect global transportation in the years to come? What is Customs' "24-hour rule" for loading cargo aboard ships destined for the United States?

2. Acquaint yourself with the *Harmonized Tariff Schedules of the United States*. Be sure that you understand how products and commodities are arranged in the schedules, and that you know how to use the schedules. The schedules are maintained by the U.S. International Trade Commission and can be found at http://dataweb.usitc.gov or through a link on the Customs' site. Be sure to find the full legal text, by chapter. The schedules will appear in a "pop-up" box using PDF format files (Adobe Reader© required).

   a. Know how to use the *General Rules of Interpretation* and the *General Notes*.

   b. Which countries receive GSP tariff preference treatment?

   c. Which countries qualify for duty-free treatment as "least developed beneficiary developing countries?"

   d. Which countries qualify for the *Andean Trade Preference Act*? The *African Growth and Opportunity Act* preferences?

   e. A good portion of the schedule is devoted to the dutiable status of goods moving in North America. NAFTA is the subject of the next chapter. Can you locate the NAFTA rules of origin, known as the "tariff shift" rules, in the schedules?

   f. Choose several products with which you are familiar, and attempt to classify them using the schedules.

3. The primary body of U.S. Customs law is found in Title 19 of the *United States Code*. The regulations are found in the *Code of Federal Regulations*. You can access the CFR either through Customs' Web site, through Cornell University's site, http://cfr.law.cornell.edu/cfr, or

through the Government Printing Office site, http://www.access.gpo.gov/nara/cfr. Can you find Customs' recordkeeping rules? What are the rules for filing a protest with U.S. Customs? Can you find the rules of origin, including those for textile imports?

4. Inner Secrets entered 2,000 dozen boxer-style shorts from Hong Kong. The boxer shorts are made of cotton flannel in a plaid pattern, with a waistband that is not enclosed or turned over, a side length of 17 inches, and two small nonfunctional buttons on the waistband above the fly. Two seams have been sewn horizontally across the fly, dividing the fly opening into thirds. The boxers do not have belt loops, inner or outer pockets or pouches, or button or zipper fly closures. They are marketed under the label "No Excuses." Customs classified the garments as outerwear shorts under HTSUS 6204.62.4055: "Women's or girls' suits, ensembles, suit-type jackets and blazers, dresses, skirts, divided skirts, trousers, bib and brace overalls, breeches and shorts. . . . Trousers, bib and brace overalls, breeches and shorts . . . of cotton . . . 17.7%. The Customs Service based its decision on its determination that the boxers will be worn by women as outer clothing. Inner Secrets maintains that the items are not outerwear, as Customs claims, but are actually *underwear* properly classified under HTSUS 6208.91.3010: "Women's or girls' singlets and other undershirts, slips, petticoats, briefs, panties, nightdresses, pajamas, negligees, bathrobes, dressing gowns and similar articles . . . of cotton . . . 11.9%." Inner Secrets filed a protest with the agency, which was denied. Inner Secrets brought this action with the Court of International Trade. What is the proper classification of the boxers? How would a camisole worn under a sport jacket or a slip worn as a dress be classified? *Inner Secrets v. United States,* 885 F. Supp. 248 (CIT 1995). *See also, St. Eve International v. United States,* 267 F. Supp. 1371 (CIT 2003).

5. Sports Graphics imported soft-sided "Chill" coolers from Taiwan. The coolers consist of an outer shell of a vinyl-coated nylon material; an insulating core of approximately 1/2-inch-thick polymer-based closed cell foam; a top secured by a zippered interlocking flap; an inner liner of vinyl; a handle or shoulder strap of nylon webbing and plastic fixtures as a means of carrying the merchandise; and exterior pockets secured by VELCRO or zippered closures. Customs classified the merchandise under the luggage provision, which included "Trunks . . . satchels, suitcases, overnight bags, traveling bags, knapsacks, and like articles designed to contain . . . personal effects during travel . . . and brief cases, golf bags, and like containers and cases designed to be carried with the person. . . . Luggage and handbags, whether or not fitted with bottle, dining, drinking . . . or similar sets . . . and flat goods . . . of laminated plastics . . ." at a 20 percent rate of duty. Sports Graphics contended that the imported soft-sided coolers were properly classifiable as "Articles chiefly used for preparing, serving, or storing food or beverages" at a rate of 4 or 3.4 percent *ad valorem.* What is the proper classification? Does the use of this product have a bearing on its classification? *Sports Graphics, Inc. v. United States,* 24 F.3d 1390 (Fed. Cir. 1994).

6. It is post-September 11th America and the spirit to buy American-made products is high. You enter a large, mass merchandising retail store in your home town. As you walk down the aisles of clothing, you spy small American flags proudly displayed atop every circular rack of shirts and jackets. You purchase a jacket and take it home, feeling good about your decision. Later, to your surprise, you notice that the jacket is labeled "Made in China." Actually, you had never really thought much about where the jacket was made. Do you feel that the store management should not have allowed the flags to fly in such close proximity to the clothing or was it just a patriotic gesture? What is your attitude toward purchasing foreign-made products? What do you think the attitude is of most Americans? In 2003, there was wide talk about boycotting French products because of the French lack of support for the U.S. war in Iraq. Do you think consumer boycotts are generally successful?

Managerial Implications

Your firm is one of the last remaining manufacturers of bicycles in the United States. Z-Mart is a U.S. retail chain with nearly 1,000 stores in fifteen countries. Z-Mart has asked you to prepare a proposal for a large number of bicycles to be sold at discount prices under the Z-Mart brand name. They must have a U.S. retail price of no more than $100. Z-Mart would also like to sell these bikes through its stores in France and Italy in order to compete with the European bikes made in that market. You begin to analyze your costs of materials and production. The first step of production is the sourcing of a tubular frame, a major component. You can purchase the bare frames in the United States, Canada, or Taiwan. You must clean and paint the frames before assembly. The high-performance wheels, another major component, are made from an aluminum alloy. The aluminum is made in Japan and shipped in the form of strips and rods to the Philippines, where it is cut into lengths, molded into wheel parts, and assembled. They will arrive at your plant covered in a film of oil to protect them during shipping. The tires are available from companies in Japan or Brazil. Most of the component parts, such as brakes, gears, and chains, are available directly from firms in the United States and Canada.

At a meeting of management, you are asked to prepare a plan for the production of the bicycles that will price them for Z-Mart's discount stores. In doing so, you must give consideration to the following questions. (You may make certain assumptions as to the relative costs of materials and labor if necessary.)

1. Explain how U.S. trade and tariff laws would affect your plans for bicycle production. What influence would U.S. tariff preference laws have on the sourcing of component parts? Explain how the rules-of-origin might affect the importation of the tubular frame. Would NAFTA have any impact on how you structure your operations?

2. What factors would be taken into consideration in determining where to assemble the finished bicycles? In the United States? In Taiwan? In the Philippines? You have heard that U.S. automakers are assembling cars in Mexico using workers that are paid about $10 a day. What factors would influence your decision to assemble in Mexico? What processes could you do or not do in Mexico in order to obtain the most favorable tariff treatment? What are the advantages and disadvantages of assembling there?

3. Evaluate the potential for using a foreign trade zone. What advantages or disadvantages would your firm experience in this case?

4. Determine the applicability of U.S. marking and labeling requirements with regard to the finished bicycles sold in the United States.

CHAPTER 13

NORTH AMERICAN FREE TRADE LAW

Up to this point, this text has discussed international trade law, including the basic principles of GATT law and the WTO, laws regulating import competition and unfair trade, and laws governing access to foreign markets. It has examined how the growth of free trade principles, or trade liberalization, has led to increased trade in goods and services, and an improved quality of life for people around the world. The preceding few chapters have focused on trade liberalization at the global level, through GATT and the WTO. Yet, GATT clearly encourages countries to cooperate on trade liberalization at the regional level as well. The European countries, over a period spanning fifty years, reduced barriers to trade, investment, and the free movement of people, money, information, and technology. What began in the 1950s as the "European Common Market," later became the European Economic Community, and today the EU. As the name changes signify, each step along the way increased the economic and social ties between European countries.

GATT recognizes the formation of regional free trade blocs despite an apparent conflict between regionalism and multilateralism. GATT Article 24 states that "[T]he provisions of the Agreement shall not prevent . . . the formation of a customs union or of a free trade area." These trading blocs allow members to grant each other even more favorable trade terms than those granted to WTO members with whom they have normal trade relations. Of course, GATT cautions that "the purpose of a customs union or of a free trade area should be to facilitate trade between the constituent territories and not to raise barriers to the trade of other [WTO member countries]." The WTO has the authority to deal with conflicts and complaints that regional groups have become too protectionist.

This chapter examines how Canada, Mexico, and the United States have formed a regional trading bloc in North America. These countries share trade privileges with each other beyond what is required by GATT or the WTO. For instance, although Canada might impose a 15 percent import duty on a certain product coming from another WTO country, it may admit similar products from the United States or Mexico at a lower tariff rate, or for no tariff at all. Thus, the world of doing business is greatly affected not only by global trading rules, but by regional rules as well. The trading bloc between Canada, Mexico, and the United States is known as the *North American Free Trade Area*. The purpose of the North American Free Trade Area is to spur trade and investment in North America, and to improve the standard of living throughout the continent. Later in the chapter we will see that the three countries have not just agreed on important trade issues. They also have created mechanisms to protect the North American environment, improve working conditions for laborers and promote "cross-border" investments.

> **http://www.dfait-maeci.gc.ca**
> Canadian Department of Foreign Affairs and International Trade Web site.

THE NORTH AMERICAN FREE TRADE AREA

Canada, Mexico, and the United States each have separate economic and political systems as well as different cultures, geographies, and climates. Nevertheless, the three countries have a long history of close trading relations. Together, they encompass the largest free trade area in the world, with a market of over 425 million people and a combined gross domestic product of over $11 trillion. (References to dollars in this chapter refer to U.S. dollars, or their equivalent.) Canada and the United States are far more similar to each other than to their southern neighbor. They are in advanced stages of economic development, with comparable levels of productivity and *per capita* gross domestic product. One of the reasons that it has been easy to integrate the U.S.–Canadian market is that their economies are so much alike. Mexico, on the other hand, is a developing country with a *per capita* GDP that is one-fifth that of the United States, and with an unequal distribution of income (20 percent of the population accounts for 55 percent of the income). Also, Mexico has had a history of greater government control over industry, higher tariffs, and greater barriers to foreign investment than has either the United States or Canada.

Canada–U.S. Trade. Canada and the United States are each other's largest trading partner, with two-way trade totaling $371 billion in 2002—over one billion dollars a day. Many people are surprised to learn that the United States actually exports more goods to Canada ($160 billion in 2002) than to all the countries of the EU combined, and more than three times as much as to Japan. From 1993 to 1999, U.S. exports to Canada increased 60 percent, while U.S exports to the entire world increased by only 49 percent during the same period. The United States purchased slightly more from Canada in 2002 ($210 billion) than from all the EU countries combined, and more than from any other single country, with China and Japan about tied for second. Of Canada's total imports, about 65 percent come from the United States. Canada has a population of 32 million (compared to 290 million in the United States).

Mexico–U.S. Trade. Since 1993, the date that Mexico entered into the North American Free Trade Area with the United States and Canada, U.S. trade with Mexico has grown faster than it has with any other country. From 1993 to 1999, trade between the two countries doubled, although

it decreased somewhat by 2002. Mexico has taken the lead over Japan as the United States' number two trading partner, with total two-way trade of $232 billion in 2002. In 2000, the United States accounted for 88 percent of Mexico's exports and provided 73 percent of Mexico's imports. The United States exports more goods and services to Mexico than it does to all other countries in Latin America combined. In 2002, the United States sold $97 billion to Mexico and imported $134 billion. Mexico's entrance into the North American Free Trade Area has clearly boosted its export and import trade. From 1993 to 1999, Mexico's exports to the United States increased by 237 percent. Most Mexican products enter the United States duty free or at a very low tariff rate. Over 80 percent of U.S. goods enter Mexico duty free. Mexico offers U.S. firms low production costs, plentiful labor, easy transportation to the U.S. market, employees who respect and want to work for U.S. firms, and consumers that respect U.S. product brand names. Mexico's population is 105 million people, with almost three-quarters living in urban areas.

---

http://www.cbo.gov
For a 2003 report by the Congressional Budget Office on *The Effects of NAFTA on U.S.–Mexican Trade and GDP*, link to "Publications."

For many decades, Mexico had a tightly controlled and protected economy. Its policies restricted imports and discouraged foreign investment. Many key industries were (and some remain) in the hands of government-owned monopolies. Foreign companies that wanted to do business there have had to break through a mass of government bureaucracy, red tape, trade barriers, corruption, and an outdated highway, transportation, and telecommunications infrastructure. Hampered by inefficient industries, Mexico during the 1970s and early 1980s suffered low productivity, staggering rates of inflation (as high as several hundred percent a year), and overwhelming foreign debt. Its foreign income was almost totally dependent on exports of oil and petroleum products. New government policies in the late 1980s and 1990s opened the Mexican economy to trade and investment. In 2000, Mexico announced that it had signed a trade agreement with the EU allowing European products to enter Mexico at reduced tariff rates. Privatization and deregulation also continued into this decade. Railroads, airports, natural gas transportation, telephone companies, banks, and power generation have all benefited from privatization. Benefiting from an influx of foreign capital, technology, and management skills, Mexican companies have become far more efficient than before. Mexican-made products have improved in quality and are now competitive in world markets. By 2000, inflation was down to the single-digit range and unemployment was at an all time low. As a result, Mexico has become less dependent on oil exports and now has a broader based economy. It is safe to say that much of Mexico's economic success since 1993 has been attributable to political and economic reform and to factors other than just NAFTA.

The United States has considerable cross-border investment in both Canada and Mexico. Some of this has been fostered by NAFTA. The largest U.S. investors in those countries are GM, Ford, and Daimler-Chrysler, followed by a host of companies in the oil industry, computers, supermarkets, fast-food and other franchising, telecommunications, pharmaceuticals, retailing, and beverages.

---

http://www.usmcoc.org/
United States–Mexico Chamber of Commerce (Cámara de Comercio México–Estados Unidos) Web site.

What Is NAFTA?

The North American Free Trade Area was created on January 1, 1994, by the *North American Free Trade Agreement,* both of which are called NAFTA. A *free trade area* is a group of two or more sovereign countries in which import duties and other trade barriers are reduced or eliminated. NAFTA is not a customs union or common market, as is the EU. A *customs union* is a free trade area with a common external tariff; the EU goes beyond a free trade area with its common economic and agricultural policies. On trade issues, the EU deals with other countries as outsiders, and represents its members in trade negotiations at the WTO. NAFTA does not. NAFTA fosters trade and investment between Canada, Mexico, and the United States by reducing tariffs and nontariff barriers. It also facilitates trans-

portation of goods, provision of services, and financial transactions between the three countries. Each country will generally continue to maintain its own tariff rates and quotas on imports from outside the area. (Actually, NAFTA countries have agreed to adopt a common external tariff on certain computer parts after 2004, but NAFTA is still not considered a customs union.) Each country will continue to establish its own economic policies and each country will represent itself in the WTO system.

---

www.nafta-sec-alena.org
Home page of the NAFTA Secretariat.

Survey of NAFTA's Coverage. Historically, trade agreements focused on the lowering of tariffs, but NAFTA is a trade agreement that does more than just eliminate duties between Canada, Mexico, and the United States. It liberalizes trade in goods, trade in services, cross-border investments, and more. It also addresses many regional issues that are of concern to the three countries. For instance, it contains specific provisions for protecting intellectual property rights. It makes cross-border investment easier, and serves to protect the interests of foreign investors from arbitrary government action. It allows easier access for commercial trucks and for business travel between the countries. NAFTA encourages cooperation between governments on setting antitrust policy (called *competition law* in many countries) to deal with monopolies and unfair methods of competition. NAFTA also has provisions concerning worker safety, child labor, and environmental protection. Thus, NAFTA is far broader in scope than most typical trade or investment agreements. Only the EU treaties and perhaps GATT are as broad in scope as NAFTA.

How NAFTA Came into Being. NAFTA was built upon the *U.S.–Canada Free Trade Agreement* (CFTA), which had been in effect since January 1, 1989. CFTA called for the gradual reduction of tariffs over a ten-year period and loosened restrictions on investment, government procurement, travel, and many other areas. CFTA also created a U.S.–Canadian Trade Commission and dispute settlement panels to settle trade disputes.

Regional versus Global Trade Liberalization. A major criticism raised against NAFTA, and equally applicable to any free trade area, is that it divides the world into regional trading blocs. Some people and nations fear that regional protectionism will threaten GATT's global trade liberalization achievements. Despite GATT's qualification that free trade areas not be used as a barrier to trade, goods not produced in the area will be discriminated against. An illustration can be found in the Caribbean countries who depend on the North American market for their exports. Caribbean countries feared that their industries would move their operations to Mexico to take advantage of NAFTA. (Actually, we saw in the last chapter that the United States now permits many Caribbean products to enter at very near "NAFTA parity.") Interestingly enough, Japanese firms are apparently concerned about the same issue. Press reports in *The Journal of Commerce* and elsewhere indicate that a number of Japanese firms have already built facilities in Mexico, rather than in other Asian countries such as Thailand, in order to take advantage of NAFTA tariff rates, Mexico's low wage rates, and its close proximity to the U.S. and Canadian markets.

---

http://www.ftaa-alca.org
Official page of the Free Trade Area of the Americas that follows the progress of FTAA negotiations.

Free Trade Area of the Americas. Since 1994, thirty-four countries of the Western Hemisphere have been negotiating the *Free Trade Area of the Americas* (FTAA). This is an attempt to expand NAFTA by integrating the economies of the Western Hemisphere into a single free trade area of 800 million people and $13 trillion. In 2003, President Bush said that he hoped the agreement would be completed by 2005. There are nine negotiating groups that are developing rules for reducing tariffs and trade barriers dealing with trade in goods and services, agriculture, intellectual property, market access, customs procedures, dispute settlement, and other areas.

It is hoped that most U.S. imports from the Western Hemisphere would be duty free immediately when the FTAA becomes effective. All duties would be eliminated by 2015. In some important industries, such as electrical products, information technology, and steel and wood products, duties may be eliminated immediately. One of the biggest

issues is agricultural trade, as countries tend to protect their own farming interests. U.S. imports of textiles and apparel may possibly become duty free in just a few years, provided other countries do the same. Cross-border services, investment, and government procurement would also be covered. Given that many Latin American products already enter the United States duty free, or at very low rates, it would seem that the FTAA would be a great boon to U.S. exporters that generally face tariff rates there that are as much as five times higher than American tariffs.

Of course, it is not known whether the FTAA will ever become a reality or what its provisions might be. But the impact on international trade and investment in the Western Hemisphere would be tremendous. For this reason, we mention the prospects of the FTAA early in this chapter.

Survey of Trade and Tariff Provisions

To a certain extent, NAFTA's trade and tariff provisions pattern the GATT agreements. Many principles are similar, including national treatment, nondiscrimination, tariff reduction, and elimination of nontariff barriers. NAFTA set out a period of fifteen years for the gradual phasing out of tariffs on goods that originated in North America. That period will end in 2008. However, as of 2003, nontariff barriers and tariffs on most products had already ended. But NAFTA tariff preferences only apply if the goods are of North American origin, and, as we will see in the next section, this requires that you learn how to use the complex rules of origin.

---

http://www.cbsa-asfc.gc.ca/nafta/
The Canada Border Services Agency, NAFTA page. Canada's new customs agency was created after 2001 to enhance security.

National Treatment. NAFTA's *national treatment* principle is similar to that found in GATT. It states that once goods arrive from another NAFTA country, they must be treated without discrimination and no differently than domestically made goods. So, if the United States imports taco shells from Mexico, it cannot require that only Mexican-made taco shells contain 90 percent cornmeal without setting the same standard for U.S.-made taco shells. Of course, the rule has wide application to all U.S. laws, regulations, and taxes. This provision also applies to regulations of individual U.S. states and Canadian provinces.

Tariff Elimination.   When NAFTA became effective in 1993, it eliminated many tariffs on North American goods immediately. By 2003, almost 90 percent of all tariffs were eliminated. Canadian tariffs on U.S. products were eliminated in 1998. The remaining tariffs average less than 1 percent and are scheduled to be phased out by 2008.

Elimination of Nontariff Barriers.   Most quotas, import licenses, and other barriers are being eliminated. Of course, each country may impose import restrictions to protect human, animal, or plant life, or the environment. Other special rules permit greater restrictions in key economic sectors, including automobiles, agriculture, energy, and textiles.

NAFTA prohibits new *export taxes* on goods, unless the taxes are also applied to similar goods sold for domestic consumption. *Customs user fees*—fees imposed on importers to help fund the cost of customs enforcement and port services—were eliminated by 1999. NAFTA also addresses issues related to customs administration, the public disclosure of customs regulations, fairness-in-labeling requirements for products, and other barriers to trade. Mexico does require that all entries valued at more than $2,000 be handled by a Mexican Customs broker.

Continuing   Nontariff   Barriers.   Mexico, Canada, and the United States have all been accused of maintaining nontariff barriers despite NAFTA. Mexico has still found other ways to block or slow down U.S. imports. It has imposed antidumping duties and safeguards on agriculture and chemical products. It employs customs procedures that are not completely transparent and that are unduly burdensome. U.S firms complain that regulations change without notice and are applied unfairly toward Americans. Some types of goods can only be entered through certain ports. Goods with counterfeit U.S. trademarks easily pass into Mexico without inspection at the border. Mexico has used the sanitary and phytosanitary provisions to keep out U.S. farm products, even when health and safety was not at stake. For instance, it imposed agricultural inspections at the border, instead of in the United States at the time of packing, resulting in long delays. Some shipments were turned back at the border for mere typographical errors. In 2003, the USTR maintained that Mexico had indirectly imposed a higher rate of income tax on Mexican retailers that sold imported goods.

Similarly, according to the *2003 National Trade Estimate Report*, prepared by the USTR, the United States maintains that Canada protects its dairy farmers and subsidizes their exports. Canada has raised tariffs on cheese snack foods (to 245 percent!) and has banned the use of food coloring in margarine and dairy substitutes. According to the report, the Canadian government has kept out U.S. breakfast cereals by prohibiting foods fortified with vitamins and minerals. For instance, orange juice with calcium added is considered a drug. Many U.S. foods become more expensive in Canada because U.S. manufacturers must prepare them especially for the Canadian market. The Canadian government continues to restrict U.S. content in broadcasting media. Broadcasters must still have at least 50 percent Canadian content. Thirty-five percent of music on the radio must be Canadian. There are restrictions on U.S. films that can be shown on certain Canadian stations, and foreign investment in the movie and film industry is largely prohibited or highly regulated. In many cases, Canada claims that it is just responding to U.S. barriers on Canadian products. These are just examples of trade problems that continue despite NAFTA.

RULES OF ORIGIN

NAFTA tariff rates apply only to products that are really products of Canada, Mexico, or the United States. A foreign product cannot simply be channeled through one North American country for sale in another North American country to avoid the payment of duties. For example, European or Asian products cannot be brought into Canada and then imported duty free into the United States as a product of Canada. In order to know which products qualify for NAFTA's duty-free treatment, one will have to consult the applicable rule of origin.

Rules of origin were introduced in the last chapter and are a critical issue to importers and exporters. This is the only way to determine the rate of duty or even quotas that might apply to the product being bought or sold.

Only goods that qualify under NAFTA's rules of origin can obtain NAFTA tariff rates. The most important general rules are (1) the goods are *wholly produced or obtained* in Canada, Mexico, or the United States; and (2) the goods contain nonoriginating inputs (components or raw materials), but meet the Annex 401 tariff-shift rule of origin.

Goods Wholly Produced or Obtained in North America

NAFTA applies to goods wholly produced or obtained in North America. These goods may not contain any non-North American parts or materials. NAFTA Article 415 states that the qualifications apply only to minerals mined in North America, vegetables grown in North America, live animals born and raised in North America, fish and fish products, waste, and scrap derived from production in North America. "Produced or obtained" does not mean "purchased." The definition also includes goods produced in North America *exclusively* from the raw materials just mentioned. Thus, NAFTA applies to coal mined in Tennessee, lead mined in Canada, cotton grown in Mississippi, and cattle born in Mexico and raised in Mexico or Texas. It also includes silver jewelry made in Arizona from silver mined in Mexico or taco shells made in Mexico entirely from corn grown in Iowa. The producer, however, must be able to trace *all inputs to raw materials mined, grown, or born in North America.*

Annex 401 Tariff-Shift Rule of Origin

Chapter Twelve discussed the *substantial-transformation test* that is used to determine the country-of-origin of goods imported into the United States when the goods are produced or assembled in more than one country. This test is difficult to apply, and different courts often come up with different results. The variation in court decisions leads to great uncertainty in applying the test to any given case and complicates importers' sourcing decisions. NAFTA avoids this problem by setting out a simpler rule for when a foreign or non-North American product is "transformed" into a product of North America. NAFTA substitutes a tariff classification change for the vague substantial-transformation test. When non-North American goods or materials are brought into a NAFTA country, they can be transformed into a product of North America as long as each non-North American input undergoes a tariff classification change as specified in NAFTA Annex 401. The Annex 401 rules of origin may be based on either a *change in tariff classification,* a *regional value-content requirement,* or both, depending on the requirements for that particular product. This is known as the *tariff-shift* rule. Annex 401 rules can be found in the *General Notes* of the *Harmonized Tariff Schedules.*

Changes in Tariff Classification.   To know if a product imported into the United States has undergone a change in tariff classification, you must refer to the *General Notes* found at the beginning of the *Harmonized Tariff Schedules* of the United States. These are based on the principles in Annex 401. The following example demonstrates how a product's tariff classification can change.

The harmonized system breaks down product classifications into ten digits, as described earlier in Chapter Twelve. Countries that have adopted the HTS system have "harmonized" their classification of products internationally at the subheading level. After the first six digits, each country assigns its own numbers. For example, a down-filled comforter (HTS 9404.90.85) is classified in Chapter 94 (which covers a conglomerate of unrelated manufactured articles, including furniture), heading 9404 (covering bedding and similar furnishings, stuffed), subheading 9404.90 (other than sleeping bags), and tariff item 9404.90.85 (down-filled comforters).

To determine the import duty on a North American product, you must know the product's tariff classification at the subheading level. Imagine that you are in the business of making goose down comforters in the United States and Canada. You import unfilled cotton comforter shells from China and goose down fill from Europe. You want to know the U.S. rate of duty on the finished down comforters made at your Canadian plant. You also want to know the correct country-of-origin label to put on the comforter. So, you consult the U.S. HTS. Your main "non-originating inputs" are the European down (subheading 0505.10), and the cotton shell (subheading 6307.90). You also know that the finished comforter is classified under subheading 9404.90. You find the *General Notes* that contain the NAFTA tariff-shift rules, and read the following:

> A change to subheading 9404.90 from any other chapter, except from headings 5007, 5111 through 5113, 5208 through 5212, 5408 through 5408 or 5512 through 5516.

Because the non-originating components, the down fill, and the unfilled shell are not in Chapter 94, and are not within any of the exceptions specified, they qualify as having undergone a tariff-shift when they are changed to subheading 9494.90. Thus, we have learned that the finished down comforter may be assembled in Canada and shipped to the United States under the rate for Canadian-made comforters and are not subject to any quotas on comforters of Chinese origin (and if we do a little more research we would learn that the comforter can be labeled "Made in Canada"). But suppose we had instead imported Chinese-made cotton fabric and sewed it into an unfilled shell in Canada, filled it with down, and shipped it to the United States. Ironically, the fabric itself falls within subheading 5208 through 5212, and according to the exceptions to the above rule would *not* amount to a qualified tariff-shift.

Consider pastries that are made in Canada for shipment to the United States. Pastries, breads, cakes, and biscuits fall under subheading 1905.90. Assume their only non-North American input is flour imported from Europe. The rule of origin for pastries in heading 1905 states that the item will be treated as a North American product if it undergoes "A change to heading 1905 from any other chapter." The pastries would qualify for NAFTA tariff treatment because the European-made flour was classified outside of HTS Chapter 19. However, the baker must be careful. If the pastries had been made from a prepared mix (containing flour, shortening, sugar, baking powder, etc.), they would not qualify as a North American product because mixes are classified under Chapter 19, the same chapter as the pastries themselves.

Regional Value Content Requirement.   For most products undergoing a transformation in North America, the rule of origin will be based on its tariff classification. In limited cases, NAFTA requires a specified amount of *regional value content* (a similar rule is used for trade in automobiles and parts). For example, a rule might require that at least 50 percent of the value of a finished product be North American. Regional value may be calculated either by *transaction value* or *net cost* methods. Transaction value is the price actually paid for a good. The net cost method removes sales and marketing costs, shipping costs, and certain other expenses from the calculation. The value of non-North American materials is then subtracted from the total cost of the product. Usually the regional value content must be at least 60 percent for transaction value method and at least 50 percent for the net cost method. The value of packaging materials and containers in which a product is packaged for retail sale must be taken into account as either North American or non-North American materials, as the case may be.

Transaction Value Formula

$$RVC = \frac{TV - VNM}{TV} \times 100$$

Net Cost Formula

$$RVC = \frac{NC - VNM}{NC} \times 100$$

RVC = Percent regional value content

TV = Transaction value of good, FOB basis

VNM = Value of nonoriginating material

NC = Net cost of good

The importer may generally choose which method it wants to use. (For an example of the calculations, see Exhibit 13.1.) For automobiles and auto parts, however, only the net cost method may be used.

Goods with Minimal Amounts of Non-North American Materials.   If the amount of non-North American materials in a finished prod-uct is minimal (defined as less than 7 percent of the total cost of the product), the product will still be eligible for NAFTA tariff rates. Thus, if Japanese thread is used to sew together the sleeves on an otherwise 100 percent Mexican-made jacket, and the thread is less than 7 percent of the total cost of the jacket, the finished jacket can be exported to Canada or the United States under NAFTA tariff rates.

EXHIBIT 13.1

Rules of Origin Example

Product: Wooden Furniture (HS # 9403.50)

Non-North American Inputs: Parts of furniture classified in 9403.90

Rule of Origin:

"A change to subheading 9403.10 through 9403.80 from any other chapter; or

A change to subheading 9403.10 through 9403.80 from subheading 9403.90, provided there is a regional value-content of not less than:

a) 60 percent where the transaction value is used, or

b) 50 percent where the net-cost method is used."

Explanation: Wooden furniture can qualify for NAFTA tariff preference under two scenarios—a tariff shift, or a combination of a tariff shift and regional value content requirement.

The first option—the tariff-shift rule—requires that all non-originating inputs be classified outside of HS chapter 94 (furniture and bedding). Since the non-originating inputs (furniture parts) are classified in chapter 94, (subheading 9403.90), then the product cannot qualify based on tariff shift. However, it may still qualify based on the second part of the rule.

The second option has two components—a tariff shift requirement, and a regional value content requirement. The tariff shift requirement is satisfied since the non-originating input (furniture parts) is classified in subheading 9403.90 as specified by the rule. The product must meet its regional value content requirement using the transaction value or the net cost methodology.

Given the following values, furniture qualifies for NAFTA tariff preference using the net cost methodology. The calculation is found below, with the following example.

Producer's Net Cost	$182.00 each (not including shipping, packing royalties, etc.)
Transaction Value	$200.00 each piece
Value of Non-Originating Parts	$90.00

Transaction Value Method

$$\frac{(200-90)}{200} \times 100 = 55$$

Good does not qualify under transaction value method, because it does not have at least 60 percent regional value content.

Net Cost Method

$$\frac{(182-90)}{182} \times 100 = 50.5$$

Good qualifies under net cost regional value requirement because it has at least a 50 percent regional value content.

Source: U.S. Department of Commerce, 1995.

Understanding the Mexican Tariff Schedules

Mexico, like Canada and the United States, has adopted the HTS, which means that the classification of products, up to the six-digit subheading level, will be the same in all three countries. Of course, the tariff rates will be different until such time as they are completely eliminated. U.S. exporters can obtain information on exporting to Mexico from several U.S. government sources, particularly the U.S. Department of Commerce. But the Mexican customs broker representing the importer should be able to provide more information on product classification, tariff rates, required customs documentation, and shipping and warehousing arrangements. Also, as in the United States and Canada, the Mexican customs authorities (the *Administración Especial Jurídica de Ingresos*) issue legally binding rulings on the classification of prod-

ucts. With this in mind, the following example should aid in understanding the Mexican tariff schedules. Assume that the company, DownPillow, Inc., wants to export down comforters or pillows—with 100 percent North American content—to Mexico. The proper HTS classification subheading is 9404.90. Exhibit 13.2 is an excerpt from the Mexican tariff schedule for heading 9404. The product heading and subheadings are on the left, with the description in Spanish. The *Tasa Base* is the base rate for imports. Mexican base tariffs are generally either 5, 10, 15, or 20 percent. It is followed by two columns representing the phase-out tariffs for those products originating in the United States or Canada. The phase-out period is indicated by the codes A, B, B6, or C.

Once the exporter knows that the base rate is 20 percent and the phase-out code is B6 (for U.S. comforters), it can consult the phase-out schedule. DownPillow learns that the 1994 tariff rate was 16

ExHIBIT 13.2				
NAFT Tariff Phase-Out Schedule for Mexico				

Fracción Arancelaria	Descripción	Tasa Base	Productos de EE.UU. (I)	Canadá (II)
94.04	SOMIERES; ARTICULOS DE CAMA Y ARTICULOS SIMILA RES (POR EJEMPLO: COLCHONES, CUBREPIES, EDRE DONES, COJINES, PUFES, ALMOHADAS), CON MUELLES O BIEN RELLENOS O GUARNECIDOS INTERIORMENTE CON CUALQUIER MATERIA, INCLUIDOS LOS DE CAUCHO O DE PLASTICO CELULARES, RECUBIERTOS O NO.			
9404.10	-Somieres.			
9404.10.01	Somieres.	20	A	A
	-Colchones:			
9404.21	—De caucho o plástico celulares, recubiertos o no.			
9404.21.01	Colchones.	20	C	C
9404.21.02	Colchonetas.	20	A	A
9404.29	—De otras materias.			
9404.29.99	De otras materias.	20	C	C
9404.30	—Sacos (bolsas) de dormir.			
9404.30.01	Sacos (bolsas) de dormir.	20	A	A
9404.90	-Los demás.			
9404.90.01	Almohadas, almohadones, cojines.	20	B6	C
9404.90.99	Los demás.	20	B6	C

percent, and that the rate declines in equal amounts until it reaches zero in 1999 (similar charts are used for all codes and base rates; see Exhibit 13.3.)

In addition to the duty, Mexico currently imposes a 10 percent value-added tax for products sold in the border region and 15 percent on products sold in the interior. Mexican customs will not release the goods to the importer unless the broker can produce the receipt showing that the duties are paid. When the bank remits payment to the government, the importer reimburses the broker. Mexico has abolished its import licensing requirements for most U.S. goods.

The NAFTA Certificate of Origin

A NAFTA *certificate of origin,* or CO, (see Exhibit 13.4) is required for all shipments moving between the United States, Canada, and Mexico. It certifies that the goods qualify as having originated in North America for purposes of preferential tariff treatment under NAFTA. COs are not required for noncommercial shipments. COs are required for all *commercial* shipments entering the United States where the total line item value for a good (*not* the total shipment value) is more than $2,500 ($1,000 for Mexico, and $1,600 CAD for Canada). For goods below these values, the invoice must state that the goods qualify as an originating good for purposes of preferential tariff treatment under NAFTA. A CO may cover a single shipment or it may be a *blanket certificate* that covers multiple shipments of identical goods. A CO is not required for temporary imports, such as those sent for repair or servicing.

It is the responsibility of the exporter to provide a CO to the importer. The CO may be prepared by the exporter or by the exporter's customs agent with a written power of attorney. Frequently, the exporter is not the actual producer of the goods (as in cases where the exporter is a distributor or other intermediary). In this case, the exporter may complete and sign the certificate only with knowledge that the goods in fact originated in North America or if the producer has provided a written statement to that effect. An exporter that does not want to disclose the producer's identity to the importer may state that the producer's name is "available to Customs on request" (see field 3, Exhibit 13.4). It is unlawful to prepare or present a CO that is known to be false, inaccurate, or incorrect. If the preparer discovers an error in the certificate, it must be corrected within thirty days, with written notice of the corrections sent to all parties. COs may be completed in the language of either the exporting or importing country.

When completing the CO, follow the rules carefully. U.S Customs Form 434 contains instructions on the reverse side (not reproduced here). Field 7 *(Preference Criterion)* requires a letter code indicating the reason why the goods are entitled to NAFTA treatment (i.e., that they have been "wholly obtained or produced" in North America or that they may meet one of the rules of origin). The form looks simple, but it is not intuitive; use caution in preparing it.

U.S. importers *must be in possession* of an original CO before making entry or claiming the NAFTA tariff rate. If the importer does not have the certificate, the claim will be denied and penalties can be assessed. Faxed copies are accepted as originals. An importer who discovers errors in a certificate must notify Customs in writing within thirty days and pay any additional duties owed as a result. The importer must keep the certificate on file for five years.

Standards and Technical Barriers to Trade

All countries can maintain product regulations to protect public health, consumer safety, the

EXHIBIT 13.3						
Mexican Phase-Out for Textile Products Coded B6 (see tariff schedule to determine code)						
Tasa Base	1994	1995	1996	1997	1998	1999
20%	16%	12.8%	9.6%	6.4%	3.2%	0%

EXHIBIT 13.4

NAFTA Certificate of Origin

DEPARTMENT OF THE TREASURY
UNITED STATES CUSTOMS SERVICE

NORTH AMERICAN FREE TRADE AGREEMENT
CERTIFICATE OF ORIGIN

Please print or type   19 CFR 181.11, 181.22

1. EXPORTER NAME AND ADDRESS	2. BLANKET PERIOD (DD/MM/YY)
	FROM
	TO
TAX IDENTIFICATION NUMBER:	

3. PRODUCER NAME AND ADDRESS	4. IMPORTER NAME AND ADDRESS
TAX IDENTIFICATION NUMBER:	TAX IDENTIFICATION NUMBER:

5. DESCRIPTION OF GOOD(S)	6. HS TARIFF CLASSIFICATION NUMBER	7. PREFERENCE CRITERION	8. PRODUCER	9. NET COST	10. COUNTRY OF ORIGIN

I CERTIFY THAT:

¥ THE INFORMATION ON THIS DOCUMENT IS TRUE AND ACCURATE AND I ASSUME THE RESPONSIBILITY FOR PROVING SUCH REPRESENTATIONS. I UNDERSTAND THAT I AM LIABLE FOR ANY FALSE STATEMENTS OR MATERIAL OMISSIONS MADE ON OR IN CONNECTION WITH THIS DOCUMENT;

¥ I AGREE TO MAINTAIN, AND PRESENT UPON REQUEST, DOCUMENTATION NECESSARY TO SUPPORT THIS CERTIFICATE, AND TO INFORM, IN WRITING, ALL PERSONS TO WHOM THE CERTIFICATE WAS GIVEN OF ANY CHANGES THAT COULD AFFECT THE ACCURACY OR VALIDITY OF THIS CERTIFICATE;

¥ THE GOODS ORIGINATED IN THE TERRITORY OF ONE OR MORE OF THE PARTIES, AND COMPLY WITH THE ORIGIN REQUIREMENTS SPECIFIED FOR THOSE GOODS IN THE NORTH AMERICAN FREE TRADE AGREEMENT, AND UNLESS SPECIFICALLY EXEMPTED IN ARTICLE 411 OR ANNEX 401, THERE HAS BEEN NO FURTHER PRODUCTION OR ANY OTHER OPERATION OUTSIDE THE TERRITORIES OF THE PARTIES; AND

¥ THIS CERTIFICATE CONSISTS OF [   ] PAGES, INCLUDING ALL ATTACHMENTS.

11.	11a. AUTHORIZED SIGNATURE	11b. COMPANY
	11c. NAME (Print or Type)	11d. TITLE
	11e. DATE (DD/MM/YY)	11f. TELEPHONE NUMBER ▷ (Voice) (Facsimile)

Customs Form 434 (12179 3)

environment, and areas of public welfare. However, NAFTA encourages that standards and technical regulations not be used as a nontariff barrier. For instance, Mexico cannot set unnecessary technical regulations and long, drawn-out approval processes for the sale of telecommunications equipment only to discourage entry to the Mexican market by U.S. or Canadian firms. Technical requirements for telecommunications equipment such as telephones may only require that the equipment not harm the telephone network in order to be approved for use or sale. Standards can be set for energy efficiency in appliances, safety in automobiles, or chemical additives in food. NAFTA requires that each country notify the others when the development of a technical regulation or standard begins, give public notice of the proposed regulations, and provide a sixty-day comment period for interested firms or individuals to submit their arguments and concerns.

Standards and technical regulations in Mexico are called normas. *Normas* are either mandatory— the *Normas Oficiales Mexicanas,* or "official norms"—or voluntary, known simply as *Normas Mexicanas.* They are drafted by dozens of committees operating under the aegis of the *Secretaria de Comercio y Formento Industrial,* commonly called *Secofi,* the Mexican Ministry of Commerce and Industrial Development. *Normas* are published in the *Diario Oficial,* which is similar to the *Federal Register* in the United States. Mexico has hundreds of mandatory standards and over 6,000 voluntary ones. Many U.S. exporters argue that these are really used to discourage the sale of their goods in Mexico.

As noted earlier in the chapter, the United States has long complained that Mexican standards and regulations are used as unfair barriers to trade. The United States has cited Mexico's lack of notification to U.S. parties before changing its regulations—for instance, Mexico changed its import requirements on one day and put them into force the next day, leaving no time for companies to comply. The report also cited the inconsistency with which customs agents apply the law. Moreover, the report maintained that Mexico makes U.S. exporters submit their products for testing and certification only to Mexican labs, and requires detailed inspections of goods at border checkpoints, tying up shipments for excessively long periods.

Marking and Labeling Rules

The country-of-origin marking and labeling rules are set out in Annex 311 to NAFTA, and enacted in the national customs regulations of the United States, Canada, and Mexico. The rules are not uniform as between the three countries. As we saw in the last chapter, the country-of-origin rules for marking and labeling goods are not the same rules that determine the country-of-origin for tariff purposes. It is actually possible for an item to be deemed a product of a NAFTA country for marking purposes without being eligible for lowered NAFTA tariff rates. In an important case, the U.S. Court of Appeals held that the *Gibson-Thomsen* "name, character, or use" test is not applicable to NAFTA imports, and only the regulations enacted according to Annex 311 principles apply. *Bestfoods v. United States,* 165 F.3d 1371 (Fed. Cir. 1999). The case was strongly argued by the maker of "Skippy" brand peanut butter who wanted to be sure that its well-known "all American" product obtained a "Made in U.S.A." label. The peanut butter was made in the United States from "peanut slurry" imported from Canada. Bestfoods argued that they should be allowed to label "Skippy" as "Made in U.S.A." because the U.S. process substantially transformed the peanut slurry into a product with a "new name, character, or use." However, the court held that NAFTA Annex 311 replaced the old "name, character, or use" test for North American trade. A reading of Annex 311 shows that the processing of Canadian (or Mexican) peanut slurry into peanut butter in the United States does not result in the type of tariff change that would transform the slurry into a U.S. product.

Mexico's marking and labeling requirements have been controversial. The *Normas Oficiales Mexicanas,* promulgated by *Secofi,* contains specific labeling requirements for certain products (e.g., appliances, electronics, textiles, and food products). All others fall into the more general requirements for general merchandise. Mexico's labeling requirements are strict and often burdensome to U.S. and Canadian exporters. The cost of compliance is often so difficult that many small exporters cannot afford to sell their products there. Mexico has dictated the content, form, size, and even the appearance of product labels. The Spanish language labels must include the generic name of the product, the name and address of the importer and exporter, contents, and the country-of-origin. Instructions and warnings as to use and care of the product may be enclosed separately, but an invitation to read them must appear on the label. Product warranties must be clearly stated. The following incident illustrates the confusion of Mexican labeling laws: *Secofi* announced in the *Diario Oficial* that it would require that all labels be preprinted on the product or package itself, and not "stickers." Apparently the agency did not want Spanish language labels stuck over English language packaging. After a year of uncertainty and haggling, the *Bureau of National Affairs* reported that *Secofi* would probably accept stickers as long as they were as large and "as pretty" as the English language print. Exporters to Mexico need to seek good advice in labeling and marking products to avoid long delays in getting their goods to markets in Mexico.

Items Not Requiring Marks. Annex 301 exempts certain items from marking requirements: Items incapable of being marked, items that would be injured by marking, items that cannot be marked except at a cost disproportional to the cost of the goods, items in containers that indicate the country-of-origin to the ultimate purchaser, crude or bulk materials, personal items for use by the importer and not intended for sale, items produced more than twenty years prior to importation, original works of art, and a few others.

---

http://www.mexicanlaws.com
Fee-based access to Mexican laws in English, with limited free content.

TRADE IN GOODS: SECTORAL ISSUES

Sectoral issues are issues of concern to a particular industrial, agricultural, or service sector of the economy. Examples might be automobile manufacturing and assembly, telecommunications, agriculture, or financial services. NAFTA has specific provisions that reduce tariffs and liberalize trade and investment in these and other sectors. The most important and most controversial industry in North American trade relations is motor vehicles and parts.

Trade in Motor Vehicles and Parts

Perhaps no other sector will be affected by NAFTA as much as the automobile industry. Mexico had long tried to manage its automobile industry through strict trade and investment restrictions. For instance, prior to NAFTA, automobiles sold in Mexico had to contain a minimum of 36 percent Mexican-made parts. Tariffs on cars imported into Mexico were 20 percent, and 13.2 percent on automobile parts (as compared to a 2.5 percent tariff on the import of Mexican-made cars into the United States). The result was a Mexican auto parts industry that was largely inefficient and non-competitive in world markets. Of course, many modern automotive parts and assembly plants in Mexico are owned and operated by U.S., European, and Japanese firms. As discussed later in this chapter, cars assembled there cannot be released for sale into Mexico without meeting Mexican customs regulations and without the payment of duties. Cars assembled there from U.S. parts can only be returned to the United States at lowered tariff rates if they meet the strict requirements of U.S. customs law.

Canada and the United States eliminated duties on each other's automobiles even prior to NAFTA. By 2004, all three countries eliminated tariffs and restrictions on automobiles, trucks, buses, and automotive parts originating in North America. Restrictions on the cross-border trade in used cars will continue for many years to come.

Special Rules of Origin for Automobiles. To qualify for duty-free treatment, a motor vehicle that is made or assembled in North America must contain a specified percentage of North American content. For motor vehicles, these rules supersede the regional value content rules for other products, discussed earlier in the chapter.

Beginning in 2001, the content requirement rose to 62.5 percent. The same content requirements apply to engines and transmissions for these vehicles. Compliance with the rules requires complex calculations and the tracing of component parts throughout the supply chain. One of the major purposes of local content rules has been to encourage investment in North America. As Japanese plants began to build vehicles in North America, their use of North American parts increased.

Trade in Textiles and Apparel

The NAFTA textile provisions are of major significance because of the U.S. position as a major textile importer (with a large domestic industry arguing for protection from low-cost imports), and the role of Mexican plants in assembling apparel for sale in the United States. Imports of Mexican textiles and apparel were limited by quotas in the United States and Canada. Mexico has also had 20 percent tariffs on U.S. textile products. NAFTA provisions will take precedence over these tariffs, quotas, and other laws applicable to the textile trade.

Canada, Mexico, and the United States will have phased out all tariffs on textile and apparel goods that meet the North American rules of origin by 2004. All U.S. quotas on imports of Mexican textiles were immediately eliminated, and no new quotas can be used except in "emergency" situations. As discussed in the last chapter, there are specific rules of origin covering trade in textiles. They are complex and arcane, based largely on political considerations. Even the most experienced textile manufacturers and importers require an expert customs attorney or customs broker to move textiles and apparel in North America.

Trade in Agriculture

NAFTA either eliminates each country's tariffs immediately or phases them out over fifteen years. Most tariffs will have been eliminated earlier, by 2004. The *more import-sensitive products* will be controlled for the longer periods through the use of *tariff-rate quotas*—no tariff is assessed if only small quantities have been imported in a given year, but the tariff rate increases as imports rise. Agricultural products are included in this category. For instance, Canada will maintain tariffs over the imports of wheat and dairy products; the United States will maintain tariffs on imported orange juice, sugar, eggs, and poultry; and Mexico will continue tariffs on corn, beans, and dairy products. Mexico also pledged an immediate elimination of burdensome import licensing requirements for U.S. agricultural products, replacing them with tariffs that will be phased out over ten years. As noted earlier, this has not happened and is an area of constant dispute. The U.S. government estimates that the lifting of restrictions will cause a tremendous growth in agricultural trade in the future.

Government Procurement

Like many of the topics of this chapter, the basic principles of government procurement were examined in earlier chapters. NAFTA will allow North American companies to compete for contracts for the supply of goods and services to agencies of the three governments. NAFTA's government procurement rules apply to contracts for goods and services greater than $50,000, and construction contracts greater than $6.5 million. The agreement does not cover weapons, equipment, and systems needed for national defense.

When a government agency announces its request for submission of bids, it must publish the technical specifications, qualifications of suppliers, and the time limits for submission. Bids from suppliers in all NAFTA countries must be treated without discrimination. Each country has established a bid protest system that allows firms to challenge procurement procedures and awards. Countries will exchange information on bidding procedures to encourage cross-border bidding, particularly from small and medium-sized firms.

Emergency Action to Protect Domestic Industry (NAFTA Safeguards)

When NAFTA was negotiated it was clear that increased competition from foreign firms would cause some economic disruption and job loss, particularly to inefficient, uncompetitive, and outdated companies. NAFTA permits the United States, Canada, or Mexico to take very limited *emergency action* to safeguard a domestic industry. Emergency action may be taken only where increased quantities of a particular good are a *substantial cause of serious injury, or threat thereof, to a domestic industry producing a like or directly competitive good*, and only with the *consent* of the country from which the goods were exported. Generally, the right to invoke emergency safeguards under NAFTA is more limited than under GATT/WTO rules. For example, the importing country is limited to postponing any further tariff decreases under NAFTA, or to increasing the import duty as is needed to remedy the injury, but in no case higher than the MFN level. In addition, the country imposing the safeguard must agree with the exporting NAFTA country on *trade compensation*. Recall from earlier chapters, that trade compensation is a temporary reduction of duties on other products from the exporting NAFTA country equivalent in monetary terms to the safeguard action taken. For instance, if the United States seeks to impose higher duties on imports of, say, lightbulbs from Mexico, in order to save the U.S. lightbulb industry, then it will have to reduce duties on some other Mexican product, such as Mexican beer, in an equal amount.

If a NAFTA country imposes emergency safeguards on certain imported goods arriving from all WTO member countries worldwide, then these *global safeguards* may be applied to the products entering from another NAFTA country only if they comprise a *significant share of the total imports* of that type of good and contribute importantly to the serious injury.

TRADE IN SERVICES

NAFTA provisions on cross-border services are aimed at facilitating trade in services in North America. The provisions affect a wide range of service providers, including transportation and package delivery, consulting, banking and insurance, and others. The principles of national treatment and MFN trade apply. No NAFTA country may require a North American service provider to have a residence or office within its borders. Each country will be able to continue to certify and license professionals, such as doctors, lawyers, and accountants; however, the countries are working to recognize the foreign credentials of a professional, especially foreign lawyers and engineers. For instance, many professional organizations from NAFTA countries are negotiating *mutual recognition agreements*. Once ratified by state and federal governments, they will permit recognition of professional licenses in all three countries. Citizenship requirements to obtain a professional license have been eliminated.

Financial Services

U.S.–Canadian cross-border investment in financial services was largely opened in 1989. Thus, the most important impact of NAFTA's financial services provisions is that they open Mexican financial service industries to investment by U.S. and Canadian companies. Banks, insurance companies, securities firms, and other financial service providers will be able to open branches and offices throughout North America. Most restrictions were phased out by 2000, permitting a full 100 percent foreign ownership of Mexican financial institutions. Similar provisions apply to insurance companies (100 percent U.S. ownership of some Mexican insurance companies was permitted as early as 1996), and other finance companies (commercial credit, real estate lending, leasing, and credit card services).

Transportation

Almost 90 percent of goods sold across the 2,000-mile U.S.–Mexican border moves by rail or truck transportation—some five million truckloads a year. In the past, Mexican truck regulations have severely limited U.S. truck access there. Typically, U.S. carriers have had to hand over their cargo to Mexican truckers at the border. The border is known for traffic congestion and delays. Mexican truckers have been limited to a 20-mile incursion across the border. NAFTA significantly frees up cross-border transportation and opens trucking companies to foreign investment.

NAFTA does not affect regulations applied to purely domestic truck or bus transportation, and drivers will always be bound by the "rules of the road" in any foreign country in which they operate a vehicle. NAFTA did, however, provide limited cross-border truck and bus access in 1995 and full access by 2000. U.S. and Canadian trucking companies will be able to make deliveries and pickups in Mexico, and Mexican trucking companies will have similar access to their customers north of the border. The three countries are developing common safety standards for vehicles—tires, brakes, truck and cargo weight, etc.—and driver's license certifications, including testing. After 2001, U.S. and Canadian companies will be able to own a 51 percent majority interest in Mexican trucking companies, and a 100 percent ownership interest after 2004.

The Clinton administration refused to admit Mexican trucks beyond the border zone until

In the Matter of Cross Border Trucking
No. USA-MEX-98–2008–01 (2001)
(North American Free Trade Agreement Arbitral Panel Established Pursuant to Article 20)

BACKGROUND AND FACTS

To move goods between the U.S. and Mexico, shippers must typically deal with three trucking firms. Goods are shipped to a storage facility in a border town. The trailer is detached from the tractor and picked up by a drayage company that moves it across the border, where a truck in that country picks it up to haul it to its final destination. The process is inefficient and the border delays are a trucker's nightmare. This "handing-off" of cargo is necessary because the U.S. has prohibited Mexican trucks from carrying goods through to their U.S. destination for safety reasons. According to U.S. government studies, as many as 40 percent of the five million Mexican trucks that entered the U.S. in 1999 failed to meet U.S. safety requirements. Mexico does not have the same rigorous standards for driver regulation and truck inspections as does the United States, nor does it register or track safety statistics on its carriers. U.S. trucks must undergo periodic safety inspections by qualified personnel employed by the trucking company. Canadian regulations are similar to those in the U.S. and Canadian drivers have been permitted on U.S. highways for decades. The U.S. maintains that because it can inspect less than 1 percent of the Mexican trucks arriving in the U.S., it cannot open its border to Mexican trucking companies until Mexico also adopts comprehensive regulatory standards as tough as those in the United States and Canada. Mexico acknowledges that when its trucks operate in the U.S. they must comply with U.S. standards, but that the U.S. cannot dictate Mexican regulatory standards. The United States also restricts Mexican investment in U.S. trucking firms. Mexico argues that the U.S. does not treat Mexican trucks as favorably as it does trucks from the United States and Canada, and that the U.S. has violated NAFTA open investment rules by prohibiting Mexican ownership of U.S. trucking firms. The U.S. counters that under NAFTA Mexican trucks must be treated the same as U.S. and Canadian trucks only where there are "like circumstances," and that Mexican regulations are so unlike those in the U.S. and Canada that more restrictive treatment of Mexican trucks is warranted. An arbitral panel was convened to hear the dispute in 2000.

FINAL REPORT OF THE PANEL

Mexico asserts that no NAFTA provision entitles a party to impose its own laws and regulations on the other. This would be an unacceptable interference in the sovereignty of another state, and certainly not something to which any party to NAFTA has committed. Therefore, Mexico [argues that it] is under no obligation under NAFTA to enforce U.S. standards, despite cooperation between the United States and Mexico to make the regulatory systems compatible [since 1995]. However, according to Mexico, the United States has made adoption of an identical system of motor carrier regulation a condition of NAFTA implementation, even though NAFTA contemplates that harmonization would not be a condition.

According to the United States . . . Mexico cannot identify its carriers and drivers so that unsafe conduct can be properly assigned and reviewed. Without such carrier safety performance history, the United States cannot conduct a meaningful safety fitness review of Mexican carriers at the application stage. The United States also contends that it would be futile to try to perform inspections of Mexican carriers in Mexico because "Mexican carriers are not required to keep the types of records that are typically reviewed in these inspections." In contrast to Mexico's system, the United States notes that "Canada's truck safety rules and regulations are highly compatible with those of the United States." Thus, "when Canadian-based commercial trucks cross into the United States, federal and state transportation authorities can have a high level of confidence that those trucks comply with U.S. standards and requirements at least to the same degree as U.S.-based trucks. That confidence level is bolstered by a fully functioning, computerized bilateral data exchange program." Given all of these considerations, the "United States has . . . concluded that the 'circumstances' relevant to the treatment of Mexican-based trucking firms for safety purposes are not 'like' those applicable to the treatment of Canadian and U.S. carriers." Accordingly, "the United States maintains that it may apply more favorable treatment to U.S. and Canadian trucking firms than to their Mexican counterparts without running afoul of Chapter Twelve's national treatment or most-favored-nation rules."

continued

continued

Article 1202 [national treatment] provides: *Each Party shall accord to service providers of another Party treatment no less favorable than it accords, in like circumstances, to its own service providers.* Similarly, Article 1203 [most-favored-nation] states: *Each Party shall accord to service providers of another Party treatment no less favorable than it accords, in like circumstances, to service providers of any other Party or of a non-Party.* In its most succinct terms, the disagreement between the United States on the one hand, and Mexico and Canada on the other, is over whether the "in like circumstances" language permits the United States to deny access to all Mexican trucking firms on a blanket basis, regardless of the individual qualifications of particular members of the Mexican industry, unless and until Mexico's own domestic regulatory system meets U.S. approval.

[T]he Panel is of the view that the proper interpretation of Article 1202 [and 1203] requires that differential treatment should be no greater than necessary for legitimate regulatory reasons such as safety.... Similarly, the Panel is mindful that a broad interpretation of the "in like circumstances" language could render Articles 1202 and 1203 meaningless. If, for example, the regulatory systems in two NAFTA countries must be substantially identical before national treatment is granted, relatively few service industry providers could ultimately qualify. Accordingly, the Panel concludes that the U.S. position that the "in like circumstances" language permits continuation of the moratorium on accepting applications for operating authority in the United States from Mexican owned and domiciled carriers is an overly-broad reading of that clause.

The United States claims that Mexico does not even allege that there is any interest on behalf of Mexican nationals to invest in U.S. trucking firms.... [T]he prohibition on allowing Mexican investors to acquire U.S. companies that already have operating authority, on its face, violates... NAFTA Articles 1102 and 1103 ... even if Mexico cannot identify a particular Mexican national or nationals that have been rejected.

Decision. The panel unanimously held that the U.S. restrictions on the Mexican trucking industry violate NAFTA. The inadequacies of the Mexican safety regulations are not sufficient reason for the United States to refuse applications from Mexican-owned trucking companies to operate on U.S. highways. The ruling preserved the right of the U.S. to hold Mexican trucks to the same regulations, safety standards, and inspections as any other vehicle on U.S. roads. Mexican drivers can be required to meet the same licensing and performance standards as U.S. drivers and observe all "rules of the road." Under special situations, the U.S. may establish different procedures to assure that Mexican trucks and drivers comply with U.S. law, so long as the procedures are in good faith and not more restrictive to trade than necessary. The U.S. restrictions on investment are not valid because investment does not raise a safety issue.

Comment. Was the U.S. position strictly motivated by safety concerns? American truckers and organized labor have generally been opposed to opening the border. Mexican drivers make less than their American counterparts, and the border opening places them in competition with American drivers. Do you think this affected the U.S. government's position in the 1990s?

Mexican safety standards were on par with those in the United States and Canada. In the following 2001 decision, a NAFTA arbitral panel ruled that the United States was in violation of NAFTA. As you read, consider the regulatory nightmare of enforcing U.S. safety standards on millions of Mexican trucks arriving in the United States every year.

In response to this case, President Bush and Congress cooperated in an effort to give Mexican trucks full access to American highways. The Department of Transportation passed regulations to ensure that Mexican trucks complied with the same regulations that apply to American trucks.

For example, the regulations require that all trucks comply with safety, environmental, and fuel efficiency standards. Mexican trucks are required to undergo reasonable registrations, safety inspections, and equipment checks. Drivers must be properly licensed in Mexico and comply with all safety regulations, including those limiting the number of hours of continuous driving. Mexican trucking companies must implement drug and alcohol testing, maintain insurance, and keep safety-related records. Mexican trucks may enter only at authorized points of entry when inspectors are present.

The Trucking Environmental Snafu. Labor and environmental groups continue to find ways to keep Mexican trucks off U.S. roads. In *Public Citizen v. Department of Transportation,* 316 F.3d 1002 (9th Cir. 2003), a federal court of appeals put the Mexican trucking regulations on hold, ruling that the Department of Transportation had failed to properly consider the environmental impact of the rules under the *Clean Air Act* and other environmental laws. It was widely reported in the press that during these delays in implementing the regulations, U.S. trucking firms have been quietly buying ownership interests in Mexican trucking companies. It is not until Mexican trucks gain access that U.S. trucks will have reciprocal rights to enter Mexico.

Telecommunications

NAFTA eliminates all tariffs on telephones, cellular phones, and trade in telecommunications equipment by 2004. Given that the number of telephones per capita in Mexico is only a fraction of the per capita number of phones in the United States, Mexico is considered a giant untapped market for all forms of communications equipment and services. NAFTA provides that Canadian, Mexican, and U.S. telecommunications companies have nondiscriminatory access to all North American public telecommunications networks. They must be granted access to public and private (leased) lines and networks only upon conditions that are reasonable and necessary. Access to public telecommunications networks must be at rates related to the cost of operations. Technical standards may be imposed only for safety or to prevent damage to the equipment.

Mexico's telephone system had been operated as a government-owned monopoly, *Telefonos de Mexico.* Today the company has considerable private investment and is even traded on the New York Stock Exchange. Mexico has been developing a telecommunications law that would set limits on foreign investment and otherwise regulate foreign firms entering its market. During the mid-1990s, U.S. firms such as AT&T, MCI, and Sprint, and Canada's Northern Telecom, teamed up in partnerships with many Mexican companies to take advantage of growing opportunities in the telecommunications market.

CROSS-BORDER INVESTMENT

Prior to the late 1980s, Mexico had a history of strictly regulating or even prohibiting foreign investment. For instance, Mexico required that foreign investors include local participants—Mexican stockholders or partners—in any new factory or investment venture. If a foreign firm wanted to purchase an interest in a local company, Mexico usually limited them to a minority, noncontrolling interest. Mexico, as with many developing countries, has required foreign manufacturing firms located there to export finished goods to other countries for foreign currency. Investors in manufacturing companies were required to use a certain portion of domestic content in the finished goods, thus discouraging imports. Limits were placed on how much money could be transferred out of the country. A common requirement was that foreign investors had to introduce their most advanced technology to the host country. In the 1980s, Mexico turned away from the philosophies of government control as in the best interest of the country and of seizing property through *expropriation* and *nationalization;* it became more hospitable and adopted forward-thinking liberal policies toward foreign investment. It still exercises some control over foreign investment, particularly in the energy and petroleum industries, but not to the extent it did in the past.

NAFTA's Investment Provisions

NAFTA's investment provisions are found in Chapter Eleven and summarized here:

- NAFTA investors must be treated fairly, equitably, and in full accordance with basic principles of international law;
- NAFTA investors must be granted the basic protections of *most-favored-nation status* (to be treated at least as favorably as investments from outside North America), *nondiscrimination,* and *national treatment* (that NAFTA investors be treated without discrimination and no less favorably than a country's own investors or domestically owned firms are treated);
- NAFTA governments must adopt *open investment policies* and eliminate most restrictions on private investment from firms based in other NAFTA countries;

- Private property of a NAFTA investor may not be expropriated by the government without due process of law and the payment of fair compensation;
- Private investors may request an arbitral tribunal to hear an *investor claim* for money damages against a NAFTA country for violating the NAFTA investment provisions. NAFTA countries may invoke other procedures for settling investment disputes between themselves.

NAFTA's Open Investment Policies.

Investors from all three countries can now establish new companies and purchase existing ones across North American borders. In addition, NAFTA sets limits on the government regulation of North American owned companies (provisions intended largely to break down the investment barriers in Mexico). No NAFTA country can require a minimum level of local participation, or ownership by nationals (other than in certain industries in which exceptions to this rule have been reserved). No NAFTA country may place restrictions on the conversion of foreign exchange and transfer of money between accounts in another NAFTA country. Similarly, no country may either require or prohibit a firm from transferring profits earned by a subsidiary in one NAFTA country to another NAFTA country. There can be no *performance requirements* on a NAFTA investor, including no minimum export requirements (i.e., where the host government requires foreign-owned firms to export a certain percentage of goods or services produced by the local subsidiary) and no domestic content or purchasing requirements (i.e., the host government requires that a minimum percentage of raw materials used in local operations be purchased from local companies). Governments may not require that parent companies in one NAFTA country transfer advanced technology (via patents, licensing, or "know-how" agreements) to a subsidiary in another NAFTA country, and they may not require that senior managers and corporate directors be of any particular nationality.

Environmental Measures Applicable to Investments.

Mexico does not have the strict environmental laws that the United States has. For many U.S. firms, compliance with U.S. laws can be costly. When NAFTA was negotiated, heated debate surrounded the issue of whether U.S. companies, especially polluting ones, would flock to open plants in Mexico to avoid U.S. law. As a compromise in the negotiations, NAFTA provides that "it is inappropriate to encourage investment by relaxing domestic health, safety, or environmental measures. Accordingly, a [NAFTA country] should not waive . . . such measures as an encouragement for the establishment, acquisition, expansion or retention in its territory of an investment."

Exceptions to the Investment Agreement.

Canada reserved the right to review acquisitions of local companies of $150 million (Canadian) or more under the *Investment Canada Act*. Mexico also retained the right to review acquisitions worth $150 million or more. Mexico also may restrict ownership of land, cable television companies, air and land transportation, oil production and refining, and retail sales of gasoline and oil. The United States excluded investments in nuclear power, broadcasting, mining, customs brokerages, and air transportation, and may block the takeover of U.S. firms on the basis of national security.

Protecting Investors from Expropriation.

Readers from the United States and most other countries are familiar with constitutional requirements that governments must compensate property owners whose property is taken for public use. This almost universal idea is based on the notion that at times, governments must take property for public purposes, or for uses like conservation or environmental protection, and that the property owners should not have to shoulder the cost of the public welfare. Article 1110 states that no NAFTA country may expropriate property of a NAFTA investor, unless it is done pursuant to internationally accepted rules: that private property may only be taken for a public purpose or for public use on a nondiscriminatory basis, utilizing procedures that are open and fair, and in accordance with due process of law, and with the payment of fair compensation according to the market value of the property taken. The following case, *Metalclad Corp. v. The United Mexican States,* is one of the most interesting and controversial cases to come out of Chapter 11. This is a case involving a U.S. firm that attempted to build a hazardous waste landfill in Mexico. It was told that all permits necessary to build the facility had been obtained. After making significant progress to complete the project, the local municipality claimed one additional permit was missing and the state issued a decree turning

Metalclad Corporation v. The United Mexican States
International Centre for the Settlement of Investment Disputes No. ARB(AF)/97/1
Award of the Arbitral Tribunal (August 30, 2000)

BACKGROUND AND FACTS

In 1993, a Mexican firm, Coterin, received a permit from the Mexican government to build a hazardous waste treatment plant in the La Pedrera valley, in the state of San Luis Potosi, near the city of Guadalcazar. Metalclad, a U.S. company, was interested in acquiring Coterin. Several Mexican government authorities assured Metalclad that Coterin had obtained all required construction permits for the facility. One month later Metalclad purchased Coterin. In 1994, amid much opposition to the plant from local residents and environmental protestors, the city of Guadalcazar ordered a halt to construction, claiming that no municipal permit had been obtained. Metalclad responded that the Mexican federal government had told it that no further state or municipal permits were needed. Metalclad even promised to create a reserve for native species, create a local scientific advisory council, give discounts for local waste, contribute to local charities and provide some free medical services to local residents. But, without reason, the city informed Metalclad that it could not begin operation. In 1997, the state governor issued a decree designating the landfill as a protected ecological and wildlife area, putting an end to Metalclad's business there. Having expended $16.5 million on the project, Metalclad requested that a NAFTA Chapter 11 arbitral tribunal be convened to resolve the dispute. The company maintained that it had not been given fair and equitable treatment, that the Mexican regulations lacked transparency, and that Mexico had in fact expropriated their property without payment of fair compensation.

AWARD OF THE ARBITRAL TRIBUNAL

For the reasons set out below, the Tribunal finds that Metalclad's investment was not accorded fair and equitable treatment in accordance with international law, and that Mexico has violated NAFTA Article 1105(1).

Prominent in the statement of principles and rules that introduces NAFTA is the reference to "transparency." The Tribunal understands this to include the idea that all relevant legal requirements for the purpose of initiating, completing and successfully operating investments made, or intended to be made, under NAFTA should be capable of being readily known to all affected investors. There should be no room for doubt or uncertainty on such matters. . . . The absence of a clear rule as to the requirement or not of a municipal construction permit, as well as the absence of any established practice or procedure as to the manner of handling applications for a municipal construction permit, amounts to a failure on the part of Mexico to ensure the transparency required by NAFTA. Metalclad was entitled to rely on the representations of federal officials and to believe that it was entitled to continue its construction of the landfill. Moreover, the permit was denied at a meeting of the Municipal Town Council of which Metalclad received no notice, to which it received no invitation, and at which it was given no opportunity to appear. The Town Council denied the permit for reasons which included, but may not have been limited to, the opposition of the local population, the fact that construction had already begun when the application was submitted . . . and the ecological concerns regarding the environmental effect and impact on the site and surrounding communities. None of the reasons included a reference to any problems associated with the physical construction of the landfill or to any physical defects therein. The Tribunal therefore finds that the construction permit was denied without any consideration of, or specific reference to, construction aspects or flaws of the physical facility.

Mexico failed to ensure a transparent and predictable framework for Metalclad's business planning and investment. The totality of these circumstances demonstrates a lack of orderly process and timely disposition in relation to an investor of a Party acting in the expectation that it would be treated fairly and justly in accordance with the NAFTA. The Tribunal therefore holds that Metalclad was not treated fairly or equitably under the NAFTA and succeeds on its claim under Article 1105.

NAFTA provides that "no party shall directly or indirectly . . . expropriate an investment . . . or take a measure tantamount to . . . expropriation . . . except: (a) for a public purpose; (b) on a nondiscriminatory basis; (c) in accordance with due process of law and Article 1105(1); and (d) on payment of

continued

continued

compensation. Thus, expropriation under NAFTA includes not only open, deliberate and acknowledged takings of property, such as outright seizure or formal or obligatory transfer of title in favor of the host State, but also covert or incidental interference with the use of property which has the effect of depriving the owner, in whole or in significant part, of the use or reasonably to be expected economic benefit of property even if not necessarily to the obvious benefit of the host State. By permitting or tolerating the conduct of Guadalcazar . . . Mexico must be held to have taken a measure tantamount to expropriation in violation of NAFTA.

NAFTA provides for the award of monetary damages and applicable interest where a Party is found to have violated a Chapter Eleven provision. With respect to expropriation, NAFTA specifically requires compensation to be equivalent to the fair market value of the expropriated investment immediately before the expropriation took place. However, where the enterprise has not operated for a sufficiently long time to establish a performance record or where it has failed to make a profit, future profits cannot be used to determine going concern or fair market value. Rather, the Tribunal agrees with the parties that fair market value is best arrived at in this case by reference to Metalclad's actual investment in the project. For the reasons stated above, the Tribunal hereby decides that the Respondent shall pay to Metalclad the amount of $16,685,000.

Decision.   Through the actions of city, state, and federal officials, Mexico had violated Metalclad's investor rights. The Mexican regulations were not transparent, the procedures were unfair, and Mexico's actions were an indirect expropriation of Metalclad's property. As a U.S. investor in Mexico, Metalclad was not granted fair and equitable treatment.

Comment.   The tribunal also found that under the Mexican Constitution the city municipality lacked the authority to issue or deny a permit for a hazardous waste landfill, and that the protection of the environment was a matter only for the Mexican federal government. This finding concerned all three governments, because the tribunal was attempting to interpret a domestic law under a national constitution. Mexico challenged the tribunal award before the Supreme Court of British Columbia, Canada (technical jurisdictional issues placed the challenge in British Columbia). As of early 2001, no ruling had yet been issued.

---

the property into a wildlife refuge. Work was ordered stopped and Metalclad requested that an arbitral tribunal award damages.

Investor Claims and Dispute Settlement Procedures.

Investor claims are actions for damages brought by a NAFTA investor before an arbitral tribunal against a host NAFTA government for having violated NAFTA investment rules. Investor suits may be brought either under the arbitration rules of the UN Commission on International Trade Law (UNCITRAL) or, as in the *Metalclad* award, the International Centre for the Settlement of Investment Disputes (ICSID). The ICSID is an organization closely allied with the World Bank, headquartered in Washington, DC. Investor suits may be brought either by citizens or corporations of another NAFTA country, or by investors from other countries that have substantial business activities in a NAFTA country. For example, if a parent company in Sweden owns an incorporated subsidiary company in the United States, then the U.S. subsidiary may make investments in Canada or Mexico according to the open investment policies of NAFTA. Investors may bring suits for monetary damages (no punitive damages allowed) or restitution of property, but not to force a government to change its laws or policies (as can a WTO panel wherein the cases are brought by complaining governments). There are usually three arbiters selected by the parties and their awards are binding on the parties. The awards are effective only for that case and do not establish binding rules that countries must follow in future disputes. NAFTA governments may also bring dispute actions against each other, not for damages, but to compel compliance with NAFTA rules.

---

http://www.worldbank.org/icsid
The International Centre for the Settlement of Investment Disputes. See for documents, panel decisions, and information on investment treaties. Includes NAFTA investment awards.

OTHER NAFTA PROVISIONS

In negotiating NAFTA, the United States was able to see the broader implications of free trade and investment in North America. For instance, what if an unscrupulous company in Mexico produces counterfeit software and smuggles it across the border in violation of the copyrights of a U.S. company? Or suppose that a firm emits poisonous gas or pollutants from a smokestack at its Mexican plant, and they are carried by air currents to the United States? What if the top management of several competing companies meet in Denver or Mexico City and fix prices to consumers for a product that they each make? Although these problems undoubtedly occurred before NAFTA, and are tremendous issues that no one trade agreement is likely to change, the U.S. negotiators of the agreement used the opportunity to address them openly.

Intellectual Property Rights

Intellectual property rights (IPRs) are generally protected by national law, but as discussed in previous chapters, IPRs are the subject of several international conventions (e.g., the *Berne Convention*) and agreements (e.g., GATT/TRIPS). Intellectual property is covered in greater detail in Part Four of this book. NAFTA adopts the basic tenets of these international agreements and builds upon them. NAFTA's provisions protect the IPRs of North American firms. No country can make citizenship a requirement for IPR protection. Applicants for trademarks, copyrights, and patents must be treated equally and without discrimination. NAFTA guarantees that any IPR is freely transferable by the owner to another party.

Trademarks. Trademarks and service marks will be protected for ten years, and can be renewed indefinitely. The owner of a registered trademark has the right to prevent others from using identical or similar signs for goods or services if it would result in a likelihood of confusion (and a *likelihood of confusion* is presumed unless the offender can prove otherwise). Specific provisions prohibit the use of the names of geographical regions (e.g., Tennessee Whiskey), unless the products are actually derived from that area. Actual use of a trademark cannot be a condition

for filing an application for registration. NAFTA requires fair procedures for obtaining a trademark, including notice and an opportunity to be heard. Registration may be canceled if the trademark is not used for an uninterrupted period of at least two years.

Copyrights. Copyrights will be protected equally in all three countries. Computer programs will be protected as literary works, and motion pictures and sound recordings protected for fifty years. (Canada has made some exceptions for "cultural industries.") NAFTA prohibits the importation of copies of a sound recording made without the producers' authorization.

Patents. Patents must be made available for any invention "in all fields of technology" (including pharmaceuticals), whether it is a product or process. It must be new, result from an inventive step (i.e., be "nonobvious"), and be capable of industrial application (i.e., be "useful"). They are effective for a period of twenty years from the date of application, or seventeen years from the date when the patent was granted.

Enforcement and Penalties. NAFTA requires that each country enforce its IPR laws, both internally and at the border to prevent smuggling of counterfeit items. IPR owners will be able to protect their rights through administrative action and judicial relief. Courts will have the authority to order seizure and destruction of infringing items, to issue injunctions against their sale, and to permit lawsuits for damages against infringers. The NAFTA countries must provide criminal penalties for cases in which willful trademark counterfeiting or copyright piracy occurs on a commercial scale. Penalties may include imprisonment or monetary fines, or both.

Environmental Cooperation and Enforcement

The *North American Agreement on Environmental Cooperation* (NAAEC) does not set environmental or ecological standards, as does national law, but it does call for the three countries to cooperate in protecting the environment. The countries have promised to enforce their laws more effectively. They also promise to develop environmental emergency procedures and to share information on protecting the environment. They are also working to develop common environmental standards. All countries must notify the others before banning a pesticide or chemical, and afterward, all are urged to prohibit the export of such products to other countries.

---

http://www.cec.org
The North American Commission for Environmental Cooperation. Information on the spread of pesticides and pollutants, endangered wildlife, cross-border air pollution, the conservation of biodiversity, etc. The environmental agreement and national environmental laws are available here.

The NAAEC created the *North American Commission for Environmental Cooperation* (CEC) to oversee this portion of the agreement. The commission is headed by a council made up of three cabinet-level officers of the three governments. The commission may convene panels to resolve disputes between countries. The arbitral panels can authorize tariff increases against a country that fails to enforce its environmental laws or is otherwise found in violation of the environmental provisions of the agreement or impose a monetary penalty (fine). In one of NAFTA's first environmental cases, *The Journal of Commerce* reported in 1995 that the commission was investigating the death of 40,000 wild birds in Mexico. The commission acted quickly to determine the cause— apparently the birds died from the industrial dumping of either chromium or red dye—and made recommendations in order to protect other migratory birds that were due to return to the area. Mexico took quick action as a result of the commission's investigation. It was the first time in North America that authorities from other countries investigated an environmental disaster solely within another country. However, no one knows yet how willing Canada, Mexico, and the United States will be to opening these types of incidents to NAFTA investigations.

Labor Cooperation and Worker Rights

Many people worried that NAFTA would cause U.S. companies to move to Mexico to take advantage of cheap labor and weakly enforced labor laws. With this in mind, the United States insisted

on a side agreement called the *North American Agreement on Labor Cooperation* (NAALC), intended to make labor policies more uniform by promoting the following basic labor principles in the region:

- Freedom of association and right to organize
- Right to bargain collectively
- Right to strike
- Prohibition of forced labor
- Protection for children and young persons
- Minimum working conditions
- Elimination of employment discrimination
- Equal pay for women and men
- Prevention of accidents and occupational disease and injuries, and compensation to workers
- Protection of migrant workers

NAFTA does not set specific rules or domestic labor standards, but requires countries to enforce those standards that they already have. A *North American Labor Commission for Labor Cooperation* was created to oversee the agreement and to promote cooperation in labor issues. The commission is headed by a council, consisting of the U.S. Secretary of Labor and labor ministers from the other countries. An arbitral panel may be convened to investigate issues involving worker health or safety, the abuse of child labor, or the failure to enforce minimum wage laws, and it may make recommendations for solutions and impose fines.

There is some criticism of the efficacy of this agreement. One attorney quoted in *The Wall Street Journal* who litigated five cases before the NAO (National Administrative Office) noted:

> Technically speaking in all cases we won. But in all cases workers are left with a piece of paper that says "you were right." Not a single worker was ever reinstated, not a single employer was sanctioned, no union was ever recognized.

At best, the agreement provides a forum to discuss disputes. Many labor groups are poised to push vigorously for new safeguards in any future agreements.

---

http://www.naalc.org
North American Commission for Labor Cooperation. Studies and reports on labor relations law, migrant workers, employment of women, and other labor issues in North America. Access to the agreement and to the work of the commission.

Antitrust and Competition Policy

Antitrust laws, also called *competition law,* prohibit illegal monopoly control of industries, price fixing and a range of anticompetitive and unfair business practices. Both the United States and Canada have long had strong antitrust laws. Mexico adopted an antitrust law in 1993. NAFTA countries agreed to cooperate in the enforcement of these antitrust laws, including mutual legal assistance, consultations, and exchange of information. For industries in which the countries permit legal monopolies, such as Mexico's state-owned oil company, NAFTA sets rules to minimize the anticompetitive impact of the monopoly on other industries.

Rights to Temporary Entry

Unlike the EU, NAFTA does not create a common market in labor. Each country will still determine its own qualifications for employment and its own immigration policies. NAFTA countries, however, have agreed to give businesspeople easy access to their customers, clients, factories, and offices across the borders. NAFTA permits temporary entry in the following cases:

1. Business visitors engaged in international business activities related to research, manufacturing, marketing, sales, and distribution; those who are service providers; and those servicing products after-the-sale (repair or maintenance of products after the sale must be done pursuant to a warranty or other service contract on the products).
2. Traders employed by a company in a NAFTA country, and those who are buying and selling substantial amounts of goods and services.
3. Potential investors.
4. Management or executive employees transferred to subsidiary companies in another NAFTA country.
5. Qualified professionals (in sixty-three professions, ranging from teachers and lawyers to hotel managers) entering to do business (separate licensing qualifications must also be met if they intend to practice a profession).

Mexico requires these travelers to obtain the FMN card (*Formularia Migratorio* NAFTA), which is valid for thirty days. Special visas are available for periods of stay longer than thirty days. Normal tourist cards are still available.

ADMINISTRATION AND DISPUTE SETTLEMENT

NAFTA does not have the type of lawmaking institutions that the EU has. However, an administrative body oversees implementation of the agreement, and a dispute resolution process is available to NAFTA countries. The dispute resolution process is similar to that at the WTO.

NAFTA Fair Trade Commission

The *Fair Trade Commission* supervises the implementation of the agreement and attempts to resolve disputes that may arise regarding its interpretation or application. One cabinet-level official from each of the three governments, supported by an administrative staff and committees, form the commission.

Arbitral Panels. When one NAFTA country accuses another of violating NAFTA's principles, it must first attempt to negotiate a settlement. If a settlement is not reached, then the countries can seek dispute resolution. When the issue falls under both NAFTA and GATT, the countries must agree on whether it will be heard by the NAFTA Fair Trade Commission or the WTO. If they cannot agree on which forum, the case will normally be heard before the Fair Trade Commission. If a settlement is not reached, the commission may convene an *arbitral panel,* which consists of five members who are experts in trade or law. They decide whether one country has violated NAFTA and recommend a solution. If the recommendations of the arbitral panel are not followed, and no agreement is reached within thirty days, the complaining country may retaliate by raising tariffs, but no panel has the authority to tell a country to actually change its laws or policies. For example, if a panel rules that a regulation of the U.S. Consumer Product Safety Commission, the National Park Service, or other agency is violating NAFTA, an individual cannot obtain a court order compelling the agency to alter its decision solely on the basis of the panel report.

Antidumping and Countervailing Duty Cases.

The Fair Trade Commission also hears cases involving countervailing and antidumping duties. These cases are treated differently from other disputes. Recall that *countervailing duties* are imposed on imported goods that received an unfair price advantage because a part of their cost of production was subsidized by the exporting country. *Antidumping duties* are imposed on "dumped" products. Dumping, another unfair trade practice, is the selling of goods in a foreign market for less than the price charged in the country in which they were produced. Antidumping and countervailing duties are only imposed pursuant to an order of an administrative agency in the importing country. This practice will continue under NAFTA; however, the appellate process has been changed greatly. In the United States, an appeal of an agency decision in an international trade case normally goes to the U.S. Court of International Trade, but appeals from administrative orders in NAFTA cases now go to NAFTA *binational panels*, not to courts of law. The role of the panel, and *its standard of review,* in reviewing agency decisions is limited. Binational panels apply the same standard of review as would a court of law convened in the country where the case originated. Because it is not an appellate court, a panel does not make law in the traditional sense, but applies the existing law of the country from which the case was appealed. This legal process is quite unusual and controversial, because private businesses will be bound by the decision of an intergovernmental panel with no recourse to judicial review. The *Synthetic Baler Twine* case illustrates the appellate function of a binational panel in a dumping case.

Synthetic Baler Twine with a Knot Strength of 200 lbs or Less Originating in or Exported from the United States of America
CDA–94–1904–02
(NAFTA Binational Panel, 1995)

BACKGROUND AND FACTS
Poli-Twine and other Canadian twine manufacturers filed an antidumping complaint in Canada against synthetic baler twine imported from the United States. The Canadian International Trade Tribunal found that the twine was causing material injury to the production of like goods in Canada. Bridon Cordage, a U.S. exporter of twine, challenged the Tribunal's decision on the grounds that the Tribunal committed an error in applying a Canadian statute, the *Special Import Measures Act* (SIMA). A NAFTA binational panel was requested. Three aspects of the panel's decision are discussed here: (1) the standard of review; (2) whether the Tribunal properly determined that the dumping had injured Canadian industry; and (3) whether the Tribunal properly determined that the dumped goods are likely to cause injury in the future. The panel applied Canadian law because it was reviewing a decision of a Canadian government agency.

DECISION OF THE PANEL
This Binational Panel was constituted pursuant to Chapter 19 of the North American Free Trade Agreement (NAFTA) to review a finding of the Canadian International Trade Tribunal (the Tribunal). The Tribunal found that the dumping of synthetic baler twine exported from the United States of America had caused, and was likely to cause material injury to the production of like goods in Canada.

I. Standard of Review
Binational Panels are directed by NAFTA Article 1904(3) to apply the standard of review set out in the general legal principles that a court of the importing party [Canada] otherwise would apply to a review of a determination of the competent investigating authority. In the case of Canada . . . the standard of review is set forth in the [Canadian] *Federal*

continued

continued

Court Act. . . . [The Act] provides that the Tribunal's decisions will be reviewed on the grounds that it: (a) acted without jurisdiction, acted beyond its jurisdiction or refused to exercise its jurisdiction; (b) failed to observe a principle of natural justice, procedural fairness or other procedure that is required by law to observe; (c) erred in law in making a decision or order, whether or not the error appears on the face of the record; (d) based its decision or order on an erroneous finding of fact that it made in a perverse or capricious manner or without regard for the material before it; (e) acted, or failed to act, by reason of fraud or perjured evidence; or (f) acted in any other way that was contrary to law.

Complainants contend that, because binational Panels are themselves expert in international trade, the Tribunal is not entitled to the same degree of deference that ordinarily would be accorded to it by the [Canadian] Federal Court. The Panel disagrees. Pursuant to the NAFTA binational Panel review replaces judicial review by domestic courts in certain defined circumstances. NAFTA provides: The Panel shall apply the standard of review set out in NAFTA Annex 1911 and the general legal principles that a court of the importing Party otherwise would apply to a review of a determination of the competent investigating authority. NAFTA Annex 1911 states that the standard of review for Canada means "the grounds set out in subsection 18.1(4) of the Federal Court Act." Under section 18.1(4) the Federal Court is obliged by law to give "considerable deference" to the decisions of the Tribunal. In fulfilling their mandate to "apply the standard of review . . . that a court of the importing Party otherwise would apply" binational Panels are obliged to apply the same standard that would be used by the Federal Court.

The Panel holds that the requirement that Panelists be familiar with international trade law under paragraph 1 of the NAFTA, Annex 1902.2 is not intended to modify the standard of deference that is ordinarily accorded an expert tribunal. The requirement that Panelists be familiar with international trade law assists Panelists to fulfil their mandate by making it easier for them to understand the types of issues that are dealt with by the Tribunal. . . .

II. Errors of Law and Fact

Complainants contend that the Tribunal erroneously violated its legal duty under the Special Import Measures Act (SIMA) by failing to [determine all possible factors that could have caused injury to the Canadian twine industry]. This would have essentially required the Tribunal to quantify each and every factor that might be a cause of material injury, not limited to dumped goods from the United States. . . .

It is true that the effects of dumping must be segregated from other causes, and the Tribunal is required under SIMA to determine whether the dumped goods are a cause of material injury. However, neither SIMA, nor the GATT rules as incorporated in SIMA, require that the other causes be calculated or quantified beyond what is necessary to assure that injury from dumped goods is not being attributed to those other causes. . . . Of course, there may be other factors which may have contributed to the injury. As a matter of common sense, it seems to me that there almost always will be. Such matters as efficiency [of Canadian twine producers], quality, cost control, marketing ability, accuracy in forecasting, good luck and a host of others come to mind. It is the function of a specialized tribunal such as the Canadian International Trade Tribunal to weigh and balance those factors and to decide the importance to be given to each.

III. Future Injury

The amount of evidence required in order to sustain the Tribunal's findings of fact is modest. This, however, does not mean the Tribunal's determination will be upheld in the absence of any evidence in the record to support its conclusions. Such is the situation we find here.

While . . . it may be logical to assume that injury will continue as long as conditions remain the same, we are unwilling to hold that such an assumption is the equivalent of evidence. The Tribunal here based its conclusion on the "belief" that Poli-Twine will [in the future] be faced with the same market conditions as in the recent past . . . and the view that as long as the U.S. has excess production, injury will continue. These assertions may or may not be true, and if so would appear to support a conclusion of future injury, but there are not—on the basis of anything that has been brought to our attention in the briefs or oral argument—in the record as established facts. The references in the record offered in support amount to conjecture, falling short of evidence.

continued

---

continued

Decision. The Panel affirmed the Canadian Tribunal's determination that the sale of U.S. twine in Canada at unfairly low prices caused past injury to Canadian twine producers. But the Panel held that there was not sufficient evidence to support the Tribunal's conclusion that injury would continue in the future. The case was remanded to the Tribunal to reconsider new evidence on the question of future injury. The Panel applied the same standard of review that a Canadian appellate court would have applied if a court had been reviewing the case.

Comment. When reviewing an order from a U.S. agency, a NAFTA Panel applies U.S. standards for judicial review. In *Live Swine from Canada,* USA-94-1904-01 (May 30, 1995), a NAFTA panel stated that, "The Panel steps into the shoes of the Court of International Trade and the Court of Appeals for the Federal Circuit and is to apply the standards and the substantive law that those courts apply when they review a . . . determination by the Department of Commerce. This in turn means that the Panel is to hold unlawful 'any determination, finding or conclusion found . . . to be *unsupported by substantial evidence.*' . . . The Panel is not to substitute its own judgment, and the only question before it is whether the agency's action had appropriate support in fact and/or law."

Extraordinary Challenge Committees. Appeals of a binational panel decision may be taken only to a NAFTA *Extraordinary Challenge Committee,* and not to courts of law. A challenge committee examines a case only to see if a panelist was biased or guilty of misconduct, or whether the panel departed from a fundamental rule of procedure, or *exceeded its powers, authority, or jurisdiction.* A binational panel must apply the correct standard of review. Under NAFTA, a binational panel that fails to apply the correct standard of review would be considered to have exceeded its powers, authority, or jurisdiction.

Panelists for binational panels and extraordinary challenge committees are chosen from a roster of impartial judges or former judges whenever possible.

ASSEMBLY PLANTS AND THE MEXICAN *MAQUILADORA*

Long before NAFTA existed, other trade preferences had a tremendous impact on the North American region. As mentioned in Chapter Twelve, many Mexican goods shipped to the United States received special tariff preferences under the GSP, or *Generalized System of Preferences,* which were available to any developing country that qualified under the GSP law. They had either a low tariff, or no tariff at all. Canada offered similar preferences for Mexican goods. The purpose of these programs was to encourage trade with developing countries to aid in their economic growth.

Another U.S. government program not a part of NAFTA, that has had a tremendous impact on U.S.-Mexican trade business is found in Section 9802 of the *Harmonized Tariff Schedule.* This law contains a special provision allowing U.S.-made articles or component parts to be shipped to factories in a foreign country, assembled there, and returned to the United States with duties assessed only on the value of the newly assembled product *less the value of the U.S.-made article or component parts.* The law thus permits U.S. firms, such as automakers, to purchase auto parts from U.S. suppliers and assemble them in foreign plants using low-cost labor. Assembly plants can be established in all areas of the world and owned by companies from all countries. For instance, a Japanese automaker can produce cars in a Mexican assembly plant, using parts sourced from countries around the world, and then export the Mexican-made car to the United States. The car will be dutied on the value of the car less the value of the U.S. component parts. In one Ford Motor Company plant, steel from Japan is stamped into body parts, assembled together with Japanese-made engines and U.S. component parts, and the finished car is exported to the United States (much to the chagrin of U.S. autoworkers). Because of the nature of the operation, the process is sometimes called *production sharing.* It is intended to create U.S. jobs by encouraging the use of U.S.-made components when assembly of a product takes place in a foreign country. The automobile industry has invested heavily in plants in Japan, Canada, Sweden, Germany, and Mexico; the electronics industry in Asia; and the textile industry in Mexico and the Caribbean. These plants are often called *offshore assembly plants, in-bond plants,* or *border plants.* The Spanish term is *maquiladora,* derived from the word *maquila.*

Mexican Customs Rules

For the past twenty-five years, Mexico has used the *maquiladora* industry as a means of attracting foreign investment and increasing jobs, without having an influx of foreign-made goods. As of 2001, the Mexican government allows the temporary, duty-free import of articles originating in the United States or Canada, brought into Mexico for assembly *if the assembled product is returned to the United States or Canada or exported to a third country* within two years. If the finished goods are not exported within two years, or are sold for Mexican consumption, the duties become payable on the original materials. The rules are different when non-North American parts or materials are imported into Mexico for assembly in a *maquiladora* plant. As a general rule, these are dutiable when they arrive in Mexico. However, on re-export to the United States or Canada, the Mexican importer is entitled to a waiver or refund of duties in an amount equal to the lesser of the duties actually paid to Mexico or the duties assessed by the United States or Canada when the assembled product is re-exported there. This means that the Mexican importer or *maquiladora* will receive no refund of Mexican import duties if the assembled product is later shipped duty free to the United States or Canada. This gives a great incentive to *maquiladoras* to use parts and materials that originate in North America because they face paying full Mexican import duties on non-North American components. Finally, if the assembled product is sold within Mexico or is exported to a non-North American country, there is no waiver or refund at all on the original Mexican duties paid on the parts or materials.

Maquiladoras are exempt from Mexico's value-added tax.

Assembly Plant Tariff Treatment in the United States

Section 9802 tariff treatment is available only where (1) the imports were assembled in the for-

eign plant from U.S.-made fabricated components, (2) that had been exported "ready for assembly without further fabrication," and (3) that have not lost their physical identity and have not been advanced in value or improved in condition abroad except by being assembled and except "by operations incidental to the assembly process," (such as cleaning, trimming, calibrating, or lubricating). Examples of fabricated components that would qualify as being ready for assembly without losing their physical identity include transistors, machine parts, semiconductors, precut parts of wearing apparel, lug nuts, and automobile engines or tires. Bolts of fabric sent abroad to be cut into parts of shirts do not qualify as an assembly, but the sewing of two sleeves to the body of a shirt does. It is not an assembly when lumber, leather, or plastic is sent abroad to be formed into component parts. Section 9802 applies only to assembly operations, which includes any method of joining together, such as welding, gluing, or sewing. Combining chemicals, liquids, gases, or food ingredients is not considered an assembly. In addition to automobiles and clothing, other representative products include telecommunications and electronic equipment, computers, televisions, sausage casings, miniblinds, and stuffed toys—almost any product capable of assembly. In the case *Samsonite Corp. v. United States,* the operations of the plant were held to be a fabrication and not a mere assembly.

The Mexican *Maquiladora* Industry

Most Section 9802 assembly plants have been built in Mexico, due to its close proximity to the United States. U.S. firms are also able to take advantage of Mexico's lower wage rate. (However, Mexican plants often require more supervisory personnel, higher quality control costs, and have higher worker training costs than in the United States.) Almost 900,000 people are employed in several thousand Mexican *maquiladoras.* Many of them are concentrated along Mexico's border with the United States, which means lowered inventory requirements and transportation costs. Many firms also use their Mexican plants as a base for shipments to South America. *Maquiladoras* will most likely have far less importance under NAFTA than they did before the free trade pact went into effect. Of course, the plants will continue operation, but their reliance on special customs laws is

Samsonite Corp. v. United States
889 F.2d 1074 (1989)
United States Court of Appeals (Fed.Cir.)

BACKGROUND AND FACTS

Samsonite Corporation assembles luggage in Mexico for import into the United States. Many component parts used in the assembly process are made in the United States. Samsonite had shipped steel strips from the United States to Mexico for use as luggage handles. When the strips left the United States, they were five inches long, straight, and bearing a coat of oil. Their value ranged from 95 cents to $1.26. In Mexico, the strips were bent by machine into a form resembling a square-sided letter *C*, cleaned, covered with a vinyl sheath, and riveted to plastic frame assemblies. The assemblies were then placed in, and fastened to, bags of vinyl to make soft luggage. On import into the United States, the Customs Service dutied the luggage, including the value of the steel strips at the rate of 20 percent *ad valorem*. The Court of International Trade upheld the government's contention that the steel strips had not been "exported in a condition ready for assembly" and that the process in Mexico amounted to a fabrication and more than a mere assembly. Samsonite appealed.

SENIOR CIRCUIT JUDGE FRIEDMAN

To obtain a deduction for American-fabricated articles assembled abroad, the components

a. must have been exported from the United States "in condition ready for assembly without further fabrication,"
b. not have lost their physical identity in the articles by change in form, shape, or otherwise, and
c. not have been advanced in value or improved in condition "except by being assembled" and except "by operations incidental to the assembly process such as cleaning, lubricating, and painting."

As the Court of International Trade correctly pointed out, since the "foregoing three conditions for a deduction are set forth in the conjunctive, . . . each must be satisfied before a component can qualify for duty-free treatment." We agree with that court that the steel strips involved in this case did not meet those conditions.

The critical inquiry is whether the bending and shaping that the strips underwent constituted "fabrication" or mere assembly and operations incidental to the assembly process. We hold that what was done to the strips in Mexico was fabrication and not mere assembly.

When the steel strips were exported from the United States, they were just that: five-inch strips that could not serve as the frame of the luggage without undergoing a complete change in shape. Prior to assembling the luggage, the strips were bent by machine into a carefully and specially configured rectangular shape that was necessary before the original strip would serve its ultimate function as part of the frame of the luggage.

In short, what emerged after the bending operation was a different object from that which left the United States. The latter was a steel strip, the former was a metal frame for a piece of luggage. The transformation of the strip in this manner into a luggage frame was a fabrication. The strips therefore had not been exported from the United States "in condition ready for assembly without further fabrication."

Samsonite contends, however, that prior decisions of the Court of Customs and Patent Appeals require a contrary conclusion. It relies particularly on *General Instrument Corp. v. United States,* 499 F.2d 1318 (CCPA 1974). That case involved wire wound on spools that had been exported from the United States to Taiwan. There the wire was removed from the spools, formed into a horizontal coil by a winding machine, taped to prevent unraveling, dipped in cement, dried, precision shaped, removed from the spools, and wound around a core. The end product made from the wire was a component of a television set that was imported into the United States.

The Court of Customs and Patent Appeals held that: "The steps performed upon the wire after its exportation to Taiwan are not 'further fabrication' steps, but rather assembly steps within the meaning of [the statute]."

Samsonite argues that far more was done to the wire in *General Instrument* than was done to the steel strips in this case. It argues that if the processing the wire underwent in *General Instrument* was not "fabrication," a fortiori "the one simple-minded act of bending a straight frame into a C was neither a further fabrication nor a nonincidental operation."

continued

continued

The critical inquiry in determining whether fabrication rather than mere assembly took place here, is not the amount of processing that occurred in the two cases, but its nature. In *General Instrument,* the wire, when it left the United States and when it returned as part of a finished product, was a coil. The wire was taken directly from the supply spool on which it was wound and, after processing, was used in assembling the TV set components. The wire underwent no basic change in connection with its incorporation into the television set component.

In contrast, in the present case the steel strips had to undergo a significant change in shape before the actual assembly of luggage could begin. Until the steel strips had been made into C shapes they could not be used as a part of the luggage. Unlike the "assembly" that the court in *General Instrument*

held the processing of the wire involved, here "further fabrication" of the steel strips was required in order to change them into frames for luggage, before the assembly of the luggage could take place.

Decision.   The Court of Appeals upheld the decision of the lower court. The bending and processing of the steel strips in Mexico was fabrication and not a mere assembly and therefore did not qualify for duty-free treatment under Section 9802.

Comment.   In *United States v. Haggar Apparel Co.,* 526 U.S. 380, 119 S. Ct. 1392 (1999), the United States Supreme Court upheld regulations of the U.S. Customs Service (19 C.F.R. 10.16) that permapressing of men's pants was an additional step in manufacturing, and not a minor operation incidental to assembly.

being replaced by NAFTA's general tariff preferences. In 2002, *maquiladoras* accounted for almost half of Mexico's exports.

The Social Responsibility of U.S. Firms in the *Maquiladora* Industry

Maquiladoras have had a tremendous economic and social impact on the people of Mexico—and on sections of California and Texas as well—and account for the second-largest source of income, next to oil, for Mexicans. The *maquiladora* industry presents many of the same social, political, and economic issues faced by multinational firms operating anywhere in the developing world. Mexico desires the economic opportunities created by foreign plants situated there, poised on the doorstep of the U.S. market. To attract foreign investment, it offers many economic and regulatory incentives. On the other hand, Mexico expects these companies to be good citizens and to operate within the law. Most firms do understand their responsibility to comply with Mexican regulations and to contribute to the betterment of Mexican society, but managers face many perplexing problems. For instance, should a U.S. firm operating a maquila in, say, Chihuahua City provide a clinic for dealing with employee drug or alcohol problems engendered by the many workers who have left their

homes and traveled to northern Mexico in search of jobs? Should they provide these facilities even though Mexican law may not require them to do so? Should a U.S. firm in Mexico operate voluntarily under the same health and safety standards that they are expected to conform to in the United States, or merely conform to the minimum standards required under Mexican law? Should the U.S. company introduce the latest technologies to the Mexican plants and fund worker training programs? With new investment opportunities made possible by NAFTA, U.S. and Canadian companies operating throughout Mexico will face these kinds of ethical issues.

---

http://www.cocef.org/
The Border Environment Cooperation Commission (follow link for English). Created by the U.S. and Mexico to assist local communities within 62 miles of the border to develop and finance environmental infrastructure projects, such as sewage treatment and waste disposal.

No issue is more pressing in the border regions than the degradation the plants have caused to the environment. In the early 1990s, the governments of the United States and Mexico began negotiations on protecting the Rio Grande, and on building municipal sewer systems, water treatment plants, and solid-waste disposal sites. Their greatest concern is how to deal with hazardous waste. The two governments are attempting to devise ways of tracking hazardous waste and regulating disposal sites. Mexico has reportedly closed hundreds of plants for environmental violations. Complicating the problem are the thousands of trucks that cross the border daily, causing severe air pollution and damage to roads and bridges. Governments will spend hundreds of millions of dollars, at a minimum, in dealing with these social and environmental problems. Industry investors will bear an increasing share of these costs in the future. Hopefully, the new environmental cooperation spawned by NAFTA will relieve some of the problems in this fast growing border region.

international accents

Mexico

The People

Mexico is a very class-conscious society where social stratifications are well-defined. Upper class Mexicans will not dirty their hands with tasks they find beneath them. A sense of fatalism is quite strong among many Mexicans, who feel that their path through life is largely preordained.

Meeting and Greeting
- Shake hands or give a slight bow when introduced.
- Bow when greeting a Mexican woman. Shake hands only if she extends her hand first.

Body Language
- Mexicans generally stand close together when conversing. Don't show signs of discomfort, which would be considered rude by your Mexican counterpart.
- Mexicans often "hold" a gesture (a handshake, a squeeze of the arm, a hug) longer than Americans and Canadians do.
- Don't stand with your hands on your hips; this signifies anger. It is considered rude to stand around with your hands in your pockets.

Corporate Culture
- Punctuality is expected of foreign businesspeople. Your Mexican counterpart may be late or keep you waiting. Thirty minutes past the scheduled meeting time is considered punctual by Mexicans.
- Spanish is the language of business. You may need to hire an interpreter (preferably a native speaker who understands the language as it is spoken in Mexico).

- Meet with top executives first. Top-level Mexican executives may not attend subsequent meetings, which often take place with middle-level management and technical people. Don't feel insulted; this shows that discussions are proceeding positively.
- Negotiations move slowly. Be patient. For Mexicans, the building of a personal relationship comes before the building of a professional one.
- Expect approximately ten to fifteen minutes of small talk before getting down to business.
- If offered something to drink (usually coffee), don't refuse. This would be seen as an insult.
- Take some time for consideration before agreeing to anything. Quick decisiveness is often seen as hasty.
- A promise does not mean that your request will be carried out. You should always ask for written confirmation of any agreement or commitment.
- Management or other important people may sometimes make unreasonable or overly aggressive demands to demonstrate their importance within or to their own group. Be aware of such hidden agendas.
- Personalize everything. Explain how all proposals will benefit a Mexican's country, community, family and, most important, the Mexican personally.
- Deal-making almost never occurs over the phone (and rarely by letter). Mexicans prefer to do business in person.
- Your local contact person or representative is very important and should be chosen very carefully. A low-level representative will be taken as an affront by status-conscious Mexicans, who will assume that you are not really serious.

continued

- The status of your hotel accommodations, the quality of your clothes and watch, and whether or not you arrive in a chauffeured limousine or in a taxi will be critically appraised by your Mexican counterparts.
- Be persistent! Don't give up if you don't receive a response to your phone calls or letters right away or if your meetings are continually postponed or canceled. If you give up, your Mexican counter-

parts might assume that you weren't serious in the first place.

The continuation of this document is at http://schaffer.westbuslaw.com, Chapter 13.

Reprinted with permission. Excerpted from "Put Your Best Foot Forward" by Mary Murray Bosrock. © 2003 International Education Systems, St. Paul, MN. For more information about IES products, please visit http://www.MaryBosrock.com

CHAPTER SUMMARY

The *North American Free Trade Agreement* encompasses the largest free trade area in the world—Canada, Mexico, and the United States. The agreement became effective on January 1, 1994, and will have far-reaching effects well into the next century. NAFTA was based on the earlier *U.S.–Canadian Free Trade Agreement* of 1989. NAFTA was agreed to by the legislatures of the three countries only after heated debate. Proponents of the agreement saw it as a means of expanding trade opportunities for North American products, spurring cross-border investment, increasing the number of high-paying U.S. jobs in export industries, and bringing greater economic and social stability to Mexico. Opponents argued that it would result in large-scale loss of U.S. and Canadian jobs to low-wage workers in Mexico. Since the agreement went into effect, some U.S. factories have moved to Mexico, but many Asian manufacturers have also moved operations to Mexico to give them a jumping-off platform to the Americas. In the short time that NAFTA has been in effect, trade and cross-border investment in North America has grown. Although Mexico suffered a severe financial crisis in 1994, most businesspeople, investors, and traders are optimistic about the future of business there.

NAFTA is more than just a trade agreement. It contains broad provisions affecting a wide range of topics—trade in goods and services, cross-border investment, the protection of intellectual property, the protection of the environment, the health and safety of workers, and more. It calls on each of the three countries to harmonize their laws in these areas.

North American trade and investment laws are complex. Anyone buying or selling goods must be

keenly aware of the complicated customs procedures that must be followed in moving goods across borders. For instance, a product is qualified for NAFTA trade preferences or advantages only if it originated in North America. To know its country-of-origin, the exporter and importer must have a working knowledge of the rules of origin applicable to that product. Special rules apply to key industries, such as automobiles and telecommunications. NAFTA also sets out special rules for cross-border trade in services that affect banking, insurance, and transportation. Although NAFTA generally makes investment in Mexican firms easier, when starting new companies or purchasing existing ones, potential investors must have good legal advice covering investment rules as well as good advice on how they might be affected by future economic or political changes.

Finally, keep in mind that NAFTA is a part of a wider free trade movement encompassing the entire Western Hemisphere. No sooner was NAFTA effective than did the Caribbean countries ask to join. They feared being left behind as free trade leads to economic growth in the hemisphere. They were concerned that investors from the United States and other countries would relocate their factories to Mexico to qualify for NAFTA treatment. Admission to NAFTA would mean access to North American markets for their products and increased investment from sources worldwide.

Thirty-four nations of the Western Hemisphere are negotiating a *Free Trade Agreement of the Americas*. It is hoped that it can be concluded by 2005. It would result in the world's largest free trade area—a market of $13 trillion and 800 million people. Although the movement to free trade and investment policies can be derailed by any number of events, such as political change and economic cri-sis, the beginning of the twenty-first century seems a time of trade liberalization in the Americas.

Questions and Case Problems

1. Based on discussions in this chapter and Chapter Three, explain how a free trade area differs from a common market. Give examples of each.
2. Consider a study of doing business in Mexico. How does the economic, cultural, social, and political climate affect a business there? Describe Mexico's form of government. How are business relations conducted there? Are they more or less formal than in other Western countries? Describe how Mexico's policies toward trade and investment have changed over the years. Do you believe that Mexico provides a stable climate for trade and investment? What products or industries would seem to do well in the Mexican market?
3. Given the evidence about the ineffectiveness of the labor and environmental side agreements to NAFTA, do you think they should be included in any expansion of NAFTA? In a different form? Explain.
4. Your company produces "Big Duster" tires. Your most popular styles are the ones with the raised white lettering on the outside of the tire. You would like to export tires to Mexico, but cannot pass the Mexican labeling and marking requirements. Among the many other requirements, to remold the tires in Spanish would be costly. You do not think the regulations are fair. Do the requirements violate NAFTA? What course of action should you take?
5. Your company distills Kentucky bourbon. A Canadian competitor is also selling Kentucky bourbon in Ontario, but their bourbon is made in Canada. Canada's liquor control agency has looked the other way and ignored your requests to enjoin the sale. Does the sale violate NAFTA? GATT? Would

this action be heard before the NAFTA Free Trade Commission or the WTO? What steps can be taken to force Canada to enjoin the sale? What remedies are available? If the Canadian products are exported to the United States, can they be stopped at the border?
6. Compare and contrast other trade preference programs such as the GSP and the Caribbean Basin Initiative, with NAFTA. If the Caribbean countries already receive trade preferences under the CBI, why would many of them want admission to NAFTA?
7. How does the function of a NAFTA arbitral panel differ from that of a binational panel? What is the standard of review in binational panel decisions? Describe the role of an extraordinary challenge committee. Why does NAFTA recommend that panelists on binational panels and extraordinary challenge committees be judges or former judges whenever possible, but arbitral panelists may be specialists in international business or trade?
8. What is a rule of origin? Why is it important to the operation of a free trade area?
9. Discuss the social responsibility of a Canadian or U.S. manager working in Mexico. If a certain course of action were illegal in the manager's own country, but lawful and accepted in Mexico, which standard should the manager follow? Describe the social responsibility of firms operating in Mexico in regard to environmental protection, worker health and safety, and corrupt practices.
10. As you read this, what progress has been made toward wider Western Hemisphere free trade? In the Caribbean? In Central and South America?

Managerial Implications

Consider the following NAFTA management problem in a global business context.

DownPillow, Inc., a small U.S. manufacturer of down comforters and pillows, sells nationally through high-quality retailers. The company is known for its quality of materials and production. Its raw materials include cotton fabric, unfilled cotton shells, and down

fills. These materials are not produced in the United States in sufficient quantities to meet the needs of the U.S. market. The HTS classification for unfilled comforter shells is 6307.90. The classification for finished down comforters is HTS 9404.90.

For many years, DownPillow purchased materials from Europe and paid in foreign currency. Gradually, costs rose because European suppliers faced higher labor and overhead costs. A declining U.S. dollar made goods more costly, but as costs rose, the company couldn't pass them on in price increases. When the U.S. market became more competitive in the early 1990s, DownPillow looked to China for cheaper materials. China is the world's leading producer of cotton textiles and down fill. Chinese textiles enter the United States under strict quota limits, enforced by U.S. Customs. Quota category 362 includes unfilled shells, comforters, quilts, bedspreads, and other top-of-the-bed products. DownPillow negotiated with a Chinese manufacturer for low-cost materials, priced in dollars. The new products were introduced to U.S. customers in 1993 at competitive prices. The new lower-priced goods quickly became an important part of the company's line.

In the following year the political situation changed. The United States accused China of illegally transshipping textiles through third countries to "get around" the U.S. quota. In response, the United States reduced the quota on category 362. In 1994, the annual quota closed in early fall. Goods anticipated for shipment during the Christmas season sat in a customs-bonded warehouse at the port until released by U.S. Customs on January 2, 1995. By 1995, the largest U.S. importers of comforters and bedspreads had bought their merchandise early, and the quota closed on March 6. DownPillow was barely able to obtain sufficient unfilled shells for its production needs. When it tried to switch its customers back to the higher-priced merchandise made from European materials, they balked. Many threatened to take their business elsewhere.

1. Management is desperate for a solution. It has learned that Canada will permit the entry of Chinese textiles. They also know that Canadian trade negotiators put a little-known rule of origin in NAFTA providing that a product that undergoes a change from category 6307.90 to category 9404.90 will become a product of North America. (Tariff shifting is not generally available for textile articles, but widely available for many other manufactured and processed goods.) They would like your opinion on answers to the following questions:

   a. May they bring the Chinese cotton shells into Canada, and ship them to the United States despite the quota? What processes would have to take place in Canada to do this? If they did, what would the tariff rate be? Would they see any net tariff savings?

   b. Production in Canada would give ready access to the Canadian home-fashions market. Should the company explore the possibility of investment in a plant in Canada? What are the pros and cons of such a move? How would they be affected by NAFTA investment provisions?

   c. Canada is a good supplier of goose down. Would it make a difference if they used down from Canadian geese, as opposed to down plucked from geese in, say, Poland?

   d. Every state requires that comforters may only be sold if they are manufactured or imported by licensed bedding manufacturers. Does NAFTA prohibit the application of these rules to Canadian and Mexican companies? What is the purpose of these rules?

   e. The company also has had some interest from buyers in Mexico. Would any import duties apply on shipments of either its U.S.- or Canadian-made products to Mexico? What would the tariff rate be? What special textile labeling rules are applicable, and how would they affect the company's ability to market there?

   f. Management is concerned about meeting foreign health standards applicable to a natural product like down and feathers. Where would they go for information on foreign regulations?

2. Discuss the wisdom of DownPillow's decision to switch sources of supply to China. Describe the impact of customs and tariff law on a North American firm's strategy. Describe how this small company was affected by international political events out of its control. Do you think the company underestimated its customers and its market?

CHAPTER 14

THE EUROPEAN UNION AND OTHER REGIONAL TRADE AREAS

Europe's history is a long and tumultuous one with alliances formed and dissolved over a thousand years. A significant trend in the post-World War II period has been the development of regional economic alliances to facilitate trade, as well as to maintain peace and security and contain communism. These regional agreements have significant impact on the conduct of business.

Historical precedents for economic integration can be traced back as far as Charlemagne; however, the devastation of Europe by World War II and efforts to rebuild were the major forces in bringing the original six European countries—Belgium, West Germany (now called Germany), France, Italy, Luxembourg, and the Netherlands—together to form the Common Market or European Community, the forerunner of the European Union or EU. The EU in 2003 numbers fifteen countries with ten slated to join in 2004. The four freedoms—free movement of capital, persons, goods, and services—are a cornerstone of the plan for economic integration as well as the introduction of a single currency, the euro, and a monetary union.

The tumultuous events since the 2001 World Trade Center terrorist attack in New York and subsequent attacks in Bali have caused reverberations throughout the world. The war in Afghanistan and the 2003 war in Iraq or Gulf War II to oust Saddam Hussein and to find weapons of mass destruction (WMD) have affected economies and strained old alliances. Britain, Poland, Spain, Italy, Portugal, and the Czech Republic aligned with the United States and Australia in waging war in Iraq while neither Germany nor France supported the action. This confirmed the not-surprising reality that although a "union," the EU was not of one voice on foreign policy and defense. This also foreshadows divisions that may lurk beneath the surface on other matters.

This chapter examines the structure and operation of the EU and the ramifications for business. It also examines the unification process with regard to laws and the introduction of the single currency, as well as the impact of this on business. It examines the development of other trade areas in the world (the *North American Free Trade Agreement* will be discussed in a separate chapter) including Mercosur, and efforts in Central America, South America, Africa, the Arab world, and Asia.

> **http://europa.eu.int/
> index.htm**
> See for policies, institutions, and other information on the EU.

THE PHILOSOPHY OF ECONOMIC INTEGRATION

Of the numerous paradigms of economic integration, some involve more comprehensive economic and political integration, while others are more limited in scope. The United States offers a good starting point for analysis.

Federal Model

The U.S. model of federalism involves fifty states cooperating and agreeing to have one currency, army, and foreign policy managed by the federal executive branch. The states have autonomy on other matters. The president is the Commander in Chief of the Armed Forces and state law is subordinated to federal law under the Supremacy Clause of the U.S. Constitution. Remember, when the

Constitution was drafted, many states were concerned about losing their independence and being subsumed by a national identity. The smaller states were concerned about being overpowered by a large federal nation state as well as the larger former colonies. The Tenth Amendment, adopted in 1791 as part of the Bill of Rights, addressed this concern. It states, "The powers not delegated to the United States by the Constitution, nor prohibited to it by the States are reserved to the States respectively, or to the people." In the vernacular, this statement is called the "states' rights" clause.

The U.S. Constitution is a remarkable document; it managed to allay many concerns by creating a balance of power between the branches of government as well as between federal government and the states. Each state has two senators regardless of its size, while representation in the House of Representatives is based on population. Thus, more populated states have more representatives.

Article I, Section 8 of the Constitution states that Congress shall have the power "to make all laws which shall be necessary and proper for carrying into execution the foregoing." In return, the states agreed to one currency, free movement of people between states, the principle of nondiscrimination among states, as well as federal courts to deal with conflict between states, and ceded the power to Congress to regulate commerce. The individual states have also given their authority over international trade to Congress. For purposes of foreign policy, the country acts as one unit. For example, Massachusetts would not send troops to Rwanda without authorization from the federal government. Despite political differences, the states within the country act as one nation.

The U.S. experiment is now over two hundred years old and is unquestionably a success; however, this system is not for every constellation of countries. The U.S. model took recently settled colonies, often no more than one hundred years old, and politically united them, laying the foundation for future economic cooperation. Other models start from quite the opposite direction, beginning with economic cooperation and moving into political cooperation and possible unification (see Exhibit 14.1).

Free Trade Area

In contrast to the federal model, a Free Trade Area (FTA) develops when two or more countries agree

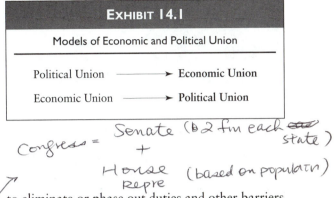

EXHIBIT 14.1

Models of Economic and Political Union

Political Union ——————▶ Economic Union

Economic Union ——————▶ Political Union

[handwritten: Congress = Senate (2 fm each state) + House Repre (based on population)]

to eliminate or phase out duties and other barriers to trade among the member countries. The FTA does not attempt to control relations of member countries to third countries. Thus, a country can be a member of an FTA and still have separate bilateral relations with other countries. FTAs vary greatly and have different approaches in handling intercountry disputes. A good dispute settlement mechanism is critical to the success of an FTA. An FTA and a federal system represent the two distinct ends on the continuum of integration.

Customs Union

A *customs union* is more ambitious in scope than an FTA. Not only does it reduce tariffs between member countries, but the customs union members also agree to deal similarly with nonmembers. The goal is to encourage trade between members just as in the FTA; however, the customs union begins to exhibit fortress-like characteristics that could lead to the erection of barriers to entry for companies and products from nonmember countries.

Common Market

A *common market* or *economic community* goes further than a customs union by trying to make uniform standards and laws among the member countries. The goal of a common market is the free movement of people, goods, services, and capital within the market. A court with jurisdiction and power to enforce its rulings is a critical element in the effectiveness of the members' compliance with the standards and laws. Without effective enforcement, each member state can continue to operate its own protectionist barriers. Yet even in 2003, this goal is not achieved easily. See the International Accents article and the *Italian Republic* case.

Britain wins EU Chocolate Battle

Luxembourg—British confectioners have won a "sweet victory" in a European court, ending a 30-year battle over what constitutes chocolate. Spain and Italy have restricted sales of British-made chocolate because it contains up to 5 percent vegetable fat instead of pure cocoa butter. But European judges ruled their efforts illegal on Thursday, saying UK chocolate was entitled to free access to all EU markets. "For the Cadbury's factory making Dairy Milk in Birmingham, and people in York putting Terry's Chocolate Oranges together, a positive ruling will be a sweet victory indeed," said Gary Titley, the UK's Labour Party leader in the European Parliament.

Italian and Spanish consumers would now be "liberated to choose old favourites like Crunchies, Double Decker, Wispa and Flake on an equal footing with local products as familiar as Ferrero Rocher," Titley told the UK Press Association. The European Commission took Spain and Italy to court after they defied a 2000 EU-wide agreement allowing a small amount of vegetable fat in chocolate as long as it was listed in the ingredients. The European Court of Justice in Luxembourg found both countries guilty of breaching EU trade laws by insisting that British chocolate be labelled as "chocolate substitute." The judgment also applies to other EU countries which market chocolates with vegetable fat—Ireland, Denmark, Portugal, Sweden and Finland. Their products have all been wrongly prohibited from being marketed under the name "chocolate," the judges said, rejecting Spanish and Italian claims that the chocolate restrictions were "based on the need for consumer protection." "The addition of those fats does not alter the nature of the product, and an indication in the label would inform consumers of their presence," the judges said. Trying to force manufacturers to label their products as "chocolate substitute" imposed extra costs on companies and "may adversely affect

how customers perceive those products. That would lead to restrictions on the free movement of goods," the judges added.

Top European chocolate makers Nestle SA and Cadbury Schweppes PLC said they were pleased with the ruling, the Associated Press reported. The ruling will help achieve "a unified market for chocolate across Europe," Nestle spokesman Marcel Rubin said.

'Family chocolate'

The chocolate war began in 1973 when Britain joined the EU. To continental Europeans, milky British chocolate with its vegetable fat was seen as less than the real thing. But London's EU membership negotiators made it clear that Britain would not adopt EU chocolate standards, which at the time required chocolate to contain only cocoa ingredients.

Britain, Ireland and Denmark won an exemption to continue making their own chocolate, while other EU countries could ban vegetable fats in chocolate if they wished. The result was the absence of familiar British brands—Mars bars, Kit Kats and Cadbury's milk chocolate—in eight countries: Belgium, France, Italy, Spain, Luxembourg, Germany, Greece and Holland. Efforts to settle the issue included suggestions to call British chocolate "household milk chocolate" or even "vegelate." A deal was finally reached in March 2000: British milk chocolate containing up to 20 percent milk—far more than many continentals consider civilised—could be exported to all EU countries if labelled as "family milk chocolate." And British chocolate, with up to 5 percent vegetable fat, could be exported to all EU countries as long as the fat was listed in the ingredients. Those rules come into force in June, but Spain and Italy decided to continue the fight to the bitter end.

SOURCE: Find this article at http://www.cnn.com/2003/WORLD/europe/01/16/chocolate.war/index.html
Copyright ©2003 CNN. Reprinted with permission.

Compatibility of Trade Areas with the WTO and GATT

At first glance, the principles underlying the formation of trade areas seem to contradict the basic principles of the WTO and GATT, which require nondiscrimination and reciprocity among all members. How can members of an FTA or customs union treat those members more favorably

Commission of the European Communities v. Italian Republic
Case C-14/00 (2003)
European Court of Justice

BACKGROUND AND FACTS

Italy required that chocolate products manufactured in other member states that contained vegetable fats other than cocoa butter be sold in Italy as "chocolate substitutes." The Commission claimed that Italy had failed to fulfill its obligation under Article 30 of the EC treaty (now, after amendment, Article 28). Council Directive 73/241/EEC of July 24, 1973, on the approximation of the laws relating to cocoa and chocolate products, states in part "the use of vegetable fats other than cocoa butter in chocolate products is permitted." * * *

Italian law no. 351 of April 30, 1976, states that food preparations containing cocoa whose "texture, consistency, color, and taste are similar to those of chocolate but whose composition does not correspond to the definition of one of the products listed in the annex to the present law, constitutes a 'chocolate substitute.'" The products referred to in that annex do not contain vegetable fats other than cocoa butters.

An Italian Ministry of Health circular of March 15, 1996, . . . stated that cocoa and chocolate products containing vegetable fats other than cocoa butter originating in the United Kingdom, Ireland, and Denmark, can be marketed within Italian territory only if their composition satisfies the rules of the state of origin and if their sales name corresponds to . . . chocolate substitute. The Italian government refused to change its interpretation of the Directive or the Italian law.

* * *

The Commission states that chocolate containing vegetable fats other than cocoa butter up to a maximum of 5 percent of the total weight of the product is manufactured under the name "chocolate" in six member states (Denmark, Ireland, Portugal, Sweden, Finland, and the United Kingdom) and that it is accepted under that name in all member states with the exception of Spain and Italy.

* * *

The Commission considers that it is not possible to claim that the addition of vegetable fats other than cocoa butter to a chocolate product that contains the minimum contents required under Directive 73/241 substantially changes the nature of the product to the point where the use of the name "chocolate" would create confusion as regards its basic characteristics.

FINDINGS OF THE COURT

First of all, it must be held that the Commission's complaint based on the fact that the Italian legislation is not in compliance with Community law, inasmuch as it places restrictions on the free movement of cocoa and chocolate products containing vegetable fats other than cocoa butter, raises the question of the extent of the harmonisation achieved under Directive 73/241.

While the parties agree that the use of such vegetable fats in cocoa and chocolate products was not harmonised by the directive, they disagree as regards the consequences of the fact for the marketing of products which contain such fats.

Since it considers that the absence of harmonisation as regards the use of vegetable fats other than cocoa butter in cocoa and chocolate products cannot exclude the marketing of products containing such fats from the application of the principle of the free movement of goods, the Commission claims that any measures restricting the free movement of those products must be considered in the light of Article 30 of the Treaty.

By contrast, the Italian Government maintains that Directive 73/241 fully regulates the marketing of the cocoa and chocolate products to which it refers, thereby precluding the application of Article 30 of the Treaty in so far as, first, it sets out the principle that the use of vegetable fats other than cocoa butter is prohibited in the manufacture of cocoa and chocolate products and, secondly, it establishes a system of free movement under the name 'chocolate' only for cocoa and chocolate products which do not contain such vegetable fats.

The Italian Government therefore contends that Directive 73/241 enables Member States whose national law prohibits the addition of vegetable fats other than cocoa butter to products manufactured within their territory also to prohibit the marketing within their territory, under the name 'chocolate', of products whose manufacture does not comply with their national legislation.

* * *

First, as regards the objectives of the provisions in question and the context in which they occur, it is clear

continued

continued

that Directive 73/241 was not intended to regulate definitively the use of vegetable fats other than cocoa butter in the cocoa and chocolate products to which it refers.

* * *

The Community legislature clearly indicated that, in the light of the disparities between Member States' legislation and the insufficient economic and technical data available, it could not, at the time the directive was adopted, take a final position on the use of vegetable fats other than cocoa butter in cocoa and chocolate products.

* * *

It must also be pointed out that, as is made clear by the case-file, the reference in the same recital to certain Member States where the use of those other vegetable fats was at that time not merely permitted but, moreover, extensive, referred to three Member States which had acceded to the Community shortly before the adoption of Directive 73/241, namely the Kingdom of Denmark, Ireland and the United Kingdom, and which traditionally permitted the addition to cocoa and chocolate products manufactured within their territory of such vegetable fats up to a maximum of 5% of total weight.

In those circumstances, the Council merely established, for the use of vegetable fats other than cocoa butter, provisional rules which were to be re-examined, in accordance with the second sentence of Article 14(2)(a) of Directive 73/241, at the end of a period of three years from its notification.

* * *

. . . Article 30 of the Treaty prohibits obstacles to the free movement of goods, in the absence of harmonisation of national laws, which are the consequence of applying to goods coming from other Member States, where they are lawfully manufactured and marketed, rules that lay down requirements to be met by those goods (such as those relating to their name, form, size, weight, composition, presentation, labelling and packaging), even if those rules apply to national and imported products alike.

* * *

That is all the more so in view of the fact that the name 'chocolate substitute', which the Italian law requires the traders concerned to use, may adversely affect the consumer's perception of the products in question, inasmuch as it denotes substitute, and therefore inferior, products.

* * *

In addition, it must be pointed out that, since Directive 73/241 explicitly permits Member States to authorise the use, in the manufacture of cocoa and chocolate products, of vegetable fats other than cocoa butter, it cannot be claimed that the products to which those fats have been added, in compliance with that directive, are altered to the point where they no longer fall into the same category as those which do not contain such fats.

Therefore, the addition of vegetable fats other than cocoa butter to cocoa and chocolate products which satisfy the minimum contents required by Directive 73/241 cannot substantially alter the nature of those products to the point where they are transformed into different products.

It follows that the inclusion in the label of a neutral and objective statement informing consumers of the presence in the product of vegetable fats other than cocoa butter would be sufficient to ensure that consumers are given correct information.

In those circumstances, the obligation to change the sales name of those products which is imposed by the Italian legislation does not appear to be necessary to satisfy the overriding requirement of consumer protection.

It follows that that legislation, to the extent that it requires the name of products which are lawfully manufactured and marketed in other Member States under the sales name 'chocolate' to be altered for the sole reason that they contain vegetable fats other than cocoa butter, is incompatible with Article 30 of the Treaty.

In the light of all the foregoing considerations, it must be held that, by prohibiting cocoa and chocolate products which comply with the requirements as to minimum content laid down in point 1.16 of Annex I to Directive 73/241 to which vegetable fats other than cocoa butter have been added, and which are lawfully manufactured in Member States which authorise the addition of such fats, from being marketed in Italy under the name used in the Member State of production, and by requiring that those products may only be marketed under the name 'chocolate substitute', the Italian Republic has failed to fulfil its obligations under Article 30 of the Treaty.

Costs

Article 69(2) of the Rules of Procedure provides that the unsuccessful party is to be ordered to pay the costs if they have been applied for in the successful party's pleadings. Since the Commission has applied for costs and the Italian Republic has been unsuccessful, the Italian Republic must be ordered to pay the costs.

continued

continued

On those grounds,

THE COURT (Sixth Chamber),

hereby:

1. Declares that, by prohibiting cocoa and chocolate products which comply with the requirements as to minimum content laid down in point 1.16 of Annex I to Council Directive 73/241/EEC of 24 July 1973 on the approximation of the laws of the Member States relating to cocoa and chocolate products intended for human consumption to which vegetable fats other than cocoa butter have been added, and which are lawfully manufactured in Member States which authorise the addition of such fats, from being marketed in Italy under the name used in the Member State of production, and by requiring that those products may only be marketed under the name 'chocolate substitute', the Italian Republic has failed to fulfil its obligations under Article 30 of the Treaty (now, after amendment, Article 28 EC);

2. Orders the Italian Republic to pay the costs.

Decision and Comment.   The court allowed chocolate products with vegetable fat to be sold as chocolate. This was another victory in the battle against national regulation, which impedes trade and can be construed as protectionist.

---

than other GATT members? Article XXIV of the GATT agreement cryptically states:

> Accordingly, the provisions of this Agreement shall not prevent, as between the territories of contracting parties, the formation of a customs union or of a free-trade area or the adoption of an interim agreement necessary for the formation of a customs union or of a free-trade area; Provided that: (a) with respect to a customs union, or an interim agreement leading to the formation of a customs union, the duties and other regulations of commerce imposed at the institution of any such union or interim agreement in respect of trade with contracting parties not parties to such union or agreement shall not on the whole be higher or more restrictive than the general incidence of the duties and regulations of commerce applicable in the constituent territories prior to the formation of such union or the adoption of such interim agreement, as the case may be.

This section has been used to lower the rates of external tariffs within a trade area for the benefit of non-FTA, WTO members. This achieves the goals of GATT for the benefit of WTO members.

The following section looks at the example of the EU and its movement from a customs union to common market to the EU and the current uncertainty about future integration efforts.

EUROPEAN UNION

The EU of today did not spring forth fully developed in its current form. Rather, it developed over a period of years and with successive modifications. Understanding the present issues requires an examination of the Union's past history.

History

Winston Churchill, former prime minister of Great Britain, stated in 1946 that postwar Europe needed a

> . . . Sovereign remedy . . . to recreate the European family, or as much of it as we can, and provide it with a structure under which it can dwell in peace and safety and freedom. We must build a kind of United States of Europe.

Jean Monnet, who held a number of different positions in the French government and is credited as the founding father of the EU, said that "the states of Europe must form a federation." George Marshall, Secretary of State for the United States, supported this concept as a way to rebuild Europe after World War II and to enable the United States to work with both the victors and the vanquished in Europe as strong strategic allies. They hoped this type of partnership would obviate the possibility of a third world war.

The EU was preceded by several earlier and less ambitious attempts at regional cooperation. The European Coal and Steel Community (ECSC), established in 1952, included the six founding countries and centered on combined price and output controls, investment subsidies, tariff protection, and competition rules. Many of the European coal and steel industries were and are government owned. The ECSC and the respective governments were instrumental in rebuilding the industries after the war and in protecting those industries from competition.

Treaty of Rome. The European Community (EC as it was called) was formed by the signing of the *Treaty of Rome* on March 25, 1957, which created the Common Market. The six member countries (Belgium, West Germany, France, Italy, Luxembourg, and the Netherlands) hoped to build on the success of the ECSC and use the organization to advance all of the countries economically without sacrificing their individuality, culture, or sovereignty.

The *Treaty of Rome* stated the original objectives of the Community (see Exhibit 14.2).

These principles were based on the creation of a customs union that would both eradicate the internal tariffs and restrictions and create a uniform external tariff for nonmembers. The Community committed to achieving the free movement of people, goods, services, and capital; and to eradicating the barriers to the establishment of business by establishing a single, integrated common market. The goals of the community are often stated as a commitment to the "Four Freedoms"—that is, to the free movement of capital, goods, people, and services.

In 1965, the *Merger Treaty* integrated the ECSC and the EURATOM (European Atomic Energy Commission, which was dedicated to the peaceful development and application of nuclear energy) into the organizational structure of the EC. Denmark, Ireland, and the United Kingdom joined in 1973, Greece in 1981, Portugal and Spain in 1986, and Austria, Sweden, and Finland in 1995.

1992 and the *Single European Act.* The ensuing years saw some progress toward the ambitious goals stated in the *Treaty of Rome,* but the dream of free movement of capital, goods, people, and services was not a reality between the member countries.

EXHIBIT 14.2

Treaty of Rome

Article 2

The Community shall have as its task, by establishing a common market and progressively approximating the economic policies of Member States, to promote throughout the Community a harmonious development of economic activities, a continuous and balanced expansion, an increase in stability, an accelerated raising of the standard of living, and closer relations between the States belonging to it.

Article 3

For the purposes set out in Article 2, the activities of the Community shall include, as provided in this Treaty and in accordance with the timetable set out therein.

A. the elimination, as between Member States, of customs duties and of quantitative restrictions on the import and export of goods, and of the other measures having equivalent effect;
B. the establishment of a common customs tariff and of a common commercial policy towards third countries;
C. the abolition, as between Member States, of obstacles to freedom of movement for persons, services, and capital;
D. the adoption of a common policy in the sphere of agriculture;
E. the adoption of a common policy in the sphere of transport;
F. the institution of a system ensuring that competition in the common market is not distorted;
G. the application of procedures by which the economic policies of Member States can be coordinated and disequilibria in their balances of payments remedied;
H. the approximation of the laws of Member States to the extent required for the proper functioning of the common market;
I. the creation of a European Social Fund in order to improve employment opportunities for workers and to contribute to the raising of their standard of living;
J. the establishment of a European Investment Bank to facilitate the economic expansion of the Community by opening up fresh resources;
K. the association of the overseas countries and territories in order to increase trade and to promote jointly economic and social development.

Even today, fewer than two percent of the EU population lives outside of the country of their birth.

In the 1980s, the members of the EC realized that because of their growth in membership and strong national allegiances and the accompanying protectionism, they had not achieved the goals of the *Treaty of Rome*. In 1985, the members called "for the abolition of barriers of all kinds, harmonization of rules, approximation of legislation and tax structures, strengthening of monetary cooperation, and the necessary . . . measures to encourage European firms to work together." The members acknowledged the need to eliminate physical barriers—such as custom checks at borders, veterinary and plant checks, technical standards and building codes, and services and professional standards—and to revamp VAT (Value Added Tax) collection. As a result of this realization and the promise of increased competitiveness upon the elimination of these barriers, the twelve existing members enacted the *Single European Act* (SEA), effective July 1, 1987. The purpose of the SEA was to strengthen the EC institutions and enable them to act and thus to achieve the goals of the *Treaty of Rome*. The SEA also set the deadline December 31, 1992, to achieve economic integration.

The SEA signalled a dramatic move away from business as usual. The members abandoned the requirement of unanimous consent to move forward and adopted the concept of qualified majority voting. This change meant that for proposals related to the internal market all the countries did not have to agree—the Community could make decisions despite some objection.

The Euro and Monetary Union: *Maastricht Treaty*.

After the passage of the SEA, the pace of change within the Community quickened. Members began to think about and discuss the next steps of integration, including a single currency, a central bank, and a unified foreign and security policy, at meetings in 1989 and 1990. The leaders were divided in their vision of Europe. Britain, as voiced by former Prime Minister Margaret Thatcher, saw a limited role for the Community and zealously guarded the autonomy of members. Other countries, notably Germany, pressed for a more unified Europe. Part of the conflict centered around the vision of a federal Europe or how far toward a United States of Europe the Community would move. Students in the United States are familiar

with the division of power and allocation by the Constitution between state and federal government. For the British, however, *federal* was a dirty word, signaling a loss of control over domestic matters.

The recession had been slower to hit Europe than the United States, and so the buoyancy of an expanding economy led to optimism about the future. Also, the sheer enormity of incorporating East Germany into Germany after the 1989 fall of the Berlin Wall had not been absorbed. Nor did European nations fully appreciate the growing pressures of nationalism that were set free along with the crumbling of communism.

The twelve leaders hammered out an agreement in 1991 at Maastricht, Netherlands, that enshrined the next significant step of accepting a single currency for the Community. The treaty ratified in 1993 set 1999 as the target date. However, countries could choose not to join that segment as the UK, Sweden, and Denmark did. The treaty also created the framework for a European Central Bank. The following timetable was agreed to:

- May 1998: determination of which countries meet the criteria (see Exhibit 14.3), exchange rates set
- January 1, 1999: euro—single currency is introduced
- 1999–2002: national currencies continue to exist until 2002, work in parallel with euro
- February 22, 2002: euro becomes sole currency of the twelve participating countries

The countries were also obligated to adhere to the Maastricht criteria, which were designed for "sustainable convergence" or Eurospeak to help grow the economies responsibly. (See Exhibit 14.3.)

The entire unification process has been complicated by the fears that member countries will lose autonomy, but the principle of "subsidiarity" enshrined in the *Maastricht Treaty* assuages some of these concerns. *Subsidiarity* means that the EU will only take action in those areas that are particularly appropriate for community-level action and that whenever possible the individual country will be able to address the issue itself.

The treaty "marks a new stage in the process of creating an ever closer union between peoples in Europe in which decisions are taken as closely as possible to the citizen." The goals are stated in Title I, Article B, shown in Exhibit 14.4. The *Maastricht Treaty* also increases the use of qualified

---

EXHIBIT 14.3

Maastricht Criteria

- Budget deficit no greater than 3 percent of GDP. GDP is defined as gross domestic product, which includes consumer spending, business investment, government purchases, and net exports.
- Public debt no more than 60 percent GDP
- Price stability—inflation within 1.5 percent of the three best countries
- Long-term interest rates within two percent of the three best countries
- Exchange rate stability—two years within the exchange rate mechanism

Many of the European countries feared that through the connection to each other by the euro, when one country stumbled into recession the others would follow automatically. Furthermore, given that the Central Bank would handle interest rates and the currency, previously available national coping mechanisms (changing interest rates and easing money supply) would no longer be available. When the United States is in a recession, many people pack up and follow the jobs to other parts of the country least affected by the downturn, but this is less palatable to many Europeans who do not view Italy and Sweden as fungible environments. Thus, the dangers of an EU recession must be offset by the overall perceived and demonstrable gains of increased investment and stimulation of economic growth.

The previous holdout countries have not yet been convinced of the necessity of using the euro. As of 2003, Britain had postponed the discussion about joining the monetary union. The Swedish voters rejected the proposal to use the euro in September 2003 just as the Danish voters did in 2000. Furthermore, even Germany and France, that have joined, were struggling to meet the criteria, particularly the applicable budget deficit criteria, as were some of the smaller countries like Portugal. This deviation will not portend well for the admission of the ten new countries that are supposed to try to meet the criteria in 2004. The economies all over Europe, like much of the world, are struggling to recover from a recession.

To ensure the monetary union would succeed, in 1997, the EU adopted the Stability and Growth Pact (SGP). The SGP should ensure that each member country continues sound fiscal policy after the implementation of the euro. The program includes an agreement to have a national budget surveillance process and a commitment to "immediate corrective actions" if the budget deficit exceeds 3 percent of GDP. There is also the possibility of sanctions, but to date these have not been used.

EXHIBIT 14.4

Goals of the *Maastricht Treaty*

Title I

Common Provisions
The Union shall set itself the following objectives:

- to promote economic and social progress which is balanced and sustainable, in particular through the creation of an area without internal frontiers, through the strengthening of economic and social cohesion and through the establishment of economic and monetary union, ultimately including a single currency in accordance with the provisions of this treaty.
- to assert its identity on the international scene, in particular through the implementation of a common foreign and security policy including the eventual framing of a common defense policy, which might in time lead to a common defense.
- to strengthen the protection of the rights and interests of the nationals of its Member States through the introduction of a citizenship of the Union.
- to develop close cooperation on justice and home affairs.
- to maintain in full the "acquis communautaire" and build on it with a view to considering, through the procedure referred to in Article N(2), to what extent the policies and forms of cooperation introduced by this treaty may need to be revised with the aim of ensuring the effectiveness of the mechanisms and the institutions of the Community.

The objectives of the Union shall be achieved as provided in this treaty and in accordance with the conditions and the timetable set out therein while respecting the principle of subsidiarity as defined in Article 3b of the treaty establishing the European Community.

majority voting, which limits the ability of countries to deadlock the Union.

Treaty of Amsterdam (1999). The treaty incorporated the principle of freedom of movement from the *Schengen Agreement.* The treaty had other amendments like authorizing appropriate action based on discrimination (race, sex, religion, age, disability, sexual orientation). It generally expanded jurisdiction over asylum, immigration, and visa matters.

Treaty of Nice (2000). The Intergovernmental Conference concluded in December 2000 with a new treaty covering a number of issues. The treaty established voting rights for new members and reallocates votes of existing members in the Council of Ministers. The Commission President's power is expanded with the ability to fire commissioners. In 2005, the countries that have two commissioners (Germany, France, Britain, Italy, and Spain) will drop one commissioner. The size of the Commission should not exceed twenty-seven. The treaty extends majority voting to development and regional aid and trade negotiations on services, but not to immigration, tax, and social security. They postponed any decision on a European Constitution. The treaty needs to be ratified by all members and may take 1½ years to complete (see Exhibit 14.5).

The treaty was ratified by Ireland, the last member country, in 2002. The commission voted to approve ten members joining by May 2004: Poland, Lithuania, Estonia, Latvia, Hungary, Czech Republic, Slovenia, Slovakia, Malta, and Cyprus. This must be approved by the fifteen existing members, as well as the ten proposed new members. If all the countries do join, the EU's population will swell to over 440 million, eclipsing the 387 million in NAFTA. This will no doubt have implications for businesses that could locate in one of the new member countries and receive the benefits of being within an EU member state.

Treaty Establishing a Constitution for Europe. For almost two years, a group of individuals including the former president of France, Valery Giscard d'Estaing, have labored to bring together all the previous treaties into a Constitution of Europe. In June 2003, a draft was presented to the Union members and will be debated. The draft constitution is 253 pages with an opening quotation from Thucydides stating: "Our constitution . . . is called a democracy because power is in the hands not of a minority but

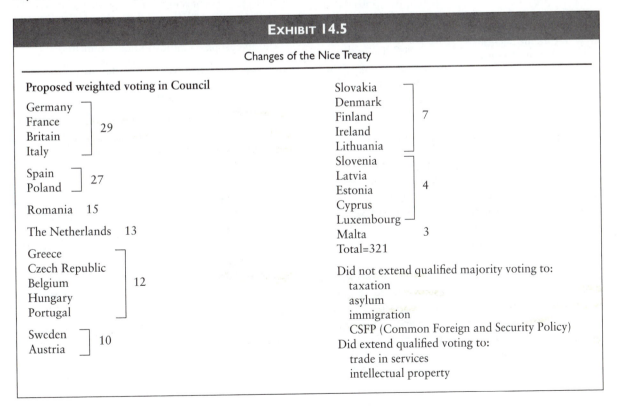

EXHIBIT 14.5

Changes of the Nice Treaty

Proposed weighted voting in Council

Germany, France, Britain, Italy	29
Spain, Poland	27
Romania	15
The Netherlands	13
Greece, Czech Republic, Belgium, Hungary, Portugal	12
Sweden, Austria	10
Slovakia, Denmark, Finland, Ireland, Lithuania	7
Slovenia, Latvia, Estonia, Cyprus, Luxembourg	4
Malta	3
Total=321	

Did not extend qualified majority voting to:
    taxation
    asylum
    immigration
    CSFP (Common Foreign and Security Policy)
Did extend qualified voting to:
    trade in services
    intellectual property

of the greatest number." After the governments review the document, it must be approved by a number of country referendums and could not go into effect until 2006 at the earliest. The draft steered clear of many of the more controversial proposals such as directly electing a president by popular vote. Instead, it is proposed the EU presidency not rotate every six months as now, but be for a term of five years. It also proposes the creation of a position of EU Foreign Minister. One of the striking differences as compared to the United States Constitution is its specificity. For example, under the title of "Freedoms," the concept of the Four Freedoms (free movement of goods, capital, people, and services) has been incorporated, as well as the "protection of personal data," "freedom of expression," and "respect for his or her private and family life." One wonders what precisely is meant by all these phrases. Under a separate title of "Dignity" is the statement: "right to life" and "no one shall be condemned to the death penalty or executed." Under the title "Equality," sexual orientation is mentioned as protected against discrimination. The Vatican is reportedly very concerned that the constitution does not mention either God or the historic role of Christianity in Europe. Whether this new constitution will be approved is in question, but the balance of 2003 and 2004 will be critical in the future of this constitution.

---

http://europa.eu.int/en/record/mt/top.html
This is the site of the text and provisions of the Maastricht Treaty.

Structure of the European Union

The *Treaty of Rome* allocated power between the Council of Ministers, the Commission, the Assembly or Parliament, and the Court of Justice. This structure was not disturbed by the *Maastricht Treaty*; however, new members changed the seats allocated to each country.

The Council.   The Council is located in Brussels, Belgium. It is composed of one representative of each member state. The position of president of the Council rotates among the membership every six months. The purpose of the Council is to coordinate economic policies of member states and "to make decisions," which includes approving legislation and international agreements. The Council shares some legislative power with the Parliament in matters. The Council also works on developing a Common Foreign and Security Policy (CFSP), but the states still have independent control over these.

With the accession of Finland, Austria, and Sweden the member countries include Belgium, Denmark, Germany, Greece, Spain, France, Ireland, Italy, Luxembourg, the Netherlands, Austria, Portugal, Finland, Sweden, and the United Kingdom for a total of eighty-seven votes.

Qualified majority voting was introduced by the SEA. A qualified majority requires sixty-two votes (71 percent). Currently the number of votes needed to block legislation equals twenty-six votes.

The rules for qualified majority voting change after November 1. According to official sources:

> From 1 November 2004, a qualified majority will be reached
>
> - if a majority of member states (in some cases a two-thirds majority) approve AND
> - if a minimum of votes is cast in favour—which is 72.3% of the total (roughly the same share as under the previous system).
>
> In addition, a member state may ask for confirmation that the votes in favour represent at least 62% of the total population of the Union. If this is found not to be the case, the decision will not be adopted. (http://europa.eu.int/institutions/council)

How this will work, remains to be seen.

The Commission.   The Commission, serving as the Union's executive body, consists of twenty members who theoretically represent the Community rather than specific national interests. The twenty seats are apportioned with France, Spain, Germany, Italy, and the United Kingdom each having two and the remainder having one. After November 1, 2004, there will be one commissioner per country. However, the countries are supposed to devise a rotational system so the number does not exceed 27. Each member, appointed by the Council, serves a four-year term and may be reappointed. The Commission is the most ambitious attempt to become supranational and to forge a Community identity. The Commission elects a president from among its members. The president must be approved by the Parliament. Each commissioner is in charge of a special area based in part on the country's interest. The commissioners head up the directorates and are staffed by the cabinets. The commissioners are named to coordinate such areas as agriculture, competition, single-market, common-trade policies, transport, and the various geographic regions themselves. For example, the EU Competition Commissioner is looking at changing the competition rules that affect how cars are sold in Europe. Existing regulations, which expired in 2002, forced car buyers to pay much more for a car in Britain than on the continent. Car dealers are preparing to battle the Commissioner on this, fearing an erosion of profits. Given the Internet economy, it seems unimaginable that consumers will tolerate major price differences for much longer. The directorates serve as support to the commissioners. Much of the work of the Commission is done in the directorates, where policies are developed. The Commission proposes regulations to the Council.

The Court of Justice.

The European Court of Justice (ECJ) in Luxembourg functions as the final arbiter of EU law. Fifteen justices are appointed by the Council for a term of six years (there may also be one or two extensions of three years each); one justice is appointed from each country. Eight advocates general are also appointed. After the new countries join, there still will be one judge per country, however, the court may sit as a "grand chamber" with only 13 judges. The court is fashioned in the civil law tradition because most of the judges come from civil, rather than common law, jurisdictions. The court's procedure reflects civil law influences. More specifically, unlike the United Kingdom or Ireland, the court itself calls witnesses, demands the production of documents, and hires necessary experts. The court recently has allowed limited cross-examination by the parties. (See Exhibit 14.6.)

Several other features serve to distinguish this court. First the decisions of the court are issued without any dissenting opinions. This practice does not indicate total agreement among the justices; however, the public is not privy to it as in the United States where the public, press, and legal scholars examine dissenting opinions to divine the theoretical differences between the judges and to predict future outcomes on different cases. This EU process helps to protect the national judges from pressure within their state, an issue about which U.S. Supreme Court judges, appointed for life, do not have to worry.

> **EXHIBIT 14.6**
>
> Court of Justice Jurisdiction
>
> **Court of Justice Jurisdiction Includes:**
>
> Proceedings for
>
> - Failure to meet an obligation.
> - Annulment of community legislation.
> - Failure to act by community institution.
> - Action for damages by community institution.
> - Appeals.
> - Preliminary ruling—clarification of community law.

The court also has positions of advocates general, a position unfamiliar in the United States or Britain, but found in France, for example. Both the parties, as well as the Advocate General, submit their positions on the case to the court. Often, although not required, the court bases its opinion on the material from the Advocate General.

National courts are obligated to follow Community law and the ECJ decisions. An English court recognized this authority in a famous opinion noting the difference between English and Community law, but nonetheless followed the controlling Community law. Lord Denning in *Bulmer v. Bollinger* (1974) stated

> **http://europa.eu.int/cj/en/index.htm**
> The home page for the Court of Justice of the EC.

The (EC) Treaty is quite unlike any of the enactments to which we have become accustomed. . . . It lays down general principles. It expresses its aims and purposes. All in sentences of moderate length and commendable style. But it lacks precision. It uses words and phrases without defining what they mean. An English lawyer would look for an interpretation clause, but he would look in vain. There is none. All the way through the Treaty there are gaps and lacunae. These have to be filled in by the judges, or by the regulations or directives. It is the European way. . . . Seeing these differences, what are the English courts to do when they are faced with a problem of interpretation? They must follow the European pattern. No longer must they argue about the precise grammatical sense. They must divine the spirit of the Treaty and gain inspiration from it. If they find a gap, they must fill it as best they can. . . . These are the principles as I understand it, on which the European Court acts.

The Court of Justice must also interpret Community law and is the ultimate authority for these conflicts.

The Court of the First Instance was established and went into operation in September 1989 to help reduce the workload of the European Court of Justice. It has jurisdiction over appeals of the Commission's decisions on mergers and acquisitions, as well as penalties imposed for price fixing and other actions taken by the Commission. It will also hear cases between EU institutions and their respective employees. If this court functions well, its jurisdiction may be expanded in the future to include certain trade disputes, much as the Court of International Trade functions in the United States.

The existence of the EU Court of Justice does not eliminate the recourse to national courts. The important and irksome role of national courts was illustrated in the recent French court's ruling that Yahoo! needed to block French web surfers from auction sites with Nazi paraphernalia. France has a very strict law on racist material. Yahoo! capitulated and prohibited the sale of Nazi material in its auction site, despite the legality of selling such items in the United States.

The Parliament.   The Parliament is served by elected representatives from each state. Originally the members were each appointed for a five-year term but now they are elected directly by the people for terms set by state law. The current number of representatives has increased to 626 because of additional seats added by the inclusion of the former East Germany into Germany. The accession of Finland, Austria, and Sweden added 16, 21, and 22 seats, respectively. The Parliament will expand again in 2004.

The Parliament meets in Brussels, Belgium, but also must meet a number of times a year in Strasbourg, France. This is both inefficient and costly but the practice continues.

The Parliament is divided between political factions that create alliances across national boundaries including the Socialists, Christian Democrats, European Democrat Alliance, Communists, Rainbow Group, Rightist, and Unaligned. The Parliament elects a president as well. Originally, the powers of

	1999–2004	2004–2007	2007–2009
Belgium	25	24	24
Bulgaria	-	-	18
Cyprus	-	6	6
Czech Republic	-	24	24
Denmark	16	14	14
Germany	99	99	99
Greece	25	24	24
Spain	64	54	54
Estonia	-	6	6
France	87	78	78
Hungary	-	24	24
Ireland	15	13	13
Italy	87	78	78
Latvia	-	9	9
Lithuania	-	13	13
Luxembourg	6	6	6
Malta	-	5	5
Netherlands	31	27	27
Austria	21	18	18
Poland	-	54	54
Portugal	25	24	24
Romania	-	-	36
Slovakia	-	14	14
Slovenia	-	7	7
Finland	16	14	14
Sweden	22	19	19
United Kingdom	87	78	78
(MAX) TOTAL	**626**	**732**	**786**

the Parliament were limited to a general consultative role but with the power to censure the commission and force their resignation by a two-thirds majority vote. They have never used this power. They also had the power to reject the budget.

The *Maastricht Treaty* significantly strengthened the role of Parliament. The Parliament now approves the appointment of members of the European Commission. It must approve international agreements. It has new co-decision powers with the Council of Ministers on measures dealing with the single market and other significant areas such as consumer protection, the environment, health, education, and culture.

European Central Bank.   Located in Frankfurt, Germany, and founded in 1998, its mission is to promote "price stability" and "to define and implement the monetary policy of the euro zone, conduct foreign exchange operations, issue notes, and promote the smooth operation of payment systems."

Distinction between Institutions. Non-Europeans have some difficulty following developments in the EU because of the lack of clarity about the institutions. The Council of Ministers can be confused with the Council of Europe, or the Conseil de l'Europe. The latter is separate from the EU, but it meets in the same building as the Parliament in Strasbourg, France, called the Palais de l'Europe. The Council has all the EU members plus a number of other countries, including Switzerland. To be a member, a country must be a parliamentary democracy and recognize human rights. The Council has a European Court of Human Rights that hears complaints about violations of the *European Convention on Human Rights* and the *Anti-Torture Convention*. The Council works to support democracy and human rights and to address the issues facing Europe. Russia was recently rejected as a member because it did not meet the criteria for membership at this stage in its development.

Similarly, one should not confuse the Court of Justice in Luxembourg with the International Court of Justice (annexed by statute to the United Nations Charter) or the European Court of Human Rights. The Luxembourg Court, an EU institution, hears cases dealing with the interpretation of the *Treaty of Rome, Maastricht Treaty,* or EU legislation and with conflicts between EU and national law.

Harmonization: Directives and Regulations

Much of the work of achieving the goal of a barrier free internal market is accomplished through the process of harmonization or approximation of laws. In other words, the member countries strive to make their laws similar in order to have a common legal environment. Article 189 of the *Treaty of Rome* states that

- A regulation shall have general application. It shall be binding in its entirety and directly applicable in all member states.
- A directive shall be binding as to the result to be achieved upon each member state to which it is addressed but shall leave to the national authorities the choice of form and methods.
- A decision shall be binding in its entirety upon those to whom it is addressed.
- Recommendations and opinions shall have no binding force.

Thus, the Council, Commission, and Parliament have several avenues open to them. Regulations having a direct effect on the states, without the necessity of passing national legislation, have been used in the agriculture and competition areas and most recently in the area of merger regulations. The Merger Regulation gave great power to the EU Commissioner in charge of Competition Policy (antitrust). See discussion in Chapter Twenty-Two.

Another example of a regulation is the December 2002 Regulation 2368/2002 to block traffic in "blood diamonds."

Directives, in contrast to regulations, require that members bring their laws into harmony with the standard stated in the directive. This approach has been used in the environmental and products liability areas, to mention two. Politically, directives allow members more autonomy to implement the legislative program. Frequently directives allow a country three years to implement the required measures. The problem attendant with a directive, however, is that national legislation may not comply with the directive, forcing the Commission to initiate action (in the Court of Justice) to force compliance of the member state. One EU lawyer commented that this part of implementation was like "slogging through mud," trying to bring the member nations into compliance on a number of issues.

Recently, many directives have focused on employment-related issues. The Fixed-Term Workers Directive, Burden of Proof in Sex Discrimination Claims Directive, Extended Working Time Directive, National Information and Employee Consultation Directive are just a few.

Privacy. Many countries in the EU have long cherished privacy and have even managed to preserve a modicum of privacy for public officials, in stark contrast to the United States. For example, former French President Mitterrand had a mistress for a number of years, as well as a child with her, and this was not written about in the press. When he died, his wife and sons, as well as his mistress and daughter, were at the funeral. It was only then that the European press discussed the story. Former President Clinton only wished that the press had such a hands-off policy regarding personal behavior. This attitude is enshrined in a number of legislative efforts. For example, the EU has a Directive on Privacy and Electronic Communication (2002/58/EC) and a Data Protection Directive. These directives have tremendous implications for financial companies, as well as any company that shares customer information with its European counterpart. In 2000, the EU and the United States reached agreement about how U.S. companies would comply with the directive through "safe harbor" provisions. The following is a list of a few of the directives connected to e-commerce and privacy:

- E-Commerce Directive
- Directive on Privacy and Electronic Communication
- Directive on the Harmonization of Certain Aspects of Copyright and Related Rights in the Information Society

- Directive on Money Laundering
- Directive Concerning Distance Marketing of Consumer Financial Services
- Directive Authorization of Electronic Communication Networks and Services
- Directive on the Prevention of the Use of Financial Systems for Purpose of Money Laundering

These directives must be implemented by national legislation, which means that it will take time so there will not be immediate uniformity across member countries. The laws also have an economic cost to businesses trying to comply with the myriad requirements (see International Accents article).

international accents

Lawyers and Technology Facing the Burden of E.U. Privacy Protections

By Tjeerd Monasch and Thomas Claassens

When eBay Inc., the California-based online auction service, acquired iBazar, the French online auctioneer in 2001, it made perfect business sense. When it wanted to transfer customer data from iBazar Netherlands to the United States, however, it ran headlong into European Union Directive 95/46/EC, which governs protections of personal data throughout the European Union, and the Netherlands' Personal Data Protection Act [Wet Bescherming Persoonsgegevens, or WBP to the Dutch] that became effective Sept. 1, 2001.

The Dutch WBP is based on the mandate of the 1995 directive, which required all E.U. states to implement national legislation with protections for personal data and its use. As long as it conforms to the directive, national privacy law can be as strict as E.U. states wish.

For U.S. companies, including New York-based industries such as financial services, media and communications, the full effects of the E.U. directive have not yet been realized.

As European states like the Netherlands write their own laws to conform to the E.U. directive, U.S. businesses face an increasing burden of compliance issues. In this sense, the eBay case is instructive because the Dutch privacy law typifies European rules and controls.

The directive requires all member states to permit transfers of personal data to countries outside the

European Union only where there is adequate protection for such data, unless one of a limited number of specific exemptions applies. The rationale is that without such rules, the high standards of data protection established by the directive would quickly be undermined, especially given the ease with which data can move across international networks. So, the Dutch WBP itself prohibits data transfer to third countries that have a so-called inadequate level of data protection.

To comply in late 2001 with what was then a new Dutch law, eBay proposed to the Netherlands Data Protection Authority, an independent agency, that the transfer of iBazar's Netherlands data be allowed unless the customer opposed it—a so-called "opt out" structure—and that the data would subsequently only be used by eBay in the United States once the customer gave his or her permission. In addition, eBay claimed the country to which the data would be transferred—the United States—had adequate personal data protection.

According to European standards, however, the United States, which has no federal data protection legislation, does not have an adequate level of data protection. Instead, the European Union and the United States reached a "safe harbor" agreement that is enforced through the U.S. Federal Trade Commission. But, there are concerns about the commission's ability to impose penalties.

continued

continued

In any case, the vast majority of companies in New York's principal industries have, so far, not signed the safe harbor agreement. As of Jan. 14, only 30 New York companies had signed it, among them a few household names like IBM, Foot Locker and Publisher's Clearing House.

In other states, the number is even lower. In Delaware, for example, none have agreed to it. And in 2001, eBay had not joined the agreement. eBay is a "controller" under the Dutch WBP law and is under the obligation to register with the Netherlands Data Protection Authority. The WBP applies to the processing of all personal data [the collection, recording, organization, storage, updating or modification, retrieval, consultation, use, distribution or making available in any other form, merging, linking, as well as blocking, erasure or destruction of data] carried out on behalf of the controller.

Registration involves extensive notification. The controller must do so before he starts processing, and therefore also before he starts collecting data. The Netherlands Data Protection Authority records this notification in a public register [with the exception of the information the controller must provide on data security]. The controller must also inform the person whose data is processed and this person must be able to trace what happens to it. The information provided to the data subject must in any event include [i] who the controller is and [ii] the reasons why the controller is collecting and processing the data. The controller must verify that the data subject has actually received this information. The controller must also take all precautions to secure the data, for example, by allowing only a limited number of people access to it. The more sensitive the data, the higher the standard of security. The security measures must be described to the Netherlands Data Protection Authority. Further, the WBP grants each person the right to object to the use of his or her personal information for direct marketing. The controller is obligated to verify he has told the subject about his rights and the controller may not use the data if the person objects.

The WBP imposes conditions for the lawful processing and transfer of personal data. For one, it applies to the processing of personal data by responsible parties outside the European Union when the equipment in use is situated in the Netherlands [unless these means are used only for forwarding personal data].

U.S. multinationals should note that the European personal data legislation in most cases also applies to their employees in Europe, not just customers and prospects. After all, multinational companies usually operate unified data processing systems for their personnel administration. In most cases, they also have databases that are accessible by all employees. Think, for example, of intranet sites that contain personnel directories.

As befits compliance with the E.U. directive, Dutch privacy law sets strict conditions. First, personal data may only be collected for specific, explicitly defined and legitimate purposes. This means the controller must demonstrate that the purpose is legitimate and necessary [Can I achieve the same purpose with less data?]. On the other hand, the controller may not change or extend these purposes during the processing. Further, the controller must always be able to base its data processing on one of the six grounds provided by the WBP:

- The data subject [the person to whom the personal data relate] has freely and unambiguously given his consent for the processing [which does not necessarily have to be in writing];
- The processing is necessary for the performance of a contract. For example, a magazine publisher may want to process personal data to complete delivery;
- The processing is necessary for compliance with a legal obligation to which the controller is subject. For example, the registration of "unusual monetary transactions" as defined by Dutch law;
- The processing of personal data is necessary in order to protect the vital interest of the data subject. For example, the transfer of personal data in a medical emergency;
- The processing of personal data is necessary for the proper performance of a public law or duty; or
- The processing of personal data is necessary for the purpose of a legitimate interest of the controller. For example, the sound management of the controller's business, including the distribution of publicity about new products.

If a controller cannot base notification on one of these six grounds, he is not allowed to process personal data at all.

Furthermore, personal data may not be further processed in a way that is incompatible with the defined and listed purposes. For example, if they have been obtained for the purpose of, say, keeping a personnel administration, they may not be used for commercial activities. The further processing of personal data for historical, statistical or scientific purposes is, however, not regarded as

continued

continued

incompatible—provided that the responsible party has made the necessary arrangements to ensure that the further processing is carried out solely for these specific purposes. Personal data may only be processed when the data are correct, accurate, adequate, relevant and not excessive. In other words, the controller may not process data that are too detailed if this is not really necessary for the intended purpose. If, for example, a collecting agency processes data in order to be able to demand payment from debtors and to collect money, this purpose does not require a detailed processing of data on the products or services the relevant debtor has bought.

The WBP in principle prohibits the processing of so-called "special personal data." Special personal data concern a person's religion, philosophy of life, race, political opinion, health, sex life and trade union membership. Also, special personal data are personal data regarding a person's criminal behavior, or other unlawful behavior. However, certain limited exceptions apply to this prohibition. The Dutch prescribe a number of remedies for non-compliance that may include collections of damages, injunctions, administrative coercion or criminal prosecution.

The most important ways to realize a relatively smooth and legitimate transfer of data from the Netherlands to the United States are by:

- Joining the safe harbor agreement;
- Notifying the Netherlands Data Protection Authority and obtaining the necessary permits in combination with the use of E.U. standard contracts; or
- Obtaining the individual consent from each relevant data subject.

As eBay found out, dealing with European privacy protections requires forethought, precise planning and exact execution.

If New York companies can meet the Dutch standard, it is likely those lessons will be well served in the rest of Europe and in the United States, where the legal issues of personal privacy protections are gathering steam.

The Common Agricultural Policy. The Community has been committed to the establishment of a Common Agricultural Policy (CAP). The CAP has been central to the EU since its inception in 1956. Its goals are enshrined in Article 39 of the *Treaty of Rome:*

1. to increase agricultural productivity
2. to ensure a fair standard of living
3. to stabilize markets
4. to guarantee regular supplies
5. to ensure reasonable prices in supplies to consumers.

In the past, it utilized several means including government price supports and support for agricultural production that are not uncommon in many countries. In 1972, the CAP accounted for over 80 percent of the Community budget whereas now it is under 50 percent.

The CAP has been divisive within the Community because the financial burden falls heaviest on countries that do not directly benefit, specifically, the United Kingdom and Germany. Although the CAP has helped to provide food at consistent prices and to maintain small firms, its cost includes surpluses and encouraging noncompetition in the farm sector. Because their way of life is threatened by any change in the CAP, militant farmers have for years engaged in creative and sometimes violent demonstrations (unloading sheep to clog the roads) to make their point. The CAP has led to major inefficiencies, including the infamous "butter mountain" where one million tons of butter were stockpiled and the CAP paid for the storage.

There have been numerous efforts to reform and revise the CAP over the years. In June 2003, a new agreement led to a commitment to reduce farm subsidies and to channel money to encourage farmers to protect the environment, as well as care for the animals. The new change signals that beginning in 2005 "single farm payments" will be made independent of farm production. This "decoupling" will help to classify the payments as "non-trade distorting" according to international standards. The payments will be linked to safety and environmental and animal health issues rather than production.

The EU now describes its goals in agriculture as "transparency, quality and safety and a farm sector in tune with the environment and animal welfare . . . A sustainable farm and food sector for the future." This will be challenging in terms of integrating the ten new members into the Community, including direct payments to farmers. The expansion of the EU could lead to an increase in agricultural land by up to 50 percent, which will no doubt create pressure on the CAP. The expansion of the EU to twenty-five members will dramatically increase the number of farmers in the EU, thus placing budgetary pressures on the CAP.

An example of how the EU dealt with the concern about BSE (bovine spongiform encephalopathy) or mad cow disease emanating from the UK illustrates some of the problems with the implementation of the single market. In 1996, the Commission banned exports of beef and other meat products from the UK because of a concern for BSE. In 1998, the ban was lifted but not all countries felt comfortable with British imports. France continued to balk at compliance with the court decision in the *National Farmers' Union* case.

National Farmers' Union and Secrétariat général du gouvernement (France) C-241/01 (2002)

BACKGROUND AND FACTS
Following the discovery of a probable link between a variant of Creutzfeldt-Jakob disease, a disease affecting human beings, and bovine spongiform encephalopathy (hereinafter 'BSE'), which was widespread in the United Kingdom at the time, the Commission adopted Decision 96/239/EC of 27 March 1996 on emergency measures to protect against bovine spongiform encephalopathy, . . . prohibiting the United Kingdom from exporting from its territory to the other Member States and third countries, in particular, live bovine animals, meat of bovine animals and products obtained from bovine animals.

ARTICLE 14
The Commission shall carry out Community inspections on-the-spot in the United Kingdom to verify the application of the provisions of this decision, in particular in relation to the implementation of official controls.

ARTICLE 15
The United Kingdom shall send the Commission every month a report on the application of the protective measures taken against BSE, in accordance with national and Community provisions.

By its third question, the national court seeks to ascertain whether a Member State is justified in invoking Article 30 EC in order to prohibit imports of agricultural products and live animals, inasmuch as Directives 89/662 and 90/425 cannot be regarded as harmonising the measures needed in order to attain the specific objective of protecting the health and life of humans provided for by that article.

FINDINGS OF THE COURT
According to settled case-law, where Community directives provide for the harmonisation of the measures necessary to ensure the protection of animal and human health and establish Community procedures to check that they are observed, recourse to Article 30 EC is no longer justified and the appropriate checks must be carried out and the measures of protection adopted within the framework outlined by the harmonising directive.
* * *

The Court has also held that even where a directive does not lay down any Community procedure for monitoring compliance or any penalties in the event of breach of its provisions, a Member State may not unilaterally adopt, on its own authority, corrective or protective measures designed to obviate any breach by another Member State of rules of Community law. . . .

It should indeed be made clear that in the European Community, which is a community based on law, a Member State is bound to comply with the provisions of the Treaty and, in particular, to act within the framework of the procedures provided for by the Treaty and by the applicable legislation.

It is in the light of those various factors that it is necessary to determine whether the French Government was able, at the date of the implicit decisions at

continued

continued

issue in the main proceedings, to invoke Article 30 EC in order to maintain the prohibition on imports of beef and veal from the United Kingdom.

Although Regulation No 999/2001 no doubt achieved full harmonisation of the rules relating to the prevention, control and eradication of certain transmissible spongiform encephalopathies, it should be noted, as has the Advocate General in points 91 to 94 of his Opinion, that Decisions 98/256 and 98/692, defining the DBES, laid down the rules necessary for the protection of public health upon the resumption of exports of beef and veal from the United Kingdom to the other Member States.

Those decisions, which are additional to the general legislation already in existence, specify the requirements of eligibility and traceability of animals liable to be used under the DBES, the requirements to be satisfied by slaughterhouses and the conditions specific to the cutting of meat, which are imposed as a supplement to the provisions in force relating to the withdrawal of specific offal.

Moreover, Article 14 of Decision 98/256 as amended provides that Community inspections must be carried out by the Commission in the United Kingdom to verify the application of the provisions of that decision, while Article 15 thereof provides for the United Kingdom to send to the Commission every month a report on the application of the protective measures taken against BSE.

As regards the obligations of the Member States other than the United Kingdom, Article 17 of Decision 98/256 as amended provides that they are to adopt the necessary measures to comply with that decision and are immediately to inform the Commission thereof.

Furthermore, as was stated in paragraph 38 of this judgment, Article 16 of Decision 98/256 as amended specifies that that decision must be reviewed regularly in the light of new scientific information and that any amendments are to be made in accordance with the procedure laid down in Article 18 of Directive 89/662.

Examination of these various provisions show that, in addition to the harmonisation of the measures necessary to ensure the protection of human health, Decision 98/256 as amended lays down procedures for monitoring compliance with it and specifies, by reference to Directive 89/662, the appropriate procedure for making the amendments which might be made essential by the development of scientific knowledge.

As regards the emergency measures liable to be taken by a Member State in the event of a serious hazard to human health, it is important to note that Decision 98/256 was adopted on the basis of Directives 89/662 and 90/425, and Decision 98/692 on the basis of Directive 89/662 alone.

Directive 89/662 describes, in Article 7, 8 and 9, the measures which may be adopted by a Member State of destination, in particular where its competent authorities establish that the goods imported do not meet the conditions laid down by Community legislation. Article 7 authorises the destruction or return of those goods and Article 9 authorises in particular the adoption, by that Member State, of interim protective measures on serious public-health or animal-health grounds.

It is in accordance with those provisions, which require the measures adopted to be notified without delay to the other Member States and to the Commission and close to collaboration between the Member States and the Commission, that a Member State must act when faced with a situation endangering the health of its population. . . .

It is moreover the application of the interim protective measures referred to in Article 9 of Directive 89/662 which is envisaged by the 13th recital in the preamble to Decision 98/692 in the event that it is discovered, after the dispatch of products which were believed to fulfil the conditions of the DBES, that those products came from an animal subsequently found to be ineligible under that scheme.

Examination of all these provisions shows that the existing legislation and, in particular, Directive 89/662 and Decisions 98/256 and 98/692 provide for the harmonisation necessary to ensure the protection of public health upon the resumption of exports of beef and veal from the United Kingdom to the other Member States and lay down Community procedures to monitor compliance with them.

It is true that, in paragraph 134 of *Commission v France,* cited above, the Court noted that there were difficulties in interpreting Decision 98/256 as amended in respect of the Member States' obligations relating to the traceability of products. Suffice it to state, however, that, as paragraph 135 of that judgment shows, those difficulties of interpretation had disappeared by the date of the implicit decisions refusing to lift the ban at issue in the main proceedings.

As regards products subject to the DBES which have been cut, processed or rewrapped in another

continued

continued

Member State and subsequently exported to France without the affixing of a distinct mark, suffice it to state that the main proceedings do not concern such products and that, in any event, the French Government has never prevented their importation.

It follows from all the foregoing that, since Directive 89/662 and Decision 98/256 as amended lay down the rules necessary for the protection of public health upon the resumption of exports of beef and veal from the United Kingdom to the other Member States, lay down a Community procedure to monitor compliance with that decision and a procedure for amending it in the light of new scientific information and provide the

appropriate legal framework for the adoption of interim protective measures by a Member State of destination for the purpose of protecting public health, a Member State is not entitled to invoke Article 30 EC in order to prevent the resumption of imports to its territory of beef and veal from the United Kingdom which were carried out in accordance with Decisions 98/256 as amended and 1999/514.

Decision and Comment. The UK was allowed to ship beef and veal outside the country. France finally complied in the face of heavy fines.

In another example of concern for food safety, the EU continues to press its concerns about genetically modified organisms (GMO). In 2001, the Commission issued regulations on GMO. The United States is angered about this continuing ban and could opt to press its case before the WTO. This would only add to the tension created by the EU's concern over the U.S. export tax breaks and tariffs on imported steel. The United States and the EU have a number of trade issues to sort out in 2004 against the backdrop of lingering tensions over the split on the Iraq war.

The Business Implications of the European Union

Businesses hoping to penetrate or to grow in the European market are dramatically affected by the developments in the EU. As harmonization and standardization continues, companies can more easily gain access to separate markets such as Italy and Portugal. A company can centralize or at least regionalize offices rather than having a separate office for each country. Obviously, national, cultural, and linguistic differences must still be respected. As regulations become more uniform, they benefit both Europeans and non-Europeans who want to do business there. Clearly, the most significant development has been the implementation of the European Monetary Union. This offers tremendous opportunities to non-European business as well.

In 2000, the EU Court of Justice in *Imperial Tobacco Ltd. v. European Parliament & Council,* C-74/79 Article 234EC, overturned the 1998 phase

out of tobacco advertising. This case is significant because it shows some of the impediments to business in navigating the single market as well as the difficulty the EU faces in trying to implement uniform requirements. The ban, overturned by the court, applied to both the cinema and posters/billboards. However, in December 2002, the EU banned newspaper, radio, magazine, and Internet tobacco advertising, effective August 2005. There already exists a television ban. Britain went ahead and banned tobacco advertising in 2003. These are significant measures because an estimated one-third of Europeans are smokers. Businesses will have to be cognizant of different countries' regulations in a number of areas. There may be subsequent limits on tar content and requirements for warning labels on tobacco products. The dramatic impact of EU regulations can also be seen in the recent change scheduled to go into effect October 2003 that eases restrictions on car dealer sales and after-sale service. This should dramatically increase cross-border competition and benefit consumers seeking lower prices. Thus businesses must keep abreast of these developments at several levels.

It is not only the directives and regulations of the EU that impact on business. The EU's efforts to negotiate with other countries may affect one's business plan. For example, in 2000, the EU negotiated a bilateral agreement with Mexico. Agreements and treaties similar to this could affect tariff rates and taxation, which might be a significant factor in any business decision.

Many businesses find themselves caught in the trade skirmishes between the United States and the

EU. For example, in April 1999, the United States placed $191 million in sanctions over the EU banana import practices. Then, in July 1999, the United States added $116 million in sanctions because of the EU ban on hormone-treated beef. In February 2000, the WTO ruled on a different matter—the U.S. Foreign Sales Corporation tax treatment by the U.S. Code gave an unfair export subsidy to U.S. companies using offshore tax havens to reduce taxes. Consequently, in November 2000, the EU petitioned the WTO for $4.04 billion in trade sanctions on U.S. goods in retaliation. The WTO will hold a hearing in 2001. The EU agreed to wait for a ruling. Currently, the EU and the United States are trying to resolve these issues. The U.S. position is that Congress passed legislation that remedied the FSC problem. However, many businesspeople anxiously await the outcome of these issues because their whole import or export plan could be dramatically affected by subsequent sanctions. This debate has continued and is exacerbated by the tensions between the United States and Germany and France over the Iraq war in 2003.

Another recent example of how a business may find itself entangled in EU policies is the EU Commission's investigation into Microsoft and its licensing practices. The Commission is examining whether Microsoft's contracts discriminate against competitors in violation of EU law. The case involves an interpretation of the 1991 European Software Directive that contains a provision for decompilation or reverse engineering. Sun Microsystems is very involved and is arguing that the same arrangement that IBM agreed to in 1984 ("licensing compatibility information regarding its mainframe computers to all comers for a flat fee") should be applied to Microsoft. While there has been a partial settlement in the United States as of September 2003, there had been no decision in the EU.

Businesses must monitor legal developments in any country where they may do business. Knowledge of the legal environment can be a strategic advantage for a business and may assist in the formulation of a business plan. Yet, it is not only law that is important. An understanding of politics can be a real business asset as well. For example, anticipating which countries are likely to join the EU and when may lead to lucrative business opportunities in the future.

OTHER REGIONAL TRADE AREAS

The EU and the United States, Canada, and Mexico in NAFTA, are not the only countries that have experimented with economically integrated trade areas.

Other countries, spurred on by the EU and NAFTA and wanting to stimulate development and investment in their own regions, are accelerating their own integration efforts. The next section looks briefly at some of these other examples.

MERCOSUR: Southern Common Market

Argentina, Brazil, Paraguay, and Uruguay agreed to form the Southern Common Market in 1991. This area encompasses 230 million people. The countries were committed to opening their markets as well as pushing exports dubbed "open regionalism." In 1994, they committed further to pushing integration toward a customs union model with a common external tariff. Some hope eventually for the free movement of labor and capital as well. A common market group forms the executive branch. Notably absent, however, is a court, an integral part of the EU and the United States. Annex III of the Agreement outlines how disputes will be handled. The first step is direct negotiation between the states. Second, is referral to the common market group. Third, if no solution can be reached, the council should propose a settlement. Without a final authority to issue binding rulings, the thorny problems of regional integration and national autonomy will not be solved easily. To date, Brazil has blocked any arbitration. In 2000, Argentina acknowledged a Mercosur arbitration panel decision that found its textile quotas unfair.

This common market has been successful and experienced a 250 percent increase in trade since 1990. Problems have surfaced since the 1998 recession and Brazil's currency devaluation in 1999.

On January 1, 1995, tariffs on approximately 95 percent of goods traded between the four countries were ended. They created a customs union by enacting a common tariff of 12 percent on goods coming from a nonmember. In 2000, they agreed to phase out restrictions by 2006 on trade in autos and parts. This is still on track. Trade has tripled since the inception of the pact. Brazil, formerly an enemy, is now Argentina's largest trading partner. Bilateral agreements have been negotiated with Chile, Bolivia, and Peru.

Since 2000, with economic conditions improving, Argentina and Brazil have been working to revitalize Mercosur and discussing a "mini-Maastricht" agreement. What will result from these talks (convergence criteria, common currency plan, court) is not clear. However, the difficult economic conditions of 2002–3 have slowed some progress. The collapse of the trade talks in Cancun, Mexico, in 2003, where developing countries like those in MERCOSUR pushed the United States and EU for farm subsidy reductions, were disappointing.

Caribbean Response to NAFTA

Many Caribbean countries believed that NAFTA had a great impact on investment in their countries. President Clinton signed the Caribbean Basin Initiative/Sub-Saharan Africa trade bill effective October 1, 2000, for a duration of eight years. This will cut tariffs on clothing from 5.8 percent to zero and will offer competition to Mexico and Asia. The *maquila* sector that takes exported U.S. material and assembles and exports it back to the United States will benefit.

Andean Community of Nations

The Andean Common Market (CAN), or Andean Group, includes Bolivia, Venezuela, Colombia, Ecuador, and Peru. It was founded in 1969 by the *Cartagena Agreement* and involves 100 million people. Venezuela joined in 1973; Chile withdrew in 1977. Peru temporarily suspended its membership in 1992 but has since rejoined.

Its legal structures include the Commission, Junta, Andean Development Bank and Reserve Fund, and the Andean Court of Justice. Initially, the countries hoped to exclude the other countries' products and to buy only from one another. This exclusionary practice meant that the population was paying excessive prices for goods.

CAN has moved toward integration, but national interests have kept these countries from moving as far on the continuum as the EU. They had hoped to create a common market by 2005 and to implement an integrated tariff.

The Commission (one representative from each country) functions as an executive branch, makes policy, appoints Junta members, approves and vetoes legislation, and ensures compliance with the agreement. The Junta (three members) supervises and implements the Commission's decisions. The Bank assists in financial development spurred both by members' contributions and foreign capital. It also assists with balance of payments problems. The *Court of Justice Treaty* (drafted in 1979; ratified in 1983) created the court, which sits in Quito, Ecuador. The protocol of Cochabamba established new procedures and expanded the powers of the court.

The Andean Parliament (in Lima, Peru) plans to have direct regional elections, but has not done so to date. This format parallels the EU, which only recently adopted this reform. The Parliament issues recommendations to achieve the goals of the *Cartagena Agreement*; thus, its power is limited. An agreement between CAN and MERCOSUR to merge has been postponed.

Free Trade in the Americas Area (FTAA)

In December 1994, thirty-four countries agreed to work toward the creation of a Western Hemisphere agreement creating a free trade area by 2005. The countries, including the United States, talked about reducing tariffs and dealing with bribery, drug trafficking, and the liberalization of capital markets. This date is in question as of this writing. Working groups continue to meet and work on issues. As one official noted, "we reiterate that FTAA can coexist with bilateral and subregional agreements." The FTAA, with 784 million people, could be the largest trade area in the world. However, the contentious issues of agricultural subsidies and Iraq as well as the U.S. presidential race in 2004, may distract the United States from aggressively pursuing these negotiations. Nevertheless, the prospect of an alliance comprised of 823 million people and 3.4 trillion dollars in trade is an enticing goal.

> http://www.ftaa_alca.org
> A Web site for the *Free Trade in the Americas* organization.

The initial euphoria of the prospect of such a large regional organization has been dimmed by the recent lack of momentum. President Clinton was denied authority (see Chapter Eight) to negotiate such an agreement during the 1996 election campaign. Then, President Clinton was unable to secure approval to start negotiations. President Bush was given authority in August 2002 with the passage of Trade Promotion Authority (TPA) legislation.

Central American Common Market

Guatemala, El Salvador, Costa Rica, Nicaragua, Honduras, and Panama signed a new agreement in October 1993 to create a common market, but the efforts to implement a uniform tariff have been unsuccessful as individual countries seek to implement separate tariffs to address domestic problems. The Bush administration is negotiating with all but Panama on a *Central American Free Trade Agreement* (CAFTA).

African Trade Areas

The development of Africa in the next century will be critically important. Ravaged by civil wars and famine after the end of the colonial occupation, many countries are trying to rebuild their economies. Just as many South American countries realized that centralized planning did not work and have moved toward restructuring internally and free trade models, so too will many African states. In 1990, 12.1 percent of world population was African. If the trend continues, by 2150, 25 percent of world population will be African and another 25 percent will be Chinese. President Bush has proposed the extension of the *African Growth and Opportunity Act* (originally introduced by President Clinton) beyond 2008. As a result of this act, textile imports increased by one-third. This allows duty-free entry for many goods.

African Economic Community. This proposed fifty-one-member group contemplates a six-phase implementation of an African common market over a twenty-year period. The official languages will be English, French, and Portuguese. The agreement will enter into effect after two-thirds of the members ratify the Agreement.

COMESA: Common Market for Eastern and Southern Africa. This 1982 treaty involves twenty-three African states. The trade area encompasses 220 million people. The group recently set a five- to seven-year goal to achieve the common market. To date they have created "standard customs documents and a dispute tribunal," but not with the powers of the EU Court of Justice.

Southern African Development Community. The SADC, formed on August 17, 1992, involves Angola, Botswana, Lesotho, Malawi, Mozambique, Namibia, Swaziland, Tanzania, Zambia, Zimbabwe, Mauritius, and South Africa, representing 135 million people. The group sees itself working in concert with the African Economic Community to develop "regional economic communities," building blocks for the continental community. Although in embryo stage, the agreement sketches cooperation on human resources, science and technology, food, security, natural resources, environment, infrastructure and services, finance, investment, trade, peace, and security. To date, however, they have issued a statement of purpose but have no structure and power necessary to develop and implement law and policy. There is hope because both Botswana and Mauritius have had economic growth of 15 percent.

The major change in Africa centers around the transformation of South Africa and the end of apartheid. Privatization in some countries has spurred a GDP growth of 6 percent. Many hope that these regional agreements will assist Africa's economic development in the way it has benefited Europe and South America. Before free trade can exist, however, there must be an infrastructure (i.e., roads, telecommunications systems, and education) to support development.

U.S.–Israel *Free Trade Agreement*

The United States has agreement with Israel as well as with the EU. Even though Israel has had a free trade agreement with the EU since 1975, which became operational in 1989, the United States and Israel signed a *Free Trade Agreement* in 1985. This agreement was the first such attempt for the United States, although prior to this, Israel enjoyed beneficial trading privileges with the United States. The pact offered continued access to the U.S. market for Israel and allowed the United States to compete with the EU for access to Israel's markets. Politically, it was also advantageous because if free trade stabilized Israel, it would be less dependent on U.S. aid. The agreement can be terminated on twelve months' notice. A subsequent pact, eliminating duties in phases, was implemented in 1995. The United States and Israel also have an agricultural agreement to reduce trade barriers.

APEC: Asia Pacific Economic Cooperation Group

Founded in 1989, the current twenty-one-member group, including the United States, Japan, Australia, Canada, South Korea, Mexico, China, and Indonesia, issued the Bogor Declaration (named after a town in Indonesia) to achieve "free and open trade and investment" by the year 2020 and in industrialized nations by 2010. This agreement is historic—though without powers of enforcement—in that half the world has agreed to be tariff free by 2020.

http:www.apec.org
Web site of the *Asia Pacific Economic Cooperation Group.*

CARICOM

This alliance comprises fifteen English-speaking Caribbean countries. The Caribbean Community, or CARICOM, was created to form a single market.

ASEAN

The Association of South East Asian Nations (ASEAN) was formed in 1967 by Indonesia, Malaysia, the Philippines, Singapore, Thailand, and Brunei (joined in 1984) with the Bangkok Declaration. Myanmar, Laos, and Cambodia were admitted, and finally Vietnam, now encompassing 500 million people. Unlike the EU and CAN, the Declaration does not set up a legal mechanism to enforce its goals of economic growth and development through trade and industry. On a continuum, as shown in Exhibit 14.7, ASEAN would fall closer to the less integrated end than any of the groups previously discussed. The structures within ASEAN are less formal too. It has a standing committee of ministers from each state. In 1976, a secretariat was formed, seated in Jakarta, Indonesia, which functions as an organizational center. ASEAN, rocked by the terrorist bombing in Bali at a nightclub, called a terrorist summit and issued a Declaration on November 2002. Terrorism threatens the stability of the region and the economies of all member countries.

http://www.aseansec.org
This address will link you to sites for APEC, ASEAN, Australia, Bangladesh, Bhutan, and Brunei.

Commonwealth of Independent States

The Council for Mutual Economic Assistance, or Comecon (also called CMEA), consisted of the USSR, Hungary, Poland, Romania, Bulgaria, East Germany, Cuba, Czechoslovakia, Mongolia, and Vietnam. Founded in 1949, Comecon served as the association of Soviet-aligned countries that negotiated annual and long-term trade agreements and dealt with balance of trade problems caused by currencies (rubles, zlotys) that were not freely traded or convertible. The group disbanded officially in

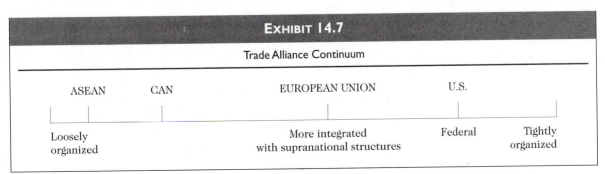

EXHIBIT 14.7

Trade Alliance Continuum

ASEAN   CAN   EUROPEAN UNION   U.S.

Loosely organized | More integrated with supranational structures | Federal | Tightly organized

1991. The Commonwealth of Independent States, begun in 1991, which is struggling with issues of economic survival after the break-up of the Soviet Union, will be interesting to follow. The twelve members are Armenia, Azerbaijan, Belarus, Georgia, Kazakhstan, Kyrgystan, Moldova, Russia, Tajikistan, Turkmenistan, Ukraine, and Uzbekistan. The Baltic States, once part of the Soviet Union, opted to ally with the EU. Several republics, including the Slavic ones of Russia, Byelorussia, and Ukraine, have signed an agreement to "coordinate domestic and foreign trade policy as well as joint activity in customs and migration policies, and the development of transport and communications systems." These republics have 70 percent of the former USSR's population, but are not centers for agricultural production. The religious and ethnic differences in the diverse land of the former Soviet Union may ultimately precipitate the balkanization of the republics, thus dissolving the single currency and the foreign policy and economic cooperation that Europe is ironically trying to achieve. However, the former Soviet model was built on military and political coercion, not cooperation. Also, some of the former Soviet republics have applied for membership in the EU.

Gulf Cooperation Council

Saudi Arabia, Kuwait, Bahrain, Qatar, the United Arab Emirates, and Oman formed the Gulf Cooperation Council (GCC) in 1981. The GCC has focused on standardizing subsidies, unifying rates for eliminating trade barriers, and negotiating with other regional groups like the EU to achieve favorable treatment. It recently set 2005 as the beginning of a Customs Union, with a 2010 deadline for a common currency. There is an agreement to have a common tariff on most products. In fact, tariff rates are scheduled to drop to 5.5–7.5 percent from 15–20 percent in 2005.

Arab League

The Arab League was founded in 1945 and currently has twenty-two members (Algeria, Bahrain, Djibouti, Egypt, Iraq, Jordan, Kuwait, Lebanon, Libya, Mauritania, Morocco, Oman, Palestine, Qatar, Yemen, Saudi Arabia, Somalia, Sudan, Syria, Tunisia, the United Arab Emirates, and the Yemen Arab Republic). The League is "involved in political,

economic, cultural, and social programs designed to promote the interests of member states." In September 2003, the Arab League allowed Iraq's new foreign minister to represent the country. There had been a dispute because of the U.S. role in occupying Iraq. The Foreign Minister stated, "The new Iraq will be based on diversity, democracy, constitution, law, and respect for human rights."

The *Cotonou Agreement:* Europe's Future Partnership with Developing Countries

For over twenty-five years, Europe's business relationship with developing countries was largely determined by two European trade programs: the Generalized System of Preferences and the *Lome Convention*. As of 2000, Europe and the developing countries of Africa, the Pacific, and the Caribbean chartered a new course of cooperation to bolster their economic partnership and political ties in the years to come.

The EU Generalized System of Preferences (GSP). Since 1971, the EU GSP program has provided tariff preferences for European imports of goods from developing countries. The specific rate depends on how "import sensitive" the product is. Once an industry in a developing country no longer requires the tariff preference in order to maintain its export level, tariff rates will gradually be raised. This will allow other lesser developing countries an opportunity to increase their exports to Europe. As in the United States, the most economically advanced beneficiary countries will "graduate" from the program. Even lowered duties apply to countries that observe international standards for workers' rights and for the conservation of tropical forests.

Europe and the African, Caribbean and Pacific Countries (ACP). The European countries have long had special trade relationships with the ACP developing countries because many of them were European colonies at one time. By 1975, the EU had undertaken a program for 78 of the poorest, or least developed, ACP nations. Known as the *Lome Convention,* this preference program was more generous and broader in scope than the U.S. or EU GSP programs. It did not only lower tariff rates, but addressed such issues as the transport of radioactive waste and human rights. Over 650 million people live in the ACP countries, most of them in absolute poverty.

In 2000, the *Lome Convention* was replaced by a new, comprehensive, trade and foreign aid agreement known as the *Cotonou Agreement* (Cotonou, Benin, West Africa). The focus of the agreement is to build EU-ACP partnerships to reduce poverty. The current *Lome* preferences will last until 2007, and then be replaced by a set of new "partnership agreements" that will cover a wide range of issues. Trade preferences will continue, although some of the ACP countries (not the poorest) will have to reciprocate and provide trade preferences of their own for European-made goods. This will encourage them to remove trade barriers and attract investment.

But *Cotonou* is about more than trade. The ACP countries will be encouraged to develop their own principles of "good governance." This applies to issues like enhancing the democratic process and the equality of men and women, managing natural resources, combating bribery and corruption of government officials, ending indiscriminate weapons trade, and encouraging spending on health care and other social programs rather than on armaments or war. Critics warn that the EU must not simply "throw money" at the problem. But the *Cotonou Agreement* is a pledge by the EU and the ACP countries to create a social and political environment in the ACP countries that will permit good economic policies to work and that will improve the quality of life for those living there. The agreement will become effective when approved by the European Parliament and the ACP countries. It is scheduled to last twenty years. Cuba had requested to join, but as a result of the crackdown, in March 2003, on dissidents, the EU has suspended consideration.

African Development Groups

Other organizations exist as well. The African Union, a fifty-three-member group known formerly as Organization of African Union, started in 1963 and achieved its major goals of ending apartheid and decolonization. Its new agenda includes advocacy for democracy, human rights, and economic development. NEPAD, New Partnership for Africa's Development, is a program of the AU. It is targeting corporate governance, management, and socioeconomic development within the area.

The South African Customs Union (SACU) is comprised of Botswana, Lesotho, Namibia, South Africa, and Swaziland, as well as the South African Free Trade and Development Agreement (SAFTDA) with the same members.

Hopefully, at least several organizations will really be able to affect change in African countries and begin the process of sustained economic development so needed in the area.

CHAPTER SUMMARY

The development of integrated trade areas reflects an age-old desire to maximize each country's strength and to grow and prosper. The United States is a successful model of such an effort. Regional trading blocs raise issues about regional protectionism and the conflict with the GATT and WTO. Members are acutely aware of both benefits as well as threats of integration, but are driven by the need to compete internationally.

In reaction to EU unification, other countries have been stimulated to consider cooperative efforts to reduce trade barriers as a counterbalance to the threat of "Fortress Europe."

States are motivated to form trade areas to improve their own economic position and to secure the future. Numerous forms of alliances are possible but the conflicts perennially remain. The persistent question is how to subordinate state interests so as to achieve unity. What national interests can be deferred, and what are the tradeoffs?

Only a little over 140 years ago the United States was ripped apart by the Civil War. Although the United States has been reunified, one cannot forget how regional differences may place a great stress on unity. The regional groups discussed here have strived to form lasting alliances despite major differences in ideology, culture, and language.

These regional efforts should be watched closely to see how they progress toward economic and possibly political integration. The speed and the depth of integration will vary. The groups may even splinter into subgroups progressing at different speeds or choosing to cooperate only on some issues. The divisive issue of nationalism will hinder some groups' efforts. The delicate balance between promoting trade and economic growth and protectionism may either prompt great trade rivalries between "mega" associations or open the way to truly free trade for all nations.

Questions and Case Problems

1. Rewe, a limited liability company with an office in Germany, imported goods from the EU countries. In 1976, Rewe applied to a German agency for permission to import Cassis de Dijon. The agency responded that only spirits with 32 percent alcohol could be marketed in Germany in addition to beer. Cassis had only 15–20 percent spirit content and could not be imported. The German court referred the case to the ECJ to deal with conflicts between German law and Article 30 and 37 of the *Treaty of Rome* (see *Commission v. Federal Republic of Germany*, C-178/84, March 12, 1987). The German government argued that they were trying to protect public health and consumers. How did the court rule? Why? Did this settle the issue for the future?

2. Germany has had laws addressing the regulation of beer since 1516. Germany had a law that prohibited additives in beer. The Community tried to harmonize its laws on additives and passed several directives on additives. The Commission notified Germany in 1982 that its beer law created barriers to member states that wanted to import beer into Germany, thus Germany's law violated Article 30 and 36 of the *Treaty of Rome*. Germany argued that to sell a beer with additives would mislead consumers and there are resultant public health concerns. How did the Court of Justice rule? Why didn't the *Cassis de Dijon* (see *Rewe–Zentral* [Cassis de Dijon], C-120/78, February 20, 1979) case preclude the necessity of this case? Why did the community need to address such a similar issue nine years after *Rewe*? Does the court still have to address similar issues today? Give an example from your reading. Find a case on the Internet.

3. The UK has not decided, as of July 2003, whether it will join in a monetary union. How will this decision affect business? Sweden faces a referendum in September 2003 on this issue. What is the reaction of European political leaders? European business leaders? American businesspeople? How workable will a monetary union be without three members?

4. The EU passed the Electronic Signature Directive in 2000. It is technology neutral. Germany already has a law that requires a specific encrypted form. Is this a conflict? How does this impact on business? How does it compare to the U.S. law?

5. Compare the EU approach to privacy and the U.S. approach. How are they different and similar? What are the ramifications to business for each? Which approach is better?

6. How does the EU's approach to GMOs differ from the United States? How does this affect international business? Find an update for the controversy. What role may the WTO play? How interrelated are the other trade disputes?

7. May Germany require that waste that is shipped to another member state be disposed of according to Germany's environmental protection laws? See *Daimler Chrysler AG v. Land Baden—Wurttemberg* (C-324/99) 2001. What impact does this ruling have on business? Does the result suggest a need for more Community standards? Why or why not?

8. What is the difference between a directive, a regulation, and a recommendation? Why would the EU choose one over the other? Give examples. What impact does this decision have on businesses?

9. There are a number of developments on the African continent in terms of efforts to build a customs union and integrated trade areas. Which ones seem most successful? Why? Do you think a court is essential? Compare with NAFTA.

10. What progress has the Gulf Cooperation Council made in moving toward the stated goal of a customs union? What impact might that have on the Arab League and neighboring countries? How does this balance with the WTO obligations?

11. Go to the EU Web site and review the "Treaty Establishing a Constitution for Europe." How does this compare to the U.S. Constitution? How might it affect business, if at all?

Managerial Problems

1. You have an office in Spain. You have hired a worker, Ms. Jimenez, for a fixed term and have renewed her contract twice. You have just renewed her contract and discover that she will be giving birth within three months. You send her a notice stating that she is terminated effective in one month (which is two months before her due date). You believe that since she was only on a limited term contract she cannot expect to be treated like a more permanent employee and given all maternity benefits. Are there any legal concerns

here? What impact might this decision have on the advancement of women in employment? How will this affect your hiring practices?

2. You are engaged in the competitive perfume business and decide you want to protect your intellectual property in an aggressive way. You decide to try to register the odor or olfactory mark of a "balsami-cally fruity scent with a hint of cinnamon" in the EU. You have the chemical formula as well as a descrip-tion. You argue that Directive 89/104/EEC of December 21, 1988, allows registration of "acoustic marks, colors, holograms and other non-traditional marks." Will this be a successful strategy? What else can you do? (See *Ralf Sieckmann v. Deutches Patent-und Markenamt*, C-273/00, Dec. 12, 2002).

3. Your company is expanding to Europe. You must pick a location for your office and have two loca-tions to choose between.
   a. How will you make this decision?
   b. Will whether the country has joined the Single Currency have an impact on your decision?
   c. Would you be discouraged from locating to a country that has had a poor track record of implementing Directives?
   d. What about considering placement in one of the countries that plan to join sometime after 2005?

4. Labco is a small manufacturing company that wants to do more business exporting to the EU. They dis-cover that the Commission is considering a Directive that might limit their ability to do business in those countries.
   a. What can they do? The president of the company has asked you to research this matter and outline a plan of action.
   b. What difference does it make if your company is a very large, publicly traded corporation?
   c. What are your options if the EU implements a Directive or regulation that you believe discrimi-nates against you as a foreign business?

5. Imagine that you are a student intern, assigned to the Vice President of International Sales at the firm where you are working for a semester. Up until now, the firm's primary markets are in the United States and Canada. The toys are designed in the United States, with manufacturing contracted to firms in China. At a meeting with the Vice President's design and marketing people, he asks about opening new markets in Europe. He explains that, in the United States, the design and sale of children's toys is highly regulated by the U.S. Consumer Products Safety Commission. Indeed, some other companies have had their toys removed from store shelves for non-compliance with federal regulations. He feels there must be some consumer safety regulations in effect in Europe that will act as a barrier to his firm's access to European markets. After all, if the regulations are very different from those in the United States, he is concerned about the cost of redesigning the toys to comply with the European standards. After the meet-ing, the Vice President asks you to find answers to the following questions:
   a. Are there any standards or technical regulations in effect in Europe covering the sale of toys? Where can he locate the regulations on the design, manufacture, and marketing of children's toys in Europe? Can you give a specific web address so he can look at them himself?
   b. Do the toys have to meet different requirements in every single European country, or is there some standard covering all of Europe?
   c. What toys do they apply to, and what, if any, toys are exempt?
   d. What are the design and manufacturing standards for toys covered by the regulations, and what is the standard for safety? Are there any specific provisions covering the toys' physical or mechani-cal properties?
   e. Do the toys have to be tested in advance for com-pliance with safety regulations?
   f. What are the labeling requirements? Is there a certain label, or mark, that will let consumers know that the toy has been tested for safety?

CHAPTER 15

THE REGULATION OF EXPORTS

This chapter continues the discussion of laws and regulations relating to the movement of goods. First, the discussion focused on imports, now this chapter turns to focus on exports. Prior to 9-11, Western European and North American countries had a relatively free inflow of technology. However, as a result of the increased risk and vigilance because of terrorism, monitoring has increased. More countries around the world are now paying greater attention to both imports and exports. The regulation of exports continues; in some instances it is enhanced to prevent the terrorist from acquiring key components and technology and in other instances it is more relaxed to reward a valued trade partner that is cooperating in the war against terrorism.

Historically, the United States has been concerned about its technology and weaponry falling into the hands of its enemies. The "enemy" has been defined differently from decade to decade as allegiances shifted, but the conviction that one should provide neither a military nor an economic advantage to the current enemy has remained constant. Therefore, the United States, in conjunction with its allies, has chosen to regulate the export and re-export of arms, technology, commodities with military applications, and other strategic commodities including technical data, component parts, and chemicals.

Initially, the focus was on controlling technology moving from "West to East" to communist countries. The emphasis has shifted because of the collapse of the USSR and the end of the Cold War to "North-South" concerns or movement of technology to belligerent or unstable Third World countries. Nonetheless, controls still exist to the former communist countries as well.

Export controls are not simply a U.S. unilateral initiative either. Other countries participate in multilateral efforts through several organizations to control exports to terrorists or certain destinations or end users. These will be discussed in this chapter.

The U.S. government agencies that handle the control of exports have overlapping jurisdiction: Bureau of Industry and Security within the Commerce Department (BIS), Department of State Office of Defense Trade Controls, Department of Treasury offices of Foreign Assets Controls (OFAC), International Traffic Arms Regulations (ITAR), U.S. Munitions List, Missile Technology Control Regime, Department of Homeland Security with the Bureau of Customs and Border Protection (Customs-Trade partnership against terrorism), Department of Defense (Defense Threat Reduction Agency-Technology Security), Department of Energy, and the intelligence community (e.g., FBI Joint Terrorism Task Force (JTTF)). The BIS plays the greatest role in the control of "dual use" technology—those that have both a business use as well as a potential military application. The breadth covered by the export control regulations is expansive, ranging from formulas to making toxic chemicals to technology.

Controlling exports is not as simple as, say, a basketball game where the object is to keep the ball from the other side and to score points for one's team. The United States and its allies, including Japan, are theoretically on the same team, yet each has concerns about sharing technology with teammates or allies. For example, pitched battles were waged over agreements to cooperate with Japan in developing specialized missile systems because some people feared the agreements would give some economic advantage to the already powerful Japan. Lurking behind the economic argument lay concern about delivering a military advantage to a current ally but a former formidable enemy. Friendly nations also compete to develop particular kinds of technology (e.g., high-definition television) so that one country may enjoy the economic rewards of being first.

Many items are routinely allowed to be exported without an individual export license because of the decontrol of technology, however, knowing which ones are still controlled requires attention. Thus, for the first-timer, as well as the seasoned exporter, a review of how the law and regulations will affect their product is essential.

This chapter examines the history of U.S. export controls, the current export laws, the international efforts toward multilateral controls, and the enforcement of these laws. It concludes with an assessment of the effectiveness and necessity of such controls, and their impact on business.

HISTORY OF EXPORT CONTROLS

The rationale for controlling exports is not a complicated one. An example with hypothetical countries illustrates the problem: If the country, Igo, is an "enemy" of Mabu, then it is reasonable that Igo does not want Mabu to have any advantage supplied directly or indirectly by Igoan businesspeople that will adversely affect Igo militarily or economically. Yet, if Mabu can buy the same technology from Rowa, doesn't that only hurt Igoan business?

Therein lies the dilemma of export controls: If one refuses to supply the desired goods to the "enemies," then someone else will. As a consequence, not only will the hostile country have the technology, but U.S. businesses will have lost a sale. Yet, no one wants to assist in fulfilling Lenin's alleged prophecy that "The capitalists will sell us the rope we need to hang them." As the definition of "enemy" changes and becomes less clear-cut (and is by no means uniformly agreed upon), the task is made more difficult. Even within the United States, significant disagreements arise within the business community and the defense establishment on these issues. Knowing the law is the key to effective export managment.

The Development of the Legal Framework

During the American Revolution, Congress outlawed exports to Britain. The United States utilized export controls during the early 1900s in response to both war and emergency conditions. They were reintroduced during World War II and were intended to last only until the war ended. When hostilities ceased, the justification of preventing critical shortages of necessary goods was no longer relevant, but the Cold War tensions developed in which old allies of World War II, the Soviet Union and United States, who had fought the common enemy of Germany, themselves became enemies. The archetypal battle between democracy and communism had begun in earnest, and export controls were a way to ensure that the West proffered no economic or military help to the Eastern Bloc. The *Export Control Act of 1949* reflected this philosophy.

The *Export Control Act.*   This act controlled the exporting of commodities with military application to communist countries and gave the president power to restrict exports based upon three criteria: national security, foreign policy, or the preservation of materials in short supply. Thereafter, Congress renewed the powers of the president under this act and in subsequent acts. Congress has the power under the U.S. Constitution "to regulate commerce with foreign nations." Article I, Section 8. Under the law, Congress delegated power to the president, who in turn delegated it to the secretary of commerce.

The United States was not alone in its efforts to control exports. Concurrently, in 1949, the United States and six European countries formed the *Coordinating Committee for Multilateral Export Controls* (COCOM).

In the United States, many revisions and acts followed the original *Export Control Act*. In 1951, the *Battle Act (Mutual Defense Assistance Act),* which controlled arms exports, made official the U.S. role in COCOM and tied foreign aid to compliance with the goals of export controls. This act was followed by the *Mutual Security Act* of 1954.

The *Export Administration Act*. In 1962, because of escalating U.S.–Soviet tensions relating to Cuba, the *Export Control Act* was strengthened to authorize the denial of export licenses to ship goods "detrimental to the national security and welfare of the United States." Subsequent enactments of the *Export Administration Acts* of 1969, 1972, 1974, 1977, and 1979, stated that the purpose was "to restrict the export of goods and technology which would make a significant contribution to the military potential of any other nation or nations which would prove detrimental to the national security of the United States."

At the same time export controls were being strengthened, the law reflected a growing recognition that the United States and allied countries must be able to export in order to be competitive. In 1979, Congress enacted the *Export Administration Act* (EAA), which acknowledged the necessity of balancing the need for trade and exports with national security interests. Subsequent changes were made by the *Export Administration Act Amendments of 1985* and the *Export Enhancement Act of 1988* (part of the *Omnibus Act*). The 1988 law substantially liberalized U.S. export controls, easing license restrictions and decontrolling some items while increasing penalties and reinforcing the enforcement process. These controls expired in 1990.

Subsequently, Congress enacted extensions of the EAA. In April 1993, Congress extended the Act through June 30, 1994. When the extension expired—Congress was stymied on a more controversial overhaul of the entire export system proposed by the Clinton administration—President Clinton was forced to use powers granted under IEEPA *(International Emergency Economic Powers Act)* and extend the provisions of the EAA. Congress could not agree on a revision, but renewed the EAA in 2000, although it was set to expire again in 2001. President Bush, just as President Clinton, was forced to use his authority under IEEPA to extend the Export Administration Act as amended. The EAA was extended by Executive Order 13222 and extended annually by presidential notice in the *Federal Register*. Congress continues to struggle to try to pass legislation overhauling this complex area. Newspapers, seeking confidential information about applications for exports, have sought to use the lapse in the EAA to argue unsuccessfully that the confidentiality provisions were no longer in effect (see the following case, *Times Publishing Co. v. United States*).

Export controls have been dramatically reshaped by a number of factors. The end of the Cold War and the struggle to identify who is the "enemy," as well as two Gulf Wars and continued threats of terrorism, have had a significant impact. The apparent ease with which Saddam Hussein was able to acquire so much military equipment before and after the first Gulf War in 1991 caused a reevaluation of export controls. The terrorist attack of 9/11 and subsequent attacks around the world, as well as the second Gulf War, have heightened the importance of focusing on the end user of military technology. As a result of this heightened awareness, in 2003, Bushnell Corporation was sentenced to a $650,000 criminal fine and five years of probation for exporting over five hundred Night Ranger night vision devices to Japan and fourteen other countries without the required export licenses. This sentence served as a warning to manufacturers, distributors, and exporters of night vision equipment that has potential military use. Under the *International Emergency Economic Powers Act*, optical sensors such as the Night Rangers are controlled for national security and foreign policy reasons.

The *USA PATRIOT Act*. Other controls include the *USA PATRIOT Act*. Title III makes banks and other financial intermediaries responsible for monitoring lists of persons and utilizing a compliance program to catch money launderers and suppliers to foreign terrorist networks. Banks, money service firms, and securities brokers and dealers—as well as foreign banks with correspondent accounts in the United States—are now within the scope of such laws.

While there were restrictions on money laundering prior to 9/11, in its aftermath, there has been increased emphasis on stopping terrorists' supply of money. Passed in October 2001, the *USA PATRIOT Act* strengthened existing treasury department regulation of banks and other institutions dealing with parties listed on government watch lists. This could impact on trade in several ways. If a foreign purchaser uses a letter of credit, the bank may have to hold the money and notify the government. This also provides a business opportunity for the many companies that will design and

Times Publishing Co. v. United States
236 F.3d 1286 (2001)
United States Court of Appeals (11th Cir.)

BACKGROUND AND FACTS

The Department of Commerce (DOC) appeals the District Court's grant of summary judgment for the Times on their Freedom of Information claim to release applications for export licenses to Cuba granted between 1996–1999. The DOC denied the request under the Export Administration Act (EAA). The Times argued that because the EAA had lapsed, the provision of the EEA, Section 12(c), was not in effect. The DOC argued that even though the statute lapsed, the Executive Order maintained "the effectiveness of the EAA" and this provision.

CIRCUIT JUDGE HULL

* * *

President Clinton exercised the authority given to him under the IEEPA to issue Executive Order No. 12,924 on August 19, 1994, on the eve of the expiration of the EAA, to allow that, "to the extent permitted by law, the provisions of the EAA, as amended, . . . shall be carried out under this order so as to continue in full force and effect and amend, as necessary, the export control system heretofore maintained by the Export Administration Regulations issued under the EAA, as amended."

* * *

Congressional intent to maintain the confidentiality of government information is the cornerstone of Exemption 3. With respect to the export licensing information Appellees seek, Congress has acted specifically to design a statutory provision to maintain confidentiality. Although Congress has permitted the statute containing this provision to lapse on a number of occasions, Congress has authorized the President, also by means of statute, to maintain the force of the confidentiality provision by way of executive order and has acted in accordance with the continued confidentiality of such information during those times of lapse. Further, Congress has renewed the confidentiality provision each time it has renewed the EAA. Finally, on November 2, 2000, Congress renewed the EAA of 1979 through August 20, 2001. In renewing the Act and ending the most recent period of lapse, Senator Gramm, Chairman of the Senate Committee on Banking, Housing and Urban Affairs, stated that "replacing the 1994 expiration date with a 2001 expiration date will make

clear that Commerce's authority to apply the 12(c) confidentiality provisions of the 1979 act is to be considered as covering any information regarding license applications obtained during that time period, as if there had been no interruption of authority." . . . In signing the amendment on November 13, 2000, President Clinton also stated: "the reauthorization confirms the Department's ability to keep export licensing information obtained during the lapse of the EAA from public disclosure, which is a critical part of the Department's export control system and protects sensitive business information and commercial interests of U.S. exporters." Statement by the President, November 13, 2000. This subsequent legislative history and comment by the executive branch specifically demonstrate Congress' intent to preserve the confidentiality of the precise export license information sought in this case pursuant to executive order during periods of lapse. . . . ("[T]he subsequent legislative history accompanying the enactment of the Export Administration Amendments Act of 1985 supports the validity of the regulation.").

Where Congress has made plain its intention to exclude the information sought by Appellees from public disclosure under FOIA, the purpose of Exemption 3—to ensure that "basic policy decisions on governmental secrecy are made by the Legislative rather than the Executive branch"—is satisfied. . . . In addition, where there is no dispute that Congress granted the President authority to extend the provisions of the EAA containing the statutory exemption and that the President has exercised this authority in signing Executive Order 12,924, an overly technical and formalistic reading of FOIA to disclose information clearly intended to be confidential would undermine the Supreme Court's direction that the FOIA exemptions are to be given meaningful reach and application. In light of Congress' clear expression of its intent to protect the confidentiality of the requested export licensing information, it would be truly nonsensical to protect such information submitted to the Department through August 20, 1994, release identical information submitted between August 21, 1994 and November 13, 2000, and again protect such information from November 14, 2000

continued

continued

forward. The confidentiality of the export licensing information sought by Appellees, provided by section 12(c) of the EAA, was maintained by virtue of Executive Order 12, 924.

We conclude that the comprehensive legislative scheme as a whole—the confidentiality provision of the EAA, the intended and foreseen periodic expiration of the EAA, and the Congressional grant of power to the President to prevent the lapse of its important provisions during such times—exempts

from disclosure the export licensing information requested by Appellees. We, therefore, reverse the grant of summary judgment in favor of Appellees and remand to the district court for the entry of judgment in favor of the Appellant.

Comment.   This case signals the problems that happen when Congress can not work together to enact laws. Nonetheless, the Court was able to keep the applications private in keeping with the original EAA.

sell software to manage such compliance programs and cross-check all depositors on government lists of terrorists and other watch lists.

Multilateral Export Control

The Coordinating Committee for Multilateral Export Controls (COCOM) was formed in 1949 to coordinate the exports of technology to communist countries. Seventeen countries were members including Australia, Belgium, Canada, Denmark, Germany, Greece, Italy, the United Kingdom, France, Japan, Luxembourg, the Netherlands, Norway, Portugal, Spain, Turkey, and the United States. Several countries, Ireland, Sweden, Switzerland, Finland, Austria, Singapore, and New Zealand, had agreements to enforce export controls and thus share some of the benefits of more liberal intramember exporting. Under COCOM, members reviewed certain licenses.

The end of the Cold War also signalled a major reassessment of export controls by the members. COCOM ceased to exist on March 30, 1994. The *Wassenaar Arrangement* formed in 1996 (named after a suburb of the Netherlands near the Hague) does not have the single-country veto, as COCOM did. The thirty-three current member countries include the United States, countries of Europe, Russia, Japan, Turkey, and many Eastern European countries. Taiwan is not a member but agreed to abide. Thus, the United States cannot veto another country's decision to issue an export license. This loose arrangement reflects the lack of consensus about the level of control necessary in today's world. There is a serious question about the utility of any export controls imposed by only one country. It is interesting to note that in such an

important matter, there is no treaty; essentially there is a notice requirement wherein member countries will give another country the opportunity to object to the issuance of an export license.

The Australia Group.   The Australia Group is another group of countries that have agreed to cooperate in halting the spread of chemical and biological weapons (CBW). It was formed in 1985 with fifteen countries inspired by the use of chemical weapons by Iraq against Iran and now has thirty-three member countries. Additionally, countries participate in the Missile Technology Control Regime (MTCR) founded in 1987. One of the oldest groups, The Nuclear Suppliers Group, founded in 1975 with forty members because of India's 1974 nuclear explosion, tries to limit the use of nuclear material for peaceful domestic ventures.

The problem with all of these multilateral efforts is that they are voluntary and without enforcement powers. Nonetheless, since 9-11, countries have redoubled their efforts to work cooperatively to address this worldwide terrorism threat.

The EU recently passed new legislation, EC No. 1334/2000, "setting up a community regime for the control of dual use items and technology." Similarly the UK passed a new export control act in 2002. To date, the United States has not been able to put aside political differences and focus on this task of overhauling the export law.

The Purpose of the Export Regulation

The purpose of the export regulation was captured in the 1979 EAA:

It is the policy of the United States that export trade by United States citizens be given a high priority and not be controlled except when such controls (A) are necessary to further fundamental national security, foreign policy, or short supply objectives. . . .

The mission of the BIS is defined as:

To advance U.S. national security, foreign policy and economic interests. BIS's activities include: regulating the export of sensitive goods and technologies in an effective and efficient manner; enforcing export control, antiboycott and public safety laws; cooperating with and assisting U.S. industry to comply with international arms control agreements, monitoring the viability of the U.S. defense industrial base; and promoting federal initiatives and public–private partnerships to protect the nation's critical infrastructures.

It could be estimated that approximately 80 percent of the controls are concerned with national security and foreign policy. Adherence to the goals of nuclear nonproliferation and noncooperation with boycotts are also goals of the legislation.

Controls apply to four types of transactions:

1. Export of commodities and technical data from the United States.
2. Re-exports of U.S.-origin commodities and technical data among foreign countries.
3. Exports and re-exports from a foreign country of products with U.S.-origin parts.
4. Exports and re-exports from a foreign country of products based on U.S. technical data (prod-

ucts designed from U.S.-origin research and technical data; re-exports include goods shipped from the United States to Singapore, for example, and from Singapore to India).

Thus, shipments out of the United States as well as from foreign countries are affected by this law.

It is important to understand that a demonstration of controlled technology to a foreign national within the United States can be deemed an export as well as an email sent abroad. Currently, the U.S. government is working with immigration to better track unauthorized access to technology within the United States. Clearly, this is a huge undertaking.

Antiboycott Provisions

Antiboycott law provisions are also included in the EAA. The section on foreign boycotts makes it illegal to "comply . . . [with or] support any boycott fostered or imposed by a foreign country against a country which is friendly to the United States." This provision was primarily aimed at Middle Eastern countries that tried to orchestrate a boycott of Israel. The following case addresses a challenge to the constitutionality of both the *Export Administration Act* and the *Antiboycott Regulations* published in the *Code of Federal Regulations.*

Other countries' companies do cooperate with the boycott. Companies have honestly indicated that their internal sales policy forbids transactions with Israel. In *Israel Aircraft Industries Ltd. v.*

Briggs & Stratton Corp. v. Baldridge
539 F. Supp. 1307 (E.D. Wis. 1982) aff'd, 728 F.2d 915 (1984)
United States Court of Appeals (7th Cir.)

BACKGROUND AND FACTS
In December 1954, the League of Arab States called for an economic boycott of Israel. Under the "General Principles" worked out by the Arab states, a firm could be blacklisted if it traded with Israel.

The plaintiff manufactures internal combustion engines. Its products are often used as component parts. Briggs has been blacklisted because of dealing with Israel.

In May of 1977, Briggs received a letter from its Syrian distributor telling it that it had been blacklisted and

refused an import license. He also received a questionnaire, which was translated as follows:

1. Has the company now or in the past had main or branch factories in Israel?
2. Has the company now or in the past had general offices in Israel for its regional or international works?
3. Has it granted now or in the past the right of utilizing its name or trademarks or patents to persons or

continued

continued

establishments or Israel works inside or outside Israel?

4. Does it share in or own now or in the past shares in Israel works or establishments inside or outside Israel?
5. Does it now or did it offer in the past any technical assistance to any Israeli work or establishment?
6. Does it represent now or did it represent in the past any Israel establishment or work inside or outside Israel?
7. What are the companies which it shares in or with, their nationality and the size or rate of this share?

Briggs answered the questions "no," but did not have it authenticated because of the new antiboycott regulations. The blacklisting continued, but subsequently the company was removed from the blacklist. Briggs was unquestionably injured economically by the blacklisting. Briggs brought an action against the officials charged with enforcing the act and regulations, claiming that they violated the First, Fifth, and Ninth Amendments to the U.S. Constitution.

DISTRICT JUDGE GORDON

. . . The Commerce Department regulations are consistent with this express policy to require persons to refuse to furnish information which would have the effect of furthering a boycott against a nation friendly to the United States. Thus the regulations are not inconsistent with the policies of the act.

I also reject Briggs' argument that the regulations permit a firm to supply information in the absence of a questionnaire that it cannot supply if it gets one. Example (ix) following the intent regulation reads:

U.S. company A is on boycotting country Y's blacklist. In an attempt to secure its removal from the blacklist, A wishes to supply to Y information which demonstrates that A does at least as much business in Y and other countries engaged in a boycott of X as it does in X. A intends to continue its business in X undiminished and in fact is exploring and intends to continue exploring an expansion of its activities in X without regard to Y's boycott.

A may furnish the information, because in doing so it has no intent to comply with, further, or support Y's boycott. 15 C.F.R. 369.1(e), Examples of Intent.

Briggs' interpretation of this example goes too far. The example merely permits a company on its own initiative to demonstrate non-discriminatory conduct. . . .

Briggs argues that because the regulations cause Briggs to be blacklisted, and thus affect its worldwide sales, the government has totally destroyed Briggs' rights to its foreign trade. Briggs likens the effect to a restriction on private property which "forc[es] some people alone to bear public burdens which, in all fairness and justice, should be borne by the public as a whole."

In *Andrus v. Allard,* the Supreme Court held that the denial of one traditional property right, where the others were not disturbed, did not always amount to a taking. In *Andrus,* there was no physical invasion or restraint on the property in question; the regulation only prohibited the sale of the property. The Court did not find dispositive the fact that the regulations prevented the most profitable use of the property.

When we review regulation, a reduction in the value of property is not necessarily equated with a taking. . . . [L]oss of future profits—unaccompanied by any physical property restriction—provides a slender reed upon which to rest a takings claim.

The reed is equally slender here. The regulations apply to all Americans equally. It is possible that they have a somewhat greater impact on Briggs than they do on others, but that does not constitute a taking. Briggs has lost some profits because it has lost some sales, but its property has not been seized or restrained by the government. There is no restriction by the challenged regulation on Briggs' efforts to export its products. In prohibiting Briggs from answering certain questions, the government has not taken Briggs' property in violation of the Fifth Amendment.

Therefore, IT IS ORDERED that the motion of the plaintiffs for summary judgment be and hereby is denied.

IT IS ALSO ORDERED that the defendant's motion for summary judgment be and hereby is granted.

IT IS FURTHER ORDERED that this action be and hereby is dismissed upon its merits.

Decision.   Thus, the antiboycott regulations were upheld by the court despite the difficulty business may have in complying with them.

Israel Aircraft Industries Ltd. v. Sanwa Business Credit Corp. & the Sanwa Bank, Ltd.
16 F.3d 198 (1994)
United States Court of Appeals (7th Cir.)

BACKGROUND AND FACTS

Sanwa Business Credit Corporation, the principal lender to Fairchild Aircraft Corporation, is the American subsidiary of a Japanese bank. After Fairchild entered bankruptcy, Israel Aircraft Industries, Ltd. (an Israeli corporation) and Quadrant Management, Inc., formed a joint venture to acquire Fairchild. They were unwilling to pay off Fairchild's debts at face value and asked Sanwa to accept the joint venture in lieu of Fairchild as the borrower under a revised credit arrangement. According to the complaint Sanwa said no, on instructions of its parent, for the sole reason that Sanwa Bank will not deal with any Israeli corporation so long as the League of Arab States maintains its boycott of Israel. The district court dismissed the complaint, holding that § 8 of the Export Administration Act does not create a private right of action in favor of victims of foreign boycotts.

EASTERBROOK, CIRCUIT JUDGE

. . . A look beneath the surface of this legislation reinforces the inferences from its text and structure. When Congress enacted the statute in 1977, it recognized that there would be no private enforcement.

The Senate Committee wrote of "[t]he danger of unwarranted allegations in this highly sensitive area." What makes the subject especially "sensitive" is that it concerns the foreign relations of the United States. Nations use boycotts and other forms of commercial pressure to achieve diplomatic and military ends. The United States uses the device frequently (at the moment, commerce with Cuba, Haiti, Iran, Iraq, Vietnam, and Yugoslavia is severely limited) and has no objection to the principle of international boycotts. Whether to recognize or instead to resist a boycott announced by some other nation—and what form any resistance will take—depends on the degree of friendliness between the United States and its target, and on the other options available to the United States. This nation recognizes not only that foreign nationals may be under pressure by their home governments to comply with boycotts we seek to break, but also that diplomatic overtures may be more successful than awards of damages in undermining unwelcome boycotts. Our case, a suit by an Israeli corporation against a Japanese bank to obtain damages on account of the bank's decision to respect a boycott by the Arab League, exposes some of the complications. Would the State Department find it as easy to enlist Japanese aid in bringing about harmony between the Palestinians and Israel—a subject on which mighty strides have been made while this case was in progress—if American courts were compelling Japanese firms and their subsidiaries to pay large sums? Whatever bargaining space the State Department enjoys could be curtailed by the presence of actors (judges and private litigants) beyond the influence of U.S. negotiators. No surprise, then, that Congress left implementation of § 8 to the President, who establishes the foreign policy of the United States. It would be imprudent for a court to create rights of action that might interfere with the conduct of foreign policy. . . .

Israel Aircraft makes a claim under state law in addition to §8. It contends that by refusing to advance credit to the joint venture, Sanwa tortiously interfered with its business opportunities—whether with Israel Aircraft's opportunity to deal with Quadrant, or the joint venture's ability to acquire Fairchild's assets, the complaint is not quite clear. . . .

Sanwa did not induce any third party to cease dealing with Israel Aircraft. It simply refused to lend any money to the joint venture. Israel Aircraft and Quadrant could have borrowed from any of a hundred other lenders and purchased Fairchild's assets in bankruptcy. Because the joint venture was unwilling to pay off Fairchild's loans in full (and apparently feared that it would not be the highest bidder at an auction in bankruptcy), it sought concessions from Sanwa, Fairchild's principal creditor. Sanwa balked. Israel Aircraft has not cited, and we could not find, any case holding a financial institution liable in tort for failing to make a concession that would have facilitated an extension of credit. By refusing to lend money, a bank does not "tortiously interfere" with the use the borrower would make of the funds. Other ways of characterizing Sanwa's conduct are possible but do not change the result under state law.

Affirmed.

Decision.   Israel Aircraft was not successful in using the U.S. courts against Sanwa.

Sanwa Business Credit Corp. & the Sanwa Bank, Ltd., an Israeli corporation unsuccessfully tried to use U.S. law to coerce a U.S. subsidiary of a Japanese bank to lend it money.

Many companies choose to accept the proposed governmental penalties rather than fight the case in court. Even if a company believes it did nothing wrong, it may, as a business decision, accept the penalty without a trial because the penalty will be less costly and is a certain outcome.

An example of a recent antiboycott case that settled in 2003 involved Rockwell Automation, a successor to Reliance Electric, which had two foreign subsidiaries. The subsidiary of Reliance allegedly did not report a Kuwaiti inquiry about whether goods had originated in Israel and failed to keep adequate records. Furthermore, a subsidiary actually did furnish information to other potential buyers about blacklist status. As a result, a $9,000 civil penalty was imposed after the company both voluntarily disclosed the events and cooperated with the investigation. It is important to remember that a company cannot answer "no" regarding questions about its dealing with Israel; it must report these inquiries. Answering "no" is viewed as cooperating with the boycott.

There are a number of other kinds of requests that companies may face that also should be reported. For example, these statements on purchase orders should be reported: "This order is placed subject to the suppliers not being on the Israel boycott list published by the central Arab League" or "The seller shall not supply goods or materials that have been manufactured or processed in Israel nor shall the services of any Israeli organization be used in handling or transporting the goods or materials."[1]

DEVELOPMENTS IN THE LAW

The major changes in Poland, Hungary, and the Czech Republic have logarithmically raised expectations of future trade partnerships. U.S. allies, as well as the countries that are former members of the Warsaw Pact, will increase their demands for an easing of restrictions on trade (export controls), as well as on licensing and investment. If countries feel that the former Soviets are no longer a threat waiting to pounce at the borders (as they did in the past in Prague and Afghanistan), then their concern will

be transformed into a desire to sell and profit from the transfer of technology to these technologically hungry markets. Former President Clinton continued in the footsteps of President G. H. Bush in decontrolling many items. Computers and high-tech equipment were significantly decontrolled in 1993. In March of 1994 the old Cold War bans on selling telecommunications and computer equipment to the former Soviet Union and China were ended. In 1997, to prevent a former Soviet Republic from selling off military equipment to Third World countries, the United States purchased them instead. This subsidization may have to substitute for a weaker multilateral export control regime. The U.S. has continued the decontrol of technology (with the exception of satellites) and recently allowed the sale of encryption software.

It is not surprising that 9/11 prompted a reassessment of how to improve the efficacy of controls despite the fact that the tragedy of the World Trade Center did not involve illegal exports. The tension for reform in the law involves two equal pushes: to decontrol items for allies and to increase controls for suspect users and end users.

Several developments resulted from these disparate efforts. In 2003, changes were made to the encryption policy, allowing certain persons to "take personal use encryption commodities and software to countries not listed in Group E:1." In general, the other section allows more flexibility in traveling with laptops and so on. The government notes that "there will be no licensing or post-export reporting requirements related to the export or reexport of such mass market encryption products" after the initial review.

Another example of decontrol is the major shift in exporting regulations application to India. In March 2003, the United States and India signed the *U.S.–India High Technology Cooperation Agreement.* This signals a continuing shift in the relationship between the two countries. For example, in 1999, 45 percent of all export applications for shipments to India were denied, but in 2002, only 10 percent were denied. Presumably, the agreement will further reduce this number. The Entity List of companies (involved in proliferation activities) previously had one hundred fifty-nine Indian companies on it, but now has only two Indian companies, which is a significant reduction in the level of scrutiny to be applied. Nuclear and missile controlled items destined for India have been moved from a "policy of denial" to a case-by-case review.

In 2002, President Bush revised controls on "high performance computers" (represented by ECCN 4A003) that have a "composite theoretical performance" (CTP) of up to 190,000 millions of theoretical operations per second (MTOPS)— these can now be exported to most places with a License Exception. This includes China, Russia, and India. Previously, the cutoff was 28,000 MTOPS. This relaxation of rules did not affect shipments to so-called terrorist supporting countries. Additionally, the government agreed to limit export controls on "general purpose microprocessors" in conformance with *Wassenaar* countries. Despite decontrol, some companies' expansion plans are limited by export law (see the International Accents article).

An example of trying to tighten controls involves the Department of Commerce Transship-ment Country Export Control Initiative (TECI). This initiative works on two levels: government to government and government to the private sector. The initiative tries to minimize the cost imposed on industry, while ensuring enforcement and multi-country cooperation. It works with Export Control and Border Security (EXBS), Container Security Initiative (CSI), Customs Trade Partnership against Terrorism (C-TPAT), Operation Shield America, and the Dangerous Materials Initiative.

MECHANICS OF THE LAW

This section examines in greater detail the mechanics of how the law and accompanying regulations contained in the *Code of Federal Regulations* are applied. The Export Administration Regulations (EAR) begin with some basic questions. What is the item? Where is it going? Who will be the end user? What will they do with it?

international accents

TI Rules Out Plants in Mainland

Tim Culpan in Taipei

Texas Instruments has no plans to set up chip fabrication plants on the mainland for its semiconductors which go into mobile phones. The world's fourth-largest chipmaker with US $6.9 billion in sales last year said yesterday China was becoming increasingly important to the electronics manufacturing industry but there was no compelling reason for it to manufacture its chips in the country. Chairman and chief executive Tom Engibous said Texas Instruments sub-contracted some of its production to Shanghai-based Semiconductor Manufacturing International Corp (SMIC), which he described as a "very good source of wafers."

Chips made within China receive favourable treatment, compared with imports, such as breaks on the value-added tax. To take advantage of the benefit, it would make more economic sense to outsource to companies such as SMIC rather than spending money to set up a new manufacturing facility in China. At the same time, foreign companies such as Texas Instruments are prevented by the Wassenaar Arrangement from establishing state-of-the-art fabrication facilities in China.

Most mainland foundries produce chips etched at a line-width measuring 0.25 micron, but smaller line-widths used by leading edge manufacturers are off-limits to China. "Export controls in the United States would not allow us to build a 0.13 micron or 0.09 micron wafer fab," Mr. Engibous said. "Until that changes, it's not going to be probable that people are going to go in and build a real wafer fab." But Mr. Engibous was positive on the long-term prospects for the mainland chip industry. "I think the first phase of Chinese contributions to the semiconductor industry will be very high quality foundries, and those will be great assets to us," he said.

Copyright © 2003 *South China Morning Post*, reprinted with permission.

http://

http://www.aesdirect.gov
For online filing of Shipper's Export Declarations.
http://www.tradenet.gov
See for export information.

There are a number of possible reasons for controlling the export of an item:

AT	Anti-Terrorism
CB	Chemical and Biological Weapons
CC	Crime Control
CW	Chemical Weapons Convention
EI	Encryption Items
FC	Firearms Convention
MT	Missile Technology
NS	National Security
NP	Nuclear Nonproliferation
RS	Regional Stability
SS	Short Supply
XP	High Performance Computers
SI	Significant Items

The regulations outline a number of steps the exporter must take:

Step 1: Determine whether your item is subject to the exclusive jurisdiction of another federal agency.

Step 2: If software, determine if it is publicly available technology and software. This step is relevant for both exports and reexports.

Step 3: Determine if the items are reexports of U.S.-origin items. This step is appropriate only for reexporters. For an item in a foreign country, you should determine whether the item is of U.S. origin.

Step 4: Determine if items are foreign-made and incorporate less than the *de minimis* level of U.S. parts, components, and materials. This step is appropriate only for items that are made outside the United States and not currently in the United States.

Step 5: Determine if the items are foreign-made and incorporate more than the *de minimis* level of U.S. parts, components, or materials. If the incorporated U.S. parts exceed the relevant *de minimis* level, then the export from abroad is subject to the EAR.

Step 6: Determine if the items are foreign-made and produced with certain U.S. technology for export to specified destinations. This step is appropriate for foreign-made items in foreign countries.

There are other steps as well. Step 7 requires a classification of the item on the Commerce Control List (CCL). Step 8 looks at the country destination, while Step 9 cross-checks by chart whether a license is required.

The exporter is then directed through a number of other checks and screens: (10) foreign-made items incorporating U.S.-origin items and the *de minimis* rule, (11) foreign-produced direct product, (12) persons denied export privileges, (13) prohibited end uses and end users, (14) embargoed countries, (15) proliferation, (16) in transit, (17) review denial orders, (18) know your customer, and (19) review general prohibitions.

The following general prohibitions describe certain exports, reexports, and other conduct, subject to the scope of the EAR, in which an exporter may not engage without a license from the BIS or a License Exception from each applicable general prohibition:

1. Export and re-export of controlled items to listed countries.
2. Re-export and export from abroad of foreign-made items with more than a *de minimis* amount of controlled U.S. content.
3. Re-export and export from abroad of the foreign-produced direct product of U.S. technology and software.
4. Action prohibited by denial order.
5. Export or re-export to prohibited end-use or end-user.
6. Export to embargoed destination.
7. Export supporting proliferation activity.
8. Violation of orders, terms, or conditions.
9. Proceeding with transaction with knowledge that a violation has occurred or is about to occur. (See Exhibit 15.1)

The regulations continue to monitor, in theory, the re-export of goods. Thus, if a controlled product moves from the United States to Thailand to India, the U.S. law purports to cover this transaction, even after a lapse of time. This extraterritorial application of U.S. law offends many countries. Its effectiveness may also be questioned in light of the Wassenaar arrangement supplanting COCOM.

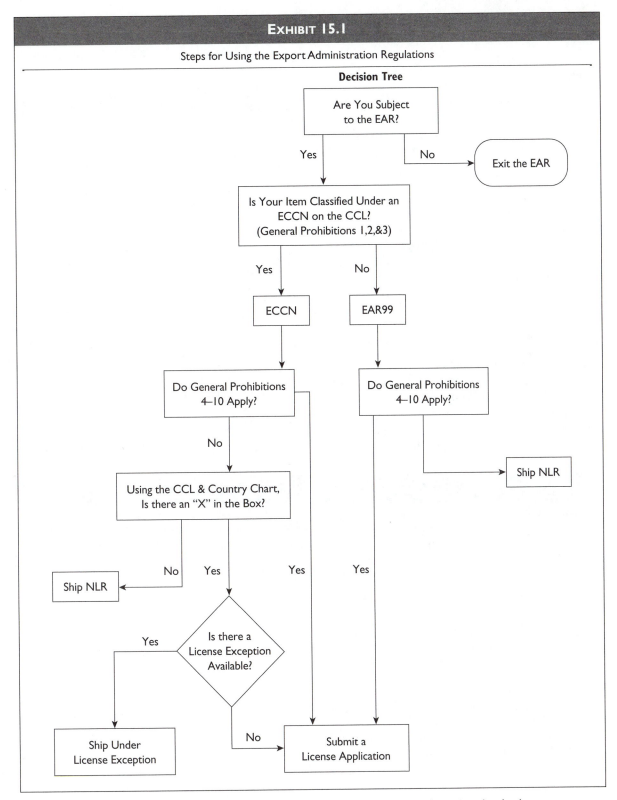

EXHIBIT 15.1

Steps for Using the Export Administration Regulations

Decision Tree

SOURCE: Bureau of Industry and Security, U.S. Dept. of Commerce, http://w3.access.gpo.gov/bis/ear/ear_data.html

For a list of some commonly asked questions, see Exhibit 15.2.

License

If an item is controlled, then the exporter must apply for a license. The exporter must use the ECCN, along with the Commerce Control List and Country Chart. There may be special exceptions based on item, country, license, or special conditions.

If no license is required, then *NLR* (no license required) is reported on the Shipper's Export Declaration (SED).

A new license, called the *Special Comprehensive License* (SCL) replaces earlier distribution and service supply licenses.

An exporter who does not know the ECCN, can request a classification. It is also possible to ask for an advisory opinion from the BIS. (See Exhibit 15.3 for a summary of the ECCN system.)

Extraterritorial Application. A little-known fact is that the export control law covers the movement of U.S.-origin commodities and technical data or products containing U.S.-origin parts from one foreign country to another. This extraterritorial application of the law has caused some

political problems for the United States. Its allies, including the United Kingdom, were not pleased that the United States (prior to 1989) did not have

---

EXHIBIT 15.2

Export Counseling Questions and Answers

- Do I need a license to export to Puerto Rico?
- How do I find out about duties and taxes for exporting to certain countries?
- The Shipper's Export Declaration (SED) requires a Schedule B number. Can you furnish me with that number?
- How do I know if my software has encryption capability?
- What is the "official" version of the Export Administration Regulations?
- Is there an embargo on Sudan?
- I've been told that the embargoes on Iran, Libya and Sudan have been abolished, is this true?
- If I have an export license for a computer at 10,000 CTP, may I ship a computer at 7,500 under that license?
- Our company does little exporting now, but we are anticipating a much higher volume in the near future. I am interested to know whom I could contact for training information on general export compliance?

SOURCE: http://www.bis.doc.gov/licensing/ExporterFAQ.

EXHIBIT 15.3

Summary of Commerce Control List Numbering System Making Up the ECCN (Export Control Classification Number)

(1) The CCL is divided into ten general categories, indicated by the first character, numbered from 0 to 1, as follows:

0—Nuclear Materials, Facilities and Equipment, and Miscellaneous
1—Materials
2—Materials Processing
3—Electronics
4—Computers
5—Telecommunications and Information Security
6—Sensors and Lasers
7—Avionics and Navigation
8—Marine Technology
9—Propulsion Systems and Transportation Equipment

(2) Five groups of products fall within each category; the second character is identified by the letters A through E as follows:

A—Equipment, Assemblies, and Components
B—Production and Test Equipment
C—Materials
D—Software
E—Technology

SOURCE: 15 C.F.R. §736

sufficient faith in each allied country's export control system.

The extraterritorial application of the law means that to move U.S.-origin goods controlled by export laws from India to Taiwan, one needs a U.S. export license. The law also covers the movements or the export and re-export of foreign products from a foreign country when the product is based on U.S.-origin technical data. Under these provisions, the United States has been pursuing high-level discussions with Israel for allegedly violating the *Export Control Law* by sharing what the United States believes was U.S.-origin technical data with South Africa for use in constructing a bomb.

Licensing Review Process

One of the difficulties exporters face is that of trying to comply with the law in a way that allows them to do business in a timely manner and meet the demands of their clients. The Bureau of Industry and Security (BIS) must review and rule on licenses within ninety days or send the matter to the president. This problem is compounded by the overlapping jurisdictions of the various U.S. agencies that administer the U.S. export laws, a situation that results in confusion over which agency has jurisdiction over a particular question.

Once the application for a type of validated license is received, the Office of Export Licensing reviews the application. If it is complete, the specialist will either make a determination about the license or refer the application to the relevant agency:

- Department of Defense (national security)
- Department of Energy (nuclear nonproliferation)
- Department of State (reviews both the equipment and end-user for foreign policy concerns) (OTC—Office of Defense Trade Control)
- Intelligence Community (end-user checks dealing with weapons of mass destruction)
- Department of the Treasury (can also become involved in dealing with embargoed countries as well as tobacco and firearms)
- OFAC (Office of Foreign Assets Control)

If the departments cannot reach consensus, the application goes through several layers of interagency committees including the Operating Committee, Advisory Committee on Export Policy (ACEP), Export Administration Review Board

(EARB), culminating in a final decision by the president. Time limits prescribe when a matter must move to the next level, but no limits are placed on the total time the government can take to consider the application. At any time, an agency may send the matter out to the National Security Council for review.

If your item is not listed on the CCL, then it may be an EAR99, which is an item that does not need a license unless it is going to an embargoed destination or a prohibited end use. A business deal that cannot be consummated because $10 million worth of goods are waiting for a license to be shipped can cause the calmest executive to have "a Maalox moment." In fiscal year 2002, BIS received almost 11,000 applications and approved approximately 80 percent of them. The average time until approval was thirty-nine days. If the application did not have to be referred to another agency for review, then it only took eleven days. It took forty-four days on average for referred applications. There were nine applications for an SCL license.

Deemed Exports

When technology is released to a foreign national, even within the United States, it is considered a "deemed export" that requires a license. Technology is considered "released" when it can be visually inspected. Any foreign national is covered, including businesspeople, tourists, and students, but does not include those with a "green card" or who are U.S. citizens.

Foreign Availability

Finally, authorities in the United States are beginning to recognize that if a product is available from another source besides the United States, export controls make little sense. The Office of Foreign Availability within the Department of Commerce allows U.S. companies to petition for a review of the foreign availability of products and technology. If the office determines that a non-U.S. item of comparable quality is available for the proscribed country buyer, making the controls ineffective, the Department of Commerce may recommend decontrol of the item. Decontrol does not happen immediately, however, because the president may override the office's finding for national security reasons.

Export Management System

One of the problems companies face is how to comply with the ever-changing export regulations. The need for management controls that are not exorbitantly expensive nor stifling to business development is clear. (See Exhibit 15.4 for an example.) There are now more lists to check for the exporter. See Exhibit 15.5.

EXHIBIT 15.4

Menu of Export Management System Elements

- A clear statement of management policy communicated to all levels of the firm involved in export/reexport sales, traffic and related functions, emphasizing the importance of compliance with the Export Administration Regulations (EAR).
- Identification of positions and specific individuals responsible for compliance with the EAR.
- A program for recordkeeping as required by the EAR.
- A continuing program for educating people who require knowledge of the EAR.
- An internal review program to verify compliance with the firm's EMS and the EAR.
- A system for consulting the Bureau of Export Administration (BXA) when questions arise regarding the propriety of specific report transactions.
- An order processing system that documents employee clearance of transactions in accordance with the requirements of the firm's EMS.
- Screening Elements:
  1. Denied Persons Screen
  2. Product Classification/License Determination Screen
  3. Diversion-Risk Screen
  4. Nuclear Screen
  5. Missile Screen
  6. Chemical and Biological Weapons Screen

SOURCE: http://www.bis.doc.gov/exportmanagementsystems/pdf/

EXHIBIT 15.5

Lists to Check

Denied persons
Unverified
Entity
Specially designated nationals
Debarred

Management must create a system that maintains the required records for at least two years including invoices, shippers export declarations, bills of lading, and air waybills. (Keeping the records longer may be advisable because the statute of limitations is five years for criminal actions.) A company should have a policy in place, with trained personnel to implement the policy, as well as a system of internal audits and notification of the BIS in case of irregularity. A significant part of the process is an effective screening operation that searches orders for prospective problems.

These requirements place a burden on the seller to ensure that the buyer does not violate the EAA. Weekly readings of the *Federal Register* to update the companies barred from doing business are essential.

A firm's voluntary disclosure of export violations to the BIS discovered as the result of an internal audit may lessen the ultimate penalties imposed. For example, Sigma Designs, a California computer component company, concluded, based upon an independent audit, that they had violated the law 237 times between 1988 and 1990 with computer parts shipments worth more than $9 million. In January 1994, Sigma signed a consent agreement that levied a civil fine of $750,000. The company, however, paid only $237,000; the remaining $513,000 was suspended for two years and will be waived if Sigma does not violate the law during that period. An export management system may have avoided the errors and the resulting fine. Nonetheless, the prompt action taken allowed Sigma to reduce the damage of its violation.

---

http://www.bis.doc.gov
Provides information and links relevant to export licenses and controls and country-specific exporting.
http://www.bis.doc.gov/licensing/index/html
See this address on country-specific export counseling.

DIVERSION

Diversion refers to the illegal placement of goods or commodities in the hands of an individual(s) for whom an export license would not be granted either because of country group, end-use of the product, or the product itself. Although diversion stories might seemingly belong in a Grade B movie, with North Korean agents in trench coats walking around with briefcases full of cash, such stories are not so far from the truth. Both the newspapers and enforcement agencies are replete with accounts of schemes to divert sensitive technology to a prohibited destination. One case involved a "sting" operation in which agents substituted two hundred pounds of kitty litter for avionic equipment sent from the United States to England and then to Iran.

Another example of diversion is the reported scheme to ship U.S.-origin helicopters to North Korea through a West German firm, Delta-Avia Fluggerate, GmbH. Although a number of them were shipped, finally the U.S. was able to intercede and prevent the final fifteen from reaching their destination. The company was denied export privileges by the Department of Commerce while an investigation of the incident proceeded.

Many companies face the problem of how to determine when a buyer may be planning to divert the goods to an ultimate buyer who would not have been able to purchase the same item directly. The Department of Commerce has published *Indications of Potential Illegal Exports*, which should assist exporters in identifying when a buyer may have a diversion scheme in mind (see Exhibit 15.6).

An exporter who had reason to know that an end-user was going to direct the products to an embargoed destination is liable. This liability places a burden and duty on the exporter to inquire about the projected buyer and the anticipated uses for the product. Thus, the pressure to make a fast sale must be tempered by judicious inquiry.

ENFORCEMENT

Recent export cases detail aggressive enforcement actions:

- In 2001, an aircraft manufacturer paid a $2.12 million civil fine. This settled charges that license applications in 1994–95 for exports to China had false information about machine tools.
- In 2002, a Massachusetts company sold $435,000 worth of lab equipment to a company in the United Arab Emirates. The company subsequently learned that the equipment had been disassembled in Jabal and shipped to Iran. This would have required reauthorization of OFAC. The company was denied export privileges for ten years.
- A company paid a $414,000 criminal fine for exporting oil field processing equipment to Iran. Its London affiliate was fined $448,000 and there were additional civil fines against both entities. Additionally, both entities were placed on the denial of export privilege list, although

---

EXHIBIT 15.6

BIS's Red Flags

Possible indicators that an unlawful diversion might be planned by your customer include the following:

1. The customer or purchasing agent is reluctant to offer information about the end-use of a product.
2. The product's capabilities do not fit the buyer's line of business; for example, a small bakery places an order for several sophisticated lasers.
3. The product ordered is incompatible with the technical level of the country to which the product is being shipped. For example, semiconductor manufacturing equipment would be of little use in a country without an electronics industry.
4. The customer has little or no business background.
5. The customer is willing to pay cash for a very expensive item when the terms of the sale call for financing.
6. The customer is unfamiliar with the product's performance characteristics but still wants the product.
7. Routine installation, training or maintenance services are declined by the customer.
8. Delivery dates are vague, or deliveries are planned for out-of-the-way destinations.
9. A freight forwarding firm is listed as the product's final destination.
10. The shipping route is abnormal for the product and destination.
11. Packaging is inconsistent with the stated method of shipment or destination.
12. When questioned, the buyer is evasive or unclear about whether the purchased product is for domestic use, export or reexport.

US Judge Overturns Executives' Convictions

By Andrea Estes, Globe Staff

A federal judge has thrown out the eight-year-old convictions of two defense company executives who sold technology that helped India build better nuclear missiles, finding that even though their conduct was "reprehensible," it was not criminal.

In a stunning finale to a decade-long drama, US District Court Judge Douglas Woodlock overturned the jury convictions last month of Walter Lachman of Concord and Maurice Subilia of Kennebunkport, Maine, but sealed the decision until yesterday.

The top executives of two related high-tech companies were found guilty of violating Department of Commerce export rules, intended to stop the spread of nuclear weapons, by shipping a device without a special license.

The jury found that the men believed they needed a permit, but Woodlock said he was persuaded by the defense lawyers' argument.

In a 66-page decision, Woodlock found that the men's actions were morally wrong, but not criminal.

"It is difficult to conceive an area in which the danger to the public interest is more critical," Woodlock wrote.

"I have no doubt . . . that the defendants here sought—for their own private economic advantage and heedless of the national security interests of this country—to exploit imprecision in the regulatory regime for controlling exports," he wrote.

Yet, Woodlock found that he could not uphold the convictions.

The judge credited evidence offered by the posttrial defense team of Harvard professor Alan Dershowitz, Harvey Silverglate, Andrew Good, and Michael Schneider, who argued that even Commerce Department employees had differing views as to what the regulation meant and whether the device involved was covered.

The jury found that Lachman and Subilia sold equipment that helped India improve its Agni medium range nuclear missile.

They faced up to 10 years in federal prison and $5 million in fines.

But Woodlock never sentenced the men or responded to their motions for a new trial or a judgement of acquittal—until July 18. Then he voided the convictions.

The case—involving Fiber Materials Inc. of Biddeford, Maine, and Materials International of Acton—spanned a decade, and had many twists and turns.

Prosecutors, who are mulling over an appeal, said they were "perplexed," by the reversal, especially in light of security concerns after the Sept. 11, 2001, attacks.

"We're extremely disappointed," said US Attorney Michael Sullivan. "The jury heard the evidence with very specific instructions related to the meaning of the statute itself and concluded these defendants violated the act. He knew they did it and what they were doing is wrong—that's irreconcilable," Sullivan said.

Neither the defendants nor their lawyers would comment on the decision.

The defendants, whose companies have continued to receive millions of dollars in government defense contracts since their convictions, had asked the federal government to reimburse them for the costs of defending against the charges.

In the late 1980s and early 1990s, the men sold India a complete plant for processing carbon-carbon—fibers that when applied to missiles make them strike more accurately because they can withstand the heat of atmospheric reentry.

The 1993 indictment charged that the companies and executives sold India a control panel for a "hot isostatic press," a device that processes the carbon-carbon before it is applied to missiles. The controls regulated heat and pressure.

The regulations barred the export without a license of a control panel "specially designed" for a large isostatic press—one that could be used in the production of nuclear missiles.

The defendants sent a control panel for a large isostatic press and added a switch so it could be adapted for use with a small isostatic press—equipment used for research, not missile-making.

They said that during the 2½ week trial it was intended for use with the small isostatic press and did not require a license.

continued

continued

Prosecutors contended that the companies jury-rigged the device to make it look as if it was intended to control the small isostatic press.

Defense lawyers argued that a control panel was "specially designed" and subject to a license only if it were used exclusively to operate a large isostatic press.

Fiber Materials Inc. and Materials International were awarded more than $28 million in contracts between fiscal year 1996 and fiscal year 2002, according to records of the Federal Procurement Data Center.

FMI is working on the AEGIS and Tomahawk cruise missile, the Trident sea-launch ballistic missile and the National Missile Defense program, according to Woodlock's decision, which was sealed because it referred to classified government information. The opinion was declassified this week.

FMI had asked government agencies it does business with to reimburse its legal fees, including $1 million just for lawyers' fees in fiscal years 1995 and 1996, according to court documents.

In addition, FMI has filed additional claims for legal fees every year since then, according to Daniel McGinty, a spokesman for the Defense Contract Management Agency, which oversees defense contracts. McGinty could not provide a dollar amount on the additional requests.

A hearing is scheduled for January, he said.

---

with portions of the penalty suspended—the end result was a one-year denial of export privileges for the UK subsidiary.

- An example of a smaller case is the $30,000 civil penalty placed on a German company because it reexported 1,550 U.S.-origin shotguns from Germany to Poland.
- In March 2002, the president of a company pleaded guilty and was given eighteen months' probation and a criminal fine of $5,000 for falsifying export documents. She had undervalued computers on invoices and when she forwarded them to freight forwarders, they had listed false information on the Shipper's Export Declarations.
- A recent settlement announced in 2002 involved a fine of $1,760,000 for exporting biological toxins. A multinational corporation had acquired a company in 1997 that had previously exported these toxins to Europe without a license. The company's exporting contined after the acquisition. The penalty could have been much worse but the end use did not involve weapons.
- Another case illustrates the cooperation between BIS and state terrorism task forces. In 2003, a company agreed to settle a case of shipping "liquid injectors" to Iran through Belgium. The company paid $44,000 and lost export privileges for two and one half years. The CEO paid $4,500 and lost export privileges for seven years. There was a criminal plea as well, with a

$50,000 corporate fine and a $2,000 individual fine together with probation for three years.

The penalties for violation of the export laws can be severe. For willful violation of the EAR, one can be fined five times the value of the export or $1 million, as well as be charged with violations of other statutes like conspiracy, mail and wire fraud, and money laundering. One can also face ten years in prison, as well as have the goods in question seized and face forfeiture, debarment, and being placed on the denial orders list. Civil penalties can be $250,000 per violation. There are also stiff penalties for violations of the *Arms Export Control Act* and *Trading with the Enemy Act*. (See http://www.bis.doc.gov/Enforcement/Case Summaries/default. htm for summaries of other, more recent cases.)

The Act also makes room for civil penalties and administrative sanctions. An entity may be denied exporting privileges via a temporary denial order.

Current Issues

The major issues in export control remain: Who is the enemy? Will there be effective multilateral controls? What will be controlled? If there are no multilateral controls, what about unilateral controls? Can the Department of Commerce both promote and control exports?

The worldwide incidents of terrorism may be the catalyst needed to remind countries that they need to work together to address this problem rather than unilaterally. Within the United States, perhaps Congress may find the resolve to address and simplify the export law after the next presidential election.

CHAPTER SUMMARY

Within the United States, regardless of the agency structure, the pursuit of both export promotion and control will always be a deliberate balance between trade growth and national security and foreign policy interests. Internationally, forging a consensus and enforceable regulations becomes more difficult as countries' perceptions and definitions of the "threat" evolve. When the United States unilaterally imposes export controls, as it did in 1999 on the commercial satellite industry, European companies are quick to take advantage of this supply gap. The efficacy of the *Wassenaar Arrangement* will be tested in the future. The U.S. Congress must come together to enact a comprehensive export administration act. Failure to do so will relegate the United States to a purely reactive mode and place U.S. businesses at a great disadvantage internationally.

Questions and Case Problems

1. "Unilateral export controls are expensive, serve no purpose, and only injure our own business. It's like borrowing a gun to shoot yourself in the foot, or more like in the heart." Agree or disagree with this statement. Give support for this answer. Who is most likely to have said something like this? Who is most likely to disagree?

2. Explain the difference between unilateral and multilateral export controls. How has the end of the Cold War affected the multilateral export control system?

3. What is a "deemed export"? How can this impact your business in the United States?

4. Daniel Bernstein, a UC graduate student, developed an encryption program called "snuffle" and wanted to post it on the Internet. The U.S. government said he needed a license. What result?

5. Is it ethical to hold a businessperson legally responsible if he or she sells controlled technology to a second party that is then diverted to a third prohibited end-user? What factors will influence your answer?

6. In May 1994, the Atlanta branch of an Italian bank, BNL, agreed to pay a civil penalty of $475,000 for 104 alleged violations of EAA and regulations based on the antiboycott provisions. BNL, in seeking reimbursement on letters of credit, provided information to Iraqi banks on the company's business dealings with Israel. These events occurred between 1987 and 1990. The Georgia state courts had ordered the bank to pay $17 million owed to a German manufacturer on a letter of credit after being presented with the appropriate documents, despite language on the documents that stated, "We declare that the goods are neither of Israeli origin nor do they contain Israeli materials nor are they being exported from Israel." The bank filed a petition for certiorari with the U.S. Supreme Court on June 16, 1994. What ruling do you think the Court made? Why? Is this a "Catch-22" for the bank? What could they do to avoid this problem?

7. How has the *USA PATRIOT Act* affected export controls? Find an update from the Internet within the last six months on this subject.

8. Does the shipment of electric cattle prods require a license? Why?

9. Have decontrol efforts continued despite concerns over terrorism? Give examples.

Managerial Implications

1. Your company, AJAX Pharmaceutical, based in New Jersey, is approached by an agent for a company in Egypt and Jordan about participating in several joint ventures in the Middle East and Asia. The agent inquires about the status of your investment in Israel. You currently have an offer from a newly formed Israeli investment group to purchase your 30 percent share of Drugisco, an Israel-based company. How do you respond? What is your legal obligation? What other information do you need to answer the question?

   You are also asked about your ability to ship certain chemicals that are controlled. Do you have any obligation to report this inquiry? You initially ship the requested items to Japan. You discover through a late-night meeting in a Karaoke bar that those items were being sold through a middleman and are now headed to Afghanistan. What is this called and do you have any legal responsibility? Ethical? What managerial controls can you implement to reduce the likelihood of this happening in the future?

2. Your company, Enzyme, Inc., manufactures both biological and chemical agents that have potential military uses. You understand that Congress is considering the contentious issue of how to revamp the entire export control regime. Prepare a letter to your state's senators, articulating your company's position about decontrol. Do you think your company should take an active position in lobbying for a new law? What are the risks associated with such a position? Will you discuss these issues with your board of directors?

Note

1. See http://www.bis.doc.gov/AntiboycottCompliance for other sample inquiries.

PART 4

Regulation of the International Marketplace

The issues addressed in Parts Two and Three of this text are applicable to any U.S. enterprise wishing to export its goods to another country, even if that enterprise is located inside the United States. Part Two considered international commercial law, which creates a reliable framework assuring exporters and importers in different parts of the world reception money for goods and services. International trade law, discussed in Part Three, involved the framework of barriers and openings to trade among nations. In Part Four, the focus turns to the legal complications that arise when one actually moves a portion of one's enterprise outside the United States.

Many business factors may prompt a business to take this step. First, most businesses—from Madagascar to Minnesota—find that one sells more goods if one employs a local sales representative. A business that wishes to promote sales abroad will be greatly advantaged if it retains the services of an individual abroad to promote sales. If such a retention proves successful, the business may then wish to establish an office in that country. Indeed, the business might eventually generate greater profits from making and selling its product abroad—or even exporting it back into the United States.

When the U.S. business first establishes a presence abroad, it becomes subject to regulation by the foreign country being "penetrated" and to a series of U.S. laws that apply to such "penetrators." As the presence in such a "host country" progresses from local office phase through manufacturing plant, the level of host country regulation becomes more intense. For instance, a U.S. company that builds a factory in a foreign nation may become subject to national and provincial: labor laws; environmental laws; tax laws; technology transfer laws; laws governing the appropriate level of foreign ownership of businesses; laws governing the repatriation of profits to the United States; possible nationalization by the foreign country; the U.S. *Foreign Corrupt Practices Act*; and a plethora of U.S. and foreign country antitrust laws.

Part Four treats this immense body of law in a general, thematic way, as the great diversity of local laws governing investment demands. In contrast to international commercial law—in which great consistency has developed over millions of commercial transactions—and to trade law—in which substantial harmonization has emerged through GATT and WTO, laws governing foreign investment are peculiarly reflective of local culture and attitudes. Like culture, these laws vary widely among the more than 200 nations of the planet. Further, these laws—like the attitudes they reflect—are constantly evolving. Many countries, including the United States, have fluctuated from the extreme of being aggressively hostile to foreign investment and back to a friendlier attitude.

The position on this spectrum of any given country at any given time depends upon mercurial international and domestic political conditions.

For instance, from the 1950s through the mid-1970s, many developing countries grew progressively more antagonistic toward foreign investment, reflecting emerging national self-esteem and wariness of former colonial masters. But when anti-foreign investment laws caused those economies to run out of capital resources in the late 1970s and early 1980s, many of the governments reversed course and passed more investment-friendly laws, including laws that permitted the privatization of former government enterprises. Finally, as subsidies for former state activities ended and new foreign owners raised prices in the late 1990s and early in the twenty-first century, some governments began to swing back to more xenophobic state policies.

In short, no one can predict precisely what foreign investment laws will be tomorrow. One can, however, identify different approaches that nations have taken in regulating foreign business penetration. A working knowledge of these approaches provides a framework that a businessperson can employ to analyze different aspects of the legal environment in the country in which investment is considered.

Part Four begins at the least intrusive and, hence, least regulated, foreign presence and moves through increasingly substantial and regulated forms of establishment. Chapter Sixteen reviews issues that arise once the enterprise retains an agent or a representative abroad. Such retention triggers the host country's requirements for agency relationships, as well as its laws relating to advertising and marketing. It also unleashes one of the principal concerns of U.S. business abroad, the U.S. *Foreign Corrupt Practices Act*. Chapter Seventeen reviews licensing and other arrangements through which a U.S. enterprise is paid for permitting a foreign entity to use its intellectual property. Many host countries closely regulate these arrangements as they wish to capture the intellectual property for their own nationals. Chapter Eighteen turns to the legal peculiarities of operating in another country—subjecting oneself to the full array of the host country's corporate, currency, and tax laws. Chapter Nineteen considers the political risk associated with committing capital resources in a foreign country: nationalization or expropriation of one's investment by the foreign sovereign. The end of Chapter Nineteen explores the flip side of nationalization, the emerging process of privatization, and reviews the different ways in which formerly public assets are transferred to private hands. Most assets nationalized in the twentieth century have now been privatized, although there is pressure in many nations to "re-nationalize." Chapter Twenty discusses labor laws, which mirror the broadly varying concepts of the proper relationship between employees and their places of work. Chapter Twenty-One provides an in-depth treatment of international environmental law, one of the most dynamic legal disciplines in recent years. Finally, Chapter Twenty-Two addresses the pinnacle of foreign penetration, situations in which U.S. investors have come to so dominate the relevant country that they become subject to its antitrust or competition laws.

As the foregoing summary suggests, confronting foreign law is a bit like taking on Hydra, the many-headed monster of Greek mythology. In these succeeding chapters, the student may find that every time he or she cuts off one of the law monster's heads, like Hydra, the monster will replace it with two new heads.

INTERNATIONAL MARKETING LAW: SALES REPRESENTATIVES, ADVERTISING, AND ETHICAL ISSUES

As noted in Chapter Five, an American business can sell its goods abroad by simply delivering them FOB a U.S. port onto an ocean-bound vessel. If the business sells its products abroad in that fashion and does not otherwise have any contacts with the country to which its goods are bound, it will generally escape regulation by the foreign country. Why then, would a U.S. business place a representative abroad and enmesh itself in foreign regulation?

First, a business can expand the geographic market by expanding the geographic scope of its marketing. If a company advertises popcorn poppers only in Topeka, Kansas, it will sell popcorn poppers only to Zimbabwean buyers who happen by Topeka or who stumble onto its Internet site. If, on the other hand, the company markets in Harare, Zimbabwe, the enterprise will encounter more prospective Zimbabwean buyers. Thus, the enterprise that believes Zimbabwe is a "hot" prospective market for poppers will retain the services of a sales representative located in Zimbabwe.

Second, a local presence permits the Topeka enterprise to maintain the popcorn poppers sold abroad. Zimbabweans are more likely to buy a Topeka popper through the Internet if they know they can get it repaired in Harare rather than have to send it back to Topeka for maintenance. Thus, if the initial sales efforts bear some fruit, the Topeka enterprise may wish to establish a sales and service facility in Harare.

http://www.ita.doc.gov
Provides information and links on market access and compliance.

Before embarking on these initiatives, however, the Topeka enterprise should review the Zimbabwe law affecting representatives of foreign enterprises.

REGULATION OF RELATIONSHIPS WITH REPRESENTATIVES

Relationships with representatives take two basic forms: the agency and the independent contract. An *agency* is a business arrangement in which one party, the agent, performs a variety of functions on behalf and at the direction of another party, the principal. Most employees of a corporation, for example, are agents of that corporation for one purpose or another.

Independent contractors, who are also often known as *independent agents* outside the United States, perform general tasks for the business, but retain substantial discretion and independence in carrying them out. Consultants to a corporation are often viewed as independent contractors. Under U.S. law, the main importance of the distinction between agents and independent contractors is that third parties can generally sue the principal for acts of an agent, but not for those of an independent contractor. This distinction is important to principals because they wish to avoid paying for their representatives' injuries to third parties. The distinction does not, however, change the deal between the agent and principal; the substantive terms of the agreement are those developed between the principal and the agent.

The United States places few restrictions on the substantive terms of the representative–principal relationship. Two sophisticated parties can agree on virtually any compensation they wish, from a few dollars to an ownership interest in the principal's enterprise. They can decide on the extent to which one will indemnify the other. They can expand or restrict the representative's scope of discretion as they mutually deem appropriate. Accordingly, a U.S. enterprise is accustomed to shaping representative–principal relationships without worrying about governmental intervention. The enterprise assumes it will make its own deal with the agent; the government will not alter that arrangement.

Supersession of Agreement with Representative

In many countries, that assumption would be in error. Nations often have laws calculated to protect local representatives irrespective of the deal that the representative has negotiated. In effect, local law may state that, notwithstanding the written agreement between the principal and the representative, negotiated terms are superseded to protect the representative. Stated another way, even if the representative agrees to a 1 percent commission with the U.S. principal, the principal might find that it is obligated to pay the representative no less than 2 percent. Little surprises like

this commission requirement can greatly affect the profitability of a foreign venture.

This supersession problem is particularly acute when the U.S. business terminates the agency arrangement. Irrespective of what the contract provides, the U.S. investor may need to make a large payment to the representative in order to terminate, or the U.S. principal may not have a right to terminate the agent at all. For example, the *Voyageur, Representant et Placier* (VRP)—a type of representative—is entitled to special protection under the French labor code; every representative is assumed to be a VRP unless the written agreement specifies otherwise. Similarly, under Council Directive 86/653 of the European Union, parties may agree to a fixed-term contract. But if the parties continue their relationship after the stated term, it becomes an *evergreen contract*—one that may be terminated only by a three-month written notice for any relationship that has lasted for three years or more.

To American eyes, this web of laws favoring local representatives has the stench of bald protectionism. But host countries view such laws quite differently. They regard them as providing a level playing field for local small businessmen against multinational giants. In the following case, Paraguay's Supreme Court of Justice stated the case for such laws quite capably.

Electra-Amambay S.R.L. v. Compañía Antártica Paulista Ind. Brasileira de Bebidas E Conexos
Order No. 827 (November 12, 2001)
Paraguay Supreme Court of Justice

BACKGROUND AND FACTS
The Paraguayan government has enacted a law that specifically protects Paraguayan representatives of foreign companies. Among other things, the law requires a foreign company to make an extraordinarily large payment to the Paraguayan representative if the *representative* is terminated for some reason other than "just cause." Just cause is narrowly defined in the Paraguayan statute. There is no similar law protecting Paraguayan distributors or other representatives of Paraguayan-based enterprises.

Compañía Antártica, a Brazilian firm, terminated Electra-Amambay, its Paraguayan representative. Electra-Amambay argued that the termination was not for good cause and sought its statutory penalty. Compañía Antártica countered by arguing that the Paraguayan statute was an unconstitutional discrimination based on national origin.

JUDGE CARLOS FERNANDEZ GADEA
Compania Antártica advances the objection that [the] Articles . . . of the Law No. 194/93, on which

continued

continued

the [Electra-Amambay] bases its lawsuit, is unconstitutional.
* * *

The objection maintains that articles 1, 4, 5, 6, 7, and 8 constitute an unjust and arbitrary discrimination against foreign manufacturers and companies.... They establish obligations, assumptions, and sanctions only and exclusively against foreign manufacturers and firms, but not against persons domiciled within the country. [The objection is that] this inequality violates Articles 46 and 47, paragraph 2 of the National Constitution.
* * *

This Law, 194/93, is of a special character, regulating the relationships between foreign manufacturers and firms and their representatives, agents, and distributors of their products domiciled in the country. And in the case of the termination of these relationships without a statement of just cause, it sets forth how the amount of damages should be calculated. It is customary that a foreign firm which contracts for the services of physical and legal persons domiciled in Paraguay lays down the ground rules of said relationship, establishing the rights and obligations of both parties. With the promulgation of this law, the parties are placed on an equal footing, establishing the damages that should be paid by the foreign firm in the case of a rupture of the contractual bond without just cause. The firm or persons who find themselves in the country, for the promotion, sale, or placement within the republic of products or services provided by the foreign firm necessarily had to incur expenses in investments so that the referred product would have success in the local market. However, it is necessary to underscore that if there exists just cause, the foreign firm or provider has suitable and appropriate means at its disposal to seek exoneration from liability for the damages.

[Compañía Antártica makes the further point] that Article 2 of the mentioned law ... in defining the different types of contractual relationships, abusively exceeds the intention, will and interest of the

manufacturers who simply wish to export their products without creating any contractual relationship other than that of the simple purchase and sale of goods. [Moreover, it notes] Article 9 [of the law] presumes to rise to the level of "public order" [but] in this case, the social order is not implicated. The implicated interests involve a small minority of the population and not the general interest.
* * *

With respect to this point, I believe that it is not logical to think that the foreign manufacturers have an interest only in a simple purchase and sale transaction. The relationship between the parties can go much further than a single transaction. Such a relationship should be found to exist [before the statute applies]. As to Article 9 ... the law was clothed as a matter of "public order" when it was enacted as such by the public legislative power.
* * *

Finally, it is important to emphasize that this law does not reflect an exaggerated protectionism of the State, but rather legal security and equality, bearing in mind that one of the parties (the foreign company) is in better economic condition than its local representative and that the latter finds itself in a unequal state, whether for lack of technical training, economic resources or qualified personnel. It is because of this that the State intervenes in this relationship, setting forth precise rules with which the parties must comply, especially when the foreign enterprise unilaterally decides to terminate this relationship, without cause. It is in this situation, when the national representative is economically prejudiced, that [the law] compensates for this prejudice in some way by an award of damages.... As has been said, there exist causes that are justifications exempt from the obligation to pay damages through which the foreign enterprise can exonerate itself from this responsibility. These causes are found itemized in the law.

Decision. The Court rejected the objection as inadmissible and charged Compañía Antártica with all costs.

In the European Union (EU), Council Directive 86/653 on agency requires each EU member state to pass consistent national laws on representatives. These include a few mandatory provisions that may seem odd to Americans. For instance, it provides for an *economic conditions alarm:* The principal must notify the agent if it expects that the agent's volume of business—and thus the agent's commission—will be "significantly lower" than what the agent "normally" expects. The Directive also requires payment of a commission not only when a transaction is concluded because of the agent's efforts, but also whenever a transaction is made between the principal and a party the agent previously acquired as a customer. Further, a *commission override* is included: Whenever a principal makes a sale in a territory or a market sector reserved for the agent, the principal must pay the agent a commission, whether or not the agent actually participated in the sale, no matter what the agency agreement provides. Under the Directive, these commissions accrue when the customer "should have [executed its part of the transaction] if the principal has executed his part of the transaction." Thus, commissions must be paid even if the deal is not done.

Tax and Labor Regulation and Principal Liability: The Dependent–Independent Distinction

The retention of a representative often leads to principal liability and triggers tax and labor law requirements. The burdensomeness of these regulations frequently increases upon a finding by the host country that the representative is a *dependent agent* rather than an *independent agent.*

For tax purposes, the principal is often viewed as having opened an office once it hires a dependent agent within the host country. Upon such an office opening, the principal's transactions become subject to the host country's corporate tax laws.

Similarly, a dependent agent is viewed as an employee for purposes of the host country's labor law. As in the United States, having an *employee* subjects a company to pension law, tax withholding law, labor negotiations law, and other legal consequences. But, in many countries, such a determination can also affect the control of the U.S. investor's foreign enterprise. For example, as Chapter Twenty explains, in many countries employees may have statutory rights to representation on the company's board of directors.

Finally, if an agent is *dependent,* the principal will be vicariously liable to third parties for the agent's misdeeds. In the context of *product liability*—responsibility to consumers for defects in one's product—the agent–principal relationship is not a critical consideration. As long as the U.S. manufacturer's product enters the foreign market, the manufacturer is likely to be in the "chain of distribution" and subject to suit whether it does business through a dependent or independent agent. But it makes a difference if the U.S. manufacturer has no hand in the agent's liability-creating act. If the entrepreneur's Nairobi dependent agent runs over a law student in the agent's delivery truck, the entrepreneur may be liable in Kenya for a lifetime of lost income. If the agent is independent, the entrepreneur probably has no such liability.

In hiring a representative, therefore, a firm must determine whether the arrangement will be characterized as creating a dependent agent or an independent agent. Unfortunately, this distinction is not based on any single definitive test. Instead, courts review a variety of factors and determine whether a dependent agency, on balance, has been created.

The more flexibility and discretion the representative has, the more likely the representative is to be considered independent. Representatives who personally organize, pursue, and set the schedule for the marketing program—that is, those who have great discretion in organizing their time and work—are more likely to be considered independent. If, on the other hand, the U.S. principal creates the marketing program in detail and the representatives simply carry it out, the representatives are likely to be dependent. Similarly, agents who have an obligation to follow the specific instructions of the principal are likely to be dependent. In contrast, agents who are given a task to perform, but no obligation to follow the principal's instructions in carrying out that task, are more likely to be viewed as independent. The EU Agency Directive, for example, simply defines independent agents as those with "continuing authority to negotiate the sale or purchase of goods" on behalf of the principal. A compensation package that is based solely on commissions, rather than on periodic payments or a fixed salary with reimbursement of overhead expenses, is also indicative of independence. Independent agents typically rent their own office space and hire subagents to carry out the tasks. Finally, representatives who serve more than one principal are more likely to be considered independent. Exhibit 16.1 lays out these considerations in graphic form.

Of course, the U.S. investor may not wish to give an agent the level of discretion required to be an independent agent. The U.S. company may wish to have a greater level of quality control and a greater share of the entrepreneurial profits in the

EXHIBIT 16.1		
The Distinction Between Independent and Dependent Agents		
	Independent	Dependent
Scheduling	Details created by agent within principal's general requirements	Details provided by principal
Work Organization	Principal identifies strategic objectives; agent determines tactics and has continuing authority for achieving objectives	Principal is involved in working out details
Instructions	Principal does not instruct; change in direction causes change in compensation	Agent is always subject to change in instructions
Compensation	Commissions; fixed amount of money	Hourly pay or salary
Expenses	Included in compensation amount	Specific expense reimbursement
Number of Principals	Works for many clients	Works for one client

venture. These benefits of a dependent agent often outweigh the costs of greater regulation. But in weighing the business benefits of retaining a dependent agent, the U.S. investor should thoroughly understand the local legal costs it will incur.

REGULATION OF ADVERTISING ABROAD

If the Topeka enterprise wishes to sell its popcorn poppers to the Zimbabwean public, hiring an agent in Zimbabwe may not be enough. The enterprise will need to determine how best to advertise its poppers to the Zimbabwean consumer. This will require development of marketing strategies attractive to the local culture. Obviously, the soccer-loving Zimbabweans will be unimpressed by endorsements from U.S. football players. Just as cultural differences affect what advertising is attractive to foreign consumers, they affect what advertising is forbidden. Marketing abroad requires a sensitivity to the limits that foreign law can place on marketing efforts.

The marketer may not place just anything on the television screens or in the newspapers. These local legal limits do not always correspond with local interests. For instance, a commercial that features an explicit sexual message might well spur sales both in Denmark and in Saudi Arabia; after all, a significant percentage of individuals in all cultures have an interest in things prurient. In

Denmark, the authorities would take no interest in such a commercial. In Saudi Arabia, however, the "religious police" might mete out corporal punishment to one's local representative. An ineffective advertising campaign may simply prove unprofitable, but an *illegal* advertising campaign may lead to an unexpected stay at a local prison facility.

Truth in Advertising

One of the founding concepts of libertarian capitalism is that of *caveat emptor* (let the buyer beware). According to this precept, government should not intervene in commercial relations. Buyers should investigate the seller's claims or obtain contractual representations and warranties. If they fail to do so and the claims turn out to be false, they have only themselves to blame. Under classic capitalist theory, the *invisible hand* of the market will, in time, ferret out consistently dishonest sellers and consistently careless buyers.

Ultimately, the Ninth Commandment—thou shalt not bear false witness—has decisively triumphed over caveat emptor; virtually every nation, at least formally, now prohibits false advertising. The European Union, for example, specifically excludes fraudulent advertising from its general protection of commercial speech. Even during the late nineteenth century—the high water mark of libertarian capitalist thought—courts found ways to

Carlill v. Carbolic Smoke Ball Co.
1 Q.B. 256 (1983)
Queen's Bench

BACKGROUND AND FACTS

The defendants, proprietors and vendors of a medical preparation called the "Carbolic Smoke Ball," inserted the following advertisement in the *Pall Mall Gazette* on November 13, 1891:

> £100 reward will be paid by the Carbolic Smoke Ball Company to any person who contracts the increasing epidemic influenza, colds, or any disease caused by taking cold, after having used the ball three times daily for two weeks according to the printed directions supplied with each ball. £1000 is deposited with the Alliance Bank, Regent Street, showing our sincerity in the matter. During the last epidemic of influenza many thousand carbolic smoke balls were sold as preventives against this disease, and in no ascertained case was the disease contracted by those using the carbolic smoke ball.

The plaintiff was a lady who, relying on this advertisement, bought one of the balls at a chemist's shop, and used it as directed, three times a day, from November 20, 1891 to January 17, 1892, when she was attacked by influenza.

LORD JUSTICE LINDLEY

The first observation I will make is that we are not dealing with any inference of fact. We are dealing with an express promise to pay £100 in certain events. Read the advertisement how you will, and twist it about as you will, here is a distinct promise expressed in language which is perfectly unmistakable—"£100 reward will be paid by the Carbolic Smoke Ball Company to any person who contracts the influenza after having used the ball three times daily for two weeks according to the printed directions supplied with each ball."

We must first consider whether this was intended to be a promise at all, or whether it was a mere puff which meant nothing. Was it a mere puff? My answer to that question is No, and I base my answer upon this passage: "£1000 is deposited with the Alliance Bank, showing our sincerity in the matter." Now, for what was that money deposited or that statement made except to negate the suggestion that this was a mere puff and meant nothing at all. . . .

Then it is contended that it is not binding. In the first place, it is said that it is not made with anybody in particular. Now that point is common to the words of this advertisement and to the words of all other advertisements offering rewards. They are offers to anybody who performs the conditions named in the advertisement, and anybody who does perform the condition accepts the offer. . . .

[I]t is said that this advertisement is so vague that you cannot really construe it as a promise—that the vagueness of the language shows that a legal promise was not intended or contemplated. The language is vague and uncertain in some respects, and particularly in this, that the £100 is to be paid to any person who contracts the increasing epidemic after having used the balls three times daily for two weeks. It is said, When are they to be used? According to the language of the advertisement no time is fixed, and, construing the offer most strongly against the person who has made it, one might infer that any time was meant. . . . I do not think that business people or reasonable people would understand the words as meaning that if you took a smoke ball and used it three times daily for two weeks you were to be guaranteed against influenza for the rest of your life, and I think it would be pushing the language of the advertisement too far to construe it as meaning that . . . [I]t strikes me that there are two, and possibly three, reasonable constructions to be put on this advertisement, any one of which will answer the purpose of the plaintiff. Possibly it may be limited to persons catching the "increasing epidemic" or any colds or diseases caused by taking cold, during the prevalence of the increasing epidemic. That is one suggestion; but it does not commend itself to me. Another suggested meaning is that you are warranted free from catching this epidemic, or colds or other diseases caused by taking cold, whilst you are using this remedy after using it for two weeks. If that is the meaning, the plaintiff is right, for she used the remedy for two weeks and went on using it till she got the epidemic. Another meaning, and the one which I rather prefer, is that the reward is offered to any person who contracts the epidemic or other disease within a reasonable time after having used the smoke ball. . . . What is a reasonable time? It has been suggested that there is no standard of reasonableness;

continued

---

continued

that it depends upon the reasonable time for a germ to develop! I do not feel pressed by that. It strikes me that a reasonable time may be ascertained in a business sense and in a sense satisfactory to a lawyer. . . . It strikes me, I confess, that the true construction of this advertisement is that £100 will be paid to anybody who uses this smoke ball three times daily for two weeks according to the printed directions, and who gets the influenza or cold or other diseases caused

by taking cold within a reasonable time after so using it; and if that is the true construction, it is enough for the plaintiff.

Decision.   The Queen's Bench found that the advertisement was, in the parlance of contract law, a definite and operative offer that the plaintiff had accepted through her performance. It entered judgment of £100 on her behalf.

---

protect the unwary. In a country with no consumer protection laws, English courts protected consumers by stretching ancient contract law principles to newspaper advertising. If one promises that one's product can specifically do something, they reasoned, one is liable in contract if the product fails to live up to the promise.

The universal distaste for deceptive advertising illustrated in *Carbolic Smoke Ball* is shared to varying degrees throughout the world. But some cultures are less tolerant of "puffing"—vagueness and exaggeration—in advertising than other cultures. The Teutonic penchant for accuracy, for example, prevented a German snack food marketer from making an unspecific claim that its potato chips contained "40 percent less fat." When a competitor sued, a German court interpreted the ambiguous statement to be a representation that the chips contained 40 percent less fat than *any* existing brand. Finding that the chips did not, the court enjoined the entire advertising program.

to take advantage of such greater latitude abroad. But the trend is clear: In most countries, the authorities are catching up to the philosophical descendants of the *Carbolic Smoke Ball* medical science entrepreneurs.

The sanctions for false advertising vary from place to place. Of particular interest is the South Korean requirement of a public apology. Although to a Westerner such a sanction would be little more than a slap on the wrist, the ignominy of a public apology caused an advertiser to appeal the public apology sentence to the High Court of Seoul. The Seoul court found that the advertiser was guilty of deception, but it also found extenuating circumstances in the case. Therefore, it reversed the sentence of a public apology, finding it too harsh a penalty.

---

http://www.intelproplaw.com
This site provides information about international patent, trademark, and copyright law.

---

http://www.adageglobal.com
See this address for news and information on international advertising and marketing.

The exacting standards of the Japanese are similarly intolerant of exaggeration. In Japan, the Fair Trade Committee prevented PepsiCo, Inc. from advertising its cola drink as "the choice of the neXt generation" as it does in the United States. After all, members of the Japanese regulators ruled, Pepsi was second to Coca-Cola in the Japanese market.

Other nations are far more flexible. In some countries, hucksters have been victimizing others for centuries. While investors can, they may wish

Content-Specific Regulations

Advertising can also be outlawed even if its content is perfectly true. Advertising aimed at children, for example, is closely and diversely regulated. More than forty countries prohibit or greatly limit such advertising, reasoning that children cannot intelligently assess the content of commercials. Many of these bans reflect idiosyncratic cultural values. This is particularly illustrated in case of the different approaches in advertising to children. The following article illustrates how some of these differences clash when different nations try to agree on common advertising laws.

international accents

Europe Puts Mute on Kid Ads

Peter Ford, Staff writer for
The Christian Science Monitor

With the pre-Christmas TV advertising blitz in full swing, and your kids presenting you with computer printouts of their holiday wish list, you think there is no escape from Pokemon, LEGO, Teletubby, and Barbie ads? Think again. Think Sweden. Or Norway, or Austria. Those countries all ban ads before, during, or after children's television programs. And there are signs that other European governments are thinking of following suit. "The debate seems to be going in favor of more restrictions on advertising to children all across Europe," says Lionel Stanbrook, deputy director of the Advertising Association, which represents British advertisers. In Britain, where the average child watches nearly 18,000 ads a year, some parents might welcome such restrictions.

In Sweden, the law forbidding all TV advertising aimed at children under 12 is overwhelmingly popular among the public and politicians. (In the United States, children watching three hours of TV a day—the norm—see about 25,000 spots a year. Any attempt to restrict them would be challenged under First Amendment guarantees of free speech.) There are no Continent-wide rules: In Norway, Austria, and the Flemish part of Belgium no advertising is allowed around children's programs; toy ads are banned on Greek TV, while Italy, Poland, Denmark, and Latvia are studying plans for tighter regulations.

The European Commission, the European Union's ruling body, is to launch a continent-wide study of the issue next month. "The idea," says Commission official Aviva Silver, "is that the study would form the basis for any revision [of EU rules] that was seen to be necessary."

Sweden is pushing hard for its ban on children's advertising to be extended across Europe. "Young children do not understand what advertising is all about," says Axel Edling, Sweden's consumer ombudsman. "Our research has shown that a child can't distinguish between commercials and programs until they are 5 or 6, and that they don't really understand the commercial purpose behind advertising until they are 10 or 12."

Advertisers challenge that. "I don't think we have any way of really knowing whether ads are distinguishable or not in a child's mind," says Mr. Stanbrook. "Ads that take advantage of children should not be broadcast. . . . The key point is, are they being ripped off?"

Studies have shown that children pay much more attention to advertisements than grownups and that they are three times more likely than their parents to remember a brand name from an ad. "Children are much easier to reach with advertising. They like ads and they pick up on them really fast," said Stephen Colegrave, marketing director for Saatchi and Saatchi, a leading international ad agency, on British television last month. "Quite often we can exploit that relationship and get them pestering their parents."

Although in the holiday season, of course, toys and games are filling the airwaves. For the rest of the year the bulk of the ads on European television aimed at children tout candy, breakfast cereals, fast foods, and snacks.

A recent study by Consumers International, a London-based watchdog organization, found that 95 percent of ads on British TV aimed at children were for foods that are high in fat, sugar, or salt.

"TV advertising tends to persuade kids to eat all the wrong things," says Peta Cottee, projects director for Sustain, a British umbrella organization of citizens' groups concerned about food and health. "TV is a very powerful tool in persuading kids what they want, and to pester their parents as they go round supermarkets."

"Pester power" is not meant to rule unchecked: an EU directive regulating TV advertising prohibits anything that "directly encourage[s] minors to persuade their parents or others to purchase the goods or services being advertised." But you don't have to spend long in a French supermarket listening to conversations between parents and their offspring to know that few children appear to have read the EU directive.

Even in countries where the law is not draconian, the "TV Without Frontiers" directive specifies that "advertising shall be readily recognizable as such." For Lars Maren, deputy director of the media division in the Swedish Culture Ministry, "If it is true that

continued

---

continued

children under a certain age don't understand what advertising is all about, any advertisement aimed at those children is violating the rules."

Mr. Maren says Sweden is preparing to use its presidency of the EU, starting in January 2001, to press its case on fellow EU members. "As president you have some power over part of the agenda. . . . One issue Sweden finds important is the situation of children in the new media landscape."

Stanbrook is already fighting back, organizing lobbying sessions with members of the European Parliament and Commission officials. He foresees a "lively debate," and expects to be able to ward off a Europe-wide ban on TV advertising to children.

Maren is not so sure. "When [Swedish Culture Minister] Marita Ulvskog first began pushing this question, there was no interest at all among her European colleagues," he says. "But at last month's meeting of European culture ministers, she said she found half of them sympathetic."

Take note, Pikachu.

This article first appeared in *The Christian Science Monitor* on December 16, 1999 and is reproduced with permission. Copyright © 1999 The Christian Science Monitor. All rights reserved. Online at http://www.csmonitor.com

---

In some nations, *language laws* can complicate cross-border advertising. In Indonesia, the municipal government of Jakarta, worried about cultural invasion from ethnic minorities, bans languages other than Indonesian from billboards and jails violators for up three months. The marketing difficulties created by this law become apparent when one considers that, for most of the 180 million people in the Indonesian islands, Indonesian is a second language.

France is famous—or infamous perhaps—for its aggressive policing of language laws. In France, every word used in advertising must be French, even if the French population more commonly uses the English word. For example, although virtually all French businesspeople prefer to use the simple English term *cash flow,* the language law recently required them to reflect the concept in its seldom-used French incarnation of "marge brute d'auto-financement." If similar laws prevailed in the United States, advertisers would have to refer to *paté* by its less appetizing English equivalent, *ground goose liver.* Most recently, in October 2003, the French government, in an effort to prevent the use of English, the predominant language of technology, banned its civil service from using the term "email," a term used by people of all languages the world over. All government ministries, Web sites, publications, and documents must now use "courriel"—a shortening of "courrier electronique"—when referring to the messages sent via the Internet.

The advertising laws in some of the relatively new Eastern European democracies indicate a remaining socialist distrust of capitalist advertising. The Czech Republic bans "hidden seduction" and insists that advertising be based on the "specific features of the goods." And Hungary formerly demanded that the advertiser have sufficient inventories of advertised goods on hand before beginning an advertising campaign.

Other advertising regulations are aimed at specific types of products. For instance, almost all countries limit the advertising of "sin" products—tobacco and alcohol. As in all advertising, however, regulations reflect the customs of the countries that enact them.

Starting in 1993, France banned all tobacco advertising and most liquor advertising—direct or indirect—including sponsorship of sports events. The only exception: French wine. With a ferocity mindful of its recent totalitarian heritage, Bulgaria has banned all tobacco advertising outside of tobacco shops and threatened violators with a $50,000 fine per violation. The antiauthoritarian Brits, on the other hand, do not forbid tobacco advertising, but insist on self-imposed and highly subjective industry guidelines. This approach led to the banning of an ad campaign featuring two overweight, balding, middle-aged men whom the industry watch group deemed "too appealing" to young people. Belgium permits cigarette advertising, but only those that focus on the package or on part of its design. Even more curious, Belgium generally permits advertising of alcoholic beverages, but not for absinthe drinks. The Belgian enmity to the green liquor may not be intuitively obvious to Americans. And even the definition of "sinful liquor" can be counterintuitive. In 1995, Iran's spiritual leader ruled that foreign soft drinks such as Coca-Cola and Pepsi-Cola were forbidden because they somehow advance Zionism.

As the following excerpt from Senegal demonstrates, all of these "anti-sin" laws in developed nations have caused a migration of "sin" products to people in the Third World.

The central point in advertising abroad is that the U.S. enterprise must seek legal advice from local practitioners and fashion local advertising appropriately. Indeed, in many countries, the guiding norms are not in laws at all but in industry codes observed by the local marketing organizations. The rules in this area are as diverse and arbitrary as human culture itself and as transitory as political opinion. Perhaps the primary general principle is that no useful general principles apply to all cultures.

international accents

Tobacco Firms Busily Enticing New African Smokers

by Peter Masebu, PANA, SENEGAL
May 29, 1999

DAKAR, Senegal (PANA)—Khady is not a football fan but she attends weekend football league matches at Dakar's Leopold Sedar Senghor stadium, where she distributes free cigarettes made by her tobacco company. Interestingly, most of those who accept the "poisoned" present are youths. These would likely have seen the cigarette brand's advertisements which abound in the Senegalese dailies and elsewhere. Lately, tobacco firms have also erected beautiful retail selling stations at busy strategically located bus stops and other places in the seaside Senegalese capital.

Khady's work does not always end at the stadium if there is a big conference taking place in Dakar that weekend. As part of vigourous marketing, her company ensures that she sells the silent killer to delegates addicted to tobacco, a known or probable cause of some 25 diseases. The graceful 19-year old Khady does not smoke, but takes offence when someone tries to interfere in her work. At a football match one day, she rebuked a journalist who called her "the merchant of death" for enticing young smokers to join the 1.1 billion who were already using tobacco in the world at the beginning of the 1990s. Out of these, says the World Health Organization (WHO), 800 million were in developing countries compared with 300 million in developed countries. . . .

The WHO has expressed serious concern that smokers in most Third World countries are not informed about how it is almost impossible to quit smoking after being addicted to nicotine, the powerful additive contained in tobacco.

While advertising tobacco during sports events is common in Dakar because tobacco companies are their major sponsors, there is no attempt to disclose the dangers posed by the chemical additives like nicotine, as happens in developed countries like the United States. . . .

Asked why the number of smokers keeps rising in Senegal and other African countries, a medical practitioner who spoke on the condition of anonymity said: "The issue is that most governments keep a blind eye to advertising because the more cigarettes the companies sell the more tax they pay. Consequently, the tobacco firms have become even more aggressive, erecting selling posts all over and advertising at will. . . ."

WHO estimates that . . . "if current trends continue, 500 million people alive today will be killed by tobacco." The UN health agency is urging governments to start reducing that by banning tobacco advertising and promotion, the sale of cigarettes to children and to impose health warnings on all tobacco products. "This might be very difficult because tobacco firms are running away from the developed world to Africa and the Third World in order to escape those stringent rules," said the anonymous Senegalese medical doctor. . . .

Nonetheless, while governments hesitate to take bold steps to ensure the tobacco industry takes the health aspect more seriously, nicotine addiction and tobacco-related death toll will continue rising, albeit silently, with people like Khady playing her part in the process.

Marketing Considerations: The Nestlé Infant Formula Case

An enterprise that seeks to market a product in a new nation must be alert to unanticipated risk associated with the product in the new environment. If such risk exists, even if a marketing campaign is technically lawful, the law, public scorn, or both will in time catch up with the entrepreneur. The Nestlé infant formula case is an excellent illustration of this problem.

Infant formula manufacturers have long provided hospitals with free or low-cost formula as a marketing technique. The concept is that the mother develops a brand loyalty from the child's birth that is unlikely to change over time. In addition, formula manufacturers promoted their products, like all other merchants, through mass media. Some have argued that these marketing techniques have the effect of discouraging mothers from breast-feeding, which is widely regarded to be superior to infant formulas. This discouragement is said to be particularly influential in the Third World, where mothers are less educated and more impressionable.

Critics argue that in such developing countries, forsaking breast-feeding can have especially grim consequences. Outside hospitals, the water supply may not be sanitary and mothers may not understand usage instructions. Improper use can lead to malnutrition, diarrhea, and gastroenteritis.

Nestlé, S.A., a Swiss concern with over 40 percent of the $3 billion baby formula market, became a lightning rod for criticism. Critics charged that Nestlé was luring uneducated Third World mothers from breast-feeding through its marketing activities. These critics organized a series of boycotts against all Nestlé products throughout developed countries.

In response, Nestlé changed its promotional practices and, in 1976, phased out mass media advertising. But still Nestlé did not escape criticism because it continued to provide free and low-cost formula. The World Health Organization promulgated an "International Code of Marketing of Breast Milk Substitutes," which many countries have implemented as law. Nestlé voluntarily agreed to follow the code in 1982, agreeing to supply formula only upon request by hospital administrators. Third World administrators, however, continued to order formula and give it to virtually all mothers. Accordingly, in 1989, several groups in Britain, Ireland, and Sweden reactivated the boycott because of what they viewed as continued promotion. Finally, in January 1991, Nestlé committed to stop supplying free and low-cost formula completely.

In short, although Nestlé acted in conformance with the law, it still found itself in a vortex of controversy that adversely affected its profitability throughout the world. Marketing often involves understanding that corporations may be held to a higher standard than that mandated by law.

THE *FOREIGN CORRUPT PRACTICES ACT*

In most nations, the government is far more immersed in the day-to-day functioning of commerce than is the government of the United States in its economy. Particularly in emerging nations, favorable government action or inaction is frequently a prerequisite to concluding a transaction. Naturally, such government action or inaction results from the exercise of discretion by government officials, giving such officials greater influence in commercial transactions than their North American counterparts. Many of these foreign government officials are not above informing their discretion with a bribe. Indeed, in many countries, bribery of public officials has historically been a way of life.

This is the case even though almost every nation in the world formally outlaws bribery of its own officials. For example, the Russian Federation has enacted a complex legal framework prohibiting official corruption. Since April 1992, Presidential Decree 351 has, as a prophylactic measure, barred civil servants from participating in entrepreneurial activities, managing commercial activities, or accepting foreign business trips paid by commercial entities. The Russian *Federal Anti-Monopoly Law* restricts government officials from owning enterprises or serving in a voting capacity in a commercial enterprise. Penalties for violation include fines, dismissal from office, and imprisonment. Nonetheless, while these laws have been in full effect, Russia has earned a dubious reputation for omnipresent official corruption that has recently deterred foreign investment.

South Korea also has an impressive and strict antibribery legal framework. Article 129 of the

Korean *Criminal Code* prohibits not only receipt or solicitation of a bribe, but also "manifestation of a will to deliver" a bribe. In August 1996, two former South Korean presidents were convicted of criminal bribery—having accepted hundreds of millions of dollars from business enterprises. One was sentenced to death, while the other was sentenced to twenty-two years and six months in prison. Yet, in 1998, massive official corruption came to public light and South Korea experienced a near-collapse of its financial system.

A foreign investor who makes a payoff to a foreign official therefore risks criminal prosecution by the official's country. But in many countries, this risk is not great. For instance, prior to very recent events, South Korean prosecutors had enforced bribery laws only against lower-level officials and had exercised their prosecutorial discretion to avoid actions against politically powerful high-level officials. In fact, for the foreign investor, there is often a much greater risk of official persecution if the corrupt payment is *not* made.

A few countries in the world also outlaw bribes by its citizens to public officials in *other* countries. Because one of those countries is the United States, every American who retains an agent abroad should be familiar with the *Foreign Corrupt Practices Act* (FCPA).

---

http://www.usdoj.gov/criminal/fraud/fcpa.html
http://www.ita.doc.gov/legal/fcpanew.html
Information on the FCPA.

Origins of the FCPA and Other Antibribery Measures

In the mid-1970s, the press in the United States uncovered a number of instances of U.S.-based corporations making payments to foreign leaders for official favors. An aircraft manufacturer was widely alleged to have made payments to the Japanese prime minister and a Dutch prince in exchange for assistance in obtaining government contracts. At the same time, alleged payments to a number of members of the Italian government caused its president to resign.

Concerned by these embarrassing incidents, the U.S. Securities and Exchange Commission instituted a voluntary disclosure program to assess the frequency of the phenomenon. Firms were invited to tell of their payoffs abroad under a loose understanding of nonprosecution.

The volume of the response was remarkable. More than four hundred U.S. companies revealed that they had bribed foreign public officials. The amounts paid aggregated into the hundreds of millions of dollars. Although corporations based in other countries allegedly engaged in the same practices, no nation had ever publicly confessed to such a massive pattern of corrupting behavior.

The U.S. public was in no mood to condone such frank admissions of immorality. Scarcely a year before, the president of the United States had resigned because of the so-called Watergate cover-up. Nor had any nation ever faced the embarrassment of admitting such an extensive pattern of corrupt activity. U.S. public opinion and the world's disdain demanded prompt and decisive action. They got it. By December 1977, Congress had passed and the president had signed the world's first law outlawing its citizens' bribes to officials of another nation.

For two decades, the United States was alone in forbidding its citizens from bribing foreign officials. Indeed, some nations permitted tax deductions for such payments. But the tide has finally turned. In February 1999, the *Convention on Combating Bribery of Foreign Public Officials in International Business* became effective. The Convention obligated the member states of the Organization for Economic Cooperation and Development (OECD) to enact a law making the bribery of foreign public officials a criminal act; as of mid-2003, thirty-four countries had ratified the Convention, including all major European countries and Latin American economic powers such as Argentina, Brazil, Chile, and Mexico. Like the FCPA, the *OECD Convention* also mirrors the accounting provisions of the FCPA, which require detection of corrupt payments. The Convention is particularly significant because the nations that have ratified it are home to virtually all large international corporations. The *OECD Convention* is limited to active corruption of foreign public officials and does not impose the higher FCPA standards. In most respects, however, the *OECD Convention* is consistent with the FCPA; indeed, the FCPA was amended in 1998 to harmonize its terms with that of the *OECD Convention*.

Other international legal efforts are also afoot. In late 2003, the United Nations General Assembly adopted the *U.N. Convention Against Corruption.* The *U.N. Convention* was formulated through negotiations involving 125 countries, including many less developed nations. While the Convention is unlikely to enhance existing enforcement mechanisms, it provides additional international focus on the problem as a serious obstacle to development. Separately, the Council of Europe has promulgated a *Criminal Law Convention*— adopted in November 1998 by the Council of Ministers—that includes a more encompassing definition of corruption. Like the FCPA, the *Criminal Law Convention* covers active and passive bribery and transnational bribes. The European Union has enacted four treaties and protocols focused on criminalization of transnational bribery. Under the *First Pillar Provisions of Community Law,* the European Commission is trying to prepare a community-wide law against corruption; this effort includes consideration of explosive issues, such as tax treatment of bribes and audit rules.

In the developed countries, the movement against bribe-givers is gathering force. To understand how these anti-bribe giver statutes work, this study now turns in depth to the law that applies to U.S. enterprises, the FCPA.

Structure of the FCPA

The *Foreign Corrupt Practices Act* seeks to punish bribery of foreign officials and to establish internal accounting mechanisms that will prevent such bribery. Criminal punishment is accomplished through the so-called *antibribery* provisions. The prevention function is accomplished through provisions that seek to detect illegal payments by examining the *accounting and recordkeeping systems* of the enterprise.

The Antibribery Provisions. In essence, the antibribery provisions prohibit U.S. firms from "corruptly" paying or offering to pay a "foreign official" for assistance in obtaining or retaining business. It also prohibits payments to a person, such as a foreign agent, when the payer knows that a portion of the payment will go to a public official. In light of the increasing importance of multinational organizations, in March 2002, the president signed an executive order designating European Union officials and officials of public international organizations as within the definition of "foreign official."

Violating antibribery provisions is a serious offense. Any individual convicted can be jailed for up to five years and fined up to $100,000. In November 2002, the U.S. Sentencing Commission promulgated amendments making FCPA violations subject to the same sentencing guidelines as domestic bribery cases. Any corporation convicted can be fined $2 million per violation. Unfortunately, the law does not clearly define what one has to do to commit this serious criminal act. It contains three principal points of ambiguity: the "routine governmental action" exception, the "corruptly" requirement, and the "knowing" requirement.

Congress recognized that in many countries petty graft is so common that to forbid U.S. companies from engaging in it would be tantamount to forbidding them from doing business there. Accordingly, Congress excluded from the coverage of the FCPA any payment that is a "facilitating or expediting payment . . . the purpose of which is to expedite or secure the performance of a routine governmental action." Such "routine actions" can include the granting of qualification to do business, processing of visas, providing police and mail service, or providing basic utilities or transportation services.

The routine governmental action exception is limited—few government actions do not involve some discretion, particularly in countries outside the United States. As discussed in other chapters, foreign statutes tend to lay out broad general outlines and allow government officials to fill in the interstices. In short, U.S. executives largely must guess whether the role of any given government official will ultimately be determined by some court to be "routine." And if they guess wrong, they can go to jail. Under such circumstances, taking chances is not advisable.

Where gratuity payments to customs officials are routine, the U.S. investor must make a careful assessment of its potential FCPA liability vis-à-vis its ability to operate effectively without making facilitating payments. Many U.S. companies have simply determined that the profits of operating in such countries are not worth the risk. U.S. investments in Russia, for example, have largely vanished.

Although the word *corrupt* is used in a number of criminal statutes, the legal concept is not well defined. Someone who is simply negligent in making a payment is not generally considered corrupt. Thus, a businessperson who, through lack of sophistication, fails to realize that part of a payment to a local foreign agent is in fact going to a government official may not have the corrupt state of mind required for a violation of the antibribery provision. (Such a businessperson might, however, be in violation of the accounting provisions, which have no "corruptness" requirement.) Corruptness requires that the businessperson display a reckless or conscious disregard for the consequences of personal actions. In other words, even if payers do not have actual knowledge that a payment is being made, they are corrupt if they act as if they do not care whether it is going to a government official.

The corruptness requirement does not excuse the victim of extortion. Even if a foreign official is extorting a payment from a U.S. investor, the firm is corrupt if it makes the payment. When faced with an extortion request in a country in which a U.S. firm already has substantial assets, therefore, the firm must refuse to make the payment and suffer the consequent losses. The situation, of course, again suggests that the investor should carefully review the business climate in the foreign country before entering it.

The ambiguities that accompany the "corruptness" concept are similar to those that surround the "knowing" requirement. Although Congress has now made clear that "mere foolishness" is insufficient for liability, the standard is intended to cover "any instance where 'any reasonable person would have realized' the existence of the circumstances or result and the [person] has 'consciously chosen not to ask about what he had reason to believe he would discover.'" The danger is that a foreign agent might be asking for a commission that will ultimately end up in the hands of a foreign official. If a firm discovers that its agent made a payment to a government, the U.S. prosecutors would review the circumstances surrounding the payment to the agent to determine whether the firm "knew" of the agent's bribe. Suffice it to say that whenever an agent asks for an unusually big fee or commission, a U.S. investor has reason to be nervous.

The Accounting and Recordkeeping Requirements.   The FCPA also requires a U.S. investor to "make and keep books, records, and accounts which, in reasonable detail, accurately and fairly reflect the transactions and dispositions of its assets." It further requires an investor to "devise and maintain a system of internal accounting controls sufficient to provide reasonable assurances" that all transactions are authorized and that access to assets is tracked. These are commonly referred to as the *accounting and recordkeeping provisions.*

The principal objection to the accounting provisions is that they fail to incorporate any concept of *materiality*. U.S. businesses are not normally expected to unearth every fact in their financial statements; aside from its impracticality, the reader of the financial statements would drown in a sea of detail. Thus, accounting systems are generally geared to tracking "material" facts—facts that a prudent investor in the company should know. A $5,000 problem in a $5 billion company, for instance, would not normally be perceived as material.

By not including a concept of materiality, the accounting provisions of the FCPA require the U.S. company's accounting system to be able to identify bribery irrespective of how small it may be. Although $5,000 might be a great deal of money to an individual, tracking every such problem represents a formidable task for a multibillion-dollar company. Nevertheless, as a technical matter, ignoring such a task is a possible violation of the FCPA.

The Department of Justice Review Process

Before entering a transaction raising a possible FCPA issue, an investor can seek an interpretation of these somewhat ambiguous provisions from the U.S. Department of Justice (DOJ). But the investor may not like the process.

The inquiring firm first submits all relevant details of the proposed transaction to the DOJ, including appropriate documentation—the Department will not respond to hypothetical fact situations. The firm must be willing to risk the confidentiality of the deal—all documents in the DOJ's possession are subject to the *Freedom of Information Act,* which permits any American, including journalists, to request disclosure of documents in the government's possession. Even when the specifics of the deal are afforded confidential treatment, the

DOJ will always issue a release that describes the general nature of the transaction and the identity of the parties involved. Thus, the procedure has the initial disadvantage of subjecting the transaction to the scrutiny of the public at large, including the U.S. firm's competitors. These competitors may be attracted to the opportunity and lure the U.S. firm's proposed business partners away with a more attractive deal. Disclosure of the deal has other adverse side effects. The public officials involved may resent having their integrity publicly questioned. Indeed, such public disclosure might well have adverse effects on the officials' standing in their own home country.

The DOJ will respond in thirty days unless it requires the submission of additional information. If it does require such additional information, the Department will have an additional thirty days from the time of receipt of that information. At the end of this two-month period, the DOJ will either express an interest to pursue or not to pursue a prosecution under the FCPA—or simply decline to state any position. This delay is not very satisfactory in most business transactions. While the parties await a response, market conditions may change so as to make the deal less attractive or entirely unattractive for one of the parties.

Perhaps because of these problems, the DOJ review procedure is used quite infrequently. Although millions of foreign transactions have occurred since the procedure was instituted in 1980, only a few dozen requests have been made under the DOJ procedure. In the overwhelming majority of cases, U.S. firms are choosing not to avail themselves of the procedure. This is not because FCPA issues are not surfacing.

The saving grace of this ambiguous criminal statute is that it is seldom enforced. Prosecutors do not have to seek a criminal indictment for every possible alleged impropriety; they generally have discretion not to bring action when the evidence of a crime is not strong. U.S. authorities are implementing prosecutorial discretion in deciding not to go after businesses in borderline cases. Although the FCPA is now nearly a quarter century old, U.S. authorities have seldom actually initiated formal enforcement actions in connection with alleged payment of foreign officials.

A 1993 FCPA investigation, relating to alleged payments by Northrop Corporation to South Korean officials as persuasion for purchases of F-20 fighter planes, was dropped with no action. The first grand jury indictment under the FCPA in years was returned in April 2003. The alleged violation did not involve subtle interpretations of "knowing" or "corruptness"; in fact, it did not even involve an employee of a U.S. company. A U.S. citizen, who acted as counselor to the government of Kazakhstan was accused of diverting fees paid by oil companies into Swiss bank accounts for the benefit of Kazak officials. It appears prosecutors are not going to spend their time on close questions.

While FCPA is almost certainly to remain on the books, as time goes on without significant enforcement, it becomes less menacing. It seems somewhat clear, after all these years, that the DOJ will exercise its prosecutorial discretion to enforce the spirit of the law vigorously rather than an unrealistically broad interpretation to go after legitimate U.S. businessmen.

Despite the FCPA and the increasing acceptance of the *Convention on Combating Bribery of Foreign Public Officials in International Business,* the battle against corruption is far from won. As the following article makes clear, in many places bribery is still the rule.

As we have seen, most other developed countries are now also moving to punish bribe-givers. The OECD and the European Union are enacting their own anticorruption statutory frameworks. The International Monetary Fund (IMF) has said that IMF officials would henceforth regard it as their duty to press for anticorruption reforms in countries seeking to borrow money. The World Bank noted that if it finds evidence of corruption in any projects it finances, it will cancel the project. Now, the underdeveloped world has weighed in through the *U.N. Convention Against Corruption.* As the following case reflects, courts will give no refuge to a bribe-giver, no matter how sympathetic its circumstances.

Prudent Behavior for the U.S. Businessperson

Achieving greater profits for one's company is certainly not worth a five-year prison sentence, improbable as prosecution may be. Further, any detection of any corruption will increasingly lead to a termination of financing from multilateral institutions, leading to disastrous consequences for the investor. Therefore, the best course of action for the U.S.

Some Countries Are Bad to the Bone on Bribery: But New Initiatives and Laws May Be Leading to a Global Cleanup

By Peter Reina *enr.construction.com,* June 30, 2003

With middlemen diverting cash into the Swiss bank accounts of a corrupt southern African official, the Lesotho Highlands Water project epitomizes graft in international construction. Continuing court activity this month and next will ensure that Lesotho remains a symbol of international construction's murky side and may help clean up the industry globally.

In Lesotho, a former government project director of the multibillion dollar Highland's dam and tunnel scheme is entering his second year in prison. He will stay there until 2020, barring parole. A key middleman died before facing the law and another local consultant pleaded guilty a few weeks ago. Two international design firms have been found guilty of bribery and a leading French contractor faces trial. More actions may follow.

The eruption of activity in Lesotho has become a "landmark" for growing intolerance to corruption, says Neil Stansbury, a British lawyer with long construction experience. "I think we are going to start to see more publicity around global corruption," adds Tony Boswell, the Houston, Texas-based senior vice president of global ethics for AMEC plc, London.

By taking on international companies and their teams of lawyers, Lesotho earned star billing at the high-level eleventh International Anti-Corruption Conference in South Korea in late May. The government wanted to "set an example for other countries," said Lesotho Attorney General Fine Maem.

Across the globe in London, a number of top international contractors met confidentially under the auspices of the independent anti-corruption body Transparency International (TI), based in Berlin and having national chapters in over 80 countries. . . .

TI has compiled a corruption index for countries based on 15 surveys and polls by nine organizations that asked business people, country analysts and residents about their perceptions of corruption (see table) Bangladesh and Nigeria are the most corrupt, according to TI.

Among bigger international players, companies from Russia and China were found to bribe "on an exceptional and intolerable scale," with Taiwanese and South Koreans following closely behind, says CRG (Control Risks Group).

Despite having the oldest law criminalizing corruption abroad, U.S. firms were found to "have a high propensity to pay bribes to foreign government officials," on par with Japanese companies, says TI. Firms from France, Spain, Germany, Singapore and the U.K. were cleaner. And those from Australia, Sweden, Switzerland, Austria, Canada, the Netherlands and Belgium were least likely to bribe, says TI.

Among more corrupt regions, the former Communist Europe and Soviet Union remain prominent, according to a survey by the European Bank for Reconstruction and Development and the World Bank. It found "bribe taxes" exceeding 3% of company sales, with corruption most widespread in Russia. "I've heard stories [in Eastern Europe] of people who wanted to do business on the straight and narrow but [who] were forced out of the market," says Michael Mix, infrastructure business development manager at Bechtel Ltd., London.

In Asia, Indonesia remains notorious for corruption, according to a new survey of 1,000 expatriates by Hong Kong-based Political and Economic Risk Consultancy Ltd. India ranked almost as bad, followed by Vietnam, Thailand, China, The Philippines, Taiwan, Malaysia and South Korea. Singapore emerged as the cleanest country, ahead of Australia and the U.S.

Corruption is more than "brown envelopes paid to a civil servant," says Jean Pierre Méan, EBRD's chief compliance officer. "In a certain Western European city, there was an apartment made available to civil servants on an hourly basis," he says.

However, incidents witnessed by Stansbury . . . involved intermediaries. Commonly, a person claiming influential contacts would emerge, offering help with a bid for a fee. "Ten to twenty million dollars is not surprising," says Stansbury.

continued

continued

RANK IN 2002	COUNTRY	SCORE 10=highly clean 0=highly corrupt	HIGH-LOW RANGE	RANK IN 2002	COUNTRY	SCORE 10=highly clean 0=highly corrupt	HIGH-LOW RANGE
1	Bangladesh	1.2	0.3 - 2.0	46	Colombia	3.6	2.6 - 4.6
2	Nigeria	1.6	0.9 - 2.5	47	Sri Lanka	3.7	3.3 - 4.3
3	Paraguay	1.7	1.5 - 2.0	48	Slovak Republic	3.7	3.0 - 4.6
4	Madagascar	1.7	1.3 - 2.5	49	Morocco	3.7	1.7 - 5.5
5	Angola	1.7	1.6 - 2.0	50	Latvia	3.7	3.5 - 3.9
6	Kenya	1.9	1.7 - 2.5				
7	Indonesia	1.9	0.8 - 3.0				
8	Azerbaijan	2	1.7 - 2.4				
9	Uganda	2.1	1.9 - 2.6				
10	Moldova	2.1	1.7 - 3.0				
11	Haiti	2.2	0.8 - 4.0				
12	Ecuador	2.2	1.7 - 2.6				
13	Cameroon	2.2	1.7 - 3.2				
14	Bolivia	2.2	1.7 - 2.9				
15	Kazakhstan	2.3	1.7 - 3.9				
16	Vietnam	2.4	1.5 - 3.6				
17	Ukraine	2.4	1.7 - 3.8				
18	Georgia	2.4	1.7 - 2.9				
19	Venezuela	2.5	1.5 - 3.2				
20	Nicaragua	2.5	1.7 - 3.4				
21	Guatemala	2.5	1.7 - 3.5				
22	Albania	2.5	1.7 - 3.3				
23	Zambia	2.6	2.0 - 3.2				
24	Romania	2.6	1.7 - 3.6				
25	Philippines	2.6	1.7 - 3.6				
26	Pakistan	2.6	1.7 - 4.0				
27	Zimbabwe	2.7	2.0 - 3.3				
28	Tanzania	2.7	2.0 - 3.4				
29	Russia	2.7	1.5 - 5.0				
30	India	2.7	2.4 - 3.6				
31	Honduras	2.7	2.0 - 3.4				
32	Cote d'Ivoire	2.7	2.0 - 3.4				
33	Argentina	2.8	1.7 - 3.8				
34	Uzbekistan	2.9	2.0 - 4.1				
35	Malawi	2.9	2.0 - 4.0				
36	Panama	3	1.7 - 3.6				
37	Senegal	3.1	1.7 - 5.5				
38	Turkey	3.2	1.9 - 4.6				
39	Thailand	3.2	1.5 - 4.1				
40	El Salvador	3.4	2.0 - 4.2				
41	Egypt	3.4	1.7 - 5.3				
42	Ethiopia	3.5	3.0 - 4.0				
43	Dominican Republic	3.5	3.0 - 3.9				
44	China	3.5	2.0 - 5.6				
45	Mexico	3.6	2.5 - 4.9				

Using such "middlemen" is a practice the construction industry, "in particular," has tolerated, says John Bray, CRG's Tokyo-based director. . . .

Crooked middlemen were at the heart of the Lesotho case, climaxing with last year's trial and sentencing of the Highlands Development Authority's chief executive, Masupha Sole. He was found guilty of taking bribes from intermediaries of international firms. The representative agreements "were nothing more than bribe agreements," says Maem.

But law alone is not enough for Boswell, hired this year to improve AMEC's ethics strategy. "This is a cultural issue. . . . If [company] leaders do not establish the culture . . . the people are going to find ways around [the law]," he says. "What we need to do is train." Bechtel is seemingly content with its strategy. Its guidance outlines the laws, urging staff to consult company lawyers before starting relationships with anyone "who might be considered to be a foreign official." Staff must get assurances that no inducements will be paid through foreign associates, whose appointments need senior approval. Staff must account for all payments they make, and whistleblowers have telephone help lines in 16 countries.

Voluntary pacts and codes are not enough, says Stansbury. "The export credit agencies need to start investigating," he says. With TI support, Stansbury will soon publish a report on the danger signs of corruption. Central to his recommendations will be a dramatic increase in government investigations, which "must be followed by prosecutions and imprisonment," he says. "It's been a surprise to me . . . how prevalent corruption is and how accepted it is by people who would otherwise be reasonably moral."

entrepreneur abroad is vigilance against foreign corruption. First, direct payments to government officials, other than those associated with the most ministerial tasks of clearing customs, should be completely avoided. They should be avoided even if the foreign official is wrongfully extorting money by threatening to terminate existing business with the U.S. firm. These considerations suggest that the

Adler v. The Federal Republic of Nigeria
219 F.3d 869 (2000)
United States Court of Appeals (9th Cir.)

BACKGROUND AND FACTS

James Adler, a United States citizen, and El Surtidor, a Mexican corporation of which Adler was controlling shareholder, brought action against the Federal Republic of Nigeria, the Central Bank of Nigeria ("CBN"), and seventeen Nigerian officials.

In August 1992, Adler received a letter signed by Chief Abba Ganna. The letter proposed a "business transaction" between Adler, Ganna and the Chief Accountant of the Nigerian National Petroleum Corporation ("NNPC"). Ganna explained the transaction as follows:

> [D]uring the last civilian regime here in Nigeria, the elected members of the ruling party used their positions and formulated companies and awarded themselves contracts which were fantastically over-invoiced in various government ministries.
>
> On the overthrow of the regime by the present military government, an inquiry was set to this. Findings and recommendations were made to the government who has given its blessing for the payment of these contracts half/fully executed. You can now see that there is a good deal for these government officials presently in office hence the ousted notable party stalwarts can not come forward for some of the claims.

Ganna requested that Adler send (1) four signed and stamped copies of El Surtidor letterhead and pro forma invoices; and (2) the number of a foreign bank account. In addition, Adler would be responsible for purchasing first-class airplane tickets for Nigerian officials to travel to Mexico to collect their share of the money. In exchange for providing these services, Adler would earn a forty percent commission. The remaining sixty percent of the funds would be divided between "miscellaneous expenses" (ten percent) and "the government officials" (fifty percent). Adler performed as requested.

In September 1992, Adler traveled to Nigeria and visited the home of the Minister of Finance and an office of the CBN where he met with various individuals who identified themselves as Nigerian government officials. Among these "officials" was John Olisa, Deputy Governor of the CBN. Olisa told Adler that the Nigerian government had assigned to El Surtidor rights under a contract between the NNPC and Strabarg Company, another foreign company, for the computerization of Nigerian oil fields. Olisa also showed Adler a bank draft

for sixty million dollars made out to El Surtidor and Jaime Adler, and had Adler sign the assignment Olisa told Adler that he would give him a copy of the contract after Adler deposited funds to cover the difference in the exchange rate between the U.S. dollar and the Nigerian nira ("shortfall deposit funds").

Beginning with Olisa's request for the shortfall deposit funds, individuals, whom Adler believed to be officials of the Nigerian government, repeatedly requested payments from Adler. They described these payments variously as shortfall deposit funds, taxes, processing fees, confirmation fees, surcharges, legal fees, travel expenses, and gratification. Almost every time that someone requested a payment from Adler, that individual told Adler that as soon as he made that payment, the sixty million dollars would be deposited into his account. The payments totaled $5,180,000.

Between August 1992 and July 1994, Adler corresponded, by mail and by telephone, with a variety of individuals who represented themselves as officials of the Nigerian government. In addition, Adler made two more trips to Nigeria prior to filing this lawsuit. In December 1992, he visited Olisa's residence. On the April 1994 trip, Adler met with Paul Ogwuma, Governor of the CBN.

It all turned out to be a scam on Adler by the Nigerian government officials. The promised $60 million never came. Adler ultimately sued in the United States to recover the funds he had advanced the Nigerian government officials.

After trial, the United States District Court for the Southern District of California held, in relevant part, that (1) Adler paid bribes totaling 2.11 million dollars to Nigerian officials in violation of the *Foreign Corrupt Practices Act*, (2) at least one official of the Nigerian government, CBN Governor Paul Ogwuma, participated as a co-conspirator in the fraud against Adler; and (3) the Nigerian government permitted other co-conspirators to use the CBN offices to further the fraud. On these facts, the district court barred Adler from recovering the money he paid to Nigerian government officials because he came to the Court with "unclean hands." Both sides appealed.

HARRY PREGERSON, CIRCUIT JUDGE

We . . . affirm the district court's factual findings, and its application of the clean hands defense to bar Adler's recovery.

continued

continued

On appeal, defendants ask us to reverse several of the district court's factual findings. Specifically, defendants challenge the following findings of fact: (1) Adler met CBN Governor Paul Ogwuma and Ogwuma was a co-conspirator in the conspiracy to defraud Adler; (2) Ogwuma sent Adler letters requesting payments; (3) Adler paid Ogwuma $50,000; (4) Adler met the Nigerian Minister of Finance at the Minister's home; (5) Adler met John Olisa and Olisa is a Deputy Governor of the CBN; (6) Adler received a Revenue Collector's Receipt showing payment of $300,000; (7) the Nigerian government required a shortfall payment of $570,000; (8) Adler paid various fees and taxes to the Nigerian government; (9) Brigadier Ball Peters was Unit Commander for the Presidential Task Force on Trade Malpractices of CBN; and (10) Dr. Clement Odozi was the Deputy Governor of the CBN. . . . We may not reject the district court's "account of the evidence [if it] is plausible in light of the record viewed in its entirety." Here, the district court's factual findings present a plausible account of the evidence, and therefore defendants' challenge fails to satisfy the clear error standard.

On cross-appeal, Adler argues that the district court erred in applying the unclean hands doctrine. The unclean hands doctrine "closes the doors of a court of equity to one tainted with inequitableness or bad faith relative to the matter in which he seeks relief, however improper may have been the behavior of the defendant. . . ." Under this doctrine, plaintiffs seeking equitable relief must have "acted fairly and without fraud or deceit as to the controversy in issue." . . . The district court decided that Adler dirtied his hands by intentionally attempting to aid and abet the Nigerian officials' scheme to steal from the government treasury and by paying bribes. . . .

Nevertheless, Adler puts forth a variety of arguments in an attempt to persuade this court that inequity results from the district court's exercise of discretion. He asserts that he and the Nigerian officials are not equally at fault; that the Nigerian officials will be unjustly enriched if they do not return the funds to Adler; and that this court should grant Adler a remedy because, by doing so, it will discourage Nigerian officials from perpetrating such schemes in the future. Whatever the merits of these arguments, the district court did not abuse its discretion in reaching the opposite conclusion.

First, it is not clear that Adler is any less blameworthy than the Nigerian officials. The Nigerian officials proposed the criminal scheme, but Adler voluntarily participated in it. And while the Nigerian officials successfully defrauded Adler of over five million dollars, Adler attempted to steal sixty million dollars from the Nigerian government. Second, the fact that the defendants will receive a windfall is not an absolute bar to the unclean hands defense. . . . Finally, it is not clear that justice would be served by compelling the Nigerian government to return the money to Adler. Making a judicial remedy available when the bribe fails to accomplish the intended result would reduce the risk inherent in paying bribes, and encourage individuals such as Adler. In short, public policy favors discouraging frauds such as the one perpetrated on Adler, but it also favors discouraging individuals such as Adler from voluntarily participating in such schemes and paying bribes to bring them to fruition. . . .

Decision. The Ninth Circuit held that the district court properly exercised jurisdiction over this case; the district court's factual findings are not clearly erroneous; and the district court did not abuse its discretion in applying the unclean hands defense to bar Adler's recovery.

businessperson may wish to avoid nations in which such extortion is known to be likely to occur. Such situations put the U.S. firm between a rock and a hard place: if they accept the extortion demand, they risk U.S. criminal conviction; if they refuse the demand, they face a substantial business loss in the country of the corrupt official.

Second, foreign agents should be carefully selected and even more carefully paid. Preferably, the U.S. businessperson should build an ample file of the references upon which the foreign agent was retained and of investigations into the person's char-

acter. Commissions and other payments should conform to customary rates in that nation. "Premium" transactions should be avoided in nations with suspect reputations. And appropriate inquiry should be made with respect to the government officials whose discretion is involved in any given transaction.

CHAPTER SUMMARY

If a U.S. enterprise chooses to expand into a foreign nation by hiring an independent agent, it may avoid much of the foreign regulation inherent in establishing a full corporate presence or in cross-border licensing. It will, however, need to take care that the independent agent is indeed recognized as independent. Further, the enterprise will benefit from a familiarity with the statutory framework of rights that protect the agent, irrespective of any agreement between them.

Once armed with a local agent, the U.S. enterprise must be mindful of advertising and promotional efforts abroad and their regulatory requirements that reflect the sensitivities of the local culture. And it must be particularly careful that such "promotion" does not include a quaint local custom of official bribery.

Questions and Case Problems

1. Suppose that Roger Sobodka, a U.S. executive stationed in Paris, wishes to build a support office for his firm's technicians in the suburb of Asnieres. He enters into an agreement with Francois Demblans, a homebuilder, to do the work for $100,000. M. Demblans may, however, seek reimbursement of costs created by unforeseen circumstances. The agreement further specifies that the office building will be completed in nine months, and that M. Demblans will modify his work upon Mr. Sobodka's reasonable instructions. Assuming that French agency law is consistent with that discussed in this chapter, is M. Demblans a dependent or an independent agent for Mr. Sobodka?

2. After conducting a market survey, Penton Intergalactic, Ltd., a manufacturer of plows, believes that there is pent-up demand for its product in the expanding agricultural economy of Paraguay. Penton retains Saul Ortiz, a Paraguayan with a substantial business selling agricultural implements. Penton's New York City advertising agency develops the ad campaign and strategy for introduction of the product, including a rather precise time schedule. Sr. Ortiz is to follow Penton's instruction as the project develops. Sr. Ortiz will use the same employees that he uses in his business operations, except that a few Penton employees will be on site to assist him. He will be paid a commission on each plow sold, plus reimbursement of marketing expenses identifiable as related to the Penton program. Assuming that Paraguayan agency law is consistent with that discussed in this chapter, is Sr. Ortiz a dependent or an independent agent?

3. Jordan Motors, Inc. opens a dealership in Frankfurt, West Germany, selling American cars. In its advertising campaign, Jordan claims that for the next two weeks only, it will beat the price on any comparable German car by 1,000 Deutsche marks. Faced with this threat to its market share, Hartman Autos, A. G. slashes its prices to cost. Andrea Giebbels comes to Jordan's showroom with a written quote of Hartman's price for its bottom-of-the-line German car and demands that Jordan sell her twenty of its bottom-of-the-line cars for a substantial loss. Jordan refuses. If Fraulein Giebbels brings an action, will she be able to enforce Jordan's offer? If Hartman sues, can it have Jordan's advertising campaign enjoined?

4. Borges Meat Marketing, Inc., a Nebraska corporation, wishes to establish a network of gourmet butcher shops in India. It has a well-developed introductory advertising campaign that it has employed in establishing similar butcher shops in the United States and does not wish to go to the expense of developing a new one. What should it do?

5. Joseph Supersonic Company, a U.S. jet fighter manufacturer, is eager to sell its aircraft to the state-owned airline of the Republic of Platano and wishes to retain a local representative to assist it. Maria de la Concepcion Casañas y Diaz is reputed to have the best government contracts in Platano; her clients have been successful in garnering contracts a high percentage of the time. Accordingly, she is more in demand than other local representatives, and her fee is the highest in the country. What are the implications of hiring Srta. Casañas y Diaz?

6. Assume the facts in Question 5 and assume further that a reference check has uncovered rumors that Srta. Casañas y Diaz has had intimate relations with Platano's assistant secretary for government procurement, although there are no plans for a more permanent relationship. What are the FCPA implications now?

7. Assume that Srta. Casañas was retained, but Joseph failed to obtain the contract. To Joseph's chagrin, however, it subsequently learns that Srta. Casañas y Diaz used part of her fee to make a $10,000 payment to a government official. If Joseph has total assets of $5 billion, should the episode be reported on its financial statement?

Managerial Implications

Your firm, Flyboy, Inc. is a successful U.S. manufacturer of aircraft. Flyboy would like to expand its market to Pamonia, a small, oil-rich kingdom that was once an Italian colony. The principal purchaser of aircraft in Pamonia is the government, although some private families have the resources to purchase the product. The same private families are, not coincidentally, also the nobility of the Pamonian kingdom. For a new entrant like Flyboy, breaking into the market without a local representative is not possible. You are also aware that local custom includes "grease payments" and lavish gifts to customers in Pamonia.

1. Prepare a paper considering the pluses and minuses of entering the Pamonian market, focusing on the legal risks posed by the proposed investment and how Flyboy might avoid them.
2. Describe the arrangements into which you would enter with your Pamonian agent.
3. Evaluate the possibility of using an Italian firm as your distributor in the country. What would be the FCPA implications if Flyboy simply delivered the aircraft FOB Pamonia and had no involvement in marketing? What implications would this have for Flyboy's profit margin?

CHAPTER 17

LICENSING AGREEMENTS AND THE PROTECTION OF INTELLECTUAL PROPERTY RIGHTS

REASONS FOR INTELLECTUAL PROPERTY TRANSFER ARRANGEMENTS

The most rapidly growing method of doing business abroad is to transfer *intellectual property rights* (IPRs)—technological know-how or artistic work—to a foreign business in exchange for a fee or other form of remuneration. Like the simple engagement of a representative discussed in the preceding chapter, IPR transfers need not involve any capital investment abroad. They usually involve manufacturing or merchandising one's product or service in the foreign country. By engaging a foreign party to do this manufacturing or merchandising, the U.S. investor can avoid the substantial risks and legal entanglements of capital investments abroad, discussed in chapters to follow.

IPR owners transfer them for a broad variety of reasons. The U.S. firm might, for a fee—sometimes called a *royalty*—grant a *license* to a foreign company that would permit it to use the U.S. firm's trademarks, copyrights, or know-how in making products for sale in the vicinity of the foreign company's country. Alternatively, the U.S. company might provide the IPR and components to a foreign manufacturing plant that will fabricate the product for re-export back to the U.S. concern. In many cases, the foreign product is itself a component of the U.S. company's product. Upon receipt, the U.S. company will integrate it into the ultimate product in the United States. In addition, a U.S. firm can use a transfer of technology as its contribution to a joint venture abroad in exchange for a share of the joint venture. The joint venture would use the technology to manufacture and, perhaps, market the product.

A U.S. company typically enters into one of these arrangements because it provides market or other opportunities that the firm otherwise could not exploit efficiently. The firm may already be producing at the full extent of its domestic manufacturing capacity and may not have the resources to expand significantly. Licensing or teaming with a foreign company with adequate capital and perhaps other attractive assets—for instance, a ready marketing network in desired export markets—is a way to expand the company's market without raising substantial additional capital.

Other U.S. firms have ample funds and a good product, but an inadequate *research and development* (R&D) capability. Confronting the need to improve its technology quickly before it is nudged out of market share by competing technologies, such a company may wish to team with a foreign company that has a strong R&D staff in order to expand to new geographic markets in the short term, while developing enhanced products for the future.

Still other companies possess a utility patent that has a broad range of potential applications, but lack the breadth of management capabilities, developmental resources, or marketing skills to exploit all applications simultaneously. After such a company reserves for itself the patent applications that seem most consistent with its skills and orientation, the company might license the basic technology to other firms, each of which is authorized to develop a specified product or geographic market.

The appeal of substantially cheaper labor costs in a host country is a chief enticement to shifting production offshore. The U.S. company may not, however, know its way around the foreign country or may fear the risk of nationalization. In such a situation, the U.S. firm might prefer contracting with a local firm for its production requirements, rather than setting up its own factory abroad.

In short, there are many reasons for an IPR owner to transfer its intellectual property. Regardless of the motivation for a transfer, the risk is the same—the risk of losing control of one's IPRs and helping to establish a competitor. For example, a small U.S. chemical manufacturer may provide its basic patent to a large French manufacturer through a joint venture in the hope of exploiting the European market and obtaining added R&D capacity. But in doing so, it may simply be giving the powerful foreign firm an opportunity to research around the patent and develop non-infringing alternatives— or infringing products that cannot be proved to infringe. With such products, the French firm may come to dominate Europe, as well as pose a threat in the U.S. firm's own home market.

INTELLECTUAL PROPERTY RIGHTS: TRANSFER ARRANGEMENTS

The heart of any IPR transfer is a grant of license that permits the other party to use the relevant right. The conditions of and compensation for that use form the balance of the agreement.

Right to Use and Conditions of Use

The licensor often agrees to provide services to facilitate the anticipated activities, such as assistance in setting up an assembly line or other training and technical support. The licensor generally seeks to restrict the licensee's use of the transferred IPR. Common restrictions include *geographic limitations:* For example, a licensor of a "name brand" doll may limit the licensee's sale of that doll within a specific nation. *Field of use limitations* restrict the applications for which the licensee may employ the IPR. For example, the licensor of a laser technology might permit one licensee to use the technology only in connection with medical applications, while retaining for itself the right to use the technology for communications applications and other uses. Other potential restrictions might be *output or customer restrictions,* especially if the licensor plans to use the licensee as a source of products for the licensor's own distribution requirements.

When the licensor's economic return depends on the licensee's marketing success, the licensor may seek to impose various obligations on the exploitation of the licensed IPR. The licensee usually will be expected to pledge to use its "best efforts" to develop a market for the products manufactured with the IPR. Many licensors go further, demanding that the licensee comply with specific marketing quotas under pain of losing its license.

Competitive Circumstances

When exploitation of the licensed IPR requires significant financial or other resources of the licensee, it will often demand *exclusive rights* in the IPR within some geographic area in order to enhance its chances of earning an adequate return on its investment. The licensor, on the other hand, may not want to "put all of its eggs in one basket." A licensee could fail for many reasons, such as lack of commitment, inability to secure financing, or marketing inadequacies. Meanwhile, competing technologies may come into the market, the licensor's patents may expire, or other events may intrude to reduce the long-term prospects for the venture. Licensors who are concerned about such risks sometimes grant rights to two or more licensees who are willing to compete to develop the target market. Licensees faced with this situation will probably attempt to negotiate some compensating advantage, such as a reduced royalty obligation.

Setting the royalty level for a particular IPR can be a difficult proposition, especially when the degree of market demand for the IPR may not yet be clear. Setting the royalty level too high may boost the total price for the end products to a level that is not competitive with substitute products available in the market. Demand may be high in Dijon for a hamburger sold using McDonalds' trademarked materials and quality control practices, justifying a higher price; but at some point, consumers will be happier with a Brand X hamburger produced by someone who does not pay royalties. At that point, sales—and royalties—will decline, hurting licensor and licensee alike. The trick is to identify a royalty level that allows both licensor and licensee to optimize their respective returns.

Confidentiality and Improvements

Another key license provision will be the clause setting forth the licensee's obligation to keep the licensed technology confidential so that third parties cannot exploit the technology. Such provisions are critical when the IPR being licensed is technology protected primarily by trade secret procedures rather than patent law. The licensee often will try to limit the length of the period during which it must maintain confidentiality, while the licensor's interest is to preserve confidentiality for the anticipated useful life of the trade secret. The parties may also bargain over the specific means by which the licensee will be expected to safeguard the confidential technology. For instance, the licensor may demand that the licensee's employees enter into confidentiality and non-exploitation agreements the licensor could enforce in the event of a breach. The licensor might also demand that only employees who "need to know" the technology be informed of it.

The parties will also usually negotiate over ownership and use rights if the licensee develops improvements in the licensed technology or creates new inventions based on that technology. Reasoning that the licensee would not have had the opportunity to develop these useful technologies without the know-how supplied by the licensor, the licensor may seek a *grant back* to itself of ownership in or, at a minimum, the right to use—often without compensation—such new technology.

Licensors and licensees also haggle about termination issues. These principally focus on the period of time during which the licensee may exploit the licensed IPR, what events may cause the license to be terminated before the end of the scheduled term of the license, and the rights of the licensee in the IPR, if any, after termination. Thus, the licensor will try to be sure that the licensee agrees not to use the IPR in competition with the licensor or to disclose it to a potential competitor. The licensee, on the other hand, will try to keep royalties low and minimize or abbreviate the noncompetition or nondisclosure provisions.

Many of the conflicts discussed here are often at issue during negotiations of IPR transfer agreements, whether domestic or international. The principal difference in the international scenario is that the host government often creates circumstances that favor the local licensee.

INTERNATIONAL PROTECTION FOR PATENTS, TRADEMARKS, AND OTHER INTELLECTUAL PROPERTY

Host countries can promote or undermine potential transfers of IPRs through a variety of direct and indirect means. Without laws protecting patents, copyrights, trade secrets, and trademarks, foreign owners of IPRs will be unwilling to share their valuable intangible assets with citizens in the host country because of the possibility that their IPRs will be stolen.

During the last century, nations struggled to establish a consistent international legal system of intellectual property, with only limited success. The benefits of open trade in IPRs were often outweighed by a desire not to permit foreigners to profit through the sale of mere ideas. Progress was slow when intellectual property was a less important engine of wealth than industrial organization. The personal computing/telecommunications/Internet revolution, however, made intellectual property the principal source of product value. Not surprisingly, the creators of this new value have moved rapidly to protect it through a comprehensive series of treaties. These treaties streamline and make procedures uniform, expand the geographic scope of protection and, ultimately, create an international IPR enforcement network.

Paris Convention

The first international property treaty was the *International Convention for the Protection of Industrial Property,* better known as the *Paris Convention.* The *Paris Convention,* originally prepared in 1883 and since revised many times, guarantees that in each signatory country, foreign trademark and patent applications from other signatory countries receive the same treatment and priority as domestic applicants: "Nationals of each of the [signatory] countries . . . shall, as regards the protection of industrial property, enjoy in all the other countries . . . the advantages that their respective laws now grant, or may hereafter grant, to nationals. . . ." In other words, no signatory country can give intellectual property protection to its own citizens unless it provides the same protection to the citizens of the other signatories. This principle of "national treatment"—an animating principle of all intellectual property treaties—eliminated the potential discrimination against foreigners in obtaining patents.

---

http://www.wipo.int or http://www.wto.org
These Web sites have links to the full text of each treaty.

The *Paris Convention* also gives a trademark holder in any signatory country a "right of priority." The Convention provides that the date of an applicant's foreign application is deemed the same as the date of the applicant's original application on the same invention, so long as the foreign application was filed before the first anniversary of the original application. Because in most countries the first to file is the patent holder, this principle prevented a "race to the patent office" in other countries after the original filing.

There are two main problems with the *Paris Convention* scheme. First, the Convention does not require any minimum substantive standard of patent protection. Thus, if a nation has no pharmaceutical R&D capability, it can decide that it is "immoral" to permit pharmaceutical patents and deny patent protection to pharmaceuticals. Although as a practical matter such a law is aimed at foreigners—because no locals have pharmaceutical patents—it is in compliance with the *Paris Convention*.

A further drawback of the Convention is its lack of an enforcement mechanism. Disputes under the treaty are to be resolved by the International Court of Justice, but most signatory countries either do not recognize that court's jurisdiction or ignore rulings with which it does not agree. Consequently, there is no real procedure for enforcing verdicts other than voluntary compliance. In the 1990s, the developed nations determined to resolve these two defects of the *Paris Convention*. The result was the *TRIPS Agreement,* discussed later.

Patents

In 1970, *The Patent Cooperation Treaty* (PCT) supplemented the *Paris Convention* by establishing a centralized utility patent application process. The PCT application is filed on a standard form with the World Intellectual Property Organization

(WIPO). The WIPO, a United Nations agency headquartered in Geneva, Switzerland, processes the common application and forwards it to the countries designated by the applicant. The PCT gives a patent applicant in a signatory country a *priority claim* once it files an international application in the standard PCT format. After the filing, the applicant then has up to thirty months to begin the administrative processing (prosecution) of the application in the countries in which it wishes to obtain protection. This allows the applicant business to lock in an application date while giving it time to raise capital on the basis of the patent filing. If capital cannot be raised—suggestive of inadequate commercial interest—the applicant can walk away without having spent needless sums in worldwide patent prosecution.

The only place with a consolidated multinational patent application is the EU. Since 1978, one has been able to obtain protection in all countries of the Union by filing a single application under the *European Patent Convention*. This system was enhanced in December 1989 when the member states signed the *Agreement Relating to Community Patents,* which created a unitary system for the application and grant of European patents and a uniform system for the resolution of litigation concerning patent infringement. Under this system, all persons seeking a European patent complete the same PCT application form with the European Patent Office (EPO), located in Munich, Germany. The EPO's *Revocation Division* and a *Patent Administration Division* grant and revoke patents for the entire EU. Infringement actions are brought in *Community Patent Courts of First Instance* and *Second Instance,* with all appeals to a single *Common Patent Appeal Court* for the entire Union. As a further bit of streamlining, the EPO filing is coordinated with the PCT process. An applicant can complete the PCT standard filing and designate the EPO as a "country" of origin to obtain both EPO and PCT protection.

The PCT system applies only to "utility" patents, but there is a similar emerging treaty system for design patents. The *New Act of the Hague Agreement Concerning the International Registration of Industrial Designs* establishes a single standard application and single design patent filing process. The United States signed this act in July 1999.

Trademarks

As previously noted, registered trademarks are assured national treatment by the *Paris Convention*. The *Paris Convention* also confers a "right of priority" to a trademark holder if the foreign registrations are made within six months after the original registration. Trademark prosecution, however, is usually based on the law of the country where registration is sought.

One exception to this nation-by-nation process is the EU's single multinational trademark registration system. Since 1996, the Community Trademark Regulation, administered by the Office for Harmonization in the Internal Market (OHIM), has allowed a single trademark registration enforceable throughout the EU. The Trademark Regulation also provides a unified enforcement authority; infringement in any member state can be prosecuted within OHIM.

The other exception is the new system of the 1989 protocol to the *Madrid Agreement Concerning the International Registration of Marks of 1891 (Madrid Protocol)*. Like the PCT, the Protocol provides a centralized filing system on a standard form and a designation of the countries in which trademark registration is sought. The WIPO also administers the prosecution and notifies designated countries. Although many countries have ratified the Protocol, the United States and many others have not.

The War of "Geographic Indications"

Notwithstanding these attempts to standardize the law, a "mark" in one nation may still be a generic name in another. Until the recent attempts to standardize practice take effect, the determination of whether an item is generic requires an analysis of the conditions in the country where a mark is sought. This is particularly well illustrated in the context of "geographic indications"—where a product, particularly a wine or liquor, is marketed by reference to a geographic region. For example, there has long been a dispute as to whether it is appropriate to label a sparkling wine made in the style developed in Champagne, France, as "champagne." The following case illustrates this "geographic indications" dispute, while underscoring just how narrowly national the focus in trademark law can be.

Comite Interprofessionel du Vin de Champagne v. Wineworths Group, Ltd.
2 N.Z.L.R. 432 (1991)
High Court of Wellington

BACKGROUND AND FACTS

An Australian company sought to sell sparkling wine, made in Australia from grapes grown in Australia, in New Zealand in bottles that included the word "champagne" on the label. The *Comite Interprofessionel du Vin de Champagne* (the CIVC), a group of champagne producers from the French department of Champagne, sought an injunction to prevent the Australians from "passing off" Australian sparkling wine as wine actually produced in the region of Champagne.

JUDGE JEFFRIES

These proceedings are brought by the plaintiffs to protect their claimed property right in the word "Champagne." As an editorial policy in this judgment I am using the word champagne with a capital when it refers to the district and the wine from the district.

The plaintiffs seek in effect to prevent the defendant from importing into New Zealand sparkling wine from Australia labeled champagne. . . .

Champagne . . . is relatively new, having its origin in time at the end of the seventeenth century but its final development was a nineteenth century phenomenon. Dom Perignon of the Benedictine Abbey of Hautvillers near Epernay in the Champagne district is credited with its beginning. . . . The two features of Champagne of prime importance for its uniqueness are the soil and climate in which the grapes are grown, and the method of manufacture by skilled personnel. . . . For the production of grapes for Champagne there are strict geographical limitations imposed by law. . . . By [French] law the wine allowed to carry the appellation Champagne must be produced exclusively within precise zones. . . . The essence of the methode

continued

continued

champenoise is that the process of second fermentation takes place in the bottle in which it is sold. . . .

This proceeding is about New Zealand law and the understanding of its people so it is appropriate to say something of the wine industry and wine drinking by New Zealanders. Viticulture commenced with the first settlers 150 years ago and never abated, but New Zealanders did not early develop a widespread interest in and use of wines either locally made or imported. This was in contrast to Australia where indigenous wine manufacture and drinking became a more integral part of the lifestyle of that country. . . . New Zealanders' attitude toward wine underwent a marked change commencing from about thirty years ago. . . . The population became markedly more knowledgeable on wines and the demand for information was met principally by newspaper columns and books on wine.

Champagne has been exported to New Zealand from about the middle of the last century in small quantities until 1979, and increasingly in the 1980s. It is certain there were quite small volume exports of Australian champagne from 1977 onwards. . . . New Zealand has, apart from the foregoing, no history of material consumption, or manufacture, of sparkling wine prior to 1980. . . . In about 1981 Montana Wines, Ltd., which is New Zealand's largest maker, launched a sparkling wine produced by methode champenoise and labeled it "Lindauer New Zealand Champagne." Proceedings were issued in 1982 against Montana and after four years were settled by a consent order of the Court issuing an injunction generally restraining the use of the word champagne on that defendant's products.

[In Australia,] [s]parkling wine calling itself champagne made from grapes grown in Australia by the methode champenoise, and by other methods, has been entirely accepted and without direct challenge from the CIVC. The plaintiffs recognize, and although reluctantly accept, for Australia, like Canada and the United States of America, there is no legal protection available to them over the use of the appellation champagne.

The sparkling wine market in New Zealand changed dramatically with the introduction here from Australia in 1986 of Yalumba Angas Brut Champagne. The wine was of good quality and reasonably priced. It was a stunning success and other wine importers began a serious search in Australia for competitors. . . .

It is appropriate here to emphasize the plaintiffs' view of what makes the product and therefore the name of Champagne so special. The product is a quality one and by virtue of the cost of manufacture it is necessarily expensive, which is part of its exclusivity. From the quality product the reputation has developed, which reflects the specialness of the wine itself arising from factors outlined above. Whilst it has developed a reputation as a quality sparkling wine the consumption of it has also become widely associated with certain types of human activity which are mobilized around celebration and joy. Champagne is appropriate as a wine with which to celebrate (a characteristic is that it palpably agitates in the glass) and that is reinforced by exotic origin (for all but the French) and its cost. The plaintiffs say the excellent wine, whose quality is secured by the law of France, is rolled up with its deserved reputation and the name is a valuable right to them as owners. . . .

It is appropriate here to deal with a phenomenon which is occurring in Australia . . . whereby [s]parkling wines at the lower end of the price range not made from the classic Champagne grape varieties and using the transfer method are continued to be called champagne but those at the upper end of the price range made by methode champenoise are tending not to be called champagne, but given a brand name with the label showing it was produced by methode champenoise. That trend clearly suggests that the word champagne has been so devalued in the market in Australia that the public now needs a word, or words, that will convey the excitement and quality surrounding the word champagne say in New Zealand or the United Kingdom.

What the defendant [says] is that the word *champagne* has in New Zealand lost its distinctive significance so as to be properly defined now as a generic term having generic use within the wine market. . . .

The task of the Court is to decide how the adult population of New Zealand as a group perceives the word. One has only to frame the task in that way to demonstrate its immense difficulty.

The Court holds [market research] studies supporting the contention that there is significant evidence that champagne is not a generic word by usage in New Zealand. . . . From the evidence of the wine experts emerged two other observations worth making. If Australian wine interests were able to export sparkling wines to New Zealand it would have overall a deleterious effect by setting back the desirable

continued

continued

goal of attainment of the maximum accuracy and fair labeling on wine bottles. . . . The countries who are members of the Common Market strictly adhere to France's proprietary right in the word Champagne. . . . There was a conscious attempt to supply [restaurant wine] lists encompassing a wide range of restaurants from the select and expensive ones downwards . . . the great majority make the distinction between sparkling wines and Champagne. [T]he Court's decision is that the word champagne in New Zealand is not generically used to describe any white sparkling wine.

The word *champagne* does, in my view, have a special impact or impression on ordinary, average New Zealanders for whom wine drinking generally plays no significant part in their lives. This nonexpert, phlegmatic, even uninterested representative New Zealander does have a definite response to the word *champagne* over and above noting it to be a white sparkling wine, or one with bubbles in it. That response if pushed to articulation might be, a wine

for celebration, expensive, of French origin, special method of manufacture, name of district in France, consumed by a certain social class, a wine ships are launched with or crowds are sprayed with after a major sporting event is won. . . .

The question for the Court is whether importation into New Zealand, as aforesaid by the defendant advertising and selling Seaview Champagne, is deceptive in the way complained of by the plaintiffs. The Court's decision is that it is deceptive. To begin with the finding of the Court is that the word *champagne* is distinctive and that in New Zealand it has not passed into generic territory. Having found it is not generic then to use it in the market previously described is deceptive. . . . By using the word *champagne* on the label the defendant is deceptively encroaching on the reputation and goodwill of the plaintiffs.

Decision. The Court enjoined the Australian defendants from using the word *champagne* in New Zealand.

For a time, these worldwide liquor name wars resulted in an armistice of sorts between the United States and the EU. In a bilateral agreement concluded in 1994, the United States agreed to prevent its companies from labeling U.S.-made liquor as *Scotch whisky, Irish whiskey, cognac, Armagnac, Calvados,* or *brandy de Jerez.* In exchange, Europeans may not label European-made products as *bourbon* or *Tennessee whiskey.* The debate over trademarks for geographic locations of products, however, has recently grown very heated. In October 2003, the WTO agreed to establish a panel to examine EC Council Regulation 2081/92, which creates restrictive rules on the protection of trademarks and geographical indications for geographical products and foodstuffs. Regulation 2081/92 does not allow a nation to register its geographical indications in the EU's Register of Protected Designations of Origin and Protected Geographical Designations (EU's Geographical Designations Register) unless the nations provide the same enhanced protection as the EU. The United States and Australia each complained about the Regulation and a panel was established.

The United States and Australia argued that by not permitting the names of agricultural products from non-EU member countries to be registered without reciprocity in the EU's Geographical Designations Register, the EU is violating its national treatment and most favored nation obligations under the GATT and TRIPS. Further, the terms of the Regulation mean that the EU does not grant the advantages that EU products receive to products of non-EU member countries. For example, EC Council Regulation 2081/92 grants certain monitoring and enforcement benefits to geographical indications of EU members, but does not grant the same benefits to non-EU member countries.

In addition, the United States and Australia complained that EC Council Regulation 2081/92:

1. Diminishes legal protection for trademarks (including preventing the use of an identical or similar sign that is likely to confuse) provided by Articles 1, 2, 16, 20, 24.5, 41, and/or 42 of TRIPS.
2. Does not provide the legal means for countries to prevent the misleading use of a geographical

indication or to prevent any use of a geographical indication that constitutes unfair competition within the meaning of Article 10b of the *Paris Convention* (1967) and is contrary to Articles 1 and 22.2 of the TRIPS Agreement.

3. Does not define a geographical indication in a manner consistent with the definition provided in TRIPS.

4. Is not applied in a transparent manner, contrary to Articles 1, 63.1, and 63.3 of TRIPS.

5. Does not provide adequate enforcement procedures and has been prepared, adopted, or applied with the effect of creating unnecessary obstacles to trade, being more trade-restrictive than necessary to fulfill a legitimate objective, contrary to Articles 2.1 and 2.2 of the *Technical Barriers to Trade Agreement*.

Geographical Indications Under the *Doha Development Agenda*

The battle of "geographical indications" is not limited to the developed worlds of North America, Australia, and Europe and, now, is not limited to wines and liquors. The Development Agenda of the Doha Ministerial Conference has also included two issues relating to geographical indications: (a) creating a multi-register for wines and spirits and (b) extending the higher or enhanced level of protection accorded to wines and spirits under Article 23 of TRIPS to other products.

The negotiations for the creation of a multi-register for geographical indications for wines and spirits are required under Article 23.4 of TRIPS and covered under paragraph 18 of the *Doha Declaration*. There are two main arguments in the negotiations. On one hand, countries led by the United States, Argentina, Australia, and Japan propose a voluntary system where notified geographical indications would be registered in a database. Under this proposal, governments choosing to participate would have to consult the database when making decisions on protection in their countries. Countries that do not wish to participate would simply be "encouraged" but not "obliged" to consult the database. In contrast, the so called "EU proposal" suggests that the registration would establish a "presumption" that the geographical indication is to be protected in all countries. The presumption of protection can be

challenged on certain grounds, but once a name or term has been registered, a nation can no longer refuse protection to the registered name or term unless the name or term is challenged within eighteen months from registration.

A number of countries have requested extending the enhanced protection given to wines and spirits by Article 23 of TRIPS to other products. Advocates of an extension of the enhanced level for products other than wines and spirits include the EU, China, Thailand, Pakistan, and Nigeria. They argue that a key component of the value of certain agricultural products (such as basmati rice and parma ham) is the well-established link to the regions where these goods are produced. As in the case of wines and spirits, the demand for these products provides opportunities for producers from those regions. To protect these producers from usurpation, the extension advocates argue that safeguards similar to those of wines and spirits need to be in place. The opponents of the extension—including the United States, Japan, Canada, Australia, and New Zealand—argue that the existing level of protection under Article 22 of TRIPS is adequate and that providing the enhanced protection would be expensive to enforce. The opponents of enhanced protection also argue that the usurpation claim is flawed, especially since the world has seen a great number of immigrants taking the methods of producing or making these products with them to their new home countries.

Domain Name Trademarks. The protection of Internet domain names with trademark law is unsettled. After much international negotiation, in August 1999, the Internet Corporation for Assigned Names and Numbers (ICANN) adopted the *Uniform Domain Name Dispute Resolution Policy*. The Policy set forth general "first to file" rules for domain names, but excepted "bad faith" filings. It also created an innovative dispute resolution process that submitted complaints and replies electronically over the Internet to a WIPO Arbitration and Mediation Center. In January 2000, the first case was decided under the Policy. The WIPO panel determined that the defendant "cybersquatter" had registered the domain name "world-wrestlingfederation.com" in bad faith and ordered him to cease using it. The new process certainly meted out swift justice: it took only six weeks to go from submission of the initial complaint to the ultimate decision. In the years since, the WIPO process has continued to provide a refreshingly quick and uncomplicated way of resolving Internet IPR disputes.

Copyrights

The *Berne Convention for the Protection of Literary and Artistic Works,* better known as the *Berne Convention,* deals with the granting of copyrights among signatory nations. Like the *Paris Convention,* the *Berne Convention* is based on a *national treatment* scheme: each signatory nation must afford foreigners the same treatment as its own citizens. Unlike the *Paris Convention,* however, the *Berne Convention* requires all signatory nations to enact certain minimum substantive laws. These *minima* include prohibitions against copying literary and artistic works and granting authors exclusive rights to adaptations and broadcasts of works. In contrast to the fragmented patent and trademark system, there is no filing requirement. All an author needs to do is affix the symbol © and the year of authorship to provide copyright protection throughout the world. The *Berne Convention* signatories agree to grant national treatment to copyright holders from other signatories automatically from the moment of creation rather than the time of filing.

The coming of the computer revolution and the Internet has brought software copyright issues to the forefront. First, there was a significant dispute as to whether computer programs were copyrightable subject matter. This was resolved in late December 1996, when WIPO approved the *Draft Treaty on Certain Questions Concerning the Protection of Literary and Artistic Works,* providing that: "Computer programs are protected as literary works within the meaning of Article 2 of the Berne Convention. Such protection applies to the expression of a computer program in any form." This treaty, also known as the *WIPO Copyright Treaty* or the *Protocol to the Berne Convention,* expands the scope of broadcasts that an author must permit to include "any communication to the public of their works, by wire or wireless means, including the making available to the public of their works in such a way that members of the public may access these works from a place and a time individually chosen by them." Natu-

rally, this is carefully crafted to include access through the Internet. Together with the *Performances and Phonograms Treaty,* passed at the same time, the Protocol sought to tighten international law by requiring signatory nations to provide adequate legal protection against the circumvention of technological security measures, effective remedies against the knowing removal of electronic rights-management information and the related acts of distribution, and necessary measures to permit effective action against any act of infringement of rights covered by the treaties.

The United States wanted to go even further, seeking to cover even temporary reproduction of copyrighted material unless the nation enacted certain minimum standards of protection. Because the Internet works by sending packets of data into a computer's temporary memory, this would have created significant issues as to Internet "browsing." The dispute was resolved through an *Agreed Interpretation of a Treaty* provision, and that interpretation has been implemented in different contexts.

All of these provisions had dubious significance in the context of the *Berne Convention.* Like the *Paris Convention,* it has been very difficult to enforce the *Berne Convention* effectively. This enforcement problem was one of the principal forces that drove negotiations on the *TRIPS Agreement.*

TRIPS

As intellectual property became increasingly valuable, the developed world—which created virtually all such property—increased pressure to cure the defects of the *Paris* and *Berne Convention* systems. These efforts bore fruit in the GATT *Agreement on Trade-Related Aspects of Intellectual Property Rights* (TRIPS), which became effective as to most nations on January 1, 2000. TRIPS obligates its signatories to enact minimum substantive standards of protection and creates a viable enforcement mechanism. In effect, TRIPS causes developing countries to adopt intellectual property laws that mirror those of Europe and North America and adds a system to enforce them.

TRIPS requires every member of the World Trade Organization (WTO) to abide by the *Paris and Berne Conventions*—including the recent protocols to those treaties—and apply the treaties' national treatment requirements so that all foreign

IPR owners receive the same protection as local nationals. It establishes fifty-year copyright protection pursuant to the *Berne Convention.* All WTO members must recognize the patent holders' right to assign or license their patents and the term of patent protection must be at least twenty years.

Further, patent protection is now to be available for "any new inventions, whether products or processes, in all fields of technology, provided that they are new, involve an inventive step (*nonobvious*) and are capable of industrial application (*useful*)." TRIPS even established minimum standards for trade secret protection along the lines of uniform trade secret statutes in the United States.

> http://lexmercatoria.net
> See for the TRIPS agreement.

TRIPS seeks to remedy some of the acknowledged problems of the *Paris* and *Berne Conventions.* First, unlike the *Paris Convention,* TRIPS sets minimum standards of intellectual property protection. A nation can no longer comply with international intellectual property law by having its law provide no protection. Second, TRIPS requires signatory countries to "ensure that enforcement procedures as specified in this Part are available under their laws so as to permit effective action against any act of infringement of intellectual property rights covered by this Agreement, including expeditious remedies to prevent infringements and remedies which constitute a deterrent to further infringements." If one nation believes that another is out of compliance, it can initiate a dispute proceeding before a WTO panel.

Because most industrialized countries had effective patent, copyright, and trademark systems in place before TRIPS, these systems became compliant with minor adjustments. TRIPS required emerging nations, however, to enact a whole new statutory scheme, including an adequate domestic enforcement mechanism. TRIPS was the first WTO agreement to impose "positive" obligations on WTO signatories to adopt the new law; previously, WTO agreements had relied on negative prohibitions.

TRIPS has drawbacks. The developed nations accepted an "escape clause" to the minimum substantive standards in Article 8 of TRIPS. Signatory nations may:

> exclude from patentability inventions, the prevention within their territory of the commercial exploitation of which is necessary to protect *ordre public* or morality, including to protect human, animal or plant life or health or to avoid serious prejudice to the environment.

Thus, although any actions taken under Article 8 must be "consistent with the provisions" of the TRIPS, Brazil may again refuse to grant pharmaceutical patents if they are at odds with the *ordre public.* Developed nations counter that the exception was intended to be narrow, permitting patent infringement only for: (1) noncommercial purposes, (2) research, (3) experimentation for testing or improvement, and (4) educational purposes. Litigation on the issue seems likely, for many emerging countries are not inclined to pay vast royalties on intellectual property.

Emerging nations fear that high tech exports protected by intellectual property rights will increase their trade deficits and slow development of their own industry. These fears easily translate into massive domestic political pressure, leading signatory governments to reinterpret their commitments. Thus, to the extent these nations seek to comply at all, they do so in the least restrictive way possible.

The Philippines, for example, created a TRIPS compliant system for patenting and trademarking foreign drugs. The legislature then took away most of the system's economic value by requiring brand drug manufacturers to produce generic versions of their drugs. Another example of an attempt at reinterpretation is Canada's assault on Article 33, which provides a twenty-year term for patents. In the *Canada 17–20* case, Canada defended its term of seventeen years from grant for certain patents as sufficiently "consistent" with the term of twenty years from filing. Canada contended that seventeen- and twenty-year terms were equivalent, and that if Canada's term was shorter in some instances, it was due to circumstances within the control of the applicant. In May 2000, a WTO Panel rejected Canada's position, but the Canadians' willingness to pursue it shows that little is clear in this area. See, *Canada—Term of Patent Protection,* WTO Doc. No. 00-1695 (May 5, 2000), available at http://www.wto.org/english/tratop_e/disu_e/distabase_wto_members1_e.htm.

The following case illustrates how a party not wishing to comply with TRIPS might seek to reinterpret it.

India—Patent Protection for Pharmaceutical & Agricultural Chemical Products
AB-1997-5, WTO Doc. No. 97-5539 (December 19, 1997)
World Trade Organization Appellate Body

BACKGROUND AND FACTS

The United States brought a complaint under TRIPS. It asserted that India had violated its obligations to provide a "means" for patent protection and exclusive marketing rights for pharmaceutical and agricultural chemical products during the transition period from when the TRIPS Agreement was entered into (1 January 1995) and when developing countries were obligated to have enacted TRIPS-compliant IPR laws for those products (1 January 2005). India took the position that certain "administrative instructions" from the executive branch to the Patent Office—on which there would be no action until 1 January 2000—were a sufficient "means" for purposes of TRIPS. As to exclusive marketing rights, it took the position that it had no obligation to provide any until after it processed patent applications, which would not begin until after 1 January 2005, when determination of patents for the "sensitive" pharmaceutical and agricultural products would begin.

The WTO Panel ruled against India, and India appealed to the WTO Appellate Body.

MESSRS. LACARTE-MUR, BACCHUS, AND BEEBY

India asserts that it has established, through "administrative instructions," "a means" by which applications for patents for pharmaceutical and agricultural chemical products (often referred to as "mailbox applications") can be filed and filing dates assigned to them. . . . India argues that the function . . . of the TRIPS Agreement is to ensure that the Member concerned receives patent applications as from 1 January 1995 and maintains a record of them on the basis of which patent protection can be granted as from 2005.

India argues that . . . the obligation to provide exclusive marketing rights to a pharmaceutical or agricultural chemical product for which a patent application has been made arise only after the events specified in the provision have occurred. India maintains that there is nothing . . . that creates an obligation to make a system for the grant of exclusive marketing rights system generally available in the domestic law before [the determination of patents referred to above].

* * *

Article 27.1 of the TRIPS Agreement provides generally:

Subject to the provisions of paragraphs 2 and 3, patents shall be available for any inventions, whether products or processes, in all fields of technology, provided that they are new, involve an inventive step and are capable of industrial application. Subject to Article 65 and paragraph 8 of Article 70 . . . patents shall be available and patent rights enjoyable without discrimination as to the place of invention, the field of technology and whether products are imported or locally produced.

* * *

With respect to patent protection for pharmaceutical and agricultural chemical products, certain specific obligations are found in Articles 70.8 and 70.9 of the TRIPS Agreement. Article 70.8 states:

Where a Member does not make available as of the date of entry into force of the WTO Agreement patent protection for pharmaceutical and agricultural chemical products commensurate with its obligations under Article 27, that Member shall:

(a) . . . provide as from the date of entry into force of the WTO Agreement a means by which applications for patents for such inventions can be filed;

* * *

The issue before us in this appeal is: what precisely is the "means" for filing mailbox applications that is contemplated and required by Article 70.8(a)?

India is entitled, by the "transitional arrangements" in paragraphs 1, 2 and 4 of Article 65, to delay application of Article 27 for patents for pharmaceutical and agricultural chemical products until 1 January 2005. In our view, India is obliged, by Article 70.8(a), to provide a legal mechanism for the filing of mailbox applications that provides a sound legal basis to preserve both the novelty of the inventions and the priority of the applications as of the relevant filing and priority dates. . . .

But what constitutes such a sound legal basis in Indian law? To answer this question, we must recall first an important general rule in the TRIPS Agreement. Article 1.1 of the TRIPS Agreement states, in pertinent part: "Members shall be free to determine the appropriate method of implementing the provisions of this Agreement within their own legal system and practice." Members, therefore, are free

continued

continued

to determine how best to meet their obligations under the TRIPS Agreement within the context of their own legal systems. And, as a Member, India is "free to determine the appropriate method of implementing" its obligations under the TRIPS Agreement within the context of its own legal system. . . .

India contends that it has established, through "administrative instructions," a "means" consistent with Article 70.8(a) of the TRIPS Agreement. According to India, these "administrative instructions" establish a mechanism that provides a sound legal basis to preserve the novelty of the inventions and the priority of the applications as of the relevant filing and priority dates consistent with Article 70.8(a) of the TRIPS Agreement. According to India, pursuant to these "administrative instructions," the Patent Office has been directed to store applications for patents for pharmaceutical and agricultural chemical products separately for future action pursuant to Article 70.8, and the Controller General of Patents Designs and Trademarks ("the Controller") has been instructed not to refer them to an examiner until 1 January 2005. According to India, these "administrative instructions" are legally valid in Indian law. . . .

Whatever their substance or their import, these "administrative instructions" were not the initial "means" chosen by the Government of India to meet India's obligations under Article 70.8(a) of the TRIPS Agreement. The Government of India's initial preference for establishing a "means" for filing mailbox applications under Article 70.8(a) was the Patents (Amendment) Ordinance (the "Ordinance") promulgated by the President of India on 31 December 1994. . . . In accordance with . . . India's Constitution, the Ordinance expired on 26 March 1995, six weeks after the reassembly of Parliament. This was followed by an unsuccessful effort to enact the Patents (Amendment) Bill 1995 to implement the contents of the Ordinance on a permanent basis. . . . From these actions, it is apparent that the Government of India initially considered the enactment of amending legislation to be necessary in order to implement its obligations under Article 70.8(a). However, India maintains that the "administrative instructions" issued in April 1995 effectively continued the mailbox system established by the Ordinance, thus obviating the need for a formal amendment to the Patents Act. . . .

Section 5(a) of the Patents Act provides that substances "intended for use, or capable of being used,

as food or as medicine or drug" are not patentable. "When the complete specification has been led in respect of an application for a patent," section 12(1) requires the Controller to refer that application and that specification to an examiner. Moreover, section 15(2) of the Patents Act states that the Controller "shall refuse" an application in respect of a substance that is not patentable. We agree with the Panel that these provisions of the Patents Act are mandatory. And, like the Panel, we are not persuaded that India's "administrative instructions" would prevail over the contradictory mandatory provisions of the Patents Act. We note also that, in issuing these "administrative instructions," the Government of India did not avail itself of the provisions . . . of the Patents Act, which allows the Central Government "to make rules for carrying out the provisions of [the] Act" or section 160 of the Patents Act, which requires that such rules be laid before each House of the Indian Parliament. We are told by India that such rulemaking was not required for the "administrative instructions" at issue here. But this, too, seems to be inconsistent with the mandatory provisions of the Patents Act.

We are not persuaded by India's explanation of these seeming contradictions. Accordingly, we are not persuaded that India's "administrative instructions" would survive a legal challenge under the Patents Act. And, consequently, we are not persuaded that India's "administrative instructions" provide a sound legal basis to preserve novelty of inventions and priority of applications as of the relevant filing and priority dates. . . .

Article 70.9 of the TRIPS Agreement reads:

> Where a product is the subject of a patent application in a Member in accordance with paragraph 8(a), exclusive marketing rights shall be granted, notwithstanding the provisions of Part VI, for a period of five years after obtaining marketing approval in that Member or until a product patent is granted or rejected in that Member, whichever period is shorter, provided that, subsequent to the entry into force of the WTO Agreement, a patent application has been filed and a patent granted for that product in another Member and marketing approval obtained in such other Member.

India argues that Article 70.9 establishes an obligation to grant exclusive marketing rights for a product that is the subject of a patent application

continued

continued

under Article 70.8(a) after all the other conditions specified in Article 70.9 have been fulfilled. . . . India maintains that the Panel's interpretation of Article 70.9 has the consequence that the transitional arrangements in Article 65 allow developing country Members to postpone legislative changes in all fields of technology except the most "sensitive" ones, pharmaceutical and agricultural chemical products. India claims that the Panel turned an obligation to take action in the future into an obligation to take action immediately. . . .

* * *

By its terms, Article 70.9 applies only in situations where a product patent application is filed under Article 70.8(a). . . . Article 70.9 specifically refers to Article 70.8(a), and they operate in tandem to provide a package of rights and obligations that apply during the transitional periods contemplated in Article 65. It is obvious, therefore, that both Article 70.8(a) and Article 70.9 are intended to apply as from the date of entry into force of the WTO Agreement.

India has an obligation to implement the provisions of Article 70.9 of the TRIPS Agreement effective as from the date of entry into force of the WTO Agreement, that is, 1 January 1995. India concedes that legislation is needed to implement this obliga-

tion. India has not enacted such legislation. To give meaning and effect to the rights and obligations under Article 70.9 of the TRIPS Agreement, such legislation should have been in effect since 1 January 1995.

For these reasons, we agree with the Panel that India should have had a mechanism in place to provide for the grant of exclusive marketing rights effective as from the date of entry into force of the WTO Agreement, and, therefore, we agree with the Panel that India is in violation of Article 70.9 of the TRIPS Agreement.

Decision. The Appellate Body upheld the Panel's conclusions that (a) India has not complied with its obligations under Article 70.8(a) to establish "a means" that adequately preserves novelty and priority in respect of applications for pharmaceutical and agricultural product patents during the transitional periods of the TRIPS Agreement; and (b) that India has not complied with its obligations under Article 70.9 of the TRIPS Agreement. Accordingly, the Appellate Body recommended that India bring its legal regime for patent protection of pharmaceutical and agricultural chemical products into conformity with India's obligations under Articles 70.8 and 70.9 of the TRIPS Agreement.

India has not been alone in imaginatively seeking to delay implementation deadlines. Faced with domestic legislatures as uncooperative as India's, many noncompliant developing countries have tried to extend these deadlines and to renegotiate aspects of the TRIPS Agreement. More developed countries have refused formal extensions or new negotiating mandates, but are widely understood to have agreed to exercise restraint in bringing cases to the WTO. If the delay brought by this restraint does not result in compliance, one can expect a torrent of WTO litigation.

The *Doha Declaration* on **TRIPS** and **Public Health**

Due to the exponential increase in the number of HIV/AIDS sufferers from developing countries, worldwide debate focused on the connection between the cost of pharmaceuticals and the wors-

ening public health of citizens from developing countries. In November 2001, ministers of WTO member countries agreed to approve what is known as the *Doha Declaration on the TRIPS Agreement and Public Health (Doha Declaration).* The final text of the *Doha Declaration* recognizes the "gravity of the public health problems afflicting many developing and least-developed countries especially those resulting from HIV/AIDS, tuberculosis, malaria and other epidemics" and the "need for TRIPS to be a wider national and international action to address these problems." The WTO ministers stressed the importance of the implementation and interpretation of the TRIPS Agreement in a manner that supports public health through improving access to existing medicines and formulating new medicines. The Declaration provides for the extension of a transition period until January 1, 2016, during which least-developed countries would be exempt from providing patent and trade secrets protection for pharmaceuticals. The least-developed countries were also permitted to retain their right to apply for further extensions.

One key issue that was not resolved at the time of the Doha Ministerial Conference involved the interpretation of Section 31 of TRIPS, which permitted governments to issue compulsory licenses to allow companies to make patented products or use a patented process under license without the consent of the patent owners, but only under certain conditions intended to protect the legitimate interests of the patent holder. Article 31(f) of TRIPS states that products made under compulsory licensing must be "predominantly for the supply of the domestic market." While this section directly applies to countries that have the resources or host companies that have the capability to manufacture these pharmaceuticals, it indirectly affects less developed countries not equipped to manufacture pharmaceuticals by effectively limiting their ability to import cheaper generic drugs from countries producing pharmaceuticals under the compulsory licensing provisions of TRIPS.

The *Doha Declaration* assigned to the TRIPS Council the task of determining whether to provide additional flexibility so that countries unable to produce pharmaceuticals domestically could import patented drugs made under compulsory licensing. In August 2003, the TRIPS Council decided to allow any WTO member country to export pharmaceuticals made under compulsory licenses. The TRIPS Council decision took the form of an "interim waiver" that allowed countries producing generic copies of patented products under compulsory licenses to export the products to eligible importing countries. The waiver is intended to last until the relevant portion of TRIPS is amended. All WTO member countries are permitted to import pharmaceuticals under the TRIPS council decision, however, twenty-three developed countries announced that they would voluntarily not avail themselves of this provision to import pharmaceuticals.

Government Policies in Emerging Nations

Industries in emerging nations are typically in great need of technological know-how. The significant research and development that leads to technological innovation is generally the product of substantial capital investment, long lead times, and a strong educational infrastructure. Less developed countries have a great shortage of these commodities. To industrialize, such nations—whether modern Brazil or postwar Japan—must rely on important technology.

Nevertheless, emerging countries have historically not tolerated unrestricted technology transfer. First, poorer nations typically husband hard currency reserves with great care. They permit the outflow of hard-currency royalties only for particularly attractive technologies. Such nations are understandably reluctant to squander foreign exchange so that their citizens may have a higher-quality soft drink. And such nations often severely restrict or prohibit trademark royalties that are not combined with a right to use accompanying technology. Indeed, the central banks of these countries will sometimes unilaterally restrict remittances of hard-currency royalty payments. Peru, for instance, froze all such hard-currency royalty remittances without warning during the late 1980s and early 1990s. Whenever possible, the intellectual property owner should make firm arrangements with the relevant government authorities in advance about royalty arrangements.

One way for the foreign owner to avoid this repugnance to hard-currency royalties is to raise the price of production equipment, input materials, or other goods that the licensee is contractually obligated to purchase from the owner to produce the end product. In more comprehensive arrangements, the licensee can accept a lower commission for distributing the end product in the host country, or perform assembly or other manufacturing functions for other goods at a reduced rate. In these ways, the owner obtains the same financial yield without having any part of the money placed in the royalty category. When these solutions do not lead to the same return, the owner can consider deferring royalties during the initial years of the agreement until the licensee can earn substantial hard currency through exports and use those earnings to pay the owner.

Second, the host country may be concerned about the anticompetitive effects of a licensing agreement. If the foreign entity is not forced to license the technology to local competitors, it might enjoy a local monopoly on the product. If so, one would expect that its pricing policies would reflect its monopolistic market position, to the detriment of the local economy. Largely based on the strength of this anticompetitive rationale, the *Andean Common Market* issued its Decision 220, which, *inter alia,* forbade provisions in technology transfer agreements that (1) attempted to fix the price of goods manufactured with the licensed technology, (2) prohibited the licensee from using competing technologies, (3) required the use of goods sold by the technology owner, which in turn blocked one of the methods for avoiding restrictions on royalties, or (4) limited the volume of end products manufactured with the technology.

Third, the local government might simply wish to obtain the long-term benefits of the technology for its own nationals by wresting control of it from foreign hands. This objective is often justified with the argument that royalties are redundant because the cost of technology should be included in the cost of the products sold. In the context of trademarks, this argument has been extended to say that, because trademarks do not produce value in and of themselves, trademark royalties are inherently exploitative. These arguments, of course, disregard the benefits of encouraging technological innovation or of creating a reputation for quality in a trademark.

If local entrepreneurs are given an opportunity to employ foreign technology, they might become dominant not only in the local economy but against the original licensor throughout the world. The Japanese success in the period after World War II is largely attributable to an ability to cause the transfer of technology. The Japanese philosophy was essentially that a transfer of technology contract is a "sale" rather than a temporary lease of the technology. At the end of the term of the license, the licensee should be free to use the technology.

This former Japanese philosophy was followed by Brazil's technology transfer watchdog, the National Institute of Industrial Policy (INPI). Regardless of what a technology agreement stated, INPI regarded a technology transfer agreement as a sale of the technology rather than a license. In other words, at the end of the term the Brazilian licensee could, in INPI's eyes, freely use the technology to make end products for the local Brazilian market or for *export into the technology owner's home market.*

Unfortunately for Brazil, technology owners had also learned a lot from the Japanese appropriation of technology in the postwar era. The Brazilian policy did little more than catch a few uninitiated owners unaware. Most technology owners did not repeat the error of their postwar counterparts and merely steered clear of Brazil, inhibiting that nation's industrial development. In time, INPI changed its approach.

Prior to TRIPS, many nations used these philosophical foundations to restrict license terms and cap royalty payments, all to the benefit of local licensees. In India, for example, licenses once could not last longer than eight years—and in many types of technologies, less than that. In Colombia, all agreements had to be approved by the Royalties Committee, which allowed agreements to last only three to five years. In both nations, royalties were limited to a percentage cap. Another outgrowth of this philosophy is that local subsidiaries are sometimes forbidden to send royalty payments home. This policy assures that the foreign technology owner must part with its technology to a locally controlled entity in order to pull any royalties out of the nation.

Over time, these practices have damaged local developing economies as much as the potential licensors, who now simply avoid such economies as too dangerous for licensing. It was this change in attitude—which threatened to leave emerging nations without IPR and consequently at a grave competitive disadvantage—that largely persuaded developing countries to sign TRIPS.

Policies Influenced by Marxist Ideology

Marxist theory has historically complicated intellectual property policy in communist countries. Marxism regards intellectual innovation as a product of society that is manifested through individuals. Because the society is the true author of the creation, the individual should have no independent right to the profits from the creation—all such benefits should be owned by the state. Communist intellectual property regulation has greatly restricted the monetary benefits individuals receive from their inventions and has discouraged the recognition of compensable IPRs.

These policies had negative effects on innovation in communist nations. To be blunt, individuals are far more likely to be innovative if they will grow rich as a result of their innovation; few individuals are motivated to be innovative for the greater good of the homeland. The disastrous economic consequences of Marxist disincentives eventually caused communist governments to develop regulatory schemes that reward individual initiative while bowing to Marxist tradition. For instance, the Chinese have afforded certain inventions eligibility for *certificates of authorship.* Although the ownership right in the invention remains in theory in the state, the inventors are entitled to a monetary award by virtue of their certificate of authorship. The Chinese have grown more comfortable with permitting "collective" bodies, such as corporations—even if owned by few individuals—to obtain trademark and other intellectual property protection.

As on other subjects, different views on the protection of intellectual property are prevalent among the remaining Marxist countries. Nevertheless, the few nations that remain in the Marxist camp are devising methods that, while paying homage to tradition, protect the benefits to the individual inventors that are so necessary to technological innovation.

Attitudes in Developed Nations

National chauvinism does not end once a country becomes developed. The tendencies of licensing laws to favor local licensees persist in developed countries. In many high-technology electronic fields, for instance, European nations have been well behind U.S. firms. Not coincidentally, significant disputes have arisen between the *European Telecommunication Standards Institute* (ETSI)—which must certify all electronic products in the European market for safety and compatibility purposes—and U.S. computer hardware manufacturers. Purportedly to assist its technical research efforts, ETSI sought to require all firms seeking to sell equipment in Europe to sign an "undertaking" agreeing to grant licenses to any other merchant for patented technology necessary to implement ETSI standards. U.S. manufacturers immediately complained, noting that this presented them with the Hobson's choice of agreeing to forego potential licensing income or being excluded from the European market. The U.S. government soon stepped in on behalf of its manufacturers, and the dispute turned into a nation-against-nation fight.

As local licensees become more capable of defending their own interests, however, the cloak of protectionism does not wear as well. More important, as local enterprises become more sophisticated, they require greater amounts of IPR. The same local enterprises that once may have relied on government intervention to procure more favorable terms become impatient at the delays and obstacles inherent in having the government involved in the transfer of much needed technology.

Perhaps the clearest example of this evolution is the transformation of Japan's policy toward technology licensing over the past several decades. Through the 1960s, every technology transfer agreement required governmental approval. As discussed previously, the Japanese government ministries used this process to negotiate a better deal for the Japanese licensees than the licensees had been able to do in their own negotiations. The Japanese government could do this because under its system it could simply prevent a technology transfer agreement by taking no action on a request for approval.

As Japan became an economic powerhouse, however, this system increasingly became an impediment to Japanese industrialists. Even today, Japan is a net importer of technology; in light of the vastly increased number of such agreements and the need for greater speed in international transactions, the approval process grew to be a hindrance. Moreover, in light of the great economic strength of Japanese corporations, the pro-Japan function of government approval had become archaic. And by the 1970s, Japan certainly had no difficulty in conserving foreign exchange reserves. To accommodate these new realities, the Japanese system was transformed in the late 1970s to *notification* only. The government had a number of days within which to object to an approval for a technology transfer agreement; if it took no action, the agreement was approved.

This trend is also being reflected in other newly developed countries such as South Korea. In cases in which the need for protection of fledgling domestic enterprises has waned and the need for additional technology has waxed, the more restrictive policies relating to technology transfer tend to be eased.

Continuing TRIPS Turmoil on Biodiversity

Beginning in 1999, the TRIPS Council commenced its review of Article 27.3 of TRIPS that relates to biotechnological inventions. Article 27.3

of TRIPS permits countries to *exclude* plants, animals, and biological processes from patent protection (although microorganisms and non-biological and microbiological processes are eligible for patents). Article 27.3(b), however, requires member countries to provide for the protection of plant varieties either by patents or through a system created specifically for that purpose (*sui generis*), or a combination of both.

The TRIPS Council's discussions include a variety of controversial topics. First, how should the existing TRIPS provisions on the patentability or non-patentability of plant and animal inventions actually be and should these provisions be modified. Second, the Council addressed the interpretation of effective protection for new plant varieties, including a discussion on the effects of other laws such as the *International Union for the Protection of New Variety of Plants*. Third, it focused on the handling of certain moral and ethical issues such as the extent to which invented life forms shall be eligible for patent protection. Finally, the Council considered the issue of traditional knowledge and genetic material, and the rights of communities or countries where this knowledge or genetic material originates.

A key topic under consideration by the TRIPS Council is whether there exists a conflict between TRIPS and the UN *Convention on Biological Diversity* (CBD). Those who argue that a conflict exists claim that while the CBD appears to grant sovereignty in biological resources to the countries that possess them, TRIPS permits these resources to be patented. Consequently, there is currently a dispute as to whether rights and benefits given to the resource holders under the CBD are taken away by TRIPS.

In November 2001, the *Doha Declaration* linked the issues of biotechnology, biodiversity, and traditional knowledge and declared that further work by the TRIPS Council on these reviews should be guided by the TRIPS objectives and principles and must take development into account.

Since the Doha Ministerial Conference, a number of proposals have been submitted for dealing with these complex subjects on biodiversity. On October 17, 2002, the EU submitted a paper that includes a proposal to examine the requirement that patent applicants disclose the origin of genetic material. Switzerland submitted a proposal on May 28, 2003, suggesting an amendment to WIPO's *Patent Cooperation Treaty*, which in essence would require domestic law to ask patent applicants to disclose the origins of genetic resources and traditional knowledge. Under this proposal, a failure to disclose required information could delay the grant of patent protection or affect its validity.

Similar proposals have been submitted by the nations that are home to the biological resources. A paper submitted by Brazil, Cuba, Ecuador, India, Peru, and Venezuela in June 2003 develops earlier proposals on disclosure of the origins of biological resources and traditional knowledge, "prior informed consent" for exploitation, and equitable benefit sharing. Under this proposal, the TRIPS section on biodiversity will be amended to make disclosure of the origins of genetic resources obligatory. Also in June 2003, the African Group submitted a paper that proposes to prohibit the patenting of all life forms (plants, animals, and microorganisms) and prefers *sui generis* protection for plant varieties to preserve farmers and breeders rights to use and share harvested seeds. This paper recommends disclosure obligations similar to that submitted on June 24, 2003, to the TRIPS Council.

Several developed countries—the owners of the intellectual property that creates these medical improvements—have opposed additional requirements to disclose traditional knowledge, the source of genetic material, and information on prior informed consent and benefit sharing. These countries argue that further legislation on these subjects is not necessary as these issues could be adequately addressed in contractual agreements between the researching entities and the communities that own these genetic materials and traditional knowledge.

The outcome of all these proposals remains to be seen.

NONENFORCEMENT OF IPR LAWS

As seen throughout this book, the varying attitudes of nations are generally reflected in the text of their laws. In the IPR context, however, TRIPS now mandates what each country's laws must say; attitudes in this context are now more accurately reflected in how the words of these laws are actually enforced.

It is one thing to enact laws as TRIPS requires and quite another to enforce them. A number of countries—particularly in Asia, Latin America,

Africa, and the Middle East—have a panoply of laws designed to protect domestic and foreign IPR, but fail to enforce the laws or do not have adequate procedures to enable foreign parties to take advantage of the laws. After NAFTA, for example, Mexico adopted most internationally accepted standards with respect to IPR. To this day, however, Mexico City streets are littered with pirated music and videos because Mexico has not devoted many of its scarce resources to enforcing those laws.

Still others enforce their laws in a discriminatory fashion so that foreign parties do not have confidence that their rights will be vindicated against clear infringement. Indeed, some nations tacitly encourage piracy of such IPR by their citizens. In South Korea, the government once published details of pharmaceutical and pesticide formulations to facilitate their copying by locals. In China, after a great deal of prodding from developed nations, the Chinese government enacted modern copyright infringement legislation and even created special IPR tribunals. But in the meantime, China allowed construction of twenty-six compact disk plants with the capacity to manufacture over fifty million compact disks a year—despite the fact that China has a relatively small number of consumers who can purchase CDs and that virtually no Western companies have licensed the reproduction of their products in China. A particularly flagrant violation occurred in 1994, when a relative of the Chinese premier opened a huge laser disk and compact disk factory with the capacity to manufacture 5.5 million CDs and 1.5 million laser disks a year. Despite open violations of the ostensible IPR protection laws, Chinese authorities refused to permit even an inspection of the facility by Westerners.

This piracy is very big business. The Motion Picture Association of America estimates that the American movie industry alone loses $150 million a year due to piracy. In recent years, the U.S. government and leaders of its domestic "high-tech" and entertainment industries have focused a great deal of attention on the interrelation between the quality of foreign intellectual property protection and the vitality of U.S. trade in foreign countries and, indeed, the U.S. domestic market. Many international firms from developed nations joined to form the *International Counterfeiting Coalition* to pressure governments into enforcing IPR laws.

At the urging of these industry groups, the U.S. government has become active in promoting the adoption and effective enforcement of intellectual property laws by its various trading partners. As noted previously, the TRIPS Agreement requires WTO countries to ensure that IPR laws are enforced and to call for the seizure of goods infringing upon IPR rights; a failure to enforce such laws now can give rise to a WTO trade proceeding. Taiwan, once an internationally notorious haven of piracy, largely eliminated piracy after the United States was on the verge of enacting retaliatory tariffs on Taiwanese products. When the United States threatened to block hundreds of millions of Brazilian products from entering the United States, the government of Brazil agreed to a strict timetable for implementing patent and copyright reforms. U.S. movie industry officials, in partnership with the U.S. government, have used the threat of *Super 301* trade proceedings against Italian products to prod Italian officials into more diligent enforcement of its copyright laws. And, prior to China's accession into the WTO in December 2001, the United States was instrumental in preventing China from being admitted into the WTO as long as it continued to be an IPR outlaw. The following case illustrates that this relentless pressure has resulted in some enforcement even in the People's Republic of China.

THE MECHANICS OF IPR TRANSFER REGULATIONS

Three basic types of regulatory schemes provide the format for IPR transfer agreements. They range from preapproval to notification–registration to no regulation. The third scheme is obviously the most beneficial to the U.S. entrepreneur. Because the absence of law is somewhat uninteresting to one studying legal issues, however, the text focuses on the preapproval and registration–notification systems in selected countries.

Prior-Approval Schemes

The requirement of substantive prior approval from a government agency is the more intrusive government regulatory scheme and is indicative of a relatively protectionist government policy. The degree to which it intrudes on private enterprise

Walt Disney Co. v. Beijing Publishing Press
Zhongjing zhichu No. 141 (1994)
Beijing First Intermediate Court

BACKGROUND AND FACTS

Beijing Publishing Press, Beijing Children's Publishing Press, and the Beijing Distribution Office of New World Bookstore Distribution Center published and distributed a series of books called *Collection of Disney Moral Tales*. The collection included reproductions of many Disney cartoon characters, although these Chinese firms had not received authorization from the copyright holder, the Walt Disney Company. Disney brought action in Chinese court against the Chinese entities for infringement of copyright.

Beijing Publishing Press and its corporate affiliate, Children's Press, countered that use rights for the cartoon likenesses had been obtained through a "Contract for Assignment of Simplified Versions" executed with Maxwell Communications Corporation plc. Maxwell had since gone bankrupt.

Beijing Publishing Press and Children's Press further relied on an agreement with Maxworld (China) Publishing Corp., Ltd., a joint venture between Children's Press and Maxwell, under certification that the foreign party had confirmed publishing rights to the collection. Beijing Publishing Press and Children's Press took the view that, in light of this latter agreement, they had no obligation to contact the foreign party regarding copyright matters. They brought in Maxwell as a third party defendant.

Beijing Distribution Office asserted that it was merely a distributor, not a publisher, and was under no obligation to investigate the legality of copyright of books and periodicals.

CHIEF JUDGE SU CHI

[P]rocedures for registration of copyright for the Mickey Mouse likeness were completed . . . in the United States, and the copyright belonged to the Disney Company. The Beijing Publishing Press, in each of August 1991, November 1992 and November 1993, printed and published "Bambi," "Dumbo," "101 Dalmatians," "Alice in Wonderland," "Lady and the Tramp," "Sleeping Beauty," "Cinderella," "Snow White," and "Peter Pan" in which the cartoon likeness were exactly the same as those appearing in the original versions provided by the plaintiffs. . . .

The Disney Company and the Maxwell Company signed an agreement on 19 August 1987 which provided: "Disney Company licenses to Maxwell Company exclusive rights to publish and sell within China Chinese-language publications based on Disney World characters. The license granted under this License Agreement may not be assigned by the Licensees to any third party". . . . [T]he Maxwell Company signed the "Contract for Assignment of Simplified Versions" with the Children's Press on 21 March 1991, which contract provided: "Under authorization from the Disney Company, the Maxwell Company possesses an exclusive right to publish Chinese language versions of Disney children's reading materials and to represent the Disney Company in regard to copyright trading of such publications. Maxwell Company assigns the authorization from the Disney Company to the Children's Press." On the same day, the Children's Press and the Maxworld Company, in order to implement the "Contract for Assignment of Simplified Versions," signed an agreement whereby the Children's Press entrusted the Maxworld Company to finalize, arrange composition of, and make printing plates for and of the text of Disney children's reading materials. . . . Maxworld also undertook to provide to the Children's Press confirmation by the foreign party of the copyright contract relating to the Disney Collection, which would serve as the legal basis for possession within China of the copyright by the Children's Press. Following this, the Maxworld Company obtained film costs for the Collection in the amount of RMB 69,750 yuan, which, after deducting costs of RMB 59,312.40 yuan, resulted in a profit of RMB 10,437.60 yuan.

On 11 March 1992, the Children's Press delivered the "Contract for Assignment of Simplified Versions" to the Beijing Municipal Copyright Authority for examination and approval. Because no authorization had been issued by the Disney Company, this Authority could not complete registration procedures. No supplemental registration procedures were ever completed by the Children's Press.

[T]he Beijing Publishing Press and the Beijing Distribution Office signed a working agreement on 1 February 1991 which provided . . . "Where it publishes foreign products and books, the publishing press shall enter into a publishing contract with the copyright owner and shall register the contract with

continued

continued

the Copyright Registration Authority. After obtaining a registration number, the book shall be passed to the Beijing Distribution Office for pre-selling and publication. Failing this, the publishing press shall be responsible for any disputes that may arise regarding publication, distribution and selling of foreign copyrighted materials. . . ."

After entry into force of the 17 March 1992 Sino–U.S. Memorandum of Understanding, the Beijing Publishing Press published 118,200 volumes of the Collection, of which it published 41,779 volumes on its own, stored 33,341 volumes, and entrusted the Beijing Distribution Office to distribute 43,080 volumes . . . gross profits were RMB 5,999.04 yuan. . . .

This Court, based on the provisions of the Sino–U.S. Memorandum of Understanding, concludes that, effective 17 March 1992, products of United States nationals have received the protection of Chinese law. Disney Company, in regard to the cartoon likeness germane to this matter—Mickey Mouse, Cinderella, Snow White, Peter Pan, Bambi, Dumbo, 101 Dalmations, Alice, Lady, etc.—enjoys copyright protection. Absent authorization by the Disney Company, commercial use of these cartoon likenesses constitutes infringement.

Although the Disney Company had previously authorized the Maxwell Company to publish and print an album of cartoon likenesses in China, it never authorized the Maxwell Company to assign such publishing and printing rights to third parties. Accordingly, assignment by the Maxwell Company of its publishing and printing rights in respect of these products . . . to the Children's Press constitutes, on the one hand, an infringement of Disney's rights and, on the other hand, is a fraud on the Children's Press. The Contract by which this assignment was made is void as a matter of law.

From a legal perspective, the Maxwell Company's use of fraudulent means to sign the "Contract for Assignment of Simplified Versions" was the main cause of this infringement of rights. . . . [C]onsidering that the Maxwell Company became bankrupt in July 1993, this Court will not offer any opinion regarding the liability of the Maxwell Company in this matter.

That the Children's Press, without having first investigated whether the Maxwell Company had any right to assign publication rights to the Disney Company products, nonetheless concluded a publishing agreement with it, was extremely reckless. [In a publication of] the State Copyright Administration, . . .

there is a provision as follows: "Effective 1 March 1988, any unit or individual entering into publishing trading contract with Taiwan, Hong Kong or Macao, and regardless of whether it provides for licensing out of copyrights or for authorizing use or for taking assignment of authorizations, shall be submitted to the Copyright Administration Authority for review and registration. Where a contract has not been reviewed and registered, it shall, prior to 1 March 1990, be submitted to the review and registration authority in accordance with procedures. Contracts not reviewed and registered shall be void."

The Children's Press, after being refused permission by the relevant department of the State Copyright Administration to register this contract on the ground that it could show no legal proof of copyright, did not conduct any inquiry, and did not implement registration procedures in accordance with relevant national legislation, and proceeded to publish picture albums containing likenesses of Disney cartoon characters. That it was aware it was at fault in so doing is clear. Since the Children's Press is not an independent legal person, its liability shall be borne by the Beijing Press. . . . Both of the . . . occasions on which the Beijing Publishing Press published the products occur following entry into force of the Sino–U.S. Memorandum of Understanding, and constituted infringement for which the Beijing Publishing Press should assume responsibility.

The Beijing Distribution Office participated in marketing the second and third publications by the Beijing Publishing Press of the Collection. In accordance with . . . "Implementing Regulations of the People's Republic of China on the Law of Authorship Rights," marketing, regardless of whether it takes the form of "consignment sales" or "distribution" is a form of publishing. . . . A publisher has a legal responsibility to know whether or not the publications it handles are legally defective. The cooperative agreement signed by the Beijing Distribution Office and the Beijing Publishing Press provides that, where foreign products or books are published, the Beijing Publishing Press and the owner of the copyright shall sign a publishing agreement and register it with the Copyright Administration Authority. . . . In fact, whether or not the Beijing Distribution Office ever obtained a registration number from the Copyright Administration Authority was not investigated. This demonstrates clearly that the Beijing Distribution Office, at the time it signed the agreement, took

continued

continued

notice of the regulations of relevant State departments but did not implement them. We hold that the Beijing Distribution Office was aware of its fault in this regard and that it should accept responsibility for infringement in publishing the infringed books. . . .

This Court is of the view that the profits or losses of actual business operations are not always the same as the illegal benefits it can obtain. Profits, as a legal matter, should be determined based on the total amount made by the Beijing Publishing Press from publication of infringed works minus reasonable costs (of printing and for payment of taxes). At the same time, the amount payable to the plaintiff as compensation should be this amount plus reasonable bank interest and reasonable fees of the plaintiff incurred in the course of prosecuting this lawsuit.

Decision. The Beijing First Intermediate Court entered an order providing, among other things, that (1) Beijing Publishing Press and the Beijing Distribution Office should cease all publication and distribution of the *Collection of Disney Moral Tales* and that all volumes in their possession should be confiscated, along with the colored films thereof; (2) Beijing Publishing Press should make a public apology to the Walt Disney Company in a Chinese newspaper published and printed throughout China; (3) Beijing Publishing Press should make a one-time compensation payment to the Disney Company of RMB 227,094.14 yuan and pay a fine of RMB 50,000 yuan; (4) RMB 5,000.04 yuan in illegal income earned by the Beijing Distribution Office should be confiscated; and (5) the defendants should bear RMB 40,000 yuan of Disney's attorneys' fees.

---

depends largely on the attitude and mandate of the relevant regulatory agencies.

In India, for example, licensing agreements must be approved by the Indian Foreign Investment Board. But before the board can give that approval, it is required to seek the opinion of each governmental ministry that may be concerned with the product involved. Depending on the product, this process can include quite a number of agencies. Moreover, the guidelines for approval are quite demanding. The Indian licensee should be free to sublicense the technical know-how to local Indian companies, sometimes eviscerating the licensor's nondisclosure provisions. Further, the Indian government forbids payment of a minimum guaranteed royalty to a foreign licensor. And the Indian party to the agreement should be able to export the products it makes with the license—the greatest fear of the licensor that fears competition from the licensee in other markets.

Most prior-approval schemes are not so detailed in their delegation of authority. Instead, the laws are written in general terms with broad interpretive powers vested in the bureaucracy. Some nations call for the exercise of this discretion by giving government officials a broad range of reasons for disapproving a transfer of technology. As noted earlier, the Royalties Committee in Colombia could refuse to register a technology transfer agreement if the proposed license continued confiden-

tiality obligations after its term, or if the term extended for more than three to five years.

Other countries have taken an approach that depends even more on discretion: All transfer-of-technology agreements are prohibited unless a specific reason can be found for them to be permitted. The Japanese *gensoku kinshi* (prohibited in principle) system was a good example. In this system, the principal variable was not any doctrine of law, but bureaucratic practice over time that decided what transactions should be exempted from the presumption of prohibition. The key "legal" insight to the foreign investor would come from those familiar with the personalities administering the process.

These discretionary systems are well adapted to reject requests for technology transfers by mere delay. In its heyday, the Japanese approval mechanism once held up a request for a technology transfer by Texas Instruments, Inc. to a proposed Texas Instruments subsidiary in Japan for more than four years. While Texas Instruments was stalemated, Japanese competitors were able to develop technologies that would help them combat the Americans once they arrived. And many companies not as dogged as Texas Instruments were simply driven away by delay.

Delay is also used as a weapon in technology transfers that require a patent. For instance, in some Latin American countries, the patent process sometimes took eight years from start to finish.

During that entire period, all fees payable to the owner of the patent were held up.

Notification–Registration Schemes

A notification or registration system is more open to technological transfer. The Japanese *gensoku kinshi* (prohibited in principle) system was transformed over time to the *gensoku jiyu* (free in principle) system. Similar instances may be found in South Korea, Venezuela, and Mexico, where prior-approval schemes have been replaced by a simple registration procedure. Countries with a general system of notification often make exceptions for areas of heightened concern, such as technology agreements between foreign companies and their controlled subsidiaries. Because of the patent inequality in bargaining position in such situations, many countries with a notification–registration system will still require specific approval of technology transfer agreements between such companies.

A danger in notification–registration countries is that some provisions of a registered contract might not be enforceable under those countries' laws. Thus, license royalties in a given contract might be retroactively ruled excessive and recharacterized as taxable income to the foreign company. Indeed, in some Chinese special economic zones, the foreign investor must compensate the local licensee for losses incurred in sales of products manufactured by the transferred technology.

A significant danger in any approval or notification system is that the government bureaucracy can make an unauthorized disclosure of the foreign party's intellectual property. Some commentators have suggested that, notwithstanding its advanced new laws, Mexico is not acquiring the most modern industrial technology because foreign investors do not wish to risk piracy of their IPRs. In Japan, foreign investors cast a wary eye on the Japanese government's continuing requirements for specificity in describing transferred technology even under a notification system. Although Japanese authorities respond that such information is necessary for statistical purposes, and that any disclosure by a government official could lead to criminal sanctions, foreign investors remain concerned about possible leaks from government ministries to Japanese firms.

A relevant provision of U.S. trade law is Section 337 of the *Tariff Act,* which prohibits, among other things, the importation of articles that infringe a U.S. patent, trademark, or copyright. For example, if someone tries to import "fake" Rolex watches into the United States from a country that does not enforce its IPR laws, the Rolex trademark holder may seek to exclude the fakes through Section 337. The International Trade Commission (ITC) carries out investigations under this provision upon the filing of a complaint by the trademark holder or by the ITC on its own initiative. If the ITC determines that an article is being imported in violation of Section 337, U.S. Customs may stop the article from entering the United States or, upon subsequent violation, the property may be seized and forfeited to the U.S. government. Proof of injury is not required in order to block the imported items. After the TRIPS was accepted by other nations effective in 1995, Congress amended Section 337 in the *Uruguay Round Agreement Act* to respond to concerns about allegedly discriminating aspects of the provision.

THE GRAY MARKET

As noted earlier, the prospective U.S. licensor fears that the IPR that it licenses abroad may come back into its home market to compete with the licensor's goods. After a license's anticompetition restrictions expire, the licensee might take the product it makes with the IPR and invade the U.S. market. But even before that occurs, a licensor must contemplate the danger that a completely unrelated party—with whom the licensor has no anticompetition agreement—will purchase the licensed product and import it back into the United States. This importation of merchandise produced and sold abroad and then imported back into the United States for sale in competition with the U.S. trademark owner is referred to as the *gray market* or *parallel trade.* The products imported back are *gray market goods* or *parallel imports.*

The Nature of the Problem

The gray market principally threatens the U.S. licensor if the product is sold at a lower price abroad than in the United States, which can happen for a variety of reasons. The U.S. licensor might have established such a reputation of quality in the U.S. market that it can command a substantial premium for its product there. But before its product builds a similar reputation abroad, the licensor will not be able to charge a similar premium. In the meantime, the gray marketer could simply purchase the goods abroad more cheaply, transport them back to the United States, and place them in direct competition with the U.S. licensor.

The gray market is also stimulated by international currency fluctuations. Relative currency values vary minute by minute during each business day. Retailers and wholesalers of goods are much slower to react, however. Thus, upon a negative movement by, say, the Mexican peso, a nimble arbitrageur can purchase the U.S. product in Mexico at a price that is a bargain in U.S. dollars.

Holders of trademarks are opposed to the gray marketers. They note that some products sold abroad under their trademarks are actually different from the domestic products. For instance, soft drinks sold in the Far East are sweetened more than their U.S. counterparts. U.S. licensors argue that sale of the foreign product in the United States could have a detrimental impact on the reputation of their domestic product.

U.S. licensors also argue that gray marketers receive a "free ride" on their U.S. marketing efforts. They point out that a substantial investment in time, effort, and capital is required to develop the sort of reputation that commands a premium in the United States market. Consequently, they argue, the gray marketer who comes in without making any payment to the U.S. trademark holder is stealing some of the return on the holder's investment.

Consumers, on the other hand, are generally delighted by the gray market. It often enables them to obtain goods of the same or comparable quality as well-known brands at a lower price. Thus, U.S. consumer advocates and merchandise retailers favor the gray market.

Resolution of the Dispute

In this hotly debated area, courts have gone in a variety of directions. Moreover, national legislatures, including the U.S. Congress, are often called upon to provide assistance to one side or the other in the struggle.

Under one view, the trademark holder has no right to control goods after it sells them in commerce. After such a sale, the trademark holder has *exhausted* its control, and once its control has been exhausted, the trademark holder cannot complain of competition by others. The exhaustion doctrine would create a wide-open gray market.

Courts seem to have accepted the proposition, however, that if a gray market product is so different as to call into question the quality of the domestic product, the licensor should be granted relief, especially if the seller of the domestic product has independently developed goodwill in its home country. Justice Oliver Wendell Holmes wrote one of the opinions that formed the foundation for analysis in this area.

In situations with relatively little possibility of confusion, in which the quality of the gray market product is indistinguishable from the domestic product, U.S. courts have not been solicitous of the rights of licensors. In such cases, courts prize the benefits of price competition over concerns about a free ride for the gray marketer. More recent Supreme Court cases confirm this trend favoring gray market forces where there is little chance of confusion. In *K Mart Corp. v. Cartier, Inc.,* 486 U.S. 281 (1988), the U.S. Supreme Court allowed the entry of gray market imports if the foreign manufacturer and the domestic trademark owner are subject to common control.

Recently, the European Court of Justice has charted a different course. In the cases of *Sebago Inc. v. GB Unic, SA,* [1999] E.T.M.R. 681 and *Silhouette International Schmied GmbH & Co. KG v. Hartlauer Handelsgesellschaft mbH,* [1999] E.C.R. 1–4799, the ECJ interpreted the EU's Trademark Directive as permitting reimport from one Union country to another, but forbidding reimport from other countries into the European Union. This "regional trademark exhaustion" principle was calculated to protect free access to markets within the Union while protecting the integrity of the common market from nonmembers.

Paradoxically, in its *Maglite* advisory opinion of December 3, 1997, [1997] EFTA Court Report 197, the court of the European Free Trade Association—to which a number of EU members belong—interpreted the very same Trademark Directive to require "international exhaustion"—that is, free reimport whether or not there was a danger of confusion. In doing so, the EFTA court emphasized the importance of promoting free trade.

The parallel import issue, which most believe was left open in the TRIPS Agreement—although some disagree even there—will probably be ultimately resolved in the context of the WTO.

A. Bourjois & Co. v. Katzel
360 U.S. 689 (1923)
United States Supreme Court

BACKGROUND AND FACTS

A French company with a business in the U.S. sold the U.S. business to the U.S. company, A. Bourjois & Co., along with their trademark for face powder. A. Bourjois reregistered the trademark and continued with the face powder business, using the same box and trademark for the product. Katzel bought a quantity of the same powder in France and sold it in the U.S. in boxes closely resembling the A. Bourjois boxes, but with their own labels. The plaintiff, A. Bourjois, sued for copyright infringement.

JUSTICE HOLMES

In 1913 A. Bourjois & Cie., E. Wertheimer & Cie., Successeurs, doing business in France and also in the United States, sold the plaintiff for a large sum their business in the United States, with their good will and their trade marks registered in the Patent Office. The latter related particularly to face powder, and included the above words. The plaintiff since its purchase has registered them again and goes on with the business that it bought, using substantially the same form of box and label as its predecessors and importing its face powder from France. It uses care in selecting colors suitable for the American market, in packing and in keeping up the standard, and has spent much money in advertising, so that the business has grown very great and the labels have come to be understood by the public here as meaning goods coming from the plaintiff. The boxes have upon their backs: "Trade Marks Reg. U.S. Pat. Off. Made in France—Packed in the U.S.A. by A. Bourjois & Co., Inc., of New York, Succ'rs. in the U.S. of A. Bourjois & Cie., and E. Wertheimer & Cie."

The defendant, finding that the rate of exchange enabled her to do so at a profit, bought a large quantity of the same powder in France and is selling it here in the French boxes which closely resemble those used by the plaintiff except that they have not

the last quoted statement on the backs, and that the label reads, "Poudre de Riz de Java," whereas the plaintiff has found it advisable to strike out the suggestion of rice powder and has "Poudre Java" instead. There is no question that the defendant infringes the plaintiff's rights unless the fact that her boxes and powder are the genuine product of the French concern gives her a right to sell them in the present form.

After the sale the French manufacturers could not have come to the United States and have used their old marks in competition with the plaintiff. . . . If for the purpose of evading the effect of the transfer, it has arranged with the defendant that she should sell with the old label, we suppose that no one would doubt that the contrivance must fail. There is no such conspiracy here, but, apart from the opening of a door to one, the vendors could not convey their goods free from the restriction to which the vendors were subject. . . . It deals with a delicate matter that may be of great value but that easily is destroyed, and therefore should be protected with corresponding care. It is said that the trade mark here is that of the French house and truly indicates the origin of the goods. But that is not accurate. It is the trade mark of the plaintiff only in the United States and indicates in law, and, it is found, by public understanding, that the goods come from the plaintiff although not made by it. It was sold and could only be sold with the good will of the business that the plaintiff bought. It takes the reputation of the plaintiff upon the character of the goods.

Decision.   The plaintiff sought a preliminary injunction restraining the defendant from infringing its copyrights. The U.S. Supreme Court reversed the decision of the U.S. Court of Appeals not to grant such a preliminary injunction.

FRANCHISING: LICENSING OUTSIDE THE TECHNOLOGICAL CONTEXT

Franchising seldom involves technological complexity. It is an arrangement in which the licensor permits the licensee to sell certain goods under the

licensor's trademark or service mark under a franchising agreement. To prevent devaluation of its trademark, the licensor will typically condition its use on the licensee's observance of certain quality standards. Thus, a Muscovite who wishes to open a McDonald's restaurant will contract with McDonald's Corporation for a franchise; a condition of the franchise will likely be that the franchisee follow specified processes in cooking hamburgers.

Several observations may be made about franchises. First, although franchising seldom involves significant patent law or other technological issues, many of the considerations noted in other licensing contexts apply with equal force. The franchiser will often wish to condition retention of the franchise on the franchisee meeting defined marketing quotas. The franchisee will attempt to obtain exclusive rights within some geographic area, while the franchiser will resist granting such rights or will try to narrow the geographic area. Franchisers must make the same balancing considerations as other licensors in arriving at an appropriate royalty level. And the duration of the franchise will be hotly disputed.

Second, although patent law protection is generally not a significant issue in franchising, trademark protection is. Quite often, the most valuable asset that the franchisee purchases is the right to use the franchiser's good name and trademarks on what are otherwise local products. If trademark protection or enforcement is lax in the local jurisdiction, the value of the franchise accordingly declines.

Third, as discussed in the succeeding chapter on antitrust and competition laws, *competition* laws have greatly affected a number of these issues. For instance, the European Commission has invalidated franchisers' *quality assurance* provisions when they were deemed unduly restrictive of the franchisee's ability to compete. Franchisers must also be concerned about the application of competition laws to *tied-purchase* clauses that require the franchisee to buy certain goods from the franchiser. Such provisions are sometimes difficult to justify on quality control grounds. And geographic exclusivity will not be permitted if it unduly restricts competition within the host country.

Fourth, because franchisees typically sell to the local domestic market and generate few exports, franchisers face special difficulties repatriating profits from soft currency countries. This problem is solved by creating sections within franchise stores within which the identical products are sold for hard currency at relatively favorable exchange rates. Even if this is a small part of the total sales, as long as it is equal to the franchisee's payments due to the franchiser, it can largely relieve the problem. Another approach has been *countertrade* pay-

ments to the franchiser with goods instead of hard currency. Thus, PepsiCo, Inc. is partially paid for its cola products by its Russian co-venturers with mushrooms for the pizzas of PepsiCo's Pizza Hut subsidiary. But the potential for countertrade is limited in most soft currency countries; goods from such nations are often not competitive with those from hard currency countries.

Fifth, in a few nations, a number of laws are specifically directed at the franchising phenomenon. The franchiser must be alert for *franchise tax* laws, which can impose taxes based on the franchiser's worldwide operations—even if the local operations fizzle. Such taxes may sometimes be avoided by structuring the franchise agreement in accordance with local preferences.

Sixth, *system* franchisers—those with a prepackaged program of instruction and initiation for prospective franchisees—should take care to avoid the entanglements of *language politics*. A few countries contain regions in which business must be conducted in a certain language. A prominent example is in the province of Quebec in Canada; the law there requires that business is done in French. A U.S. franchiser that brings its standard English-language package into such an area may be subject to significant civil penalties.

Finally, some nations impose stringent disclosure requirements on who may be a franchiser and what must be disclosed to prospective franchisees. These restrictions include registration requirements for highly detailed disclosure about the franchiser's business that the franchiser may not wish to make.

> **http://www.franchise.org**
> See for information from the International Franchise Association.

CHAPTER SUMMARY

In general, licensing provides a firm with intellectual property with a means for increasing the returns yielded by that property by permitting someone else to exploit it. In the international context, this capability is particularly useful: a U.S. concern with little or no experience in Nepal can contract with someone with such experience to exploit the Nepalese market. In the normal course, licensor and licensee will negotiate over matters such as conditions and extent of use, compensation, and confidentiality. The negotiations between licensor and licensee are complicated in the international context. Many countries seek to assist local licensees in their efforts to acquire advanced technology. Local legislation may supersede contractual provisions in order to permit host-country nationals to possess the intellectual property more rapidly. Lax enforcement of local legislation may provide a further source of mischief. Under some approval systems, nothing is likely to happen without cooperation of a local licensee.

Fortunately, the achievement of the TRIPS Agreement should greatly standardize and improve the situation. After it is fully implemented, TRIPS should provide minimum standards of intellectual property

protection and a reliable worldwide system of enforcement. It will take a while for the parties to work through continuing disagreements on TRIPS implementation.

If all these complications were not bad enough, the U.S. firm that sends goods abroad may find them exported back to its local market. The trend among developed countries has been to permit such increased competition.

Notwithstanding all of these hazards, the logic of efficiency and accelerating technical advances that underlie licensing makes it a rapidly expanding and highly profitable form of doing business abroad. It is, however, an endeavor that must be pursued cautiously.

Questions and Case Problems

1. Hirt Systems Company is a U.S. company that has a strong market in the United States for its "securing" of computer terminals; that is, enveloping such terminals with lead so as to prevent the emission of microwaves that can be picked up by "spy receivers." The key to Hirt's success is its know-how in design. Because the application is labor intensive, models produced abroad are significantly cheaper. Hirt has been affected by these lower-priced models, though it has held its own because of the superiority of its design. As part of its expansion program, Hirt is considering construction of a new assembly plant. Discuss the relative benefits and risks of building it as a Hirt-owned concern in a Third World country under the direction of Hirt's U.S. management as opposed to building it in the United States.

2. Assuming the same facts as in Question 1, what would be the advantages and disadvantages of a joint venture with a major foreign company abroad compared to the alternatives discussed in Question 1?

3. Scott Hill, a U.S. inventor, has developed and patented a revolutionary new running shoe that increases one's speed significantly. His invention has achieved considerable success in his native American Midwest. Two European companies have offered him joint venture packages to take his invention to the track-happy Europeans. Barthelemy Plus Grande, S.A. is a French sportswear giant with a marketing and distribution system that includes every major city in Western Europe and massive capital resources. Pék Társaság, a recently privatized

Hungarian firm, offers substantially lower labor costs. Which should Mr. Hill choose as a joint venture partner? Why?

4. Mr. Hill's marketing experts advise him that the Japanese market is hungry for his shoes. Focusing on technology transfer issues, discuss whether he should seek a Japanese joint venture partner or enter through a wholly owned subsidiary.

5. Analyze the same issues raised in Question 4, but assume Mr. Hill is considering entry into a "prior-approval" country.

6. Laffite Enterprises, Inc., a U.S. firm, has purchased the right to use the trademark of Wellington Imperial, Ltd., in the United States for a high-quality line of Napoleonic War reproductions. Wellington has a cheap line of Napoleonic trinkets that it sells in France. Degas Magazines, S.A., a French firm, begins to import the low-priced Wellington line into the United States. If Laffite brings an action against Degas, how would a U.S. court address the policy considerations presented?

7. Geyer Schokolade, A.G. makes the bonbon of choice for the German yuppie; its product's cachet permits Geyer to charge a hefty premium at home. Geyer expands into the U.S. market—where no one has heard of its bonbons—and charges a more reasonable price to garner market share. Henry Joseph, a U.S. entrepreneur, reimports the bonbons into Germany and offers them at a substantial saving below Geyer's price. What will be the result of Geyer's attempt to stop Mr. Joseph at the EEC Court of Justice?

Managerial Implications

1. You work for Wilbur Intergalactic, Ltd., a leading North Carolina processor and purveyor of North Carolina-style pork barbecue. Certain areas of North Carolina centered around Wilson, N.C., are known for producing superior pork barbecue because of the peculiar nature of the soil in which the pigs wallow and because of the method for preparing barbecue developed in that area. Soon, Limited Wilbur and other purveyors begin to refer to their barbecue as "Wilson-Style Barbecue" as a promotional name for their product. In 1999, the North Carolina legislature designates Wilson County as a special barbecue area and prohibits anyone from using the designation "Wilson-Style Barbecue" for barbecue not made from Wilson-bred hogs, in Wilson, pursuant to the Wilson method. Soon thereafter, the Professional Committee of Wilson Barbecue secures the U.S. trademark "Wilson-Style Barbecue" for Limited Wilbur and its other members.

   In 2001, Limited Wilbur management learns that at France's Euro Wally World, a French firm has been selling pork barbecue with the words "Method Wilson" on the label. The barbecue is made from local French hogs, but pursuant to the Wilson method of barbecuing. The committee has not secured trademark protection in France.

   a. Explain how a French court would analyze the issue of whether the French barbecuers are infringing upon Limited Wilbur's property rights. In this analysis, discuss whether "Wilson-Style Barbecue" is too generic to receive protection and what Limited Wilbur's rights are under the various intellectual property treaties.

   b. Develop a plan for expanding Limited Wilbur's product marketing to France, giving consideration to steps that it should take to preserve its "Wilson-Style Barbecue" trade name.

2. Undertake a study of the trade war between China and the United States over intellectual property rights. After years of trying to get China to protect American IPRs, an agreement was reached between the two countries in 1992. Reports of copyright and trademark violations continued, and in June 1994, an investigation was initiated under *Special 301*. China was identified as a priority country in July 1994 (59 FR 35558). A determination was made to take action against China on February 7, 1995 (60 FR 7230). The nation's press covered the story daily, describing how it would cost U.S. consumers billions of dollars a year. China embarked on its own public relations campaign, with U.S. television showing bulldozers crushing thousands of bootlegged and counterfeit CDs on a street in China. A month later, on March 7, 1995, the USTR announced that China had agreed to take the needed action to protect IPRs of U.S. film, recording, and software companies.

   a. What is the annual cost of Chinese IPR violations to U.S. companies? How have IPR violations affected the decision of American companies to do business there? What has been the response of private firms to these violations and how have they tried to control them?

   b. What positive actions has China taken to correct the problem? What new laws have been passed for the protection of IPRs and how are they enforced?

   c. Consider specifically the problems of U.S. software companies in China. Can you find any information about Microsoft's position on doing business in China? What has been their strategy to tap into the potentially huge Chinese market, while assuring that their copyrights on software remain protected? If the Chinese government views IPR violations as a legitimate way to make a profit, would bringing the government in as a joint venture partner be one way to get the Chinese to see the need for IPR protection?

3. L'anza Research Inc. manufactures high-quality hair care products in California. Copyrighted labels are attached to all products and packaging. In the United States, L'anza sells exclusively to authorized distributors who resell within limited geographic areas and then only to authorized retailers such as hair salons. Exports to foreign distributors are sold at a 40 percent discount. L'anza sold three shipments containing several tons of merchandise to its distributor in the United Kingdom, Quality King, who resold them to a buyer in Malta. L'anza later discovered that the products had been resold to a U.S. buyer for less than the wholesale price, and were being sold at discounted prices by unauthorized retailers in California. L'anza complained that since it held the right to the copyrighted language and design of the labels, the unauthorized resale violated U.S. copyright laws. The lower courts agreed. The U.S. Supreme Court reversed, unanimously holding that under the "first sale" doctrine, once a copyright owner places an authentic, copyrighted item in the stream of commerce, it has no further right to control its distribution or reimportation. Thus any lawful purchaser of

the products may dispose of them as they please without further obligation. This decision does not apply to counterfeited, pirated, or illegally copied goods shipped into the United States in violation of the copyright or trademark laws. What should L'anza have done to protect itself? Why is a foreign distributorship agreement important? What specific areas of concern should it address? See, *Quality King Distributors v. L'anza Research Int'l. Inc.*, 523 U.S. 135 (1998).

CHAPTER 18

HOST-COUNTRY REGULATION: CORPORATE LAW, TAXATION, AND CURRENCY RISK

A business that operates in a foreign country must comply with the laws of that country. This "rule" of international business has significant implications for U.S. business managers. A projected high profit margin may be meaningless if local law prevents repatriation of profits to the United States. Low per-hour labor costs will be less attractive if local law dictates that employees control 50 percent of the local board of directors. The anticipated capital cost of building a factory may be grossly in error if the manager fails to consider that he is in an Islamic country in which it is more difficult to arrange short-term financing. These legal differences are not all bad for U.S. companies; many foreign nations attract investment precisely because of less demanding laws.

For better or worse, foreign law is almost always different from U.S. law. First, as noted in earlier chapters, the U.S. common law system, based on Anglo-Saxon antecedents, is fundamentally different from the legal system in all non-English-speaking nations. Second, these fundamental differences in approach to law are compounded by cultural and political differences that are reflected in law. For instance, the United States strongly favors the free flow of capital in and out of the country, and its laws impose relatively few barriers to that flow. Countries that are concerned about their foreign reserves or that favor central governmental control place many more restrictions on the flow of capital.

Business managers trained in the business environment of the United States must become familiar with the legal schemes created by foreign cultures before subjecting their companies to them. This chapter reviews the limits on foreign investment imposed by host-country corporate laws and tax laws.

HOST-COUNTRY CORPORATE LAW AFFECTING FOREIGN INVESTMENT

Nationalization—a government's taking of a private business—once seemed like a quick route for a host government to gain dominance over enterprises operating in its country, but it had very adverse long-term effects. Once a nation nationalizes its industries, potential foreign investors stay away and capital resources dry up. Further, because the government that takes over the enterprises—like all governments—lacks the entrepreneurial skills necessary for the business to prosper, the business soon stalls. An economy filled with such moribund businesses then goes into a funk. Citizens find themselves without employment, living standards fall, and the government faces a different, more intense pressure.

Accordingly, most countries now focus on preventing a resurgence of foreign economic domination rather than impeding the flow of foreign investment. This is done through host nation regulations on the form and substance of foreign investment under a wide assortment of domestic corporate laws. These laws often reflect the nation's preoccupation with foreign economic domination that previously led to nationalization. This concern is particularly visible in strategic industrial sectors.

Those nations more concerned with the potential for foreign domination tend to have more restrictive laws against foreign penetration of their economies. For example, the massive U.S. economy has relatively little fear of being dominated by outsiders and has few obstacles to foreign investors. By contrast, developing economies that can be easily overwhelmed by more sophisticated and well-heeled capitalists place many preconditions to such investment. Within these more restrictive countries, regulation tends to be more stringent as the level of an enterprise's foreign ownership or foreign operational control grows. Nations in transition to entrepreneurial systems—where privatization is proceeding—find vestiges of suspicion of foreign penetration even as they try to enact free enterprise legal systems.

Corporate control is, therefore, a principal line of demarcation in studying different schemes of corporate law. This chapter first discusses foreign investment in businesses owned by local nationals, and then turns to those businesses controlled from abroad. In its examination of the former, the text addresses corporate requirements associated with all investments, irrespective of control considerations. In the discussion of the latter, the chapter addresses the additional considerations that arise once foreign ownership exceeds 50 percent of an enterprise.

MINORITY OWNERSHIP INVESTMENTS

Among minority investments, it is useful to distinguish between "passive" and "active" investments. For our purposes, a *passive investment* is one in which the investor limits its involvement to providing equity or debt capital in an enterprise managed by another. The classic passive investment is the acquisition of a noncontrolling amount of stock in or a loan to a company with no participation in the management of the enterprise. This is an investment that relies on the managerial efforts of others, not unlike an investor's purchasing of stock on a public exchange. With an *active investment*, the investor participates in the management of the enterprise. The prototype of an active minority investment is an international joint venture. Under these circumstances, each investor brings substantial operational experience to the new company along with its capital contribution.

Because passive minority investments create the least risk of foreign control, they are the least regulated of foreign investments. Active minority ownership investments, on the other hand, begin to raise the specter of "outsider" influence and thus are the subject of greater governmental regulation.

Passive Debt Investments

Perhaps the least intrusive of all investments is the extension of credit. In a loan, the foreign investor analyzes the proposed foreign activity and evaluates its commercial prospects and "political risk." If the activity seems profitable and capable of repaying the loan, the foreign lender will make its advance in exchange for repayment at an agreed-upon interest rate before any equity owners in the enterprise are repaid. Because lenders are *senior* to other investors, they are willing to accept a fixed, lower return than others and to participate very little in management. Indeed, any significant participation in management can, in some countries, lead to *lender liability,* a partial or total forfeiture of the lenders' special status.

Because it is relatively unintrusive, the international lender faces little government regulation. For the international lender, the principal form of risk apart from *enterprise risk* is *currency risk*. Legal and administrative restrictions on the conversion of local currency into hard currency and on the transfer of hard currency out of the country can endanger loan repayment. Currency fluctuation can also create difficulties. Because international loans are typically made in the currency of the lender's home country, if the value of the local currency is dropping vis-à-vis that of the lender's home currency, the borrower may suddenly be unable to repay the loan even if its business is operating as expected. Issuing the loan in the home currency does not solve this problem from the foreign lender's perspective. While this reduces the risk of borrower default, it simply shifts currency risk directly on the lender The lender, after all, had to get the funds it lent from its home. The lender's depositors, shareholders, and bondholders will expect to be repaid in hard currency.

To ameliorate this currency fluctuation issue, *currency arbitrageurs* now offer *currency swaps* and other "hedges" against currency fluctuation. Arbitrageurs are intermediaries who limit a party's risk by agreeing—pursuant to standard contracts sanctioned by the International Swap Dealers Association—to deliver a certain amount of a stated currency at a specified future date in exchange for a current payment of another currency. This limits the risk of the purchaser of the swap, transferring it to the arbitrageur. The arbitrageur will then try to find someone who wants to enter into a balancing swap to supply him the currency needed for the first swap. If the arbitrageur does its job properly, it will satisfy matching needs for currency, taking relatively little risk.

In the Islamic world, religious law adds additional complications to the passive foreign lender. The Koran prohibits making money from the lending of money. Because bank financing is necessary for effective business, however, lenders have devised an interesting array of financing techniques that do not violate Islamic scripture. The following article explains this fascinating phenomenon.

international accents

Unlocking Islamic Finance

By Sara Khalile

Infrastructure Finance

> Those who consume interest shall not rise again, except as one arises whom Satan has prostrated by the touch; that is because they have said: "Bargaining is the same as interest." God has permitted bargaining but has forbidden interest. Sura 2: 275–276, The Koran.

The Oil Boom

The first Islamic bank was incorporated in Egypt in the mid-1960s. But it wasn't until a decade later and following the oil boom that the concept took on a more visible role. Devout Muslims in the Persian Gulf region and other oil-rich Arab states realized that instead of putting their new wealth in conventional banks, they could build a business catering to depositors like themselves who shunned interest, yet sought profits.

However, Islamic banks soon realized that many depositors had little taste for risk-taking and long-term investments. As a result, many of these banks began focusing on products that provide predetermined rates of return in the short term, such as commodities and trade financing. In these transactions the banks would arrange for a trader to buy goods on the banks' behalf and resell them to clients at a markup.

In searching for new investment products, Islamic banks and their *shari'a* boards (which assess the religious acceptability of the bank's transactions) have found a natural fit with project finance. "Philosophically, there are a lot of similarities between the two," says Isam Salah, attorney. "In project finance, you are basing the success of your loan on the success of the project [because the lender cannot sue the borrower but must rely on the project for repayment], as opposed to a conventional loan, where you are not necessarily tied in to the success of the venture. That is what Islamic finance principles call for—that you share the risks as well as the rewards."

For example, *ijara,* the Islamic leasing structure, fits well with nonrecourse finance. Using an *ijara* contract, Islamic project financiers purchase the assets of a power plant and lease them back to the project sponsor at a markup and on a deferred-payment basis during the life of the lease. This is not only compatible with Islamic law, it is often a favored approach of conventional banks financing independent power projects.

Another alternative is the *istisna* structure, which resembles a suppliers credit or a preproduction facility for advanced funding of a large project. In this case, the Islamic bank funds the project's major suppliers, acquires title to the equipment, and passes the title on to the project company on the basis of an agreed-upon deferred-payment structure.

The applicability of Islamic finance to large infrastructure projects was first demonstrated in 1993 with the 1,292-megawatt (MW) Hub River power project in Pakistan. The project set a precedent by obtaining religious approval for an Islamic bridge financing, arranged by ANZ Grindlays, to be used alongside conventional project financing.

Richard Duncan, director of global Islamic finance at ANZ Investment Bank in London, explains that efforts to raise medium-term funds were bogged down in lengthy negotiations, leaving the project

continued

continued

stalled. At that point, Saudi Arabia's Al Rajhi Banking & Investment Corp. stepped in and provided a $92 million in *istisna* preproduction financing.

Al Rajhi bought the rights to equipment (turbines) that had not yet been manufactured, and sold these rights to the project company on a markup basis. Although the cost was comparable to the cost of a standard short-term trade finance facility, a conventional financing alternative was not available at the time. The *istisna* facility was extended twice before it was finally repaid when financing closed on the project in 1994.

Islamic Instruments

Structuring a limited-recourse or nonrecourse project finance transaction with Islamic capital requires the use of several Islamic financing instruments. . . . The short-term needs and working-capital requirements of a project are best addressed by *murabaha* financing contracts (cost-plus financing), in which the Islamic bank buys equipment, fuel or raw materials and sells them to the project company at a markup and on a deferred-payment basis. The *murabaha* is then taken out by an *istisna* financing (preproduction facility), which in turn is taken out by an *ijara* financing—which resembles conventional lease financing. Once the *ijara* contract has expired, the project company takes title to the assets.

All of these Islamic financing mechanisms get around the prohibition on interest payments by having the financiers take ownership of assets and lease or resell them to the project company.

The *shari'a* court, explains Citibanks' Rehman, is about 1,500 years old and is not clear on many issues. "A lot," he says, "is subject to interpretation." There is growing enthusiasm among Islamic scholars for industry-wide standards, but that may take years to develop.

A Guide to Islamic Banking

Halal: Practices permitted under Islamic law

Harram: Practices forbidden under Islamic law

Ijara: A leasing structure based on risk sharing. The financier acquires title to the asset and leases it at a predetermined fee. Title is passed on to the client once the lease expires.

Istisna: A supplier's credit or preproduction facility. The financier acquires equipment and passes the title on to the client on a predetermined deferred-payment basis.

Modaraba: A partnership agreement where one party contributes financing and the other contributes assets (i.e., property, equipment or expertise). Profit sharing is predetermined. Losses are borne by the financier.

Murabaha: A short-term commercial finance agreement. The financier acquires goods on behalf of the client, who purchases and takes title to the goods at an agreed-upon date and at a price that includes a predetermined markup.

Musharaka: A joint-venture agreement where both financier and client contribute capital and share the profits and losses in proportion to their investment.

Riba: Interest charged by a lending institution

Shari'a: Doctrines regulating Islam

---

http://www.islamic-banking.com
http://www.islamic-finance.com/indexnew.htm
See these sites for more on Islamic business practices.

Passive Equity Investments

The capital markets of North America, Western Europe, and Japan are becoming increasingly unified. Investors from each area have increasing confidence in their investments in securities issued in the other areas. Consequently, "foreign" money has become an important segment of each of these markets. In fact, one can monitor the price quotations of an internationally traded stock on the different stock exchanges in order to seek the best price. As long as the foreign investors do not try to accumulate a block sufficient in size to exert control in the governance of the company, their money is welcome. Through *American Depository Receipts (ADRs)*—certificates held by U.S. trust institutions representing interests in stock held by a bank in a foreign country—many non-U.S. companies have become available to U.S. investors. ADRs permit Americans to invest in foreign firms in very much the same way that they can invest in companies listed on U.S. stock exchanges. And Americans can do more than invest abroad; they can now offer their securities to investors abroad by listing their stock in European and other foreign markets. Indeed, the phenomenon of transnational takeovers—as between companies in developed economies—has become more common, with European and Japanese investors taking over U.S. concerns and U.S. investors taking over European companies. In Europe, many national firms are merging across borders to form multinational concerns better suited to competing in the continent-wide competitive environment of the EU.

In this world market, a U.S. investor needs to investigate nuances of overseas equity markets. One of the major differences abroad is in the regulation of trading in securities by people with access to nonpublic information, or *insider trading*. In the United States, insider trading is a criminal violation. In the corporate scandals of 2001–02, participation in insider trading resulted in the incarceration of a number of senior corporate officers. In stark contrast, many foreign nations view insider trading as "a mere violation of the rules of ethics," rather than a violation of law. Further, some nations, such as Japan, have anti-insider trading laws on the books, but its authorities are generally perceived not to enforce them. Thus, U.S. investors must approach a purchase of securities in certain countries carefully; the sellers may have adverse nonpublic information about what they are selling.

Because regulated, honest markets tend to attract more investors, however, the international trend is now decisively toward the U.S. "high disclosure" model of securities regulation. The EU moved aggressively to prod national legislatures to improve uniform standards of investor protection through a series of binding directives: the Directive on Admission of Securities in the Stock Market, the Directive on Prospectuses, and the Directive on Semi-Annual Reports. These directives set the stage for the development of pan-European stock markets with reliable market information. Virtually all western European nations have now outlawed insider trading. Even infant securities markets such as those in China are seeking to implement regulatory schemes that ensure broad dissemination of information about companies whose shares are publicly traded. This trend toward disclosure is not motivated by a reverence for honesty; it is a calculated realization that, in the long run, honest markets increase capital investment and the wealth of all market participants.

Other peculiarities of foreign equity markets are more subtle. In certain Swiss industries, for instance, a company's capital stock is divided into bearer shares (*inhaberaktien*) and registered shares (*namensaktien*). Although both kinds of shares are publicly traded, only Swiss citizens may purchase registered shares. Because registered shares most often hold the majority of the Swiss company's voting power, this system generally assures Swiss control.

In some countries, legal structures do not create formal impediments to foreign equity investments; however, the country's tradition can frustrate attempts to convert a passive investment into a more active holding. In Japan, efforts by large minority U.S. stockholders to gain greater influence have been unsuccessful. In the absence of a mutually acceptable joint venture arrangement, minority investment in Japan is often viewed as permanently passive.

Active Investments

For the U.S. investor that wishes to exercise a measure of control over its minority investment—the active investor—joint ventures are often the vehicle of choice. A foreign investor may enter into a joint venture by combining with a national of the host country to create a new entity or by acquiring a portion of an existing local entity. The four basic forms of a joint venture are: (1) a foreign corporation, (2) a foreign partnership, (3) a U.S. corporation with a foreign branch, or (4) a U.S. partnership with a foreign branch.

The precise shape of the joint venture depends largely on the participants' relative treatment under the tax laws of the host country and the United States, and whether the countries have entered into a tax treaty that might affect the application of those laws. In many cases, for instance, remittances from branches may be taxed at higher rates than dividends from a foreign subsidiary. This is because taxes are generally deferred until dividends are declared.

In some strategic sectors of the economy, however, many nations strictly limit foreign investment.

Even in the United States—with the world's largest economy and most powerful armed forces and presumably the least fear of outside influence—foreign nationals may not hold more than a 25 percent voting interest in an airline or a company that owns an earth station or microwave license. Some of these restrictions led Australian Rupert Murdoch to become a U.S. citizen before completing his acquisition of the Fox television network. Foreigners are also prevented from controlling U.S. defense contractor producing technologies deemed important to the national security. In countries even more fearful of overseas domination, foreigners are excluded from a larger number of sectors. Prior to its conversion to the privatization doctrine, Argentina required prior approval of any investments in defense or national security, electricity, gas, telecommunications, public utilities, radio and television stations, insurance companies, or financial entities. In many of these cases, the government's inability to run these sectors effectively without private initiative, foreign capital, and expertise ultimately caused restrictive governments to open up these sectors through privatization.

Even if a foreign entity cannot control a joint venture directly by owning a majority of its voting equity, it may control it indirectly by entering into one or more key contracts with the joint venture that tie up the venture with obligations to the foreigner. For example, if the joint venture is to assemble components manufactured in the United States under terms that give substantial discretion over whether to continue supplying them, the U.S. investor retains significant control even if the investor owns few shares and names few directors to the board; the U.S. investor, after all, controls the supply of components. Similarly, a U.S. investor can exercise control through supply contracts, marketing agreements, management contracts, and veto powers in the joint venture agreements.

These contractual means of control have led some nations to initiate full substantive preapproval procedures for active foreign investment. India, one of the nations formerly most wary of foreign influence, once had a particularly elaborate example of this preapproval procedure. Foreign investment proposals in India were evaluated by the Project Approval Board comprised of representatives of relevant government agencies. The Project Approval Board submitted the proposal to a variety of committees that acted as arms of the board in determining whether the proposed joint venture complied with five different Indian laws governing foreign investment. Needless to say, the administrative difficulties and expense involved in such a process discourage foreign investment. Many foreign investors shunned India, retarding the nation's development.

India also provides an example of how such preapproval procedures have been reformed to encourage investment. In the mid-1990s, India changed the clearance procedure for all foreign investments of less than $120 million. As long as the foreign investor limits its equity stake to 51 percent or less in thirty-four selected industries, the only approval necessary would be from the Reserve Bank of India. This simplification and centralization of the approval process created a boom in foreign investment in India. Indeed, approving projects through a single unified entity has now become accepted throughout the Third World, from Egypt's semiautonomous Investment Authority to Kenya's Foreign Investment Agency.

Conversely, many countries give preferences and incentives to certain types of foreign investments, especially high-technology companies and export-oriented industries. For instance, in India, export-oriented businesses are granted special relief from duties normally imposed on foreign components and are given assistance in obtaining import licenses. The People's Republic of China tries to make up for its poor infrastructure by giving high-technology firms priority access to its public utilities.

Local Assistance

The great variety and complexity of laws and regulations affecting foreign investment make it particularly important for the U.S. investor to retain the assistance of host-country nationals familiar with local law and customs. For example, acquisition of a Brazilian export license once took approximately 1,470 separate legal acts. Few U.S. investors would be able to work their way through such extensive bureaucracy without someone familiar with the process and the people who administer it. Despite simplifications brought by NAFTA, paperwork for truck shipments into Mexico is notoriously complex: a Mexican customs broker is a must. In Germany, businesses must be members of a

Handelskammer, a society of merchants. Because many registered Handelskammer members have been working together for decades, for practical purposes, an investor cannot conduct business without someone who has an established relationship within that circle. In short, the foreign investor may have to navigate around legal obstacles with substantial cultural overtones. Typically, the only way the investor can do this is by enlisting the assistance of local experts.

MAJORITY OWNERSHIP INTERESTS

There are a number of important business reasons why an enterprise would prefer to establish an entity it controls through majority ownership rather than an entity in which it owns a minority interest. For instance, the firm that greatly fears disclosure of its software know-how would be reluctant to enter into any venture that it did not fully control, whether the potential co-venturer was a Mongolian or a Virginian. The international context places an additional layer of complexity over the businessperson's decision process. For example, certain nations simply do not permit 100 percent foreign ownership of software manufacturers—or they impose taxes that make such ownership extremely unattractive.

Establishing a Foreign Branch or Subsidiary

An enterprise that wishes to establish an entity abroad under its control may create a subsidiary or a branch. This step is not to be taken lightly. Whether the company establishes a subsidiary or a branch, it may waive rights of protection under the bilateral investment protection agreements of the United States. In many cases, the company subjects itself completely to the foreign nation's corporate tax laws.

Certain differences separate the subsidiary approach from the branch approach. If a company chooses to establish a branch abroad, it faces greater potential vicarious liability. In essence, the company is directly accountable for any liabilities of a branch, while it is not for a separate corporation that is a subsidiary. Thus, if the foreign activity involves potential product liability or environmental liability, a subsidiary corporation is indicated.

On the other hand, the establishment of a branch rather than a subsidiary may have significant consequences under local tax law and U.S. tax law. Because tax laws often distinguish between different forms of an enterprise, such laws often dictate the establishment of a U.S. branch, a U.S. partnership, a foreign corporation, or a foreign partnership.

Tax Issues Associated with Foreign Branches and Subsidiaries

Tax issues are as varied as local tax laws and the circumstances of the individual ventures. Despite tax treaties between nations, methods of calculating income, deductions, and depreciation differ significantly. Further complications occur when these different systems are applied to multinational transactions. A general international business law textbook could not possibly address the tax systems of all nations in the world. Indeed, the U.S. Internal Revenue Service by itself is the subject of numerous different courses in American law schools. The U.S. investor should, however, be aware of the more important provisions of the U.S. tax law that affect international transactions.

Foreign Tax Credits. Under U.S. tax law, corporations are taxed on all income, including income from foreign sources, regardless of where it is earned. The United States, however, does not tax foreign subsidiaries of U.S. companies on the income that they earn abroad; U.S. law taxes income that is repatriated or paid as a dividend to the U.S. parent. Thus, if the tax systems of different countries were not coordinated to some degree, companies would face double taxation on the same business profits: once by the host country when the foreign subsidiary earns it and a second time by the United States when the parent receives it from the subsidiary as a return on investment.

Because such double taxation discourages international transactions, different nations have developed their own systems for avoiding it. France and the Netherlands, for example, completely exempt the foreign source income of their firms. The United States uses a tax credit method, allowing a 100 percent credit for foreign income taxes paid. If the foreign tax is lower than the U.S. tax, the U.S. company must pay the difference. If the foreign tax is greater, the U.S. company does not get a refund, but need not pay any U.S. tax on the foreign source income.

The strength of international pressure to compel cooperation on these tax issues can be decisive. In recent years, the state of California defied international convention by taxing the foreign income of foreign affiliates of companies with a California presence. Because this "worldwide reporting method" did not correspond with the usual taxation of income "where earned," it created a double taxation problem for all foreign firms doing business in California. Accordingly, these firms sent their U.S. lawyers to challenge the constitutionality of the worldwide reporting method. California successfully defended its system against this attack for years, finally winning in the United States Supreme Court in the 1994 case of *Barclays Bank v. Franchise Tax Board of California*, 512 U.S.298. But the British Exchequer and the Organization for Economic Cooperation and Development condemned the California tax system and threatened retaliatory action against California firms. With this threat to California's business community—why would a firm stay in California rather than Utah if it would be substantially disadvantaged in its international business—California backed down. Its legislature enacted "water's edge" legislation that limited taxation to the activities of a firm within the United States.

One recurring tax issue revolves around the U.S. investor's ability to credit taxes it has paid to a foreign country against taxes it would have to pay on its U.S. tax return. In essence, a U.S. enterprise receives a credit for appropriate foreign taxes against its U.S. taxes with respect to income from foreign sources. Thus, an investor needs to consider the tax rates applicable to a particular form of organization and whether the foreign impositions are creditable taxes for U.S. purposes. Because the issue of whether foreign impositions are creditable taxes for U.S. purposes is so central to the investment decision, it may be instructive to review how the courts resolved one such controversy in the following case.

Bank of America Nat'l. Trust & Savings Assn. v. United States
459 F.2d 513 (1972)
United States Court of Claims

BACKGROUND AND FACTS
Plaintiff Bank of America conducted a general banking business in the Kingdom of Thailand, the Republic of the Philippines, and the Republic of Argentina. With respect to this business, Bank of America paid the three jurisdictions various types of taxes. Bank of America demanded a credit for most of these assessments either on its federal income tax returns or by refund claim.

The Internal Revenue Service disallowed a number of the credits claimed and Bank of America appealed to a trial commissioner. The trial commissioner held for the Bank of America with respect to the Thailand Business Tax, Type 1 and Type 2; the Philippine Tax of Banks; and the City of Buenos Aires Tax on Profit-Making Activities. The matter was appealed to the Court of Claims.

JUDGE DAVIS
For a domestic corporation, §901(a) and (b)(1) of the Internal Revenue Code . . . allows a credit against federal income taxes of "the amount of any income, profits, and excess profits taxes paid or accrued during the taxable year to any foreign country or to any possession of the United States." It is now settled that the question of whether a foreign tax is an "income tax" within §901(b)(1) must be decided under criteria established by our revenue laws and court decisions, and that the foreign tax must be the substantial equivalent of an income tax as the term is understood in the United States. . . .

[T]he Thailand Business Tax . . . states that . . . persons engaged in business have the duty to pay business tax on the "gross takings" for each tax month at [rates ranging from 2.5 percent to 10.5 percent]. "[G]ross takings" from the business of banking [are] (a) interest, discounts, fees, or service charges, and (b) profit, before the deduction of any expense, from the exchange, purchase, or sale of currency, issuance, purchase, or sale of notes or foreign remittances.

The City of Buenos Aires Tax on Profit-Making Activities . . . imposes a tax on the gross receipts of

continued

continued

banks, insurance, savings and loan, and security and investment companies, and . . . provides that, in the case of banks and other lending institutions, "the taxable amount shall be composed of interest, discounts, profits from nonexempt taxable securities, and other revenue, resulting from profits and remuneration for service received in the course of the last business year."

The Philippines Tax on Banks provides . . . that there shall be collected a tax of 5 percent on the gross receipts derived by all banks doing business in the Philippines from interest, discounts, dividends, commission, profits from exchange, royalties, rentals of property, real and personal, and all other items treated as gross. . . . For none of the three taxes was the taxpayer permitted to deduct from gross income the costs or expenses of its banking business or of producing its net income.

The problem, then, is whether such imposts on gross banking income . . . are "income taxes" under the foreign tax credit—"income taxes" as we use that term in the federal system under our own revenue laws.

There is consensus on certain basic principles, in addition to the rule that the United States notion of income taxes furnishes the controlling guide. All are agreed that an income tax is a direct tax on gain or profits, and that gain is a necessary ingredient of income. . . . Income, including gross income, must be distinguished from gross receipts which can cover returns of capital. . . . Only an "income tax," not a tax which is truly on gross receipts, is creditable.

[W]e cannot accept the position that all foreign gross income taxes, no matter whether or not they tax or seek to tax profit or net gain, are covered by that provision. [F]rom 1913 on, Congress has always directed the domestic levy at some net gain or profit, and for almost sixty years the concept that the income tax seeks out net gain has been inherent in our system of taxation. That is the "well-understood meaning to be derived from an examination of the [United States] statutes which provide for the laying and collection of income taxes"—the basic test . . . for determining whether a foreign tax is an "income tax" under the foreign tax credit. . . . Where the gross income levy may not, and is not intended to, reach profit (net gain), allowance of the credit would serve only haphazardly to avoid double taxation of net income, since only the United States tax—under the concept followed since 1913—would necessarily fall upon such net gain. There would not then be any

significant measure of commensurability between the two imposts (except by chance).

We do not, however, consider it all-decisive whether the foreign income tax is labeled a gross income or a net income tax, or whether it specifically allows the deduction or exclusion of the costs or expenses of realizing the profit. The important thing is whether the other country is attempting to reach some net gain, not the form in which it shapes the income tax or the name it gives. In certain situations a levy can in reality be directed at net gain even though it is imposed squarely on gross income.

For instance, it is almost universally true that a wage or salary employee does not spend more on expenses incident to his job than he earns in pay. A foreign tax upon the gross income of an employee from his work should therefore be creditable by the employee under 901(b)(1) despite the refusal of the other jurisdiction to permit deduction of job-related expenses. The reason is, of course, that in those circumstances the employee would always (or almost always) have some net gain and, accordingly, the tax, though on gross income, would be designed to pinch net gain in the end—and would in fact have that effect. In those circumstances, a loss (excess of expenses over profit) is so improbable, and some net gain is so sure, that the tax can be placed on gross income without any real fear or expectation that there will be no net gain or profit to tax.

Our review of the [law] persuades us that the term "income tax" in 901(b)(1) covers all foreign income taxes designed to fall on some net gain or profit, and includes a gross income tax if, but only if, that impost is almost sure, or very likely, to reach some net gain because costs or expenses will not be so high as to offset the net profit. . . .

Do the three foreign taxes we are now discussing . . . meet this test? Each of the taxes is levied on gross income from the banking business and allows no deductions for the costs or expenses of producing the income. Any taxpayer could be liable whether or not it operated at a profit during the year. The only question is whether it is very unlikely or highly improbable that taxpayers subject to the impost would make no profit or would suffer a loss. Obviously, plaintiff and the other institutions subject to the taxes had substantial costs in their banking business, salaries and rent being the major items. The covered banks must also have had bad debts and defaults, and these would have to be taken into account in calculating annual net gain. . . .

continued

continued

Nor can one say on this record that the three governments felt that net gain would always (or nearly so) be reached by these special banking levies, or that they designed these particular taxes to nip such net profit. Each of the three jurisdictions had a general net income tax (comparable to ours, and admittedly creditable) which the Bank of America and other banks had to pay. That was the impost intended to reach net gain. We cannot say, therefore, that there was only a minimal risk that the combination of a bank's expenses plus its debt experience (and other losses) would outbalance its net gain or profits in any particular year—or that the foreign countries so considered.

Decision. The United States Court of Claims dismissed Bank of America's petitions for a tax credit.

Taxation of E-Commerce. Products and services sold over the Internet to a foreign nation are subject to that nation's taxation. For a time, this fact was obscured by the sheer ease with which the World Wide Web crosses borders and the U.S. government's treatment of the Internet as a tax-free zone. The moratorium on taxation of the medium is now over. An e-company marketing abroad has to consider the foreign tax liability incurred in such transactions.

All European Union purchases are subject to a value-added tax, or VAT, similar to U.S. states' sales taxes on retail goods. Each of the EU member states has its own VAT rate, from 15 to 25 percent of the price of the item sold. This application of land-based law on Internet transactions has odd consequences. For example, a U.S. customer who buys a product over the Internet from a European vendor owes no VAT at the time of purchase. If he or she later visits Europe, he or she will owe the VAT upon arrival. And then, he or she is reimbursed the VAT upon leaving European territory! Obviously, authorities are not enforcing VAT against U.S. consumers. The provision was enacted to impose a tax obligation on U.S.-based merchants selling to European consumers; all such suppliers with over 100,000 euros in sales to an EU nation must file returns and pay VAT on all sales.

More controversially, the EU treats sales of downloadable music or software as services for tax purposes. Because services are taxed at higher VAT rates than goods and most Internet music and software originate in the United States, this was clearly a political decision aimed at American business. An immediate international confrontation broke out between the United States and Europe on the issue. The dispute was resolved apolitically. Under VAT rules, services—unlike goods—are taxed at the place where they are provided. Therefore, there was no way to enforce the law without U.S. government cooperation. The EU recognized that no tax was due on such VAT sales from a non-EU supplier because it was impossible for the EU tax authorities to enforce such transactions. It continues to work with the United States for a resolution, though these measures have not yet proven to be successful. More debates like this are likely to unfold before nations' e-commerce tax systems are coordinated in the same way that we have seen on income taxation.

Transfer Pricing. Another major recurring international tax issue is generally referred to as *transfer taxes* or the *transfer-pricing* provisions. The transfer-pricing provisions are an attempt by the Internal Revenue Service to prevent U.S. firms from avoiding U.S. taxes by structuring deals with foreign affiliates so that an affiliate in a low tax foreign jurisdiction gets most of the profit. When a U.S. corporation enters into a contract with a foreign subsidiary that it controls, it may obviously structure the transaction so that only the subsidiary profits from the deal. If international firms had free rein to do this, they would price their transactions so that all profit would be realized by subsidiaries in low-tax or no-tax jurisdictions, depriving Uncle Sam of his cut of the action.

To prevent this type of tax avoidance, transfer-pricing provisions require that pricing in such inter-company transactions be conducted at "arm's-length" prices—the prices that would have resulted from negotiation between unrelated parties. Failure to achieve such pricing allows the Internal Revenue Service to reconstruct retroactively what the arm's-length price should have been and to impose penalties based upon that recomputation. Virtually all developed nations have also adopted similar transfer-pricing provisions, with the same objective of preventing tax avoidance through manipulation of inter-company transactions.

In the *Compaq* case, the U.S. Tax Court delineated the limits of the discretion of the IRS in this area, decisively underscoring the pre-eminence of market-based transactions over cost-plus methodologies in transfer-pricing cases.

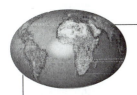

Compaq Computer Corp. Subsidiaries v. Commissioner of Internal Revenue
113 T.C. 214
United States Tax Court

BACKGROND AND FACTS

Petitioner Compaq Computer Corporation manufactures personal computers (PCs). Printed circuit assemblies (PCAs) are the electronic circuitry inside the PC's central processing unit that allows the PC to operate. Compaq set up a PCA manufacturing subsidiary in Singapore. The petitioner purchased PCAs from its Singapore subsidiary at actual market prices based on purchases of similar PCAs from unrelated subcontractors that were primarily located in the United States, with a "turnkey equivalent" adjustment based not on actual transactions, but on industry practice. The Internal Revenue Service took the position that such pricing resulted in too much profit being left in Singapore, a low tax jurisdiction. The IRS argued that a "cost-plus" approach—which would place more profit in the United States—should have been used. Accordingly, the IRS declared a deficiency in Compaq's consolidated returns. Compaq appealed to the Tax Court.

COHEN, CHIEF JUDGE

The issue addressed in this opinion is whether income relating to printed circuit assemblies (PCA's) should be reallocated . . . to petitioner from its Singapore subsidiary for its 1991 and 1992 fiscal years. . . . Unless otherwise indicated, all section references are to the Internal Revenue Code. . . .

Compaq U.S. bought 3.6 million PCA's worth $597 million on a turnkey equivalent basis from unrelated subcontractors. The PCA's were nearly identical to PCA's sold by Compaq Asia to Compaq U.S. After adjustment for differences in physical property and circumstances of the sales, the prices that Compaq U.S. paid to the unrelated subcontractors for PCA's were comparable to the prices that Compaq U.S. paid to Compaq Asia for PCA's.

The issue that we are considering here is whether the transfer prices for PCA's that were charged

between Compaq U.S. and Compaq Asia meet the arm's-length standard. . . . Petitioner asserts that [the IRS] notice determinations are unacceptable and that comparable transactions between unrelated parties prove that the transfer prices satisfy the arm's-length standard. . . . [The IRS] asserts that petitioner has not presented comparable uncontrolled prices to prove that its transfer pricing system should be upheld. . . . [The IRS] primary argument is that petitioner's turnkey equivalent analysis is not based on actual transactions. . . .

Section 482 gives [the IRS] broad authority to allocate gross income, deductions, credits, or allowances between two related corporations if the allocations are necessary either to prevent evasion of taxes or to reflect clearly the income of the corporations. . . . The applicable standard is arm's-length dealing between taxpayers unrelated by ownership or control. . . .

> The purpose of section 482 is to prevent the artificial shifting of the net incomes of controlled taxpayers by placing controlled taxpayers on a parity with uncontrolled, unrelated taxpayers.
>
> * * *
>
> the regulations attempt to identify the "true taxable income" of each entity based on the taxable income which would have resulted had the entities been uncontrolled parties dealing at arm's length.* * *

When [the IRS] has determined deficiencies based on section 482, the taxpayer bears the burden of showing that the allocations are arbitrary, capricious, or unreasonable. . . . [The IRS] section 482 determination must be sustained absent a showing of abuse of discretion. . . . "Whether respondent has exceeded its discretion is a question of fact."* * * In reviewing the reasonableness of respondent's determination, the Court focuses on the reasonableness of the result, not on the details of the methodology used.

continued

continued

[The IRS] used unrealistic material, labor, and overhead markups in applying its formulas. If markups in the range of industry markups are used, the results of [IRS] analysis bear no recognizable relation to [the IRS] notice amounts. [Compaq's] analysis establishes an arm's-length price for PCA purchases by Compaq U.S. from Compaq Asia that is approximately $232 million greater than [the IRS] determination in the notice. Due to the significant difference in these arm's-length prices and [the IRS] determination in the notice of deficiency, we conclude that [the IRS] allocations lead to an unreasonable result and are thus arbitrary, capricious, and unreasonable.

In addition to proving that the deficiencies set forth in the notice are arbitrary, capricious, or unreasonable, petitioner must also prove that the prices charged by Compaq Asia were consistent with arm's-length pricing. . . . The regulations set forth three pricing methods to determine whether there is an appropriate arm's-length price. First, if comparable uncontrolled sales exist, the regulations mandate that the CUP method be used. If there are no comparable uncontrolled sales, the resale price method must be utilized if the standards for its application are met. If the standards for the resale price method are not satisfied, either that method or the cost-plus method may be used, depending upon which method is more feasible and is more likely to result in an accurate estimate of an arm's-length price. Where none of the three methods can be reasonably applied, some other appropriate method may be used.

Under the CUP method, the arm's-length price of a controlled sale is equal to the price paid in comparable uncontrolled sales including necessary adjustments. "Uncontrolled sales" are sales in which the seller and the buyer are not members of the same controlled group. . . . Uncontrolled sales are considered "comparable" to controlled sales if the physical property and circumstances involved in the uncontrolled sales are identical to the physical property and circumstances involved in the controlled sales or if such properties and circumstances are so nearly identical that differences either have no effect on price or such differences can be reflected by a reasonable number of adjustments to the price of the uncontrolled sales. Adjustments can be made only where such differences have a definite and reasonably ascertainable effect on price. Some of the differences listed in the regulations as possibly affecting price are differences in quality, terms of sale, intangible property associated with the sale, level of the market, and geographic market in which the sales take place. Whether differences render sales noncomparable depends upon the particular circumstances and property involved. . . .

Petitioner has presented substantial evidence of uncontrolled transactions with unrelated subcontractors. Petitioner's CUP analysis is predicated on Compaq U.S. purchases of 3.6 million PCA's from unrelated subcontractors between 1990 and 1993. The aggregate purchase price of these PCA's totaled $597 million on a turnkey equivalent basis and was 93.1 percent of the Compaq U.S. standard cost. In addition, the purchases occurred in the regular course of business and were substantial in both frequency and amount. . . . Although these transactions were not identical to the controlled transactions involving Compaq Asia, we conclude that they are sufficiently similar to provide a reliable measure of an arm's-length result. Thus, the purchases from unrelated subcontractors identified by petitioner qualify as comparable uncontrolled sales for purposes of application of the CUP method.

Compaq U.S. purchases of PCA's from unrelated subcontractors, however, differ in some respects from the PCA purchases from Compaq Asia. Accordingly, within the context of [tax regulations] and the particular facts in this case, the specific differences between the Compaq U.S. purchase of PCA's from Compaq Asia and unrelated subcontractors must be examined to determine "Whether and to what extent differences in the various properties and circumstances affect price. . . ." The record demonstrates that the only differences in PCA's within each product category were the particular components used on each individual PCA and the time required to process PCA's on the manufacturing line. We are persuaded that these differences can be corrected with adjustments to Compaq U.S. standard costs. . . .

Based on the uncontrolled purchases of 3.6 million PCA's, the turnkey equivalent price of PCA's purchased from unrelated subcontractors was 93.1 percent of the Compaq U.S. standard costs weighted to the Compaq Asia production amount. Compaq Asia turnkey prices were 93.9 percent of the Compaq U.S. standard cost. Thus, the relationship between Compaq Asia prices and unrelated subcontractors prices is definite, and a reasonably accurate adjustment can be made using these ratios. . . .

continued

continued

Ultimately, [the IRS] argues that, because the CUP method cannot be applied, a profits-based fourth method is the appropriate method of determining arm's-length prices in this case. The Court was faced with the same "prices v. profit" argument [in a prior case]. This Court held:

> The fact that B&L Ireland could, through its possession of superior production technology, undercut the market and sell at a lower price is irrelevant. Petitioners have shown that the $7.50 they paid for lenses was a "market price" and have thus "earned the right to be free from section 482 reallocations." * * *

The same is true in the present case. The CUP method establishes arm's-length prices for PCA's that were sold by Compaq Asia, and a large profit margin does not prevent use of the CUP method.

Decision. The Tax Court found that petitioner satisfied its burden of proving that the prices in the intercompany transactions were consistent with arm's-length prices and ordered the IRS to reduce its deficiency notices accordingly.

---

http://www.wto.org
Go to this site for links on related topics through the WTO.

In the 1992 U.S. presidential elections, abuse of transfer pricing by foreign corporations became a significant campaign issue. It seems that foreign firms collectively reported a return on assets that was only one-third of comparable domestic competitors—suggesting widespread underreporting. As a result of the notoriety that the problem received, the Internal Revenue Service enacted new regulations to increase reporting in the area in order to permit detection of evasion. But the basic structure of transfer pricing remained in place. And despite much discussion of "minimum taxes" against foreign corporations doing business in the United States, the threat of foreign retaliation against U.S. firms cooled legislators' ardor.

Foreign Sales Corporations. Virtually all nations provide incentives to companies that export. In the United States, tax incentives are provided in part through the "extraterritorial income" provisions of the Internal Revenue Code. Under this law, U.S. firms may create a foreign subsidiary, informally called a foreign sales corporation, to handle their export taxation. The U.S. parent may sell goods directly to this entity, which will resell them in export markets, or the parent may export directly overseas and pay a commission to the entity for assisting in making the sale. The earnings of the entity are called extraterritorial income. Of the extraterritorial income earned, just over one-

third is taxable to the entity at regular corporate rates. The earnings can be repatriated to the U.S. parent without incurring further tax liability.

Companies involved in a shared foreign sales corporation can sometimes obtain export trading company immunity from U.S. antitrust laws so that they may divide export territories, use common export marketing plans, share export pricing information, and engage in other joint marketing activities. They do not normally share profits or bear the risks of the sale of each other's products.

Laws Prohibiting Foreign Control

Virtually every country prohibits entities controlled by foreigners in particularly sensitive sectors. As noted previously, the United States outlaws foreign control in "security-sensitive" fields such as telecommunications, air transportation, and military procurement. Governments that feel more insecure about foreigners tend to exclude foreign-controlled investments from more sectors of their economies. Until NAFTA and the privatizations of the 1990s, Mexico generally prohibited 100 percent foreign investment, permitting it only in thirty-four designated industrial activities. The Mexican government permitted its bureaucracy to add to or subtract from that list, depending on changing conditions. Recently, these laws have been changed to give government officials discretion to permit 100 percent foreign ownership in many industries and majority shares in even more.

Other countries are even more restrictive, permitting foreign control only in sectors in which they have the greatest interest in development. India and China, for example, have until recent years generally permitted full foreign ownership only in firms that manufacture exclusively for export. Such firms were tolerated because they earned needed foreign exchange for the host country. India and China also permitted high levels of foreign majority ownership in high-technology firms. In that instance, the overwhelming desire for modernization outweighed distrust of foreign control.

Finally, a few nations such as North Korea have been so xenophobic that they do not permit foreign majority ownership at all. However, the collapse of the communist system and the extreme unavailability of capital to isolationist nations in the 1990s pushed nearly all countries to accept foreign majority ownership in the twenty-first century. Nominally communist nations such as Cuba and Vietnam now permit foreigners to own and control investments within their borders.

An example of the evolution in anti-majority ownership laws was seen in the former Soviet Union republics. The joint venture law passed in the Soviet Union in January 1987 limited foreign ownership in a joint venture to 49 percent or less. Although the law sought to promote foreign investment and was widely publicized and discussed in the West, restrictions on ownership and other barriers to foreign investment continued to limit the number of entrepreneurs willing to risk investing in the Soviet Union. In December 1988, responding to criticisms of its 1987 law, the Soviet Union passed another law that, among other things, eliminated the 49 percent ownership requirement. Since that time, the foreign investment laws of the Russian Federation and most of the former Soviet Republics have become even more accepting of foreign participation in all sectors of the economy.

Effects of Prohibition of Control

As noted above, investors prize control highly. Firms interested in the long-term growth of the joint venture are vitally interested in guiding the venture's progress through its startup period and in holding the reins as the venture matures. Investors that have valuable technology or know-how fear that it could be transferred into unfriendly hands.

Accordingly, investor reaction to legal measures prohibiting control has always been negative. India's enactment of a general 40 percent limitation on for-

eign ownership, for example, led to a 55 percent drop in foreign investment between 1975 and 1987. Similarly, Mexico's enactment of a 49 percent foreign investment limit—since modified in most industries other than the petroleum sector—led to an abrupt reduction of foreign investment from over 10 percent of all private investment to about 3 percent. In short, the need for foreign capital—which, as we will see in Chapter Nineteen, completely reversed the trend to nationalization—has reversed the movement to broad prohibition of foreign control. The U.S. investor now seldom sees a much greater tolerance for foreign-controlled private entities and a larger number of sectors of foreign economies in which they can invest. Indeed, through the process of privatization, U.S. investors increasingly are buying into sectors of the economy recently owned by the state.

CONTROLLING CURRENCY RISK

One of the most distinctive aspects of doing business outside of the United States is currency risk. *Currency risk* simply does not exist in domestic transactions. An entrepreneur who makes an investment in a domestic business is principally concerned with its operational profitability. If the investment is in an enterprise that will be earning foreign currency, however, the entrepreneur must also consider the two forms of currency risk: fluctuation risk and inconvertibility risk.

Fluctuation risk is the possibility that the currency of the country in which the U.S. investor has put its money will devalue against the U.S. dollar. For example, in 2000, the pressure of massive imports from Brazil drove the Argentine government suddenly to abandon its 10-year-old policy of pegging the Argentine peso to the U.S. dollar. The Argentine currency abruptly devalued over 50 percent against the U.S. dollar. When a foreign currency devalues against the dollar, the value of the investment's profit—and the rate of return on the entrepreneur's dollar investment—declines. If the U.S. investor borrowed the U.S. dollars that it invested abroad, a devaluation of the foreign currency may prevent the investment from generating enough U.S. dollars to even repay the debt. A sudden variation in the exchange rate can ruin an operationally successful business investment.

Inconvertibility risk is the risk that the government of a country with soft currency will hinder the foreign entrepreneur from trading the foreign currency back into U.S. dollars or another hard currency. A *soft currency* is one that is not freely exchangeable on public markets for currencies of other nations, generally this is because its fluctuation risk is viewed as too great. To obtain hard currencies such as the U.S. dollar in soft-currency countries, one must generally go through the country's government, which will exchange the local currency for dollars at an "official rate," often very favorable to the government.

In a soft-currency nation, hard currency is in short supply. At the time of the initial investment, the U.S. investor must often hand over its dollars to the local central bank, which will incorporate them into the government's hard currency reserves and exchange them for the local currency. To get dollars back for the local soft currency, the U.S investor must fill out an application and await a response. The government then decides who gets to exchange the local soft currency for its supply of hard currency.

Through a wide variety of diverse and imaginative ceilings, prohibitions, and controls, such governments can limit access to hard currency for foreigners seeking to take profits out of the local economy. The local country may, for instance, require central bank approval of all remittances, permitting the bank to place a moratorium on remittances during periods that the government's hard currency needs exceed its resources. The nation may impose a large surtax on out-of-country royalty fee remittances. It may prohibit remittances on returns on capital for a period of years after the initial investment. Remittances of fees from local subsidiaries to U.S. parent corporations may be limited or proscribed altogether. An effective unofficial technique is for the government simply to sit on the investor's application indefinitely. Because inconvertibility controls can effectively destroy profit, investors need to understand how to limit this risk.

Minimizing Fluctuation Risk: Currency Swaps

The U.S. entrepreneur's principal concern is how to limit the risk posed by the fact that the investment will be earning some other currency from an investment made in U.S. dollars. A broad assortment of financial instruments, generically known as *currency swaps*, may be purchased to hedge against

fluctuation risk. For example, a party who will need dollars in the future will enter into an agreement to deliver a certain number of Argentine pesos in the future to a currency arbitrageur or other financial intermediary. The number of pesos to be delivered to the financial intermediary in the future will implicitly reflect anticipated fluctuation rates and a profit for the intermediary. In other words, the currency swap transfers the risk of fluctuation to the intermediary, leaving the investor with only the risk of the business itself. The intermediary will then seek to "hedge" its risk by a matching transaction with another, unrelated party in which the intermediary agrees to deliver the Argentine pesos it receives in the first transaction for the U.S. dollars the intermediary has agreed to deliver in the first transaction. Done properly, the intermediary matches business parties' needs and takes a spread. To facilitate these transactions, the International Swap Dealers Association has developed a standard form agreement so that all legal terms in these deals are matched as well. In addition to hedging, a number of legal approaches can further minimize fluctuation and inconvertibility risks.

Arrangements with the Soft-Currency Country

The most direct way of assuring access to hard currency is to obtain that access from the government of the soft-currency country. The essential problem in soft-currency countries is the great demand for a limited amount of hard currency. Accordingly, the queue for hard currency is long, and when the investor finally gets to the front of the queue, it receives only its ration of foreign currency.

If the investor proposes bringing a desired industry to the soft-currency nation—a high technology plant or a hard-currency earner—it can negotiate with the government in advance for preferential access to hard currency. The resulting *currency exchange rights* can solve the inconvertibility problem for the foreign investor.

If preferential currency exchange rights are not available, the U.S. investor may seek *import substitution rights* from the government. These rights are available when the new venture will manufacture a product in the soft-currency country that the nation had previously imported. Through import substitution rights, the government permits the U.S. investor to repatriate profit up to the amount of money the country would have otherwise spent importing what the new venture is providing. Again, however, an investor must reach this agreement before actually committing capital to the soft-currency nation.

Payment and Price Adjustment Approaches

In most situations, the government will not be willing or legally able to provide the foreign investor either currency exchange or import substitution rights. The investor must therefore create legal structures for its investment that will maximize the foreign venture's U.S. dollar resources. One way to protect against currency risk is through the structure of payments back to the U.S. investor.

First, whenever possible, the investor should negotiate for lump-sum, hard-currency payments as early as possible rather than a series of future installments, even in situations where one would normally extend installment financing in the domestic context. Thus, even in a royalty deal for intellectual property, the investor may opt for a single payment for the present value of the anticipated income stream. This up-front payment avoids the uncertainty of whether the foreign customer will receive hard currency allocations in future years—a function not only of the nation's foreign exchange success but also of the investor's political prowess. Hard currency today is the best antidote to fluctuation and inconvertibility risk.

The obvious drawback with this approach is that most foreign customers and foreign investments cannot yield immediate cash. Many foreign ventures are startup operations, relying on future earnings to pay a return. And the approach does not work at all for a U.S. firm that plans to generate revenue by selling its products abroad for foreign currency.

A second approach is to build currency adjustment mechanisms into contractual payment terms through *profit margin preservation* provisions or *unitary index adjustment* factors. Under the profit margin preservation approach, the price or payment to the U.S. investor will be adjusted periodically to maintain the same profit margin by contractually identifying a cost structure in the relevant currency and agreeing to modify the price as the cost of the cost structure's elements changes over time. Profit margin preservation, however, discloses the U.S. company's cost structure, which

is often valuable information to its competitors and therefore highly confidential.

This serious problem does not exist if the parties provide for formulaic adjustment of payment terms based on an accepted unitary index. This index can be a commonly accepted measure of relative currency value or national inflation. The drawback of indexes is that they are frequently independent of the facts of the transaction. And many public indexes relating to soft-currency values are notoriously unreliable. Finally, neither the profit margin preservation nor the unitary index adjustment approaches address the issue of repatriation. In other words, if one's cost structure is stated in zlotys or adjusted to an acceptable index, one may be technically protected against 300 percent devaluation against the dollar, but one has no way of exchanging one's many zlotys for dollars.

Structuring of Hard-Currency Obligations and Revenues

Another series of methodologies for dealing with currency risk involves structuring transactions so as to conserve U.S. dollar resources. An investor can achieve this type of risk reduction by avoiding dollar-denominated obligations and by conserving hard currency earned by the venture.

Few investments are funded entirely through contributions of equity from the entrepreneur. In most cases, the entrepreneur borrows a significant portion of the capital necessary to launch the venture. An important rule in currency risk avoidance in a venture that will be generating local currency revenues is to borrow that money, to the greatest extent possible, in local currency. In that way, the local outpost will be able to use its local revenues directly to service its obligations without exposure to the vagaries of the international currency markets or the whims of local authorities who control access to hard currencies.

The Argentine devaluation of the early 2000s illustrates this point. In view of Argentina's decade-long commitment to maintaining fiscal stability by maintaining parity between the peso and the U.S. dollar, many North American entrepreneurs came to regard the peso's exchange rate to the dollar as relatively stable. Many such businesses invested in Argentine power plant and other infrastructure projects, borrowing money in lower interest U.S. dollar loans. But when the peso crashed, the pesos the Argentine power plants earned were suddenly worth 50 percent less in dollars; many ventures could no longer make their debt payments and went into bankruptcy. By contrast, those investors who had borrowed in pesos did not face this financial problem: The peso had dropped in value relative to the dollar, but within Argentina, it still was the unit of exchange; the ventures could simply continue to use their pesos within Argentina to pay their debts. In fact, because devaluation was accompanied by some inflation, those with fixed interest rate debt actually had to devote less of their cash flow to debt service. Of course, the U.S. dollar value of their profits did fall, but many used the excess pesos to focus on the impact on their business of the attendant economic crisis in Argentina, itself no easy task.

The same rule applies with respect to contracts between the venture and *trade creditors,* the entities that sell supplies or services to the venture. To the greatest extent possible, the venture should buy locally so that it can pay for the goods and services in local currency. This again conserves the enterprise's hard-currency resources so that as much of these resources as possible can be available for transfer back to the U.S. investor.

If the investor anticipates that the foreign venture will experience significant hard-currency earnings, it should take steps to prevent the hard currency from reentering the soft-currency country. Instead of transferring payment for the foreign venture's products directly to the venture, hard-currency customers would be instructed to pay the U.S. investor directly. The investor takes what the foreign venture owes it in debt payments, fees, or dividends and transfers the balance to the foreign venture.

Through a related approach, the U.S. investor "calls" a percentage of the foreign venture's production. In other words, the investor actually finds hard-currency customers, sells the product to them, obtains the payment, takes its agreed-upon share, and transfers the remaining share to the venture. This practice is particularly common in situations in which the foreign venture is the manufacturing or assembling arm of the U.S. investor.

Countertrade

Countertrade is another popular way of dealing with currency inconvertibility. In countertrade, local currency earnings are used to purchase local products, which are then exported to a hard-currency country for sale. The proceeds of the hard-currency sale are then converted into dollars and returned to the U.S. investor.

An example of countertrade was used by Pepsi Cola Corporation in Russia. Pepsi was faced with the prospect of holding a large amount of volatile rubles for the sales of its soft drink products in the Russian Federation, which it wished to exchange promptly for dollars. To resolve its dilemma, Pepsi structured a multiparty transaction whereby rubles were used to purchase Russian mushrooms for Pepsi's Pizza Hut affiliate. Pizza Hut then paid Pepsi for the mushrooms the dollar amounts that it would have otherwise had to spend.

The principal difficulty with countertrade is that the U.S. investor must find a supply of quality local goods that are in demand in hard-currency countries. After all, if the country had many such goods, it probably would not be a soft-currency country.

Informal Consortia or Parallel Exchanges

In some soft-currency countries, foreign investors form consortia to trade local soft currency. At various times, some members of a consortium would have more of the local currency than they can get rid of, while others may need more than they can earn to develop profitable business. By broadening the base of foreign investors, a private *parallel exchange* is thereby formed in countries without formal currency exchanges.

One of the most notable of these consortia was the American Trade Consortium formed in the Russian Federation in the spring of 1988, which permitted U.S. firms to freely exchange currencies between themselves. This consortium permitted U.S. firms to exchange currency at market, rather than artificial official rates, and provided immediate availability in the midst of fiscal chaos.

Similar parallel exchanges have existed among hard-currency investors in Latin American countries. As Latin American currencies become freely convertible, however, their incidence has declined. The key to participating in these informal exchanges is to be sure that the U.S. investor does not inadvertently violate local currency exchange laws.

Inconvertibility Insurance

A final alternative for the U.S. investor is an *inconvertibility* or *"non-transfer" insurance* policy. Such policies can be purchased for *hard blockages*—when the government actually passes a law that prevents conversion or transfer. For a somewhat higher fee, a businessperson may purchase a policy that also protects against *soft blockages,* which are excessive delays in processing a request to convert or transfer by the local government authorities. Protected items can include repatriation of profits, dividends, local repayments, management and royalty fees, technical assistance fees, and any other form of income considered to be earnings or return on capital. Inconvertibility insurance is a type of political risk insurance and is provided to companies in the same manner as other forms of political risk insurance (described in Chapter Nineteen).

CHAPTER SUMMARY

Companies operating in other countries must abide by those nations' laws. The level of foreign investment regulation in a given country depends on a number of factors, including the amount of foreign currency reserves, whether the government favors central control, and their fear of foreign control. In minority ownership investments (owning less than 50 percent of the enterprise), an investor can have either an active investment and participate in managing the enterprise, or a passive investment that provides only equity capital to be managed by others. Many countries create a legal structure that limits foreign majority control of businesses. For the more active investor, a joint venture is often the best form of foreign investment. Local traditions, regulations, and tax laws all influence what form of joint venture is most attractive.

Currency risk in cross-border business transactions comes in two forms: fluctuation and inconvertibility. Fluctuation risk for a U.S. investor is the possibility that the value of a given foreign currency will decrease against the value of the U.S. dollar. Inconvertibility risk occurs in soft-currency countries. Governments whose currency is not exchanged in public international markets often lack a supply of hard currency they can use in conducting international business. Because of their low reserves of easily exchangeable currency, these countries often limit repatriation of foreign profits through a wide range of regulations, such as central bank approvals for money transfers, surtaxes, and legal prohibitions.

These risks can be minimized by hedging with a variety of financial instruments, or through legal approaches such as currency swaps, prior arrangements with the soft-currency government, payment and price adjustments, countertrade, consortia or parallel exchanges, and inconvertibility insurance.

Questions and Case Problems

1. Keefe Energy, Inc., a U.S. firm, enters into a joint venture with Energia Guerra, S.A., a Mexican firm, to build and operate a coal-fired electric-power-generating plant with an estimated useful life of thirty-five years. The building and land will be owned by G/K, S.A., a company 80-percent owned by Guerra and 20-percent owned by Keefe. G/K will enter into an agreement with Keefe under which Keefe is to build and operate the plant and receive 95 percent of the projected profit from the plant for the first twenty years of its operation. Is Keefe making a minority investment? What sort of scrutiny is the joint venture likely to receive from government officials?

2. Assume the same facts as in Question 1, except that the joint venture is to build and operate a computer microcircuit manufacturing plant. What different considerations come into play in government review? What is the likely outcome?

3. What financing alternatives would be available to a U.S. firm that was interested in investing in a proposed manufacturing plant in a small country that recently left the communist bloc and did not wish to invest much of its own resources?

4. If a U.S. company establishes a 100 percent subsidiary in another country, what three general aspects of U.S. income tax law should the company be sure it has addressed?

5. What are the implications for an American who purchases shares in a German company on the basis of inside information?

Managerial Implications

You work for Luree Intergalactic, Inc., a Montana Alpine ski manufacturer. Because of attractive relative labor costs found in Latvia, Luree joins forces with Aivars, AG, a Latvian firm, to build a new factory in Riga to serve the European market. Together, Luree and Aivars establish Udris, Ltd., a Latvian joint-stock company that will own the factory and sell products from it. Udris will be free to sells its skis to anyone, but expects to sell most of its initial output to Luree and Aivars. Under an agreement between Luree and Aivars, Luree will purchase skis from Udris for resale in Europe east of Ukraine, and in North and South America, New Zealand, and Japan; Aivars will market the remaining portion of Udris's production to the rest of the world.

1. Because Luree has greater financial resources than does Aivars, its capital contribution will entitle it to 90 percent of Udris. Aivars also recognizes that it has received the less attractive ski markets. It expects to derive most of its income from a special contract with Udris to test new ski models on mogul runs. Prepare a memorandum that anticipates what principal corporate law concerns will need to be addressed in this arrangement.

2. Aivars suggests that, as compensation for being Udris's first customers, Luree and Aivars receive a discount off the price that Udris charges other purchasers. Analyze the transfer-pricing issues raised by this proposal.

CHAPTER 19

NATIONALIZATION, EXPROPRIATION, AND PRIVATIZATION

The preceding chapters discussed the gradual progression of commitment by a U.S. investor in a nation—from appointment of a representative, through the transfer of intellectual property rights, to commitment of capital resources abroad. Up to now, the discussion has covered the increasing vulnerability to regulation under the laws of the host country. In a sense, the differences in risk from doing business in the United States are only of degree and local peculiarity. After all, the United States often has similar regulations.

Political risk is an altogether different kind of risk. Perhaps the most elementary and important distinction between investment in the United States and investment abroad is that the foreign government may through *nationalization* or an *expropriation* simply take one's investment without paying full compensation. Concerns about nationalization and expropriation were paramount through most of the twentieth century. In the early twentieth century, communist and socialist governments aggressively nationalized industries in Europe; in the 1960s and 1970s, emerging and newly independent governments took over foreign-owned enterprises in Latin America, Asia, and Africa. Questions about the level of adequate compensation for such takings were vital.

Then, in the late 1980s, communism died and governments ran nationalized industries into the ground. Suddenly, the government was selling the assets back to the private sector. *Privatization,* the transfer of government-owned assets to the private sector, is simply the reverse of the nationalization–expropriation process; it illustrates that trends in international law, like the political environment that law reflects, are cyclical. This chapter begins with a discussion of the legal issues surrounding nationalization and proceeds through the unwinding of nationalization in the privatization movement.

THEORIES RELATING TO TAKINGS OF FOREIGN PROPERTY

Although nationalization became important only in the twentieth century, Western legal scholars have been debating the propriety of the takings of foreign property for hundreds of years. This dialectic can be summarized in two major theories: the *traditional* theory and the *modern-traditional* theory.

The Traditional Theories

Traditional theory prohibits all takings of foreign property, while modern-traditional requires prompt, adequate, and effective compensation for such takings. The modern-traditional requirement of adequate compensation has been questioned or rejected in some parts of the world, particularly in socialist countries that adhere to the theory of preeminence of the sovereign rights of the state. In order to understand how to limit risks, the foreign investor must be aware of their extent in all parts of the globe.

The classic doctrine on the taking of the property of foreign citizens was developed in Europe beginning in the seventeenth century. Because the

European states were capital exporters during that period, the doctrine was predictably protective of foreign investment. The fundamental principle was that foreign investors—unlike local merchants—should be exempt from the sovereign's condemnation rights: "The right of subjects then differs from the right of foreigners in this, that over those who are in no way subject, the power of eminent domain has no control." The local investor was subject to expropriation by the sovereign under the legal doctrine of *eminent domain*. For example, the government can condemn a U.S. citizen's land if it needs the land to build a highway, so long as it compensates that citizen for the fair value of the land. Under the traditional theory, however, the foreign investor would have been exempt from such takings. This made some sense in the context of the pre-twentieth century international system in which citizens of the advanced mercantile or industrial countries were considered to be wholly immune from the judicial power of the less-developed host state. Thus, in the nineteenth century, Britain dispatched gunboats to Venezuela to compel restitution of expropriated property of British subjects.

As the sovereign equality of nations became accepted in the twentieth century, the traditional doctrine became indefensible and evolved into the *modern-traditional theory*. This theory recognizes the sovereign's right to nationalize foreign-owned property, but places conditions on the proper exercise of that right. The exercise of the right must be (1) for a public purpose; (2) nondiscriminatory, not directed specifically against a foreign person; and (3) accompanied by *prompt, adequate, and effective compensation*. Thus, a sovereign cannot take foreign property for harassment, personal aggrandizement, or other nonpublic purposes, and cannot target the property of one nationality discriminatorily. And compensation must be paid. To modern-traditional thinkers, "adequate" compensation meant fair market value as a going concern, including future earnings and intangibles; "prompt" meant as soon as reasonable, and "effective" meant cash or a commodity immediately available and freely convertible to cash. This modern traditionalism was eloquently advanced by Secretary of State Cordell Hull in his response to the expropriations triggered by the Mexican Revolution (see Exhibit 19.1).

Modern-traditional theory is accepted as customary international law by the countries that have historically been capital exporters: the North American and Western European nations. In the 1970s and 1980s, arbitrations arising out of the expropriation of foreign oil holdings led to pronouncements by the Iran–United States Claims Tribunal in The Hague confirming that modern-traditional theory remains the accepted international standard.

Thus, although an overseas investment is normally subject to the host country's sovereign right to expropriate, in developed countries the investor should be entitled, under customary international law, to full compensation—at least if the investor can obtain arbitration of the dispute. But the modern-traditional theory, by far the majority view, has not been accepted everywhere.

Non-Western Theories of Takings

The first intellectual counterpoint to the traditional theory came from Latin America in the nineteenth century through the so-called *Calvo Doctrine*. The Calvo Doctrine placed the sovereign ahead of the foreign investor within the sovereign's territory and challenged any intervention by foreign states in investment disputes as a violation of the territorial jurisdiction of the host country. Calvo proponents argue that nationalization is a legitimate exercise of the sovereign's preeminent right to restructure the economy and is not subject to the law of any other jurisdiction, including international law. The appropriate recourse of the foreign investor should be no greater than that of any domestic investor: to appeal to the courts or political branches of the sovereign nation taking the "nationalizing" action. No foreign nation or entity had any right to impose itself simply because the investor happened to be of foreign origin.

Calvo's emphasis on the primacy of the state corresponded nicely with the concept of state property inaugurated by the Bolshevik Revolution. To communists, the theory that the sovereign state had a right to restructure its own economy was consistent with the expropriations that followed the revolution. Other communist states followed the Soviet example.

Finally, when Europe's former Asian and African colonies became politically independent in the years

---

EXHIBIT 19.1

Diplomatic Note from the Secretary of State of the United States
of America to the Minister of Foreign Affairs of Mexico
July 21, 1938
United States Department of State

Background and Facts

Agrarian expropriations began in Mexico in 1915. As of August 30, 1927, 1,621 moderate-sized properties of American citizens had been taken. Subsequent to 1927, additional properties, chiefly farms of a moderate size, with a value claimed by their owners of $10,132,388 were expropriated by the Mexican government. The claims of their owners were referred to a General Claims Commission established by agreement between the two governments, but as of 1938, when Secretary Hull sent his letter, not a single claim had been adjusted and none had been paid.

Secretary of State Cordell Hull

The taking of property without compensation is not expropriation. It is confiscation. It is no less confiscation because there may be an expressed intent to pay at some time in the future. If it were permissible for a government to take the private property of the citizens of other countries and pay for it as and when, in the judgment of that government, its economic circumstances and its local legislation may perhaps permit, the safeguards which the constitutions of most countries and established international law have sought to provide would be illusory. Governments would be free to take property far beyond their ability or willingness to pay, and the owners thereof would be without recourse. We cannot question the right of a foreign government to treat its own nationals in this fashion if it so desires. This is a matter of domestic concern. But we cannot admit that foreign government may take the property of American nationals in disregard of the rule of compensation under international law. Nor can we admit that any government unilaterally and through its municipal legislation can, as in this instant case, nullify this universally accepted principle of international law, based as it is on reason, equity and justice. . . .

The whole structure of friendly intercourse, of international trade and commerce, and many other vital and mutually desirable relations between nations indispensable to their progress rest upon the single and hitherto solid foundation of respect on the part of governments and of peoples for each other's rights under international justice. The right of prompt and just compensation for expropriated property is a part of this structure. It is a principle to which the government of the United States and most governments of the world have emphatically subscribed and which they have practiced and which must be maintained. It is not a principle which freezes the status quo and denies changes in property rights but a principle that permits any country to expropriate private property within its borders in furtherance of public purposes. It enables orderly change without violating the legitimately acquired interests of the citizens of other countries.

---

following World War II, they came to view nationalization as a necessary part of economic independence. In their view, as long as foreigners controlled the economy, they effectively controlled the country, irrespective of who occupied the political apparatus. These newly emerging states could not begin to pay full compensation for such nationalizations because they simply lacked the tax base to do so. Hence, the communist sovereign state counter-theories seemed quite useful.

In short, during the twentieth century, much of the world rejected modern traditional theory and adopted theories that in one way or another asserted that the state had a right to take foreign property for what purposes it chose and upon payment of less than full compensation. Whatever the intellectual

basis for the takings, for the foreign investor, the results were the same: Its property was taken and the investor was paid less than the property was worth.

In recent years, the number of adherents to sovereign rights theories has been in a steep decline. When Latin American countries defaulted on their loans from North American and European banks, capital for their economies dried up. In order to attract new capital investment—in many cases for the re-privatization of assets Latin governments had nationalized—they were compelled to assure prospective foreign investors that future investments would be treated under the modern-traditional theory. This was accomplished both through domestic legislation and international treaties. Similarly, when the Eastern European communist bloc collapsed in the 1989–1991 period, the new democracies adopted the modern-traditional theory in a series of bilateral treaties and national legislation so as to attract foreign investment. In the 1990s, most former colonies also accepted the modern-traditional theory as a prelude to attracting foreign capital. Nonetheless, the sovereign rights theory remains alive—if dormant—as an intellectual force. In many of these nations, it may be no farther away than another change in the international economic climate.

Public Purpose, Nondiscrimination, and the Expropriation–Nationalization Distinction

Sovereign rights proponents like Professor Calvo rejected the modern-traditional theory's "prerequisites" of public purpose and nondiscrimination. They argue that the right to take foreign property is an attribute of national sovereignty and, as such, cannot be conditioned on whether an international tribunal characterizes the taking as discriminatory or as furthering a private purpose. In essence, the sovereign has a right to take foreign property without having outsiders impose preconditions.

Paradoxically, sovereign rights states nevertheless incorporated public purpose concepts in deciding whether a taking is one that merits full compensation—as in an expropriation—or one that merits less compensation—as in nationalization. The classic *expropriation* is a taking of an isolated item of property. The foreign investor is singled out as the target of governmental action in a fashion that might be viewed as discriminatory and not part of a national public plan. By contrast, a *nationalization* is the taking of an entire industry or a natural resource as part of a plan to restructure the nation's economic system. In a nationalization, the values underlying sovereign rights theories are most strongly implicated, and full compensation is not required by those theories.

One of the few nations that has not been precluded by treaty from espousing sovereign rights theories is the Islamic Republic of Iran. The *INA Corp.* arbitration demonstrated that some jurists still accept sovereign rights concepts.

The approach suggested by the panel in the *INA* case—less than full compensation in the event of any large scale nationalization—remains a distinct minority view. Most international tribunals, including most panels of the Iran–United States Claims Tribunal, adhere to the modern-traditional theory. But no less an authority than the *Restatement (Third) of Foreign Relations Law*—which ostensibly reflects the consensus view—states that less than full compensation may be acceptable in "exceptional circumstances" such as agricultural land reform. Modern-traditional theory continues to be under attack.

Level of Compensation. Once it has been determined that a taking was a "nationalization," sovereign rights advocates uniformly reject the traditional formula of "prompt, adequate, and effective compensation." First, they often disavow the obligation to provide fair market value compensation. With respect to the taking of lands or natural resources, for instance, they argue that the state already owns the resource and need pay only for the foreign owners' improvements to the land or resources.

If one scratches the surface of these arguments, one will uncover the practical point that the government that is taking the good cannot afford its fair market value. If, in the view of such a nation, a taking of foreign property is necessary for effective political independence, those imperatives override mere commercial considerations. Thus, a number of sovereign rights states have favored measures of compensation that bear only an attenuated relationship to fair value. An example is *net book value* of the nationalized asset, that reflects the depreciated cost of assets—using accounting depreciation conventions—without regard to whether there has in fact been depreciation. Many assets, for example, actually appreciate over time because of appreciation in the value of what they produce or because the business of which it is a part has a "going concern value" over and above the value of the asset in isolation.

Second, sovereign rights states generally insist on the right to schedule payment of the compensation over time. This installment method has sometimes been accomplished through devices such as the issuance of national bonds payable in the local currency. In addition to being paid less than market value, the victim of nationalization must bear the fluctuation risk associated with the local currency;

INA Corp. v. Islamic Republic of Iran
8 Iran–U.S. Claims Tribunal Reports 373 (1985)
Iran–United States Claims Tribunal

BACKGROUND AND FACTS
On May 3, 1978, a subsidiary of INA Corporation (INA), INA International Insurance Company, Ltd. (INA International), acquired 20 percent of the shares of Bimek Shargh, an Iranian insurance company. The proposed investment by INA International was approved by Central Insurance of Iran (CII), the government body responsible for the regulation of insurance activities in Iran, by a letter to Shargh of December 27, 1977. INA International paid 20 million rials for the shares of Shargh.

On June 25, 1979, the Law of Nationalization of Insurance and Credit Enterprises was enacted in Iran. Article 1 provided as follows:

> To protect the rights of the insured, to expand the insurance industry and the entire State and to place it at the service of the people, from the date of this law, all insurance enterprises in Iran are proclaimed nationalized with acceptance of the principle of legitimate ownership.

INA claimed what it alleged to be the going value of its Shargh shares, together with interest and legal costs.

JUDGE LAGERGREN
The essence of the dispute between the Parties lies not in the fact of nationalization having taken place, which is agreed, but in the determination of the level of compensation, if any, which should be paid to the shareholders of Shargh as a consequence. No compensation has been paid to date, INA argues for compensation that is "prompt, adequate and effective," on the basis both of general principles of international law and the Treaty of Amity, Economic Relations, and Consular Rights of 15 August 1955. INA asks the Tribunal to accept the amount of its initial investment in Shargh as the best available indicator of the value of the company as a going concern at the time of nationalization just over one year later.

The respondent government concedes that, in principle, the working of Article I of the nationalization law does, in appropriate cases, envisage the payment of compensation to private shareholders of nationalized insurance companies, but that this must be based on the "net book value" of the company.

It has long been acknowledged that expropriations for a public purpose and subject to conditions provided for by law—notably that category which can be characterized as "nationalizations"—are not *per se* unlawful. A lawful nationalization will, however, impose on the government concerned the obligation to pay compensation.

This case presents, in addition, a classic example of a formal and systematic nationalization by decree of an entire category of commercial enterprises considered of fundamental importance to the nation's economy. During the course of the post-Revolutionary economics restructuring in Iran. . . . The insurance companies, including Bimek Shargh, were nationalized by decree on 27 June 1979. . . . Such measures number among the risks which investors must be prepared to encounter.

In the event of such large-scale nationalizations of a lawful character, international law has undergone a gradual reappraisal, the effect of which may be to undermine the doctrinal value of any "full" or "adequate" (when used as identical to "full") compensation standard as proposed in the case.

However, the Tribunal is of the opinion that in a case such as the present, involving an investment of a rather small amount shortly before the nationalization, international law admits compensation in an amount equal to the fair market value of the investment.

Decision. The Iran–United States Claims Tribunal awarded INA Corporation the amount it sought plus simple interest at 8.5 percent per annum from the date of nationalization.

as discussed in Chapter Eighteen, the value of soft currencies—and of a bond promising to pay a certain number of units of that currency in the future—can change dramatically. Further, there is a substantial risk with the local country's ability to repay—many emerging nations have defaulted on their international debts. Because of these risks, such bonds might be transferable to others only at a massive discount, if at all.

Creeping Expropriation. Short of outright expropriation, the foreign nation may impose regulations that gradually limit the exercise of ownership rights—so-called *creeping expropriation.* Creeping expropriation regulations include discriminatory taxes, legislative controls over management of the firm, price controls, forced employment of nationals, license cancellation, and, as discussed in Chapter Eighteen, restrictions on currency convertibility. Unlike straightforward expropriation, creeping expropriation requires a determination as to whether a "taking" or mere regulation has occurred before any compensation is deemed to be justified, making it even more dangerous to the foreign investor.

Investors in emerging nations need also concern themselves with the business consequences of politically unstable environments. For example, the Indonesian government's refusal to comply with International Monetary Fund mandates caused an economic crisis that sparked destructive Jakarta riots in the spring of 1998. Apart from causing widespread *physical damage* to business assets, such *"political violence"* created *business interruptions* to enterprises with operations in Indonesia. The violence and government countermeasures, in many cases, led to *forced abandonment* of projects by firm employees racing out of the country for their lives. All of these occurrences are *"casualties"* against which the prudent business manager may wish to insure.

GUARDING AGAINST POLITICAL RISK

As Latin American and Eastern European countries accept the modern-traditional theory, the sovereign rights approaches recede as a threat. Indeed, former communist nations turned so completely from the sovereign rights approach that they created procedures for compensating Western firms for nationalizations that occurred decades earlier. The U.S. Foreign Claims Compensation Commission, which resolves claims by U.S. citizens against countries that have nationalized their assets without adequate compensation, has aggressively pursued U.S. claims in the new democracies.

If economic conditions do not improve, today's modern traditionalist might be tomorrow's nationalizing government. In March 2001, the South African government announced a plan to expropriate one-third of farmland to black ownership from white owners, including foreign investors. The plan called for "adequate compen-

sation" to the white owners, but this was redefined to mean something other than the land's current fair market value. In late 2003, the government of Argentina announced that it considered all bilateral investment treaties that agreed to "full, adequate, and effective" compensation in international arbitration to be unconstitutional and unenforceable. Nations that in the 1990s led the way to privatization now seem to be considering selective re-nationalization.

The bottom line is that the U.S. investor in countries that once espoused the sovereign rights theory is exposed to risk of loss from political action. Its investment can be taken for a fraction of its true value.

Having defined the problem, the investor must determine how to guard against it. He or she may do so either by purchasing insurance against the event before it happens or bringing legal action against the wrongdoer after it happens.

Political Risk Insurance

Entrepreneurs normally assume the risk that their business will fail because their product is unable to find an adequate market. However, the entrepreneurs will usually try to avoid the risk of failure caused by events beyond their control, such as fire, earthquake, or employee dishonesty. To cover those risks, they normally contract with an insurance company, which assumes this risk for a fee called a *premium,* based on an actuarial assessment of the probability of loss among all of the company's insureds. From this practice arose the concept of insurance against political risk. Entrepreneurs who are unwilling to hazard the risk of a foreign government taking will pay a premium to a public or private insurance company.

Obviously, the cost of this insurance is a disincentive to investment abroad. In order for the U.S. or Western European investor to justify foreign investment, the anticipated increased marginal returns on the emerging market venture—as compared to a comparable U.S. or Western European investment—must be greater than the cost of the insurance. If political risk and the cost of insurance become too great, the emerging market investment becomes financially unjustifiable. Indeed, the historic commitment of the United States to protecting private property from public seizure—eliminating political risk and political risk insurance—is one of

international accents

Time Bomb of Litigation Delays Threatens Russian Privatizations

By Virginie Coulloudon and Victor Yasmann
July 25, 2003
Russia Weekly, Johnson's Russia
List RFE/RL Newsline

Self-exiled tycoon Boris Berezovskii blasted President Vladimir Putin in an open letter published in "Kommersant-Daily" . . . accusing him of pursuing a "creeping anti-constitutional coup" by attempting to redistribute private property almost 10 years after it was privatized under President Boris Yeltsin's administration. Berezovskii argued that Putin has considerable support within the state bureaucracy and that possible expropriations by the state could lead to a civil war. . . .

[P]rominent businessmen and even politicians are increasingly emotional when describing the situation that has arisen as a result of the lawsuits brought against the oil giant Yukos [the privately owned fourth largest oil company in the world]. . . . The Yukos affair has reminded all investors that ownership is not a sacrosanct right in today's Russia. [M]any Russian businessmen openly fear that the latest developments are a sign that some privatization bids could be revised in the next few months.

[T]he Prosecutor-General's Office opened seven cases against Yukos just a few months before the "litigation delay"—the 10-year period for challenging the outcome of the privatization tender—expires. When then-First Deputy Prime Minister Anatolii Chubais launched the privatization program in 1994, most strategic privatization deals stipulated a 10-year litigation delay. Ten years after, that time bomb is about to explode and poses a serious threat to private ownership in Russia.

The privatization of state enterprises officially started in 1991–92 and was conducted in two phases. . . . On 22 July 1994, Yeltsin issued a decree on the second phase of privatization: the remaining state holdings were to be sold for cash at competitive auctions, with part of the proceeds going to the companies as capital for their restructuring and the rest going to the government. . . . Now, 10 years on Russia faces a crucial challenge as the legal deadlines for challenging tender results approach. This loophole in the privatization legislation now opens the way for the country's most strategic enterprises to be selectively targeted. [O]ne can expect to see charges filed against private, strategic enterprises that are not controlled by the power elite. As is now traditional in Russia, this process will develop both at the federal and regional levels, thus allowing the power elite to strengthen its position. This is bad news for all Russian investors who attempted to eliminate the omnipresent clan logic and implement rules of transparent business.

[Economic Development and Trade Minister German Gref] recently told "Vedomosti" that "one should keep in mind that there is no clear boundary between a revision of history and a crime investigation. If there were [economic] crimes committed during the privatization process, nobody will be able to stop their investigation until the litigation delay is over." . . . This is precisely what investors are afraid of—that the Russian state will expropriate their businesses while they are asked to "remain calm."

the qualities that makes it one of the world's most attractive investment markets.

Political Risk Insurance from Government Agencies.　A number of capital-exporting nations have established government corporations that provide political risk insurance, such as the United States' *Overseas Private Investment Corporation*

(OPIC). In essence, national agencies like OPIC hope to promote exports to foreign countries by providing coverage to firms of its own nation for expropriation (including creeping expropriation), nationalization, revolution, insurrections, and currency inconvertibility. Thus, the underlying purpose is both good and bad for the U.S. investor; insurance is provided at rates that do not include a significant profit for the insurer, but the availability of insurance is sometimes subject to politically motivated conditions that exclude many projects. For example, when India tested nuclear weapons in May 1998, OPIC funding for projects based in India immediately became unavailable. Further, investments must not adversely affect the U.S. balance of payments or U.S. employment; the host country must not impose performance regulations that are likely to reduce "positive trade benefits likely to accrue to the United States." A manufacturing joint venture that makes nothing but components for export back to the United States may not meet this requirement. OPIC also gives preference to investments in countries with relatively low per capita annual income. This condition targets the insurance coverage to the poorest countries, which coincidentally also have the least viable infrastructure. It is precisely in those countries where the commercial risk is often so high that the foreign investor would not wish to enter, irrespective of the political risk. Finally, OPIC can operate only in a country with which the United States has concluded a bilateral investment agreement. Because, under these bilateral investment agreements, the host country effectively agrees to waive its sovereign rights views on takings in disputes with the United States, some nations have not entered into them.

Other developed nations have public institutions similar to OPIC that promote investment from their own countries. These include Japan's Bank for International Cooperation, Germany's Hermes Kreditversicherung-AG, France's Compagnie francaise d'Assurance pour le commerce extérieur, and the Export Development Corporation of Canada. The conditions and limitations of these political risk programs are quite similar to those of OPIC. In some projects, a number of these national *export credit agencies* will pool their efforts.

A similar but internationally based investment insurance company is the *Multilateral Investment Guarantee Agency* (MIGA). Started in early 1988 as an independent affiliate of the World Bank, MIGA issues insurance guarantees to protect a foreign investor from expropriation, war, revolution, or other noncommercial risks. MIGA guarantees are granted for a fifteen-year term. To qualify, both the investor's home country and the country into which it is investing must be parties to the MIGA convention.

Private Political Risk Insurance. Two principal markets provide private political risk insurance. Lloyds of London insurance *syndicates*—pools of money provided by investors to insure specific projects—provide such insurance on a case-by-case basis. In this market, the U.S. investor engages a broker for a specific transaction, and the broker negotiates terms with heads of syndicates specializing in political risk insurance. The syndicate heads then obtain commitments from other syndicates in order to spread the risk exposure.

Alternatively, the investor can approach a lead underwriter of a group operating under a *reinsurance treaty*, an agreement among insurers whereby the underwriter leading the group spreads the risk among its members. Under the terms of the reinsurance treaty, the lead underwriter can commit the resources of the entire group after negotiating the transaction with the U.S. investor.

Private insurance has many advantages. First, private insurers have no political agendas and therefore have no special political prerequisites to issuing insurance. The host country need not be extremely poor and the foreign investor can hail from anywhere. In addition, the private insurance approval process can be faster than is the case with public agencies.

Private insurers, however, are in business for profit. Accordingly, their coverage can be quite expensive as compared to the government programs. Second, private syndicates will often not enter particularly politically volatile areas without a public agency as a partner. Third, the term of private insurance policies is generally limited to five to seven years, longer than in the past but still too short for an adequate return from larger capital-intensive construction projects.

In recent years, trends toward the modern-traditional theory and international investment treaties and codes have lowered the perceived risk of political risk insurance. The result has been an explosion in the availability of such insurance.

Resolving Investment Disputes with Foreign Nations

Foreign investors must understand the risks associated with seeking relief from U.S. or international forums if the prospective investment is nationalized. The first alternative for a victim of nationalization would be to seek relief in the courts of the country where the property was nationalized. In countries with well-developed traditions of an independent judiciary, this alternative is feasible. As German or Japanese investors in the United States will testify, however, even there the foreigner is at a disadvantage as a stranger in the other party's "home court." Even worse, countries with significant political risk tend not to have judiciaries as independent as that of the United States. Finally, if the country happens to ascribe to sovereign right principles, recourse to its judiciary would be rather fruitless for the injured U.S. investor. Nevertheless, under traditional international law principles, an injured investor may need to exhaust local remedies before invoking diplomatic or international adjudication.

A second possibility would be for the investor to sue the host state in the United States. After all, most governments have assets in the United States that would be subject to attachment by U.S. courts. The Boeing 747 of a state-run airline on the tarmac of O'Hare Airport can satisfy most judgments. But there are serious obstacles to this course of action. First, under the *Foreign Sovereign Immunities Act of 1976*, a federal court would not have jurisdiction over the foreign nation unless the court finds that the state's acts fall within a *commercial activity exemption* to immunity. Second, even if the court had jurisdiction over the foreign state, it might abstain from exercising it under principles of abstention referred to as the *Act of State Doctrine*. Finally, if the investor can get a U.S. court to hear the case, the investor should be prepared to rely on a treaty or powerful international law argument because U.S. courts will decline to hear a case if most of the evidence is abroad. In light of these difficulties, the foreign investor may wish to bring its case to an international arbitration. To do this, however, the host nation must have consented to such dispute resolution in advance.

The *Foreign Sovereign Immunities Act.*

In 1976, Congress enacted the *Foreign Sovereign Immunities Act* (FSIA). Under FSIA, foreign states are generally immune from the jurisdiction of U.S. courts, save for seven exceptions: (1) waiver by the foreign state; (2) the state's action constitutes "commercial activity" carried on by the state; (3) rights in property are taken in violation of international law; (4) rights in property are acquired through inheritance or gifts in the United States; (5) noncommercial torts within the United States;

(6) maritime liens based on the foreign state's "commercial activity"; and (7) certain types of counterclaims if the foreign state is the one that starts the lawsuit against a U.S. citizen. In light of the rising terrorist threat, Congress amended FSIA to allow a U.S. citizen to bring suit against a foreign state in a U.S. court for damages resulting from a state-sponsored act of terrorism. The U.S. Supreme Court has held that these are the only exceptions to FSIA's grant of immunity and has interpreted these exceptions narrowly.

The most significant of these exceptions to FSIA is the "commercial activity" exception. In relevant part, the exception provides that "a foreign state shall not be immune from the jurisdiction of the United States or the states in any case . . . in which the action is based . . . upon an act outside the territory of the United States in connection with the commercial activity of the foreign state elsewhere and it causes a direct effect on the United States." This exception is principally aimed at situations in which the state enters into a commercial contract with an investor and is acting as a private commercial party. One of the most comprehensive analyses by the Supreme Court on what constitutes "commercial activity" under the FSIA is found in the *Saudi Arabia v. Nelson* case. Writing for a slim majority of the Court, Justice Souter was careful to contrast the actions charged against Saudi Arabia with the *Republic of Argentina v. Weltover, Inc.* case, where Argentina had clothed its actions in official enactments.

In the wake of the terrorist attacks on September 11, 2001, the "state-sponsored terrorism" exception to the FSIA has received increased attention. This exception requires a plaintiff to satisfy a number of prerequisites. First, the plaintiff must seek money damages, not injunctive relief, for personal injury or death resulting from "an act of torture, extrajudicial killing, aircraft sabotage, hostage taking, or the provision of material support . . . for such an act." Second, the plaintiff must be a U.S. national when the act of terrorism occurs. Third, the defendant sovereign nation must be designated a "state sponsor of terrorism" by the State Department at the time the act occurs. Finally, if the terrorism occurred in the defendant state's territory, the plaintiff must have first tried to seek an international arbitration. In *Acree v. Iraq,* a respected federal court applied this statute against the government of Iraq for its actions in the first Gulf War.

Saudi Arabia v. Nelson
507 U.S. 349 (1993)
Supreme Court of the United States

BACKGROUND AND FACTS

The Nelsons, a married couple, filed an action for damages against the Kingdom of Saudi Arabia, a Saudi hospital, and the hospital's purchasing agent in the United States. The purchasing agent had, at the direction of the Saudi government, recruited the husband through advertising in the United States to work at a hospital in Saudi Arabia. The plaintiffs alleged that, once in Saudi Arabia, the Saudis had unlawfully detained and tortured the husband. They also based their suit on the defendants' negligent failure to warn him of the possibility of severe retaliatory action if he attempted to report on-the-job hazards. The Court of Appeals found subject matter jurisdiction, concluding that the husband's recruitment and hiring were "commercial activities" of Saudi Arabia and the hospital, carried on in the United States and that the Nelsons' action was "based upon" these activities within the meaning of the statute. There was, the Court of Appeals reasoned, a sufficient nexus between those commercial activities and the wrongful acts that had allegedly injured the Nelsons.

JUSTICE SOUTER

The Foreign Sovereign Immunities Act of 1976 entitles foreign states to immunity from the jurisdiction of courts in the United States . . . subject to certain enumerated exceptions. One is that a foreign state shall not be immune in any case "in which the action is based upon a commercial activity carried on in the United States by the foreign state." . . . The Act defines such activity as "commercial activity carried on by such state and having substantial contact with the United States" . . . and provides that a commercial activity may be "either a regular course of commercial conduct or a particular commercial transaction or act," the "commercial character of [which] shall be determined by reference to its "nature," rather than its "purpose." . . .

We begin our analysis by identifying the particular conduct on which the Nelsons' action is "based" for purposes of the Act. . . . In denoting conduct that forms the "basis," or "foundation," for a claim . . . the phrase is read most naturally to mean those elements of a claim that, if proven, would entitle a plaintiff to relief under his theory of the case. . . . Earlier . . . we noted that [the commercial activity

exception] contains two clauses following the one at issue here. The second allows for jurisdiction where a suit "is based . . . upon an act performed in the United States in connection with a commercial activity of the foreign state elsewhere," and the third speaks in like terms, allowing for jurisdiction where an action "is based . . . upon an act outside the territory of the United States in connection with a commercial activity of the foreign state elsewhere and that act causes a direct effect in the United States." . . . Congress manifestly understood there to be a difference between a suit "based upon" commercial activity and one "based upon" acts performed "in connection with" such activity. The only reasonable reading of the former term calls for something more than a mere connection with, or relation to, commercial activity. (We do not mean to suggest that the first clause of [the exception] necessarily requires that each and every element of a claim be commercial activity by a foreign state, and we do not address the case where a claim consists of both commercial and sovereign elements. We do conclude, however, that where a claim rests entirely upon activities sovereign in character, as here, jurisdiction will not exist under that clause regardless of any connection the sovereign acts may have with commercial activity.)

In this case, the Nelsons have alleged that petitioners recruited Scott Nelson for work at the hospital, signed an employment contract with him, and subsequently employed him. While these activities led to the conduct that eventually injured the Nelsons, they are not the basis for the Nelsons' suit. Even taking each of the Nelsons' allegations about Scott Nelson's recruitment and employment as true, those facts alone entitle the Nelsons to nothing under their theory of the case. The Nelsons have not, after all, alleged breach of contract . . . but personal injuries caused by petitioners' intentional wrongs and by petitioners' negligent failure to warn Scott Nelson that they might commit those wrongs. Those torts, and not the arguably commercial activities that preceded their commission, form the basis for the Nelsons' suit. Petitioners' tortious conduct itself fails to qualify as "commercial activity" within the meaning of the Act. . . . [T]he Act defines "commercial activity" as "either a regular course of commercial conduct or a

continued

continued

particular commercial transaction or act," and provides that "[t]he commercial character of an activity shall be determined by reference to the nature of the course of conduct or particular transaction or act, rather than by reference to its purpose." . . . If this is a definition, it is one distinguished only by its diffidence; as we observed in our most recent case on the subject, it "leaves the critical term 'commercial' largely undefined." *Republic of Argentina v. Weltover, Inc.* . . . We do not, however, have the option to throw up our hands. The term has to be given some interpretation, and congressional diffidence necessarily results in judicial responsibility to determine what a "commercial activity" is for purposes of the Act.

We took up the task just last Term in *Weltover* . . . which involved Argentina's unilateral refinancing of bonds it had issued under a plan to stabilize its currency. Bondholders sued Argentina in federal court, asserting jurisdiction under the third clause of [the exception]. In the course of holding the refinancing to be a commercial activity for purposes of the Act, we observed that the statute "largely codifies the so-called 'restrictive' theory of foreign sovereign immunity first endorsed by the State Department in 1952." We accordingly held that the meaning of "commercial" for purposes of the Act must be the meaning Congress understood the restrictive theory to require at the time it passed the statute.

Under the restrictive, as opposed to the "absolute," theory of foreign sovereign immunity, a state is immune from the jurisdiction of foreign courts as to its sovereign or public acts (jure imperii), but not as to those that are private or commercial in character (jure gestionis). . . . We explained in *Weltover* . . . that a state engages in commercial activity under the restrictive theory where it exercises "only those powers that can also be exercised by private citizens," as distinct from those "powers peculiar to sovereigns." Put differently, a foreign state engages in commercial activity for purposes of the restrictive theory only where it acts "in the manner of a private player within" the market. . . . We emphasized in *Weltover* that whether a state acts "in the manner of" a private party is a question of behavior, not motivation:

> [B]ecause the Act provides that the commercial character of an act is to be determined by reference to its "nature" rather than its "purpose," the question is not whether the foreign government is acting with a profit motive or instead with the aim of fulfill-

ing uniquely sovereign objectives. Rather, the issue is whether the particular actions that the foreign state performs (whatever the motive behind them) are the type of actions by which a private party engages in "trade and traffic or commerce."

We did not ignore the difficulty of distinguishing "purpose" (i.e., the reason why the foreign state engages in the activity) from "nature" (i.e., the outward form of the conduct that the foreign state performs or agrees to perform), but recognized that the Act "unmistakably commands" us to observe the distinction. Because Argentina had merely dealt in the bond market in the manner of a private player, we held, its refinancing of the bonds qualified as a commercial activity for purposes of the Act despite the apparent governmental motivation.

Unlike Argentina's activities that we considered in *Weltover,* the intentional conduct alleged here (the Saudi Government's wrongful arrest, imprisonment, and torture of Nelson) could not qualify as commercial under the restrictive theory. The conduct boils down to abuse of the power of its police by the Saudi Government, and however monstrous such abuse undoubtedly may be, a foreign state's exercise of the power of its police has long been understood for purposes of the restrictive theory as peculiarly sovereign in nature. . . . Exercise of the powers of police and penal officers is not the sort of action by which private parties can engage in commerce.

The Nelsons . . . urge us to give significance to their assertion that the Saudi Government subjected Nelson to the abuse alleged as retaliation for his persistence in reporting hospital safety violations, and argue that the character of the mistreatment was consequently commercial. . . . But this argument does not alter the fact that the powers allegedly abused were those of police and penal officers. In any event, the argument is off the point, for it goes to purpose, the very fact the Act renders irrelevant to the question of an activity's commercial character. Whatever may have been the Saudi Government's motivation for its allegedly abusive treatment of Nelson, it remains the case that the Nelsons' action is based upon a sovereign activity immune from the subject-matter jurisdiction of United States courts under the Act.

In addition to the intentionally tortious conduct, the Nelsons claim a separate basis for recovery in petitioners' failure to warn Scott Nelson of the hidden dangers associated with his employment. The

continued

continued

Nelsons allege that, at the time petitioners recruited Scott Nelson and thereafter, they failed to warn him of the possibility of severe retaliatory action if he attempted to disclose any safety hazards he might discover on the job. . . . In other words, petitioners bore a duty to warn of their propensity for tortious conduct. But this is merely a semantic ploy. For aught we can see, a plaintiff could recast virtually any claim of intentional tort committed by sovereign act as a claim of failure to warn, simply by charging the defendant with an obligation to announce its

own tortious propensity before indulging it. To give jurisdictional significance to this feint of language would effectively thwart the Act's manifest purpose to codify the restrictive theory of foreign sovereign immunity.

Decision. The Supreme Court reversed the judgment of the Court of Appeals, dismissing the case. This meant that the Nelsons could not bring suit in an American court over the alleged actions in Saudi Arabia.

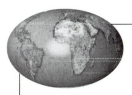

Acree v. The Republic of Iraq
2003 WL 21537919 (2003)
United States District Court (D.D.C.)

BACKGROUND AND FACTS

Plaintiffs are former prisoners of war and other detainees held by the Iraqi government of Saddam Hussein during the first Gulf War. While in detention, the plaintiffs were subjected to brutal forms of physical torture including severe beatings, mock executions, threatened castration, threatened dismemberment, electrical shocks, starvation, sleep denial, and confinement in dark and filthy conditions.

JUDGE ROBERTS

The FSIA's enumerated exceptions to sovereign immunity are the basis for subject matter jurisdiction over foreign states and their agencies and instrumentalities. . . . The Court has jurisdiction pursuant to the exception set forth in 28 U.S.C. §1605(a)(7) over suits against states designated by the Department of State as terrorist states with respect to certain acts in which either the claimant or the victim were nationals of the United States. The first statutory element for subject matter jurisdiction pursuant to §1605(a)(7), as amended, is that "money damages are sought against a foreign state for personal injury . . . caused by an act of torture . . . or the provision of material support or resources . . . for such an act if such act or provision of material support is engaged in by an official, employee, or agent of such foreign state while acting within the scope of his or her office, employment, or agency." This case is such an action for personal injury

caused by the torture and the provision of material support and resources for such torture by officials and employees of Iraq while acting within the scope of their office or employment. For purposes of §1605(a)(7) actions, "torture" is defined in §1605(e)(1) of the FSIA by reference to §3 of the Torture Victim Protection Act of 1991. That section defines torture to include: "any act, directed against an individual in the offender's custody or physical control, by which severe pain or suffering . . . , whether physical or mental, is intentionally inflicted on that individual for such purposes as obtaining from that individual or a third person information or a confession, punishing that individual for an act that individual or a third person has committed or is suspected of having committed, intimidating or coercing that individual or a third person, or for any reason based on discrimination of any kind." . . . The treatment of the POW plaintiffs by their Iraqi captors falls squarely within this definition of torture.

The second element under §1605(a)(7) is that the foreign state was designated as a state sponsor of terrorism at the time the act occurred. The Republic of Iraq was designated by the Department of State as state sponsor of terrorism in September 1990, prior to defendants' torture and mistreatment of the American POWs and their families. . . .

The third requirement for subject matter jurisdiction is that, if the act occurred in the foreign state

continued

continued

against which the claim has been brought, then the claimant must afford the foreign state a reasonable opportunity to arbitrate the claim in accordance with accepted international rules of arbitration. The plaintiffs in this case repeatedly offered the defendants an opportunity to arbitrate their claims in accordance with accepted international rules of arbitration, yet the defendants did not accept plaintiffs' offers.

The final element for jurisdiction under §1605(a)(7) is that either the claimant or the victim must be a national of the United States. Plaintiffs in this case are all nationals of the United States. Because this case was filed pursuant to the Flatow Amendment, there is a further requirement that United States officials, employees or agents would be liable for such acts if carried out within the United

States. . . . American officials, employees or agents would be liable for similar acts of torture if carried out in the United States. . . .

All of the requirements contained in §1605(a)(7) are satisfied in this case and the Court, therefore, has subject matter jurisdiction. Because the Court has subject matter jurisdiction, the service of process achieved here pursuant to §1608 of the FSIA provides personal jurisdiction over the defendants in this case. . . .

Decision. The court, having jurisdiction, entered a judgment against the government of Iraq for $653 million in compensatory damages and $306 million in punitive damages. The plaintiffs are seeking sources of assets to satisfy this judgment.

For a U.S. entrepreneur, the act becomes relevant if it is considering doing business, directly or indirectly, with a nation that is on the State Department's list of "state sponsors of terrorism." For example, there are over 6,000 claims against Cuba alone. If any of the claimants can show that the entrepreneur owes an account payable to such a "state sponsor of terrorism," it might find itself to be the recipient of an order of attachment, seizing funds ostensibly owed to the terrorist sponsor. Doing business in such nations has become very risky indeed.

http://www.travel.state.gov/
fsia.html
See for the FSIA.

Acts of State Doctrine.   If a court decides that, under the FSIA, it can hear the U.S. investor's case against the sovereign state, the investor must still persuade the court to exercise this jurisdictional power despite the *Act of State Doctrine*. The doctrine was historically referred to as a choice-of-law doctrine under which, for reasons of *comity* among nations—friendly relations marked by mutual recognition of laws—a U.S. court will refuse to inquire into the validity of any act of a foreign government. In a more recent case, however, the U.S. Supreme Court has narrowed the impact of the doctrine by abandoning the comity rationale.

The Act of State Doctrine is also inapplicable if the foreign state has entered into an investment treaty that effectively waives the policy as regards U.S. investors. Indeed, this principle permits U.S. agencies to rely on bilateral investment treaties to exert significant influence on foreign governments not to take adverse political action against U.S. investment.

Justice Scalia suggested in the *Kirkpatrick* case that "some Justices have suggested" a possible exception to the Act of State Doctrine for commercial activity—specifically, the plurality opinion of Justice Byron White in *Alfred Dunhill of London, Inc. v. Cuba,* 425 U.S. 682 (1976). As recently as 2002, Judge Garland of the District of Columbia Circuit observed that this question had not yet been resolved in *World Wide Minerals Ltd. v. Republic of Kazahkstan,* 296 F.3d 1154, 1166 (D.C. Cir.). Other lower courts have split on the question of whether such an exception exists. Until the Supreme Court again addresses the issue, the matter will remain open.

International Adjudication.   If it is too difficult to proceed in either the host country or in the United States, the investor should look into the possibility of dispute resolution in an international tribunal—a subject addressed in Chapter Three. As pointed out there, however, arbitration is by nature a voluntary action. If one is concerned

W.S. Kirkpatrick v. Environmental Tectronics Corp.
110 S. Ct. 701 (1990)
United States Supreme Court

BACKGROUND AND FACTS

The government of Nigeria awarded a military contract to W. S. Kirkpatrick & Co. The losing bidder, Environmental Tectronics Corporation (ETC), investigated the circumstances under which the contract had been awarded and learned that the winner had bribed key government officials who were responsible for making the award. Ultimately, the U.S. Department of Justice conducted an investigation that confirmed ETC's findings, and high Kirkpatrick officials pled guilty to violations of the *Foreign Corrupt Practices Act.* Thereafter, ETC brought a civil lawsuit against Kirkpatrick in the United States under the *Racketeer Influenced Corrupt Organizations Act* and the United States antitrust laws. Kirkpatrick moved to dismiss the lawsuit on the basis that the act of state doctrine prohibited the federal court from considering the matter. The district court granted Kirkpatrick's motion, but the Court of Appeals reversed the district court.

JUSTICE SCALIA

This Court's description of the jurisprudential foundation for the act of state doctrine has undergone some evolution over the years. We once viewed the doctrine as an expression of international law, resting upon "the highest considerations of international comity and expediency." We have more recently described it, however, as a consequence of domestic separation of powers, reflecting "the strong sense of the Judicial Branch that its engagement in the task of passing on the validity of foreign acts of state may hinder" the conduct of foreign affairs. . . .

We find [that] the factual predicate for application of the act of state doctrine does not exist. Nothing in the present suit requires the Court to declare invalid, and thus ineffective as "a rule of decision for the courts of this country," the official act of a foreign sovereign.

In every case in which we have held the act of state doctrine applicable, the relief sought or the defense interposed would have required a court in the United States to declare invalid the official act of a foreign sovereign performed within its own territory. In the present case, by contrast, neither the claim nor any asserted defense requires a determination that Nigeria's contract with Kirkpatrick International was, or was not effective. Petitioners point

out, however, that the facts necessary to establish respondent's claim will also establish that the contract was unlawful. Specifically, they note that in order to prevail respondent must prove that petitioner Kirkpatrick made, and Nigerian officials received, payments that violate Nigerian law, which would, they assert, support a finding that the contract is invalid under Nigerian law. Assuming that to be true, it still does not suffice. The act of state doctrine is not some vague doctrine of abstention but a "principle of decision binding on federal and state courts alike." "The act within its own boundaries of one sovereign State . . . becomes . . . a rule of decision for the courts of this country." Act of state issues only arise when a court must decide—that is, when the outcome of the case turns upon—the effect of official action by a foreign sovereign. When that question is not in the case, neither is the act of state doctrine. That is the situation here. Regardless of what the court's factual findings may suggest as to the legality of the Nigerian contract, its legality is simply not a question to be decided in the present suit, and there is thus no occasion to apply the rule of decision that the act of state doctrine requires.

Petitioners insist, however, that the policies underlying our act of state cases—international comity, respect for the sovereignty of foreign nations on their own territory, and the avoidance of embarrassment to the Executive Branch in its conduct of foreign relations—are implicated in the present case because, as the District Court found, a determination that Nigerian officials demanded and accepted a bribe "would impugn or question the nobility of a foreign nation's motivations," and would "result in embarrassment to the sovereign or constitute interference in the conduct of foreign polity of the United States." The United States, as amicus curiae, favors the same approach to the act of state doctrine, though disagreeing with petitioners as to the outcome it produces in the present case. We should not, the United States urges, "attach dispositive significance to the fact that this suit involves only the 'motivation' for, rather than the 'validity' of, a foreign sovereign act," and should eschew "any rigid formula for the resolution of act of state cases generally." . . .

continued

---

continued

But what is appropriate in order to avoid unquestioning judicial acceptance of the acts of foreign sovereigns is not similarly appropriate for the quite opposite purpose of expanding judicial incapacities where such acts are not directly (or even indirectly) involved. It is one thing to suggest, as we have, that the policies underlying the act of state doctrine should be considered in deciding whether, despite the doctrine's technical availability, it should nonetheless not be invoked; it is something quite different to suggest that those underlying policies are a doctrine unto themselves, justifying expansion of the act of state doctrine (or, as the United States puts it, unspecific "related principles of abstention") into new and uncharted fields.

The short of the matter is this: Courts in the United States have the power, and ordinarily the obligation, to decide cases and controversies properly presented to them. The act of state doctrine does not establish an exception for cases and controversies that may embarrass foreign governments, but merely requires that, in the process of deciding, the acts of foreign sovereigns taken within their own jurisdictions shall be deemed valid. That doctrine has no application to the present case because the validity of no foreign sovereign act is at issue.

Decision. The U.S. Supreme Court affirmed the decision of the Court of Appeals, permitting ETC to proceed with its lawsuit against Kirkpatrick.

---

about a hostile sovereign act, the time to seek the host state's consent to arbitration is before the investment is made, not after it has been expropriated. A carefully drawn arbitration clause in a contract with a government agency can provide reasonable assurance that an expropriation will be adjudicated according to the prevailing principles of international law requiring full compensation.

When contracting with a government agency, the entrepreneur should not blindly rely on the arbitration provision in the contract (the *clause compromissoire*) because the government official agreeing to the provision might have no power to do so. In many nations, national legislation or the national constitution supersedes contractual provisions under which an arbitrator would be passing judgment on the exercise of sovereign state powers or would affect public institutions. In other cases, certain areas of law are excluded from coverage. For example, *Andean Pact Decision 24* once excluded foreign investment contracts and foreign transfer of technology contracts from the jurisdiction of any foreign court or arbitrator. Similarly, Article 100 of the Argentine Constitution prohibits the state from submitting to arbitration on issues arising out of remittance of capital or profits abroad. Generally speaking, relatively straightforward matters such as the payment of damages to the entrepreneur upon the state's breach of an agreement not to take property is deemed by the legislature to be within an arbitrator's power.

The entrepreneur should also be on the alert for special procedural requirements imposed by national laws. Perhaps the most common of these in the context of arbitration is the requirement of a document (the *compromise*), signed by the parties to the *clause compromissoire,* which submits the specific dispute at issue to arbitration. The theory of the compromise is that the parties will begin to come together through the process of framing the dispute for the arbitrator. Obviously, a recalcitrant party can instead make this process the source of unnecessary delay.

These national procedural requirements are as diverse as nations themselves. In the following case, a foreign investor neglected to structure its contract with a government entity so as to assure that its choice of an international arbitral tribunal would be honored under local law. The result was very bad for the foreign investor.

Many countries have agreed to arbitration in cases of investment disputes in *foreign investment codes.* Another source of consent to arbitration is by treaty. The United States has negotiated bilateral investment treaties with a large number of its trading partners under which the host countries consent to arbitration in case of dispute with U.S. investors. The arbitration agreement can provide for *ad hoc* arbitration, as under the United Nations' UNCITRAL Rules, or may refer to an arbitral institution. Perhaps the most significant arbitration agreement involving a government is the *Convention on the*

National Thermal Power Corp. v. The Singer Co.
1993 Y.B. Com. Arb. 403 (1992)
The Supreme Court of India

BACKGROUND AND FACTS

The National Thermal Power Corporation of India (NTPC) entered into a contract with The Singer Company, a British concern, to supply equipment and erect certain projects in India. A dispute arose and Singer sought arbitration under International Chamber of Commerce (ICC) rules in London, as provided in the contract. Singer won the arbitration and was granted an award by the ICC tribunal. Singer then sought to enforce the award in India under the Indian Foreign Awards Act, which limits the role of Indian courts to recognition and enforcement of the foreign arbitral award. NTPC argued against enforcement of the award, claiming that because the contract was governed by Indian law, it was not a "foreign award" under the *Foreign Awards Act* and that, despite the contract's clear submission to ICC arbitration, the whole case should be re-tried in India under the *Indian Arbitration Act.* The Delhi High Court dismissed NTPC's application and NTPC appealed to the Supreme Court of India.

JUSTICE THOMMEN

The General Terms and Conditions of Contract . . . are expressly incorporated in the agreements and they state: "the laws applicable to this Contract shall be the laws in force in India. The Courts of Delhi shall have exclusive jurisdiction in all matters arising under the contract." [Another clause] of the agreement deals with arbitration in respect of a foreign contractor. The latter provision says:

> In the event of foreign Contractor, the arbitration shall be conducted by three arbitrators . . . all Rules of Conciliation and Arbitration of the International Chamber of Commerce shall apply to such arbitrations. The arbitration shall be conducted at such places as the arbitrators may determine.

The fundamental question is whether the arbitration agreement contained in the contract is governed by the law of India so as to save it from the ambit of the Foreign Awards Act and attract provisions of the Arbitration Act. . . .

[Counsel for Singer contends] that while the main contract is governed by Indian law, as expressly stated by the parties, arbitration being a collateral contract and procedural in nature, it is not necessarily bound by the proper law of the contract. . . . London having been chosen in accordance with the ICC Rules to be the seat of arbitration, English law is the proper law of arbitration, and all proceedings connected with it are governed by that law . . .

[I]f the parties have specifically chosen the law governing the conduct and procedure of arbitration, the arbitration proceedings will be conducted in accordance with that law so long as it is not contrary to the public policy or the mandatory requirements of the law of the country in which the arbitration is held. . . . Where . . . the parties have, as in the instant case, stipulated that the arbitration between them will be conducted in accordance with the ICC Rules, those rules, being in many respects self-contained or self-regulating and constituting a contractual code of procedure, will govern the conduct of the arbitration. . . .

The proper law of the contract in the present case being expressly stipulated to be the laws in force in India and the exclusive jurisdiction of the courts in Delhi in all matters arising under the contract having been specifically accepted, . . . the proper law governing the arbitration agreement is indeed the law in force in India, and the competent courts of this country must necessarily have jurisdiction over all matters concerning arbitration. Neither the rules of procedure for the conduct of arbitration contractually chosen by the parties (the ICC Rules) nor the mandatory requirements of the procedure followed in the courts of the country in which the arbitration is held can in any manner supersede the overriding jurisdiction and control of the Indian law and the Indian courts. . . .

A "foreign award," as defined under the Foreign Awards Act means an award made . . . on differences arising between persons out of legal relationships . . . which are considered to be commercial under the law in force in India. To qualify as a foreign award under the Act, the award should have been made in pursuance of an agreement in writing for arbitration to be governed by the New York Convention or the Recognition and Enforcement of Foreign Arbitration Awards . . . and not to be governed by the law of India. . . . An award is "foreign" not merely because it

continued

continued

is made in the territory of a foreign State, but because it is made in such a territory on an arbitration agreement not governed by the law of India. An award made on an arbitration agreement governed by the law of India, though rendered outside India, is . . . not treated in India as a "foreign award." . . .

Such an award necessarily falls under the Arbitration Act and is amenable to the jurisdiction of the

Indian Courts and controlled by the Indian system of law just as in the case of any other domestic award. . . .

Decision. The Supreme Court of India set aside the judgment of the Delhi High Court, ordering a re-trial of the entire case in India, effectively finding that if Indian law governs a contract, an international arbitration provision is void.

Settlement of Investment Disputes Between States and Nationals of Other States, to which the United States is a party. The Convention provides a forum and a set of rules for the arbitration of disputes between U.S. citizens and signatory countries. Both the citizen and the host country agree that the Convention governs and that all disputes will be resolved by the *International Centre for the Settlement of Investment Disputes* (ICSID).

HISTORICAL DEVELOPMENT OF PRIVATIZATION

Although privatization is the opposite of nationalization, the two are historically intertwined. In the Middle Ages, the national monarch owned the great bulk of property. Indeed, the monarch's grant of fiefs in that property formed the basis for the feudal system and, in time, for the nation-state. Not until the rise of the merchant and industrial classes did private property become important. It was at that time that Grotius and others shaped the limitations on the powers of a sovereign to "nationalize" the property of a foreign merchant.

Some sovereigns began to realize that if they transferred property to private parties who would better develop and manage it, sovereigns would realize tax revenues from otherwise valueless assets. One of the first "sovereigns" to do so extensively was the United States of America, a nation possessed of vast undeveloped natural resources. For example, the right of millers to dam a river was favored over the rights of downstream property owners because of the pro-development effects of mills. Similarly, entrepreneurs were given concessions to build and collect tolls from canals they built. *Homestead Acts*

transferred government land to those who farmed it, federal land management laws permitted private ranchers to graze on government land at low fees. A similar privatization trend was taking place throughout the world, particularly in Europe's colonial possessions. By the end of the nineteenth century, the bulk of the world's wealth was in private hands.

This trend was reversed by Marx's indictment of the excesses of capitalist economics. Marxist views were fully or partially accepted in Russia and other communist countries, newly independent African and Asian nations, and newly elected labor or other leftist governments in Western Europe and Latin America. These governments nationalized or expropriated all or large parts of the private sector—especially those parts of the private sector owned by foreigners.

But sovereigns' ability to develop property had not improved in the intervening centuries. Without the engine of the individual profit incentive, nationalized enterprises grew inefficient and flaccid. The nationalized enterprise gradually went from producing profits for the government to requiring subsidies from the government to cover its losses. Not surprisingly, the nationalization trend collapsed and privatization returned. In the late 1970s and the 1980s, Great Britain's Thatcher government began sales of government assets, reversing the nationalizations of industry effected by Labour governments decades earlier. Mrs. Thatcher's ideas became fashionable in other developed nations and the privatization process took hold—countries as diverse as France, Japan, and Argentina had soon effected privatizations of their own. Upon the fall of the communist bloc in 1989, privatization expanded to transform the economies of former non-market economies. Even mainland China and Vietnam, the last major bastions of communism, developed business forms that transferred control of assets to private entrepreneurs, especially foreign investors. The focus of this chapter now turns to the specifics of the structure of the privatization process.

PREPARATION FOR PRIVATIZATION

Privatization takes many forms. Indeed, each combination of assets, sellers, and purchasers requires its own particular structure for privatization. Although in many ways privatization can be like the acquisition of a division of a private company, the steps that sellers take to prepare for privatization, the patterns of those sales, and the legal concerns that they raise tend to be different from those of other asset transfers. To understand the principal considerations at issue, a description of the process of preparing government assets for privatization is presented entailing four generic models of privatization.

At the outset, the industry to be privatized is a functioning unit of the national government. Whether it is a major steel manufacturer or an individual power plant, its purpose is to further national interests, as defined by the government's political leaders. These interests are most frequently to increase volume of output or number of persons employed. Profit is only incidentally one of these interests—in fact, in many former communist countries the concept of profit was unknown. The fact that the expenses associated with bloated employee numbers overwhelmed the enterprise's revenues was not a source of concern. All revenues went into the state and all expenses were covered by the state. Government employees, whose purpose is public service, not private gain, staffed the government enterprise. The equipment of the enterprise may have been chosen to maximize employment, rather than to minimize unit cost. If the enterprise received free supplies or natural resources from other government divisions, those supplies may have been used in a wasteful manner.

If such an enterprise were immediately put on the block, it may not attract a buyer. The private entrepreneur would not have reliable financial information from which to make a risk assessment. Privatizing governments soon discovered that they needed to prepare the asset for sale before privatizing.

Similarly, the legal infrastructure for private investment must be created. International investors require a functioning commercial code. They require an understandable regulatory regime governing the newly privatized enterprise. They need to understand competitive requirements. Preparation of national assets for privatization has become a critical and standardized part of the process.

The Creation and Organization of an Independent Government Corporation

The privatization process typically begins with a functioning unit of the government: the national telecommunications ministry, the national steel manufacturing ministry, or some other governmental unit. The assets that are necessary for the unit to function are segregated and transferred to a new corporate entity, the stock of which is wholly owned by the government. Thus, the Telecommunications Administration of the Ministry of Communication becomes Telco, Inc., a government-owned company.

This transfer is generally followed by a transitional period during which the new entity begins to operate as a private enterprise. It will record its expenses and its revenues separately from those of the government and develop financial statements that will permit potential purchasers to assess its performance. The framework of non-fair market value exchanges with other government units and lax accounting practices is disassembled. During this transitional period, the government continues to fund net capital needs of the fledgling enterprise. This process takes much of the guesswork out of privatization acquisitions, permitting the right investor to come into the company at the right price.

Preparation of a Legal System for Privatization

Before foreign investors acquire an interest in former government assets, they will want a solid legal infrastructure in place. This infrastructure creates clear rights of property and enforceability of contracts.

"Clearing" of Expropriation Claims. Before any transfer of assets to private hands can occur, the government must develop a property system that permits *clearing of title* to such assets. Many assets owned by governments were once "nationalized" from private parties. The people who owned the assets before the government nationalized them—and who may have a claim against the government for a wrongful nationalization or expropriation—may have a restitution claim against the government. Without clearing of title, that claim might be available against the purchaser of the asset.

To solve this problem, governments frequently create a legal network whereby the victim of expropriation must either assert its claim within a specified period or waive it. If the period passes without a claim, the government can transfer the asset with clear title. If restitution claims are asserted, a system is put in place for prompt rulings.

If a quick sale is desired, the government may forego a title-clearing procedure and assume responsibility for the possible adverse claim. For example, Germany's privatization trust, the Treuhand, issued an Investment Preference Decision (*Investitionsvorrangbescheid*) when it wished to promote investment in a priority sector. Upon the investor's compliance with the conditions of the decision—such as a specified level of investment—the restitution claim is blocked. In *blocked claims,* the government often limits the expropriation victim to the proceeds of the sale of the asset if the sale is deemed to have been conducted under reasonable commercial terms.

The investor must be sure that the government office with the authority to waive these restitution liabilities has approved the transaction; frequently that office is different from the office actually selling the asset.

Property and Contract Law.

In former communist countries, the state was the only legitimate repository of wealth. Expropriation and nationalization was so complete that there was no longer a legal concept of private property. The recognition of private property rights is essential to privatization. Without clear assurance to the investor of its right to own the property as it is developed, the incentive is diminished.

A functioning system of private property requires establishment of laws governing the acquisition and transfer of title, filing registries for real property mortgages, systems for acquiring and recording chattel mortgages, and other unglamorous mechanics. Russia, for example, passed a law on mortgages in 1991, but was very slow to establish the filing registries necessary to implement the law. Without the registries, mortgage financing—a bedrock of capital investment in the West—can operate only with great complexity, unnecessary expense, and substantial risk.

A free market maximizes value by permitting and enforcing voluntary exchanges between independent merchants. Contract law based on capitalist economics performs this exchange function. Before launching privatization, therefore, a government must implement a modern contract law system.

Methods of Distribution

The final preparation for privatization is the development of a plan to distribute shares. Shares can be distributed through private or public equity, a voucher system, or debt-for-equity swaps.

Private and Public Equity Placements.

The simplest transfer of ownership is to a single group of investors. Typically such an investment is part of a strategic entry into the local market or acquisition of new manufacturing capacity. The deal is worked out in direct negotiations between government and investor group and made firm in a shareholders' agreement between them. The government may also sell to the passive investing public through the sale of part of the enterprise's stock on local stock exchanges, and direct another portion for sale in foreign equity markets through American Depository Receipts or other similar securities.

Voucher Systems.

Governments also occasionally transfer public assets to their citizens for free. The concept underlying these *voucher* systems is that, in order for capitalism to take hold, stock ownership should be widespread among the national population. In populations in which the standard of living is low, most people do not have the resources to invest, so the objective of wide distribution can only be achieved through free distribution. Further, the theory continues, the people have paid for their shares through years of laboring for a state-owned system.

This type of distribution typically begins with the issuance of voucher coupon booklets that contain points for bidding on shares in state firms to the entire population or to a portion of the population with a specific interest in the enterprise being privatized, such as its workers or citizens of a region greatly affected by the enterprise.

Often private citizens entrust their vouchers to large private investment funds that pool vouchers. These funds then bid against one another to acquire specific entities being privatized. After a fund or group of funds acquires the asset, they, as the owners of the enterprise, enter into transactions with foreign investors. With the financial assistance of multilateral banks, many of these funds actually finance and direct the process of preparing the former public entity for the subsequent transfer of interests to international investors. In this way, the investment funds effectively take the place of the government in privatizing the enterprise.

Voucher systems do not always work well. In Russia, private citizens—lacking knowledge about capital markets and often in dire need of cash—promptly sold their vouchers to unscrupulous individuals at low prices. Massive numbers of vouchers were soon concentrated in the hands of people with few entrepreneurial credentials. Similar experiences led subsequent voucher programs, such as Poland's National Investment Fund program, to require a modest payment for the vouchers from eligible members of the public. In Hungary, the government has permitted payment of the modest sum over a number of years and does not transfer the vouchers until final payment is made. Other nations simply make the vouchers personal and not transferable during the transitional period.

Debt-for-Equity Swaps. A popular mechanism in selling state assets is the *debt-for-equity swap.* One popular type of debt swap involves the exchange of external sovereign debt for internal equity. In essence, the government permits foreign investors to pay for the government's equity in the entity to be privatized with debt instruments of that government.

The debt of many governments, of course, is in default and may be purchased at a substantial discount from current holders. If the investor can purchase a government's debt for twenty cents on the dollar, it can buy $1 million of the government's debt for only $200,000, thereby conserving its hard currency. By pursuing such a strategy in its many privatizations, the Argentine government drastically slashed the amount of the country's debt. In a second type of swap, local investors exchange

external debt for internal debt. Host country investors obtain debt instruments of the government being traded abroad at a discount with their hard currency assets, convert them into local currency-denominated debt, and resell them in the host country as internal debt. This latter approach has the positive side effect of reversing capital flight from the host country. By allowing residents to use assets abroad to purchase external debt and convert it to domestic debt, privatization of a company actually improves the nation's balance of payments.

MODELS OF PRIVATIZATION

Privatizations can be organized into four groups or "models" to facilitate one's understanding of the various important characteristics. Few real-world transactions will be "pure" examples of any one of the models, but will include elements of more than one model.

Sale of a Noncontrolling Interest

The least radical type of privatization involves the sale of a substantial but *noncontrolling interest* in the enterprise to private investors. The predominant feature of this model is that control will remain in the hands of the government employees who formerly managed the asset for the government, and the government retains a substantial equity interest in the new enterprise (see Exhibit 19.2).

A noncontrolling interest is often sold to a single strategic investor. In such cases, the purchaser can try to ameliorate the downside of continued government control through the shareholder agreement between the government—in its capacity as a shareholder—and the private shareholder. Such shareholder agreements lay out terms, under which shareholder takes the stock, that give it specified rights and protections greater than those of a typical minority investor.

If the sale does not involve a strategic investor, however, the privatization of a minority holding will not bring in new expertise. The passive investor, after all, is interested in picking a manager for its investment and then looking for other investments. Private investors typically do not wish to put their money in an enterprise in which critical decisions affecting profit will be made by

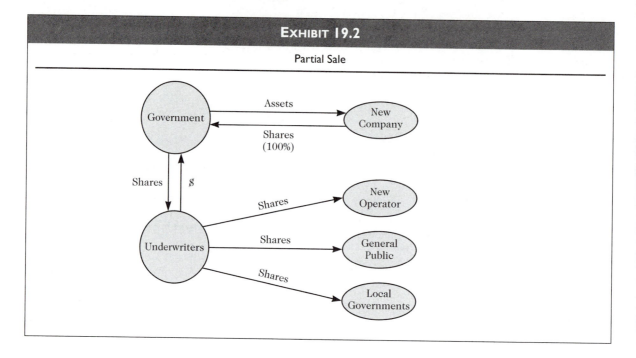

EXHIBIT 19.2

Partial Sale

The Trade Sale

an entity that does not react to the profit motive. Such a sale does not, therefore, achieve the objective of injecting entrepreneurship into the entity, and typically results in lower private investor interest and a smaller capital investment.

Some governments retain some control even after selling a majority interest in the enterprise by a stock interest called a *golden share*. The golden share gives no economic rights, but can limit the private investors' voting rights to a certain set threshold, place government appointees on the company board, or give the veto power over board decisions in certain specified areas. At times, this veto power is stated in general "wherever necessary to further national interest" terms. The government does not wish to turn a significant source of national employment and manufacturing over to people outside its control—in short, it is reluctant to cede power.

Another way for the government to retain control while transferring a majority interest is to reserve a substantial portion of the shares for local or provincial governments or labor unions. Unless the private entrepreneur is well connected with the local polity, the local government can be expected to vote in a manner consistent with the national government, particularly on issues of employment reduction.

The Trade Sale

At the opposite end of the privatization spectrum is the *trade sale* model, the transfer of control of the unit's assets to a single private investor or group of investors. The distinguishing feature of this model is that when the smoke clears, the purchaser controls the use of the assets. It decides which of the former employees are kept and what capital plant improvements are to be made. The government may pursue the trade sale either as a stock sale or as a sale of assets (see Exhibit 19.3).

If the former government unit primarily provided services, the government may achieve privatization through *management contracts*. The government contracts with a private firm to perform services—as diverse as maintenance of port facilities to trash pickup—formerly provided by the government. Contracting out in this way may mean that some state-owned assets can be sold off because they are no longer needed now that the contractor is handling the enterprise's function.

A variation of this asset trade sale concept occurs when a private firm is sold the right, or *concession*, to provide a service or infrastructure over which the state can exercise substantial control. The concession is discussed in greater depth in the following section.

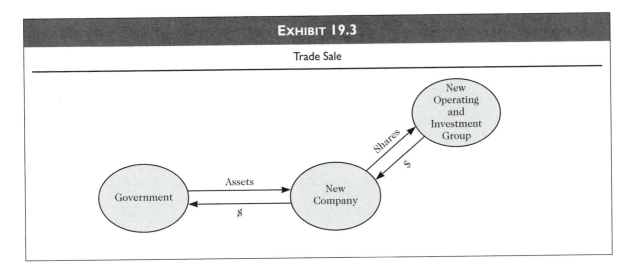

EXHIBIT 19.3

Trade Sale

Advantages and Disadvantages of the Trade Sale.

A trade sale has many advantages. First, of course, it is the capitalist ideal of privatization. It brings assets into the hands of private entrepreneurs with a strong financial incentive in transforming the former state entity into one that can function in a competitive market. Second, it is the speediest way to effect privatization, reducing the need for government interference during any transitional period. Third, it is especially useful in selling small companies for which demand is low in equity markets. In countries such as the Czech Republic, small shops were simply transferred to the individuals or families who had previously operated them for the state.

The trade sale, however, also presents disadvantages. First, the complete takeover by a foreign entity of a national company can lead to backlash from the local population. When Spanish-owned Iberia Airlines acquired Aerolineas Argentinas, many Argentines condemned a "new Spanish colonialization." Such publicity was unhelpful to a firm such as Aerolineas Argentinas, an airline that relied primarily on the patronage of Argentines. Thus, in a trade sale, the new entrepreneur group can often benefit by including significant local participation.

Second, a trade sale also places a great deal of responsibility on private entrepreneurs who may not have the capital resources necessary to pull off a successful privatization. In fact, some would-be privatizers have collapsed into bankruptcy soon after the sale. Thus, the government has a stake in

carefully exploring the financial depth of the buyer in a trade sale.

The Sale to Employees

Privatization can also be structured as a transfer to the enterprise's former employees, without retention of control by the government. Under this model, existing management and employees become the new owners, most often in conjunction with a group of outside private investors (see Exhibit 19.4).

Within the private sector in developed economies, acquisitions of companies by their management and supporting investment groups are known as *leveraged buyouts* (LBOs). In that context, management enlists private investors to purchase a private company as majority partners. These investors give the members of management a minority equity stake because of the value they add to the assets of the company and to give management a financial incentive to make the enterprise succeed.

In the context of public enterprises, giving the current senior government employees an equity stake in the new enterprise serves the same objectives, as well as others peculiar to privatizations. First, privatizations are necessarily political transactions that require broad support within the government. Senior government officials with a financial stake in privatization as future shareholders will favor it more readily than if they have none. Second, lower-level employees will generally be asked to make wage, pension, and work rule concessions to the new private entity. Resistance from government

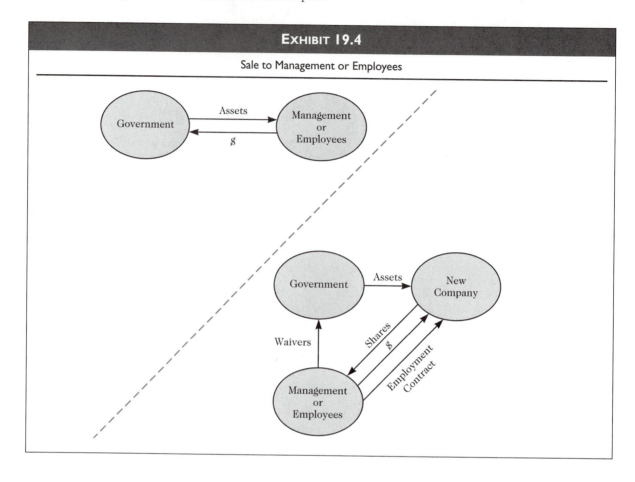

employees is perhaps the greatest barrier to privatization. In many Latin American countries, for example, union representatives of these employees have used their considerable political influence to prevent or retard privatization. In such circumstances, a significant employee ownership element in the privatization structure may be necessary as a way of moderating opposition from employee groups. Third, in the case of Eastern Europe not all traces of socialist ideology have been erased from consciousness; the concept of excluding workers from ownership remains politically unattractive. Russian lawmakers have entertained legislation that called for leasing of state property to workers' collectives with a subsequent option to purchase. Similarly, the Czech and Slovak privatizations issued a percentage of shares to workers for free. In a privatization of a Polish chocolate waffle manufacturer by a Swiss concern, 20 percent of the new company's privatization order specifically provides for sale of equity to workers at half price.

This LBO model has occurred in a relatively pure form in some developed nations, such as in the privatization of British Telecomm. But in less-developed nations, it occurs principally as a facilitating element. Most government units are being privatized largely because they are poorly managed; existing upper government officials are not viewed as adding significant value to the underlying assets. As for the rank and file, privatization is often a prelude to "streamlining" of enterprises—the dismissal of large segments of the bureaucracy that cannot be justified under a regime in which expenses are principally incurred to generate revenues. In that context, placing substantial numbers of shares in the hands of ex-employees could prove to be bad policy. Nonetheless, foreign investors can expect to issue a small number of shares to employees of the old government unit in privatizations as a necessary part of concluding the acquisition of government assets.

Argentina developed an innovative Employee Stock Ownership Plan (ESOP) model that illustrates an important approach in this area. The government sets aside 10 percent of each company in trust for the employees. The workers do not immediately pay for their shares, but the purchase price is paid with the shares' dividends over time. The workers elect representatives to administer the trust, and the trust is allowed one board seat.

Concessions: BOTs and BOOs

A different sort of privatization involves the "conceding" to private parties the right to perform a function traditionally reserved to the government. The most common of these is the right to build different types of infrastructure—electric generation plants, ports, airports, highways, bridges, tunnels, mineral extraction facilities, and the like—and the accompanying right to collect revenues generated by the infrastructure project. In contrast to other privatizations, the government is not transferring an existing asset, but instead, a right to earn revenues in order to encourage the building of a new asset.

BOTs and BOOs.
There are two basic types of concessions. In the more common concession, the government grants the right to collect revenues for a number of years. After the term of the concession, the right, together with the asset built by the concessionaire reverts back to the state. Under this model, often referred to as a *Build-Operate-Transfer* (BOT) transaction and shown in Exhibit 19.5, the government obtains an infrastructure asset that promotes development of the economy without making any current capital expenditures.

The term of the BOT concession is generally sufficient for the investor group to repay the debt it incurred and recoup its equity outlay with a substantial profit. This time period can vary widely depending upon the project: the period in the British Channel Tunnel is fifty years; the period in the Malaysian North/South Expressway is thirty years; power generation projects often have periods of fifteen to twenty-five years. At times, rather than a fixed term of years, the parties will use benchmarks, such as the repayment of debt financing.

In the second major type of concession, the government actually sells the concessionaire a "permanent" concession. These transactions, called *Build-Operate-Own* (BOO) deals, are common in infrastructure projects that involve particularly

high risk and therefore require particularly high incentive. For example, the high risk normally associated with doing business in many less developed African nations often requires that the BOO model be followed. Similarly, in countries with an emphatic history of state intervention in the economy, governments pursue BOO projects as an added measure of assurance to the private investment community that the move to privatization is not a passing political phase.

---

http://www.public-policy.org/~ncpa/pd/pdint173.html
Visit this site for material on privatization attempts in China.

http://

The Concession and Anticompetitive Considerations. Because the government is granting a right to perform an activity in which it has a monopoly, the recipient of the right will expect to receive at least some part of the monopoly right for some period of time. For example, a concessionaire will not assume the risk of building a railroad line if the government is then free to use the roadbed that the concessionaire has graded to build a competing line.

Because infrastructure projects by their nature generally involve modifying the environment in a way that facilitates later competitive investment, such monopoly concessions are common. The concession to the company that built the English Channel Tunnel specified that England and France could not take any steps to facilitate any other transportation connection until the year 2000. Even more significantly, the two governments agreed that during the fifty-year term of the concession, they would not help finance, through public funds or public guarantees, any such connection. Without such state help, any competitor would face a difficult road.

The government must take steps to prevent abuse of the economic power a monopoly implies. This includes not only pricing abuses, but asset maintenance and service issues as well. In the absence of a free market to ensure good service through safe equipment at fair prices, the government must devise reasonable alternatives. These concerns are addressed through controls on the concessionaire's pricing, either through regulation or in the concession contract itself. For example, if

Exhibit 19.5

BOT Transaction

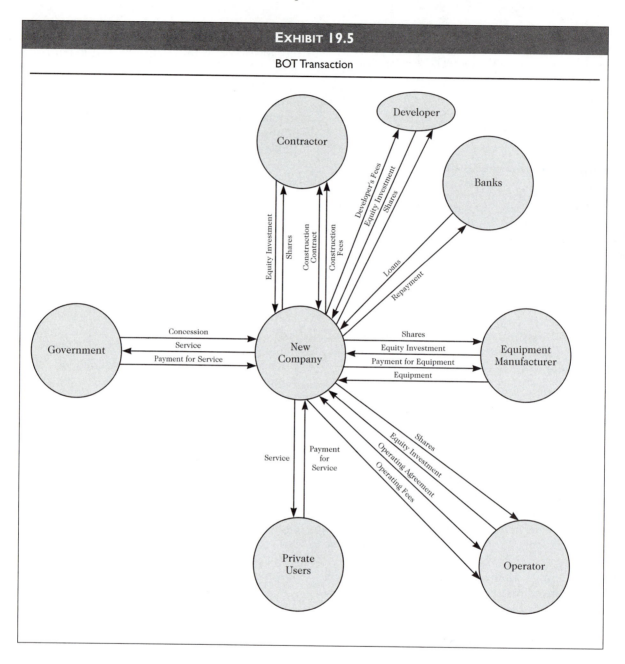

the project suffers cost overruns due to the fault of the consessionaire, it must not be permitted to recover that overrun through price increases. When the government lacks the resources to put up infrastructure that the society needs to advance the general economic good, innovative compromises are the government's best alternative.

The best remedy to monopoly power is to end

it. Accordingly, governments have been increasingly aggressive in limiting the term of monopoly rights to reasonable periods for the repayment of debt and return on investment.

Advantages and Disadvantages of the Concession. In granting a concession, the government cedes control for the duration of the concession over a crucial aspect of the national economy—its infrastructure—to people who may not have the interests of the nation foremost in their minds. There are, however, substantial advantages that counter the drawbacks.

First, the government adds an infrastructure asset to the nation without having to spend any sums from the national treasury. Better infrastructure in turn attracts other forms of investment to boost the economy. An international shoe manufacturer is more likely to locate in a nation with a reliable power supply to run its equipment and good roads and port facilities to bring in components and ship out product. Each of these new investors will employ citizens; both employer and employees will pay taxes. Instead of an outflow from threadbare public coffers to prop up unproductive public enterprises, there is a substantial positive inflow of taxes from successful private firms. As sovereigns discovered centuries ago, development is advanced while enriching the treasury.

Second, the cost of services is shifted from taxpayers to users of the services. Instead of a road that is paid for equally by those who never use it and those who routinely send fifty-ton semitrailers over them, there is a toll road that charges by use. This, in turn, introduces market discipline. If the road concessionaire is to keep winning his customers over from their free alternatives, he must deliver well-maintained roads worth the price of admission.

Third, in some transactions, the government may be able to negotiate an equity share of the project company. In such cases, the government can actually earn a profit from its own concession. When the Turkish State decided to create a new telecommunications network, it felt that, given the potential market, it should receive $500 million for its telephony license offering. When it found no takers, it accepted a $100 million BOT proposal to build the system. To make up for what it viewed as lost value, it retained a nonvoting participation in 52 percent of the project's profits. That interest is projected to bring the Turkish State more than its first "fixed price" deal.

Fourth, by offering an equity interest in the project, the government can more readily attract foreign capital. Typical "turnkey" construction projects do not present the entrepreneurial potential of a long-term BOT project. Therefore, the former typically attracts such interest only if the government offers the foreign firms a high, fixed profit margin. BOT projects can generate interest at lower initial rates with the potential entrepreneurial payoff resulting from good long-term service and client development.

Fifth, at the end of the term of a BOT transaction, the government receives an infrastructure asset of substantial value. Some equipment assets, such as roads and bridges, may actually appreciate in value over time.

Finally, concessions enhance the nation's physical and human technological infrastructure. Such projects bring in and improve the use of modern technology and train local citizens in the use of such technology.

The government's loss of control over its infrastructure can be ameliorated. First, the government can control the central network into which these infrastructure projects join. An independent electric power producer must generally sell all or a substantial portion of its output into the national grid, a bridge services the national road system, and so on. By controlling the concessionaire's access—and conditioning the terms of that access—the government can maintain a measure of control over the concessionaire. Second, the concession may contain performance requirements. If the concessionaire fails to achieve certain project completion benchmarks or specified plant generation goals within stated periods, it pays significant penalties or forfeits the concession. The same can be done with safety and employment concerns. Finally, the government can do what the United States has historically done with its private utility, telecommunications, transportation, and health care sectors. It can regulate.

The Models in Combination

As noted at the outset, the models of privatization discussed here seldom occur in a pure form. For instructive purposes, a review of a few "impure" variations is helpful.

The Joint Venture Privatization. A government may compromise its desire for control enough to grant the investor group an even share of the new enterprise, but not enough to give it minority control. The resulting joint venture privatization is really a mix of the trade sale model and the noncontrolling interest model (see Exhibit 19.6).

Because of the ensured equity deadlock in the joint venture structure, most of the important issues are addressed in the shareholders' agreement

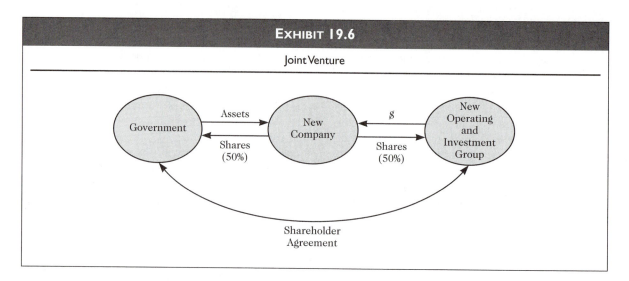

EXHIBIT 19.6

Joint Venture

between the parties. In a typical government–foreign investor joint venture, such a shareholder agreement will grant the investor control over most day-to-day operating matters. The government maintains control over certain issues in which it has a special interest, such as minimum production or employment levels. Finally, in other areas both parties have an equal say—and the ability to deadlock the firm.

Example of Privatization Mixing Models.

Some privatization deals include a little of everything. The following model, outlined in Exhibit 19.7, addresses a number of issues.

The transaction begins with the government transferring public assets, including a concession, to a new company for 40 percent of the shares and a waiver of some pension and other rights from its former employees. Simultaneously, the private operator makes a significant capital contribution in the new firm in exchange for 50 percent of the new company. At the same time, the employees enter into a labor contract with the new firm on more favorable terms than their former contract with the government and waive rights against the government in exchange for 10 percent of the new company.

To obtain cash for the national treasury immediately, the government sells three-fourths of its holding—30 percent of the new company—to underwriters for distribution to the general public. As a condition of the sale, the government may require that the underwriters resell a portion of the stock to the local national public on local stock exchanges. In addition to generating revenue

for the public coffers, the offering gives a broad segment of the citizenry a stake in the venture. The government maintains a 10-percent interest in order to retain a voice in the affairs of the firm and to realize some of the long-term equity growth associated with a successful new venture.

Similarly, the operator reduces its capital exposure by reselling part of its stake—20 percent of the new company—to the public in an underwritten offering. The sale to the international public market ensures the highest possible return to the operator. The operator retains a 30-percent block, which is sufficient in light of the wide holding of the balance of the stock. After the smoke clears, the passive investing public holds 50 percent of the stock, assuring the operator of continued effective control with its 30-percent block. The transaction is essentially a trade sale, but has broad elements of the employee purchase, noncontrolling interest, and concession financing models. In short, privatization soup.

---

http://www.ncpa.org/~ncpa/pi/internat/intdex7.html
Contains links to privatization information on several countries, including Peru, the Czech Republic, and Poland.

As privatization has encompassed more and more industries, a real debate has arisen as to the proper limits of this technique. Are there not, after all, some government activities that ought not be run for profit? The issues underlying this debate are concisely set forth in the following International Accents, which addresses President George W.

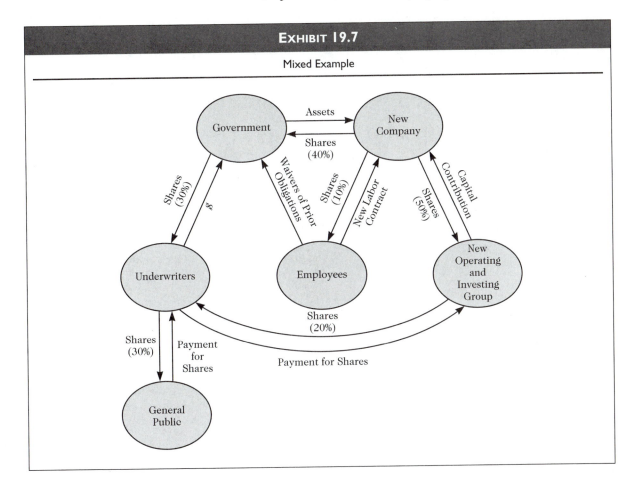

EXHIBIT 19.7

Mixed Example

Bush's plan to privatize air traffic control in the United States.

CHAPTER SUMMARY

U.S. citizens who invest in sovereign rights countries—even those privatizing government assets or services—need to consider seriously the possibility that the foreign sovereign will take their investment. All such investors must decide whether they wish to assume the risk of litigating such a taking or whether they wish to obtain political risk insurance to cover it. Those investors who choose the former will wish to place themselves in the best position possible by having appropriate international arbitration or litigation provisions that both establish the measure of compensation due and identify the arbiter that will do the measuring. Arbitration or litigation is perhaps best done in a nation where the ground rules have been set by a bilateral investment treaty between the foreign nation and the United States. If the investors decide to obtain insurance covering political risk, they will wish to avail themselves of the alternative with the best mixture of cost and flexibility. In making these decisions, investors should consider the fact that the law in this area is in a state of evolution; risk is enhanced by the element of unpredictability.

The privatization of formerly state-run enterprises is the most important development in international corporate law in recent memory. Its dramatic rise has virtually eliminated non-market economies and has made the private corporation or partnership the most important economic factor in the international marketplace. With its rise, nations have lost direct control over labor and environmental issues and have turned to regulation as a way to curb capitalism's less attractive tendencies.

international accents

US ATC Privatisation Is a Thorny Issue

November 6, 2003
By Jim Smith, *Jane's Transportation* Fortnightly Editor

In their respective draft versions of the $62 billion Federal Aviation Administration (FAA) authorisation bill, both the House of Representatives and the Senate have said no to privatising ATC because it is a critical service. Under private operation, a company may decide to make a few more bucks, putting the public in harm's way in the process, Congress maintains.

Following suit, members of Congress representing the areas in which the remaining 69 airports are located went ballistic. Not in my backyard! The union representing air traffic controllers also went berserk. But while the bill passed last week by the House takes out any mention of specific airports, it does not prohibit the president from privatising ATC at his discretion. . . .

One side of the argument maintains that rather than trying to save money by privatisation, the Bush administration should stack the FAA with competent managers. Another view is that the private sector operates more efficiently across the board—whether the job is removing rubbish or operating gaols. As far as ATCs are concerned, other governments have privatised at no peril to air travellers. Let the FAA exercise stringent oversight.

Still another opinion points at failure in the UK to provide safe, essential and cheaper train services, by privatising rail service and maintenance. That argument maintains that privatisation is congruent with peril. But the high cost of the US government's provision of ATC services probably rests with the usual bureaucracy that is not pandemic in the private sector.

Air traffic controllers—in spite of protestations from unions—could probably land better-paying jobs working in an environment that rewards the deserving. Private sector operators could cut much of the fat currently associated with the government operation of ATC.

Anyone who has had the misfortune of dealing with the US government bureaucracy has to believe in Adam Smith's "Invisible Hand" philosophy.

Reproduced with permission from Jane's Information Group—
Jane's Transport Finance.

Questions and Case Problems

1. Pursuant to Bulgaria's new joint venture program, Zasada, Inc., a U.S. firm, constructs a football helmet manufacturing facility in Sofia to produce helmets for export to the United States. Four years later, a change in the Russian Parliament leads to domestic policy reversals. Russia annexes Bulgaria as a member of its federation and takes possession of all Bulgarian factories that employ more than twenty-five people, including Zasada's helmet facility. Was this a nationalization or an expropriation? How would the *INA Corp.* tribunal assess the appropriate compensation to Zasada? How would the *traditional* theory court measure that compensation? How would the *modern-traditional* theory court measure that compensation? What do these decisions suggest about the development of compensation theory?

2. Economic development in the Republic of Costa Azul is perceived to be hindered by the ownership of all farmland by a few families and firms—some of which are U.S.-owned. A new government is democratically elected on a platform of land redistribution; the government, however, has no currency to buy such land and lacks the credit necessary to borrow significant sums. If Costa Azul cannot afford to pay "prompt and just" compensation for foreign private property, should it refrain from initiating social change? Does it make a difference if Costa Azul refrains from taking the land and instead increases property taxes on lots greater than twenty-five hectares by a hundred times?

3. How should the FSIA apply if a government purchases private property as an embassy and violates

local ordinances in its operation? What if a government-owned airline sells a tour package to a private citizen, then detains and refuses her entry into the country as an undesirable? What if the government retains a consulting firm to develop a national agricultural development plan and then refuses to pay because its agricultural policy changes?

4. Was the "confiscation" of all cigar manufacturers by the Cuban government in the early 1960s an expropriation or a nationalization? Was this confiscation commercial activity in which a private businessperson could engage? Was the Cuban government's assertion of rights to post-intervention sums paid for cigars a commercial act? Is the analysis any different with respect to pre-intervention shipments?

5. Maria Hartman, a U.S. investor, owns a toy assembly plant in the Kingdom of Fromage Vert. At a tennis match between a leading U.S. player and a star Fromagian, Maria irritates the king by cheering for the American. The next day, the king issues an edict taking Ms. Hartman's plant for the kingdom. Ms. Hartman sues Fromage Vert in U.S. District Court for the Southern District of New York, where the kingdom's airline owns an office. Would the U.S. court have jurisdiction in the absence of a treaty? Do you think the Fromagian taking of the toy assembly plant was a commercial activity? Was it an "act of state"?

6. Is privatization a recent phenomenon? Why has it become more prominent in recent years? What triggered the move to more privatization in Latin American countries? In former communist nations?

7. Briefly describe the partial sale model of privatization. What is the predominant characteristic of the partial sale? How can a minority private investor try to protect itself from abuse by the majority government owner?

8. Briefly describe the trade sale model of privatization. What is the distinguishing feature of the trade sale? How is privatization achieved through management contracts?

9. List three reasons why giving employees an equity share in the new private entity makes sense. Give a reason that is principally applicable in Eastern Europe. What are two disadvantages associated with transferring shares to employees? What are two types of consideration that employees can be asked to give in exchange for their shares?

10. Briefly describe the concession model of privatization. How long should the term of the concession be?

11. Name four types of adjustments to regulations that are often addressed in the context of privatizations. Explain how they may be addressed.

12. Ernesto Ortiz, famed American corporate raider, initiates a hostile takeover of Bundesbank Freidumia (BF), the largest commercial bank in Freidumia. In purchasing 70 percent of BF's shares, Ortiz pays a substantial premium for control. After he concludes the transaction, Freidumia outlaws any foreigner or person under foreign control from voting shares in a commercial bank corporation, thereby wresting control from Mr. Ortiz. Has a nationalization taken place? An expropriation?

Managerial Implications

Your firm, Lloyd Aviation Company, is a leading U.S. manufacturer of helicopters. While on a trip to Moscow, you met Gennady Tupolev, the head of the former Soviet Air Force division that once manufactured military helicopters. The Russian government has no funds to finance further operations for the Tupolev Division and he needs to privatize its operations. The Russian government is reluctant to cede control over an industry that is so central to its national security; however, its conversion to commercial production will require thorough

control by Lloyd. The division has a strong research and development department. Many of the division's lower-level employees, however, will need to be laid off if it is to be a commercially viable operation.

1. Prepare a memorandum to Lloyd's board of directors outlining your plan for privatizing the Tupolev Division.
2. What regulatory arrangements should Lloyd make with the Russian government?

CHAPTER 20

LABOR AND EMPLOYMENT DISCRIMINATION LAW

Corporations are lifeless entities with one principal objective: maximizing profit for their stockholders. To be sure, many corporate leaders find it good business to be thoughtful of those who work for the firm. Unless government intervenes, however, corporations will often subordinate the interests of their workers to those of their stockholders. Accordingly, virtually all societies have enacted laws that protect workers from abusive or discriminatory practices.

This regulation varies widely from place to place. For example, the protective framework that safeguards and enfranchises German workers is extremely different from the United States' emphasis on individual achievement by workers and on control by managers. This chapter examines different approaches in this important area and their effect on international business transactions.

GENERAL DIRECTIONS OF LABOR LAW ABROAD

Any active investment, whether controlled by investors from the United States or from some other country, relies on employees and is thus influenced by the host country's labor laws. Because these laws are often different from those encountered in the United States, investors must review them and the attitudes they reflect. Although a more detailed study would reveal countless differences between U.S. and foreign labor laws, a review of three principal areas gives a general sense of the distinctions.

First, many nations' laws require employee consultation or participation in management decisions that Americans view as being central to the manage-

rial prerogative. Second, many countries place legal constraints on employee dismissal that are completely unfamiliar to the U.S. investor. Third, when the U.S. investor acquires a foreign business, by operation of law, it may also be acquiring the foreign industry's labor arrangements.

Employee Participation in Strategic Decisions

A current controversy in managerial theory involves the level of discretion owners and management should have in making strategic decisions and whether labor should participate in such decisions. A nation's laws on these issues have historically been shaped by its socio-political traditions. One of the interesting phenomena of modern labor law is how these approaches are merging as the world's economies merge.

The U.S. View. Notwithstanding legislative initiatives such as the *Worker Adjustment, Retraining, and Notification Act*—which at times requires sixty days' notice of the closing of a plant with more than one hundred employees—U.S. companies come from an environment that allows them great flexibility. Traditionally, U.S. management, completely by itself and in secret, makes strategic decisions such as whether to close a plant or reduce manpower levels. In the United States, management decides and labor carries out those decisions at an agreed hourly rate.

U.S. law mirrors this perspective: the U.S. Supreme Court has squarely held that an employer need not bargain with its employees over whether to shut down part of its business. The Court viewed this prerogative as akin to the closing down of a business, where "an employer has the absolute right to terminate his entire business for any reason he pleases."

The German Approach.

Europeans have traditionally viewed the role of workers quite differently. The law in many continental countries grants workers a right of consultation about or notice before the implementation of decisions resulting in workforce reductions. German law illustrates these worker rights of participation. Each plant with more than five employees must have a *Betriebsrat* (*works council*) to represent that plant's interest. In contrast to any U.S. counterpart, these works councils are independent from trade unions. They represent the interests of plant employees as distinct from those of the employer or those of the trade unions.

Under the *German Works Constitution Act,* the employer must fully inform the works council in "due time" of any plant changes that might result in "substantial disadvantages for employees" and consult with it on such proposals. In the course of that consultation, the employer solicits the works council's approval of the employer's method of selecting persons to be terminated as a result of the plant change. If the employer and the works council cannot resolve a dispute through this methodology, they then appear before an arbitration committee. In addition, the employer notifies the regional office of the Federal Employment Institute. If this office believes the plant change would strain local resources, it can delay the change until two months after notice. As these examples illustrate, U.S. companies can be confronted with a radically different labor situation once they go abroad.

Mandatory Employee Representation on Boards of Directors

A number of countries require substantial employee representation on the corporate board of directors. This is often accomplished by mandating a two-tiered board: a large supervisory board (the *Aufsichtsrat*) and a management board (the *Vorstand*). The *Aufsichtsrat* is responsible for representing shareholder interests, while the *Vorstand* manages the firm from day to day.

In Germany, the Netherlands, and Luxembourg, employees have direct representation in the *Aufsichtsrat*. Indeed, in Germany, companies that employ more than two thousand workers must establish *Aufsichtsrat* representation that is 50 percent labor and 50 percent shareholders. In companies with more than five hundred workers, one-third of the *Aufsichtsrat* must be composed of workers.

This focus on worker participation in corporate decisions has proved attractive to former communist nations that for fifty years emphasized the rights of workers. New laws in the Czech Republic and Poland, among others, have followed the German law model of worker boards.

The implications for U.S. investors are important. All significant strategic decisions require supervisory board approval. Thus, the *Vorstand* must present persuasive reasons for a strategic plan that involves workforce reductions. In short, the flexibility of management is not as great in German model countries as in the United States.

In Japan, management–labor strife is rare because of traditional and structural factors that blur distinctions between management and workers. Union leadership is a stepping stone to management; nearly 15 percent of union officials rise to serve as executives of the company. Consequently, union leaders have little incentive to take strident labor positions against those responsible for their advancement. Labor laws are generally inoffensive.

Impediments to Dismissal

Prevailing national norms also create different legal frameworks on the issue of employee dismissal. National attitudes toward the proper relationship between manager and employee heavily color the content of national law.

Underlying Philosophical Foundations.

People in the United States, perhaps the most capitalist of nations, do not commonly believe that anyone is entitled to a job. Once an individual ceases to be productive, her future employment is in jeopardy. Legally required severance pay is low, as it is viewed as a humane cushion to help the discharged until they can find new employment.

Europeans, on the other hand, feel that employees acquire a property interest in their jobs over time. Thus, the more senior an employee, the greater is his or her property interest. Accordingly, severance pay is legally required as compensation for the taking of this substantial property, and it increases as the employee becomes more senior. For the most senior employees, the high severance level can be so prohibitive as to strongly discourage involuntary dismissal. This system is often criticized as creating a very senior workforce with little incentive to perform.

The traditional Japanese view is that one's job is a central part of her place in society and that a job largely defines the person. An individual is expected to hold a job for the same company for a lifetime. In Japan, the focus is not on the conditions of dismissal but on the propriety of dismissal in the first place. Other nations tend to fall within one of these models or between them.

Legal Frameworks Reflecting Philosophy.   In the United States, employers historically have been able to terminate employees with little notice. Without a collective bargaining agreement in place, U.S. management was not limited in its employee termination options. This picture has changed somewhat as U.S. businesses have been influenced by European and Japanese practices. Relatively recent federal legislation now gives employees unpaid leave to care for family members, guarantees workers their jobs back after such leave, and requires a warning of plant closings. More and more U.S. managers now take a page from Japanese companies and seek ways of providing greater assurance of employment. Nonetheless, U.S. law gives entrepreneurs great flexibility to do as they wish with their employees. Those U.S. businessmen face quite a different legal world beyond their shores.

United Kingdom law mandates that an employer consult with the appropriate trade union before making a dismissal. If the workforce is to be reduced by ten or more employees, a consultation must take place sixty days prior to termination. Under German law, the works council must approve any dismissal. If it does not, the employer may appeal to a labor court, but is likely to lose the appeal. Indeed, the *Betriebsrat* can affirmatively call for the dismissal of employees even without a request from the employer.

Japan is perhaps the most interesting case. There the written law seems to permit relatively free dismissal of employees. But tradition, embodied in decisional law, protects the employee (see the *Kochi Hoso* case that follows).

A similar attitude was reflected in Japan's approach to plant closings. Japanese companies in financial stress seldom closed factories. Instead, plants were taken over by friendly affiliates in good financial condition, or workers were turned over to local successful firms. Again, discretion implicit in Japanese labor law was interpreted to enforce these cultural traditions. U.S. companies, such as Proctor & Gamble and Chase Manhattan Bank, have faced court proceedings from local unions challenging plant shutdowns in Japan as "unfair labor practices." This has occurred even when the U.S. firms offered the dismissed employees new jobs in different locations.

Just as U.S. employment practices are being influenced by those of Europe and Japan, the Japanese are being influenced by Westerners. During the long recession of the 1990s and early twenty-first century, giants such as Nippon Telephone & Telegraph, NKK Corporation, and Nissan Corporation all successfully implemented reductions in their workforces. These companies did not actually lay off employees, but effected the reductions through normal attrition, intracompany transfers, and transfers to subsidiaries. Because many employees rejected unattractive transfers and many of the subsidiaries went out of business, this shift proved to be significant. At the same time, surveys of Japanese executives indicated a broad consensus that the days of lifetime employment and strict seniority advancement systems were numbered. In short, the differences between nations as to the permanence of employment are still quite significant. However, over time they are becoming less profound.

Assumption of Employment Arrangements

> http://www.mac.doc.gov/tcc
> See for links to specific labor/employment topics through the TCC.

To a far greater extent than in the United States, many foreign nations—particularly European countries—compel corporate acquirers to adhere to existing employment arrangements. In other words, when acquiring a manufacturing plant, one may be

Kochi Hoso (Broadcasting Co.)
Rokeisoku No. 937 (1977)
Supreme Court of Japan

BACKGROUND AND FACTS

Like all Japanese firms with more than ten employees, Kochi Hoso was required to maintain rules of employment that specified the conditions under which an employee might be discharged. Kochi Hoso, a radio broadcasting company, clearly specified that tardiness for a broadcast was cause for dismissal. No contractual provision excused such tardiness.

The plaintiff, a radio announcer, had twice failed to arrive at the studio in time for a news broadcast. After the second offense, Kochi Hoso discharged the plaintiff, pointing to the unambiguous rules. Plaintiff sought reinstatement, arguing that although the discharge was within the rules, it was unreasonable or contrary to public policy. The Supreme Court found no reasonable cause for termination.

PER CURIAM

Even when an employee's conduct constitutes a cause for a discharge, an employer may not always discharge the employee. It should be noted that when the said discharge is found to be significantly unreasonable under the specific situation so that it could be hardly approved as being appropriate in the light of the socially accepted view, such a discharge should be considered to be an abusive exercise of an employer's power to discharge employees and, thus, to be invalid.

Decision. The Supreme Court of Japan ordered that the radio announcer be reinstated in his job.

---

acquiring the collective-bargaining agreement that the seller had negotiated with the trade union prior to the purchase of the company. Thus, a U.S. investor must assess this inherited liability before acquiring a foreign company.

EMPLOYMENT DISCRIMINATION OUTSIDE THE UNITED STATES

The United States almost certainly has the most comprehensive set of laws against discrimination of all sorts in employment. Because most other countries were created as the geographic homes of homogeneous ethnic groups, they have experienced relatively little need to develop antidiscriminatory schemes. Germany, after all, is where ethnic Germans live and Japan is where ethnic Japanese live. There has not been a perception of a need to protect against ethnic discrimination. At the opposite extreme, the Baltic countries, formerly part of the Soviet Union, have passed laws mandating discrimination against the ethnic Russian minority.

Foreign laws are becoming more important as international transportation brings ethnic minorities to virtually every nation, and the issue of discrimination against women comes to the fore. The principal employment discrimination issue for U.S. companies, however, remains whether U.S. laws apply to their overseas operations.

The Extraterritorial Application of U.S. Employment Discrimination Law

There has been significant disagreement in Congress and the legal community concerning the extent to which U.S. discrimination laws apply abroad and how they could apply if they did. For instance, how can a U.S. company operate in Islamic countries that legally require discrimination against Christians and Jews if it has to treat everyone equally? In 1991, the U.S. Supreme Court first gave some direction in this area.

Soon after the Supreme Court had spoken, Congress sought to overrule the *Aramco* case by at least partially extending U.S. employment law overseas. Congress expressly extended Title VII to firms operating outside the United States under the "control" of a U.S. entity (see Exhibit 20.1).

And as the *Aramco* Court predicted, Congress made an exception for situations where compliance

Equal Employment Opportunity Commission v. Arabian American Oil Co.
499 U.S. 244 (1991)
United States Supreme Court

BACKGROUND AND FACTS

The respondents are two Delaware corporations, Arabian American Oil Company (Aramco) and its subsidiary, Aramco Service Company (ASC). Aramco's principal place of business is Dhahran, Saudi Arabia, and it is licensed to do business in Texas.

In 1979, Boureslan was hired by ASC as a cost engineer in Houston. A year later he was transferred, at his request, to work for Aramco in Saudi Arabia. Boureslan remained with Aramco in Saudi Arabia until he was discharged in 1984. He instituted this suit in the United States District Court for the Southern District of Texas against Aramco and ASC. He sought relief under Title VII of the *Civil Rights Act* on the ground that he was harassed and ultimately discharged by respondents on account of his race, religion, and national origin.

CHIEF JUSTICE REHNQUIST

Both parties concede, as they must, that Congress has the authority to enforce its laws beyond the territorial boundaries of the United States. Whether Congress has in fact exercised that authority in this case is a matter of statutory construction. It is our task to determine whether Congress intended the protections of Title VII to apply to United States citizens employed by American employers outside of the United States.

It is a long-standing principle of American law "that legislation of Congress, unless a contrary intent appears, is meant to apply only within the territorial jurisdiction of the United States." It serves to protect against unintended clashes between our laws and those of other nations which could result in international discord.

Title VII prohibits various discriminatory employment practices based on an individual's race, color, religion, sex, or national origin. An employer is subject to Title VII if it is "engaged in an industry affecting commerce." "Commerce," in turn, is defined as "trade, traffic, commerce, transportation, transmission, or communication among the several States; or between a State and any place outside thereof." . . .

Petitioners . . . assert that since Title VII defines "States" to include States, the District of Columbia, and specified territories, the clause "between a State and any place outside thereof" must be referring to areas beyond the territorial limit of the United States. The language relied upon by petitioners—and it is they who must make the affirmative showing—is ambiguous, and does not speak directly to the question presented here. The intent of Congress as to the extraterritorial application of this statute must be deduced by inference from boilerplate language which can be found in any number of congressional acts, none of which have ever been held to apply overseas.

If we were to permit possible, or even plausible interpretations of language such as that involved here to override the presumption against extraterritorial application, there would be little left of the presumption.

Petitioners argue that Title VII's "alien exemption provision . . . clearly manifests an intention" by Congress to protect U.S. citizens with respect to their employment outside of the United States. The alien exemption provision says that "the statute" shall not apply to an employer with respect to the employment of aliens outside any State. Petitioners contend that from this language a negative inference should be drawn that Congress intended Title VII to cover United States citizens.

If petitioners are correct that the alien-exemption clause means that the statute applies to employers overseas, we see no way of distinguishing in its application between United States employers and foreign employers. Thus, a French employer of a United States citizen in France would be subject to Title VII—a result at which even petitioners balk. The EEOC assures us that in its view the term "employer" means only "American employer," but there is no such distinction in this statute.

It is also reasonable to conclude that had Congress intended Title VII to apply overseas, it would have addressed the subject of conflicts with foreign laws and procedures. In amending the Age Discrimination in Employment Act of 1967 to apply abroad, Congress specifically addressed potential conflicts with foreign law by providing that it is not unlawful for an employer to take any action prohibited by the ADEA "where such practices involve an employee in a workplace in a foreign country, and compliance

continued

continued

with the ADEA would cause such employer . . . to violate the laws of the country in which such workplace is located." Title VII, by contrast, fails to address conflicts with the laws of other nations.

Decision. Petitioners failed to present sufficient affirmative evidence that Congress intended Title VII to apply abroad. Accordingly, the judgment of the Court of Appeals was affirmed.

EXHIBIT 20.1

Extension of Title VII to Foreign Operations of U.S. Firms
Civil Rights Act of 1991 Pub. L. No. 102–166, 105 Stat. 1071, 1077–78 (1991)
United States Congress
Sec. 109. Protection of Extraterritorial Employment

a. Definition of Employee. [The Civil Rights Act and the Americans with Disabilities Act] are each amended by adding to the end the following: "With respect to employment in a foreign country, such term includes an individual who is a citizen of the United States." . . .
b. "It shall not be unlawful under [the Civil Rights Act] for an employer (or a corporation controlled by an employer), . . . to take any action otherwise prohibited . . . with respect to an employee in a workplace in a foreign country if compliance with such section would cause such employer (or such corporation), . . . to violate the law of the foreign country in which such workplace is located."
c. 1. If an employer controls a corporation whose place of incorporation is a foreign country, any practice prohibited by section 703 or 704 engaged in by such corporation shall be presumed to be engaged in by such employer.
   2. Sections 703 and 704 shall not apply with respect to the foreign operations of an employer that is a foreign person not controlled by an American employer.
   3. For purposes of this subsection, the determination of whether an employer controls a corporation shall be based on:
   A. the interrelation of operations;
   B. the common management;
   C. the centralized control of labor relations; and
   D. the common ownership or financial control of the employer and the corporation.

---

with Title VII would violate the law of the country where the firm is located.

Congress' action did not prove to be the last word. A few years after the enactment of the Act, (Title VII), the *Equal Employment Opportunity Commission* (EEOC) sought to give some direction to U.S. employers in its Enforcement Guidance Memorandum No. 915.002. In doing so, the EEOC also enunciated its views on the extraterritorial application of the *Americans with Disabilities Act* (ADA). But U.S. courts did not accept EEOC's "guidance." When the EEOC tried to expand the applicability of the ADEA to all persons applying for employment in the United States, the Fourth Circuit Court of Appeals, through the respected Judge Wilkinson, rejected the effort.

Thus, there are three principal defenses to U.S. challenges of employment decisions abroad. These

are whether (1) the decision is made by "a foreign person not controlled by an American employer," (2) the U.S. Title VII and the *Age Discrimination in Employment Act* (ADEA) conflict with a host country's laws, so that the employer faces "foreign compulsion" because to comply with U.S. law would violate the host country's laws, and (3) the performance of the job requires a trait such as a specific religion or gender, allowing the employer the "bona fide occupational qualification" defense. Each of these will be reviewed in turn.

Control by a Foreign Person

When Congress passed the ADEA amendments, there was still some hope of clearly defining the nationality of a corporation's controlling person. As the stock of international business is simultaneously

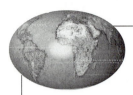

Reyes-Gaona v. North Carolina Growers Ass'n, Inc.
250 F.3d 861 (2001)
United States Court of Appeals (4th Cir.)

BACKGROUND AND FACTS

Plaintiff Luis Reyes-Gaona was a Mexican national over the age of forty. Defendant North Carolina Growers Association (NCGA) was an American corporation that assists agricultural businesses in North Carolina in securing farm labor through a legal federal program. Defendant Del-Al was an agent of NCGA that recruits workers for NCGA and its members. Reyes-Gaona went to a Del-Al office in Mexico and asked to be placed on a list of workers seeking employment in North Carolina. Del-Al told Reyes-Gaona that NCGA would not accept workers over forty years old unless that person had worked for NCGA before. With the support of the United States Equal Employment Opportunity Commission, Reyes-Gaona filed suit against NCGA and Del-Al, alleging age discrimination in violation of the *Age Discrimination in Employment Act.*

WILKINSON, CHIEF JUDGE

This case requires us to decide whether the Age Discrimination in Employment Act (ADEA) covers foreign nationals who apply in foreign countries for jobs in the United States. We hold that the Act does not cover such persons. . . .

Plaintiff is a foreign national who applied in a foreign country for work in the United States. Accordingly, we begin, as we must, by acknowledging the "longstanding principle of American law 'that legislation of Congress, unless a contrary intent appears, is meant to apply only within the territorial jurisdiction of the United States.' " . . . This interpretive canon is an especially important one as it "serves to protect against unintended clashes between our laws and those of other nations which could result in international discord." . . . Thus, the presumption against extra-territorial application of a federal statute can be overcome only if there is an "affirmative intention of the Congress clearly expressed." . . . Since this determination is necessarily "a matter of statutory construction," we begin with the text of the ADEA itself.

The ADEA makes it unlawful "for an employer" to "fail or refuse to hire" or "otherwise discriminate against any individual with respect to his compensation, terms, conditions, or privileges of employment, because of such individual's age." The term "employer" means any company "engaged in an industry affecting commerce who has twenty or more employees" and includes the agents of such companies. . . . The term "employee" means "an individual employed by any employer," and "includes any individual who is a citizen of the United States employed by an employer in a workplace in a foreign country." . . . Prior to 1984, the ADEA did not contain the language regarding U.S. citizens employed in foreign workplaces. To the contrary, [the ADEA] adopted language from the Fair Labor Standards Act (FLSA) excluding from coverage any individual "whose services during the workweek are performed in a workplace within a foreign country." . . .

Based on the exclusionary language adopted from the FLSA, many courts held that, before 1984, the ADEA had a purely domestic focus and did not cover American citizens working for American companies in foreign countries. . . . The presumption against the extra-territorial application of American laws required this result because absent a clear statement from Congress, the scope of American law is limited to "the territorial jurisdiction of the United States." . . . Thus the presumption prevented the ADEA from regulating events taking place in foreign countries even when they involved citizens of the United States. And the Act certainly could not have reached the even more attenuated situation of a foreign national applying in a foreign country for work in the United States.

In 1984, Congress partially closed this gap. Congress [amended] the ADEA to give it limited extra-territorial application. The definition of "employee" was amended to include "any individual who is a citizen of the United States employed by an employer in a workplace in a foreign country." . . . This new statutory language explicitly expanded the ADEA to prohibit U.S. companies from discriminating against U.S. citizens employed in foreign countries. Congress also included an accompanying provision outlawing such discrimination by subsidiaries of U.S. corporations. . . . The language was "carefully worded to apply only to citizens of the United States" who worked for a U.S. company or its subsidiary because Congress recognized that the "well-established principle of sover-

continued

continued

eignty" prohibited the United States from imposing "its labor standards on another country." . . . These amendments demonstrated that "when it desires to do so, Congress knows how to" expand "the jurisdictional reach of a statute." . . . Notably missing from the 1984 amendments, however, is any provision regulating the conduct at issue here. Congress explicitly gave the ADEA extra-territorial application with respect to certain U.S. citizens while simultaneously declining to extend coverage to foreign nationals like Reyes-Gaona. Nothing in the amendments regulates age discrimination by U.S. corporations against foreign nationals in foreign countries. And the doctrine of expressio unis est exclusio alterius instructs that where a law expressly describes a particular situation to which it shall apply, what was omitted or excluded was intended to be omitted or excluded. . . . Thus, a faithful reading of the plain text of the statute, especially in light of the 1984 amendments, compels the conclusion that Reyes-Gaona's claim is not sustainable under the ADEA.

Reyes-Gaona and the EEOC disagree. They claim that this case does not require extra-territorial application of the ADEA because the job Reyes-Gaona applied for was in the United States. The crux of their argument is that when determining whether a suit requires extra-territorial application of the ADEA, courts always look to the place of employment rather than the place where the decision was made. Because Reyes-Gaona applied for a job in the United States, they argue, the presumption against extra-territoriality is not implicated by this suit. In support they note that the ADEA itself contains the term "workplace." For example, "employee" is defined to include U.S. citizens employed "in a workplace in a foreign country." . . . And the Act excepts from its reach employees "in a workplace in a foreign country" where compliance would conflict with the laws of the country "in which such workplace is located."

We are not persuaded. All of these statutory references come from the 1984 amendments to the ADEA which, as previously explained, do not cover Reyes-Gaona. Nothing in the ADEA provides that it shall apply anytime the workplace is in the United States regardless of the nationality of the applicant or the country in which the application was submitted. And the fact that the 1984 amendments refer to workplace does not mean that the Act focuses on work situs to the exclusion of the situs of the application or the nationality of the applicant. . . .

The simple submission of a resume abroad does not confer the right to file an ADEA action. Indeed, such a broad reading of the Act could have staggering consequences for American companies. Expanding the ADEA to cover millions of foreign nationals who file an overseas application for U.S. employment could exponentially increase the number of suits filed and result in substantial litigation costs. If such a step is to be taken, it must be taken via a clear and unambiguous statement from Congress rather than by judicial fiat.

The Supreme Court has instructed the lower courts to take seriously the presumption against extra-territorial application of U.S. laws. In keeping with these instructions, many lower courts, including this one, held that the ADEA had no extra-territorial application prior to 1984. Congress responded by amending the Act to provide for limited extra-territorial reach. Since these amendments do not reach the case at bar, there remains nothing in the text of the ADEA to rebut the presumption against extending it to cover Reyes-Gaona. And the limited nature of the 1984 amendments indicates that foreign nationals in foreign countries are not covered by the ADEA, regardless of whether they are seeking employment in the United States or elsewhere.

Decision.   The Fourth Circuit Court of Appeals affirmed the district court's dismissal of Mr. Reyes-Gaona's suit.

---

offered in many international exchanges—in each of which people of all nationalities may anonymously purchase stock—it becomes virtually impossible to identify the nationality of owners in industrialized countries. Courts have, however, prevented the EEOC and U.S. citizens from bringing suit against foreign firms with very substantial U.S. operations.

The courts provided additional guidance on the limits of extraterritorial application of U.S. anti-

discrimination laws in the District of Columbia in *Shekoyan v. Sibley Int'l Corp.,* 217 F. Supp.2d 59 (D.D.C. 2002). In *Shekoyan*, the court excluded a permanent U.S. resident alien who worked abroad for a U.S. government contractor from the extra-territorial protection of Title VII and the ADEA. In *Shekoyan,* the court held that although the employee was a U.S. resident and employment and training occurred in the United States he was an alien not protected by U.S. antidiscrimination laws when the job was solely located abroad.

The Foreign Compulsion Defense

Congress also intended to provide a "foreign compulsion" defense, permitting U.S. firms flexibility when the enforcement of U.S. employment laws overseas would result in a violation of foreign law.

As in all things legal, however, interesting questions arise in difficult cases. In the following case, the U.S. Court of Appeals for the District of Columbia found that where U.S. law would cause a U.S. firm to violate a foreign collective bargaining agreement—not a law, strictly speaking—the foreign compulsion defense nonetheless applied. Again, a court rejected the EEOC view.

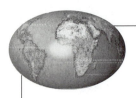

Mahoney v. RFE/RL, Inc.
47 F.3d 447 (1995)
United States Court of Appeals
(D.C. Cir.)

BACKGROUND AND FACTS

RFE/RL, Inc. is a Delaware nonprofit corporation that is funded but not controlled by the federal government and is best known for its broadcast services, Radio Free Europe and Radio Liberty. RFE/RL's principal place of business is Munich, Germany. In 1982, the company entered into a collective bargaining agreement with unions representing its employees in Munich. One of the provisions of the labor contract, modeled after a nationwide agreement in the German broadcast industry, required employees to retire at age sixty-five.

After Congress amended the *Age Discrimination in Employment Act* (ADEA) to cover American citizens working for American corporations overseas, RFE/RL thought its American employees in Munich would no longer have to retire at the age of sixty-five, as the collective bargaining agreement provided, and could continue to work if they chose. In order to implement this understanding, the company applied to the "Works Council" for limited exemptions from its contractual obligation. Rejecting RFE/RL's requests, the Works Council determined that allowing only those employees who were American citizens to work past the age of sixty-five would violate not only the mandatory retirement provision, but also the collective bargaining agreement's provision forbidding discrimination on the basis of nationality. RFE/RL appealed the Works Council's decisions with respect to the plaintiffs to the Munich Labor Court and lost. The Labor Court agreed with the Works Council that RFE/RL must uniformly enforce the mandatory retirement provisions because exemptions would unfairly discriminate against German workers. The Labor Court also held that the company's retaining

employees over the age of sixty-five despite the collective bargaining agreement would be illegal. The company terminated plaintiff De Lon in 1987, and plaintiff Mahoney in 1988. Both plaintiffs were working for the company in Munich, both were U.S. citizens, and both were discharged pursuant to the labor contract because they had reached the age of sixty-five.

CIRCUIT JUDGE RANDOLPH

If an American corporation operating in a foreign country would have to "violate the laws" of that country in order to comply with the Age Discrimination in Employment Act, the company need not comply with the Act. The question here is whether this "foreign laws" exception . . . applies when the overseas company, in order to comply with the Act, would have to breach a collective bargaining agreement that foreign unions. . . .

The parties agree that RFE/RL thereby violated the ADEA unless the "foreign laws" exception applied. The Act prohibits employers from discriminating against employees on the basis of age. "Employee" includes "any individual who is a citizen of the United States employed by an employer in a workplace in a foreign country;" and it is common ground that the Act covers RFE/RL.

The "foreign laws" exception to the Act states: It shall not be unlawful for an employer, employment agency, or labor organization—(1) to take any action otherwise prohibited under subsections (a), (b), (c), or (e) of this section where . . . such practices involve an employee in a workplace in a foreign country, and compliance with such subsections would cause such

continued

continued

employer, or a corporation controlled by such employer, to violate the laws of the country in which such workplace is located. The district court held [the provision] inapplicable because the mandatory retirement provision is part of a contract between an employer and unions—both private entities—and has not in any way been mandated by the German government. Second, the provision does not have general application, as laws normally do, but binds only the parties to the contract. . . .

If RFE/RL had not complied with the collective bargaining agreement in this case, if it had retained plaintiffs despite the mandatory retirement provision, the company would have violated the German laws standing behind such contracts, as well as the decisions of the Munich Labor Court. In the words of [the foreign compulsion defense], RFE/RL's "compliance with [the Act] would cause such employer . . . to violate the laws of the country in which such workplace is located." Domestic employers of course would never face a comparable situation; the Supremacy Clause of the Constitution would force any applicable state laws to give way, and provisions in collective bargaining agreements contrary to the Act would be superseded. Congressional legislation cannot, however, set aside the laws of foreign countries. When an overseas employer's obligations under

foreign law collide with its obligations under the Age Discrimination in Employment Act, [the foreign compulsion defense] quite sensibly solves the dilemma by relieving the employer of liability under the Act. . . .

We recognize that RFE/RL's collective bargaining agreement is legally enforceable, which necessarily means that breaching the agreement in order to comply with the Act would . . . "cause" RFE/RL "to violate the laws of" Germany. Plaintiffs complain that RFE/RL could have bargained harder for a change in the labor contract. But application of [the foreign compulsion defense] does not depend on such considerations. The collective bargaining agreement here was valid and enforceable at the time of plaintiffs' terminations, and RFE/RL had a legal duty to comply with it. There is not, nor could there be, any suggestion that RFE/RL agreed to the mandatory retirement provision in order to evade the Age Discrimination in Employment Act. Such provisions are, the evidence showed, common throughout the Federal Republic of Germany, and RFE/RL entered into this particular agreement before Congress extended the Act beyond our borders.

Decision. The Court of Appeals reversed the District Court opinion and remanded the case back with instructions to dismiss the matter.

The Bona Fide Occupational Qualification Defense

The bona fide occupational qualification defense (BFOQ), both in Title VII and the ADEA, provides that an employer may engage in discrimination if it is "reasonably necessary to the normal operation of the particular business or enterprise." This is not much of a "safe harbor" for U.S. employers; what is "reasonably necessary" for one person may not be for another. For example, when an American hospital refused to send Jewish anesthesiologists to Saudi Arabia, a court held that the BFOQ defense to the Jewish doctors' suit did not apply. The court found that the employer had not made appropriate efforts to determine the Saudi Arabian policy regarding the entry of Jewish doctors into the country and that the Saudi government had never directed the employer that American Jews could not participate in the program. Another court found the BFOQ defense did not justify a refusal to

promote a woman to a senior position. The court found inadequate the company's reasoning that she would have to deal with men in Latin America, where, they argued, businesspeople believe that women belong in the home. The BFOQ defense might be useful to the litigator trying to defend company action after the fact, but it seems too uncertain to be a useful tool for business planning.

Antidiscrimination Laws Outside the United States

The history of the United States is peppered with the successive immigrations by various ethnic groups, each seeking civic and economic freedom. Even the framers of the Constitution, while virtually all of British ancestry, were products of four different migrations from different parts of Britain, with distinctly different religious traditions. Not surprisingly, the United States has a highly developed legal system proscribing discrimination based on religion, ethnicity, or national origin. As we have seen in the preceding section, this body of law has in turn given rise to related legal principles prohibiting discrimination based on other criteria that have become socially unacceptable bases for differentiation, such as age and gender.

The multiethnic makeup of the United States has been relatively unusual. As F. Scott Fitzgerald elegantly noted, "France was a land, England was a people, but America having about it that quality of the idea, was harder to utter. . . . It was a willingness of the heart." Most Europeans and Asians lived in geographic regions inhabited by their ethnic brethren. The same has been true to a lesser extent in Africa, where traditional ethnic groups remain dominant in regions of multi-tribal nations created by European colonists. Even today, the competing desires of ethnic groups to dominate a geographically contiguous zone are a primary cause of civil strife in these continents. "Ethnic cleansing" in Bosnia and post-1999 "counter-cleansing" in Kosovo were efforts to create geographic regions where only one ethnic group resides. Although Latin America does not have the same tie to the land as do the peoples of Europe, Asia, and Africa, the dominance of the Spanish culture in Hispanic America and of the Portuguese culture in Brazil has prevented legal developments similar to those in the United States. Few discrimination laws were the legal result of these social conditions.

The revolution in transport and communications, however, is ending ethnic homogeneity in the Old World. Ethnic North Africans work in Paris, ethnic Pakistanis in London, and ethnic Turks in Frankfurt; and women are not as willing to accept discrimination in the workplace.

Discrimination Based on National Origin or Religion. In a few countries, the law actually requires discrimination based on religion or national origin. When a country is synonymous with an ethnic group, that ethnic group sometimes justifies preservation of ethnic identity by the methodical exclusion of those outside it. Thus, Estonia has created citizenship laws, the plain intent of which is to deny citizenship to ethnic Russians who arrived during the seventy years of Soviet rule. Because Estonia confers employment and other benefits on the basis of citizenship, its citizenship law is a device for favoring ethnic Esto-

nians over ethnic Russians in employment opportunities. Dominant ethnic groups in small, wealthy nations threatened by large numbers of industrious ethnic outsiders often enact laws to prevent those outsiders from holding certain types of jobs. For example, ethnic Kuwaitis and Jordanians have thus excluded Palestinian co-religionists from key jobs and properties. Likewise, when a nation does not distinguish between religion and the state, the law often calls for discrimination against infidels. In the twenty-first century, these laws are somewhat less widespread. Pro-discrimination laws are most frequently found in Middle Eastern Islamic countries such as Pakistan, Iran, and Saudi Arabia. One may also encounter such pro-discrimination statutes in countries where atheism is the state religion, such as Cuba and North Korea.

Obviously, there are no such pro-discrimination laws in the United States. Nonetheless, the U.S. investor must take such laws into account in staffing foreign operations. Because they are rooted in deep cultural or political fear of outside influence, violations of their terms generally lead to very adverse action by the local government.

The U.S. investor must now also understand foreign laws prohibiting ethnic discrimination, similar but different from U.S. models. Articles 7, 48, 52, and 59 of the *European Union Treaty* forbid different types of discrimination within the Union on the basis of nationality. The motivating principle behind these provisions is that nationals from each Member country should be free to pursue their economic interests anywhere within the unified European economy without fear of differential treatment. The following case demonstrates the Community's commitment to protect even the oldest of professions.

EU antidiscrimination law has not historically prohibited discrimination against ethnic individuals who are not Member State nationalities. But this is changing. The EU's *Group on Treaty Amendment and Community Competence* has in recent years noted that measures prohibiting racism and xenophobia should become part of the EU's discussion on EU treaty amendments. Among the measures discussed have been the granting of legal status to resident non-EU citizens and granting third country nationals EU-citizen status upon completion of a five-year lawful residency requirement in one of the Member States.

Bezguia Adoui v. Belgian State & City of Liège; Cornuaille v. Belgian State
1982 E.C.R. 1665
Court of Justice of the European Communities

BACKGROUND AND FACTS

On 3 June 1980, Miss Adoui, a French national, submitted an application to the City of Liège for a permit to reside in Belgium. The Minister of Justice denied her application and ordered her to leave the country because her personal conduct made her residence undesirable. This order was based on the Minister's finding that she worked in a bar in which waitresses displayed themselves in the window and were able to be alone with their clients for sexual encounters. Such conduct was contrary to the laws of Liège. She was not actually found to have so displayed herself, however.

Miss Adoui refused to comply with the expulsion order, asserting that she was the victim of discrimination based on national origin. In essence, Miss Adoui took the position that no similar action was taken against Belgian women merely suspected of engaging in display activities in furtherance of the business of prostitution. She sought relief from a court with jurisdiction over the Minister of Justice, the Tribunal de Premiere Instance at Liège.

Miss Cornuaille, another French national, was similarly accused of being a waitress of questionable moral character who "in scant dress displays herself to clients" for purposes of prostitution. The Committee of Aliens Office issued an opinion recommending her expulsion, without having taken account of the matters which had been the subject of the complaint to the criminal authorities. Like Ms. Adoui, Miss Cornuaille summoned the Committee to the Liège Tribunal, alleging discrimination on the basis of national origin.

The President of the Liège Tribunal stayed the proceedings in both cases and to refer to the Court of Justice under Article 177 of the *Treaty of Rome,* questions for a preliminary ruling to determine whether a foreign national could be expelled on the basis of conduct for which a citizen was not normally reprimanded.

J. MERTEN DE WILMARS, PRESIDENT; G. BOSCO AND A. TOUFFAIT, PRESIDENTS OF CHAMBERS; P. PESCATORE, LORD MACKENZIE STUART, A. O'KEEFE, T. KOOPMANS, U. EVERLING, AND A. CHLOROS, JUDGES

The questions were raised in actions brought against the Belgian State by the Plaintiffs in the main proceedings, who are of French nationality, in connection with the refusal by the administrative authority to issue a permit enabling them to reside in Belgian territory, on the ground that their conduct was considered to be contrary to public policy by virtue of the fact that they were waitresses in a bar which was suspect from the point of views of morals.

The Belgian Law of 21 August 1948 terminating official regulation of prostitution prohibits soliciting, incitement to debauchery, exploitation of prostitution, the keeping of a disorderly house or brothel, and living on immoral earnings. The police regulation of the City of Liège of 25 March 1957 and subsequent orders provide that persons engaged in prostitution may not display themselves to passers-by, that the doors and windows of the premises where they pursue their activity are to be closed and covered so that it is impossible to see inside, and that those persons may not stand in the street near such premises.

[The questions referred to the Court] are essentially concerned with the question whether a Member State may, by virtue of the reservations contained in Articles 48 and 56 of the EEC Treaty, expel from its territory a national of another Member State or deny him access to that territory by reason of activities which, when attributable to the former State's own nationals, do not give rise to repressive measures.

Those questions are motivated by the fact that prostitution as such is not prohibited by Belgian legislation, although the Law does prohibit certain incidental activities, which are particularly harmful.

The reservations contained in Articles 48 and 56 of the EEC Treaty permit Member States to adopt, with respect to the nationals of other Member States measures which they cannot apply to their own nationals, inasmuch as they have no authority to expel the latter from the national territory or to deny them access thereto. Although that difference of treatment, which bears upon the nature of the measures available, must therefore be allowed, it must nevertheless be stressed that, in a Member State, the authority empowered to adopt such measures must not base the exercise of its powers on assessments of certain conduct which would have the effect of

continued

continued

applying an arbitrary distinction to the detriment of nationals of other Member States.

Although Community law does not impose upon the Member States a uniform scale of values as regards the assessment of conduct which may be considered as contrary to public policy, it should nevertheless be stated that conduct may not be considered as being of a sufficiently serious nature to justify restrictions on the admission to or residence within the territory of a Member State or a national of another Member State in a case where the former Member State does not adopt, with respect to the same conduct on the part of its own nationals, repressive measures or other genuine and effective measures intended to combat such conduct.

The answer to [the questions referred to the Court] should therefore be that a Member State may not, by virtue of the reservation relating to public policy contained in Articles 48 and 56 of the Treaty, expel a national of another Member State from its territory or refuse him access to its territory by reason of conduct which, when attributable to the former State's own nationals, does not give rise to repressive measures or other genuine and effective measures intended to combat such conduct.

Decision.   On those grounds, the court, in answer to the questions referred to it by the President of the Tribunal de Premiere Instance, Liège, hereby rules:

[A] Member State may not, by virtue of the reservation relating to public policy contained in Articles 48 and 56 of the Treaty, expel a national of another Member State from its territory or refuse him access to its territory by reason of conduct which, when attributable to the former State's own nationals, does not give rise to repressive measures or other genuine and effective measures intended to combat such conduct.

The notification of the grounds relied upon to justify an expulsion measure or a refusal to issue a residence permit must be sufficiently detailed and precise to enable the person concerned to defend his interests.

The person concerned must be entitled to put forward to the competent authority his arguments in defense and to be assisted or represented in such conditions as to procedure as are provided for by domestic legislation. Those conditions must not be less favorable to the person concerned than the conditions applicable to proceedings before other national authorities of the same type.

Discrimination Based on Gender.   The movement to abolish discrimination based on gender is relatively new. Until the twentieth century, few nations even granted women the right of suffrage. The great majority of nations imposed many restrictions on work outside the home.

During the twentieth century, women's legal status changed radically. Gender discrimination laws were largely replaced with antidiscrimination provisions. Legal restrictions on women's roles in the workplace are now principally limited to a few fundamentalist Islamic nations.

Notwithstanding these legal advances, gender discrimination remains almost universal—at different levels—in the twenty-first century. In Japan, women earn only 63 percent of what men earn. In the United States, the figure is 74 percent. Northern European nations are among the best—in Sweden and Denmark, the figures are 87 and 88 percent, respectively. But others are measurably worse; Chile's booming economy has done little to improve the ratio of fifty-four cents for women to

every dollar men make. Discriminatory access to educational opportunity is not the explanation. In Latin America, on the average, a woman needs fifteen years of education to make the same amount as a man with eleven years of education. Similarly, a 2003 study of gender discrimination in the Ukraine found widespread discrimination against women in all employment sectors despite broad legal guarantees of equal protection. The discrimination included job announcements that specified male applicants only and job announcements requiring an attractive appearance for female applicants. In addition, the study found discrimination against unmarried women and women with small children.

Lawmakers have particularly focused on the issue of maternity leave. An EU directive now provides for a minimum of fourteen weeks' maternity leave and an allowance of at least 75 or 80 percent of net salary. It further stipulates that pregnant workers cannot be fired. In Hong Kong, a new law provides for ten weeks' maternity leave at two-thirds of the woman's latest salary. India requires six weeks' leave at full pay. The Ukraine allows ten weeks' pre-birth and eight weeks' post-birth salaried maternity leave, as well as additional unpaid leave until the child reaches age three. The up-to-age-three leave allows the mother to collect benefits from the state.

There has also been change in the area of equal pay for equal work. Article 119 of the EU treaty and Community Directives 75/117 and 76/207 require equal pay for equal work and equality in access to employment. As noted in the *Bilka-Kaufhaus* case, compliance with these principles is determined through a practical "effect-oriented" test.

Bilka-Kaufhaus GmbH v. Karin Weber von Hartz
1986 E.C.R. 1607
Court of Justice of the European Communities

BACKGROUND AND FACTS

By order of 5 June 1984, the Bundesarbeitgericht (German Federal Labour Court) referred the following question to the court for a preliminary ruling: May there be an infringement of Article 19 of the EEC Treaty in the form of "direct discrimination" where a department store which employs predominantly women excludes part-time employees from benefits under this occupational pension scheme although such exclusion affects disproportionately more women than men?

LORD MACKENZIE STUART, CHIEF JUDGE; KOOPMANS, EVERLING, BAHLMANN, AND JOLIET, PPC; BOSCO, DUE, GALMOT, AND KAKOURIS, JUDGES

By order of 5 June 1984, received by the Court on 2 July 1984, the Bundesarbeitsgericht (Federal Labour Court) requested a preliminary ruling pursuant to Article 177 of the EEC Treaty . . . concerning the interpretation of Article 119 of the Treaty.

The questions have arisen in the context of an action brought against Bilka Kaufhaus GmbH (Bilka) by its previous employee, Karin Weber von Hartz, concerning her entitlement to a retirement pension under the supplementary pension scheme set up by Bilka for its employees.

It appears from the file that Bilka has for several years had a supplementary pension scheme (occupational pension) for its employees. . . . According to the version in force from 26 October 1973, part-time employees qualify under the scheme only if they have been in full-time employment for fifteen years out of a total of twenty.

Mrs. Weber was employed by Bilka as a sales assistant from 1961 to 1976. After working full-time, she opted to work part-time from 1 October 1972

up to the date when her contract of employment came to an end. As she had not worked a minimum of fifteen years full-time Bilka refused her an occupational pension.

Mrs. Weber challenged the legality of Bilka's refusal in the German labour courts on the ground, inter alia, that the occupational pension scheme was in breach of the principle of equal pay for men and women, enshrined in Article 119 of the EEC Treaty. On this point Mrs. Weber argued that the requirement, for receiving an occupational pension, of a minimum period of full-time employment is to the detriment of female workers who, in order to be able to take care of their family and children, are more likely to be induced to choose part-time work than their male colleagues.

Bilka, on the other hand, maintained that it could not be accused of violating the principle of equal pay because the decision to exclude part-time employees from the occupational pension scheme was based on objectively justified economic grounds. In this connection it emphasized that the employment of full-time workers, by comparison with part-time workers, involves fewer ancillary costs and permits staff to be used for the whole period during which stores are open.

In the first question on which it seeks a preliminary ruling, the national court asked whether the staff policy of a department store company, consisting in excluding part-time employees from an occupational pension scheme, constitutes discrimination prohibited by Article 119 if the exclusion affects far more female workers than males.

For a reply to this question, reference should be made to the judgment of 31 March 1981. In that judgment the Court considered the question whether a pay practice consisting in fixing a lower hourly rate

continued

continued

of pay for part-time work than for full-time work is compatible with Article 119. A practice of this kind is comparable to that referred to by the national court in the present case because, although Bilka makes no distinction in relation to hourly pay as between part-time or full-time employees, it grants an occupational pension only to employees in the latter category. As an occupational pension is within the definition of pay given by paragraph 2 of Article 119, as shown above, it follows that the global pay given by Bilka to full-time employees is higher than that for part-time employees, assuming an equal number of hours worked.

It follows that, if it were found that a considerably smaller percentage of women than men work full-time, the exclusion of part-time workers from the occupational pension scheme would be contrary to Article 119 of the Treaty if, taking account of the difficulties encountered by women arranging matters so as to be able to work full-time, this measure cannot be explained by factors excluding discrimination based on sex.

However, if the enterprise is able to show that its pay practice can be explained by objectively justified factors which are unrelated to discrimination based on sex, it would not be possible to find a breach of Article 119. Therefore the reply to the first question by the national court should be that Article 119 of the EEC Treaty is infringed by a department store company which excludes part-time employees from its occupational pension scheme where that exclusion affects a much greater number of women than men, unless the enterprise shows that the exclusion is based on objectively justified factors which are unrelated to any discrimination based on sex.

In the second question the national court aims in substance to establish whether the reasons put forward by Bilka to explain its pay policy can be considered "objectively justified economic reasons" within the meaning of the judgment of 31 March 1981, when reasons of commercial expediency in the department store sector do not necessitate such a policy.

It falls to the national court, which alone is competent to assess the facts, to decide whether, and if so to what extent, the grounds put forward by an employer to explain the adoption of a pay practice which applies irrespective of the employee's sex, but which in fact affects more women than men, can be considered to be objectively justified for economic reasons. If the national court finds that the means chosen by Bilka meet a genuine need of the enterprise, that they are suitable for attaining the objective pursued by the enterprise and are necessary for that purpose, the fact that the measures in question affect a much greater number of women than men is not sufficient to conclude that they involve a breach of Article 119.

Therefore the answer to question 2(a) should be that, according to Article 119, a department store company may justify the adoption of a pay policy involving the exclusion of part-time employees from its occupational pension scheme, regardless of sex, by contending that it seeks to employ as few workers of this kind as possible, if it is found that the means chosen to attain this objective meet a genuine need of the enterprise, are suitable for attaining the objective in question and are necessary for that purpose.

Finally the national court, in question 2(b), asks whether the employer is compelled, pursuant to Article 119 of the Treaty, to organize the occupational pension scheme for employees in such a way as to take account of the fact that the family commitments of female employees prevent them from fulfilling the conditions for entitlement to a pension.

It should be observed that the ambit of Article 119 is limited to the problem of discrimination in pay between men and women. On the other hand, problems connected with other conditions of work and employment are envisaged generally by other provisions of Community law, particularly Article 117 and 118 of the Treaty, with a view to harmonization of the social systems of Member States and approximation of their legislation in this field.

This imposition of an obligation of the kind described by the national court in its question goes beyond the ambit of Article 119 and has no other basis in Community law as it stands at present.

Therefore the reply to question 2(b) must be that Article 119 does not have the effect of compelling an employer to organize the occupational pension scheme for employees in such a way as to take account of the special difficulties encountered by employees with family commitments in fulfilling the conditions entitling them to such as pension.

Decision. The Court of Justice remanded the case to the German Federal Labor Court for proceedings consistent with the foregoing rulings.

Gender discrimination cases have found only mixed success in Japan. In July 1990, a Tokyo District Court ruled for the first time that female employees had been improperly denied promotions due to gender discrimination. Although the court awarded eighteen women $640,000, consistent with Japan's respect for the integrity of the workplace, the court declined to direct promotions because such action would interfere with personnel decisions. As noted in the following article, however, in November 2003, the Tokyo District Court found that different, lower pay for women was acceptable. Notwithstanding occasional setbacks, movement on gender discrimination issues seems consistent throughout the world.

FOREIGN LAWS PERMITTING DIFFICULT WORK CONDITIONS

One of the principal reasons for locating a plant abroad is relative cost advantage. Particularly in low-skill manufacturing, one's dollars go farther paying salaries in an economy with a weak currency and a low cost of living. Many Third World countries lack burdensome work rules that add unnecessary costs.

international accents

Women Lose Kanematsu Wage-Bias Suit

November 6, 2003
The Japan Times

The Tokyo District Court rejected a damages suit [on November 5, 2003] against Kanematsu Corp. by six women who said they suffered gender-based wage discrimination at the trading house.

In their lawsuit, the women, three of whom still work for the company, had sought a combined 319 million yen in damages. They said the firm's policy of paying men and women different wages is not only illegal but also irrational and discriminatory. The plaintiffs said they performed the same jobs as their male colleagues. The damages they were seeking included compensation, the lump-sum difference between the wages of men and women, and the wages between April 1992 and last July, when the trial ended.

Presiding Judge Yukio Yamaguchi acknowledged that setting different hiring courses and wage systems violates the Constitution's ban on gender discrimination and its stipulation that all are equal before the law. However, "such actions only become illegal and void when the discrimination is irrational and runs counter to public order," he said. Given that as of 1985, the Equal Employment Law only obliged firms to "make efforts" to stop discriminatory hiring and treatment, Kanematsu's actions at the time could not be deemed illegal, the judge ruled. . . .

According to the court, Kanematsu had a policy of paying men and women differently until 1985, when it launched a wage system in which all workers were paid according to their jobs. Men thereafter were paid for providing general services and women for their clerical services.

The company argued that men worked in its core positions dealing with corporate services, while women engaged in support services and were hired based on their duties. It said the gender wage gap was the result of hiring procedures appropriate for the time. The Equal Employment Law was amended in June 1997 to ban discriminatory treatment against women, and Kanematsu introduced a new personnel system in April that year that made it easier for female employees to change career tracks and move to higher-paying jobs. The court ruled that this new system was rational and that the firm's wage system in the end did not go against public order. . . .

In February 2002, Judge Yamaguchi ordered Nomura Securities Co. to pay 56 million yen in damages to 12 female employees who were denied promotions because it discriminated against female workers. The court said Nomura's actions were illegal and discriminatory since the policy was still maintained even after the revised law on equal job opportunities for men and women took effect in 1999. . . .

Other nations boast smooth labor–management relations that avoid expensive disputes. In some cases, cost savings are attributable to work conditions that, while lawful in the host country, are not legal in industrialized Western nations. In some instances, the local labor practices may not even be legal under local law. U.S. companies almost never directly engage in illegal employment practices; rather, they often place orders for a product or a component with a foreign buying agent that submits a low bid. These agents procure foreign suppliers to assemble the products or components in accordance with the U.S. company's specifications. These suppliers in turn subcontract parts of the product to smaller shops. Typically, the worst abuses occur in these low-cost small shops—several steps removed from the U.S. purchaser.

A U.S. firm, even if operating legally within the host country, must concern itself with whether those practices violate nonbinding standards issued by the *International Labor Organization* (ILO) and other international standards. And if unaware of dubious labor practices, but using foreign buying agents, it should conduct due diligence to satisfy itself that such practices are not in use. As will be seen, a failure to do so can have adverse consequences in the U.S. firm's target markets.

Unsafe Labor Conditions

In developed countries, government agencies such as the U.S. Occupational Safety and Health Administration regulate conditions in the workplace. In many emerging nations, there is no such legal framework and working conditions can become quite hazardous. One of the more common and dangerous of these practices is the blocking and locking of all exits in manufacturing facilities as a low-cost measure to prevent pilfering. This practice has caused thousands of workers to be trapped and burned alive when fire broke out in such buildings. For example, a fire in a locked toy factory near Bangkok killed more than 240 workers and injured hundreds of others. In a separate incident, a fire in a locked facility killed eighty young women in Dongguan, China. The lack of ventilation in such factories also increased the incidence of tuberculosis and sinusitis among workers.

A second common safety issue is the use of antiquated and poorly maintained equipment. Such equipment causes the rate of work injuries to balloon. Indeed, in many emerging nations, work-related injuries have doubled in the last five years.

Harsh work rules—legal in many developing nations—are a third major concern. In order to maximize output per worker and thereby reduce cost per unit, some manufacturers permit assembly line workers to use the restroom only three times in a twelve-hour day. This practice not only subjects workers to great physical discomfort, it increases the incidence of urinary tract infections.

Prison Labor

Prison labor exists to some extent in virtually all countries. Prisoners manufacture most of the license plates in the United States. In a few nations including the People's Republic of China, however, it is legal for prisoners to work in traditionally commercial forms of manufacturing. If developed nations have difficulty competing with low-cost labor in underdeveloped countries, they have even less chance of competing with free, involuntary labor from such nations. The use of such labor is simply unacceptable to Western governments.

With close relations in China between government and business, the practice of prison labor became particularly prevalent in the late 1980s. In 1992, the United States stepped up the pressure on China to exclude prison labor products from exports to the United States. The result was the diplomatic Memorandum of Understanding shown in Exhibit 20.2. As is often the case in matters of international trade, the matter did not end with the signing of an agreement. Two-and-one-half years after the Memorandum of Understanding, the United States received renewed reports of prison labor generating exports to the United States. The United States threatened trade sanctions to enforce the Memorandum before a new agreement was concluded in 1994.

http://policy.house.gov/html/china_bills.html
Information on China prison labor.
http://www.cecc.gov
Information on human rights from the Congressional–Executive Commission on China.

EXHIBIT 20.2

U.S. Memorandum on Prison Labor in China

Memorandum of Understanding Between the United States of America and

the People's Republic of China on Prohibiting Import and Export Trade in Prison Labor Products

---

31 *International Legal Materials* 1071 (August 7, 1992)

The Government of the United States of America and the Government of the People's Republic of China (hereinafter referred to as the Parties)

Considering that the Chinese Government has noted and respects United States laws and regulations that prohibit the import of prison labor products, has consistently paid great attention to the question of prohibition of the export of prison labor products, has explained to the United States its policy on this question, and on October 10, 1991, reiterated its regulations regarding prohibition of the export of prison labor products;

Considering that the Government of the United States has explained to the Chinese Government U.S. laws and regulations prohibiting the import of prison labor products and the policy of the United States on this issue; and

Noting that both Governments express appreciation for each other's concerns and previous efforts to resolve this issue,

Have reached the following understanding on the question of prohibiting import and export trade between the two countries that violates the relevant laws and regulations of either the United States or China concerning products produced by prison or penal labor (herein referred to as prison labor products).

The Parties agree:

1. Upon the request of one Party, and based on specific information provided by that Party, the other Party will promptly investigate companies, enterprises or units suspected of violating relevant regulations and laws, and will immediately report the results of such investigations to the other.
2. Upon the request of one Party, responsible officials or experts of relevant departments of both parties will meet under mutually convenient circumstances to exchange information on the enforcement of relevant laws and regulations and to examine and report on compliance with relevant regulations and laws by their respective companies, enterprises, or units.
3. Upon request, each Party will furnish to the other Party available evidence and information regarding suspected violations of relevant laws and regulations in a form admissible in judicial or administrative proceedings of the other Party. Moreover, at the request of one Party, the other Party will preserve the confidentiality of the furnished evidence, except when used in judicial or administrative proceedings.
4. In order to resolve specific outstanding cases related to the subject matter of this Memorandum of Understanding, each Party will, upon request of the other Party, promptly arrange and facilitate visits by responsible officials of the other Party's diplomatic mission to its respective companies, enterprises or units.

This Memorandum of Understanding will enter into force upon signature.

Child Labor

Because wages for children tend to be quite low, child labor is common, if illegal, in "low-cost" nations. For instance, although work during school hours is illegal for anyone under fourteen years of age in both Sri Lanka and Mexico, 500,000 children under fourteen work in Sri Lanka, 700,000 work in Zambia, and millions work in Mexico. Children form the labor foundation for Bangladesh's garment industry and India's carpet industry. In 2002, the ILO reported that 246 million children worldwide were engaged in some form of child labor, with 171 million in dangerous work conditions, including the worst forms of child labor, such as prostitution, slavery, and drug trafficking.

Naturally, children who are employed cannot attend school and receive formal education. And children are not as resistant to disease in unsanitary environments. Children in Indian carpet shops, for example, have a high incidence of tuberculosis, worm infestation, skin disease, and enlarged lymph glands.

Consequences of Participation in Illegal or Harsh Work Conditions

Participating in illegal or harsh work conditions might ultimately raise more than a philosophical dilemma; the U.S. investor might have to see the workers on the other end of a summons in the United States. In *Dow Chemical v. Domingo Castro*

Nepal Not Doing Enough to End Child Labour

The Times of India, November 21, 2000

KATHMANDU: Rights activists have charged successive governments in Nepal with paying mere lip service to the cause of eliminating child labour.

Prime Minister Girija Prasad Koirala on Sunday pledged to free Nepal of child labor and expressed his government's commitment towards an International Labor Organization (ILO) convention to eliminate child labor. Nepal's Parliament is expected to approve the convention in its winter session next year.

"His Majesty's government is devoted to build a Nepali society free from children's exploitation and provide them every possible opportunities for their healthy upbringing and bright future," Koirala said.

According to estimates, there are 2.6 million child laborers under the age of 14 in Nepal, of which 1.7 million work full-time. These children have been forced to work due to poverty. Many of them are engaged in the worst forms of child labor like prostitution, drug trafficking and debt bondage. Many children are employed in the carpet industry, a major foreign exchange earner for Nepal, even though foreign buyers insist that children be not employed in making the rugs.

A leading carpet manufacturer told IANS on condition of anonymity that the small and deft fingers of children are most efficient in carpet weaving. He said though he feels sorry for the children as they work at an age they ought to be in school, his efforts alone cannot help solve the problem.

"If I kick them out of from my factory, they will be on the streets tomorrow and nobody will take care of them," the carpet manufacturer said. The government, he alleged is just "selling slogans" on the issue of child labor. He said, "Some people in the government and some non-governmental organizations might benefit from these slogans, but not the children."

Government officials concede that the situation has not improved. Ten years have passed since Nepal signed the Convention on the Rights of Children, but little has been done to improve the children's lot, said Bhubaneshwari Satyal, a member of the Central Child Welfare Committee. "Many have expressed commitment to fight for the rights of the children but it has remained only on paper," she said.

An ILO convention adopted in June 2000 calls on nations to prohibit and eliminate the worst forms of child labor urgently to cover all persons under the age of 18 years. Nepal's Child Development Forum president Sharad Sharma said: "There are about 300 nongovernmental organizations and international nongovernmental organizations working for the rights of children, but the weakness in the implementation of policies has hampered in the process to reach the desired goal." ILO has selected Nepal as one of the countries to run a pilot project for the elimination of the worst forms of child labor.

Alfaro, 786 S.W.2d 674 (Tex. 1990), the Texas Supreme Court found that eighty Costa Rican banana plantation workers could sue the U.S. manufacturers of a pesticide in Texas for alleged medical injuries. This decision—rendered in a products liability context—opens the door to the massive tort liability associated with U.S. forums like Texas.

In the firms' markets, they may also face consumer boycotts. Labor organizations and other increasingly active opponents of dubious labor practices are identifying and targeting companies involved—directly or indirectly—in such practices. The threat of such protests has proved a potent incentive for investors to avoid them.

International trade treaties increasingly threaten these practices. Most developed nations have attempted to make nonenforcement of employment laws a violation of international trade agreements, just as dumping or subsidies discussed in Chapter Ten. The United States has proposed amendments to the WTO trade rules that tie labor standards to international trade. These amendments were stalled and the delegates decided that labor issues should instead be discussed in the context of the ILO, where discussion has not been particularly effectual. In its effort, the United States has focused on providing a tool for enforcing ILO conventions on unsafe working conditions, minimum age for child labor, and forced labor, without addressing any issues on minimum wages. Developing nations cried foul, asserting that such standards would be misused by the developed world to bar their products from developed markets. Although this matter remains under intense negotiation, some nations have agreed to combat trade practices like child labor in order to secure trade deals with the United States.

The U.S. Congress has reacted to the stalled effort to tie labor standards to international trade by entertaining a unilateral expansion of its own trade laws. Under a proposed revision of *Section 301* of the *Trade Act of 1974,* discussed in Chapter Eleven, the harsh *Section 301* sanctions and retaliatory measures would be available if it could be proved that an importer is violating an established set of labor standards. Because such a measure is not addressed in the global trade rules, however, the law might itself have been deemed a violation of the international trade agreement. In October 1997, Congress did pass the *Sanders Amendment,* which bans the import of any product made by forced child labor. In addition, Congress established the Child Labor Command Center, located at U.S. Customs headquarters, which acts as a clearinghouse for information and provides 24-hour "hotline" telephone service to a wide variety of audiences in order to provide a venue for allegations about prohibited importations. The initiative increases foreign staffing by assigning three additional special agents to areas where forced child labor is the most common. In addition, Customs is to engage in outreach programs with the trade, government, and nongovernment organizations to achieve successful enforcement of the *Sanders Amendment.*

A private initiative is also making significant progress. Some U.S. firms—of which Levi Strauss & Co. is particularly prominent—have instituted global "sourcing guidelines" to determine with whom they will do business. Levi Strauss requires a certification from suppliers that they are in compliance with the guidelines. If Levi Strauss has reason to believe that a supplier or its subcontractors have violated one of these guidelines, it will investigate the matter. If it finds a violation, it will terminate its contract with the supplier. As a result of this program, Levi Strauss stopped manufacturing jeans in China in 1993. Finally, as seen in the next article, by April 1998, China had made sufficient concessions to human rights to permit Levi Strauss to return. Such a guidelines approach, if adopted by more firms, would go a long way to eradicating questionable working conditions.

Chapter Summary

Labor law poses particular difficulties for the U.S. investor because of markedly different attitudes toward employer–employee relations in other nations. Especially surprising are laws that require employee input into strategic decisions, prescribe employee representation on boards of directors, and place impediments to dismissals. The investor must also familiarize itself with the different approaches to employment discrimination abroad and coordinate such approaches with requirements of the United States on such operations. Finally, the U.S. investor abroad should avoid harsh work conditions that are illegal in the West. Such practices may come back to haunt the investor in his home jurisdiction through personal injury lawsuits and consumer boycotts.

It's All in the Jeans as Levi Returns to China

The Birmingham Post, April 11, 1998

Millions of Levi Strauss jeans—the real ones—will be rolling out of Chinese factories next year for the first time since the company pulled out of the country in 1993.

Privately-owned Levi Strauss & Co. of San Francisco, the world's largest brand-name apparel manufacturer, has claimed it has perceived improvements in human rights in China and plans to resume product sourcing operations there.

The company quit manufacturing in China five years ago over human rights concerns at a time when demand for jeans there was soaring and China turned out 836 million square meters of denim a year—one third of global denim output.

But Levi is going back in, its president and chief operating office Mr. Peter Jacobi has said. . . . "We are going to re-engage in China for a number of reasons. One, we believe that the environment has improved to the point that we can operate consistent with what we are. Part of that's because the human rights environment has improved." He said Levi Strauss is confident it will find contracting partners in China who fitted the ethical and business standards set down in the company's sourcing guidelines. He expected Levi Strauss products to start coming off Chinese production lines again in 1999. The company produced 2.8 million items a year in China from third party contractors at the time of its dramatic high-profile withdrawal five years ago.

Levi has diversified its products in recent years, and classic blue jeans are no longer its only sought after apparel. . . .

Levi Strauss has no plan to become an owner-operator of factories in China, Mr. Jacobi said, but would rely on partners. "We'll go through contractors, we're not going to owner operate. There's no reason to," he said. "We believe there are contractors that can be good partners working with us with our sourcing guidelines." . . .

Levi quit China to safeguard its global image at a time when China's human rights record was widely condemned. "The major concern was that we couldn't conduct our business in a way that was consistent with our sourcing guidelines because of the (human rights) environment," Mr. Jacobi said. "We felt that because of our reputation, because of our desire to run our business consistent with what we care about and what we value, that the environment was hostile to that.

"We felt it was better that we begin the process of winding our business there and extricating ourselves." But he said the company now felt able to find partners in tune with Levi's guidelines, which cover issues ranging from ethics and employment standards to legal requirements and a ban on using child labour or prison convicts.

Levi announces no profit figures but it reported global sales last year of GBP4.2 billion, down 3.9 per cent from record 1996 sales. It also announced last November the closure of 11 North American plants in a bid to stay competitive.

Questions and Case Problems

1. Would a U.S. court, like the Supreme Court of Japan, overrule an employer's contractual rights because of a countervailing "socially accepted view"? What if the employment contract was between a drug lord and his "trigger man"? Do you think that the relative homogeneity of a national culture affects the breadth of issues on which society has a "socially accepted view"?

2. Susan Currie is a U.S. manufacturer of tear gas, which she sells to various governments for crowd control. To reduce transportation costs to the interested governments, Ms. Currie is considering building a new plant in Germany. The plant will employ 2,500 people. What foreign labor law considerations should she take into account?

Managerial Implications

Your firm is Crystallina, a U.S. mineral water producer and distributor. A strong market for mineral water is South Moravia, a nation dominated by a fundamentalist state religion that prohibits drinking any alcohol or carbonated beverages. Market studies indicate that if Crystallina established offices in South Moravia, it would reap rich profits. If employees of a company like Crystallina violate South Moravian religious law, however, the company is liable for severe fines.

1. South Moravian religious law prohibits women from engaging in gainful employment. Accordingly, if Crystallina establishes an office there, it will not be able to offer any of its women executives an opportunity to work there. What U.S. legal issues are raised for Crystallina? Should Crystallina establish an office in South Moravia?

2. Now assume that South Moravian religious law permits women to work, but strictly prohibits homosexual behavior of any kind. Accordingly, if Crystallina establishes an office there, it will not be able to offer any of its gay executives an opportunity to work there. Are there any U.S. legal issues raised for Crystallina? Should Crystallina establish an office in South Moravia?

3. Now assume that South Moravian religious law permits women to work and has no particular concern about private homosexual behavior, but strictly prohibits Christian worship of any kind. Because Roman Catholics recognize a duty to worship on Sundays and holy days, if Crystallina establishes an office in South Moravia, it will not be able to offer any of its Catholic executives an opportunity to work there. What U.S. legal issues are raised for Crystallina? Should Crystallina establish an office in South Moravia?

CHAPTER 21

ENVIRONMENTAL LAW

Laws protecting the environment once deserved only brief mention in a book about laws affecting foreign investments. In recent years, however, there has been extraordinary activity in international environmental law. There have been large-scale international environmental disasters, and concern over the possible thinning of the ozone layer and "global warming" has intensified. "Green" political parties have formed around environmental issues; in some important nations they have become part of governing coalitions. Consequently, nations have been furiously enacting legislation and entering into treaties concerning the environment. Although this body of international law is not yet as well developed as other centuries-old legal subjects, its impact on commercial activity has become noteworthy.

CONSIDERATION OF VARYING ENVIRONMENTAL REQUIREMENTS

Virtually all human activity alters the environment in some way. The central problem of environmental law is determining which activities alter the environment to an unacceptable degree. Those determinations, like all human judgments, vary depending on the circumstances of the person making them. Cutting down huge forests is as acceptable to Brazilian pioneers as it was to the North American pioneers—such as Abraham Lincoln—who turned the virgin forests of Illinois and Indiana into the heart of the grain belt. However, in the twenty-first century, most North Americans find Brazilian tree cutting unacceptable, even though none have proposed a reforestation of Peoria.

All things being equal, most people favor a clean and aesthetic environment. But all things are not equal. Poorer nations tend to oppose extensive international environmental regulation because it impairs their ability to profit from less-sophisticated production procedures. Wealthy countries tend to favor environmental protection, not only because they can afford to, but also because they profit from it. Wealthy nations are the ones that design and manufacture complex equipment, which makes production pollution-free. Wealthy nations sometimes use environmental and health issues as a pretext for keeping price-competitive foreign competition at bay. Understanding the reasons for differences in environmental views between nations is critical to understanding the dynamics of traditional and emerging legal remedies.

Differences in Regulatory Schemes

Differences in nations' circumstances and views lead to differences in their environmental laws. First, the cost–benefit analysis as to any environmental modification often varies from country to country. A country with an opportunity to profit from a sulphur-belching power plant is more likely to think that the plant's modification of the environment is acceptable than a neighbor nation, which does not profit from the plant but suffers from its acid rain. Second, countries that are happy with the economic status quo are more inclined to favor environmental measures. Wealthy nations tend to have more laws to reduce pollution from industrial processes than countries plagued with malnutrition. Third, some nations lack the technological infrastructure to produce without pollution. In a strict economic sense, enacting a regulatory scheme that mandates buying such infrastructure greatly benefits wealthier nations—which manufacture and sell such equipment—and hampers less-developed nations that must spend scarce resources to purchase it. Finally, some governments permit officials to profit from environmental modifications. Thus, a nation may be lax in regulating hazardous waste disposal if the families of government officials greatly profit from the activity.

Obviously, many of these factors tend to place the wealthier, more developed democracies on the side of international environmental regulation and the less-developed nations in opposition to such regulation. This dichotomy between the rich "North" and the poor "South" forms the principal dividing line in virtually all issues relating to international environmental law.

For foreign investors, these differences have meant advantages in locating their facilities in countries with fewer environmental restrictions. A steel factory will cost millions less to build in South Korea than if it were built in the United States, where sophisticated antipollution equipment would be required. A hazardous waste dump is easier to locate in Ghana than in Germany because Germany has a more comprehensive legal framework protecting groundwater from such waste.

These incentives have not been lost on countries pursuing conservation. First, because nature does not recognize political boundaries, one nation's ban of chlorofluorocarbons (CFCs) only postpones depletion of the ozone layer if its neighbors continue to produce them. Canada's laws against acid rain are not fully effective if its populous southern neighbor does not enact similar laws. Second, the environmental regulations of the conservation-minded nation will make its products more expensive, placing it at a competitive disadvantage vis-à-vis countries less concerned about the environment. Accordingly, conservationists have sought legal relief through international dispute resolution, import bans, and multilateral treaties.

Foreign investors must consider the risk that the host country's less-restrictive environmental laws will be changed through this international action. This risk can be substantial. The installation of antipollution devices after a plant is built, for example, can be vastly more expensive than including them during construction. In many circumstances, the better choice for the risk-averse investor is to build on the assumption that local environmental laws will evolve to First World standards.

Environmental Law as an Anticompetitive Tool

"Environmentally responsible" nations are not without sin. Such nations often enact strict local environmental laws not so much to save the environment as to prevent foreign competition.

The EU has been accused of doing this to protect its meat and dairy products industry, which has been battered by foreign competition. In 1993, the EU traced an outbreak of hoof and mouth disease in Italian livestock to Croatia. Rather than banning Italian meat or Croatian meat, the Union banned meat from the entire former East bloc. Needless to say, the arbitrariness of banning meat from half a continent on the basis of a disease outbreak in a region of one small nation, especially while not banning meat from the only country where the disease had actually occurred, struck many producers as unfair. Eastern block meat was, however, cheaper. Similarly, members of the EU banned U.S. beef because many U.S. producers enhanced their livestock through bovine growth hormones. No proof that the hormones had any adverse effect on the meat has yet been offered. U.S. meat was, however, demonstrably less expensive and more popular among European consumers.

The United States has also been accused of using environmentally disguised trade barriers. The EU has complained of a variety of U.S. taxes and fines that they assert are disproportionately directed at European auto imports. In the mid-1990s, the United States enacted *Corporate Average Fuel Efficiency* (CAFE) standards and "gas-guzzler" surtaxes ostensibly to encourage fuel conservation and reduce air pollution. At the same time, the United States enacted a luxury tax on certain high-priced vehicles. The taxes nominally apply to domestic cars as well as European autos. Interestingly, however, European automakers pay about 90 percent of the combined gas-guzzler taxes, luxury taxes, and CAFE fines, although they hold only about 4 percent of the U.S. automobile market. Another instance of U.S. discrimination may be seen in the *Reformulated Gasoline* case on page 630.

An amusing example of alleged "environmental" anticompetitive behavior was seen in the French resort town of Grenoble. The city's leaders banned Bermuda shorts in public pools and encouraged bathers to wear bikinis and other skimpy traditional French bathing suits. They argued that the added material in the Bermuda shorts polluted their pools. Interestingly, all Bermuda shorts were foreign made.

TRADITIONAL INTERNATIONAL REMEDIES

The Polluter Pays: Responsibility for Pollution

In the absence of an agreement, the only way a country may address its neighbor's environmental pollution is through the dispute resolution mechanisms available under international law. Binding adjudica-

---

The Trail Smelter Arbitration
3 R. Int'l Arb. Awards 1938 (1941)
Trail Smelter Arbitral Tribunal

MESSRS. HASTIE, GREENSHIELDS, AND WARREN

This Tribunal is constituted under, and its powers are derived from and limited by, the Convention between the United States of America and the Dominion of Canada signed at Ottawa, April 15, 1935. . . . The controversy is between two governments involving damage occurring or having occurred, in the territory of one of them (the United States of America) and alleged to be due to an agency situated in the territory of the other (the Dominion of Canada). As between the two countries involved, each has an equal interest that if a nuisance is proved, the indemnity to damaged parties for proven damage shall be just and adequate and each has also an equal interest that unproven or unwarranted claims shall not be allowed. For, while the United States' interests may now be claimed to be injured by the operations of a Canadian corporation, it is equally possible that at some time in the future Canadian interests might be claimed to be injured by an American corporation. The Columbia River has its source in the Dominion of Canada. At a place in British Columbia named Trail, it flows past a smelter located in a gorge, where zinc and lead are smelted in large quantities. From Trail, its course is easterly and then it swings in a long curve to the international boundary line, at which point it is running in a southwesterly direction; and its course south of the boundary continues in that general direction. The distance from Trail to the boundary line is about seven miles as the crow flies or about eleven miles, following the course of the river. . . .

In 1906, a smelter was started under American auspices near the locality known as Trail, B.C. In 1936, the Consolidated Mining and Smelting Company of Canada, Limited, obtained a charter of incorporation from the Canadian authorities, and that company acquired the smelter plant at Trail as it then existed. Since that time, the Canadian company, without interruption, has operated the smelter, and from time to time has greatly added to the plant until it has become one of the best and largest equipped smelting plants on the American continent. . . . This increased production resulted in more sulphur dioxide fumes and higher concentrations being emitted into the air.

From 1925, at least, to 1937, damage occurred in the State of Washington resulting from sulphur dioxide emitted from the Trail Smelter [by adversely affecting agricultural activities]. The second question under Article III of the Convention is as follows:

> In the event of the answer to the first part of the preceding question being affirmative, whether the Trail Smelter should be required to refrain from causing damage in the State of Washington in the future, and, if so, to what extent?

Damage has occurred since January 1, 1932, as fully set forth in the previous decision. To that extent, the first part of the preceding question has thus been answered in the affirmative.

As Professor Eagleton puts it . . . "A state owes at all times a duty to protect other states against injurious acts by individuals from within its jurisdiction." . . . But the real difficulty arises rather

continued

continued

when it comes to determine what, *pro subjecta materie,* is deemed to constitute an injurious act.

The Tribunal . . . finds that, under the principles of international law . . . no state has the right to use or permit the use of its territory in such a manner as to cause injury by fumes or in the territory of another or the properties or persons therein, when the case is of serious consequence and the injury is established by clear and convincing evidence.

Considering the circumstances of the case, the Tribunal holds that the Dominion of Canada is responsible in international law for the conduct of the Trail Smelter. Apart from the undertakings in the

Convention, it is, therefore, the duty of the government of the Dominion of Canada to see to it that this conduct should be in conformity with the obligation of the Dominion under international law as herein determined.

Decision. The Tribunal held that so long as the existing conditions in the Columbia River Valley prevailed, the Trail Smelter would be required to refrain from causing any damage through fumes in the State of Washington. It further found that the indemnity for such damage should be fixed in such manner as the governments, acting under the Convention, should agree.

---

tion has not been common because, until treaties recently implemented with Europe, the alleged polluter would not consent to jurisdiction in such cases. An instance in which the polluter did consent to arbitration involved a Canadian smelter that was sending fumes into the United States in the 1930s. The case remains one of the more complete statements of the environmental obligations between nations.

> **http://www.ciel.org**
> See for links and information at the site for the Center for International Environmental Law.

Regulation of Products that Violate Environmental Objectives

Because international binding arbitration of environmental disputes such as in the *Trail Smelter* case are rare, a more frequent method for counterattack is for the conservation-minded nation to enact domestic legislation outlawing import of the offending product. These regulations take two basic forms: regulations against a product because the product itself violates environmental norms in the regulating country, and regulations against a product because it is manufactured through a process that is environmentally objectionable.

This type of domestic counterattack is somewhat restricted by the *General Agreement on Tariffs and Trade* (GATT), but GATT restrictions do not prevent nations from excluding products that are environmentally offensive by their very nature.

Thus, if meat or a bathing suit poses a health or other environmental threat under local standards, and local standards are applied in a nondiscriminatory way, GATT presents no difficulty. In the following case, the United States was able to keep out Canadian lobsters because they did not meet U.S. minimum-size requirements designed to protect the lobster population. This "nondiscriminatory internal regulation" was upheld although lobsters that reside in colder Canadian waters are by nature smaller and therefore disproportionately affected by the regulation. One should especially focus on the tribunal's explanation of GATT restrictions and how the United States avoided them; the minority view is also instructive in pointing to gray areas in these GATT restrictions.

As the *Canadian Lobster* case demonstrates, states have a great deal of flexibility in excluding products that are by their own nature contrary to local environmental standards. In fact, the flexibility is so great that nations at times misuse facially neutral standards—such as "no baggy swimsuits"—to give preference to local products. But if nothing is wrong with the product itself, a country will have more difficulty excluding the product on an environmental basis.

Regulation of Products with Environmentally Objectionable Production Processes

The *Canadian Lobster* case is an example of trade restriction based on a threat to the environment

Lobsters from Canada
1990 WL 299945
United States–Canada Free Trade Agreement Binational Panel

BACKGROUND AND FACTS

The American lobster is only found in U.S. and Canadian waters in the western Atlantic Ocean. It grows by shedding its external shell, a process called "molting." American lobsters molt about 20 to 25 times between birth and sexual maturity. Water temperature affects how often lobsters molt. In cold waters, it may take a lobster up to ten years to reach sexual maturity; in warm waters, lobsters reach sexual maturity in as little as five years. Canadian waters tend to be colder than U.S. waters.

In 1989, the United States Congress passed an "environmental" amendment to the *Magnuson Fishery Conservation and Management Act* that prohibited the transport of whole live lobsters smaller than a certain minimum size. Canada sought relief against the United States before the Free Trade Agreement Binational Panel, alleging that the amended *Magnuson Act* was actually a restriction on importation of lobsters from Canada, in violation of Article XI of GATT. The United States argued that the amendment was not a "restriction on importation" but an "internal measure" subject only to GATT Article III. The United States further argued that even if Article XI applied, the *Magnuson Act* fell within an exception to Article XI found in Article XX(g), which permits restrictions on importation if they relate to conservation of an exhaustible natural resource.

CHAIRMAN NORWOOD, MESSRS. CLINGAN, LATIMER, AND POLLER, AND MS. WEST

The Majority View. The pertinent part of Article XI . . . reads:

> No prohibitions or restrictions other than duties, taxes or other charges . . . shall be instituted or maintained by any contracting party on the importation of any product of the territory of any other contracting party. . . .

Article III, in summary, prohibits the use of any form of [nontariff barrier] (NTB) to afford protection to domestic production. . . . Article III sets forth the principle of nondiscrimination or equal treatment or, more precisely, "national treatment" between imported and domestic products[:]

The products of the territory of any contracting party imported into the territory of any other contracting party shall be accorded treatment no less favorable than accorded to like products of national origin in respect of all laws, regulations and requirements affecting their internal sale, offering for sale, purchase, transportation, distribution or use.

Article XI is the principle GATT Article containing the general ban against the use of QRs [qualitative restrictions] to limit importation. The Article itself contains exceptions, such as that for certain QRs on agricultural and fisheries products.

Article III is the principal GATT Article limiting the use of "border" and "internal" measures on imported goods. The rule of "national" treatment that it specifies to carry out the competition principle noted earlier bars a country from extending internal measures to imported goods in a way that bears more onerously on the imported products than on the like domestic products. . . .

As between Articles XI and III. . . . [t]he trade effects on Canadian lobsters will not differ if the U.S. measures are determined to fall under one of these Articles rather than the other. Whether as Article XI measures on importation or as Article III measures on internal marketing, the U.S. limits on Canadian lobsters will have identical effects: imports of subsized lobsters will be zero.

The import counterpart of some of these measures would presumably be permitted by one of the general exceptions listed in Article XX, for example, any that could be justified as necessary to protect human, animal, or plant life or health. But many such prohibitions or restrictions affecting imported goods clearly would not. The internal marketing counterparts of these measures therefore would not be permissible under GATT if they were to fall under Article XI. Article III, on the other hand, was structured to permit governments to impose internal regulatory measures, subject to the national treatment standard, whether or not such measures met the specific exceptions of Article XX.

The Panel concluded that the appropriate principle to be used in determining whether the U.S. measures

continued

continued

were covered by Article III was the nonprotection principle of . . . that Article.

The Panel determined that the U.S. measures imposed on live U.S. and Canadian lobsters were covered by Article III and not by Article XI. In particular, they considered that the measures, as now applied in the U.S. internal market, or as they might be imposed at the border, came within the scope of "laws, regulations requirements affecting the internal sale, offering for sale, purchase, transportation, distribution or use of products."

The Minority View: That Article XI Is Applicable. Some members of the Panel concluded that [w]hat is determinative is the practical effect of the measure. . . . Measures couched in terms leading the reader to Article III may in truth and substance and effect be measures which the GATT signatories intended to prohibit by Article XI. . . . In any event, it is one thing to make an exporter's competition in the importing country's market prohibitively expensive, by discriminatory requirements, but it is quite another to bar entry into the market; the 1989 amendment fits into the latter category.

In view of the effect of the 1989 amendment (effect which is exactly the intent of those drafting it: to exclude Canadian sub-sized lobsters from the American market), and in view of the language of Article XI and of the analysis of GATT Panel precedents, some members of the Panel concluded that the 1989 amendment is prohibited by Article XI. It is a prohibi-

tion or restriction on international commerce, in effect on importation. Its intended and practical effect is to deny to Canadian, and some domestic, sub-sized lobsters the access they had to the American market until January of 1990. Taking all this into consideration, the members of the Panel who concluded that the U.S. measures were in conflict with Article XI were able to conclude only that the objectives of the 1989 amendment were both of a conservation nature and a trade restriction. Due to the fact that there was no persuasive evidence to support the assertion that the amendment's primary objective was conservation, and the limited discussion of alternatives, these members were unable to draw a conclusion that the amendment was "primarily aimed at" conservation. The United States, for example, did not address the reasons for which its conservation objectives could not be met by special marking of Canadian small lobsters, requirements that lobsters be sorted by size prior to importation into the United States, particular documentary requirements as to sub-sized lobsters of Canadian origin, increased penalties for the possession of sub-sized lobsters, more vigilant enforcement efforts, or possibly other requirements.

Decision. The majority ruled that the U.S. lobster size regulations were "internal measures" and therefore did not violate GATT's prohibition against restrictions that apply only to imports. The United States was permitted to continue applying its minimum-size rules.

---

inherent in a product itself—the sale of premature lobsters. The environment is more frequently injured, however, not by the product itself but by the process used to make the product. Nothing about finished steel is environmentally harmful. But if the plant that manufactures the steel has no pollution-control devices, the plant will destroy the ecosystems in bodies of water surrounding it, darken the atmosphere, and contribute to acid rain. Ironically, Articles III and XI of GATT—which in *Canadian Lobsters* were found to permit very discriminatory restrictions if the very foreign product *itself* threatened the environment—have been found to forbid such restrictions if targeted at an environmentally offensive process used to create the product, unless the proscribing party is flexible in the application of standards.

As the *Shrimp* case makes clear, the WTO Appellate Body is quite tolerant of a nation that attempts to force foreign producers to comply with the same environmentally conscious procedures as required within the nation, so long as the importing nation is flexible in accepting other nations' approaches to achieving the same environmental objective. But when a nation attempts to create different standards for foreign parties—as in the *Reformulated and Conventional Gasoline* case—the WTO can be very demanding.

Litigation Against Polluters in an Affected Country

If the polluting foreign investor is subject to the jurisdiction of the conservationist nation's courts,

United States—Import Prohibition of Certain Shrimp and Shrimp Products
Recourse to Article 21.5 of the DSU by Malaysia
WT/DS58/AB/RW, 10-21-2001
WTO Appellate Body

BACKGROUND AND FACTS

To protect endangered sea turtle populations from further decline by reducing their incidental mortality in commercial shrimp trawling, U.S. commercial shrimp trawlers are required to use Turtle Excluder Devices (TEDs) approved in accordance with standards established by the United States National Marine Fisheries Service. In 1989, the U.S. Congress enacted Section 609 of Public Law 101-162, under which the Department of State was to certify whether nations that export shrimp to the United States had adopted programs to reduce the incidental capture of sea turtles in their shrimp fisheries that were comparable to the program in effect in the United States. If the State Department did not certify a nation, that nation would be banned from exporting shrimp to the United States. In practice, the State Department effectively required that other countries adopt a TEDs requirement. In 1998, the WTO Appellate Body found the U.S. measure to be a forbidden prohibition on imports that was not justified under Article XX(b)'s exception for measures taken to protect animal life "not applied in a manner which would constitute a means of arbitrary or unjustifiable discrimination between countries." In essence, the Appellate Body found that the U.S. de facto insistence on a U.S. excluder device was "unjustifiable discrimination" and therefore recommended that the United States bring Section 609 into conformity with the GATT.

Congress did nothing to the law, but the State Department revised the guidelines it used in enforcing the law. Where the government of a harvesting country requested certification on the basis of having adopted a program based on TEDs, certification was to be granted if the program included a requirement that commercial shrimp trawlers use TEDs that are "comparable in effectiveness" to those used in the United States, and a credible enforcement effort that includes monitoring for compliance. In May 1998, the State Department certified that sixteen nations had indeed adopted such programs. It also certified that the fishing environments in twenty-three other countries do not pose a threat of the incidental taking of sea turtles protected under Section 609. Under Section 609, shrimp imports from any nation not certified were prohibited effective May 1, 1998.

Malaysia was not certified and challenged the revised procedure. The WTO panel ruled that, as enforced under the revised State Department guidelines, Section 609 no longer constituted an "unjustified discrimination." Malaysia appealed to the WTO Appellate Body.

CHAIRMAN BACCHUS AND MESSRS. GANESAN AND LACARTE-MURÓ

In 2000, Malaysia informed the [WTO Dispute Settlement Body] DSB that it was not satisfied that the United States had complied with the recommendations and rulings of the DSB, and announced that it wished to seek recourse to a panel . . .

[In this appeal, the] issue was whether the Panel had erred in finding that the measure at issue was now applied in a manner that no longer constituted a means of "arbitrary or unjustifiable discrimination between countries where the same conditions prevail" and was, therefore, within the scope of measures permitted under Article XX of the GATT 1994. To answer this question, the Appellate Body analyzed (1) the nature and extent of the duty of the United States to pursue international cooperation in the protection and conservation of sea turtles and (2) the flexibility of the Revised Guidelines. Regarding the issue of international cooperation, the Panel reached the conclusion that the United States had an obligation to make serious good faith efforts to reach an agreement before resorting to the type of unilateral measure currently in place. Following, the Appellate Body stated the chapeau of Article XX, whereas

> subject to the requirement that such measures are not applied in a manner which would constitute a means of arbitrary or unjustifiable discrimination between countries where the same conditions prevail, or a disguised restriction on international trade, nothing in this Agreement shall be construed to prevent the adoption or enforcement by any contracting party of measures: [. . .]

The Appellate Body also mentioned its conclusion in the *United States—Shrimp* case that the United States had to provide all exporting countries "similar opportunities to negotiate" an international agreement to

continued

continued

avoid "arbitrary or unjustifiable discrimination." . . . With respect to that measure, the United States could conceivably respect that obligation, and the conclusion of an international agreement might nevertheless not be possible despite the serious, good faith efforts of the United States. Requiring that a multilateral agreement be concluded by the United States in order to avoid "arbitrary or unjustifiable discrimination" in applying its measure would mean that any country party to the negotiations with the United States, whether a WTO Member or not, would have, in effect, a veto over whether the United States could fulfill its WTO obligations. Such a requirement would not be reasonable. The Appellate Body concluded that the United States could not be held to have engaged in "arbitrary or unjustifiable discrimination" under Article XX solely because one international negotiation resulted in an agreement while another did not. The Appellate Body upholds the Panel's finding. . . .

Afterwards, the Appellate Body turned to the analysis of the next issue, the flexibility of the Revised Guidelines. Malaysia claimed that the United States unilaterally imposed its domestic standards on exporters. Moreover, Malaysia disagreed with the Panel that a measure could meet the requirements of the chapeau of Article XX if it would be flexible enough, both in design and application, to permit certification of an exporting country with a sea turtle protection and conservation programme comparable to that of the United States. The Appellate Body stated that "conditioning access to a Member's domestic market on whether exporting Members comply with, or adopt, a policy or policies unilaterally prescribed by the importing Member may, to some degree, be a common aspect of measures falling within the scope of one or another of the exceptions (a) to (j) of Article XX." However, a separate question arises, when examining under the chapeau of

Article XX, a measure that provides for access to the market of one WTO Member for a product of other WTO Members conditionally.

In *United States—Shrimp*, the Appellate Body concluded that the measure at issue there did not meet the requirements of the chapeau of Article XX relating to "arbitrary or unjustifiable discrimination" because, through the application of the measure, the exporting members were faced with "a single, rigid and unbending requirement to adopt essentially the same policies and enforcement practices as those applied to, and enforced on, domestic shrimp trawlers in the United States." In this dispute, on the other hand, the Panel found that the new measure is more flexible than the original measure and had been applied more flexibly than was the original measure. The new measure, in design and application, did not condition access to the United States market on the adoption by an exporting Member of a regulatory programme aimed at the protection and the conservation of sea turtles that was essentially the same as that of the United States.

The Appellate Body noted that the Revised Guidelines contained provisions that permitted the United States authorities to take into account the specific conditions of Malaysian shrimp production, and of the Malaysian sea turtle conservation programme, should Malaysia decide to apply for certification. It concluded that the provisions of the Revised Guidelines, on their face, permitted a degree of flexibility that would enable the United States to consider the particular conditions prevailing in Malaysia if, and when, Malaysia applied for certification.

Decision. The Appellate Body upheld the finding of the Panel and therefore made no recommendations to the DSB with respect to Section 609.

it might be hailed into court there. This scenario is quite possible where the pollution directly affects the territory of the conservationist nation.

An interesting example involves international emissions from a nuclear plant. The Supreme Court of Austria held that Austrian landowners could sue the former Czechoslovakia in Austrian courts for the environmental effects of such emissions. Note especially the court's reliance on the absence of a valid claim under Czech law.

Litigation Against Polluters in Polluter's Home

Another traditional approach to obtaining relief against a polluter is to sue it in its home jurisdiction. In many countries, this approach is not practical: the local judges would be disinclined to rule against a significant local enterprise. Even in a neutral forum, however, such a suit can run into significant difficulties. In *Aguinda v. Texaco, Inc.*,

United States—Standards for Reformulated and Conventional Gasoline
WT/DS2/AB/R, 4-29-1996
WTO Appellate Body

BACKGROUND AND FACTS

The *Clean Air Act* of 1990 (the CAA) established two programs to control pollution from gasoline combustion. The first program created large metropolitan ozone "nonattainment areas" that had experienced the worst summertime ozone pollution. All gasoline sold to consumers in these nonattainment areas must be "reformulated." The second program concerned "conventional" gasoline, which may be sold to consumers in the rest of the United States. The sale of conventional gasoline in nonattainment areas was not allowed.

The U.S. Environmental Protection Agency (EPA) enacted the "Gasoline Rule" to implement these programs, which relied heavily on the use of 1990 baselines as a means of determining compliance. Baselines could be either individual (established by the entity itself) or statutory (established by the EPA and intended to reflect average 1990 United States gasoline quality), depending on the nature of the entity concerned. The Gasoline Rule did not provide individual baselines for foreign refiners. The statutory baseline requirement was not imposed on domestic refiners. In short, foreign refiners had to comply with industry averages, while domestic refiners could, if they chose, look to their individual circumstances.

Venezuela challenged the Gasoline Rule as an "arbitrary or unjustifiable discrimination" under the chapeau of GATT Article XX. A WTO Panel ruled in favor of Venezuela and the United States appealed.

CHAIRMAN FELICIANO AND MESSRS. BEEBY AND MATSUSHITA

[The Appellate Body] came to the question of whether [the Gasoline] rules would also meet the requirements of the chapeau of Article XX. The Appellate Body stated that the chapeau was animated by the principle that while the exceptions of Article XX may be invoked as a matter of legal right, they should not be so applied as to frustrate or defeat the legal obligations of the holder of the right under the substantive rules of the [GATT]. Put otherwise, if those exceptions were not to be abused or misused the measures falling within the particular exceptions must be applied reasonably, with due regard both to the legal duties of the party claiming the exception and the legal rights of the other parties concerned.

The Appellate Body noted that there was more than one alternative course of action available to the United States in promulgation regulations implementing the CAA. These included the imposition of statutory baselines without differentiation as between domestic and imported gasoline. Such an approach, if properly implemented, could have avoided any discrimination at all. Moreover, the United States could have made available individual baselines to foreign refiners as well as domestic refiners.

In explaining why individual baselines for foreign refiners had not been put in place, the United States laid heavy stress upon the difficulties related to anticipated administrative problems that individual baselines for foreign refiners would have generated which the EPA would have had to face. The Appellate Body, following the reasoning of the Panel, denied these arguments. It acknowledged that the anticipated difficulties concerning verification and subsequent enforcement would be doubtless real to some degree, but they viewed them as insufficient to justify the denial to foreign refiners of individual baselines permitted to domestic refiners. There are established techniques for checking, verification, assessment and enforcement of data relating to imported goods, techniques which in many contexts are accepted as adequate to permit international trade—trade between territorial sovereigns—to go on and grow.

The United States also explained why the statutory baseline requirement was not imposed on domestic refiners as well. The United States concluded that the application of the statutory baseline to domestic producers of reformulated and conventional gasoline in 1995 would have been physically and financially impossible because of the magnitude of the changes required in almost all United States refiners. As the Appellate Body noted, while the United States counted the costs of its domestic refiners of statuary baselines, there was nothing in the record to indicate that it did other than disregard that kind of consideration when it came to foreign refiners.

The Appellate Body found that the resulting discrimination must have been foreseen, and was not merely inadvertent or unavoidable.

continued

continued

Decision. The Appellate Body came to the conclusion that the baseline establishment rules in the Gasoline Rule, in their application, constitute "unjustifiable discrimination" and a "disguised restriction on international trade." It thus held that the baseline establishment rules, although within the terms of Article XX(g), were not entitled to the justifying protection afforded by Article XX as a whole. The Appellate Body recommended that the Dispute Settlement Body request the United States to bring the baseline establishment rule into conformity with its obligations under the General Agreement.

Judgment of February 23, 1988
39 Österreichische Zeitschrift für Öffentliches Recht und Völkerrecht 360
Supreme Court of Austria

BACKGROUND AND FACTS

The plaintiff, an owner of real estate in Austria near the former Czechoslovakia, brought action in Austrian courts seeking to prevent the construction of a nuclear power plant 115 kilometers away in Czechoslovakia. The plaintiff alleged that the plant had not been properly licensed and that the effects of radionuclides generated during the plant's normal operation—and especially in case of an accident—threatened his real estate. Plaintiff alleged that the operation of the plant was not possible without the emissions of radioactive-contaminated water vapor and of excessive warmth.

The Court of First Instance denied plaintiff's claim, holding that it lacked *jurisdiction ratione loci*—geographic jurisdiction over the matter. On appeal, the Court of Second Instance affirmed the lower court decision. The Oberste Gerichtshof (Supreme Court) of Austria, however, disagreed with the courts below.

PER CURIAM

The Court of First Instance—affirmed by the Court of Second Instance—has disavowed its [own] *jurisdiction ratione loci* . . . but the Supreme Court is of the opinion that [the statute governing venue of claims related to real estate] also provides *jurisdiction ratione loci* for Austrian courts over claims . . . of real estate owners affected by emissions [of a foreign state]. No treaty rules exist in the case in question with respect to Czechoslovakia.

It is unreasonable to require the claimant to pursue legal proceedings in Czechoslovakia, which obviously are not possible because there the problem under consideration is treated as a public law problem and acts *jure imperii* [official acts] cannot give rise to civil law obligations. This view is not consistent with Austrian law [under which] foreign states can be sued for acts *jure gestionis* [commercial activity] before courts [of another state]; and the question whether acts of the state are acts *jure imperii* or *jure gestionis* is not to be determined by the national law in question but according to general international law. Under such international law, the construction and the operation of a . . . plant for the generation of electricity are not within the scope of *jure imperii*, but are *jure gestionis* and therefore not excluded from the national [Austrian] jurisdiction. . . .

It cannot be said that legal proceedings in Austria would only lead to a judgment which is not enforceable and therefore would only have academic, and not protective, importance; although in the absence of a treaty on execution of judgments with the state in question, an execution of the judgment would presumably not be possible in Czechoslovakia, the pecuniary penalties imposed to enforce the claim . . . could probably be enforced in Austria and a violation by the defendant of the restraining order of a court could be a legal ground for possible claims of damages by the plaintiff.

As all conditions for Austrian jurisdiction exist but the *jurisdiction ratione loci* has been rejected by the court which would have been competent according to [Austrian law], the Supreme Court . . . is competent to designate a Court of First Instance as the court having *jurisdiction ratione loci* in this case.

Decision. The Supreme Court of Austria reversed the finding of the Court of Second Instance that Austrian courts lacked jurisdiction over the plaintiff's claim. It remanded the matter to the trial court where the plaintiff's real estate was situated for further litigation.

Aguinda v. Texaco, Inc.
1994 WL 142006
United States District Court (S.D.N.Y.)

BACKGROUND AND FACTS

Plaintiffs were Ecuadoran citizens residing in the tropical rain forest of Eastern Ecuador. They sought to represent a class of 30,000 Ecuadorans against Texaco, Inc., alleging that Texaco had engaged in environmental abuse for decades until 1990. The alleged misdeeds included large-scale disposal of inadequately treated hazardous wastes and destruction of tropical rain forest habitats. These activities, the plaintiffs asserted, caused harm to indigenous peoples living in the rain forest, to their property, and to the stability of Amazon basin habitats. The plaintiffs sought damages for their injuries and an injunction preventing the defendant from continuing or renewing its polluting activities.

Texaco moved to dismiss the case, arguing that courts of the United States were an inconvenient forum for adjudicating the claims and that some of the counts should be thrown out in any case.

JUDGE BRODERICK

Pursuit of individualized monetary relief for a large class of persons in a foreign country growing out of events implemented abroad presents substantial difficulties, even though those events were partially initiated in the United States. These difficulties are sufficient to make a forum in New York inconvenient, and to cause litigation of such claims here to run counter to the goal of "just, speedy and inexpensive" judicial administration . . . provided necessary steps are taken to assure availability of an alternate forum for such claims in Ecuador. Disputes over class membership, determinations of individualized or common damages, and the need for large amounts of testimony with interpreters, perhaps often in local dialects, would make effective adjudication in New York problematic at best. Most [factors] appear to favor resolution of damage claims in Ecuador. These include access to proof, availability of witnesses, possible viewing of sites, local interest, administrative difficulties, problems of choice of law and application of foreign law.

Appropriate caution in making any final determination requires that prior to dismissal of any part of this case on *forum non conveniens* or other grounds raised by Texaco, Texaco must:

a. Execute a binding acceptance of personal jurisdiction over it in Ecuadoran courts and

b. Provide binding acceptance of such jurisdiction by any Texaco subsidiaries having assets derived from the operations in Ecuador at issue, or waiver of the corporate veil by Texaco, or

c. Post an adequate bond to cover any liability imposed by the Ecuadoran courts.

If these requisites are met, consideration may be given to (a) absolute dismissal of plaintiffs' individualized monetary and class action claims or (b) stay of litigation of such claims in this court to permit their pursuit in Ecuador.

Many of the factors discussed above which may favor dismissal of plaintiffs' individual and class action damage claims on *forum non conveniens* grounds are less applicable insofar as injunctive relief is concerned, particularly if the demand for such relief is based on allegedly initiatory events in the United States. There is no known currently ongoing litigation between the parties in Ecuador, nor is there supervision of any entity located in Ecuador, nor is there [anything] which would be disrupted were jurisdiction over such equitable claims . . . to be exercised by this court.

The existence or nonexistence of events in this country which may be related to alleged injury in Ecuador may be explored based on documents or other information received in or sent from this country, minutes or recollections of consultations conducted with management in the United States, and evidentiary support from U.S. sources for types of conduct challenged by plaintiffs. . . .

In *Sequihua v. Texaco* . . . the court dismissed environmental pollution claims against Texaco also involving Ecuador on grounds of comity and *forum non conveniens*. That case differs from the one at bar as set forth in plaintiffs' complaint . . . in that in *Sequihua* the "challenged activity . . . occurred entirely in Ecuador," the "enforcement . . . of any judgment" was assumed to be required to be pursued in Ecuador, and relevant witnesses were expected to be solely those located in Ecuador. By contrast, decision making on the part of the defendant in the United States may or may not turn out to support some or all of plaintiffs' claims in the present case. . . .

Texaco moves to dismiss several claims as based on the "local action" doctrine under which actions

continued

continued

involving specific real property . . . must be tried where the land is located.

Further information is necessary to determine whether or not the current case falls within this category. If any injury caused by defendant's conduct is confined to specifiable real estate, the core concerns underlying the local action doctrine would be applicable. Large-scale industrial pollution in liquid form by contrast, may spread in widening circles not limited to any specific properties. . . . If discovery indicates that actionable steps were initiated in the United States, the local action concept might be inapplicable. . . .

Texaco moves to dismiss count VIII alleging violation of the Alien Tort statute . . . which was originally enacted in 1789 and by its terms is applicable to private as well as governmental actors. The Alien Tort statute provides:

> The district courts shall have original jurisdiction of any civil action by an alien for a tort only, committed in violation of the law of nations or a treaty of the United States.

Plaintiffs rely on the Alien Tort statute as a source of substantive law. Ordinarily governmental abuses such as official torture are the subject of suits under the Act, but the absence of such a limitation was explicitly noted as significant in *Argentine Republic v. Hess*. . . . No violation of a treaty has been alleged. The law of nations is, by contrast, customary in nature, to be defined by the usages, solemn commitments and clearly articulated principles of the international community. Participation of the United States in formulation of such usages, commitments and principles is, of course, of particular importance—and may indeed be necessary—where the courts of the United States are asked to enforce them.

Non-treaty international law may be treated as the "sober second thought of the community" upon which, as stated by [Justice] Harlan F. Stone, . . . all law ultimately rests. No single document can create it, but the unanimity of view as well as consistency with domestic law and its objectives are highly relevant. . . .

Although many authorities are relevant, perhaps the most pertinent in the present case is the Rio Declaration on Environment and Development (1992). Principle 2 on the first page of the document recognizes that states have "the sovereign right to exploit their own resources pursuant to their own environmental and developmental policies," but also have "the responsibility to ensure that activities within their jurisdiction or control do not cause damage to the environment of other States or areas beyond the limits of national jurisdiction." The Rio Declaration may be declaratory of what it treated as pre-existing principles just as was the Declaration of Independence.

Environmental damage is recognized in the domestic law of the United States as subject to legal restrictions. See among numerous other provisions, the National Environmental Policy Act [and] Endangered Species Act. . . . Indeed, an entire title of the United States Code (Title 16) is devoted explicitly to conservation. The totality of these enactments bespeak an overall commitment to responsible stewardship toward the environment. . . .

Decision concerning the possible applicability of [U.S. law] to this case must await additional information after further discovery focusing on events, if any, initiated or assisted in the United States which might violate international law. . . .

Decision. The court reserved judgment on each of Texaco's motions, pending the results of discovery on the extent to which events giving rise to the harm occurred in the United States or were carried out in response to directives issued in the United States. Texaco did not immediately agree to Ecuadoran jurisdiction, so the damages case proceeded, pending discovery, in the United States.

---

a U.S. court found that the victims of environmental misdeeds abroad could sue in the United States to seek legal redress. But such a ruling depended on the demonstration that significant activities had occurred in the United States. While reading the *Aguinda* case, note that, as in the *Judgment of February 23, 1988,* the court focuses on the availability of a remedy in the Ecuadoran court system.

An approach centered on the jurisdiction of U.S. courts may be effective against U.S. companies, but it seems ultimately doomed to be ineffective because it cannot provide relief if none of the acts relating to environmentally suspect action occurred in the United States. A U.S. investor could, for example, ensure that all discussion relating to a specific polluting project take place in the country with the most forgiving environmental laws. For an approach to be effective in furthering conservation, therefore, it needs to be multinational in scope.

Inadequacies of the Traditional International Pollution-Control System

Existing international remedies can be effective in specific instances, but they are unlikely to be effective in transforming the international environmental legal system. International arbitration can proceed only if both parties have consented. Such consent is infrequent in the environmental context, because a nation usually does not voluntarily subject itself to a proceeding about pollution generated from its own territory. As we have seen, trade sanctions must be couched in product defects. But most environmental damage is caused by manufacturing processes and, as we saw in the *Import Prohibition of Certain Shrimp and Shrimp Products* decision, such processes are largely exempt from regulation under GATT. Litigation in the affected conservationist nation can be effective against investors, but the affected nation must be sufficiently close to suffer a direct physical adverse effect. Litigation in the polluter's home country can be circumvented by having all actions and decisions occur in the less conscientious nation. Accordingly, new approaches are being pursued to address the problem of global pollution.

EMERGING PROBLEMS AND SOLUTIONS

In light of the perceived shortcomings of traditional legal methodologies for addressing environmental controversies, environmentalists have been developing regional and global solutions. We survey a representative group of the more important of these approaches.

Regional Approaches

The most regional approach to environmental protection is in national environmental regulations of exports. Even if GATT constrains a nation from excluding imports created in environmentally suspect ways, the nation can certainly regulate its exports. The U.S. law relating to the export of environmentally hazardous materials is an excellent case in point.

National Constraints on Exports. The cornerstone of U.S. environmental regulation of the export of hazardous materials is the principle of prior informed consent (PIC). The export of pesti-

cides, for example, is regulated by the U.S. Environmental Protection Agency (EPA) under the *Federal Insecticide, Fungicide, and Rodenticide Act* (FIFRA). FIFRA requires that before a U.S. seller can export pesticides that are not registered for use in the United States, it must obtain the PIC of the purchaser and give notice to the appropriate official in the receiving country. The restrictions of the *Resource Conservation and Recovery Act* (RCRA) are even more demanding on the export of hazardous waste. RCRA requires the exporter to provide notice to the EPA of any forthcoming shipment. Then, the government of the receiving country must expressly accept the shipment and provide written notice to the EPA of that consent. Special manifest requirements apply to the shipment, and the exporter has annual reporting obligations to the EPA.

U.S. legislation also seeks to assure that the foreign government's consent is thoroughly informed. The *Toxic Substances Control Act* (TSCA) imposes reporting and record-keeping requirements on all chemical substances. In international transactions, TSCA requires exporters to notify the EPA of the export of any chemical or article containing a chemical that is or has been subject to testing under the statute. The EPA must then notify the foreign government of the EPA action with respect to the chemical.

The United States has many laws regulating pesticide use within the United States, but no law exists that forbids manufacturers from exporting banned pesticides to countries with less stringent or poorly enforced laws. This creates the so-called "Circle of Poison"—U.S.-banned pesticides are exported to the Third World and are used on crops, which are then exported back to the United States. These pesticides then reenter the United States as residues on food products.

Seeing the inherent inadequacy of domestic legislation, the "Circle of Poison" problem motivated the developed world to seek global solutions to the international distribution of toxins. As discussed later, they are now turning to international treaties. The following excerpt illustrates the "Circle of Poison" problem through a case study of the problem in Mexican agricultural imports to the United States.

In certain areas, national legislation—even of a nation as large as the United States—has virtually no

The "Circle of Poison" Issue

By Colleen Tighe, American University

1. The Issue

Although considerable controversy exists concerning the exportation of pesticides, the United States continues to export banned or unregistered pesticides to Mexico. The detrimental consequences are twofold. First, pesticide exports create a "circle of poison" situation in which US banned pesticides are exported to the Third World and are used on crops whose produce is then sent back to the US. Second, considerable evidence exists concerning the harmful health effects of pesticides on agricultural workers in the Third World.

2. Description

The United States relies heavily on the importation of food produced from Third World countries, particularly from Mexico: 25 percent of all fresh and frozen produce in the US is imported, 50 percent of which comes from Mexico. Furthermore, these figures are increasing. From 1989 to 1990, fruit imports from Mexico increased by $100 million and by $200 million for vegetables. . . .

While the US increases its reliance on Mexican produce, Mexico has increased its reliance on pesticide imports and is currently the second largest pesticide importer in Latin America (Tansey, 56). In turn, the US chemical industry has increased its pesticide production and exportation to meet growing demand. From 1990 to 1991, production increased by 3.5% and sales reached $7.6 billion with one billion pounds of pesticides produced. Pesticide exports accounted for nearly one-third of sales, 25 percent of which were not registered by the EPA. . . . Furthermore, US customs records show that exports of chlordane, one of the most toxic pesticides ever formulated, increased tenfold between 1987 and 1990. . . . 26 pesticide ingredients banned from use in the US are exported to the Third World, six of which are used in Mexico. . . .

[F]irst, toxicity threatens US consumers in the "circle of poison" effect in which unregistered or banned pesticides are exported to Mexico and sprayed on crops whose produce is then exported back to the US. . . . The

EPA ranks pesticide residues as one of the leading health problems in the US. A study conducted by the National Academy of Scientists estimates that in the next 70 years, one million additional cases of cancer in the US will be caused by pesticide residues. . . .

In the early 1980s, 15 percent of beans and 13 percent of peppers imported from Mexico exceeded FDA limitations for pesticide residues. . . . Currently, FDA tests on imported foods reveal that contamination by illegal pesticides account for only five percent of imports; however, contamination rates are higher for imported carrots, pineapples, rice, peas and pears. . . . Moreover, the FDA only tests one or two percent of imports . . . while the rest wind up in US grocery stores.

In June 1990, the US Senate Agricultural Committee voted to ban the export of unsafe pesticides. The panel adopted the legislation as part of the 1990 farm bill and hoped that the House of Representatives would address the issue. Strong objection to the bill came from the National Agricultural Chemicals Association, a trade group consisting of pesticide manufacturers, whose 1989 export sales totaled $2.2 billion. The bill was never enacted and, although the issue continues to be debated, it is largely ignored. . . .

Critics argue that most pesticide exports are merely unregistered in the US rather than banned. Many pesticides formulated in the US are never tested for approval because they are of no use to US agricultural needs and are sent directly to countries with suitable soils or who grow produce that can utilize the chemicals. Critics also argue that, with a ban, countries will seek out other countries who are willing to supply the banned pesticides. . . .

The second consequence is the health hazards that Mexican workers face when using banned or unregistered pesticides Since 1990, the Mexican government has made environmental standards much more strict yet does very little to enforce them. Furthermore, inspection of pesticides and pesticide residue is almost unheard of. . . .

Improper pesticide use has been found to cause various forms of cancer, birth defects, miscarriages, sterility, and deaths. The Third World uses 80 percent

continued

continued

of the world's pesticides and the World Health Organization estimates that all of the 220,000 annual pesticide related deaths occur in the Third World. . . . Moreover, agricultural workers are rarely given sufficient information on the risks involved and thus do not take proper protective measures when using pesticides. As a result, pesticide poisoning is thirteen times higher for Latin American workers than for US workers. . . .

In the Culiacan Valley in Sinaloa, Mexico three thousand field workers are hospitalized each year from pesticide intoxication alone. Contrary to widespread belief, the North American Free Trade Agreement (NAFTA) has not reduced the level of pesticide use in Mexico. . . .

Source: http://gurukul.ucc.american.edu/ted/mexpest.htm
Reprinted with permission.

---

effect. For most environmental issues, global and regional problems require multinational solutions.

North American Environmental Treaties. In North America, progress toward common environmental standards has been through bilateral treaties and the *North American Free Trade Agreement* (NAFTA). NAFTA's *Environmental Side Agreements* established the North American Commission for Environmental Cooperation (CEC), headquartered in Montreal. Although the North American Free Trade Commission is normally to consider all trade disputes, including disputes with environmental implications, the CEC determines whether any party to NAFTA has shown a "persistent pattern of failure" to "effectively enforce its environmental law." A finding of such a pattern can result in a broad range of sanctions, including suspension of NAFTA benefits. Thus, nongovernmental organizations now have an international forum to challenge the anticonservation activities of the three signatory governments (Canada, Mexico, and the United States). The following case discusses the requirements in one such challenge.

Under the Treaty, the three nations also agreed to jointly finance a variety of border wastewater and water pollution projects. Further, NAFTA creates permanent committees for Standards-Related Measures and for Sanitary and Phytosanitary Measures to harmonize the environmental laws of the three nations. The objectives of these efforts, together with the Commission on Environmental Cooperation (CEC), are to convert such regulation into acceptable standards in NAFTA countries and ultimately to remove such standards as an impediment to trade.

In addition to resolving enforcement disputes, the Commission has conducted studies as to proposed developments in border areas. For example, in January 1998, the Commission selected a ten-member panel to review the findings of the commission study of the San Pedro River. The concept of the study was to help "guide and inform policymakers, local residents and the North American public about the conservation of this shared asset." Similar small "eco-projects" have been supported by the Commission.

http://www.cec.org/home/index.cfm?varlan=english
Web site for the North American Commission for Environmental Cooperation

The work of the CEC has been more that of a development agency than of an environmental cop. For example, at its latest annual meeting in 2003, the CEC Council discussed conservation of biodiversity, management of freshwater, sound management and tracking of hazardous waste, and promoting cooperation in environmental enforcement. Other topics included the promotion of public–private partnerships to encourage voluntary initiatives to attain higher levels of environmental protection and the enhancement of "the availability of financially relevant environmental information" to explore voluntary mechanisms through which environmental information can be made available to financial investors. The emphasis is on voluntary action even though most effective compliance is achieved through involuntary means.

It is plain, therefore, that NAFTA mechanisms still do not permit the United States and Canada to

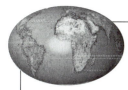

Hudson River Audubon Society of Westchester, Inc. & Save Our Sanctuary Committee:
United States
Determination of Submission SEM 00-003 (12 April 2000)
Secretariat of the Commission for Environmental Cooperation

BACKGROUND AND FACTS

The Submitters, Hudson River Audubon Society of Westchester, Inc. and Save Our Sanctuary Committee filed with the Secretariat of the North American Commission for Environmental Cooperation a submission on enforcement matters pursuant to Article 14 of the *North American Agreement on Environmental Cooperation* ("NAAEC" or "Agreement"). They alleged that the United States Department of Interior–National Park Service, was failing to enforce and proposing to violate: (i) the *Migratory Bird Treaty Act* (MTBA), a U.S. statute that prohibits the killing of migratory birds without a permit from the U.S. Fish and Wildlife Service; and (ii) the *Endangered Species Act of 1973* (ESA), which prohibits the taking of endangered and threatened species, requires the protection of such species "whether by protection of habitat and food supply," and requires the designation of "critical habitat." The Department of Interior was alleged to be doing this by proposing to construct a paved, multi-purpose bicycle path through the Jamaica Bay Wildlife Refuge, which is part of the Gateway National Recreational Area located in Queens, New York. The Submitters asserted that the construction of this pathway through the Jamaica Bay Wildlife Refuge would destroy critical habitat for endangered and threatened species and will result in the taking of migratory birds (including nests) and will therefore be in violation of both the MTBA and the ESA.

DIRECTOR MARKELL

A. Overview

Article 14 of the NAAEC directs the Secretariat to consider a submission from any non-governmental organization or person asserting that a Party to the NAAEC is failing to effectively enforce its environmental law. When the Secretariat determines that a submission meets the Article 14(1) requirements, it then determines whether the submission merits requesting a response from the Party named in the submission based upon the factors contained in Article 14(2). . . .

The Secretariat . . . has determined that the submission does not presently meet the criteria in Article 14 for further consideration.

B. The Governing Legal Framework

The opening sentence of Article 14(1) authorizes the Secretariat to consider a submission "from any non-governmental organization or person asserting that a Party is failing to effectively enforce its environmental law. . . ." Following this first sentence, Article 14(1) lists six specific criteria relevant to the Secretariat's consideration of submissions. The Secretariat must find that a submission:

(a) is in writing in a language designated by that Party in a notification to the Secretariat;

(b) clearly identifies the person or organization making the submission;

(c) provides sufficient information to allow the Secretariat to review the submission, including any documentary evidence on which the submission may be based;

(d) appears to be aimed at promoting enforcement rather than at harassing industry;

(e) indicates that the matter has been communicated in writing to the relevant authorities of the Party and indicates the Party's response, if any; and

(f) is filed by a person or organization residing or established in the territory of a Party.

C. Application of the Governing Legal Framework

As noted above, the opening sentence of Article 14(1) authorizes the Secretariat to consider a submission "from any non-governmental organization or person asserting that a Party is failing to effectively enforce its environmental law. . . ." The submission, filed by the Hudson River Audubon Society of Westchester, Inc. (Hudson River) and Save Our Sanctuary Committee, meets the requirement in the opening sentence of Article 14(1) that it be filed by a "non-governmental organization." It also meets the requirement that it focus on an asserted failure to enforce a Party's environmental laws, rather than on a deficiency in the law itself. Further, both the Endangered Species Act and the Migratory Bird Treaty Act qualify as environmental laws. The submission, however, does not meet the requirement in the first sentence that the assertion focus on an alleged ongoing failure to enforce.

continued

continued

Article 14(1) requires that a submission allege that a Party "is failing" to effectively enforce its environmental law. The process presupposes in a case such as this one, where the submission identifies a particular government action as the source of the alleged enforcement failure, that the Party involved actually has taken the action at issue or made some final decision. Absent such a final action or decision, any allegation of a failure to effectively enforce is based on speculation.

Although the submission alleges that the National Park Service "is failing to enforce" the MBTA and the ESA, it also alleges that the NPS is "proposing to violate" these statutes. Based on the Secretariat's understanding of the status of the potential bicycle path project that is the focus of the submission, it appears that the submission focuses on a prospective rather than on an ongoing asserted failure to effectively enforce. It therefore fails to comply with Article 14(1)'s requirement that the submission assert that a Party "is failing" to effectively enforce its environmental laws. . . .

The information supplied in the submission and the attachments to it do not reflect that the NPS has made a final decision to construct a bicycle path through the Refuge in any particular form or location. Indeed, the information provided with the submission suggests that the government is currently engaged in evaluating the appropriate location and other details of such a bicycle path. . . . Because the submission does not identify a final government decision on the bicycle path, the assertion that the content of that decision constitutes a failure to effectively enforce is premature.

Further, . . . the submission . . . does not meet the requirement in Article 14(1)(c) of the NAAEC that a submission provide sufficient information to allow the Secretariat to review the submission, including any documentary evidence on which the submission may be based. The activity that allegedly constitutes a failure to enforce both the MBTA and the ESA involves construction of a bicycle path that, according to attachments to the submission, is tentatively planned to be 10 feet wide with one-foot shoulders. The submission does little to support its assertion that construction of the path "will destroy critical habitat" for endangered and threatened species and thereby violate the ESA. The submission, for example, does not indicate what endangered or threatened species are found within the Refuge. It similarly does not indicate where "critical habitat" exists within the Refuge or the portion of such habitat (if any) which purportedly will be destroyed by the proposed bicycle path. Concerning the Migratory Bird Treaty Act, the submission alleges that construction of the path will result in the taking of migratory birds (including nests). It adds that the construction and resulting recreational use of the path will disrupt nesting and feeding of migratory birds and destroy nests and feeding areas in violation of the MBTA.

The Submitters cite to recent CEC publications that identify the Refuge as a key conservation site and an important bird area. The submission, however, does not provide support for its assertion that the path, in light of its location and other details, will cause disruption or destruction that violates the MBTA. Absent further information to support the existence of a connection between construction of the bicycle path and the types of impacts that would violate the ESA and/or the MBTA, the submission fails to satisfy Article 14(1)(c). . . .

Decision. The Secretariat terminated the Article 14 process with respect to this submission, effectively finding that the Submitters did not have a right to be heard under the Treaty.

---

impose their policies on less-developed Mexico. In fact, the Commission has broadly declared it has no right to investigate actions by legislatures of NAFTA countries even if those actions effectively nullify other laws. The lure of free trade was effectively employed to persuade Mexico to make its laws more protective of the environment and, for the first time, a multinational structure was created to enforce environmental standards. Through a variety of actions before the Commission, non-governmental organizations have tried to make enforcement of this new legal scheme in Mexico more satisfactory.

European Union Environmental Initiatives. In December 1985, within the EU the *Single European Act* made the environment an official responsibility of the EU, amending Section 13 of the *Treaty of Rome* with a new Title VII on "Environment." In October 1987, the European Council enacted a comprehensive environmental action program. In all, the Council of Ministers of the European Communities has adopted more than 125 different directives on environmental protection that the member states are obliged to implement through national legislation. Further, the European

Commission has pursued hundreds of infringement procedures against member nations to compel implementation of these directives. As a result of this aggressive approach, many EU members now exceed the United States in thoroughness of environmental protection schemes.

The European Commission has also issued a number of "Green Papers" in its attempt to advance Union-wide environmental standards. First, it proposed a uniform system of civil liability for damage to the environment. The proposal would standardize the principles under which firms have to pay to repair environmental damage. It specifies situations under which strict liability concepts apply and compensation mechanisms for cases in which the responsible party cannot be identified. In 2000, the Commission issued its Green Paper on Greenhouse Gas Emissions Trading Within the European Union. In that paper, it sought to create an emissions trading system for the energy sector and large industrial installations and to target measures to reduce emissions on a Union-wide basis. A similar trading system currently exists in the United States. Later, the Commission issued a Green Paper on the Environmental Issues of PVC, which tried to reconcile conflicting measures between the member states with respect to PVC. PVC, which has been associated with adverse effects on human health and the environment, had been the source of bitter controversy as different states developed conflicting positions. On environmental issues, the Commission is increasingly in the position of clearinghouse and arbiter for policy differences within the EU.

In January 2003, the European Parliament issued a Directive to assure that, on environmental matters, the public has full access to whatever information it needs to petition the Commission on these policy matters. The legislation creates an inherent public right to such information and a presumption that disclosure of information is the general rule. By creating this unusual right to information, the Directive seeks to achieve greater awareness of environmental matters, a free exchange of views, and more effective participation by the public in environmental decision making in all the nations of the European Union. The Commission will be pressed to continue in its efforts.

Regional Marine Treaties. Nations sharing bodies of water have cooperated significantly on environmental issues. Marine environmental protection was pioneered in 1972 by the *London Convention for the Prevention of Marine Pollution by Dumping from Ships and Aircraft,* which prohibited the dumping of specified hazardous wastes from ships at sea, and required permits for the dumping of others. The *Helsinki Convention on the Protection of the Marine Environment of the Baltic Sea Area* improved on the *London Convention* by providing for an effective international inspection and enforcement network. The *Barcelona Convention for the Protection of the Mediterranean Sea from Pollution* took matters further by enlarging the *London Convention's* list of prohibited substances. In November 2003, the Ministers of the Environment of the Mediterranean countries signed a declaration "to speed up the eradication of the at-risk single hull vessels which travel to and from across the Mediterranean." Similar convention arrangements have been concluded for the Red Sea and the Gulf of Aden, the Caribbean, the Southeast Pacific, and the South Pacific.

Developments in South Asia and the South Pacific. Countries in South Asia and the South Pacific are not renowned for vigilant enforcement of environmental policy. Nations in this region have emphasized industrial development rather than reduction of environmentally adverse by-products of that development. Indeed, as discussed later, China and India are leaders of the emerging countries' resistance to global attempts to outlaw technologies believed to deplete the ozone layer and cause global warming. Further, the serious East Asian financial crisis of 1997 reduced even more the limited resources committed to environmental efforts. Nevertheless, some nations have made efforts at regional environmental cooperation in the region.

A number of countries in the region have entered into the *ASEAN Agreement on the Conservation of Nature and Natural Resources,* under which each of the parties recognize "the responsibility of ensuring that activities under their jurisdiction or control do not cause damage to the environment or the natural resources under the jurisdiction" of other nations. In addition, a number of regional environmental programs have been established to coordinate policy: (1) the South Asia Cooperative Environment Program (Afghanistan, Bangladesh, India, Iran, Maldives, Nepal, Pakistan, and Sri Lanka); (2) ASEAN (Singapore, Thailand, and Brunei); and (3) the South

Pacific Regional Environment Program (with participation of twenty-one South Pacific island nations).

Developments in Eastern Europe and Central Asia.

During Eastern Europe's communist years, it was the most environmentally devastated region in Europe. The corruption and poverty of the communist system did not leave funds to protect the environment. In the first years after the fall of the Berlin Wall, Eastern Europe was preoccupied with economic recovery and did not expend significant resources on environmental compliance and monitoring. Now, finally, Eastern Europe has joined the "green" movement.

In May 2003, the Czech Republic, Hungary, Montenegro, Poland, Romania, Serbia, Slovakia, and the Ukraine adopted the *Convention on Environment Protection and Sustainable Development of the Carpathians*. The *Carpathian Convention* creates treaty obligations among the signatories to protect, maintain, and sustainably manage the natural resources of that mountain region. The Treaty specifically adopts: (a) the precaution and prevention principles, (b) the "polluter pays" principle, articulated in the *Trail Smelter* case, and (c) public participation and stakeholder involvement in development initiatives in each country, ending the "race to the bottom" among these emerging European economic participants. By creating a multinational approach to the problem, the Carpathian nations seek to restore their collective environment. At the Pan-European Ministers' Conference, the Environment Ministers of the region expressed their support of the Carpathian effort, noting their intent to contribute to improving environmental conditions by strengthening the efforts of these countries in environmental protection and by facilitating partnership and cooperation between these countries and other European countries.

At the Kyiv Conference in 2003, twenty-two European countries, including eleven nations formerly in the Eastern Bloc, signed the *Protocol on Civil Liability and Damage Caused by the Transboundary Effects of Industrial Accidents*. The Protocol arose from the accident at a dam at Baia Mare (Romania) in January 2000, which sent 100,000 tons of waste water with highly toxic pollutants, including cyanide, into rivers in Hungary, Yugoslavia, and Romania. This Protocol gives affected individuals a legal claim for compensation and fills in the major gap in remedies reflected in the *Judgment of February 23, 1988*. A wronged party in one signatory nation can now make the polluter pay in another nation. Memories are long, however: the Czech Republic, target of the *Judgment of February 23, 1988*, did not sign the Protocol.

---

http://www.kyiv-2003.info/main/index.php?mode=1
See for information on the Kyiv Conference.

http://www.unece.org/
See for environmental information on the United Nations Economic Commission for Europe site.

Initiatives by Multilateral Agencies.

Multilateral agencies have advanced the effort by applying uniform environmental standards to projects that they finance. The World Bank, for example, has published a 460-page volume of environmental guidelines for its personnel to use in evaluating the adequacy and effectiveness of pollution control measures for industrial projects. If a country wishes to obtain financing for its projects from the World Bank or its private project finance affiliate, the International Finance Corporation (IFC), the characteristics of the project must fall within accepted world environmental standards. In light of the importance of these financing sources in the Third World, the impact on both public and private projects has been very substantial.

---

http://sedac.ciesin.org/entri/texts/asean.natural.
resources.1985.html
ASEAN natural resources agreement.

Global Solutions

The United Nations began its work in the environmental arena in December 1972 when it adopted the *Stockholm Declaration on the Human Environment* and founded the *United Nations Environmental Programme* (UNEP). UNEP has now been the catalyst for the formulation and adoption of almost thirty binding multilateral instruments and ten sets of nonbinding environmental guidelines and principles.

---

http://www.unep.org/
Web site for the United Nations Environment Programme.

The World Trade Organization. As demonstrated in the *Reformulated Gasoline* and *Shrimp* cases, GATT affirmatively prevents a conservationist nation from imposing its environmental policies on others through trade law. Environmentalists are working hard to reverse this by adding provisions to GATT to be implemented in the context of the successor to GATT, the WTO.

As with other international environmental initiatives, most developed nations favor the creation of a permanent trade and environment committee to advance and implement pro-environment proposals, while less-developed countries resist the concept strongly. Most proposals likely to come out of an environmental committee would, in their view, adversely affect their exports into the developed world. Some structure seems inevitable, but years of discussion have created little more than commissions to further study the possibility.

One proposal advanced is that of an additional *ad valorem* tax on all imports to promote environment-friendly development in poorer nations. This proposal addresses the inability of the Third World to pay for the technology necessary to implement a cleaner environment. But poor countries are not enthusiastic about the proposal. First, paying a tax on their exports would make them less competitive with domestic products in developed countries. Second, the funds would ultimately find their way back to the richer countries that manufacture the antipollution infrastructure.

During debate on the *Convention on Biological Biodiversity,* the less-developed countries have offered their own suggestion: that the richer nations simply make the technology available for no charge. This triggered strong opposition from the United States, the home of most inventors and manufacturers of that equipment. The less-developed world also was willing to assure that species important to biomedical research would be kept alive. But, in return, the owners of intellectual information would have to share that information for free. Not surprisingly, the United States, the home country of most firms with important biomedical intellectual property, did not support that portion of the Convention either. The crafting of provisions that left some of the more difficult questions open for another day allowed the United States to join in the Convention.

Another set of proposals focus on uniform WTO accepted standards for labeling and packaging. The concept is to establish standards that protect the environment and yet prevent nations from using such standards as a trade barrier. During the Ministerial Conferences in Doha (2001) and Cancún (2003), the Ministers instructed the Committee on Trade and Environment to give attention to the impact of eco-labeling on trade and to examine whether existing WTO rules stand in the way of eco-labeling policies.

Environmentalists were quite active among the groups that rioted at the December 1999 WTO ministerial meetings in Seattle, Washington. The protests had relatively little impact on the trade-oriented group, but they did reflect long-term pressure from "green" constituencies that the WTO is taking into account. The continuing North–South conflict on these questions has nonetheless prevented significant progress to date in that forum. More heartening news has come from other global gatherings.

Finally, at the Ministerial Conference in Cancún, the Ministers agreed to launch negotiations on how WTO rules are to apply to WTO members that are parties to environmental agreements. Today, about twenty out of approximately two hundred multilateral environmental agreements contain trade provisions. According to the Ministers, the objective of the new negotiations will be a clarification of the relationship between trade measures taken under the environmental agreements and WTO rules. The Ministers also agreed to negotiations on the reductions or elimination of tariff and nontariff barriers to environmental goods and services.

---

http://www.wto.org/english/tratop_
e/envir_e/envir_e.htm
See for environmental information on the WTO site.

Global Ban on Toxic Substances. As noted earlier, domestic legislation such as TSCA has banned certain toxic substances domestically, and somewhat limited their circulation abroad. But so long as developing nations permit the use of these substances, their adverse effect is felt throughout the world. Beginning in 1998, nations began to discuss global solutions to the issue of proliferation of toxins.

These negotiations did not go easily. The environmental effects of toxins in the developed world are alarming. Because toxins drain into the world's waters, effects are often contracted through the eating of fish. American researchers have documented learning and behavioral problems in children exposed prenatally to PCBs through mothers who ate Great Lakes fish. In Japan, high dioxin levels have been found in whale and dolphin meat sold there. Research has detected toxins in animals thousands of miles from where the pollutant is used. But toxins are often effective in controlling pests and permitting more abundant crops in areas where food is otherwise scarce. In light of its recurring history of famine, it is understandable that Ethiopia has 250 sites of dangerous pesticides, including 1,500 tons of aldrin, chlordane, and DDT.

In December 2000, negotiators from 122 countries signed the first global ban on the use of specified chemical compounds. The banned substances were the acknowledged "dirty dozen" of chemical contamination linked to birth defects and genetic abnormalities: PCBs, DDT, dioxins, and furans. The industrialized nations agreed to pay poor countries $150 million annually to help them find alternatives and permitted the limited use of DDT for public health reasons, such as malaria control.

**http://www.wcl.american.edu/environment/
iel/treaty.cfm**
Web site for international environmental treaties.

The *Basel Convention.*

One of the best examples of multinational cooperation in environmental matters is the *Basel Convention on Transboundary Movements of Hazardous Wastes and Their Disposal,* which was adopted by 116 nations under the auspices of UNEP. The Basel system is not as stringent, but it is broader in scope than the U.S. law on movement of hazardous waste discussed previously.

As the volume of waste ballooned in the 1980s, a substantial trade developed in the transport of wastes from the United States and Western European countries to developing nations. Because of strict environmental restrictions on disposal in the developed countries, and low or no restrictions in developing nations, waste generators could dispose of hazardous waste at a much lower cost by simply sending it on a barge to a less-developed country. For example, Guinea Bissau entered into contracts valued at more than $600 million over five years—about the size of its entire gross national product—to receive U.S. and European garbage. The downside of this system, of course, is that unpremeditated hazardous wastes enter the world's ecosystem just as surely whether they are dumped in Bissau, Guinea Bissau, or in Champaign, Illinois. The emerging countries, which were realizing substantial revenues, were reluctant to change the arrangement.

The *Basel Convention* regulates the transport of wastes that display certain "hazardous characteristics." Transport is prohibited unless the disposer notifies the governments of the receiving and transit nations of the nature and amount of wastes in a shipment. These governments must then authorize the shipment; the receiving nation must also confirm that arrangements are in place for the "environmentally sound management of the wastes in question." During shipment, the refuse must be clearly manifested with the contents of the shipment. Upon completion of disposal, the exporter must notify the receiving nation; if completion is not effected, the exporting nation must accept a return of the wastes. And to prevent the development of "waste outlaw" nations, all signatories are prohibited from permitting the transport of wastes to non-signatories.

The Convention is hampered by a lack of consensus on a number of critical definitional issues. No widely accepted definition of what is "hazardous" has been determined. Nor has a universal agreement on what management is sufficient to *remediate* wastes (i.e., render them harmless to the environment) been established. The difficulties in these areas are exacerbated by the substantial incentive that officials in receiving nations have in allowing unrestricted transport of refuse, which can make them less demanding than officials in developed nations. If the governing elites in the receiving countries— many of which are not democratic—are unenthusiastic in enforcement, the *Basel Convention* does not work well. UNEP and others continue to work on these difficult definitional and enforcement issues.

---

http://www.nato.int/ccms/swg12/docs/amepp6b.htm
http://www.mac.doc.gov/nafta/1126.htm
http://www.med.govt.nz/ers/environment/
hazardous/index.html
See these sites for more on the import/export
of hazardous material.

The *Convention on International Trade in Endangered Species.* The *Convention on International Trade in Endangered Species of Wild Fauna and Flora* (CITES), which was enacted about two decades ago and is now in force in 152 nations, is an example of how well a treaty can work when it has broad political support. CITES created a system for identifying and listing endangered and threatened species. It forbids the import or export of such species unless a "scientific authority" finds that the import or export will not aggravate the species' situation. It currently governs trade in more than 30,000 protected plant and animal species.

Noncompliant nations—whether parties or nonparties to the Convention—face potentially severe multilateral trade sanctions for violations. For example, CITES has identified certain species of Caspian Sea sturgeon as endangered; leading exporters such as Russia and Iran must demonstrate that the caviar trade is not detrimental to sturgeon or it would ban such exports to all markets. Because of the broad support for CITES in both developed and most less-developed nations, the Treaty is generally judged to be effective. The former outlaw nations have been brought to heel by overwhelming political pressure.

The *Montreal Protocol.* UNEP has sponsored a particularly comprehensive example of a global solution to a global environmental problem in the *Montreal Protocol on Substances That Deplete the Ozone Layer.* The *Montreal Protocol* calls for a gradual reduction of substances feared to damage the ozone layer by imposing a freeze on consumption and a 10-percent limit on increases in production beginning in 1990, a 20-percent reduction in both consumption and production by 1993, and a further 30-percent reduction in production by 1998. The Protocol uses the same sanction as used in CITES against violators: all signatories to the Protocol are pledged to impose trade sanctions against violators.

The Protocol assuaged the concerns of the less developed countries by permitting them greater flexibility in compliance with the Protocol than the more-developed countries. In other words, the developed countries have to reduce their chlorofluorocarbon (CFC) levels before the emerging countries. For a period, factories in the emerging countries would have less demanding standards than those in other nations. The idea is that, over time, the production levels of chlorofluorocarbons (CFCs) in the developed world would tend to become more equal with those in the less developed world, and, eventually, all would decline.

This inequality in treatment created a significant political issue in the United States. As manufacturers and workers discovered the difficulties of competing with foreign-based firms that can use less expensive, dirtier equipment and processes, they objected loudly to the disparity in treatment. In fact, U.S. corporations in affected industries increasingly move manufacturing facilities to such lower cost nations triggering adverse reactions from unions. The future of the *Montreal Protocol* may rest with how industrialized nations cope with this transitional period of inequality.

The *Climate Control Convention.* Difficult as resolving the issues of the ozone layer has proved to be, agreement is even more difficult in the context of "global warming," addressed in the *U.N. Framework Convention on Climate Change.* After all, CFCs and halons are rather obscure chemicals that make life somewhat easier but are not critical to industrial development. However, if the earth really is experiencing a global warming, resolution of such a problem requires a substantial reduction in thermal energy use. At issue are not only the internal combustion engines of automobiles and lawn mowers; most electric power in the United States is generated through burning of fossil fuels.

Because energy use is central to economic growth, the less-developed countries are not likely to agree quickly to any limitations that could restrict their economic development. And the less-developed world is not alone in its opposition. The United States, Canada, and the United Kingdom, all of which rely heavily on fossil fuels for their energy needs, have steadfastly—through both "liberal" and "conservative" administrations—opposed proposed quantitative or temporal goals for carbon dioxide emissions. Matched against this alliance are the "green-influenced" governments of continental Europe and Japan, which rely on carbon dioxide-free nuclear power. The latter nations are impatient to push for hard restrictions, especially on the United States.

To complicate matters further, global warming would not affect all nations adversely. A rise in the ocean levels from arctic ice melt may flood much of Southeast Asia and drought would occur in some currently fertile areas. On balance, however, a warmer, moister climate would provide longer, frost-free growing seasons. According to a UNEP study, a 1.5 Celsius degree temperature increase in the Central European section of the former Soviet Union would result in a 30-percent increase in its wheat yield.

Finally, scientists continue to disagree about whether the thickening blanket of greenhouse gases is, in fact, increasing world temperatures. Various theories as to the circulation of air in the atmosphere and theories about the cooling effect of other synthetic airborne materials—such as sulfate particles that impede sunlight's penetration of the atmosphere—give significant substance to the arguments of those nations that oppose a global warming treaty.

At the 1992 United Nations Rio Conference on Environment and Development, the world community took its first tentative step toward a multilateral resolution of this problem with the *Framework Convention on Climate Change*. The Convention does not resolve any of the foregoing disputes or require any measures from its parties. Rather, it established a framework for later discussions leading to more specific treaties on the issue. The Convention identifies harmonization of national regulation and disguised discrimination against imports as areas to be addressed. In December 1997, the *Kyoto Protocol* to the Convention went a step further, setting quantitative targets for the reduction of greenhouse gases by 5 percent below 1990 levels. The EU agreed to reduce emissions by 8 percent, the United States by 7 percent, and Japan by 6 percent.

Then, from 1998 through November of 2000, officials from all corners of the globe fought over how to measure such reductions. The United States and Canada argued that they should be allowed to purchase "pollution credits" from countries with low emissions rather than meeting the goals immediately. They also argued that they should be allowed to deduct from their emission totals "carbon sinks"—areas such as forests and farmlands that absorb carbon compounds. In November 2000, the EU rejected these arguments, accusing the North Americans of evading their Kyoto commitments. There matters stood as the George W. Bush administration took power in the

United States. In 2001, the administration quickly took the position that the carbon dioxide commitments were not enforceable against the United States in the absence of a pollution credit scheme.

Little progress has occurred in the intervening years. In late 2003, nations again met to confer on the Convention on climate change. While the Ministers passed a resolution "that climate change remains the most important global challenge to humanity and that its adverse effects are already a reality in all parts of the world," there was no further agreement on enforcement apparatus. Instead, two funds were developed to support developing countries' efforts in the area, the Special Climate Change Fund and the Least Developed Countries Fund. These funds support technology transfer, adaptation projects, and other activities. Several countries renewed an earlier pledge to contribute US$ 410 million annually to developing countries. Obviously, in light of the magnitude of the problem, this is not very much money.

---

http://unfccc.int/
See this site for information on United Nations Framework Convention on Climate Change.

General Prospects for Global Environmental Solutions. In a world where emerging public opinion strongly favors environmental protection, one should not underestimate the potential for global solutions. A relatively short time ago, for example, the differences between whaling nations and environmentalists in nonwhaling nations were thought to be intractable. The force of public opinion in the whalers' own countries led to an agreement to permit international regulation. Today, commercial hunting of whales is regulated by the International Whaling Commission, which meets periodically to determine how much, if any, whaling is to be allowed. From 1986 through 1992, the commission effectively banned whaling, with an increase in whale stocks that brought the threatened mammal from the edge of extinction to the point where limited hunting has begun again.

For "First World" investors, agreements like the *Montreal Protocol*—if it stays in force despite political pressure—mean that their Third World manufacturing plants will need to comply with international standards at some point in the future.

Further, because the Protocol also prohibits trade in CFCs between parties to the Protocol and nonparties, foreign investors that manufacture products in the less-developed world for export to the developed world, must expect that those export markets are likely to be closed to them if their plants are located in a country that is not a party to the agreement. The bottom line for foreign investors is that differences in environmental regulations are becoming increasingly difficult to exploit.

CHAPTER SUMMARY

Environmental law is an area of rapidly increasing regulation as conservationism becomes an accepted goal of groups across the political spectrum. As this trend is internationalized through bilateral and multilateral treaties, the investor who seeks to avoid environmental protection laws runs the risk of being trapped abroad with an unusable investment.

Questions and Case Problems

1. What would the Austrian Supreme Court have done if a private cause of action had been available in Czechoslovakia? How do you think the court would handle complaints about a nuclear accident such as Chernobyl?

2. How would an Austrian judgment for money damages against the Czechoslovak government be enforced? What type of injunctive relief would be possible?

3. If a U.S. company is presented with the opportunity to build a plant in a former communist country with less stringent laws on carbon dioxide emissions, what factors should it take into consideration before proceeding with the project? To what extent is the long-term investment interest of the company's shareholders to be considered? Are any other issues relevant to management's consideration? Would the company's president, who bypassed this low-risk opportunity to realize profit for the shareholders because of personal political views, have fulfilled management's fiduciary obligations to the shareholders?

4. Assume that a democratically elected government, after a favorable vote in a popular referendum, launches a program to clear 150,000 acres of tropical rain forest in order to promote economic development. To carry out the will of the people, the government issues a request for proposals to international engineering firms for a contract to help clear the acreage. A number of international firms have

indicated that they will bid on the project. Prepare a memo to your U.S. firm expressing your views on whether the firm should submit a bid.

5. Despite the *Montreal Protocol,* the nation of Livy continues to produce CFC-emitting refrigerators and to export them to nations throughout the world. A number of governments object to Livy's practices and ban its exports, pursuant to the Protocol. Livy brings an action under GATT, alleging that under the principles stated in the *Shrimp Excluded Devices* case, this is an attempt to impose conservationist policies on Livy. How should the GATT panel rule?

6. The Kingdom of Carolinium has a strong commitment to the preservation of wild horse herds. The neighboring Republic of Giles Run is a major dog food manufacturer and regularly uses wild horse meat in its products. These products are exported to and marketed in Carolinium. In accordance with its principles, Carolinium enacted the Horse Conservation and Health Act (HCHA) banning the use of all horse meat in any animal or human food products. Carolinium justified the HCHA on conservationist and health grounds. The evidence for any health hazard from horse meat is limited to a few scattered cases of botulism. The Carolinium ban effectively terminated all dog food exports from Giles Run. In response, Giles Run called for the creation of a GATT panel to consider the HCHA violation of GATT. How should the GATT panel rule?

Managerial Implications

Your employer, Ortiz-Hartman Steel Limited, is a specialty U.S. steel manufacturer. Over the past several years, Ortiz-Hartman has been underpriced in its specialty steel submarket by a manufacturer from the Bish-

opric of Saul, a nation that has virtually no environmental laws. Steel plants in Saul spew pollutants into the air and the rivers. Some of the pollutants damage the property and health of Saul subjects, but no cause of action in Saul affords them relief. Other pollutants damage the environment in neighboring countries. Faced with crippling competition, some members of Ortiz-Hartman management recommend that Ortiz-Hartman build a plant in Saul and take advantage of the more forgiving pollution laws.

1. Your employer asks you to prepare a memorandum summarizing the potential liability to Ortiz-Hartman associated with building a plant in Saul under current law. In your assessment, address all possible sources of liability, even those that you consider to be unlikely. Explain the detailed reasoning for your assessments.

2. Prepare a memorandum summarizing long-term risk in light of emerging international environmental legal standards.

CHAPTER 22

REGULATING THE COMPETITIVE ENVIRONMENT

An enterprise with great market power must be concerned with the limits that antitrust or competition laws place on extensions of that power. Such extensions include not only the introduction of products but also franchise and licensing arrangements.

Unlike other bodies of law reviewed in Part Four of this book, the general substance of competition laws is markedly similar from nation to nation. The way in which that law is implemented, however, differs significantly from place to place.

HISTORICAL DEVELOPMENT OF INTERNATIONAL COMPETITION LAW

"Antitrust" law has been important in the United States since the end of the nineteenth century. At that time, Congress passed the *Sherman Antitrust Act* and the *Clayton Act* to permit "trust-busters" to break up a number of "trusts" and cartels that used their size to crush their competition. These laws, with strong populist support and developed independently in American courts, are the foundation of an economic system that relies on maximizing competition to permit free market forces to operate.

After the Second World War, the European equivalent of antitrust law—*competition law*—developed rapidly. Under Articles 81 (formerly 85) and 82 (formerly 86) of the *Treaty of Rome*, the members of the European Union pledged to regulate anticompetitive actions within the Union and outlaw the abuse of dominant market power. These articles, now implemented by the Commis-

sion of the European Communities, form the bedrock upon which the highly sophisticated competition law of the EU is based. In recent years, the Commission's Directorate-General COMP (DG-COMP)—the EU's version of a combination of the Federal Trade Commission and the U.S. Department of Justice in antitrust enforcement matters—has prepared numerous regulations for adoption by the European Council of Ministers and issued a host of decisions and exemptions. Competition law has also become an important activity for the European Court of Justice, which hears appeals of Commission decisions and referrals from the courts of the EU member states on competition law issues. The European approach, however, has less confidence in market forces and is more fearful of unrestrained competition. The Europeans are more willing to rely on direct government action and less willing to count on litigation.

About seventy other nations around the world now have enacted competition policy-based national merger notification and review regimes. From South Korea to Brazil to the Czech Republic, all nations are concerned with private domination of sectors of the national economy.

Even as competition laws multiply, their content becomes more diverse. Some nations follow the U.S. model, some follow the EU model, some combine the approaches, and some opt for new ideas. The U.S. Attorney General's International Competition Policy Advisory Committee has sought to promote substantive convergence among competition law schemes and procedural "best practices," but has concluded that ". . . agreement on specific substantive rules is unlikely in the foreseeable future" and that "[c]omplete harmonization will be achieved only in the long run, if ever."

Thus, businesses today face conflicting trends in competition law. To understand how these affect businessmen, this chapter begins with a review of the basic structure of antitrust/competition law.

---

http://www.ipanet.net

Register here and select Business Conditions: Quick Reference under Databases for links to competitive information.

BASIC REGULATORY FRAMEWORK

The form of antitrust laws differs somewhat from nation to nation. Germany's competition legislation—the *Gesetzgegen Wettbewerbsbeschrankungen*—is highly detailed and addresses many issues in advance so as to limit the discretion of the administering agency and the courts to define and develop the law. In stark contrast, but consistent with its reliance of government policy implementation, the Korean *Monopoly Regulation and Fair Trade Act* is drafted in more general terms. It leaves to administrative regulations the specification of what is prohibited and how it is prohibited. The Japanese *Antimonopoly Law* facially resembles the U.S. law from which it is largely drawn, but is administered by the Japanese Fair Trade Commission, more like EU law. Consistent with its litigious tradition, antitrust laws in the United States are stated in general terms, with the details worked out in court.

Despite these differences in form and enforcement, the substance of competition law is remarkably similar in its focus on two types of activity. First, competition laws tend to prohibit agreements between competitors that restrict competition. From this general principle flows a whole range of specific prohibitions against anticompetitive clauses in licensing, franchising, and other types of agreements. Second, such laws prohibit the abuse of a dominant market position. From this general principle come a variety of concepts such as bans against predatory pricing and refusals to deal.

Prohibitions Against Agreements to Restrict Competition

Article 81 of the *Treaty of Rome* and Section 1 of the *Sherman Act* both prohibit concerted anticom-

petitive conduct. The *Sherman Act* does so in broad, unspecific language. Article 81(1) flatly prohibits all "agreements between undertakings [firms], decisions by associations of undertakings or concerted parties which may affect trade between the Member States of the European [Union] and which have as their object or effect the prevention, restriction, or distortion of competition within the Common Market." Article 81(2) automatically voids all agreements that violate Article 81(1), and Article 81(3) authorizes the European Commission to grant exemptions from this prohibition. Similar regulatory schemes may be found in competition law provisions of other nations.

Prohibitions against agreements that restrict competition are ordinarily the most relevant to international transactions. As noted in Chapter Seventeen (Licensing Agreements and the Protection of Intellectual Property Rights), a principal objective of every licensor is to prevent its licensee from competing with it. Left to its own devices, the licensor would seek pledges of eternal noncompetition throughout the Milky Way Galaxy. But the licensor must moderate its demands consistent with local competition law.

This principle is implemented differently under different systems. Some nations require governmental review of virtually all such "vertical" arrangements between firms and their distributors, customers, or suppliers. For example, Chile generally prohibits the establishment of exclusive distribution systems that restrict trade. Because exclusive distribution agreements always restrict trade, this prohibition means that one must review all such arrangements with officials from the *Fiscalía Nacional Económica*, the Chilean competition law enforcer, to obtain discretionary pre-clearance.

The United States characteristically looks at such arrangements in the context of determining whether they enhance or inhibit the workings of a competitive marketplace. The regulators and courts will allow vertical restraints if a reasonable case can be made that they foster better service and hence enhance inter-brand competition, encourage innovation, or do not foreclose a substantial part of the market to others.

In the EU, the Commission is more likely to intervene to prevent vertical restraints. In the area of patent licensing, DG-COMP is forgiving of some anticompetitive restrictions but not as forgiving as U.S. authorities would be, particularly with respect to products that include both patented and un-patented components. U.S. policy tends to accept a patent holder's restrictions in the hope of giving greater encouragement to innovation.

A significant difference exists between the ways that the EU and the United States analyze competition issues raised by patent licenses. U.S. anti-trust experts tend to view enhanced profit for the patent holder as a desirable incentive to innovation. By contrast, the Europeans increasingly view the monopoly inherent in a patent as a danger to competition that should be minimized as much as possible.

The European Commission is more flexible with respect to know-how transfer agreements than patent licenses. The rationale is that because the owner of know-how does not have any legally cognizable right to its knowledge, it can rely only on secrecy. And the only way to protect secrecy is through restrictive provisions prohibiting the licensee from competing against the licensor or from disclosing the know-how to any third party. If the Commission could not give the potential licensor of know-how confidence that its know-how would be kept secret, the licensor would be left with little incentive to enter into any agreement. The result would be anticompetitive because no one but the licensor would have the know-how.

The EU and other competition authorities also show flexibility in reviewing franchise agreements. Franchise agreements involve peculiar considerations because the franchiser must have substantial control over the franchisee. Like other licensors, the franchiser must protect its know-how. In addition, the franchiser must assure that the franchisee is producing and marketing the product in a manner consistent with the franchiser's good name. One franchisee's poor performance can have adverse effects on the franchiser's operations internationally. Indeed, the franchiser may wish to prevent the franchisee from charging prices that are inconsistent with the pricing practices of other franchisees. The European Court of Justice has considered these unusual attributes of the franchiser–franchisee relationship and, in general, has given franchisers and franchisees great flexibility in structuring their relationships.

Japan's consensus-oriented tradition has historically encouraged collaboration rather than competition among its major corporations. Consistent with this tradition, Japan permitted development of tightly wound *keiretsu* networks of suppliers and distributors. Although these networks competed against one another in Japan, their control over the means of distribution through highly restrictive distribution agreements prevented foreign firms from effectively entering the Japanese market. In fact, when they could enter the market at all, foreign companies were compelled to enter into a single, exclusive distributorship agreement for all of Japan. Obviously, the single distributor was able to exact quite favorable terms, and the Japanese consumer was confronted with relatively high prices. In 1990, the Japan Fair Trade Commission ruled that companies with at least a 25 percent share of the Japanese market are prohibited from signing exclusive import distribution contracts. Enforcement of these restrictions has not, however, been aggressive.

Abuse of Dominant Market Position

Article 82 of the *Treaty of Rome,* Section 2 of the *Sherman Act,* and their counterparts in other national competition statutes address the problem of monopolies and the abuse of monopoly power. To be in violation of such monopoly provisions, a company must first have a dominant market position, which is defined differently in different countries and in different industries. Second, the dominant party must be found to have abused this position.

In smaller countries, where, by definition, fewer entities can survive in the relevant markets, market domination tends to be more widely tolerated. Thus, in Canada, where industry is considerably more concentrated than in the United States, optimal levels of industrial concentration are likely to be relatively higher than in the United States. Moreover, cultural and historical factors are also of considerable importance. For instance, in Germany and France, refusals to deal (*refus de vente*) are closely proscribed, even if the refuser has a relatively low level of market dominance.

The EU Merger Regulation

The foregoing commentary describes traditional enforcement mechanisms that are familiar to U.S. businesspeople—the parties acted and the authorities subsequently reacted. Some exceptions will be discussed in the following section. Beginning September 21, 1990, however, the Council of the

European Communities enacted Regulation 4064/89, better known as the EU Merger Regulation. Under the Merger Regulation, parties to all mergers, acquisitions, joint ventures, and other business combinations having a *community dimension* must provide pre-transaction notification to the Commission.

The EU Merger Regulation has historically been administered by the Commission's Merger Task Force in rapid-fire fashion. Under the Regulation, deals "notified" to the Commission are automatically suspended for the first three weeks of the merger inquiry. During the three-week period, the Task Force intensively studies the competitive effects of the proposed transaction. It also entertains the views of third parties if they can demonstrate a sufficient interest in the proposed merger. The Task Force generally renders a decision within the suspension period, although it will extend it in complex cases.

The Commission begins with an analysis of the materials submitted by the parties seeking approval. It also has broad investigative powers under the Merger Regulation, including the ability to request information, to examine business records, to ask "for oral explanations on the spot," and to conduct on-site investigations. In fact, the Commission has broad powers to levy fines for noncompliance or failure to cooperate during the investigative process.

In any inquiry, the Commission first attempts to determine "*community dimension*" in cases of any dispute on the issue. Such a dimension exists when (1) the aggregate worldwide sales of all the firms being combined exceed 5 billion European currency units or *euros* and (2) the aggregate sales of the firms within the Union exceeds 250 million euros. (The value of the euro varies widely against the U.S. dollar, but one euro is usually worth somewhat more or less than one dollar.) Even if these tests are satisfied, a concentration does not have a community dimension if more than two-thirds of the aggregate community-wide profit is in only one member state. If the proposed concentration has a "community dimension," then only the Commission is to examine the transaction; member states cannot interfere with or contradict the Commission's findings.

Once the Task Force determines that the transaction has a community dimension, it then determines whether the concentration is *compatible* with the common market. In essence, a concentration that creates or strengthens a dominant position so as to "significantly impede" effective competition within the Union is "incompatible" with the common market.

The criteria employed in assessing compatibility include market share—compatibility is presumed if joint market share in the common market does not exceed 25 percent—legal or practical barriers to entry, notice of supply and demand in relevant markets, competition from firms outside the Union, and the structure of the markets.

In essence, the Commission undertakes a two-step analysis to determine whether an "undertaking" in a merger creates or strengthens a dominant position. First, it defines the "relevant markets" affected by the merger—both in terms of product line and geography. Second, the Commission determines the effect of the merger on the market so defined.

If a proposed transaction does not have a community dimension, it is jointly regulated by the Commission and member state enforcement authorities. The boundary between regulation under the Merger Regulation and "normal" DG-COMP review under Articles 81 and 82 is hazy. If a proposed joint venture is "concentrative"—if it will "independently and permanently perform all of the functions of an autonomous economic entity," without "coordination of the competitive behavior of the parties amongst themselves or between them and the joint venture,"—it is deemed to be subject to review under the Merger Regulation. If on the other hand, it is merely "cooperative," regular review is appropriate.

---

http://www.parliament.the-stationery-office.co.uk/
Select the U.K. parliament publications database, and initiate a search for the EU Merger Regulation.

A trio of cases decided in 2002 by the European Court of First Instance (CFI) in Luxembourg ushered in a more hospitable climate for mergers within the European Community. In often scathing language, the CFI vetoed the Merger Task Force's decisions blocking the unions. Altogether, the three cases suggest that, at least as of late 2003, EC regulatory power over mergers has been severely curtailed, and that any Merger Task Force rejection of a proposed merger will be held to a stringent standard of proof.

Airtours v. Commission of the European Communities
Case T-342/9 (2002)
European Court of First Instance

BACKGROUND AND FACTS

A UK-based travel company, Airtours (now MyTravel) sought to purchase a travel agency known as First Choice, announcing its planned merger to EC authorities in April, 1999. In September, 1999, the Merger Task Force blocked that proposed merger, asserting that such a proposed combination of travel powerhouses would necessarily create a "collective dominant" position in the UK market for so-called short-haul travel vacations. The Merger Task Force asserted that this would lead to higher prices for consumers as well as the elimination of smaller, less visible agencies. Airtours appealed to the Court of First Instance.

PRESIDENT JUDGE LINDH

The prospective analysis which the Commission has to carry out in its review of concentrations involving collective dominance calls for close examination in particular of the circumstances which, in each individual case, are relevant for assessing the effects of the concentration on competition in the reference market. . . . [W]here the Commission takes the view that a merger should be prohibited because it will create a situation of collective dominance, it is incumbent upon it to produce convincing evidence thereof. The evidence must concern, in particular, factors playing a significant role in the assessment of whether a situation of collective dominance exists, such as, for example, the lack of effective competition between the operators alleged to be members of the dominant oligopoly and the weakness of any competitive pressure that might be exerted by other operators. . . .

Finally, contrary to the Commission's contention . . . the fact that to some extent (30 to 40% of the shares) the same institutional investors are found in Airtours, First Choice and Thomson cannot be regarded as evidence that there is already a tendency to collective dominance in the industry. It is sufficient to point out in that regard that . . . there is no suggestion in the Decision that the group of institutional shareholders forms a united body controlling those quoted companies or providing a mechanism for exchange of information between the three undertakings. Furthermore, the Commission cannot contend that those shareholders are a further force for cautious capacity management, unless it has examined to what extent they are involved in the management of the companies concerned. Finally, even assuming that it were proved they are capable of exercising some influence on the management of the undertakings, since the concerns of the common institutional investors with respect to growth (and thus capacity) merely reflect a characteristic inherent in the relevant market, the Commission would still have to establish that the fact that institutional investors hold shares in three of the four leading tour operators amounts to evidence that there is already a tendency to collective dominance. . . .

It is apparent from the foregoing that, since it did not deny that the market was competitive, the Commission was not entitled to treat the cautious capacity planning characteristic of the market in normal circumstances as evidence substantiating its proposition that there was already a tendency to collective dominance in the industry. . . .

In the light of all of the foregoing, the Court concludes that the Decision, far from basing its prospective analysis on cogent evidence, is vitiated by a series of errors of assessment as to factors fundamental to any assessment of whether a collective dominant position might be created. It follows that the Commission prohibited the transaction without having proved to the requisite legal standard that the concentration would give rise to a collective dominant position of the three major tour operators, of such a kind as significantly to impede effective competition in the relevant market.

Decision. The CFI annulled the Merger Task Force's decision prohibiting the merger. This was the first instance that the CFI had overruled such a merger ban by the EC.

In *Airtours,* the CFI frequently criticizes the Merger Task Force for not meeting the requisite standard of proof, affording the EC none of the deference normally accorded an administrative agency's decision. Indeed, the CFI stated that the Task Force did "not give the slightest indication that there is no competition between the main tour operators." Such harsh criticism was particularly damning when one considers that, under the Merger Regulation's scheme, businesses do not take the risk of going forward without the agency's approval.

The *Airtours* CFI did agree that the so-called "collective dominance" test was the proper analytic framework for analyzing mergers, but it redefined the test to make it more difficult to stop mergers. Specifically, mergers must have "the direct and immediate effect of creating or strengthening a position of [collective dominance], which is significantly and lastingly to impede competition in the

relevant market." The CFI emphasized that if no competitive effects were immediately created, then the merger must be allowed.

Airtours was only the first in a series of bad news for the Merger Task Force. In the *Schneider* decision, the CFI annulled an EC decision because it had not followed its own procedural rules. This CFI decision served notice that it was henceforth going to require strict compliance with procedural safeguards in the preapproval process.

In addition to noting this procedural error, the

Schneider Elec. SA v. Commission of the European Communities
2002 Eur. Ct. Rep. II 04201 (2002)
European Court of First Instance

BACKGROUND AND FACTS
Schneider Electric SA ("Schneider"), a company incorporated under French law, is the parent company of a group engaged in the manufacture and sale of products and systems in the electrical distribution, industrial control, and automation sectors. Legrand SA is a company incorporated under French law, which specializes in the manufacture and sale of electrical equipment for low-voltage installations. Schneider launched its bid to acquire Legrand on January 15, 2001, in a $6.43 billion purchase offer. In accordance with the requirements in the Merger Regulation, Legrand notified the Commission of Schneider's proposal to make a public exchange offer for all shares of Legrand held by the public. Due to French merger rules, Schneider proceeded with its purchase of Legrand before the Merger Task Force ruled on the propriety of the merger. The Commission ultimately decided, however, in August 2001, that the transaction would create an anticompetitive dominant position in a number of key markets. The CFI then considered the Schneider case under new fast-track provisions designed to hasten judicial review of such merger decisions.

PRESIDENT JUDGE VESTERDORF
The Court considers . . . the claim that Schneider's rights of defence have been infringed in that the Commission included in the Decision a specific objection which was not clearly expressed in the statement of objections. . . .

According to well-established case-law, the Decision need not necessarily replicate the statement of objections. Thus, it is permissible to supplement the

statement of objections in the light of the parties' response, whose arguments show that they have actually been able to exercise their rights of defence. The Commission may also, in the light of the administrative procedure, revise or supplement its arguments of fact or law in support of its objections. . . .

Nonetheless, the statement of objections must contain an account of the objections cast in sufficiently clear terms to achieve the objective ascribed to it by the Community regulations, namely to provide all the information the undertakings need to defend themselves properly before the Commission adopts a final decision. . . .

In addition, in the procedures for reviewing concentrations, the statement of objections is not solely intended to spell out the complaints and give the undertaking to which it is addressed the opportunity to submit comments in response. It is also intended to give the notifying parties the chance to suggest corrective measures and, in particular, proposals for divestiture and sufficient time, given the requirement for speed which characterises the general scheme of Regulation No 4064/89, to ascertain the extent to which divestiture is necessary with a view to rendering the transaction compatible with the common market in good time. . . .

The Commission was consequently required to explain all the more clearly the competition problems raised by the proposed merger, in order to allow the notifying parties to put forward, properly and in good time, proposals for divestiture capable, if need be, of rendering the concentration compatible with the common market.

continued

continued

It is not apparent on reading the statement of objections that it dealt with sufficient clarity or precision with the strengthening of Schneider's position vis-à-vis French distributors of low-voltage electrical equipment as a result not only of the addition of Legrand's sales on the markets for switchboard components and panel-board components but also of Legrand's leading position in the segments for ultra-terminal electrical equipment. The Court observes in particular that the general conclusion in the statement of objections lists the various national sectoral markets affected by the concentration, without demonstrating that the position of one of the notifying parties on a given product market would in any way buttress the position of the other party on another sectoral market. . . .

Competitive overlap is conceivable only within a single national sectoral market and is thus different in nature from the mutual support provided at distribution level where two undertakings hold leading positions in one country in two distinct but complementary sectoral markets.

It follows that the statement of objections did not permit Schneider to assess the full extent of the competition problems to which the Commission claimed the concentration would give rise at distributor level on the French market for low-voltage electrical equipment.

Decision. The CFI annulled the Merger Task Force's prohibition on the merger because of the Force's defective procedural handling of the case.

CFI specifically criticized the finding that the merged entity's dominance in France would necessarily imply dominance in other countries. Indeed, the court suggested that the Merger Task Force likely inflated the merged entity's probable strength.

The ultimate blow for the Task Force in the autumn of 2002 was the *Tetra Laval* case. There, the CFI rejected the Force's factual analysis of the likely negative horizontal and vertical impacts of the merger at issue. Further, in the CFI's first comment on the leveraging analysis adopted by the Merger Task Force, it redefined the "leveraging" theory of concentration to virtual uselessness.

In essence, the CFI noted that the leveraging theory—while still a viable theory—was nonetheless speculative in its actual impact. Notably, the CFI elsewhere criticized the Merger Task Force for failing to presume that the merged firm would at least attempt to behave in a legal fashion (i.e., the prospect of being branded a criminal would be a strong deterrent on the merged entity's leadership). Just because a conglomerate can leverage its dominance, the CFI reasoned, is not tantamount to having a realistic incentive for doing so. In considering a "leveraging" theory, the Commission was to consider the extent to which the incentive to act illegally would be reduced due to the illegality of the conduct in question, the likelihood of its detection, the action taken by the competent authorities, and the financial penalties that could result.

Thus, leveraging as a concept remains a viable force in merger review, but the CFI signaled that the Merger Task Force will have to come up with more tangible proof regarding such leveraged effects. Specifically, "the proof of anti-competitive conglomerate effects of such a merger calls for a precise examination, supported by convincing evidence, of the circumstances which allegedly produce those effects."

This string of decisions resulted in suggestions that the European Union should abandon the present model of endowing the investigatory EC Merger Task Force with enforcement powers in favor of the U.S. antitrust regulatory model, which requires a court judgment to block a merger. As a result of such pressures, the EC adopted a set of fundamental reforms regarding mergers, commonly known as the "Green Paper." The reform package includes a more flexible timeframe regarding merger investigations and guidelines regarding horizontal mergers, with guidance regarding key concepts such as how to analyze anticompetitive behavior, and greater fact-finding powers for the Merger Task Force. Specifically, the Green Paper explored the merits of both the "dominance" test and the "substantial lessening of competition" (SLC) test for assessing anticompetitive effects, but failed to embrace the SLC test. In April 2003, the EC itself announced it planned to dismantle the crippled EC Merger Task Force by the spring of 2004. In the future, the investigatory

Tetra Laval BV v. Commission of the European Communities
Cases T-5/02 and T-80/02 (Ct./ First Instance Oct. 25, 2002)
European Court of First Instance

BACKGROUND AND FACTS

Tetra Laval, a Swedish company that is the world's largest carton packaging manufacturer, decided to expand into the field of plastic bottle plugs. It sought to buy the French company Sidel, which makes the equipment that blows plastic plugs into milk and soft drink bottles, commonly known as PET technology. The proposed deal was valued at 1.7 billion euros. Tetra purchased Sidel prior to EC approval. The EC Merger Task Force later prohibited the merger on the grounds that the union would be able to "leverage" its dominance in carton packaging to also become dominant in the PET packaging equipment market, thus reducing competition horizontally and vertically. This so-called "leveraging" theory had also been used earlier by the Merger Task Force to reject the highly controversial GE/Honeywell merger, despite the fact that the U.S. does not utilize the concept in antitrust review.

PRESIDENT JUDGE VESTERDORFF

Whilst it is true that the modified merger would enable Sidel, through Tetra's presence in the market for plastic bottle capping systems, to offer almost totally integrated PET lines, it is obvious that the vertical effects of Sidel's entry into that market through the merged entity, and Sidel's concomitant disappearance as a potential customer of the other operators active on that market, would be minimal in the light of the relatively weak position held by Tetra on that market. In addition, the global capacity of the merged entity, compared with Sidel's current capacity, to offer such integrated PET lines would not be strengthened by the modified merger, because Tetra would divest itself of its PET preforms

activities. The Sidel annual report shows that sales of those lines accounted for only around 20% of Sidel's SBM machine sales in 2001, despite the alleged exponential growth of 30% between 1999 and 2000 to which the Commission refers in its defence.

As for the alleged effects on the EBM machines market, the contested decision expressly acknowledges that, in the light of Tetra's reply of 1 October 2001 to the supplemental statement of objections, the position of other players allayed concerns about dominance in a potential market for machines producing aseptic HDPE bottles with handles. . . . It is thus clear that the modified merger would not have significant negative effects on the position of converters active in the HDPE market. That market would, post-merger, remain a highly competitive market.

Consequently, it has not been shown that the modified merger would result in sizeable or, at the very least, significant vertical effects on the relevant market for PET packaging equipment. In those circumstances, the Court finds that the Commission made a manifest error of assessment in so far as it relied on the vertical effects of the modified merger to support its finding that a dominant position on those PET markets would be created for the merged entity through leveraging. . . .

It follows from the foregoing that the Commission committed manifest errors of assessment in relying on the horizontal and vertical effects of the modified merger to support its analysis of the creation of a dominant position on the relevant PET markets.

Decision.   The CFI rejected the Merger Task Force's decision essentially for a lack of evidence.

---

watchdog's powers will be split among the antitrust units of the EC's general competition directorate.

DISTINCTIONS OF NON-U.S. COMPETITION LAW

Foreign competition law is similar to U.S. law in substance, but it is enforced quite differently. The most obvious distinction—and the primary reason for the absence of much competition law litigation

outside the United States—is in the sanctions for violating the law.

Private Causes of Action for Damages and Criminal Prosecution

Although the Department of Justice has brought marquee cases such as *United States v. Microsoft,* 87 F. Supp.2d 30 (D.D.C. 2000), U.S. law is enforced principally by "private attorneys general"—private parties ostensibly injured by the antitrust violation. Such plaintiffs are encouraged by the United States' recognition of a private cause of action for violations of antitrust rules and the award of treble damages to successful litigants. With this large pot of gold at the end of the litigation rainbow, and relatively little downside exposure (U.S. litigants need not pay the other side's lawyer's fees if they lose), plaintiffs are encouraged to take their shot. Similarly, risk-averse defendants are encouraged to settle out of court before trial.

In Europe, EU competition laws may be enforced only in national courts; a private party may not go to the pan-European forums of the EU. Thus, a private party must generally play in the alleged violator's "home court," where the judiciary might be inclined to favor local interests. There is no equivalent to the U.S. federal court system. In Japan, for example, there are few remedies available to plaintiffs, and local courts are very reluctant to rule against large enterprises.

In all countries outside the United States, if the plaintiff loses, it must pay the defendants' substantial attorneys' fees. Further, outside the United States, no treble-damage awards are available. Thus, plaintiffs have much greater risk, less probability of success, and less reward if they succeed. The result is drastically less litigation.

In fact, many countries provide no private cause of action at all. In Germany, enforcement of competition law is in the hands of the *Bundeskartellamt* (Federal Cartel Office); in Korea, the Minister for the Economic Planning Board enforces the act. In the European Union, Article 81(2) declares void any agreement that violates the terms of Article 81(1), but does not provide for a private cause of action for damages.

U.S. antitrust law also poses the possibility of criminal liability, which is not possible under the European or Japanese models. This is not an idle threat: In 2000, the Department of Justice reported that it had no fewer than thirty pending grand jury investigations involving alleged international cartels. Those who approach the U.S. market have to tread gingerly in anticompetitive activity.

U.S. antitrust lawyers might be somewhat bemused by the punishment meted out in South Korea. When the three largest Korean manufacturers of color televisions were conclusively found to have engaged in a price-fixing scheme, they were ordered to end the scheme and to offer a public apology to the Korean people. The manufacturers appealed!

Article 81(3) and the Rule of Reason

The analytical framework established by U.S. antitrust law distinguishes between actions that are *per se* wrong and actions to which the *rule of reason* applies. Simply put, per se violations are those that no amount of explanation can make legal, while actions subject to the rule of reason can be legal if, upon analysis, they are not found to be anticompetitive.

A raging dispute surrounds the issue of whether the rule of reason is an appropriate mode of analysis under EU competition laws. The language of Article 81(2) does not lend itself to the suggestion that some literally restrictive agreements may nonetheless be valid because of overarching procompetitive effects. Nonetheless, the Commission has flirted with that interpretation of the language in some of its decisions.

It is clear, however, that the Commission may, under Article 81(3), exempt agreements that violate the terms of Article 81(1) by a "comfort letter," an individual exemption, or a negative clearance. The Commission's actions in these processes has functioned much like the rule of reason analysis. Employing similar analysis, the Commission also grants block exemptions to entire classes of contracts.

An *individual exemption* essentially allows an agreement that would otherwise violate Article 81 because it has favorable economic effects overall. For example, an individual exemption might be granted if the proposed agreement improves the production of goods or promotes technological economic progress, imposes only restrictions indispensable to such product improvement, and does not eliminate competition as to a substantial part of the products in question. This weighing of public benefit against public loss from anticompetitive activity has been adopted in the antitrust laws of each of the formerly Communist nations of Central and Eastern Europe.

A *negative clearance*, on the other hand, is confirmation that the proposed agreement does not fall within Article 81(1) at all. It requires the Commission's analysis of whether, in fact, the proposed agreement will impair competition. The disadvantage of the negative clearance is that, if the facts as to competition turn out to be different from those represented on the application, the parties can nonetheless be fined.

Finally, the *block exemption* also involves a rule of reason analysis by the Commission. Under the terms of the block exemption, the Commission identifies the type of agreement eligible for exemptions and the types of anticompetitive provisions permitted in such agreements. In considering each provision to be included in a block-exemption contract, the Commission weighs the European Union's interest in promoting productive cooperation between parties against the costs of somewhat reduced competition. Three existing block exemptions are exclusive distribution, exclusive purchasing (including special arrangements for beer), and oil-and-gas franchising.

Preapproval Procedures Versus Litigation

The preceding examination of non-U.S. antitrust laws reveals another difference between the U.S. system and various foreign systems. In their exemption system and the EU Merger Regulation, Europeans have structured their system to provide for a resolution of competition law issues prior to the transaction taking place, typically through administrative action. The parties to the request may generally rely on the European Commission's negative clearance. Other non-U.S. systems have similar pre-clearance procedures on which parties can rely, which significantly reduce the amount of private litigation to enforce competition law outside the United States.

If the European Commission had to clear every potentially anticompetitive action in Europe, however, it would need more people than are in DG-COMP. It has tried to ameliorate this problem through its *de minimis* exceptions and granting block exemptions. The *de minimis* exception essentially provides that Article 81(1) is not violated if (1) the parties to the agreement in question have combined gross annual revenues of less than 200 million euros, and (2) the products covered by the agreement do not account for more than 5 percent of the volume in the relevant market. And as noted previously, the EU Merger Regulation has a much higher "community dimension" threshold.

Thus, with the *de minimis* exception, the majority of agreements within the European Union are not considered to be anticompetitive. The Commission will on occasion also issue "comfort letters" that tell companies that their anticipated transaction, if implemented as represented, is not likely to infringe competition rules.

The Commission also issues block exemptions applicable to entire industries or types of agreements. The broad number of subject areas permit companies to proceed with confidence in not violating Article 81(1) as long as they follow the highly specific instructions of the Commission to form their agreements. The parties whose agreements in these categories precisely follow the wording approved by the Commission need not seek approval from the Commission in order to have their transaction considered exempt.

The great benefit of the preapproval approach pursued by the European Union and many other governments is that the parties can consummate the transaction without risk of subsequent nullification and fines. The preapproval approach, however, has costs of its own. First, even with block exemptions, *de minimis* rules, and comfort letters to reduce the flow of work, the Commission has been overwhelmed. Over time an enormous backlog has developed at the Commission; disposition of pending requests has become famously slow. In contexts where the passage of time would kill the commercial objective of the transaction, firms go forward and take their chances on a rule of reason analysis. Second, the block exemption approach effectively prohibits virtually everything, then exempts large areas. Businesses are burdened with trying to write agreements that fit the rigid categories of the exemptions. Such an approach greatly hinders innovation in fashioning contractual arrangements, restricting the flexibility of entrepreneurs. This is a substantial cost. One of the engines of capitalism is that different parties invent mutually beneficial arrangements that permit them to service customers better. All efforts to address these problems in the Commission preapproval system have been widely judged insufficient.

In late September 2000, the Commission effectively proposed an end to its preapproval system for transactions under the Merger Regulation threshold. The Commission would eliminate any requirement that such transactions notify the Commission. Instead, parties would, as in the United States, decide for themselves whether an arrangement violates competition law, based on Commission precedent. DG-COMP would use its scarce resources for enforcement actions. In that enforcement, DG-COMP would have broader investigative powers—such as unannounced "dawn raids"—and stiffer penalties for violations. Also, national competition enforcement authorities would be granted broader powers to investigate and prosecute violations of national law. The proposal must be debated by the European Parliament and approved by the member states. Some member states are opposed to this abandonment of the traditional system, but the Commission's proposal underscores the difficulties of preapproval systems in this context.

The United States does not have an analogous preapproval system. The closest parallel is the review process created by the *Hart–Scott–Rodino Act,* under which certain mergers, joint venture agreements, and similar transactions must be brought before the Department of Justice before they are concluded. The DOJ's permission to conclude the transaction does not, however, preclude the Department from later litigating the issues, nor does it prevent any private party from bringing such a suit. In fact, in *California v. American Stores Co.,* 495 U.S. 271 (1990), the U.S. Supreme Court held that private parties and state authorities may sue in federal court for divestiture of a merger even after it has been approved by the DOJ or the Federal Trade Commission. On the whole, antitrust policy in the United States is developed in the courts in the context of litigation.

Another area in which the United States differs from European Union countries is the extent to which statutes are given extraterritorial application. This difference has engendered such international hostility that it deserves separate treatment.

EXTRATERRITORIAL EFFECT OF COMPETITION LAWS

In an increasingly interdependent world, no country or continent operates in isolation. Anticompetitive behavior in Costa Rica may well have an adverse effect on the price of bananas in the United States. The basic question is whether U.S. law can or should do anything to prevent Costa Rican

monopolistic action. Though the trend is now changing somewhat, Europeans have historically been reluctant to apply their competition law outside the Common Market. Conversely, Americans have tended to apply their antitrust law to every corner of the globe.

http://english.peopledaily.com.cn/home.html
Try this site for articles on foreign competition.

The U.S. Effects Test

The United States started with a limited concept of extraterritorial jurisdiction, but has since developed it in a way that accords U.S. antitrust law a substantial extraterritorial effect. The issue was first examined in *American Banana Co. v. United Fruit Co.,* 213 U.S. 347 (1909), by the great Justice Oliver Wendell Holmes. This case was resolved in a fashion with which most Europeans would feel comfortable.

In *American Banana,* the plaintiff, a U.S. corporation, alleged that a rival U.S. corporation had caused the Costa Rican government to seize the plaintiff's banana plantation and prevent the completion of the plaintiff's railway. The plaintiff argued that these acts prevented it from competing in the production and sale of bananas for export to the United States in violation of the *Sherman Antitrust Act.* Justice Holmes dismissed the complaint, interpreting the *Sherman Act* "as intended to be confined in its operation and effect to the territorial limits over which the lawmaker has general and legitimate powers." Because the United States could not control what happened in Costa Rica, Justice Holmes reasoned that Congress did not intend to regulate what happened there.

Justice Holmes's elegant prose was not long the law in the United States. Court decisions after *American Banana* tended to acknowledge it and its reasoning, but applied the ruling in odd ways. In time, ignoring the importance of the decision rendered it a nullity and opened the way for a new interpretation of the intent of Congress in the *Sherman Act,* thus creating the so-called U.S. *effects doctrine,* which was developed in the landmark case of *United States v. Aluminum Co. of America.*

Although careful to require consequences in the United States, Judge Hand, in *Alcoa,* pushed the

United States v. Aluminum Co. of America
148 F.2d 416 (1948)
United States Court of Appeals (2nd Cir.)

BACKGROUND AND FACTS

In 1931, a group of aluminum producers, one French, two German, one Swiss, one British, and one Canadian (Limited) formed a Swiss corporation named "Alliance." Each of the producers was a shareholder of Alliance.

In 1936, the shareholders instituted a system of royalties centered around Alliance. Each shareholder was to have a fixed production quota for every share it held, but as its production exceeded the sum of its quotas, it was to pay a royalty, graduated in proportion to the excess, to Alliance. Alliance then distributed the royalties as dividends to the shareholders in proportion to their shares. The effect was to create a cartel that controlled aluminum supplies and therefore kept prices high. Imports into the United States were included in the quotas.

The cartel ended in 1939 when the German shareholders became enemies of the French, British, and Canadian shareholders.

JUDGE HAND

Did the agreement . . . of 1936 violate Section 1 of the [Sherman] Act? [W]e are concerned only with whether Congress chose to attach liability to the conduct outside the United States of persons not in allegiance to it. That being so, the only question open is whether Congress intended to impose the liability, and whether our own Constitution permitted it to do so: as a court of the United States, we cannot look beyond our own law. Nevertheless, it is quite true that we are not to read general words, such as those in this act without regard to the limitations customarily observed by nations upon the exercise of their powers; limitations which generally correspond to those fixed by the "Conflict of Laws." . . . We should not impute to Congress an intent to punish all whom its courts can catch, for conduct which has no consequences within the United States. On the other hand, it is settled law . . . that any state may impose liabilities, even upon persons not within its allegiance, for conduct outside its borders that has consequences within its borders which the state reprehends; and these liabilities other states will ordinarily recognize. It may be argued that this act extends further. Two situations are possible. There

may be agreements made beyond our borders not intended to affect imports, which do affect them, or which affect exports. Almost any limitation of the supply of goods in Europe, for example, or in South America, may have repercussions in the United States if there is trade between the two. Yet when one considers the international complications likely to arise from an effort in this country to treat such agreements as unlawful, it is safe to assume that Congress certainly did not intend to act to cover them. Such agreements may on the other hand intend to include imports into the United States, and yet it may appear that they have had no effect upon them. That situation might be thought to fall within the doctrine that intent may be a substitute for performance in the case of a contract made within the United States; or it might be thought to fall within the doctrine that a statute should not be interpreted to cover acts abroad which have no consequence here. We shall not choose between these alternatives; but for argument we shall assume that the act does not cover agreements, even though intended to affect imports or exports, unless its performance is shown actually to have had some effect upon them. [The agreement] would clearly have been unlawful, had [it] been made within the United States; and it follows from what we have just said that [it was] unlawful, though made abroad, if [it was] intended to affect imports and did affect them. . . . [T]he change made in 1936 was deliberate and was expressly made to accomplish [a restraint on exportation of aluminum to the United States for sale in competition with Alcoa]. . . . The first of the conditions which we mentioned was therefore satisfied; the intent was to set up a quota system for imports.

[A] depressant upon production which applies generally may be assumed . . . to distribute its effect evenly upon all markets. Again, when the [shareholders of Alliance] took the trouble specifically to make the depressant apply to a given market, there is reason to suppose that they expected that it would have some effect, which it could have only by lessening what would otherwise have been imported. . . .

There remains only the question whether this assumed restriction had any influence upon

continued

---

continued

prices. . . . [A]n agreement to withdraw any substantial part of the supply from a market would, if carried out, have some effect upon prices, and was as unlawful as an agreement expressly to fix prices. The underlying doctrine was that all factors which contribute to determine prices, must be kept free to operate unhampered by agreements. For these reasons we

think that the agreement of 1936 violated Section 1 of the [Sherman Antitrust] Act.

Decision. The U.S. Court of Appeals for the Second Circuit reversed the district court decision and remanded the case to it for further proceedings consistent with its opinion.

---

reach of U.S. antitrust law farther toward extraterritoriality than Justice Holmes. In subsequent cases, this trend intensified. U.S. courts interpreted the *Sherman Act* to require an ever decreasing "effect" on the United States before it was applicable. Other courts soon turned to the question of whether actions by Americans affecting foreign markets could somehow satisfy the "effects" test.

Perhaps the crowning touch in this expansion came in *Joseph Muller Corp., Zurich v. Societe Anonyme De Gerance Et D'Armament,* 508 F.2d 814 (2d Cir. 1974), when a Swiss corporation sued a French corporation in the United States claiming a violation of U.S. antitrust laws, even though no U.S. companies or consumers were directly affected by any of the acts in question. Further, a Franco–Swiss treaty required that any suits between French and Swiss citizens were to be brought in the defendant's country. Nevertheless, the U.S. trial court found the requisite effects for jurisdiction over the dispute. U.S. courts, in applying the "effects" test of *Alcoa,* effectively displaced foreign treaties and laws on the basis of minimal U.S. connections.

By the 1970s, some federal courts of appeal had grown disenchanted with the *Alcoa* test because of its failure to take into account the legitimate interests of foreign nations. These courts developed a *jurisdictional rule of reason* that took into account (1) whether the action had some effect on U.S. commerce, (2) whether the restraint was of a type and magnitude to be considered a violation of the U.S. antitrust laws, and (3) the comity (goodwill) interests of the foreign nation against the interests of the United States in antitrust enforcement. Courts did not universally accept this approach, however, and U.S. court intervention continued to spark international friction. Thus, in 1982, the U.S. Congress finally clarified its intent in the *Sherman Act,* adopting a strict version of the "effects"

test in the *Foreign Trade Antitrust Improvements Act.* In essence, the act provides that U.S. antitrust law does not apply to conduct unless such conduct has a "direct, substantial, and reasonably foreseeable effect on United States commerce or on the business of a person engaged in exporting goods from the United States to foreign nations."

The *Foreign Trade Antitrust Improvements Act* did not end disagreement. As the following case makes clear, five of the members of the U.S. Supreme Court continue to have a rather sweeping view of the scope of the *Sherman Act's* applicability. This case has not been qualified in any way since it was decided and remains the law of the United States.

As the operations and investments of U.S. and foreign businesses have become increasingly enmeshed, the DOJ and the Federal Trade Commission have been obliged to develop enforcement guidelines so that businesspeople would have a better sense of when they might expect prosecution. In 1995, they revised these Antitrust Enforcement Guidelines for International Operations, expressing a great "interest in international cooperation," and set forth fourteen illustrative examples. Despite these protestations, however, the agencies showed that they intend to be aggressive. The 1995 Guidelines cite the *Hartford Fire* holding to support the U.S. government view that interest balancing is a discretionary matter of comity.

U.S. courts similarly continue to be aggressive in the assertion of their jurisdiction over transactions concluded in foreign nations. In 1995, a federal judge ruled that a Danish company doing business in Great Britain could sue a British company in the United States for alleged anticompetitive conduct in Great Britain because the British company's activity would prevent the Danish company from exporting goods to the United States.

Hartford Fire Insurance Co. v. California
113 S.Ct. 2891 (1993)
United States Supreme Court

BACKGROUND AND FACTS

Nineteen states and numerous private parties brought antitrust suits against U.S. insurers, U.S. and foreign rein-surers based in London, and insurance brokers. The insurers, reinsurers, and brokers were alleged to have agreed to boycott commercial general liability (CGL) insurers that refused to change the terms of their stan-dard domestic CGL insurance policies to conform with the policies the defendant insurers wanted to sell. The plaintiff States asserted that the practical effect of the policies that the defendant insurers wanted to sell was that (1) occurrence CGL coverage would become unavailable for many risks; (2) pollution liability coverage would become almost entirely unavailable for the vast majority of casualty insurance purchasers; and (3) cover-age of seepage, pollution, and property contamination risks would be limited.

The U.S. District Court for the Northern District of California dismissed the suits because it refused to exer-cise *Sherman Act* jurisdiction over foreign reinsurers under principles of international comity. The Court of Appeals for the Ninth Circuit reversed this decision of the District Court.

JUSTICE SOUTER

[W]e take up the question . . . whether certain claims against the London reinsurers should have been dis-missed as improper applications of the Sherman Act to foreign conduct. . . .

At the outset, we note that the District Court undoubtedly had jurisdiction of these Sherman Act claims. . . . Although the proposition was perhaps not always free from doubt, see *American Banana Co. v. United Fruit Co.,* . . . it is well established by now that the Sherman Act applies to foreign conduct that was meant to produce and did in fact produce some substantial effect in the United States. . . . Such is the conduct alleged here: that the London reinsur-ers engaged in unlawful conspiracies to affect the market for insurance in the United States and that their conduct in fact produced substantial effect. . . . According to the London reinsurers, the District Court should have declined to exercise such jurisdic-tion under the principle of international comity. The Court of Appeals agreed that courts should look to

that principle in deciding whether to exercise jurisdic-tion under the Sherman Act. . . . But other factors, in the court's view, including the London reinsurers' express purpose to affect United States commerce and the substantial nature of the effect produced, outweighed the supposed conflict and required the exercise of jurisdiction in this case. . . .

When it enacted the Foreign Trade Antitrust Improvements Act of 1982 . . . Congress expressed no view on the question whether a court with Sherman Act jurisdiction should ever decline to exercise such jurisdiction on grounds of international comity. . . .

We need not decide that question here, however, for even assuming that in a proper case a court may decline to exercise Sherman Act jurisdiction over for-eign conduct (or, as Justice Scalia would put it, may conclude by the employment of comity analysis in the first instance that there is no jurisdiction), inter-national comity would not counsel against exercis-ing jurisdiction in the circumstances alleged here.

The only substantial question in this case is whether "there is in fact a true conflict between domestic and foreign law." . . . The London reinsur-ers contend that applying the Act to their conduct would conflict significantly with British law, and the British Government, appearing before us as *amicus curiae,* concurs. . . . They assert that Parliament has established a comprehensive regulatory regime over the London reinsurance market and that the conduct alleged here was perfectly consistent with British law and policy. But this is not to state a conflict. "[T]he fact that conduct is lawful in the state in which it took place will not, of itself, bar application of the United States antitrust laws," even where the foreign state has a strong policy to permit or encourage such conduct. . . . No conflict exists, for these purposes, "where a person subject to regulation by two states can comply with the laws of both." . . . Since the London reinsurers do not argue that British law requires them to act in some fashion prohibited by the law of the United States . . . or claim that their compliance with the laws of both countries is other-wise impossible, we see no conflict with British law. . . . We have no need in this case to address other considerations that might inform a decision to refrain

continued

continued

from the exercise of jurisdiction on grounds of international comity.

JUSTICE SCALIA, DISSENTING

I dissent from the Court's ruling concerning the extraterritorial application of the Sherman Act. . . .

[V]arious British corporations and other British subjects argue that certain of the claims against them constitute an inappropriate extraterritorial application of the Sherman Act. It is important to distinguish two distinct questions raised by this petition: whether the District Court had jurisdiction, and whether the Sherman Act reaches the extraterritorial conduct alleged here.

On the first question, I believe that the District Court had subject-matter jurisdiction over the Sherman Act claims against all the defendants. . . . The respondents asserted nonfrivolous claims under the Sherman Act, and [the U.S. judicial code] vests district courts with subject-matter jurisdiction over cases "arising under" federal statutes. . . .

The second question—the extraterritorial reach of the Sherman Act—has nothing to do with the jurisdiction of the courts. It is a question of substantive law turning on whether, in enacting the Sherman Act, Congress asserted regulatory power over the challenged conduct. . . . If a plaintiff fails to prevail on this issue, the court does not dismiss the claim for want of subject-matter jurisdiction—want of power to adjudicate; rather, it decides the claim, ruling on the merits that the plaintiff has failed to state a cause of action under the relevant statute. See, . . . *American Banana Co. v. United Fruit Co.*

There is, however, a type of "jurisdiction" relevant to determining the extraterritorial reach of a statute; it is known as "legislative jurisdiction," . . . or "jurisdiction to prescribe." . . . This refers to "the authority of a state to make its law applicable to persons or activities," and is quite a separate matter from "jurisdiction to adjudicate." . . . There is no doubt, of course, that Congress possesses legislative jurisdiction over the acts alleged in this complaint: Congress has broad power under [the Constitution] "[t]o regulate Commerce with foreign Nations," and this Court has repeatedly upheld its power to make laws applicable to persons or activities beyond our territorial boundaries where United States interests are affected. . . . But the question in this case is whether, and to what extent, Congress has exercised that undoubted legislative jurisdiction in enacting the Sherman Act.

Two canons of statutory construction are relevant in this inquiry. The first is the "long-standing principle of American law 'that legislation of Congress, unless a contrary intent appears, is meant to apply only within the territorial jurisdiction of the United States.'" . . . We have, however, found the presumption to be overcome with respect to our antitrust laws; it is now well established that the Sherman Act applies extraterritorially. See, . . . *United States v. Aluminum Co. of America.* . . .

But if the presumption against extraterritoriality has been overcome or is otherwise inapplicable, a second canon of statutory construction becomes relevant: "[A]n act of congress ought never to be construed to violate the law of nations if any other possible construction remains." . . . Though it clearly has constitutional authority to do so, Congress is generally presumed not to have exceeded those customary international-law limits on jurisdiction to prescribe.

Consistent with that presumption, this and other courts have frequently recognized that, even where the presumption against extraterritoriality does not apply, statutes should not be interpreted to regulate foreign persons or conduct if that regulation would conflict with principles of international law. . . . "The controlling considerations" in this choice-of-law analysis were "the interacting interests of the United States and of foreign countries." . . .

The solution . . . adopted [by the Court in a maritime personal injury case] was to construe the statute "to apply only to areas and transactions in which American law would be considered operative under prevalent doctrines of international law." . . . [T]he principle was expressed in *United States v. Aluminum Co. of America* . . . the decision that established the extraterritorial reach of the Sherman Act. . . .

The "comity" [authorities] refer to is not the comity of courts, whereby judges decline to exercise jurisdiction over matters more appropriately adjudged elsewhere, but rather what might be termed "prescriptive comity": the respect sovereign nations afford each other by limiting the reach of their laws. That comity is exercised by legislatures when they enact laws, and courts assume it has been exercised when they come to interpreting the scope of laws their legislatures have enacted. . . . Comity in this sense includes the choice-of-law principles that, "in the absence of contrary congressional direction," are assumed to be incorporated into our substantive laws having extraterritorial reach. . . . Considering comity in this way is just part

continued

continued

of determining whether the Sherman Act prohibits the conduct at issue. . . .

Under the Restatement [of Foreign Relations Law], a nation having some "basis" for jurisdiction to prescribe law should nonetheless refrain from exercising that jurisdiction "with respect to a person or activity having connections with another state when the exercise of such jurisdiction is unreasonable." . . . The 'reasonableness' inquiry turns on a number of factors including, but not limited to: "the extent to which the activity takes place within the territory [of the regulating state], . . . the connections, such as nationality, residence, or economic activity, between the regulating state and the person principally responsible for the activity to be regulated, . . . the character of the activity to be regulated, the importance of regulation to the regulating state, the extent to which other states regulate such activities, and the degree to which the desirability of such regulation is generally accepted, . . . the extent to which another state may have an interest in regulating the activity, . . . [and] the likelihood of conflict with regulation by another state." . . .

Rarely would these factors point more clearly against application of United States law. The activity relevant to the counts at issue here took place primarily in the United Kingdom, and the defendants in these counts are British corporations and British subjects having their principal place of business or residence outside the United States. Great Britain has established a comprehensive regulatory scheme governing the London reinsurance markets, and clearly has a heavy "interest in regulating the activity." . . . Finally, section 2(b) of the McCarran-Ferguson Act allows state regulatory statutes to override the Sherman Act in the insurance field, subject only to [a] narrow "boycott" exception . . . suggesting that "the importance of regulation to the [United States]" . . . is slight. Considering these factors, I think it unimaginable that an assertion of legislative jurisdiction by the United States would be considered reasonable, and therefore it is inappropriate to assume, in the absence of statutory indication to the contrary, that Congress has made such an assertion. . . .

If one erroneously chooses, as the Court does, to make adjudicative jurisdiction (or, more precisely, abstention) the vehicle for taking account of the needs of prescriptive comity, the Court still gets it wrong. It concludes that no "true conflict" counseling nonapplication of United States law (or rather, as it thinks, United States judicial jurisdiction) exists unless compliance with United States law would constitute a violation of another country's law. . . . That breathtakingly broad proposition . . . will bring the Sherman Act and other laws into sharp and unnecessary conflict with the legitimate interests of other countries—particularly our closest trading partners.

[T]here is clearly a conflict in this case.

Decision. The Supreme Court affirmed that part of the judgment of the Court of Appeals that reversed the District Court's refusal to exercise jurisdiction over foreign reinsurers.

Eskofot A/S v. Du Pont (U.K.) Ltd.
872 F. Supp. 81 (1995)
United States District Court (S.D.N.Y.)

BACKGROUND AND FACTS
Eskofot A/S, a Danish company, was a large producer of equipment for the graphic arts and printing industry. It had average annual sales of approximately $75 million, $12 million of which was derived from sales in the United States. Du Pont UK was an English corporation with a printing and graphic arts division in England, more than 90 percent of whose total sales were in Britain. Du Pont UK conducted no business in the United States; had no office, employees, bank accounts, books, or records there; and was not licensed to do business in the United States.

Howson-Algraphy Division of Vickers PLC ("Howson") was the indirect predecessor of Du Pont UK.

Eskofot and Howson began work on a new printing system in 1987, and formalized their relationship with a written agreement in November 1987. In May 1989, Howson was sold to Du Pont, a U.S. corporation, and its name was changed to Du Pont-Howson Limited ("DPH"). DPH accepted the assignment of Eskofot's contract and executed two additional agreements with Eskofot relating to materials for the development of plate making systems.

In 1992, Du Pont UK acquired DPH, and in June

continued

continued

1992, Du Pont UK notified Eskofot that it wanted to cancel the agreements. Eskofot alleged that Du Pont retained full control of the plates, processors, and chemicals, and that the defendants intensified their worldwide sales and marketing efforts for the printing systems. In April 1993, Eskofot instituted an action against Du Pont UK in England (the "English action") for breach of its agreement and for damages stemming from Du Pont's alleged abuse of its dominant market position, pursuant to Article 82 of the *Treaty of Rome.*

Four months after bringing the English action, Eskofot brought an action in New York under the *Sherman Act* against E.I. Du Pont De Nemours & Company and Du Pont UK. Eskofot alleged that the defendants had monopolized the domestic and international market for certain printing equipment and materials. It further alleged that the defendants had engaged in systematic, intentional conduct in restraint of trade.

JUDGE LEISURE

Defendants maintain that the Court's jurisdiction to hear antitrust claims brought by foreign competitors derives from the Foreign Trade Antitrust Improvements Act, 15 U.S.C. S §6a (the "FTAIA"). Defendants note that the FTAIA was intended to exempt from U.S. antitrust law conduct that lacks the necessary level of domestic effect.... Defendants contend that Eskofot's complaint pleads no facts from which the Court can conclude that defendants' conduct had a direct, substantial, and reasonably foreseeable effect in the United States.... Plaintiff argues that the FTAIA does not apply to a claim that trade, involving foreign nations, has affected the import commerce of the United States.... Eskofot further argues that the instant dispute relates directly to import commerce. Consequently, Eskofot concludes, this case should not be considered under the FTAIA "direct, substantial and reasonably foreseeable" standard....

This Court notes that the FTAIA, by its own terms, clearly states that the provisions of the Sherman Act do not apply to conduct involving trade or commerce, "other than import trade or import commerce," with foreign nations. The implication that the Sherman Act provisions continue to apply to import trade and import commerce is unmistakable. Plaintiff contends that defendants' actions have precluded it from exporting goods into the United States. Consequently, plaintiff's pleading alleges an impact on import trade and import commerce into the United States.

Rather than the FTAIA's "direct, substantial and reasonably foreseeable" standard, the Court must determine whether the challenged conduct has, or is intended to have, any anti-competitive effect upon United States commerce.... Eskofot alleges that defendants' actions have had a significant anti-competitive effect upon United States commerce. Moreover, Eskofot alleges facts which, if true, amply support its contention. As a result, this Court has subject matter jurisdiction.

Eskofot alleges that both it and Du Pont always planned to market and sell, respectively, the Proff Print and Silverlith systems and their component parts in the United States. Eskofot further asserts that it would have sold its Proff Print system in the United States if it were not for defendants' conduct, and that defendants still intend to market their Silverlith system in the United States. Defendants dispute these assertions and contend that they are merely conclusory allegations that should be accorded little weight in determining whether to apply American antitrust laws.

The Court notes that, in the present posture of this action, factual questions must be resolved in favor of plaintiff. The instant allegations, for example, require a careful investigation of the records of the various parties before they can be resolved.... Certainly Eskofot and defendants have the capacity to sell their systems in the United States, and both Du Pont and Eskofot currently sell a certain percentage of their products in the United States. Whether Du Pont or Du Pont U.K. has sold, developed plans to sell, or harbors ambitions of selling the Silverlith system in the United States are questions of fact. Resolving these questions and other factual questions in favor of the plaintiff, this Court finds that plaintiff has sufficiently demonstrated that defendants' conduct impacted the import trade of the United States....

In sum, plaintiff has alleged that: its sale of the Proff Print system in the United States was precluded by defendants' actions, defendants intend to sell Silverlith in the United States, defendants have already initiated marketing activities in the United States to facilitate future sales, and that consumers in the United States will be negatively affected by the higher prices and reduced output that flow from the emergence of a monopoly....

[T]his Court cannot even conclude that the conduct alleged by plaintiff has not had a direct, actual, and foreseeable effect in the United States.

Decision. The Court denied the defendants' motion to dismiss the lawsuit and permitted the case to proceed in the United States.

continued

The European "Implementation" Test

Most nations take a more restrained approach to extraterritorial antitrust jurisdiction than the United States. Under the *territorial* theory of jurisdiction, which is widely accepted throughout the world, a nation may clearly assert jurisdiction over a merger involving a firm based in its territory. Thus, the People's Republic of Mozambique would be within its internationally recognized rights in asserting jurisdiction over a merger between a Mozambique company and a Canadian firm.

A more controversial situation arises when a subsidiary of a foreign-based company seeks to engage in a transaction within the host country's jurisdiction. Although this situation does not involve questions as to jurisdiction over the subsidiary under the territorial theory, if the host country cannot also obtain authority over the foreign parent, that parent could evade the host country's competition laws merely by conducting all of its activities in the host country through a controlled subsidiary. Faced with this difficulty, the European Court of Justice devised the *single economic unit* concept, under which the court imputes the behavior of a controlled subsidiary to the parent. This concept also permits the court to consider the parent's level of market dominance in determining whether the subsidiary's actions are monopolistic. The court has expanded this concept in the *Philip Morris* judgment (*BAT Reynolds v. Commission,* [1987] E.C.R. 4487), to find jurisdiction not only when actual voting control is acquired, but also when the foreign acquirer would achieve "material influence" over an erstwhile European competitor.

The farthest reach of the accepted territorial jurisdiction doctrine is the principle of *objective territoriality*. Under this principle, a state may exercise jurisdiction over conduct commenced outside its territory when the act or effect of the act is physically completed inside its territory. However, many nations have vigorously resisted the extension of this effects test beyond physical effects in the host country to mere consequences that result in a nation, such as the effects from anticompetitive conduct.

The more restricted European effects test has meant that companies can conspire to limit competition in exports to a nation without that nation being able to claim jurisdiction over the conspiracy. For example, in Germany, each exportkartell unifies the marketing power of German corporations in a single industry for potent export activity outside the Common Market.

As Europeans have begun to develop their own massive multinational market, however, they have become more flexible in defining what constitutes a "physical completion" of an act within a territory. In the following case, commonly referred to as the *Wood Pulp* case, the European Court of Justice found that the European Commission could assert jurisdiction over foreign companies with *no* presence in the Union but which exported to the Union through independent distributors. The court justified jurisdiction on the basis that the firms had engaged in price-fixing activity that was "implemented" within the Union.

The court in the *Wood Pulp* decision expressly declined to adopt the U.S. effects test, setting forth a new "implementation within the Community" test. The EU Merger Regulation literally applies to companies outside the Union: the definition of "community dimension" measures aggregate worldwide sales of the two merged entities, not whether the assets are located inside the Union. So long as the two foreign firms have sales in the Union in excess of 250 million euros and worldwide sales in excess of 5 billion euros, they would be caught. If two large U.S. firms with significant sales to European distributors merge in the United States, must they comply with the regulation? While it is a logical extension of *Wood Pulp*, such an exercise of jurisdiction would convert the "implementation" test into a thinly veiled European "effects test."

Blocking Legislation

A necessary upshot of the U.S. effects doctrine is that the U.S. litigation system and pro-competition policies are carried into many foreign nations; the United States, after all, is by far the world's largest market. And, as noted earlier, both the U.S. system of litigation and the U.S. pro-competition policies are quite inconsistent with the systems and policies in other nations. The clash triggered a rash of dueling legislation. In an antitrust action brought by the Justice Department against the uranium production industry, an American producer alleged that uranium producers outside the United States had formed a cartel to raise the price of uranium. As the producer sought discovery

A. Ahlstrom Osakeyhtio v. Commission of the European Communities
1987–88 Tfr. Binder Common Mkt. Rep. (CCH) 14,491 (1988)
Court of Justice of the European Communities

BACKGROUND AND FACTS

Wood pulp is the principal raw material used in production of paper and paperboard. In 1988, member states produced only a small fraction of their requirements for wood pulp. Virtually all of the product purchased in the Union originated from producers in countries that were then not members of the Union: Finland, Sweden, Canada, and the United States.

Many of these wood pulp producers had no presence in the Union. They sold their products to independent distributors and users located in the Union.

In each of these countries, the wood pulp producers organized into associations for export. In the United States, this group was the *Pulp, Paper, and Paper Board Export Association of the United States* (known as KEA), formed under the *Webb–Pomerene Act,* which exempts associations of U.S. exporters from U.S. antitrust laws. Each of these associations engaged in discussions on pricing policy regarding exports to the Union.

The European Commission brought action against the members of the associations under the *Treaty of Rome,* found them guilty of anticompetitive activity under Article 81 of the Treaty and imposed fines on them. The associations appealed to the Court of Justice, asserting that the Commission lacked jurisdiction over them.

PRESIDENT LORD MACKENZIE STUART

All the applicants that made submissions regarding jurisdiction maintain first of all that by applying the competition rules of the Treaty to them the Commission has misconstrued the territorial scope of Article 81. They note that . . . the Court of Justice did not adopt the "effects doctrine" but emphasized that the case involved conduct restricting competition within the Common Market because of the activities of subsidiaries that could be imputed to the parent companies. The applicants add that even if there is a basis in [Union] law for applying Article 81 to them, the action of applying the rule interpreted in that way would be contrary to public international law, which precludes any claim by the [Union] to regulate conduct restricting competition adopted outside the territory of the [Union] merely by reason of the economic repercussions which that conduct produces within the [Union].

The applicants which are members of the KEA further submit that the application of [Union] competition rules to them is contrary to public international law insofar as it is in breach of the principle of noninterference. They maintain that in this case the application of Article 81 harmed the interest of the United States in promoting exports by United States undertakings as recognized in the Webb–Pomerene Act of 1918, under which export associations, like the KEA, are exempt from United States antitrust laws.

Insofar as the submission concerning the infringement of Article 81 of the Treaty itself is concerned, it should be recalled that under that provision all agreements between undertakings and concerted practices which may affect trade between Member States and which have as their object or effect the restriction of competition within the Common Market are prohibited.

It should be noted that the main sources of supply of wood pulp are outside the [Union]—in Canada, the United States, Sweden, and Finland—and that the market therefore has global dimensions. Where wood pulp producers established in those countries sell directly to purchasers established in the [Union] and engage in price competition in order to win orders from those customers, that constitutes competition within the Common Market.

It follows that where those producers concert on the prices to be charged to their customers in the [Union] and put that concentration into effect by selling at prices that are actually coordinated, they are taking part in concertation that has the object and effect of restricting competition with the Common Market within the meaning of Article 81 of the Treaty.

Accordingly, it must be concluded that by applying the competition rules in the Treaty in the circumstances of this case to undertakings whose registered offices are situated outside the [Union], the Commission has not made an incorrect assessment of the territorial scope of Article 81. The applicants have submitted that the decision is incompatible with public international law on the grounds that the application of the competition rules in this case was founded exclusively on the economic repercussions

continued

continued

within the Common Market of conduct restricting competition which was adopted outside the [Union].

It should be observed that an infringement of Article 81, such as the conclusion of an agreement that has had the effect of restricting competition within the Common Market, consists of conduct made up of two elements: the formation of the agreement, decision, or concerted practice and the implementation thereof. If the applicability of prohibitions laid down under the competition law were made to depend on the place where the agreement, decision, or concerted practice was formed, the result would obviously be to give undertakings an easy means of evading those prohibitions. The decisive factor therefore is the place where it is implemented.

The producers in this case implemented their pricing agreement within the Common Market. It is immaterial in that respect whether or not they had recourse to subsidiaries, agents, sub-agents, or branches within the [Union] in order to make their contacts with purchasers within the [Union].

Accordingly, the [Union's] jurisdiction to apply its competition rules to such conduct is covered by the territoriality principle as universally recognized in public international law.

As regards the argument based on the infringement of the principle of non-interference, it should be pointed out that the applicants who are members of KEA have referred to a rule and the effect of those rules is that a person finds himself subject to contradictory orders as to the conduct he must adopt, each State is obliged to exercise its jurisdiction with moderation.

There is not, in this case, any contradiction between the conduct required by the United States and that required by the [Union] since the Webb–Pomerene Act merely exempts the conclusion of export cartels from the application of United States antitrust laws but does not require such cartels to be concluded.

Decision. The Court of Justice affirmed the Commission's imposition of fines on the foreign companies that had coordinated their pricing policies.

---

against foreign producers to document its charges, foreign nations cried foul. They asserted that the uranium litigation was an attempt by the United States to enforce its economic policies abroad.

In short order, Canada, Australia, France, the Netherlands, New Zealand, Switzerland, Germany, and the United Kingdom enacted *blocking legislation*. Essentially, these statutes contain provisions that block the discovery of documents located in their countries and bar the enforcement of foreign judgments there. In addition, some contain *clawback provisions* under which the foreign companies can sue in their own country to recover against local U.S. assets all or part of the amount of an antitrust judgment rendered in the United States.

These blocking laws are tantamount to international legal warfare. Blocking legislation is still a useful tool in other contexts. For example, many nations reacted against the *Cuban Democracy Act of 1992*, a U.S. law that prohibits foreign subsidiaries of U.S. corporations from doing business in Cuba by forbidding those subsidiaries from obeying the act. Blocking legislation again appeared when the Clinton Administration set forth its somewhat more aggressive international antitrust stance.

Chapter Summary

One of the prices of business success is regulation by antitrust laws. In recent years, antitrust/competition law, which had its roots in the United States, has spread around the world. This has created a new area for American entrepreneurs to consider when engaging in business activities.

Questions and Case Problems

1. The Slobovian Confederation's five producers control 95 percent of the world's supply of "goom," the key ingredient in the production of goomey bears. To maximize the Slobovian standard of living, the government passed a law creating a cartel among the five producers and forbidding access to Slobovian goom by any other entity. The price of goomey bears skyrocketed in the United States. Giggles Consolidated, U.S. candy manufacturer, attempted to purchase a goom mine in Slobovia but was rejected by the cartel. As a result, Giggles brought an antitrust action against the cartel members in a U.S. district court. Does U.S. law apply? If the U.S. court finds for Giggles, how can U.S. courts enforce such a judgment?

2. In the case in Question 1, if a U.S. court sought to enforce U.S. laws on Slobovia's leading export, how would U.S.–Slobovian relations be affected? What if a key U.S. naval base was located in Slobovia? How well equipped are courts to conduct such relations?

3. In *Alcoa*, Judge Hand points out that even agreements to restrict trade only in Europe and South America would have anticompetitive repercussions in the United States. What additional element did he require before giving U.S. antitrust law extraterritorial effect?

4. If Judge Hand had written his decision in December 1941, at the beginning of World War II, rather than in 1945, at its successful end, would he have handed down a judgment against the national aluminum company of a principal ally of the United States? Should a decision affecting the nation's relations with an ally reflect such considerations? Do you think the U.S. role in that war affected judges' perceptions of the relative importance of U.S. law?

5. Why would a British company bring a competition lawsuit under U.S. antitrust laws rather than British competition law? What advantages does a company have in alleging an antitrust conspiracy? Describe the differences between U.S. law and British law in the areas of pretrial discovery, attorneys' fees, and potential damage awards.

6. As Sir Donaldson pointed out, English courts have no authority to interpret treaties, whereas U.S. courts do. What arguments suggest that the English approach is preferable? What arguments indicate that the U.S. approach is better?

7. U.S. antitrust law reflects U.S. economic policy. If U.S. antitrust law resolves an economic dispute among British companies, has U.S. economic policy been extended to Britain? What are the implications of the United Kingdom's requirement that British companies use its own policy in resolving such disputes?

Managerial Implications

Your firm, Ellis Pets Consolidated, has developed a state-of-the-art process for producing see-through plastic hamster cages. The plastic is thin, so as not to distort the pet owner's view of the hamster, yet hard enough to resist the hamster's gnawing, and quite inexpensive in a market with great price elasticity. The Ellis process is strictly know-how; on advice of patent counsel, Ellis has not sought any patent protection. Ellis has achieved a dominant share in the U.S. market with its line of see-through hamster cages. A large international plastics manufacturer headquartered in Lyon, France—Vivian Plastique, S.A.—wishes to license the process from Ellis to apply it to other uses.

1. Vivian sees the process as so valuable that it is willing to agree never to use the process for applications within the pet industry anywhere in the world. In fact, Vivian is willing to agree never to enter the pet industry in any way. Analyze for Ellis the enforceability of these proposed agreements by Vivian. Include in your analysis alternatives that would be preferable for Ellis.

2. The hamster cage manufacturers of Europe suddenly become aware of the threat posed by Ellis. They agree to apply concerted pressure on pet stores throughout Europe to shut Ellis out. Ellis brings an antitrust action in the U.S. District Court for the Southern District of Florida. Does the court have jurisdiction over the European hamster cage manufacturers? Will Ellis be able to enforce discovery requests in Europe?

UNITED NATIONS CONVENTION ON CONTRACTS FOR THE INTERNATIONAL SALE OF GOODS[1]

The States Parties to this Convention,

Bearing in mind the broad objectives in the resolutions adopted by the sixth special session of the General Assembly of the United Nations on the establishment of a New International Economic Order,

Considering that the development of international trade on the basis of equality and mutual benefit is an important element in promoting friendly relations among States,

Being of the opinion that the adoption of uniform rules which govern contracts for the international sale of goods and take into account the different social, economic and legal systems would contribute to the removal of legal barriers in international trade and promote the development of international trade,

Have agreed as follows:

PART ONE: SPHERE OF APPLICATION AND GENERAL PROVISIONS

Chapter I. Sphere of Application

Article I

(1) This Convention applies to contracts of sale of goods between parties whose places of business are in different States:
   (a) when the States are Contracting States; or
   (b) when the rules of private international law lead to the application of the law of a Contracting State.

(2) The fact that the parties have their places of business in different States is to be disregarded whenever this fact does not appear either from the contract or from any dealings between, or from information disclosed by, the parties at any time or at the conclusion of the contract.

(3) Neither the nationality of the parties nor the civil or commercial character of the parties or of the contract is to be taken into consideration in determining the application of this Convention.

Article 2

This Convention does not apply to sales:
   (a) of goods bought for personal, family or household use, unless the seller, at any time before or at the conclusion of the contract, neither knew nor ought to have known that the goods were bought for any such use:
   (b) by auction;
   (c) on execution or otherwise by authority of law;
   (d) of stocks, shares, investment securities, negotiable instruments or money;
   (e) of ships, vessels, hovercraft or aircraft.
   (f) of electricity.

Article 3

(1) Contracts for the supply of goods to be manufactured or produced are to be considered sales unless the party who orders the goods undertakes to supply a substantial part of the materials necessary for such manufacture or production.

(2) This Convention does not apply to contracts in which the preponderant part of the obligations of the party who furnishes the goods consists in the supply of labour or other services.

Article 4

This Convention governs only the formation of the contract of sale and the rights and obligations of the seller and the buyer arising from such a contract. In particular, except as otherwise expressly provided in this Convention, it is not concerned with:
   (a) the validity of the contract or of any of its provisions or of any usage;
   (b) the effect which the contract may have on the property in the goods sold.

Article 5

This Convention does not apply to the liability of the seller for death or personal injury caused by the goods to any person.

---

[1]Source of text: U.N. Document A/CONF.97/18, Annex I, English version reprinted in 52 Fed. Reg. 6264 (1987) and in 19 I.L.M. 668 (1980)

Article 6

The parties may exclude the application of this Convention or, subject to article 12, derogate from or vary the effect of any of its provisions.

Chapter 2. General Provisions

Article 7

(1) In the interpretation of this Convention, regard is to be had to its international character and to the need to promote uniformity in its application and the observance of good faith in international trade.

(2) Questions concerning matters governed by this Convention which are not expressly settled in it are to be settled in conformity with the general principles on which it is based or, in the absence of such principles, in conformity with the law applicable by virtue of the rules of private international law.

Article 8

(1) For the purposes of this Convention statements made by and other conduct of a party are to be interpreted according to his intent where the other party knew or could not have been unaware what that intent was.

(2) If the preceding paragraph is not applicable, statements made by and other conduct of a party are to be interpreted according to the understanding that a reasonable person of the same kind as the other party would have had in the same circumstances.

(3) In determining the intent of a party or the understanding a reasonable person would have had, due consideration is to be given to all relevant circumstances of the case including the negotiations, any practices which the parties have established between themselves, usages and any subsequent conduct of the parties.

Article 9

(1) The parties are bound by any usage to which they have agreed and by any practices which they have established between themselves.

(2) The parties are considered, unless otherwise agreed, to have impliedly made applicable to their contract or its formation a usage of which the parties knew or ought to have known and which in international trade is widely known to, and regularly observed by, parties to contracts of the type involved in the particular trade concerned.

Article 10

For the purposes of this Convention:

    (a) if a party has more than one place of business, the place of business is that which has the closest relationship to the contract and its performance, having regard to the circumstances known to or contemplated by the parties at any time before or at the conclusion of the contract;

    (b) if a party does not have a place of business, reference is to be made to his habitual residence.

Article 11

A contract of sale need not be concluded in or evidence by writing and is not subject to any other requirements as to form. It may be proved by any means, including witnesses.

Article 12

Any provision of article 11, article 29 or Part II of this Convention that allows a contract of sale or its modification or termination by agreement or any offer, acceptance or other indication of intention to be made in any form other than in writing does not apply where any party has his place of business in a Contracting State which has made a declaration under article 96 of this Convention. The parties may not derogate from or vary the effect of this article.

Article 13

For the purposes of this Convention 'writing' includes telegram and telex.

Part Two: Formation of the Contract

Article 14

(1) A proposal for concluding a contract addressed to one or more specific persons constitutes an offer if it is sufficiently definite and indicates the intention of the offeror to be bound in case of acceptance. A proposal is sufficiently definite if it indicates the goods and expressly or implicitly fixes or makes provision for determining the quantity and the price.

(2) A proposal other than one addressed to one or more specific persons is to be considered merely as an invitation to make offers, unless the contrary is clearly indicated by the person making the proposal.

Article 15

(1) An offer becomes effective when it reaches the offeree.

(2) An offer, even if it is irrevocable, may be withdrawn if the withdrawal reaches the offeree before or at the same time as the offer.

Article 16

(1) Until a contract is concluded an offer may be revoked if the revocation reaches the offeree before he has dispatched an acceptance.

(2) However, an offer cannot be revoked:

(a) if it indicates, whether by stating a fixed time for acceptance or otherwise, that it is irrevocable; or

(b) if it was reasonable for the offeree to rely on the offer as being irrevocable and the offeree has acted in reliance on the offer.

Article 17

An offer, even if it is irrevocable, is terminated when a rejection reaches the offeror.

Article 18

(1) A statement made by or other conduct of the offeree indicating assent to an offer is an acceptance. Silence or inactivity does not in itself amount to acceptance.

(2) An acceptance of an offer becomes effective at the moment the indication of assent reaches the offeror. An acceptance is not effective if the indication of assent does not reach the offeror within the time he has fixed or, if no time is fixed, within a reasonable time, due account being taken of the circumstances of the transaction, including the rapidity of the means of communication employed by the offeror. An oral offer must be accepted immediately unless the circumstances indicate otherwise.

(3) However, if, by virtue of the offer or as a result of practices which the parties have established between themselves or of usage, the offeree may indicate assent by performing an act, such as one relating to the dispatch of the goods or payment of the price, without notice to the offeror, the acceptance is effective at the moment the act is performed, provided that the act is performed within the period of time laid down in the preceding paragraph.

Article 19

(1) A reply to an offer which purports to be an acceptance but contains additions, limitations or other modifications is a rejection of the offer and constitutes a counter-offer.

(2) However, a reply to an offer which purports to be an acceptance but contains additional or different terms which do not materially alter the terms of the offer constitutes an acceptance, unless the offeror, without undue delay, objects orally to the discrepancy or dispatches a notice to that effect. If he does not so object, the terms of the contract are the terms of the offer with the modifications contained in the acceptance.

(3) Additional or different terms relating, among other things, to the price, payment, quality and quantity of the goods, place and time of delivery, extent of one party's liability to the other or the settlement of disputes are considered to alter the terms of the offer materially.

Article 20

(1) A period of time for acceptance fixed by the offeror in a telegram or a letter begins to run from the moment the telegram is handed in for dispatch or from the date shown on the letter or, if no such date is shown, from the date shown on the envelope. A period of time for acceptance fixed by the offeror by telephone, telex or other means of instantaneous communication, begins to run from the moment that the offer reaches the offeree.

(2) Official holidays or non-business days occurring during the period for acceptance are included in calculating the period. However, if a notice of acceptance cannot be delivered at the address of the offeror on the last day of the period because that day falls on an official holiday or a non-business day at the place of business of the offeror, the period is extended until the first business day which follows.

Article 21

(1) A late acceptance is nevertheless effective as an acceptance if without delay the offeror orally so informs the offeree or dispatches a notice to that effect.

(2) If a letter or other writing containing a late acceptance shows that it has been sent in such circumstances that if its transmission had been normal it would have reached the offeror in due time, the late acceptance is effective as an acceptance unless, without delay, the offeror orally informs the offeree that he considers his offer as having lapsed or dispatches a notice to that effect.

Article 22

An acceptance may be withdrawn if the withdrawal reaches the offeror before or at the same time as the acceptance would have become effective.

Article 23

A contract is concluded at the moment when an acceptance of an offer becomes effective in accordance with the provisions of this Convention.

Article 24

For the purposes of the Part of the Convention, an offer, declaration of acceptance or any other indication of intention 'reaches' the addressee when it is made orally to him or delivered by any other means to him personally, to his place of business or mailing address or, if he does not have a place of business or mailing address, to his habitual residence.

Part Three: Sale of Goods

Chapter 1. General Provisions

Article 25

A breach of contract committed by one of the parties is fundamental if it results in such detriment to the other party as substantially to deprive him of what he is entitled to expect under the contract, unless the party in breach did not foresee and a reasonable person of the same kind in the same circumstances would not have foreseen such a result.

Article 26

A declaration of avoidance of the contract is effective only if made by notice to the other party.

Article 27

Unless otherwise expressly provided in this Part of the Convention, if any notice, request or other communication is given or made by a party in accordance with this Part and by means appropriate in the circumstances, a delay of error in the transmission of the communication or its failure to arrive does not deprive that party of the right to rely on the communication.

Article 28

If, in accordance with the provisions of this Convention, one party is entitled to require performance of any obligation by the other party, a court is not bound to enter a judgement for specific performance unless the court would do so under its own law in respect of similar contracts of sale not governed by this Convention.

Article 29

(1) A contract may be modified or terminated by the mere agreement of the parties.

(2) A contract in writing which contains a provision requiring any modification or termination by agreement to be in writing may not be otherwise modified or terminated by agreement. However, a party may be precluded by his conduct from asserting such a provision to the extent that the other party has relied on that conduct.

Chapter 2. Obligations of the Seller

Article 30

The seller must deliver the goods, hand over any documents relating to them and transfer the property in the goods, as required by the contract and this Convention.

Section I. Delivery of the Goods and Handing over of Documents

Article 31

If the seller is not bound to deliver the goods at any other particular place, his obligation to deliver consists:

(a) if the contract of sale involves carriage of the goods—in handing the goods over to the first carrier for transmission to the buyer;

(b) if, in cases, not within the preceding subparagraph, the contract relates to specific goods, or unidentified goods to be drawn from a specific stock or to be manufactured or produced, and at the time of the conclusion of the contract the parties knew that the goods were at, or were to be manufactured or produced at, a particular place—in placing the goods at the buyer's disposal at that place;

(c) in other cases—in placing the goods at the buyer's disposal at the place where the seller had his place of business at the time of the conclusion of the contract.

Article 32

(1) If the seller, in accordance with the contract or this Convention, hands the goods over to a carrier and if the goods are not clearly identified to the contract by markings on the goods, by shipping documents or otherwise, the seller must give the buyer notice of the consignment specifying the goods.

(2) If the seller is bound to arrange for carriage of the goods, he must make such contracts as are necessary for carriage to the place fixed by means of transportation appropriate in the circumstances and according to the usual terms for such transportation.

(3) If the seller is not bound to effect insurance in respect of the carriage of the goods, he must, at the buyer's request, provide him with all valuable information necessary to enable him to effect such insurance.

Article 33

The seller must deliver the goods:

(a) if a date is fixed by or determinable from the contract, on that date;

(b) if a period of time is fixed by or determinable from the contract, at any time within that period unless circumstances indicate that the buyer is to choose a date; or

(c) in any other case, within a reasonable time after the conclusion of the contract.

Article 34

If the seller is bound to hand over documents relating to the goods, he must hand them over at the time and place and in the form required by the contract. If the seller has handed over documents before that time, he may, up to that time, cure any lack of conformity in the documents, if the exercise of this right does not cause the buyer unreasonable inconvenience or unreasonable expense. However, the buyer retains any right to claim damages as provided for in this Convention.

Section II. Conformity of the Goods and Third Party Claims

Article 35

(1) The seller must deliver goods which are of the quantity, quality and description required by the contract and which are contained or packaged in the manner required by the contract.

(2) Except where the parties have agreed otherwise, the goods do not conform with the contract unless they:

(a) are fit for the purposes for which goods of the same description would ordinarily be used;

(b) are fit for any particular purpose expressly or impliedly made known to the seller at the time of the conclusion of the contract, except where the circumstances show that the buyer did not rely, or that it was unreasonable for him to rely, on the seller's skill and judgement;

(c) possess the qualities of goods which the seller has held out to the buyer as a sample or model;

(d) are contained or packaged in the manner usual for such goods or, where there is no such manner, in a manner adequate to preserve and protect the goods.

(3) The seller is not liable under subparagraphs (a) to (d) of the preceding paragraph for any lack of conformity of the goods if at the time of the conclusion of the contract the buyer knew or could not have been unaware of such lack of conformity.

Article 36

(1) The seller is liable in accordance with the contract and this Convention for any lack of conformity which exists at the time when the risk passes to the buyer, even though the lack of conformity becomes apparent only after that time.

(2) The seller is also liable for any lack of conformity which occurs after the time indicated in the preceding paragraph and which is due to a breach of any of his obligations, including a breach of any guarantee that for a period of time the goods will remain fit for their ordinary purpose or for some particular purpose or will retain specified qualities or characteristics.

Article 37

If the seller has delivered goods before the date for delivery, he may, up to that date, deliver any missing part or make up any deficiency in the quantity of the goods delivered, or deliver goods in replacement of any non-conforming goods delivered or remedy any lack of conformity in the goods delivered, provided that the exercise of this right does not cause the buyer unreasonable inconvenience or unreasonable expense. However, the buyer retains any right to claim damages as provided for in this Convention.

Article 38

(1) The buyer must examine the goods, or cause them to be examined, within as short a period as is practicable in the circumstances.

(2) If the contract involves carriage of the goods, examination may be deferred until after the goods have arrived at their destination.

(3) If the goods are redirected in transit or redispatched by the buyer without a reasonable opportunity for examination by him and at the time of the conclusion of the contract the seller knew or ought to have known of the possibility of such redirection or redispatch, examination may be deferred until after the goods have arrived at the new destination.

Article 39

(1) The buyer loses the right to rely on a lack of conformity of the goods if he does not give notice to the seller specifying the nature of the lack of conformity within a reasonable time after he has discovered it or ought to have discovered it.

(2) In any event, the buyer loses the right to rely on a lack of conformity of the goods if he does not give the seller notice thereof at the latest within a period of two years from the date on which the goods were actually handed over to the buyer, unless this time-limit is inconsistent with a contractual period of guarantee.

Article 40

The seller is not entitled to rely on the provisions of articles 38 and 39 if the lack of conformity relates to facts of which he knew or could not have been unaware and which he did not disclose to the buyer.

Article 41

The seller must deliver goods which are free from any right or claim of a third party, unless the buyer agreed to take the goods subject to that right or claim. However, if such right or claim is based on industrial property or other intellectual property, the seller's obligation is governed by article 42.

Article 42

(1) The seller must deliver goods which are free from any right or claim of a third party based on industrial

property or other intellectual property, of which at the time of the conclusion of the contract the seller knew or could not have been unaware, provided that the right or claim is based on industrial property or other intellectual property:

(a) under the law of the State where the goods will be resold or otherwise used, if it was contemplated by the parties at the time of the conclusion of the contract that the goods would be resold or otherwise used in that State; or

(b) in any other case, under the law of the State where the buyer has his place of business.

(2) The obligation of the seller under the preceding paragraph does not extend to cases where:

(a) at the time of the conclusion of the contract the buyer knew or could not have been unaware of the right or claim; or

(b) the right or claim results from the seller's compliance with technical drawings, designs, formulae or other such specifications furnished by the buyer.

Article 43

(1) The buyer loses the right to rely on the provisions of article 41 or article 42 if he does not give notice to the seller specifying the nature of the right or claim of the third party within a reasonable time after he has become aware or ought to have become aware of the right or claim.

(2) The seller is not entitled to rely on the provisions of the preceding paragraph if he knew of the right or claim of the third party and the nature of it.

Article 44

Notwithstanding the provisions of paragraph (1) of article 39 and paragraph (1) of article 43, the buyer may reduce the price in accordance with article 50 or claim damages, except for loss of profit, if he has a reasonable excuse for his failure to give the required notice.

SECTION III. REMEDIES FOR BREACH OF CONTRACT BY THE SELLER

Article 45

(1) If the seller fails to perform any of his obligations under the contract or this Convention, the buyer may:

(a) exercise the rights provided in articles 46 to 52;

(b) claim damages as provided in articles 74 to 77.

(2) The buyer is not deprived of any right he may have to claim damages by exercising his right to other remedies.

(3) No period of grace may be granted to the seller by a court or arbitral tribunal when the buyer resorts to a remedy for breach of contract.

Article 46

(1) The buyer may require performance by the seller of his obligations unless the buyer has resorted to a remedy which is inconsistent with this requirement.

(2) If the goods do not conform with the contract, the buyer may require delivery of substitute goods only if the lack of conformity constitutes a fundamental breach of contract and a request for substitute goods is made either in conjunction with notice given under article 39 or within a reasonable time thereafter.

(3) If the goods do not conform with the contract, the buyer may require the seller to remedy the lack of conformity by repair, unless this is unreasonable having regard to all the circumstances. A request for repair must be made either in conjunction with notice given under article 39 or within a reasonable time thereafter.

Article 47

(1) The buyer may fix an additional period of time of reasonable length for performance by the seller of his obligations.

(2) Unless the buyer has received notice from the seller that he will not perform within the period so fixed, the buyer may not, during that period, resort to any remedy for breach of contract. However, the buyer is not deprived thereby of any right he may have to claim damages for delay in performance.

Article 48

(1) Subject to article 49, the seller may, even after the date for delivery, remedy at his own expense any failure to perform his obligations, if he can do so without unreasonable delay and without causing the buyer unreasonable inconvenience or uncertainty of reimbursement by the seller of expenses advanced by the buyer. However, the buyer retains any right to claim damages as provided for in this Convention.

(2) If the seller requests the buyer to make known whether he will accept performance and the buyer does not comply with the request within a reasonable time, the seller may perform within the time indicated in his request. The buyer may not, during that period of time, resort to any remedy which is inconsistent with performance by the seller.

(3) A notice by the seller that he will perform within a specified period of time is assumed to include a request, under the preceding paragraph, that the buyer make known his decision.

(4) A request or notice by the seller under paragraph (2) or (3) of this article is not effective unless received by the buyer.

Article 49

(1) The buyer may declare the contract avoided:

    (a) if the failure by the seller to perform any of his obligations under the contract or this Convention amounts to a fundamental breach of contract; or

    (b) in case of non-delivery, if the seller does not deliver the goods within the additional period of time fixed by the buyer in accordance with paragraph (1) or article 47 or declares that he will not deliver within the period so fixed.

(2) However, in cases where the seller has delivered the goods, the buyer loses the right to declare the contract avoided unless he does so:

    (a) in respect of late delivery, within a reasonable time after he has become aware that delivery has been made;

    (b) in respect of any breach other than late delivery, within a reasonable time:

        (i) after he knew or ought to have known of the breach;

        (ii) after the expiration of any additional period of time fixed by the buyer in accordance with paragraph (1) of article 47, or after the seller has declared that he will not perform his obligations within such an additional period; or

        (iii) after the expiration of any additional period of time indicated by the seller in accordance with paragraph (2) of article 48, or after the buyer has declared that he will not accept performance.

Article 50

If the goods do not conform with the contract and whether or not the price has already been paid, the buyer may reduce the price in the same proportion as the value that the goods actually delivered had at the time of the delivery bears to the value that conforming goods would have had at that time. However, if the seller remedies any failure to perform his obligations in accordance with article 37 or article 48 or if the buyer refuses to accept performance by the seller in accordance with those articles, the buyer may not reduce the price.

Article 51

(1) If the seller delivers only a part of the goods or if only a part of the goods delivered is in conformity with the contract, articles 46 to 50 apply in respect of the part which is missing or which does not conform.

(2) The buyer may declare the contract avoided in its entirety only if the failure to make delivery completely or in conformity with the contract amounts to a fundamental breach of the contract.

Article 52

(1) If the seller delivers the goods before the date fixed, the buyer may take delivery or refuse to take delivery.

(2) If the seller delivers a quantity of goods greater than that provided for in the contract, the buyer may take delivery or refuse to take delivery of the excess quantity. If the buyer takes delivery of all or part of the excess quantity, he must pay for it at the contract rate.

Chapter 3. Obligations of the Buyer

Article 53

The buyer must pay the price for the goods and take delivery of them as required by the contract and this Convention.

SECTION I. PAYMENT OF THE PRICE

Article 54

The buyer's obligation to pay the price includes taking such steps and complying with such formalities as may be required under the contract or any laws and regulations to enable payment to be made.

Article 55

Where a contract has been validly concluded but does not expressly or implicitly fix or make provision for determining the price, the parties are considered, in the absence of any indication to the contrary, to have impliedly made reference to the price generally charged at the time of the conclusion of the contract for such goods sold under comparable circumstances in the trade concerned.

Article 56

If the price is fixed according to the weight of the goods, in case of doubt it is to be determined by the net weight.

Article 57

(1) If the buyer is not bound to pay the price at any other particular place, he must pay it to the seller:

    (a) at the seller's place of business; or

    (b) if the payment is to be made against the handing over of the goods or of documents, at the place where the handing over takes place.

(2) The seller must bear any increase in the expenses incidental to payment which is caused by a change in his place of business subsequent to the conclusion of the contract.

Article 58

(1) If the buyer is not bound to pay the price at any other specific time, he must pay it when the seller

places either the goods or documents controlling their disposition at the buyer's disposal in accordance with the contract and this Convention. The seller may make such payment a condition for handing over the goods or documents.

(2) If the contract involves carriage of the goods, the seller may dispatch the goods on terms whereby the goods, or documents controlling their disposition, will not be handed over to the buyer except against payment of the price.

(3) The buyer is not bound to pay the price until he has had an opportunity to examine the goods, unless the procedures for delivery or payment agreed upon by the parties are inconsistent with his having such an opportunity.

Article 59

The buyer must pay the price on the date fixed by or determinable from the contract and this Convention without the need for any request or compliance with any formality on the part of the seller.

SECTION II. TAKING DELIVERY

Article 60

The buyer's obligation to take delivery consists:

(a) in doing all the acts which could reasonably be expected of him in order to enable the seller to make delivery; and

(b) in taking over the goods.

SECTION III. REMEDIES FOR BREACH OF CONTRACT BY THE BUYER

Article 61

(1) If the buyer fails to perform any of his obligations under the contract or this Convention, the seller may:

(a) exercise the rights provided in articles 62 to 65;

(b) claim damages as provided in articles 74 to 77.

(2) The seller is not deprived of any right he may have to claim damages by exercising his right to other remedies.

(3) No period of grace may be granted to the buyer by a court or arbitral tribunal when the seller resorts to a remedy for breach of contract.

Article 62

The seller may require the buyer to pay the price, take delivery or perform his other obligations, unless the seller has resorted to a remedy which is inconsistent with this requirement.

Article 63

(1) The seller may fix an additional period of time of reasonable length for performance by the buyer of his obligations.

(2) Unless the seller has received notice from the buyer that he will not perform within the period so fixed, the seller may not, during that period, resort to any remedy for breach of contract. However, the seller is not deprived thereby of any right he may have to claim damages for delay in performance.

Article 64

(1) The seller may declare the contract avoided:

(a) if the failure by the buyer to perform any of his obligations under the contract or this Convention amounts to a fundamental breach of contract; or

(b) if the buyer does not, within the additional period of time fixed by the seller in accordance with paragraph (1) of article 63, perform his obligation to pay the price or take delivery of the goods, or if he declares that he will not do so within the period so fixed.

(2) However, in cases where the buyer has paid the price, the seller loses the right to declare the contract avoided unless he does so:

(a) in respect of late performance by the buyer, before the seller has become aware that performance has been rendered; or

(b) in respect of any breach other than late performance by the buyer, within a reasonable time:

(i) after the seller knew or ought to have known of the breach; or

(ii) after the expiration of any additional period of time fixed by the seller in accordance with paragraph (1) of article 63, or after the buyer has declared that he will not perform his obligations within such an additional period.

Article 65

(1) If under the contract the buyer is to specify the form, measurement or other features of the goods and he fails to make such specification either on the date agreed upon or within a reasonable time after receipt of a request from the seller, the seller may, without prejudice to any other rights he may have, make the specification himself in accordance with the requirements of the buyer that may be known to him.

(2) If the seller makes the specification himself, he must inform the buyer of the details thereof and must fix a reasonable time within which the buyer may make a different specification. If, after receipt of such a communication, the buyer fails to do so within the time so fixed, the specification made by the seller is binding.

Chapter 4. Passing of Risk

Article 66

Loss of or damage to the goods after the risk has passed to the buyer does not discharge him from his obligation to pay the price, unless the loss or damage is due to an act or omission of the seller.

Article 67

(1) If the contract of sale involves carriage of the goods and the seller is not bound to hand them over at a particular place, the risk passes to the buyer when the goods are handed over to the first carrier for transmission to the buyer in accordance with the contract of sale. If the seller is bound to hand the goods over to a carrier at a particular place, the risk does not pass to the buyer until the goods are handed over to the carrier at that place. The fact that the seller is authorized to retain documents controlling the disposition of the goods does not affect the passage of the risk.

(2) Nevertheless, the risk does not pass to the buyer until the goods are clearly identified to the contract, whether by markings on the goods, by shipping documents, by notice given to the buyer or otherwise.

Article 68

The risk in respect of goods sold in transit passes to the buyer from the time of the conclusion of the contract. However, if the circumstances so indicate, the risk is assumed by the buyer from the time the goods were handed over to the carrier who issued the documents embodying the contract of carriage. Nevertheless, if at the time of the conclusion of the contract of sale the seller knew or ought to have known that the goods had been lost or damaged and did not disclose this to the buyer, the loss or damage is at the risk of the seller.

Article 69

(1) In cases not within articles 67 and 68, the risk passes to the buyer when he takes over the goods or, if he does not do so in due time, from the time when the goods are placed at his disposal and he commits a breach of contract by failing to take delivery.

(2) However, if the buyer is bound to take over the goods at a place other than a place of business of the seller, the risk passes when delivery is due and the buyer is aware of the fact that the goods are placed at his disposal at that place.

(3) If the contract relates to goods not then identified, the goods are considered not to be placed at the disposal of the buyer until they are clearly identified to the contract.

Article 70

If the seller has committed a fundamental breach of contract, articles 67, 68 and 69 do not impair the remedies available to the buyer on account of the breach.

Chapter 5. Provisions Common to the Obligations of the Seller and of the Buyer

SECTION I. ANTICIPATORY BREACH AND INSTALLMENT CONTRACTS

Article 71

(1) A party may suspend the performance of his obligations if, after the conclusion of the contract, it becomes apparent that the other party will not perform a substantial part of his obligations as a result of:
  (a) a serious deficiency in his ability to perform or in his creditworthiness; or
  (b) his conduct in preparing to perform or in performing the contract.

(2) If the seller has already dispatched the goods before the grounds described in the preceding paragraph become evident, he may prevent the handing over of the goods to the buyer even though the buyer holds a document which entitles him to obtain them. The present paragraph relates only to the rights in the goods as between the buyer and the seller.

(3) A party suspending performance, whether before or after dispatch of the goods, must immediately give notice of the suspension to the other party and must continue with performance if the other party provides adequate assurance of his performance.

Article 72

(1) If prior to the date for performance of the contract it is clear that one of the parties will commit a fundamental breach of contract, the other party may declare the contract avoided.

(2) If time allows, the party intending to declare the contract avoided must give reasonable notice to the other party in order to permit him to provide adequate assurance of his performance.

(3) The requirements of the preceding paragraph do not apply if the other party has declared that he will not perform his obligations.

Article 73

(1) In the case of a contract for delivery of goods by instalments, if the failure of one party to perform any of his obligations in respect of any instalment constitutes a fundamental breach of contract with respect to that installment, the other party may declare the contract avoided with respect to that instalment.

(2) If one party's failure to perform any of his obligations in respect of any instalment gives the other party good grounds to conclude that a fundamental breach of contract will occur with respect to future instalments, he may declare the contract avoided for the future, provided that he does so within a reasonable time.

(3) A buyer who declares the contract avoided in respect of any delivery may, at the same time, declare it avoided in respect of deliveries already made or of future deliveries if, by reason of their interdependence, those deliveries could not be used for the purpose contemplated by the parties at the time of the conclusion of the contract.

Section II. Damages

Article 74

Damages for breach of contract by one party consist of a sum equal to the loss, including loss of profit, suffered by the other party as a consequence of the breach. Such damages may not exceed the loss which the party in breach foresaw or ought to have foreseen at the time of the conclusion of the contract, in the light of the facts and matters of which he then knew or ought to have known, as a possible consequence of the breach of contract.

Article 75

If the contract is avoided and if, in a reasonable manner and within a reasonable time after avoidance, the buyer has bought goods in replacement or the seller has resold the goods, the party claiming damages may recover the difference between the contract price and the price in the substitute transaction as well as any further damages recoverable under article 74.

Article 76

(1) If the contract is avoided and there is a current price for the goods, the party claiming damages may, if he has not made a purchase or resale under article 75, recover the difference between the price fixed by the contract and the current price at the time of avoidance as well as any further damages recoverable under article 74. If, however, the party claiming damages has avoided the contract after taking over the goods, the current price at the time of such taking over shall be applied instead of the current price at the time of avoidance.

(2) For the purposes of the preceding paragraph, the current price is the price prevailing at the place where delivery of the goods should have been made or, if there is no current price at that place, the price at such other place as serves as a reasonable substitute, making due allowance for differences in the cost of transporting the goods.

Article 77

A party who relies on a breach of contract must take such measures as are reasonable in the circumstances to mitigate the loss, including loss of profit, resulting from the breach. If he fails to take such measures, the party in breach may claim a reduction in the damages in the amount by which the loss should have been mitigated.

Section III. Interest

Article 78

If a party fails to pay the price or any other sum that is in arrears, the other party is entitled to interest on it, without prejudice to any claim for damages recoverable under article 74.

Section IV. Exemptions

Article 79

(1) A party is not liable for a failure to perform any of his obligations if he proves that the failure was due to an impediment beyond his control and that he could not reasonably be expected to have taken the impediment into account at the time of the conclusion of the contract or to have avoided or overcome it or its consequences.

(2) If the party's failure is due to the failure by a third person whom he has engaged to perform the whole or a part of the contract, that party is exempt from liability only if:
   (a) he is exempt under the preceding paragraph; and
   (b) the person whom he has so engaged would be so exempt if the provisions of that paragraph were applied to him.

(3) The exemption provided by this article has effect for the period during which the impediment exists.

(4) The party who fails to perform must give notice to the other party of the impediment and its effect on his ability to perform. If the notice is not received by the other party within a reasonable time after the party who fails to perform knew or ought to have known of the impediment, he is liable for damages resulting from such nonreceipt.

(5) Nothing in this article prevents either party from exercising any right other than to claim damages under this Convention.

Article 80

A party may not rely on a failure of the other party to perform, to the extent that such failure was caused by the first party's act or omission.

Section V. Effects of Avoidance

Article 81

(1) Avoidance of the contract releases both parties from their obligations under it, subject to any damages which may be due. Avoidance does not affect any provision of the contract for the settlement of disputes or any other provision of the contract governing the rights and obligations of the parties consequent upon the avoidance of the contract.

(2) A party who has performed the contract either wholly or in part may claim restitution from the other party of whatever the first party has supplied or paid under the contract. If both parties are bound to make restitution, they must do so concurrently.

Article 82

(1) The buyer loses the right to declare the contract avoided or to require the seller to deliver substitute goods if it is impossible for him to make restitution of the goods substantially in the condition in which he received them.

(2) The preceding paragraph does not apply:
   (a) if the impossibility of making restitution of the goods or of making restitution of the goods substantially in the condition in which the buyer received them is not due to his act or omission;
   (b) if the goods or part of the goods have perished or deteriorated as a result of the examination provided for in article 38; or
   (c) if the goods or part of the goods have been sold in the normal course of business or have been consumed or transformed by the buyer in the course of normal use before he discovered or ought to have discovered the lack of conformity.

Article 83

A buyer who has lost the right to declare the contract avoided or to require the seller to deliver substitute goods in accordance with article 82 retains all other remedies under the contract and this Convention.

Article 84

(1) If the seller is bound to refund the price, he must also pay interest on it, from the date on which the price was paid.

(2) The buyer must account to the seller for all benefits which he has derived from the goods or part of them:
   (a) if he must make restitution of the goods or part of them; or
   (b) if it is impossible for him to make restitution of all or part of the goods or to make restitution of all or part of the goods substantially in the condition in which he received them, but he has nevertheless declared the contract avoided or required the seller to deliver substitute goods.

Section VI. Preservation of the Goods

Article 85

If the buyer is in delay in taking delivery of the goods or, where payment of the price and delivery of the goods are to be made concurrently, if he fails to pay the price, and the seller is either in possession of the goods or otherwise able to control their disposition, the seller must take such steps as are reasonable in the circumstances to preserve them. He is entitled to retain them until he has been reimbursed his reasonable expenses by the buyer.

Article 86

(1) If the buyer has received the goods and intends to exercise any right under the contract or this Convention to reject them, he must take such steps to preserve them as are reasonable in the circumstances. He is entitled to retain them until he has been reimbursed his reasonable expenses by the seller.

(2) If goods dispatched to the buyer have been placed at his disposal at their destination and he exercises the right to reject them, he must take possession of them on behalf of the seller, provided that this can be done without payment of the price and without unreasonable inconvenience or unreasonable expense. This provision does not apply if the seller or a person authorized to take charge of the goods on his behalf is present at the destination. If the buyer takes possession of the goods under this paragraph, his rights and obligations are governed by the preceding paragraph.

Article 87

A party who is bound to take steps to preserve the goods may deposit them in a warehouse of a third person at the expense of the other party provided that the expense incurred is not unreasonable.

Article 88

(1) A party who is bound to preserve the goods in accordance with article 85 or 86 may sell them by any appropriate means if there has been an unreasonable delay by the other party in taking possession of the goods or in taking them back or in paying the price or the cost of preservation, provided that reasonable notice of the intention to sell has been given to the other party.

(2) If the goods are subject to rapid deterioration or their preservation would involve unreasonable expense, a party who is bound to preserve the goods in accordance with article 85 or 86 must take reasonable measures to sell them. To the extent possible he must give notice to the other party of his intention to sell.

(3) A party selling the goods has the right to retain out of the proceeds of sale an amount equal to the reasonable expenses of preserving the goods and of selling them. He must account to the other party for the balance.

Part Four: Final Provisions

Article 89

The Secretary-General of the United Nations is hereby designated as the depositary for this Convention.

Article 90

This Convention does not prevail over any international agreement which has already been or may be entered into and which contains provisions concerning the matters governed by this Convention, provided that the parties have their places of business in States parties to such agreement.

Article 91

(1) This Convention is open for signature at the concluding meeting of the United Nations Conference on Contracts for the International Sale of Goods and will remain open for signature by all States at the Headquarters of the United Nations, New York until 30 September 1981.

(2) This Convention is subject to ratification, acceptance or approval by the signatory States.

(3) This Convention is open for accession by all States which are not signatory States as from the date it is open for signature.

(4) Instruments of ratification, acceptance, approval and accession are to be deposited with the Secretary-General of the United Nations.

Article 92

(1) A Contracting State may declare at the time of signature, ratification, acceptance, approval or accession that it will not be bound by Part II of this Convention or that it will not be bound by Part III of this Convention.

(2) A Contracting State which makes a declaration in accordance with the preceding paragraph in respect of Part II or Part III of this Convention is not to be considered a Contracting State within paragraph (1) of article 1 of this Convention in respect of matters governed by the Part to which the declaration applies.

Article 93

(1) If a Contracting State has two or more territorial units in which, according to its constitution, different systems of law are applicable in relation to the matters dealt with in this Convention, it may, at the time of signature, ratification, acceptance, approval

or accession, declare that this Convention is to extend to all its territorial units or only to one or more of them, and may amend its declaration by submitting another declaration at any time.

(2) These declarations are to be notified to the depositary and are to state expressly the territorial units to which the Convention extends.

(3) If, by virtue of a declaration under this article, this Convention extends to one or more but not all of the territorial units of a Contracting State, and if the place of business of a party is located in that State, this place of business, for the purposes of this Convention, is considered not to be in a Contracting State, unless it is in a territorial unit to which the Convention extends.

(4) If a Contracting State makes no declaration under paragraph (1) of this article, the Convention is to extend to all territorial units of that State.

Article 94

(1) Two or more Contracting States which have the same or closely related legal rules on matters governed by this Convention may at any time declare that the Convention is not to apply to contracts of sale or to their formation where the parties have their places of business in those States. Such declarations may be made jointly or by reciprocal unilateral declarations.

(2) A Contracting State which has the same or closely related legal rules on matters governed by this Convention as one or more non-Contracting States may at any time declare that the Convention is not to apply to contracts of sale or to their formation where the parties have their place of business in those States.

(3) If a State which is the object of a declaration under the preceding paragraph subsequently becomes a Contracting State, the declaration made will, as from the date on which the Convention enters into force in respect of the new Contracting State, have the effect of a declaration made under paragraph (1), provided that the new Contracting State joins in such declaration or makes a reciprocal unilateral declaration.

Article 95

Any State may declare at the time of the deposit of its instrument of ratification, acceptance, approval or accession that it will not be bound by subparagraph (1)(b) of article 1 of this Convention.

Article 96

A Contracting State whose legislation requires contracts of sale to be concluded in or evidenced by writing may at any time make a declaration in accordance with article 12 that any provision of article 11, article 29, or Part II of this Convention, that allows a contract sale or its modification or termination by agreement or any offer, acceptance, or other indication of intention to be made in any form other than in writing, does not apply where any party has his place of business in that State.

Article 97

(1) Declarations made under this Convention at the time of signature are subject to confirmation upon ratification, acceptance or approval.

(2) Declarations and confirmations of declarations are to be in writing and be formally notified to the depositary.

(3) A declaration takes effect simultaneously with the entry into force of this Convention in respect of the State concerned. However, a declaration of which the depositary receives formal notification after such entry into force takes effect on the first day of the month following the expiration of six months after the date of its receipt by the depositary. Reciprocal unilateral declarations under article 94 takes effect on the first day of the month following the expiration of six months after the receipt of the latest declaration by the depositary.

(4) Any State which makes a declaration under this Convention may withdraw it at any time by a formal notification in writing addressed to the depositary. Such withdrawal is to take effect on the first day of the month following the expiration of six months after the date of the receipt of the notification by the depositary.

(5) A withdrawal of a declaration made under article 94 renders inoperative, as from the date on which the withdrawal takes effect, any reciprocal declaration made by another State under that article.

Article 98

No reservations are permitted except those expressly authorized in this Convention.

Article 99

(1) This Convention enters into force, subject to the provisions of paragraph (6) of this article, on the first day of the month following the expiration of twelve months after the date of deposit of the tenth instrument of ratification, acceptance, approval or accession, including an instrument which contains a declaration made under article 92.

(2) When a State ratifies, accepts, approves or accedes to this Convention after the deposit of the tenth instrument of ratification, acceptance, approval or accession, this Convention, with the exception of the Part excluded, enters into force in respect of that State, subject to the provisions of paragraph (6) of this article, on the first day of the month following the expiration of twelve months after the date of the deposit of its instrument of ratification, acceptance, approval or accession.

(3) A State which ratifies, accepts, approves or accedes to this Convention and is a party to either or both the Convention relating to a Uniform Law on the Formation of Contracts for the International Sale of Goods done at The Hague on 1 July 1964 (1964 Hague Formation Convention) and the Convention relating to a Uniform Law on the International Sale of Goods done at The Hague on 1 July 1964 (1964 Hague Sales Convention) shall at the same time denounce, as the case may be, either or both the 1964 Hague Sales Convention and the 1964 Hague Formation Convention by notifying the Government of the Netherlands to that effect.

(4) A State party to the 1964 Hague Sales Convention which ratifies, accepts, approves or accedes to the present Convention and declares or has declared under article 92 that it will not be bound by Part II of this Convention shall at the time of ratification, acceptance, approval or accession denounce the 1964 Hague Sales Convention by notifying the Government of the Netherlands to that effect.

(5) A State party to the 1964 Hague Formation Convention which ratifies, accepts, approves or accedes to the present Convention and declares or has declared under article 92 that it will not be bound by Part III of this Convention shall at the time of ratification, acceptance, approval or accession denounce the 1964 Hague Formation Convention by notifying the Government of the Netherlands to that effect.

(6) For the purpose of this article, ratifications, acceptances, approvals and accessions in respect of this Convention by States parties to the 1964 Hague Formation Convention or to the 1964 Hague Sales Convention shall not be effective until such denunciations as may be required on the part of those States in respect of the latter two Conventions have themselves become effective. The depositary of this Convention shall consult with the Government of the Netherlands, as the depositary of the 1964 Conventions, so as to ensure necessary coordination in this respect.

Article 100

(1) This Convention applies to the formation of a contract only when the proposal for concluding the contract is made on or after the date when the Convention enters into force in respect of the Contracting States referred to in subparagraph (1)(a) or the Contracting State referred to in subparagraph (1)(b) of article 1.

(2) This Convention applies only to contracts concluded on or after the date when the Convention enters into force in respect of the Contracting States referred to in subparagraph (1)(a) or the Contracting State referred to in subparagraph (1)(b) of article 1.

Article 101

(1) A Contracting State may denounce this Convention, or Part II or Part III of the Convention, by a formal notification in writing addressed to the depositary.

(2) The denunciation takes effect on the first day of the month following the expiration of twelve months after the notification is received by the depositary. Where a longer period for the denunciation to take effect is specified in the notification, the denunciation takes effect upon the expiration of such longer period after the notification is received by the depositary.

DONE at Vienna, this day of eleventh day of April, one thousand nine hundred and eighty, in a single original, of which the Arabic, Chinese, English, French, Russian and Spanish texts are equally authentic.

IN WITNESS WHEREOF the undersigned plenipotentiaries, being duly authorized by their respective Governments, have signed this Convention.

THE GENERAL AGREEMENT ON TARIFFS AND TRADE[1]

55 U.N.T.S. 194 (1947)
(SELECTED PROVISIONS)

PART ONE:

Article I
General Most-Favoured-Nation Treatment

1. With respect to customs duties and charges of any kind imposed on or in connection with importation or exportation or imposed on the international transfer of payments for imports or exports, and with respect to the method of levying such duties and charges, and with respect to all rules and formalities in connection with importation and exportation, and with respect to all matters referred to in paragraphs 2 and 4 of Article III, any advantage, favour, privilege or immunity granted by any contracting party to any product originating in or destined for any other country shall be accorded immediately and unconditionally to the like product originating in or destined for the territories of all other contracting parties.

* * *

Article II
Schedules of Concessions

1. (a) Each contracting party shall accord to the commerce of the other contracting parties treatment no less favourable than that provided for in the appropriate Part of the appropriate Schedule annexed to this Agreement.

   (b) The products described in Part I of the Schedule relating to any contracting party, which are the products of territories of other contracting parties, shall, on their importation into the territory to which the Schedule relates, and subject to the terms, conditions or qualifications set forth in that Schedule, be exempt from ordinary customs duties in excess of those set forth and provided for therein. Such products shall also be exempt from all other duties or charges of any kind

imposed on or in connection with importation in excess of those imposed on the date of this Agreement or those directly and mandatorily required to be imposed thereafter by legislation in force in the importing territory on that date.

PART TWO:

Article III
National Treatment on Internal Taxation and Regulation

1. The contracting parties recognize that internal taxes and other internal charges, and laws, regulations and requirements affecting the internal sale, offering for sale, purchase, transportation, distribution or use of products, and internal quantitative regulations requiring the mixture, processing or use of products in specified amounts or proportions, should not be applied to imported or domestic products so as to afford protection to domestic production.

2. The products of the territory of any contracting party imported into the territory of any other contracting party shall not be subject, directly or indirectly, to internal taxes or other internal charges of any kind in excess of those applied, directly or indirectly, to like domestic products. Moreover, no contracting party shall otherwise apply internal taxes or other internal charges to imported or domestic products in a manner contrary to the principles set forth in paragraph 1.

* * *

4. The products of the territory of any contracting party imported into the territory of any other contracting party shall be accorded treatment no less favourable than that accorded to like products of national origin in respect of all laws, regulations and requirements affecting their internal sale, offering for sale, purchase, transportation, distribution or use. The provisions of

---

[1]All references to "Contracting Parties" now refers to Members of the World Trade Organization.

this paragraph shall not prevent the application of differential internal transportation charges which are based exclusively on the economic operation of the means of transport and not on the nationality of the product.

5. No contracting party shall establish or maintain any internal quantitative regulation relating to the mixture, processing or use of products in specified amounts or proportions which requires, directly or indirectly, that any specified amount or proportion of any product which is the subject of the regulation must be supplied from domestic sources. Moreover, no contracting party shall otherwise apply internal quantitative regulations in a manner contrary to the principles set forth in paragraph 1.

* * *

7. No internal quantitative regulation relating to the mixture, processing or use of products in specified amounts or proportions shall be applied in such a manner as to allocate any such amount of proportion among external sources of supply.

8. (a) The provisions of this Article shall not apply to laws, regulations or requirements governing the procurement by governmental agencies of products purchased for governmental purposes and not with a view to commercial resale or with a view to use in the production of goods for commercial sale.

   (b) The provisions of this Article shall not prevent the payment of subsidies exclusively to domestic producers, including payments to domestic producers derived from the proceeds of internal taxes or charges applied consistently with the provisions of this Article and subsidies effected through governmental purchases of domestic products.

* * *

Article VI
Anti-dumping and Countervailing Duties

1. The contracting parties recognize that dumping, by which products of one country are introduced into the commerce of another country at less than the normal value of the products, is to be condemned if it causes or threatens material injury to an established industry in the territory of a contracting party or materially retards the establishment of a domestic industry. For the purposes of this Article, a product is to be considered as being introduced into the commerce of an importing country at less than its normal value, if the price of the product exported from one country to another

   (a) is less than the comparable price, in the ordinary course of trade, for the like product when destined for consumption in the exporting country, or,

   (b) in the absence of such domestic price, is less than either
      (i) the highest comparable price for the like product for export to any third country in the ordinary course of trade, or
      (ii) the cost of production of the product in the country-of-origin plus a reasonable addition for selling cost and profit.

   Due allowance shall be made in each case for differences in conditions and terms of sale, for differences in taxation, and for other differences affecting price comparability.

2. In order to offset or prevent dumping, a contracting party may levy on any dumped product an anti-dumping duty not greater in amount than the margin of dumping in respect of such product. For the purposes of this Article, the margin of dumping is the price difference determined in accordance with the provisions of paragraph 1.

3. No countervailing duty shall be levied on any product of the territory of any contracting party imported into the territory of another contracting party in excess of an amount equal to the estimated bounty or subsidy determined to have been granted, directly or indirectly, on the manufacture, production or export of such product in the country-of-origin or exportation, including any special subsidy to the transportation of a particular product. The term 'countervailing duty' shall be understood to mean a special duty levied for the purpose of offsetting any bounty or subsidy bestowed, directly or indirectly, upon the manufacture, production or export of any merchandise.

4. No product of the territory of any contracting party imported into the territory of any other contracting party shall be subject to antidumping or countervailing duty by reason of the exemption of such product from duties or taxes borne by the like product when destined for consumption in the country-of-origin or exportation, or by reason of the refund of such duties or taxes.

5. No product of the territory of any contracting party imported into the territory of any other contracting party shall be subject to both anti-dumping and countervailing duties to compensate for the same situation of dumping or export subsidization.

6. (a) No contracting party shall levy any anti-dumping or countervailing duty on the importation of any product of the territory of another contracting party unless it determines that the effect of the dumping or subsidization, as the case may be, is such as to cause or threaten material injury to an established domestic industry, or is such as to retard materially the establishment of a domestic industry.

* * *

Article VII
Valuation for Customs Purposes

1. The contracting parties recognize the validity of the general principles of valuation set forth in the following paragraphs of this Article, and they undertake to give effect to such principles, in respect of all products subject to duties or other charges or restrictions on importation and exportation based upon or regulated in any manner by value. Moreover, they shall, upon a request by another contracting party review the operation of any of their laws or regulations relating to value for customs purposes in the light of these principles. The CONTRACTING PARTIES may request from contracting parties reports on steps taken by them in pursuance of the provisions of this Article.

2. (a) The value for customs purposes of imported merchandise should be based on the actual value of the imported merchandise on which duty is assessed, or of like merchandise, and should not be based on the value of merchandise of national origin or on arbitrary or fictitious values.

   (b) "Actual value" should be the price at which, at a time and place determined by the legislation of the country of importation, such or like merchandise is sold or offered for sale in the ordinary course of trade under fully competitive conditions. To the extent to which the price of such or like merchandise is governed by the quantity in a particular transaction, the price to be considered should uniformly be related to either (i) comparable quantities, or (ii) quantities not less favourable to importers than those in which the greater volume of the merchandise is sold in the trade between the countries of exportation and importation.

   (c) When the actual value is not ascertainable in accordance with subparagraph (b) of this paragraph, the value for customs purposes should be based on the nearest ascertainable equivalent of such value.

* * *

Article VIII
Fees and Formalities Connected with Importation and Exportation

1. (a) All fees and charges of whatever character (other than import and export duties and other than taxes within the purview of Article III) imposed by contracting parties on or in connexion with importation or exportation shall be limited in amount to the approximate cost of services rendered and shall not represent an indirect protection to domestic products or a taxation or imports or exports for fiscal purposes.

   (b) The contracting parties recognize the need for reducing the number and diversity of fees and charges referred to in sub-paragraph (a).

   (c) The contracting parties also recognize the need for minimizing the incidence and complexity of import and export formalities and for decreasing and simplifying import and export documentation requirements.

2. A contracting party shall, upon request by another contracting party or by the CONTRACTING PARTIES, review the operation of its laws and regulations in the light of the provisions of this Article.

3. No contracting party shall impose substantial penalties for minor breaches of customs regulations or procedural requirements. In particular, no penalty in respect of any omission or mistake in customs documentation which is easily rectifiable and obviously made without fraudulent intent or gross negligence shall be greater than necessary to serve merely as a warning.

4. The provisions of this Article shall extend to fees, charges, formalities and requirements imposed by governmental authorities in connexion with importation and exportation, including those relating to:

   (a) consular transactions, such as consular invoices and certificates;

   (b) quantitative restrictions;

   (c) licensing;

   (d) exchange control;

   (e) statistical services;

   (f) documents, documentation and certification;

   (g) analysis and inspection; and

   (h) quarantine, sanitation and fumigation.

Article IX
Marks of Origin

1. Each contracting party shall accord to the products of the territories of other contracting parties treatment with regard to marking requirements no less favourable than the treatment accorded to like products of any third country.

2. The contracting parties recognize that, in adopting and enforcing laws and regulations relating to marks of origin, the difficulties and inconveniences which such measures may cause to the commerce and industry of exporting countries should be reduced to a minimum, due regard being had to the necessity of protecting consumers against fraudulent or misleading indications.

3. Whenever it is administratively practicable to do so, contracting parties should permit required marks of origin to be affixed at the time of importation.

4. The laws and regulations of contracting parties relating to the marking of imported products shall

be such as to permit compliance without seriously damaging the products, or materially reducing their value, or unreasonably increasing their cost.

5. As a general rule, no special duty or penalty should be imposed by any contracting party for failure to comply with marking requirements prior to importation unless corrective marking is unreasonably delayed or deceptive marks have been affixed or the required marking has been intentionally omitted.

6. The contracting parties shall co-operate with each other with a view to preventing the use of trade names in such manner as to misrepresent the true origin of a product, to the detriment of such distinctive regional or geographical names of products of the territory of a contracting party as are protected by its legislation. Each contracting party shall accord full and sympathetic consideration to such requests or representations as may be made by any other contracting party regarding the application of the undertaking set forth in the preceding sentence to names of products which have been communicated to it by the other contracting party.

Article X
Publication and Administration of Trade Regulations

1. Laws, regulations, judicial decisions and administrative rulings of general application, made effective by any contracting party, pertaining to the classification or the valuation of products for customs purposes, or to rates of duty, taxes or other charges, or to requirements, restrictions or prohibitions on imports or exports or on the transfer of payments therefor, or affecting their sale, distribution, transportation, insurance, warehousing, inspection, exhibition, processing, mixing or other use, shall be published promptly in such a manner as to enable governments and traders to become acquainted with them. Agreements affecting international trade policy which are in force between the government or a governmental agency of any contracting party and the government or governmental agency of any other contracting party shall also be published. The provisions of this paragraph shall not require any contracting party to disclose confidential information which would impede law enforcement or otherwise be contrary to the public interest or would prejudice the legitimate commercial interests of particular enterprises, public or private.

* * *

Article XI
General Elimination of Quantitative Restrictions

1. No prohibitions or restrictions other than duties, taxes or other charges, whether made effective through quotas, import or export licences or other measures, shall

be instituted or maintained by any contracting party on the importation of any product of the territory of any other contracting party or on the exportation or sale for export of any product destined for the territory of any other contracting party.

* * *

Article XII
Restrictions to Safeguard the Balance of Payments

1. Notwithstanding the provisions of paragraph 1 of Article XI, any contracting party, in order to safeguard its external financial position and its balance of payments, may restrict the quantity or value of merchandise permitted to be imported, subject to the provisions of the following paragraphs of this Article.

2. (a) Import restrictions instituted, maintained or intensified by a contracting party under this Article shall not exceed those necessary:

   (i) to forestall the imminent threat of, or to stop, a serious decline in its monetary reserves, or

   (ii) in the case of a contracting party with very low monetary reserves, to achieve a reasonable rate of increase in its reserves.

* * *

Article XIII
Non-discriminatory Administration of
Quantitative Restrictions

1. No prohibition or restriction shall be applied by any contracting party on the importation of any product of the territory of any other contracting party or on the exportation of any product destined for the territory of any other contracting party, unless the importation of the like product of all third countries or the exportation of the like product to all third countries is similarly prohibited or restricted.

* * *

Article XIX
Emergency Action on Imports of Particular Products

1. (a) If, as a result of unforeseen developments, and of the effect of the obligations incurred by a contracting party under this Agreement, including tariff concessions, any product is being imported into the territory of that contracting party in such increased quantities and under such conditions as to cause or threaten serious injury to domestic producers in that territory of like or directly competitive products, the contracting party shall be free, in respect of such product, and to the extent and for such time as may be necessary to prevent or remedy such injury, to suspend the obligation in whole or in part or to withdraw or modify the concession.

* * *

2. Before any contracting party shall take action pursuant to the provisions of paragraph 1 of this Article, it shall give notice in writing to the CONTRACTING PARTIES as far in advance as may be practicable and shall afford the CONTRACTING PARTIES and those contracting parties having a substantial interest as exporters of the product concerned an opportunity to consult with it in respect of the proposed action. When such notice is given in relation to a concession with respect to a preference, the notice shall name the contracting party which has requested the action. In critical circumstances, where delay would cause damage which it would be difficult to repair, action under paragraph 1 of this Article may be taken provisionally without prior consultation, on the condition that consultation shall be effected immediately after taking such action.

* * *

Article XX
General Exceptions

Subject to the requirement that such measures are not applied in a manner which would constitute a means of arbitrary or unjustifiable discrimination between countries where the same conditions prevail, or a disguised restriction on international trade, nothing in this Agreement shall be construed to prevent the adoption or enforcement by any contracting party of measures:

(a) necessary to protect public morals;

(b) necessary to protect human, animal or plant life or health;

(c) relating to the importation or exportation of gold or silver;

(d) necessary to secure compliance with laws or regulations which are not inconsistent with the provisions of this Agreement, including those relating to customs enforcement, the enforcement of monopolies operated under paragraph 4 of Article II and Article XVII, the protection of patents, trade marks and copyrights, and the prevention of deceptive practices;

(e) relating to the products of prison labour;

(f) imposed for the protection of national treasures of artistic, historic or archaeological value;

(g) relating to the conservation of exhaustible natural resources if such measures are made effective in conjunction with restrictions on domestic production or consumption;

(h) undertaken in pursuance of obligations under any intergovernmental commodity agreement which conforms to criteria submitted to the CONTRACTING PARTIES and not disapproved by them or which is itself so submitted and not so disapproved;

(i) involving restrictions on exports of domestic materials necessary to ensure essential quantities of such materials to a domestic processing industry during periods when the domestic price of such materials is held below the world price as PART of a governmental stabilization plan; Provided that such restrictions shall not operate to increase the exports of or the protection afforded to such domestic industry, and shall not depart from the provisions of this Agreement relating to non-discrimination;

(j) essential to the acquisition or distribution of products in general or local short supply;

* * *

Article XXII Consultation

1. Each contracting party shall accord sympathetic consideration to, and shall afford adequate opportunity for consultation regarding, such representations as may be made by another contracting party with respect to any matter affecting the operation of this Agreement.

* * *

Article XXIII
Nullification or Impairments

1. If any contracting party should consider that any benefit accruing to it directly or indirectly under this Agreement is being nullified or impaired or that the attainment of any objective of the Agreement is being impeded as the result of

   (a) the failure of another contracting party to carry out its obligations under this Agreement, or

   (b) the application by another contracting party of any measure, whether or not it conflicts with the provisions of this Agreement, or

   (c) the existence of any other situation, the contracting party may, with a view to the satisfactory adjustment of the matter, make written representations or proposals to the other contracting party or parties which it considers to be concerned. Any contracting party thus approached shall give sympathetic consideration to the representations or proposals made to it.

2. If no satisfactory adjustment is effected between the CONTRACTING PARTIES concerned within a reasonable time, or if the difficulty is of the type described in paragraph 1 (c) of this Article, the matter may be referred to the CONTRACTING PARTIES. The CONTRACTING PARTIES shall promptly investigate any matter so referred to them and shall make appropriate recommendations to the CONTRACTING PARTIES which they consider to be concerned, or give a ruling on the matter, as appropriate. The CONTRACTING PARTIES may consult with CONTRACTING PARTIES, with the Economic and Social Council of the

United Nations and with any appropriate intergovernmental organization in cases where they consider such consultation necessary. If the CONTRACTING PARTIES consider that the circumstances are serious enough to justify such action, they may authorize a contracting party or parties to suspend the application to any other contracting party or parties of such concessions or other obligations under this Agreement as they determine to be appropriate in the circumstances. If the application to any contracting party of any concession or other obligation is in fact suspended, that contracting party shall then be free, not later than sixty days after such action is taken, to give written notice to the Executive Secretary to the CONTRACTING PARTIES of its intention to withdraw from this Agreement and such withdrawal shall take effect upon the sixtieth day following the day on which such notice is received by him.

Part Three:

Article XXIV
Territorial Application—Frontier Traffic—Customs
Unions and Free-trade Areas
* * *

4. The contracting parties recognize the desirability of increasing freedom of trade by the development, through voluntary agreements, of closer integration between the economies of the countries parties to such agreements. They also recognize that the purpose of a customs union or of a free-trade area should be to facilitate trade between the constituent territories and not to raise barriers to the trade of other contracting parties with such territories.

5. Accordingly, the provisions of this Agreement shall not prevent, as between the territories of CONTRACTING PARTIES, the formation of a customs union or of a free-trade area or the adoption of an interim agreement necessary for the formation of a customs union or of a free-trade area; Provided that:

(a) with respect to a customs union, or an interim agreement leading to the formation of a customs union, the duties and other regulations of commerce imposed at the institution of any such union or interim agreement in respect of trade with CONTRACTING PARTIES not parties to such union or agreement shall not on the whole be higher or more restrictive than the general incidence of the duties and regulations of commerce applicable in the constituent territories prior to the formation of such union or the adoption of such interim agreement, as the case may be;

(b) with respect to a free-trade area, or an interim agreement leading to the formation of a free-

trade area, the duties and other regulations of commerce maintained in each of the constituent territories and applicable at the formation of such free-trade area or the adoption of such interim agreement to the trade of CONTRACTING PARTIES not included in such area or not parties to such agreement shall not be higher or more restrictive than the corresponding duties and other regulations of commerce existing in the same constituent territories prior to the formation of the free-trade area, or interim agreement, as the case may be; and
* * *

Article XXVIII Tariff Negotiations

1. The CONTRACTING PARTIES recognize that customs duties often constitute serious obstacles to trade; thus negotiations on a reciprocal and mutually advantageous basis, directed to the substantial reduction of the general level of tariffs and other charges on imports and exports and in particular to the reduction of such high tariffs as discourage the importation even of minimum quantities, and conducted with due regard to the objectives of this Agreement and the varying needs of individual CONTRACTING PARTIES, are of great importance to the expansion of international trade. The CONTRACTING PARTIES may therefore sponsor such negotiations from time to time.

2. (a) Negotiations under this Article may be carried out on a selective product-by-product basis or by the application of such multilateral procedures as may be accepted by the CONTRACTING PARTIES concerned. Such negotiations may be directed towards the reduction of duties, the binding of duties at then existing levels or undertakings that individual duties or the average duties on specified categories of products shall not exceed specified levels. The binding against increase of low duties or of duty-free treatment shall, in principle, be recognized as a concession equivalent in value to the reduction of high duties.
* * *

Article XXXVII Commitments

1. The developed CONTRACTING PARTIES shall to the fullest extent possible . . . (a) accord high priority to the reduction and elimination of barriers to products currently or potentially of particular export interest to less-developed CONTRACTING PARTIES, including customs duties and other restrictions which differentiate unreasonably between such products in their primary and in their processed forms;
* * *

MULTILATERAL AGREEMENTS ON TRADE IN GOODS (SELECTED PROVISIONS)[1]

General Agreement on Tariffs and Trade
April 15, 1994

GENERAL AGREEMENT ON TARIFFS AND TRADE 1994

* * *

1. The General Agreement on Tariffs and Trade 1994 ("GATT 1994") shall consist of:
   (a) the provisions in the General Agreement on Tariffs and Trade, dated 30 October 1947 . . . as amended or modified by the terms of legal instruments which have entered into force before the date of entry into force of the WTO Agreement;
   (b) the provisions of the legal instruments . . . that have entered into force under the GATT 1947 before the date of entry into force of the WTO Agreement:
       (i) protocols and certifications relating to tariff concessions;
       (iv) other decisions of the Contracting Parties to GATT 1947;
   (c) the Understandings [set forth in the Uruguay Round Agreements];
   (d) the Marrakesh Protocol to GATT 1994.
2. Explanatory Notes
   (a) The references to "contracting party" in the provisions of GATT 1994 shall be deemed to read "Member" . . . .

UNDERSTANDING ON BALANCE-OF-PAYMENTS

* * *

3. Members shall seek to avoid the imposition of new quantitative restrictions for balance-of-payments purposes unless, because of a critical balance-of-payments situation, price-based measures cannot arrest a sharp deterioration in the external payments position. In those cases in which a Member applies quantitative restrictions, it shall provide justification as to the reasons why price-based measures are not an adequate instrument to deal with the balance-of-payments situation. A Member maintaining quantitative restrictions shall indicate in successive consultations the progress made in significantly reducing the incidence and restrictive effect of such measures. It is understood that not more than one type of restrictive import measure taken for balance-of-payments purposes may be applied on the same product.

4. Members confirm that restrictive import measures taken for balance-of-payments purposes may only be applied to control the general level of imports and may not exceed what is necessary to address the balance-of-payments situation. In order to minimize any incidental protective effects, a Member shall administer restrictions in a transparent manner. The authorities of the importing Member shall provide adequate justification as to the criteria used to determine which products are subject to restriction. . . .

MARRAKESH PROTOCOL TO GATT 1994

* * *

2. The tariff reductions agreed upon by each Member shall be implemented in five equal rate reductions, except as may be otherwise specified in a Member's Schedule. The first such reduction shall be made effective on the date of entry into force of the WTO Agreement, each successive reduction shall be made effective on 1 January of each of the following years,

---

[1]Certain complex agreements have not been included here. They include the Subsidies Agreement, the Agreement on Agriculture, the Agreement on Rules of Origin, and the Understanding on Rules and Procedures Governing the Settlement of Disputes.

and the final rate shall become effective no later than the date four years after the date of entry into force of the WTO Agreement, except as may be otherwise specified in that Member's Schedule.

3. The implementation of the concessions and commitments contained in the schedules annexed to this Protocol shall, upon request, be subject to multi-lateral examination by the Members.

AGREEMENT ON THE APPLICATION OF SANITARY AND PHYTOSANITARY MEASURES

* * *

1.1. This Agreement applies to all sanitary and phytosanitary measures which may, directly or indirectly, affect international trade.

2.1. Members have the right to take sanitary and phytosanitary measures necessary for the protection of human, animal or plant life or health, provided that such measures are not inconsistent with the provisions of this Agreement.

2.2. Members shall ensure that any sanitary or phytosanitary measure is applied only to the extent necessary to protect human, animal or plant life or health, is based on scientific principles and is not maintained without sufficient scientific evidence. . . .

2.3. Members shall ensure that their sanitary and phytosanitary measures do not arbitrarily or unjustifiably discriminate between Members where identical or similar conditions prevail, including between their own territory and that of other Members. Sanitary and phytosanitary measures shall not be applied in a manner which would constitute a disguised restriction on international trade.

5.2. In the assessment of risks, Members shall take into account available scientific evidence; relevant processes and production methods; relevant inspection, sampling and testing methods; prevalence of specific diseases or pests; existence of pest- or disease-free areas; relevant ecological and environmental conditions; and quarantine or other treatment.

AGREEMENT ON TEXTILES AND CLOTHING

* * *

1.1. This Agreement sets out provisions to be applied by Members during a transition period for the integration of the textiles and clothing sector into GATT 1994.

2.1. All quantitative restrictions within bilateral agreements maintained under the MFA . . . shall . . . be

notified in detail, including the restraint levels, growth rates and flexibility provisions, by the Members maintaining such restrictions to the Textiles Monitoring Body provided for [herein]. Members agree that as of the date of entry into force of the WTO Agreement, all such restrictions maintained between GATT 1947 contracting parties, and in place on the day before such entry into force, shall be governed by the provisions of this Agreement.

5.1. Members agree that circumvention by trans-shipment, re-routing, false declaration concerning country or place of origin, and falsification of official documents, frustrates the implementation of this Agreement to integrate the textiles and clothing sector into GATT 1994. Accordingly, Members should establish the necessary legal provisions and/or administrative procedures to address and take action against such circumvention. Members further agree that, consistent with their domestic laws and procedures, they will cooperate fully to address problems arising from circumvention.

5.6. Members agree that false declaration concerning fibre content, quantities, description or classification of merchandise also frustrates the objective of this Agreement. Where there is evidence that any such false declaration has been made for purposes of circumvention, Members agree that appropriate measures, consistent with domestic laws and procedures, should be taken against the exporters or importers involved.

AGREEMENT ON TECHNICAL BARRIERS TO TRADE

* * *

2.1. Members shall ensure that in respect of technical regulations, products imported from the territory of any Member shall be accorded treatment no less favourable than that accorded to like products of national origin and to like products originating in any other country.

2.2. Members shall ensure that technical regulations are not prepared, adopted or applied with a view to or with the effect of creating unnecessary obstacles to international trade. For this purpose, technical regulations shall not be more trade-restrictive than necessary to fulfil a legitimate objective, taking account of the risks non-fulfilment would create. Such legitimate objectives are, inter alia: national security requirements; the prevention of deceptive practices; protection of human health or safety, animal or plant life or health, or the environment. In assessing such risks, relevant elements of consideration are, inter alia: available scientific and technical information, related processing technology or intended end-uses of products.

2.3. Technical regulations shall not be maintained if the circumstances or objectives giving rise to their adoption no longer exist or if the changed circumstances or objectives can be addressed in a less trade-restrictive manner.

2.4. Where technical regulations are required and relevant international standards exist or their completion is imminent, Members shall use them, or the relevant parts of them, as a basis for their technical regulations except when such international standards or relevant parts would be an ineffective or inappropriate means for the fulfilment of the legitimate objectives pursued, for instance because of fundamental climatic or geographical factors or fundamental technological problems.

2.8. Wherever appropriate, Members shall specify technical regulations based on product requirements in terms of performance rather than design or descriptive characteristics.

2.11. Members shall ensure that all technical regulations which have been adopted are published promptly or otherwise made available in such a manner as to enable interested parties in other Members to become acquainted with them.

AGREEMENT ON TRADE-RELATED INVESTMENT MEASURES

* * *

1. This Agreement applies to investment measures related to trade in goods only (referred to in this Agreement as "TRIMs").
Illustrative List of Prohibited Restrictions:

2. TRIMs that are inconsistent with the obligation of national treatment . . . include those which are mandatory or enforceable under domestic law or under administrative rulings, or compliance with which is necessary to obtain an advantage, and which require:
   (a) the purchase or use by an enterprise of products of domestic origin or from any domestic source, whether specified in terms of particular products, in terms of volume or value of products, or in terms of a proportion of volume or value of its local production; or
   (b) that an enterprise's purchases or use of imported products be limited to an amount related to the volume or value of local products that it exports.

3. TRIMs that are inconsistent with the obligation of general elimination of quantitative restrictions . . .

include those which are mandatory or enforceable under domestic law or under administrative rulings, or compliance with which is necessary to obtain an advantage, and which restrict:
   (a) the importation by an enterprise of products used in or related to its local production, generally or to an amount related to the volume or value of local production that it exports;
   (b) the importation by an enterprise of products used in or related to its local production by restricting its access to foreign exchange to an amount related to the foreign exchange inflows attributable to the enterprise; or
   (c) the exportation or sale for export by an enterprise of products, whether specified in terms of particular products, in terms of volume or value of products, or in terms of a proportion of volume or value of its local production.

GATT 1994 ANTIDUMPING AGREEMENT

* * *

2.1. For the purpose of this Agreement, a product is to be considered as being dumped, i.e. introduced into the commerce of another country at less than its normal value, if the export price of the product exported from one country to another is less than the comparable price, in the ordinary course of trade, for the like product when destined for consumption in the exporting country.

2.2 When there are no sales of the like product in the ordinary course of trade in the domestic market of the exporting country or when, because of the particular market situation or the low volume of the sales in the domestic market of the exporting country, such sales do not permit a proper comparison, the margin of dumping shall be determined by comparison with a comparable price of the like product when exported to an appropriate third country, provided that this price is representative, or with the cost of production in the country of origin plus a reasonable amount for administrative, selling and general costs and for profits.

2.4. A fair comparison shall be made between the export price and the normal value. This comparison shall be made at the same level of trade, normally at the ex-factory level, and in respect of sales made at as nearly as possible the same time. Due allowance shall be made in each case, on its merits, for differences which affect price comparability, including differences in conditions and terms of sale, taxation, levels of trade, quantities, physical characteristics, and any other differences which are also demonstrated to affect price comparability.

2.6   Throughout this Agreement the term "like product" shall be interpreted to mean a product which is identical, i.e., alike in all respects to the product under consideration, or in the absence of such a product, another product which, although not alike in all respects, has characteristics closely resembling those of the product under consideration.

3.4.   The examination of the impact of the dumped imports on the domestic industry concerned shall include an evaluation of all relevant economic factors and indices having a bearing on the state of the industry, including actual and potential decline in sales, profits, output, market share, productivity, return on investments, or utilization of capacity; factors affecting domestic prices; the magnitude of the margin of dumping; actual and potential negative effects on cash flow, inventories, employment, wages, growth, ability to raise capital or investments. This list is not exhaustive, nor can one or several of these factors necessarily give decisive guidance.

3.5   It must be demonstrated that the dumped imports are, through the effects of dumping . . . causing injury within the meaning of this Agreement [defined as "material injury to a domestic industry, threat of material injury to a domestic industry or material retardation of the establishment of such an industry"].

AGREEMENT ON CUSTOMS VALUATION

* * *

1.   The customs value of imported goods shall be the transaction value, that is the price actually paid or payable for the goods when sold for export to the country of importation . . . provided:

(c)   that no part of the proceeds of any subsequent resale, disposal or use of the goods by the buyer will accrue directly or indirectly to the seller . . . ; and

(d)   that the buyer and seller are not related, or where the buyer and seller are related, that the transaction value is acceptable for customs purposes under the provisions of paragraph 2.

2.   (a)   In determining whether the transaction value is acceptable for the purposes of paragraph 1, the fact that the buyer and the seller are related . . . shall not in itself be grounds for regarding the transaction value as unacceptable. In such case the circumstances surrounding the sale shall be examined and the transaction value shall be accepted provided that the relationship did not influence the price.

AGREEMENT ON PRESHIPMENT INSPECTION

* * *

1.3.   Preshipment inspection activities are all activities relating to the verification of the quality, the quantity, the price, including currency exchange rate and financial terms, and/or the customs classification of goods to be exported to the territory of the user Member.

2.1.   User Members shall ensure that preshipment inspection activities are carried out in a nondiscriminatory manner, and that the procedures and criteria employed in the conduct of these activities are objective and are applied on an equal basis to all exporters affected by such activities. They shall ensure uniform performance of inspection by all the inspectors of the preshipment inspection entities contracted or mandated by them.

2.3.   User Members shall ensure that all preshipment inspection activities, including the issuance of a Clean Report of Findings or a note of non-issuance, are performed in the customs territory from which the goods are exported or, if the inspection cannot be carried out in that customs territory given the complex nature of the products involved, or if both parties agree, in the customs territory in which the goods are manufactured.

2.4.   User Members shall ensure that quantity and quality inspections are performed in accordance with the standards defined by the seller and the buyer in the purchase agreement and that, in the absence of such standards, relevant international standards apply.

2.5.   User Members shall ensure that preshipment inspection activities are conducted in a transparent manner.

2.15.   User Members shall ensure that preshipment inspection entities avoid unreasonable delays in inspection of shipments.

AGREEMENT ON IMPORT LICENSING PROCEDURES

* * *

1.3.   The rules for import licensing procedures shall be neutral in application and administered in a fair and equitable manner.

1.9.   The foreign exchange necessary to pay for licensed imports shall be made available to license holders on the same basis as to importers of goods not requiring import licences.

AGREEMENT ON SAFEGUARDS

* * *

2.1. A Member may apply a safeguard measure to a product only if that Member has determined . . . that such product is being imported into its territory in such increased quantities, absolute or relative to domestic production, and under such conditions as to cause or threaten to cause serious injury to the domestic industry that produces like or directly competitive products.

2.2. Safeguard measures shall be applied to a product being imported irrespective of its source.

5.1. A Member shall apply safeguard measures only to the extent necessary to prevent or remedy serious injury and to facilitate adjustment. If a quantitative restriction is used, such a measure shall not reduce the quantity of imports below the level of a recent period which shall be the average of imports in the last three representative years for which statistics are available, unless clear justification is given that a different level is necessary to prevent or remedy serious injury. Members should choose measures most suitable for the achievement of these objectives.

5.2. In cases in which a quota is allocated among supplying countries, the Member applying the restrictions may seek agreement with respect to the allocation of shares in the quota with all other Members having a substantial interest in supplying the product concerned.

7.1. A Member shall apply safeguard measures only for such period of time as may be necessary to prevent or remedy serious injury and to facilitate adjustment. The period shall not exceed four years, unless it is extended. . . .

AGREEMENT ON GOVERNMENT PROCUREMENT

* * *

3.1. With respect to all laws, regulations, procedures and practices regarding government procurement by this Agreement, each Party shall provide immediately and unconditionally to the products, services and suppliers of other Parties offering products or services of the Parties, treatment no less favorable than:
(a) that accorded to domestic products, services and suppliers; and
(b) that accorded to products, services and suppliers of any other Party.

7.2. [Government] entities shall not provide to any supplier information with regard to a specific procurement in a manner which would have the effect of precluding competition.

8 (b). Any conditions for participation in tendering procedures shall be limited to those which are essential to ensure the firm's capability to fulfil the contract in question.

16.1. [Government] entities shall not, in the qualification and selection of suppliers, products or services, or in the evaluation of tenders and award of contracts, impose, seek or consider offsets.

19.1. Each Party shall promptly publish any law, regulation, judicial decision, administrative ruling . . . regarding government procurement. . . .

20.2. Each party shall provide non-discriminatory, timely, transparent and effective procedures enabling suppliers to challenge alleged breaches of the Agreement arising in the context of procurements which they have, or have had, an interest.

General Agreement on Trade in Services (Selected Provisions)

April 15, 1994

Article I
Scope and Definition

1. This Agreement applies to measures by Members affecting trade in services.

Article II
Most-Favoured-Nation Treatment

1. With respect to any measure covered by this Agreement, each Member shall accord immediately and unconditionally to services and service suppliers of any other Member treatment no less favourable than that it accords to like services and service suppliers of any other country.

Article III
Transparency

1. Each Member shall publish promptly and, except in emergency situations, at the latest by the time of their entry into force, all relevant measures of general application which pertain to or affect the operation of this Agreement. International agreements pertaining to or affecting trade in services to which a Member is a signatory shall also be published.

Article VI
Domestic Regulation

1. In sectors where specific commitments are undertaken, each Member shall ensure that all measures of general application affecting trade in services are administered in a reasonable, objective and impartial manner. . . .

4. With a view to ensuring that measures relating to qualification requirements and procedures, technical standards and licensing requirements do not constitute unnecessary barriers to trade in services, the Council for Trade in Services shall, through appropriate bodies it may establish, develop any necessary disciplines. Such disciplines shall aim to ensure that such requirements are, inter alia:

   (a) based on objective and transparent criteria, such as competence and the ability to supply the service;

   (b) not more burdensome than necessary to ensure the quality of the service;

   (c) in the case of licensing procedures, not in themselves a restriction on the supply of the service. . . .

6. In sectors where specific commitments regarding professional services are undertaken, each Member shall provide for adequate procedures to verify the competence of professionals of any other Member.

Article VII
Recognition

1. For the purposes of the fulfilment, in whole or in part, of its standards or criteria for the authorization, licensing or certification of services suppliers . . . a Member may recognize the education or experience obtained, requirements met, or licenses or certifications granted in a particular country. Such recognition, which may be achieved through harmonization or otherwise, may be based upon an agreement or arrangement with the country concerned or may be accorded autonomously.

3. A Member shall not accord recognition in a manner which would constitute a means of discrimination between countries in the application of its standards or criteria for the authorization, licensing or certification of services suppliers, or a disguised restriction on trade in services.

Article X
Emergency Safeguard Measures

1. There shall be multilateral negotiations on the question of emergency safeguard measures based on the principle of non-discrimination. The results of such

negotiations shall enter into effect on a date not later than three years from the date of entry into force of the WTO Agreement.

Article XI
Payments and Transfers

1. Except under the circumstances envisaged in Article XII, a Member shall not apply restrictions on international transfers and payments for current transactions relating to its specific commitments.

Article XIX
Negotiation of Specific Commitments

1. In pursuance of the objectives of this Agreement, Members shall enter into successive rounds of negotiations, beginning not later than five years from the date of entry into force of the WTO Agreement and periodically thereafter, with a view to achieving a progressively higher level of liberalization. Such negotiations shall be directed to the reduction or elimination of the adverse effects on trade in services of measures as a means of providing effective market access. This process shall take place with a view to promoting the interests of all participants on a mutually advantageous basis and to securing an overall balance of rights and obligations.

Article XX
Schedules of Specific Commitments

3. Schedules of specific commitments shall be annexed to this Agreement and shall form an integral part thereof.

AGREEMENT ON TRADE-RELATED ASPECTS OF INTELLECTUAL PROPERTY RIGHTS

General Agreement on Tariffs and Trade April 15, 1994

PART ONE: GENERAL PROVISIONS AND BASIC PRINCIPLES

Article 3 National Treatment
1. Each Member shall accord to the nationals of other Members treatment no less favourable than that it accords to its own nationals with regard to the protection of intellectual property, subject to the exceptions already provided in, respectively, the Paris Convention (1967), the Berne Convention (1971), the Rome Convention or the Treaty on Intellectual Property in Respect of Integrated Circuits.

Article 4
Most-Favoured-Nation Treatment
With regard to the protection of intellectual property, any advantage, favour, privilege or immunity granted by a Member to the nationals of any other country shall be accorded immediately and unconditionally to the nationals of all other Members.

Article 7
Objectives
The protection and enforcement of intellectual property rights should contribute to the promotion of technological innovation and to the transfer and dissemination of technology, to the mutual advantage of producers and users of technological knowledge and in a manner conducive to social and economic welfare, and to a balance of rights and obligations.

PART TWO: STANDARDS CONCERNING THE AVAILABILITY, SCOPE AND USE OF INTELLECTUAL PROPERTY RIGHTS

SECTION I: COPYRIGHT AND RELATED RIGHTS

Article 9
Relation to the Berne Convention
1. Members shall comply with . . . the Berne Convention (1971). . . .
2. Copyright protection shall extend to expressions and not to ideas, procedures, methods of operation or mathematical concepts as such.

Article 10
Computer Programs and Compilations of Data
1. Computer programs, whether in source or object code, shall be protected as literary works under the Berne Convention (1971).

Article 11
Rental Rights
In respect of at least computer programs and cinematographic works, a Member shall provide authors and their successors in title the right to authorize or to prohibit the commercial rental to the public of originals or copies of their copyright works. A Member shall be excepted from this obligation in respect of cinematographic works unless such rental has led to widespread copying of such works which is materially impairing the exclusive right of reproduction conferred in that Member on authors and their successors in title. In respect of computer programs, this obligation does not apply to rentals where the program itself is not the essential object of the rental.

Article 12
Term of Protection
Whenever the term of protection of a work, other than a photographic work or a work of applied art, is calculated on a basis other than the life of a natural person, such term shall be no less than 50 years from the end of the calendar year of authorized publication, or, failing such authorized publication within 50 years from the making of the work, 50 years from the end of the calendar year of making.

Article 14
Protection of Performers, Producers of
Phonograms (Sound Recordings) and Broadcasting
Organizations
1. In respect of a fixation of their performance on a phonogram, performers shall have the possibility of preventing the following acts when undertaken without their authorization: the fixation of their unfixed performance and the reproduction of such fixation. Performers shall also have the possibility of preventing the following acts when undertaken without their authorization: the broadcasting by wireless means and the communication to the public of their live performance.
5. The term of the protection available under this Agreement to performers and producers of phonograms shall last at least until the end of a period of 50 years computed from the end of the calendar year in which the fixation was made or the performance took place. The term of protection granted pursuant to paragraph 3 shall last for at least 20 years from the end of the calendar year in which the broadcast took place.

Section II: Trademarks

Article 15
Protectable Subject Matter
1. Any sign, or any combination of signs, capable of distinguishing the goods or services of one undertaking from those of other undertakings, shall be capable of constituting a trademark. Such signs, in particular words including personal names, letters, numerals, figurative elements and combinations of colours as well as any combination of such signs, shall be eligible for registration as trademarks. Where signs are not inherently capable of distinguishing the relevant goods or services, Members may make registrability depend on distinctiveness acquired through use. Members may require, as a condition of registration, that signs be visually perceptible.
3. Members may make registrability depend on use. However, actual use of a trademark shall not be a condition for filing an application for registration.

An application shall not be refused solely on the ground that intended use has not taken place before the expiry of a period of three years from the date of application.
4. The nature of the goods or services to which a trademark is to be applied shall in no case form an obstacle to registration of the trademark.
5. Members shall publish each trademark either before it is registered or promptly after it is registered and shall afford a reasonable opportunity for petitions to cancel the registration. In addition, Members may afford an opportunity for the registration of a trademark to be opposed.

Article 16
Rights Conferred
1. The owner of a registered trademark shall have the exclusive right to prevent all third parties not having the owner's consent from using in the course of trade identical or similar signs for goods or services which are identical or similar to those in respect of which the trademark is registered where such use would result in a likelihood of confusion. In case of the use of an identical sign for identical goods or services, a likelihood of confusion shall be presumed. The rights described above shall not prejudice any existing prior rights, nor shall they affect the possibility of Members making rights available on the basis of use.

Article 18
Term of Protection
Initial registration, and each renewal of registration, of a trademark shall be for a term of no less than seven years. The registration of a trademark shall be renewable indefinitely.

Article 19
Requirement of Use
1. If use is required to maintain a registration, the registration may be cancelled only after an uninterrupted period of at least three years of non-use, unless valid reasons based on the existence of obstacles to such use are shown by the trademark owner. Circumstances arising independently of the will of the owner of the trademark which constitute an obstacle to the use of the trademark, such as import restrictions on or other government requirements for goods or services protected by the trademark, shall be recognized as valid reasons for non-use.
2. When subject to the control of its owner, use of a trademark by another person shall be recognized as use of the trademark for the purpose of maintaining the registration.

Article 20
Other Requirements
The use of a trademark in the course of trade shall not be unjustifiably encumbered by special requirements, such as use with another trademark, use in a special form or use in a manner detrimental to its capability to distinguish the goods or services of one undertaking from those of other undertakings. This will not preclude a requirement prescribing the use of the trademark identifying the undertaking producing the goods or services along with, but without linking it to, the trademark distinguishing the specific goods or services in question of that undertaking.

Article 21
Licensing and Assignment
Members may determine conditions on the licensing and assignment of trademarks, it being understood that the compulsory licensing of trademarks shall not be permitted and that the owner of a registered trademark shall have the right to assign the trademark with or without the transfer of the business to which the trademark belongs.

Section III: Geographical Indications

Article 22
Protection of Geographical Indications
1. Geographical indications are, for the purposes of this Agreement, indications which identify a good as originating in the territory of a Member, or a region or locality in that territory, where a given quality, reputation or other characteristic of the good is essentially attributable to its geographical origin.
2. In respect of geographical indications, Members shall provide the legal means for interested parties to prevent: (a) the use of any means in the designation or presentation of a good that indicates or suggests that the good in question originates in a geographical area other than the true place of origin in a manner which misleads the public as to the geographical origin of the good; (b) any use which constitutes an act of unfair competition within the meaning of Article 10b is of the Paris Convention (1967).
3. A Member shall, ex officio if its legislation so permits or at the request of an interested party, refuse or invalidate the registration of a trademark which contains or consists of a geographical indication with respect to goods not originating in the territory indicated, if use of the indication in the trademark for such goods in that Member is of such a nature as to mislead the public as to the true place of origin.
4. The protection under paragraphs 1, 2 and 3 shall be applicable against a geographical indication which, although literally true as to the territory, region or locality in which the goods originate, falsely represents to the public that the goods originate in another territory.

Article 23
Additional Protection for Geographical Indications for Wines and Spirits
1. Each Member shall provide the legal means for interested parties to prevent use of a geographical indication identifying wines for wines not originating in the place indicated by the geographical indication in question or identifying spirits for spirits not originating in the place indicated by the geographical indication in question, even where the true origin of the goods is indicated or the geographical indication is used in translation or accompanied by expressions such as "kind," "type," "style," "imitation" or the like.

Section IV: Industrial Designs

Article 25
Requirements for Protection
1. Members shall provide for the protection of independently created industrial designs that are new or original. Members may provide that designs are not new or original if they do not significantly differ from known designs or combinations of known design features. Members may provide that such protection shall not extend to designs dictated essentially by technical or functional considerations.

Article 26
Protection
1. The owner of a protected industrial design shall have the right to prevent third parties not having the owner's consent from making, selling or importing articles bearing or embodying a design which is a copy, or substantially a copy, of the protected design, when such acts are undertaken for commercial purposes.
3. The duration of protection available shall amount to at least 10 years.

Section V: Patents

Article 27
Patentable Subject Matter
1. Subject to the provisions of paragraphs 2 and 3, patents shall be available for any inventions, whether products or processes, in all fields of technology, provided that they are new, involve an inventive step and are capable of industrial application. Subject to paragraph 4 of Article 65, paragraph 8 of Article 70 and

paragraph 3 of this Article, patents shall be available and patent rights enjoyable without discrimination as to the place of invention, the field of technology and whether products are imported or locally produced.

2. Members may exclude from patentability inventions, the prevention within their territory of the commercial exploitation of which is necessary to protect the public order or morality, including to protect human, animal or plant life or health or to avoid serious prejudice to the environment, provided that such exclusion is not made merely because the exploitation is prohibited by their law.

3. Members may also exclude from patentability: (a) diagnostic, therapeutic and surgical methods for the treatment of humans or animals; (b) plants and animals other than micro-organisms, and essentially biological processes for the production of plants or animals other than non-biological and microbiological processes. However, Members shall provide for the protection of plant varieties either by patents or by an effective sui generis system or by any combination thereof. The provisions of this subparagraph shall be reviewed four years after the date of entry into force of the WTO Agreement.

Article 28
Rights Conferred

1. A patent shall confer on its owner the following exclusive rights: (a) where the subject matter of a patent is a product, to prevent third parties not having the owner's consent from the acts of: making, using, offering for sale, selling, or importing for these purposes that product; (b) where the subject matter of a patent is a process, to prevent third parties not having the owner's consent from the act of using the process, and from the acts of: using, offering for sale, selling, or importing for these purposes at least the product obtained directly by that process.

2. Patent owners shall also have the right to assign, or transfer by succession, the patent and to conclude licensing contracts.

Article 29
Conditions on Patent Applicants

1. Members shall require that an applicant for a patent shall disclose the invention in a manner sufficiently clear and complete for the invention to be carried out by a person skilled in the art and may require the applicant to indicate the best mode for carrying out the invention known to the inventor at the filing date or, where priority is claimed, at the priority date of the application.

2. Members may require an applicant for a patent to provide information concerning the applicant's corresponding foreign applications and grants.

Article 31
Other Use Without Authorization
of the Right Holder

Where the law of a Member allows for other use of the subject matter of a patent without the authorization of the right holder, including use by the government or third parties authorized by the government, the following provisions shall be respected: (a) authorization of such use shall be considered on its individual merits; (b) such use may only be permitted if, prior to such use, the proposed user has made efforts to obtain authorization from the right holder on reasonable commercial terms and conditions and that such efforts have not been successful within a reasonable period of time. This requirement may be waived by a Member in the case of a national emergency or other circumstances of extreme urgency or in cases of public non-commercial use. In situations of national emergency or other circumstances of extreme urgency, the right holder shall, nevertheless, be notified as soon as reasonably practicable. . . .

Article 32
Revocation/Forfeiture

An opportunity for judicial review of any decision to revoke or forfeit a patent shall be available.

Article 33
Term of Protection

The term of protection available shall not end before the expiration of a period of twenty years counted from the filing date.

PART THREE: ENFORCEMENT OF INTELLECTUAL PROPERTY RIGHTS

Article 41

1. Members shall ensure that enforcement procedures as specified in this Part are available under their law so as to permit effective action against any act of infringement of intellectual property rights covered by this Agreement, including expeditious remedies to prevent infringements and remedies which constitute a deterrent to further infringements. These procedures shall be applied in such a manner as to avoid the creation of barriers to legitimate trade and to provide for safeguards against their abuse.

2. Procedures concerning the enforcement of intellectual property rights shall be fair and equitable. They shall not be unnecessarily complicated or costly, or entail unreasonable time-limits or unwarranted delays.

3. Decisions on the merits of a case shall preferably be in writing and reasoned. They shall be made available at least to the parties to the proceeding without undue delay. Decisions on the merits of a case shall be based only on evidence in respect of which parties were offered the opportunity to be heard.

4. Parties to a proceeding shall have an opportunity for review by a judicial authority of final administrative decisions and, subject to jurisdictional provisions in a Member's law concerning the importance of a case, of at least the legal aspects of initial judicial decisions on the merits of a case. However, there shall be no obligation to provide an opportunity for review of acquittals in criminal cases.

Article 44
Injunctions
1. The judicial authorities shall have the authority to order a party to desist from an infringement, inter alia to prevent the entry into the channels of commerce in their jurisdiction of imported goods that involve the infringement of an intellectual property right, immediately after customs clearance of such goods. Members are not obliged to accord such authority in respect of protected subject matter acquired or ordered by a person prior to knowing or having reasonable grounds to know that dealing in such subject matter would entail the infringement of an intellectual property right.

Article 45
Damages
1. The judicial authorities shall have the authority to order the infringer to pay the right holder damages adequate to compensate for the injury the right holder has suffered because of an infringement of that person's intellectual property right by an infringer who knowingly, or with reasonable grounds to know, engaged in infringing activity.

Article 48
Indemnification of the Defendant
1. The judicial authorities shall have the authority to order a party at whose request measures were taken and who has abused enforcement procedures to provide to a party wrongfully enjoined or restrained adequate compensation for the injury suffered because of such abuse. The judicial authorities shall also have the authority to order the applicant to pay the defen-

dant expenses, which may include appropriate attorney's fees.

Article 51
Suspension of Release by Customs Authorities
Members shall, in conformity with the provisions set out below, adopt procedures to enable a right holder, who has valid grounds for suspecting that the importation of counterfeit trademark or pirated copyright goods may take place, to lodge an application in writing with competent authorities, administrative or judicial, for the suspension by the customs authorities of the release into free circulation of such goods. Members may enable such an application to be made in respect of goods which involve other infringements of intellectual property rights, provided that the requirements of this Section are met. Members may also provide for corresponding procedures concerning the suspension by the customs authorities of the release of infringing goods destined for exportation from their territories.

Article 57
Right of Inspection and Information
Without prejudice to the protection of confidential information, Members shall provide the competent authorities the authority to give the right holder sufficient opportunity to have any goods detained by the customs authorities inspected in order to substantiate the right holder's claims. The competent authorities shall also have authority to give the importer an equivalent opportunity to have any such goods inspected. Where a positive determination has been made on the merits of a case, Members may provide the competent authorities the authority to inform the right holder of the names and addresses of the consignor, the importer and the consignee and of the quantity of the goods in question.

Article 59
Remedies
Without prejudice to other rights of action open to the right holder and subject to the right of the defendant to seek review by a judicial authority, competent authorities shall have the authority to order the destruction or disposal of infringing goods in accordance with the principles set out in Article 46. In regard to counterfeit trademark goods, the authorities shall not allow the re-exportation of the infringing goods in an unaltered state or subject them to a different customs procedure, other than in exceptional circumstances.

Article 60
De Minimis Imports
Members may exclude from the application of the above provisions small quantities of goods of a non-commercial

nature contained in travellers' personal luggage or sent in small consignments.

Section V: Criminal Procedures

Article 61

Members shall provide for criminal procedures and penalties to be applied at least in cases of wilful trademark counterfeiting or copyright piracy on a commercial scale. Remedies available shall include imprisonment and/or monetary fines sufficient to provide a deterrent, consistently with the level of penalties applied for crimes of a corresponding gravity. In appropriate cases, remedies available shall also include the seizure, forfeiture and destruction of the infringing goods and of any materials and implements the predominant use of which has been in the commission of the offence. Members may provide for criminal procedures and penalties to be applied in other cases of infringement of intellectual property rights, in particular where they are committed wilfully and on a commercial scale.

Part Seven: Institutional Arrangements

Article 68
Council for Trade-Related Aspects of Intellectual Property Rights
The Council for TRIPS shall monitor the operation of this Agreement and, in particular, Members' compliance with their obligations hereunder, and shall afford Members the opportunity of consulting on matters relating to the trade-related aspects of intellectual property rights.

NORTH AMERICAN FREE TRADE AGREEMENT

Between the Government of the United States of America, the Government of Canada and the Government of the United Mexican States (Selected Provisions) Effective January 1, 1994

PART ONE: GENERAL PART

Article 101
Establishment of the Free Trade Area
The Parties to this Agreement, consistent with Article XXIV of the General Agreement on Tariffs and Trade, hereby establish a free trade area.

Article 103
Relation to Other Agreements
1. The Parties affirm their existing rights and obligations with respect to each other under the General Agreement on Tariffs and Trade and other agreements to which such Parties are party.
2. In the event of any inconsistency between this Agreement and such other agreements, this Agreement shall prevail to the extent of the inconsistency, except as otherwise provided in this Agreement.

PART TWO: TRADE IN GOODS

Article 301
National Treatment
1. Each Party shall accord national treatment to the goods of another Party in accordance with Article III of the General Agreement on Tariffs and Trade (GATT) . . .

Article 302
Tariff Elimination
1. Except as otherwise provided in this Agreement, no Party may increase any existing customs duty, or adopt any customs duty, on an originating good.
2. Except as otherwise provided in this Agreement, each Party shall progressively eliminate its customs duties on originating goods in accordance with its Schedule. . . .

Article 305
Temporary Admission of Goods
1. Each Party shall grant duty-free temporary admission for: (a) professional equipment necessary for carrying out the business activity, trade or profession of a business person who qualifies for temporary entry . . . , (b) equipment for the press or for sound or television broadcasting and cinematographic equipment, (c) goods imported for sports purposes and goods intended for display or demonstration, and (d) commercial samples and advertising films, imported from the territory of another Party, regardless of their origin and regardless of whether like, directly competitive or substitutable goods are available in the territory of the Party. . . .

Article 306
Duty-Free Entry of Certain Commercial Samples and Printed Advertising Materials
Each Party shall grant duty-free entry to commercial samples of negligible value, and to printed advertising materials, imported from the territory of another Party, regardless of their origin, but may require that: (a) such samples be imported solely for the solicitation of orders for goods, or services provided from the territory, of another Party or non-Party; or (b) such advertising materials be imported in packets that each contain no more than one copy of each such material and that neither such materials nor packets form part of a larger consignment.

Article 307
Goods Re-Entered after Repair or Alteration
1. [N]o Party may apply a customs duty to a good, regardless of its origin, that re-enters its territory after that good has been exported from its territory

to the territory of another Party for repair or alteration, regardless of whether such repair or alteration could be performed in its territory.

2. [N]o Party may apply a customs duty to a good, regardless of its origin, imported temporarily from the territory of another Party for repair or alteration.

Article 309
Import and Export Restrictions

1. Except as otherwise provided in this Agreement, no Party may adopt or maintain any prohibition or restriction on the importation of any good of another Party or on the exportation or sale for export of any good destined for the territory of another Party, except in accordance with Article XI of the GATT, including its interpretative notes, and to this end Article XI of the GATT and its interpretative notes, or any equivalent provision of a successor agreement to which all Parties are party, are incorporated into and made a part of this Agreement.

2. The Parties understand that the GATT rights and obligations incorporated by paragraph 1 prohibit, in any circumstances in which any other form of restriction is prohibited, export price requirements and, except as permitted in enforcement of countervailing and antidumping orders and undertakings, import price requirements.

3. In the event that a Party adopts or maintains a prohibition or restriction on the importation from or exportation to a non-Party of a good, nothing in this Agreement shall be construed to prevent the Party from: (a) limiting or prohibiting the importation from the territory of another Party of such good of that non-Party; or (b) requiring as a condition of export of such good of the Party to the territory of another Party, that the good not be re-exported to the non-Party, directly or indirectly, without being consumed in the territory of the other Party. . . .

Article 316
Consultations and Committee on Trade in Goods

1. The Parties hereby establish a Committee on Trade in Goods, comprising representatives of each Party.

2. The Committee shall meet on the request of any Party or the Commission to consider any matter arising under this Chapter.

Chapter 4. Rules of Origin

Article 401
Originating Goods

Except as otherwise provided in this Chapter, a good shall originate in the territory of a Party where: (a) the good is wholly obtained or produced entirely in the territory of one or more of the Parties . . . (b) each of the non-originating materials used in the production of the good undergoes an applicable change in tariff classification set out in Annex 401 as a result of production occurring entirely in the territory of one or more of the Parties, or the good otherwise satisfies the applicable requirements of that Annex where no change in tariff classification is required, and the good satisfies all other applicable requirements of this Chapter; (c) the good is produced entirely in the territory of one or more of the Parties exclusively from originating materials; or (d) except for a good provided for in Chapters 61 through 63 of the Harmonized System, the good is produced entirely in the territory of one or more of the Parties but one or more of the non-originating materials provided for as parts under the Harmonized System that are used in the production of the good does not undergo a change in tariff classification because (i) the good was imported into the territory of a Party in an unassembled or a disassembled form but was classified as an assembled good pursuant to General Rule of Interpretation 2(a) of the Harmonized System, or (ii) the heading for the good provides for and specifically describes both the good itself and its parts and is not further subdivided into subheadings, or the subheading for the good provides for and specifically describes both the good itself and its parts, provided that the regional value content of the good, determined in accordance with Article 402, is not less than 60 percent where the transaction value method is used, or is not less than 50 percent where the net cost method is used, and that the good satisfies all other applicable requirements of this Chapter.

Chapter 8. Emergency Action

Article 801
Bilateral Actions

1. [During] the transition period only, if a good originating in the territory of a Party, as a result of the reduction or elimination of a duty provided for in this Agreement, is being imported into the territory of another Party in such increased quantities, in absolute terms, and under such conditions that the imports of the good from that Party alone constitute a substantial cause of serious injury, or threat thereof, to a domestic industry producing a like or directly competitive good, the Party into whose territory the good is being imported may, to the minimum extent necessary to remedy or prevent the injury: (a) suspend the further reduction of any rate of duty provided for under this Agreement on the good; (b) increase the rate of duty on the good to a level not to exceed the lesser of (i) the most-favored-nation (MFN) applied rate of duty in effect at the time the action is taken,

and (ii) the MFN applied rate of duty in effect on the day immediately preceding the date of entry into force of this Agreement; or (c) in the case of a duty applied to a good on a seasonal basis, increase the rate of duty to a level not to exceed the MFN applied rate of duty that was in effect on the good for the corresponding season immediately preceding the date of entry into force of this Agreement. . . .

4. The Party taking an action under this Article shall provide to the Party against whose good the action is taken mutually agreed trade liberalizing compensation in the form of concessions having substantially equivalent trade effects or equivalent to the value of the additional duties expected to result from the action. . . .

Article 802
Global Actions

1. Each Party retains its rights and obligations under Article XIX of the GATT or any safeguard agreement pursuant thereto except those regarding compensation or retaliation and exclusion from an action to the extent that such rights or obligations are inconsistent with this Article. Any Party taking an emergency action under Article XIX or any such agreement shall exclude imports of a good from each other Party from the action unless: (a) imports from a Party, considered individually, account for a substantial share of total imports; and (b) imports from a Party, considered individually, or in exceptional circumstances imports from Parties considered collectively, contribute importantly to the serious injury, or threat thereof, caused by imports.

PART THREE: TECHNICAL BARRIERS TO TRADE

Article 904
Basic Rights and Obligations

1. Each Party may, in accordance with this Agreement, adopt, maintain or apply any standards-related measure, including any such measure relating to safety, the protection of human, animal or plant life or health, the environment or consumers, and any measure to ensure its enforcement or implementation. . . .

2. Notwithstanding any other provision of this Chapter, each Party may, in pursuing its legitimate objectives of safety or the protection of human, animal or plant life or health, the environment or consumers, establish the levels of protection that it considers appropriate. . . .

4. No Party may prepare, adopt, maintain or apply any standards-related measure with a view to or with the effect of creating an unnecessary obstacle to trade between the Parties. An unnecessary obstacle to

trade shall not be deemed to be created where: (a) the demonstrable purpose of the measure is to achieve a legitimate objective; and (b) the measure does not operate to exclude goods of another Party that meet that legitimate objective.

Article 905
Use of International Standards

1. Each Party shall use, as a basis for its standards-related measures, relevant international standards. . . .

2. A Party's standards-related measure that conforms to an international standard shall be presumed to be consistent with Article 904(3) and (4).

PART FIVE: INVESTMENT, SERVICES AND RELATED MATTERS

Article 1102
National Treatment

1. Each Party shall accord to investors of another Party treatment no less favorable than that it accords, in like circumstances, to its own investors with respect to the establishment, acquisition, expansion, management, conduct, operation, and sale or other disposition of investments.

2. Each Party shall accord to investments of investors of another Party treatment no less favorable than that it accords, in like circumstances, to investments of its own investors with respect to the establishment, acquisition, expansion, management, conduct, operation, and sale or other disposition of investments.

3. The treatment accorded by a Party under paragraphs 1 and 2 means, with respect to a state or province, treatment no less favorable than the most favorable treatment accorded, in like circumstances, by that state or province to investors, and to investments of investors, of the Party of which it forms a part. . . .

Article 1103
Most-Favored-Nation Treatment

1. Each Party shall accord to investors of another Party treatment no less favorable than that it accords, in like circumstances, to investors of any other Party or of a non-Party with respect to the establishment, acquisition, expansion, management, conduct, operation, and sale or other disposition of investments.

2. Each Party shall accord to investments of investors of another Party treatment no less favorable than that it accords, in like circumstances, to investments of investors of any other Party or of a non-Party with respect to the establishment, acquisition, expansion, management, conduct, operation, and sale or other disposition of investments.

Article 1106
Performance Requirements

1. No Party may impose or enforce any of the following requirements, or enforce any commitment or undertaking, in connection with the establishment, acquisition, expansion, management, conduct or operation of an investment of an investor of a Party or of a non-Party in its territory: (a) to export a given level or percentage of goods or services; (b) to achieve a given level or percentage of domestic content; (c) to purchase, use or accord a preference to goods produced or services provided in its territory, or to purchase goods or services from persons in its territory; (d) to relate in any way the volume or value of imports to the volume or value of exports or to the amount of foreign exchange inflows associated with such investment; (e) to restrict sales of goods or services in its territory that such investment produces or provides by relating such sales in any way to the volume or value of its exports or foreign exchange earnings; (f) to transfer technology, a production process or other proprietary knowledge to a person in its territory, except when the requirement is imposed or the commitment or undertaking is enforced by a court, administrative tribunal or competition authority to remedy an alleged violation of competition laws or to act in a manner not inconsistent with other provisions of this Agreement; or (g) to act as the exclusive supplier of the goods it produces or services it provides to a specific region or world market.

Article 1107
Senior Management and Boards of Directors

1. No Party may require that an enterprise of that Party that is an investment of an investor of another Party appoint to senior management positions individuals of any particular nationality.
2. A Party may require that a majority of the board of directors, or any committee thereof, of an enterprise of that Party that is an investment of an investor of another Party, be of a particular nationality, or resident in the territory of the Party, provided that the requirement does not materially impair the ability of the investor to exercise control over its investment.

Article 1110
Expropriation and Compensation

1. No Party may directly or indirectly nationalize or expropriate an investment of an investor of another Party in its territory or take a measure tantamount to nationalization or expropriation of such an investment ("expropriation"), except: (a) for a public purpose; (b) on a non-discriminatory basis; (c) in accordance with due process of law and Article 1105(1); and (d) on payment of compensation in accordance with paragraphs 2 through 6.
2. Compensation shall be equivalent to the fair market value of the expropriated investment immediately before the expropriation took place ("date of expropriation"), and shall not reflect any change in value occurring because the intended expropriation had become known earlier. Valuation criteria shall include going concern value, asset value including declared tax value of tangible property, and other criteria, as appropriate, to determine fair market value.
3. Compensation shall be paid without delay and be fully realizable.

Article 1114
Environmental Measures

1. Nothing in this Chapter shall be construed to prevent a Party from adopting, maintaining or enforcing any measure otherwise consistent with this Chapter that it considers appropriate to ensure that investment activity in its territory is undertaken in a manner sensitive to environmental concerns.
2. The Parties recognize that it is inappropriate to encourage investment by relaxing domestic health, safety or environmental measures. Accordingly, a Party should not waive or otherwise derogate from, or offer to waive or otherwise derogate from, such measures as an encouragement for the establishment, acquisition, expansion or retention in its territory of an investment of an investor.

Chapter 12. Cross-border Trade in Services

Article 1201
Scope and Coverage

This Chapter does not apply to: (a) financial services, (b) air services. . . .

Article 1202
National Treatment

1. Each Party shall accord to service providers of another Party treatment no less favorable than that it accords, in like circumstances, to its own service providers.
2. The treatment accorded by a Party under paragraph 1 means, with respect to a state or province, treatment no less favorable than the most favorable treatment accorded, in like circumstances, by that state or province to service providers of the Party of which it forms a part.

Article 1205
Local Presence
No Party may require a service provider of another Party to establish or maintain a representative office or any form of enterprise, or to be resident, in its territory as a condition for the cross-border provision of a service.

Chapter 14. Financial Services

Article 1403
Establishment of Financial Institutions
1. The Parties recognize the principle that an investor of another Party should be permitted to establish a financial institution in the territory of a Party in the juridical form chosen by such investor.
2. The Parties also recognize the principle that an investor of another Party should be permitted to participate widely in a Party's market through the ability of such investor to: (a) provide in that Party's territory a range of financial services through separate financial institutions as may be required by that Party; (b) expand geographically in that Party's territory; and (c) own financial institutions in that Party's territory without being subject to ownership requirements specific to foreign financial institutions.

Article 1404
Cross-Border Trade
1. No Party may adopt any measure restricting any type of cross-border trade in financial services by cross-border financial service providers of another Party that the Party permits on the date of entry into force of this Agreement, except to the extent set out in Section B of the Party's Schedule to Annex VII.

Article 1405
National Treatment
1. Each Party shall accord to investors of another Party treatment no less favorable than that it accords to its own investors, in like circumstances, with respect to the establishment, acquisition, expansion, management, conduct, operation, and sale or other disposition of financial institutions and investments in financial institutions in its territory.
2. Each Party shall accord to financial institutions of another Party and to investments of investors of another Party in financial institutions treatment no less favorable than that it accords to its own financial institutions and to investments of its own investors in financial institutions, in like circumstances, with respect to the establishment, acquisition, expansion, management, conduct, operation, and sale or other disposition of financial institutions and investments.

Chapter 15. Competition Policy, Monopolies and State Enterprises

Article 1501
Competition Law
1. Each Party shall adopt or maintain measures to proscribe anti-competitive business conduct and take appropriate action with respect thereto, recognizing that such measures will enhance the fulfillment of the objectives of this Agreement. To this end the Parties shall consult from time to time about the effectiveness of measures undertaken by each Party.
2. Each Party recognizes the importance of cooperation and coordination among their authorities to further effective competition law enforcement in the free trade area. The Parties shall cooperate on issues of competition law enforcement policy, including mutual legal assistance, notification, consultation and exchange of information relating to the enforcement of competition laws and policies in the free trade area.
3. No Party may have recourse to dispute settlement under this Agreement for any matter arising under this Article.

Chapter 16. Temporary Entry for Business Persons

Article 1603
Grant of Temporary Entry
1. Each Party shall grant temporary entry to business persons who are otherwise qualified for entry under applicable measures relating to public health and safety and national security. . . .
2. A Party may refuse to issue an immigration document authorizing employment to a business person where the temporary entry of that person might affect adversely: (a) the settlement of any labor dispute that is in progress at the place or intended place of employment; or (b) the employment of any person who is involved in such dispute. . . .

Part Six: Intellectual Property

Article 1701
Nature and Scope of Obligations
Each Party shall provide in its territory to the nationals of another Party adequate and effective protection and enforcement of intellectual property rights, while ensuring that measures to enforce intellectual property rights do not themselves become barriers to legitimate trade.

Article 1705
Copyright
1. Each Party shall protect the works covered by the Berne Convention, including any other works that

embody original expression within the meaning of that Convention. In particular: (a) all types of computer programs are literary works within the meaning of the Berne Convention and each Party shall protect them as such; and (b) compilations of data or other material, whether in machine readable or other form, which by reason of the selection or arrangement of their contents constitute intellectual creations, shall be protected as such. The protection a Party provides under subparagraph (b) shall not extend to the data or material itself, or prejudice any copyright subsisting in that data or material.

2. Each Party shall provide to authors and their successors in interest those rights enumerated in the Berne Convention . . . including the right to authorize or prohibit: (a) the importation into the Party's territory of copies of the work made without the right holder's authorization; (b) the first public distribution of the original and each copy of the work by sale, rental or otherwise; (c) the communication of a work to the public; and (d) the commercial rental of the original or a copy of a computer program.

4. Each Party shall provide that, where the term of protection of a work, other than a photographic work or a work of applied art, is to be calculated on a basis other than the life of a natural person, the term shall be not less than 50 years from the end of the calendar year of the first authorized publication of the work or, failing such authorized publication within 50 years from the making of the work, 50 years from the end of the calendar year of making.

Article 1706
Sound Recordings

2. Each Party shall provide a term of protection for sound recordings of at least 50 years from the end of the calendar year in which the fixation was made.

Article 1708
Trademarks

1. For purposes of this Agreement, a trademark consists of any sign, or any combination of signs, capable of distinguishing the goods or services of one person from those of another, including personal names, designs, letters, numerals, colors, figurative elements, or the shape of goods or of their packaging. Trademarks shall include service marks and collective marks, and may include certification marks. A Party may require, as a condition for registration, that a sign be visually perceptible.

2. Each Party shall provide to the owner of a registered trademark the right to prevent all persons not having the owner's consent from using in commerce identical or similar signs for goods or services that are identical or similar to those goods or services in respect of which the owner's trademark is registered, where such use would result in a likelihood of confusion. In the case of the use of an identical sign for identical goods or services, a likelihood of confusion shall be presumed. The rights described above shall not prejudice any prior rights, nor shall they affect the possibility of a Party making rights available on the basis of use.

3. A Party may make registrability depend on use. However, actual use of a trademark shall not be a condition for filing an application for registration. No Party may refuse an application solely on the ground that intended use has not taken place before the expiry of a period of three years from the date of application for registration. . . .

7. Each Party shall provide that the initial registration of a trademark be for a term of at least 10 years and that the registration be indefinitely renewable for terms of not less than 10 years when conditions for renewal have been met.

8. Each Party shall require the use of a trademark to maintain a registration. The registration may be canceled for the reason of non-use only after an uninterrupted period of at least two years of non-use, unless valid reasons based on the existence of obstacles to such use are shown by the trademark owner. Each Party shall recognize, as valid reasons for non-use, circumstances arising independently of the will of the trademark owner that constitute an obstacle to the use of the trademark, such as import restrictions on, or other government requirements for, goods or services identified by the trademark.

11. A Party may determine conditions on the licensing and assignment of trademarks, it being understood that the compulsory licensing of trademarks shall not be permitted and that the owner of a registered trademark shall have the right to assign its trademark with or without the transfer of the business to which the trademark belongs.

13. Each Party shall prohibit the registration as a trademark of words, at least in English, French or Spanish, that generically designate goods or services or types of goods or services to which the trademark applies.

Article 1709
Patents

1. [E]ach Party shall make patents available for any inventions, whether products or processes, in all fields of technology, provided that such inventions are new, result from an inventive step and are capable of industrial application. For purposes of this Article, a Party may deem the terms "inventive step" and "capable of

industrial application" to be synonymous with the terms "non-obvious" and "useful," respectively.

5. Each Party shall provide that: (a) where the subject matter of a patent is a product, the patent shall confer on the patent owner the right to prevent other persons from making, using or selling the subject matter of the patent, without the patent owner's consent; and (b) where the subject matter of a patent is a process, the patent shall confer on the patent owner the right to prevent other persons from using that process and from using, selling, or importing at least the product obtained directly by that process, without the patent owner's consent.

Article 1711
Trade Secrets

1. Each Party shall provide the legal means for any person to prevent trade secrets from being disclosed to, acquired by, or used by others without the consent of the person lawfully in control of the information in a manner contrary to honest commercial practices, in so far as: (a) the information is secret in the sense that it is not, as a body or in the precise configuration and assembly of its components, generally known among or readily accessible to persons that normally deal with the kind of information in question; (b) the information has actual or potential commercial value because it is secret; and (c) the person lawfully in control of the information has taken reasonable steps under the circumstances to keep it secret.

2. A Party may require that to qualify for protection a trade secret must be evidenced in documents, electronic or magnetic means, optical discs, microfilms, films or other similar instruments.

3. No Party may limit the duration of protection for trade secrets, so long as the conditions in paragraph 1 exist.

Article 1712
Geographical Indications

1. Each Party shall provide, in respect of geographical indications, the legal means for interested persons to prevent: (a) the use of any means in the designation or presentation of a good that indicates or suggests

that the good in question originates in a territory, region or locality other than the true place of origin, in a manner that misleads the public as to the geographical origin of the good; (b) any use that constitutes an act of unfair competition within the meaning of the Paris Convention.

2. Each Party shall, on its own initiative if its domestic law so permits or at the request of an interested person, refuse to register, or invalidate the registration of, a trademark containing or consisting of a geographical indication with respect to goods that do not originate in the indicated territory, region or locality, if use of the indication in the trademark for such goods is of such a nature as to mislead the public as to the geographical origin of the good.

Chapter 22. Institutional Arrangements and Dispute Settlement Procedures

Article 2001
The Free Trade Commission

1. The Parties hereby establish the Free Trade Commission, comprising cabinet-level representatives of the Parties or their designees.

2. The Commission shall: (a) supervise the implementation of this Agreement . . . (c) resolve disputes that may arise regarding its interpretation or application; (d) supervise the work of all committees and working groups established under this Agreement . . .

Article 2005
GATT Dispute Settlement

[D]isputes regarding any matter arising under both this Agreement and the General Agreement on Tariffs and Trade, any agreement negotiated thereunder, or any successor agreement (GATT), may be settled in either forum at the discretion of the complaining Party.

Article 2021
Private Rights

No Party may provide for a right of action under its domestic law against any other Party on the ground that a measure of another Party is inconsistent with this Agreement.